4

Pro Oracle Database 11*g* RAC on Linux

Steve Shaw
Martin Bach

Apress®

Pro Oracle Database 11*g* RAC on Linux

ISBN-13 (pbk): 978-1-4302-2958-2

ISBN-13 (electronic): 978-1-4302-2959-9

Printed and bound in the United States of America (POD)

President and Publisher: Paul Manning
Lead Editor: Jonathan Gennick
Technical Reviewer: Bernhard Cock Buning and Sandesh Rao
Editorial Board: Clay Andres, Steve Anglin, Mark Beckner, Ewan Buckingham, Gary Cornell, Jonathan Gennick, Jonathan Hassell, Michelle Lowman, Matthew Moodie, Duncan Parkes, Jeffrey Pepper, Frank Pohlmann, Douglas Pundick, Ben Renow-Clarke, Dominic Shakeshaft, Matt Wade, Tom Welsh
Coordinating Editor: Anita Castro
Copy Editor: Patrick Meader and Mary Ann Fugate
Compositor: Bytheway Publishing Services
Indexer: BIM Indexing & Proofreading Services
Artist: April Milne
Cover Designer: Anna Ishchenko

Distributed to the book trade worldwide by Springer Science+Business Media, LLC., 233 Spring Street, 6th Floor, New York, NY 10013. Phone 1-800-SPRINGER, fax (201) 348-4505, e-mail orders-ny@springer-sbm.com, or visit www.springeronline.com.

For information on translations, please e-mail rights@apress.com, or visit www.apress.com.

Apress and friends of ED books may be purchased in bulk for academic, corporate, or promotional use. eBook versions and licenses are also available for most titles. For more information, reference our Special Bulk Sales–eBook Licensing web page at www.apress.com/info/bulksales.

Contents at a Glance

Contents

ix

About the Author

■ **Steve Shaw** is the database technology manager for Intel Corporation in EMEA (Europe, the Middle East, and Africa). Steve leads the initiative for migrating databases from RISC systems running UNIX operating systems to Intel Linux servers with a focus on helping customers get the best out of Oracle and open source database solutions on leading-edge technologies. He has over 13 years of experience of working with Oracle on Intel systems and 10 years with Oracle on Linux. Steve is the author and maintainer of Hammerora, the leading open source Oracle and MySQL Load Test Tool and an acknowledged expert on real-world database benchmarks and performance. Steve is a popular speaker at Oracle- and Linux-related events worldwide, including Oracle Openworld, Linuxcon, and the UKOUG and DOAG conferences. He also speaks regularly at SIGs, seminars, and training events and contributes articles to database- and Linux-related publications and web sites. He is an Oracle Certified Professional and holds a master of science degree in computing from the University of Bradford, UK.

■ **Martin Bach** is an independent Oracle consultant and author. He has specialized in the Oracle Database Management System since 2001, with his main interests in high availability and disaster recovery solutions for mission critical 24x7 systems. Martin is a proud member of the Oracle Certified Master community, having successfully passed the exam for Database 10g Release 2. Additionally, he has been nominated as an Oracle Ace, based on his significant contribution and activity in the Oracle technical community. With this accreditation, Oracle Corporation recognized his proficiency in Oracle technology as well as his willingness to share his knowledge and experiences with the community.

When not trying to get the best out of the Oracle database for his customers, or working on understanding its internals, Martin can be found attending Oracle usergroup meetings. Martin also maintains a successful weblog at `martincarstenbach.wordpress.com`, which is regularly updated with his latest research results and information about this book. Martin holds a German degree, "Diplom Betriebswirt (FH)," obtained at the University of Applied Sciences in Trier, Germany.

About the Technical Reviewer

■ **Bernhard de Cock Buning** is a co-founder of Grid-It. Within the partnership, he works as a DBA/consultant. In this role, he specializes in high availability (Real Application Cluster, Dataguard, MAA, Automatic Storage Management). He has around 12 years of experience with Oracle RDBMS products. He started his career with Oracle Support in the Netherlands, where he worked for seven years. He is still reaping the benefits from Oracle Support in the Netherlands from 1999 to 2006, where he was part of an HA team. He prefers to work with advising, implementing, and problem-solving with regards to the more difficult issues and HA topics. In addition to this, Bernhard enjoys giving various high availability training courses and presentations for different clients and usergroups.

■**Sandesh Rao** is a director running the RAC Assurance development team within RAC Development at Oracle Corporation, specializing in performance tuning, high availability, disaster recovery, and architecting cloud-based solutions using the Oracle stack. With 12 years of experience in the HA space and having worked on several versions of Oracle with different application stacks , he is a recognized expert in RAC and Database Internals; most of his work involves solving tough problems in the implementation of projects for financial, retailing, scientific, insurance, and biotech industries, among others. His current position involves running a team that develops best practices for the Oracle Grid Infrastructure, including products like RAC (Real Application Clusters), Storage (ASM, ACFS), and the Oracle Clusterware.

Prior to this position, Sandesh ran the Database Enterprise Manager BDE (Bugs Diagnostics and Escalations) organization within Oracle Support, which screens for defects that are raised with customer SRs. Sandesh has more than a decade of onsite and back-office expertise backed by an engineering degree in computer science from the University of Mumbai, India. He can also be found on Linkedin (www.linkedin.com/pub/sandesh-rao/2/956/1b7).

Acknowledgments

We would like to thank the people who assisted in all stages of the researching, testing, writing, reviewing, and publication of this book. In particular, we would like to thank the Apress team of Lead Editor Jonathan Gennick and Coordinating Editor Anita Castro for their invaluable advice, guidance, and knowledge. We would like to thank Copy Editor Patrick Meader for the skill involved in blending our technical writing into a finished book. For the technical review, we would like to thank Bernhard de Cock Buning, Sandesh Rao, and Chris Barclay for their time in reading, commenting, and improving the meaning that we wished to convey. We would also like to thank Julian Dyke for his assistance in sharing research and seeing the project through to completion, and Markus Michalewicz, Frits Hoogland, Joel Goodman, Martin Widlake, and Doug Burns for inspiration and their help in putting the material together. Finally, we would like to recognize the contribution of the Oracle User Group in the UK and Europe and, in particular, contributors to the UKOUG Oracle RAC SIG: David Burnham, Dev Nayak, Jason Arneil, James Anthony, Piet de Visser, Simon Haslam, David Kurtz, Thomas Presslie, and Howard Jones.

Steve Shaw and Martin Bach

I would like to thank my wife, Angela, my daughter, Evey, and my sons, Lucas and Hugo, for their unwavering support, understanding, and motivation in enabling this edition of the book to be completed. I would also like to thank my parents, Ron and Carol, for their help in providing the time and space to write. On the technical side, I would like to thank my managers and colleagues of Intel enterprise software enabling for databases: Michael Vollmer, Alex Klimovitski, Andrew G. Hamilton, and Mikhail Sinyavin, and the Intel Winnersh UK team of Evgueny Khartchenko, Hugues A. Mathis and Nadezhda Plotnikova. I would also like to thank Christian Rothe and Jonathan Price of Oracle for assistance with Oracle Enterprise Linux and Oracle VM. Finally, I would like to thank Todd Helfter, the author of Oratcl, and the many of users of Hammerora worldwide for their contribution to the Oracle, Linux, and open source community.

Steve Shaw

I would like to thank my wife and son for their great patience and support during the time I was busy researching and writing this book. Without your support, it would not have been possible to finish it in time. I would, of course, thank a few people who have helped me get to where I am now.

Invaluable support at the university was provided by Prof. Dr. Steinbuß, who first started my enthusiasm for the Oracle Database and Sushi. I can't forget Jens Schweizer, Timo Philipps, Axel Biesdorf, and Thorsten Häs for countless good hours in H105. I would like to thank the members of the technical team I worked with in Luxemburg: Michael Champagne, Yves Remy, and especially Jean-Yves Francois. Without you, I would have found it very hard to develop the same professional attitude to problem-solving and managing time pressure. I would also like to thank Justin and Lisa Hudd, Kingsley Sawyers, Pete Howlet, Dave Scammel, Matt Nolan, and Alex Louth for a lot of support during my first years in England. Also, for the work I did in London: Shahab Amir-Ebrahimi, David Marcos, Peter Boyes, Angus Thomas, James Lesworth, Mark Bradley, Mark Hargrave, and Paul Wright.

Martin Bach

CHAPTER 1

■ ■ ■

Introduction

In this chapter, we will discusses reasons for deploying Oracle Real Application Cluster to protect your database-based application from an unplanned outage and giving your application high availability, fault tolerance, and many other benefits that cannot be obtained from running your application against a single-instance Oracle database. This chapter will also cover the history of RAC and the evolution of Oracle clustering products, culminating with the product we know now.

Introducing Oracle Real Application Clusters

Oracle Real Application Clusters (RAC) is an option that sits on top of the Oracle database. Using the shared disk architecture, the database runs across a set of computing nodes offers increased availability, allows applications to scale horizontally, and improves manageability at a lower cost of ownership. RAC is available for both the Enterprise Edition and the Standard Edition of the Oracle database.

When users think of RAC, Oracle also wants them to think of *the grid*, where the grid stands for having computing power as a utility. With Oracle's tenth major release of the database, the focus changed from the *i* for *Internet* users were so familiar with (e.g., Oracle 9*i*) to a *g* for *grid computing* (e.g., Oracle 10*g*). The trend in the industry away from comparatively expensive proprietary SMP servers to industry-standard hardware running on the Linux operating system seems to support the idea that users want to treat computing power as a utility. And indeed, some of the largest physics experiments conducted today, including those that rely on the Large Hadron Collider (LHC) at the Centre for Nuclear Research CERN in Geneva, are using industry-standard hardware and Oracle RAC for data processing.

The RAC option has been available since Oracle 9*i* Release 1 in the summer of 2001. Prior to that, the clustered Oracle database option was known as the *Oracle Parallel Server* option. RAC offers fundamental improvements over Oracle Parallel Server—and the introduction of Cache Fusion has helped improve application scalability and inter-instance communication, as well as propelled RAC into mainstream use.

In a study published by the Gartner Group, analysts suggested that Oracle RAC in 9*i* Release 1 required skilled staff from various departments for successful RAC implementations. At the time, the analysts rated RAC as a reliable option, allowing users to increase scalability and availability; however, they also said that its complexity was an inhibitor to widespread adoption.

Since then, Oracle has worked hard to address these concerns. Key new features were added in Oracle 10*g* Release 1 that built on the successful components introduced previously. For example, Oracle Automatic Storage Management provided the functionality of a clustered logical volume manager, removing the dependency that required Oracle users to license such functionality from third-party software vendors (and thereby increasing the desire of Oracle's customers to implement it).

10*g* Release 1 also included Oracle Clusterware, a unified, portable clustering layer that performed tasks that often required third-party clustering software previously. Prior to 10*g* Release 1, Oracle Clusterware was available only on Windows and Linux; however, 10*g* Release 1 marked its release for all major platforms. Of course, non-Oracle cluster-management software can still be used if needed, depending on Oracle's certification with a given stack.

These successful components have been further enhanced with the 11.2 release of the database. Increasing emphasis has been put on computing as a utility. Computing as a utility in this context means less administrator intervention and more automatically performed actions. For example, the new Grid Plug And Play deployment option allows users to easily add and remove nodes from a cluster. Clusters can be logically divided into subunits referred to as *server pools*. Such a server pool can be declared the home for a RAC database—shrinking and expanding the number of servers in the server pool automatically causes the database to adapt to the new environment by adding or removing database instances.

To summarize, Oracle 11g Release 2 Enterprise Edition RAC promises the following benefits to users:

- *High availability:* The shared-everything architecture guarantees that node failures do not imply loss of service. The remaining nodes of the cluster will perform crash recovery for the failed instance, guaranteeing availability of the database.

- *Scalability:* Multiple nodes allow an application to scale beyond the limits imposed by single-node databases

- *Manageability:* Multiple databases can be consolidated into a RAC cluster.

- *Reduced cost of ownership:* RAC can be deployed on industry standard hardware, offsetting the licensing cost with lower hardware cost.

In addition to the aforementioned features, Oracle 11g Release 2 also includes a product called *RAC One Node*. Oracle has recognized the fact that some RAC deployments have been installed purely for high availability; it has also discovered that other (virtualization) products are increasingly being used. To counter that trend, RAC One Node builds on the RAC technology stack: Oracle Clusterware, Oracle Automatic Storage Management, and the Oracle database. Oracle RAC One Node will be discussed in more detail in Chapter 3.

Examining the RAC Architecture

Figure 1-1 provides an overview of the RAC technology stack (see Chapter 3 for a much more in-depth discussion of the RAC architecture).

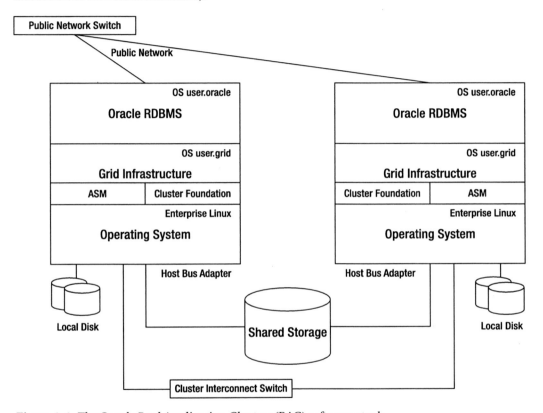

Figure 1-1. The Oracle Real Application Clusters (RAC) software stack

As you can see in Figure 1-1, Oracle RAC is based around the following software components:

- Oracle RAC runs on top of an operating system.
- Oracle RAC builds on the Oracle software stack.
  - Oracle recommends installing Grid Infrastructure—the clustering software layer—with a dedicated user, usually **grid**. This account has to be created on the operating system level

- In the releases preceding 11*g* Release 2, it was possible to install the storage layer with a dedicated operating system account. With 11*g* Release 2, Oracle began bundling its cluster aware logical volume manager software, Automatic Storage Management (ASM), into the cluster software stack. Note that this approach no longer allows a strict separation of duties, as was the case before. The Oracle RDBMS binaries are traditionally installed under the **oracle** account.

- Depending on the choice of storage, Oracle provides libraries to facilitate the discovery and management of shared storage in form of RPMs.

- The Oracle Cluster aware layer is a prerequisite for running clustered Oracle databases. It must be installed before the database binaries are installed

- Oracle Real Application Clusters requires shared storage for the database files, such as online redo logs, control files, and data files. Various options are available for users to choose from. It appears that Oracle's strategic choice is to use ASM, its own cluster-aware logical volume manager.

- Finally, the database binaries are installed.

- A database is created after the software stack is installed and configured.

From Oracle 10*g* Release 1 to Oracle 11*g* Release 1, Oracle's software components could be installed on certified cluster file systems such as Oracle's own OCFS2, a so-called shared Oracle home. Beginning with Oracle 11*g* Release 2, only the RDBMS software binaries can be installed as a shared home, Grid Infrastructure, the cluster foundation, can no longer be installed on a shared file system.

As also illustrated in Figure 1-1, you can see the following differences between single instance of Oracle database and a two-node RAC:

- A private interconnect is used for intercluster communication; this interconnect relies on a private interconnect switch.

- A public network is used for all client communication with the cluster.

- To speed up detection of failed nodes, Oracle RAC employs virtual IP addresses as cluster resources. When a node fails, its virtual IP migrates to another node of the cluster. If that were not the case, clients would have to wait for TCP/IP timeouts (which can be very long) before trying the next node of the cluster. When migrated to another host, the virtual IP address can immediately signal that the node is down, triggering the client to try the next host in the local naming file.

- Shared storage is required for the database files.

Deploying RAC

As we have seen, systems based on RAC offer a number of advantages over traditional single-instance Oracle databases. In the upcoming sections, we will explore such systems in more depth, focusing on the hallmarks of the RAC option: high availability, scalability, manageability and cost of ownership.

Maintaining High Availability

Compute clustering aims to provide system continuity in the event of (component) failure, thus guaranteeing a high availability of the service. A multitude of ideas have been developed over the past decades to deal with sudden failure of components, and there is a lot of supporting research. Systems fail for many reasons. Most often, aging or faulty hardware causes systems to become unusable, which leads to failures. However, operator errors, incorrect system specifications, improper configuration, and insufficient testing of critical application components can also cause systems to fail. These should be referred to as soft failures, as opposed to the hard failures mentioned previously.

Providing Fault Tolerance by Redundancy

The most common way to address hardware faults is to provide hardware fault tolerance through redundancy—this is common practice in IT today. Any so-called *single point of failure*—in other words, a component identified as critical to the system—should have adequate backup. Extreme examples lie in space travel-the space shuttles use four redundant computer systems with the same software, plus a fifth system with a different software release. Another example is automated control for public transport, where component failure could put lives at risk. Massive investment in methods and technology to keep hardware (processor cycles, memory, and so on) in sync are justified in such cases.

Today, users of Oracle RAC can use industry standard components to protect against individual component failures; a few milliseconds for instance recovery can usually be tolerated.

Most storage arrays are capable of providing various combinations of striping and mirroring of individual hard disks to protect against failure. Statistically, it's known that hard drives manufactured in batches are likely to fail roughly around the same time, so disk failure should be taken seriously when it happens. The connections between the array(s) and the database host should also be laid out in a redundant way, allowing multiple paths for the data to flow. This not only increases throughput, but failure of a host-based adaptor or a SAN switch can't bring down the system, either.

Of course, all critical production servers should also have redundancy for the most important internal components, such as power supply units. Ideally, components should be hot swappable, but this is becoming less of an issue in a RAC environment because servers can be easily added and removed from the cluster for maintenance, and there are few remaining roadblocks to performing planned maintenance in a rolling fashion.

One of the key benefits of Oracle RAC has always been its ability to provide a highly available database platform for applications. Oracle RAC uses a software layer to enable high availability; it accomplishes this by adding database instances that concurrently access a database. In the event of a node failover, the surviving node(s) can be configured to take the workload over from the failed instance. Again, it is important to design the cluster to allow the surviving node to cope with the workload; otherwise, a complete loss of database service could follow an individual node failure.

Making Failover Seamless

In addition to adding database instances to mitigate node failure, Oracle RAC offers a number of technologies to make a node failover seamless to the application (and subsequently, to the end user), including the following:

- Transparent Application Failover

- Fast Connect Failover

Transparent Application Failover (TAF) is a client-side feature. The term refers to the failover/reestablishment of sessions in case of instance or node failures. TAF is not limited to RAC configurations; active/passive clusters can benefit equally from it. TAF can be defined through local naming in the client's **tnsnames.ora** file or, alternatively, as attributes to a RAC database service. The latter is the preferred way of configuring it. Note that this feature requires the use of the OCI libraries, so thin-client only applications won't be able to benefit from it. With the introduction of the Oracle Instant client, this problem can be alleviated somewhat by switching to the correct driver.

TAF can operate in two ways: it can either restore a session or re-execute a select statement in the event of a node failure. While this feature has been around for a long time, Oracle's net manager configuration assistant doesn't provide support for setting up client-side TAF. Also, TAF isn't the most elegant way of handling node failures because any in-flight transactions will be rolled back—TAF can resume running select statements only.

The fast connection failover feature provides a different way of dealing with node failures and other types of events published by the RAC high availability framework (also known as the Fast Application Notification, or FAN). It is more flexible than TAF.

Fast connection failover is currently supported with Oracle's JDBC implicit connection cache, Oracle's Universal Connection Pool, and Oracle Data Provider for .Net session pools, as well as OCI and a few other tools such as CMAN. When registered with the framework, clients can react to events published by it: instead of polling the database to detect potential problems, clients will be informed by way of a push mechanism—all sessions pertaining to a failed node will be marked as invalid and cleaned up. To compensate for the reduction in the number of available sessions, new sessions will be created on another cluster node. FAN uses the Oracle Notification Services (ONS) process or AQ to publish its events. ONS is created and configured by default during a RAC installation on all of the RAC nodes.

An added benefit: It's possible to define user callouts on the database node using FAN events to inform administrators about node up/down events.

Putting the Technology Stack in Perspective

A word of caution at this stage: Focusing on the technology stack up to the database should never be anything other than the first step on the way to a highly available application. Other components in the application stack also need to be designed to allow for the failure of components. There exist cases where well designed database applications adhering to all the criteria mentioned previously are critically flawed because they use only a single network switch for all incoming user traffic. If the switch fails, such an application becomes inaccessible to end users, even though the underlying technology stack as a whole is fully functional.

Defining Scalability

Defining the term *scalability* is a difficult task, and an all-encompassing definition is probably out of scope for this book. The term is used in many contexts, and many database administrators and developers have a different understanding of it. For RAC systems, we normally consider a system to scale if the application's response time or other key measurement factors remains constant as the workload increases.

Scoping Various Levels of Scalability

Similar to a single point of failure, the weakest link in an application stack—of which the database is really just one component—determines its overall throughput. For example, if your database nodes are connected using Infiniband for storage and the interconnect, but the public traffic coming in to the web servers only uses 100Mbit Ethernet, then you may have a scalability problem from the beginning, even if individual components of the stack perform within the required parameters.

Therefore, we find that scalability has to be considered from all of the following aspects:

- Hardware scalability

- Storage scalability

- Operating system scalability

- Database scalability

- Application scalability

You will learn more about each of these scalability levels in later chapters of this book.

Scaling Vertically vs. Horizontally

Additional resources can be added to a system in two different ways:

- *Scale up*: Before clustered computing became a widely spread option, database servers were usually upgraded and/or extended to offer better performance. Often, *big iron* was purchased with some of the CPU sockets unpopulated, along with other methods that allowed room for growth. When needed, components could be replaced and extended, all within the same system image. This is also known as scaling vertically.

- *Scale out*: The design advantage RAC offers over SMP servers lies in the fact that additional nodes can be added to the cluster to increase the overall throughput, whereas even the most powerful SMP server will run out of processor sockets eventually. This is also known as *scaling horizontally*.

Please bear in mind that, for certain workloads and applications, RAC might not be the best option because of the overhead associated with keeping the caches in sync and maintaining global locks. The CPU processing power available in industry standard hardware continues to increase at an almost exponential rate due to the fundamentals of Moore's Law (see Chapter 4 for more information about this topic).

Changing the underlying hardware can in principle have three different outcomes:

- The throughput increases.

- The throughput remains constant.

- The throughput decreases.

Architects aim for linear scalability, where the throughput remains constant under additional workload—in other words, doubling the number of nodes should also double the throughput of the application. Technical overhead, such as the cache synchronization and global locking, prevent exact linear scalability in RAC; however, a well designed application—one that uses business logic inside the database, bind variables, and other techniques equally applicable to single-instance Oracle systems—will most likely benefit greatly from RAC.

Generally speaking, the scalability achieved with RAC varies according to the application and database design.

Increasing Manageability

The cost of licensing RAC can be partly offset by the improved manageability it offers. For example, the technology behind the RAC technology stack makes it an ideal candidate for database consolidation. Data center managers are increasingly concerned with making optimal use of their available resources, especially with the more recent focus on and interest in *green IT*.

Achieving Manageability Through Consolidation

Server consolidation comes in many forms. Current trends include the consolidation of databases and their respective applications through virtualization or other forms of physically partitioning powerful hardware. Oracle RAC offers a very interesting avenue for Oracle database server consolidation. One of the arguments used in favor of consolidation is the fact that it is more expensive (not only from a license point of view) to support a large number of small servers, each with its own storage and network connectivity requirements, than a large cluster with one or only a few databases. Also, users can get better service-level agreements, monitoring, and backup and recovery from a centrally managed system. Managers of data centers also like to see their servers working and well utilized. Underutilized hardware is often the target of consolidation or virtualization projects.

Several large companies are implementing solutions where business units can request access to a database, usually in the form of a schema that can then be provisioned with varying levels of service and resources, depending on the requirements. It is possible to assume a scenario where three clusters are employed for Gold, Silver, and Bronze levels of service. The infrastructure department would obviously charge the business users different amounts based on the level and quality of the service provided. A very brief description of such a setup might read as follows:

- *Gold*: This cluster would be very closely monitored. It would also include multiple archive log destinations, standby databases, and 24x7 coverage by DBAs. Flashback features would be enabled, and multiple standby databases would be available in data centers located in secure remote locations. Frequent backups of the database and archived logs would guarantee optimal recoverability at any time. Such a cluster would be used for customer-facing applications that cannot afford downtime, and each application would be configured so that it protected against node failures.

- *Silver*: This cluster would offer a similar level of service, but it would be limited to business hours. It would be used for similarly important applications, with the exception that there will be no users connecting to them after business hours.

- *Bronze*: This cluster would be intended for quality assurance, development, or test environments. Response times for the DBA team would be lower than for Silver or Gold levels, and there wouldn't be backups because frequent refresh operations would allow testers and developers to roll out code.

The preceding examples don't represent strict implementation rules, obviously; your business requirements may be vastly different—hence an evaluation of your requirements should always precede any implementation.

Users of a database could specify their requirements in a very simple electronic form, making the provisioning of database access for applications quite easy and more efficient; this approach offers a high degree of automation.

Note that the Gold-Silver-Bronze scenario assumes that it doesn't matter for many applications if they have multiple schemas in their own database or share one database with other projects. The more static an application's data, the more suited that app is for consolidation.

A different approach to server consolidation is to have multiple databases run on the same cluster, instead of employing one database with multiple schemas. Tom Kyte's web site (`http://asktom.oracle.com`) includes an ongoing discussion where participants have been debating whether running multiple instances on the same physical host is recommended—the discussion is mostly centered on the fact that some Oracle background processes run in the real-time scheduling class, which could potentially starve other processes out of CPU time. Today's modern and powerful hardware, such as eight-core and above x86-64 processors, have somewhat diminished the weight of such arguments.

Enabling Database Consolidation

Several features in the Oracle database help to make server consolidation successful:

- The Resource Manager
- Instance Caging
- Workload management

The Resource Manager allows the administrator to use a variety of criteria to group users into a resource consumer group. A resource consumer group defines how many resources in a database can be assigned to users. Since Oracle 10, users can be moved into a lower resource consumer group when they cross the threshold for their allowed resource usage. Beginning with Oracle 11, they can also be upgraded once their calls are completed. This is especially useful in conjunction with connection pooling and web applications where one session can no longer be directly associated with an individual, as it was in the days of dedicated server connections and Oracle Forms applications. In the connection pooling scenario, the application simply grabs a connection out of the pool of available connections, performs its assigned task, and then returns the connection to the pool. Often these operations are very short in nature. Connection pooling offers a huge advantage over the traditional way of creating a dedicated connection each time a user performs an operation against the database, greatly reducing the overhead associated with establishing a dedicated server process.

Instance caging is a new Oracle 11.2 feature. It addresses a scenario where multiple databases run on the same cluster (instead of the single database/multiple schemas design discussed previously). In a nutshell, instance caging allows administrators to limit the number of CPUs available to the database instance by setting an initialization parameter. In addition, a resource manager plan needs to be active for this feature to work in cases where resource usage is further defined.

Finally, *workload management* allows you to logically subdivide your RAC using the concept of services. Services are a logical abstraction from the cluster, and they permit users and applications to connect to a specific number of nodes. Services are also vital for applications to recover from instance failure—a service can be defined to fail over to another node in case the instance it was running on has failed. Oracle allows the administrator to set up a list of nodes as the preferred nodes—nodes where the application preferably connects to. Oracle also allows the administrator to specify available nodes in case one of the preferred nodes fails. Services can also be used for accounting. For example, you might use them to charge a business for the use of a cluster, depending on its resource consumption.

Consolidating Servers

Server consolidation is a good idea, but it shouldn't be used excessively. For example, running the majority of business critical applications on the same cluster in the same data center is not a good idea.

Consolidation also requires input from many individuals, should the system have to switch to the Disaster Recovery (DR) site. Scheduled DR tests can also become difficult to organize as the number of parties increases. Last but not least, the more data is consolidated in the same database, the more difficult it becomes to perform point-in-time recoveries in cases of user error or data corruption, assuming there is a level of data dependence. If you have a situation where 1 product in 15 consolidated on a RAC system needs to revert back to a particular point in time, it will be very difficult to get agreement from the other 14 products, which are perfectly happy with the state of the database and their data.

Assessing the Cost of Ownership

As discussed previously in the section on manageability, many businesses adopt RAC to save on their overall IT infrastructure cost. Most RAC systems in the UK are deployed on industry-standard components running the Linux operating system. This allows businesses to lower their investment in hardware, while at the same time getting more CPU power from their equipment than was possible a few years ago.

However, RAC can contribute considerably to the cost of the Oracle licenses involved, unless Standard Edition is deployed. However, the Oracle Standard Edition doesn't include the Data Guard option, which means users must develop their own managed recovery solutions, including gap resolution.

Choosing RAC vs. SMP

Undeniably, the hardware cost of deploying a four-node RAC system based on industry-standard Intel x86-64 architecture is lower than the procurement of an SMP server based on a different processor architecture that is equipped with 16 CPUs. Before the advent of multicore systems, industry-standard servers were typically available with up to 8 CPU socket configurations, with each socket containing a single-processing core. Currently, systems are available with 64 cores in a single 8-socket x86-64 server that supports multiple terabytes of memory. Such configurations now enable Oracle single-instance processing capabilities on industry-standard hardware that was previously the domain of dedicated RISC and mainframe environments.

Further economies of scale could be achieved by using a standard-hardware model across the enterprise. Industry-standard x86-64 systems offer many features that modern databases need at a relatively low cost. Once the appropriate hardware platform is adopted, the IT department's Linux engineering team can develop a standardized system image to be distributed through local software repositories, making setup and patching of the platform very easy. Additionally, by using similar hardware for e-mail, file sharing, and databases, the cost for training staff such as data center managers, system administrators and to a lesser degree database administrators can also be reduced. Taken together, these benefits also increase efficiency. Hardware maintenance contracts should also be cheaper in such a scenario because there is a much larger similar base for new systems and spares.

The final argument in favor of RAC is the fact that nodes can be added to the cluster on the fly. Technologies such as Grid Plug and Play introduced with Oracle 11.2 make this even simpler. Even the most powerful SMP server will eventually reach its capacity limit; RAC allows you to sidestep that problem by adding more servers.

Evaluating Service-Level Agreements

Many businesses have agreed to levels of service with other parties. Not meeting the contractually agreed level of service usually implies the payment of a fee to the other party. Unplanned downtime can contribute greatly to overrunning service-level agreements, especially if the mean time to recovery (MTTR) is high. It is imperative that the agreed service levels are met at all times. Depending on the fees involved, the party offering the service for others might need to keep engineers for vendor support on hot standby—in other words, as soon as components fail—so that the on-site engineers can replace or fix such components. Needless to say, that level if service comes at a premium.

The use of RAC can help reduce this cost. As described earlier in this introduction, Oracle RAC is a shared-everything environment, which implies that the failure of a node doesn't mean the complete loss of the service, as was the case in the earlier scenario that covered a single instance of Oracle. Further enhancements within the Oracle cluster layer make it truly possible to use computing as a utility. With server pools, *hot spare* servers can be part of the cluster without actively being used. Should a server pool running an Oracle RAC database fall below the minimum number of usable nodes, spare servers can be moved into the server pool, restoring full service in very little time. Grid Infrastructure is also able to take out a node from a different server pool with a lower priority to satisfy the minimum number of nodes requirement of the higher priority server pool; this enables powerful capacity management and is one of the many improvements offered by Oracle 11.2, which pushes the idea of grid computing to entirely new levels.

However, it should be noted that RAC doesn't protect against site failure, except for the rare case where an extended distance cluster is employed.

Improving Database Management

When done right, server or database consolidation can offer great benefits for the staff involved, and economies of scale can be achieved by reducing the cost of database management. Take backups, for example: instead of having to deploy backup agents to a large number of hosts to allow the tape library to back up databases, only a few distinct systems need to be backed up by the media management library. Patching the backup agents will also become a much simpler task if fewer agents are involved. The consolidated backup can be much simpler to test and verify, as well.

With a consolidated RAC database, disaster-recovery scenarios can also become simpler. Many systems today are using data outside their own schema; in Oracle, database links are often employed in case different databases are used. Add in new technologies such as Service Oriented Architecture or BPEL, and it becomes increasingly difficult to track transactions across databases. This is not so much of a problem if the *master* database only reads from other sources. As soon as writing to other databases is involved, (disaster) recovery scenarios became very difficult. So instead of using multiple federated databases, a consolidated RAC system with intelligent grants across schemas can make recovery much simpler. Site failures could also be dealt with in a much simpler way by implementing failover across a couple of databases instead of dozens.

Factoring in the Additional Hardware Cost

Deploying RAC involves a more elaborate setup than running a single-instance Oracle database. In the most basic (but not the recommended) way, all that's needed to run an Oracle database is a server with sufficient memory and internal disk capacity running under an employee's desk—and you might be surprised by how many production systems are run that way! With RAC, this is not the case (we are omitting the case of running RAC in a virtual environment for this discussion).

To deploy RAC in a production environment with high availability requirements, you need the following:

- *A sufficiently robust data center environment*: This data center must have enough power, rack space, cooling, and security.

- *A storage subsystem*: This should be configured to provide redundancy for its disks.

- *A storage infrastructure*: The predominant deployment configuration of RAC is on 4 or 8 Gbit/s fiber-channel based storage array networks (SANs), but you also find RAC deployed using NFS, iSCSI, and fibre channel over Ethernet or protocols such as Infiniband.

- *Multiple host bus adapters*: These depend on the technology chosen, but they effectively allow communication between the database server and the storage backend.

- *Multipathing software*: Multipathing software supports channel failover and multiple paths to the storage backend, thereby increasing throughput and offering fault tolerance. The Linux kernel offers the device-mapper-multipath toolset out-of-the-box, but most vendors of host bus adapters (HBAs) have their own multipathing software available for Linux.

- *Networking infrastructure*: A private interconnect is required for RAC for inter-cluster communication, as is a public interface to the RAC database. As with the connection to the storage backend, network cards should be teamed (*bonded*, in Linux terminology) to provide resilience.

- *Management and monitoring software*: The monitoring of a RAC database should be proactive, users of the system should never be the first ones to alert the administrators of problems with the database or application.

- *Backup software*: Being able to back up and restore an Oracle database is the most important task of a database administrator. The most brilliant performance-tuning specialist would be at a loss if he couldn't get the database back on line. Enterprise-grade backup solutions often have dedicated agents to communicate directly with the database through RMAN; these agents need to be licensed separately.

- *Operating system support*: The Linux distribution must be certified for the use with your Oracle release. You should also have vendor support for your Linux distribution.

Many sites use dedicated engineering teams that certify a standard-operation build, including the version and patch level of the operating system, as well as all required drivers, which makes the roll-out of a new server simple. It also inspires confidence in the database administrator because the prerequisites for the installation of RAC are met. If such a validated product stack does not exist, it will most certainly be created after the decision to roll out RAC has been made.

USING RAC FOR QUALITY ASSURANCE AND DEVELOPMENT ENVIRONMENTS

A question asked quite frequently concerns RAC and quality assurance environments (or even RAC and development environments). After many years as a RAC administrator, the author has learned that patching such a sensitive system is probably the most nerve-racking experience you can face in that role.

It is therefore essential to be comfortable with the patching procedure and potential problems that can arise. In other words, if your company has spent the money, time, and effort to harden its application(s) against failures using the Real Application Clusters option, then it should also be investing in at least one more RAC cluster. If obtaining additional hardware resources is a problem, you might want to consider virtualizing a RAC cluster for testing. This is currently supported with Oracle's own virtualization technology, called *Oracle VM*, which is free to download and use. Consequently we discuss RAC and virtualization with Oracle VM in Chapter 5. Alternatively, you could opt for virtual machines based on VMWare or another virtualization provider; however, bear in mind that such a configuration has no support from Oracle.

Assessing the Staff and Training Cost

One of the main drawbacks cited against RAC in user community forums is the need to invest in training. It is true that RAC (and to a lesser degree, the introduction of Automatic Storage Management) has changed the requirements for an Oracle DBA considerably. While it was perfectly adequate a few years ago to know about the Oracle database only, the RAC DBA needs to have a broad understanding of networking, storage, the RAC architecture in detail, and many more things. In most cases, the DBA will know the requirements to set up RAC best, and it's her task to enlist the other teams as appropriate, such as networking, system administration, and storage. A well-versed multiplatform RAC DBA is still hard to find and naturally commands a premium.

Clustering with Oracle on Linux

In the final part of this chapter, we will examine the history of Oracle RAC.

Oracle RAC—though branded as an entirely new product when released with Oracle 9*i* Release 1— has a long track record. Initially known as Oracle Parallel Server (OPS), it was introduced with Oracle 6.0.35, which eventually was renamed Oracle 6.2. OPS was based on the VAX/VMS distributed lock manager because VAX/VMS machines essentially were the only clustered computers at the time; however, the DLM used proved too slow for OPS due to internal design limitations. So Oracle development wrote its own distributed lock manager, which saw the light of day with Oracle 6.2 for Digital.

The OPS code matured well over time in the Oracle 7, 8, and 8*i* releases. You can read a remarkable story about the implementation of OPS in *Oracle Insights: Tales of the Oak Table* (Apress, 2004).

Finally, with the advent of Oracle 9.0.1, OPS was relaunched as Real Application Clusters, and it hadn't been renamed since. Oracle was available on the Linux platform prior to 9*i* Release 1, but at that time no standard enterprise Linux distributions as we know them today were available. Linux—even though very mature by then—was still perceived to be lacking in support, so vendors such as Red Hat and SuSE released road maps and support for their distributions alongside their community versions. By 2001, these platforms emerged as stable and mature, justifying the investment by Oracle and other big software players, who recognized the potential behind the open source operating system. Because it runs on almost all hardware, but most importantly on industry-standard components, Linux offers a great platform and cost model for running OPS and RAC.

At the time the name was changed from OPS to RAC, marketing material suggested that RAC was an entirely new product. However, RAC 9*i* was not entirely new at the time; portions of its code were leveraged from previous Oracle releases.

That said, there was a significant change between RAC and OPS in the area of cache coherency. The basic dilemma any shared-everything software has to solve is how to limit access to a block at a time. No two processes can be allowed to modify the same block at the same time; otherwise, a split brain situation would arise. One approach to solving this problem is to simply serialize access to the block. However, that would lead to massive contention, and it wouldn't scale at all. So Oracle's engineers decided to coordinate multiple versions of a block in memory across different instances. At the time, parallel cache management was used in conjunction with a number of background processes (most notably the distributed lock manager, DLM). Oracle ensured that a particular block could only be modified by one instance at a time, using an elaborate system of locks. For example, if instance B needed a copy of a block instance A modified, then the dirty block had to be written to disk by instance A before instance B could read it. This was called block pinging, which tended to be slow because it involved disk activity. Therefore, avoiding or reducing block pinging was one of Oracle's design goals when tuning and developing OPS applications; a lot of effort was spent on ensuring that applications connecting to OPS changed only their own data.

■ **Tip** Oracle documentation for older releases is still available; you can find more detail about the PCM concepts available from this URL: http://download.oracle.com/docs/cd/A58617_01/server.804/a58238/ch9_pcm.htm.

The introduction of Cache Fusion phase I in Oracle 8*i* proved a significant improvement. Block pings were no longer necessary for consistent read blocks and read-only traffic. However, they were still needed for current reads. The Cache Fusion architecture reduced the need to partition workload to instances. The Oracle 8.1.5 "New Features" guide states that changes to the interinstance traffic includes:

> "... a new diskless ping architecture, called cache fusion, that provides copies of blocks directly from the holding instance's memory cache to the requesting instance's memory cache. This functionality greatly improves interinstance communication. Cache fusion is particularly useful for databases where updates and queries on the same data tend to occur simultaneously and where, for whatever reason, the data and users have not been isolated to specific nodes so that all activity can take place on a single instance. With cache fusion, there is less need to concentrate on data or user partitioning by instance."

This document too can be found online at: `http://download-west.oracle.com/docs/cd/A87862_01/NT817CLI/server.817/a76962/ch2.htm`.

In Oracle 9*i* Release 1, Oracle finally implemented Cache Fusion phase II, which uses a fast, high speed interconnect to provide cache-to-cache transfers between instances, completely eliminating disk IO and optimizing read/write concurrency. Finally, blocks could be shipped across the interconnect for current and consistent reads.

Oracle addressed two general weaknesses of its Linux port with RAC 9.0.1: previous versions lacked a cluster manager and a cluster file system. With Oracle 9*i*, Oracle shipped its cluster manager, called *OraCM for Linux and Windows NT* (all other platforms used a third-party cluster manager). OraCM provided a global view of the cluster and all nodes in it. It also controlled cluster membership, and it needed to be installed and configured before the actual binaries for RAC could be deployed.

Cluster configuration was stored in a sever-management file on shared storage, and cluster membership was determined by using a quorum file or partition (also on shared storage).

Oracle also initiated the Oracle Cluster File System (OCFS) project for Linux 2.4 kernels (subsequently OCFS2 has been developed for 2.6 kernels, see below); this file system is released under the GNU public license. OCFS version one was not POSIX compliant; nevertheless, it allowed users to store Oracle database files such as control files, online redo logs, and database files. However, it was not possible to store any Oracle binaries in OCFS for shared Oracle homes. OCFS partitions are configured just like normal file systems in the **/etc/fstab** configuration file. Equally, they are reported like an ordinary mount point in output of the **mount** command. The main drawback was the inherent fragmentation that could not be defragmented, except by reformatting the file system.

■ **Note** The file system fragmentation problem is described in My Oracle Support note 338080.1.

With the release of Oracle 10.1, Oracle delivered significant improvements in cluster manageability, many of which have already been discussed. Two of the main new features were Automatic Storage Management and Cluster Ready Services (which was renamed to Clusterware with 10.2 and 11.1, and is now called *Grid Infrastructure*). The *ORACM* cluster manager, which was available for Linux and Windows NT only, has been replaced by the Cluster Ready Services feature, which now offers the same "feel" for RAC on every platform. The server-management file has been replaced by the Oracle Cluster Registry, whereas the *quorum disk* is now known as the *voting disk*. With 10*g* Release 2, voting disks could be stored at multiple locations to provide further redundancy in case of logical file corruption. In 10.1, the files could only reside on raw devices; since 10.2, they can be moved to block devices, as well. The Oracle 11.1 installer finally allows the placement of the Oracle Cluster Registry and voting disks on block devices without also having to use raw devices. Raw devices have been deprecated in the Linux kernel in favor of the **O_DIRECT** flag. With Grid Infrastructure 11.2, the voting disk and cluster registry should be stored in ASM, and they are only allowed on block/raw devices during the migration phase. ASM is a clustered logical volume manager that's available on all platforms and is Oracle's preferred storage option—in fact, you have to use ASM with RAC Standard Edition.

In 2005, Oracle released OCFS2, which was now finally POSIX compliant and much more feature rich. It is possible to install Oracle binaries on OCFS2, but the binaries have to reside on a different partition than the datafiles because different mount options are required. It is no longer possible to install Grid Infrastructure, the successor to Clusterware, as a shared Oracle home on OCFS; however, it is possible to install the RDBMS binaries on OCFS2 as a shared Oracle home.

Since the introduction of RAC, we've seen the gradual change from SMP servers to hardware, based on the industry-standard x86 and x86-64 architectures. Linux has seen great acceptance in the industry, and it keeps growing, taking market share mainly from the established UNIX systems, such as IBM's AIX, HP-UX, and Sun Solaris. With the combined reduced costs for the hardware and the operating system, RAC is an increasingly viable option for businesses.

Running Linux on Oracle

A considerable advantage of choosing Oracle over many alternative commercial database environments has always been the wide availability of Oracle on different hardware and operating system environments. This freedom of choice has enabled Oracle's customers to maintain their competitive advantage by selecting the best technology available at any single point in time. No other operating system exemplifies this advantage more than Linux. Linux has proven to be a revolutionary operating system, and Oracle has been at the forefront of the revolution with the first commercial database available on the platform. And the Oracle commitment to Linux shows no sign of abating, given that the company's most recent high-profile announcements at the annual Oracle Openworld conference all had a Linux component. In 2006, Oracle announced the release of the first operating system to be directly supported by Oracle: Oracle Enterprise Linux. This was followed in 2007 by the release of Oracle VM, an Oracle Enterprise Linux-based virtualization product. In 2008, Oracle introduced its first two hardware products: the Exadata Storage Server and the HP Oracle Database Machine. Both of these are built on an Oracle Enterprise Linux foundation.

Linux has broken the trend of running Oracle on proprietary operating systems only available on hardware at significant expense from a single vendor. Similarly, clustered Oracle solutions were beyond the reach of many Oracle customers due to the requirement to purchase hardware interconnect technology and clustering software from the same vendors.

Linux offers a higher standard and a greater level of choice to Oracle customers who want to select the best overall environment for their needs. The wide adoption of this new standard is illustrated by the fact that in the year following the publication of the first edition of this book, analyst market research showed that deployments of Oracle on Linux grew at the rate of 72 percent, with more than half of all new RAC implementations being installed on Linux.

The openness of Linux also means that, for the first time, affordable clustered Oracle database solutions eliminate the requirement for third-party clustering software and hardware interconnects. By removing these barriers to entry for clustered database solutions, the increasing popularity of RAC has been closely related to the adoption of Linux as the platform of choice for Oracle customers.

If you run Oracle on Linux, examining the origins of the operating system and its historical context in terms of its relationship to commercial UNIX operating systems is useful. Possessing a level of knowledge about the nature of the GNU General Public License and open source development is also beneficial because it helps you more fully leverage the license models under which Linux and related software is available. We cover these topics in the sections that follow.

Understanding the Role of Unix

To truly understand Linux, you need to start by looking at the background of the Unix operating system. Unix was created in 1969 by Ken Thompson, a researcher at Bell Laboratories (a division of AT&T). It was designed from the outset to be an operating system with multitasking and multiuser capabilities. In 1973, Unix was rewritten in the new C programming language from Dennis Ritchie to be a portable operating system easily modified to run on hardware from different vendors. Further development proceeded in academic institutions to which AT&T had made Unix available for a nominal fee.

AT&T took this course of action, as opposed to developing Unix as a commercial operating system, because, since 1956, AT&T was bound by a consent decree instigated from a complaint made by Western Electric in 1949. This decree prevented AT&T, as a regulated monopoly in the telephony industry, from engaging in commercial activity in other non-telephony markets such as computing. The consent decree is often attributed with being a significant milestone in the birth of the open source movement, enabling the wide and rapid dissemination of Unix technology. For example, one of the most important derivatives of Unix, Berkeley Software Distribution (BSD), was developed at the University of California, Berkeley, as a result.

The judgment on which the consent decree was based was vacated in 1982 when Bell was removed from AT&T, and AT&T developed and sold UNIX System III as a commercial product for the first time. In addition, all Unix derivatives now required a license fee to be paid to AT&T. AT&T combined features from the multiple versions of Unix in distribution, such as BSD, into a unified release of UNIX called System V Release 1, which was released in 1983. Subsequent commercial versions of UNIX were developed under a license from this System V code base, with improvements from releases incorporated into System V eventually resulting in the seminal release of System V Release 4 (SVR4) in 1989. Commercial variants of Unix licensed from AT&T source code were distinguished by the capitalization of the word UNIX, and examples of UNIX included Hewlett Packard's HP-UX, IBM's AIX, and Sun Microsystems's Solaris.

In 1991, AT&T formed the company UNIX System Laboratories (USL), which held the rights and source code to UNIX as a separate business entity. AT&T retained majority ownership until Novell acquired USL in 1993. A year later, the rights to the UNIX trademark and specification, now known as the *Single UNIX Specification*, were transferred by Novell to the X/Open Company. This marks the point at which the UNIX trademark was separated from the source code. In 1996, the X/Open Company merged with the Open Software Foundation (OSF) to form The Open Group. A year earlier (1995), certain licensing agreements regarding the UNIX source code and UnixWare operating system were purchased from Novell by SCO. In 2003, SCO filed a lawsuit against IBM and Sequent (which was subsequently acquired by IBM), claiming that IBM had copied a small section of the source code of UNIX into Linux; SCO sought damages for the unauthorized use of its intellectual property. In addition, SCO also sent a number of "Dear Linux User" letters to enterprise Linux users, warning them that the use of Linux violated SCO's UNIX copyright. However, Novell disputed the claim that in their agreement SCO had actually purchased the copyright to the UNIX source code. In 2007, the court case was ruled in Novell's favor, establishing Novell and not SCO as the rightful owner of the UNIX copyright. Hence, this ruling also ended SCOs claims against IBM and Linux users. At the time of writing, the Open Group owns the trademark UNIX in trust, while Novell, which owns SUSE Linux, retains the copyright to the UNIX source code.

Because the UNIX source code is separate from the UNIX trademark, there can be and are multiple implementations of UNIX. For an operating system to be defined as UNIX, it must adhere to the standards dictated by The Open Group's Single UNIX Specification; it must also license the rights from The Open Group to use the UNIX trademark. You can view a list of compliant UNIX operating systems on The Open Group's web site (**www.opengroup.org**).

Liberating Software

At the same time that AT&T began developing Unix commercially, Richard Stallman, a programmer at MIT, initiated a project to construct a Unix-like operating system for which the source code was to be freely available. Stallman's system was named the *GNU Project*, with the recursive acronym standing for *GNU's Not Unix*. To guarantee the freedom of the software, Stallman created the Free Software Foundation (FSF); the definition of "free" in this case is related to the concept of liberty (i.e., freedom), as opposed to lack of revenue.

This concept of freedom for software is encapsulated in the GNU General Public License (GPL), which incorporates a modified form of copyright known as *copyleft*. The GNU GPL, which has become the most popular license for free software, grants its recipients the following rights:

- The freedom to run the program for any purpose

- The freedom to study how the program works and modify it (implying that the source code must be made freely available)

- The freedom to redistribute copies

- The freedom to improve the program and release the improvements to the public

GNU GPL–licensed software is always released in conjunction with the source code. As the recipient of software distributed with such a license, you are free to modify and distribute the software as you wish; however, you must subsequently grant the same rights for your version of the software that you received from the original. Therefore, you may not, for example, take GNU GPL software and modify it, copyright it, and subsequently sell executable-only versions.

The first major output of the GNU Project was the GNU C Compiler (GCC), whose release was followed by numerous other tools and utilities required for a fully functional Unix operating system. The Hurd project was also underway to create the kernel of this free Unix operating system; however, it was still far from completion when Linux originated.

Developing Linux

In 1991, Linus Torvalds, then a student at the University of Helsinki, bought a PC with an Intel 80386 processor and installed a commercially available operating system called Minix (miniature Unix), which had been developed by Andrew Tanenbaum, to fully exploit the potential of his new PC. Torvalds began to rewrite parts of the software to introduce desired operating system features; in August 1991, version 0.01 of the Linux kernel was released. Version 0.01 actually still ran wholly under the Minix operating system, and version 0.02 enabled a small number of GNU utilities, such as the **bash** shell, to be run. The first stable version of the Linux kernel, version 1.0, was released in 1994. *Kernel* refers to the low-level system software that provides a hardware abstraction layer, disk and file system control, multitasking, load balancing, networking, and security enforcement. Torvalds continues to this day to oversee the development of the Linux kernel. Since the initial Linux version, thousands of developers around the world have contributed to the Linux kernel and operating system.

Linux is written almost entirely in C, with a small amount of assembly language. The Linux kernel is released under the GNU GPL and is therefore free software.

Major releases of the Linux kernel in recent years have included Linux 2.4.0 in January 2001 and 2.6.0 in December 2003. Linux kernel version numbers have the following format:

```
<kernel_version>.<major version>.<minor_version>.<patch>
```

For example, recent versions have been numbered 2.4.37 and 2.6.28.7, and the latest versions can be found at **www.kernel.org/**. Until recently, only the kernel and major and minor version numbers were used. The patch number was added during version 2.6.

Within the Linux kernel version format, the kernel version number is changed least frequently—only when major changes in the code or conceptual changes occur. It has been changed twice in the history of the kernel: in 1994 (version 1.0) and in 1996 (version 2.0).

The second number denotes the major revision of the kernel. Even numbers indicate a stable release (i.e., one deemed fit for production use, such as 2.4 or 2.6); odd numbers indicate development releases (such as 2.5) and are intended for testing new features and drivers until they become sufficiently stable to be included in a production release.

The third number indicates the minor revision of the kernel. Prior to version 2.6.8, this was changed when security patches, bug fixes, new features, or drivers were implemented in the kernel. In version 2.6.8 and later, however, this number is changed only when new drivers or features are introduced; minor fixes are indicated by the fourth number.

The fourth number, or patch number, first occurred when a fatal error, which required immediate fixing, was encountered in the NFS code in version 2.6.8. However, there were not enough other changes to justify the release of a new minor revision (which would have been 2.6.9). So, version 2.6.8.1 was released, with the only change being the fix of that error. With version 2.6.11, the addition of the patch number was adopted as the new official versioning policy. Bug fixes and security patches are now managed by this fourth number, and bigger changes are implemented only in minor revision changes (the third number).

Our emphasis here has been on the Linux kernel, but it is important to note that a Linux operating system should more correctly be viewed as a GNU/Linux operating system—without the GNU tools and utilities, Linux would not be the fully featured Unix operating system on which Oracle RAC installations can and do provide all the features that make it comparable (and more!) to commercial operating systems.

Clarifying the distinction between Linux and commercial UNIX is also worthwhile. Because the Linux community has not licensed the use of the UNIX trademark and is not fully compliant in all aspects with the Single UNIX Specification, it is by definition not a UNIX operating system. Similarly, no version of UNIX is available under GPL licensing. Later versions of **glibc** (the GNU Project's C standard library), however, do include levels of functionality as defined by the Single UNIX Specification, and the close relationship and common heritage between Linux and UNIX are readily apparent. Therefore, it is normal to see Linux referred to as a "Unix" or "Unix family" operating system, where the use of initial capitalization is intended to draw the distinction between the registered trademark UNIX held by The Open Group and the historical concepts and origins of the Unix operating system from which Linux emerged.

Expanding the Concept of Free with Open Source

Partly based on the growing popularity of free software development that was inspired by the success of Linux, the term "open source" was coined in 1998 to clarify and expand on the definition of what had previously been described as "free" software. *Open source* is defined by the following nine rules:

- *Free redistribution*: Open source software cannot prevent someone from using the software in a larger aggregated software bundle, such as a Linux distribution that is subsequently sold or given away.

- *Source code*: The source code for any open source software must be available either bundled with the executable form of the software or with the executable form easily accessible. The source code must remain in a form that would be preferential to the author for modification and cannot be deliberately obfuscated.

- *Derived works*: This stipulation of open source is directly inherited from free software and ensures that redistribution of modified forms of the software is permitted under the same license as the original.

- *Integrity of the author's source code*: This condition enables a greater level of restriction than that of free software by ensuring that it is possible to prevent the redistribution of modified source, as long as modifications are permitted in the form of patch files. The license may also prevent redistribution of modified software with the same name or version number as the original.

- *No discrimination against persons or groups*: Open source licenses cannot discriminate against individuals or groups in terms of to whom the software is available. Open source software is available to all.

- *No discrimination against fields of endeavor*: Open source licenses cannot place limitations on whether software can be used in business or commercial ventures.

- *Distribution of license*: The license applied to open source software must be applicable as soon as the software is obtained and prohibits the requirement for additional intermediary licensing.

- *License must not be specific to a product*: The license that applies to the open source software must apply directly to the software itself and cannot be applied selectively only when that software is released as part of a wider software distribution.

- *License must not restrict other software*: The license cannot place requirements on the licensing conditions of other independent software that is distributed along with the open source software. It cannot, for example, insist that all other software distributed alongside it must also be open source.

For software to be correctly described as open source, it must adhere to each and every one of the preceding criteria. In some cases, software is described as open source to simply mean that the source code has been made available along with the executable version of the software. However, this form of open source is often accompanied by restrictions relating to what can be done with the source code once it has been obtained, especially in terms of modification and redistribution. Only through compliance with the preceding rules can software be officially termed *open source*; the software included in distributions of the Linux operating system are genuinely defined as open source.

Combining Oracle, Open Source, and Linux

In 1998, the Oracle database became the first established commercial database to be available on Linux. Oracle Corporation's commitment to Linux has continued with all Oracle products being made available on the operating system.

At the time of writing, Oracle RAC is supported on the following Linux releases: Oracle Enterprise Linux, Red Hat Enterprise Linux, Novell's SUSE Linux Enterprise Server, and Asianux. For users based in the Americas, Europe, the Middle East, and Africa, the choice is between Oracle Enterprise Linux, Red Hat Enterprise Linux, and Novell's SUSE Linux Enterprise Server. Asianux, on other hand, is also supported, but in the Asia Pacific region only. We do not advocate any of these distributions over the others—all are ideal Linux platforms for running Oracle.

■ **Note** If you wish to know whether a particular Linux distribution is certified by Oracle and therefore qualifies for support, the definitive source of information is the My Oracle Support web site (support.oracle.com).

Although the Oracle database on Linux remains a commercial product that requires the purchase of a license for production installations in exactly the same way as the Oracle database on other, commercial operating systems, Oracle maintains a much deeper relationship with Linux. Within Oracle Corporation is a Linux Projects development group responsible for the development of free and open source software. Oracle continues to work with the existing Linux distributors Red Hat and Novell to certify Oracle software on Red Hat Enterprise Linux and SUSE Linux Enterprise Server; however, the immediate recipient of Oracle Linux support is Oracle Enterprise Linux. That said, the open source nature of any development for the Linux platform ensures that the improvements for one version of Linux can subsequently benefit all Linux distributions. In addition to Oracle Enterprise Linux and Oracle VM, Oracle also releases a number of products under open source licenses and develops software for incorporation into the Linux kernel, such as the second version of the Oracle Cluster File System (OCFS2).

Drilling Down on Unbreakable Linux

Unique among platforms supported by Oracle, the Linux operating system is backed by Oracle's Unbreakable Linux initiative, which provides Oracle worldwide support for Oracle Enterprise Linux, a derivative version of Red Hat Enterprise Linux that Oracle makes available via download for free. It is important to distinguish between the Unbreakable Linux initiative based around Oracle Enterprise Linux and the previous Unbreakable Linux program, for which was Oracle providing first-level support for selected Linux distributions of Red Hat Enterprise Linux, Novell's SUSE Linux Enterprise Server, and Asianux.

The Oracle Database and RAC continues to be supported on these distributions; however, Linux support issues must now be raised in the first instance with the Linux distributor in question and not with Oracle. Oracle provides Linux operating system support only for Oracle Enterprise Linux. Another difference: in the previous incarnation of the Unbreakable Linux initiative, it was a pre-requisite to have a support contract with Oracle for Oracle products, as well as a standard support subscription contract for the operating system with Red Hat or Novell (or an Asianux alliance member in the Asia Pacific region). With the Unbreakable Linux initiative based on Oracle Enterprise Linux, it is not a pre-requisite to have any level of support contract for the Linux operating system in conjunction with an Oracle Database support contract. In other words, as with the Oracle Database on other operating systems, Linux support is arranged and managed separately from the Oracle Database. You can use Oracle Enterprise Linux for free without support while still receiving support for the Oracle Database, or you can subscribe to Oracle Unbreakable Linux and receive support directly from Oracle for the Oracle Enterprise Linux operating system. You can also subscribe to Oracle Unbreakable Linux and receive support for Oracle Enterprise Linux without using other Oracle software, or you can use an alternative certified Linux distribution to run Oracle software and arrange support accordingly for both Linux and Oracle—the choice is entirely at the customer's discretion.

For those who choose Unbreakable Linux for the associated Linux support from Oracle, the choice of hardware platforms is more defined than it is for other hardware platforms for which the Oracle Database 11g is available on Linux. Unbreakable Linux support is available for the x86/x86-64 and Itanium hardware platforms only.

In this book, our emphasis is on Oracle Enterprise Linux and the hardware platforms supported by Oracle under the Unbreakable Linux initiative. The most compelling reason to focus on this platform is the fact that the installable CD images of Oracle Enterprise Linux are available without restriction, and therefore provide the most accessible Linux platform release applicable to the widest number of Oracle RAC on Linux deployments. However, as we discuss in the following section, from a practical viewpoint Oracle Enterprise Linux and Red Hat Enterprise Linux are the same, and therefore every detail discussed is applicable to both versions of what is essentially a Red Hat Enterprise Linux distribution. Similarly, although we do not discuss installation or configuration of SUSE Linux Enterprise Server or Asianux in depth, it is important to note that all Linux distributions run the Linux kernel, so they all share more similarities than differences. Some of the minor implementation details may differ; however, the majority of features and their usage will be the same, no matter which Linux distribution you use. As long as your particular Linux release is certified by Oracle, then the choice between distributions should be based on business decisions, such as how well the support for a given distribution is tailored to your unique requirements. In other words, you would not choose a given distribution based on the significant technical superiority of any particular release.

Creating and Growing Red Hat Enterprise Linux

In 1994, Marc Ewing released his own distribution of Linux, which he called Red Hat Linux. The following year, ACC Corporation, a company formed by Bob Young in 1993, merged with Ewing's business and the resulting company became Red Hat Software.

Red Hat grew steadily over the next few years, expanding into Europe and Japan; and introducing support, training, and the Red Hat Certified Engineer (RHCE) program.

In July 1998, Oracle announced support for Red Hat Linux. However, at the time, Linux was perceived by some as a complex platform to work with due to the rapid pace of development and number of releases available at any one time. The open source mantra of "release early, release often" presented difficulties for enterprise environments used to the slower, more genteel development cycles of commercial operating systems.

In March 2002, Red Hat announced its first enterprise-class Linux operating system, Red Hat Linux Advanced Server. Oracle, along with the hardware vendors Dell, IBM, and Hewlett-Packard, announced support for the platform. A policy was put in place to stabilize releases on this version for 18 months in order to allow partners such as Oracle to port, test, and deploy their applications. This policy has largely been successful, although Red Hat's quarterly updates still often contain significant changes. Red Hat has also undertaken to support each major release of Red Hat Enterprise Linux for seven years from the point of its initial release.

In March 2003, the Red Hat Enterprise Linux family of operating system products was launched. Red Hat Linux Advanced Server, which was aimed at larger systems, was rebranded Red Hat Enterprise Linux AS (Advanced Server). In addition, two more variants were added: Red Hat Enterprise Linux ES (Edge Server or Entry-level Server) for medium-sized systems and Red Hat Enterprise Linux WS (Workstation) for single-user clients.

Since 2003, Red Hat has focused on the business market and Red Hat Enterprise Linux. Red Hat Linux 9 was the final consumer release; this was eventually supplanted by the Fedora Project.

In Red Hat Enterprise Linux 3, Red Hat backported many of the features from the Linux 2.5 development kernel to the version of the Linux 2.4 kernel on which the release was based. Red Hat Enterprise Linux 3 was followed in February 2005 by Red Hat Enterprise Linux 4, which was based on the Linux 2.6 kernel. In March 2007, Red Hat Enterprise Linux 5 was released. Red Hat Enterprise Linux 4 is the earliest supported release for the Oracle Database 11g. With Red Hat Enterprise Linux 5, the terminology was also changed once more for the different variations of the release. Red Hat Enterprise Linux AS became Red Hat Enterprise Linux Advanced Platform, Red Hat Enterprise Linux ES became just Red Hat Enterprise Linux, and Red Hat Enterprise Linux WS became Red Hat Enterprise Linux Desktop.

Table 2-1 summarizes the major Red Hat Enterprise Linux releases to date.

Table 2-1. *Red Hat Enterprise Linux Releases*

Version	Release Date
2.1 AS (Pensacola)	March 2002
2.1 ES (Panama)	May 2003
3 (Taroon)	October 2003
4 (Nahant)	February 2005
5 (Tikanga)	March 2007

Red Hat subscription pricing is dependent on the number of processor sockets and the level of support provided. At the time of writing, two support packages are offered for Red Hat Enterprise Linux Advanced Platform as Standard or Premium subscription for systems with more than two processor sockets with an additional Basic package for Red Hat Enterprise Linux with two processor sockets or less. Subscriptions are charged on a per-system basis for one or three years, and installable software is only available for download to subscribed customers only.

CentOS and Scientific Linux are examples of popular derivatives of Red Hat Enterprise Linux that are compatible with the Red Hat Enterprise Linux versions freely available for download.

Extending Red Hat with Oracle Enterprise Linux

Like CentOS and Scientific Linux, Oracle Enterprise Linux is known as a clone or derivative of Red Hat Enterprise Linux Advanced Platform. Oracle Enterprise Linux is made possible by the GNU GPL, under which the software included in Red Hat Enterprise Linux is released. Therefore, Oracle is able to redistribute a Linux operating system that has full source and binary compatibility with Red Hat Enterprise Linux. In other words, Oracle Enterprise Linux is in fact Red Hat Enterprise Linux, except with respect to Red Hat copyrighted material, such as logos and images, which have been removed. Consequently, from a technical standpoint, the implementation of the operating systems delivered by Red Hat and Oracle are indistinguishable from each other. This is because Oracle Enterprise Linux features full kABI (Kernel Application Binary Interface) compliance with Red Hat Enterprise Linux. In the default installation, the kernel is unmodified from the Red Hat version. However, Oracle Enterprise Linux includes an additional kernel in which Oracle fixes bugs from the initial release; this version is available for manual RPM install if you wish to do so.

Where the difference does lie between the releases is in terms of the support programs available. As detailed in the earlier section on Unbreakable Linux, Oracle offers a support program for Oracle Enterprise Linux direct from Oracle, without the involvement of a third-party Linux distributor. An additional significant difference is in the availability of the software. Oracle enables the download of installable software from `http://edelivery.oracle.com/linux`. It also allows the use of Oracle Enterprise for free, without restrictions. This accessibility means that you are entitled to run Oracle Enterprise Linux on as many systems as you wish, including production systems, and without having purchased a support subscription. It is also possible to copy, redistribute, and use the software as freely as you wish. This makes Oracle Enterprise Linux the only certified Enterprise Linux release available for download in both installable and source form without the prior purchase of a subscription. Oracle also provides additional levels of support. First, it provides an option to subscribe to the Unbreakable Linux Network for software updates between releases. Second, it offers what it calls Basic support (with varying charges for systems with up to two processors) and Premier support (with varying charges for systems with more than two processors).

Drilling Down on SuSE Linux Enterprise Server

SuSE was originally a German company founded in 1992 as a UNIX consulting group by Hubert Mantel, Burchard Steinbild, Roland Dyroff, and Thomas Fehr. *SuSE* is a German acronym that stands for *Software und System Entwicklung*, which translates to "software and system development" in English.

The company started by distributing a German version of Slackware Linux, but eventually decided to release its own distribution. The Jurix distribution developed by Florian LaRoche was used as a basis for the first SuSE distribution, released in 1996 as SuSE Linux 4.2.

May 2002 saw the formation of the United Linux consortium, in which SuSE played a prominent role. United Linux was a collaboration among a number of Linux distributors; the goal of this consortium was to create a single Linux enterprise standard to unify their distributions around in terms of development, marketing, and support. The members of United Linux were SuSE, Turbolinux, Conectiva, and the SCO Group. The initial version (1.0) of United Linux was based on the 2.4.18 kernel; however, various factors resulted in United Linux ultimately being unsuccessful in its aims of unification, despite support for the Oracle database being available with the initial release.

During this period, SuSE continued to release its own distributions of Linux. SuSE Enterprise Linux 8.0 (SLES8), based on the 2.4 kernel, was released in May 2002. This release provided a solid foundation on which to run Oracle9*i*.

In October 2003, SuSE released SLES9, based on the 2.6 kernel. SLES9 includes support for the Native POSIX Thread Library, a key feature of Linux 2.6 releases that significantly boosts the performance of multithreaded Linux applications.

The termination of the United Linux consortium was announced in January 2004 and coincided with the completion of Novell's acquisition of SuSE. Around this time, SuSE was renamed as *SUSE*. SLES9 was followed in July 2006 by SLES10, which was the earliest supported SLES release for the Oracle Database 11*g* and SLES 11 in March 2009.

Table 2-2 summarizes the major SUSE Linux Enterprise Server releases.

Table 2-2. SUSE Linux Enterprise Server Releases

Version	Release Date
8.0	April 2002
9.0	October 2003
10.0	July 2006
11.0	March 2009

SLES subscription pricing is charged per server for terms of one or three years, and it is available for Basic, Standard, and Priority levels of support.

UNDERSTANDING THE RESTRICTIONS OF ENTERPRISE LINUX AND OPEN SOURCE

It is important to be aware that, no matter which Linux distribution you choose, all of the software included in an enterprise Linux distribution remains open source, and the Linux kernel, as well as all of the utilities and applications included with the distribution, are free software. No single Linux distributor is responsible for more than a small contribution to what remains a community developed operating system. Therefore, when you purchase a license for an enterprise edition of Linux, you are purchasing the prepackaged distribution of that software; and, most importantly, a subscription to the vendor's Linux support services. You are not purchasing or licensing the Linux software in a manner similar to which you purchase an Oracle software license, for example. Enterprise Linux versions may or may not be available for download from the Linux vendors in an installable form; however, they are always available as stipulated by the conditions of open source as source code and remain freely distributable.

Taking Linux to Asia

Asianux, as its name suggests, is a Linux operating system available in the Asia Pacific region. Asianux is the result of an alliance among five of Asia's leading Linux distributors to produce an enterprise Linux standard in the region. The distributors are China's Red Flag Software; Japan's Miracle Linux, which is over 50% owned by Oracle; Korea's Haansoft; Vietnam's VietSoftware; and Thailand's WTEC. Aisanux Server 2.0 is the earliest supported release for Oracle Database 11g.

As our focus in this book is on the Linux distributions with the widest global Unbreakable Linux support provided by Oracle, we do not cover Asianux in subsequent chapters. However, Asianux is also based on Red Hat Enterprise Linux, so many of the implementation details discussed will be applicable.

Summary

In this chapter, we introduced Oracle Real Application Clusters and the reasons for implementing this database option. In particular, we explained the differences between a single-instance Oracle database and its limitations when it comes to an instance failure. We also discussed aspects of RAC, especially high availability considerations such as the scalability of a RAC solution compared to symmetric multiprocessor machines. Manageability improvements can be a huge advantage when databases are consolidated into a RAC system. We also touched on the various aspects regarding the total cost of ownership of a RAC system. Finally, we concluded with an overview over the history of Oracle clustering technology.

In the Linux part of the chapter, we examined the history of and concepts behind the Linux operating system, with a focus on understanding the features of the Linux platform that distinguish it from the alternative proprietary operating systems on which Oracle RAC is available. In particular, the aim of this chapter was to clarify the meaning of the terms *free software* and *open source*, as well as the relationship of Oracle to open source. In addition, we introduced the different versions of Linux on which you may consider deploying your Oracle RAC environment, paying particular attention to Oracle Enterprise Linux.

CHAPTER 2

■ ■ ■

RAC Concepts

Chapter 1 provided an introduction to Real Application Clusters; in this chapter, we will move on to discuss the concepts behind RAC in more detail. The topics introduced in this chapter form the basis of a successful implementation of a stable and highly available RAC environment.

We will begin with a look at cluster concepts in general, and then see which of them are available in RAC. Next, we will introduce the cluster layer foundation itself—Oracle Grid Infrastructure—before taking a closer look at the clustered database. Towards the end of this chapter, we will introduce some of the more interesting 11*g* Release 2 features from a RAC database administrator's point of view.

There is a lot of important information to be absorbed—information that will serve as the foundation for the following chapters, where we will dig deeper into the topics raised here.

Clustering Concepts

A computer cluster abstracts the fact that it consists of multiple nodes from a cluster's users. From an outside point of view, a cluster is really just a single entity. Clustering has a long history, and Digital Equipment Corporation's VAX operating system is often credited as being one of the pioneers in supporting clustering. Clusters address the problem that a single unit can't provide the needed throughput and performance an enterprise needs. They also prevent a total outage of a service in the event of a node failure. Therefore, clusters are used to for reliability, scalability, and availability. Computer clusters exist for many purposes, from providing supercomputing power for the systems listed in the top 500 list for ultra-complex calculations, to protecting a web server from crashes. Before we explore RAC in the broader context of clustering, we will introduce the most common clustering concepts first.

Configuring Active/active Clusters

Clusters configured in an *active/active* role feature cluster members that *all* serve user requests—none of them is idly waiting on standby. In most setups, the hardware of the cluster members is identical to prevent skewed performance and to facilitate effective load balancing across the cluster. Active/active clusters require more complex management software to operate because access to all resources, such as disk and memory, needs to be synchronized across all nodes. Most often, a private interconnect will be employed as a heartbeat mechanism. The cluster management software will have to detect problems with nodes, such as node failures and intercluster communication problems.

The so-called "split-brain" is a dreaded condition in clustering where the communication between cluster members is interrupted while all the cluster nodes are still running. Adhering to its programming, the cluster software in each of the cluster halves will try to fail over resources of the nodes it considers crashed. The danger of data corruption looms here: if the application communicates with effectively unsynchronized cluster halves, different data can be written to disk. A split brain scenario is a well-known threat to clustering, and vendors of cluster management software have got the right tools to prevent this from happening.

Oracle's cluster management software is referred to as Cluster Ready Services in 10*g* Release 1 and Clusterware in 10*g* Release 2. In 11*g* Release 2, it was finally rebranded as *Grid Infrastructure*, and it uses the cluster interconnect and a quorum device, called a *voting disk*, to determine cluster membership. A voting disk is shared by all nodes in the cluster, and its main use comes into play when the interconnect fails. A node is evicted from the cluster if it fails to send heartbeats through the interconnect and the voting disk. A voting disk can also help in cases where a node can't communicate with the other nodes via the interconnect, but still has access to the voting disk. The subcluster elected to survive this scenario will send a node eviction message to the node. Clusterware performs node eviction using the STONITH algorithm. This is short for *shoot the other node in the head*—a software request is sent to the node to reboot itself. This can be tricky if the node to be rebooted is hung, and responding to a software reset might not be possible. But luckily, the hardware can assist in these cases, and Grid Infrastructure has support for IPMI (intelligent platform management interface), which makes it possible to issue a node termination signal. In the event of a node failure or eviction, the remaining nodes should be able to carry on processing user requests. Software APIs should make the node failure transparent to the application where possible.

Implementing Active/passive Clusters

An active/passive cluster operates differently from an active/active cluster. Hardware in an active/passive cluster is also identical or nearly identical, but only one of the two nodes is processing user requests at a time. The cluster management software constantly monitors the health of the resource(s) in the cluster. Should a resource fail, the cluster-management layer can try to restart the failed resource a number of times before it fails it over to the standby node.

Depending on the setup, the cluster resource can be located on shared storage or a file system that is also failed over as part of the resource failover. Use of a shared file system offers advantages over the use of an unshared file system, which might have to be checked for corruption through fsck(8) before being remounted to the standby node. Veritas Cluster Suite, Sun (Oracle) Cluster, and IBM HACMP are examples for cluster managers that allow the setup of active/passive clusters.

A little known fact is that using Oracle Grid Infrastructure makes it very simple to set up a cost effective active/passive cluster. Leveraging the Grid Infrastructure API and Oracle's Automatic Storage Management as a cluster logical volume manager makes it easy to constantly monitor a single instance Oracle database. In case of a node failure, the database will automatically be relocated to the standby node. Depending on the fast_start_mttr _target initialization parameter and the size of the recovery set, the failover to the standby node can be very quick; however, users will be disconnected from the database as part of the failover process.

Configuring a Shared-All Architecture

A cluster in which all nodes have concurrent access to shared storage and data is termed a *shared-all* or *shared-everything* configuration. Oracle RAC is an example of a shared-everything architecture: a single database located on shared storage is accessed by multiple database instances running on cluster nodes. In the Oracle terminology, an instance refers to the non-persistent memory structures, such as the shared global area (SGA) background- and foreground-user processes. In contrast, the database is the persistent information stored in data files on disk. With RAC, unlike a shared-nothing design, instance failure doesn't translate to a loss of access to the information mastered by that instance. After an instance failure, one of the remaining instances in the cluster will perform instance recovery, which you'll learn more about in Chapter 3, which covers RAC Architecture. If this happens, all remaining instances will continue to be accessible to users. Using high availability technologies such as Fast Connection Failover for connection pools or Transparent Application Failover can mask the instance failure from the user to varying degrees. The failed instance will eventually rejoin the cluster and reassume its share of the workload.

Configuring a Shared-Nothing Architecture

A shared-nothing database cluster is configured as a number of members in a cluster, where each node has its own private, individual storage that is inaccessible to others in the cluster. The database is vertically partitioned between the nodes; result sets of queries are returned as the unioned result sets from the individual nodes. The loss of a single node results in the inability to access the data managed by the failed node; therefore, a shared-nothing cluster is often implemented as a number of individual active/passive or active/active clusters to increase availability. MySQL Cluster is an example for a shared-nothing architecture.

Exploring the Main RAC Concepts

A Real Application Clusters (RAC) database is an active/active cluster employing a shared-everything architecture. To better understand what RAC is, as well as which components are employed, this chapter will introduce each of the following components involved from the bottom up:

- Cluster nodes
- Interconnect
- Oracle Grid Infrastructure
- Automatic Storage Management
- Real Application Cluster
- Global Resource Directory
- Global Cache Service
- Global Enqueue Service
- Cache Fusion

    It should be noted at this point that the software stack has evolved, and some of the concepts we discuss in this chapter have changed with Oracle 11g Release 2. We have dedicated a section at the end of this chapter to the new features; this section will provide you with a more complete picture about what's new in the latest release. Before doing that, however, let's have a closer look at each of the concepts just mentioned.

Working with Cluster Nodes

The basic building block of any cluster is the individual cluster node. In Oracle RAC, the number of nodes you can have in your cluster is version dependent. Publicly available documentation states that Oracle 10.2 Clusterware supports 100 nodes in a cluster, while 10.1 Cluster Ready Services supported 63 instances. Even though RAC-based applications continue to be available when individual nodes fail, every effort should be made to ensure that individual components in the database server don't prove to be a single point of failure (SPOF).

Hot swappable components, such as internal disks, fans, and other components should be found on the part list when procuring new hardware. Additionally, power supplies, host bus adapters, network cards, and hard disks should be redundant in the server. Where possible, components should be logically combined, either by hardware in form of RAID controllers or software. Examples of the latter would be software RAID, network bonding, or multipathing to the storage area network. Attention should also be paid to the data center, where the nodes are hosted—you should use an uninterruptible power supply, sufficient cooling, and professional racking of the servers as a matter of course. A remote lights-out management console should also be added to the item list—sometimes a node hangs for whatever reason, and it urgently needs troubleshooting or rebooting.

Leveraging the Interconnect

The cluster interconnect is one of the main features in Oracle RAC. Not only does the interconnect allow the cluster to overcome the limitations by the block pinging algorithm when transferring data blocks from one instance to another, it can also be used as a heartbeat and general communication mechanism. Interconnect failure will result in a cluster reconfiguration to prevent a split-brain situation: one or more cluster nodes will be rebooted by Grid Infrastructure.

It is possible to have a different interconnect for RAC and Grid Infrastructure, in which case you need to configure RAC to use the correct interconnect. The interconnect should always be private—no other network traffic should ever be sent across the wires. Users of RAC can choose from two technologies to implement the interconnect: Ethernet and Infiniband.

Using an Ethernet-based Interconnect

The use of 10 Gigabit Ethernet for the cluster interconnect is probably the most common setup in existence. The cluster daemons (we will cover these in detail later in this chapter) use TCP/IP as a means for communication. The Cache Fusion traffic used for cache coherence, which is different from the daemon communication, will make use of the User Datagram Protocol (UDP). UDP is found on the same transport layer as the better known Transmission Control Protocol (TCP). Where the latter is connection-oriented and uses explicit hand-shaking to guarantee that network packets arrive in order and that lost packets are retransmitted, UDP is stateless: it is a fire-and-forget protocol. UDP simply sends a packet (*datagram*) to the destination. The main advantage of UDP over TCP is that it's comparably lightweight, which is the reason it was chosen as the transport protocol.

■ **Note** Please refrain from using cross-over Ethernet cables in a two-node cluster; the cluster interconnect must be switched, so the use of cross-over cables is explicitly not supported!

Efficiency and performance of the cluster interconnect can be increased by using so-called jumbo frames. Ethernet frames come in various sizes, usually limited to 1500 bytes by what is referred to as the maximum transmission unit (MTU). The frame size determines how much data can be transported with a single Ethernet frame—the larger the frame, the higher the payload. Storing a larger payload inside an Ethernet frame means that less work must be done on the server and switch, providing more efficient communication overall. Many switches allow a higher than the standard MTU range of 1500-9000 bytes to be sent in one frame, making it a jumbo frame. Note that jumbo frames aren't routable; unfortunately, this means they can't be used on a public network. When deciding to use jumbo frames, it is important to ensure that all cluster nodes use the same MTU.

We explained in the introduction on individual database server nodes that components should be redundant, and that the network interface cards should definitely be among those redundant components. Combining multiple network ports to a logical unit is referred to as *bonding* in Linux. Unlike many other operating systems, network cards can be bonded without having to purchase additional software. A new master device, bond, will be created that enslaves two or more network cards. Once completed, the bonded network device will route all network traffic into and out of the server. You should not bond network ports of the same network interface card.

Implementing an Infiniband-based Interconnect

Infiniband is a popular implementation of a remote direct memory access architecture (RDMA). It is a high-speed interconnect commonly associated with high-performance computing (HPC) environments. According to http://openfabrics.org/, the majority of all clusters in the Top500 HPC list use this implementation. RDMA enables parallel, direct, memory-to-memory transfers between the nodes in the cluster, and it requires dedicated RDMA adapters, switches, and software. It also avoids the CPU processing and context switching overheads associated with Ethernet-based implementations.

There are two different ways to implement Infiniband interconnects on Linux. The first way is referred to as *IP over Infiniband* (IPoIB) and—speaking in greatly simplified terms—it replaces Ethernet for the media access control and link-layer control layers. Since the Internet Protocol remains, the network protocol use of IPoIB is completely transparent to applications. The IPoIB implementation offers significant performance improvements over Ethernet connections.

Another option is to use Reliable Datagram Sockets over Infiniband. This option is available beginning with Oracle 10.2.0.3. RDS is available through the Open Fabric Enterprise Distribution (OFED) for Linux and Windows, developed by the Open Fabrics Alliance. As of version 2.6.30, RDS has found its way into the Linux kernel, with Oracle playing a major role as a contributor. The key characteristics of RDS are low-latency, low-overhead, and a high bandwidth—basically, all you could ask for in RAC!

You can find a compatibility matrix available online at www.oracle.com/technology/products/database/clustering/certify/tech_generic_linux_new.html.

This matrix lists RDS as supported for Linux with QLogic/SilverStorm switches on Oracle 10.2.0.3 and newer. Open Fabrics Enterprise Distribution (OFED) 1.3.1 and newer for RDS v2 is supported from Oracle 11.1 onwards with QLogic, HP, and Voltaire switches. My Oracle Support note 751343.1 has a direct link to the required patches for Oracle Enterprise Linux/Red Hat Enterprise Linux 5. Unfortunately, there does not seem to be a deployment instruction for RDS on SuSE Linux Enterprise Server. Oracle advises customers to monitor the certification page for updates.

The Oracle Database Machine and Exadata Storage server drive the use Infiniband to the extreme, offering up to 40Gb/s for communication within the cluster, which is impossible to beat with Ethernet. An Infiniband solution has the great advantage of higher performance of than the ever-so-present Gigabit Ethernet interconnect, but it also comes at a higher cost and introduces another technology set into the data center.

Clusterware/Grid Infrastructure

Grid Infrastructure is tightly integrated with the operating system and offers the following services to RAC:

- Internode connectivity
- Cluster membership
- Messaging
- Cluster logical volume manager
- Fencing

Grid Infrastructure is required to run RAC, and it must be installed in its own, non-shared Oracle home, referred to as ORA_CRS_HOME or CRS_HOME. Oracle Grid Infrastructure will contain the binaries to run the Automatic Storage Management component, as well.

Oracle's Cluster software has gone through a number of name changes, as already indicated in other sections of this chapter, which Table 2-1 details. As we explained in this chapter's introduction, one of the purposes of clustering multiple computers is to make them appear as a single entity to the cluster's users. The cluster management software is responsible for doing exactly this, and Oracle Grid Infrastructure is remarkable because it means Oracle development has come up with unified cluster management software for all RAC-supported platforms.

Table 2-1. Oracle Cluster Software Naming

Product Name	Corresponding Version	Terminal Release	Release Date	Comments
Cluster Ready Services	10g Release 1	10.1.0.5	2003	No patch set update (PSU) is available.
Clusterware	10g Release 2	10.2.0.5	2005	The latest PSU available at the time of writing is 10.2.0.4.3; terminal release is not out yet.
Clusterware	11g Release 1	11.1.0.7	2007	11.1.0.7.2 is the latest available PSU at the time of writing.
Grid Infrastructure	11g Release 2	Not yet known	2009	11.2.0.1.1 are the latest PSUs available at the time of writing for database and Grid Infrastructure.

Until Oracle 9*i*, vendor-specific clusterware was used to provide the same services that Oracle Clusterware provides today. So why did Oracle reinvent the wheel? The foreword by one of the ASM architects in the excellent *Oracle Automatic Storage Management: Under-the-Hood & Practical Deployment Guide* by Nitin Vengurlekar et al (McGraw Hill, 2007) gives you a hint at how Oracle works internally. The foreword writer noted that Oracle was not satisfied by the cluster file systems available from third-party vendors. There was also the problem that any improvement suggested by Oracle would also benefit Oracle's competitors. Hence, Oracle came up with an entirely new product (ASM) that only the Oracle database could use.

Similar thoughts may have played a role with the creation of unified cluster management software. The use of third-party cluster software is still possible, but it's getting less and less common since Oracle's Grid Infrastructure provides a mature framework. Should you decide to use a third-party cluster solution, then Grid Infrastructure must be installed on top of that. Multi-vendor solutions, especially in the delicate area of clustering, can lead to a situation where none of the vendors takes responsibility for a problem, and each blames the other parties involved for any problems that occur. By using only one vendor, this blame-game problem can be alleviated.

Planning a RAC Installation

When planning a RAC software installation, you first install Grid Infrastructure, then the Oracle RDBMS binaries, followed by the application of the latest patches to the new installation. The install process of all Oracle-clustered components, including Grid Infrastructure, follows the same process: once the software is made available to one of the cluster nodes, you start Oracle Universal Installer. Its task is to copy and link the software on the local node first. It then copies all files needed to all the other cluster nodes specified. This saves the installer from linking components on each node. After the software is distributed to all nodes, a number of scripts need to be executed as root, initializing the Grid Infrastructure stack and optionally starting ASM to mount the predefined disk groups. Once this step is complete, the Oracle Universal Installer performs some more internal initialization tasks before running a final verification check. The Oracle Universal Installer (OUI) will prompt you for the installation of a clustered Oracle home only if the installation of Grid Infrastructure succeeded when you run OUI to install the database binaries.

You must meet a number of prerequisites before you can install Grid Infrastructure. Public and private networks need to be configured, and SSH user equivalence or password-less logins across all cluster nodes must be established. Grid Infrastructure also requires kernel parameters to be set persistently across reboots, and it checks for the existence of required software packages—mainly compiler, linker, and compatibility libraries—before the installation. A great utility, called *cluster verification tool* or *cluvfy*, assists system and database administrators in meeting these requirements. In version 11.2 of the software, some of the detected problems are fixable by running a script cluvfy generates.

Grid Infrastructure cannot be installed into a shared Oracle home: all nodes of the cluster need their own local installation. The utility cluvfy checks for this, as well as for sufficient disk space. Not being able to use a shared Oracle home for Grid Infrastructure marks a change from previous versions of Clusterware.

With the installation finished, Grid Infrastructure will start automatically with every server restart, unless specifically instructed not to.

USING A GRID IN SINGLE-INSTANCE ORACLE

The use of Grid Infrastructure is not limited to clusters—it also provides high availability to single-instance Oracle deployments, as well. The *standalone* Grid Infrastructure installation was previously called Single Instance High Availability (SIHA), but it was renamed to Oracle Restart in the public release. With Oracle Restart, you shouldn't need startup scripts to start and stop databases and services because single-instance Oracle is managed in a way very similar to RAC. For example, you get FAN events as an added benefit when services go down (unexpectedly) or as part of a Data Guard broker-controlled failover operation.

Choosing a Process Structure

Once installed, a number of daemons are used to ensure that the cluster works as expected and communication to the outside world is possible. Some of these are started with root privileges if the Linux platform requires it. For example, any change to the network configuration requires elevated rights. The other daemon processes are executed with the Grid software owner's permissions. Table 2-2 introduces the main Clusterware and Grid Infrastructure daemons.

Table 2-2. Main Clusterware/Grid Infrastructure Daemons and Their Use

Daemon process	Description
Oracle High Availability Service (OHAS)	The Oracle High Availability Service is the first Grid Infrastructure component started when a server boots. It is configured to be started by init(1), and it is responsible for spawning the agent processes.
Oracle Agent	Two oracle agents are used with Grid Infrastructure. The first one, broadly speaking, is responsible for starting a number of resources needed for accessing the OCR and voting files. It is created by the OHAS daemon.
	The second agent is created by the Cluster Ready Services Daemon (CRSD—see below), and it starts all resources that do not require root access on the operating system. The second Oracle Agent is running with the Grid Infrastructure software owner's privileges, and it takes over the tasks previously performed by the racg process in RAC 11.1.
Oracle Root Agent	Similar to the Oracle Agent, two Oracle Root Agents are created. The initial agent is spawned by OHAS, and it initializes resources for which the Linux operating system requires elevated privileges. The main daemon created is CSSD and CRSD. The Cluster Ready Services daemon CRSD in turn will start another Root agent.
	The agent will start resources that require root privileges, which are mainly network related.
Cluster Ready Services Daemon (CRSD)	The main Clusterware daemon uses the information stored in the Oracle Cluster Registry to manage resources in the cluster.
Cluster Synchronization Services Daemon (CSSD)	The CSS processes manage cluster configuration and node membership.
Oracle Process Monitor Daemon (OPROCD)	The oprocd daemon is responsible for I/O fencing in Clusterware 11.1. It was introduced for Linux with the 10.2.0.4 patch set. Before this patch set, the kernel hangcheck-timer module was responsible for similar tasks. Interestingly, oprocd had always been used on non-Linux platforms.
	Grid Infrastructure replaced oprocd with the cssdagent process.

Daemon process	Description
Event Manager Daemon (EVM)	The EVM daemon is responsible for publishing events created by Grid Infrastructure.
Cluster Time Synchronization Service (CTSS)	The CTSS service is used as an alternative to the Network Time Protocol server for cluster time synchronization, which is crucial for running RAC. The Cluster Time Synchronization Services daemon can run in two modes: observer or active. It will run in observer mode whenever NTP is available; however, it will be actively synchronizing cluster nodes against the master node it runs on in the absence of NTP.
Oracle Notification Service (ONS)	This is the primary daemon responsible for publishing events through the Fast Application Framework.

The startup sequence of Grid Infrastructure changed significantly in RAC 11.2—the startup sequence in RAC 11.1 was pretty much identical to the process in Oracle 10.2. Instead of starting cluster ready services, cluster synchronization services, and event manager directly through `inittab(5)`, the Oracle High Availability Service now takes care of creating agent processes, monitoring their siblings' health, and spawning cluster resources.

Among the non-Oracle managed daemons, NTP takes a special role. For each cluster, it is imperative to have clock synchronization, and Grid Infrastructure is no exception.

Tables 2-3 and 2-4 list the main daemons found in Clusterware 11.1 and Grid Infrastructure respectively.

Table 2-3. *Clusterware 11.1 Main Daemons*

Component	Linux Process	Comment
CRS	`crsd.bin`	Runs as root.
CSS	`init.cssd`, `ocssd`, and `ocssd.bin`	Except for `ocssd.bin`, all these components run as root.
EVM	`evmd`, `evmd.bin`, and `evmlogger`	`evmd` runs as root.
ONS	`Ons`	
ORPOCD	`oprocd`	Runs as root and provides node fencing instead of the hangcheck timer kernel module.
RACG	`racgmain`, `racgimon`	Extends clusterware to support Oracle-specific requirements and complex resources. It also runs server callout scripts when FAN events occur.

Table 2-4. Grid Infrastructure 11.2 Main Daemons

Component	Linux Process	Comment
CRS	crsd.bin	Runs as root.
CSS	ocssd.bin, cssdmonitor, and cssdagent	
CTSS	octssd.bin	Runs as root.
EVM	evmd.bin, evmlogger.bin	
Oracle Agent	oraagent.bin	
Oracle Root Agent	orarootagent	Runs as root.
Oracle High Availability Service	ohasd.bin	Runs as root through init, the mother of all other Grid Infrastructure processes.
ONS/eONS	ons/eons	ONS is the Oracle Notification Service; eONS is a java process.

The following example lists all the background processes initially started by Grid Infrastructure after a fresh installation:

```
[oracle@node1 ~]$ crsctl status resource -init -t
--------------------------------------------------------------------------------
NAME          TARGET  STATE     SERVER            STATE_DETAILS
--------------------------------------------------------------------------------
Cluster Resources
--------------------------------------------------------------------------------
ora.asm
      1       ONLINE  ONLINE    node1             Started
ora.crsd
      1       ONLINE  ONLINE    node1
ora.cssd
      1       ONLINE  ONLINE    node1
ora.cssdmonitor
      1       ONLINE  ONLINE    node1
ora.ctssd
      1       ONLINE  ONLINE    node1             OBSERVER
ora.diskmon
      1       ONLINE  ONLINE    node1
ora.drivers.acfs
      1       ONLINE  ONLINE    node1
ora.evmd
      1       ONLINE  ONLINE    node1
```

```
ora.gipcd
     1              ONLINE   ONLINE          node1
ora.gpnpd
     1              ONLINE   ONLINE          node1
ora.mdnsd
     1              ONLINE   ONLINE          node1
```

You may have noticed additional background processes in the output of this list. We'll discuss those in Chapter 8, which covers Clusterware.

Configuring Network Components

Grid Infrastructure requires a number of network addresses to work correctly:

- A public network address for each host

- A private network for each host

- A virtual (not yet assigned) IP address per host

- One to three unassigned IP addresses for the Single Client Access Name feature.

- If Grid Plug and Play is used, another non-used virtual address for the Grid Naming Service

Every host deployed on the network should already have a public IP address assigned to it that users can connect to, so that requirement is easy to satisfy. The private network has been already been discussed in this chapter's "Interconnect" section, and it's an absolute requirement for Grid Infrastructure. Again, it should be emphasized that the private interconnect is used exclusively for Grid Infrastructure/RAC Cache Fusion—adding iSCSI or NFS traffic over it does not scale well!

Node virtual IP addresses are one of the most useful additions to Oracle clustering. They need to be on the same subnet as the public IP address, and they are maintained as cluster resources within Grid Infrastructure. Let's think back to what it was like in the 9*i* days: in the case of a node failure, the public node address didn't reply to any connection requests (it couldn't because the node was down). If a client session tried to connect to the failed node, it had to wait for the operating system to time the request out, which can be a lengthy process. With the virtual IP address, things go considerably quicker: when a node fails, Grid Infrastructure fails the node's virtual IP address over to another node of the cluster. When a client connects to the failed over virtual IP address, Grid Infrastructure knows that this particular node is down and can send a reply back to the client, forcing it to try to connect to the next node in the cluster.

Another requirement calls for one to three IP addresses, regardless of the cluster size. This requirement is new to Grid Infrastructure. A new address type called *single client access name* (SCAN) abstracts from the number of nodes in the cluster. The SCAN is initiated and configured during Grid Infrastructure upgrades or installations. Before starting the installation, you need to add the IP addresses for the SCAN to DNS for a round-robin resolution to the single client access name.

In case you decide to use the Grid Naming Service, you need to allocate a virtual IP address on the public network for it.

■ **Note** The Grid Naming Service is explained in detail in the "11*g* Release 2 New Features" section later in this chapter.

Setting up Shared Grid Infrastructure Components

In addition to the software daemons mentioned previously, Grid Infrastructure uses two different types of shared devices to manage cluster resources and node membership: the so-called Oracle Cluster Registry OCR and voting disks. Oracle 11.2 introduced a new, local-only file called *Oracle Local Registry* (OLR). All these components will be explained in their respective sections later in this chapter.

Implementing the Oracle Cluster Registry and Oracle Local Registry

The first of the shared persistent parts of Grid Infrastructure is the Oracle Cluster Registry. Shared by all nodes, it contains all the information about cluster resources and permissions that Grid Infrastructure needs to operate. To be sharable, the OCR needs to be placed either on a raw device, a shared block device, a cluster file system such as OCFS2, or Automatic Storage Management. With Grid Infrastructure, the use of non-ASM storage (or alternatively, a clustered file system) for the OCR is only supported for upgraded systems. All new installations either have to use a supported clustered file system or ASM. The OCR can have one mirror in RAC 10 and 11.1, and up to five copies can be defined in Grid Infrastructure for added resilience.

The OCR is automatically backed up every four hours by Grid Infrastructure, and a number of backups are retained for recoverability. RAC 11.1 introduced the option to manually back up the Cluster Registry, and additional checks of its integrity are performed when running diagnostic utilities as the root user. Clusterware 11.1 simplified the deployment of the Cluster Registry on shared block devices through Oracle Universal Installer. Prior to this, a manual procedure for moving the OCR to block devices was needed. When using raw devices in RAC 11.1 and Red Hat 5 or SLES 10, manual configuration of the raw devices through udev was necessary. Notes on My Oracle Support explain the procedure, which differs depending upon whether single or multipathing is used to connect to shared storage.

In some rare cases, the OCR can become corrupted, in which case a restore from a backup may be needed to restore service. Depending on the severity of the corruption, it might be sufficient to restore one of the mirrors to the primary location; otherwise, a backup needs to be restored. The administration and maintenance of the OCR is only supported through the use Oracle-supplied utilities—dumping and modifying the contents of the OCR directly will result in Oracle support refusing to help you with your configuration problem.

An additional cluster configuration file has been introduced with Oracle 11.2, the so-called *Oracle Local Registry* (OLR). Each node has its own copy of the file in the Grid Infrastructure software home. The OLR stores important security contexts used by the Oracle High Availability Service early in the start sequence of Clusterware. The information in the OLR and the Grid Plug and Play configuration file are needed to locate the voting disks. If they are stored in ASM, the discovery string in the GPnP profile will be used by the cluster synchronization daemon to look them up. Later in the Clusterware boot sequence, the ASM instance will be started by the cssd process to access the OCR files; however, their location is stored in the /etc/ocr.loc file, just as it is in RAC 11.1. Of course, if the voting files and OCR are on a shared cluster file system, then an ASM instance is not needed and won't be started unless a different resource depends on ASM.

Configuring Voting Disks

Voting disks are the second means of implementing intercluster communication, in addition to the cluster interconnect. If a node fails to respond to the heartbeat requests of the other nodes within a countdown-threshold, the non-responsive node will eventually be evicted from the cluster.

Similar to the Oracle Cluster Registry, the voting disk and all of its mirrors (up to 15 voting disks are supported in Grid Infrastructure, vs. three in Clusterware 11.1) need to be on shared storage. Raw devices, a clustered-file system, or Automatic Storage Management are possible locations for the voting disks. Again, and this is exactly the same as with the OCR, not storing the voting disks in a clustered file system or ASM in Grid Infrastructure is supported only for upgraded systems. Block and raw device support for these files will be deprecated in Oracle 12.

It is strongly recommended by Oracle to use at least three voting disks located in different locations. This is for resilience. When using ASM to store the voting disks, you need to pay attention to the redundancy level of the disk group and the failure groups available. Note that all copies of the voting disk will be in only one disk group—you can't spread the voting disks over multiple disk groups. With an external redundancy disk group, you can only have exactly one voting disk, a number that can't be increased by specifying multiple disk groups with external redundancy. Disk groups with normal redundancy need at least three failure groups to be eligible for storing exactly three voting disks; high redundancy is more flexible because it lets you support up to five voting disks.

Leveraging Automatic Storage Management

Automatic Storage Management was introduced to the RAC software stack as part of Oracle 10*g* Release 1. Oracle ASM is a cluster-aware logical volume manager for Oracle's physical database structures. Files that can be stored in ASM include control files, database files, and online redo logs. Until 11*g* Release 2, it was not possible to store any binaries or other type of operating system files—neither was it a suitable option for installing a shared Oracle home.

■ **Note** The complete list of files supported by ASM changes from release to release. You can find the current list in the "Administering Oracle ASM Files, Directories, and Templates" chapter in the *Storage Administrator's Guide*. The short version is this: you can store anything but plain text (e.g., traces, logs, and audit files), classic export, and core dump files.

ASM is built around the following central concepts:

- ASM disk

- Failure groups

- ASM disk groups

A number of individual ASM disks—either physical hard drives or external storage provided to the database server—form an ASM disk group. There is an analogy with LVM in that ASM disks correspond with physical volumes (see the *PV* in Figure 2-1). ASM disks sharing a common point of failure such as a disk controller can be grouped in a failure group for which there is no equivalent in LVM. An ASM disk group can be used to store physical database structures: data files, control files, online redo logs and other file types. In contrast to Linux's logical volume manager, LVM2, no logical volumes are created on top of a disk group. Instead, all files belonging to a database are logically grouped into a directory in the disk group. Similarly, a file system is not needed; this explains why ASM has a performance advantage over the classic LVM/file system setup (see Figure 2-1 for a comparison of LVM2 and ASM).

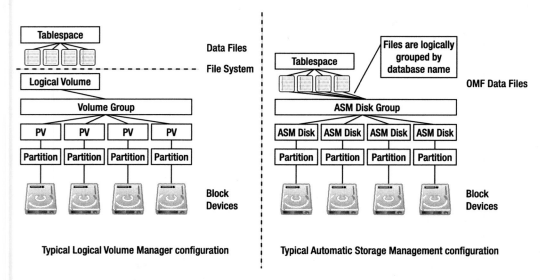

Figure 2-1. A comparison between Linux LVM and Automatic Storage Management

The restriction to store general purpose files has been lifted in Grid Infrastructure, which introduces the ASM Cluster File System (ACFS). We will discuss this in more detail in the "11*g* Release 2 New Features" section later in this chapter. ASM uses a stripe-and-mirror-everything approach for optimal performance.

The use of ASM and ACFS is not limited to clusters; single-instance Oracle can benefit greatly from it, as well. In fact, with Oracle Restart, the standalone incarnation of Grid Infrastructure will provide ASM as an added benefit—there is no longer any reason to shy away from this technology. Initially met with skepticism by many administrators, this technology has (at least partly) moved responsibility for storage from the storage administrators to the Oracle database administrator.

Technically, Oracle Automatic Storage Management is implemented as a specific type of Oracle instance—it has its own SGA, but no persistent dictionary. In RAC, each cluster node has its own ASM instance—and only one. When starting, each instance will detect the ASM disk group resources in Grid Infrastructure, through an initialization parameter in Clusterware. Each instance will then mount those disk groups. With the correct permissions granted—ASM 11.2 introduced Access Control Lists (ACLs)—databases can access their data files. Using ASM requires using Oracle Managed Files (OMF), which implies a different way of managing database files. Initialization parameters in the RDBMS instance such as db_create_file_dest and db_create_online_dest_n, as well as db_recovery_file_dest to an extent, define which disk group data files, online redo logs/control files and files for the flash recovery area are created. When requesting the creation of a new file, Oracle Managed Files will create a filename based on the following format:

```
+diskGroupName/dbUniqueName/file_type/file_type_tag.file.incarnation
```

ame might look like this:

```
293.699134381
```

...ed way of storing the database in Standard Edition RAC. This shows that
...ly. ASM allows you to perform many operations online; as an added benefit,
...upgraded in a rolling fashion, minimizing the impact on the database

...v partition level; LVM2 logical volumes should be avoided for production
...ASM is supported over NFS, as well. However, instead of mounting the
...ler directly, zero-padded files created by the *dd* utility have to be used as
...FS, you should also check with your vendor for best practice documents. We
...NFS for ASM for reasons of practicality.
...al requirements, such as very large databases with 10TB and more of data,
...e extent sizes defined on the disk group level. A common storage
...ves using only the outer regions of disk platters, which offer better
...he platter. ASM Intelligent Data Placement allows administrators to define
...regions with greater speed and bandwidth. Frequently accessed files can be specifically placed into
these areas for overall improved performance. Hard disk manufacturers are going to ship hard disks with
4k sector sizes soon, increasing storage density in the race for ever faster and larger disks. ASM is
prepared for this, and it provides a new attribute for disk groups called *sector size* that can be set to either
512bytes or 4096bytes.

A typical workflow for most installations begins with the storage administrator presenting the
storage to be used for the ASM disk to all cluster nodes. The system administrator creates partitions for
the new block devices and adds necessary configuration into the multipathing configuration. Either
ASMLib or udev can be used to indicate the new partitioned block device as a candidate disk. After
handover to the database team, the Oracle administrator uses the new ASM disk in a disk group. All of
these operations can be performed online without having to reboot the server.

Working with ASM Disks

An *ASM disk* is the basic building block of ASM. A *disk* is a shared block device presented to all nodes of
the cluster, and it is made available to the ASM instance either as a raw device or through the services of
ASMLib. ASM disks are generally multipathed, but they can also be single-pathed.

The use of raw devices is only supported in Oracle 11.1; the Oracle 11.2 documentation explicitly
states that raw devices are deprecated. Oracle follows the Linux kernel developers who officially
deprecated raw devices with kernel 2.6. Presenting ASM disks to the database servers can be difficult at
times. From an administration point of view the use of ASMLib is far easier to use than raw devices.
Regardless of which method is used, the new LUN is recognized as a candidate for addition into an ASM
disk group.

As soon as an ASM candidate disk is added to a disk group, meta information is written into its
header. This allows the ASM instance to recognize the disk and to mount it as part of a disk group.

Disk failure is a common occurrence when dealing with storage arrays. Individual hard disks are
mechanical devices that undergo high levels of usage. It's normal for them to fail. In most cases, a
storage array uses protection levels to mirror disk contents or uses parity information to reconstruct a
failed disk's data.

Disk failures in ASM are not very common because most deployments will use LUNs with storage
array protection. However, should a disk fail in an ASM protected disk group, urgency is required to
replace the failed disk to prevent it from being dropped. A new parameter introduced in ASM 11.1 called

disk repair time allows administrators to fix transient disk failures without incurring a full rebalance operation. A rebalance operation occurs when a disk is added or (forcibly) removed from an ASM disk group, restriping the contents of the disk groups across the new number of ASM disks in the disk group. Depending on the size of the ASM disk group, this rebalancing can be a lengthy operation. If the administrators are lucky enough to get the ASM disk back into the disk group before rebalancing occurs, the resilvering of the disk group is magnitudes faster because a only dirty region log needs to be applied to the disk, instead of a full rebalance operation.

Depending on the storage backend used, the LUN can either be protected internally on the array by a RAID level, or it can be an aggregation of unprotected storage (*JBOD*). This has implications for the protection on the ASM disk group level; we will discuss this topic next.

PRESENTING ASM DISKS: UDEV AND ASMLIB

ASMLib and udev(7) both address the problem of device name persistence. In Linux, the order in which devices are detected and enumerated is not static. This is in contrast to Solaris, for example, where the disk device names (cxtxdxpx) do not change unless a disk is physically moved within the array. A reconfiguration on the storage array can prove a big problem in Linux if no multipathing software is used: a device previously presented to the operating system as /dev/sda can be mapped as /dev/sdg after a reboot, simply because it has been detected a little later than during the last boot. Raw device mappings based on a device name are bound to fail.

Enter *udev* to the rescue. In udev, an integral part of the Linux operating system, rules are defined to leverage the fact that a SCSI device's world-wide-ID (WWID) does not change. The rule creates a mapping—it defines that device /dev/raw/raw1 will always be mapped to the LUN with SCSI ID abcd. The main problem with udev is that its configuration is not intuitive or easy to use. The udev configuration needs to be maintained by the administrator on all nodes of the cluster because udev doesn't replicate its configuration.

This problem does not exist for multipathed storage, where another software layer (e.g., the device-mapper-multipath package) or vendor-specific software might create a logical device combining each path to the storage.

ASMLib takes another approach. The ASMLib tools are freely available for download from http://oss.oracle.com, and they make the administration of ASM disks very easy. ASMLib consists of three RPMs: a kernel module, the actual ASMLib, and support tools. Before making use of a LUN as an ASM disk, you use the ASMLib tools to stamp it, which you accomplish by assigning a name to the LUN that writes meta information into the disk header. ASM will then be able to identify the new LUN as a potential candidate for addition to an ASM disk group. During a reboot, ASMLib will scan the system for ASM disks and will identify all of those presented to the operating system, regardless of the disk's physical device name assigned during the boot process. This ensures device-name stability at a very low cost.

ASMLib will explicitly use asynchronous I/O, but it doesn't make this visible through populating the kio-buffers in the kernel memory structures. As we said before, ASMLib is a kernel module, and it allocates its memory structures internally; unfortunately, it does not populate the slabinfo file in the proc file system. It can deal with single- and multipathing configurations.

Exploiting ASM Disk Groups

When all ASM disks are made available to the operating system—for simplicity, we assume this is accomplished through ASMLib—we can use them. Multiple ASM disks can be aggregated to disk groups, just as in classical LVM, where multiple physical volumes are aggregated into volume groups. Like LVM volume groups, disk groups can be named and take attributes. Depending on the protection level of the individual ASM disk/LUN, three different redundancy levels can be defined:

- External redundancy
- Normal redundancy
- High redundancy

When creating a disk group with external redundancy, ASM will assume that the storage array takes care of protection from individual hard disk failure, and it won't perform any mirroring. However, it will stripe extents of a default size of 1M across all ASM disks available to the disk group. A write error to an ASM disk will force the disk to be dismounted. This has severe implications because no copies of the extents stored on the disk are available, and the whole disk group becomes unavailable.

With normal redundancy ASM will stripe and mirror each extent. For each extent written to disk, another extent will be written into another failure group to provide redundancy. With ASM 11.2, individual files can be defined to be triple-mirrored; two-way mirroring is the default. Normal redundancy can tolerate the failure of one ASM disk in the disk group.

Even higher protection is available with high redundancy, which provides triple-mirroring by default. With triple-mirroring, two additional copies of the primary extent are created. The loss of two ASM disks can be tolerated in disk groups with high redundancy.

Configuring Failure Groups

Failure groups are a logical grouping of disks that fail in their entirety if a component fails. For example, the disks belonging to a single SCSI controller form a failure group—should the controller fail, all disks will become unavailable. Failure groups are used by ASM to store mirror copies of data in normal and high redundancy disk groups. If not explicitly configured, each ASM disk forms its own failure group.

Normal redundancy disk groups need to consist of at least two failure groups, while high redundancy disk groups require at least three fail groups. However, it is recommended that you use more than the minimum number of fail groups for additional data protection.

ASM by default reads the primary extent from an ASM disk group. In extended distance clusters (see Chapter 3), this could cause a performance penalty if the primary extent is on the remote storage array. ASM 11.1 addresses this problem by introducing a preferred mirror read: each ASM instance can be instructed to read the local copy of the extent, regardless of whether it's a primary or copied extent.

Weighing Your ASM Installation and Administration Options

Until Oracle 11.1, the best practice was to install ASM as a separate set of binaries. This offered the advantage of being able to upgrade Clusterware and ASM independently of the database. For example, Clusterware and ASM could be upgraded to 11.1.0.7 while the database remained on the base release. If adhered to, this best practice resulted in a typical three Oracle home installation:

- Clusterware

- Automatic Storage Management

- Database

If required, ASM 11.1 can be installed under a different operating system account than the one used for the installation of the RDBMS binaries. Oracle accounted for the fact that role separation between the database and storage administrators is common practice on many sites.

ASM is administered either through SQL*Plus, Enterprise Manager (dbconsole), or the Database Configuration Assistant (dbca). A major surprise awaited the early adopters of Oracle 11g Release 2: ASM is now part of Grid Infrastructure, both for single-instance and RAC environments. A new configuration assistant—asmca—has taken over and extended the functionality the database configuration assistant offered in 11.1. ASM can no longer be started out of the RDBMS Oracle home, either. The new ASM configuration assistant adds support for another new ASM feature called *ASM Cluster File System*; we will discuss this feature in more detail in the "Oracle 11.2 New Features" section.

The introduction of ASM to an Oracle environment—whether single instance or RAC—frequently devolves into a political debate, rather than remaining focused around what ASM can do for the business. Storage administrators often struggle to relinquish control over the presentation of storage from the fabric to Oracle DBAs. Role separation has been made possible with the introduction of a new super-user role called *SYSASM*, as opposed to the *SYSDBA* role we're familiar with since Oracle 9i. You can tie the SYSASM privilege to a different role than the SYSOPER or SYSDBA users.

Installing Real Application Clusters

With the setup and configuration of Grid Infrastructure completed, it is time to turn our attention towards the clustered Oracle software installation. As we just saw, Grid Infrastructure provides the framework for running RAC, including intercluster communication links, node fencing, node-membership services, and much more. Automatic Storage Management is Oracle's preferred way of storing the database. RAC uses all of these concepts and extends the basic services where necessary. In the following sections, we will discuss installation considerations for RAC; the difference between RAC and single-instance Oracle storage considerations for the RAC database; and finally, Cache Fusion and internal RAC metadata information.

Sorting Through Your Installation Options

After a successful Grid Infrastructure/Clusterware installation, Oracle Universal Installer will detect that a cluster is present and will offer the option to install the binaries with the RAC option on the entire cluster or a user-defined subset of the cluster. This is the easy part of the installation process. The Grid Infrastructure installation was the hard part, and now it is time to relax a little. It is good practice to use cluvfy, the cluster-verification tool, to check that all the requirements for the RDBMS installation are fulfilled. Just as with the cluster layer, Oracle Universal Installer will copy and link the software on the first node and then push the Oracle home to the other nodes specified in the installation setup.

Unlike Grid Infrastructure, Oracle RDBMS binaries can be installed on a shared file system such as OCFS2 or the brand new ASM Cluster File System ACFS, which has its own set of advantages and disadvantages. The addition of new nodes to the cluster is simplified because no new software has to be installed on the new node. Patching will be simplified as well—only one Oracle home has to be patched. However, patches cannot be installed in a rolling fashion, so downtime is inevitable.

For some time now, Oracle has used Oracle Configuration Manager (OCM) to simplify the integration of systems with My Oracle Support. Creation of service requests can use the information transmitted by OCM to fill in information about the system; previously, this was tedious at best after the fifth request for the same system has been filed. OCM can operate in an offline and online mode, depending on the security policy on the customer's site. Oracle claims that the information transmitted by OCM can speed up resolutions to service requests. In the relevant section, all you need to supply is a login to My Oracle Support and a password. It's probably good practice to create a dedicated account in My Oracle Support for this purpose.

During the installation process, Oracle Universal Installer will prompt the administrator to create/upgrade a database or install just the binaries. If patch sets are to be installed as soon as Oracle 11.2.0.2 is out, it is prudent to install the binaries only, patch the setup, and then create the database.

Choosing Between a Single Instance and a RAC Database

An Oracle RAC database is different from a single instance database in a number of key aspects. Remember that in RAC, a single database on shared storage is concurrently accessed by multiple database instances on different server hosts. Database files, online redo log files, control files and server parameter files must all be shared. Additionally, flashback logs, archived redo logs, a Data Pump dump, and Data Guard broker configuration files can also be shared, depending on your configuration—this is optional, but it's also highly recommended. When using ASM, you will also find a local parameter file (*pfile*) on each RAC instance pointing to the server parameter file in its respective disk group. Another locally stored file is the Oracle password file. Users of a cluster file system usually keep these files in a shared location with instance-specific symbolic links to $ORACLE_HOME/dbs.

As you will see in the following sections, a RAC database also contains all the structures you expect to find in single-instance Oracle databases, extending them to take the database's special needs for cluster operations into account.

Working with Database Files

Database files contain all the data belonging to the database, including tables, indexes, the data dictionary, and compiled PL/SQL code, to mention just a few. In a RAC database, there is only one copy of each data file that is located on shared storage and can be concurrently accessed by all instances. The data files are identical to those found in a single-instance database. Datafiles are not mirrored by Oracle by default. Most users choose to implement redundancy at the storage level to prevent the loss of datafiles due to media failure. Oracle Automatic Storage Management can provide redundancy in case the storage array does not provide this facility.

Storing Information in Control Files

As you know, the control files store information about the physical structures of the database, as well as their status. Depending on your use of the Recovery Manager RMAN, the controlfile can also contain information about RMAN backups in the absence of a dedicated RMAN catalog database. In single-instance Oracle and RAC, control files should be mirrored to provide protection against corruption and storage failures. When using ASM together with a flash recovery area, this multiplexing is automatically done for you. By default, Oracle multiplexes the control file to the disk group specified by the db_create_file_dest initialization parameter and the flash recovery area specified by the db_recovery_file_dest parameter. The control_files parameter, which indicates the location of the control files and all copies, is automatically updated for you when using a server parameter file in this case. Be aware that control files can become a point of contention in RAC because they are frequently updated. So be sure not to mirror too many copies of the controlfile and also locate them on fast storage.

Leveraging Online Redo Logs and Archiving

In RAC, each database instance has its own set of online redo log files, called a *thread*. Online redo log files are aggregated into groups within their instance's thread. In case you were wondering: single-instance Oracle behaves the same way, although you do not normally notice it! Thread 1 belongs to the instance (there is a one to one mapping between instance and database in this setup). Information about the thread number is available in V$LOG and related views.

You need two groups of online redo logs per thread, and you should also consider manually multiplexing the groups' members if not using ASM and a flash recovery area. The mapping between the instance and the thread is performed in the server parameter file: the initialization parameter "thread" maps the thread number to the instance. The convention is to map instance n is mapped to thread n; however, this is not required. In other words, you will find prod1.thread=1 in the spfile. An additional online redo thread is required when adding an instance to the cluster—this can be done in one of two ways. First, the administrator can use the alter database add logfile group x thread y SQL command in administrator-managed databases. Second, it can be done automatically by Oracle in policy-managed databases. A thread also needs to be enabled to be used by Oracle.

■ **Note** A policy-managed database is a new way of managing a RAC database; it is explained in more detail in the "11.2 New Features" section later in this chapter.

Online redo logs in RAC function just as they do in single-instance Oracle. The lgwr background process flushes the redo buffer, a part of the SGA, to the online redo logs that belong to the instance the transaction was committed. Online redo logs need to be on fast storage, or they might become a point of contention, especially for systems with high commit rates. A common tuning techniques applied to poorly designed applications is to reduce the commit rate and to move at least the online redo logs and control files to fast storage, eliminating some of the worst performance bottlenecks. Systems with a high log switch rate can benefit from additional redo log groups per thread to give the archiver process more time to archive the used online redo log. This technique is also beneficial in situations when the archiver is responsible for shipping an archived redo log to a standby database; however, most modern systems use the Log Network Service (LNSn) process to asynchronously send a redo to the standby database's Remote File Server (RFS) process. There is one LNS process per destination in Oracle 10.2 and 11.1. In Oracle 11.2, the LNSn processes were replaced by the NSSn and NSAn background processes. The NSSn process will be used for synchronous shipping of redo; likewise, NSAn will be used for asynchronous shipping of redo. The size of each individual online redo log should be such that log switches don't occur too frequently—the Automatic Workload Repository, or *statspack reports*, help administrators identify an appropriate size for the online redo logs. Oracle 11.2 even allows administrators to choose the block size of online redo logs, accounting for the fact that modern storage units use 4kb sector sizes instead of 512b.

In case of an instance failure in RAC, which you'll learn more about in Chapter 3, all threads are merged to help create the recovery set for the roll-forward/roll-back operation performed by the server monitor process.

Once filled by the `lgwr` process, one of the `archiver` processes will copy the used online redo log to the specified destination.

■ **Note** You are correct if you're thinking that the `archiver` process copies redo logs only if the database is in archive log mode; however, we can't think of a RAC production database that does not operate in this mode!

The flash recovery area introduced with Oracle 10*g* Release 1 seems to be the favorite destination for archived redo logs. If you are not using one, we recommend storing the archived redo logs on a shared-file system that is accessible to all nodes. As with single-instance Oracle, the archived logs are essential for a point in time recovery processes. The difference between RAC and single instance deployments is that in RAC, Oracle needs all the archived logs from all threads of the database. You can verify that Oracle is using all log files for each thread in the alert log of the instance that performs media recovery.

Managing Undo Tablespaces

Similar to online redo log threads, each cluster database instance has its own undo tablespace. Again, the 1:1 mapping between the instance and the undo tablespace name is performed in the server parameter file. This mapping doesn't mean that the undo tablespace is permanently tied only to the instance. All other instances can access the undo tablespace to create read-consistent images of blocks.

When adding a new instance to the cluster, an additional undo tablespace needs to be created and mapped to the new instance, the same requirement that applies to the online redo logs. In the case of policy-managed databases, Oracle does this for you; otherwise, the administrator has to take care of this task.

Although it is still possible to use manual undo management, we strongly recommend using Automatic Undo Management (AUM).

Weighing Storage Options for RAC Databases

An Oracle RAC database has to be stored on shared storage, as discussed previously. Administrators can choose from the following options:

- *Automatic Storage Management*: This is Oracle's preferred storage option and the only supported configuration for RAC Standard Edition.

- *Oracle Cluster File System 2* (OCFS2). A POSIX compliant cluster file system developed by Oracle to store arbitrary files

- *Raw Devices*: We recommend not using raw devices; not only are they deprecated in the Linux kernel, but they are also deprecated with Oracle 11.2.

- *Network File System*: This checks the certification matrix on My Oracle Support for support of your NFS filer.

- *Red Hat Global File System*: This is supported for Red Hat and Oracle Enterprise Linux only; it can be used for the Flash Recovery Area and database files alike.

It should be pointed out that Oracle recommends Automatic Storage Management for use with RAC in all parts of the documentation. Judging by the fact that ASM receives numerous improvements in each new release, it's probably a good time to get started with the technology, if you haven't already done so.

OCFS2 was discussed in more detail in Chapter 1; it is a POSIX-compliant file system for Linux kernel 2.6 and newer. It overcomes many of the initial OCFS limitations and allows users to store binaries and database files needed for RAC. Interestingly, Oracle RAC 11.2 also supports the use of Red Hat's (formerly Sistina's) Global File System.

■ **Note** If you are planning to use a RAC over NFS, your filer needs to be explicitly supported by Oracle.

Drilling Down on a RAC Database Instance

A RAC database consists of two or more instances. Each instance usually resides on a different cluster node and consists of a superset of the shared memory structures and background processes used to support single-instance databases.

It is possible to install RAC on only one node for testing, without having to pay for the interconnect hardware or shared storage; however, such a setup is not recommended for production. Even though only a single database instance is used and no data will be shipped over an interconnect, operations routinely performed have to go through additional code paths not required for a single-instance database, which creates overhead.

■ **Note** Not all nodes of a RAC database have to be up and running-the ability to run on a subset of physical nodes is integral to the instance recovery process and cluster database startup.

Each instance has its own set of shared memory called *Shared Global Area* (SGA), and it is allocated at instance startup. The SGA is comprised of multiple sub-pools and a fixed portion that is platform dependent. The buffer cache, shared pool, log buffer, streams, and many other pools take up the memory of the SGA. For some time now, Oracle has introduced technologies to automatically manage and tune the different SGA components. Oracle 10*g* gave administrators Automatic Shared Memory Management to handle most of the SGA components. Oracle 11 also introduced Automatic Memory Management (AMM) to handle the Program Global Area (PGA) in the set of automatically managed memory. However, AMM is not compatible with Linux huge pages, which can be a problem for systems with large memory.

Oracle has to synchronize access to shared memory locally and across the cluster. You might recall that, thanks to the RAC technology stack, all database instances can access other database instances' SGAs.

The methods employed by the Oracle kernel to protect shared memory in RAC are not different from single-instance Oracle. Latches and locks are used in both cases. A *latch* is a low level, lightweight serialization device. Processes trying to acquire a latch do not queue—if a latch cannot be obtained, a process will *spin*. Spinning means that the process will enter a tight loop to prevent being taken off the CPU by the operating system's scheduler. Executing a tight loop should prevent the process from being taken off the CPU. If the latch still can't be acquired, the process will eventually sleep and try again at regular intervals. Latches are local to the instance; however, there are no cluster wide latches.

On the other hand, locks are obtained for a longer period, and they are more sophisticated than the simple latch we just discussed. Locks can be shared or exclusive—with interim stages—and processes trying to acquire locks will have to wait on a first in, first out (FIFO) basis. Access to locks is controlled by so-called enqueues, which maintain a list of processes waiting for access to a given resource. Unlike latches, enqueues are maintained cluster wide.

Locking and latching are well known and understood in single-instance Oracle; however, the requirements for cache coherency in Oracle RAC mean that locking and latching are significantly more complex in RAC. As with single-instance Oracle, access to data blocks in the buffer cache and enqueues must be managed within the local instance; however, access by remote instances must be managed, as well. For this reason, Oracle uses the Global Resource Directory (GRD) and a number of additional background processes.

■ **Note** Oracle has amended V$-views for cluster-wide use by adding an instance identifier to each view and renaming it to *GV$*. Think of a GV$ view as a global view that encompasses the dynamic performance views from all instances in the cluster.

Using the Global Resource Directory (GRD)

Additional background processes are used in Real Application Clusters for cache synchronization—remember that RAC uses the Cache Fusion architecture to simulate a global SGA across all cluster nodes. Access to blocks in the buffer cache needs to be coordinated for read consistency and write access, and enqueues to shared resources are now global across the cluster. These two main concepts are implemented in the Global Cache Service (GCS), for accessing the common buffer cache; and the Global Enqueue Service (GES), for managing enqueues in the cluster.

Both GCS and GES work transparently to applications. The meta structure used internally is the previously mentioned Global Resource Directory (GRD), which is maintained by the GCS and GES processes. The GRD is distributed across all nodes in the cluster and part of the SGA, which is why the SGA of a RAC database is larger than a single instance's equivalent. Resource management is negotiated by GCS and GES. As a result, a particular resource is managed by exactly one instance, referred to as the resource master. Resource mastering is not static, however. Oracle 9*i* Release 2 (to a degree) and subsequent versions of Oracle implemented dynamic resource mastering (DRM). In releases prior to Oracle 9*i* Release 2, resource premastering would only happen during instance failure, when the GRD was reconstructed. Resource mastering in newer releases can happen if Oracle detects that an instance different from the resource master accesses a certain resource more than a given number of times during a particular interval. In this case, the resource will be remastered to the other node. Many users have reported problems with dynamic remastering, which can add undesired overhead if it happens too frequently. Should this happen, DRM can be deactivated.

■ **Note** The GRD also records which resource is mastered by which instance—a fact that will come in very handy during recovery, should an instance fail.

Figure 2-2 provides an overview of how the GCS and GES background processes work hand-in-hand to maintain the GRD; other RAC background processes have been left out intentionally.

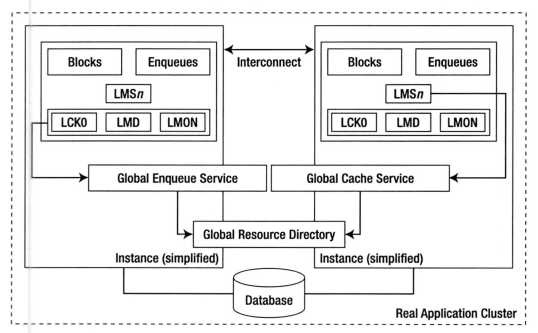

Figure 2-2. *The Global Resource Directory in the context of Global Enqueue Services and Global Cache Services*

Maintaining Cache Coherence with Global Cache Services (GCS)

The Global Cache Service uses the LMS*n* background processes to maintain cache coherency in the global buffer cache. As we already discussed in Chapter 1, multiple copies (but only one current version!) of the same block can exist in the global SGA .GCS keeps track of the status and the location of data blocks. GCS will also ship blocks across the interconnect to remote instances.

Managing Global Enqueues with Global Enqueue Services (GES)

Similar to GCS, which works on the block level, GES manages global enqueues in the cluster. As a rule of thumb, if an operation doesn't involve mastering/transferring blocks within the global buffer cache, then it is most likely handled by GES. The Global Enqueue Service is responsible for all inter-instance resource operations, such as global management of access to the dictionary and library cache or transactions. It also performs intercluster deadlock detection. It tracks the status of all Oracle enqueue mechanisms for resources that are accessed by more than one instance. The Global Enqueue Service Monitor (LMON) and Global Enqueue Service Daemon (LMD) form part of the Global Enqueue Services.

The Lock Process (LCK0) process mentioned in Figure 2-2 is responsible for non-Cache Fusion access, such as library and row cache requests.

Transferring Data Between Instances with Cache Fusion

Cache Fusion is the most recent evolution of inter-instance data transfer in Oracle. Instead of using the block ping mechanism implemented through Oracle 8*i*, Oracle uses a fast interconnect to transfer data blocks for reads and writes across all cluster nodes.

⧉ **Note** Cache Fusion was partially implemented in Oracle 8*i* as well, but completed in 9*i* Release 1, which also saw the rebranding of Oracle Parallel Server to Real Application Clusters.

The block ping method of transferring blocks between instances was hugely expensive; at the time, it was strongly advised that you tie workloads to instances to ensure a minimum amount of inter-instance block transfer. In Oracle Parallel Server, when an instance other than the one holding a current block requested the current block for modification, it signaled that request to the holding instance, which in turn wrote the block to disk, signaling that the block could be read. The amount of communication and the write/read operation to disk were hugely undesirable.

Cache Fusion block transfers rely on the Global Resource Directory, and they never require more than three hops, depending on the setup and the number of nodes. Obviously, if there are only two cluster nodes, then there will be a two-way cache transfer. For more than two nodes, a maximum of three hops will be necessary. Oracle has instrumented communication involving the cache with dedicated wait events ending either in two-way or three-way cache transfers, depending on the scenario.

When an instance requests a data block through Cache Fusion, it first contacts the resource master to ascertain the current status of the resource. If the resource is not currently in use, it can be acquired locally by reading from the disk. If the resource is currently in use, then the resource master will request that the holding instance passes the resource to the requesting resource. If the resource is subsequently required for modification by one or more instances, the GRD will be modified to indicate that the resource is held globally. The resource master, requesting, and holding instance can all be different, in which case the maximum of three hops must be used to get the block.

The previously mentioned two-way and three-way block transfers are related to how resources are managed. In case the resource master holds the requested resource, then the request for the block can be satisfied immediately and the block shipped, which is a two-way communication. In a three-way scenario, the requestor, resource master, and holder of the block are different—the resource master needs to forward the request, introducing a new hop.

From this discussion, you can imagine that the effort to coordinate blocks and their images in the global buffer cache is not to be underestimated. In a RAC database, Cache Fusion usually represents both the most significant benefit and the most significant cost. The benefit is that Cache Fusion theoretically allows scale-up, potentially achieving near-linear scalability. However, the additional workload imposed by Cache Fusion can be in the range of 10% to 20%.

Achieving Read Consistency

One of the main characteristics of the Oracle database is the ability to simultaneously provide different views of data. This characteristic is called *multi-version read consistency*. Queries will be read consistently; writers won't block readers, and vice versa. Of course, multi-version read consistency also holds true for RAC databases, but a little more work is involved.

The *System Change Number* is an Oracle internal timestamp that is crucial for read consistency. If the local instance requires a read-consistent version of a block, it contacts the block's resource master to ascertain if a version of the block that has the same SCN, or if a more recent SCN exists in the buffer cache of any remote instance. If such a block exists, then the resource master will send a request to the relevant remote instance to forward a read-consistent version of the block to the local instance. If the remote instance is holding a version of the block at the requested SCN, it sends the block immediately. If the remote instance is holding a newer version of the block, it creates a copy of the block, called a *past image*, applies undo to the copy to revert it to the correct SCN; and sends it over the interconnect.

Synchronizing System Change Numbers

System Change Numbers are internal time stamps generated and used by the Oracle database. All events happening in the database are assigned SCNs, and so are transactions. The implementation Oracle uses to allow read consistency relies heavily on SCNs and information in the undo tablespaces to produce read-consistent information. System change numbers needs to be in sync across the cluster. Two different schemes to keep SCNs current on all cluster nodes are used in Real Application Clusters: the *broadcast-on-commit* scheme and the *Lamport* scheme.

The broadcast-on-commit scheme is the default scheme in 10*g* Release 2 and newer; it addresses a known problem with the Lamport scheme. Historically, the Lamport scheme was the default scheme—it promised better scalability as SCN propagation happened as part of other (not necessarily related) cluster communication and not immediately after a commit is issued on a node. This was deemed sufficient in most situations by Oracle, and documents available on My Oracle Support seem to confirm this. However, there was a problem with the Lamport scheme: It was possible for SCNs of a node to lag behind another node's SCNs—especially if there was little messaging activity. The lagging of system change numbers meant that committed transactions on a node were "seen" a little later by the instance lagging behind.

On the other hand, the broadcast-on-commit scheme is a bit more resource intensive. The log writer process LGWR updates the global SCN after every commit and broadcasts it to all other instances. The deprecated max_commit_propagation_delay initialization parameter allowed the database administrator to influence the default behavior in RAC 11.1; the parameter has been removed in Oracle 11.2.

Exploring the New Features of 11*g* Release 2

The final section of this chapter provides an overview of the most interesting new features introduced with Oracle 11*g* Release 2, both for Grid Infrastructure and for RAC. Many of these have already been mentioned briefly in previous sections in this chapter, as well as in Chapter 1.

Leveraging Grid Plug and Play

Many new features in 11*g* Release 2 aim to make maintenance tasks in Oracle RAC simpler, and Grid Plug and Play (GPnP) is no exception. It seems to the authors that another design goal of Oracle software is to provision support for tasks and services that were traditionally performed outside the DBA department. Simplifying the addition of cluster nodes to provide true grid computing where computing power is a utility seems to have also been a contributing factor to the design decisions made with RAC 11.2. There is a big demand in the industry for consolidation. Making maximum use of existing hardware resources has become very important, and RAC is well suited for this role. Grid Plug And Play helps administrators maintaining the cluster. For example, a number of manual steps previously required when adding or removing nodes from a cluster are automated with GPnP.

■ **Note** GPnP focuses on the Grid Infrastructure layer—it does not address the addition of instances to a RAC databases. Adding and removing nodes to or from a RAC database is done through server pools.

Grid Plug and Play is not a monolithic concept; rather, it relies on several other new features:

- Storing cluster information in a XML configuration file

- Cluster time synchronization (CTSS)

- The Grid Naming Service (GNS)

- Single Client Access Name (SCAN)

- Server Pools

Grid Plug and Play works behind the scenes. You will most likely notice the absence of configuration dialogs when performing cluster maintenance. For example, you won't be prompted for information such as a new node's name or its virtual IP address.

GPnP defines a node's meta data-network interfaces for public and private interconnect, the ASM server parameter file, and CSS voting disks. The profile, an XML file, is protected by a wallet against modification. If you have to manually modify the profile, it must first be unsigned with $GRID_HOME/bin/gpnptool, modified, and then signed again with the same utility. Don't worry, though; the profile is automatically updated without administrator intervention when using cluster management tools such as oifcfg.

The CTSS daemon, part of Grid Infrastructure, synchronizes time between cluster nodes in the absence of a network accessible network time protocol (NTP) server. This could remove the dependency on an NTP server, however we recommend using NTP wherever possible—you might otherwise end up with incorrect (but consistent!) system time on all nodes.

Prior to Oracle 11.2, a node's public and virtual IP addresses had to be registered in a Domain Name Server (DNS) for clients to connect to the database correctly and to support connect time load balancing. Cluster maintenance, such as adding or removing nodes, requires changes in DNS that can be a burden if such maintenance is performed often. The idea behind Grid Naming Service is to move the mapping of IP addresses to names and vice versa out of the DNS service and into Clusterware. Technically, Clusterware runs its own little nameserver, listening on yet another virtual IP address using a method called *subdomain delegation*. In simple terms, you create a new subdomain (e.g., ebsprod) to your domain (example.com) and instruct the root name server for your domain to hand off all requests for the subdomain (ebsprod.example.com) to GNS. During subsequent steps of the installation, you won't be asked to supply virtual IP addresses and names—only public and private network information has to be supplied. The addresses GNS uses have to come from a dynamic host configuration protocol (DHCP) server on the public network. Table 2-5 gives an overview of addresses and their use, their default names, and details on which part of the software stack is responsible for resolving them. The only dependency on DNS exists during the initial cluster installation, when the GNS virtual address is allocated and assigned in the DNS.

Table 2-5. Network Addresses with Active GNS

Address used by/for	Default Name	Assigned Type	Assigned by	Resolved by
Global Naming Service virtual address	clustername-gns.example.com	virtual	DNS administrator	DNS
public node address	assigned hostname	public	assigned during OS installation	GNS
node virtual address	publicName-vip	virtual	address assigned through DHCP	GNS
node private address	publicName-priv	private	fixed	hosts file
SCAN virtual IP 1	clustername-gns.example.com	virtual	assigned through DHCP	GNS
SCAN virtual IP 2	clustername-gns.example.com	virtual	assigned through DHCP	GNS
SCAN virtual IP 3	clustername-gns.example.com	virtual	assigned through DHCP	GNS

We recommend defining the private IP addresses for the cluster interconnect in the /etc/hosts file on each cluster node; this will prevent anyone or anything else from using them.

▪ **Caution** The use GNS is optional; at the time of writing, a number of bugs related to GNS are reported against the base release.

You choose to use GNS during the installation of Grid Infrastructure by ticking a small box and assigning a subdomain plus a virtual IP address for GNS. The instruction to DNS to perform subdomain delegation needs to be completed prior to the installation.

The next feature in our list is called *Single Client Access Name* (SCAN), which we will discuss later. SCAN helps with abstracting the number of nodes from client access. The addition and deletion of nodes is completely transparent—the SCAN relates to the cluster rather than the database.

To minimize additional effort after the addition of a node to the cluster, server pools have been introduced to simplify the addition and removal of database instances to a RAC database. We will discuss server pools next.

Modeling Resources with Server Pools

Server pools are an interesting new feature. They provide a new way of modeling resources in Clusterware. They allow you to subdivide a cluster into multiple logical subunits that can be useful in shared environments. All nodes in Clusterware 11.2 are either implicitly or explicitly part of a server pool. By default, two pools exist after a fresh installation: the free pool and the generic pool. The generic pool is used for backward compatibility, and it stores pre-11.2 databases or administrator-managed 11.2 databases. The free pool takes all non-assigned nodes.

Server pools are mutually exclusive and take a number of attributes, such as the minimum and maximum number of nodes, an importance, and a name. The importance attribute in a server pool ensures that low priority workloads don't starve out more important ones for resources. It is possible to reallocate servers from one pool to another, which can lead to very interesting scenarios in capacity management. Clusterware can automatically move servers from other server pools to meet an important server pool's minimum size requirement.

Server Pools go hand-in-hand with a new way of managing RAC databases. Prior to Oracle 11.2, administrators were responsible for adding and removing instances from a RAC database, including the creation and activation of public online redo log threads and undo tablespaces. Server pools—and the use of Oracle Managed Files as in ASM—automate these tasks through the use of the form of policy managed databases. *Administrator-managed databases* are, as the name suggests, managed entirely by the database administrator. In other words, this is the RAC database until to Oracle 11.1. Policy-managed databases use automated features for adding and removing instances and services. The number of nodes a policy-managed database starts is configured by the server pool's cardinality; in other words, if you need another instance, then all you need to do is to assign a new node to the database's server pool, and Oracle will do the rest.

■ **Note** See Chapter 11 to learn more about the implications of services on policy-managed databases.

In conjunction with server pools, Grid Infrastructure introduced another feature called *Role Separated Management*. In shared environments, administrators should be restricted to managing their respective server pool. Access Control Lists are implemented for Clusterware resources, including server pools, to govern access to resources. A new role, the *cluster administrator*, is introduced. By default, the Grid Infrastructure software owner "grid" and the root user are permanent cluster administrators. Additional operating system accounts can be promoted to cluster administrators, each of which can have a set of permissions on resources, types, and server pools. Separation of duties now seems to be possible on the cluster level—but bear in mind that the grid owner and root users are all powerful.

Ensuring POSIX Compliance with ACFS

ASM has been discussed at great length in this chapter in relation to shared storage for the RAC database. Oracle 11.2 extends ASM so it not only stores database-related file structures, but also provides a POSIX compliant cluster file system called ACFS. POSIX compliance means that all the operating system utilities we use with ext3 and other file systems can be used with ACFS. A space efficient read-only, copy-on-write snapshot mechanism is available as well, allowing for up to 63 snapshots to be taken. ASM Cluster File System uses 64-bit structures internally; it is a journal file system, and it uses metadata checksums to ensure data integrity. ACFS can be resized online, and it uses all the services ASM offers, even (most importantly) I/O distribution.

ACFS solves a problem users had in RAC. Database directory objects and external tables can now point to ACFS file systems, allowing a single view on all the external data in the cluster. In the real world, users of external tables had to make sure to connect to the correct instance to access the underlying data in the external table or directory object. With ACFS, it is no longer necessary to connect to a specific node. Presenting the file system to all nodes solves the problem. ACFS also addresses the fact that the use of an additional cluster file system—OCFS2, for example—could cause problems on RAC systems because it meant the existence of a second set of heartbeat processes.

ACFS is not limited to RAC. Another scenario for ACFS is a web server farm protected by the Grid Infrastructure high availability framework that uses ACFS to export the contents of the web site or application code to the server root directories.

ACFS can store database binaries, BFILEs, parameter files (pfiles), trace files, logs, and, of course, any kind of user application data. Database files are explicitly not supported in ACFS, and Oracle won't allow you to create them in an ACFS mount point. However, Oracle does explicitly support installing the Oracle binaries as a shared home in ACFS; the mounting of the file system can be integrated into Clusterware, ensuring that the file system is available before trying to start the database.

ACFS uses the services of the ASM Dynamic Volume Manager (ADVM). It provides volume management services and a standard device driver interface to its file system clients, such as ACFS and ext3. The ACFS file system is created on top of an ADVM volume, which is a specific ASM file type that differentiates it from other ASM managed-file types, such as datafiles, controlfiles, and so on. Figure 2-3 details the relationship between ASM disks, the ASM disk group, a dynamic volume, and ACFS file system:

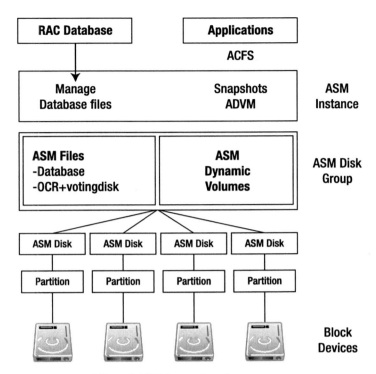

Figure 2-3. ACFS and ASM dynamic volumes

Management of ACFS and ADVM volumes is tightly integrated into Enterprise Manager, the ASM Configuration Assistant (ASMCA), and command line utilities, as well as into SQL*Plus.

Using Oracle Restart Instead of RAC

Oracle Restart, or Single Instance High Availability as it was called previously, is the standalone version and counterpart for Grid Infrastructure for RAC. Similar to its big brother, Oracle Restart keeps track of resources such as (single-instance) databases; the ASM instance and its disk groups; and listener and other node applications, such as Oracle Notification Service. It also uses the Oracle High Availability Service (OHAS) and its child processes to monitor the state of registered resources and restarts failed components if necessary. Oracle Restart's meta information is stored in the Oracle Local Registry (OLR), and it also runs a CSSD instance you don't need to create through a call to localconfig add for ASM up to Oracle 11.1. The great thing about Oracle Restart is its integration with ONS and the resource administration through the commands already known from RAC. Finally, database administrators don't need to worry about startup scripts—Oracle Restart will start a database when the server boots. Dependencies defined in Oracle Restart ensure that a database doesn't start before ASM is up, and so on. This means that mistakes such as forgetting to start the listener should be a problem of the past. Managed service providers will appreciate that Oracle Restart is identical across all platforms, thereby providing a uniform way of managing databases and their startup scripts.

Oracle Restart reduces the number of recommended Oracle homes by one—all you need is a Grid Infrastructure home that contains the binaries for ASM and the RDBMS software home. Unlike Grid Infrastructure, Oracle Restart can share the ORACLE_BASE with the database binaries. The installation is very similar to the clustered installation, minus the missing copy to remote locations. Another benefit: It doesn't require the definition of an OCR or voting disk locations. The execution of the root.sh script initializes the OLR and creates the ASM instance with the disk groups specified.

After installing Oracle Restart, you will see the following list of resources in your system:

```
[oracle@devbox001 ~]$ crsctl status resource -t
--------------------------------------------------------------------------
NAME            TARGET  STATE       SERVER              STATE_DETAILS
--------------------------------------------------------------------------
Local Resources
--------------------------------------------------------------------------
ora.LISTENER.lsnr
                ONLINE  ONLINE      devbox001
ora.DATA.dg
                ONLINE  ONLINE      devbox001
ora.REDO.dg
                ONLINE  ONLINE      devbox001
ora.FRA.dg
                ONLINE  ONLINE      devbox001
ora.asm
                ONLINE  ONLINE      devbox001          Started
--------------------------------------------------------------------------
Cluster Resources
--------------------------------------------------------------------------
ora.cssd
      1         ONLINE  ONLINE      devbox001
ora.diskmon
      1         ONLINE  ONLINE      devbox001
```

As you can see, ASM disk groups are resources, both in clustered and single-instance installations, which makes it far easier to mount and unmount them. Disk groups are automatically registered when first mounted; you no longer need to modify the asm_diskgroups initialization parameter.

Once Oracle Restart is configured, you can add databases to it just as you do in RAC, but with one important difference: no instances need to be registered. Databases can be configured with their associated disk groups, creating a dependency: if the disk group is not mounted when the database starts, Oracle Restart will try to mount the disk group(s) first.

Services are defined through a call to srvctl—again, just as in the RAC counterpart. Do not set the initialization parameter service_names to specify a database's services.

By default, Oracle Restart won't instantiate the Oracle Notification Service. Adding the daemons is useful in conjunction with the Data Guard broker, which can send out FAN events to inform clients of a failover operation. FAN events are also sent for UP and DOWN events, but the lack of high availability in single-instance Oracle limits the usefulness of this approach.

Simplifying Clusterd Database Access with SCAN Listener

The Single Client Access Name is a new feature that simplifies access to a clustered database. In versions prior to Oracle 11.2, an entry in the tnsnames.ora file for a n-node RAC database always referenced all nodes in the ADDRESS_LIST section, as in the listing that follows:

```
QA =
  (DESCRIPTION =
    (ADDRESS_LIST =
      (LOAD_BALANCE = ON)
      (FAILOVER = ON)
      (ADDRESS = (PROTOCOL = tcp)(HOST = london1-vip.examle1.com)(PORT =
          1521))
      (ADDRESS = (PROTOCOL = tcp)(HOST = london2-vip.examle1.com)(PORT =
          1521))
      (ADDRESS = (PROTOCOL = tcp)(HOST = london3-vip.examle1.com)(PORT =
          1521))
      (ADDRESS = (PROTOCOL = tcp)(HOST = london4-vip.examle1.com)(PORT =
          1521))
    )
    (CONNECT_DATA =
      (SERVICE_NAME = qaserv)
    )
  )
```

Adding and deleting nodes from the cluster required changes in the ADDRESS_LIST. In centrally, well managed environments, this might not be much of a problem; however, for certain environments, where clients are distributed across a farm of application servers, this process might take a while and is error prone. The use of a SCAN address removes this problem—instead of addressing every single node as before, the SCAN virtual IP addresses refer to the cluster. Using the SCAN, the preceding connection entry is greatly simplified. Instead of listing each node's virtual IP address, all we need to do is enter the SCAN scanqacluster.example1.com. Here's the simplified version:

```
QA =
  (DESCRIPTION =
    (ADDRESS_LIST =
      (ADDRESS = (PROTOCOL = tcp)(HOST = scanqacluster.examle.com)(PORT = 1521))
    )
    (CONNECT_DATA =
      (SERVICE_NAME = qaserv)
    )
  )
```

As a prerequisite to the installation or upgrade of Grid Infrastructure, at least one but preferably three previously unused IP addresses in the same subnet as the public network must be allocated and registered in DNS. Alternatively, in case you decide to use the Grid Naming Service (GNS), the GNS daemon will allocate three IP addresses from the range of addresses offered by the DHCP server. The IP addresses are *Address* (*A*) records in DNS that resolve to the SCAN name in a round robin fashion; you also need to make sure a reverse lookup is possible. Oracle Universal Installer will create new entities called *SCAN listeners*, along with the SCAN virtual IP addresses. The SCAN listeners will register with the local database listeners. A SCAN listener and a SCAN virtual IP address form a resource pair—both will be relocated to a different cluster node if a node fails. In case you ever need to, you can use the server control utility to administer the SCAN listener and IP.

The SCAN listeners are responsible for connect time load balancing, and they will hand off connections to the least loaded node offering the service the client requested. Figure 2-4 shows how these listeners fit into the overall RAC picture.

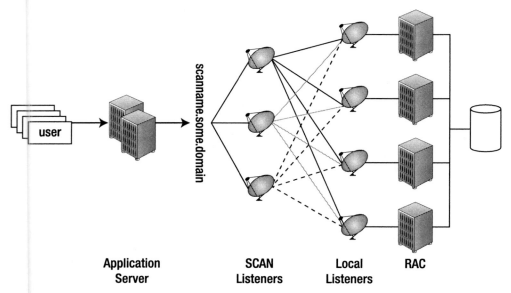

Figure 2-4. *SCAN listeners in the context of Real Application Clusters*

Figure 2-4 demonstrates the use of the SCAN. Assuming a three-tier application design and a manual—a non-GNS configuration, in other words—the application server's sessions connect to the SCAN *scanname.examle.com* on behalf of users. A DNS server is contacted to resolve the SCAN, and it will return one of the three IP addresses defined; this helps when spreading the load to all three SCAN listeners. The SCAN listener in turn will redirect the request to the local listener of the least loaded node, offering the service requested by the client. At this stage, the process is no longer different from the pre-SCAN era: the client resolves the virtual IP address of the node and establishes the connection.

The transition to the use of SCAN addresses is not mandatory—you can continue to use the old connection strings unless you would like to connect to a policy-managed database.

Summary

In this chapter, we discussed the relevant concepts behind Real Application Clusters that are necessary for understanding of the remaining chapters of the book. We began by introducing the various cluster concepts; there are differences in how many nodes serve requests, as well as in how the data served to clients is managed in the cluster. RAC takes the best of all worlds: all nodes serve requests, and they all access all the data concurrently.

We also discussed the cluster interconnect used extensively by Clusterware and Grid Infrastructure. Grid Infrastructure is the foundation for RAC databases, providing the necessary infrastructure service for the node membership management and intercluster communication that RAC needs. Next, we looked at Oracle's preferred storage option for the cluster database, Automatic Storage Management. ASM is a mature, cluster aware logical volume manager used to store all physical database structures. Oracle is pushing ASM heavily, and we recommend taking a closer look at this technology if you have not already done so. ASM uses techniques similar to other logical volume managers, making it easy to understand the concepts.

We also described RAC and how this technology is different from single-instance Oracle databases. The Cache Fusion architecture allows the definition of a cluster-wide shared global area. A number of additional structures maintained by each database instance ensure cache coherency in the global buffer cache; enqueue mastering is also globally performed.

Finally, we focused on some of the interesting new features introduced by Oracle 11g Release 2.

## CHAPTER 3

RAC Architecture

This chapter discusses features of the Oracle database that influence the architecture during the design stage of a highly available application based on Oracle Real Application Clusters (RAC). We will also point out where the availability can be limited, such as when a patch or a major upgrade must be performed. We will then have a look at intersite availability, discussing Data Guard for disaster recovery and Oracle Streams for message sharing and replication. A RAC solution is not an island; many components play a role, and many technologies can be leveraged to achieve a robust, highly available, and scalable application.

Availability Considerations

Many users chose a RAC solution because they need their application to be available to their users continuously and to be tolerant for to certain types of failures that could otherwise interrupt service. In the age of multitiered, Internet-facing applications, availability and application scalability are crucial to keeping a loyal user base. Research has shown that users can be very impatient. If the web page they are browsing doesn't render completely in the browser in less than approximately 10 seconds, they tend to move on and rarely come back.

Once implemented, the availability of a system can essentially be compromised by two different types of outages: planned and unplanned. The Oracle technology stack offers a wealth of complementary technologies that can protect against almost any type of outage. Table 3-1 lists some technologies that can save you from an unplanned outage when it occurs. Table 3-2 lists technologies that can help you prevent outages from occurring to begin with.

Table 3-1. Technologies that Counter Unplanned Outages

Failure	Technology	Mean time to recovery (estimated)
Node failure	Real Application Clusters	No downtime, but review table for implications of instance recovery
Failure occurring on the storage layer	Automatic Storage Management	No downtime when using normal or high redundancy for disk groups

Failure	Technology	Mean time to recovery (estimated)
Human error	Flashback Database/Flashback Table	No database downtime for recovering dropped tables
		Duration of the "flashback database" depends on the amount of data changed
	Data Guard with delayed redo application	Very little downtime during failover operation to standby database
Data Corruption	Data Guard	Very little downtime during failover to disaster recovery site; can be automated with fast start failover
Site failure	Data Guard	Very little downtime during failover to disaster recovery site

Table 3-2. Options to Minimize Planned Outages

Operation	Technology	Mean Time To Recovery (estimated)
Operating System changes, such as when applying security patches	Oracle RAC	No downtime when patching the OS one node at a time; use dynamic service relocation to active nodes
Changes to Oracle cluster layer	Data Guard graceful switchover	Very little downtime, assuming all standby databases are in sync with production
SAN migration	Oracle ASM	No downtime if database servers are connected simultaneously to both SANs; ASM disks can be dropped and added to an ASM disk group online and concurrently in one operation

64

Operation	Technology	Mean Time To Recovery (estimated)
Extending storage	Oracle ASM	No downtime as additional storage can be added to ASM disk groups; ASM will automatically start a rebalancing operation to restripe and mirror the data across all new disks
Database patch	RAC	Refer to section "Online Maintenance and Patching" for a detailed discussion of database patching and its implications
Database major release upgrade	Oracle RAC and Data Guard logical standby database	Users report downtime of 5 to 30 minutes
Platform migration	Transportable database, transportable tablespace, Oracle Streams, and Golden Gate	Highly project-specific downtime, mainly depending on the I/O subsystem and the number/size of data files
Data Changes	Many, including dbms_redefinition, online index rebuilds, and edition based redefinition	Little downtime, depending on the type of change

Deciding the Number of Nodes

A large number of RAC systems consist of only two nodes. You often see this demonstrated during the opening show of hands at Oracle user group meetings in the United Kingdom. Often such systems are used in a way similar to active/passive clusters, where RAC is deployed purely as a high availability solution.

The discussion about the appropriate number of cluster nodes should not be limited the live production system. Before users adopt RAC, they should also consider the number of nodes for the pre-production environment such as staging or quality assurance, as well as by the disaster recovery solution. For many reasons, it is beneficial to have the pre-production environment equivalent to your production environment. Otherwise, you might experience unpleasant surprises when your code is released. You should also test on an exact copy of your production database-if your data is out of sync with production; any testing is likely to be inaccurate. Having a non-production RAC cluster is essential for rolling out patches to production because patches definitely need to be tested to avoid unplanned outages or corruption of the Oracle binaries.

If no additional hardware or budget is available to create a RAC system just for testing, you might create a virtualized RAC system on a spare server. Oracle VM is a free hypervisor that can be used to host a RAC system (you can learn more about virtualization in Chapter 5).

The capabilities of the disaster recovery (DR) site should also be equal to those of the production site; the last thing the DBAs and management need in a crisis situation, such as when the disaster recovery site needs to be activated, is to find out that the DR site can't handle the workload. The common practice of "recycling" the old production environment for DR is definitely not recommended.

Two-Node RAC Clusters

There are a number of advantages to operating two-node RAC installations. First, licensing costs are lower compared to multinode configurations. Second, using only two nodes makes global cache transfers simpler because three-way communication can't happen. The licensing conditions for the Standard Edition RAC don't seem to allow for more than two nodes equipped with recent processor types, so your topology is not as flexible as with the Enterprise Edition.

When designing and implementing such a setup, each individual cluster node needs to be able to cope with the full workload in case of a node failure. Alternatively, the workload has to be reduced in such a scenario; do this by informing users to perform essential operations only if possible. This used to be a much bigger problem when individual RAC nodes were less powerful than they are now, when many production RAC nodes now are equipped with 64GB of RAM and two or more quad core CPUs. These setups should be more than capable of handling a full workload.

Oracle RAC One Node

With Oracle 11.2, a hybrid RAC between RAC and active/passive configuration has been introduced to the user community. This hybrid is known as *RAC One Node*. It features a complete installation of the Oracle RAC software stack that makes a later transition to full blown RAC simple in case you need to scale up. One of the main intentions of RAC One Node is to allow for planned downtime. For example, a running database instance can be migrated to another host using the *omotion* utility with very little impact, and maintenance can take place on the host the instance was originally running on. In contrast to a RAC system, there is only one instance actively servicing user connections; nevertheless, the database will be created as a RAC database.

■ **Note** This is the main difference between active/passive clusters where a single instance database is protected by a high availability framework.

This single instance is registered in Oracle Grid Infrastructure, the metadata repository and high availability framework for Oracle clusters. This approach means that the RDBMS instance benefits from the high availability options Grid Infrastructure provides, namely failure detection and protection, online rolling patches, and rolling upgrades to the underlying operating system.

The base release for *RAC One Node*, 11.2.0.1, will only be available for Linux. It is not supported with Data Guard, nor is it available with the default installation. Users interested in *RAC One Node* will have to download MyOracle Support patch 9004119. Administrators of other platforms will have to wait for the first patch set to be released before they can use RAC One Node. The user guide also suggests that RAC One Node won't support third-party cluster software such as Veritas Storage Foundation for RAC or HP Serviceguard. Once the RAC database has been created on a node, a set of tools installed as part of the aforementioned patch allows the user to convert the system to a RAC One Node database. You need to call `raconeinit` to convert the database to RAC One Node. Once the tool finishes, you will notice that the database instance has been renamed to `instanceName_1`.

As mentioned previously, a new utility called *omotion* allows users to migrate a RAC One Node instance to another node in the cluster. Migrating the instance is useful for planned maintenance or if your cluster node is running out of resources and can no longer accommodate the database. To mitigate disruption to application users, the use of either Transparent Application Failover or Fast Connect Failover is required (you will learn about both of these later in this chapter). If none of these technologies is used, ongoing transactions will be allowed to complete within a certain user definable window; however, then users will be disconnected from the database and receive an ORA-3113 "End of line on communication channel" error. This error is caused by a shutdown of the database instance that commences after the grace period.

If you decide that there is a business case for updating from RAC One Node to "full" RAC, another tool called *racone2rac* can make the transition simple. Just select your RAC One Node database from a text-based menu and allow the tool to convert it to a RAC database. The result of the conversion looks similar to what you would get with a so-called policy-managed RAC database. Policy-managed databases are new with Oracle 11*g* Release 2, and they mark a shift away from the traditional RAC database, where the database administrator was responsible for administering all aspects of the RAC database, such as initialization parameters, online redo threads, and other structural changes. With policy-managed databases, the DBA only has to define how many nodes he'd like the database to have, and Oracle will take care of the rest. Any missing database components will be created as needed.

Multi-Node RAC Systems

Multinode systems are much more likely than the more common two-node cluster to support the whole workload if an individual node should fail. A correctly designed RAC system should have sufficient redundant capacity available to guarantee the application can continue with as little interruption as possible. Many enterprises therefore implement Real Application Clusters with more than two nodes. In the ideal case, when designing an *n*-node cluster, the same cluster should be able to support the workload with *n*-1 nodes available. This implies that there is a completely redundant last node available to the cluster. The redundant node does not have to be idle. For example, it could be used for backup and reporting; the only requirement is that all of its capacity can be made available to the cluster at short notice.

Beginning with Oracle 10.1, it is possible to add nodes to the cluster on-the-fly if your business or management teams come to the conclusion that the existing number of nodes is insufficient to support the workload. With Oracle 11.2, this has been improved and simplified with the introduction of Grid Plug and Play and policy-managed databases.

Online Maintenance and Patching

Regardless of how careful the testing for a new system was prior to its rollout, sooner or later every environment will require patches. This can be due to many reasons; the most common are listed here:

- An internal error is causing application unavailability.

- The currently used version is going out of support. For example, Oracle 10*g* Release 2 is moving out of premier support in 2010 (but Oracle is waiving the fees for extended support for an additional year), which could be a reason for businesses to move on to the next release.

- A critical security patch needs to be applied.

- Contractual requirement to perform scheduled maintenance.

Patches can have an effect on availability, even though Oracle has improved the situation by providing online patches and a rolling patch application mechanism. The primary tool for patch application in Oracle is *opatch*. However, *point* (major) release changes cannot be performed with opatch, so you have to use Oracle Universal Installer (OUI) for such tasks.

■ **Caution** With critical, highly available systems, it is important not to patch systems just for the sake of patching them!

Any patching of a system is inherently risky, regardless of how much testing has been performed beforehand. Almost any database administrator can tell a story about a patch application that went wrong. Patching can also mean you have to incur downtime to the node while the cluster binaries are modified on that node.

In the Oracle database universe, there are a number of different types of patches (see Table 3-3 for a list of them).

Table 3-3. Oracle Patch Types

Patch Type	Patch description
One-off patch	This is a single patch to fix a specific problem.
Merge level request patch (MLR)	If a one-off patch conflicts with an already installed patch, Oracle development can be asked to provide a merged set of these patches.
Critical Patch Updates (CPU)	Critical Patch Updates are released quarterly and address security issues with Oracle products. Note that CPUs are not restricted to the RDBMS. Most CPUs require users to be on the last or next to last patch set, so you should regularly check Oracle's web site at www.oracle.com/technology/deploy/security/alerts.htm for more information about critical patches.
Patch Set Updates (PSU)	Patch Set Updates bundle previously separate patches in given product areas together. For instance, the first PSU for 10g Release 2 (its contents were published in My Oracle Support note 8576156.8) included, among other items, a RAC Recommended Patch Bundle, a Data Guard Logical Recommended Patch Bundle, and a Data Guard Physical Recommended Patch Bundle. Oracle assures users in My Oracle Support note 854428.1 that Patch Set Updates are intended to be low risk and RAC rolling installable. Oracle also claims in the same note that the patch is well tested. Don't take this as an excuse not to test. Patch Set Updates include the latest Critical Patch Update, as well.

Patch Type	Patch description
Bundle Patch	Bundle patches were used before Patch Set Updates, and they bundled a number of patches per product area. Bundle patches were available for Data Guard logical and physical standby databases, the Data Guard broker, Clusterware, RAC, and other areas. There don't seem to be new bundle patches at the time of writing because they have been replaced by PSUs.
Patch set	A patch set is used to apply a point release to the database, such as patching a 11.1.0.6 system to 11.1.0.7. At the time of writing, there was no patch set for 11*g* Release 2 yet. The patch set contents are to be installed into an existing Oracle home. Rolling application of patch sets is possible for Cluster Ready Services/Clusterware/Grid Infrastructure since 10.1.0.2 (see "Oracle Clusterware (formerly CRS) Rolling Upgrades" on MOS 338706.1). Oracle Automatic Storage Management can be upgraded in a rolling fashion as well, beginning with 11.1.0.6. Note that there is a high probability of hitting unpublished bug 7436280 when upgrading clustered ASM 11.1.0.6 to 11.1.0.7 when issuing the command to stop the rolling upgrade. One of patches is available for 32-bit and 64-bit Linux, as well as some other platforms; this one-off patch is also included in the 11.1.0.7.1 Patch Set Update. RDBMS instances can't be patched in a rolling fashion. Also bear in mind that the cluster layer needs to be patched to an equal or higher version than the RDBMS and ASM binaries in RAC.
Major release update	A major database release change requires downtime and a lot of testing! An example of a major release change is the migration from 11*g* Release 1 to 11*g* Release 2 or from 10*g* Release 2 to 11*g* Release 2. You need to check the upgrade guide of your destination release for information about your upgrade paths. In any case, such a release requires you to install the new software into a separate Oracle Home. The downtime required to migrate to the new release can be minimized by using a (transient) logical standby database.

Patching Real Application Clusters Using opatch

In the past, patching a system most often meant downtime. But now, opatch supports rolling upgrades of the cluster, which minimizes the interruption to service availability. Before trying to apply any patch, it is important to verify that the Oracle Inventory containing the metadata about all nodes in the cluster and their patch levels is not corrupt. The global inventory is maintained during all patch operations and lists the available Oracle Homes on a RAC cluster, as well as the patches applied. You run the opatch utility with the `lsinventory` option to verify that the inventory is not corrupted, as in the following example:

```
[grid@london1 ~]$ $ORACLE_HOME/OPatch/opatch lsinventory
Invoking OPatch 11.2.0.1.2

Oracle Interim Patch Installer version 11.2.0.1.2
Copyright (c) 2010, Oracle Corporation.  All rights reserved.
```

```
Oracle Home        : /u01/app/grid/product/11.2.0/crs
Central Inventory  : /u01/app/oraInventory
   from            : /etc/oraInst.loc
OPatch version     : 11.2.0.1.2
OUI version        : 11.2.0.1.0
OUI location       : /u01/app/grid/product/11.2.0/crs/oui
Log file location  : /u01/app/.../opatch/opatch2010-06-14_16-00-57PM.log

Patch history file: /u01/app/.../opatch/opatch_history.txt
Lsinventory Output file location : /u01/app/...opatch/lsinv/lsinventory2010-06-14_16-00-
57PM.txt
--------------------------------------------------------------------------
Installed Top-level Products (1):
Oracle Grid Infrastructure                              11.2.0.1.0
There are 1 products installed in this Oracle Home.
Interim patches (2) :
Patch  9343627      : applied on Fri Apr 30 13:11:32 BST 2010
Unique Patch ID:  12381846
   Created on 15 Apr 2010, 11:28:38 hrs PST8PDT
   Bugs fixed:
     9343627, 9262748, 9262722
Patch  9352237      : applied on Fri Apr 30 13:06:29 BST 2010
Unique Patch ID:  12381846
   Created on 25 Mar 2010, 00:05:17 hrs PST8PDT
   Bugs fixed:
     8661168, 8769239, 8898852, 8801119, 9054253, 8706590, 8725286, 8974548
     8778277, 8780372, 8769569, 9027691, 9454036, 9454037, 9454038, 8761974
     7705591, 8496830, 8702892, 8639114, 8723477, 8729793, 8919682, 8818983
     9001453, 8475069, 9328668, 8891929, 8798317, 8820324, 8733749, 8702535
     8565708, 9036013, 8735201, 8684517, 8870559, 8773383, 8933870, 8812705
     8405205, 8822365, 8813366, 8761260, 8790767, 8795418, 8913269, 8897784
     8760714, 8717461, 8671349, 8775569, 8898589, 8861700, 8607693, 8642202
     8780281, 9369797, 8780711, 8784929, 8834636, 9015983, 8891037, 8828328
     8570322, 8832205, 8665189, 8717031, 8685253, 8718952, 8799099, 8633358
     9032717, 9321701, 8588519, 8783738, 8796511, 8782971, 8756598, 9454385
     8856497, 8703064, 9066116, 9007102, 8721315, 8818175, 8674263, 9352237
     8753903, 8720447, 9057443, 8790561, 8733225, 9197917, 8928276, 8991997,
     837736

Rac system comprising of multiple nodes
  Local node = london1
  Remote node = london2
  Remote node = london3
  Remote node = london4
--------------------------------------------------------------------------
OPatch succeeded.
```

You can find the important lines here near the bottom of the output; the opatch utility discovered correctly that the system in question is a four-node RAC system. The utility also correctly detected that the command was run from the local node, london1. Do not proceed with a patch if the information reported by opatch is inaccurate because then opatch won't be able to properly register the patch information in the global inventory.

Opatch Operation Modes

OPatch can operate in four different modes for Real Application Clusters:

- All node patch

- Rolling patch

- Minimum Downtime patch

- Local patch

All Node Patch Mode

Opatch treats the cluster exactly as a single instance and patches all nodes while the database is down in this mode. This patch mode has the heaviest impact on availability, and can only be applied during an agreed downtime window. Otherwise this patch mode is not really suitable for a RAC system.

Rolling Patch Mode

All nodes in the cluster are patched, but only one at a time to avoid downtime. Process-wise, the first node is brought down for patching. When patched, it's started again. OPatch will ask you if you want to continue with the next node, and so on until all nodes are patched. There is no downtime because there is always at least one node up and servicing user requests.

Unfortunately not all patches are rolling patches. To find out if a patch is a rolling patch, you can use opatch's query option, as in this example:

```
[grid@london1 PSU1]$ $ORACLE_HOME/OPatch/opatch query \
> -is_rolling_patch 9343627/

Invoking OPatch 11.2.0.1.2
Oracle Interim Patch Installer version 11.2.0.1.2
Copyright (c) 2010, Oracle Corporation.  All rights reserved.

Oracle Home       : /u01/app/grid/product/11.2.0/crs
Central Inventory : /u01/app/oraInventory
   from           : /etc/oraInst.loc
OPatch version    : 11.2.0.1.2
OUI version       : 11.2.0.1.0
OUI location      : /u01/app/grid/product/11.2.0/crs/oui
Log file location : /u01/.../opatch/opatch2010-06-14_16-41-58PM.log
Patch history file: /u01/.../cfgtoollogs/opatch/opatch_history.txt
-------------------------------------------------------------------
Patch is a rolling patch: true
OPatch succeeded.
```

Minimum Downtime Patch Mode

Another patching mechanism is referred to as *minimum downtime patching*. With this patching strategy, you divide your cluster into two sets of nodes. When patching, the first set of nodes is shut down and patched. Once the patching is completed, the second set of nodes is shut down. Now the previously patched first set of nodes is started, followed by the patch application to the second set. Once the patch to the second set of nodes is completed, the second set of nodes is brought up again, resulting in a patched cluster.

Local Patch Mode

Finally, individual nodes in the cluster can be patched by specifying the -local flag with the opatch command. A strategy similar to the rolling patch can be employed with this approach. In the end, you should verify that the patch information is correctly recorded in the Oracle inventory of each node.

Which patch you should use depends on the availability requirements and the preference of the user or the business. Minimum downtime patching and rolling patching are similar in the way they make the cluster partially unavailable. Some businesses have the luxury of a weekend downtime window, so they can use an all-node patch, which saves time and resources.

Instance Recovery in RAC

Another actor influencing availability of a RAC system is instance recovery. As noted previously, instance failure won't cause a complete outage of the application as with single-instance Oracle, where availability drops to nothing straight away, and users will notice the failure. In the single-instance scenario, the memory structures that make up the Oracle shared global area (SGA) will be gone and need to be reinitialized when the instance starts. Once that happens, the system monitor (SMON) process will have to perform instance recovery to get the database back into a consistent state and available to users. Unfortunately, this can take some time.

Instance recovery in RAC is very different than in the single-instance scenario, and it won't cause an outage. The instance failure will be detected by another instance in the cluster. Once detected, there is a window where the RAC system briefly will appear frozen for users, while the background processes remaster failed resources across the cluster. The time window while the system is unavailable or partially unavailable depends on the activity of the system, the number of blocks mastered in the failed instance, and the number of global resources such as enqueues that were held by the failed instance.

Instance recovery will be managed by any other instances on behalf of the failed instance. There are two streams of work that need to be done:

Enqueue Remastering: The Global Enqueue Service Monitor has to recover global resources such as enqueues (mainly TX and TM-transaction and table modification enqueues) and cache resources from the buffer cache.

Database Recovery: The SMON process performs database recovery similar to how it's handled in a single-instance crash scenario.

Some of these operations can be performed in parallel.

Enqueue Remastering

The first step during instance recovery is to remaster global enqueues. This task is performed by the Global Enqueue Service (GES). You can think of enqueues as global locks; some of the enqueue metadata held in the global resource directory is lost as consequence of the instance crash, and it has to be recovered by the surviving instances that are working together to do so. It's the LMON Global Enqueue Services Monitor process that is responsible for this work.

The global resource directory (GRD) is maintained jointly by all cluster nodes in their SGA. Cluster operations requiring access to resources in the cluster are synchronized, and this is exactly with the GRD is for. The GRD is maintained by the global cache service daemon and global enqueue service daemon, which are responsible for managing blocks in the shared SGA and global locks. Each resource in the cluster is mastered by a specific instance, and all other instances know the resource master for a resource.

The time it takes to recover the global enqueues depends on workload of the system, as well as on the number of failed instances and pending work. On a busy system, you will most likely find that TM and TX enqueues, which are table/partition modification enqueues and transaction enqueues respectively, take the longest to remaster. In the past—that is, in the days of Oracle Parallel Server— users experimented with setting the initialization parameter dml_locks to 0. You also occasionally find this advice on the Internet, but be careful! While this setting effectively disables enqueues, which makes remastering a quick process, it also imposes several restrictions that make such an approach untenable for today's environments. Specifically, setting dml_locks to 0 imposes the following restrictions:

- You cannot use drop table or create index statements.

- Explicit lock statements are no longer allowed. For example, you cannot issue a LOCK TABLE statement.

- You cannot use Enterprise Manager on any instance with dml_locks set to 0.

The tradeoffs here make experimenting with the parameter not worth your while. As discussed previously, RAC instance recovery can have an effect on your application. Therefore, you should thoroughly test your application's exposure to instance failure before rolling it out into production.

The second step during instance recovery is to remaster global cache resources, which are the blocks in the buffer cache. The Global Cache Service daemon, GCS, is responsible for this task. To speed the process up, only those resources that have lost their master will be remastered. This approach marks an evolution from earlier releases, where all resources were remastered; obviously, the earlier approach took longer to complete. While resources are remastered, the LMS Global Cache Services process doesn't handle additional requests for accessing blocks in the buffer cache. Any sessions that are lucky enough to have the handles they need, but also don't need any further requests for resources (blocks), can carry on working. All other sessions must wait until the instance recovery process has finished.

Database Recovery

While the global cache resources (database blocks) are being remastered, the server monitor process starts building what is referred to as a recovery set. The *recovery set* is a set of blocks that need recovery; the SMON server monitor process needs to merge the online redo logs of all threads to complete the recovery set.

SMON also performs the next stage of instance recovery. The resources that were previously identified by SMON in need for recovery, the recovery set, need to be claimed to prevent other instances from accessing them while they wait to be recovered.

At this stage, the global resource directory is unfrozen. The global resources have been remastered (distributed among the surviving cluster nodes), and all the blocks in need of recovery are locked down for SMON to apply a redo to them. You are ready to roll forward now. All other blocks in the buffer cache are now accessible to users, and the system becomes partially available. As with single instance Oracle, some blocks are *dirty* because their corresponding transactions have not completed. Changes to those blocks need to be rolled back by applying *undo information* to them. The system will be fully available again as soon as all the blocks in the recovery set are actually recovered and the resource handles to them have been released.

This lengthy discussion illustrates why you probably want to keep the instance recovery process as short as possible. First and foremost, you'd prefer to keep users connected and able to carry out work in the application. Unfortunately, there is no RAC equivalent to the `fast_start_mttr_target` parameter we set in single-instance Oracle to govern a target time for instance startup after a database crash. The `fast_start_mttr_target` parameter supersedes the `log_checkpoint_interval`, `log_checkpoint_timeout`, and `fast_start_io_target` parameters, so it should be used instead. Setting `fast_start_mttr_target` allows Oracle to populate the V$INSTANCE_RECOVERY view, which can give the administrator an indication about the probable instance recovery time.

■ **Note** As with any recovery scenario, you can set `recovery_parallelism` to a non-default value to spawn multiple recovery slaves during the recovery process (this requires `parallel_max_servers` to be > 0) to speed things up.

Oracle 10*g* introduced an underscore parameter called `_fast_start_instance_recovery_target` that allows you to influence the time needed to perform instance recovery. As with any underscore parameter, you need to check with Oracle support first to see whether setting it has any negative effects. The `_fast_start_instance_recovery_target` parameter governs the maximum amount of time between the point when an instance recovery starts and the rolling forward ends; in other words, it governs the time interval for which the system is not available.

Failover Considerations

When designing a RAC-based application, developers and architects need to address the fact that even the best hardware is not 100% reliable. Using RAC mitigates the implications of an instance failure, but some additional measures need to be taken on the application side to mask such a failure from the application and ultimately the user accessing it.

Unfortunately, not all applications are RAC aware. Commercial, off-the-shelf packages often don't come with RAC support. In such scenarios, an active/passive cluster (see Chapter 2 for more details) or a RAC One Node system might be a suitable alternative if the vendor can't be persuaded to certify a RAC installation.

Applications available with RAC support provided by the vendor or internally developed applications can use various high-availability technologies to mask instance failure. These technologies include Transparent Application Failover (TAF) and Fast Connection Failover (FCF).

Often applications are developed on single-instance Oracle. This is not a problem because an application can always be enabled to run on RAC. But it should be immediately apparent that it is easier to add failover support to applications developed in-house or to applications for which source code is available. When designing a new application, failover should be considered right from the start because the cost of introducing such features during a redesign can be huge.

Transparent Application Failover

As explained in Chapter 1, TAF allows database sessions to use OCI libraries to fail over to one of the surviving nodes of the cluster in the case of a node failure. Applications using the JDBC thin driver cannot benefit from this feature because that driver does not use OCI. TAF is a client-side feature: in the event of a node failure, notifications are sent out to trigger actions on the client side.

Failover Modes

Transparent Application Failover can be configured to work in two modes, or it can be deactivated. If we count *deactivated* as a mode, it means TAF can be assigned the following three options:

- Session failover
- Select failover
- None (default)

The *session failover* mode is probably the most basic case because it doesn't require any code changes for implementation. All that is required is a suitable local naming definition in the form of a tnsnames.ora file or a TAF policy attached to a database service. TAF will automatically reconnect the user session using the same connection string if a node failure occurs.

The *select failover* mode allows clients to continue fetching rows from an open cursor after the session has been re-established on another node. Internally, TAF will re-execute the same query, discarding the rows already returned to the user and thereby making the failover transparent. There is a slight overhead associated with this because Oracle has to keep track of which data has already been transmitted.

If you explicitly specify *none* as the failover type, you prevent any failover from happening. The only reason to specify none, rather than omitting the FAILOVER_MODE clause altogether, is to explicitly deactivate TAF.

■ **Note** Any DML changes that are created by transactions in progress can't be recovered by TAF. In such a scenario, the not-yet-committed transaction will be rolled back when the session is re-established on another instance.

In addition to node failures, TAF can also be configured to work with Data Guard configurations and active/passive clusters, thereby providing a failover capability in Data Guard scenarios.

Failover Methods

With the failover mode specified, users can further define a method that dictates exactly how TAF will re-establish the session on the other instance. A failover method can be defined independently of the failover type. The failover method determines how the failover works; the following options are available:

- Basic
- Preconnect

As its name suggests, the *basic* option instructs the client to establish a new connection only after the node failed. This can potentially lead to a large number of new connection requests to the surviving instance. In the case of a two-node RAC, this might cause performance degradation until all user connections are re-established. If you consider using this approach, you should test for potential performance degradation during the design stage.

The *preconnect* option is slightly more difficult to configure. When you specify the preconnect parameter, the client is instructed to preconnect a session to a backup instance to speed up session failover. You need to bear in mind that these preconnections increase the number of sessions to the cluster. In addition, you also need to define what the backup connection should be.

Fast Connection Failover and Fast Application Notification

Fast Connection Failover provides a means to transparently recover from instance failures for clients with support for Fast Application Notification (FAN). *FAN* is a framework for publishing UP and DOWN events for cluster reconfiguration. Such events could be changes to the availability of database services and instances.

The following clients that have integrated support for Fast Connection Failover:

- Java Database Connection Driver (JDBC)
- Oracle Universal Connection Pool UCP
- Clients using the Oracle Call Interface
- Oracle Data Providers for .Net

The easiest way to use FAN is to use one of the preceding clients. That way, no code changes have to be made to the application because these clients have integrated support for FAN events. In addition to protection from node failures, applications based on FAN and FCF can also use the load balancing advisory introduced in Oracle 10*g* Release 2 to make best use of resources in the cluster.

The great advantage of using FAN lies in its design. Instead of requiring the application to poll the database for information, the notification framework advises the application of cluster changes. It is less likely that an application will connect to hung or otherwise overloaded nodes, or try to use a stale connection pointing to a failed database instance.

Database services need to be defined to enable FAN. A database service is the primary tool for workload management in Real Application Clusters. It allows users to group similar workloads together or subdivide the cluster into disjoint units. Batch services, reporting services, payroll services are all examples of the sort of service we are talking about. Services are always associated with database instances. They can also be associated with specific attributes to enable high availability technologies such as TAF and FAN.

■ **Note** You can learn more about database services in Chapter 11, which discusses workload management.

Fast Connection Failover is based on the high availability framework. Clients with support for FAN events receive and process them depending on the event sent. Technically, FAN and FCF rely on events published by the Oracle Notification Services background process, which is automatically installed and configured as part of the node apps in RAC. A JDBC connection pool is an example of a client that uses these events. Upon receiving a DOWN event from the framework, connections in the pool pertaining to the failed instance or service will be marked as invalid by the connection pool and then cleared up. To make up for the reduced number of sessions, additional sessions will be established on the other cluster nodes, as defined by the service. The prerequisites for using FCF are simple, and they can be met by standalone Java applications or connection pools.

Beginning with Oracle 11.1.0.7, the implicit connection cache previously required for FCF to work is deprecated. As with most Oracle features, it won't go away in the next release, but you can expect to see it removed eventually. The new feature called Universal Connection Pool (UCP) supercedes the implicit connection cache's functionality.

When specifying the db_domain initialization parameter, it is possible that FCF does not work in 11g Release 2's base release. This is due to an unpublished bug: "8779597 - [11GR2-LNX-090731] A NUMBER OF JDBC CONNECTION IS INCORRECT WITH FAN UP EVENT." A one-off patch is available, and the bug will be fixed in the first patch set to 11.2.0.2.

Interestingly, FCF is not limited to events published within the cluster. The Data Guard broker also publishes FAN events after a failover operation. Even single-instance Oracle, when registered with Oracle Restart, can receive events. Setting your connection string properly to reference primary and standby database host can make session failover after Data Guard role changes extremely efficient and elegant.

Scalability Considerations

One of the best definitions of scalability (a term which is used in many contexts) is found in the Oracle Performance Tuning Guide for database 11g Release 2. It states the following:

> *Scalability is a system's ability to process more workload, with a proportional increase in system resource usage. In other words, in a scalable system, if you double the workload, then the system uses twice as many system resources.*

> —Oracle Database Performance Tuning Guide 11g Release 2 (11.2)
> Chapter 2 "Understanding Scalability"

Any system designed should adhere to the principles of scalability. Designing scalable RAC applications is not too different than designing efficient single-instance Oracle database applications. An application that scales well in a non-clustered configuration is likely to scale well on RAC, too. The requirement for writing a scalable application is always a given, even if only a small user base is expected initially.

Scalability Enhancers

Any application accessible over the Internet 365 days a year 24 hours a day poses special challenges to the architect. Many requirements are unclear at first, and usage patterns are difficult to predict until the application has reached an equilibrium state, at which time usage statistics can be interpolated into the future. Many application development cycles tend to be very short: the goal is to stay competitive in a highly volatile market. Similarly, testing time is limited. The short cycles and limited testing time require prudent planning and modern software development technologies to ensure that new releases don't compromise the overall system performance.

The Oracle RAC option potentially offers greatly increased scalability. In a correctly designed RAC cluster, additional hardware resources should yield increases in overall throughput. In other words, if you add another server to the cluster, it will either be able to handle an increased workload, or response times will be reduced. In addition, many large tasks can be divided into subtasks and executed concurrently on multiple nodes. Database services are the primary tool for mapping workloads to database nodes.

■ **Note** The following discussion assumes that the hardware stack is adequately sized and does not include a limiting factor. Scalability cannot be viewed for isolated components in the application stack: every part of the architecture needs to be able to deal with the anticipated workload.

The introduction of the Cache Fusion cluster interconnect algorithm in Oracle 9*i* puts RAC a quantum leap ahead of Oracle Parallel Server, allowing most applications to run on RAC with little or no modification. With Cache Fusion, the cluster uses one shared SGA across all database instances. Resources such as blocks in the buffer cache and (global) enqueues are mastered by individual nodes and are controlled through the Global Resource Directory. In Oracle 8*i* OPS and earlier, it was important to isolate workloads from one another because inter-instance block transfers using the block ping method (you can learn more about this method in Chapter 1) were very resource intensive and to be avoided, if possible. The only way to avoid such block transfers was by assigning similar workloads to the same instance. Cache Fusion addresses the problem of workload isolation to instances by allowing transactions to run on multiple nodes without fear of cache transfers. High speed interconnects such as Infiniband or 10Gigabit Ethernet further reduce cache transfer times. However, RAC users should still be cautious when employing parallel operations across cluster nodes because this can potentially lead to interconnect congestion. Cache Fusion mainly helps when scaling OLTP-like workloads.

Today's databases tend to grow increasingly larger, and this trend doesn't only apply to data warehouses. With the decreased cost for storage and the demand by businesses for storing highly detailed information as opposed to aggregates, the maintenance of tables and indexes has become a challenge. Databases should therefore undergo careful capacity planning in the design stage, especially in terms of expected data growth. Segments that are expected to grow considerably should be partitioned right from the start to allow better performance and/or manageability. If you find out that some segments are growing quicker than initially expected, you can introduce partitioning to them by employing the DBMS_REDEFINITION package for an online table redefinition.

Long-running batches in data warehouses and hybrid workloads can benefit from the parallel execution feature, which is discussed in great detail in Chapter 14. Parallel execution makes maximum use of the available resources in order to complete a task, such as a data load or a long-running report.

To help cope with data growth, Oracle 11*g* Release 1 simplified the compression functionality already present in the database kernel with the advanced compression feature. Prior to Oracle 11*g*, compression offered a way to deal with rapid data growth, but it required bulk inserts or direct loads to compress data and did not work on large objects and some user defined data types. Targets for compression were tables, table partitions, and materialized views. The compression feature extended the index compression that was already part of the RDBMS kernel. The easiest ways to use compression in data warehousing was to use the SQL loader command-line tool for direct path loads or to reorganize objects using CREATE TABLE AS SELECT statements. Alternatively, data could be inserted either in parallel with the APPEND hint or by using DBMS_REDEFINITION to compress tables/partitions online. Compressing data in tables can save space, improve cache efficiency, and reduce I/O operations when retrieving data. However, there was an overhead associated with the compression and decompression of the data blocks.

Oracle 11g lifted many restrictions in the advanced compression option, making compression useful for OLTP workloads by introducing support for insert and update operations. Instead of being compressed when filled, blocks are now compressed in batch operations to minimize the impact on the system.

■ **Note** Advanced compression offers far more than table compression. For example, it allows for Secure File de-duplication and compression, Data Pump compression, and the compression of the redo stream in Data Guard, topics that are outside the scope of this book.

The Oracle database offers many additional features that can improvement scalability for RAC clusters, including the following:

- Automatic memory management

- Reverse key indexes

- Automatic Segment Space Management

- Sequence caching

- Locally Managed Tablespaces

- Automatic Storage Management

- Result Cache

Most of these features can simply be implemented by the database administrator. In the case of third-party applications, however, it is important to confirm with the vendor that the application will be still supported if you use them.

Scalability Inhibitors

There are some pitfalls you must avoid when developing applications in RAC. Let's ignore unsuitable and non-scalable hardware for the moment, and look at some other causes for this. For example, poor application design contributes massively to poor scalability. The following paragraphs list some common problems that should be avoided.

Many developers are taught object oriented-programming languages such as Java or C#, which allow designers to develop abstract base types and use features such as inheritance to subclass these types for their individual needs. The object-oriented approach to developing needs to be translated into the relational model when using a database as a backend. There are many frameworks available to perform this task, but many of these tend to be generic in nature, and typically they don't fully support the capabilities of a modern database management system. In fact, many frameworks use the database as little more than a glorified file system, which makes tuning applications based on these frameworks difficult.

When developing applications for the Oracle database, it is important to pay attention to schema design. Oracle offers a wealth of data and segment types to choose from, depending upon usage requirements. Suboptimal schema design can cause queries to be expensive or to use lots of physical and logical I/Os, which ultimately hampers scalability. As a rule of thumb, the application schema should be normalized. However, it is sometimes acceptable to de-normalize the schema for performance reasons. However, we want to emphasize that suitable schema design yields the greatest performance benefit.

Caching information in the application server layer is a design approach that we often encounter. Such caching is done with performance is mind. It is well intended, but typically it only masks the underlying problem in the short term. The problem leading to the creation of the cache will return when the volume of data exceeds the cache's size.

Ineffective transaction design is another performance inhibitor. Ineffective design often manifests itself in the form of LOCK TABLE and SELECT FOR UPDATE statements. These can cause locking and serialization problems that only get worse in a RAC environment.

Some applications that use legacy technology can present scalability problems. Web servers that serve dynamic content utilizing the Common Gateway Interface to connect to a RDBMS instance often establish new connections to the database for each web page served to the client. The pattern in these applications is to connect, perform a little bit of work, and then disconnect. Unsurprisingly, such applications can cause a considerable load on the database server. Prior to Oracle 11g, this load could somewhat be alleviated by using multiple shared servers and dispatchers. A better way to support these applications, however, is to configure the Database Resident Connection Pool (DRCP) that came with Oracle 11g Release 1. The DRCP has specifically been designed to care for applications that do not or cannot use connection pooling. DRCP works by providing a pool of dedicated connections within the database, rather than in the middle-tier. Oracle's Real User Experience Insight product uses DRCP with great effect to connect the user interface (written in PHP) to the repository database. DRCP memory requirements can be lowered compared to both dedicated server and shared server connections. This allows applications to scale well for large user numbers.

Unsuitable or incorrectly specified hardware can also contribute to scalability problems. Saturated storage controllers or write caches that are undersized can lead to degraded IO performance of the system. For example, overcommitting memory on a database server can lead to a situation where the kernel daemon responsible for freeing memory drives the load average so high that the system becomes unresponsive and has to be rebooted.

REAL WORLD EXAMPLE: ADDRESSING PERFORMANCE ISSUES

Some time ago, we were asked to help troubleshoot application performance for a web-based application that connects to an Oracle active-passive cluster based on Oracle Clusterware. Users were complaining about the application "hanging" and a slow response time.

Upon investigation, the following became apparent:

- Bad transaction design severely limited scalability.

- The application code accessing the database was built using an inflexible development framework.

- The application was not stateless, as one would expect from a web-based tool.

- The connection pool was oversized.

The worst part—and a problem that is nearly impossible to fix (because it originated from the application development framework)—was the transaction design. Whenever a user modified data in the frontend, the connection her application grabbed from the connection pool would turn every subsequent select into a `select for update` statement. Even though the number of users was not huge, the `select for update` commands from multiple sessions effectively introduced massive enqueue problems that resulted in the hanging or slow performance situation. Oracle deadlock detection alleviated this problem a little from a database point of view by rolling back a few transactions, but otherwise this problem required a major application rewrite to fix. Lesson learned: Any application design should address scalability right from the outset.

Standby Databases

Real Application Clusters is primarily a high availability and scalability solution. Among its main benefits: It protects the system from loss of service in case of instance failure, which would otherwise cause an unplanned outage in a single-instance setup.

However, a catastrophic site failure is usually not covered by RAC, except for the case of a rare implementation of extended distance clusters. Also, common human errors such as the following can cause logical corruption in the database:

- Dropping a table with the deactivated Flashback Table feature

- Updating data with an incorrectly specified where clause

- Confusing the production development with the development or test environment

Without standby databases, either a *flashback database* call or a point-in-time restore is needed to recover from such mishaps. With today's large database systems, a point-in-time restore is usually not an option due to the large mean time to recovery associated with a full restore and recovery operation. Adding in the fact that RAC has been chosen in many cases for high availability highlights why a few hours of downtime cannot be tolerated. The Flashback Database feature introduced in Oracle 10*g* has greatly reduced the recovery time in many cases. In fact, the Flashback Database feature has become invaluable, not only for recovery of the production live database, but as we will see later in this chapter, for Data Guard scenarios as well.

Introduction to Oracle Standby Databases

To protect from site failures or human error, an additional precaution needs to be taken in a RAC environment to provide disaster recoverability. Oracle Enterprise Edition has offered a feature called Oracle Data Guard since version 7.3 to address this requirement.

In Oracle 7 and 8/8*i*, this feature was referred to as a *standby database*. The principle behind the technology is simple yet effective: an identical copy of the live (or primary) database (AKA the standby database) is instantiated in a remote data center. The standby database is constantly in the state of media recovery, unless opened for read-only access. Without the Active Data Guard option introduced in Oracle 11.1, there is an additional caveat you need to be aware of: while the database is opened in read-only mode, it doesn't apply changes received from the primary database.

While not a problem per se, the fact that changes are not being applied can extend the time needed to transition to the standby database. This is because additional archived redo logs have to be applied unless you are willing to incur data loss. Without Active Data Guard, the database has to be in mount state for managed recovery to work. The mount state prevents users, except for those with sysdba privilege, from connecting to the database. Any attempt to do so will result in an ORA-1033 "Oracle initialization or shutdown in progress" message.

When the standby feature was introduced in Oracle 7.3, maintaining a standby database was a highly manual process: the database administrator was in charge of transferring archived redo logs generated on the primary database to the standby site using utilities such as rcp or ftp (rsync). Once the logs were on the standby site, the standby database had to be placed in recovery mode. The only possible action the administrator could take was to activate the standby database in order for it to assume the primary role. This process where the DBA copied logs was referred to as *manual* recovery.

Beginning with Oracle 8*i*, the standby database uses *managed* recovery to stay in sync with the primary database. Using Oracle Net*8 communication, the primary database ships changes to the standby database, which are subsequently applied to the data files to keep the systems in sync. The application of changes can be delayed to protect the system from the aforementioned user errors. A standby database can also used for reporting or backing up data; this removes some of the load from the primary database.

A further milestone was reached with Oracle 9*i*, which introduced the logical standby database and graceful switchover operations. It was also in Oracle 9*i* that the standby database feature was renamed to Data Guard. Users of Data Guard were also given another choice for transmitting redo information to the standby. In addition to the `archiver`, which traditionally shipped information to the standby database after an online redo log was archived, the log writer process could be used to perform the same task. Standby redo logs were introduced as the counterpart to the primary database's online redo logs. Instead of having to wait for a complete archived redo log to arrive, the redo stream could be written into a standby redo log, thus reducing the risk of data loss. Oracle 9*i* Database also introduced the Data Guard broker with support for Enterprise Manager, as well as a command-line tool to simplify the setup and management of standby databases.

Another noteworthy evolution came with Oracle 10*g*, when the Real Time Apply feature was integrated into the database kernel. Using standby redo logs on the standby database server, the redo stream arriving on the destination could be applied to the standby database immediately, without having to wait for the standby redo log to be archived and applied. This further reduces the possibility of data loss.

Figure 3-1 illustrates the concepts for Oracle 11*g*, where redo generated by user activity on the primary database is transported via the Log Network Server (LNS0) process—not the log writer, as in previous versions—to the standby database's Remote File Server (RFS) process. In turn, the RFS process writes the redo stream into standby redo logs. The managed recovery process (MRP0) on the standby database applies the new information as soon as it arrives. Once filled, the standby redo log is archived by one of the standby database's archiver processes.

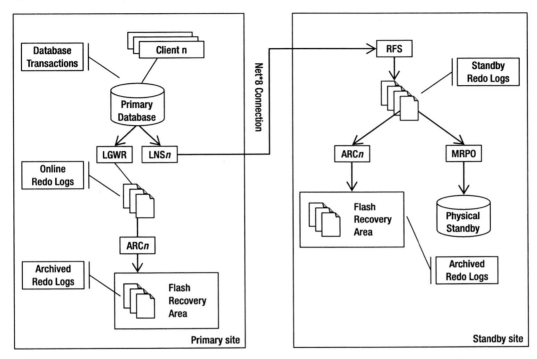

Figure 3-1. *This figure shows the Data Guard physical standby configuration with asynchronous redo transport and real time apply under 11.1; note that 11.2 uses NSAn instead of LSNn to ship redo asynchronously.*

Provision of support for data corruption has been introduced in Oracle 11g Release 1. Setting the new db_lost_write_protect parameter helps prevent lost writes, and Data Guard will also try re-fetching corrupt blocks detected during the redo apply to a physical standby database, and vice versa. This is referred to as Automatic Block Media Recovery.

With Oracle 11g Release 2, the previous limit of 10 archive log destinations (both local and remote) has been lifted, and up to 30 standby databases can now form part of a Data Guard configuration. A cascaded standby database configuration in which a standby database passes on redo to another standby database is not possible (read: supported) if the primary database is a RAC 11.2 database.

Types of Standby Database

You can choose from the following four different types of standby databases:

- Physical standby database
- Snapshot standby database

- Logical standby database
- Transient logical standby database

Each of these will be covered in more detail in the sections that follow.

Physical Standby Database

The physical standby database was the first standby database option available. In all aspects, a physical standby database is an identical bit-for-bit copy of the primary database. All schema structures, database users, and segments are identical down to the block level.

A physical standby database is kept in sync with production through the application of redo (referred to as "redo apply"). The process employed is the same one that a database administrator would use to recover a live database after a media failure. Apart from disaster recovery scenarios, a standby database can be used for reporting and backup. With a little bit of manual effort, a physical standby database can also be used for testing hot fixes on production systems. You do this by activating it for read-write access after having taken it out of the Data Guard configuration. Once the testing of the hot fix on like-for-like production data is complete, the Flashback Database feature can be used to flash the database back to the point in time prior to its activation, followed by its conversion back to a physical standby. The downside to this procedure is that, while the database is open for read-write access, it won't receive any archived logs from the (real) primary database. This can cause a lot of network traffic once the database has been converted back to a physical standby.

Snapshot Standby Database

The snapshot standby database achieves the exact same result as the physical standby database opened read-write for testing, as just described. However, the snapshot database doesn't require that the administrator worry about the fine print and all the details. The snapshot standby will receive archived logs from production, significantly reducing the overhead during gap resolution. However, the archived redo logs received from production aren't applied until after the snapshot standby database has been converted back to a physical standby database, so the time it takes for the standby database to get back in sync with production is proportional to the amount of redo to be applied.

When upgrading a database with a standby database(s) in place, the redo transport mechanism will ensure that the dictionary changes are propagated to all destinations for as long as the catalog upgrade script is executing on the primary site. This is true for both physical and snapshot standby database configurations. All you need to do is ensure that the Oracle binaries on the standby servers exactly match the binaries on the primary database.

You can have both single-instance standby databases and multi-node RAC systems for your disaster recovery solution. However, bear in mind that your standby database must to be able to cope with the workload in a disaster recovery situation. You are well advised to use identical hardware for both production and standby environments. If you use identical hardware, and your standby database is a RAC database as well, then all instances can receive redo from the primary database, thereby spreading the load. However, only one instance can *apply* redo.

Logical Standby Database

A logical standby database differs from a physical standby database in that it is not an exact 1:1 copy of the live database. Every logical standby database starts its existence exactly like a physical standby database, but it is then converted for read-write access. At this stage, the primary database and logical standby deviate. Physical (and snapshot) standby databases stay synchronized through the application of redo logs. However, a logical standby database stays synchronized by having it execute all the same SQL statements as the primary database. This mechanism is often referred to as *SQL Apply*.

Internally, SQL Apply uses the log miner feature to extract SQL statements from the redo stream. It then applies SQL statements rather than redo to the standby database. Therefore, a logical standby database has the same data structure as the primary database, but the physical representation of the data in the database is likely to be different. There are also some restrictions as to which data types are supported on the primary database, and this list keeps growing from release to release.

Another big difference between a physical and logical standby database is the fact that a logical standby database is open read-write while it still receives changes from production. A logical standby database is unlikely to be used for disaster recovery purposes. Its main purpose is to provide an environment in which reporting can be offloaded from production as changes from the live system are fed into the database. This provides a high degree of data accuracy. The fact that the logical standby database is open read-write means that additional data structures such as indexes and materialized views can be created to speed up queries that would otherwise be too expensive to maintain on the primary database.

Finally, logical standby databases can be used as part of the process to upgrade primary databases to newer releases or to apply patch sets to a system with almost no downtime. This little used technique is referred to as a *rolling upgrade* in the Oracle documentation. The transient logical standby database discussed in the next section is what you really want to use in cases where you want to apply a rolling upgrade in your own environment.

Transient Logical Standby Database

Oracle has recognized that few businesses are willing to set up a logical standby database only for the rolling upgrade of an Oracle database. Setting up a logical standby database is not a trivial task, and maintaining a logical standby database requires close monitoring to check that all transactions have been applied. For this reason, Oracle 11g Release 1 provides the capability to transiently convert a physical standby database into a logical standby database for the duration of a rolling upgrade. After the upgrade, the logical standby database is converted back to its original role as a physical standby database.

This type of standby database is not listed under the name *transient logical standby* in the documentation; however, it is mentioned in Chapter 12 of the *Oracle Data Guard Concepts and Administration Guide*. Chapter 12 in that guide covers how to perform rolling upgrades of a database. The rolling upgrade steps are identical to using a logical standby database for the upgrade process; however, the setup of the logical standby database is greatly simplified.

Active Data Guard

The majority of standby databases are probably physical standby databases running in remote disaster recovery data centers waiting to be activated. Many users of such configurations have remarked that this isn't the best use of resources. While it is possible to use the standby database as a source for backups, the tapes must be shipped from the DR site to the primary site if something occurs. The other option, using the standby database for reporting and ad-hoc queries that couldn't possibly be executed on the primary database, also has a downside: while the database is open for read-only mode, no archived logs are applied, which causes the primary and the standby databases to go out of sync and the data to become stale.

Beginning with 11*g* Release 1, Oracle addressed these concerns with the Active Data Guard option, which needs to be acquired on top of Enterprise Edition. When purchased, this option offers the following benefits over and above what Data Guard already provides:

- Physical Standby databases in read-only mode can have managed recovery enabled. This allows users to offload their queries to current production data, thus combining the best of both worlds. Oracle refers to this feature as *Real Time Query*.

- This option also allows the use of block change tracking for faster incremental backups on the standby database.

Active Data Guard can also be used as a scalability tool for web-based content. For example, multiple standby databases opened read-only with the Active Data Guard option enabled to provide real time data access to web servers. This significantly scales data access. Updates to the data occur only on the primary database through a controlled user interface, and changes are immediately propagated to the reader farm through Real-Time Query.

Role Transitions

Data Guard supports two types of role transitions: a graceful switchover and a failover. During a switchover operation, the primary database ensures that no data loss occurs by performing a log switch and waiting for the redo to be applied on all databases that form part the Data Guard configuration. Only then will it transform into a standby database itself. At this stage, *all* the databases forming part of the Data Guard configuration are physical standby databases. The administrator then chooses one of the other standby databases to assume the primary role.

A switchover is an elegant solution that helps to minimize time required for performing the following maintenance operations:

- Replacing hardware

- Migrating to another storage technology, such as Automatic Storage Management

- Migrating to another storage array

- Moving the data center

- Changing the word size of a database

- Upgrading database and Clusterware versions

- Upgrading the operating system

Although not entirely free of downtime, a switchover provides a proven technology for performing such tasks.

REAL WORLD EXAMPLE: SWITCHING OVER GRACEFULLY

While working on a long-overdue hardware upgrade project, we successfully employed a graceful switchover. In one case, we increased the number of cluster nodes from two to three, upgraded the operating system, modified the underlying storage, and changed the database word size.

The system to be replaced consisted of a two-node, 32-bit Red Hat 3.9 installation relying on a 10.2.0.3 RAC cluster using OCFS version 1. The new system consisted of three nodes, with 10.2.0.4 Clusterware and ASM/RDBMS binaries running Red Hat Enterprise Linux 5 update 3 in 64-bit mode. In lieu of OCFS1, we moved to Automatic Storage management. At the same time, an identical hardware configuration for the standby database was enabled in a remote data center.

Counting the time for preparation and sanity checking, the whole operation took only a little longer than one hour.

A failover indicates a more severe situation in which the primary database is no longer available for a switchover, possibly because of a site failure or the loss of the storage backend. In such a situation, the administrator should try salvaging as many outstanding archived logs as possible. The DBA should also minimize or, preferably, eliminate the gap to be resolved on the standby database before activating one of the standby databases for read-write access. Data loss may occur, depending on the protection mode the Data Guard configuration is using.

Prior to the introduction of the Flashback Database feature, activating a standby database always implied that the primary database had to be completely rebuilt by restoring from a backup. Today, however, if the failed primary database has flashback enabled, then the time and effort required for a reinstantiation of the database can be greatly reduced, assuming that it can be started up without problems. For example, once the failed database has been restarted after a complete data center power outage, it is possible to flash it back to the system change number that existed prior to the activation of the new primary. From there, the database can be converted to a physical standby with only a few commands. When the situation clears, the former primary database can then be the target of a graceful switchover to restore service to before the failover.

Role transitions are slightly different, depending on the type of standby database (logical or physical) to assume the primary role, and each database administrator should be familiar with the steps necessary to carry out the different role transitions. Regular disaster recovery tests should be performed to ensure that the standby database(s) and the entire dependent infrastructure, such as load balancers and application servers, can execute the workload in the disaster recovery center. Easily accessible documentation is important because it can help the more junior team members perform this task and keep a cool head during a crisis.

■ **Note** Switchover operations involving RAC used to require that all but one instance were shut down prior to issuing the switchover command sequence. This was true until Oracle 11.2, when this restriction was partially removed.

Data Protection Modes

Data Guard offers three different data protection modes. Depending on the business requirements, Data Guard can be set up for maximum performance without affecting the operation of the primary database; alternatively, it can be set up to ensure zero data loss. There are advantages and disadvantages to all three options (see Table 3-4 for a description of available modes).

Table 3-4. The Data Guard Operation Modes

Operation Mode	Description
Maximum Protection	This mode provides the highest level of protection from data loss, ensuring that there will be zero data loss if the primary database fails. To achieve this level of protection, the standby database has to acknowledge that the redo generated by a transaction on the primary database has been written into its standby redo logs (in addition to the primary database's online redo logs) before the transaction can be committed on the primary database. If the primary database can't write to the standby database's standby redo logs, it will shut down to prevent data loss from occurring. Obtaining a zero data loss guarantee comes at a price: the application's commit time can increase compared to a different protection mode, and the primary database may shut down as a consequence of a network problem.
Maximum Performance	This mode dictates that the performance and availability of the primary database are not affected by the standby database. The default protection mode, maximum performance, has no redo write dependency between the primary and standby databases; in other words, the primary database commits transactions independently of the standby database. Because of this, many businesses introduce regular, forced log switches on the primary database using the ARCHIVE_LAG_TARGET initialization parameter.
Maximum Availability	This is a hybrid mode that strikes a balance between the other two modes. For transactions to commit on the primary database, at least one synchronized standby database must have received the redo in its standby redo logs. If it's not possible to write the redo stream to at least one synchronized database, the primary will perform as if it were configured in maximum performance mode.

The Data Guard Broker

The Data Guard broker is an integral part of the replication framework that lets you define Data Guard configurations, including support for all types of standby databases. The broker is installed by default with the RDBMS binaries. Its architecture was added to Data Guard in Oracle 9*i*, and it is a mature but little-used feature. From a user's point of view, the Data Guard broker simplifies the setup, maintenance, and monitoring of Data Guard configurations, as well as role transitions; RAC, of course, is fully supported. The tight integration into Enterprise Manager (not DBConsole!) also allows the creation of physical and logical standby database through simple mouse movements and a few key strokes. The usability of the Enterprise Manager integrated broker is higher than the command line interface alternatively available to the administrator. Enterprise Manager is more feature rich but requires additional infrastructure.

When used, Data Guard broker will rely on its own binary configuration files and additional background processes to configure the relevant initialization parameters upon instance start; it will also monitor the databases in the configuration. In RAC, the configuration files need to be on shared storage. ASM, raw devices, and cluster file systems are suitable candidates to store the files. You don't have to replicate the configuration on each database. Rather, the broker will automatically preserve the single image view of your Data Guard configuration by replicating changes to all database involved. You should not try to issue SQL commands through *sqlplus* to modify the Data Guard configuration because your changes are likely to be overwritten the next time the Data Guard broker starts: once the broker, always the broker.

Conceptually, the main objects the Data Guard broker operates on are configurations, databases, instances, and properties. To begin, a configuration is created with the primary database only. Up to 30 standby databases can then be added, along with their respective attributes. Data Guard broker will automatically detect whether a database is made up of multiple instances and register them with their database. Once all databases are added in and the administrator is happy with the setup, the configuration can be enabled. From there, the Data Guard broker takes command over the Data Guard environment.

The database object has properties and state information associated with it. As noted earlier, you no longer set initialization parameters directly. Instead, you change the state of the database to enable/disable log shipping or enable/disable managed recovery. The list of database properties you can either read or modify has grown with the evolution of Data Guard. Important properties you can modify include the following (among other options):

- Synchronous or asynchronous sending of redo to the standby database

- The delay for the application of a redo to the standby database; this setting is useful for preventing data corruption caused by human error in a multi-standby database environment

- Compression of the redo. Beginning with Oracle 11.1, archived logs could be compressed during gap resolution; Oracle 11*g* Release 2 introduces compression for the redo stream, but a license for the Advanced Compression option is required.

- Database file name conversion

- Log file name conversion

- The preferred apply instance for RAC

- Apply parallelism

When using Enterprise Manager, you don't have to remember the property names. Instead, you use the graphical user interface (GUI) to manage your Data Guard configuration.

The Data Guard broker has built-in support to modify redo transport and apply services for RAC and single-instance installations. As an additional benefit, the Data Guard broker allows you to set up automatic failover for unsupervised Data Guard configurations. This is referred to as *Fast Start Failover*. With this feature, an observer process running on hardware separate from the database servers monitors the primary database, and it can be configured to automatically fail over to the standby based on conditions. In the context of RAC, the Data Guard broker assumes that the RAC database is available, as long as at least one instance responds to user requests. Beginning with Oracle 11*g* Release 1, an API to control the Fast Start Failover option is available in form of the DBMS_DG package. After the failover is complete, the Data Guard broker will post a Fast Application Notification event indicating that the new primary database is ready for use. FAN uses the Oracle Notification Services process to post the event, so the database needs to either be a RAC database or single-instance database integrated with Oracle Restart.

■ **Note** Oracle Restart is a new feature that was introduced in Grid Infrastructure 11.2. In simple terms, it allows the registration of resources, such as ASM disk groups, ASM, and RDBMS instances in Clusterware. This works similarly to the way it works in RAC. The aim is to make custom startup scripts obsolete by starting all resources and their dependencies on a database server through Grid Infrastructure. Oracle Restart was also known as single instance high availability (SIHA).

Extended Distance Clusters

Extended distance clusters, or stretch clusters, are a special form of RAC system. Most RAC systems are designed to reside in a single data center, with the database servers, application servers, switches, and storage located close to one another. As the name suggests, extended distance clusters are different. Figure 3-2 illustrates some of the key concepts that apply.

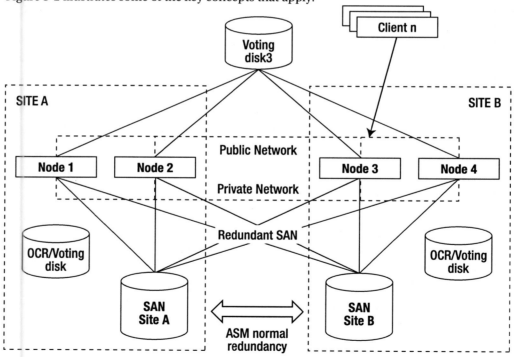

Figure 3-2. An architectural overview of an extended distance RAC

Using the same basic building blocks as "normal" clusters, individual nodes are geographically dispersed, offering protection from (local) site failure. Extended distance clusters compete with Data Guard as a means to protect users from site failure; however, Data Guard physical standby databases will be located further away from the primary under normal circumstances. When configured correctly, they can satisfy the disaster recover requirements better than an extended distance cluster.

The extended distance cluster relies on a dedicated low latency, high throughput cluster interconnect even more than a RAC cluster in the same cabinet does. Such a dedicated interconnect becomes increasingly more expensive to lease as the distance between the nodes grows.

Extended distance clusters are set up using two sites in most scenarios. Each site has its own storage and is mirrored on the SAN level or through Automatic Storage Management. In case of ASM, all disks in the local SAN are aggregated in a single failure group. ASM also needs to use normal redundancy for the disk groups used by the cluster. The extended distance cluster feature became usable for practical purposes with the release of Oracle 10.2.0.3 Enterprise Edition. Oracle 11g Release 1 lifted the requirement that hardware had to be located in the same server room or cabinet for Standard Edition RAC, allowing users to roll-out extended distance clusters with a Standard Edition license. Oracle 11.1 also introduced an ASM feature called *Preferred Mirror Read*. This feature allows the local instance to read data from the local SAN. In Oracle 10g, ASM could only ever read the primary copy of an extent that could be located on the remote SAN, thus introducing unneeded latency.

Special attention is required for the deployment and configuration of voting disks that are used among other tasks to manage node membership. Since Oracle 10g Release 2, it's been possible to define three voting disks in the cluster. For extended RAC, voting disks should to be configured to reside on each local storage array for the first and second voting disks. The third voting disk can be placed on inexpensive storage, such as an NFS on an independent (i.e. non-cluster) system to provide quorum.

Oracle Streams

Oracle Streams is a highly flexible messaging system built into the Oracle database Enterprise Edition. To a lesser degree, it is also available with Standard Edition since Oracle 11g Release 1. Using the Oracle Streams technology, it is possible to capture, propagate, and apply data definition changes, data manipulation changes, and user-defined messages from a source database to one or multiple destinations. It is even possible to use Oracle Streams to send data back to the source database; however, we, the authors, struggle to identify a use case for this. Oracle Streams also offers support for heterogeneous messaging, and you could also employ it to send data to a non-Oracle database.

It might help you to think of Oracle Streams as a technology similar to Data Guard's logical standby database because it uses similar concepts under the hood. However, Oracle Streams provides more flexibility for sharing information with other databases. It also allows you to share information across platform boundaries. Cross platform data support exists for Data Guard physical standby databases, as well; however, you cannot use this feature to replicate a subset of the database. Therefore, Oracle Streams is an excellent tool for platform migrations and database consolidation, far more suitable than the classical export/import method so often used traditionally. Oracle Streams also offers advantages over the transportable tablespace/database feature because it allows the source database to stay online and remain usable while the changes applied to it are applied to the new destination database.

There are many other uses for Oracle Streams as a technology. For one, it is vastly superior to the old Advanced Replication toolset, but it can also be employed to trickle-feed data warehouses. For another, it can be used for platform migration, as well as for notification services and message exchange in general. It is possible to modify the data stream at almost any stage using flexible rule sets or handler functions, which makes data transformation on-the-fly possible. Interestingly, Oracle Streams also provides the foundation for other Oracle technologies, such as Change Data Capture (CDC).

The remainder of this section will focus on Oracle Streams as a replication and high availability tool. Replicating data from a source to a destination database is performed in three major processing steps:

1. Capturing messages

2. Propagating messages to the destination(s)

3. Applying messages

Depending on the capture type, the propagation step can be omitted. Unlike with a Data Guard configuration, Enterprise Manager DBConsole allows the configuration and maintenance of an Oracle Streams setup.

Streams Processing

Capturing data marks the beginning of the stream's data flow. Capture can be performed either on the source database or on the destination database. Capturing data on the source is referred to as *local capture*, whereas capturing data on the destination database is referred to as *downstream capture*. The capture process uses the log miner functionality to extract SQL commands from the redo logs, hence its the similarity to a Data Guard logical standby database.

■ **Note** Oracle 11*g* provides another capture type called synchronous capture. This chapter does not discuss this feature because it has a number of limitations, such as not being able to capture DDL changes. However, this feature is available in Standard Edition and Standard Edition 1.

Supplemental logging onto the captured object (or, depending on the scope of the replication, the whole database) places the additional information necessary for the capture process to construct the logical change records into the redo logs. A logical change record is an internal representation of a database change, such as a DDL or DML command. This supplemental information is required by the apply process to merge the LCR to the destination database (this will be covered in more detail momentarily). Supplemental logging creates overhead; sufficient testing should ensure that the database can handle the new load.

Regardless of whether a local or downstream capture process is used, user-definable rules determine which information should be captured from the redo logs. It's this freedom to choose what information gets captured that makes Oracle Streams more flexible than a logical standby database. The user defines which tablespace, schema, or tables to capture changes from; the user can also define negative rules to filter information. Once extracted, the capture process transforms the information into a logical change record (LCR) and enqueues it into a buffered queue that draws its memory from the SGA.

Oracle Streams uses queueing to propagate or stage LCRs extracted from the redo logs. The queues are buffered, but their contents can "spill" to disk if too much memory is consumed. Again, you can define rules to filter out particular LCRs and exclude them from propagation. Oracle employs a throttling mechanism if the enqueue rate is too high.

Propagation between source and destination queues is handled by the database scheduler jobs, and Oracle Streams guarantees message delivery. Propagation uses database links to transmit the information from the source to the destination for a configuration if local capture is used. When employing downstream capture, propagation is not necessary because the apply process will dequeue messages the capture process added to the local queue.

Once the information reaches the destination database queue, the apply process can dequeue the LCRs and apply them to the database. Alternatively, it is possible to use your own code to which a LCR can be passed before it is applied to the database for inspection or modification. Such a processing set is referred to as an *apply handler* in the Oracle documentation, and it is especially useful for data warehouse feeds or complex requirements where data must be cleansed. You can have such handlers for data manipulation changes, data definition changes, and other user-defined message types. Identical to the capture and propagation processes, you can define a rule set to discard certain LCRs before application to the database objects.

The apply process is a critical part of the Oracle Streams high availability and replication framework. Many views exist to monitor its performance. Viewing the contents of LCRs is especially useful in error situations. By default, the apply process will stop when it encounters an error, such as a foreign key violation or a tablespace with no space left in it. All errors will be reported to the so-called *error queue*, where they are available for review by the administrator. It is possible to retry individual transactions or all of the enqueued erroneous transactions after the underlying problem has been fixed.

Oracle Streams Prerequisites

Technically, Oracle Streams uses an administrator account most often named *strmadmin*. (You might remember the earlier *repadmin* account for advanced replication.) However, if your environment has strict security requirements, individual accounts can be used for capturing, propagating, and applying data. Next, bi-directional database links need to be configured between source and destination to serve two purposes:

1. During the initial setup, Data Pump can be used to initialize the streams configuration. In this case, the database links serve as the equivalent to the command-line `network_link` parameter.

2. Streams allows bi-directional replication.

At this stage, the capture and propagation processes are created to capture changes prior to the next step: object instantiation. Once the prerequisites are in place, you need to instantiate the objects to be replicated on the destination database. Data volumes permitting this can be implemented using Data Pump on-the-fly or through other techniques, such as RMAN. Finally, the apply process is created to receive changes from the source database. Once the propagation is enabled, data will start to flow. *The Oracle Streams Replication Administrator's Guide* also recommends creating a dedicated tablespace for the streams administration account to separate the I/O workload if messages spill to disk, which happens when the propagation can't keep up or flow control is enabled for other reasons.

In addition to the Enterprise Manager Grid Control/DBConsole GUI, Oracle introduced the DBMS_STREAMS_ADM package in 10*g* Release 2. It offers a number of procedures to combine the instantiation of streams after the database links and *strmadm* administrator accounts have been created. It is highly recommended that you take a look at this package. Note that many of the instantiation procedures have a `perform_action` parameter that can be set to `false`. The result of the call will be a text file that contains the steps necessary to implement streams. Using DBMS_STREAMS_ADM offers another benefit: if anything in the execution of the script goes wrong, the problem and progress are listed in DBA_RECOVERABLE_SCRIPT_ERRORS, and they can be resumed at the stage where it failed.

Before using Oracle Streams, it is important to review the My Oracle Support notes about Oracle Streams patches. The main document seems to be note 437838.1, which is titled "Streams Specific Patches." A number of notes have been written that advise those who adopted Oracle Streams to apply patches on top of their patch set. This can be difficult because the introduction of PSUs complicates this approach. Additional one-off patches can cause patch conflicts, and they may have to be replaced by merge level request (MLR) patches. Oracle recommends always applying the latest PSU. You should also consult My Oracle Support for the recommended setup information for your database version and Oracle Streams.

Cluster Topologies

We've covered a lot of introductory information so far. Now it's time to bring it all together for the big picture. Consider a common multitiered, web-based application acting as a company's intranet. Figure 3-3 shows a simplified view of such an application. The necessary DR environment and network switches/firewalls that you'd undoubtedly find have been omitted for clarity. Also, the number of load balancers, webservers, and RAC nodes is arbitrary, so you might find that your application needs more (or possibly less) computing power.

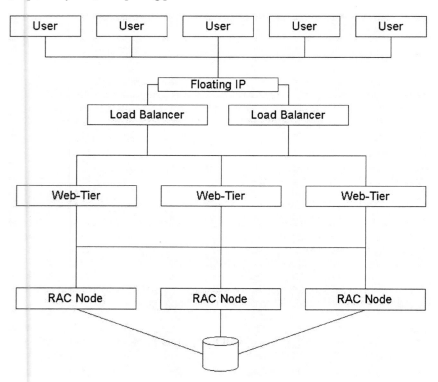

Figure 3-3. A simplified view of a three-tiered application

First, you have the "outside" world, where clients are located that connect to the public network switch and grant access to the load balancing layer. Load balancers should be employed to evenly distribute the incoming connection requests to the web server layer. This should prevent a single application server from being overloaded with requests while others are idle. Many load balancers employ a DNS round-robin algorithm, whereas a few products are capable of recording the load on the web server and routing the request to the least-loaded webserver.

If network encryption is used, it can be extremely beneficial to use load balancers with hardware encryption to support offloading a lot of the CPU power required to decode the incoming data stream.

Second, you have the next layer, where you find the web application servers. A multitude of products is available to perform this task. It will be necessary to choose which programming language to write the application in. There are limitations governing which platform can be used, especially with respect to Microsoft's .NET framework, where platform independence exists only in a rudimentary fashion. For example, the Mono framework on Linux lags several versions behind the current Windows version (4.0). More choice is available for Java-based applications because the Java Development Kit is available on most platforms. Solutions range from small servlet and Java Server Pages (JSP) containers such as Apache Tomcat; to Java Enterprise Edition capable web application servers such as JBoss or commercial solutions such as Weblogic (formerly known as BEA); to IBM's WebSphere, among other application servers. Oracle seems to have discontinued its own application server in favor of acquiring BEA.

At the bottom end of the application stack, we find the Oracle RAC database and the storage area network.

Depending on your security requirements, additional firewalling can be found between the different application layers, but they have been omitted from discussion in this chapter for the sake of clarity.

Summary

In this chapter, we investigated a number of topics relevant to the deployment of an Oracle RAC-based application. The most important subject designers and developers should have on their agenda is the continuous availability of the application, regardless of failure. RAC is an excellent high availability option, but it requires a little effort to enable applications to make the best use of it. This is easier to do for applications developed in-house applications than for applications that rely on third-party tools, especially if no access to the source code is available and no agreement has been made with the third-party vendor to RAC-enable the application.

If packaged applications can't use connection pools to benefit from events published by the FAN framework, Transparent Application Failover in session mode can provide at least a little bit of resilience, provided that the application uses the Oracle Call Interface libraries.

Instance recovery is another factor influencing application availability. As we saw, a failure of a busy instance can impact other nodes until the global resource directory is reconstructed, and the recovery set is applied to the database.

Writing a scalable application should be the design goal for any architect or developer. Experience has taught us that scalability is difficult to retrofit into an existing codebase; therefore it should be addressed from the outset. The Oracle database provides many features that can be used to improve scalability, depending on a given environment's requirements. Unfortunately, many application development frameworks don't allow fine-grained access to the generated code, which can make it difficult to ensure scalability.

We discussed intercluster failures in depth in the Instance Recovery in RAC section; however, what if the entire site fails? Oracle Data Guard standby databases are well suited to provide protection in the case of such scenarios. To a lesser extent, these standby databases are suited for extended distance clusters, as well. Finally, we examined Oracle Streams and how they can help you achieve high availability of applications.

The contents presented in the chapter should aide you in designing a highly available and scalable protected application on RAC maximizing your investment in this new technology.

CHAPTER 4

■ ■ ■

Hardware

In this chapter, we will review the technology decisions to be made in terms of the hardware required for a RAC cluster. The question of hardware is often neglected by DBAs; however, for a well-tuned application, the potential performance improvements offered by the latest server, interconnect, and storage architectures running the current versions of Linux is greater than those achievable by upgrades or software tuning on previous generations of technology. For this reason, hardware is a crucial topic of consideration for designing the best RAC configurations; this is particularly true for understanding how all of the components operate in conjunction for optimal cluster performance.

Knowing your hardware is also essential for assessing the total cost of ownership of a clustered solution. A proper assessment considers not just the costs of hardware alone, but also the significant potential savings offered in software acquisition and maintenance by selecting and sizing the components correctly for your requirements. In a RAC environment, this knowledge is even more important because, with a requirement for increased capacity, you are often presented with a decision between adding another node to an existing cluster and replacing the cluster in its entirety with updated hardware. You also have the choice between a great number of small nodes and a small number of large nodes in the cluster. Related to how you make this choice is how the network communication between the nodes in the cluster is implemented, so this chapter will also discuss the implementation of input/output (I/O) on the server itself in the context of networking. Knowing the hardware building blocks of your cluster is fundamental to making the correct decisions; it can also assist you in understanding the underlying reasons of how to configure the Linux operating system to achieve optimal Oracle RAC performance for installing and configuring Linux (see Chapter 6 for more details).

In addition to the Linux servers themselves, a crucial component of any RAC configuration is the dedicated storage array separate from any of the individual nodes in the cluster upon with the Oracle database is installed and shared between the nodes (see in Chapter 2); therefore, we also cover the aspects of storage I/O relating to RAC. In the context of RAC, I/O relates to the reads and writes performed on a disk subsystem, irrespective of the protocols used. The term *storage* encompasses all aspects relating to this I/O that enable communication of the server serving as the RAC node with nonvolatile disk.

Considering hardware presents a challenge in that, given the extraordinary pace of development in computing technology, reviewing the snapshot of any particular cluster configuration, in time, will soon be made obsolete by the next generation of systems and technologies. So, rather than focus on any individual configuration, we will review the general areas to consider when purchasing hardware for RAC that should remain relevant over time. With this intent, we will also refrain from directly considering different form factors, such as blade or rack-mounted servers. Instead, we will consider the lower-level technology that often lies behind a form factor decision.

The aim of this chapter is to provide a grounding to build a checklist when selecting a hardware platform for RAC on Linux. This will enable you to make an optimal choice. However, one factor that should be abundantly clear before proceeding is that this chapter will not tell you precisely what server, processor, network interconnect, or storage array to purchase. No two Oracle environments are the same; therefore, a different configuration may be entirely applicable to each circumstance.

Oracle Availability

Before beginning the selection of a hardware platform to run Oracle RAC on Linux, your first port of call should be Oracle itself, to identify the architectures on which Oracle releases the Oracle database for Linux with the RAC option.

At the time of writing, the following four architectures using Oracle terminology have production releases of the Oracle Database on Linux:

- *x86*: A standard 32-bit Intel compatible x86 processor

- *x86-64*: A 64-bit extended x86 processor (i.e., Intel EM64T, AMD64)

- *Itanium*: The Intel Itanium processor

- *Power*: The IBM Power processor

- *zSeries*: The IBM mainframe

In this chapter, our focus is on the first two architectures because of the availability of Oracle Enterprise Linux for these platforms as discussed in Chapter 1, and the additional availability of Oracle Database 11*g* Release 2.

In addition to simply reviewing the software availability, we also recommend viewing the RAC Technologies Matrix for Linux Platforms technology matrix to identify platform-specific information for running Oracle RAC in a particular environment. With the advent of the most recent generation of online Oracle support called *My Oracle Support*, Oracle Product Certification Matrices are no longer available for public access without a support subscription. It is therefore necessary to have a valid login at https://support.oracle.com to access the RAC Technologies Matrix.

If you have a valid My Oracle Support login at the top-level menu, click the More... tab, followed by Certifications.

On the Certification Information page, enter the search details in the dropdown menus under the Find Certification Information heading. For example, under Product Line, select Oracle Database Products. Under both Product Family and Product Area, select Oracle Database. Under Product, select Oracle Server – Enterprise Edition. And under Product Release, select 11gR2RAC. Leave the other options at their default selections and press the Search button to display the Certification Information by Product and Platform for Oracle Server - Enterprise Edition. Select the Certified link next to the platform of interest to display the Certification Detail. Now click Certification Notes, and the page displayed will include a link to a RAC Technologies Compatibility Matrix (RTCM) for Linux Clusters. These are classified into the following four areas:

- Platform Specific Information on Server/Processor Architecture

- Network Interconnect Technologies

- Storage Technologies

- Cluster File System/Volume Manager

It is important to note that these technology areas should not be considered entirely in isolation. Instead, the technology of the entire cluster should be chosen in a holistic manner. For example, the importance of the storage-compatibility matrix published by the storage vendors you are evaluating is worth stressing. Many storage vendors perform comprehensive testing of server architectures running against their technology, often including Oracle RAC as a specific certification area. To ensure compatibility and support for all of your chosen RAC components, the servers should not be selected completely independently of the storage—and vice versa.

An additional subject you'll want to examine for compatible technology for RAC is cluster software, which, as a software component, is covered in detail in Chapter 8.

In this chapter, we will concentrate on the remaining hardware components and consider the selections of the most applicable server/processor architecture, network interconnect, and storage for your requirements.

Server Processor Architecture

The core components of any Linux RAC configuration are the servers themselves that act as the cluster nodes. These servers all provide the same service in running the Linux operating system, but do so with differing technologies. One of those technologies is the processor, or CPU.

As you have previously seen, selecting a processor on which to run Oracle on an Oracle Linux supported platform presents you with two choices. Table 4-1 shows the information gleaned from the choices' textual descriptions in the Oracle technology matrix.

Table 4-1. *Processor Architecture Information*

Server/Processor Architecture	Processor Architecture Details
Linux x86	Support on Intel and AMD processors that adhere to the 32-bit x86 architecture.
Linux x86-64	Support on Intel and AMD processors that adhere to the 64-bit x86-64 architecture. 32-bit Oracle on x86-64 with a 64-bit operating system is not supported. 32-bit Oracle on x86-64 with a 32-bit operating system is supported.

x86 Processor Fundamentals

Although the processor architecture information in Table 4-1 describes two processor architectures, the second, x86-64 is an extension to the instruction set architecture (ISA) of x86. The x86 architecture is a complex instruction set computer (CISC) architecture and has been in existence since 1978, when Intel introduced the 16-bit 8086 CPU. The de facto standard for Linux systems is x86 (and its extension, x86-64) because it is the architecture on which Linux evolved from a desktop-based Unix implementation to one of the leading enterprise-class operating systems. As detailed later in this section, all x86-64 processors support operation in 32-bit or 64-bit mode.

Moore's Law is the guiding principle to understand how and why newer generations of servers continue to deliver near exponential increases in Oracle Database performance at reduced levels of cost. Moore's Law is the prediction dating from 1965 by Gordon Moore that, due to innovations in CPU manufacturing process technology, the number of transistors on an integrated circuit can be doubled every 18 months to 2 years. The design of a particular processor is tightly coupled to the silicon process on which it is to be manufactured. At the time of writing, 65nm (nanometer), 45nm, and 32nm processes are prevalent, with 22nm technologies in development. There are essentially three consequences of a more advanced silicon production process:

- *The more transistors on a processor, the greater potential there is for the CPU design to utilize more features:* The most obvious examples of this are multiple cores and large CPU cache sizes, the consequences of which you'll learn more about later in this chapter.

- *For the same functionality, reducing the processor die size reduces the power required by the processor:* This makes it possible to either increase the processor clock speed, thereby increasing performance; or to lower the overall power consumption for equivalent levels of performance.

- Shrinking the transistor size increases the yield of the microprocessor production process: This lowers the relative cost of manufacturing each individual processor.

As processor geometries shrink and clock frequencies rise, however, there are challenges that partly offset some of the aforementioned benefits and place constraints on the design of processors. The most important constraint is that the transistor current leakage increases along with the frequency, leading to undesired increases power consumption and heat in return for gains in performance. Additionally, other constraints particularly relevant to database workloads are memory and I/O latency failing to keep pace with gains in processor performance. These challenges are the prime considerations in the direction of processor design and have led to features such as multiple cores and integrated memory controllers to maintain the hardware performance improvements that benefit Oracle Database implementations. We discuss how the implications of some of these trends require the knowledge and intervention of the DBA later in this chapter.

One of the consequences of the processor fundamentals of Moore's Law in an Oracle RAC environment is that you must compare the gains from adding additional nodes to an existing cluster on an older generation of technology to those from refreshing or reducing the existing number of nodes based on a more recent server architecture. The Oracle DBA should therefore keep sufficiently up-to-date on processor performance that he can adequately size and configure the number of nodes in a cluster for the required workload over the lifetime of the hosted database applications.

Today's x86 architecture processors deliver high performance with features such as being superscalar, being pipelined, and possessing out-of-order execution; understanding some of the basics of these features can help in designing an optimal x86-architecture based on Oracle RAC environment.

When assessing processor performance the clock speed is often erroneously used as a singular comparative measure. The *clock speed*, or *clock rate*, is usually measured in gigahertz, where 1GHz represents 1 billion cycles per second. The clock speed determines the speed at which the processor executes instructions. However, the CPU's architecture is absolutely critical to the overall level of performance, and no reasonable comparison can be made based on clock speed alone.

For a CPU to process information, it needs to first load and store the instructions and data it requires for execution. The fastest mode of access to data is to the processor's registers. A *register* can be viewed as an immediate holding area for data before and after calculations. Register access can typically occur within a single clock cycle, for example assume you have a 2GHz CPU: retrieving the data in its registers will take one clock cycle of ½ a billionth of a second (½ a nanosecond). A general-purpose register can be used for arithmetic and logical operations, indexing, shifting, input, output, and general data storage before the data is operated upon. All x86 processors have additional registers for floating-point operations and other architecture-specific features.

Like all processors, an x86 CPU sends instructions on a path termed the *pipeline* through the processor on which a number of hardware components act on the instruction until it is executed and written back to memory. At the most basic level, these instructions can be classified into the following four stages:

1. *Fetch*: The next instruction of the executing program is loaded from memory. In reality, the instructions will already have been preloaded in larger blocks into the instruction cache (we will discuss the importance of cache later in this chapter).

2. *Decode*: x86 instructions themselves are not executed directly, but are instead translated into microinstructions. Decoding the complex instruction set into these microinstructions may take a number of clock cycles to complete.

3. *Execute*: The microinstructions are executed by dedicated execution units, depending on the type of operation. For example, floating-point operations are handled by dedicated floating-point execution units.

4. *Write-back*: The results from the execution are written back to an internal register or system memory through the cache.

This simple processor model executes the program by passing instructions through these four stages, one per clock cycle. However, performance potentially improves if the processor does not need to wait for one instruction to complete write-back before fetching another, and a significant amount of improvement has been accomplished through *pipelining*. Pipelining enables the processor to be at different stages with multiple instructions at the same time; since the clock speed will be limited by the time needed to complete the longest of its stages, breaking the pipeline into shorter stages enables the processor to run at a higher frequency. For this reason, current x86 enterprise processors often have between 10- to 20-stage pipelines. Although each instruction will take more clock cycles to pass through the pipeline, and only one instruction will actually complete on each core per clock cycle, a higher frequency increases the utilization of the processor execution units—and hence the overall throughput.

One of the most important aspects of performance for current x86 processors is out-of-order execution, which adds the following two stages to the simple example pipeline around the execution stage:

- *Issue/schedule*: The decoded microinstructions are issued to an instruction pool, where they are scheduled onto available execution units and executed independently. Maintaining this pool of instructions increases the likelihood that an instruction and its input will be available to process on every clock cycle, thereby increasing throughput.

- *Retire*: Because the instructions are executed out of order, they are written to the reorder buffer (ROB) and retired by being put back into the correct order intended by the original x86 instructions before write-back occurs.

Further advancements have also been made in instruction-level parallelism (ILP) with superscalar architectures. ILP introduces multiple parallel pipelines to execute a number of instructions in a single clock cycle, and current x86 architectures support a peak execution rate of at least three and more typically four instructions per cycle.

Although x86 processors operate at high levels of performance all of the data stored in your database will ultimately reside on disk-based storage. Now assume that your hard-disk drives have an access time of 10 milliseconds. If the example 2GHz CPU were required to wait for a single disk access, it would wait for a period of time equivalent to 20 million CPU clock cycles. Fortunately, the Oracle SGA acts as an intermediary resident in random access memory (RAM) on each node in the cluster. Memory access times can vary, and the CPU cache also plays a vital role in keeping the processor supplied with instructions and data. We will discuss the performance potential of each type of memory and the influence of the CPU cache later in this chapter. However, with the type of random access to memory typically associated with Oracle on Linux on an industry-standard server, the wait will take approximately between 60 and 120 nanoseconds. The time delay represents 120 clock cycles for which the example 2GHz CPU must wait to retrieve data from main memory.

You now have comparative statistics for accessing data from memory and disk. Relating this to an Oracle RAC environment, the most important question to ask is this: "How does Cache Fusion compare to local memory and disk access speeds?" (One notable exception to this question is for data warehouse workloads as discussed in Chapter 14). A good average receive time for a consistent read or current block for Cache Fusion will be approximately two to four milliseconds with a gigabit-Ethernet based interconnect. This is the equivalent of 4 to 5 million clock cycles for remote Oracle cache access, compared to 120 clock cycles for local Oracle cache access. Typically, accessing data from a remote SGA through Cache Fusion gives you a dramatic improvement over accessing data from a disk. However, with the increased availability of high performance solid-state based storage, Flash PCIe cards, and enterprise storage that utilizes RAM based caching (as discussed later in this chapter), it may be possible that disk-based requests could complete more quickly than Cache Fusion in some configurations. Therefore the algorithms in Oracle 11*g* Release 2 are optimized so that the highest performing source of data is given preference, rather than simply assuming that Cache Fusion delivers the highest performance in all cases.

Similarly, you may consider supported interconnect solutions with lower latencies such as Infiniband, which you'll learn more about later in this chapter. In this case, *Cache Fusion* transfers may potentially reduce measurements from milliseconds to microseconds; however, even a single microsecond latency is the equivalent of 2000 CPU clock cycles for the example 2GHz CPU, and it therefore represents a penalty in performance for accessing a remote SGA compared to local memory.

x86-64

The 64-bit extension of x86 is called x86-64 but can also be referred to as x64, EM64T, Intel 64, and AMD64; however, the minor differences in implementation are inconsequential, and all of these names can be used interchangeably.

Two fundamental differences exist between x86, 32- and x86-64, 64-bit computing. The most significant is in the area of memory addressability. In theory, a 32-bit system can address memory up to the value of 2 to the power of 32, enabling a maximum of 4GB of addressable memory. A 64-bit system can address up to the value of 2 to the power of 64, enabling a maximum of 16 exabytes, or 16 billion GB, of addressable memory—vastly greater than the amount that could be physically installed into any RAC cluster available today. It is important to note, however, that the practical implementations of the different architectures do not align with the theoretical limits. For example, a standard x86 system actually has 36-bit physical memory addressability behind the 32-bit virtual memory addressability. This 36-bit physical implementation gives a potential to use 64GB of memory with a feature called Page Addressing Extensions (PAE) to translate the 32-bit virtual addresses to 36-bit physical addresses. Similarly, x86-64 processors typically implement 40-bit or 44-bit physical addressing; this means a single x86-64 system can be configured with a maximum of 1 terabyte or 16 terabytes memory respectively. You'll learn more about the practical considerations of the impact of the different physical and virtual memory implementations later in this chapter.

In addition to memory addressability, one benefit from moving to 64-bit registers is the processors themselves. With 64-bit registers, the processor can manipulate high-precision data more quickly by processing more bits in each operation.

For general-purpose applications x86-64 processors can operate in three different modes: 32-bit mode, compatibility mode, or 64-bit mode. The mode is selected at boot time and cannot be changed without restarting the system with a different operating system. However, it is possible to run multiple operating systems under the different modes simultaneously within a virtualized environment (see Chapter 5). In 32-bit mode, the processor operates in exactly the same way as standard x86, utilizing the standard eight of the general-purpose registers. In compatibility mode, a 64-bit operating system is installed, but 32-bit x86 applications can run on the 64-bit operating system. Compatibility mode has the advantage of affording the full 4GB of addressability to each 32-bit application. Finally, the processor can operate in 64-bit mode, realizing the full range of its potential for 64-bit applications.

This compatibility is indispensable when running a large number of 32-bit applications developed on the widely available x86 platform while also mixing in a smaller number of 64-bit applications; however, Oracle's published certification information indicates that 32-bit Oracle is not supported on a 64-bit version of Linux on the x86-64 architecture. That said, the architecture may be used for 32-bit Linux with 32-bit Oracle or for 64-bit Linux with 64-bit Oracle. The different versions cannot be mixed, though, and compatibility mode may not be used. To take advantage of 64-bit capabilities, full 64-bit mode must be used with a 64-bit Linux operating system, associated device drivers, and 64-bit Oracle—all must be certified specifically for the x86-64 platform.

The single most important factor for adopting 64-bit computing for Oracle is the potential for memory addressability beyond the capabilities of a 32-bit x86 system for the Oracle SGA. Additionally, the number of users in itself does not directly impact whether a system should be 32- or 64-bit. However, a significantly large number of users also depend on the memory handling of the underlying Linux operating system for all of the individual processes, and managing this process address space also benefits from 64-bit memory addressability. For this reason, we recommend standardizing on an x86-64 processor architecture for Oracle RAC installations. In addition, memory developments such as NUMA memory features are only supported in the 64-bit Linux kernel; therefore, the advantages of 64-bit computing are significantly enhanced on a server with a NUMA architecture as discussed later in this chapter.

Multicore Processors and Hyper-Threading

Recall for a moment the earlier discussion of Moore's Law in this chapter. Whereas improvements in manufacturing process have produced successive generations of CPUs with increasing performance, the challenges—especially those related to heat and power consumption—have resulted in the divergence of processor design from a focus on ever-advancing clock speeds. One of the most significant of these developments has been the trend towards multicore processors (see Figure 4-1). A *multicore processor* is one that contains two or more independent execution cores in the same physical processor package or socket.

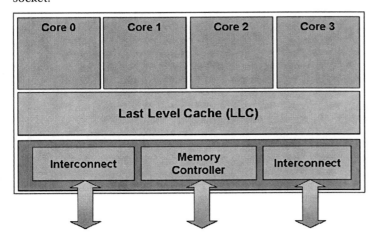

Figure 4-1. A multicore processor

For example, a quad-core processor can execute four processes completely independently and simultaneously without contending for CPU resources, such as registers. In other words, the design aims to achieve higher performance and greater power efficiency in the same profile platform, as opposed to utilizing the same manufacturing technology to produce a single-core processor with a higher clock speed. The trend toward multicore processors is but one example of a reduced emphasis on attempting to increase processor performance solely by increasing this clock frequency; instead, the multicore approach attempts to achieve greater performance by implementing more parallelism by leveraging a greater number of shorter pipelines than earlier processor architectures.

It is important to note that, in an Oracle environment, the workload of a typical Oracle user session will be scheduled and executed on one physical core only. Therefore, the best way to achieve better performance is to improve throughput and scalability by making resources available to process the workload of multiple sessions, the Oracle Database, and operating system processes concurrently. This approach improves performance more than processing these tasks more quickly, but in a serial fashion. The notable exception to this occurs with Oracle Parallel Execution, where a Parallel Query can take one complex query; however, such a query almost always requires full table scans and breaking the query into tasks completed by a number of Parallel Execution Servers on multiple cores across all of the CPUs in a RAC environment (as noted previously, we discuss Parallel Execution in more depth in Chapter 14).

From a scalability perspective, it is important to note that not all of the processor resources are entirely independent within a multicore processor. Advantages may be leveraged by sharing some resources between the cores, such as the CPU LLC (Last Level Cache). Typically the distinction can be drawn between the processor cores themselves are being within the core block and the shared resources being identified as the uncore block.

At the time of writing, processors to run Linux with one, two, four, six, and eight cores are available. From a design perspective, multicore processors complement RAC architectures by enabling a greater level of processing power in increasingly lower profile platforms with fewer CPU sockets. When architecting a grid solution based on RAC, multicore processors present more options to increase the parallelism available within an individual server, as well as by adding additional servers across the cluster. This approach presents more design options for a finer level of granularity within the nodes themselves and across the entire cluster.

Simultaneous Multi-Threading (SMT), also known as Hyper-Threading (HT), is a feature distinct from multicore processing that appears on some processors. HT makes a single execution core appear to the operating system as two processors. For example, a quad-core CPU with HT will appear as eight processors. This appearance is a logical representation, and the number of physical processors remains the same. HT enables more efficient usage of the execution units of single processor core by scheduling two threads onto the same processor core at the same time. This usage model means that, in a multiprocess environment, the processor is more likely to process two simultaneous threads more rapidly than it would process the same two threads consecutively, resulting in higher performance and throughput. This approach is not to be confused with Switch-on-Event Multi-Threading (SoEMT), which is employed on alternative architectures. In that approach, only one process or thread executes on the core at a single time. However, upon encountering an event where that thread would stall, such as to read another scheduled thread from memory, the thread is switched to run on the processor.

HT can be enabled and disabled at the BIOS level of the server. However, where this feature is typically available, it can prove beneficial to Oracle workloads. We recommend that this feature be enabled by default, unless you're testing in a particular environment where it proves to have a detrimental impact upon performance. The main benefit of HT for Oracle is thatthroughput will improve by scheduling more processes to run, thus ensuring that all the processors are utilized while other processes are waiting to fetch data from memory.

The number of physical and logical CPUs presented to the operating system can be viewed in /proc/cpuinfo. The following extract shows some of the information for the first CPU, processor 0, on a system:

```
[root@london1 ~]# cat /proc/cpuinfo
processor       : 0
vendor_id       : GenuineIntel
cpu family      : 6
model           : 26
model name      : Intel(R) Xeon(R) CPU        X5570  @ 2.93GHz
stepping        : 5
cpu MHz         : 2933.570
cache size      : 8192 KB
physical id     : 0
siblings        : 4
core id         : 0
cpu cores       : 4
apicid          : 0
fpu             : yes
fpu_exception   : yes
cpuid level     : 11
wp              : yes
flags           : fpu vme de pse tsc msr pae mce cx8 apic sep mtrr pge
mca cmov pat pse36 clflush dts acpi mmx fxsr sse sse2 ss ht tm syscall
nx rdtscp lm constant_tsc ida pni monitor ds_cpl vmx est tm2 cx16 xtpr
popcnt lahf_lm
bogomips        : 5871.08
clflush size    : 64
cache_alignment : 64
address sizes   : 40 bits physical, 48 bits virtual
power management:
```

To correctly map the processor viewed at the Linux operating system level to the processor, you can use thread software available from the CPU manufacturers to determine the correct topology. The example output in Table 4-2 is generated on a two-processor socket Quad-Core Xeon processor based system with HT enabled.

Table 4-2. Processor Thread Mapping

Socket/Core	OS CPU to Core Mapping			
Socket 0				
OScpu#	| 0 8	| 1 9	| 2 10	| 3 11 |
Core	|c0_t0 c0_t1	|c1_t0 c1_t1	|c2_t0 c2_t1	|c3_t0 c3_t1 |
Socket 1				
OScpu#	| 4 12	| 5 13	| 6 14	| 7 15 |
Core	|c0_t0 c0_t1	|c1_t0 c1_t1	|c2_t0 c2_t1	|c3_t0 c3_t1 |

The output illustrates that, against the 16 processors, the operating system identifies the mapping of the Hyper-Threads of the first four set of cores as corresponding to CPUs 0 to 3 and 8 to 11. The second set of four cores are mapped to CPUs 4 to 7 and 12 to 15, respectively. As we shall see later in this chapter when we discuss memory performance, understanding the correct mapping on your system may help you create a more efficient scheduling of the workload.

CPU Cache

If the memory, Cache Fusion, or disk access speeds were the maximum at which the CPU could fetch the data and instructions it requires, the CPU would spend much of its clock cycles stalling, waiting for them to be retrieved. Therefore, the crucial components of the processor for Oracle workloads are the faster units of memory on the processor itself (i.e., the CPU cache).

The CPU cache stores the most commonly accessed areas of main memory in terms of data, executable code, and the page table entries in the transaction look-aside buffer (TLB). For example, the RDBMS kernel executable size for Oracle 11g on Linux x86-64 is more than 200MB. This means you will gain immediate benefits from a large cache size that stores as much of this executable as possible, while also providing more rapid access to data.

Cache is usually (although not always) implemented in a hierarchy with the different levels feeding each other. Typically Level 1 (L1) cache can be accessed in anything from 1 clock cycle to 5 clock cycles, or up to 2.5 nanoseconds at 2GHz. L2 cache can be accessed in 5–10 clock cycles, or up to 5 nanoseconds at 2GHz. L3 cache, or the LLC in a shared cache processor architecture, can usually be accessed in anything from 10 to 40 clock cycles depending on implementation, which is equivalent to 20 nanoseconds at 2GHz. Therefore, data stored in cache can be accessed at least three times faster than data stored in main memory, providing a considerable performance improvement. Also, as with registers, the more cache there is within the CPU, the more likely it is that it will perform efficiently by having data available to process within its clock cycles. The data in cache is ultimately populated with the data from main memory. When a requested byte is copied from memory with its adjacent bytes as a memory block, it is stored in the cache as a *cache line*. A *cache hit* occurs when this data is requested again, and instead of going to memory, the request is satisfied from the cache. By implementing a hierarchical system, the need to store the most-requested data close to the processor illustrates one of the reasons why maintaining an optimal Oracle indexing strategy is essential. Unnecessary full-table scans on large tables within the database are guaranteed to challenge even the most advanced caching implementations.

Of course, this view of caching provides an oversimplification for the implementation of a mulitcore or multiprocessor system (and uniprocessor systems using direct memory access [DMA] for I/O) because every read from a memory address must always provide the most up-to-date memory from that address, without fail. When multiple processors all share the same memory, they may all may have their own copies of a particular memory block held in cache, and if these are updated, some mechanism must be employed to guarantee consistency between main memory and the cache lines held on each and every single processor. The more processors you have, the greater the workload required for ensuring consistency. This process for ensuring consistency is termed *cache coherency*. Cache coherency is one of the reasons why features such as hash clusters, where Oracle stores the rows for multiple tables in the same data blocks; or Index-Organized Tables (IOTs), where the data is stored in the same blocks as the index; can bring significant performance benefits to transactional systems.

At the most basic level, CPU caches operate in one of two modes: *write-through* or *write-back*. In write-through mode, when the processor modifies a line in the cache, it also writes that date immediately to the main memory. For performance, the processor usually maintains a valid bit to determine whether the cache line is valid at any one time. This valid bit is the simplest method to maintain coherency. In write-back mode, the cache does not necessarily write the value back to another level of the cache hierarchy or memory immediately. This delay minimizes the performance impact, but it also requires a more complex protocol to ensure that all values are consistent across all processors. When processors employ different levels of cache, they do not necessarily employ the same mode or protocol for each level of cache.

All of the architectures of interest implement what is termed a *snooping protocol*, where the processor monitors the system bus for signals associated with cache reads and writes. If an individual processor observes activity relating to a cache line that it has loaded and is currently in a valid state, then some form of action must take place to ensure coherency. If a particular cache line is loaded on another processor, but not modified (e.g., if multiple users select the same rows from the Oracle database), the cache line will be valid, but some action must be taken to ensure that each processor is aware that it is not the only one with that particular piece of data. In addition, if a cache line is in a modified state on another processor, then one of two things must happen. First, that particular line will need to be either written back to main memory to be reread by the requesting processor. Or second, it will be transferred directly between caches. For RAC, the performance potential for cache-to-cache transfers is an important reason why you're typically better off with fewer cluster nodes with more processors, as opposed to more nodes with fewer processors.

The most basic form of the snooping protocol to implement cache coherency is the Modified Shared Invalid (MSI) protocol. This protocol is applied to each and every line loaded in cache on all of the processors in the system; it is also applied to the corresponding data located in main memory. A cache line can be in a modified state on one processor and one processor only. When it is in this state, the same data in cache on another processor and main memory must always be in an invalid state. The modified state must be maintained until the main memory is updated (or the modified state is transferred to another processor) to reflect the change and make it available to the other processors. In the shared state, one or more caches have the same cache line, all of which are in the valid state, along with the same data in memory. While a cache line is in a shared state, no other cache can have the data in a modified state. If a processor wishes to modify the cache line, then it must change the state to modified and render all of the corresponding cache lines as invalid. When a cache line is in a shared state, the processor is not required to notify the other processors when it is replaced by other data. The shared state guarantees that it has not been modified. The invalid state determines that the cache line cannot be used, and it does not provide any information about the state of the corresponding data in main memory.

Table 4-3 illustrates the permitted states available for an example cache line within two caches. Note that more than a passing similarity exists between the way that cache coherency is maintained at the processor level and the way that Cache Fusion operates between the Oracle RAC nodes. This comparison illustrates how, in a RAC environment, you are in fact operating in an environment that implements multiple levels of coherency at both the individual system and cluster levels.

Table 4-3. MSI Cache States

	INVALID	SHARED	MODIFIED
INVALID	Invalid	Shared	Modified
SHARED	Shared	Shared	Not Permitted
MODIFIED	Modified	Not Permitted	Not Permitted

Although theoretically simple to implement, the MSI protocol would require all state changes to be atomic actions and, therefore, would prove impractical to implement on a real system running software such as Oracle. Additionally if using a point-to-point interconnect as opposed to a shared system bus between processors there is no longer a single point to resolve cache coherency. Instead, additional exclusive, owner and forwarding states are added for the architectures of interest to realize the Modified Exclusive Shared Invalid (MESI) protocol, the Modified Exclusive Shared Invalid Forwarding (MESIF) protocol and the Modified Owned Exclusive Shared Invalid (MOESI) protocol. The exclusive state is similar to the shared state, except that the cache line is guaranteed to be present in one cache only. This limitation enables the processor to then change the state of the cache line, for example, from an Oracle UPDATE statement to modified, if required, without having to notify the other processors across the system bus. The addition of the exclusive state is illustrated in Table 4-4.

Table 4-4. *MESI Cache States*

	INVALID	SHARED	EXCLUSIVE	MODIFIED
INVALID	Invalid	Shared	Exclusive	Modified
SHARED	Shared	Shared	Not Permitted	Not Permitted
EXCLUSIVE	Exclusive	Not Permitted	Not Permitted	Not Permitted
MODIFIED	Modified	Not Permitted	Not Permitted	Not Permitted

The owner state signifies that the processor holding a particular cache line is responsible for responding to all requests for that particular cache line, with the data in main memory or other processors being invalid. This state is similar to the modified state; however, the additional state is a necessity when an architecture implements the concept of individual CPUs being privately responsible for a particular section of main memory.

Later in this chapter, we will discuss implementations of memory architectures, including the attributes of cache coherent non-uniform memory architectures (ccNUMA) which are becoming the standard implementation for x86 platforms. A MESI protocol implemented in a ccNUMA architecture would result in a higher level of redundant messaging traffic being sent between the processors, which would impact latency and system performance. For this reason, the MESI protocol has been adapted to both the MESIF and MOESI protocols for efficiency. For example, in the MESIF protocol, that additional Forwarding state is added, and the Shared state is modified. In MESIF, only one cache line may be in the Forwarding state at any one time. Additional cache lines may hold the same data; however, these will be in the Shared state, and the response to any snoop request is satisfied by the cache line in the Forwarding state only. Because the cache lines in a Shared state do not respond to read requests, cache coherency messaging is significantly reduced when the same data is held in multiple cache lines. Once the cache line in the Forwarding state is copied, the new copy is then designated as the sole cache line to be in the Forwarding state, and the previous copy reverts back to a Shared status. This ensures that the single cache line in the Forwarding state is unlikely to be aged out of an individual cache by other requests. If a particular cache line has multiple requests, the workload and bandwidth to satisfy these requests is evenly distributed across all of the processors in the system.

CPU Power Management

Power management is of increasing importance in a data center environment. As processors and other server components reach greater clock frequencies, power management can present two challenges: using increased amounts of power and generating increased levels of heat. First, power always comes at a cost, and the levels of power that can be supported in any particular data center environment will always have a finite limit. Second, all of the heat generated requires that it be dissipated to keep all of the computing components within recommended operating temperatures. For these reasons, CPU power utilization is an important component of achieving power management goals. In a RAC environment, however, it is important to balance the power demands of the processor against the power requirements of the entire server. For example, as will be discussed later in this chapter, different implementations of memory and storage technology will also have an impact on the power consumption of a server. You should consider power as a criteria that you measure across an entire cluster, as opposed to focusing strictly on the power consumption of the individual components. Entire server power utilization can then be used as an additional factor in determining the appropriate size and number of nodes in the cluster.

For power management, a standard interface, the Advanced Configuration and Power Interface (ACPI), is implemented across all server architectures to give the operating system a degree of control over the power utilization of the system components. For the CPU itself, a number of technologies are employed to manage power utilization. For example, Intel processors have four power management states, the most important of which to an Oracle installation are the P-states that govern power management when the CPUs are operational and C-states when the CPUs are idle. P-states are implemented by dynamic CPU voltage and frequency scaling that steps processor voltage and frequency up and down in increments. This scaling up and down occurs in response to the demands for processing power. The processing demands are determined by the operating system. Hence, it is Linux that requests the P-states at which the processors operate. If this feature is available on a platform, it can be determined within the CPU information of the basic input/output system (BIOS) with an entry such as P-STATE Coordination Management. The output of the dmesg command should display information regarding the CPU frequency under an ACPI heading, such as the following:

```
ACPI: CPU0 (power states: C1[C1] C2[C3])
ACPI: Processor [CPU0] (supports 8 throttling states)
```

Once enabled, the frequency can be monitored and set by the cpuspeed daemon and controlled by the corresponding cpuspeed command based on the temperature and external power supplies of CPU idle thresholds. The processor frequency can also be controlled manually by sending signals to the cpuspeed daemon with the kill command. The current active frequency setting for a particular processor can be viewed from the CPU MHz entry of /proc/cpuinfo. For example, at the highest level of granularity, the cpuspeed daemon can be disabled as follows:

```
[root@london1 ~]# service cpuspeed stop
Disabling ondemand cpu frequency scaling:                    [  OK  ]
```

When the daemon is disabled, the processors run at the level of maximum performance and power consumption:

```
[root@london1 ~]# cat /proc/cpuinfo | grep -i MHz
cpu MHz          : 2927.000
cpu MHz          : 2927.000
```

Conversely, the daemon can be enabled as follows:

```
[root@london1 ~]# service cpuspeed start
Enabling ondemand cpu frequency scaling:                     [  OK  ]
```

By default, the processors run at a reduced frequency; hence, they have reduced performance and power consumption:

```
[root@london1 ~]# cat /proc/cpuinfo | grep -i MHz
cpu MHz         : 1596.000
cpu MHz         : 1596.000
```

From this initial state, the processors are able to respond dynamically to demands for performance by increasing frequency and voltage at times of peak utilization and lowering them when demand is lower. It is important to note that individual cores in a multicore processor can operate at different frequencies depending on utilization of the cores in question. You can see this at work in the following example:

```
[root@london1 ~]# cat /proc/cpuinfo | grep -i MHz
cpu MHz         : 1596.000
cpu MHz         : 2927.000
```

In an HT environment where two threads run on a core simultaneously, the core will run at a frequency determined by the demands of the highest performing thread.

When a CPU is idle, it can be instructed to operate in a reduced power state. It is possible to halt the clock signal and reduce power or shut down units within the CPU. These idle power stats are called C-states. Like P-states, C-states are implemented in a number of steps. A deeper state conserves more energy. However, it also requires additional time for the CPU to re-enter a fully operational state. C-states can also be observed under the ACPI:

```
[root@london1 processor]# cat /proc/acpi/processor/CPU0/power
active state:           C2
max_cstate:             C8
bus master activity:    00000000
states:
   C1:                      type[C1] promotion[C2] demotion[--] latency[000]
 usage[00011170] duration[00000000000000000000]
  *C2:                      type[C3] promotion[--] demotion[C1] latency[245]
 usage[00774434] duration[00000000001641426228]
```

It is important to reiterate that, in a RAC environment, power management should be measured holistically across the entire cluster and not on an individual component level. Moreover, CPU power management should be handled the same way. Performance demands and power utilization is governed at the operating system level on an individual node. Hence, awareness is not extended to the level of the Oracle Database software. For this reason, there is the potential that power saving operations on one node in the cluster may negatively impact the performance of another, and you should therefore monitor the use of power management techniques against desired performance. For example, if levels of utilization are low on some nodes, you should consider at a design level whether reducing the number of nodes in the cluster or using virtualization can increase the utilization of individual CPUs to the level desired without requiring CPU power management enabled. If so, you will be able reduce the number of individual nodes, thereby saving in the overall power demands of the cluster.

Virtualization

All of the latest CPU architectures that support Oracle RAC on Linux implement additional features to support full virtualization of the operating system. This fact enables multiple instances of the operating system and nodes within a RAC cluster to be hosted on a single physical server environment. You can find in-depth details on these additional processor features in the context of virtualization with Oracle VM lin Chapter 5.

Memory

As we have progressed through the server architecture, you should clearly see that, in an Oracle RAC context, one of the most important components on each node is the RAM. Memory is where your SGA resides, and it's also the place where Cache Fusion of data blocks between the instances in the cluster takes place. Understanding how this memory is realized in hardware is essential to understanding the potentials of cluster performance.

Virtual Memory

When a process is initially created, the Linux kernel creates a set of page tables as virtual addresses that do not necessarily bear any relation to the physical memory addresses. Linux maintains the directory of page table entries for the process directly in physical memory to map the virtual memory addresses to the physical ones. For example, this translation between virtual and physical memory addresses means that, on a 32-bit system, each Linux process has its own 4GB address space, rather than the entire operating system being limited to 4GB. Similarly, on an x86-64 system with 48-bit virtual addressing, the limit is considerably greater than 256TB.

This directory of page table entries has a number of levels. When a virtual memory access is made, translating the virtual address can result in a number of physical memory accesses to eventually reach the actual page of memory required. To reduce this impact on performance within the Memory Management Unit (MMU) located on the CPU, a table exists with its own private memory—the TLB. Every request for data goes to the MMU, where the TLB maps the virtual memory addresses to the physical memory addresses based on the tables set up in the TLB. These tables are populated by the kernel according to the most recent memory locations accessed. If the page table entries are not located in the TLB, then the information must still be fetched from the page tables in main memory. Therefore, it's advantageous to ensure that highest number of memory references possible can be satisfied from the TLB.

The TLB capacity is usually small, and the standard page size on an x86 and x86-64 Linux system is 4KB. Thus, the large amount of memory required by Oracle means that most accesses will not be satisfied from the TLB, resulting in lower-than-optimal performance. Oracle uses a large amount of contiguous memory, so the references to this memory could more efficiently managed by mapping a smaller number of larger pages. For this reason, on Linux systems implementing the 2.6 kernel, Oracle 11*g* can take advantage of a huge TLB pool. You will learn how to configure these huge pages, which we strongly recommend using, in Chapter 6. When correctly implemented, huge pages increase the likelihood that an Oracle memory access will be satisfied from the TLB. This stands in contrast to traversing a number of physical memory locations to discover the desired memory address. This approach also saves CPU cycles that would otherwise be spent managing a large number of small pages. It also saves on physical memory to provide the address mappings in the first place. Additionally, huge pages are pinned in memory and not selected as candidates to be swapped to disk under conditions of memory contention.

Understanding the TLB and memory addressability can assist you in understanding why sizing the SGA too large for requirements can be detrimental, especially in a RAC environment. Sizing the SGA too large means that you could have a large number of address mappings that you do not need, increasing the likelihood that accessing the memory location that you do require will take longer by requiring that you traverse the ones you do not. For RAC, an oversized SGA has the additional impact of requiring an increased number of blocks to be mastered unnecessarily across the entire cluster. The SGA on each node in the cluster should be sized optimally, ensuring that it is not too small, but also not too large.

Physical Memory

Many different physical types of memory can be installed in computer systems, and they can vary significantly in terms of performance and capacity. Physical memory is comprised of dual in-line memory modules (DIMM) on which the RAM chips are located.

Most non-enterprise-based computer systems use single data rate RAM (SDRAM); however, enterprise class–based systems normally use double data rate RAM (DDR), which has been generally available since 2002. This technology has advanced through DDR2, available since 2004; and DDR3, which has been available since 2007.

Memory speed is measured in terms of memory clock performance. In fact, memory clock performance governs the speed of the memory I/O buffers and the rate at which data is pre-fetched, so the clock performance does not necessarily correspond directly with the speed of the memory itself, called the *core frequency*. DDR is technology extremely similar to SDRAM; however, unlike SDRAM, DDR reads data on both the rising and falling edges of the memory clock signal, so it can transfer data at twice the rate.

When reviewing a hardware specification for memory, the definition will resemble the following:

```
RAM Type - PC3-10600 DDR3-1333
```

This definition gives you both the bandwidth and the clock frequency of the memory specified. However, most memory buses are 64-bits wide (which equals to 8 bytes), so you can multiply the bus speed by 8 bytes (or 64 bits) to determine the bandwidth given in the RAM Type definition. Therefore, if you have a bus speed of 1333MHz (which is, in fact, twice the speed of 667MHz and can also be identified as *megatransfers* or MT/s), you can calculate that the following example is named PC3-10600 with the PC-3 prefix signifying the memory as DDR3:

```
2 x 667MHz x 8 bytes(64 bits) = 10667 MB/s (or 10.6 GB/s)
```

Similarly, the following memory type is named PC3-12800:

```
2 x 800MHz x 8 bytes(64 bits) = 12800 MB/s (or 12.8 GB/s)
```

Whereas DDR can transfer data at twice the core frequency rate with the examples shown (based on DDR3 memory), the total bus frequency is a factor of eight times the memory core frequency, which are 166MHz and 200MHz for these examples, respectively. DDR3 is able to operate at double the data rate of DDR2 and at four times the core memory frequency. Table 4-5 summarizes the bandwidths available for some common memory types based on DDR, DDR2, and DDR3.

Table 4-5. Common Memory Bandwidths

Bandwidth	Core Frequency	Clock Frequency	Name	Memory Type
1.6GB/s	100MHz	100MHz	PC1600	DDR200
2.1GB/s	133MHz	133MHz	PC2100	DDR266

Bandwidth	Core Frequency	Clock Frequency	Name	Memory Type
2.7GB/s	166MHz	166MHz	PC2700	DDR333
3.2GB/s	200MHz	200MHz	PC3200	DDR400
3.2GB/s	100MHz	200MHz	PC2-3200	DDR2-400
4.3GB/s	133MHz	266MHz	PC2-4300	DDR2-533
5.3GB/s	166MHz	333MHz	PC2-5300	DDR2-667
6.4GB/s	200MHz	400MHz	PC2-6400	DDR2-800
6.4GB/s	100MHz	400MHz	PC3-6400	DDR3-800
8.5GB/s	133MHz	533MHz	PC3-8500	DDR3-1066
10.6GB/s	166MHz	667MHz	PC3-10600	DDR3-1333
12.8GB/s	200MHz	800MHz	PC3-12800	DDR3-1600

From the table, you can see that, at the clock frequency of 200MHz, the throughput of 3.2GB/s is the same for both DDR and DDR2. Similarly, at a clock frequency of 400MHz, the throughput of DDR2 and DDR3 is also the same at 6.4GB/s. However, in both cases, the core frequency of the more advanced memory is lower, offering more scope to increase frequencies and bandwidth beyond the limits of the previous generation. The lower core frequency also means that the power consumption is lower, with voltages for DDR3 at 1.5V, DDR2 at 1.8V, and DDR at 2.5V. However, the trade-off is that, with a lower memory core frequency, latency times may be longer for the time taken to set up any individual data transfer.

In choosing memory for a system, you will not achieve the best possible result simply by selecting the highest level of throughput possible. There are a number of selection criteria that must be considered in terms of both the processor and the memory to optimize a configuration for either the highest levels of bandwidth or the largest amounts of capacity. In addition to configuring the correct memory capacity and bandwidth, you also need to transfer the data to the CPU itself. Typically, the memory controller is integrated in the CPU itself in the uncore block of a multicore processor, and the uncore will support a different frequency from the processing cores themselves. The uncore frequency will be available with the processor specification from the manufacturer, and it is required to be double that of the memory frequency. For example, DDR3-1333 memory requires an uncore frequency of 2.66MHz. Therefore, it is essential to ensure that the processor itself supports the memory configuration desired.

Do not confuse the role of the memory controller with the MMU discussed earlier in the context of virtual memory. In earlier generations of architectures we are discussing, the memory controller may be located in a couple different places. First, it may be located on the *Front Side Bus* (FSB), between the CPU and main memory as part of the Memory Controller Hub (MCH), also known as the northbridge of the server chipset. Second, on more recent architectures, it may be integrated on the CPU itself (as noted previously). The memory controller provides a similar translation function to the MMU, but one of its roles is to map the physical addresses to the real memory addresses of the associated memory modules.

In addition to the translation role, the memory controller counts read and write references to the real memory pages, averages the access gap for each memory bank, and manages the power states of each individual memory module. The memory controller also provides a degree of error checking and some memory reliability features.

Regardless of the location of the memory controller, the memory configuration supported will be determined by both the memory specification and the number of channels supported by the controller. For the architectures of interest, an integrated memory controller in which there is one per processor socket may support two, three, or more memory channels. For example, Figure 4-2 illustrates a dual multicore processor system with three channels per processor and three DIMMs per channel.

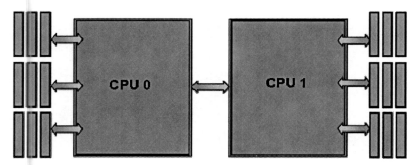

Figure 4-2. A dual, multicore processor system

Given DDR3-1333 memory with the specifications referenced in Table 4-5, and also given a processor with sufficient uncore frequency; each processor can support a maximum memory bandwidth of 32GB/s. This is equivalent to the 10.6 GB/s supported by each channel, and thus 64GB/s total for the two-processor configuration. With DDR3-1066, the maximum bandwidth per processor would be 25.5 GB/s, which is equivalent to the 8.5 GB/s supported by each channel. Typically however, we see a reduction in memory bus speeds as additional DIMMs are added to a memory channel, regardless of the speeds supported by the DIMMs themselves. Therefore, a fully populated system will deliver lower levels of bandwidth than a sparsely configured system. In this example, assuming DDR3 DIMMs are available at 2GB, 4GB, or 8GB configurations; an optimal maximum bandwidth configuration would populate 1 x 8GB DDR3-1333 DIMM per channel to deliver 48GB of memory across the system operating at 32GB/s per processor. Alternatively, an optimal maximum capacity configuration would populate 3x 8GB DDR3-800 DIMMs per channel to deliver 144GB of memory across the system, but this iteration would operate at a lower bandwidth of 19.2 GB/s per processor. All memory channels will operate at the lowest supported frequency by any one channel. Therefore, it is good practice to ensure that all memory populated within a system—and ideally across the entire cluster—is of the same type.

To verify the memory configuration in a system, the command dmidecode reports on the system hardware (as reported by the system BIOS). This report includes details about the system motherboard, processors, and the number and type of DIMMs. The output from dmidecode is extensive, so it is good practice to direct the output to a file. For example, the following extract shows the reported output for an occupied DIMM slot. This example shows the location of a DDR3-800 1GB DIMM and its relevant location in the system:

```
Handle 0x002B, DMI type 17, 27 bytes.
Memory Device
        Array Handle: 0x0029
        Error Information Handle: Not Provided
```

```
Total Width: 64 bits
Data Width: 64 bits
Size: 1024 MB
Form Factor: DIMM
Set: 1
Locator: A1_DIMM0
Bank Locator: A1_Node0_Channel0_Dimm0
Type: DDR3
Type Detail: Synchronous
Speed: 800 MHz (1.2 ns)
Manufacturer: A1_Manufacturer0
Serial Number: A1_SerNum0
Asset Tag: A1_AssetTagNum0
Part Number: A1_PartNum0
```

. In this example, which is relevant to the system and memory configuration described previously, 18 DIMM slots populated with this type of memory verifies that the system is configured to provide memory bandwidth of 19.2 GB/s per processor, or 38.4 GB/s across the entire system. As such, `dmidecode` output serves as a useful reference for assessing the capabilities of a system.

Ultimately, the memory configuration limitations should be considered against the throughput and latency of the entire cluster, the private interconnect, the workload, and the level of interconnect traffic expected. We recommend a design where sufficient memory capacity is configured on each of the individual nodes to cache data on a local basis as much as possible. Although performance may be lost against the potential memory bandwidth within the system, this will certainly be more than outweighed by the gains from minimizing Cache Fusion traffic between the nodes.

NUMA

In discussing physical memory, we considered the role of the memory controller and whether it was located on the FSB or integrated on the CPU. In a multiprocessor configuration, if the memory controller is located on the FSB, it is known as a Symmetric Multi-Processing (SMP) system. In this configuration, memory access by all processors is shared equally across the same bus. Things change with an integrated memory controller, however (see Figure 4-3 for a logical representation of the type of memory architecture implemented in a four-processor configuration).

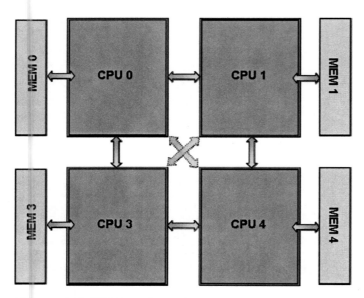

Figure 4-3. A NUMA configuration

You should be able to see how Figure 4-3 extends to four processors the physical implementation for two processors shown in Figure 4-2. , For simplicity eachmemory link is shown as a logical representation of a number of physical memory channels. The important aspect of this configuration is that it introduces the concept of local and remote memory with the integrated memory controller on each CPU being responsible for a subset of the memory of the whole system. To this extent, it implements a Non-Uniform Memory Architecture (NUMA) which on all architectures of interest to Oracle on Linux are the same as a Cache Coherent Non-Uniform Memory Architecture (ccNUMA). This means, as far as the software is concerned, local and remote memory access can be treated the same. It is also worth noting that, for a NUMA configuration, an Oracle on Linux system does not necessarily mandate an integrated memory controller. For example, some systems are based upon a cell configuration where four processors connected by a FSB and a number of DIMMs are connected together into a larger system with NUMA at a coarser granularity. These systems are typically implemented in eight-processor socket and above configurations, so they are less common in a RAC on Linux environment than the NUMA configurations on a single-system board. For this reason, the focus in this chapter is on NUMA implemented at the CPU level with an integrated memory controller that usually has two, four, or even up to eight-processor sockets per system.

As discussed previously in this chapter, Cache Fusion introduces additional latencies to access data from a remote buffer cache when compared to the data cached in local memory. In a NUMA configuration, a similar concept can be applied; however, it is applied at the CPU level, as opposed to the system level,. The communication between the processors is through dedicated point-to-point interconnects that replace the function of the shared FSB. In Intel systems, the interconnect is known as the QuickPath Interconnect (QPI); in AMD systems, it is known as HyperTransport. When a process requires access to remote memory, the communication takes place across the interconnect, and the request is serviced by the remote memory controller.

Determined by settings at the BIOS level of the system, a NUMA server can be booted in NUMA or non-NUMA mode. Typically in NUMA mode, all of the memory attached to the individual memory controllers is presented in a contiguous manner. For example, in a two-processor configuration, the first half of the system memory will map to the memory on one controller, while the second half will map to the other. In conjunction with a NUMA-aware operating system and application, this enables software to be optimized to show preference to local memory. Consequently, it is important to reiterate, as previously noted when discussing 64-bit computing, that 32-bit Linux operating systems are not NUMA-aware. Thus, they cannot take advantage of a server booted in NUMA mode. The alternative is to select a BIOS option that lets you run a NUMA server in non-NUMA mode. Typically, this means that cache line sized (64byte on the server architectures in question) allocations of memory are interleaved between all of the memory controllers in the system. For an example process running on a two-processor system booted in non-NUMA mode, this means that half of the memory accesses will be serviced by one memory controller, while the other half will be serviced by the other memory controller. A non-NUMA configuration is therefore likely to result in greater CPU interconnect traffic than a NUMA-optimized configuration at the hardware level. Additionally, as more processors are added to the configuration, interleaving memory may generally have a greater impact than when this policy is applied to a fewer number of processors. This impact does not necessarily mean that performance will be lower for any given workload because, conversely, optimizing for a NUMA aware configuration also requires additional software to implement. Typically, the benefits of NUMA awareness and optimization are realized as the number of processors increase. However, we recommend performance testing to determine the benefits for a particular environment. To determine the correct NUMA settings at the platform level, it is important to be familiar with the NUMA support available at both the Linux operating system and Oracle Database levels.

The 64-bit Linux operating systems with 2.6-based kernels that support Oracle 11*g* Release 2 include NUMA functionality, and NUMA support is enabled automatically when the operating system is booted on a system where NUMA has been enabled at the BIOS level, Even in this case however NUMA can be disabled at the operating system level by a kernel command line option in the grub.conf file. For example, consider this line:

```
kernel /vmlinuz-2.6.18-128.el5 ro root=/dev/VolGroup00/LogVol00 numa=off
```

If NUMA support is disabled, this fact is noted by the kernel:

```
dmesg | grep -i numa
Command line: ro root=/dev/VolGroup00/LogVol00 numa=off
NUMA turned off
```

Alternatively, if NUMA support is enabled either at the BIOS or kernel level, then the status is also recorded:

```
[oracle@london1 ~]$ dmesg | grep -i numa
NUMA: Using 31 for the hash shift
```

Application-level Linux NUMA functionality is provided in the numactl RPM package. This package includes a shared object library called libnuma, which is available for software-development level NUMA configuration. The numactl command provides a NUMA command-line interface and the ability to configure the preferred policy for NUMA memory allocation manually. Therefore, from an Oracle Database 11*g* perspective, utilization of the libnuma library is enabled by setting the appropriate NUMA related int.ora parameters (we will cover this in more detail later in this section). Also, the numactl command can be used both to view and set NUMA configuration, regardless of whether that Oracle level NUMA has been enabled. For example, the numactl command can be used to view the memory allocation, as in the following example, which shows a system with two memory controllers:

```
[root@london1 ~]# numactl --hardware
available: 2 nodes (0-1)
node 0 size: 9059 MB
node 0 free: 8675 MB
node 1 size: 9090 MB
node 1 free: 8872 MB
node distances:
node   0   1
  0:  10  21
  1:  21  10
```

The following output shows the current configuration policy:

```
[root@london1 ~]# numactl --show
policy: default
preferred node: current
physcpubind: 0 1 2 3 4 5 6 7 8 9 10 11 12 13 14 15
cpubind: 0 1
nodebind: 0 1
membind: 0 1
```

The preceding output introduces additional NUMA terminology: nodes and distance. A *node* refers to the units of managed memory; or, in other words, to a processor with an integrated memory controller an individual CPU. Therefore, it is important not to confuse the finer granularity of a NUMA node with the wider granularity of a RAC node. The distance is defined by the ACPI System Locality Information Table (SLIT), and determines the additional time required to access the memory on a remote node against a value of 10 for the local node. The default values will be governed by the architecture of the hardware concerned, but these values may be configured manually at the BIOS level. In the previous example, where you had two nodes, the matrix is simple. That example shows that the latency for accessing the memory on a remote node should be taken for NUMA policy as being just over twice the time as accessing local memory. Therefore, if the memory access time to local memory is 60ns, then remote memory will be just over 120ns. With four or more sockets, and depending on the architecture, memory access may require more than one hop to remote memory. Thus, for multiple hops, the matrix will be populated by access times that show higher latencies. The operating system NUMA information can also be read directly from the information in the /sys/devices/system/node directory, where NUMA details for the individual nodes are given in directories named after the nodes themselves. For example, the following shows how the distance information is derived for node0:

```
[root@london1 node0]# more distance
10 21
```

There is also basic information on NUMA statistics in this directory that records page-level access:

```
[root@london1 node0]# more numastat
numa_hit 239824
numa_miss 0
numa_foreign 0
interleave_hit 8089
local_node 237111
other_node 2713
```

These statistics can also be displayed for all nodes with the numastat command:

```
[oracle@london1 ~]$ numastat
                        node0            node1
numa_hit               394822           873142
numa_miss                   0                0
numa_foreign                0                0
interleave_hit          11826            11605
local_node             386530           854775
other_node               8292            18367
```

One of the most important areas of information in the node directory concerns the NUMA memory allocation. The details are the same as in /proc/meminfo; however, here the allocation is shown for the individual nodes, illustrating how the memory allocation is configured and utilized:

```
[root@london1 node0]$ more meminfo
Node 0 MemTotal:       9276828 kB
Node 0 MemFree:        1465256 kB
Node 0 MemUsed:        7811572 kB
Node 0 Active:          211400 kB
Node 0 Inactive:         77752 kB
Node 0 HighTotal:            0 kB
Node 0 HighFree:             0 kB
Node 0 LowTotal:       9276828 kB
Node 0 LowFree:        1465256 kB
Node 0 Dirty:               28 kB
Node 0 Writeback:            0 kB
Node 0 FilePages:       170280 kB
Node 0 Mapped:           38620 kB
Node 0 AnonPages:       199608 kB
Node 0 PageTables:       13304 kB
Node 0 NFS_Unstable:         0 kB
Node 0 Bounce:               0 kB
Node 0 Slab:             15732 kB
Node 0 HugePages_Total:   3588
Node 0 HugePages_Free:     847
```

As previously noted, in a non-NUMA configuration all memory is interleaved between memory controllers in 64-byte-sized allocations. Therefore, all memory assigned, whether it's SGA or PGA, will be implicitly distributed in such a manner. With a NUMA-aware environment, however, there are more options available for configuration. By default, memory is allocated from the memory local to the processor where the code is executing. For example, when the Oracle SGA is allocated using the shmget() system call for automatic shared memory management or the mmap() system call for 11g automatic memory management (see Chapter 6 for more details about this), by default the memory is taken contiguously from a single or multiple nodes, according to requirements.

Let's look at how this works in Oracle version 11g Release 2. If it has been NUMA-enabled (we will cover this in more depth later in this section), and it is able to create multiple shared segments dedicated to individual memory nodes, then contiguous memory allocation at the operating system level would be the preferred behavior for optimal scalability under this scheme. However, if NUMA is not enabled, or the version of Oracle creates only a single shared memory segment, then this will potentially result in an unbalanced configuration with the SGA running entirely within the memory of one processor. If that happens, the system will suffer from latency and bandwidth limitations regarding physical memory, as discussed earlier. For example, the following listing shows a default memory configuration after an Oracle instance has been started with the SGA almost entirely resident in the memory on node 1:

```
[oracle@london1 ~]$ numactl --hardware
available: 2 nodes (0-1)
node 0 size: 9059 MB
node 0 free: 8038 MB
node 1 size: 9090 MB
node 1 free: 612 MB
node distances:
node   0   1
  0:  10  21
  1:  21  10
```

For general Oracle performance, but especially when the Oracle 11*g* Database is not configured for NUMA, we recommend the use of huge pages as discussed in Chapter 6. When the huge pages are allocated at the operating system level the default policy is to allocate memory in an evenly distributed manner from all of the available memory controllers until the huge page allocation is complete. For example, consider the following test command:

```
echo 2048 > /proc/sys/vm/nr_hugepages
```

This command manually sets the number of huge pages. Their allocation can be viewed in the meminfo files under the /sys/devices/system/node directory:

```
Node 0 HugePages_Total:   1024
Node 0 HugePages_Free:    1024
Node 1 HugePages_Total:   1024
Node 1 HugePages_Free:    1024
```

It is clear that this approach is similar to the interleaving of memory in a non-NUMA configuration. However, in this case it has only been done at the coarser granularity of the huge pages from which the SGA will be allocated, rather than the entire underlying system memory map. That said, the Oracle Database NUMA configuration determines whether this allocation will be used on a per memory node basis or a more general interleaved basis.

When using huge pages on a NUMA system, we recommend allocating them at boot time. This is because, if the memory on one node has no further memory to contribute, then allocation of the rest of the huge pages will be taken from the remaining node or nodes, resulting in an unbalanced configuration. Similarly, when freeing huge pages, the requested de-allocation will take place, thus freeing the maximum amount of memory from all of the nodes in order.

You have seen that there are a number of implications for the correct set up of a NUMA system at both the BIOS and Linux operating system levels before starting Oracle. Also, the chosen settings must be considered in conjunction with the preferred NUMA policy for Oracle.

As noted previously, Oracle 11*g* Release 2 on Linux includes NUMA awareness and functionality; however, these are controlled and configured with unsupported parameters known as underscore parameters. At the highest level in Oracle 11*g* Release 2, Oracle NUMA features are determined by the parameter _enable_NUMA_support. Prior to Oracle 11*g* Release 2, there was also the NUMA-related parameter _enable_NUMA_optimization; the difference between the two is that, even if the latter parameter was manually set to FALSE in 11*g* Release 1, a degree of NUMA functionality continued to remain within the Oracle 11*g* software. Therefore, at Oracle 11*g* Release 1, despite the default setting of the NUMA parameter, Oracle recommended disabling NUMA functionality by applying patch number 8199533, rather than by setting this parameter. However, it is important to note that this original parameter has been deprecated from Oracle 11*g* Release 2. For _enable_NUMA_support, the default value of this parameter is set to FALSE, and it can be viewed with a statement such as the following:

```
SQL> select a.ksppinm "Parameter", b.ksppstvl "Session Value",
c.ksppstvl "Instance Value"
from x$ksppi a, x$ksppcv b, x$ksppsv c
where a.indx = b.indx
AND a.indx = c.indx
AND ksppinm = '_enable_NUMA_support';

_enable_NUMA_support
FALSE

FALSE
```

By default, the additional parameter _db_block_numa is also set to the value of 1, which shows that memory will be configured as if for the presence of a single memory node. Oracle NUMA support can be enabled on a system with hardware and Linux NUMA support by setting the value of _enable_NUMA_support to TRUE. For example, consider the result of running the following command with sysdba privilege and then restarting the database:

```
SQL> alter system set "_enable_NUMA_support"=TRUE scope=spfile;

System altered.
```

If successfully configured, the database alert log will report that a NUMA system has been found and that support has been enabled, as in the following example for a two-socket system:

```
NUMA system found and support enabled (2 domains - 8,8)
```

The alert log for a four-socket system would like this:

```
NUMA system found and support enabled (4 domains - 16,16,16,16)
```

Additionally the parameter _db_block_numa will have been set to the same value as the number of memory nodes or domains reported in the alert log, which will also report that _enable_NUMA_support is set to a non-default value, as in this example:

```
System parameters with non-default values:
  processes               = 150
  _enable_NUMA_support    = TRUE
```

Use the following commands to determine Oracle's success at creating a NUMA configuration:

```
SQL> oradebug setmypid
Statement processed.
SQL> oradebug ipc
Information written to trace file.
```

The generated trace file contains information on the SGA. The example that follows illustrates how to create a number of NUMA pools that correspond to the recognized number of memory nodes:

```
Area #0 'Fixed Size' containing Subareas 0-0
  Total size 000000000021eea0 Minimum Subarea size 00000000
  Owned by:  0,  1
    Area  Subarea    Shmid      Stable Addr       Actual Addr
      0        0     884737 0x00000060000000 0x00000060000000
                                Subarea size     Segment size
                                000000000021f000 0000000044000000
Area #1 'Variable Size' containing Subareas 3-3
  Total size 0000000040000000 Minimum Subarea size 04000000
  Owned by:  0,  1
    Area  Subarea    Shmid      Stable Addr       Actual Addr
      1        3     884737 0x000000638fd000 0x000000638fd000
                                Subarea size     Segment size
                                0000000040703000 0000000044000000
Area #2 'NUMA pool 0' containing Subareas 6-6
  Total size 0000000160000000 Minimum Subarea size 04000000
  Owned by:  0
    Area  Subarea    Shmid      Stable Addr       Actual Addr
      2        6     950275 0x00000204000000 0x00000204000000
                                Subarea size     Segment size
                                0000000160000000 0000000160000000
Area #3 'NUMA pool 1' containing Subareas 5-5
  Total size 000000015c000000 Minimum Subarea size 04000000
  Owned by:  1
    Area  Subarea    Shmid      Stable Addr       Actual Addr
      3        5     917506 0x000000a4439000 0x000000a4439000
                                Subarea size     Segment size
                                000000015fbc7000 0000000160000000
Area #4 'Redo Buffers' containing Subareas 4-4
  Total size 0000000000439000 Minimum Subarea size 00000000
  Owned by:  1
    Area  Subarea    Shmid      Stable Addr       Actual Addr
      4        4     917506 0x000000a4000000 0x000000a4000000
                                Subarea size     Segment size
                                0000000000439000 0000000160000000
```

If you look later in the trace file report, or if you run the ipcs command as discussed in Chapter 12; you can observe the multiple shared memory segments created to correspond to the individual memory nodes—ID's 917506 and 950275, in this case. These segments optimize the Oracle configuration to give processes local memory access to the SGA, thereby reducing memory interconnect traffic and increasing scalability as more memory nodes are added to the configuration:

```
------ Shared Memory Segments --------
key         shmid    owner    perms    bytes        nattch    status
0xa3c20e68  32768    oracle   660      4096         0
0x00000000  884737   oracle   660      1140850688   28
0x00000000  917506   oracle   660      5905580032   28
0x00000000  950275   oracle   660      5905580032   28
0xfb0938e4  983044   oracle   660      2097152      28
```

It is important to note that an Oracle NUMA configuration is supported, whether you use using automatic memory management or automatic shared memory management. Additionally, if huge pages have been configured, this is also compatible with enabling NUMA at the Oracle Database level. Therefore, we continue to recommend the use puge pages, even if enabling NUMA for performance benefits.

If _enable_NUMA_support has been set to TRUE, however, the alert reports that the parameter has been set to a non-default value. If this value is FALSE, it indicates that there has been an issue with enabling NUMA support on your system at the Oracle level. In particular, you should verify the presence of the numactl RPM package containing the libnuma library on the system and optionally the numactl-devel package. Prior to Oracle version 11.2.0.2, if the numactl-devel package is not installed it is necessary to create an additional symbolic link to the libnuma library. This enables the Oracle Database to detect the library's presence, which you accomplish as follows:

```
[root@london1 ~]# cd /usr/lib64
[root@london1 lib64]# ln -s libnuma.so.1 libnuma.so
```

If NUMA is enabled at the BIOS and Linux operating system levels, but disabled within Oracle, such as with a release prior to Oracle 11g Release 2, it should be clear that how NUMA is configured within the operating system will consequently determine how memory is allocated to the Oracle SGA on startup. If huge pages have already been configured, as you have seen by default, this is done in a NUMA-aware manner. This means Oracle can take advantage of an interleaved memory configuration implemented on its behalf. If Huge Pages have not been pre-configured, the default policy is to allocate the SGA from standard-sized memory pages. In this case, SGA will therefore be allocated contiguously across memory nodes, as previously discussed. To mitigate the potential performance impact of SGA memory not being evenly distributed , it is also possible to set an interleaved memory configuration when starting a database with sqlplus.For example, you might start sqlplus as follows:

```
[oracle@london1 ~]$ numactl --interleave=all sqlplus / as sysdba

SQL*Plus: Release 11.1.0.6.0 - Production on Sun Feb 27 00:29:09 2005

Copyright (c) 1982, 2007, Oracle.  All rights reserved.

Connected to an idle instance.

SQL>
```

The preceding example means that the SGA is interleaved across the available memory nodes, as illustrated here:

```
[oracle@london1 ~]$ numactl --hardware
available: 2 nodes (0-1)
node 0 size: 9059 MB
node 0 free: 4096 MB
node 1 size: 9090 MB
node 1 free: 4443 MB
node distances:
node   0   1
  0:  10  21
  1:  21  10
```

However, in a RAC environment, it is not possible to control the NUMA allocation policy manually on all nodes when using the srvctl command to start multiple instances across the cluster. Therefore, in an Oracle 11g Release 2 RAC environment on NUMA systems, we recommend explicitly enabling NUMA support at the instance level. This is will be particularly beneficial on systems with four or more sockets and the most memory-intensive workloads. If you do not wish to enable NUMA support, then what we recommend is an interleaved or evenly distributed SGA configuration that is implemented either at the BIOS level or, preferably, with huge pages. In all cases, you should have the same configuration on all systems in the cluster.

Memory Reliability

In the era of 64-bit Linux computing and gigabytes of data held in buffer cache, the DBA should be fully aware of the technologies and limitations of memory available in enterprise-based servers, especially in a RAC environment that uses multiple SGAs and holds much of the database in memory at the same time. If there is a memory failure on one of the nodes, depending on the frequency of the checkpointing, you risk a considerable reduction in service while one of the remaining nodes recovers from the redo logs of the failed instance. As SGAs increase in size, the potential for the time to recover increases. On Oracle 11g, the checkpointing process is self-tuning and does not require the setting of any specific parameters; however, if parameters such as FAST_START_MTTR_TARGET are not set, you have less direct control over the possible recovery time, as will be explained later in the chapter.

To mitigate against the possibility of a memory error halting the cluster for a significant period of time, all systems will include a degree of memory error detection and correction. Initially, parity-based checking afforded the detection and correction of single-bit memory errors; however, the common standard for memory is now Error Correction Code (ECC) with an extra data byte lane to detect and correct multiple-bit errors and even offline failing memory modules. Additional memory reliability features include registered DIMMs, which improve memory signal quality by including a register to act as a buffer at the cost of increased latency. Registered DIMMs are identified by the addition of an *R* to the specification, such as PC3-10600R. Unbuffered DIMMS are identified by a *U*, such as PC3-10600U. Registered DIMMs can support a larger number of DIMMs per memory channel, which makes them a requirement for high memory capacity.

Additional memory protection features are also available. For example, to protect against DIMM failure, the feature known as *Single Device Data Correction* (SDDC) or by the IBM name of *Chipkill* enables the system to recover from the failure of a single DRAM device on a DIMM. In conjunction with Chipkill, the *Memory Sparing* feature is supported by some systems. On detection of a failing DRAM device, this feature enables the channel to be mapped to a spare device. To enhance memory protection beyond Memory Sparing, some systems also support *Memory Mirroring*. In a Memory Mirroring configuration, the same data is written to two memory channels at the same time, thereby increasing reliability and enabling the replacement of failed DIMMs online, but at the cost of lowering the memory utilization to half of the overall capacity.

Additional Platform Features

There are many additional platform features present, on top of the server attributes we have already discussed. These sophisticated features are becoming increasingly important in helping to maintain the highest levels of cluster availability.

The following sections describe many of the features that may be available, depending on the platform chosen and their applicability to deploying a successful RAC environment.

Onboard RAID Storage

Later in this chapter, there is a detailed discussion of RAID storage in general, as opposed to onboard RAID in particular. The value of a server equipped with an onboard RAID storage system is resiliency. By far, the most common fault occurring within a server will be the failure of the hard disk. In a RAC environment, the failure of an unprotected drive containing the operating system or Oracle binaries will cause the ejection of the node from the cluster, as well as a lengthy reconfiguration once the drive is replaced. Wherever possible, all internal disk drives should be protected by an onboard RAID storage system. (Booting from a protected SAN or hosting the Oracle Home directories on a SAN or NAS are also viable options.) If an onboard RAID storage system is not available, then software RAID within the Linux operating system of disk drives should be configured during installation, as detailed in Chapter 6.

Machine Check Architectures

A *Machine Check Architecture* (*MCA*) is an internal architecture subsystem that exists to some extent on all x86- and x86-64–based systems. MCA exists to provide detection of and resolution for hardware-based errors. However, not all hardware errors—for example, the failing of a disk—will be reported through the MCA system.

All MCA events fall within the following two categories:

- *CPU errors*: These are errors detected within the components of the CPU, such as the following:

- External bus logic

- Cache

- Data TLB

- Instruction fetch unit

- *Platform errors*: Errors delivered to the CPU regarding non-CPU errors, and events such as memory errors.

Depending on the severity of the error detected, the following three resolutions are possible, depending on the level of MCA available:

- *Continue*: The resolution used when an error is detected and corrected by the CPU or the server firmware. This kind of error is transparent to the operating system. Examples of these errors include single- or multiple-bit memory error corrections and cache parity errors. Corrected machine check (CMC) is used to describe an error corrected by the CPU. A corrected platform error (CPE) is an error detected and corrected by the platform hardware.

- *Recover*: The resolution used when a process has read corrupted data, also termed *poisoned data*. Poisoned data is detected by the firmware and forwarded to the operating system, which, through MCA support, terminates the process. However, the operating system remains available.

- *Contain*: The resolution used when serious errors, such as system bus address parity errors, are detected, and the server is taken offline to contain them. These *noncorrected*, or *fatal*, errors can also be termed MCA, which in this case means *Machine Check Abort*.

Overstating the importance of MCA features within a RAC environment would be difficult. Within RAC, detecting errors as soon as possible is important, as is either correcting them or isolating the node. The worst possible outcome is for a failing node to corrupt the data stored on disk within the database, which is the only copy of the data in the entire cluster. To monitor the activity of the MCA the first indication of its activity will be an entry in the system log as follows.

```
Jan 17 13:22:29 london1 kernel: Machine check events logged
```
On observing this message the DBA should check the machine check event log in the file /var/log/mcelog where messages are preceded by a notice such as the following identifying the error detected.

```
MCE 30
HARDWARE ERROR. This is *NOT* a software problem!
Please contact your hardware vendor
```

We recommend gaining familiarity with the MCA available on your system.

Remote Server Management and IPMI

In any enterprise-level RAC environment, remote server management is an essential feature for helping DBAs to meet the level of responsiveness required to manage clustered systems. A method must be available to access the system remotely in terms, diagnostics, or system management board functions, as well as to administer the system from any location, regardless of the current operating system state.

In a standard environment without remote server management, if the operating system has not started successfully, accessing the system will not be possible. In a RAC environment, being fully in control of all systems that have write access to the disks on the external storage where the database is located is especially important. Unless the DBA is always in a physical location near the RAC cluster, then remote management is a necessity.

Within Oracle 11g Release 2, there exists an integrated solution that implements a standard for remote server management: Intelligent Platform Management Interface (IPMI). IPMI raises system level functionality to the operating system for operations such as monitoring system temperatures, fan speeds, and hardware events, as well as for viewing the console. In particular, IPMI enables rebooting a server either locally or remotely, regardless of the status of the operating system. For this reason, IPMI is an optional configuration method selected during the Grid infrastructure installation used within Oracle 11g Release 2 RAC for I/O fencing. Although IPMI is not a mandatory requirement, we do recommend you ensure that IPMI is supported in new hardware you evaluate for RAC because of the advantages inherent in this tool's more advanced I/O fencing. Configuration and management of IPMI using ipmitool and the OpenIPMI packages are discussed in Chapter 6.

Network Interconnect Technologies

The private interconnect is an essential component of a RAC installation. It enables high-speed communication between the nodes in a cluster for Cache Fusion traffic. In this section, we will review the hardware availability for implementing the interconnect from the I/O implementation on the server to the available protocols and their related implementations supported on the Linux operating system.

You can learn more about the supported network and private interconnect, RAC Technologies Compatibility Matrix (RTCM) for Linux Clusters, in this chapter's "Network Interconnect Technologies" section. Table 4-6 illustrates the network protocols and supported configurations in this section.

Table 4-6. Network Interconnect Technologies

Network Protocol	Supported Configuration
Ethernet	100 Mbs, 1 Gigabit, or 10 Gigabit Ethernet
Infiniband (IB)	IP over IB and OFED 1.3.1/RDS v2 over IB and higher

Based on the available technologies detailed in Table 4-6, our focus in this section is on the Ethernet and Infiniband protocols, as well as the requisite hardware choices.

Server I/O

Previously in this chapter, we walked through all of the components of server architecture relevant to Oracle, from the processor to the system memory. Beyond local memory, you can access your data blocks through Cache Fusion. Before taking into account the available interconnect technologies external to the server, we will consider the fundamentals of the system bus on the server itself, through which all network communication takes place. These input/output (I/O) attributes of the server are also relevant in connecting to the SAN or NAS subsystem, which we will also discuss later in this chapter.

The precise configuration of the I/O connectivity supported by a server will be governed by the server chipset and, in particular, the I/O Controller Hub (ICH) on the system motherboard. The ICH is also known as the southbridge, and it connects to the Memory Controller Hub (MCH) or northbridge, thereby completing the connectivity of the system components previously discussed in this chapter. Therefore, you should review the specifications of the chipset to fully determine the I/O connectivity supporting the protocols discussed in the following sections.

PCI

For nearly all of the architectures available to run Linux, server I/O will be based on the Peripheral Component Interconnect (PCI). PCI provides a bus-based interconnection with expansion slots to attach additional devices, such as Network Interface Cards (NIC) or Fibre Channel host bus adapters (HBAs). For Oracle RAC in an enterprise environment, common requirements include the following: one external network interface; one backup network interface; two teamed network interconnect interfaces; and two teamed storage-based interfaces, which must be either network- or Fibre Channel–based. Of the six connections required, some may be satisfied by dual or quad cards. In some environments, such as a blade-based system, the connections are shared between servers. The expansion slots within a particular server may also have different specifications. Therefore, DBAs need to know whether the connections and bandwidth available from a particular environment will meet their requirements. Also note whether the PCI slots available are *hot pluggable*, which means that a failed card may be replaced without requiring server downtime.

The original implementation of PCI offered a 32-bit bus running at frequency of 33MHz. The following calculation shows that this presents 133 MB/s of bandwidth:

```
33 x 4 bytes (32 bits) = 133 MB/s
```

PCI-X

The bandwidth shown for PCI is shared between all of the devices on the system bus. In a RAC environment, the PCI bus would be saturated by a single Gigabit Ethernet connection. For this reason, the original 32-bit, 33MHz PCI bus has been extended to 64 bits at 266MHz. However, the 64-bit bus has also been extended to 100MHz and 133MHz, and it is now referred to as *PCI-X*. The configurations of PCI are summarized in Table 4-7.

Table 4-7. PCI Configurations

Bus	Frequency	32-bit Bandwidth	64-bit Bandwidth
PCI	33MHz	133MB/s	266MB/s
PCI	66MHz	266MB/s	532MB/s
PCI-X	100MHz	Not applicable	800MB/s
PCI-X	133MHz	Not applicable	1GB/s

PCI-X has sufficient capability to sustain a RAC node with gigabit-based networking and 1Gb- or 2Gb-based storage links. However, like PCI, PCI-X is a shared-bus implementation. With Ethernet, Fibre Channel, and Infiniband standards moving to 10Gb-based implementations and beyond, sufficient bandwidth is likely to be unavailable for all of the connections that an Oracle RAC node requires with PCI-X.

PCI-Express

The consideration of the bandwidth requirements of 10Gb connections should be made in conjunction with selecting a platform that supports the generation of PCI called *PCI-Express*. PCI-Express should not be confused with PCI-X. In contrast to PCI-X's shared bus, PCI-Express implements a high-speed point-to-point serial I/O bus.

When reviewing a hardware specification for PCI connectivity, the relevant section will explicitly reference PCI-Express or its abbreviation of PCIe, as follows:

```
Six (6) available PCI-Express Gen 2 expansion slots
```

In contrast to PCI, a PCI-Express link consists of dual channels, implemented as a transmit pair and a receive pair, to enable bi-directional transmission simultaneously. The bandwidth of a PCI-Express link can be scaled by adding additional signal pairs for multiple paths between the two devices. These paths are defined as x1, x4, x8, and x16, according to the number of pairs. Like memory configuration, the desired PCIe configuration should also be cross-referenced against the supported configuration of the system chipset. For example, if the chipset is described as supporting 36 PCIe lanes, this means it will support two x16 links and an x4 link; one x16, two x8 links, and an x4 link; or any supported combination that is also dependent on the configuration of the physical slots available on the motherboard.

The unencoded bandwidth is approximately 80% of the encoded data transfer rate PCI-Express uses a form of encoding that utilizes the remaining 20%. The encoding enables better synchronization, error detection, and error resolution. For this reason, the transfer rate is often written as GT/s (Gigatransfers per second) to distinguish the actual Gb/s transfer rate from the rate at which the data itself is transmitted. Each link consists of dual channels and is bi-directional. In the original implementation, each lane supported 250MB/s. However, the revised PCI Express Base 2.0 specification released in 2007 doubles the clock frequency from the maximum of 1.25GHz at the original implementation to a maximum of 2.5Ghz at the revised specification, which is commonly known as Gen 2. This effectively doubles the bandwidth per lane to 500MB/s. Table 4-8 illustrates the combined bandwidth of both directions with an x1 link that supports a total bandwidth of 1Gb/s.

Table 4-8. PCI-Express Gen 2 Configurations

PCIe Implementation	Transfer Rate	Data Rate	Bandwidth
x1	10GT/s	8Gb/s	1GB/s
x4	40GT/s	32Gb/s	4GB/s
x8	80GT/s	64Gb/s	8GB/s
x16	160GT/s	128Gb/s	16GB/s

At the time of writing, PCI Express Gen 3 is under development, this specification increases the frequency to 4GHz and the bandwidth per lane to 1GB/s.

Because it is based on a point-to-point architecture, PCI-Express will support 10Gb and higher links to the interconnect and storage without sharing bandwidth. PCI-Express adapters also natively support features that are usually managed at the system-board level with PCI and PCI-X, such as hot plug, hot swap, and advanced power management. You can use the command dmidecode as described previously for memory lspci to query your platform configuration for PCI-Express support. Do so using this format:

```
[root@london1 ~]# /sbin/lspci | grep -i express
00:01.0 PCI bridge: Intel Corporation X58 I/O Hub PCI Express Root Port 1 (rev 12)
00:02.0 PCI bridge: Intel Corporation X58 I/O Hub PCI Express Root Port 2 (rev 12)
00:03.0 PCI bridge: Intel Corporation X58 I/O Hub PCI Express Root Port 3 (rev 12)
...
```

When considering Infiniband as an interconnect technology, it is important to note that Infiniband also implements a serial architecture-based protocol in its own right. Therefore, Infiniband does not, by definition, require PCI-Express connectivity with the option of Infiniband Landed on Motherboard (LOM) providing a direct system connection. That said, such configurations are not particularly common and tend to be focused more in the direction of HPC computing. More common Infiniband implementations feature Infiniband implemented with PCI-Express HBAs, which are also known as Host Channel Adapters (HCAs). The latter approach enables the selection of an industry standard server platform, while also adding Infinband as an additional technology. For this reason, we recommend systems with expansion slots that support PCI and PCI-derived technologies with bandwidth sufficient for your Oracle RAC requirements.

Private Interconnect

Building on the PCI I/O capabilities of the server platform, you can implement the cluster interconnect with a number of different technologies. As detailed previously in this section, the supported configurations are based on Ethernet and Infiniband connectivity.

Standard Ethernet Interconnects

The most popular choice for an Oracle RAC cluster interconnect is a Gigabit Ethernet switched network. Gigabit Ethernet connectivity is available through dedicated HBAs inserted into the PCI slots on a server. However, almost without exception, industry-standard servers will include at least two Gigabit Ethernet ports directly on the server motherboard. These industry-standard servers provide Ethernet connectivity without requiring additional hardware, thus leaving the additional PCI slots free for further connectivity.

Gigabit Ethernet run in full duplex mode with a nonblocking, data center class switch should be the minimum interconnect standard applied.

■ **Note** A simple network crossover cable may at first appear to be a low-cost alternative to connect a two-node cluster, enabling you to create a directly linked network between two cluster nodes. However, this alternative is not supported as an interconnect with RAC on Linux. Without the electrical isolation provided by a switch, NIC hardware errors on one of the servers could also cause hardware errors on the other server, rendering the entire cluster unavailable. This configuration also eliminates the option of a redundant networking configuration and prevents the addition of more than two nodes to the cluster.

Gigabit Ethernet theoretically supports transfer rates of 1,000Mb/s (1000 Megabits are equivalent to 100 Megabytes) and latencies of approximately 60 to 100 microseconds for shorter packet sizes. A clear difference exists between this latency and the two to four milliseconds we previously specified for the average receive time for a consistent read or current block for Cache Fusion. In addition to the Oracle workload, processing the network stack at the Linux operating system level is a major contributing factor to the latency of Cache Fusion communication.

For standard TCP/IP networking, reading from or writing to a network socket causes a context switch, where the data is copied from user to kernel buffers and processed by the kernel through the TCP/IP stack and Ethernet driver appropriate to the NIC installed. Each stage in this workload requires a degree of CPU processing, and tuning kernel network parameters (you can learn more about this in Chapter 6) can play a role in increasing network throughput.To minimize the overhead of network processing, the default protocol for Oracle 11*g* RAC on Linux is the User Datagram Protocol (UDP), as opposed to Transmission Control Protocol (TCP). UDP is a non-connection-oriented protocol that doesn't guarantee data ordering. It also places the responsibility for verifying the data transmitted on the application itself—Oracle, in this case. The benefit of this approach is this: UDP reduces the kernel networking requirements.

At the time of writing, 10 Gigabit Ethernet (10GbE) technology is becoming more widely available and has recently been supported within the RAC Technologies Matrix. As 10GbE adoption increases, driven by reduction in cost and 10GbE ports available directly on server motherboards, it is likely to become the standard implementation over time, offering improved levels of bandwidth in addition to lower latencies compared to gigabit Ethernet. Therefore, we recommend monitoring the status of 10GbE closely. Given the required levels of cost, availability, and support for 10GbE, its adoption should be viewed as a progressive development of Ethernet, and it should be adopted where reasonably possible. When implementing 10 Gigabit Ethernet over copper cabling, it is important to also use the correct cabling for such an implementation; Cat 5 or 5e is commonly used for Gigabit Ethernet, while 5e or 6 is commonly used for 10 Gigabit Ethernet.

Fully Redundant Ethernet Interconnects

In a standard environment with a two-node cluster and no resiliency, each node connects to a single interconnect (Oracle does not recommend running the Clusterware and Database interconnect on separate networks) with a single NIC, in addition to the public network and any additional networks, such as the backup network. Figure 4-4 shows the interconnect network for simplicity.

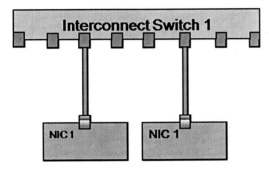

Figure 4-4. Nonredundant interconnect

If a single interconnect NIC fails, Oracle Clusterware will attempt to reconnect for a user-defined period of time before taking action to remove the node from the cluster. By default, the amount of time it will wait is defined by the 11*g* Clusterware CSS Misscount value as 30 seconds. When this happens, the master node directs the Oracle database Global Cache Service to initiate recovery of the failed instance. However, if the interconnect network fails because, for example, the network switch itself fails, then a scenario will result that is equivalent to the failure of every single node in the cluster, except for the designated master node. The master node will then proceed to recover all of the failed instances in the cluster before providing a service from a single node. This will occur irrespective of the number of nodes in the cluster.

Because the master node must first recover all instances, this process will result in a significant reduction in the level of service available. Therefore, we recommend the implementing a fully redundant interconnect network configuration.

A common conisdieration is to implement the Oracle CLUSTER_INTERCONNECTS parameter. This parameter requires the specification of one or more IP addresses, separated by a colon, to define the network interfaces that will be used for the interconnect. This network infrastructure is configured as shown in Figure 4-5.

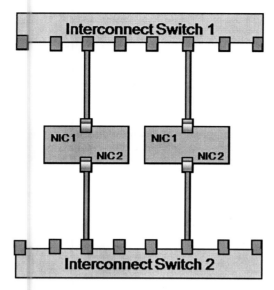

Figure 4-5. Clustered interconnects

The CLUSTER_INTERCONNECTS parameter however is available to distribute the network traffic across one or more interfaces, enabling you to increase the bandwidth available for interconnect traffic. This means it is most relevant in a data warehousing environment. The parameter explicitly does not implement failover functionality; therefore, the failure of any interconnect switch will continue to result in the failure of the entire interconnect network and a reduced level of service. Additionally, Oracle does not recommend setting the CLUSTER_INTERCONNECTS parameter, except in specific circumstances. For example, the parameter should not be set for a policy-managed database (you will learn more about workload management in Chapter 11).

To implement a fully redundant interconnect configuration requires the implementation of software termed *NIC bonding* at the operating system level. This software operates with the network driver level to provide two physical network interfaces that operate as a single interface. In its simplest usage, this software provides failover functionality, where one card is used to route traffic for the interface, and the other remains idle until the primary card fails. When a failure occurs, the interconnect traffic is routed through the secondary card. This occurs transparently to Oracle—its availability is uninterrupted, the IP address remains the same, and the software driver also remaps the hardware or MAC address of the card, so that failover is instantaneous. The failover is usually only detectable within Oracle by a minimal IPC time-out wait event. It is also possible in some configurations to provide increased bandwidth. This would deliver a similar solution to the CLUSTER_INTERCONNECTS parameter, with the additional protection of redundancy.

When implementing a bonding solution, understanding the implications of NIC failure, as opposed to failure of the switch itself, is important. Consider the physical implementation shown in Figure 4-5, where two nodes are connected separately to two switches. In this scenario, if a primary NIC fails on either of the nodes, that node will switch over to use its secondary NIC. However, this secondary NIC is now operating on a completely independent network from the primary card that still remains operational on the fully functional node. Communication will be lost, and the Oracle Clusterware will initiate cluster reconfiguration to eject the non-master node from the cluster.

Now considering the physical implementation shown in Figure 4-6, where the two nodes are connected separately to the two switches. In this case, the two switches are also connected with an interswitch link or an external network configuration, enabling traffic to pass between the two interconnect switches. As with the previous scenario, when a NIC fails, the network traffic is routed through the secondary interface. However, in this case, the secondary interface continues to communicate with the primary interface on the remaining node across the interswitch link. In a failover mode when no failures have occurred, only the primary switch is providing a service. After a failure, both switches are active and routing traffic between them.

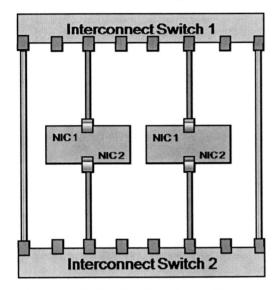

Figure 4-6. Fully redundant clustered interconnects

Crucially, this failover scenario also guards against the failure of a switch itself. While operational, if the secondary switch fails, the network traffic remains with the primary interconnect, and no failover operations are required. However, if the primary switch fails, the driver software reacts exactly as it would if all of the primary NICs on all of the nodes in the cluster had failed at exactly the same time. All of the NICs simultaneously switch from their primary to their secondary interface, so communication continues with all of the network traffic now operating across the secondary switch for all nodes. In this solution, there is no single point of failure because either a single NIC, network cable, switch, or interswitch link can fail without impacting the availability of the cluster. If these components are hot-swappable, they can also be replaced, and the fully redundant configuration can be restored without impacting the availability of the clustered database.

This form of teaming requires interaction with the network driver of the NICs used for bonding. Therefore, this approach is best implemented with channel bonding in an active-backup configuration in the widest range of cases (see Chapter 6 for more information on this subject). The implementation of NIC bonding in a broadcast configuration is not recommended for the high availability demands of an Oracle RAC configuration. In addition to a high availability configuration, a load balancing configuration may be implemented, depending upon the support for such a configuration at both the network hardware and driver levels.

Infiniband

The specifications of Infiniband describe a scalable, switched, fabric-based I/O architecture to standardize the communication between the CPU and peripheral devices. The aim of Infiniband was to unify and replace existing standards such as Ethernet, PCI, and Fibre Channel, so as to move beyond static server configurations to a dynamic, fabric-based data center environment where compute power can be added separate from the devices that provide the data to be processed.

The evolution of technologies such as PCI-Express and 10 Gigabit Ethernet testify to the fact that Infiniband did not wholly succeed in its initial design goal; however, the technology has become established as a standard for the interconnect between compute nodes in high performance computing clusters, and more recently, as the connectivity technology utilized by the Oracle Exadata Storage Server.

Infiniband is similar to PCI-Express in the way it implements a serial architecture that aggregates multiple links. Infiniband supports 2.5Gb/s per link. It also includes support for double data rate (DDR), which increases this to 5Gb/s; and quad data rate (QDR), which increases its throughput to 10 Gb/s at the same frequency. The most common system interconnect implementation uses 4x links, which results in bandwidth of 20Gb/s and 40Gb/s; however, also like PCI-Express encoding, this reduces the available bandwidth to 16 Gb/s and 32 Gb/s respectively. In addition to its bandwidth benefits, Infiniband latencies are also measured in microseconds, with a typical value of 10 microseconds. This means Infiniband offers significant latency gains over Ethernet, as well as a reduction in the CPU utilization required for I/O.

To implement Infiniband in an Oracle RAC environment, IP over Infiniband is supported. However, the optimal solution with Oracle 11g on Linux is to use the Reliable Datagram Sockets (RDS) protocol for its lower utilization of CPU, rather than Infiniband over IB. It is important to note that the supported implementation and version of RDS for Linux is the Open Fabrics Enterprise Distribution (OFED) 1.3.1 for RDS version 3, which is not included in either Red Hat or Oracle Enterprise Linux by default. This means it must be downloaded from Oracle as patch 7514146 and installed separately. It is also necessary to relink the binary when both the ASM and database instance are shutdown to use RDS, as shown in the following lines:

```
[oracle@london1 ~]$ cd $ORACLE_HOME/rdbms/lib
[oracle@london1 lib]$ make -f ins_rdbms.mk ipc_rds ioracle
```

Once relinked, Oracle RDS must be successfully configured and used. Note that both RDS and UDP cannot be configured at the same time. Therefore, returning to the default UDP settings requires relinking the binary again:

```
[oracle@london1 lib]$ make -f ins_rdbms.mk ipc_g ioracle
```

Infiniband fabrics are typically implemented with the focus on providing bandwidth in a clustered environment. For this reason, they are often configured in what is known as a Fat Tree Topology or Constant Bisectional Bandwidth (CBB) network to support a large number of nodes in a non-blocking switch configuration with multiple levels. This is in contrast to the hierarchical configuration of a typical Ethernet-based interconnect. However, it is important to note that the bandwidth requirements of Oracle RAC are typically considerably lower than the HPC supercomputing environments where Infiniband is typically deployed. Therefore, we recommend verifying the benefits of such an approach before deploying Infiniband as your interconnect technology.

Private Interconnect Selection Summary

In the absence of compelling statistical evidence that you will benefit from using a higher performance interconnect, we recommend selecting the default UDP protocol running over Ethernet at a gigabit or 10 gigabit rating for a default installation of an Oracle RAC cluster. Ethernet offers a simpler, more cost-effective interconnect method than Infiniband; and where cost is a decisive factor, implementing Infiniband should be compared against the alternative of 10 Gigabit Ethernet, coupled with high-performance server processors and the RAM to provide an adequate buffer cache on all server nodes. In other words, you need to consider your entire solution, rather than focusing on your method of interconnect entirely in isolation. To that end, we recommend comprehensive testing of your application in a RAC environment with multiple node and interconnect configurations as the basis for moving beyond a default configuration. As you have seen, Ethernet also offers greater potential for building redundancy into the interconnect configuration—and at a significantly lower cost.

There are a handful of exceptions where an Infiniband interconnect may prove a valuable investment. For example, it might make sense when implementing large data warehousing environments where high levels of inter-instance parallel processing capabilities are required. Additionally, Infiniband may prove worthwhile when looking to consolidate both the interconnect and storage fabric into a single technology with sufficient bandwidth to accommodate them both. However, in the latter circumstance, 10 Gigabit Ethernet should also be considered, to see if it can meet the increased bandwidth requirements.

Storage Technologies

In this chapter, we have progressed through the hierarchy of the RAC Technologies Compatibility Matrix (RTCM) for Linux Clusters, taking an in-depth look at the attributes of the server processor architecture, memory, and network interconnect technologies. In this section, we complete that analysis by reviewing the foundation that underpins every RAC implementation: storage technologies. As you learned in Chapter 2, you can have a single logical copy of the database shared between multiple server nodes in a RAC configuration. This logical copy may consist of multiple physical copies replicated either with ASM, alternative volume management software, or at the hardware level. However, maintaining the integrity of this single logical copy of data means that choosing the right storage solution is imperative. As with all architectural designs, if you fail to pay sufficient attention to the foundations of RAC, then it is unlikely that you will succeed in building a solution based on this technology. Table 4-9 details the storage protocols and configurations supported by Oracle in a RAC configuration. In addition to Oracle's level of support, it is also a requirement that the selected servers and storage be a supported configuration by the vendors in question.

Table 4-9. Storage Technologies

Storage Protocol	Supported Configuration
Fibre Channel	Switched Configuration or Fibre Channel Ports Integrated into Storage
Fibre Channel over Ethernet (FCoE)	Cisco FCoE supported
SCSI	Support for two nodes

Storage Protocol	Supported Configuration
iSCSI	Support for up to 30 nodes with gigabit Ethernet storage network
NFS	Supported solutions from EMC, Fujitsu, HP, IBM, NetApp, Pillar Data Systems and Sun

In the following sections, we will examine the merits of the supported storage protocols and associated storage technologies. Before doing so, however, we will first put this information into its proper context by examining how Oracle utilizes storage in a clustered environment.

RAC I/O Characteristics

The I/O characteristics of an Oracle database, including a RAC-based one, can be classified into four groups: random reads, random writes, sequential reads, and sequential writes. The prominence of each is dependent on the profile of the application; however, some generalizations can be made.

In a transactional environment, a number of random writes will be associated with the database writer (DBWRn) process (we use DBWRn to represent all of the database writer processes). These writes are in addition to the sequential writes associated with the redo logs and the log writer (LGWR) process. A level of random reads would also be expected from index-based queries and undo tablespace operations. Sequential read performance from full-table scans and parallel queries is normally more prominent in data warehouse environments, where there is less emphasis on write activity, except during batch loads.

To lay the foundation for a discussion of storage, we will begin by focusing on the read and write behavior that an Oracle cluster is expected to exhibit.

Read Activity

In this section, we have used the terms *random reads* and *sequential reads* from a storage perspective. However, the Oracle wait event usually associated with a sequential read realized on the storage is db file scattered read, whereas the Oracle wait event usually associated with a random read on the storage is db file sequential read. Therefore, clarifying the differing terminology seems worthwhile.

Within Oracle, the reading of data blocks is issued from the shadow process for a user's session. A *scattered read* is a multiblock read for full-table scan operations where the blocks, if physically read from the disk storage, are normally accessed contiguously. The operations required to read the blocks into the buffer cache are passed to the operating system, where the number of blocks to fetch in a single call is determined by the Oracle initialization parameter, DB_FILE_MULTIBLOCK_READ_COUNT. The long-standing methodology for UNIX multiple buffer operations is termed *scatter/gather*. In Linux, the SCSI generic (sg) packet device driver introduced the scatter/gather I/O in the 2.2 kernel. For Oracle on Linux, a similar methodology is employed, where scattered reads are issued with the pread() system call to read or write multiple buffers from a file descriptor at a given offset into the user session's program global area (PGA). Subsequently, these buffers are written into noncontiguous buffers in the buffer cache in the SGA. The key concept to note is that the data may be retrieved from the disk in a contiguous manner, but it is distributed into noncontiguous, or scattered, areas of the SGA. In addition to db file scattered read, in some circumstances you may also see the wait event direct path read associated with a profile of multiblock reads on the storage. The ultimate destination of the data blocks in a direct path read is the PGA, as opposed to the SGA. This is most evident when utilizing Parallel Query; hence, the typical profile on the storage is one of multiple, contiguous reads with the requests issued asynchronously by the

Parallel Execution Servers. Parallel Execution in a RAC environment is discussed in more detail in Chapter 14.

A db file sequential read event, on the other hand, is associated with index-based reads and often retrieves a single block or a small number of blocks that are then stored contiguously within the SGA. A single block read, by definition, is stored in contiguous memory. Therefore, this form of I/O is termed sequential if it's physically read from the disk storage, despite the fact that the file locations for these blocks are accessed randomly.

For the reasons previously described in this chapter, the important aspect to note in terms of read storage activity for RAC is that accessing data blocks through Cache Fusion from other nodes in the cluster is preferable to accessing them from disk. This holds true, no matter which method you employ. However, the buffer cache should always be sufficiently sized on each node to minimize both Cache Fusion and physical disk reads, as well as to ensure that as much read I/O as possible is satisfied logically from the local buffer cache. The notable exception occurs with data warehouse environments, where in-memory parallel execution is not being used. In that case, the direct path reads are not buffered in the SGA, so sufficient and usually considerable read I/O bandwidth must be available to satisfy the combined read demands of the cluster.

Write Activity

In a transactional environment, the most important aspect of storage performance for RAC in an optimally configured system will most likely be the sequential writes of the redo logs. The online redo logs will never be read as part of normal database operations, with a couple of exceptions.

■ **Note** The fact that Oracle redo logs are only ever written in a sequential manner may not hold true when the redo logs are based on a file system where direct I/O has not been implemented. In this case, the operating system may need to read the operating system block before providing it to Oracle to write the redo information, and then subsequently write the entire block back to the storage. Therefore, on a file system, a degree of read activity may be associated with disks where the redo logs are located when observed from Linux operating system utilities.

These exceptions are as follows: when one node in the cluster has failed, so the online redo logs are being read and recovered by another instance; and when the archiver (ARCn) process is reading an online redo log to generate the archive log. These activities, however, will not take place on the current active online redo log for an instance.

To understand why these sequential writes take prominence in a transactional environment, it's important to look at the role of the LGWR process. The LGWR process writes the changes present in the memory resident redo log buffer, which itself comprises a number of smaller individual buffers to the online redo logs located on disk. LGWR does not necessarily wait until a commit is issued before flushing the contents of the log buffer to the online logs; instead, by default, it will write when the log buffer is 1/3 full, _LOG_IO_SIZE is modified, every three seconds, or if posted by the DBWRn process—whichever occurs first, as long as LGWR is not already writing. Additionally, if a data block requested by another instance through Cache Fusion has an associated redo, then LGWR must write this redo to disk on the instance currently holding the block before it is shipped to the requesting instance.

Note that there are two important aspects of this activity in terms of storage utilization. First, in a high-performance OLTP environment, storage performance for redo logs is crucial to overall database throughput. Also, with Oracle 11g Release 2, the log buffer is sized automatically, so it cannot be modified from the default value. Second, issuing a rollback instead of a commit does not interrupt the sequential write activity of the LGWR process to the online redo logs. The rollback operation is completed instead from the information stored in the undo tablespace. Because these undo segments are also stored in the database buffer cache, the rollback operation will also generate redo, resulting in further sequential writes to the online redo logs.

When an Oracle client process ends a transaction and issues a commit, the transaction will not be recoverable until all of the redo information in the log buffer associated with the transaction and the transaction's system change number (SCN) have been written to the online redo log. The client will not initiate any subsequent work until this write has been confirmed; instead, it will wait on a log file sync event until all of its redo information is written.

Given sufficient activity, LGWR may complete a log file sync write for more than one transaction at a time. When this write is complete, the transaction is complete, and any locks held on rows and tables are released.

It is important to note that a log file sync is not totally comprised of I/O related activity, and it requires sufficient CPU time to be scheduled to complete its processing. For this reason, it is true that poorly performing storage will inevitably result in significant times being recorded on log file sync wait events. However, the converse is not necessarily true, that high log file sync wait events are always indicative of poorly performing storage. Scenarios associated with high CPU utilization moving to a system with a more advanced CPU or, to a lesser extent, increasing the scheduling priority of the LGWR process, can significantly increase the redo throughput of an apparently disk-bound environment.

Note that the modified blocks stored in the database buffer will not necessarily have been written to the storage at this point. In any event, these will always lag behind the redo information to some degree. The redo information is sufficient for database recovery; however, the key factor is the time taken to recover the database in the event of a failure. The more that the SCN in the online redo logs and archive logs is ahead of the SCN in the database datafiles, the longer the time that will be taken to recover.

Oracle RAC has multiple redo log threads—one for each instance. Each instance manages its own redo generation, and it will not read the log buffer or online redo logs of another instance while that instance is operating normally. Therefore, the redo log threads operate in parallel.

For RAC, all of the redo log threads should be placed on storage with the same profile to maintain equilibrium of performance across the cluster. The focus for redo should also be placed on the ability of the storage to support the desired number of I/O operations per second (IOPS) and the latency time for a single operation to complete, with less emphasis placed on the bandwidth available.

In addition to the sequential write performance associated with the redo log threads, other important storage aspects for transactional systems include the random reads and writes associated with the buffer cache and the writes of the DBWRn process. For 11g, the actual number of DBWR processes configured is either 1 or CPU_COUNT/8, whichever is greater. Like the LGWR process, DBWRn has a three-second time-out when idle. And when active, DBWRn may write dirty or modified blocks to disk. This may happen before or after the transaction that modified the block commits. This background activity will not typically have a direct impact on the overall database performance, although the DBWRn process will also be active in writing dirty buffers to disk, if reading more data into the buffer cache is required and no space is available.

For example, when a redo log switch occurs or the limits set by the LOG_CHECKPOINT_TIMEOUT or LOG_CHECKPOINT_INTERVAL parameter are reached for a particular instance, a thread checkpoint occurs, and every dirty or modified block in the buffer cache for that instance only will be written to the datafiles located on the storage. A thread checkpoint can also be manually instigated on a particular instance by the command alter system checkpoint local. A thread checkpoint ensures that all changes to the data blocks from a particular redo log thread on an instance up to the checkpoint Number, the current SCN

(System Change Number), have been written to disk. This does not necessarily mean that the resulting DBWR*n* activity is limited to the local instance. As discussed in Chapter 2, when another instance requires the data block already in use, that data block is shipped via the interconnect through Cache Fusion to the requesting instance, while the original instance maintains a copy of the original block called a past image. The past image must be held until its block master signals whether it can be written to disk or discarded. In this case, it is the DBWR*n* process of the instance with the most recent past image prior to the checkpoint Number that does the write to disk. From a storage perspective, however, this is not additional disk write activity in a RAC environment. Instead, DBWR Fusion writes are a result of the transfer of current data blocks between instances through Cache Fusion, without the modified blocks having been written to disk beforehand. Therefore, the most recent committed changes to a data block may reside on another instance. Without Cache Fusion, writes of modified blocks to disk to be read by another instance are known as *DBWR Cross-Instance writes* and involves an increased DBWR*n* workload. With DBWR Fusion writes, any additional overhead is in interconnect related messaging, as opposed to the storage level.

A full checkpoint on all instances, known as a Global Checkpoint, writes out all changes for all threads and requires the command alter system checkpoint global, which is also the default if local or global is not specified. Checkpoint details can be reported in the alert log by setting the parameter log_checkpoints_to_alert to the value of TRUE. Doing so reports that a checkpoint occurred up to a particular redo byte address (RBA) in the current redo log file for that instance.

Setting the parameter FAST_START_MTTR_TARGET to a time value in seconds of between 0 and 3600, while unsetting LOG_CHECKPOINT_TIMEOUT and LOG_CHECKPOINT_INTERVAL, calculates the correct checkpoint interval based on the desired recovery time in a process called *fast start checkpointing*. Fast start checkpointing has been available since Oracle 9*i*; therefore, setting LOG_CHECKPOINT_TIMEOUT and LOG_CHECKPOINT_INTERVAL is not recommended. Additionally, since release 10*g*, automatic checkpoint tuning is enabled if the FAST_START_MTTR_TARGET parameter is not set or is set to a sufficiently large value, which means that potentially no checkpoint related parameters are required to be set. Note that setting the FAST_START_MTTR_TARGET is not mandatory; nevertheless, we recommend setting this parameter in a RAC environment to enable fast start checkpointing. Doing so is preferable to relying entirely upon automatic checkpoint tuning because, in a RAC environment, checkpoint tuning also impacts recovery from a failed instance, in addition to crash recovery from a failed database.

It is important to be aware that the parameter FAST_START_MTTR_TARGET includes all of the timing required for a full crash recovery, from instance startup to opening the database datafiles. However, in a RAC environment, there is also the concept of instance recovery, whereby a surviving instance recovers from a failed instance. To address this issue, the _FAST_START_INSTANCE_RECOVERY_TARGET parameter was recommended by Oracle for RAC at version Oracle 10*g* Release 2 as a more specific way to determine the time to recover from the failed instance. However, this parameter was only relevant if one instance in the cluster failed, and it's no longer available for Oracle 11*g* Release 2. Therefore, we recommend setting the parameter FAST_START_MTTR_TARGET in a RAC environment. If you set this value too low for your environment and checkpointing is frequent, then the workload of the DBWR*n* process will be high, and performance under normal workloads is likely to be impacted. At the same time, the time to recover a failed instance will be comparatively shorter. If the FAST_START_MTTR_TARGET parameter is set too high, then DBWR*n* activity will be lower, and the opportunity for throughput will be higher. That said, the time taken to recover from a failed instance will be comparatively longer. FAST_START_MTTR_TARGET can be set dynamically, and the impact of different values can be observed in the column ESTIMATED_MTTR in the view V$INSTANCE_RECOVERY. For recovery from a failed instance, the instance startup time and total datafile open time should deducted from the ESTIMATED_MTTR value and can be read in the columns INIT_TIME_AVG and the number of datafiles multiplied by FOPEN_TIME_AVG in X$ESTIMATED_MTTR respectively.

During a recovery operation, the FAST_START_PARALLEL_ROLLBACK parameter determines the parallelism of the transactional component recovery operation after the redo apply. By default, this parameter is set to a value of LOW, which is twice the CPU_COUNT value. Given sufficient CPU resources, this parameter can be set to a value of HIGH to double the number of processes compared to the default value; the aim of changing this parameter is to improve the transaction recovery time.

The differing profiles of the LGWR and DBWR*n* processes on the nodes of the cluster will dictate the activity observed on the storage. There is more emphasis on LGWR activity in a transactional, as opposed to a data warehouse, environment. Some of the balance in activity between LGWR and DBWR*n* processes lies in the mean time to recover. But given redo logs of a sufficient size, a checkpoint on each node will most likely occur at the time of a log switch. This checkpoint will allow sufficient time for DBWR*n* to flush all of the dirty buffers to disk. If this flushing does not complete, then the Checkpoint Not Complete message will be seen in the alert.log of the corresponding instance, as follows:

```
Thread 1 cannot allocate new log, sequence 2411
Checkpoint not complete
  Current log# 4 seq# 2410 mem# 0: +REDO/prod/onlinelog/group_4.257.679813563
Sun Feb 27 05:51:55 2009
Thread 1 advanced to log sequence 2411 (LGWR switch)
  Current log# 1 seq# 2411 mem# 0: +REDO/prod/onlinelog/group_1.260.679813483
Sun Feb 27 05:52:59 2009
Thread 1 cannot allocate new log, sequence 2412
Checkpoint not complete
  Current log# 1 seq# 2411 mem# 0: +REDO/prod/onlinelog/group_1.260.679813483
Sun Feb 27 05:53:28 2009
Thread 1 advanced to log sequence 2412 (LGWR switch)
  Current log# 2 seq# 2412 mem# 0: +REDO/prod/onlinelog/group_2.259.679813523
```

When this error occurs, throughput will stall until the DBWR*n* has completed its activity and enabled the LGWR to allocate the next log file in the sequence. When the FAST_START_MTTR_TARGET parameter is set to a non-zero value, the OPTIMAL_LOGFILE_SIZE column in the V$INSTANCE_RECOVERY view is populated with a value in kilobytes that corresponds to a redo log size that would coincide a checkpoint with a log file switch, according to your MTTR target. Consequently, a longer recovery target will coincide with the recommendation for larger redo log files. This value varies dynamically; therefore, we recommend using this value for general guidance, but mainly to help ensure that the log files are not undersized in conjunction with expected DBWR*n* performance to the extent that Checkpoint Not Complete messages are regularly viewed in the alert log. Although the precise redo log size is dependent on the system throughput, typically a range from 512MB to 2GB is an acceptable starting value for a RAC environment.

Asynchronous I/O and Direct I/O

Without asynchronous I/O, every I/O request that Oracle makes to the operating system is completed singly and sequentially for a particular process, with the pread() system call to read and corresponding pwrite() system call for writes. Once asynchronous I/O has been enabled, multiple I/O requests can be submitted in parallel within a single io_submit() system call, without waiting for the requests to complete and subsequently be retrieved from the queue of completed events. Utilizing asynchronous I/O potentially increases the efficiency and throughput for both DBWR*n* and LGWR processes. For DBWR*n*, it also minimizes the requirement that you increase the values of DB_WRITER_PROCESSES beyond the default settings that may benefit synchronous I/O.

In an Oracle RAC on Linux environment, I/O processing is likely to benefit from enabling asynchronous I/O both in regular operations and for instance recovery. Asynchronous I/O support at the operating system level is mandatory for an Oracle 11*g* Release 2 installation, and it is a requirement for using ASM.

To utilize asynchronous I/O for Oracle on Linux, you need to ensure that the RPM package `libaio` has been installed according to the process described in Chapter 4:

```
[oracle@london1 ~]$ rpm -q libaio
libaio-0.3.106-3.2
```

The presence of the `libaio` package is mandatory, even if you do not wish to use asynchronous I/O, because the Oracle executable is directly linked against it, and it cannot be relinked with the `async_off` option to break this dependency. The additional `libaio-devel` RPM package is checked for under package dependencies during the Oracle installation; and in x86-64 environments, both the 32-bit and 64-bit versions of this RPM are required.

Asynchronous I/O can be enabled directly on raw devices. However, with Oracle 11g Release 2, raw devices are not supported by the Oracle Universal Installer (OUI) for new installs. That said, raw devices are supported for upgrades of existing installations, and they may be configured after a database has been installed. Asynchronous I/O can also be enabled on file systems that support it, such as the OCFS2, and it is enabled by default on Automatic Storage Management (ASM) instances, which we discuss in Chapters 6 and 9, respectively. For NFS file systems, the Direct NFS Client incorporated within Oracle 11g is required to implement asynchronous I/O against NFS V3 storage devices.

Where asynchronous I/O has not been explicitly disabled, by default the initialization parameter `DISK_ASYNCH_IO` is set to `TRUE`. Thus, it will be used on ASM and raw devices when the instance is started. In fact, it is important to note that ASM is not itself a file system (see Chapter 9 for more details on this topic), so the compatible I/O is determined by the underlying devices, which are typically raw devices. For this reason, setting asynchronous I/O for ASM and raw devices implies the same use of the technology.

If the `DISK_ASYNCH_IO` parameter is set to `FALSE,` then asynchronous I/O is disabled. The column `ASYNCH_IO` in the view `V$IOSTAT_FILE` displays the value `ASYNC_ON` for datafiles where asynchronous I/O is enabled.

If you're using asynchronous I/O on a supporting file system such as OCFS2, however, you also need to set the parameter `FILESYSTEMIO_OPTIONS`, which by default is set to `NONE`. Setting `FILESYSTEMIO_OPTIONS` to anything other than the default value is not required for ASM. Oracle database files are stored directly in ASM; they cannot be stored in an Automatic Storage Management Cluster File System (ACFS), so `FILESYSTEMIO_OPTIONS` is not a relevant parameter for ACFS.

On a file system, this parameter should be set to the value `ASYNCH` by executing the following commands on one instance in the cluster:

```
[oracle@london1 lib]$ srvctl stop database -d PROD
SQL> startup nomount;

SQL>  alter system set filesystemio_options=asynch scope=spfile;

SQL> shutdown immediate;

[oracle@london1 lib]$ srvctl start database -d PROD
```

Once asynchronous I/O is enabled, there are a number of ways to ascertain whether it is being used. For example, if ASMLIB is not being used when running iterations of the command `cat /proc/slabinfo | grep kio`, changing values under `kioctx` and `kiocb` show that that asynchronous I/O data structures are being used. Additionally, during testing, the output of the operating system `strace` command run against the `LGWR` and `DBWRn` processes can be viewed for the use of the `io_submit()` *and* `io_getevents()` system calls. It is important to note, however, that if you're using ASMLIB on 2.6 kernel-based systems, only the read() system call is evident, even for write events. For example, the following snippet determines the process id of the LGWR process:

```
[oracle@london1 ~]$ ps -ef | grep -i lgwr
oracle    5484     1  0 04:09 ?        00:00:00 asm_lgwr_+ASM1
oracle    5813     1  1 04:11 ?        00:02:32 ora_lgwr_PROD1
oracle   28506 13937  0 06:57 pts/2    00:00:00 grep -i lgwr
```

This process can then be traced with the output directed into a file until it is interrupted with Ctrl-C:

```
[oracle@london1 ~]$ strace -af -p 5813 -o asynctest
Process 5813 attached - interrupt to quit
Process 5813 detached
```

Viewing this output in the file shows the use of the read() system call, even for the sequential writes of LGWR:

```
read(22,"MSA\0\2\0\10\0P\0\0\0\0\0\0\0\260\306v\32\0\0\0\0\300\17q\202\
327*\0\0"..., 80) = 80
read(22, "MSA\0\2\0\10\0P\0\0\0\0\0\0\0\260\306v\32\0\0\0\0\0\0\0\0\0\0"
..., 80) = 80
```

For this reason, when using ASMLIB the only determinant of the use of asynchronous I/O is by checking the value of the column ASYNCH_IO in the view V$IOSTAT_FILE. With Linux 2.6-based kernels, the size of the asynchronous I/O operations can no longer be modified with the kernel parameter, fs.aio-max-size. Instead, the size must be determined automatically.

Asynchronous I/O should not be confused with direct I/O. Direct I/O is an Oracle parameter set to avoid file system buffering on compatible file systems, and depending on the file system in question, it may be used either independently or in conjunction with asynchronous I/O. Remember: If you're using ASM, direct I/O is not applicable.

Direct I/O can be enabled in the initialization parameter file by setting the parameter FILESYSTEMIO_OPTIONS to DIRECTIO. If enabling both asynchronous I/O and direct I/O is desired on a compatible file system, then this parameter can alternatively be set to the value of SETALL, as in this example:

```
SQL> alter system set filesystemio_options=directIO scope=spfile;
```

Alternatively, you can set the value like this:

```
SQL> alter system set filesystemio_options=setall scope=spfile;
```

This means a combination of the parameters DISK_ASYNCH_IO and FILESYSTEMIO_OPTIONS can be used to fine-tune the I/O activity for the RAC cluster, where appropriate. However, adding such support should always be referenced against the operating system version and storage.

Hard Disk and Solid State Disk Drive Performance

The previous synopsis of RAC I/O characteristics activity illustrates that the most important aspects of I/O are two-fold. First, it's essential to ensure that all committed data is absolutely guaranteed to be written to the storage. Second, the database must always recoverable in a timely and predictable manner in the event of a node, cluster, or even site failure. In terms of the permanent storage, the database is able to recover when the data is actually written to the disks themselves.

Hard disk drives tend to offer dramatically increased capacity and a degree of improved performance as newer models are introduced; however, the basic technology has remained the same since hard disks were introduced by IBM in the 1950s.

Within each drive, a single actuator with multiple heads reads and writes the data on the rotating platters. The overall performance of the drive is determined by two factors: seek time and latency. *Seek time* is the time the heads take to move into the desired position to read or write the data. Disks in enterprise storage tend to be available in configurations of up to 10,000 or 15,000 rotations per minute (rpm), with the 15,000 rpm disks utilizing smaller diameter platters. The shorter distance traveled by the heads results in a lower seek time, typically around 3.5 to 4 milliseconds. *Latency* is the time taken for the platter to rotate to the correct position once the head is in position to read or write the correct sector of data. A full rotation on a 15,000 rpm drive takes approximately four milliseconds and on a 10,000 rpm drive. Thus, it takes six milliseconds with full rotations resulting in the longest latency possible; the average latency will be approximately half this amount for all reads and writes, and the typical quoted value for latency on a 15,000 rpm drive is therefore two milliseconds. Once the head and platter are in the correct position, the time taken to actually transfer the data is negligible compared to the seek and latency times.

An additional important concept for achieving the maximum performance from a drive is that of *destroking*. Destroking is the process of storing data only on the outer sectors of the disk, leaving the inner sectors unused. The outer sectors store more information, and therefore enable the reading and writing of more data without repositioning the heads, which improves the overall access time at the cost of a reduction in capacity. Additionally, all enterprise class disk drives include a RAM memory-based buffer, typically in the order of 8MB to 16MB. This RAM improves the potential *burst rate* data transfer, which is the fastest possible data transfer a disk can sustain. This is measured by taking the time to transfer buffered data and excluding actual disk operations.

Hard disk performance seen by the Oracle Database is dependent on multiple factors, such as the drive itself, the controller, cables, and HBA. For this reason, a number of figures and terminologies are quoted in reference to overall performance, and it is beneficial to be able to identify and compare the relevant values. The first of these is the External Transfer Rate, which is usually given in megabytes per second (MB/s). For example, you might see 400MB/s for a drive with a 4Gb/s Fibre Channel interface. At first, this might initially seem to indicate that a single drive would be sufficient to sustain a 4Gb/s Fibre Channel HBA. However, this value is based on the burst rate value, so it's mostly academic with respect to Oracle database performance. Second, the internal transfer rate is given in megabits, and it's usually shown as a range from the slowest to the fastest sustained performance expected from the drive, such as 1051 to 2225. As this value is shown is megabits, and there are 8 megabits to the megabyte, it is necessary to divide by 8 to reach a comparable figure to the external transfer rate. In this example, that translates to range of 131MB/s to 278MB/s. With a 25% deduction for the disk controller, this example drive should be able to sustain a minimum transfer rate of 98.25MB/s. Third, the sustained transfer rate is the long-term read or write rate, with the former being the higher value that can be sustained for a longer period of time than the burst rate. With this example, the sustained transfer rate can be calculated as the average of the internal transfer rate values, as in this example:

```
(((1051 + 2225) /2 ) /8 ) * 0.75  = 154 MB/s
```

The sustained transfer rate quoted in a specification sheet is typically shown as a range of values around this average value, such as 110MB/s to 171MB/s, with the actual value dependent on the overall hardware configuration. Therefore, the average value is the optimal figure for calculations based on sustained transfer rates. At the time of writing, average read performance of up to 150MB/s and average write performance of up to 140MB/s were typical values for best-in-class enterprise drives. Therefore, in an ideal theoretical scenario, a minimum of three such drives would be required to sustain the bandwidth of a single 4Gb/s Fibre Channel HBA on a single node in the cluster. For an additional comparison, more than 425 such drives, coupled with the appropriate PCI and HBA configuration, would be required to approach a similar bandwidth capacity available within memory of a single two-socket node from the example given previously in this chapter, where the memory bandwidth was 64GB/s. This example is a further illustration of the importance of ensuring as much data as possible is cached in the local memory of the cluster nodes. Finally, in addition to transfer rates the value of IOPS (Input/Output Operations Per Second) is also important. Whereas transfer rates measure the data bandwidth of a drive, IOPS measures the number of individual operations that the drive can support within a second. Consequently, the actual IOPS value is dependent upon the workload, although this is typically measured on short random I/O operations, and it can be estimated from the average seek time, in addition to the average latency. Hard disk IOPS vary can also be improved by queuing technology, depending on the drive of Tagged Command Queuing (TCQ) for ATA and SCSI disks and Native Command Queuing (NCQ) for SATA disks up to values of 300-400 IOPS, with similar values for both read and write.

We recommend that even when purchasing high specification hard-disk drives and enterprise class storage for an entry level two-node cluster, a starting disk configuration should at a minimum be twelve drives in a RAID configuration (we will cover this in greater depth later in this Chapter). Taking into account RAID technologies to mitigate the risks of drive failure, as well as the requirements for the configuration of different RAID groups to account for the different storage profiles of the LGWR and DBWR*n* processes, it is likely that number of drives required will significantly exceed this number to prevent performance being negatively affected.

Solid State disk drives (SSDs) are a technology gaining prominence. They promise to enhance both disk drive performance and reduce power consumption; however, it is important to note that, as opposed to being an emerging technology, it is one that has taken decades to mature. For example, EMC Corporation began reintroducing SSDs in 2008 for the first time since 1987. Current generations of SSDs are based on NAND Flash memory, and they are either single-level cell (SLC) or multi-level cell based. SLC stores a single bit per memory cell, whereas MLC applies different levels of voltage to store multiple bits per cell. MLC-based drives offer higher capacity, whereas SLC drives bring higher levels of write performance and durability. At the time of writing, the best-in-class of both SLC and MLC SSDs offer sustained read transfer rates of 250MB/s. However, whereas SLCs also deliver a sustained write transfer rate of 170MB/s, the equivalent value for an MLC is only 70MB/s. Write performance is also superior when SSDs are below full capacity. Additionally, MLCs have a lifespan of 10,000 write-erase cycles; for SLCs, this value is 100,000 write-erase cycles. In contrast to hard disks, SSD latency varies and is dependent upon the operation. Typical latencies for read, write, and erase are 25 microseconds, 250 microseconds, and 0.5 milliseconds for SLCs; and 50 microseconds, 900 microseconds, and 3.5 milliseconds for MLCs, respectively. Nevertheless, these latencies offer a significant improvement over the seek times associated with hard disks. Also, they immediately point to the most significant gains being for random read operations, as illustrated by the associated IOPS values. For example, SLCs deliver up to 3300 write IOPS, but 35000 read IOPS. SSD IOPS values do depend more upon the transfer size when compared to hard disks, with the higher IOPs values measured at the 2Kb and 4Kb transfer sizes.SSD IOPS values approach hard disk equivalent IOPS at larger 64Kb and 128Kb transfer sizes for both read and write. Queuing technologies can also enhance SSD performance most significantly for read IOPS values and the addition of TRIM commands to identify blocks deleted at the OS level for write IOPS values. Both SLCs and MLCs have advantages for different areas of utilization. SLCs, for example, with their enhanced durability, higher write bandwidth but lower capacity, would be preferred over MLCs for redo log disks.Redo performance exceeds that of hard disks most notably due to the higher IOPS at smaller transfer sizes,MLCs with their higher capacity and SLC equivalent random I/O performance deliver comparative advantages for read-focused datafile performance such as indexes.

SSDs are a technology experiencing increasing levels of adoption. Where the opportunity arises, we recommend testing to determine whether the performance advantages are realized in your RAC environment. It is important to note performance characteristics can vary between vendors. To maximize drive lifespan, it would be advantageous to spread the write-erase cycles across the entire drive as evenly as possible. For this reason, all SSDs employ a logical block address (LBA) allocation table where each LBA is not necessarily stored in the same physical area of the disk each time it is written. Unlike a hard-disk drive, SSDs may take a period of time to optimize performance and reach a steady state of high sustained transfer rates. For this reason, it is especially important to either ensure that your use of SSDs are incorporated into a certified enterprise storage solution or that drives are correctly prepared with a low level format (LLF) before doing direct comparisons with hard-disk drive solutions.

If adopting SSD versus hard-disk technology in a disk-for-disk comparison, SSDs offer improved levels of performance, with the most significant gains delivered in random I/O operations, while the gap between the two technologies is narrower for throughput of sequential operations that are less dependent on hard disk seek times. Hard-disk drives also support much larger storage capacities and lower costs for that capacity. If you're considering power consumption across the cluster, then it is important to be aware that an active SSD will typically consume 2.4 Watts of power, compared to the 12.1 Watts for a hard-disk drive. Therefore, the impact of your choice of disk on the power consumption of the storage array should be a consideration, in addition to the total power consumption at the server level, as well as the power consumption of the CPU and memory components.

In addition to SSDs, Flash Storage technology can also be deployed in additional form factors, such as on motherboard flash modules or Flash PCIe cards. It is important to note, from an architectural perspective, that in a RAC environment these devices are local to an individual node within the cluster, whereas an SSD can be viewed as a direct replacement for a hard-disk drive across the configuration that can be integrated into an enterprise storage array shared between the nodes in the cluster. Flash PCIe cards also can connect directly into the PCIe interface on a server, whereas SSDs, if implemented directly into a host, will connect through the SATA protocol, as discussed later in this chapter. An SSD can also be used within an external storage array through an HBA (Host Bus Adapter) and a protocol such as Fibre Channel to connect the array. Both of these mediums add latency to the I/O solution, but offer greater flexibility, manageability, and reliability to enterprise environments than a single card configuration.

Flash PCIe cards in particular have relevance to an Oracle storage feature introduced with Oracle 11*g* Release 2 called the *Database Smart Flash Cache*. It is important to note, however, that in its initial release, this technology was supported by the Linux operating system, although it was disabled. Patch 8974084 was released later to resolve this issue.With its parameters DB_FLASH_CACHE_FILE and DB_FLASH_CACHE_SIZE, the Flash Cache is documented to be a second-tier buffer cache residing on Flash Storage, and it is presented by the operating system as a standard disk device. The Flash Cache can be considered in implementation in a manner similar to the CPU L2 Cache, as discussed previously in this chapter. A Flash Cache sized up to a factor of 10 greater than the buffer cache is accessed in a hierarchical manner, supplying the RAM resident buffer cache with data blocks fetched with access times in the region of 50 microsecond latencies. Although an improvement over standard hard disk access times measured in milliseconds, it should be noted accessing RAM-based memory within 100 nanoseconds is completed 500 times faster than the Flash-based access; therefore, the Flash Cache should be considered as complementing the in-memory buffer cache, as opposed to replacing it. Thus the Flash Cache provides an additional storage tier local to each node in a RAC environment between the RAM, which is also local to each node; and the disk-based storage, which is shared between all nodes.

Whereas Flash PCIe cards connect by the PCIe interface through the ICH (both the PCIe interface and ICH were covered previously in this chapter), on-motherboard flash modules offer the potential of bringing Flash memory further up the performance hierarchy, above the PCIe interface. To realize this, a number of technology companies are collaborating on a standard interface to NAND flash chips, termed the ONFI (Open NAND Flash Interface). Through this interface, a server would be equipped with a low latency interface to Flash storage directly on the motherboard of the server.

At the time of writing, testing of Database Smart Flash Cache was not possible. We see the most relevance for enhancing performance in single-instance environments. With RAC, however, there is already an additional storage tier between local RAM and shared storage—namely, through Cache Fusion by accessing data blocks across the interconnect from a remote instance. Therefore, the main consideration is whether accessing a data block stored in the Flash Cache on a remote instance with Cache Fusion would outperform the remote instance accessing the data block directly from disk, such as from an SSD storage tier. The actual benefits would ultimately depend on all the technology deployed in the solution discussed in this chapter, such as the CPU, memory, and the interconnect. If you're considering a virtualized solution with Oracle VM, which you will learn more about in Chapter 5, it is also worth noting that such a device would be accessed with drivers at the Dom0 layer, in which case accessing the second tier of the buffer cache external to Guest could have a potential impact on performance.

In a RAC environment, storage based on both hard disk and SSD is best evaluated at the shared storage level, and combinations of both SSD and hard disk drives can also be adopted to configure a hybrid storage environment to take advantage of SSD performance in conjunction with hard-disk capacity. However, whether you're adopting hard-disk drives, SSDs, or a combination of both, all RAC cluster solutions require storage solutions based on multiple disk drives, the configuration of which impacts both storage performance and capacity. For this reason, we will discuss how this is achieved with RAID.

RAID

RAID was defined in 1988 as a *Redundant Array of Inexpensive Disks* by David A. Patterson, Garth Gibson, and Randy H. Katz at the University California, Berkeley. Later use often sees the *Inexpensive* replaced with *Independent*; the two terms are interchangeable, without affecting the core concepts.

The original RAID levels defined are 1, 2, 3, 4, and 5 (and 0), with additional terminology added at later points in time, such as RAID 0+1, RAID 10, and RAID-50.

In general, the term *RAID* is applied to two or more disks working in parallel, but presented as a logical single disk to the user to provide enhanced performance and/or resilience from the storage. RAID can be implemented in one of three ways:

- *Option 1*: This option is referred to as *Just a Bunch of Disks* (JBOD). The JBOD is presented to the volume-management software running on the server that implements RAID on these devices; specifically, it is presented as logical volumes of disks to the database. RAID processing takes place using the server CPU.

- *Option 2*: A JBOD is presented to the server, but the RAID processing is done by a dedicated RAID host bus adapter (HBA) or incorporated onto the motherboard of the server itself, also known as *RAID on motherboard* (ROMB). In this case, RAID processing is done on the server, but not by the server CPU.

- *Option 3*: The server is connected to an external RAID array with its own internal RAID controller and disks, and it is presented a configurable logical view of disks. RAID processing is done completely independently from the server.

For RAC, the RAID implementation must be cluster-aware of multiple hosts accessing the same disks at the same time. This implementation restriction rules out the second RAID option and limits the choice in the first category to third-party solutions (from companies such as HP PolyServe and Symantec

Veritas) that may be overlaid with cluster file systems and Oracle ASM. A more common RAID solution for RAC is the third option, where you use an external dedicated-storage array.

Whichever implementation is used, RAID is based on the same concepts and is closely related to the Oracle stripe-and-mirror-everything (SAME) methodology for laying out a database on storage for optimal performance and resilience. Therefore, in the following sections we will look at the most popular and practical implementations of RAID.

RAID 0 Striping

RAID 0 implements striping across a number of disks by allocating the data blocks across the drives in sequential order, as illustrated in Table 4-10. This table shows a stripe set of eight disks. The blocks from A to X represent, not Oracle blocks, but logical blocks of contiguous disk sectors, such as 128KB. In this example, we have one stripe against eight disks, which makes our total stripe size 1MB (8×128KB).

Table 4-10. RAID 0

DISK1	DISK 2	DISK 3	DISK 4
BLOCK-A	BLOCK-B	BLOCK-C	BLOCK-D
BLOCK-I	BLOCK-J	BLOCK-K	BLOCK-L
BLOCK-Q	BLOCK-R	BLOCK-S	BLOCK-T
DISK 5	**DISK 6**	**DISK 7**	**DISK 8**
BLOCK-E	BLOCK-F	BLOCK-G	BLOCK-H
BLOCK-M	BLOCK-N	BLOCK-O	BLOCK-P
BLOCK-U	BLOCK-V	BLOCK-W	BLOCK-X

This implementation does not cater to redundancy; therefore, by the strictest definition, it is not RAID. The loss of a single drive within the set results in the loss of the entire RAID group. So, on one hand, this implementation offers a lower level of protection in comparison to the presentation of individual drives.

What it does offer, on the other hand, is improved performance in terms of operations per second and throughput over the use of individual drives for both read and write operations. The example in the table would in theory offer eight times the number of operations per second of an individual drive and seven times the average throughput for hard disks. The throughput is marginally lower with hard-disk drives due to the increased latency to retrieve all of the blocks in a stripe set because the heads must move in parallel on all drives to a stripe. On solid state-based storage, the average throughput is also a factor of eight.

For RAC, this implementation of RAID delivers the highest-performing solution; however, the lack of resilience makes it unsuitable for any production implementation. RAID 0 is heavily utilized, mainly for commercial database benchmarks. The combination of RAID 0 and destroking on hard-disk drives is ideal for an environment where data loss or the cost of unused disk space is not a significant consideration.

RAID 1 Mirroring

In RAID 1, all data is duplicated from one disk or set of disks to another, resulting in a mirrored, real-time copy of the data (see Table 4-11).

Table 4-11. RAID 1

DISK 1		DISK 2	DISK 3		DISK 4
BLOCK-A	=	BLOCK-A	BLOCK-D	=	BLOCK-D
BLOCK-B	=	BLOCK-B	BLOCK-E	=	BLOCK-E
BLOCK-C	=	BLOCK-C	BLOCK-F	=	BLOCK-F
DISK 5		**DISK 6**	**DISK 7**		**DISK 8**
BLOCK-G	=	BLOCK-G	BLOCK-J	=	BLOCK-J
BLOCK-H	=	BLOCK-H	BLOCK-K	=	BLOCK-K
BLOCK-I	=	BLOCK-I	BLOCK-L	=	BLOCK-L

RAID 1 offers a minor performance improvement over the use of single drives because read requests can be satisfied from both sides of the mirror. However, write requests are written to both drives simultaneously, offering no performance gains. The main benefits of this form of RAID are that, in the event of a single drive failure or possibly multiple drive failures, the mirror is broken, but data availability is not impacted. This means that performance is only marginally impaired, if at all, until the drive is replaced. At this point, however, performance is impacted by the resilvering process of copying the entire contents of the good drive to the replacement, a lengthy and intensive I/O operation.

When implemented in software using a volume manager, the CPU load from mirroring is the lowest of any form of RAID, although the server I/O traffic is doubled, which should be a consideration in comparing software- to hardware-based RAID solutions.

The most significant cost of this form of RAID comes in using exactly double the amount of storage as that which is available to the database.

RAID 10 Striped Mirrors

RAID 10 offers the advantages and disadvantages of both RAID 0 and RAID 1, first by mirroring all of the disks onto a secondary set, and then by striping across these mirrored sets. Table 4-12 shows this configuration.

Table 4-12. RAID 10

DISK 1		DISK 2	DISK 3		DISK 4
BLOCK-A	=	BLOCK-A	BLOCK-B	=	BLOCK-B
BLOCK-E	=	BLOCK-E	BLOCK-F	=	BLOCK-F
BLOCK-I	=	BLOCK-I	BLOCK-J	=	BLOCK-J
DISK 5		**DISK 6**	**DISK 7**		**DISK 8**
BLOCK-C	=	BLOCK-C	BLOCK-D	=	BLOCK-D
BLOCK-G	=	BLOCK-G	BLOCK-H	=	BLOCK-H
BLOCK-K	=	BLOCK-K	BLOCK-L	=	BLOCK-L

This form of RAID is usually only available with hardware-based RAID controllers. It achieves the same I/O rates that are gained by striping, and it can sustain multiple simultaneous drive failures in which the failures are not experienced on both sides of a mirror. In this example, four of the drives could possibly fail with all of the data, and therefore the database, remaining available. RAID 10 is very much the implementation of SAME that Oracle extols; however, like RAID 1, it comes at the significant overhead of an additional 100% requirement in storage capacity above and beyond the database.

RAID 0+1 Mirrored Stripes

RAID 0+1 is a two-dimensional construct that implements the reverse of RAID 10 by striping across the disks and then mirroring the resulting stripes. Table 4-13 shows the implementation of RAID 0 across disks 1, 2, 5, and 6, mirrored against disks 3, 4, 7, and 8.

Table 4-13. RAID 0+1

DISK 1	DISK 2		DISK 3	DISK 4
BLOCK-A	BLOCK-B	=	BLOCK-A	BLOCK-B
BLOCK-E	BLOCK-F	=	BLOCK-E	BLOCK-F
BLOCK-I	BLOCK-J	=	BLOCK-I	BLOCK-J
DISK 5	**DISK 6**		**DISK 7**	**DISK 8**
BLOCK-C	BLOCK-D	=	BLOCK-C	BLOCK-D
BLOCK-G	BLOCK-H	=	BLOCK-G	BLOCK-H
BLOCK-K	BLOCK-L	=	BLOCK-K	BLOCK-L

RAID 0+1 offers identical performance characteristics to RAID 10, and it has exactly the same storage-capacity requirements. The most significant difference occurs in the event of a drive failure. In the RAID 0+1 configuration, if a single drive fails—for example, Disk 1—then you lose access to the entire stripe set on disks 1, 2, 5, and 6. At this point, you only have to lose another disk on the stripe set on the other side of the mirror to lose access to all of the data and, thus, the database it resides on.

Therefore, you might reasonably question where a RAID 0+1 configuration would be used instead of RAID 10. If implementing RAID in hardware on a dedicated-storage array, then you would *never* use this approach; RAID 10 should always be used. However, if using software RAID, such as with Oracle ASM, in combination with any number of low-cost modular storage arrays, a RAID 0+1 configuration can be used to stripe the disks at the storage level for performance and then mirrored by software between multiple arrays for resilience.

RAID 5

RAID 5 introduces the concept of parity. In Table 4-14, you can see the eight disks striped similarly to RAID 0, except that you have a parity block at the end of each stripe. This parity block is the same size as the data blocks, and it contains the results of the exclusive OR (XOR) operation on all of the bits in every block in the stripe. This example shows the first three stripes; and if it were to continue across all of the disks, you would have seven disks of data and one disk of parity.

Table 4-14. RAID 5

DISK 1	DISK 2	DISK 3	DISK 4
BLOCK-A	BLOCK-B	BLOCK-C	BLOCK-D
BLOCK-I	BLOCK-J	BLOCK-K	BLOCK-L
BLOCK-Q	BLOCK-R	BLOCK-S	BLOCK-T
DISK 5	**DISK 6**	**DISK 7**	**DISK 8**
BLOCK-E	BLOCK-F	BLOCK-G	PARITY
BLOCK-M	BLOCK-N	PARITY	BLOCK-H
BLOCK-U	PARITY	BLOCK-O	BLOCK-P

In this RAID configuration, the data can be read directly, just as it can in RAID 0. However, changing a data block requires writing the data block, and then reading, recalculating, and subsequently rewriting the parity block. This additional overhead for writes on RAID 5 is termed the *write penalty*. Note that, from the properties of the XOR operation for a write operation, touching the data block and the parity block is only necessary for a write operation; the parity can be calculated without it being required to access all of the other blocks in the stripe. When implemented on a hardware-based RAID controller, the impact of the parity calculation is negligible compared to the additional read and write operations, and the write penalty will range from 10% to 30%, depending on the storage array used. RAID 5 is less effective when implemented as a software solution because of the requirement to read all of the data, including the parity information, back to the server; calculate the new values; and then write all of the information back to the storage, with the write penalty being approximately 50%.

Recalling our discussion of storage fundamentals for RAC, this RAID configuration may appear completely unsuited to LGWR activity from a redo thread, presenting the system with a large number of sequential writes and no reads. From a theoretical standpoint, this unsuitability is true. However, good RAID 5-storage systems can take this sequential stream of writes and calculate the parity block without first needing to read the parity block from disk. All of the blocks and the parity block are written to disk in one action, similar to RAID 0; hence, in the example shown, eight write operations are required to commit blocks A to G to disk, compared to the fourteen required for RAID 10, although these can be completed in parallel.

The primary attraction of RAID 5 is that, in the event of a disk failure, the parity block means that the missing data for a read request can be reconstructed using the XOR operation on the parity information and the data from the other drives. Therefore, to implement resiliency, the 100% overhead of RAID 10 has been significantly reduced to the lower overhead of the parity disk. Unlike RAID 10, however, the loss of another drive will lead to a total data loss. The loss of a single drive also leads to the RAID 5 group operating in a degraded mode, with the additional load of reading all of the blocks and parity in the stripe to calculate the data in the failed block increasing the workload significantly. Similarly, when all of the drives are replaced, all of the blocks and the parity need to be read to regenerate the block, so it can be written to the replaced drive.

With parity-based RAID, an important area to look at is the impact of significantly larger disk media introduced since the original RAID concepts were defined. Despite the increase in disk size, the likelihood of a disk failure remains approximately the same. Therefore, for a RAID 5 configuration of a given capacity, the chances of operating in degraded mode or even losing data are comparatively higher. This risk has led to the emergence of RAID 50–based systems with mirrored RAID 5 configurations. However, RAID 50 offers further challenges in terms of the impact on performance for RAC.

Storage Cache

In using the term *cache*, we are referring to the RAM set aside to optimize the transfer of the Oracle data from the storage, and we are primarily concerned with the storage-array controller cache. For data access, other levels of cache exist at the hardware level through which the Oracle data will pass, for example, the multiple levels of CPU cache on the processor discussed previously in this chapter, as well as the buffer cache on the hard drive itself. Note that both are usually measured in a small number of megabytes.

As we have seen previously in this chapter, for a transactional system, the storage will experience a number of random reads and writes, along with a continual stream of shorter sequential writes. Data warehouse activity will either buffer much of the data in the SGA for single threaded queries, or request long, continual streams of reads for parallel queries with minimal write and redo log activity outside of data loading times.

For write operations, the effect of cache on the storage controller can be significant to a point. If operating as a write-back cache, the write request is confirmed as complete as soon as the data is in cache, before it has been written to disk. For Oracle, this cache should always be mirrored in RAM and supplied with a backup battery power supply. In the event of failure, this backup enables the data within cache to be written to disk before the storage array shuts down, reducing the likelihood of database corruption. Write cache is also significant in RAID 5 systems because it enables the calculation of parity for entire stripes in cache, and it stores frequently used parity blocks in cache, thus reducing the read operations required.

This benefit from write cache, however, is valuable only to a certain extent in coping with peaks in throughput. In the event of sustained throughput, the data will be written to cache faster than the cached data can be written to disk. Inevitably, the cache will fill and throughput will operate at disk speed. Storage write cache should be seen as an essential buffer to enable the efficient writing of data back to disk. Allocating a large amount of cache, however, will never be a panacea for a slow disk layout or subsystem.

RAID Summary

Of the generally available RAID configurations discussed, a popular choice is RAID 5. The reasons are straightforward: RAID 0 is not practical in terms of redundancy, and RAID 1 is not suitable for performance. Although RAID 10 and RAID 0+1 offer the best performance and reliability, they have the significant cost of requiring a 100% overhead in storage compared to usable capacity. In theory, RAID 5 offers a middle ground, sacrificing a degree of performance for resilience, while also maintaining most of the storage capacity as usable.

In practice, the costs and benefits are not as well defined. With RAID 1, RAID 0, and combinations of these levels, throughput calculations tend to be straightforward. With RAID 5, however, benchmarking and tests are required to clearly establish the performance thresholds. The reason for these testing requirements is that the advantages for RAID 5 tend to be stated from the viewpoint of a single sequential write stream, combined with random reads where performance is predictable. In practice, hosting more than one database environment on a storage system is highly likely; when adding RAC into the equation with multiple redo log streams, the I/O activity tends to be less identifiable than the theory dictates.

For example, as the RAID 5 system increases in activity, you are less likely to be taking direct advantage of storing and calculating your stripes in cache and writing them together to disk in one action. Multiple, single-logical-block updates will take at least four I/O operations for the parity updates, and the increased number of I/O operations will be compounded in the event of *stripe crossing*; that is, where the cluster file system or ASM stripe is misaligned with the storage stripe. Stripe crossing will result in more than one parity operation per write compounding the effect on throughput still further.

As more systems and activity are added to the RAID 5 storage, the impact becomes less predictable, meaning that RAID 10 is more forgiving of the practice of allocating storage ad hoc, rather than laying it out in an optimal manner. This difference between the theory and practice of RAID 5 and RAID 10 tends to lead to polarity between Oracle DBAs and storage administrators on the relative merits of RAID 5 and RAID 10. Both approaches are, in fact, correct from the viewpoints of their adherents.

In summary, when determining a RAID specification for RAC, RAID 10 with hardware is the optimal choice for fault tolerance, read performance, and write performance. Where RAID 5 is used, the careful planning, layout, and testing of the database across the storage can deliver a cost-effective solution, especially where the workload is predominantly read-only, such as a data warehouse. For a transactional system, RAID 10 for the redo log threads and RAID 5 for the datafiles can provide a practical compromise.

Storage Protocols for Linux

DBAs are presented with a multitude of terminologies and techniques for selecting and configuring storage for RAC. The key determining characteristic is the requirement for simultaneous access to the storage from all of the nodes in the cluster. From a practical standpoint, however, options to satisfy this requirement on Linux include technologies such as FireWire, Small Computer System Interface (SCSI), Fibre Channel Storage Area Network (SAN), Internet Protocol (IP) SAN, and Network Area Storage (NAS).

The correct decision depends on a number of factors. And, because no two environments are identical, the factors are likely to differ on a case-by-case basis. It is also important not to consider storage entirely in isolation. As seen previously, crucial functionalities, such as RAID, can be implemented at either at the hardware or software level, and the level implemented should be determined before a purchasing decision is made.

An important point to note is that the storage protocol decision is not necessarily a decision between storage vendors. Leading storage vendors offer the same products, and these include the ability to support many different protocols, according to circumstance.

Though our prime consideration up to this point has been storage performance for RAC, additional, equally important decision criteria include cost, resilience, manageability, and supportability of the entire database stack from storage to server hardware and software. For example, ruling out any particular storage protocol due to the CPU overhead on the cluster nodes is counterintuitive, without also taking into account the predicted workload and CPU capacity available on the nodes.

Although, from a practical point of view, a RAC cluster can be built on low-cost storage with a medium such as FireWire, this configuration is not worthy of consideration in a production environment in terms of both performance and supportability. In reality, the storage and storage infrastructure will most likely be the most costly hardware components of the entire solution.

Despite the number of options available for the configuration of storage for RAC, you have, in fact, two major approaches to implementing I/O for RAC on Linux: *block I/O* and *file I/O*. Although these often are categorized as SAN and NAS, respectively, implementations such as Internet small computer system interface (iSCSI) mean that the distinctions are not necessarily clearly defined. Therefore, we will look at the protocols available, beginning with the primary foundation of block I/O, the SCSI protocol.

SCSI

Some of the confusion regarding I/O in Linux stems from the fact that SCSI defines both a medium— that is, the physical attachment of the server to the storage—and the protocol for communicating across that medium. To clarify, here we refer to the SCSI protocol operating over a standard copper SCSI cable.

The SCSI protocol is used to define the method by which data is sent from the host operating system to peripherals, usually disk drives. This data is sent in chunks of bits—hence, the term *block I/O*–in parallel over the physical medium of a copper SCSI cable. Because this SCSI data is transmitted in parallel, all bits must arrive in unison.

The original implementation of SCSI in 1986 utilized an 8-bit data path at speeds of up to 5MB/s, and it enabled up to eight devices (including the host adapter itself) to connect to a single host adapter. Because of the signal strength and the deviation from the original source being transmitted, called *jitter*, the maximum distance a SCSI device could be from the host system using a high voltage differential was effectively limited to under 25m.

SCSI has subsequently been revised and updated to speeds of 320MB/s with up to 16 devices, although at a lower bus length of 12m using a low-voltage differential.

Each SCSI device has an associated target ID, and this target can be further divided into subdevices identified by LUNs. Because a server can have several host adapters, and each one may control one or more SCSI buses, uniquely identifying a SCSI device means that an operating system must account for the controller ID, the channel (or bus) ID, the SCSI ID, and the LUN. This hierarchy is precisely the one implemented in Linux for addressing SCSI devices, and it can be viewed with the following command:

```
[root@london1 ~]# cat /proc/scsi/scsi
Attached devices:
Host: scsi0 Channel: 00 Id: 00 Lun: 00
  Vendor: ATA      Model: ST3500320NS    Rev: SN05
  Type:   Direct-Access                  ANSI SCSI revision: 05
Host: scsi5 Channel: 00 Id: 00 Lun: 00
  Vendor: Slimtype Model: DVD A  DS8A1P  Rev: C111
  Type:   CD-ROM                         ANSI SCSI revision: 05
```

```
Host: scsi6 Channel: 00 Id: 00 Lun: 00
  Vendor: DGC       Model: RAID 0          Rev: 0324
  Type:   Direct-Access                    ANSI SCSI revision: 04
Host: scsi6 Channel: 00 Id: 00 Lun: 01
  Vendor: DGC       Model: RAID 0          Rev: 0324
  Type:   Direct-Access                    ANSI SCSI revision: 04
```

From this output, you can see that on SCSI host adapter 6, there are two drives on SCSI ID 0 and SCSI ID 1. This, this output indicates that the system has a single HBA, from which the two external disks are presented. Although /proc/scsi/scsi can still be used to view the SCSI disk configuration from the Linux 2.6 kernel, the SCSI configuration is in fact maintained under the /sys directory. For example, you can view the configured block devices using this snippet:

```
[root@london1 ~]# ls -ld /sys/block/sd*
drwxr-xr-x 7 root root 0 Mar  8 23:44 /sys/block/sda
drwxr-xr-x 6 root root 0 Mar  8 23:44 /sys/block/sdb
drwxr-xr-x 6 root root 0 Mar  8 23:44 /sys/block/sdc
```

Similarly, you can use this snippet to determine the details of SCSI host adapter 6, through which the SCSI disks are connected:

```
[root@london1 ~]# cat /sys/class/scsi_host/host6/info
Emulex LPe11000-M4 4Gb 1port FC: PCIe SFF HBA on PCI bus 0e device 00 irq 169
```

Finally, you can also view the major and minor device numbers for a specific device--in this case, the major number 8 and minor number 32. This which will prove useful for cross-referencing the physical storage layout with the configured disks, as discussed later in this section:

```
[root@london1 ~]# cat /sys/class/scsi_device/6:0:0:1/device/block:sdc/dev
8:32
```

Using the /sys interface, you can also initiate a bus rescan to discover new devices, without needling to reload the relevant driver module, as in this snippet:

```
[root@london1 ~]# echo "- - -" > /sys/class/scsi_host/host6/scan
```

The names of the actual SCSI devices, once attached, can be found in the /dev directory. By default, unlike some UNIX operating systems that identify devices by their SCSI bus address, Linux SCSI devices are identified by their major and minor device numbers. In earlier static implementations, there were either 8 or 16 major block numbers for SCSI disks. The initial 8 major block numbers were as follows: 8, 65, 66, 67, 68, 69, 70, and 71. The second set of 8 major block numbers added the following list of major numbers to the initial 8: 128, 129, 130, 131, 132, 133, 134, and 135.

Each major block number has 256 minor numbers, some of which are used to identify the disks themselves, while some others are used to identify the partitions of the disks. Up to 15 partitions are permitted per disk, and they are named with the prefix *sd* and a combination of letters for the disks and numbers for the partitions.

Taking major number 8 as an example, the first SCSI disk with minor number 0 will be /dev/sda, while minor number 1 will be the first partition, /dev/sda1. The last device will be minor number 255, corresponding to /dev/sdp15. This letter and number naming convention continues with /dev/sdq for major number 65 and minor number 0; next comes /dev/sdz15 at major number 65 and minor number 159, and this continues with /dev/sdaa at major number 65 and minor number 160. Within 2.6 kernels, device configuration is dynamic with udev based on the major and minor number for a device available under /sys (we discuss udev configuration in more detail in Chapter 6). With dynamic configuration, there is no restriction when creating a large number of static devices in advance. For example, the following shows all of the created SCSI disk devices on a system:

```
[root@london1 ~]# ls -l /dev/sd*
brw-r----- 1 root disk 8,  0 Mar  8 23:44 /dev/sda
brw-r----- 1 root disk 8,  1 Mar  8 23:44 /dev/sda1
brw-r----- 1 root disk 8,  2 Mar  8 23:44 /dev/sda2
brw-r----- 1 root disk 8, 16 Mar  8 23:44 /dev/sdb
brw-r----- 1 root disk 8, 17 Mar  8 23:44 /dev/sdb1
brw-r----- 1 root disk 8, 32 Mar  8 23:44 /dev/sdc
brw-r----- 1 root disk 8, 33 Mar  8 23:44 /dev/sdc1
```

It is possible to use any available major number once the original 16 reserved major numbers have been allocated; and, as there are 4,095 major numbers, a 2.6 kernel based Linux implementation can support many thousands of disks, with the actual total number dependant on the sum total of all devices on the system. Also, /proc/partitions can be used to show the configured devices and their corresponding major and minor device numbers that correspond with the preceding directory listing:

```
[root@london1 ~]# cat /proc/partitions
major minor  #blocks  name

   8     0  488386584 sda
   8     1     104391 sda1
   8     2  488279610 sda2
   8    16  104857600 sdb
   8    17  104856223 sdb1
   8    32  313524224 sdc
   8    33  313516476 sdc1
 253     0  467763200 dm-0
 253     1   20512768 dm-1
```

Although the device-naming convention detailed is the default, one with udev device names can be changed according to user-defined rules and persistent bindings created between devices and names. In some respects, such an approach offers similar functionality to what is offered by ASMLIB.

SCSI, by itself, as a protocol and medium, is not generally associated with the term *SAN*. First, the number of devices that can be connected to a single SCSI bus is clearly limited, and a strict SCSI implementation restricts the access to the bus to one server at a time, which makes it unsuitable for RAC. Second, although using link extenders to increase the length of SCSI buses is possible, doing so is impractical in a data-center environment, especially when compared to alternative technologies.

These disadvantages have led to advancements in SCSI, most notably the development of Serial Attached SCSI (SAS) to overcome the limitations of the parallel transmission architecture and to include the support of I/O requests from more than one controller at a time. However, these developments need to be balanced against overcoming the disadvantages of the SCSI medium with alternative technologies, such as Fibre Channel (FC).

Despite these disadvantages, the SCSI protocol itself remains the cornerstone of block-based storage for Linux. Its maturity and robustness have meant that the additional technologies and protocols used to realize SANs are implemented at a lower level than the SCSI protocol; therefore, even though

SCSI cabling will rarely be used, the device naming and presentation will remain identical, as far as the operating system and Oracle are concerned.

Fibre Channel and FCoE

FC was devised as a technology to implement networks and overcome the limitations in the standard at the time, which was Fast Ethernet running at 100Mb/s. Although FC is used to a certain extent for networks, these ambitions were never fully realized because of the advent of Gigabit Ethernet. However, the development of FC for networks made it compatible with the requirements for overcoming the limitations of SCSI-based storage as follows: transmission over long distances with a low latency and error rate, and the implementation of a protocol at a hardware level to reduce the complexities and CPU overheads of implementing a protocol at the operating system level.

These features enabled the connection of multiple storage devices within the same network; hence, the terminology, *Storage Area Network*. Note that although FC and SAN are often used interchangeably, they are not synonymous—a SAN can be implemented without FC, and FC can be utilized for other reasons apart from SANs. Also, similar to SCSI, with FC it's important to distinguish between the medium and the protocol. Despite the name, FC can be realized over copper or fiber-optic cabling, and the name *Fibre Channel* is correctly used to refer to the protocol for communication over either.

The FC protocol has five levels: FC-0 to FC-4. Levels FC-0 to FC-3 define the protocol from a physical standpoint of connectivity all the way through to communication. FC-4 details how the Upper Layer Protocols (ULPs) interact with the FC network. For example, it defines how the FC Protocol (FCP) implements the SCSI protocol understood by the operating system, with the FCP functionality delivered by a specific device driver. Similarly, IPFC implements the Internet Protocol (IP) over FC. There are also three separate topologies for FC: fabric, arbitrated loop, and point-to-point. By far, the most common of these topologies for RAC is the fabric topology, which defines a switch-based network enabling all of the nodes in the cluster to communicate with the storage at full bandwidth.

Optical cabling for FC uses two unidirectional fiber-optic cables per connection, with one for transmitting and the other for receiving. On this infrastructure, the SCSI protocol is transmitted serially, which means distances of up to 10 km are supported at high transfer rates. As well as supporting greater distances, fiber-optic cabling is also insensitive to electromagnetic interference, which increases the integrity and reliability of the link. The server itself must be equipped with an FC HBA that implements the FC connectivity and presents the disk devices to the host as SCSI disks.

At the time of writing, existing FC products support transfer rates of up to 8Gb/s (800 MB/s). However, these available rates must always be considered in conjunction with the underlying disk performance. For example, you must have a minimum of three high specification hard-disk drives in the underlying storage to outperform SCSI alone.

When implementing a SAN environment in a fabric topology, a method must be in place to distinguish between the servers to present the storage to. RAC is the perfect example to illustrate that no restriction exists in the number of hosts that are presented an identical view of the same storage. To realize this lack of restriction, all devices connected to a fabric are identified by a globally unique 64-bit identifier called a *World Wide Name* (WWN). When the WWN logs into a fabric, it is assigned a 24-bit identifier that represents the device's position within the topology, and zoning is configured at the switch layer to ensure that only the designated hosts have a view of their assigned storage. This explanation is, to some extent, an oversimplification, because for resilience systems can be equipped with multiple HBAs and connected to the same storage by different paths through separate switches to guard against hardware failure. This configuration is realized at the host level by multipathing software that unifies the multiple paths into a single disk image view (see Chapter 6 for a detailed implementation of I/O Multipathing with a device-mapper).

With these advantages of performance and connectivity over SCSI, FC has become the dominant protocol for SAN. However, it does have some distinct disadvantages that can inhibit realizing these benefits. One of the most significant of these is cost. The components for FC—the server HBA, optical cabling, and infrastructure—are significantly more expensive than their copper equivalents. Concerns have also been voiced about the lack of security implemented within the FC protocol, and the supported distances of up to 10 km are still a significant constraint in some environments.

In addition, arguably the most problematic area for Fibre Channel SAN, especially for RAC, is that of interoperability and support. To Oracle and the operating system, FC is interacting with SCSI devices, possibly with a clustered-file system layered on top, and could be using asynchronous and/or direct I/O. The device driver for the server HBA implements the SCSI interaction with the storage using FCP, and it could be running multipathing software across multiple HBAs. The storage is also likely to be dealing with requests from multiple servers and operating systems at the same time. Coupled with RAC, all of the servers in the cluster are now interacting simultaneously with the same disks. For example, one node in the cluster recovering after a failure could be scanning the storage for available disks, while the other nodes are intensively writing redo log information. You can see an exponential increase in the possible combinations and configurations. For this reason, FC storage vendors issue their own compatibility matrices of tested combinations, of which clustering—Oracle RAC, in particular—is often an included category. These vendors often provided detailed information about supported combinations, such as the Oracle and Linux versions, the number of nodes in the cluster, multipathing software support, and HBA firmware and driver versions. In reality, this certification often lies behind the curve in Oracle versions, patches, and features; in Linux releases and support; in server architectures; and in many other factors, which make the planning and architecting of the entire stack for compatibility a crucial process when working on FC SAN-based systems. Storage vendors should always be consulted with respect to support at the planning stage of an FC-based RAC solution on Linux.

A recent development is the introduction of Fibre Channel over Ethernet (FCoE), which seeks to mitigate against some of the complexities of Fibre Channel, while also leveraging its advantages and dominance in SAN environments. FCoE replaces the FC-0 and FC-1 layers with Ethernet, thereby enabling Fibre Channel installations to be integrated into an Ethernet-based network. From an Ethernet-based technology perspective, 10GbE is the key driving technology, providing sufficient bandwidth for Ethernet networks to host both networking and storage traffic simultaneously—an architectural approach termed *Unified Fabrics*. This approach is of particular interest in RAC environments that require a single networking technology for both the cluster interconnect and SAN traffic, thereby increasing the flexibility of a clustered solution. A similar Unified Fabric approach can also be adopted with Infiniband, although with Ethernet as its underlying technology, FCoE integrates directly with the SAN at the network layer, as opposed to replacing both the network and SAN with a new protocol. At the time of writing, FCoE is still classed as an emerging technology, albeit one that, given sufficient levels of adoption, brings considerable potential to simplifying a Grid-based computing approach.

iSCSI

In addition to FCoE, there are three other competing protocols for transporting block-based storage over an IP-based network: Internet Small Computer Systems Interface (iSCSI), Internet FC Protocol (iFCP), and FC over TCP/IP (FCIP).

FCIP supports tunneling of FC over an IP network, while iFCP supports FCP level 4 implemented over the network. Whereas these protocols are often implemented in environments looking to interconnect or interoperate with existing FC-based SANs, the leader is iSCSI, which makes no attempt to implement FC. Instead, it defines a protocol to realize block-based storage by encapsulating SCSI into the Transmission Control Protocol (TCP) to be transmitted over a standard IP network. This native use of TCP/IP means that an existing Gigabit Ethernet infrastructure can be used for storage, unifying the hardware requirements for both storage and networking. The major benefits that stem from this unification include reducing cost of implementation, simplifying the administration of the entire network, and increasing the distance capabilities through the existing LAN or WAN—all while using well-understood IP-based security practices.

In iSCSI terminology, the client systems, which in this case are the RAC cluster nodes, require an iSCSI initiator to connect the storage target. Initiators can be realized in either software or hardware. The software initiator is, in effect, a driver that pairs the SCSI drivers with the network drivers to translate the requests into a form that can be transferred. This translation can be then be used with a standard Ethernet network interface card (NIC) connected to the storage by Category-5 cabling.

Like FC, once successfully implemented, iSCSI lets Oracle and Linux view and interact with the disks at a SCSI protocol level. Therefore, Oracle needs to be based on ASM-configured block devices or a cluster-file system on the storage presented. iSCSI software drivers for Linux are available as part of the defaultLinux install and the configuration of iSCSI is on Linux is detailed in Chapter 5, in the context of configuring storage for virtualization.

An alternative for iSCSI is the use of specialized iSCSI HBAs to integrate the entire iSCSI protocol stack of Ethernet, TCP/IP, and iSCSI onto the HBA, removing all of I/O protocol processing from the server. At the time of this writing, these HBAs are available at gigabit speeds over standard Category-5 cabling. Products supporting 10Gb speeds are available with fiber-optic cabling or the copper-based 10GBase-CX4 cable associated with InfiniBand. The downside: The costs approach those of the better-established FC, despite the improved performance.

SATA

Serial Advanced Technology Attachment (SATA) has received a degree of attention as a means of providing low-cost, high-capacity storage in comparison to SCSI- and FC-based disks. This lower cost for SATA, however, comes with some significant disadvantages when deployed with standard hard disks. SATA is based on a point-to-point architecture in which disk requests cannot be queued; therefore the maximum throughput is significantly lower compared to its higher-cost rivals, especially for random I/O. Rotational speeds are also lower, so latency tends to be higher for SATA. In its original specification, SATA supports throughput of 1.5Gb/s (150MB/s).

In addition, the maximum cable length for SATA is 1 m, introducing some physical limitations that mean, in practice, SATA–based arrays need to be connected to the target host systems by existing SAN or NAS technologies.

The most significant disadvantage cited for SATA is that the mean time between failures (MTBF) is up to three times that of SCSI- or FC-based disks. However, this measurement is based on SATA implementations of hard-disk drives. SATA is also a protocol commonly used for SSDs; therefore, the MTBF values should not be taken as applying to all SATA-based storage. It is also worth noting that, although SATA is commonly used for SSDs, it is not an exclusive requirement, and the relationship is primarily driven by the production of SSDs that are widely compatible with notebook, desktop, and server implementations. For example, SSDs are also available with a Fibre Channel interface.

In a RAID configuration with SATA, the maximum practical limit is 12 to 16 devices per controller. This means that database storage using this type of disk technology often requires the management of multiple storage arrays from the target-host level; hence, the applicability of volume-management software, such as ASM. As we noted earlier in our discussion of RAID 0 and RAID 1, using multiple storage arrays to achieve satisfactory levels of performance dictates that RAID 0+1 be used to mirror arrays at a host level of disks striped at the array level.

SATA has advanced to the SATA II specification, which has doubled the throughput to 3 Gb/s (300MB/s). There is also an additional draft specification that increases throughput to 6 Gb/s. The additional specification was introduced in 2008. When used in conjunction with SSDs, this means that SATA can also compete with SCSI and Fibre Channel disks in the performance sector. SSDs take advantage of some of the performance features available with SATA II—in particular, the Native Command Queuing (NCQ) that under the specification permits queuing up to 32 requests per device.

Using Block-Based Storage

Once the block storage is available on all of the hosts in the cluster and visible in /proc/scsi/scsi, you have a choice about how to configure the devices in a form for use by Oracle on more than one system simultaneously. Standard file systems such as ext2 or ext3 are often used for single-instance environments. However, these file systems are not applicable for use in clustered environments where data may be cached and blocks modified on multiple nodes without synchronization between them, resulting in the corruption of the data.

From a protocol standpoint, the simplest approach is for Oracle to use the devices directly as raw character devices. However, from a technical standpoint, although raw devices are supported for upgrades and can be configured from the command line with SQLPLUS, they are no longer supported within OUI for new installs. Also, Oracle has indicated that raw devices will not be supported in releases subsequent to Oracle 11g. On the other hand, block devices are the storage underlying Oracle ASM, as discussed in Chapter 9, and these devices must be used by ASM for storing database files without an intervening file system, including ACFS.

The alternative to using the block devices configured with ASM is to use the corresponding block-based device with a file system designed specifically for operating in a clustered environment that also supports the storage of database files. In Chapter 5 we look at how to configure OCFS2 in the context of virtualization.

Linux I/O Scheduling

I/O scheduling governs how the order of processing disk I/O requests is determined. In Linux, I/O scheduling is determined by the Linux kernel; with 2.6 Linux kernel releases, four different I/O schedulers are available. Selecting the most appropriate scheduler may have an influence on the performance of your block-based storage. The schedulers available are as follows:

- Completely Fair Queuing (CFQ)

- Deadline

- NOOP

- Anticipatory

The scheduler can be selected by specifying the elevator option of the Linux boot loader. For example, if you are using GRUB, the following options would be added to the /boot/grub/grub.conf file: CFQ uses elevator=cfq, Deadline uses elevator=deadline, NOOP uses elevator=noop, and Anticipatory uses elevator=as. With 2.6 kernels, it is also possible to change the scheduler for particular devices during runtime by echoing the name of the scheduler into /sys/block/devicename/queue/scheduler. For example, in the following listing we change the scheduler for device sdc to deadline while noting that device sdb remains at the default:

```
root@london1 ~]# cat /sys/block/sdc/queue/scheduler
noop anticipatory deadline [cfq]
[root@london1 ~]# echo deadline > /sys/block/sdc/queue/scheduler
[root@london1 ~]# cat /sys/block/sdc/queue/scheduler
noop anticipatory [deadline] cfq
[root@london1 ~]# cat /sys/block/sdb/queue/scheduler
noop anticipatory deadline [cfq]
```

It is important to note that such dynamic scheduler changes are not persistent over reboots.

CFQ is the default scheduler for Oracle Enterprise Linux releases, and it balances I/O resources across all available resources. The Deadline scheduler attempts to minimize the latency of I/O requests with a round robin–based algorithm for real-time performance. The Deadline scheduler is often considered more applicable in a data warehouse environment, where the I/O profile is biased toward sequential reads. The NOOP scheduler minimizes host CPU utilization by implementing a FIFO queue, and it can be used where I/O performance is optimized at the block-device level. Finally, the Anticipatory scheduler is used for aggregating I/O requests where the external storage is known to be slow, but at the cost of latency for individual I/O requests.

Block devices are also tunable with the parameters in /sys/block/devicename/queue:

```
[root@london1 queue]# ls /sys/block/sdc/queue
iosched              max_sectors_kb  read_ahead_kb
max_hw_sectors_kb  nr_requests     scheduler
```

Some of the tunable parameters include the nr_requests parameter in /proc/sys/scsi, which is set according to the bandwidth capacity of your storage; and read_ahead_kb, which specifies the data pre-fetching for sequential read access, both of which have default values of 128.

CFQ is usually expected to deliver the optimal level of performance to the widest number of configurations, and we recommend using the CFQ scheduler, unless evidence from your own benchmarking shows another scheduler delivers better I/O performance in your environment.

With the CFQ scheduler, I/O throughput can be fine-tuned for a particular process using the ionice utility to assign a process to a particular scheduler class. The process can range from *idle* at the lowest to *real-time* at the highest, with *best-effort* in between. For example to change the scheduling process of the LGWR process, you need to begin by identifying the process id for the process:

```
[root@london1 ~]# ps -ef | grep lgwr | grep -v grep
oracle    13014    1  0 00:21 ?        00:00:00 asm_lgwr_+ASM
oracle    13218    1  0 00:22 ?        00:00:00 ora_lgwr_PROD1
```

In this case, querying the process shows that no scheduling priority has been set:

```
[root@london1 ~]# ionice -p 13218
none: prio 0
```

The scheduling classes are 1, 2, and 3 for real-time, best-effort, and idle, respectively. For real-time and best-effort, there are eight priority levels, ranging from 0-7, that determine the time allocated when scheduled. The following example shows how to set the LGWR process to a real-time class with a priority level of 4:

```
[root@london1 ~]# ionice -c1 -n4 -p 13218
[root@london1 ~]# ionice -p 13218
realtime: prio 4
```

In any case, we recommend testing your RAC storage configuration and chosen I/O scheduler. If, after testing, you conclude that you would benefit from using a non-default I/O scheduler, then you should ensure that you use the same scheduler on each and every node in the cluster.

NFS and NAS

So far we have covered the realization of block-based storage for Oracle RAC, as well as the technology underlying the implementation of SANs. In contrast to SAN, there is also NAS, which takes another approach in providing storage for RAC.

Although the approach is different, many storage vendors support both a SAN and/or NAS implementation from the same hardware. By definition, iSCSI is both SAN and NAS. To draw the distinction, we will use NAS to define storage presented over a network, but provided as a file-based system, as opposed to a block-based one. For Linux and RAC, the only file system that you need to be concerned with is the Network File System (NFS) developed by Sun Microsystems. Oracle supports RAC against solutions from EMC, Fujitsu, HP, IBM, NetApp, Pillar Data Systems, and Oracle Sun StorageTek. If you're using NFS with Oracle 11g, the Direct NFS client was introduced to implement NFS connectivity directly into the Oracle software itself, without requiring the use of the Linux NFS client.

As we have seen with block-level storage, Oracle RAC can either use the block devices directly or with ASM; or, for greater manageability, it can layer a file system such as OCFS2 on top of the block devices at the operating system level. The challenge for such a clustered-file system is to manage the synchronization of access between the nodes to prevent corruption of the underlying storage when a node is ejected from the cluster. Therefore, such an approach requires a degree of communication between the nodes. With a NAS approach, however, the file system itself is presented by the storage device and mounted by the RAC nodes across the network. This means that file-system synchronization is reconciled at the storage level. NAS storage also enables further file system features such as journaling, file-based snapshots, and volume management implemented and managed at the storage level for greater efficiency.

At the hardware level, NAS is realized by a file server, and the RAC nodes communicate with the file server through standard Ethernet connectivity. We want to stress that, For a RAC cluster, this storage network should be an absolutely private, dedicated network with strictly no other non-storage-related network traffic. The RAC cluster should not be connected simply by the local LAN, with NAS configuration requiring the same respect accorded to FC. Because file servers were originally designed for file sharing, their functionality is compatible with the RAC shared-all database approach. Also, because file servers are designed for this one function only, they tend to be highly optimized and efficient compared to a generic operating system in this role. A RAC cluster should not be based on an NFS file system served by anything but specialized hardware designed for that purpose and supported under the RAC Technologies Compatibility Matrix (RTCM) for Linux Clusters.

At the connectivity level, as discussed for iSCSI, generally available Ethernet technology currently operates at gigabit speeds below that of the commonly available bandwidth for FC, although increasing adoption of 10GbE provides a more level playing field in this respect. A commonly quoted restriction is that the data is transferred from the nodes through TCP/IP, which is implemented by the server CPU, and the communication between the CPU and the NIC results in a higher number of CPU interrupts. The use of the 11g Direct NFS client and server-based network acceleration technologies such as TOEs can negate some of this impact, but the additional overhead will impact the level of performance available to some degree.

Evaluating Storage Performance

As you have seen, there are a considerable number of factors that affect storage performance in an Oracle RAC environment, from the processor and memory to process the I/O requests down through the system, to the disk drives themselves. As such, evaluating the potential storage performance of a system from an entirely theoretical standpoint can only be accurate to a certain degree; therefore, the optimal way to understand the nuances of each approach is to test and compare the solution applicable to your environment.

To draw comparisons between various I/O configurations, we recommend testing the configurations in question. Ultimately, the best way of determining a storage configuration capable of supporting an Oracle RAC configuration is to measure that storage under an Oracle Database workload. However, while noting the relevance of measuring actual Oracle Database workloads, there is also a tool called Oracle Orion available with both the Grid infrastructure software and Oracle Database software installations in Oracle 11g Release 2. This tool enables the testing of storage performance in isolation.

If you're running against block devices, Orion should be run against the block devices themselves and not a file in the file system mounted upon them. Also, the user running the software should have permission to read and write to those devices, none of which should not be in use for any software or contain data that requires preserving. Set the names of your disks in a file with the extension .lun, as in this example:

```
[root@london1 bin]# cat prod.lun
/dev/sdd
```

When running Orion, you should ensure that the LD_LIBRARY_PATH environment variable is set to include either $ORACLE_HOME/lib or the equivalent directory in the Grid Infrastructure software home. You can find details for how to do this in Chapter 6. This snippet shows how to run the Orion tool with the –help argument:

```
[oracle@london1 bin]$ ./orion -help
ORION: ORacle IO Numbers -- Version 11.2.0.1.0

ORION runs IO performance tests that model Oracle RDBMS IO workloads.
It measures the performance of small (2-32K) IOs and large (128K+) IOs
at various load levels.
...
```

There are a number of options for configuring the type of I/O workload; however, the initial preliminary set of data can be collected, as follows:

```
[root@london1 bin]# ./orion -run simple -testname prod
ORION: ORacle IO Numbers -- Version 11.2.0.1.0
prod_20091113_1511
Calibration will take approximately 9 minutes.
Using a large value for -cache_size may take longer.
```

Within the working directory, a number of data files are produced, including a summary of performance data that corresponds to the storage-related values discussed previously in this chapter, including megabytes per second throughput, IOPS, and latency:

```
Maximum Large MBPS=91.09 @ Small=0 and Large=1
Maximum Small IOPS=1454 @ Small=5 and Large=0
Minimum Small Latency=2906.70 usecs @ Small=1 and Large=0
```

Other workloads in addition to simple include normal, oltp, dss with oltp reporting, IOPS, and latency and dss focusing on megabytes per second. Also, some advanced configurations give more opportunity to fine-tune the I/O workload, such as specifying different block sizes from the default.

I/O Calibration is also available within the Oracle 11*g* database in its DBMS_RESOURCE_MANAGER package. This procedure implements a read-only workload and is run as follows by specifying the input parameters of the number of physical disks on which the Oracle Database is installed, as well as the maximum tolerated latency in milliseconds:

```
SQL> set serveroutput on
declare
  max_iops              integer;
  max_mbps              integer;
  actual_latency        integer;
begin
  dbms_resource_manager.calibrate_io (
    num_physical_disks => 15,
    max_latency        => 10,
    max_iops           => max_iops,
    max_mbps           => max_mbps,
    actual_latency     => actual_latency);
  dbms_output.put_line ('IOPS = ' || max_iops);
  dbms_output.put_line ('MBPS = ' || max_mbps);
  dbms_output.put_line ('Latency = ' || actual_latency);
end;
/
```

The procedure may take up to 10 minutes to complete, and the status of the calibration process can be viewed as follows:

```
SQL> select inst_id, status from gv$io_calibration_status;

   INST_ID STATUS
---------- -------------
         1 IN PROGRESS
         2 IN PROGRESS
```

Note that the preceding runs on one instance in the cluster only, although Oracle recommends that all instances in the cluster remain open to calibrate the read workload across the entire cluster. Finally, the output parameters are reported by the procedure, as in this example:

```
IOPS = 2130
MBPS = 186
Latency = 9

PL/SQL procedure successfully completed.
```

This output can also be viewed subsequently in the view DBA_RSRC_IO_CALIBRATE and compared against the start and end of time of individual test runs.

Summary

In this chapter, we have looked at the RAC Technologies Compatibility Matrix (RTCM) and investigated all of the components available to you for building for RAC clusters on Linux. This chapter should give you, as an Oracle DBA, the knowledge to intelligently interpret hardware specifications and drill down into the features that are required to create a successful RAC environment. It should also enable you to balance all of the components from the processor and memory to the network interconnect and storage for the purpose of determining their relative advantages and limitations within a RAC environment. The goal of this approach is to select the optimal configuration of hardware to achieve the desired performance, scalability, and reliability.

CHAPTER 5

■ ■ ■

Virtualization

Virtualization is a term used liberally within computing. In its broadest sense, *virtualization* is used to define any technology solution where a level of abstraction is applied to separate the consumers of resources from the compute resources themselves. Virtualization is a term frequently used in grid computing, and RAC is correctly identified as a virtualization technology in its own right. Within this context, RAC is the abstracting technology that enables a number of separate physical servers to appear to Oracle database resource consumers as if it were a single database.

RAC One Node is the logical extension of applying virtualization terminology to RAC. In essence, RAC One Node is an installation of RAC, within which only a single instance is active for servicing workloads at any particular time. The additional nodes provide failover functionality and an ability to upgrade and patch the initial instance. However, for installation and configuration, RAC One Node is an administration-managed RAC database installed on one node only, and it's identified with the `raconeinit` command. Therefore the technical implementation of RAC One Node for virtualization is the same as covered for RAC in general throughout this book. RAC One Node is also supported within a standard virtualized environment, as we will detail in this chapter. For this reason, we are going narrow our usage of the term virtualization to apply to platform or server virtualization and the dedicated Oracle virtualization software called Oracle VM. Oracle VM is one of the most exciting and evolving technologies for Oracle DBAs supporting clustered environments. Therefore in this chapter we explore the full capabilities of Oracle VM. We do not exclude features such as high availability that can be used for functionality similar to RAC but also where Oracle VMcomplements RAC environments.

Virtualization Definition and Benefits

In platform virtualization, the technology solution enables the hardware resources of one physical server or platform to be distributed between multiple operating system environments.

Figure 5-1 illustrates the definition of virtualization as we use the term in this chapter. The figure shows three independent operating systems deployed on a single server. From the perspective of the user, each operating system acts as if it is a complete, separate, physical machine with the virtualization software called the *Virtual Machine Monitor* (VMM), or *Hypervisor*, managing the assignment of the physical resources between the gguest operating systems.

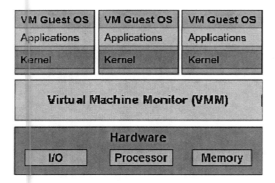

Figure 5-1. Three virtual machines running on one physical server

With virtualization thus defined, the potential benefits of this technology complementing RAC in an Oracle grid computing environment should start to become clear. With RAC abstracting resources across physical servers and virtualization abstracting within them, we have added another dimension to the Oracle database grid. Virtualization delivers the opportunity to design a grid solution based on a much finer granularity of the hardware resources discussed in Chapter 4 than in non-virtualized RAC environments.

Deploying RAC in a virtualized environment brings a number of potential advantages:

- Improved efficiency and manageability

- Reduced hardware and software cost

- Virtual RAC on a single server

However, you must also consider some additional factors when thinking about implementing virtualization:

- VMM performance overhead

- Running multiple levels of clustering Software

- Guest OS timing and scheduling

- Live migration of RAC instances

- Dynamic changes of CPU and memory resources

- Monitoring performance statistics

Improved efficiency and manageability is the key benefit touted for virtualization solutions. The benefit of decoupling the operating system from the physical hardware significantly improves the ability to respond to changes in levels of demand for resources by Oracle database services. For example, a common solution to respond to increased demand for resources has been to add an additional node to a cluster. However, adding that additional node to the cluster and migrating services to that node is a response that cannot be completed immediately. In a virtualized environment on the other hand, hardware resources such as processor and memory can be added and subtracted to the virtualized operating system environment and Oracle instance dynamically, enabling you to respond to demand without an interruption in service.

Virtualized environments also improve efficiency and manageability by significantly improving operating system installation and configuration times, thereby reducing the time it takes to deploy new database installations. Advanced virtualization features such as live migration also enable the transfer of running operating system images between servers across the network. The flexibility to move operating systems between servers has considerable benefits. For example, you might move a RAC instance to a more powerful server to meet a temporary increase in demand, conduct hardware maintenance on existing servers without interrupting the service, or even to perform rapid upgrades on new server platforms.

Virtualization can also reduce the overall cost of the solution for hardware, software, and data center requirements, such as power, cooling, and physical space. By enabling resources to dynamically respond to requirements, a smaller pool of servers running at a high level of utilization can service the same demands as a larger unvirtualized pool of servers dedicated to servicing distinct business needs. Deploying a smaller pool of servers reduces hardware and data center costs. It also reduces software costs in cases where lower software licenses can be applied to virtualized images on servers partitioned into presenting fewer resources. This enables you to manage software costs more closely against the levels of utilization.

A significant benefit that virtualization brings to RAC is the ability to build a virtual RAC cluster on a single server. For example, you might have one physical server host two Linux gguest operating systems where RAC is installed within the two gguests, and the cluster shared storage is the local disk within the server. This approach significantly lowers the hardware requirements for building a RAC environment, which makes it ideal for learning, training, testing, and development of RAC. However, it is important to note that more than one instance of a RAC cluster hosted on the same virtualized physical server in a production environment is neither recommended nor supported by Oracle.

Advantages that appear compelling must also be balanced against some potential disadvantages.

First, the virtualization software inevitably requires resources for its own operations that subsequently will not be available to the virtualized operating systems—and hence, the installed Oracle database. Consequently, one cost of virtualization is that it inevitably means that there will be a reduction in the relative level of performance available from a particular physical server compared to the same server installed natively with an operating system and the Oracle software.

Second, as with the introduction of any level of abstraction, virtualization brings more complexity to the solution, such as requiring additional testing certification above and beyond Oracle RAC on Linux within a native operating system. For example, as detailed later in this chapter, virtualization offers an additional approach to clustering with the ability to redistribute running gguest operating systems between separate physical servers. This functionality implements an independent approach to clusterware; therefore, with RAC running in a virtualized environment, it is important to manage multiple levels of clusterware at both the virtualization and the gguest/RAC layers. At the guest layer, it is also important to consider the impact of operating system timing and scheduling on the RAC clusterware to prevent node evictions from occurring due to timing differences between the guest and the VMM software. Closely related is the impact upon clusterware of this ability to live migrate guest operating systems between nodes in the cluster, as well as the ability of the RAC Clusterware to correctly detect and respond to this occurrence. Within the guest itself, virtualization also enables resources such as CPU and memory to be increased or decreased within a running operating system. Therefore, RAC must also be able to respond to these changes without impacting the level of service offered by the cluster. Oracle is also highly instrumented with detailed performance information available to both tune and troubleshoot the Oracle environment. However, in a virtualized environment, there is another layer of software to consider underneath the operating system, and the performance of the Oracle database in question may be impacted by the resource demands of distinct operating system hosted on the same physical server. With such a dynamic environment for moving loads within the grid, it may become more difficult to gather the consistent information required for Oracle performance diagnosis.

Virtualization is a technology evolving at a rapid pace. The potential advantages and disadvantages are not fixed, and the balance is shifting over time as the disadvantages are resolved. The degree to which the balance lies for a particular RAC deployment at a certain time will determine whether virtualization is applicable to each individual case at the time you consider it.

Oracle VM

In introducing virtualization, we have so far discussed the technology in generic terms. To begin deploying it, we need to narrow the scope to the virtualization software supported in a RAC environment. This software is Oracle VM.

Introduced in 2007, Oracle VM is the only virtualization software on which RAC is supported and certified; therefore if you're looking to virtualize a RAC environment, then we recommend using the officially supported choice.

Oracle VM consists of two distinct software components: Oracle VM Server, an open source server virtualization product; and Oracle VM Manager, an Oracle closed source software product that is installed on a separate server and used for managing multiple Oracle VM Server installations. Both products are free to download from http://edelivery.oracle.com.

Similar to how Oracle Enterprise Linux is based on Red Hat Enterprise Linux, Oracle VM is based on the Xen hypervisor, a well established open source virtualization solution on which Oracle sits as a member of the advisory board. Despite the fact that the underlying technology of Oracle VM is the same as that which underlies Xen, there are differences in the hardware architectures and guest operating systems supported with Oracle VM; namely, Oracle VM narrows the scope from the wider Xen support to the x86 and x86-64 architectures only and to the Linux and Windows guest operating systems only. It is also likely that the support requirements for RAC on Linux in an Oracle VM environment will be more narrowly defined than the equivalent native environment, and we therefore recommend that you check the latest supported configuration information at the design stage before proceeding with installation.

The Oracle VM Manager is a Java application that runs in a standalone distribution of Oracle Containers for J2EE (OC4J). This distribution presents a browser-based management console and stores configuration information in an Oracle database repository. Oracle VM Manager is not an essential component for deploying Oracle VM Server; however, we do recommend using it to take advantage of the increased flexibility in managing high availability features across a pool of managed servers. Although it is possible to install the Oracle VM Manager within a guest operating system on a VM Server in a production environment, we recommend maintaining a separate physical server or server cluster protected by Oracle Clusterware to ensure that all Oracle VM Servers are manageable.

Oracle VM Server Architecture

Before reviewing the design considerations for implementing RAC in a virtualized environment, it is worthwhile gaining some background about the Oracle VM Server architecture. Doing so will prove particularly beneficial in understanding the performance and management characteristics in comparison to RAC installed directly in a native server environment.

The ideal starting point for an insight into how an x86 based system can be virtualized is the protection model of the processor architecture. This model is similar to other processor architectures, and it consists of four rings of increasing privilege levels, from Ring 0 with the most to Ring 3 with the least (see Figure 5-2).

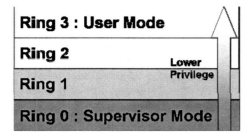

Figure 5-2. Processor protection and the rings of increasing privilege

In a standard Linux installation, the operating system kernel executes instructions in Ring 0 *kernel or supervisor mode*, and the user applications are run in ring 0 *user mode*; Rings 1 and 2 are unused. Programs that run in Ring 3 are prevented by the processor from executing privileged instructions. An attempt to execute instructions that violate the privilege level results in the processor raising a general protection fault interrupt, which is handled by the operating system and usually results in the termination of the running process. An example of such a fault is a *segmentation fault* resulting from an invalid memory access.

For the Oracle VM server to run guest operating systems, it needs to run underneath software designed to run in supervisor mode—hence, the role of the Xen hypervisor, which literally supervises the supervisor mode of the guest operating system.

When the Oracle VM Server is booted, the Xen hypervisor named xen.gz or xen-64bit.gz in Oracle VM Server is loaded into system memory and run at the protection level of Ring 0 of the processor.

It is important to note that the Xen hypervisor itself is not a Linux operating system, and other open-source virtualization projects such as KVM give the Linux kernel a hypervisor role. Instead, the Xen hypervisor that runs directly on the hardware is a lightweight operating-system environment based on the Nemesis microkernel. After booting, the hypervisor subsequently creates a privileged control domain termed *Domain 0* or *Dom0*, and it loads a modified Linux operating system into Domain 0's memory. Next, the Linux operating system boots and runs at the Ring 1 privilege level of the processor, with user and command applications running at Ring 3. In an x86-64 environment, both the guest kernel and applications run in Ring 3 with separate virtual memory page tables.

This chapter's introduction on the privilege levels of the processor architecture raises an immediate question: How can the guest operating system execute at a more restricted privilege level than the level that it was designed for? The answer: It does this through a virtualization technique called *paravirtualization*.

Paravirtualization

In paravirtualization, the guest operating system is modified so that attempts to execute privileged instructions instead initiate a synchronous trap in the hypervisor to carry out the privileged instruction. The reply returns asynchronously through the event channels in the hypervisor. These modified system calls, or *hypercalls*, essentially enable the hypervisor to mediate between the guest operating system and the underlying hardware. The hypervisor itself does not interact directly with the hardware. For example, the device drivers remain in the guest operating systems, and the hypervisor instead enables the communication between the guest and hardware to take place.

The Linux operating system in Dom0 is paravirtualized. However, it has special the privilege to interact with the hypervisor to control resources and to create and manage further guest operating systems through a control interface. The Oracle VM Agent also runs in Dom0 to serve as medium through which the Oracle VM Manager can control the Oracle VM Server. As with the operation of the Oracle VM Agent when you log into the Oracle VM Server, you log into the Oracle Enterprise Linux operating system running in Dom0 and not into the Xen hypervisor itself. Dom0 is also by default a driver domain, although the creation of further privileged driver domains is permitted. The hypervisor presents a view of all of the physical hardware to the driver domain that loads the native Linux device drivers to interact with the platform hardware, such as disk and network I/O. Dom0 also loads the back-end device drivers that enable the sharing of the physical devices between the additional guest operating systems that are created.

When guest operating system environments are to be created, unprivileged domains termed *DomUs* are created to contain them. When a domU is created, the hypervisor presents a view of the platform according to the configuration information defined by the administrator and loads the paravirtualized operating system. It is important to note that, in the paravirtualized guest operating system, the applications that run in user space such as the Oracle software do not need to be paravirtualized. Instead, this software can be installed and run unmodified.

CPU resources are presented to guests as *VCPUs* (*virtual CPUs*). These VCPUs do not have to correspond on a one-to-one basis to the physical cores (or logical for hyper-threaded CPUs). While Oracle VM Server will permit the creation of more VCPUs than physical cores, we do not recommend doing so because it may negatively impact performance. How efficiently the workload is allocated between guests is the responsibility of the CPU scheduler. The default scheduler in Oracle VM Server is the credit-based scheduler, and it can be managed with the xm sched-credit command, as shown later in this chapter. The credit scheduler implements a work conserving queuing scheme relative to the physical CPUs. This means that it does not allow any physical CPU resources to be idle when there is a workload to be executed on any of the VCPUs. By default, in a multi-processor environment CPU, cycles will be evenly distributed across all of the available processor resources, based on the credit scheme with each domain receiving an equal share. However, each domain has a weight and cap that can be modified to skew the load balancing across the system between domains. For example, Dom0 is required to service I/O requests from all domains, so it may be beneficial to give Dom0 a higher weighting. Alternatively, it is also possible to set processor affinity for VCPUs by pinning a VCPU to a physical core with the xm vcpu-pin command. Thus, dedicating a physical core to Dom0 can improve I/O throughput. Pinning of VCPUs is also a requirement for Oracle server partitioning, where Oracle VM is used to limit the number of processor cores below the number that are physically installed on the system for Oracle database licensing requirements.

In addition to CPU resources, memory management in a virtualized Oracle database environment is vital to performance. In Oracle VM Server, all memory access is ultimately under the hypervisor layer. This means, when considering SGA management, it is useful to understand some of the concepts for how this virtualized memory is managed.

In Chapter 4, we considered both physical and virtual memory in a Linux environment. The first distinction to be made between this and memory management in a virtualized environment is between physical and pseudo-physical memory. Physical memory is managed by the Xen hypervisor in 4KB pages on x86 and x86-64. However, this operates at a level beneath the guest operating system in some versions of Oracle VM, so it is not possible to take advantage of support for huge pages (see Chapter 7 for more information). For this reason, memory performance for large Oracle SGA sizes will be lower in a virtualized environment than would be the case for Linux installed on the native platform.

Oracle's requirement for addressing large amount of memory a consideration for memory allocation requires that the Xen hypervisor keeps a global page table for all of the physical memory installed on server readable by all guest domains. This page table stores the mapping from the physical memory to the pseudo-physical memory view for the guest domains. The guest operating system requires its memory to be contiguous, even though the underlying pages maintained by the hypervisor page table will be non-contiguous. Therefore, the pseudo-physical page table managed by each guest maps the guest domain memory to physical memory. In this case, the physical memory is pseudo-physical memory. Therefore, the guest domain requires a shadow page table to translate the pseudo-physical addresses into real physical memory addresses for each guest process.

The hypervisor provides the domain with the physical memory addresses during domain creation, against which the domain can build the pseudo-physical address mapping. Xen occupies the first 64MB of the address space. As discussed in Chapter 4, the guest operating system already maintains its own mapping of virtual memory to physical memory, and the small amount of private memory in the TLB of the MMU in the processor maintains a small number of these mappings to improve performance. Xen is installed in each address space to prevent the TLB from being flushed as a result of the context switch when the hypervisor is entered.

With this implementation, guest operating systems can read from memory directly. However, writing to memory requires a hypercall to synchronize the guest operating system page table and the shadow page table. These updates can be batched into a single hypercall to minimize the performance impact of entering the hypervisor for every page fault. However, there can still be a performance overhead in Oracle environments, especially in the case of intensive logical I/O and large SGA sizes.

Memory allocation is not static, and it can be increased or decreased dynamically for a domain within a maximum memory limit set at domain-creation time implemented by a balloon memory management driver.

In the context of Oracle, memory pages and shared memory structures such as the Oracle SGA cannot be shared between DomUs. However, from a technical standpoint, the Xen hypervisor permits access to the same memory between domains using the grant table mechanism. This presents interesting possibilities for the evolution of future RAC technology beyond 11*g* in the area of communication between instances in an Oracle VM virtualized environment.

In the case of I/O such as disk and network communication, shared memory between domains is already used. However, it is used only for communication between Dom0 and the DomUs. This is because none of the devices on the PCI bus are presented to the DomU these are presented to Dom0 or privileged driver domains only. Instead, the DomU loads paravirtualized front-end device drivers to interoperate with the back-end device drivers in the driver domain. Communication between front-end and back-end device drivers takes place through the shared memory rings in the hypervisor layer. The equivalent of a hardware interrupt from the hypervisor to the guest takes place through event channels. Figure 5-3 illustrates the paravirtualized Oracle VM Server environment with both Dom0 and a single DomU guest operating system.

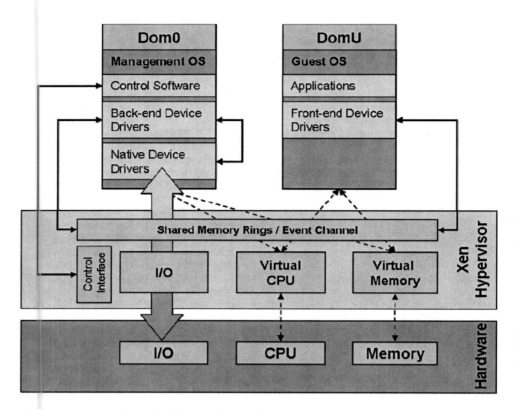

Figure 5-3. A Paravirtualized Oracle VM environment

If an I/O device is not in use at the time a DomU domain is created, then it can be presented to a DomU domain instead, which can then load the native device drivers and work with that device as if working in a standard Linux environment. However, this device can only be presented to one domain at a time and doing so will prevent further guests from using this device.

Full Virtualization

Paravirtualization delivers an efficient method by which to virtualize an environment. However, a clear disadvantage to paravirtualization is that the guest operating system must be modified to be virtualization-aware. In terms of Linux, it is now necessary to work with a different version of the operating system compared to the native environment. However, the modifications are minimal. Operating systems that are not open source cannot be paravirtualized, which means they cannot run under the Xen hypervisor in this way.

Full virtualization or hardware-assisted virtualization is a method by which unmodified non-virtualization aware operating systems can be run in an Oracle VM Server environment. With a Linux guest operating system, this means being able to run exactly the same version of the Linux kernel that would be run on the native platform. To do this requires a processor with virtualization technology features. Intel calls this technology *Intel VT*; for Oracle VM server on the x86 and x86-64 platform, the technology is called *VT-x*. The technology on AMD processors is called *AMD-V*; and although it's implemented in a different way, it's designed to achieve an equivalent result.

Most modern processors include hardware-assist virtualization features. If you know the processor number, then you can determine the processor features from the manufacturer's information. For example, for Intel processors, this information is detailed at `http://www.intel.com/products/processor_number/eng/index.htm`. If you don't have the processor details, you can run this the command at the Linux command line to determine whether hardware virtualization is supported by your processor:

```
egrep '(vmx|svm)' /proc/cpuinfo
```

For example, running this command might return the following:

```
dev1:~ # egrep '(vmx|svm)' /proc/cpuinfo
flags          : fpu vme de pse tsc msr pae mce cx8 apic sep mtrr pge mca
cmov pat pse36 clflush dts acpi mmx fxsr sse sse2 ss ht tm pbe nx lm
constant_tsc pni monitor ds_cpl vmx est tm2 cx16 xtpr lahf_lm
```

If the command returns processor information, then hardware virtualization is available. However, it may be necessary to enable virtualization at the BIOS level of the platform and to confirm its activation in the Oracle VM Server. In Oracle VM Server, multiple paravirtualized and fully virtualized guests can run side-by-side on a hardware virtualized platform as can 32- and 64-bit guests on a 64-bit hardware platform.

Once enabled, virtualization technology enables the guest operating system to run unmodified at its intended privilege level by defining two new operations: *VMX root operation* and *VMX non-root operation*. The hypervisor runs in VMX root operation, whereas the guest is presented with an environment where it runs in Ring 0. However, it is restricted in its privilege by running in VMX non-root operation. Additional processor features also exist to improve performance for hardware-assist virtualized environments. For example, some processors support *virtual-processor identifiers*, or *VPIDs*. VPIDs enable the virtual processor to be identified when running in VMX non-root mode, and it can be beneficial for TLB tagging. As discussed previously in this chapter, a number of techniques are used to increase performance by limiting the number of entries to the hypervisor layer. One of the reasons for this is to prevent a TLB flush from occurring. VPIDs can reduce the latency by tagging or associating an address translation entry with the processor id of a particular guest. This means that the valid address translations in the guests can be identified, even when a hypervisor entry has occurred and all TLB entries do not have to be flushed.

Whereas VPIDs can reduce the impact of entering the hypervisor, another feature—called *Extended Page Tables* (*EPTs*) in Intel terminology and *Nested Page Tables* (*NPTs*) by AMD—can improve memory performance by reducing the need to enter the hypervisor layer for page faults. This technology enables the direct translation of the pseudo-physical addresses into real physical memory addresses. Therefore, page faults can be managed directly by the guest operating system, without entering the hypervisor layer. This improves performance and reduces the memory required to maintain shadow page tables for each guest process. EPTs are supported from Xen version 3.4, which means they are also supported with Oracle VM version 2.2.

A fully virtualized guest interacts with devices in a different way from a paravirtualized guest. As we have seen, the paravirtualized guest loads front-end device drivers to communicate with the back-end device drivers managed by the driver domain. In a fully virtualized environment, the device drivers in the DomU interact with emulated devices managed by Dom0. The emulated device layer is created and managed by Dom0 with open-source software adapted from the QEMU project, which you can find at `http://wiki.qemu.org/Index.html`. Although full virtualization provides good performance on processor-intensive operations, device emulation means that I/O operations require a comparatively higher level of CPU resources, but result in a comparatively lower level of I/O performance when compared to the same load on an equivalent paravirtualized guest. I/O performance is particularly vulnerable when overall CPU utilization across the system is high.

In fully virtualized environments, it is necessary to employ additional virtualization hardware assist technology in the platform. This additional technology is termed the *IOMMU*. It is a platform feature, not a CPU feature, so its availability on a particular server will be determined by the chipset, as opposed to the processor itself. The IOMMU enables the system to support interrupts and *DMA*, which is the transfer of data from a device to memory, such as an Oracle physical I/O to multiple protection domains. Consequently, the address translation enables the DMA operation to transfer data directly into the guest operating system memory, as opposed to emulation-based I/O. The IOMMU implementation on Intel platforms is called *Virtualization Technology for Directed I/O* (*VT-d*); a similar implementation on AMD systems is termed *AMD I/O Virtualization Technology*.

There are clearly advantages and disadvantages for both paravirtualization and full virtualization techniques. It is also possible to configure hybrid implementations with, for example, fully virtualized guests deploying paravirtualized device drivers. We anticipate a merging of the technologies over time, to a point where Oracle VM virtualization will not distinguish between the two techniques, but instead will employ features from both to produce the optimal virtualized environment.

Oracle VM Design

In this chapter's introduction, we discussed the concepts of RAC as a virtualization technology. For the design of an Oracle VM configuration, it is also necessary to note that virtualization with Oracle VM is a clustering technology in its own right. Therefore, grid computing is terminology that can be applied equally to Oracle VM. To design an Oracle VM infrastructure to support RAC, it is necessary to focus on instances where clustering techniques can bring the greatest benefit to support the entire virtualized Oracle database configuration as a whole. From a design perspective, it is therefore necessary to determine in what areas the technologies are complementary.

Being familiar with RAC design, it is also useful to view the top-level Oracle VM configuration as a cluster configuration. The Oracle VM Servers serve as the nodes in the cluster managed by the Oracle VM Manager software installed on a dedicated server acting through the Oracle VM Agent running in Dom0 on the servers. The entire cluster is termed the Server Pool, and the role of a particular server in the cluster is determined by the VM Agent. The VM Agent role cannot be set on an individual VM Server, and all roles must be configured from the VM Manager.

There are three roles under which a VM Server can be configured through its Agent: as a Server Pool Master, as a Utility Server, and as a Virtual Machine Server. These roles are not mutually exclusive. For example, one server can provide all three functions in a deployment where the highest levels of availability are not a requirement.

Applying a concept familiar to a number of clustering implementations, a Server Pool has one Server Pool Master. Multiple Server Pool Masters are not permitted; however, the Server Pool Master can serve other roles. The Agent on the Server Pool Master has a holistic view across all servers in pool; all Agents within the pool can communicate with the Master Agent, and the Master Agent communicates with the Oracle VM Manager. The Master Agent manages clustering activities throughout the Server Pool, such as load balancing and high availability. Despite the fact there is only one Server Pool Master, the Server Pool has been designed so that there is no single point of failure across the entire cluster. Consequently, if the Management Server fails, then the Server Pool Master continues to operate within the configuration already implemented. If the entire Server Pool Master or Master Agent fails, then the entire Server Pool continues to operate as configured.

The Utility Server handles I/O intensive file copy and move operations throughout the Server Pool, such as creation, cloning, relocation, and removal of virtual machines. There can be more than one Utility Server in a Server Pool; and in this case, tasks are assigned with a priority order determined by the server with the most CPU resources available. For a high availability configuration, we recommend deploying a dedicated Utility Server. However, where a dedicated Utility Server is not available or desired, we recommend the Server Pool Master also serve as the Utility Server.

The Virtual Machine Servers in the Server Pool provide the functionality detailed in the section on VM Server Architecture covered earlier in this chapter. The Virtual Machine Server Agent conveys configuration and management information to the Oracle VM Server software from the Oracle VM Management Server. It also relays performance and availability information back to it. If the Virtual Machine Server's Agent is stopped or fails, then the Oracle VM Server and its guest operating systems and hosted software continue to operate uninterrupted. The Oracle VM Server can continue to be managed directly with the standard Xen hypervisor commands. However, it cannot be controlled by the Oracle VM Management Server. If the Virtual Machine Server Agent has failed as a result of the failure of the entire Oracle VM Server, however, then this is a detectable event and automatic high availability features can take place to restart the failed guest operating systems on alternative Virtual Machine Servers in the Server Pool.

In some ways, beginning the design process of using an Oracle VM Server Pool as a cluster is similar to getting started with RAC. In both cases, the infrastructure and technologies to share data between the nodes in the cluster act as a vital foundation upon which the reliability of the entire configuration depends. The lowest level of Oracle VM Server Pool is the storage layer. Fortunately, all of the storage features taken into consideration in Chapter 4 for RAC storage are applicable here. The Oracle VM storage can also be considered at an equal level in the hierarchy as the RAC storage. Therefore, it is an entirely acceptable approach to utilize exactly the same SAN or NAS infrastructure for the Oracle VM storage layer that is deployed for the RAC database. Alternatively, as discussed in Chapter 4, a storage pool approach can be deployed for increased flexibility and choice in the storage type and protocols for each particular layer. Whichever approach is taken, it is important to focus on the central point in the cluster that the storage takes and to ensure that no single point of failure exists within the storage layer itself. In a storage pool approach for RAC and the Oracle database (see Chapter 9 for details), the ASM software layer enables a high availability configuration between multiple storage servers by configuring Failure Groups. Within an Oracle VM built on the Linux software layer, the functionally equivalent software for volume management is *LVM* (the Logical Volume Manager). However, LVM does not support mirroring between separate physical storage arrays, which leaves the cluster vulnerable to the failure of a single storage server. It is therefore important to ensure that resilience is implemented at the storage layer below the Oracle VM software with dedicated storage management. It is also important that fully redundant networks are deployed with a dedicated network (or dedicated bandwidth) to the storage layer.

Built on a fully redundant storage configuration, the storage layer for the Oracle VM, as with RAC, must be made available to all servers in the cluster at the same time. However, unlike the active/active cluster approach implemented by RAC, Oracle VM is based on an active/passive approach. The cluster will access the same storage and same file systems at the same time. However, the same files are not shared simultaneously. The key concept here is the ability to rapidly bring up or migrate guest operating systems throughout the nodes in the cluster at will. To facilitate this approach, it is necessary to implement further clustering technologies and to ensure that a guest operating system is brought up and run on one—and only one—host at any one time. One of these enabling technologies, the Oracle Cluster file System (OCFS2), is already compatible and supported with RAC environments. OCFS2 is available for this role; because it's being incorporated into the Linux kernel, it's the appropriate clustering software layer to apply on top of the storage infrastructure.

■ **Note** Although the focus is on OCFS2 for Oracle VM design, it is also possible to build the shared storage for an Oracle VM Server Pool on a suitable highly available NFS-based infrastructure.

In an Oracle VM environment, OCFS2 implements the necessary clustering capabilities to protect the integrity of the guest operating system environments through its own cluster service called O2CB. This service implements a number of key components, including a node manager, heartbeat service, and distributed lock manager. One OCFS2 file system is mounted between all of the Oracle VM Servers in a Server Pool, and the guest operating system installations reside on that file system. Once configured, the O2CB service validates and monitors the health of the nodes in the cluster. O2CB does this by maintaining a quorum between the nodes in the cluster; the presence of an individual node in the cluster is preserved by updating a disk-based heartbeat, whereby it writes a timestamp to a shared system heartbeat file and reads that data of the other nodes in the cluster to ensure that the timestamp is incrementing according to a configurable threshold. O2CB also maintains a network connection and sends TCP keepalive packets between nodes to ensure the status of the connection. OCFS2 should therefore be configured on a private network interconnect and not across the public network. It is good design practice to configure the private network interconnect on the same network as the Oracle RAC private interconnect.

An algorithm determines the nodes in the cluster that are members of the quorum based on their heartbeat and network status. If a node no longer has a quorum, it will implement I/O fencing and exclude itself from the cluster by rebooting. This prevents the node from being able to access the same files as the systems in quorum in an unmanaged way. During normal operations, access to the individual files on the OCFS2 file system is synchronized by the Distributed Lock Manager (DLM) to prevent unmanaged, simultaneous access resulting in file corruption.

Having OCFS2 protecting the guest operating system environments on the Oracle VM Servers, but enabling these environments to be brought up on any server in the configured Server Pool, enables a number of high availability features to be implemented. First, automatic restarts can be configured to implement a traditional active/passive clustering approach at the guest operating system level. This means that if an individual guest or an entire server and multiple guests fail, they will be restarted on another server in the pool. Second, load balancing can be implemented by enabling a guest operating system environment to be started on the node with lowest utilization. Finally, live migration enables guest operating system environments to be transferred between Oracle VM Servers in the server pool while the guest operating system remains running, available, and providing a service.

The ability to implement clustered virtualized environments adds another dimension to highly available Oracle configurations. Oracle VM includes all the technologies to support the restarting of a single instance of an Oracle database, with minimal downtime in case of server failure. Multiple instances can also be run on separate Oracle VM Servers in the Server Pool with, for example, two Oracle VM Servers providing both active and passive or backup instances to its partner in the cluster. In this scenario, failure of one of the servers means that both instances for the databases in question will be running on the surviving node.

The potential is also increased with a RAC configuration overlaying the Oracle VM Server environment. RAC is able to complement Oracle VM Server by providing Oracle database services across guest operating system environments simultaneously. Oracle VM therefore enables the granularity of the Oracle Service to be smaller than the size of an individual node, while RAC enables the granularity to be larger than the size of an individual node. Oracle VM also simultaneously breaks the link between any physical individual server and a particular Oracle RAC instance.

It is important to note that, in a virtualized RAC environment, the Oracle Clusterware software is wholly contained within the guest operating system, which itself is running under the Oracle VM Server.

Therefore, the VM Server configuration should always be viewed as providing a foundation on which the Clusterware depends. Therefore, in a production environment, both for performance and resilience, two instances of the same cluster should not be run on the same node unless for a non-mission critical environment. Also, Oracle VM live migration should not take place while an Oracle RAC instance is running. This helps prevent the Oracle Clusterware from detecting the migration as a node failure, and the node in question from being ejected from the cluster. Figure 5-4 illustrates the complete Oracle VM design, including all of its infrastructure components.

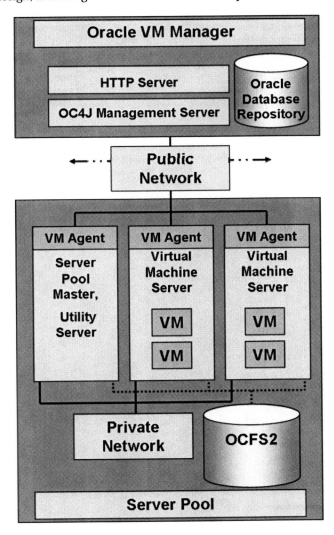

Figure 5-4. Oracle VM Design

Oracle VM Server Installation

Before installing Oracle VM Server, you should check the hardware requirements against the release notes of the Oracle VM Server software. In particular, you should allow for a more powerful processor and memory configuration than for the same server running in a native Linux environment. In particular, multi-core processors enable multiple cores to be assigned to the guest operating system environments. Therefore, eight cores or more is recommended for a flexible configuration. Additionally, memory is a crucial resource, so at least 16GB of memory or 2GB per core will permit a configurable virtualization environment.

If you decide that you wish to have hardware virtualization support, then it is necessary to enable this functionality within the processor options at the BIOS level of the server. Enabling hardware virtualization support requires a hard-reset of the server. It is possible to enable and disable hardware virtualization support after Oracle VM Server has been installed; and even when support is enabled, guestthe hardware-assist functionality will not be used if a Paravirtualized guest is installed.

You can download the Oracle VM Server package from the Oracle electronic delivery site at http://edelivery.oracle.com. Once you download the package, unzip it to produce the Oracle VM Server CD image file such as OracleVM-Server-2.2.0.iso. This file can then be burned to a CD-ROM to make a bootable installation CD-ROM. Similarly, the installation files can be copied to a USB flash memory drive that is made bootable with software such as syslinux. You can boot from the Oracle VM Server CD-ROM to display the installation screen (see Figure 5-5).

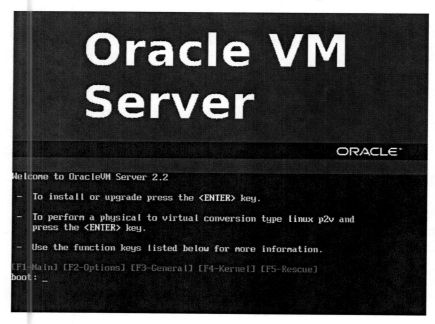

Figure 5-5. The Oracle VM Installation Weclome screen

The installation is based upon a standard Linux text-based installation procedure. Similar screens are displayed for a Linux install when the argument text is given at the boot prompt. The installation proceeds through the standard media test, language, and keyboard selection screens. If Oracle VM

Server has previously been installed, the software presents the option to upgrade the system. At the Partitioning Type screen, choose to Remove all partitions on selected drives and create the default layout. Next, accept the Warning dialog on the removal of all partitions, and then choose to Review and modify partitioning layout. By default, Oracle VM Server will partition the server disk with /swap, /boot, /, and /OVS partitions, with all unallocated storage assigned to /OVS (see Figure 5-6).

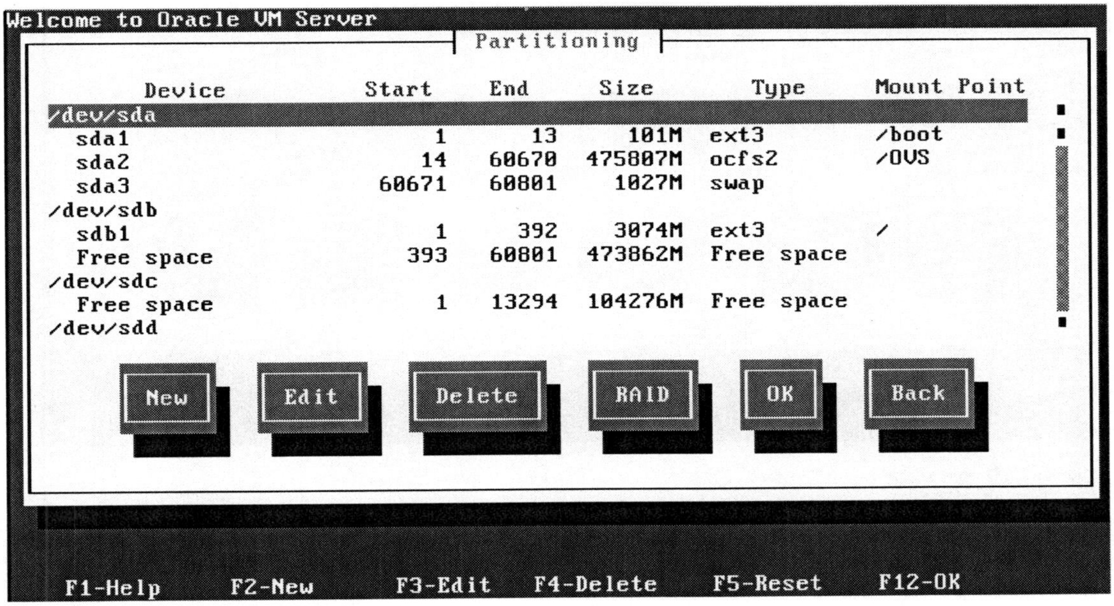

```
Welcome to Oracle VM Server
                              ┤ Partitioning ├
         Device          Start      End     Size        Type       Mount Point
/dev/sda                                                                         ▪
   sda1                      1       13      101M    ext3           /boot         ▪
   sda2                     14    60670   475807M    ocfs2          /OVS
   sda3                  60671    60801     1027M    swap
/dev/sdb
   sdb1                      1      392     3074M    ext3           /
   Free space             393    60801   473862M    Free space
/dev/sdc
   Free space               1    13294   104276M    Free space
/dev/sdd                                                                         ▪

        New      Edit      Delete      RAID      OK      Back



   F1-Help    F2-New    F3-Edit   F4-Delete   F5-Reset   F12-OK
```

Figure 5-6. Default partitioining

With a standalone configuration, you may remain with this partitioning scheme. However, with a clustered approach, /OVS will be assigned to shared storage. Therefore, the initial local /OVS partition may be unmounted or reallocated. For this reason, we recommend reversing the storage allocations to the root partition (/) and /OVS; that is, all unallocated storage should be allocated to the root partition to create a more flexible configuration once high availability has been enabled. The /OVS partition should always be formatted as file system type .ocfs2, as shown in Figure 5-7.

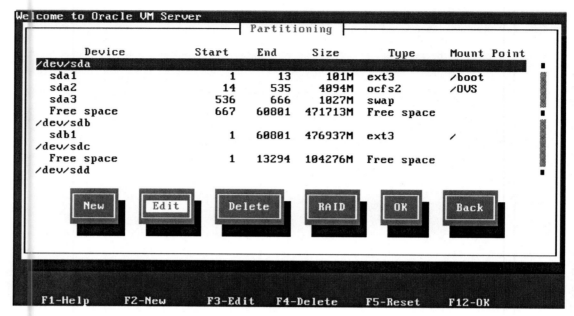

Figure 5-7. Customized partitioning

Similarly, there is the option to manually configure LVM during the partitioning stage. If hardware-level RAID is not available, then LVM may be considered for the local partitions. However, LVM should not be used for the /OVS partition. In a shared storage configuration, LVM does not support mirroring between separate physical storage arrays. Therefore, this must be implemented by the underlying storage hardware or software. At the Boot Loader Configuration screen, you install the boot loader at the Master Boot Record (MBR) location. The screen shown in Figure 5-8 determines the network configuration, with the Oracle VM Management Interface screen enabling the selection of the network interface to use for management. This screen permits the configuration of only a single interface. Therefore, you should select the interface on the public network, usually eth0. The private network interface will be configured after installation is complete. Configure the public interface with your IP address and netmask, as illustrated in Figure 5-8.

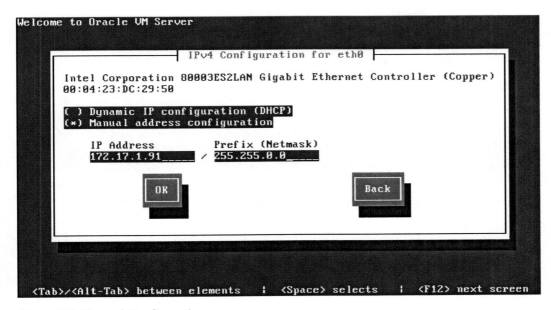

Figure 5-8. Network Configuration

On the following screen, Miscellaneous Network Settings, configure your gateway and DNS settings. Next, on the Hostname Configuration screen, enter your hostname manually, as shown in Figure 5-9.

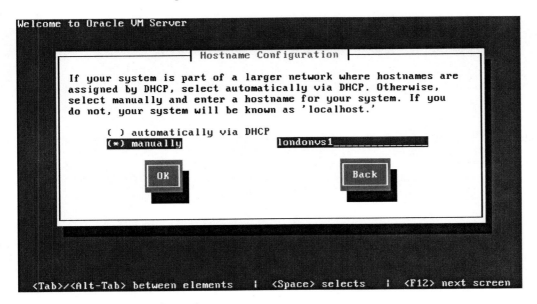

Figure 5-9. Hostname configuration

For the Time Zone Selection screen, enter the time zone of your server location and ensure that System clock *UTC* option remains selected. The following screens require the entry of passwords to be used for the Oracle VM Agent and the root user, respectively. You will need to have the Oracle VM Agent password when registering the Oracle VM Server into a Server Pool with Oracle VM Manager. Once the passwords have been entered, press *OK* on the Installation to begin screen to begin installing Oracle VM Server. Unlike a typical Linux install, there is no option available to customize the packages to be installed, and the installation proceeds to install the default package environment, as shown in Figure 5-10.

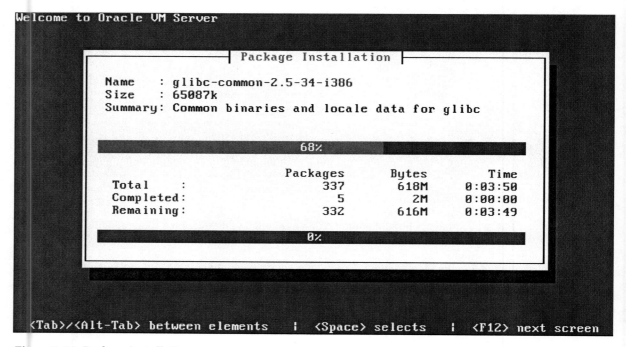

Figure 5-10. Package installation

On completion of the package install, the Complete screen is shown, prompting you to remove the installation media and to reboot the server. Press Reboot and, on the first boot only, it is necessary to accept the Oracle VM Server license agreement. Installation is now complete. You can repeat the installation procedure for the additional Oracle VM Servers in the server pool. On booting, the Oracle VM Server displays the console login prompt (see Figure 5-11).

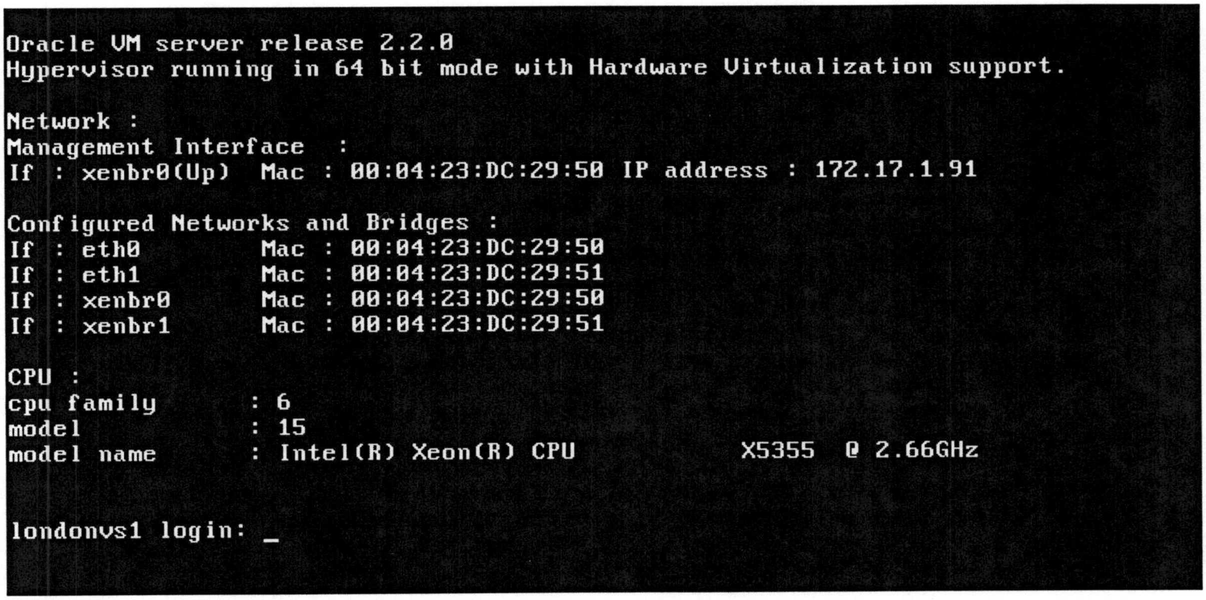

```
Oracle VM server release 2.2.0
Hypervisor running in 64 bit mode with Hardware Virtualization support.

Network :
Management Interface  :
If : xenbr0(Up)   Mac : 00:04:23:DC:29:50 IP address : 172.17.1.91

Configured Networks and Bridges :
If : eth0         Mac : 00:04:23:DC:29:50
If : eth1         Mac : 00:04:23:DC:29:51
If : xenbr0       Mac : 00:04:23:DC:29:50
If : xenbr1       Mac : 00:04:23:DC:29:51

CPU :
cpu family        : 6
model             : 15
model name        : Intel(R) Xeon(R) CPU        X5355  @ 2.66GHz


londonvs1 login: _
```

Figure 5-11. The Console Login prompt

As discussed previously, there is no graphical environment installed by default in Dom0 for which the prompt is given, and no graphical packages should be installed or configured to run in this domain. You can use the xm tools to manage the Oracle VM Server from the command prompt; these command-line tools are detailed later in the chapter. It is necessary to install and configure Oracle VM Manager if you want a supported graphical environment to manage the Oracle VM Server.

Oracle VM Manager Installation

As discussed previously in this chapter, Oracle VM Manager must be installed on a separate system from any Oracle VM Server where a supported version of Oracle Enterprise Linux has previously been installed. Oracle VM Manager is available from the Oracle edelivery site at http://edelivery.oracle.com; the unzipped package produces a CD image file, such as OracleVM-Manager-2.2.0.iso. This can be burned to a CD-ROM; alternatively, because the installation is not installing an operating system, the image can be mounted and run directly at the command line, as follows:

```
[root@londonmgr1 ~]# mount -o loop OracleVM-Manager-2.2.0.iso /mnt
[root@londonmgr1 ~]# cd /mnt
[root@londonmgr1 mnt]# ls
EULA  LICENSE  readme.txt  runInstaller.sh  scripts  source  TRANS.TBL
[root@londonmgr1 mnt]# sh ./runInstaller.sh
Welcome to Oracle VM Manager 2.2
```

```
Please enter the choice: [1|2|3]
1. Install Oracle VM Manager
2. Uninstall Oracle VM Manager
3. Upgrade Oracle VM Manager
```

Select the first choice, and the installation proceeds by installing a number of RPM packages. The first stage is the installation of a repository database. The option is given to install Oracle Express Edition on the Oracle VM Manager Server or to install the repository into an existing database. We recommend using the Oracle Express Edition installation or creating a new database to preserve the repository in a dedicated Oracle VM Management environment. The installer prompts for responses such as the port that will be used, the database listener, passwords for database accounts, and whether to start the database on boot. The default database schema is named OVS.

The installation continues with RPM installs of the ovs-manager and oc4j packages. Next, it prompts for the oc4jadmin password, keystore password for the Web Service, and whether to use HTTP or HTTPS for Oracle VM Manager. The Oracle VM Manager application is installed into the OC4J container, and the installation prompts for the password for the default administration account named admin. It is important to record this username and password combination in particular because it is used as the main login account to the Oracle VM Manager application. The installation continues by configuring the SMTP mail server to be used by the Oracle VM Manager. It is not essential for Oracle VM Manager that the SMTP server is successfully configured; however, some functionality does rely on this feature, in particular the password reminder for the Oracle VM Manager users. If this feature is not configured, no reminder can be sent. Therefore, it is beneficial to know that there is a password reset script available on the Oracle My Support site. In the OVS schema, this script updates the password field with an encrypted password in the OVS_USER table for the corresponding account name. For this reason, SMTP configuration is not absolutely essential to enabling Oracle VM Manager functionality, assuming e-mail alerts and reminders are not required. After SMTP configuration, the Oracle VM Manager installation is complete and reports the chosen configuration, as in this example:

```
Installation of Oracle VM Manager completed successfully.

To access the Oracle VM Manager 2.2 home page go to:
  http://172.17.1.81:8888/OVS

To access the Oracle VM Manager web services WSDL page go to:
  http://172.17.1.81:8888/OVSWS/LifecycleService.wsdl
  http://172.17.1.81:8888/OVSWS/ResourceService.wsdl
  http://172.17.1.81:8888/OVSWS/PluginService.wsdl
  http://172.17.1.81:8888/OVSWS/ServerPoolService.wsdl
  http://172.17.1.81:8888/OVSWS/VirtualMachineService.wsdl
  http://172.17.1.81:8888/OVSWS/AdminService.wsdl

To access the Oracle VM Manager help page go to:
  http://172.17.1.81:8888/help/help
```

The Oracle VM Manager application can be accessed by logging in through a web browser, as shown in Figure 5-12.

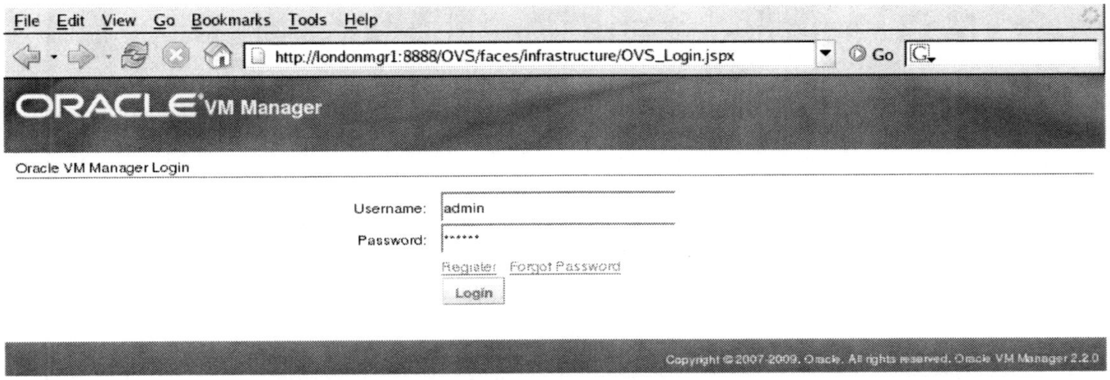

Figure 5-12. *The Oracle VM Manager Login screen*

The status of the of the Oracle VM Manager application can reviewed by checking the status of the OC4J service:

```
[root@londonmgr1 ~]# service oc4j status
OC4J is running.
```

Stopping the OC4J service requires entering the oc4jadmin password submitted during the installation:

```
[root@londonmgr1 ~]# service oc4j stop
Stopping OC4J ...
Please enter the password of oc4jadmin:

Done.
```

Restarting the OC4J service also restarts the Oracle VM Manager application:

```
[root@londonmgr1 ~]# service oc4j start
Starting OC4J ... Done.
```

The status of the underlying repository database, if installed in the default express edition database, can be checked with the command service oracle-xe status. This command reports the status of the database listener. Similar to the OC4J service, restarting the oracle-xe service restarts the repository database. It is also possible to log into the repository by setting the ORACLE_SID value to XE and the ORACLE_HOME value to /usr/lib/oracle/xe/app/oracle/product/10.2.0/server, with the default repository owner named OVS and the password given during the installation process.

Oracle supports optional additional configuration to protect the Oracle VM Manager installation with Oracle Clusterware. If the server that supports the Oracle VM Manager application fails, this configuration will fail over the application and database to an additional server. However, this configuration is not mandatory because, if required, the Oracle VM Servers can be controlled directly with the xm command line commands (you will learn more about this later in this chapter).

Oracle VM CLI Installation and Configuration

In addition to the graphical environment provided by Oracle VM Manager there is also an additional command line interface (CLI) available to interact with the Oracle VM Manager. The Oracle VM Manager installation and configuration must have previously been completed before you can use the CLI. However, the CLI lets you manage the Oracle VM management without requiring a graphical interface. It also lets you build scripts to accomplish more complex management tasks. The CLI may be installed on an Oracle Enterprise Linux server that can communicate across the network to the VM Manager.

To configure the CLI, it is necessary to download and install both the CLI and Python Web Services RPM packages. Customers of the Unbreakable Linux Network can acquire the packages, or they can be either installed directly from the public Yum repository or downloaded and installed manually. For example, the ovmcli-2.2-9.el5.noarch.rpm package is available here:

```
http://public-yum.oracle.com/repo/EnterpriseLinux/EL5/oracle_addons/x86_64/
```

Similarly, the python-ZSI-2.1-a1.el5.noarch.rpm package is available here:

```
http://public-yum.oracle.com/repo/EnterpriseLinux/EL5/addons/x86_64/
```

These packages can be installed with the rpm command:

```
[root@london5 ~]# rpm -ivh \
> python-ZSI-2.1-a1.el5.noarch.rpm ovmcli-2.2-9.el5.noarch.rpm
Preparing...                ########################################### [100%]
   1:python-ZSI             ########################################### [ 50%]
   2:ovmcli                 ########################################### [100%]
```

After installation, you complete the configuration process with the ovm config command, which, at a minimum, specifies the Oracle VM Manager host and port previously configured in this section:

```
[root@london5 ~]# ovm config
This is a wizard for configuring the Oracle VM Manager Command Line Interface.
CTRL-C to exit.

Oracle VM Manager hostname: londonmgr1
Oracle VM Manager port number: 8888
Deploy path (leave blank for default):
Location of vncviewer (leave blank to skip):
Enable HTTPS support? (Y/n): n

Configuration complete.
Please rerun the Oracle VM Manager Command Line Interface.
```

The CLI can now be used to complete Oracle VM Management tasks, without requiring a graphical environment.

Configuring Oracle VM

After installing the Oracle VM Server and Oracle VM Manager software, it is necessary to configure the environment for RAC. In particular, this means configuring high availability virtualization features across the cluster so they complement the high availability features in RAC itself. This configuration focuses on customizing the private interconnect network for optimal performance with RAC guests, configuring the server pool, and finally, configuring the Oracle Cluster File System software and enabling high availability.

Network Configuration

As detailed previously in this chapter, DomU network devices communicate through the network configured in Dom0. The configuration used is determined by the settings in /etc/xen/xend-config.sxp that call configuration scripts in /etc/xen/scripts. Scripts are available to configure bridged, routed, or NATed networks. Bridging is the most common form of network implemented in Xen, as well as the default configuration for Oracle VM Server. In the default configuration, an operating system that boots in Dom0 boots configures the network with the familiar names of devices, such as eth0 and eth1. Xend calls the wrapper script /etc/xen/scripts/network-bridges, which subsequently calls /etc/xen/scripts/network-bridge for each bridge to be configured.

After installation, only the first device, eth0, and its corresponding bridge will have been setup. The other bridges will be made available only after the underlying device has been manually configured. Through Oracle VM 2.1.5, the following occurs after the bridges are available: the standard network devices are brought down, and their configuration is copied to virtual devices, such as veth0 and veth1. The physical devices are also renamed; for example, eth0 becomes peth0. Similarly, the virtual devices are renamed, such as from veth0 to eth0. This process provides the interface names used by Dom0, as opposed to those configured for the guests. The network bridges are created with the physical interfaces connecting the bridge externally, and the virtual network interfaces (vifs) are created on the bridge. For example, the Dom0 virtual interfaces, such as veth0, which was renamed from eth0, are now connected to their corresponding vif on the bridge by the script /etc/xen/scripts/vif-bridge. Vifs are named according to their domain and device order, and they correspond to the veth devices given to the paravirtualized network devices in the DomU. Therefore, vif0.0 connects to eth0 in Dom0, while vif1.1 would connect to eth1 in the first DomU, with all connections being made through the bridge. By default, eight pairs of veth and vif connections are created, and each physical network device has a bridge, peth, veth renamed to eth, and vif in Dom0. Up to Oracle VM Server 2.1.5, veth and vif devices communicate through network loopback devices, and the number available can be increased by using the netloop.nloopbacks argument to the kernel at boot time. For hardware virtualized guests, veth devices don't connect to the vifs; instead, a tap device (such as tap0) is created by the script /etc/xen/qemu-ifup. This creates an emulated network device.

The actions required for configuring the network in a DomU guest are discussed later in this chapter, in the section that explains how to installing and configure a guest. This configuration determines the bridge to which a particular guest interface connects. To do so, it uses a new vif created on the bridge for the interface the vif-bridge script will connect to. When configured, the network interfaces in the guest are identified on the external network by MAC addresses assigned to Xen in the range 00:16:3E:xx:xx:xx. Note that the guests are not identified with the MAC addresses used by the physical devices. Figure 5-13 illustrates a simplified paravirtualized network configuration that shows the utilized network connections with only two guests in RAC environments, where both the guests are configured with a public and private network. In this illustration, the guests do not necessarily need to be members of the same cluster. While this would be a functional configuration, it is not recommended or supported for performance purposes. Instead, the guests are members of different clusters, as would be typical of a RAC development environment.

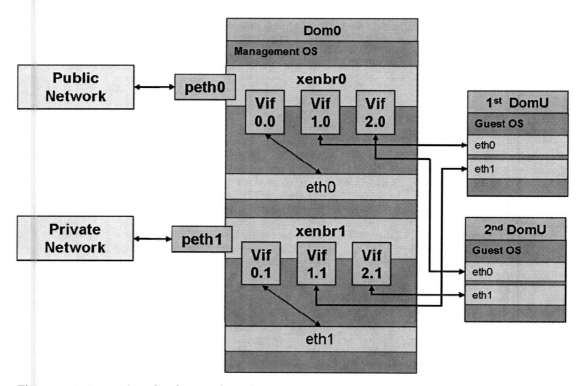

Figure 5-13. A paravirtualized network configuration

Although the bridge configuration provided by the /etc/xen/scripts/network-bridge script produces an operational environment in a clustered configuration, a practical alternative is enabling the bridge configuration at the Dom0 operating system level, as opposed to using the default script. Doing so results in a more reliable configuration, and it is compatible with advanced configurations such a network bonding, which otherwise have had issues reported with the default configuration. In Oracle VM 2.2 and later, the default network script has been modified to produce the same behavior described here. As described previously, the most important concept is that, in the default Xen networking, the default network device in Dom0 (such as eth0) was renamed to peth0. Also, the new eth0 device renamed from veth0 was created to communicate on the bridge xenbr0 through Vif0.0. In Oracle VM 2.2the IP Address is bound to the bridge itself. Also, the physical devices retain their initial name when connecting to the bridge meaning that the interface Vif0.0 is no longer created.

After installation, only the first network device of eth0 will have been configured. For an environment to support RAC, it is also necessary to configure an additional interface. Let's assume you use the command ifconfig -a in Oracle VM 2.2 later. In the example that follows, you can see that, although bridges have been configured for the interfaces eth0 and eth1, only the first bridge xenbr0 has been assigned an IP address:

```
[root@londonvs1 network-scripts]# ifconfig -a
...
xenbr0     Link encap:Ethernet  HWaddr 00:04:23:DC:29:50
           inet addr:172.17.1.91  Bcast:0.0.0.0  Mask:255.255.0.0
           UP BROADCAST RUNNING MULTICAST  MTU:1500  Metric:1
           RX packets:51582 errors:0 dropped:0 overruns:0 frame:0
           TX packets:1314 errors:0 dropped:0 overruns:0 carrier:0
           collisions:0 txqueuelen:0
           RX bytes:2983414 (2.8 MiB)  TX bytes:181128 (176.8 KiB)

xenbr1     Link encap:Ethernet  HWaddr 00:04:23:DC:29:51
           UP BROADCAST RUNNING MULTICAST  MTU:1500  Metric:1
           RX packets:85035 errors:0 dropped:0 overruns:0 frame:0
           TX packets:0 errors:0 dropped:0 overruns:0 carrier:0
           collisions:0 txqueuelen:0
           RX bytes:4479820 (4.2 MiB)  TX bytes:0 (0.0 b)
```

To configure the additional bridge and interface for the device eth1, update the configuration in /etc/sysconfig/network-scripts/ifcfg-eth1 as you would for a regular Linux network configuration:

```
[root@londonvs1 network-scripts]# more ifcfg-eth1
# Intel Corporation 80003ES2LAN Gigabit Ethernet Controller (Copper)
DEVICE=eth1
BOOTPROTO=static
HWADDR=00:04:23:DC:29:51
BROADCAST=192.168.1.255
IPADDR=192.168.1.91
NETMASK=255.255.255.0
NETWORK=192.168.1.0
ONBOOT=yes
```

The network can be restarted using the network-bridges script, as in this example:

```
[root@londonvs1 scripts]# ./network-bridges stop
Nothing to flush.
[root@londonvs1 scripts]# ./network-bridges start
net.bridge.bridge-nf-call-arptables = 0
net.bridge.bridge-nf-call-ip6tables = 0
net.bridge.bridge-nf-call-iptables = 0
Nothing to flush.
Waiting for eth0 to negotiate link.....
net.bridge.bridge-nf-call-arptables = 0
net.bridge.bridge-nf-call-ip6tables = 0
net.bridge.bridge-nf-call-iptables = 0
Nothing to flush.
Waiting for eth1 to negotiate link....
```

In this example, xenbr1 has now been assigned IP Address configured for eth1. For releases up to and including Oracle VM 2.2, you might wish to configure devices manually, without using the network bridges and network-bridge scripts. You can do so using the technique described momentarily to attain a configuration that will also support network bonding. With this approach, it is necessary to first reconfigure the interface eth0.

Begin by editing the file /etc/xen/xend-config.sxp and commenting out the section where the network-bridge script is called, as in this example:

```
#
# (network-script network-bridges)
#
```

Configure the bridges in the /etc/sysconfig/network-scripts directory. For example, bridge xenbr0 would require configuring a file /etc/sysconfig/network-scripts/ifcfg-xenbr0 as follows, where you specify the IP Address that would usually be named as eth0 and type as the bridge:

```
# Intel Corporation 80003ES2LAN Gigabit Ethernet Controller (Copper)
DEVICE=xenbr0
ONBOOT=yes
BOOTPROTO=static
IPADDR=172.17.1.91
NETMASK=255.255.0.0
NOALIASROUTING=yes
TYPE=BRIDGE
DELAY=0
```

Configure eth0 in /etc/sysconfig/network-scripts/ifcfg-eth0 as follows, specifying the bridge, but without the IP Address. For high availability, this device can also be configured as a bonded interface (see Chapter 6 for more details), instead of to eth0, as shown here:

```
# Intel Corporation 80003ES2LAN Gigabit Ethernet Controller (Copper)
DEVICE=eth0
ONBOOT=yes
BRIDGE=xenbr0
```

The steps for eth1 are exactly the same, except when specifying the private network IP address and netmask. Also, the bridge name is xenbr1. Use a kernel argument to set the number of loopback devices to zero in the file /boot/grub/grub.conf. The required vif devices can be created dynamically, and the default eight pairs are not required:

```
title Oracle VM Server-ovs (xen-64-3.1.4 2.6.18-8.1.15.1.16.el5ovs)
root (hd0,0)
kernel /xen-64bit.gz dom0_mem=834M
module /vmlinuz-2.6.18-8.1.15.1.16.el5xen ro root=LABEL=/1 netloop.nloopbacks=0
module /initrd-2.6.18-8.1.15.1.16.el5xen.img
```

Next, reboot the server for the network changes to take effect. You can see the result in the following listing, which shows a simplified and scalable network bridge configuration:

```
[root@londonvs1 network-scripts]# ifconfig -a
eth0      Link encap:Ethernet  HWaddr 00:04:23:DC:29:50
          UP BROADCAST RUNNING MULTICAST  MTU:1500  Metric:1
          RX packets:1118 errors:0 dropped:0 overruns:0 frame:0
          TX packets:465 errors:0 dropped:0 overruns:0 carrier:0
```

```
              collisions:0 txqueuelen:1000
              RX bytes:94478 (92.2 KiB)  TX bytes:63814 (62.3 KiB)

eth1          Link encap:Ethernet  HWaddr 00:04:23:DC:29:51
              UP BROADCAST RUNNING MULTICAST  MTU:1500  Metric:1
              RX packets:685 errors:0 dropped:0 overruns:0 frame:0
              TX packets:56 errors:0 dropped:0 overruns:0 carrier:0
              collisions:0 txqueuelen:1000
              RX bytes:62638 (61.1 KiB)  TX bytes:5208 (5.0 KiB)

lo            Link encap:Local Loopback
              inet addr:127.0.0.1  Mask:255.0.0.0
              UP LOOPBACK RUNNING  MTU:16436  Metric:1
              RX packets:138 errors:0 dropped:0 overruns:0 frame:0
              TX packets:138 errors:0 dropped:0 overruns:0 carrier:0
              collisions:0 txqueuelen:0
              RX bytes:23275 (22.7 KiB)  TX bytes:23275 (22.7 KiB)

xenbr0        Link encap:Ethernet  HWaddr 00:04:23:DC:29:50
              inet addr:172.17.1.91  Bcast:172.17.255.255  Mask:255.255.0.0
              UP BROADCAST RUNNING MULTICAST  MTU:1500  Metric:1
              RX packets:716 errors:0 dropped:0 overruns:0 frame:0
              TX packets:490 errors:0 dropped:0 overruns:0 carrier:0
              collisions:0 txqueuelen:0
              RX bytes:58278 (56.9 KiB)  TX bytes:66104 (64.5 KiB)

xenbr1        Link encap:Ethernet  HWaddr 00:04:23:DC:29:51
              inet addr:192.168.1.91  Bcast:192.168.255.255  Mask:255.255.0.0
              UP BROADCAST RUNNING MULTICAST  MTU:1500  Metric:1
              RX packets:117 errors:0 dropped:0 overruns:0 frame:0
              TX packets:68 errors:0 dropped:0 overruns:0 carrier:0
              collisions:0 txqueuelen:0
              RX bytes:11582 (11.3 KiB)  TX bytes:5712 (5.5 KiB
```

When a guest domain is started, vif devices showing a guest with two network interfaces will be created. They will also be shown in the network listing, as in this example:

```
vif1.0        Link encap:Ethernet  HWaddr FE:FF:FF:FF:FF:FF
              UP BROADCAST RUNNING MULTICAST  MTU:1500  Metric:1
              RX packets:419 errors:0 dropped:0 overruns:0 frame:0
              TX packets:1134 errors:0 dropped:90 overruns:0 carrier:0
              collisions:0 txqueuelen:32
              RX bytes:60149 (58.7 KiB)  TX bytes:109292 (106.7 KiB)

vif1.1        Link encap:Ethernet  HWaddr FE:FF:FF:FF:FF:FF
              UP BROADCAST RUNNING MULTICAST  MTU:1500  Metric:1
              RX packets:113 errors:0 dropped:0 overruns:0 frame:0
              TX packets:8265 errors:0 dropped:1817 overruns:0 carrier:0
              collisions:0 txqueuelen:32
              RX bytes:23325 (22.7 KiB)  TX bytes:853477 (833.4 KiB)
```

Similarly, the brctl show command displays the bridge configuration and the interfaces attached to each particular bridge:

```
[root@londonvs2 ~]# brctl show
bridge name    bridge id            STP enabled    interfaces
xenbr0         8000.000423dc1e78    no             vif1.0
                                                   eth0
xenbr1         8000.000423dc1e79    no             vif1.1
                                                   eth1
```

In addition to configuring the required bridges and interfaces, you should also ensure that the names and IP addresses used in your cluster are resolvable by all hosts, either by using DNS or by updating the /etc/hosts file. When configuring name resolution, it is important to ensure that the hostname does not resolve to the loopback address of 127.0.0.1, which will be the status of the default configuration. For example, the following details in /etc/hosts will result in errors during the subsequent cluster configuration:

```
# Do not remove the following line, or various programs
# that require network functionality will fail.
127.0.0.1              londonvs1 localhost.localdomain localhost
::1            localhost6.localdomain6 localhost6
```

Instead, the first line should resemble the following on all of the nodes in the cluster:

```
# Do not remove the following line, or various programs
# that require network functionality will fail.
127.0.0.1              localhost.localdomain localhost
172.17.1.81            londonmgr1
172.17.1.91            londonvs1
172.17.1.92            londonvs2
172.17.1.92            londonvs2
192.168.1.91           londonvs1-priv
192.168.1.92           londonvs2-priv
192.168.1.220          dss
```

In this example, londonmgr1 is the Oracle VM Manager host, londonvs1 and londonvs2 are the names of the virtual servers, and londonvs1-priv and londonvs2-priv are the private interconnect interfaces on these hosts. Finally, dss is the name of the iSCSI server to be used for shared storage for a high availability configuration.

Server Pool Configuration

Before proceeding with the server pool configuration, you need to ensure that all of the Oracle VM Servers for the cluster to be included in the same pool are installed and that the network is configured. You should also ensure that the Oracle VM agents are operational on the Oracle VM Servers by checking their status, as explained in the "Managing Domains" section later in this chapter.

The Oracle VM high availability feature and RAC are mutually exclusive. Therefore, if you choose to run RAC in a virtualized production environment, you should not use Oracle VM high availability, and vice versa. However, you may use high availability in a development or test environment or for its alternative clustering features. Depending on the version of Oracle VM, enabling high availability and configuring the Server Pool take place in different orders. Prior to Oracle VM 2.2, the Server Pool should be created first, as detailed here, and high availability should be configured later. For Oracle VM 2.2, you should omit this section and proceed with configuring high availability *before* you create the Server Pool.

The first time you log in to the Oracle VM Manager, the Server Pool Wizard is displayed and guides you through the creation of the Server Pool Master Server, as shown in Figure 5-14.

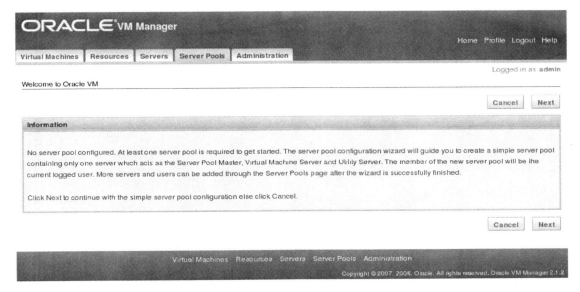

Figure 5-14. The Server Pool Configuration wizard

On the server Information page, enter the server details of the Oracle VM Server you want to act as the Server Pool Master. The Test Connection button should display this message if communication is established: "Server agent is active." Click Next and enter your chosen Server Pool Name; click Next again; and, finally, confirm your choice. The Server Pool is created at this point, as shown in Figure 5-15.

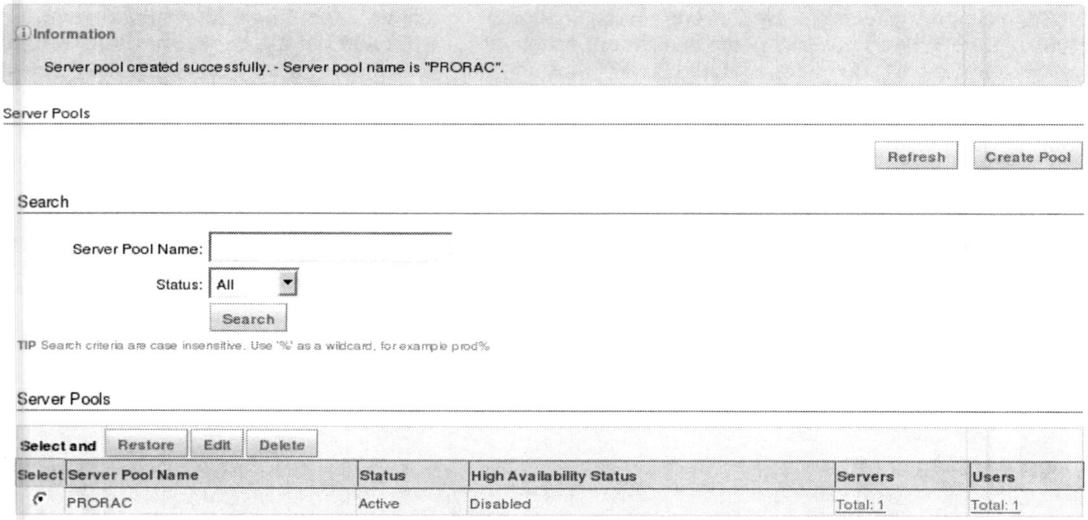

Figure 5-15. *Server Pool creation*

Once the Server Pool is created, it is possible to add additional servers to it. From the Servers tab, click Add Server, provide the Server Pool Name, and click Next. Now provide the server information and ensure that the Virtual Machine Server checkbox is selected. Optionally, you can choose Test the Connection to ensure the status of the agent on the Oracle VM Server. Next, click Add, select the server to be added under the "Servers to be Added to Server Pool" heading, and press Next. Finally, click Confirm, and the server is added to the Server Pool, as shown in Figure 5-16.

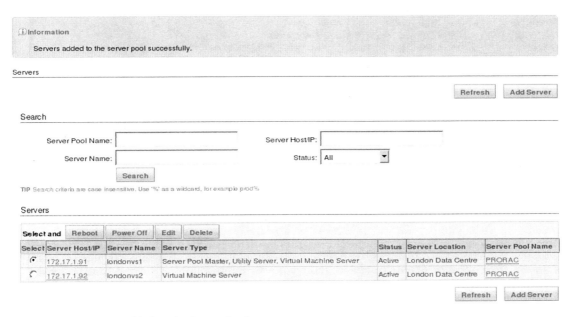

Figure 5-16. Servers added to the Server Pool

Repeat the preceding process to add all of the additional servers to be included in the Server Pool. Once of all of the nodes in the cluster are configured in the Server Pool, it is then necessary to enable high availability for the Server Pool, assuming you wish to do so.

Enabling High Availability

It is important to reiterate that, in a production environment, high availability should not be enabled with RAC due to the conflict of high availability features in both Oracle VM and RAC. However, high availability remains a valid option for a test-and-development environment, and we recommend that you learn how high availability is configured, so you can know where virtualization provides equivalent clustering capability. As with RAC, you can ensure the configuration is successful by understanding when actions are required on a single host or on all of the nodes in the cluster. In contrast to RAC, however, Oracle VM includes the concept of a Server Pool Master. Therefore, any actions run on a single host should be executed on the Server Pool Master.

Configuring Shared Storage

After a default installation, the /OVS partition is mounted as an OCFS2 file system. On a cluster file system, however, it is installed on a local device, as shown in the following example:

```
[root@londonvs1 utils]# df -h
Filesystem          Size  Used Avail Use% Mounted on
/dev/sdb1           452G  971M  427G   1% /
```

```
/dev/sda1              99M    45M    49M   49%  /boot
tmpfs                 277M     0    277M   0%   /dev/shm
/dev/sda2             4.0G   271M   3.8G   7%   /var/ovs/mount/A4AC9E8AE2214FC3ABF07904534A8777
```

In the next example, which is from Oracle VM 2.2, you don't mount /OVS directly; instead, you use a symbolic link to a Universal Unique Identifier (UUID) mount point in the directory, /var/ovs/mount:

```
root@londonvs1 ~]# ls -l /OVS
lrwxrwxrwx 1 root root 47 Dec 14 12:14 /OVS -> /var/ovs/mount/A4AC9E8AE2214FC3ABF07904534A8777
```

Prior to Oracle VM 2.2, the /OVS partition was detailed in the file /etc/fstab to be mounted directly.

To configure high availability, it is necessary for this partition to be moved to an OCSF2- or NFS-based file system that is shared between the nodes in the cluster. However, OCFS2 should not be also configured on an NFS file system. If using OCFS2, this can be configured only on a suitably highly available SAN or NAS storage option.

In this example, the storage is network based, and the disks are presented with the ISCSI protocol. By default, the ISCSI initiator software is installed on the Oracle VM Server. Specifically, the ISCSI storage is presented to all the nodes in the cluster from the dedicated storage server with the hostname dss and the IP Address 192.168.1.220. The NAS storage should either be on a separate network from that the one used by both the public network and the private interconnect, or it should be in a unified fabric environment to ensure that sufficient bandwidth is dedicated to the storage. This will help ensure that high utilization does not interfere with the clustering heartbeats of the OCFS2 or RAC software. To configure the ISCSI disks, start the ISCSI daemon service on the Oracle VM Server Pool Master Server:

```
[root@londonvs1 ~]# service iscsid start
Turning off network shutdown. Starting iSCSI daemon:
                                                          [  OK  ]
```

This snippet discovers the disks on the storage server:

```
[root@londonvs1 ~]# iscsiadm -m discovery -t st -p dss
192.168.1.220:3260,1 iqn.2008-02:dss.target0
```

Next, start the ISCSI service:

```
root@londonvs1 ~]# service iscsi start
iscsid (pid 2430 2429) is running...
Setting up iSCSI targets: Logging in to [iface: default, target: iqn.2008-02:dss.target0,
portal: 192.168.1.220,3260]
Login to [iface: default, target: iqn.2008-02:dss.target0, portal: 192.168.1.220,3260]:
successful
                                                          [  OK  ]
```

The disk discovery information can be viewed in /proc/scsi/scsi or by using the dmesg command, as follows:

```
scsi3 : iSCSI Initiator over TCP/IP
  Vendor: iSCSI     Model: DISK          Rev: 0
  Type:   Direct-Access                  ANSI SCSI revision: 04
sdf : very big device. try to use READ CAPACITY(16).
SCSI device sdf: 5837094912 512-byte hdwr sectors (2988593 MB)
```

You can partition the disk to be used for the /OVS partition with the commands fdisk or parted, as discussed in Chapter 4. This next example shows that one partition has been created on device /dev/sdf and is now available to configure for high availability:

```
[root@londonvs1 ~]# parted /dev/sdf
GNU Parted 1.8.1
Using /dev/sdf
Welcome to GNU Parted! Type 'help' to view a list of commands.
(parted) print

Model: iSCSI DISK (scsi)
Disk /dev/sdf: 2989GB
Sector size (logical/physical): 512B/512B
Partition Table: gpt

Number  Start   End     Size    File system  Name     Flags
1       17.4kB  2989GB  2989GB               primary

(parted)
```

Next, repeat the steps for disk discovery and configuration on all of the nodes in the cluster. However, do not repeat these steps for the partitioning, which should be completed on the Server Master only. The disk device is shared, so the partition information should now be visible on the rest of the nodes.

Cluster Configuration

By default, OCFS2 is installed automatically with Oracle VM Server, and it is configured by default to operate in an environment local to that server. The default configuration lends itself to being readily adapted to share the /OVS directory between multiple servers. In addition to the OCFS2 integrated into the Linux kernel, the ocfs2-tools RPM package contains the command-line tools for management. There is an additional GUI front end for these tools in an RPM package called ocfs2console; however, due to the best practice guidelines of running Dom0 with the least amount of overhead possible, there is no graphical environment available. Therefore, the GUI tools may not be installed. Thus, it is necessary to become familiar with the command-line tools for configuring OCFS2. In addition to OCFS2, the default installation also includes the o2cb service for cluster management. No additional software installations are required to extend the OCFS2 configuration into a clustered environment.

Before you can begin extending the configuration, all nodes in the cluster must ultimately share the same disk partition as the cluster root at /OVS, as in this example based on ISCSI. The default configuration has already installed an OCFS2 file system at /OVS, so it is necessary to move the existing mount point information for the /OVS directory to the shared storage. To begin creating the shared /OVS disk partition, it is necessary to format the shared storage device as an OCFS2 file system.

Before formatting the disk, you must have successfully completed the stages in Configuring Shared Storage, as described previously in this chapter. Specifically, you must have created the logical partition on a disk or shared storage system, and then provisioned it in such a way that every node in the cluster has read/write access to the shared disk. Once the disk is formatted, it can be mounted by any number of nodes. The format operation should be performed on one node only. Ideally, this node should be the one designated as the Server Pool Master. The o2cb service must be running to format a partition that has previously been formatted with an OCFS2 file system. However, if the o2cb service is not available and the file system is not in use by another server in the cluster, this check can be overridden with the –F or –force options. Volumes are formatted using the mkfs.ocfs2 command-line tool. For example, the following command creates an ocfs2 file system on device /dev/sdf1 with the OVS label:

```
[root@londonvs1 utils]# mkfs.ocfs2 -L "OVS" /dev/sdf1
mkfs.ocfs2 1.4.3
Cluster stack: classic o2cb
Overwriting existing ocfs2 partition.
mkfs.ocfs2: Unable to access cluster service while initializing the cluster
[root@londonvs1 utils]# dd if=/dev/zero of=/dev/sdf1 bs=1M count=100
100+0 records in
100+0 records out
104857600 bytes (105 MB) copied, 1.66662 seconds, 62.9 MB/s
[root@londonvs1 utils]# mkfs.ocfs2 -L "OVS" /dev/sdf1
mkfs.ocfs2 1.4.3
Cluster stack: classic o2cb
Filesystem label=OVS
Block size=4096 (bits=12)
Cluster size=4096 (bits=12)
Volume size=2988592558080 (729636855 clusters) (729636855 blocks)
22621 cluster groups (tail covers 6135 clusters, rest cover 32256 clusters)
Journal size=268435456
Initial number of node slots: 16
Creating bitmaps: done
Initializing superblock: done
Writing system files: done
Writing superblock: done
Writing backup superblock: 6 block(s)
Formatting Journals: done
Formatting slot map: done
Writing lost+found: done
mkfs.ocfs2 successful
```

After formatting the shared device as an OCFS2 file system, it is necessary to configure the cluster to mount the new OCFS2 file system and configure this file system as the cluster root on all hosts. From Oracle VM 2.2, this is done with the /opt/ovs-agent-2.3/utils/repos.py command. Prior to Oracle VM 2.2, this is done with the /usr/lib/ovs/ovs-cluster-configure command.

From Oracle VM 2.2, you will already have a local cluster root defined. This should be removed for all of the nodes in the cluster with the repos.py -d command, as shown:

```
[root@londonvs1 utils]# ./repos.py -l
[ * ] a4ac9e8a-e221-4fc3-abf0-7904534a8777 => /dev/sda2
[root@londonvs1 utils]# ./repos.py -d a4ac9e8a-e221-4fc3-abf0-7904534a8777
*** Cluster teared down.
```

The UUID will be different for all of the nodes in the cluster at this point because the nodes are defined on local storage:

```
[root@londonvs2 utils]# ./repos.py -d 5980d101-93ed-4044-baf8-aaddef5a9f3e
*** Cluster teared down.
```

At this stage, no /OVS partition should be mounted on any node, as shown in this example:

```
[root@londonvs1 utils]# df -h
Filesystem          Size  Used Avail Use% Mounted on
/dev/sdb1           452G  971M  427G   1% /
/dev/sda1            99M   45M   49M  49% /boot
tmpfs               277M     0  277M   0% /dev/shm
```

On the Server Pool Master, you should only configure the newly formatted shared OCFS2 partition as the cluster root, as shown here:

```
[root@londonvs1 utils]# ./repos.py -n /dev/sdf1
[ NEW ] 5f267cf1-3c3c-429c-b16f-12d1e4517f1a => /dev/sdf1
[root@londonvs1 utils]# ./repos.py -r 5f267cf1-3c3c-429c-b16f-12d1e4517f1a
[ R ] 5f267cf1-3c3c-429c-b16f-12d1e4517f1a => /dev/sdf1
```

Subsequently, follow the procedure detailed previously to create a Server Pool, as shown in Figure 5-17.

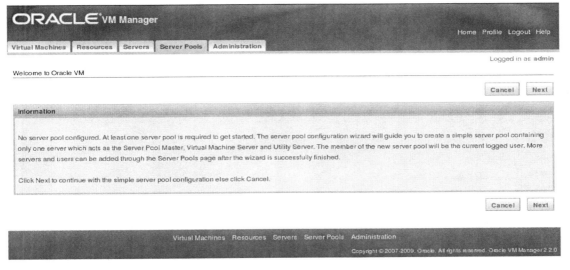

Figure 5-17. Highly available Server Pool creation

In this case, you need to ensure that the High Availability Mode checkbox is selected and click the Create button, as shown in Figure 5-18.

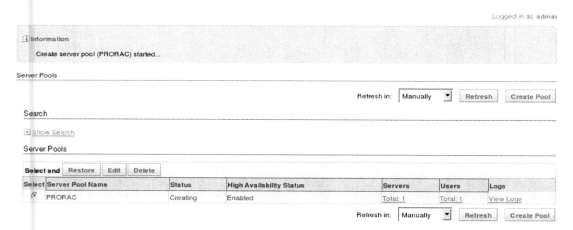

Figure 5-18. High Availability configuration

The Server Pool is created as a High Availability cluster with a single node, as shown in Figure 5-19.

Figure 5-19. The created High Availability Server Pool

On the Server Pool Master itself, the shared storage has been mounted and initialized as the cluster root under the /OVS symbolic link, as shown in this example:

```
[root@londonvs1 utils]# df -h
Filesystem          Size  Used Avail Use% Mounted on
/dev/sdb1           452G  971M  427G   1% /
```

```
/dev/sda1          99M    45M   49M   49%  /boot
tmpfs             277M      0  277M    0%  /dev/shm
/dev/sdf1         2.8T   4.1G  2.8T    1%  /var/ovs/mount/5F267CF13C3C429CB16F12D1E4517F1A
```

To add nodes to the cluster under Oracle VM Manager, click the Servers tab and then the Add Server button. Provide the server details, including the name of the Server Pool, and then click OK, as shown in Figure 5-20.

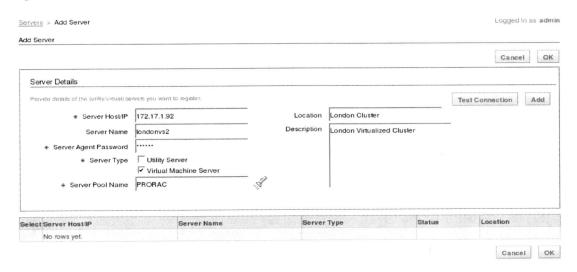

Figure 5-20. Adding a server to the Server Pool

The server is added to the Server Pool, and the cluster root partition is automatically configured and mounted as the shared storage on the additional node:

```
[root@londonvs2 utils]# df -h
Filesystem        Size   Used  Avail Use% Mounted on
/dev/sdb1         452G   971M  427G    1% /
/dev/sda1          99M    45M   49M   49% /boot
tmpfs             277M      0  277M    0% /dev/shm
/dev/sdf1         2.8T   4.1G  2.8T    1% /var/ovs/mount/5F267CF13C3C429CB16F12D1E4517F1A
```

The Server Pool is now shown as having high availability enabled with two servers (see Figure 5-21).

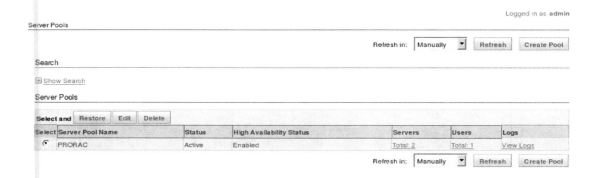

Figure 5-21. A Highly Available Server Pool with two servers

For versions of Oracle VM prior to Oracle VM 2.2, it is a more manual process to configure high availability. However, even if you're running Oracle VM 2.2, we recommend being familiar with the details in this section, so you can gain familiarity with the cluster software, even though the actual enabling commands are different.

Prior to Oracle VM 2.2, it is first necessary to unmount the existing local /OVS partition and run /usr/lib/ovs/ovs-cluster-configure on the Server Pool Master. The first operation of this command adds the following line to the file /etc/sysconfig/iptables on all of the nodes in the cluster. It also restarts the iptables service, as follows:

```
-A RH-Firewall-1-INPUT -p tcp -m state --state NEW -m tcp --dport 7777 -j ACCEPT
```

This action opens the firewall for cluster communication on the default port number of 7777. Details of the OCFS2 service are stored in the /etc/ocfs2/cluster.conf configuration file, which has a default cluster name of ocfs2. The configuration file contains the details of all of the nodes in the Server Pool, and this file is the same on each node. If making manual changes, new nodes can be added to the cluster dynamically. However, any other change, such as adding a new node name or IP address, requires a restart of the entire cluster to update information that has been cached on each node. The /etc/ocfs2/cluster.conf file contains the following two sections:

- The cluster section includes:

  - **node_count**: Specifies the maximum number of nodes in the cluster.

  - **name**: Defaults to ocfs2.

- The node section includes:

  - **ip_port**: Indicates the IP port to be used by OCFS to communicate with other nodes in the cluster. This value must be identical on every node in the cluster; the default value is 7777.

  - **ip_address**: Specifies the IP address to be used by OCFS. The network must be configured in advance of the installation, so it can communicate with all nodes in this cluster through this IP address.

- **number**: Specifies the node number, which is assigned sequentially from 0 to 254.

- **name**: Indicates the server hostname.

- **cluster**: Specifies the name of cluster.

There can be a maximum of 255 nodes in the cluster. However, the initial configuration will include all of the nodes in the Server Pool, as well as their public IP addresses. It is good practice to modify this file to use the private IP addresses as shown, and then to restart the OCFS2 and O2CB services as explained in the following section. When modifying the IP addresses, however, it is important that the hostname should remain as the public name of the host:

```
[root@londonvs2 ovs]# cat /etc/ocfs2/cluster.conf
node:
        ip_port = 7777
        ip_address = 192.168.1.91
        number = 0
        name = londonvs1
        cluster = ocfs2

node:
        ip_port = 7777
        ip_address = 192.168.1.92
        number = 1
        name = londonvs2
        cluster = ocfs2

cluster:
        node_count = 2
        name = ocfs2
```

During cluster configuration for high availability, the o2cb service is also started on each node in the cluster. This stack includes components such as the node manager, the heartbeat service, and the distributed lock manager that is crucial to cluster functionality and stability, so we recommend that you also become familiar with its parameters and operation. By default, the o2cb service is configured to start on boot up for a cluster name of ocfs2. The default configuration can be changed with the command service o2cb configure. Also, there are four parameters that can be changed to alter o2cb cluster timeout operations, depending on the cluster environment and the cluster name. Another option loads the o2cb modules at boot time. The four parameters for the o2cb service are as follows:

- O2CB_HEARTBEAT_THRESHOLD: The heartbeat threshold defines the number of heartbeats that a node can miss when updating its disk-based timestamp before it is excluded from the cluster. The value is based in iterations of two seconds each; therefore, the default value of 31 sets a timeout of 60 seconds.

- O2CB_IDLE_TIMEOUT_MS: The idle timeout, given in milliseconds, determines the maximum latency for a response on the network interconnect between the cluster nodes. The default value is 30000.

- O2CB_KEEPALIVE_DELAY_MS: The keepalive delay sets the time in milliseconds, after which a TCP keepalive packet is sent over the network when no other activity is taking place. Keepalive packets and their response ensure that the network link is maintained. Keepalive packets are short and utilize minimal bandwidth. There is default setting of 2000 milliseconds for this parameter.

- O2CB_RECONNECT_DELAY_MS: The reconnect delay has a default value of 2000 milliseconds, and it specifies the interval between attempted network connections.

The parameters can be modified by specifying new values for the configure option. While it is possible to change these values while a cluster is operational, you must not do so. The parameters must be the same on all nodes in the cluster; thus, if the O2CB_IDLE_TIMEOUT_MS value is changed dynamically when the first node in the cluster is restarted, the timeouts will be incompatible, and the node will not be able to join the cluster. Therefore, configuration changes should take place at the same time, and the o2cb modules reloaded after changes are made:

```
[root@londonvs1 ~]# service o2cb configure
Configuring the O2CB driver.

This will configure the on-boot properties of the O2CB driver.
The following questions will determine whether the driver is loaded on
boot.  The current values will be shown in brackets ('[]').  Hitting
<ENTER> without typing an answer will keep that current value.  Ctrl-C
will abort.

Load O2CB driver on boot (y/n) [y]:
Cluster stack backing O2CB [o2cb]:
Cluster to start on boot (Enter "none" to clear) [ocfs2]:
Specify heartbeat dead threshold (>=7) [31]:
Specify network idle timeout in ms (>=5000) [30000]:
Specify network keepalive delay in ms (>=1000) [2000]:
Specify network reconnect delay in ms (>=2000) [2000]:
Writing O2CB configuration: OK
Starting O2CB cluster ocfs2: OK
```

The non-default configured values for o2cb are stored in the file /etc/sysconfig/o2cb after they are changed, and the current operational values can be shown with the command service o2cb status. This command also displays the current status of the cluster:

```
[root@londonvs1 ~]# service o2cb status
Driver for "configfs": Loaded
Filesystem "configfs": Mounted
Driver for "ocfs2_dlmfs": Loaded
Filesystem "ocfs2_dlmfs": Mounted
Checking O2CB cluster ocfs2: Online
Heartbeat dead threshold = 31
  Network idle timeout: 30000
  Network keepalive delay: 2000
  Network reconnect delay: 2000
Checking O2CB heartbeat: Active
```

You can bring the cluster service online and take it offline again. To bring the cluster online, use the command service o2cb online [cluster_name], as in this example:

```
[root@londonvs1 ~]# service o2cb online ocfs2
Loading filesystem "configfs": OK
Mounting configfs filesystem at /sys/kernel/config: OK
Loading filesystem "ocfs2_dlmfs": OK
Mounting ocfs2_dlmfs filesystem at /dlm: OK
Starting O2CB cluster ocfs2: OK
```

The clustered file system can then be mounted. Using the /OVS symbolic link ensures that the correctly configured cluster root is mounted:

```
[root@londonvs1 ~]# mount /dev/sdf1 /OVS
```

To take the same ocfs2 cluster offline again, use the following command, which ensures that the clustered filesystem itself is unmounted before the service is taken offline:

```
[root@londonvs1 ~]# umount /OVS
[root@londonvs1 ~]# service o2cb offline ocfs2
Stopping O2CB cluster ocfs2: OK
Unloading module "ocfs2": OK
```

You can also stop both the ocfs2 and o2cb services individually, although the o2cb cluster service must be running with the filesystem unmounted to perform maintenance operations. As with any cluster environment, it is essential to maintain the health of the shared file system. If corrupted, the shared file system will render the entire cluster inoperational. If corruption is detected, the OCFS2 file system may operate in read-only mode, resulting in the failure of Oracle VM manager commands. You can perform a number of tuning operations on existing partitions using the tunefs.ocfs2 command-line utility. You can use the tuning tools to increase the number of node slots, change the volume label, and increase the size of the journal file. The fsck.ocfs2 tool can be used to check the health of an OCFS2 file system on an individual partition. To force a check on a file system that you suspect has errors, you can use the -f and -y options to automatically fix the errors without prompting, as in this example:

```
[root@londonvs1 ~]# fsck.ocfs2 -fy /dev/sdf1
fsck.ocfs2 1.4.3
Checking OCFS2 filesystem in /dev/sdf1:
  label:              OVS
  uuid:               cf 03 24 d4 73 78 46 b8 96 c3 45 1f 75 f5 e2 38
  number of blocks:   729636855
  bytes per block:    4096
  number of clusters: 729636855
  bytes per cluster:  4096
  max slots:          16

/dev/sdf1 was run with -f, check forced.
Pass 0a: Checking cluster allocation chains
Pass 0b: Checking inode allocation chains
Pass 0c: Checking extent block allocation chains
Pass 1: Checking inodes and blocks.
[INODE_SPARSE_SIZE] Inode 6 has a size of 4096 but has 2 blocks of
actual data. Correct the file size? y
Pass 2: Checking directory entries.
[DIRENT_LENGTH] Directory inode 6 corrupted in logical block 1 physical block
```

```
208 offset O. Attempt to repair this block's directory entries? y
Pass 3: Checking directory connectivity.
Pass 4a: checking for orphaned inodes
Pass 4b: Checking inodes link counts.
All passes succeeded.
```

Use mounted.ocfs2 to check the nodes currently mounting a specific device. Options include -d, which performs a quick detect useful in identifying the UUID for a particular device; and -f , which performs a full detect to display the mounted filesystems:

```
[root@londonvs1 ~]# mounted.ocfs2 -d
Device                FS     UUID                                     Label
/dev/sda2             ocfs2  2f77c155-017a-4830-8abb-8bc767ef7e1f
/dev/sdf1             ocfs2  cf0324d4-7378-46b8-96c3-451f75f5e238     OVS
[root@londonvs1 ~]# mounted.ocfs2 -f
Device                FS     Nodes
/dev/sda2             ocfs2  Not mounted
/dev/sdf1             ocfs2  londonvs1, londonvs2
```

For versions of Oracle VM prior to 2.2, after configuring OCFS2 it is necessary to configure the /etc/ovs/repositories file within which the cluster mount points will be maintained. This can be achieved by using /usr/lib/ovs/ovs-makerepo command, where the arguments are the device name of the partition C for cluster and a comment. This command must be run on each node in the cluster. The first run initializes the shared repository, while subsequent runs report that the shared repository is already initialized. Running this command also updates the local repository list:

```
[root@londonvs1 ovs]# ./ovs-makerepo /dev/sdf1 C "PRORAC Cluster"
Initializing NEW repository /dev/sdf1
SUCCESS: Mounted /OVS
Updating local repository list.
ovs-makerepo complete
```

After configuration, the device and OVS UUID are associated in the /etc/ovs/repositories file:

```
[root@londonvs1 ovs]# more /etc/ovs/repositories
# This configuration file was generated by ovs-makerepo
# DO NOT EDIT
@8EE876B5C1954A1E8FBEFA32E5700D20 /dev/sdf1
```

Also, the corresponding configuration stored on the device is now mounted at /OVS:

```
[root@londonvs1 ovs]# more /OVS/.ovsrepo
OVS_REPO_UUID=8EE876B5C1954A1E8FBEFA32E5700D20
OVS_REPO_SHARED=1
OVS_REPO_DESCRIPTION=PRORAC Cluster
OVS_REPO_VERSION=1
```

After configuring the /etc/ovs/repositories file, the OCFS2 mount point information should no longer be maintained in the /etc/fstab file. The command /usr/lib/ovs/ovs-cluster-check can be used to complete the cluster configuration. On the Server Pool master, use the arguments --master and --alter-fstab to complete the cluster configuration:

```
[root@londonvs1 ovs]# ./ovs-cluster-check --master --alter-fstab
Backing up original /etc/fstab to /tmp/fstab.fQOZF10773
Removing /OVS mounts in /etc/fstab
O2CB cluster ocfs2 already online
Cluster setup complete.
```

On the other nodes in the Server Pool, use only the argument --alter-fstab to complete the cluster configuration:

```
[root@londonvs2 ovs]# ./ovs-cluster-check --alter-fstab
O2CB cluster ocfs2 already online
Cluster setup complete.
```

To enable High Availability across the Server Pool, log into Oracle VM Manager and click the Server Pools tab. When the Server Pool is created, the High Availability Status field shows a status of Disabled (see Figure 5-22). Select the Server Pool and click Edit to show the Edit Server Pool page. On this page, click the Check button that corresponds to the High Availability Infrastructure field. The response chosen should be *High Availability Infrastructure works well*, as shown in Figure 5-22.

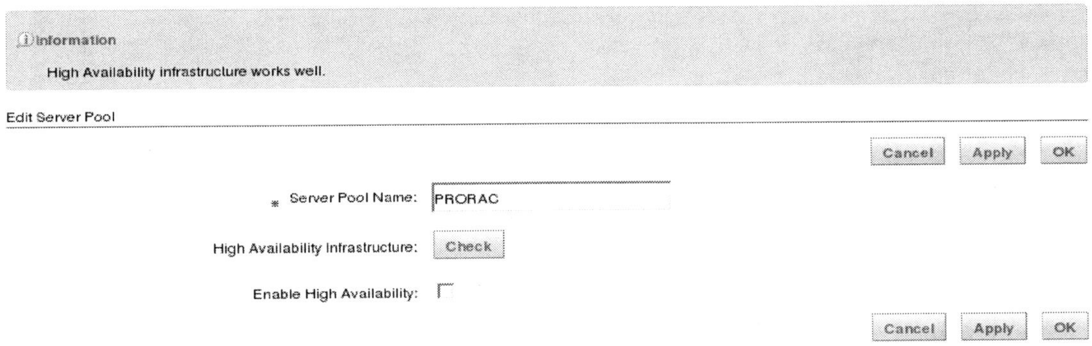

Figure 5-22. An Oracle VM 2.1.2 High Availability configuration

If the check reports an error, you need to ensure that all the steps detailed in this section have been correctly implemented on all of the nodes in the cluster. In particular, the check ensures that all the nodes in the cluster share the same /OVS partition. This means the storage can be synchronized and the cluster scripts have been correctly run on all of the nodes. The errors reported will aid in diagnosing where the configuration is incorrect. When the check is successful, select the Enable High Availability checkbox and click Apply, as shown in Figure 5-23.

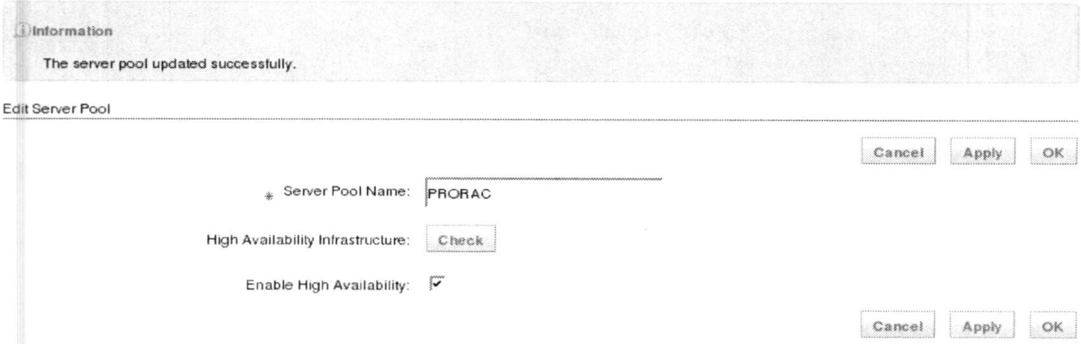

ⓘInformation

The server pool updated successfully.

Edit Server Pool

| | | | Cancel | Apply | OK |

＊ Server Pool Name: PRORAC

High Availability Infrastructure: Check

Enable High Availability: ☑

| | | | Cancel | Apply | OK |

Figure 5-23. *High Availability Enabled*

Once the Server Pool has updated, press OK. The top-level Server Pools page that shows that the High Availability Status also now shows a status of Enabled. High availability features are active across the cluster, as shown in Figure 5-24.

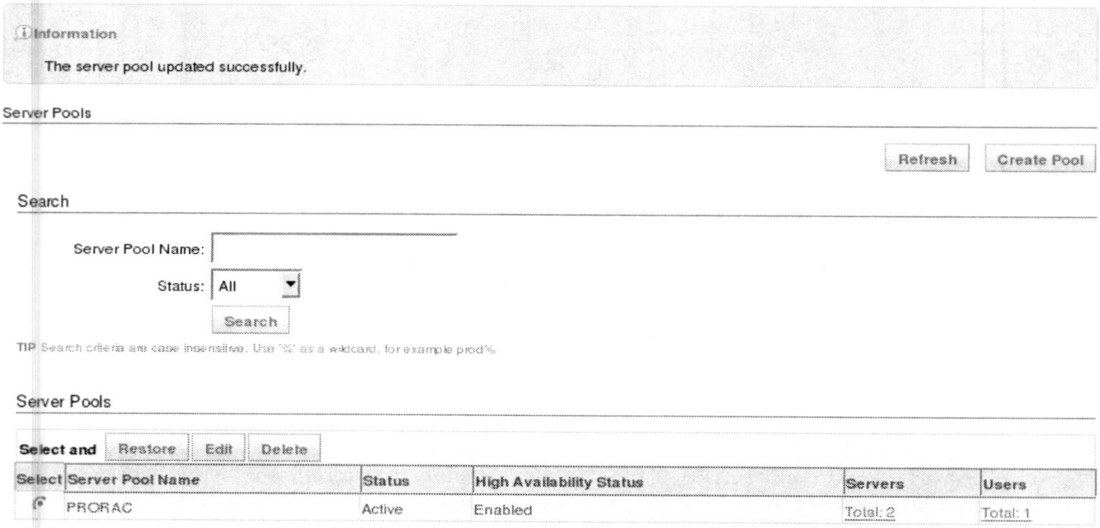

ⓘInformation

The server pool updated successfully.

Server Pools

| | Refresh | Create Pool |

Search

Server Pool Name: [   ]

Status: [All   ▼]

[Search]

TIP Search criteria are case insensitive. Use '%' as a wildcard, for example prod%.

Server Pools

Select and [Restore] [Edit] [Delete]

Select	Server Pool Name	Status	High Availability Status	Servers	Users
⦿	PRORAC	Active	Enabled	Total: 2	Total: 1

Figure 5-24. *A Highly Available Server Pool*

Installing and Configuring Guests

With the underlying Oracle VM configuration established in a high availability configuration, the next step is to create and configure DomU guest domains and to install a guest operating system environment. There are a number of ways to configure a guest both at the command line. For example, you might use the virt-install command or the Oracle VM Manager from standard installation media. For Linux environments, however, we recommend standardizing on the use of Oracle VM templates for guest installations. Oracle VM templates provide pre-configured system images of both Oracle Enterprise Linux and Oracle software environments. These environments can be imported, and guests can be created from the template without needing to undergo the operating system installation procedure. These pre-configured Oracle VM templates are available from the Oracle edelivery website. On the Media Pack Search page, you can select Oracle VM templates from the Select a Product Pack menu. For a guest to support a RAC environment, downloading the template requires only that you select the operating system, such as Oracle VM Templates for Oracle Enterprise Linux 5 Media Pack for x86_64 (64 bit).

Additionally, with Oracle Enterprise Linux JeOS, Oracle provides a freely downloadable operating system environment that enables you to build your own Oracle VM Templates for importing into Oracle VM. Therefore, adopting the use of templates enables you to maintain consistency across the installations of all of your guest environments.

Importing a Template

Whether you have created your own template or downloaded an Oracle template, the first stage to installing a guest based on this template is to import one using Oracle VM Manager. At the time of writing, there is no preconfigured Oracle RAC template, so the example will focus on the standard Linux template. On the /OVS partition shared between the Oracle VM Servers, you have a number of directories, as shown here:

```
[root@londonvs1 OVS]# ls
iso_pool  lost+found  publish_pool  running_pool  seed_pool  sharedDisk
```

When working with Oracle VM templates, you will focus on the running_pool and seed_pool; the iso_pool is for the storage of CD images. Copy the Oracle VM template file to the /OVS/seed_pool directory. If you're using the Oracle-provided templates, then also use the unzip and tar commands with the arguments zxvf to unzip and extract the template into a top-level directory named after the template. This directory will contain three files, as shown:

```
[root@londonvs1 OVM_EL5U3_X86_64_PVM_4GB]# ls
README  System.img  vm.cfg
```

Log into Oracle VM Manager and click the Resources tab to show the Virtual Machine Templates page. Click Import to show the Source page, select a template name from Server Pool, and press Next. On the General Information page, enter the details of the template to use. The templates you have extracted into the seed_pool directory are shown under the Virtual Machine Template Name dropdown menu. Now press Next. On the Confirm Information page, press Confirm to import the template. When successfully imported, the template is displayed with the status of Pending, as shown in Figure 5-25.

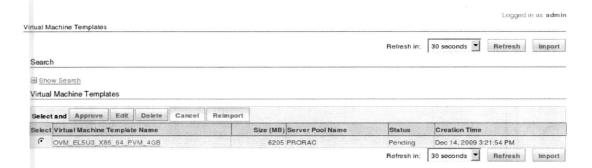

Figure 5-25. The imported template

Once the template is imported, it is necessary to approve the template before it can be used to create a guest. On the Virtual Machine Templates section, click Approve. The View Virtual Machine Template is also displayed with the status of Pending. Click Approve, and the template displays a status of *active*. This means it is ready to create a guest installation from, as shown in Figure 5-26.

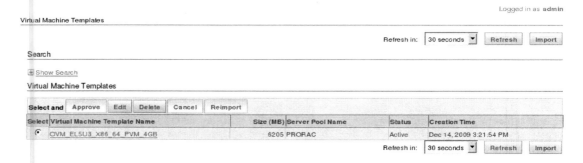

Figure 5-26. The active template

Creating a Guest from a Template

To begin creating a guest from an imported and approved Oracle VM template, log into Oracle VM Manager, click the Virtual Machines tab, and press the Create Virtual Machine button. On the Creation Method page, choose the Create virtual machine based on a virtual machine template option, and then press Next. Now select the Server Pool and the Preferred Server options. The concept of Preferred Servers is similar to that which is applied to preferred servers for RAC service management; however, in this case it specifies the preferred Oracle VM Server that will run the created guest domain if that server is available (see Figure 5-27).

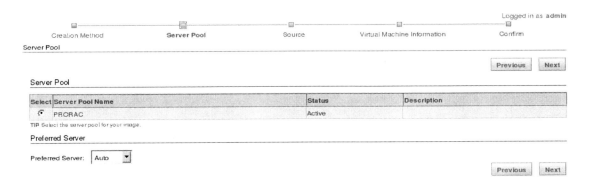

Figure 5-27. The preferred server

On the Source page, select the name of the template that was imported. Now press Next to show the Virtual Machine Information page, and then enter the details for the guest to be configured. The Virtual Machine Name will be applied to the guest domain, which may be the same as the guest operating system that runs in the domain. The console password is the password used to access the VNC interface to the guest, as discussed in the next section. It is not the root user password for the guest, which is set by default to the password of ovsroot. Under the Network Interface Card section, the first virtual interface of VIF0 is configured by default. Select Add Row, and then select the bridge on the private network. In this case, xenbr1 is chosen for the additional interface of VIF1, as shown in Figure 5-28.

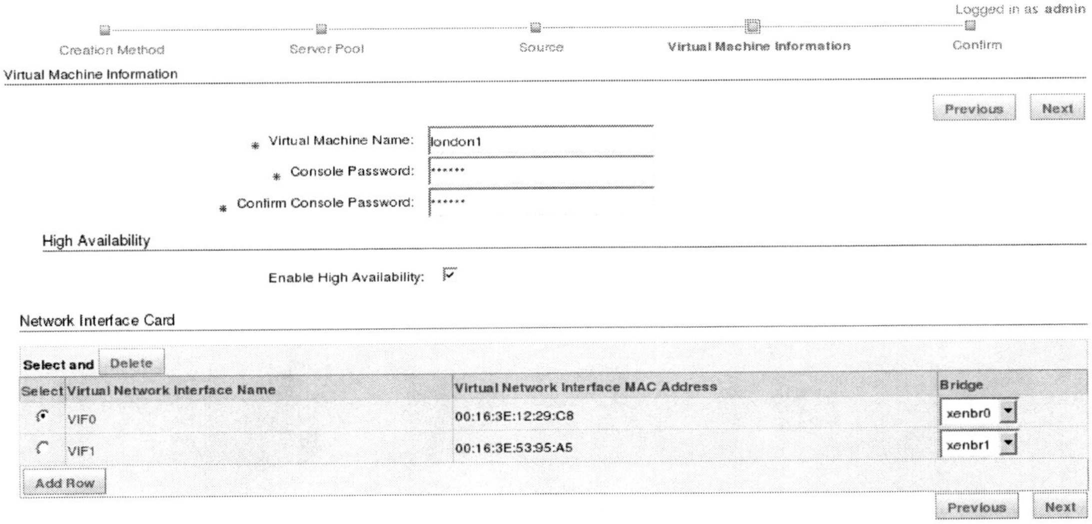

Figure 5-28. The network configuration

Press Next, and then press Next again on the Confirm Interface Screen. This creates the guest from the template. The System image file is copied from the seed_pool to the running_pool directory, as shown in Figure 5-29.

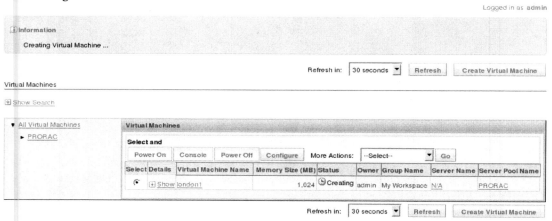

Figure 5-29. *Guest Creation*

When the creation process has completed, the guest shows a status of Powered Off. The guest can be started by pressing the Power On button.

Accessing a Guest

When the guest is running, access to the console is provided through the VNC service that is hosted by the operating system in Dom0. Once the guest network interfaces have been configured, the guest can be accessed across the network using standard tools, such as ssh. However, the console also enables accessing the guest before the network has been enabled. To find the VNC connectivity information on the Virtual Machines page, note the Oracle VM Server that the guest is running on. In the Details section, click Show and note the VNC port. In this example, the port is the VNC default of 5900 (see Figure 5-30).

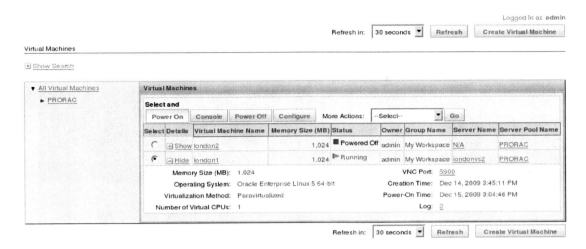

Figure 5-30. The VNC configuration

Based on this connectivity information, the guest console can be accessed using any VNC connectivity tool available in most Linux environments, such as vncviewer. Now run vncviewer with the Oracle VM Server and VNC port as arguments, as shown here:

```
[root@londonmgr1 ~]# vncviewer londonvs2:5900

VNC Viewer Free Edition 4.1.2 for X - built May 12 2006 17:42:13
Copyright (C) 2002-2005 RealVNC Ltd.
See http://www.realvnc.com for information on VNC.
```

At the graphical prompt, provide the console password entered when the guest was created. If this password has been forgotten, it can be accessed from the information stored in the Xenstore or the vm.cfg file, as detailed later in this chapter. Oracle VM Manager also provides a VNC plugin to the host web browser. Clicking the Console button under the Virtual Machines page can also display the console. In this case however, the console is embedded in the browser, as opposed to the standalone access provided by vncviewer (see Figure 5-31).

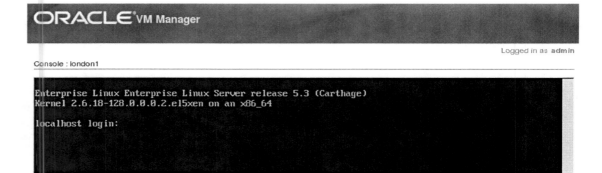

Figure 5-31. Guest Console

On first access to the guest console, you are prompted to provide the IP and hostname configuration information for the guest operating system. By default, this will configure the public eth0 interface only. Therefore, it is necessary to prepare the guest for RAC before you can log in and configure the additional private network interface.

Configuring a Guest for RAC

Once the guest template is installed, its configuration information is stored under a directory named after the guest under /OVS/running_pool. Under this directory, the file System.img is presented as a disk device to the guest when it is running. Consequently, this file should not be accessed or modified from the Oracle VM Server environment. The file vm.cfg contains the Virtual Machine configuration information, and it's where modifications can be made to change the configuration before starting the guest:

```
[root@londonvs1 12_london1]# ls -ltR
.:
total 6353708
-rw-rw-rw- 1 root root          475 Dec 15 16:07 vm.cfg
-rw-rw-rw- 1 root root          268 Dec 14 17:02 vm.cfg.orig
-rw-rw-rw- 1 root root          215 Dec 14 17:02 README
-rw-rw-rw- 1 root root 6506195968 Dec 14 17:02 System.img
```

A default vm.cfg file for a paravirtualized guest environment looks similar to the following:

```
[root@londonvs1 12_london1]# more vm.cfg
bootloader = '/usr/bin/pygrub'
disk =
['file:/var/ovs/mount/5F267CF13C3C429CB16F12D1E4517F1A/running_pool/12_london1/System.img,xvda
,w']
memory = '1024'
name = '12_london1'
on_crash = 'restart'
```

```
on_reboot = 'restart'
uuid = '6b0723e6-b2f0-4b29-a37c-1e9115798548'
vcpus = 1
vfb = ['type=vnc,vncunused=1,vnclisten=0.0.0.0,vncpasswd=oracle']
vif = ['bridge=xenbr0,mac=00:16:3E:12:29:C8,type=netfront',
'bridge=xenbr1,mac=00:16:3E:53:95:A5,type=netfront',
]
vif_other_config = []
```

In this example, the network interfaces were configured during the guest installation, and no further changes to the vm.cfg file are required. In terms of the disk devices, it can be seen that the System.img file is presented to the guest as the first block device, xvda. Using Oracle VM Manager, additional image files can be created to add disk devices to the host. However, for RAC it is necessary to pass shared physical disk devices to the guest operating systems. Although it is possible to configure an iSCSI device or NFS filesystem directly in the guest, only block devices configured from within Dom0 are supported by Oracle in a production RAC environment. If redundancy is a requirement at the disk device level, multipathing should be implemented within Dom0 (see Chapter 4 for more information). Also, udev can be used at the Dom0 level to configure device persistence or ASMLIB within the guest (again, see Chapter 4 for more information).

The physical devices must be already configured and presented to the Dom0 operating system, just as it would happen in a native Linux operating system environment. These can then be passed into the guests with a configuration, such as the one shown here:

```
disk =
['file:/var/ovs/mount/5F267CF13C3C429CB16F12D1E4517F1A/running_pool/12_london1/System.img,xvda
,w',
'phy:/dev/sdc,xvdc,w',
'phy:/dev/sdd,xvdd,w',
'phy:/dev/sde,xvde,w',
]
```

Disk devices can either be partitioned in one of two ways First, They can be partitioned within Dom0 and each partition can be passed as a device to the guest. Second, the full device can be passed to the guest and partitioned there. It is also important to note that, in some earlier versions of Oracle VM, the total number of xvd devices is limited to 16; in later versions, the limit increases to 256.

When the guest is restarted, the physical devices on which Oracle RAC can be installed and shared between the guests are available to the guest environments. These guest environments can use the physical devices exactly as would be the case for a shared disk device:

```
[root@london1 ~]# cat /proc/partitions
major minor  #blocks  name

 202    0    6353707  xvda
 202    1      32098  xvda1
 202    2    4225095  xvda2
 202    3    2088450  xvda3
 202   32  106778880  xvdc
 202   33  106775991  xvdc1
 202   48    1048576  xvdd
 202   49    1048376  xvdd1
```

```
202   64  313994880 xvde
202   65  313990393 xvde1
```

An additional configuration to prepare the guest for a RAC environment is to assign an IP address to the private network interface. This can be done exactly as you would in a standard Linux operating system environment; that is, by editing the corresponding configuration file such as /etc/sysconfig/network-scripts/ifcfg-eth1. By default, the network interfaces are configured for DHCP, and they will be automatically assigned an address if DHCP is configured in your environment. It is important to note that the MAC address for this interface is the Xen assigned MAC address, and the one used must be the MAC address shown for VIF1 during the guest creation. The same address is also shown in the vm.cfg file on the bridge, xenbr1:

```
[root@london1 network-scripts]# cat ifcfg-eth1
# Xen Virtual Ethernet
DEVICE=eth1
BOOTPROTO=static
ONBOOT=yes
IPADDR=192.168.1.1
HWADDR=00:16:3e:53:95:a5
```

It is important to note that in the standard Oracle Linux template, by default the iptables service is enabled in the guest environment. Therefore, it should also be stopped there; alternatively, you can use the service iptables stop and the chkconfig iptables off commands to prevent it from starting.

Additionally by default in a Xen configuration the time in the guest is synchronized to Dom0 and therefore the guest should be set to manage its own time with the command echo 1 > /proc/sys/xen/independent_wallclock run as root and the parameter xen.independent_wallclock=1 set in /etc/sysctl.conf. If using an template based guest then this parameter may already be set in the guest environment. If using NTP as described in Chapter 4 the guests should synchronize with the same time source.

Once all of the guest domains have been created to support the planned number of nodes for the RAC installation, it becomes possible to proceed to install and configure RAC in the guest operating system environment for a native Linux environment (see Chapter 6 for more information).

Managing Domains

One of the key features of operating in a virtualized environment is the ability to dynamically assign resources to guest operating systems according to demand. In this section, we will look at some of the tools available for managing Oracle VM, paying particular attention to managing resources. We will begin to implement this by looking at the role the Oracle VM Agent plays in communication between the VM Server and VM Manager, and then focusing on domain management with Oracle VM Manager and the xm command-line tools.

Oracle VM Agent

Earlier in this chapter, we examined the architecture of Oracle VM and the role of the Oracle VM Agent and its control interface. In doing so, we covered how this software provides an important mediation service between the Oracle VM Manager and the Oracle VM Servers in the Server Pool. Therefore, it is important to ensure that the VM Agent is correctly configured and running on each of the VM Servers.

This enables you to manage the VM Servers from a central Oracle VM Manager location. The VM Agent is installed automatically at the same time as the VM Server, enabling the VM Agent to run as a service in the Linux operating system running in the management domain. By default, it is located in /opt/ovs-agent-2.3. The VM Agent is configured to start when the Dom0 operating system is running at runlevel 3, and the command service ovs-agent status can be used to confirm its status. Using this command provides the following output, which confirms normal operations:

```
[root@londonvs1 ~]# service ovs-agent status
ok! process OVSRemasterServer exists.
ok! process OVSLogServer exists.
ok! process OVSMonitorServer exists.
ok! process OVSPolicyServer exists.
ok! process OVSAgentServer exists.
ok! OVSAgentServer is alive.
```

Each of these Agent daemons runs as a Python script from the installation location, and additional utility scripts are available under this location to interact with the agent at the command line. Various configuration options, such as setting the agent password or defining IP addresses that are permitted to communicate with the agent, are available through the command service ovs-agent configure. The Oracle VM Agent interacts with the Xen Hypervisor through the Xend daemon running in Dom0. The Xend daemon is the Xen controller daemon, and it is responsible for management functionality such as creating and configuring domains and Live Migration. The Xend daemon is also primarily written in Python; hence, this is the reason the VM Agent runs as a Python script. The status of the Xend daemon can be verified with the command service xend status:

```
[root@london1 xenstored]# service xend status
xend daemon running (pid 3621)
```

The configuration of the Xend daemon can modified with the file xend-config.sxp in the /etc/xen directory. This daemon provides modifiable configuration options for things such as the memory and CPUs for the management domain. The Xend daemon creates an additional daemon, xenstored, and makes commands available to read and write the configuration in the Xenstore. The Xenstore is the central repository for all configuration information on an Oracle VM Server, and the DomU's information can be dynamically configured by changing the information contained within it. For example, you might change its configuration to enable device discovery. The information is held in a lightweight database called a *Trivial Database* (tdb) in the form of key-value pairs. It is located in the directory, /var/lib/xenstored/tbd:

```
[root@londonvs1 xenstored]# file /var/lib/xenstored/tdb
tdb: TDB database version 6, little-endian hash size 7919 bytes
```

The entire database can be listed with the xenstore-ls command:

```
[root@londonvs1 ~]# xenstore-ls
tool = ""
 xenstored = ""
local = ""
 domain = ""
  0 = ""
   vm = "/vm/00000000-0000-0000-0000-000000000000"
```

```
  device = ""
  control = ""
   platform-feature-multiprocessor-suspend = "1"
  error = ""
  memory = ""
   target = "566272"
  guest = ""
  hvmpv = ""
  cpu = ""
   1 = ""
...
```

The hierarchical paths can be listed with the xenstore-list command. For example, you can list the uuids of the virtual machines, as in this snippet:

```
[root@londonvs1 ~]# xenstore-list /vm
00000000-0000-0000-0000-000000000000
6b0723e6-b2f0-4b29-a37c-1e9115798548
```

The xenstore-read and xenstore-write commands can be used to read and change the individual values. The command shown here details the name of the Virtual Machine that corresponds to the uuid given:

```
[root@londonvs1 ~]# xenstore-read \
> /vm/6b0723e6-b2f0-4b29-a37c-1e9115798548/name
12_london1
```

When troubleshooting configuration changes, the Xenstore determines whether information from the VM Manager and the Oracle VM Agent have been relayed to the underlying Xen software to be applied by the domains themselves. In Oracle VM the persistent storage is configured under the /OVS/running_pool directory, and there are no entries in default Xen location of /var/lib/xend/domains. That said, the configuration can be imported with the xm new command. You'll learn more about this in the "Managing Domains" section later in this chapter.

Oracle VM Manager

You have already seen from the guest operating server how, when logged into Oracle VM Manager under the Virtual Machines page, you can Power On and Power Off a guest and access the console either through the Console button or with vncviewer. By clicking the Configure button, it is also possible to modify a number of configuration parameters such as the CPU by altering the number of cores assigned to the virtual machine and the amount of memory. These values correspond to the parameters memory and vcpus in the vm.cfg file, as in this example:

```
memory = '2048'
vcpus = 2
```

These parameters can be changed in the vm.cfg file before starting a guest. However, before modifying these parameters dynamically in a production environment, it is important to check whether doing so is a supported action. Nevertheless, in an Oracle Database on Linux environment, both parameters are dynamic. This means that both CPU and memory can be added to and subtracted from an instance as it is running.

The number of cores in use by the Oracle instance is shown by the parameter cpu_count:

```
SQL> show parameter cpu_count

NAME                                 TYPE        VALUE
------------------------------------ ----------- --------------------
cpu_count                            integer     2
```

In Oracle VM Manager, if the number of cores allocated to the guest is modified and the configuration is saved, then this is reflected automatically in the cpu_count parameter in the Oracle instance running in the guest. This can immediately provide a performance increase for CPU intensive workloads, and no further configuration is needed by the DBA. However, careful consideration should be given to modifying the CPU count when parallel workloads are in operation.

Within the guest, you should not allocate more virtual CPUs than you have physical cores within the processors on your system. The exception to this rule occurs where Hyper Threading is available (as detailed in Chapter 4). In the case where this is available, the limit applies to the number of available threads, as opposed to cores. However, the performance benefits of assigning the additional virtual CPUs are not as defined, as is the case with a native implementation. Where multiple guests are configured, the total number of assigned virtual CPUs should be no more than twice the available cores or threads.

From within Oracle VM Manager, the amount of memory allocated to a guest can also be modified. However, the impact upon the guest is more dependent on the Oracle configuration than on the CPU. In Oracle 11g, Automatic Memory Management is supported by setting the parameters memory_max_size and memory_target. Consequently, memory is stored in files in the /dev/shm shared memory filesystem. However, to use this feature, the /dev/shm filesystem must be pre-configured so it is large enough to support the maximum possible size of memory_max_size. Doing so requires all memory to be assigned to the VM in advance, thereby negating any advantage of assigning memory dynamically. For this reason, we recommend not utilizing Oracle 11g Automatic Memory Management in a virtualized environment. Instead, you should use Automatic Shared Memory Management, which was introduced with 10g. Within Automatic Shared Memory Management, the SGA memory configuration is controlled by the parameters sga_max_size and sga_target. This memory cannot be assigned to the PGA, as it can with Automatic Shared Memory Management. However, and this is crucial for virtualized environments, the sga_max_size can be set to the upper memory limit to which the SGA can grow. Moreover, that memory does not need to be allocated to the guest, which means it can be set to the potential size to which memory will be dynamically assigned, as shown here:

```
SQL> show parameter sga_

NAME                                 TYPE        VALUE
------------------------------------ ----------- --------------------
sga_max_size                         big integer 12G
sga_target                           big integer 2G
```

When memory is dynamically assigned to the guest, it is not immediately assigned to the Oracle instance. It is necessary to modify the sga_target parameter up to the new memory assigned to the guest, which ensures that the Oracle RAC instance on the guest is specified, as in this example:

```
SQL> alter system set sga_target=6g scope=both sid='PROD1';

System altered.
```

When allocating memory to guests, however, you should also ensure that sufficient memory is available for Dom0. By default, this is set to the minimum value of 512MB. Where I/O activity is intensive and additional memory is available, performance can benefit from increasing this value to 1024MB, as specified in the dom0_mem kernel parameter in the grub.conf file of the Oracle VM Server.

In addition to the standard configuration options, there are several additional actions that can be performed by selecting an action from the More Actions: dropdown menu. One of the most powerful features under these options is live migration. As detailed earlier in this chapter, this option enables you to move a running guest from one Oracle VM Server to another. However, it is important to ensure that either the hardware within the hosts must be identical, or the systems must support a feature to enable migration between different platforms, such as Flex Migration on Intel platforms. Additionally, it is important to reiterate that Live Migration should not be performed while a RAC instance is running in the guest. This is because doing so will cause the node to be ejected from the cluster. Instead, it is necessary to stop the instance and restart it after migration has taken place.

When selecting the Live Migration option on the Migrate To page, select the system to migrate to and press Next. On the Confirm Information page, press Confirm and the guest is migrated, as shown in Figure 5-32.

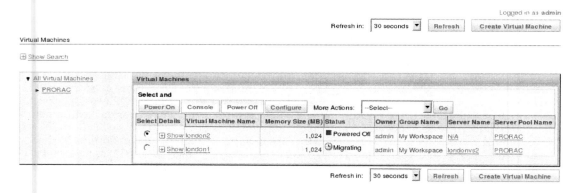

Figure 5-32. Live Migration

The time required to migrate is proportional to the memory allocated to the guest. When refreshing the Oracle VM Manager screen, the Server Name column will display the initial server first, and then the destination server. Finally, it will show the status as Running on the new server.

Oracle VM Manager CLI

In addition to functionality provided by the Oracle VM Manager's graphical environment, if you have installed and configured the CLI (as explained previously in this chapter), then you can also accomplish the same management task directly from the command line. The CLI provides a shell mode, and logging in with the username and password configured during the Oracle VM Manager installation results in an interactive prompt:

```
[root@london5 ~]# ovm -u admin -p admin shell
Type "help" for a list of commands.
ovm>
```

The help command provides details on the CLI commands available. At the top level, the help command lists all the available commands. Or, if given the argument for a particular subcommand, the command lists the next level of command options. For example, you can detail the subcommands for Server Pool management, as in this example:

```
ovm> help svrp
Server pool management:

svrp conf       ---   Configure a server pool
svrp del        ---   Delete a server pool
svrp info       ---   Get server pool information
svrp ls         ---   List server pools
svrp new        ---   Create a new server pool
svrp refresh    ---   Refresh all server pools
svrp restore    ---   Restore server pool information
svrp stat       ---   Get server pool status

"help <subcommand>" displays help message for that subcommand.
"help all" displays complete list of subcommands.
```

These subcommands can then be used to manage the environment. For example, this snippet shows the details of the Server Pool:

```
ovm> svrp ls
Server_Pool_Name Status HA
PRORAC           Active Enabled
```

The vm commands can be used to manage the guest virtual machines, while the vm ls command is available to query the configured guest environments:

```
ovm> vm ls
Name    Size(MB) Mem  VCPUs Status  Server_Pool
london1 6205     1024 1     Running PRORAC
london2 6205     1024 1     Running PRORAC
```

In the same vein, the vm info command provides full details on a particular guest:

```
ovm> vm info -n london1 -s PRORAC
                        ID: 12
      Virtual Machine Name: london1
      Virtual Machine Type: Paravirtualized
          Operating System: Oracle Enterprise Linux 5 64-bit
                    Status: Running
                Running on: londonvs1
                   Size(MB): 6205
           Memory Size(MB): 1024
   Maximum Memory Size(MB): 1024
```

```
               Virtual CPUs: 1
     VCPU Scheduling Priority: Intermediate
          VCPU Scheduling Cap: High
                 Boot Device: HDD
             Keyboard Layout: en-us
           Hign Availability: Enabled
         PVDriver Initialized: False
             Preferred Server: Auto
                   Group Name: My Workspace
                  Description: OEL5 PVM Template
```

However, the CLI is not restricted to only observing the configured environment. It can also be used to execute commands available from within the Oracle VM Manager graphical environment. For example, the following command can be used to perform live migration:

```
ovm> vm mig -n london1 -s PRORAC
Migrating.
```

It is important to note that the graphical manager will show a change in status when actions are taken with the CLI. For example, when using the preceding command, the migration initiated with the CLI will be observed as being in progress within Oracle VM Manager. This means you can use both the Oracle VM Manager and the CLI; they are not mutually exclusive.

The xm Command-Line Interface

In addition to Oracle VM Manager, there are a number of command-line tools that enable interaction with the Xen environment directly on the Oracle VM Server itself. These tools enable the creation, deletion, and management of domains. The most common management tools are xm and virsh. These tools offer similar functionality and methods to achieve the same goals by different means. We will focus on the xm tool in this chapter because xm is dedicated to managing Xen domains; whereas virsh, as part of the libvirt virtualization toolkit, is a more general purpose tool. The xm CLI is available to manage domains when logged into Dom0 with root user privileges.

Displaying Information

For a quick reference of the xm commands available, you can use xm help -l or xm help -long; these options display both the commands available and a description of each:

```
root@londonvs1 ~]# xm help -l
Usage: xm <subcommand> [args]

Control, list, and manipulate Xen guest instances.

xm full list of subcommands:

  console            Attach to <Domain>'s console.
  create             Create a domain based on <ConfigFile>.
  new                Adds a domain to Xend domain management
  delete             Remove a domain from Xend domain management.
```

```
destroy              Terminate a domain immediately.
domid                Convert a domain name to domain id.
domname              Convert a domain id to domain name.
dump-core            Dump core for a specific domain.
list                 List information about all/some domains.
...
<Domain> can either be the Domain Name or Id.
For more help on 'xm' see the xm(1) man page.
For more help on 'xm create' see the xmdomain.cfg(5)  man page.
```

In navigating with the xm CLI, the first step is to discover information about the running environment. The highest level command to display details on running domains is xm list:

```
[root@londonvs1 ~]# xm list
Name                             ID    Mem VCPUs      State   Time(s)
12_london1                        1   1024     1      -b----      0.6
30_london2                        2   1024     1      -b----      0.2
Domain-0                          0    553     8      r-----   7044.0
```

The xm list output shows the name of the domain, the domain ID, the number of VCPUs currently allocated, and the total run time. The state shows the current state of the domain, which in normal operations will be either r for running or b for blocked. The blocked state signifies a wait state, such as for an I/O interrupt, or more often, for a sleep state for an idle domain. Dom0 should always be in a running state because this will be the domain from which the xm list command is run. The other states of p for paused, c for crashed, and d for dying correspond to unavailable domains. These might be unavailable for a couple reasons. First, they might be unavailable in response to xm commands such as xm pause or xm destroy for paused and dying, respectively. Second, they might be unavailable due to an unplanned stoppage, in the case of a crash.

More detailed information, such as the domain configuration parameters, can be shown for the running domains. You do this by displaying the list in long format with the command xm list -l, as shown in the following example:

```
[root@londonvs1 ~]# xm list -l | more
(domain
    (domid 1)
    (on_crash restart)
    (uuid 6b0723e6-b2f0-4b29-a37c-1e9115798548)
    (bootloader_args -q)
    (vcpus 1)
    (name 12_london1)
    (on_poweroff destroy)
    (on_reboot restart)
    (cpus (()))
    (bootloader /usr/bin/pygrub)
    (maxmem 1024)
    (memory 1024)
    (shadow_memory 0)
    (features )
    (on_xend_start ignore)
    (on_xend_stop ignore)
    (start_time 1260894910.44)
```

```
    (cpu_time 0.626292588)
    (online_vcpus 1)
...
```

For information about the Oracle VM Server itself as opposed to the running domains, the command xm info displays information such as the processor and memory configuration of the host:

```
[root@londonvs1 ~]# xm info
host                     : londonvs1
release                  : 2.6.18-128.2.1.4.9.el5xen
version                  : #1 SMP Fri Oct 9 14:57:31 EDT 2009
machine                  : i686
nr_cpus                  : 8
nr_nodes                 : 1
cores_per_socket         : 4
threads_per_core         : 1
cpu_mhz                  : 2660
hw_caps                  :
bfebfbff:20100800:00000000:00000140:0004e3bd:00000000:00000001:00000000
virt_caps                : hvm
total_memory             : 16378
free_memory              : 13579
node_to_cpu              : node0:0-7
node_to_memory           : node0:13579
xen_major                : 3
xen_minor                : 4
xen_extra                : .0
xen_caps                 : xen-3.0-x86_64 xen-3.0-x86_32p hvm-3.0-x86_32
hvm-3.0-x86_32p hvm-3.0-x86_64
xen_scheduler            : credit
xen_pagesize             : 4096
...
```

The xm dmesg command is the primary resource for information about the Xen boot information. The command shows the version of Xen, which can be useful for cross-referencing whether known Xen features are supported in a particular version of Oracle VM:

```
[root@londonvs1 ~]# xm dmesg
```

```
(XEN) Xen version 3.4.0 (root@us.oracle.com) (gcc version 4.1.2 20080704 (Red Hat 4.1.2-46))
Fri Oct  2 12:01:40 EDT 2009
(XEN) Latest ChangeSet: unavailable
(XEN) Command line: dom0_mem=553M
...
```

You can use `xm dmesg` to learn additional information about the configuration. For example, you can use it to get detailed processor information, including feedback on whether hardware virtualization is enabled:

```
(XEN) HVM: VMX enabled
```

You can also use to determine the scheduler being used:

```
(XEN) Using scheduler: SMP Credit Scheduler (credit)
```

For performance details, you can use either the `xm top` or `xentop` command to display runtime information on the domains, including the resources they are using for processor, memory, network, and block devices. The information is displayed in a format similar to what you see with the command top when it is run in a native Linux environment:

```
xentop - 17:32:47   Xen 3.4.0
3 domains: 1 running, 2 blocked, 0 paused, 0 crashed, 0 dying, 0 shutdown
Mem: 16771152k total, 2865872k used, 13905280k free    CPUs: 8 @ 2660MHz
      NAME   STATE  CPU(sec) CPU(%)    MEM(k) MEM(%)  MAXMEM(k) MAXMEM(%) VCPUS NETS NETTX(k)
NETRX(k) VBDS   VBD_OO   VBD_RD   VBD_WR SSID
12_london1 --b---         0    0.0   1048576    6.3    1048576
   6.3    1    2        0     5708      4         0         0        72    0
30_london2 --b---         0    0.0   1048576    6.3    1048576
   6.3    1    2        2      345      1         0         4       143    0
   Domain-0 -----r      7061    6.8    566272    3.4   no limit
   n/a    8    0        0        0      0         0         0
0    0

  Delay  Networks  vBds  VCPUs  Repeat header  Sort order  Quit
```

You can use the `xm console` command to connect to the console of a running domain. For example, you can combine this command with the argument of the domain id from `xm list` to connect to the console of that VM directly from the command line:

```
root@londonvs1 ~]# xm console 2

Enterprise Linux Enterprise Linux Server release 5.3 (Carthage)
Kernel 2.6.18-128.0.0.0.2.el5xen on an x86_64

London1 login: root
Password:
[root@london1 ~]#
```

Managing Domains

Working from under /OVS/running_pool/, you can start, stop, pause, and migrate domains. If the Xenstore is unaware of a domain, you need to run the `xm create` command with the configuration file as an argument to both import the configuration and start it running:

```
[root@londonvs1 12_london1]# xm create ./vm.cfg
Using config file "././vm.cfg".
Started domain 12_london1 (id=3)
```

Similarly, a domain can be destroyed, as in the following example:

```
[root@londonvs1 12_london1]# xm destroy 12_london1
```

Under the default Oracle VM Server configuration, before you can start a domain (as opposed to creating one), you must import it. For example, attempting to start a domain shows that the Xen is not aware of the configuration:

```
[root@londonvs1 12_london1]# xm start 12_london1
Error: Domain '12_london1' does not exist.
```

The command xm new imports the configuration and stores the persistent configuration under the directory /var/lib/xend/domains. For example, importing the configuration file of the domain london1 creates the persistent configuration information for this domain. Doing so also enables the domain to be started by name:

```
[root@londonvs1 12_london1]# xm new ./vm.cfg
Using config file "././vm.cfg".
[root@londonvs1 12_london1]# xm start 12_london1
```

The corresponding command to delete this configuration is xm delete. However, deletion can only take place once a domain has been halted. Graceful shutdowns and reboots of guest operating systems in domains can be achieved with xm shutdown and xm reboot, as opposed to destroying the underlying domain. A domain can be paused and resumed in a live state using xm pause and xm unpause. That said, the domain continues to hold its existing configuration in memory, even while paused:

```
[root@londonvs1 12_london1]# xm pause 12_london1
[root@londonvs1 12_london1]# xm list 12_london1
Name              ID   Mem VCPUs     State   Time(s)
12_london1         4  1024     1     --p---      7.7
[root@londonvs1 12_london1]# xm unpause 12_london1
```

Similar commands are xm save and xm restore. However, in this case the configuration is saved to storage, and it no longer consumes memory resources. It is also possible to migrate domains between Oracle VM Server at the command line using the xm migrate command. Before doing so, you should enable the following settings in xend-config.sxp:

```
(xend-relocation-server yes)
(xend-relocation-port 8002)
(xend-relocation-hosts-allow '')
```

By default, a migration will pause the domain, relocate, and then unpause the domain. However, with the --live argument, the migration will stream memory pages across the network and complete the migration without an interruption to service. Note that it is crucial that this migration not be performed when a RAC instance is operational. Also, the database instance, respective ASM instance, and clusterware should be shutdown before migration takes place. Doing so will help you prevent an

Oracle RAC cluster node eviction. Assuming it is safe to do so, the following command initiates live migration for a domain:

```
[root@londonvs1 ~]# xm migrate 30_london2 londonvs2 --live
```

The service continues to operate on the original server while the domain is in a blocked and paused state on the target server:

```
[root@londonvs1 ~]# xm list
Name                         ID   Mem VCPUs     State   Time(s)
12_london1                    5  1024     1     -b----      0.5
Domain-0                      0   553     8     r-----   7172.0
migrating-30_london2          6  1024     1     -b----      0.0
```

Managing Resources

As discussed previously in this chapter, the scheduler is important in an Oracle VM environment because Dom0 is subject to the same scheduling as the other guest domains. However, Dom0 is also responsible for servicing physical I/O requests, which means careful management of scheduling can ensure optimal levels of throughput across all domains. Management of the scheduler should be considered in association with the other xm commands for managing CPU resources; namely, xm vcpu-list, xm vcpu-set and xm vcpu-pin. The first of these commands details the number of virtual CPUs configured on the system, and the following listing shows a system with a default configuration of Dom0 running on a system with eight physical processor cores:

```
root@londonvs1 ~]# xm vcpu-list
Name                  ID   VCPU   CPU State   Time(s) CPU Affinity
Domain-0               0      0     6  r--     1576.7 any cpu
Domain-0               0      1     7  -b-      438.6 any cpu
Domain-0               0      2     6  -b-      481.5 any cpu
Domain-0               0      3     0  -b-      217.9 any cpu
Domain-0               0      4     1  -b-      137.6 any cpu
Domain-0               0      5     5  -b-      152.3 any cpu
Domain-0               0      6     0  -b-      164.6 any cpu
Domain-0               0      7     3  -b-      102.1 any cpu
12_london1             2      0     4  -b-       36.9 any cpu
12_london1             2      1     3  -b-       23.9 any cpu
30_london2             4      0     1  -b-        5.1 any cpu
30_london2             4      1     6  -b-        5.0 any cpu
```

The second of the xm commands to modify processor resources, xm vcpu-set, lets you increase or reduce the number of VCPUs assigned to a domain. The following example decreases the number of virtual CPUs for a domain from the original setting of 2 to 1. The second VCPU displays a paused state and is unallocated to any processor:

```
[root@londonvs1 ~]# xm vcpu-set 12_london1 1
[root@londonvs1 ~]# xm vcpu-list 12_london1
Name                  ID   VCPU   CPU State   Time(s) CPU Affinity
12_london1             2      0     0  -b-       60.7 any cpu
12_london1             2      1     -  --p       31.9 any cpu
```

The number of VCPUs can be increased, although the number cannot be increased beyond the original setting when the domain was started:

```
[root@londonvs1 ~]# xm vcpu-set 12_london1 2
[root@londonvs1 ~]# xm vcpu-list 12_london1
Name                              ID  VCPU   CPU State   Time(s) CPU Affinity
12_london1                         2    0     4  -b-      61.7 any cpu
12_london1                         2    1     0  -b-      31.9 any cpu
```

As you have already seen, the VCPUs do not by default correspond directly to a physical core. This is illustrated by the section CPU Affinity, which shows that the VCPUs can run on any cpu. To set CPU affinity, the command xm vcpu-pin can be used. This command is of particular importance because it is the approved method for implementing hard partitioning for the purposes of Oracle Database licensing. Specifically, CPUs are pinned to particular guest domains and licensed accordingly; this is in contrast to licensing all of the CPUs physically installed in the server. You can use xm vcpu-pin in combination with the arguments for the domain to pin CPUs in, the VCPU to pin, and the physical CPU to pin it to. This command makes it possible to set up such a configuration, where you dedicate cores to a particular environment. For example, the following listing shows VCPU 1 being pinned to physical CPU 1 for a domain:

```
[root@londonvs1 ~]# xm vcpu-pin 12_london1 1 1
[root@londonvs1 ~]# xm vcpu-list 12_london1
Name                              ID  VCPU   CPU State   Time(s) CPU Affinity
12_london1                         2    0     3  -b-      73.1 any cpu
12_london1                         2    1     1  -b-      38.8 1
```

The same configuration can also be set in the vm.cfg configuration file at the time a domain starts. For example, the following configuration gives the domain two VCPUs pinned to physical cores 1 and 2:

```
vcpus=2
cpus=[1,2]
```

The VCPU listing displays the CPU affinity. It is important to note that the pinning is assigned across the cores and not on a 1 to 1 basis. Therefore, the listing in this case could show both of the VCPUs running on physical core 1, physical core 2, or on either of the cores, as in this example:

```
[root@londonvs1 12_london1]# xm vcpu-list 12_london1
Name                              ID  VCPU   CPU State   Time(s) CPU Affinity
12_london1                         5    0     1  -b-       2.4 1-2
12_london1                         5    1     1  -b-       3.1 1-2
[root@londonvs1 12_london1]# xm vcpu-list 12_london1
Name                              ID  VCPU   CPU State   Time(s) CPU Affinity
12_london1                         5    0     1  r--       5.2 1-2
12_london1                         5    1     2  r--       5.7 1-2
[root@londonvs1 12_london1]# xm vcpu-list 12_london1
Name                              ID  VCPU   CPU State   Time(s) CPU Affinity
12_london1                         5    0     2  -b-       5.7 1-2
12_london1                         5    1     1  -b-       6.5 1-2
```

It is important to note that that number of CPUs based on the physical core count starts at 0. For example, CPUs 0-7 will be available in an eight core system. In these examples, physical CPU 0 has been reserved for Dom0. In practice, the number of physical CPU cores to assign to Dom0 will depend on the system configuration and the processors in question. For example, as I/O demands increase, increased resources are assigned to Dom0 to ensure optimal throughput. For a RAC configuration, one or two physical cores assigned to Dom0 should be sufficient. However, I/O demands that exceed the throughput demands of a single 4Gbit Fibre Channel HBA may require more CPU resources for Dom0. Only load testing a particular environment can help you determine exactly the right settings.

Coupled with the pinning of CPUs, the command xm sched-credit is also available to fine-tune CPU resource allocation between domains. If run without arguments, the command shows the current configuration:

```
[root@londonvs1 ~]# xm sched-credit
Name                        ID Weight  Cap
Domain-0                     0    256    0
12_london1                   5    256    0
30_london2                   4    256    0
```

The output in the preceding example shows that each domain is assigned a weight and a cap value. By default, a weight of 256 and a cap value of 0 is assigned to each domain. The weight is relative, and it determines the number of CPU cycles a domain will receive. For example, a weight of 256 will proportionally receive twice as cycles as a domain with a weight of 128; in a similar vein, it would receive half as many cycles as a domain with a weight of 512. The cap value is given in percentage terms, and it defines the maximum percentage of CPU cycles that a domain may consume from a physical processor. The default value of 0 means that no cap is set for the domain. The percentage value is for a single given processor core on the system; therefore, it can exceed 100, which would cap the limit above the resources provided by just one core. You can display the weight and cap for a particular domain, as in this example:

```
[root@londonvs1 ~]# xm sched-credit -d 12_london1
Name                        ID Weight  Cap
12_london1                   5    512    0
```

You increase the weight of a domain relative to other domains like this:

```
[root@londonvs1 ~]# xm sched-credit -d 12_london1 -w 512
[root@londonvs1 ~]# xm sched-credit -d 12_london1
Name                        ID Weight  Cap
12_london1                   5    512    0
```

Similarly, the -c argument is used to modify the cap.

As discussed previously in this chapter, memory can be dynamically allocated to domains with the balloon memory management driver. The interface to this method is provided by the xm mem-set command. This command requires two arguments for the domain: the first modifies the memory allocation, while the second modifies the amount of memory, given in megabytes. In this example, the guest is allocated 4GB of memory when logged into the guest domain as root:

```
[root@london1 ~]# free
              total      used       free     shared    buffers     cached
Mem:        4096000   3219304     876696          0      65004    2299532
-/+ buffers/cache:     854768    3241232
Swap:       3047416         0    3047416
```

This example reduces the memory:

```
[root@london1 ~]# xm mem-set 12_london1 3500
[root@london1 ~]# xm list
Name                                   ID    Mem VCPUs      State   Time(s)
Domain-0                                0    834     8      r-----  3299.2
12_london1                              5   3500     2      -b----    63.1
30_london2                              4   4000     2      -b----    16.0
```

In this result, you can see that the impact is immediately registered in the guest environment:

```
[root@london1 ~]# free
             total       used       free     shared    buffers     cached
Mem:       3584000    3219552     364448          0      65004    2299676
-/+ buffers/cache:     854872    2729128
Swap:      3047416          0    3047416
```

The corresponding values in the vm.cfg file are maxmem and memory; the following values set these parameters to 6GB and 4GB, respectively:

```
maxmem = 6000
memory = 4000
```

Note that both of these values are dynamic, and they can be used conjunctively to vary the memory assigned to a domain beyond the original settings:

```
[root@londonvs1 ~]# xm mem-max 12_london1 8000
[root@londonvs1 ~]# xm mem-set 12_london1 6500
[root@londonvs1 ~]# xm list
Name                                   ID    Mem VCPUs      State   Time(s)
Domain-0                                0    834     8      r-----  3300.9
12_london1                              5   6500     2      -b----    77.4
30_london2                              4   4000     2      -b----    16.5
```

Summary

In this chapter, we have looked at the new possibilities presented by RAC when complemented with Oracle VM's virtualization. We began by covering the important concepts and reviewing the design considerations. Next, we looked at Oracle VM and the guest installation, and then at how to handle configuration for RAC guests, with a focus on enabling high availability at the virtualization layer. Finally, we detailed some of the options available for managing an Oracle VM virtualized environment.

CHAPTER 6

■ ■ ■

Linux Installation and Configuration

This chapter describes the steps required to install and configure the Linux software operating system for the Oracle Database 11*g* Release 2 RAC. As mentioned in Chapter 1, the emphasis in this book is on the Oracle Enterprise Linux distribution because the installable CD and DVD images are freely available for download and fully redistributable without cost. This combination makes Oracle Enterprise Linux the most accessible Linux operating system release supported in a RAC configuration.

As noted in Chapter 1, the differences between Oracle Enterprise Linux and Red Hat Enterprise Linux are marginal; therefore, the installation and configuration details are all directly applicable to a Red Hat Installation. Oracle Enterprise Linux provides the option of installing an Oracle modified kernel instead of the default Red Hat Kernel, with additional bug fixes by Oracle. However, we recommend reviewing the release notes to observe how applicable these fixes are to your environment before moving from the default kernel common to both the Red Hat and Oracle Enterprise Linux releases. Note that this focus on Oracle Enterprise Linux is not intended to exhibit a preference for ease of installation, use, or suitability for Oracle over the alternative supported releases of SUSE Linux Enterprise Server or Asianux, each of which may be more applicable in a particular environment. For example, there might be better choices than Oracle Enterprise Linux in cases where one of the aforementioned Linux releases has been adopted across the data center for hosting non-Oracle software applications.

The installation process is covered for the standard hardware platforms supported by Oracle Enterprise Linux and the Oracle Database 11*g* Release 2 RAC —namely x86 andx86-64.. The installation steps described in this chapter should be performed identically on each node in the cluster.

Selecting the Right Linux Software

In Chapter 4, we discussed software availability on the Certification Matrices page of Oracle's web site in the context of hardware platforms. The certification site also details the supported Linux releases at the granularity of the selected architecture, as shown for example in Table 6-1.

Table 6-1. Supported Oracle Enterprise Linux Releases for x86 and x86-64

Operating System	Products	Certified With	Version	Status
Oracle Enterprise Linux 5	11gR2	Oracle Clusterware	11*g*	Certified
Oracle Enterprise Linux 4	11gR2	Oracle Clusterware	11*g*	Certified

In Oracle Database 11*g*, all versions of the supported Linux releases are based on the 2.6 kernel with the performance and scalability benefits that this brings. Thousands of users can be handled reliably, and larger amounts of memory can be supported. Up to 64GB of memory is supported on 32-bit, x86 systems; however, on Oracle Enterprise Linux, the Hugemem kernel is required for this support.

■ **Note** The Hugemem kernel is not available on Oracle Enterprise Linux 5, and the standard SMP kernel on x86 supports up to 16GB of memory only.

On x86-64 from the Oracle Enterprise Linux 5.3 release and later, the certified maximum memory is 1TB, and the number of supported CPUs is 255.

In the first edition of this book, which focused on Oracle Database 10*g*, we detailed the installation and configuration of Red Hat Enterprise Linux 4 AS. For that reason, this edition focuses on the more recent supported version of Oracle Enterprise Linux Release 5. You should also pay particular attention to the requirements of your chosen hardware platform and its support for a particular processor or chipset.

Reviewing the Hardware Requirements

Oracle publishes a minimum set of hardware requirements for each server (see Table 6-2). Obviously, the minimum requirements must be met in order to install and configure a working Oracle database; and production environments should adhere to at least the recommended values. We strongly recommend that every node of the cluster have an identical hardware configuration, although this is not strictly mandatory, except for the CPU architecture type. The client display resolution requirements are for the system on which the Oracle Universal Installer (OUI) is displayed. You set these in the DISPLAY environment variable; therefore, the display resolution requirements do not apply to the cluster nodes themselves.

Table 6-2. Minimum and Recommended Server Requirements

Hardware	Minimum	Recommended
CPU	1 certified CPU per node	2 or more certified CPUs per node
CPU Architecture	Same on all nodes	--
Interconnect network	100Mb	Teamed 1Gb or 10Gb
External network	100Mb	1Gb or 10Gb
Backup network	100Mb	1Gb or 10Gb

Hardware	Minimum	Recommended
HBA or NIC for SAN	1Gb HBA	Dual-pathed storage vendor certified HBA iSCSI or NAS
Memory	1.5GB per node	2GB per CPU
Swap space	Between equivalent to RAM and 1.5 times RAM up to 16GB dependent on	Equivalent to RAM configured RAM size
Grid software space	4.5GB	10GB
Database software space	4GB	10GB
Temporary disk space	1GB	
Client Display Resolution	1024 x 786	--

Drilling Down on Networking Requirements

Before installing the Linux software on each node in the cluster, it is essential to fully plan and specify the network configuration and to prepare a DNS server. Depending on your requirements, you may also want a DHCP server. The planning and advance configuration requirements are determined by whether you choose to use the Oracle Grid Naming Service (GNS) or a manual IP configuration. If you have not yet selected an IP configuration scheme, then we strongly recommend that you review the concepts of GNS detailed in Chapter 2. You will need to make a choice at this point in time because the IP naming configuration required for both the network and on the operating system of the cluster nodes differs for each scheme.

Configuring a GNS or a Manual IP

Whether you're using GNS or a manual IP configuration, the availability of DNS is required to support the cluster configuration; we cover how to configure DNS to support each scheme later in this section. If using GNS, a DHCP server configuration is also required; we will also cover how to do this later in this section. As introduced in Chapter 2, GNS is an implementation of Apple's Bonjour software, the Zero Configuration Networking Standard, or Zeroconf. Avahi is similar free software that is available on Linux. However, the installation of any additional Zeroconf software is not required. GNS provides a Zeroconf service for the nodes in the cluster. It implements a system of multicast DNS to provide both the Virtual host names and IP addresses (VIP) dynamically in response to a changing cluster configuration. As a consequence, when using GNS, the requirements for the network configuration are to provide a DNS configuration and to delegate a subdomain within this configuration, so it can be managed by GNS. An additional requirement is to provide a DHCP server on the cluster subnet, from which GNS can allocate IP Addresses. The allocation of virtual names and addresses is managed by GNS when using Zeroconf, so it is important not to configure these names and addresses. Nor can you configure the Single Client Access Name (SCAN) statically, either in DNS or in the /etc/hosts file on the nodes in the cluster. DHCP is not a requirement for a manual IP configuration. However, DNS is a requirement for a manual IP configuration because it lets you resolve multiple IP addresses to the SCAN without using GNS. A manual IP configuration differs from GNS in that both the physical and virtual node names and IP addresses must be configured in both DNS and the /etc/hosts file on the cluster nodes; SCAN, on the other hand, should be configured in DNS only.

Whichever scheme you choose, we suggest that you follow a standards-driven logical naming convention that is easy to remember. If you're using a single public network, you should ensure that all public IP addresses and VIP addresses are unique within that network and located on the same subnet. If multiple public networks are required, then these may be configured and identified within the Oracle database after the Oracle software installation with the init.ora parameter, listener_networks. Note that Internet Protocol Version 6 (IPv6) is not supported with Oracle 11g Release 2 for either RAC or Clusterware. Therefore, the focus in this chapter is entirely on the standard IP addressing of IPv4. Also, IPv6 should be disabled on all hosts. Table 6-3 shows a sample network checklist for a two-node cluster with a GNS configuration.

Table 6-3. Sample GNS Network Configuration

Network Configuration	Example
DNS domain name	example.com
DNS host name	dns1.example.com
DNS server address	172.17.1.1
DHCP server address	172.17.1.1
DHCP address range	172.17.1.201 to 220
GNS sub domain	grid1.example.com
GNS host name	cluster1-gns.grid1.example.com
GNS VIP address	172.17.1.200
Cluster name	cluster1
SCAN name	cluster1-scan.grid1.example.com
SCAN addresses	Assigned by DHCP
Public Network	172.17.1.0
Public Gateway	172.17.1.254
Public Broadcast	172.17.255.255

Network Configuration	Example
Public Subnet Mask	255.255.0.0
Public Node names	london1, london2
Public IP addresses	172.17.1.101, 172.17.1.102
VIP names	Automatically assigned
VIP addresses	Assigned by DHCP
Private Network	192.168.1.0
Private Subnet Mask	255.255.255.0
Private Nodes names	london1-priv, london2-priv
Private IP addresses	192.168.1.1, 192.168.1.2
IPMI addresses	Assigned by DHCP

In a similar vein, Table 6-4 shows a sample network checklist for a two-node cluster with a manual IP configuration.

Table 6-4. Sample Manual Network Configuration

Network Configuration	Example
DNS domain name	example.com
DNS host name	dns1.example.com
DNS server address	172.17.1.1
DHCP server address	Not required
DHCP address range	Not required
GNS sub domain	Not required
GNS host name	Not required
GNS VIP address	Not required

Network Configuration	Example
Cluster name	cluster1
SCN name	cluster1-scan.example.com
SCAN addresses	172.17.1.205, 172.17.1.206, 172.17.1.207
Public Network	172.17.1.0
Public Gateway	172.17.1.254
Public Broadcast	172.17.255.255
Public Subnet Mask	255.255.0.0
Public Node names	london1, london2
Public IP addresses	172.17.1.101, 172.17.1.102
VIP names	london1-vip, london2-vip
VIP addresses	172.17.1.201, 172.17.1.202
Private Network	192.168.1.0
Private Subnet Mask	255.255.255.0
Private Nodes names	london1-priv, london2-priv
Private IP addresses	192.168.1.1, 192.168.1.2
IPMI addresses	172.17.1.10, 172.17.1.20

Configuring DNS and DHCP

As noted when we covered the networking requirements, a DNS server is a mandatory requirement, whether you're using Oracle GNS or a manual network configuration. Configuration of a fully redundant enterprise class DNS system is beyond the scope of this book, so we recommend the book *Pro DNS and Bind 10* (Apress, 2010) by Ron Aitchison if you are contemplating the installation of a full DNS configuration. But given that DNS is mandatory for proceeding with the installation of Oracle 11*g* Release 2 RAC, we deem it necessary to detail the Linux configuration of an authoritative-only Name Server. Such a server provides the minimum DNS configuration for the successfully installing and operating Oracle 11*g* Release 2 RAC in a standalone manner. *Pro DNS and Bind* provides all the information required for incorporation into a more extensive DNS System.

Before installing the DNS software, you should be aware that the DNS server should be a separate server from any of the nodes of the Oracle RAC cluster. This helps ensure that node names and IP addresses can still be resolved, irrespective of the availability of any individual node. Advanced configurations will also provide for the high availability of the DNS software. The separate server may be a physical server or a virtual server configured under Oracle VM, and the Linux software installation will either be based on an Oracle VM template or follow the approach described later in this chapter. Note that the latter approach will have no additional requirements for configuring the Oracle user, preparing for the installation of the Oracle software, or configuring the external storage. As explained in Chapter 5, an Oracle VM-based installation can provide the additional benefit of letting you base the operating system for the Name Server in a high availability environment.

In the following example, we have configured an Oracle VM-based virtual server as the DNS server dns1.example.com with the IP address 172.17.1.1. On the DNS Server, networking is enabled by default in the file /etc/sysconfig/network, and the hostname is given as the full host and domain name, as in this example:

```
[root@dns1 sysconfig]# cat network
NETWORKING=yes
NETWORKING_IPV6=no
HOSTNAME=dns1.example.com
```

The hostname and IP address of the DNS server is also configured in the /etc/hosts file:

```
[root@dns1 sysconfig]# more /etc/hosts
127.0.0.1       localhost.localdomain    localhost
172.17.1.1      dns1.example.com dns1
```

By default, the DNS Server software will not have been installed on the Linux operating system for the installation detailed in this chapter or for an Oracle VM template. Our focus here is on the standard DNS software deployed on Linux, Berkeley Internet Name Domain (BIND). BIND is installed as an RPM package from the install media, as in this example:

```
[root@dns1 ~]# rpm -ivh bind-9.3.4-10.P1.el5.x86_64.rpm
Preparing...               ########################################### [100%]
   1:bind                  ########################################### [100%]
```

After installation, the named service is installed, but not yet running, and you will get the following status message:

```
[root@dns1 ~]# service named status
rndc: connect failed: 127.0.0.1#953: connection refused
named is stopped
```

Before starting the service, it is necessary to provide the DNS configuration for your domain. The configuration provided is for an authoritative-only Name Server for the example.com domain, which can be used in a standalone environment. The top level of the configuration is set in the file /etc/named.conf, and this file specifies the names of the four required zone files for the forward and reverse look-ups of the example.com and localhost domains. The following example shows the /etc/named.conf file:

```
[root@dns1 ~]# cat /etc/named.conf
options
{
```

```
directory "/var/named";
};
zone "example.com" {
type master;
file "master.example.com";
        };
zone "localhost" {
type master;
file "master.localhost";
        };
zone  "1.17.172.in-addr.arpa" {
type master;
file  "172.17.1.rev";
};
zone "0.0.127.in-addr.arpa" {
type master;
file "localhost.rev";
};
```

Forward lookups for the example.com domain are configured in the file master.example.com, which is typically located in the directory defined in /etc/named.comf. In this example, it is called /var/named. This file details the mapping of names to IP addresses for the DNS name server itself, as well as the fixed IP address for the cluster hosts. However, additional lines can be added to resolve names to addresses for additional hosts in the domain. Also, in this case, the file provides the configuration for a subdomain to be allocated to and managed by Oracle GNS. The name server for the subdomain can be named however you wish. However, you must configure the glue record to correspond to the IP address on which the GNS service will be running after the Grid Infrastructure software installation. In this iteration of the master.example.com file, the GNS server IP Address is 172.17.1.200:

```
[root@dns1 named]# more master.example.com
$TTL    86400
@               IN SOA          dns1.example.com. root.localhost (
                                2010063000      ; serial
                                28800           ; refresh
                                14400           ; retry
                                3600000         ; expiry
                                86400 )         ; minimum
@               IN NS           dns1.example.com.
localhost       IN A            127.0.0.1
dns1            IN A            172.17.1.1
london1         IN A            172.17.1.101
london2         IN A            172.17.1.102
$ORIGIN grid1.example.com.
@               IN NS           cluster1-gns.grid1.example.com.
                IN NS           dns1.example.com.
cluster1-gns    IN A            172.17.1.200; glue record
```

For a manual IP configuration, the GNS subdomain configuration is not provided. Instead, the name to address mappings for the Public VIP addresses are required, as well as from one to three IP addresses for the SCAN name. The multiple IP addresses are returned in a round-robin manner to lookups. Note that in a manual configuration, the Public and Private IP addresses, as well as the Public

VIP addresses, must also be included in the /etc/hosts file on the cluster hosts. However, the SCAN name should only be included in the DNS configuration; the master.example.com file is configured as follows:

```
$TTL    86400
@                IN SOA      dns1.example.com. root.localhost (
                            2010063000      ; serial
                            28800           ; refresh
                            14400           ; retry
                            3600000         ; expiry
                            86400 )         ; minimum
@                IN NS       dns1.example.com.
localhost        IN A        127.0.0.1
dns1             IN A        172.17.1.1
london1          IN A        172.17.1.101
london2          IN A        172.17.1.102
london1-vip      IN A        172.17.1.201
london2-vip      IN A        172.17.1.202
cluster1-scan    IN A        172.17.1.205
                 IN A        172.17.1.206
                 IN A        172.17.1.207
```

If you are planning to perform a typical Grid Infrastructure software installation, only a manual IP configuration is available. In this case, the name of the cluster is the SCAN name, minus the domain name extension. For this reason, the SCAN name must consist of alphanumeric characters and hyphens, not be longer than 15 characters in length, and be resolved from within the DNS domain. In this example, the SCAN name for a typical installation would instead be cluster1 and fully resolved as cluster1.example.com. This restriction does not apply to an advanced installation, where the SCAN name may exceed 15 characters in length such as used here cluster1-scan. For a manual IP configuration the name is fully resolved as cluster1-scan.example.com and for GNS as cluster1-scan.grid1.example.com.

Reverse lookups are configured in the file 172.17.1.rev to provide the corresponding mappings from IP address to domain names. If you're using a manual configuration, the additional Public VIP and Manual IP addresses should also be included, as shown in the following example:

```
[root@dns1 named]# cat 172.17.1.rev
$TTL    86400
@                IN SOA      dns1.example.com. root.localhost.  (
                            2010063000      ; serial
                            28800           ; refresh
                            14400           ; retry
                            3600000         ; expiry
                            86400 )         ; minimum
@                IN NS       dns1.example.com.
1                IN PTR      dns1.example.com.
101              IN PTR      london1.example.com.
102              IN PTR      london2.example.com.
201              IN PTR      london1-vip.example.com.
202              IN PTR      london2-vip.example.com.
```

A similar configuration file is required for the local domain in the master.localhost file:

```
[root@dns1 named]# cat master.localhost
$TTL    86400
@               IN SOA  @       root (
                                2010063000      ; serial
                                28800           ; refresh
                                14400           ; retry
                                3600000         ; expiry
                                86400 )         ; minimum
                IN NS           @
                IN A            127.0.0.1
```

You must also have a zone file, such as the following example of localhost.rev, that details the reverse lookups for the local domain:

```
[root@dns1 named]# cat localhost.rev
$TTL    86400
@               IN SOA          localhost. root.localhost.  (
                                2010063000      ; serial
                                28800           ; refresh
                                14400           ; retry
                                3600000         ; expiry
                                86400 )         ; minimum
                IN NS           localhost.
1               IN PTR          localhost.
```

To direct lookups for the correct domain and Name Server, the file /etc/resolv.conf should be configured both on the Name Server and on all hosts that require name and IP addresses to be resolved by DNS. In cases where GNS will be configured, the search path should also include the GNS subdomain, as shown here:

```
[root@dns1 named]# cat /etc/resolv.conf
search example.com grid1.example.com
nameserver 172.17.1.1
options attempts: 2
options timeout: 1
```

If the iptables service is enabled, external hosts will not be able to connect to the DNS server. Therefore, you must either update the rules to permit access to the default port of 53 or stop the iptables service, as shown in this example (which approach you take will depend on your security requirements):

```
[root@dns1 ~]# chkconfig iptables off
[root@dns1 ~]# service iptables stop
Flushing firewall rules:                            [  OK  ]
Setting chains to policy ACCEPT: filter             [  OK  ]
Unloading iptables modules:                         [  OK  ]
```

Finally, the named service can be started; this will allow it to begin accepting name and IP address resolution requests for the configured domain:

```
[root@dns1 named]# service named start
Starting named:                                    [  OK  ]
```

The configuration should be verified for forward and reverse name lookups on the DNS server host, as well as for external hosts on the network within the subnet of the configured domain. The following example shows a forward name lookup:

```
[root@dns1 named]# nslookup london1
Server:         127.0.0.1
Address:        127.0.0.1#53

Name:   london1.example.com
Address: 172.17.1.101
```

And the next example shows a reverse name lookup:

```
 [root@dns1 named]# nslookup 172.17.1.101
Server:         127.0.0.1
Address:        127.0.0.1#53

101.1.17.172.in-addr.arpa        name = london1.example.com.
```

If you're planning to use a manual IP configuration, the SCAN names will resolve to the multiple allocated IP addresses at this point. For example, using the ping command to check connectivity will use each given SCAN IP address in turn. However, if using GNS, queries for the SCAN name within the subdomain are forwarded to the GNS service. For this reason, queries for names within the subdomain will only be successful after the Grid Infrastructure software has been installed. Thus we recommend verifying your DNS configuration after the installing the Grid Infrastructure software to ensure that your subdomain delegation has been successfully configured and that GNS is responding to queries, as in this example:

```
[root@london1 ~]# nslookup cluster1-scan
Server:         172.17.1.1
Address:        172.17.1.1#53

Non-authoritative answer:
Name:   cluster1-scan.grid1.example.com
Address: 172.17.1.207
Name:   cluster1-scan.grid1.example.com
Address: 172.17.1.208
Name:   cluster1-scan.grid1.example.com
Address: 172.17.1.209
```

The preceding example reiterates the point that all names within the subdomain grid1.example.com are resolved by GNS. It also illustrates that all names within the domain example.com are resolved by DNS. If GNS is not configured, then there is no subdomain in the configuration.

You may have noted that, in the manual IP configuration, the Public VIP names and SCAN names are allocated to fixed IP addresses under the DNS configuration. Note these IP addresses have not previously been defined if you're using a GNS configuration. It is for this reason that a DHCP server is not required for a manual IP configuration; however, a GNS configuration must provide the VIP and SCAN IP addresses dynamically. Host names are also configured within the subdomain by GNS, and these host names correspond to the allocated DHCP addresses automatically. The DHCP server may be on a separate server or on the same host as the DNS server. In any event, the DHCP server should not be configured on a cluster node. If the DHCP service is not already available, it may be installed as an RPM package from the install media. The DHCP configuration is detailed in the configuration file /etc/dhcp.conf, along with the desired IP address range, as in this example:

```
[root@dns1 ~]# cat /etc/dhcpd.conf
ddns-update-style interim;
ignore client-updates;
        subnet 172.17.0.0 netmask 255.255.0.0 {
        range                       172.17.1.201 172.17.1.220;
        option routers              172.17.1.254;
        option subnet-mask          255.255.0.0;
        option domain-name          "example.com";
        option domain-name-servers  172.17.1.1;
        }
```

The following snippet starts the DHCP service, so it can make the configured IP address range available for lease:

```
[root@dns1 ~]# service dhcpd start
Starting dhcpd:                                    [  OK  ]
```

After the Grid Infrastructure software is installed, you can verify the utilization of the DHCP service and the allocation of the IP addresses in the file /var/lib/dhcpd/dhcpd.leases:

```
[root@dns1 /]# cat ./var/lib/dhcpd/dhcpd.leases
...
lease 172.17.1.210 {
  starts 6 2005/06/11 04:33:14;
  ends 6 2005/06/11 16:33:14;
  tstp 6 2005/06/11 16:33:14;
  binding state free;
  hardware ethernet 00:00:00:00:00:00;
  uid "\000london1-vip";
}
lease 172.17.1.208 {
  starts 6 2005/06/11 04:33:29;
  ends 6 2005/06/11 16:33:29;
  binding state active;
  next binding state free;
  hardware ethernet 00:00:00:00:00:00;
  uid "\000cluster1-scan2-vip";
}
...
```

Within your leases file, you can also view the automatically assigned GNS host names. With your DNS and DHCP (assuming you're using GNS) services available, you're ready to install and configure the Linux operating system on the cluster nodes themselves.

Downloading the Linux Software

As discussed in the introduction to Chapter 1, Oracle Enterprise Linux can be downloaded and redistributed without cost from http://edelivery.oracle.com/linux. The registration page requires that you enter your name, company name, e-mail address, and country. You must also accept both the agreement terms and export restrictions. After the registration page, the media pack search page enables the selection of a product pack. These options include Enterprise Linux, Oracle VM, and Oracle VM Templates. You can learn more about the installation and configuration of Oracle VM and Oracle VM Templates in Chapter 5. Under Enterprise Linux, the platform menu specifies IA64 for Itanium systems and x86 32-bit and x86 64-bit for x86 and x86-64, respectively.

The timing of releases may be different for the different architectures. At the time of writing, Oracle 11g Release 2 is available for the x86 and x86-64 architectures only. Select Go for the chosen architecture, and then select an operating system release under that architecture. You will note that the Oracle database is certified to the major operating system release. However, you do have the option of selecting a number of Update releases that introduce more recent kernel versions, as well as a number of incremental updates and upgrades beyond the previous operating versions.

The precise details of the changes introduced in each release are detailed in the Oracle Enterprise Linux Release Notes. These are available at Oracle's Free and Open Source Software site at the Oracle Unbreakable Linux Support page (http://oss.oracle.com/oracle-on-linux.html). You can find these notes beneath the Key Resources heading, to the right of the bulleted item that reads *View source code*. For example, all of the Oracle Enterprise Linux Release 5 releases notes are available at this location: http://oss.oracle.com/el5/docs/. Reviewing these release notes will enable you to select the optimal point release for your requirements. It will also help you understand the differences between the Oracle Enterprise Linux release and the upstream Red Hat Enterprise Linux release on which the Oracle Enterprise Linux Release is based. Selecting the appropriate heading for a particular release presents a number of CD ISO images and a single DVD image for download. You must download either all of the CD images or the single DVD image. It is also possible to construct the DVD image from the CD images using a script called mkdvdiso.sh, which is available from http://mirror.centos.org/centos/build/mkdvdiso.sh. In other words, you don't need to download both the CD and DVD images, if both are required. Similarly, a full installation doesn't require that you download the source code for both the CD or DVD images. If you wish to either install from alternative media or run the Oracle Validated RPM as discussed later in this chapter, then we recommend downloading or constructing the DVD image for the most flexibility during installation and configuration. If you wish to install from CDs, then you need to follow a couple steps. First, unzip the CD images using an unzip utility (you can find such a handful of utilities at http://updates.oracle.com/unzips/unzips.html). Second, you need to use a DVD or CD writer to burn the correct image or images to DVD-ROM or CD-ROM. To do this, you will need to use a software utility that is capable of writing ISO files, such as cdrecord.

Preparing for a Network Install

To achieve a more rapid installation of a larger number of nodes, you may wish to install the software over a network containing the installation media. Additionally, we recommend using a network installation to configure an environment that makes running the Oracle Validated RPM as straightforward as possible. You'll learn how to do this later in this chapter.

To prepare for a network installation, it is still necessary to create either a bootable CD-ROM or USB flash drive to initiate the installation. A bootable USB flash drive can be created by copying diskboot.img from the /images directory on the first CD-ROM of the install set. Doing so ensures that the destination drive specified is the USB flash drive. For example, the following listing shows a system where the first CD is mounted on /media/cdrom and the flash disk is mounted on /media/usbdisk as device /dev/sdb1:

```
[root@londonmgr1 media]# df -h
Filesystem             Size  Used Avail Use% Mounted on
/dev/hda2               72G   44G   25G  65% /
/dev/hda1              190M   46M  135M  26% /boot
none                   252M     0  252M   0% /dev/shm
/dev/hdc               622M  622M     0 100% /media/cdrom
/dev/sdb1              964M  159M  805M  17% /media/usbdisk
```

Now note the device name of the USB disk, which you can use to unmount the file system:

```
[root@londonmgr1 ~]# umount /media/usbdisk/
```

From the /images directory of the CD-ROM, use the dd command to copy the diskboot.img file to the USB device. The following example shows an invocation of dd:

```
[root@londonmgr1 images]# ls
boot.iso      minstg2.img  README       TRANS.TBL
diskboot.img  pxeboot      stage2.img   xen
[root@londonmgr1 images]# dd if=diskboot.img of=/dev/sdb
24576+0 records in
24576+0 records out
12582912 bytes (13 MB) copied, 3.02538 seconds, 4.2 MB/s
```

Note that you must use the full device name. In the preceding example, /dev/sdb must be used and not a partition name, such as /dev/sdb1. Otherwise, the master boot record (MBR) will not be correctly written. If this is the case, the USB disk will not be bootable, and the system BIOS will report a message such as Missing Operating System when a system boot from the USB device is attempted. If the USB device has been correctly written, then by default it will run the Anaconda installer in the same mode that is specified when the argument linux askmethod is passed to the boot: installer prompt.

In Text mode, the installer will ask you to choose a language and keyboard type. Next, it will ask you to choose an installation method from the following options: Local CDROM, Hard Drive, NFS Image, FTP, or HTTP. If you're using a USB disk to boot, pressing Next at the first graphical installer screen will raise a warning like this one:

```
/dev/sdf currently has a loop partition layout.
```

This warning relates to the USB disk itself. Therefore, the option Ignore drive should be selected to prevent this drive being formatted. Alternatively, you can specify the nousbstorage option at the boot prompt to prevent this error from being raised, as in this example:

```
linux askmethod nousbstorage
```

You can use a similar approach to implement a bootable installer CD. Do so by creating an ISO image of the full isolinux/ directory from the first CD-ROM using the mkisofs utility. Next, write this image to a CD with a suitable utility, as explained previously.

If a server has been previously installed with Linux, it is also possible to locate the install image on the hard disk of that server and configure the GRUB bootloader to boot the installation image. This enables a managed upgrade of a remote server without using an external USB device or CD-ROM.

After booting the Anaconda installer, it is necessary to host the installation media with one of the methods detailed previously. We will use FTP as an efficient method for transferring files. This approach also makes it straightforward to configure an FTP daemon (such as VSFTP) to present either multiple CD disk images or a single DVD image from a remote server, as in the following example:

```
[root@ftp1 OEL5U4-x86-64]# ls
Enterprise-R5-U4-Server-x86_64-disc1.iso   mkdvdiso.sh
Enterprise-R5-U4-Server-x86_64-disc2.iso   V17795-01.zip
Enterprise-R5-U4-Server-x86_64-disc3.iso   V17796-01.zip
Enterprise-R5-U4-Server-x86_64-disc4.iso   V17797-01.zip
Enterprise-R5-U4-Server-x86_64-disc5.iso   V17798-01.zip
Enterprise-R5-U4-Server-x86_64-disc6.iso   V17799-01.zip
Enterprise-R5-U4-Server-x86_64-dvd.iso     V17800-01.zip
[root@ftp1 OEL5U4-x86-64]# mkdir -p /var/ftp/pub/el5_4_x86_64
[root@ftp1 OEL5U4-x86-64]# mount -o loop Enterprise-R5-U4-Server-x86_64-dvd.iso
/var/ftp/pub/el5_4_x86_64
```

You will be able to view the file listing under the /var/ftp/pub/el5_4_x86_64 directory. Next, it is necessary to configure and start the FTP server. If you're using the VSFTP daemon, the most direct way to do this is to edit the file /etc/vsftpd/vsftpd.conf and enable anonymous FTP with the standard /var/ftp directory as the root directory for anonymous login:

```
# Allow anonymous FTP? (Beware - allowed by default if you comment this out).
anonymous_enable=YES
anon_root=/var/ftp
#
```

There are a number of optional parameters in the vsftpd.conf file that you may also consider using. For example, by default the xferlog_enable parameter records the details of all FTP Server activity in the file /var/log/xferlog. If the local_enable option is set to YES, then you will also be able to locally test the availability of the installation media. Once you have set and reviewed the available options, you can then start the vsftpd service, as shown in this example:

```
[root@ftp1 ~]# service vsftpd start
Starting vsftpd for vsftpd:                    [  OK  ]
```

You can also verify the configuration of the settings with a local FTP login:

```
[root@ftp1 ~]# ftp localhost
Connected to ftp1.
220 (vsFTPd 2.0.1)
530 Please login with USER and PASS.
530 Please login with USER and PASS.
KERBEROS_V4 rejected as an authentication type
Name (localhost:root): anonymous
331 Please specify the password.
Password:
230 Login successful.
Remote system type is UNIX.
Using binary mode to transfer files.
ftp> ls pub/el5_4_x86_64
```

```
227 Entering Passive Mode (127,0,0,1,34,41)
150 Here comes the directory listing.
drwxr-xr-x    3 0        0            2048 Sep 16 14:24 Cluster
drwxr-xr-x    3 0        0            4096 Sep 16 14:24 ClusterStorage
-rw-r--r--    1 0        0            7037 Sep 08 22:54 EULA
-rw-r--r--    1 0        0           18390 Sep 08 22:54 GPL
-rw-r--r--    1 0        0            3957 Sep 08 22:54 README-en
-rw-r--r--    1 0        0            8394 Sep 08 22:54 README-en.html
-rw-r--r--    1 0        0           14639 Sep 08 22:54 RELEASE-NOTES-en
-rw-r--r--    1 0        0           36477 Sep 08 22:54 RELEASE-NOTES-en.html
-rw-r--r--    1 0        0            1397 Sep 08 22:54 RPM-GPG-KEY
-rw-r--r--    1 0        0            1397 Sep 08 22:54 RPM-GPG-KEY-oracle
drwxr-xr-x    4 0        0          489472 Sep 16 14:24 Server
-r--r--r--    1 0        0            4215 Sep 16 14:24 TRANS.TBL
drwxr-xr-x    3 0        0           10240 Sep 16 14:24 VT
-rw-r--r--    1 0        0            5165 Sep 08 22:54 blafdoc.css
-rw-r--r--    1 0        0            7037 Sep 08 22:54 eula.en_US
-rw-r--r--    1 0        0            3334 Sep 08 22:54 eula.py
drwxr-xr-x    4 0        0            2048 Sep 16 14:24 images
drwxr-xr-x    2 0        0            2048 Sep 16 14:24 isolinux
-rw-r--r--    1 0        0             105 Sep 08 22:54 supportinfo
226 Directory send OK.
ftp>
```

You can now boot from the install USB disk or CD and specify the FTP server as the location of the installation media. When using this installation method in Text mode, you are asked to select a preferred network interface to configure and to provide the network details necessary to configure the chosen interface on the server to be installed. If you do not have DHCP available, then select Enable IPv4 support and Manual Configuration. Next, enter your IP address, subnet mask, Gateway, and DNS Server addresses. The installer then requests the name or IP address of the FTP Server and the Enterprise Linux directory, which is /pub/el5_4_x86_64 in this case. The installer then continues in a graphical mode, unless the linux text or linux text askmethod arguments were given to the boot prompt. The installation process can then proceed according to the requirements dictated by an installation that relies on a CD-ROM, which we will cover later in this section. This approach also permits simultaneous installations of multiple nodes in the cluster—without requiring a change of installation media.

The configuration of the FTP server can also now serve as the location for your local YUM repository for running the Oracle Validated RPM after installation; you will learn more about this later in this chapter.

Another installation alternative relies on a combination of the Preboot Execution Environment (PXE) (which must be supported by the BIOS of the target server) and DHCP and TFTP servers. This combination enables the loading of the boot media across the network, but without requiring a bootable USB flash drive or CD-ROM. You can combine this approach with the Linux Kickstart utility to provide the Linux configuration information. It then becomes possible to complete an unattended installation of Oracle Enterprise Linux across the network. Kickstart can also be configured to provide default installation options for the installation methods described previously.

Your preferred installation method will depend on the number and frequency of installations you are required to perform, as well as the location of the servers to be installed. A single installation of two to four nodes in a local environment from CD-ROM or DVD will require a minimal amount of additional configuration. For example, an installation of four or more nodes, an upgrade of servers in a remote location, or a moderate frequency of installations will warrant some additional configuration for an installation method such as FTP. It will also bring the benefit of a local YUM repository. Finally, if you need to install hundreds of nodes or you need to reinstall frequently in a facility such as a training environment, then it will be well worth your time to evaluate PXE boot and Kickstart.

Installing Oracle Enterprise Linux 5

This section describes installation of Oracle Enterprise Linux version 5, and it is applicable to systems based on x86 and x86-64. Oracle Enterprise Linux version 5 is functionally equivalent to the Red Hat Enterprise Linux Advanced Platform, the full-featured release of Red Hat Enterprise Linux.

As previously discussed, the operating system software can be supplied by a number of methods, including CD-ROM, NFS, FTP, and HTTP. We will explain how to install this OS from a CD-ROM; regardless, the recommendations covered in this section are also directly applicable to the other installation methods.

Starting the Installation

To start a CD-ROM–based installation on an x86 architecture server, boot the server with the first CD-ROM of the installation set. It may be necessary to configure the BIOS to select the Boot option from CD-ROM option. The BIOS can usually be accessed when booting the server by pressing a key combination; the specific key combination depends on the BIOS vendor. Instead of a BIOS layer, more recent systems use the UEFI (Unified Extensible Firmware Interface UEFI) as the interface between the operating system and the platform firmware. EFI resides permanently in NVRAM, enabling access to the boot interface without any additional external software. EFI systems also provide the option to select the boot device from an interactive menu.

After a successful boot from CD-ROM, select the option presented by the first prompt:

```
To install or upgrade in graphical mode, Press the <ENTER> key.
Press the Enter key to run the Anaconda installer.
```

Installation Media Check

Before you begin an Oracle Enterprise Linux CD-ROM–based installation session, you are prompted to verify the installation media. We recommend that you test the media before using it for the first time. This can help you avoid unnecessary failures later in the installation process. You can test each individual CD-ROM from the installation set by selecting OK. If the media has already been verified, you can choose Skip to start the Anaconda installer.

Anaconda Installation

The Welcome page shows an Oracle Enterprise Linux splash screen and gives you the opportunity to review the release notes. When you are ready, click Next to continue.

Next, choose the language to use for the installation process and click Next. The language specified here is used during the installation process; a different language can be specified when the operating system is installed onto the system.

Now choose an appropriate keyboard and click Next. This selection can be modified once the system is operational through the System Settings menu.

Install or Upgrade

The installer searches for the existence of any previous installations of Oracle Enterprise Linux. If there has been an installation of Oracle Enterprise Linux on the system, such as version 4, the installer detects the installation and displays the option to upgrade. We recommend always doing a fresh install to achieve the most consistent installation base across all the nodes in the cluster. Choose Install Enterprise Linux and click Next. If no previous installation is detected or the Linux operating system is not an Oracle Enterprise Linux, then this page will not be displayed, and the installation will proceed to the Disk Partitioning Setup page.

If the partition table on any of the devices is unreadable, then no installation has previously taken place. Instead of the Upgrade page, you will see a warning dialog that displays the option to initialize the unreadable drives. You should do this only for drives on which you do not wish to preserve the data. For example, ASM disks previously configured on other nodes in the cluster should not be initialized. This is particularly true in cases where a node is being added to an existing cluster.

Disk Partitioning

Next, we will explain how to install an Oracle Enterprise Linux 5 system suitable for Oracle Database 11g Release 2 RAC. To ensure consistency across the cluster, we recommend accepting the default partitioning scheme.

Creating a Default Partitioning Scheme

To create a default partitioning scheme, begin by selecting the option from the dropdown menu to remove Linux partitions on selected drives. Next, create a default layout to ensure that only the internal system drives are selected. For example, you don't want to select external drives that may be shared with the other nodes in the cluster. Also, select the checkbox to review and modify the partitioning layout. You should now see something like what is shown in Figure 6-1. Click Next when you have everything right.

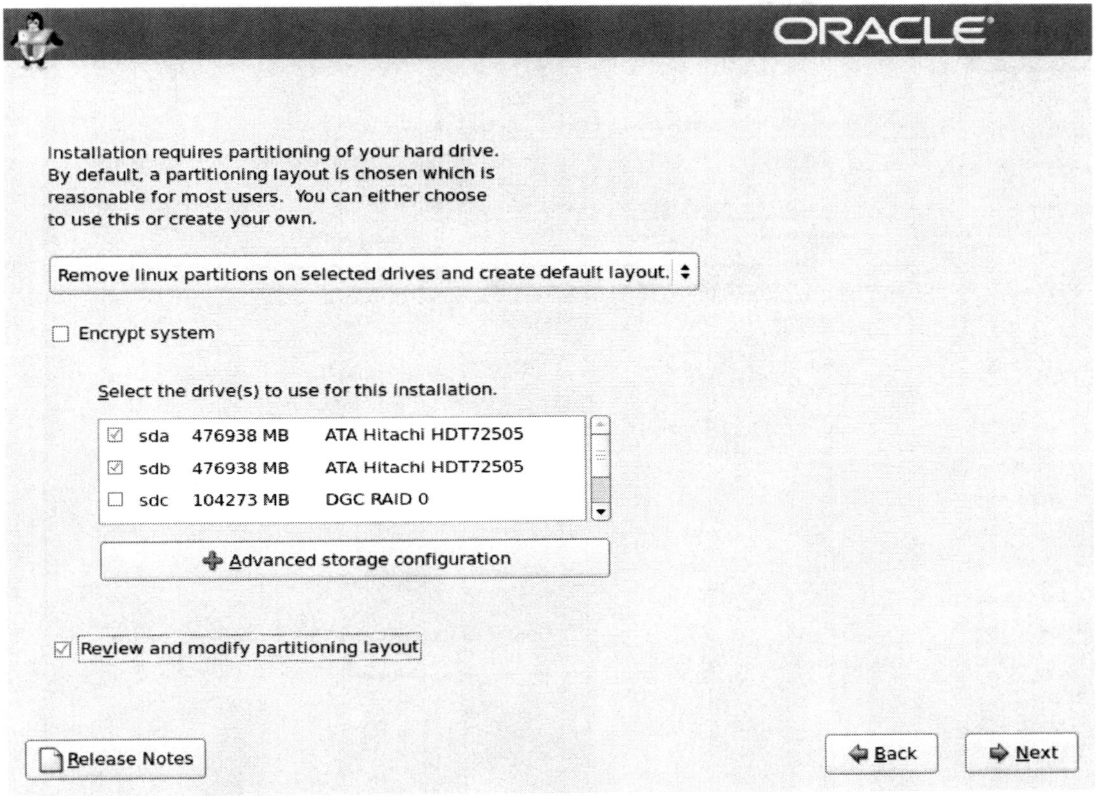

Figure 6-1. The Linux partitioning selection

A warning dialog will be displayed, indicating that proceeding will remove all partitions and data on the selected drives. Click Yes to proceed. Next, you will see the disk setup page, which includes options for partitioning (see Figure 6-2). The top pane displays the drives available and their corresponding sizes; the bottom pane shows the default partitioning scheme.

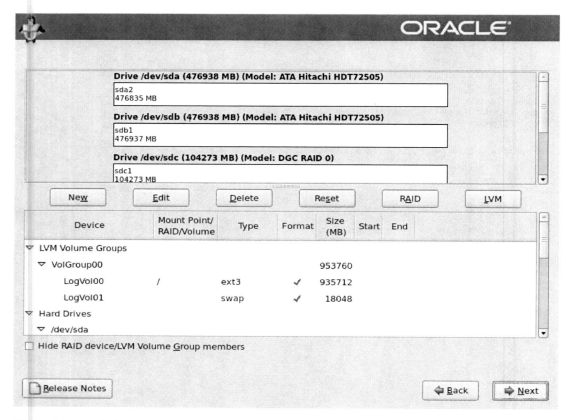

Figure 6-2. The disk setup

The default partitioning scheme illustrates how Oracle Enterprise Linux creates physical partitions and uses the Logical Volume Manager (LVM) to create a single Logical Volume Group named *VolGroup00*. This group is concatenated from the selected drives and their partitions. Under these partitions, the two logical volumes LogVol00 and LogVol01 are created for the / (root) partition and swap space, respectively. The first available drive also includes a /boot partition; this partition cannot reside on a Logical Volume because it cannot be read by the GRUB boot loader. The following snippet shows the result of a default partitioning scheme after installation:

```
Filesystem           Size  Used Avail Use% Mounted on
/dev/mapper/VolGroup00-LogVol00
                     886G  2.4G  838G   1% /
/dev/sda1             99M   13M   82M  13% /boot
tmpfs                7.9G     0  7.9G   0% /dev/shm
```

■ **Caution** There is no redundancy protection in the default configuration. Thus the failure of a single drive will result in the loss of the / (root) and /boot partitions.

We recommend that you protect your server disk drives by using a form of onboard RAID storage (see Chapter 4 for more information on RAID). If onboard RAID is not available, you should consider the options for manually configuring both RAID and the Logical Volume Manager during the disk partitioning stage, as explained later in this section.

Creating a Partition Manually

You might wish to customize the default partitioning scheme or to implement RAID and LVM manually. If so, then you have a number of options for proceeding. You also face some restrictions related to partitioning disk devices suitable for a node of Oracle Database 11*g* Release 2 RAC. As with the default configuration on systems based on Oracle Enterprise Linux 5 on x86 and x86-64, a minimum partitioning scheme without LVM must include at least the root partition (/) and swap partition (swap). If LVM is used, then the /boot partition must not be created under LVM, for the reason given in the previous section.

The choice of partitioning formats is dependent on whether the interface between the hardware and operating system is BIOS- or EFI-based; you will learn about your partitioning options in the upcoming sections.

Creating an MBR Partition

The most commonly used partitioning format on BIOS-based systems is the MS-DOS–based master boot record (MBR) format. Typically found on x86 and x86-64 systems, a BIOS-based MBR format allows up to four primary partitions to be created on each disk. One of these primary partitions can be extended and subdivided into logical partitions. The logical partitions are chained together. Theoretically, this means the maximum number of logical partitions is unlimited. However, for SCSI disks, Linux limits the total number of partitions to 15. A 2TB limit is also enforced within the MBR formatting scheme. And because the fdisk command only supports MBR formatting, fdisk also has a limit of 2TB. The MBR format stores one copy of the partition table. It also stores some system data in hidden or unpartitioned sectors, which is an important factor when trying to ensure that disk partitions are correctly aligned with external storage arrays. You'll learn more about this topic later in this chapter.

■ **Note** In Oracle Enterprise Linux 5, the Anaconda installer on x86 and x86-64 systems only supports MBR formatting. Therefore, it is not possible to create partitions larger than 2TB during installation. To create partitions of greater than 2TB, you need to use the GUID partition table (GPT) format, which you'll learn more about later in this section. Anaconda only supports the GPT format on the Itanium architecture.

Because Oracle Enterprise Linux 5 is based upon the 2.6 Linux kernel, SCSI commands support 64-bit block addresses. This means they can support individual devices beyond 2TB in size. However, the Host Bus Adapter (HBA), device driver, and the storage itself must all also support 64-bit block addressing before you can use it. If any of these components are limited to 32-bit block addresses, then a single device will also be limited to 2TB in size, regardless of the formatting scheme. Potential device and partitioning limitations aside, both the default ext3 file system and the OCFS2 file system support a maximum file system size of 16TB and a maximum individual file size of 2TB. Also, when using LVM, the maximum logical volume size is 16TB on x86 and 8EB (exabytes) on x86-64. Therefore, if you wish to create an ext3 file system larger than 2TB on a system with MBR formatting, it is possible to use LVM directly on a single disk device that has not been partitioned. It is also possible to concatenate a number of 2TB partitions with LVM, and then create the ext3 file system on the resulting logical volume.

Creating an EFI Partition

EFI-based systems were introduced with Itanium-based systems, but they are now present on some of the more recent x86 and x86-64 systems. EFI-based systems also support MBR formatting; however, you may consider using the GPT format instead for the advantages that this scheme brings. First, the GPT format is not limited to the primary and logical partitioning of the MBR; instead, it can support up to 128 partitions per disk.

Subject to using 64-bit SCSI addressing and a 2.6 kernel–based system, the GPT format can be up to 18EB in size—considerably larger than the 2TB limit. In addition, the GPT format uses primary and backup partition tables and checksum fields for redundancy and improved integrity. This can help you protect against partition table corruption. GPT partition tables also do not store any data in hidden sectors, which makes alignment offsets for external storage arrays unnecessary. Because the fdisk command does not support the GPT format, the parted command must be used instead.

The ability to implement GPT partitions after installation is not restricted to EFI-based systems. However, when using an unmodified version of GRUB, the default bootloader on x86 and x86-64, it is not possible to boot from a GPT partition. Therefore, GRUB must always be installed on an MBR-formatted partition, which means it is not possible to boot from a device with partitions larger than 2TB.

Customized Partitioning

It's possible you will want to customize the default partitioning scheme. Many system administrators prefer to partition the system with a number of partitions for distinct / (root device), swap, /boot, /home, /var, /usr /home, ORACLE_BASE, and other site-dependent configurations. Two of the main historical factors for adopting this schema were to reduce both the risk of corruption and the time required to complete file system checks in the event of a system restart when using a nonjournaled file system. We have found that Linux-based Oracle Database 11g Release 2 RAC nodes advanced, journaled file systems such as ext3 provide the most flexible approach. Therefore, we recommend the minimal configuration provided by the default installation. When installing the Oracle software, the database software is usually located in a directory tree below the ORACLE_BASE directory. Under the Optimal Flexible Architecture (OFA), the first mount point is the /u01 directory. This means that, in the default configuration, the /u01 directory can be created in the root partition. Thus we recommend that you have at least 10GB of disk space available for the Oracle software installation.

The space required for the boot device is dependent on the number of kernels compiled and configured for booting. Oracle Database 11g Release 2 RAC nodes only require the standard precompiled kernel, so space utilization rarely exceeds 30MB. The actual space used is dependent on the hardware architecture. However, if you're customizing the partition layout, then the 100MB allocated by the default configuration is sufficient.

Configuring Swap Space

Oracle's recommendations for Linux vary. For example, it recommends setting the swap size anywhere from equal to the RAM to four times the RAM. Consider the following documented example for Oracle 11*g* Release 2, which is typical. For systems with between 1GB and 2GB of RAM, Oracle recommends swap space of 1.5 times the size of RAM. For systems with between 2GB and 16GB of RAM, Oracle recommends that you set the swap size to equal the size of RAM. And for systems with more than 16GB of RAM, Oracle recommends 16GB of swap space. The size of a single swap partition in Oracle Enterprise Linux 5 is determined by the limits on the partition or the logical volume size, as discussed previously.

Swap space can be regarded as a disk-based component of virtual memory. In Linux, unlike some other UNIX operating systems, virtual memory is the sum total of RAM plus swap space. Recommendations to make the swap size one or two times the size of the RAM are often based on the requirements of traditional UNIX operating systems. This swap configuration was required because an executable program had been loaded into both swap space and RAM at the same time. Oracle's guidelines on swap allocation tend to reflect these traditional requirements. Linux, on the other hand, maintains swap space for demand paging. When an executable is loaded on Linux, it is likely that a portion of the executable will not be required, such as the error-handling code. For efficiency, Linux only loads virtual memory pages when they are used. If RAM is fully utilized and one process requires loading a page into RAM, Linux will write out the page to swap space from another process, according to a Least Recently Used (LRU) algorithm.

The performance of disk-based storage is orders of magnitude slower than memory. Therefore, you should plan to never be in the position of having pages written to swap space due to demand for RAM from competing processes. Oracle should always run in RAM, without exception. As a basic rule, you do not need a significant amount of swap space for Oracle on Linux, assuming there is enough memory installed. Every rule has an exception, however. Linux tends to be reasonably aggressive in managing swap space, maintaining as much free RAM as possible. It does this by writing out memory pages to swap space that have not been recently used, even if there is no current demand for the memory at the time. This approach is designed to prevent a greater impact on performance than doing all of the maintenance work when the space is required. This approach also frees up RAM for other potential, such as the disk buffer. The behavior of the swapping activity can be modified with the kernel parameter, vm.swappiness. A higher value means the system will be more active in unmapping mapped pages, while a lower value means that swapping activity will be reduced. However, the lower amount of swap activity comes at the expense that RAM that could potentially be freed.. The default value is 60, which you can see in /proc/sys/vm/swappiness. Note that memory allocated as huge pages is not swapped under any circumstances. The vm.panic_on_oom kernel parameter also affects virtual memory. By default this parameter is set to 0. If all virtual memory is exhausted (including the swap space), the operating system will recover memory by terminating processes with high levels of memory consumption, but low CPU activity. If the preceding kernel parameter is set to 1, a kernel panic will occur, terminating all system activity. This is the preferred approach under a RAC environment. However, you should endeavor to configure the virtual memory to ensure that the condition that provokes a kernel panic is never reached.

With this information, you can intelligently size the swap space for Oracle on Linux. You can also evaluate the correct choice between what may appear to be conflicting recommendations. First, any requirement for swap space that is two to four times the size of the RAM is an over specification based on traditional UNIX requirements. Second, although one given recommendation is for swap of 1.5 times the size of the RAM with installed RAM of 1GB to 2GB, we recommend that you install at least 2GB or RAM per installed CPU socket. Therefore, if you're meeting these guidelines, you should not plan for more swap space than you have RAM.

For the basic operating environment, swap space should not be utilized during normal usage. With enough memory, even a single 2GB swap partition will often suffice. The exception occurs in the case where many Oracle user processes or other processes are created and intersperse active periods with idle time. In this scenario, it is necessary to allocate swap space to account for cases where these processes are temporarily paged out of memory. This type of application profile may actively use more than 2GB of swap space without having any impact on overall performance; also, it can potentially increase performance by freeing RAM that is not being used. However, it is also likely under this application profile that an Oracle shared server configuration would be more efficient.

The swap space needed will depend on application requirements. Given sufficient disk space, we recommend adopting the simplest single starting point for swap space allocation for Oracle on Linux. That is, you should plan for an amount of swap space equal to the amount of RAM installed in the system. If you know that you will not create a large number of processes on the system, then you may reduce the allocation accordingly. If you do have a large number of processes but sufficient RAM, then you can evaluate using vm.swappiness to reduce the usage of swap space. If additional swap space is required, you can use the mkswap command at a later point in time. One benefit of the mkswap command: It can also be used when the system is operational. Conversely, if you have a large RAM configuration, then resizing the swap space by many tens or hundreds of gigabytes will not be detrimental to performance, as long as your swap space is equivalent to your installed RAM. However, this approach may use disk space unnecessarily. If this is the case, and you wish to conserve disk space, then you may size a swap partition smaller than the installed amount of RAM. Oracle advises a 16GB swap partition for configurations of more than 16GB of RAM. However, this does not mean that you cannot have a swap partition of more than 16GB if you wish. For example, you might use more than 16GB of swap space if you have enough disk capacity that conserving the disk space between 16GB and your available RAM size is not a concern.

Configuring RAID

If you do not have a system with onboard RAID, you may wish to consider protecting your Linux operating systems disk drives with an add-in RAID adapter. We recommend a hardware RAID solution wherever possible because it is far superior solution to its software equivalent. If you cannot configure a hardware RAID solution and wish to create a partitioning scheme with some level of redundancy, then there are two ways in which this can be achieved. First, you can use software RAID, and then use the configured RAID device as the underlying device for an LVM configuration. Second, you can use LVM to mirror devices. As previously noted, the /boot partition cannot reside on an LVM volume. When mirroring drives with a RAID 1 configuration (see Chapter 4 for more information on RAID), LVM reads from one side of the mirror only. In a software-based RAID solution, a RAID 1 configuration reads from both mirrored devices, which results in higher levels of performance.

It is also possible to configure the /boot partition on a RAID configuration with RAID 1 that uses at least one of the first two drives on the system. If the /boot directory is not a separate partition from the / (root) directory, then these conditions apply to the / (root) directory instead. For these reasons, we recommend software RAID over LVM if you're manually configuring redundancy. However—and this cannot be overemphasized—you should opt for hardware RAID wherever possible. Hardware-based RAID can protect against a drive failure transparently, but software-based software RAID may require rebooting the server if a drive fails. The advantage of the scenario just described is this: if the boot drive is in a software RAID configuration, then downtime is restricted to the time required for the reboot to take place, as opposed to the time required to restore from a backup.

The following example shows a software RAID 1 equivalent of the default partitioning scheme on the first two drives in the system. To begin configuring software RAID on the disk partitioning page, select Create custom layout from the dropdown menu and press Next. On the disk setup page, check whether there are any existing partitions or logical volumes. If so, use the Delete button to remove the disk configuration, so that the chosen drives can display free space (see Figure 6-3).

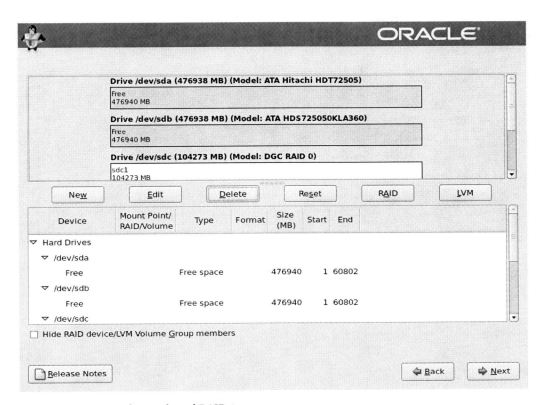

Figure 6-3. Setting up software-based RAID 1

Next, select the RAID button. This will present you with a single option: Create a software RAID partition. Press OK to display the Add Partition window. As noted previously, it is not possible for the /boot partition to reside on a logical volume. For that reason, if the / (root) and swap are to utilize LVM, then you need to independently create four software RAID partitions. Create the first two partitions on /dev/sda and /dev/sdb and make them 100MB each. Next, create two more partitions, one on each drive. This enables you to utilize the rest of the maximum allowable size. Figure 6-4 shows the created RAID partitions.

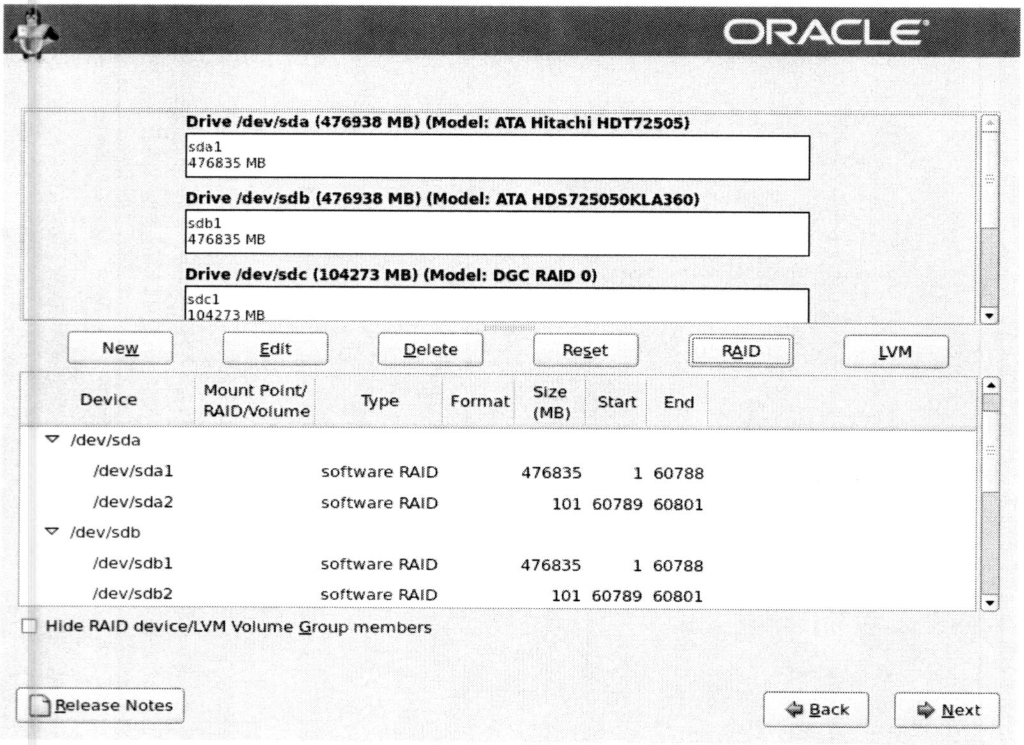

ORACLE

Drive /dev/sda (476938 MB) (Model: ATA Hitachi HDT72505)

sda1
476835 MB

Drive /dev/sdb (476938 MB) (Model: ATA HDS725050KLA360)

sdb1
476835 MB

Drive /dev/sdc (104273 MB) (Model: DGC RAID 0)

sdc1
104273 MB

New	Edit	Delete	Reset	RAID	LVM

Device	Mount Point/ RAID/Volume	Type	Format	Size (MB)	Start	End
▽ /dev/sda						
/dev/sda1		software RAID		476835	1	60788
/dev/sda2		software RAID		101	60789	60801
▽ /dev/sdb						
/dev/sdb1		software RAID		476835	1	60788
/dev/sdb2		software RAID		101	60789	60801

☐ Hide RAID device/LVM Volume Group members

Release Notes		Back	Next

Figure 6-4. *Creating the RAID partitions*

Press the RAID button again to make the following option available: Create a RAID device. This screen also shows that you now have four software RAID partitions you can use. Select the

Create a RAID device option to display the Make RAID Device window. Next, choose the following options: /boot for the Mount Point, ext3 for the File System Type, md0 for the RAID Device, and RAID 1 for the RAID Level. For the RAID members, select the two 100MB software RAID partitions created previously, and then press OK. /boot is created on /dev/md0. Repeat the process to display the Make RAID Device window. However, this time you should select a File System Type of physical volume (LVM) from the RAID Device md1 with RAID Level 1. Also be sure to select the two remaining RAID Members. Click OK to create the physical volume. Now press the LVM button to display the Make LVM Volume Group window, and then press the Add button to create the logical volumes for the / (root) and swap (see Figure 6-5).

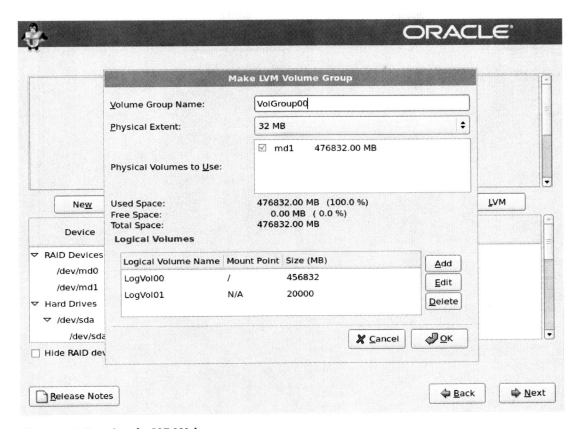

Figure 6-5. Creating the LVM Volumes

Press OK to complete the disk partitioning. At this point, you have created the default configuration with RAID 1 across the first two drives in the system (see Figure 6-6).

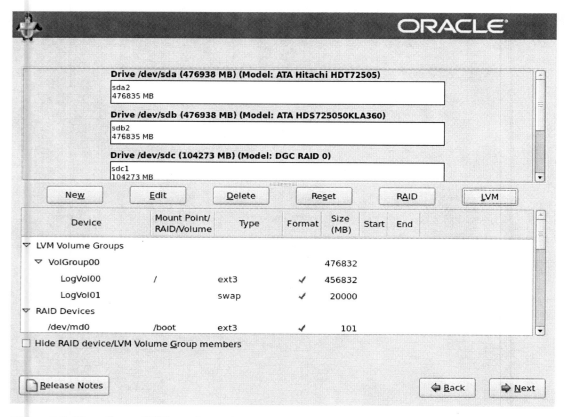

Figure 6-6. The software RAID configuration

After installation, the partitioning layout will look something like this:

```
[root@london2 ~]# df -h
Filesystem          Size  Used Avail Use% Mounted on
/dev/mapper/VolGroup00-LogVol00
                    433G  1.3G  409G   1% /
/dev/md0             99M   13M   82M  14% /boot
tmpfs               7.9G     0  7.9G   0% /dev/shm
```

After completing your chosen partitioning scheme, click Next to save the partitioning map and advance to the Boot Loader Configuration page on x86 and x86-64 systems. The disks will not be physically partitioned at this point. This won't occur until after all of the installation information has been collected, but before the installation of packages has commenced.

Configuring the Boot Loader and Network

The Boot Loader Configuration page is displayed on x86 and x86-64 systems. Accept all of the default GRUB bootloader options, and then click Next to continue to the Network Configuration page.

An Oracle Database 11*g* Release 2 RAC node needs at least two network devices, one for the external interface and one for the private interconnect network. These network devices should already have been cabled and configured for their respective networks by a network administrator. Assuming Ethernet is used, these will by default be displayed as devices with the following names: eth0, eth1, eth2, and so on. If you plan to use NIC bonding (also known as NICteaming) for interconnect resilience (see Chapter 4 for more information on this topic), the Network Configuration page will display more than the required number of devices. Teaming cannot be configured until after installation is complete, so you should only configure primary devices, leaving the Active on Boot checkbox unchecked against the planned secondary devices. The primary device configuration created at this stage will be useful when migrating to the teamed configuration.

Whether using single network devices or a teamed configuration, you need to ensure that all nodes have the same interface name for the external device. For example, if eth0 is configured as the public interface on the first node, then eth0 should also be selected as the public interface on all of the other nodes. This is a requirement for the correct operation of the VIP addresses configured during the Oracle Grid Infrastructure software installation.

On the Network Configuration page, highlight the primary external devices—for example, eth0— and click Edit. This brings up the Edit Interface dialog box for eth0. Whether you are using a GNS configuration or a manual IP configuration, we recommend that you use fixed IP addresses for the public and private interfaces on all nodes. Therefore, you should uncheck the Configure Using DHCP checkbox. If using GNS, DHCP will be used during the Oracle install to configure the VIP and SCAN addresses. However, DHCP is not required directly on the host network configuration. If you are running a network installation, then the configuration for your primary interface will already be populated from the network information given previously.

Next, you should ensure that the Activate on Boot checkbox is selected, and then complete the IP Address and Netmask according to your planned network configuration. IPv6 is not supported in a RAC configuration, so it should be disabled on all interfaces; click OK after entering the network configuration. Next, complete the information for the private interconnect device using an IP address from Table 6-5. These IP addresses have been reserved for use in private networks. For most clusters with fewer than 254 nodes, a class-C network address with a nonsegmented subnet mask (255.255.255.0) should be sufficient.

Table 6-5. IP Addresses for Private Networks

Class	Networks	Subnet Mask
A	10.0.0.0 through 10.255.255.255	255.0.0.0
B	172.16.0.0 through 172.31.0.0	255.255.0.0
C	192.168.0.0 through 192.168.255.0	255.255.255.0

If you provided the DNS Server IP Address for a network-based installation, then the DNS Server address will already be completed, and the hostname will already be configured with the full domain extension, such as london1.example.com. Alternatively, you can manually set the hostname and any gateway or DNS server addresses according to your network configuration.

Your naming conventions should allow for additional nodes, as well as for any standby databases that may be added in the future. Our example uses a geographically based naming convention, where the first node in the cluster is london1, and the second node is london2. A third node would be london3, and so on. Figure 6-7 shows how to configure host london1 using an external network configuration on eth0 and an interconnect configuration on eth1.

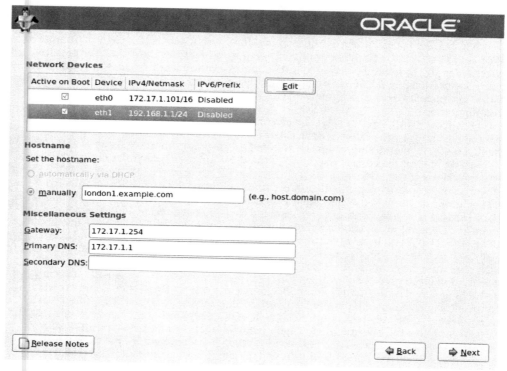

Figure 6-7. The network configuration

When you have finished updating the network settings, click Next to continue to the Time Zone Selection page.

Selecting a Time Zone

The time zone required will be determined by the geographical location of your cluster. All nodes within a cluster should have the same time zone configuration. You can select the nearest location on the interactive map or from the dropdown list beneath the map.

Oracle Enterprise Linux allows you to specify whether the hardware clock should be set to UTC/GMT time or local time. We recommend setting the system clock to UTC by checking the System Clock Uses UTC option. This enables automatic adjustment for regional daylight savings time. Setting the hardware clock to local time is useful only for systems that are configured to dual boot with other operating systems that require a local time setting. However, it is unlikely that you will want to configure dual booting for a production Oracle Database 11*g* Release 2 RAC node.

After selecting the correct system time zone, click Next to continue to the Root Password Configuration page.

Configuring the Root Password

The password for the root user account must be at least six characters in length. Enter and confirm a suitable password, and then click Next to continue to the Package Installation Defaults page.

Reviewing the Package Installation Defaults

The Package Installation Defaults page gives you a pair of options. First, you can accept a default set of packages for the Linux installation. Second, you can customize the set of packages available. Oracle provides an RPM in addition to the default installation. That RPM is termed the Oracle Validated RPM. After installation, the RPM installs any packages required for running an Oracle environment and automatically configures system settings. For example, it creates the Oracle user and related groups, as well as configuring the correct kernel parameters. The Oracle Validated RPM is included in the installation media for Oracle Enterprise Linux 5.2 and Oracle Enterprise Linux 4.7 upwards on x86 and x86-64. In addition, Oracle customers subscribed to the Unbreakable Linux Network (ULN) can retrieve the Oracle Validated RPM from there. Customers not subscribed to the Unbreakable Linux Network (ULN) can obtain the RPM from the same URL used to obtain the release notes. For example, the Oracle Validated RPM for Oracle Enterprise Linux 5 can be downloaded from this location: http://oss.oracle.com/el5/oracle-validated/.

Selecting a Package Group

The availability of the Oracle Validated RPM gives you two options for the installing Oracle Enterprise Linux. You can do either a minimal install or a default install. Running the Oracle Validated RPM after installing Oracle Enterprise Linux completes the configuration by installing the remaining Oracle required packages. You should select a minimal installation only if you require the lowest number of packages to install and run Oracle. A minimal installation also has the advantage of reducing the number of unneeded services that will run on the system. By default, it frees resources for Oracle's use. For example, even after you run the Oracle Validated RPM, using the minimal installation option does not install the X Windows server packages, which means it does not enable a graphical environment to be run directly on the server. However, the installation does include the X Windows client libraries, which enables graphical tools to be run on the local system, but displayed on a remote system with a full X Windows installation. Before choosing a minimal installation, you should also be confident that you already have or are able to configure a suitable YUM repository to resolve package dependencies when running the Oracle Validated RPM. You will learn more about configuring this repository later in this chapter. Assuming you're ready to proceed with a minimal installation (see Figure 6-8), select the Customize now checkbox at the Package Group Selection page, and then press Next.

The Package Group Selection screen includes the option to modify the package selection grouped under a number of headings, such as Desktop Environments, Applications, and Development. Under each of these headings, the right-hand pane lets you deselect all of the packages, except for the Base packages detailed under Base System. The Base system also includes the openssh package, which is required for internode communication in RAC.

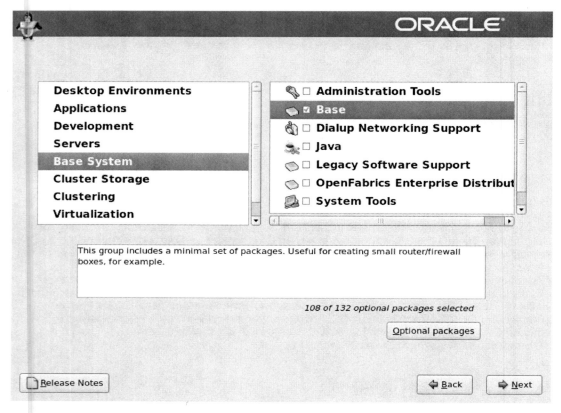

Figure 6-8. A minimal package group selection

It's possible you might wish to choose a more complete initial installation at the Package Group Selection page. If so, then leave the default selection of packages unmodified, select the Customize later checkbox, and Press Next. If you do not wish to run the Oracle Validated RPM or the RPM is not available for your architecture, then it is necessary to modify the default selection of packages at installation time. For this option, select the Software Development and the Customize now checkboxes, and then press Next. With the Development option selected in the left-hand pane, select Legacy Software Development in the right-hand pane. Next, under the heading Base System in the left-hand pane, select Legacy Software Support in the right-hand pane, and then press the Optional packages button. Now select compat-db under Packages in the Legacy Software Support window and press Close. Similarly, you should select sysstat under Packages in the System Tools window that is under the System Tools heading.

When you have selected all of the required packages for your installation, click Next and the installer will check the dependencies in the packages you have selected before continuing to the Begin Installation page.

Installing Packages

Click Next to proceed with the installation from the Begin Installation page. This will display the Required Install Media dialog box, which shows the CDs that will be needed if you're installing from CD-ROM media, depending on the packages selected. Click Continue to initiate the installation process.

The Installing Packages page shows the packages currently being installed, and it gives an estimate of the time remaining to complete the installation. If you are not performing a network installation, change the CD-ROM when prompted by the installer.

After you install the packages, you need to remove any remaining CD-ROMs or bootable USB drive, and then click Reboot.

Setting the Final Configuration

If you perform a minimal installation, on the first boot the system will present a text dialog to run a number of administrative tasks. Pressing Exit takes the system to a nongraphical login prompt. If you perform a default graphical installation, the system will call the /etc/rc.d/init.d/firstboot script the first time it system boots after installation. This enables you to set the final configuration before the installation process completes. When this script runs, the process creates the file /etc/sysconfig/firstboot, which includes the following entry: RUN_FIRSTBOOT=NO. To rerun firstboot on any subsequent reboots, it is necessary to remove this file and ensure the firstboot script is called during the boot process. You can do this by executing the command chkconfig –level 5 firstboot on. When firstboot runs, the Welcome screen is displayed. This left-hand pane for this page shows the stages required to complete the firstboot process. Click Forward to advance to the first of these stages, the License Agreement page.

Accepting the License Agreement

Browse the license agreement to be aware of the conditions, and then select Yes, I Agree to the License Agreement. You must accept the license agreement to complete the firstboot process. Click Forward to continue to the Firewall page.

Configuring the Firewall

Oracle Enterprise Linux enables you to configure varying degrees of network security. However, for an Oracle Database 11g Release 2 RAC node, enabling a firewall configuration can inhibit the correct functioning of Oracle services. For the Oracle Database 11g Release 2 RAC, we suggest you implement a dedicated firewall infrastructure on the network, but that you do not configure a firewall on any of the nodes themselves. Therefore, choose the Disabled option from the dropdown menu on the Firewall page and click Forward to continue. This will present an additional warning dialog box; click Yes to advance to the SELinux page.

Configuring SELinux

The Security Enhanced Linux (SELinux) page provides the option to configure security settings, so they comply with a number of security policies issued by regulatory bodies. Just as you did when configuring the firewall, select the Disabled option from the dropdown menu and click Forward to continue. You will see another warning dialog box that indicates no firewall has been configured; click Yes to advance to the Kdump page.

Enabling kdump

kdump is a crash-dump utility based on the system calls provided by kexec . This utility provides system state information at the time of a system crash. By default, this information is stored in /var/crash.

■ **Note** In an Oracle 11*g* Release 2 RAC environment, we do not recommend enabling kdump by default during installation. There are two reasons for this. First, the options available during installation are limited to a local crash-dump configuration. Second, the inherent stability of the overwhelming majority of Oracle 11*g* Release 2 RAC on Linux environments means that you may simply not need to consider crash-dump analysis as part of your operations.

However, if you do find that you need such a utility at a later point, then we recommend configuring a net dump server to send crash dumps to a remote server across the network. You can then configure kdump on the local system using the graphical command system-config-kdump; run this command as the root user. You can learn more about kdump configuration in the /etc/kdump.conf file, and authentication with the net dump server is enabled by the command service kdump propagate. After a reboot, kdump can then be managed as a service.

In addition to enabling kdump for debugging purposes, you may also consider setting the kernel parameter kernel.panic_on_oops to a value of 1. By default, this value is set to 0. If this parameter is left at its default value, a kernel error may cause an oops and terminate the process involved in the error. If this happens, the kernel may be left in an *uncertain state*, which means that a kernel panic occurs at a later point when the affected resources are attempted to be used, as opposed to the time when they were corrupted. Setting kernel.panic_on_oops to 1 means that the system will not attempt to continue past an error, and a kernel panic will occur at the time of the oops. This behavior might deliver better root cause analysis. For example, it might help pinpoint an error to a particular device driver.

If you choose to accept our recommendation and not enable kdump at this time, leave the Enable kdump checkbox unselected and press Forward to move to the Date and Time page.

Setting the Date and Time

The Date and Time page displays the information received from the internal system clock. Before installing Oracle Database 11*g* Release 2 RAC, it is essential that all of the nodes within the cluster be configured with exactly the same time settings. You can do this by selecting the Network Time Protocol tab. If you are setting the Network Time Protocol here, select the Enable Network Time Protocol checkbox. If you do not have specific NTP servers available, there are public NTP servers given by default at these addresses: 0.rhel.pool.ntp.org, 1.rhel.pool.ntp.org, and 2.rhel.pool.ntp.org. You have a couple options here. First, you can use these public servers. Second, you can delete the public servers from the Server listbox and instead add the names of the NTP servers you have permission to use. Click Forward and the system will contact the NTP servers specified before proceeding to the Create User page. If you do not configure NTP either at this stage or manually at a later point, then the Oracle

Software installation will report that the NTP configuration is missing. Even so, it will continue to proceed and configure the Oracle Cluster Time Synchronization Service daemon (OTCSSD)CTSS in an active state. This ensures that the time is configured identically on all nodes in the cluster. However, NTP has the advantage that this unified time will also be set to the correct clock time.

Creating a User

The Create User page lets you create a user account in addition to the standard root user on the system. However more specific details than are available here are required, in terms of the Oracle user and groups these are required to be created by the Oracle Validated RPM or manually after installation. Therefore, click Forward, and then click Continue to bypass the warning dialog box. This skips creating any additional users at this point. A subsequent page will be displayed if a sound card is detected on the system. However, it is unlikely that a sound card will be present on a server dedicated to Oracle. If one is detected, however, just click the Play button on the displayed page to test the configuration. Next, click Forward to continue to the Additional CDs page.

Installing Additional CDs

The Additional CDs page lets you install applications in addition to the standard Red Hat Enterprise Linux software. No additional software is required to be installed to complete an Oracle configuration at this stage. Click Finish to complete the installation, and then click OK at the Reboot dialog window if SELinux has been disabled.

Configuring Oracle Enterprise Linux 5

This section covers the steps required to configure the Linux operating system in preparation for an Oracle 11g Release 2 RAC installation. Our aim goes beyond simply listing the configuration changes required. Rather, we want but to explain the reasons for these changes and their effects. Doing so will enable you to optimize the each environment intelligently.

Unless stated otherwise, each configuration step should be performed by the root user on every node in the cluster. We recommend that you fully install all nodes in the cluster and confirm that the network is operational before attempting to configure the shared storage.

This chapter focuses on changes that are either essential or of great benefit for installing and operating Oracle RAC. Next, we will discuss the following configuration and verification topics:

- Configuring the Oracle Validated RPM and YUM
- Running the Oracle Validated RPM
- Verifying the Oracle Validated RPM Actions
- Post Oracle Validated RPM configuration of the Oracle user, kernel, and kernel module parameters
- Completing the Linux configuration with hostnames and name resolution
- Setting the Network Time Protocol (NTP)
- Implementing a secure shell
- Setting up shared storage, including udev and device-mapper

- Handling network channel bonding
- Configuring IPMI

All of the configuration changes described in this chapter can be made to the standard Oracle Enterprise Linux installation. However, your hardware configuration can make some steps optional. For example, you may not need to configure I/O multipathing or IPMI. This chapter will assist you in implementing the requiring settings for a successful Oracle 11*g* Release 2 RAC installation. It will also help you understand why these settings are required to achieve an optimal configuration.

Configuring a Server with the Oracle Validated RPM

The fastest way to configure an Oracle Enterprise Linux server for an Oracle database installation is to run the Oracle Validated RPM. Although that RPM is located on the installation media, by default it is not installed with the operating system. Therefore, we recommend installing and running the Oracle Validated RPM because it can help you ensure a consistent and complete installation across all nodes of the cluster. However, simply copying and running the Oracle Validated RPM after a default installation will fail because the RPM has several additional dependencies, as shown in the following example:

```
[root@london1 ~]# rpm -ivh oracle-validated-1.0.0-18.el5.x86_64.rpm
warning: oracle-validated-1.0.0-18.el5.x86_64.rpm: Header V3 DSA signature: NOKEY, key ID
1e5e0159
error: Failed dependencies:
        compat-gcc-34 is needed by oracle-validated-1.0.0-18.el5.x86_64
        compat-gcc-34-c++ is needed by oracle-validated-1.0.0-18.el5.x86_64
        libXp.so.6 is needed by oracle-validated-1.0.0-18.el5.x86_64
        libaio-devel is needed by oracle-validated-1.0.0-18.el5.x86_64
        libdb-4.2.so()(64bit) is needed by oracle-validated-1.0.0-18.el5.x86_64
        libodbc.so.1()(64bit) is needed by oracle-validated-1.0.0-18.el5.x86_64
        sysstat is needed by oracle-validated-1.0.0-18.el5.x86_64
        unixODBC-devel is needed by oracle-validated-1.0.0-18.el5.x86_64
```

There's good news and bad news. The bad news first: Resolving these dependencies manually can be a time-consuming process. The good news: Oracle Enterprise Linux comes with a tool called the Yellow dog Updater, Modified (YUM) that can help you resolve these dependencies automatically and automate the installation of the Oracle Validated RPM.

Configuring YUM

A YUM server provides a repository for RPM packages and their associated metadata. This makes installing the packages and their dependencies straightforward. Oracle provides a public YUM server at http://public-yum.oracle.com, but its server provides only the packages you have already downloaded on the installation media. Subscribers to the Unbreakable Linux Network can access additional security updates and patches on top of the content available on the public YUM server. If you do not have access to the Unbreakable Linux Network or you do not wish to use the public YUM server, it is a simple enough process to configure your own from the installation media.

Previously in this chapter, we explained how to configure VSFTP to make the installation media available across the network. Fortunately, this installation media also contains the YUM repository metadata. For example, the metadata for the Server RPMs is located under the Server/repodata directory in the file `repomd.xml`. This means you do not have to create additional metadata by building a custom repository with the `createrepo` command. You can test the readiness of the installation media for use as a YUM repository with the `wget` command. This should enable you to retrieve a selected file without any additional steps, as shown in this example:

```
[root@london1 tmp]# wget ftp://ftp1.example.com/pub/el5_4_x86_64/Server/oracle-validated*
...
2009-09-17 13:54:06 (6.10 MB/s) - `oracle-validated-1.0.0-18.el5.x86_64.rpm.1' saved [15224]
```

If you prefer, your local YUM repository can also be based on a mounted DVD-ROM. However, this repository will be local to an individual server. With the repository available, the next step is to configure YUM on the client. To do this, edit the file `/etc/yum.conf` and add the following section to the end of the file:

```
[Server]
name=Server
baseurl=ftp://ftp1.example.com/pub/el5_4_x86_64/Server/
gpgcheck=0
enabled=1
```

Setting the gpgcheck option to the value of 1 ensures that all packages are signed and that YUM will verify the signatures. As the preceding example shows, it is not strictly necessary to set this value if the YUM server is private and based on the Oracle installation media. However, you should set the value to 1 when using public YUM servers. The `baseurl` property specifies the location of the server RPMs. In the preceding example, `baseurl` property points to the FTP Server. If a local DVD is used, then `baseurl` takes the following form: `baseurl=file:///media/disk/Server/`. In this case, `baseurl` reflects the location of the mounted DVD. It is also possible to copy the DVD installation media to the local server, mount it with the `loop` option, and specify this as the file location. However, this approach is likely to be considerably more time consuming than simply configuring the FTP Server. To check the configuration, run the command `yum list`. If correctly configured, this command will list the RPMs shown as `installed`, as well as the ones listed under the Server category.

Running the Oracle Validated RPM

The system is now ready for you to install the Oracle Validated RPM with the `yum install oracle-validated` command. Once all the dependencies have been resolved, it is necessary to confirm the installation at the `Is this ok` prompt, as shown in the following truncated output:

```
[root@london1 etc]# yum install oracle-validated
Loaded plugins: security
Setting up Install Process
Resolving Dependencies
...
Is this ok [y/N]: y
...
Installed:
  oracle-validated.x86_64 0:1.0.0-18.el5

Dependency Installed:
  compat-db.x86_64 0:4.2.52-5.1
```

```
compat-gcc-34.x86_64 0:3.4.6-4
compat-gcc-34-c++.x86_64 0:3.4.6-4
elfutils-libelf-devel.x86_64 0:0.137-3.el5
elfutils-libelf-devel-static.x86_64 0:0.137-3.el5
gcc.x86_64 0:4.1.2-46.el5
gcc-c++.x86_64 0:4.1.2-46.el5
gdb.x86_64 0:6.8-37.el5
glibc-devel.i386 0:2.5-42
glibc-devel.x86_64 0:2.5-42
glibc-headers.x86_64 0:2.5-42
kernel-headers.x86_64 0:2.6.18-164.el5
libXp.i386 0:1.0.0-8.1.el5
libaio-devel.x86_64 0:0.3.106-3.2
libgomp.x86_64 0:4.4.0-6.el5
libstdc++-devel.x86_64 0:4.1.2-46.el5
sysstat.x86_64 0:7.0.2-3.el5
unixODBC.x86_64 0:2.2.11-7.1
unixODBC-devel.x86_64 0:2.2.11-7.1
```

Complete!

Once the Oracle Validated RPM installation completes, all the RPM packages and system configuration steps required for an Oracle Database 11*g* Release 2 RAC installation have also been completed. For example, the required user and groups have been created, and the necessary kernel parameters have been set. You can find the installed packages listed in /var/log/yum.log. In some combinations of the Oracle Validated RPM and Oracle Database 11*g* Release 2 on 64-bit systems, the OUI will report that some of the required packages are missing. For example, packages commonly listed as missing include libaio-devel, unixODBC, and unixODBC-devel. The error typically looks something like this:

```
This is a prerequisite condition to test whether the package
"libaio-devel-0.3.106" is available on the system. (more details)
  Check Failed on Nodes: [london2, london1]
```

This warning occurs because, on x86-64 architecture systems, the OUI checks for the presence of both the x86-64 and i386 packages, whereas some versions of the Oracle Validated RPM install only the 64-bit versions. The package versions can be verified with the following snippet:

```
[root@london1 ~]# rpm -q --queryformat "%{NAME}-%{VERSION}-%{RELEASE} (%{ARCH})\n" \
libaio-devel \
unixODBC \
unixODBC-devel
libaio-devel-0.3.106-3.2 (x86_64)
unixODBC-2.2.11-7.1 (x86_64)
unixODBC-devel-2.2.11-7.1 (x86_64)
```

You can prevent 32-bit RPMs from being reported as missing by the OUI by installing them directly with the rpm command or with the yum command. Doing so ensures that the requested architecture is fully specified by the yum install command, as in this example:

```
[root@london1 ~]# yum install unixODBC-2.2.11-7.1.i386 unixODBC-devel-2.2.11-7.1.i386 libaio-
devel-0.3.106-3.2.i386
Loaded plugins: security
Setting up Install Process
Resolving Dependencies
--> Running transaction check
---> Package libaio-devel.i386 0:0.3.106-3.2 set to be updated
---> Package unixODBC.i386 0:2.2.11-7.1 set to be updated
---> Package unixODBC-devel.i386 0:2.2.11-7.1 set to be updated
--> Finished Dependency Resolution
...
Installed:
  libaio-devel.i386 0:0.3.106-3.2           unixODBC.i386 0:2.2.11-7.1
  unixODBC-devel.i386 0:2.2.11-7.1

Complete!
```

You can now verify the subsequent presence of the correct architectures for the packages:

```
[root@london1 ~]# rpm -q --queryformat "%{NAME}-%{VERSION}-%{RELEASE} (%{ARCH})\n" \
> libaio-devel \
> unixODBC \
> unixODBC-devel
libaio-devel-0.3.106-3.2 (x86_64)
libaio-devel-0.3.106-3.2 (i386)
unixODBC-2.2.11-7.1 (x86_64)
unixODBC-2.2.11-7.1 (i386)
unixODBC-devel-2.2.11-7.1 (x86_64)
unixODBC-devel-2.2.11-7.1 (i386)
```

On NUMA based systems you may also wish to install the numactl-devel RPM package to enable full NUMA support, see chapter 4 for more details.The preceding YUM configuration provides only the Server RPM packages required by the Oracle Validated RPM. However, if you wish to continue to using YUM as a method for RPM installation, then it is also necessary to add additional categories in /etc/yum.conf under the Cluster, ClusterStorage, and VT headings (and their corresponding RPM directories). Adding these categories lets you ensure the full availability of all of the RPM packages for YUM that are present on the installation media. Alternatively, you may use the Oracle public YUM server.

Using the up2date Command

If you are a customer of the ULN, then once you have registered your system, you may also use the up2date command to install and run the Oracle Validated RPM and maintain the operating system. However, we recommend that you avoid using this command because it has been superseded by YUM. The up2date command provides functionality similar to YUM, albeit with different syntax. Specifically, this command can automatically resolve dependencies of the installed RPM packages.

■ **Note** Not only has up2date has been superseded by Yum, but it is no longer used in Red Hat Enterprise Linux 5, the upstream release for Oracle Enterprise Linux 5.

Although the up2date command is available in Oracle Enterprise Linux 5, it no longer implements the original up2date configuration. For the sake of backward compatibility, it has essentially been re-implemented as a wrapper around YUM commands by using YUM repositories. Consistency in configuration across nodes is essential for a clustered environment, so we recommend that you standardize on using only YUM commands for installing packages and resolving dependencies. To implement this approach, we also recommend that you use a local YUM repository (as described previously in this chapter) and synchronize this repository with the systems provided by the ULN. The ULN's YUM Repository Setup explains how to do this. You can then use your own YUM repository as the direct source for updating the packages on the nodes in your cluster. The benefit of this approach: You won't need to rely on an external repository where an interruption in access could render the operating system configurations on the nodes in your cluster inconsistent.

Verifying the Oracle Validated RPM Actions

In addition to installing the required RPM packages, the Oracle Validated RPM installs and runs a script to automate the configuration of the Linux operating system. This script prepares the system for the installation of the Oracle software. If you are unable to run the Oracle Validated RPM (or you choose not to), then reviewing these tasks also serves a checklist for completing the required actions manually.

The script named oracle-validated-verify is located in the /etc/sysconfig/oracle-validated directory with a symbolic link to the script located in /usr/bin. The /etc/sysconfig/oracle-validated directory also includes the file called oracle-validated.params. This file contains the input parameters for the oracle-validated-verify script. After you run this script, you can find a file called orakernel.log in the /etc/sysconfig/oracle-validated/results directory. This log contains the details of the script's actions.

The oracle-validated script's initial actions are to gather details on the system architecture, operating system kernel and distribution release, and the processor type. It uses the uname -m and uname -r commands and the /etc/issue and /proc/cpuinfo files to determine its subsequent actions. These actions are based on the values found in oracle-validated.params. The script also validates that the user running the script is the root user.

Creating the Oracle User and Groups

In some environments, one group of users will install and maintain Oracle software, while a separate group of users will utilize the Oracle software to maintain the database. Maintaining separate groups requires the creation of user groups to draw a distinction between two sets of permissions. The first set lets a group install Oracle software, which requires access to the Oracle Universal Installer (OUI) and oraInventory. The second set grants permissions for a group to accomplish general database administration tasks. These two groups are typically named oinstall and dba.

In most RAC environments, the DBA installs, maintains, and uses the Oracle software. In such cases, the oinstall group may appear superfluous. However, the Oracle inventory group is included in some preinstallation system checks; therefore, using this group for Oracle software installation is a good practice. The oracle-validated-verify script creates the dba and oinstall groups using the commands `groupadd dba` and `groupadd oinstall`, respectively. For a new installation, these groups will have the group IDs of 500 and 501, respectively. If you create these groups manually, you may specify the group ID on the command line:

```
[root@london1 root] # groupadd -g 500 dba
```

Any group ID may be used, but the same group ID should be used for the `dba` and `oinstall` groups on all nodes in the cluster. For this reason, you should ensure that no other groups are created on all the nodes in the cluster until the `oracle-validated-verify` script has been run.

After creating the groups, the script uses the following command to create the `oracle` user as a member of the `dba` and `oinstall` groups:

```
useradd -g oinstall -G dba -d /home/oracle -p $encpasswd oracle
```

Also, note how the preceding line sets the encrypted password environment variable to `oracle`.

As when creating a group, there is no cluster awareness of the user ID when creating a user. If this is the first user created after installation, then the user ID will be 500. Again, you should ensure that this is the same on all the nodes in the cluster. You can run the following command to create the `oracle` user manually:

```
[root@london1 root] # useradd -u 500 -g oinstall -G dba –d /home/oracle oracle
```

The preceding line creates a specific user ID, where the user is also a member of the `dba` and `oinstall` groups. The `oracle` user will be appended to the `/etc/passwd` file, and it will have the group ID of the `dba` group. The user will also be added to the `dba` and `oinstall` groups in the `/etc/group` file, as well as to the default home directory location of `/home/oracle`. The `oinstall` group is the primary group, while the `dba` group is a supplementary group. The `/home` directory can be in any location, but it's good practice to keep it distinct from the `ORACLE_HOME` directory, the default location for Oracle software. By default, the user is created with the default bash shell, which can be modified by using the `useradd` command with the `-s` option.

You can verify that the `oracle` user and `dba` group have been correctly configured using the `id` command, as in this example:

```
[oracle@london1 ~]$ id oracle
uid=500(oracle) gid=501(oinstall) groups=501(oinstall),500(dba)
```

After the `oracle-validated-verify` script creates the account, you should use the `passwd` command to change the default, unsecured password for the `oracle` user to something more secure:

```
[root@london1 root]# passwd oracle
Changing password for user oracle
New password:
Retype new password:
passwd: all authentication tokens updated successfully.
```

To complete the user configuration, you must also manually configure the environment variables for the `oracle` user; you'll learn how to do this later in this chapter.

Configuring Kernel Parameters

After configuring the Oracle user and groups, the Oracle Validated RPM configures the Linux kernel parameters to meet Oracle's recommendations. The updated kernel parameters are set in the file /etc/sysctl.conf; you can find a copy of the original at /etc/sysctl.conf.orabackup. Some of the kernel parameters are set according to value of the total memory in the system, which is retrieved from/proc/meminfo. Existing parameters are modified in place, while additional parameters are added to the end of the /etc/sysctl.conf. These additions are based on the values contained in oracle-validated.params. You can also manually edit the /etc/sysctl.conf file, save its contents, and then apply those settings using the following command:

[root@london1 root]# sysctl -p

The kernel parameters and their correct values for 11g Release 2 are shown in Table 6-6.

Table 6-6. The Kernel Parameter's Recommended Values

Kernel Parameter	Recommended Value
kernel.sem (semmsl)	250
kernel.sem (semmns)	32000
kernel.sem (semopm)	100
kernel.sem (semmni)	142
kernel.shmall	1073741824
kernel.shmmax	4294967295 on x86 4398046511104 on x86-64
kernel.shmmni	4096
kernel.msgmni	2878
kernel.msgmax	8192
kernel.msgmnb	65536
kernel.sysrq	1
fs.file-max	327679
fs.aio-max-nr	3145728
net.core.rmem_default	262144
net.core.rmem_max	4194304
net.core.wmem_default	262144
net.core.wmem_max	262144
net.ipv4.ip_local_port_range	1024 to 65000

The recommended Linux kernel parameter settings are very much general guidelines, but understanding these parameters and how applicable they are to your particular system is essential. You may still need to change some of the updated parameters for your configuration. These parameters can be loosely grouped into five classifications: shared memory, semaphores, network settings, message queues and open files. We will examine each of these classifications next.

Working with Shared Memory

When an Oracle instance starts, it allocates shared memory segments for the SGA. This allocation applies to RAC instances in exactly the same way as a single instance. The SGA has fixed and variable areas. The fixed area size cannot be changed, but the variable area, as the name implies, will vary according to the Oracle database parameters set in the SPFILE or init.ora file.

Within Oracle Database 11g Release 2 RAC, the memory configuration of the SGA and PGA—and consequently, the appropriate kernel parameters—are dependent on whether Automatic Memory Management (AMM), Automatic Shared Memory Management (ASMM), or even manual memory management is used. If AMM is used, then Oracle manages both SGA and PGA from one memory allocation set, according to the Oracle parameters MEMORY_TARGET and MEMORY_MAX_TARGET. If ASMM if used, however, the two most significant Oracle parameters to be aware of for sizing the SGA are SGA_TARGET and SGA_MAX_SIZE. And you must also know that session-level memory set with the PGA_AGGREGATE_TARGET parameter is not allocated from the SGA.

Setting the SGA_TARGET parameter enables Oracle to automatically set the parameters for the variable components of the SGA, such as db_cache_size and shared_pool_size; doing this does not necessarily require manually sizing these components individually. However, manually sized components such as the redo log buffer, streams pool, and nondefault database caches (e.g., the keep, recycle, and nondefault block size caches) are given priority for the allocated shared memory. Subsequently, the balance of the memory is allocated to the automatically sized components.

If you do choose to set these parameters manually, the kernel parameters required are the same as when ASMM is used. You can view the allocated shared memory segments using the ipcs -m command. The following example shows a single shared memory segment created for an SGA_TARGET and SGA_MAX_SIZE that is set to 14GB. The additional shared memory segment in this case is a single 4KB page for the ASM instance, where shmid identifies the memory mapped files in /dev/shm for the use of AMM:

```
[oracle@london1 ~]$ ipcs -m

------ Shared Memory Segments --------
key         shmid     owner     perms    bytes          nattch     status
0x6422c258  32768     oracle    660      4096           0
0x10455eac  98305     oracle    600      15034482688    31
```

You can also view the defined shared memory limits with the ipcs -lm command:

```
[root@london1 ~]# ipcs -lm

------ Shared Memory Limits --------
max number of segments = 4096
max seg size (kbytes) = 47996078
max total shared memory (kbytes) = 32388608
min seg size (bytes) = 1
```

As introduced in Chapter 4, the choice of Oracle memory management determines the operating system call to allocate memory. The shmget() system call is used for ASMM, while the mmap() system call is used for AMM. Failure to set the appropriate memory-related kernel parameters correctly could result in the Oracle instance failing to start with the correct kernel.shmall, kernel.shmmax, and kernel.shmmni parameters for ASMM. The section on Open Files should be reviewed for the parameters relevant to using AMM.

Setting the kernel.shmmax Parameter

The shmmax parameter sets the maximum size (in bytes) for a shared memory segment allowed on the system. By default on Oracle Enterprise Linux 5, shmmax is set to 68719476736, which is 64GB. This parameter limits the maximum permissible size of a single Oracle SGA shared memory segment. Typically, this should be set to exceed the value of SGA_MAX_SIZE, which itself must be greater than SGA_TARGET. If SGA_MAX_SIZE is greater than shmmax, then Oracle will fail to create the SGA in a single shared memory segment. Instead, it will use multiple, smaller shared memory segments. This most significant implications of this behavior occur when there is a NUMA-based architecture (see Chapter 4 for more information).

On NUMA architecture systems, enabling NUMA at the system, operating, and Oracle database levels results in the creation of multiple shared memory segments for the SGA, with one per memory node for an optimal NUMA configuration. (again, see Chapter 4 for information on how to accomplish this). If multiple shared memory segments are created, however, shmmax limitations may keep them from being evenly distributed.

■ **Note** shmmax determines the size of any individual shared memory segment, as opposed to the entire region of shared memory. This holds true whether you set the shmmax parameter to a value smaller than the SGA, or it is set as a result of NUMA optimization.

When creating a single shared memory segment, setting shmmax as follows will limit an Oracle SGA size that uses that single shared memory segment to 2GB:

kernel.shmmax = 2147483648

However, setting this value in excess of your desired SGA_MAX_SIZE enables Oracle to manage its own memory effectively. For example, assume you're on a system with 16GB of RAM available, an SGA_MAX_SIZE of 10GB, and an SGA_TARGET of 8GB. In this case, setting kernel.shmmax as follows enables a maximum shared memory segment of just over 10GB, which is above that required by the Oracle parameters:

kernel.shmmax = 10737418240

The Oracle Validated RPM sets the value for this parameter to 4398046511104 (4TB) on x86-64 or 4294967295 (4 GB) on x86. This helps ensure that the parameter's limit is above the architectural memory limits discussed in Chapter 4.

Setting the kernel.shmmni Parameter

The shmmni parameter specifies the maximum number of shared memory segments permissible on the entire system. For an Oracle system with one shared memory segment per SGA, this parameter reflects the maximum number of Oracle instances, including ASM instances that you wish to start on a single server. Therefore, the default value of 4096 is retained by the Oracle Validated RPM. In an operational environment, however, the number of shared memory segments is highly unlikely to ever approach this value.

Setting the kernel.shmall Parameter

Use the shmall parameter to define the maximum number of shared memory pages that can be allocated at any one time on the system; its default value is 4294967296 on x86-64 based architectures, which is equivalent to 16TB. This value is given in system pages, not in bytes, and it should be set to at least the value of shmmax/system page size. This helps ensure that sufficient memory pages are allocated to a single required SGA. Using the following Oracle Validated RPM value of on an x86-64 system, with a default 4KB page size, reduces the maximum shared memory allocation of 4398046511104 so that it is precisely equal to the 4TB limit of shmmax:

```
kernel.shmall = 1073741824
```

Therefore, the system default setting for shmall or the Oracle Validated RPM value both significantly exceed the physical memory that is supported on an x86-64 architecture system.

Using Semaphores

Semaphores are used by Oracle for resource management. They serve as a post/wait mechanism by enqueues and writers for events, such as free buffer waits. Semaphores are used extensively by Oracle, and they are allocated to Oracle at instance start-up in sets by the Linux kernel. Processes use semaphores from the moment they attach to an Oracle instance waiting on semop() system calls. Semaphores are set with the sysctl command or in the /etc/sysctl.conf file. This behavior differs from that of other Unix operating systems, where the different values are often allocated individually. You can view the semaphore limits on your system with the command ipcs -ls:

```
[root@london1 ~]# ipcs -ls

------ Semaphore Limits --------
max number of arrays = 128
max semaphores per array = 250
max semaphores system wide = 32000
max ops per semop call = 100
semaphore max value = 32767
```

You use the kernel.sem parameter to control the number of semaphores on your system. The Oracle Validated RPM sets the value of kernel.sem to the following values:

```
kernel.sem = 250 32000 100 142
```

This setting allocates values for the semmsl, semmns, semopm, and semmni parameters, respectively.

Semaphores can be viewed with the operating system command ipcs -ls .The semmsl parameter defines the total number of semaphores in a semaphore set. This parameter should be set to the Oracle Validated RPM value of 250. Setting semmsl should always be considered in terms of semmns because both parameters impact the same system resources.

The semmns parameter sets the total number of semaphores permitted in the Linux system, and 32000 is the recommended default high-range value. The previously discussed semmsl value sets the maximum number of semaphores per set, while semmni sets the maximum number of semaphore sets. This means that the overall number of semaphores that can be allocated will be the minimum value of semmns or semmsl, multiplied by the value of semmni. A default value of 32000 for semmns ensures that this value is used by the system for its total semaphore limit.

The semopm parameter defines the maximum number of semaphore operations that can be performed by the semop() system call. In Linux, semop() can set multiple semaphores within a single system call. The recommended setting for this value is 100.

The semmni parameter sets the maximum number of total semaphore sets defined, and it should have a minimum value of 128. Multiplying this value by a semmsl value of 250 precisely equals the semmns setting of 32000. Although the Oracle Validated RPM sets this value to 142, it is overridden by semmns.

Unless an extremely large number of Oracle user connections are required on each node, the Oracle Validated RPM semaphore settings should be sufficient.

Setting Network Parameters

Setting network parameters correctly is especially important in a RAC environment because of its reliance on a local high-performance network interconnect between the Oracle instances. The next section describes the kernel parameters modified by the Oracle Validated RPM.

Setting the net.ipv4.ip_local_port_range Parameter

The net.ipv4.ip_local_port_range parameter sets the range of local ports for outgoing connections. The Oracle Validated RPM changes the lower port value to 1024 and the upper port to 65000. However, the OUI for some releases of Oracle 11g Release 2 reports this as an error, and instead specifies a port range of 9000 to 65500. You may either ignore this warning and maintain the Oracle Validated RPM values or modify them to the OUI values to prevent installation warnings.

Setting the net.core.* Set of Parameters

A RAC environment includes a set of four parameters that have names that begin with net.core:

```
net.core.rmem_default, net.core.wmem_default,
net.core.rmem_max, net.core.wmem_max
```

In Linux versions based on the 2.6 kernel, you no longer strictly need to set the values of these four kernel parameters for TCP values. That's because these parameters are tuned automatically. However, because they affect all protocols, they are necessary for UDP, which is the default for protocol for the Oracle RAC interconnect communication with Gigabit Ethernet.

Values for these parameters are the default setting (in bytes) of the socket receive and send buffers, as well as the maximum sizes of these buffers. The Oracle Validated RPM modifies these values to 262144, except for net.core.rmem_max, which is set to 4194304. For some releases of Oracle 11g Release 2, the OUI reports the net.core.wmem_max setting as an error; instead, it requires a value of 1048576. You may either retain the Oracle Validated RPM value or set it to the OUI required value. Setting both the manual values and the auto-tune parameters has a different effect for both the default and maximum parameters for the TCP protocol. For TCP auto-tuning, the values of tcp_rmem and tcp_wmem specify the minimum, default, and maximum values of the socket send and receive buffers. An equivalent setting to the Oracle Validated RPM configuration would look like this:

```
net.ipv4.tcp_rmem = 4096 262144 4194304
net.ipv4.tcp_wmem = 4096 262144 4194304
```

In terms of the default parameters, the auto-tune values take precedence, so you must set them to achieve Oracle's recommended value of 262144. For the maximum values, however, the static settings take precedence, overriding the auto-tune parameters.

Message Queues

Processes that include Oracle processes can communicate in an asynchronous manner with interprocess communication (IPC) messages. These messages are placed into a message queue where they can be read by another process. An example of this in an Oracle database environment is the communication that takes place between the foreground and background processes visible through the Oracle wait events, rdbms ipc message and rdbms ipc reply. The rdbms ipc message is sent by a background process when idle and waiting for a foreground process to send a message. You can view the message queue limits on your system with the command ipcs -lq, as shown:

```
[root@london1 ~]# ipcs -lq

------ Messages: Limits --------
max queues system wide = 16
max size of message (bytes) = 65536
default max size of queue (bytes) = 65536
```

The ipcs -lq command provides information on three message queue parameters:

- msgmni: Sets the number of message queues identifiers, which is the number of individual message queues permitted on the system. The default value is 16, and the Oracle Validated RPM increases this to 2878.

- msgmax: Sets the maximum message size. The default size is 8192 bytes, and the Oracle Validated RPM preserves this value. All messages queued between processes are held in memory, and msgmax cannot be greater than the size of an individual queue.

- msgmnb: Sets the maximum combined value (in bytes) of all of the messages on an individual message queue at any one time. The default queue size is 16384, and the Oracle Validated RPM increases this to 65536 or 64KB.

Setting the Number of Open Files

The parameter that affects the number of open files is fs.file-max, and the Oracle Validated RPM sets this parameter to 327679. The fs.file-max parameter is used to set the maximum limit of open files for all processes on the system. This value is likely to be lower than the default value, which is determined dynamically based on the system memory. For example, this value is 1545510 on a x86-64 system with Oracle Enterprise Linux 5 and 16GB RAM; for 18BG of RAM, this value is 1773467. On some releases of

Oracle 11g Release 2, this value is also lower than the minimum value checked by the OUI of 6815744, although you may ignore this warning if the Oracle Validated RPM setting meets your requirements. (You may also choose to change the parameter it to the OUI required value to prevent the warnings.)

The number of open and available file handles on the system can be seen in /proc/sys/fs/file-nr. In an ASM environment, using ASMLIB will reduce the total number of file descriptors across the system. Conversely, in an AMM environment, using ASMLIB increases demand on the required file descriptors across the system.

In contrast to ASMM, using AMM means that both SGA and PGA memory are managed in a unified manner by setting the memory-related parameters, MEMORY_TARGET and MEMORY_MAX_TARGET. To manage the SGA and PGA memory together, the Oracle 11g Database on Linux uses the tmpfs file system mounted at /dev/shm for a POSIX implementation of shared memory, using the mmap() and shm_open() system calls instead of shmget().

By default, tmpfs is allocated from virtual memory. Thus it can include both physical RAM and swap space, and it is sized to half of physical memory without swap space. However, unlike huge pages, which you will learn more about later in this chapter, tmpfs memory allocation is dynamic. Therefore, if tmpfs is not used, it does not take any allocation of memory, and it does not require a change in settings if AMM is not used. When AMM is used, Oracle allocates a number of memory mapped files in tmpfs. These files are allocated with at a file, or *granule*, size ranging from 4MB to MEMORY_MAX_TARGET of 1GB and 16MB when it is greater than 1GB. The allocated files can be identified by the shmid of the corresponding single page shared memory segment. The following example shows single page shared memory segments for both an ASM instance and a database instance:

```
[oracle@london1 ~]$ ipcs -m

------ Shared Memory Segments --------
key        shmid    owner     perms     bytes     nattch     status
0x6422c258 557056   oracle    660       4096      0
0x10455eac 819201   oracle    660       4096      0
```

The allocated memory itself can be viewed in the mounted directory of /dev/shm. The zero-sized segments are mapped by Oracle processes to constitute a memory allocation up to MEMORY_MAX_TARGET, but these are not yet allocated to any of the dynamic components identified within V$MEMORY_DYNAMIC_COMPONENTS; thus they do not consume any physical memory. By default, the tmpfs file system allocates half of physical memory. Therefore, if your MEMORY_TARGET parameter exceeds this value, then the instance will fail to start with the error:

```
SQL> ORA-00845: MEMORY_TARGET not supported on this system
```

You may want to increase the size of the memory allocation in a manner that is persistent across reboots. To do this, begin by unmounting the /dev/shm file system, and then modifying the entry in /etc/fstab relating to tmpfs:

```
[root@london1 ~]# more /etc/fstab
/dev/VolGroup00/LogVol00 /              ext3    defaults         1 1
LABEL=/boot              /boot          ext3    defaults         1 2
tmpfs                    /dev/shm       tmpfs   defaults,size=15g 0 0
devpts                   /dev/pts       devpts  gid=5,mode=620   0 0
sysfs                    /sys           sysfs   defaults         0 0
proc                     /proc          proc    defaults         0 0
/dev/VolGroup00/LogVol01 swap           swap    defaults         0 0
```

Next, remount the file system to view the newly allocated space. Note that, until the memory is used, allocating a larger amount of memory to `tmpfs` does not actually result in the memory being utilized immediately:

```
[root@london1 ~]# df -h
Filesystem            Size  Used Avail Use% Mounted on
/dev/mapper/VolGroup00-LogVol00
                      433G  147G  264G  36% /
/dev/sda1              99M   13M   82M  14% /boot
tmpfs                 15G     0   15G   0% /dev/shm
```

You should keep the following in mind when working with the kernel parameter settings of the Oracle Validated RPM: when using AMM limits on memory, memory allocation is partly determined by the number of file descriptors, but it is not dependent on the shared memory parameters previously discussed in this section. Oracle recommends that the number of file descriptors be set to a value of at least 512*PROCESSES. This means that the Oracle Validated RPM setting of `fs.file-max` is sufficient for an Oracle processes value of up to 640. Failure to have a sufficient number of file descriptors will result in the following error: `ORA-27123: unable to attach to shared memory segment`. There is also a per user limit for the number of open files, in addition to the system-wide value, which by default is set to 1024. The Oracle Validated RPM modifies this per user value in the file `/etc/security/limits.conf`; you'll learn more about this in this chapter's section on PAM limits configuration.

When using AMM, there are some distinctions that you should be aware of in comparison to ASMM. First, if you're operating in a virtualized environment such as the Oracle VM (see Chapter 5), then `MEMORY_MAX_TARGET` cannot be allocated to a value greater than the memory currently allocated to the system. This limits the levels of memory that can be allocated and de-allocated to the operating system dynamically. On the other hand, `SGA_MAX_SIZE` can be set to larger than the available memory, which offers more flexibility in this case. Additionally, AMM cannot be configured in conjunction with huge pages. You should consider all of these factors when weighing the relative merits of using huge pages or AMM.

Configuring Asynchronous I/O

The parameter `fs.aio-max-nr` sets the maximum number of concurrent asynchronous I/O operations permitted on the system. By default, this parameter is set to 65536, and the Oracle Validated RPM increases this to 3145828. The actual system value can be seen in `/proc/sys/fs/aio-nr`. If `/proc/sys/fs/aio-nr` is equal to `fs.aio-max-nr`, then asynchronous I/O operations will be impacted. However, if you are using ASMLIB, then the value of `/proc/sys/fs/aio-nr` does not exceed a value of greater than 0. In this case, setting `fs.aio-max-nr` to any value has no effect. Changing the value of `aio-max-nr` does not allocate additional memory to kernel data structures, so it can be maintained at the default value.

Using Magic SysRq Keys

When the Alt+SysRq+Ctr key combination is pressed on the system console, it enables direct communication with the kernel. This functionality is primarily enabled for debugging purposes. This feature is termed the *Magic SysRq key*, and it is enabled in the Linux kernel of Oracle Enterprise Linux 5. By default, however, the parameter `kernel.sysrq` is set to 0 to disable this functionality. The Oracle Validated RPM sets this parameter to 1 to enable all of the command key combinations, although a bitmask of values between 2 and 256 can be set to limit the number of commands available. An example key combination is Alt+SysRq+b, which immediately reboots the system. The value in kernel.sysrq only enables the system request functionality when the key combination is entered on the console keyboard. The same functionality is enabled in /proc/sysrq-trigger, regardless of the value of this setting. For example, the following command from the root user will also reboot the system, even if kernel.sysrq is set to 0:

```
echo b > /proc/sysrq-trigger
```

Clusterware uses the preceding command to reset a node in the cluster.

Other notable Magic SysRq values include *t*, which provides a detailed debugging report on the activity of all processes in the system; and *m*, which provides a report on memory usage. Both of these reports can be viewed in /var/log/messages or with the dmesg command. However, because the Magic SysRq commands communicate directly with the kernel, these debugging reports should be used infrequently and not as part of commands or scripts that you run regularly for system monitoring purposes.

Setting the parameter kernel.sysrq can be a matter of choice of security policies. However, this enabled functionality requires access to the console keyboard, so it will typically mean that the user has access to the physical system, such as the power supply.

Setting PAM Limits

Linux Pluggable Authentication Modules (PAM) are responsible for a number of authentication and privilege tasks on the system. You can find a number of modules to deal with activities such as password management, and the Oracle Validated RPM in particular sets values for the pam_limits module that determines which resources on the system can be allocated by a single user session, as opposed to across the system as a whole; that is, it determines the limits that are set at the login time of a session and not cumulative values for all sessions combined. For this reason, the important session is the one that is used to start the Oracle database. These limits are set for the oracle user in the file /etc/security/limits.conf, as in the following example, which shows the settings for an x86-64 system:

```
oracle   soft   nofile   131072
oracle   hard   nofile    131072
oracle   soft   nproc     131072
oracle   hard   nproc     131072
oracle   soft   core      unlimited
oracle   hard   core      unlimited
oracle   soft   memlock   50000000
oracle   hard   memlock   50000000
```

The values can be observed at the oracle user level; use the command ulimit -a to see all parameters:

```
[oracle@london1 ~]$ ulimit -a
core file size          (blocks, -c) 0
data seg size           (kbytes, -d) unlimited
scheduling priority             (-e) 0
file size               (blocks, -f) unlimited
pending signals                 (-i) 155648
max locked memory       (kbytes, -l) 15360000
```

```
max memory size          (kbytes, -m) unlimited
open files                       (-n) 131072
pipe size            (512 bytes, -p) 8
POSIX message queues      (bytes, -q) 819200
real-time priority               (-r) 0
stack size               (kbytes, -s) 10240
cpu time                (seconds, -t) unlimited
max user processes               (-u) 131072
virtual memory           (kbytes, -v) unlimited
file locks                       (-x) unlimited
```

Alternatively, you can use the ulimit command with the relevant argument in the preceding example to see the value of an individual parameter. For all of the relevant parameters, the Oracle Validated RPM sets both the soft and hard limits to the same value. Typically, the hard value is set higher than the soft value, and the user is able to increase or decrease the session level soft value up to the hard value. However, when these values are the same, the hard limit is the single enforceable value that the user cannot exceed.

The following four parameters affect PAM limits:

- nofile: Sets the maximum number of open files at the session level. Note that this parameter is also limited by fs.file-max at the system level. However, when using features such as AMM, the user limit of 131072 will be the enforced value in the context of the maximum number of open files for the oracle user.

- nproc: Sets the maximum number of concurrent processes that a user can have running at any one time. nproc does not represent a cumulative value of all the processes created within an individual session.

- core: Sets (in KBs) a limit on the size of the core dump file generated as a result of the abnormal termination of a running program. The Oracle validated RPM sets this value to unlimited.

- memlock: Sets the maximum amount of memory that the user can lock in memory (i.e., memory allocated from physical RAM that cannot be swapped out). This parameter is particularly important in determining the memory limit (in kilobytes) that Oracle can take from a huge pages allocation. The Oracle Validated RPM sets this value (in KBs) to 50000000 (48 GB) on x86-64 and to 3500000 (3.3 GB) on x86.

Setting Kernel Boot Parameters

For AMD x86-64 architecture processors, the Oracle Validated RPM modifies the kernel boot parameters in the file /boot/grub/grub.conf to set the parameter numa=off. This parameter setting disables NUMA features (see Chapter 4 for more information); however, NUMA is not disabled on recent generations of Intel x86-64 architecture processors, which are also based on NUMA. Therefore, we recommend reviewing the NUMA section in Chapter 4 to determine the potential impact that this setting may have on different systems. We also recommend testing your configuration for its impact upon performance.

Setting Kernel Module Parameters

In addition to modifying kernel boot parameters, the Oracle Validated RPM also sets individual kernel module parameters. In particular, the script examines the file /etc/modprobe.conf for the presence of the e1000 driver, which is the device driver for Intel PRO 1000 Network Adapters. The script adds the option FlowControl=1 where this driver is present. *Flow control* is a method of using standard Ethernet pause frames to manage communication and prevent buffer overruns in cases where the sender is sending data faster than the receiver can handle it. For the e1000 driver, the FlowControl option determines whether these pause frames are both generated and responded to. The possible values are 0, which disables the feature; 1, which means receive only; 2, which means transmit only; and 3, which enables both transmitting and receiving. The Oracle Validated RPM sets this parameter for receive only. The impact of the setting can be viewed with the ethtool application with the -a argument. Note that this setting only applies to the e1000 driver for PCI and PCI-X devices. For later PCI-Express devices, the e1000e or igb drivers will be used; therefore, this setting does not apply to the later devices.

Post Oracle Validated RPM Configuration

In the next section, we review the areas where the Oracle Validated RPM has completed the base level of configuration that is applicable to both RAC and single instance environments. However, in these areas, additional changes are warranted specifically for an Oracle Database 11*g* Release 2 RAC environment.

Setting the Huge Pages Kernel Parameter

An additional kernel parameter that can bring performance benefits to an Oracle Database 11*g* Release 2 RAC on Linux configuration is vm.nr_hugepages, which implement a feature known variously as large pages, huge pages, and hugetlb.

Setting vm.nr_hugepages with sysctl configures the number of huge pages available for the system; the default value is 0. The size of an individual huge page is dependent on the Linux operating system installed and the hardware architecture. The huge page size on your system can be viewed at the end of /proc/meminfo.

The following example for an x86-64 system with Oracle Enterprise Linux 5 system shows a default huge page size of 2MB:

```
[root@london1 root]# cat /proc/meminfo
...
HugePages_Total:   0
HugePages_Free:    0
Hugepagesize:      2048kB
```

Some systems also enable the setting of a 1GB huge page size. Therefore, this page size value should always be known before setting the vm.nr_hugepages value.

Huge pages are allocated as much larger contiguous memory pages than the standard system pages. Such pages improve performance at the Translation Lookaside Buffer (TLB) level. As discussed in greater detail in Chapter 4, a larger page size enables a large range of memory addresses to be stored closer to the CPU level, increasing the speed of Oracle SGA access. This approach increases access speed by improving the likelihood that the virtual memory address of the pages that Oracle requires is already cached.

The vm.nr_hugepages parameter can be set at runtime. However, the pages are required to be contiguous. Therefore, we advise setting the required number in /etc/sysctl.conf, which is applied at boot time. Once allocated, huge pages are not pageable. This guarantees that an Oracle SGA using them will always remain resident in main memory.

The vm.nr_hugepages parameter must be set to a multiple of the huge page size to reach a value greater than the required Oracle SGA size. In addition, the Oracle user must have permission to use huge pages; this permission is granted by the memlock parameter discussed previously in this chapter.

For testing purposes, the huge page allocation can be mounted as a file system of type hugetlbfs, and memory can be utilized from this allocation using mmap(). However, at the time of writing, this mounted file system does not support AMM, nor does it support shmget() when using Oracle. Thus, there is no requirement for the hugetlbfs file system to be mounted during normal operations.

When the Oracle 11g instance starts, the shmget() call to allocate the shared memory for the SGA includes the SHM_HUGETLB flag to use huge pages, if available. If you're using ASMM or if the SGA required, then the SGA_MAX_SIZE is greater than the huge pages available. In this case, Oracle will not use any huge pages at all. Instead, it will use standard memory pages. The huge pages will still remain allocated to their pool; this will reduce the overall amount of available memory for general use on the system because huge pages will only be used for shared memory. The shmmax parameter is still applicable when using huge pages, and it still must be sized greater than the desired Oracle SGA size.

The values in the file /proc/meminfo can be viewed again to monitor the successful use of huge pages. After an Oracle instance is started, viewing /proc/meminfo will show the following:

```
HugePages_Total:   7500
HugePages_Free:     299
HugePages_Rsvd:       0
Hugepagesize:      2048 kB
```

This output shows that 7500 huge pages were created, and the Oracle instance took 14GB of this huge page allocation for its SGA. If the instance has been started and the total remains the same as the free value, then Oracle has failed to use huge pages, and the SGA has been allocated from the standard pages. You should ensure that this is the case when starting the instance with both sqlplus and the srvctl command. It is also possible to reduce the value of the vm.nr_hugepages value after the instance has been started and re-run the sysctl -p command to release remaining unallocated and unreserved huge pages.

When setting the shmall parameter, the huge pages are expressed in terms of standard system memory pages, and one single huge page taken as shared memory will be translated into the equivalent number of standard system pages when allocated from the available shmall total. The shmall value needs to account for all of the huge pages used expressed in the number of standard pages, not just the finite Oracle SGA size. setting shmall to the number of huge pages Failing to account for all of the huge pages would result in the following Oracle error when starting the instance:

```
ORA-27102: out of memory
Linux-x86-64 Error: 28: No space left on device
```

When correctly managed, huge pages can both provide performance benefits and reduce the memory required for page tables. For example, the following snippet from /proc/meminfo shows the memory consumed by page tables for a huge pages configuration on x86-64:

```
[root@london1 ~]# cat /proc/meminfo
...
PageTables:       24336 kB
...
```

```
HugePages_Total:   7500
HugePages_Free:     331
HugePages_Rsvd:       0
Hugepagesize:      2048 kB
```

This allocation is not fixed because page tables are built dynamically for all processes as required. However, if the parameter PRE_PAGE_SGA is set to true, then these page tables are built at the time of process creation. PRE_PAGE_SGA can impact both instance and session startup times, as well as memory consumption. Therefore, we only recommend setting this parameter in an environment where its impact has been assessed. For example, it may be applicable in a system where performance is being analyzed and the number of sessions created is fixed for the duration. However, this parameter is less applicable in cases where there a number of sessions that connect to and disconnect from the database in an ad-hoc manner. The following example shows a system without huge pages, where the page tables have already grown to more than 1GB in size:

```
[oracle@london1 ~]$ cat /proc/meminfo
PageTables:    1090864 kB
...
HugePages_Total:      0
HugePages_Free:       0
HugePages_Rsvd:       0
Hugepagesize:      2048 kB
```

However, there are caveats that should be kept in mind when using huge pages. As noted previously, huge pages are only used with shared memory; therefore, they should not be allocated to more than is required by the SGA. Additionally, at the time of writing, huge pages are not compatible with Oracle VM or AMM, as discussed earlier. Therefore using huge pages requires more manual intervention by the DBA for memory management. For these reasons, we recommend that you test the use of huge pages to assess whether the additional management delivers performance and memory efficiency benefits for your environment.

I/O Fencing and the Hangcheck-Timer Kernel Module

In a RAC environment, Oracle needs to rapidly detect and isolate any occurrence of node failure within the cluster. It is particularly important to ensure that, once a node has entered an uncertain state, it is evicted from the cluster to prevent possible disk corruption caused by access that is not controlled by the database or cluster software. With Oracle RAC at 10g and 11.1, eviction at the Oracle software level was managed by Oracle Clusterware's Process Monitor Daemon (OPROCD). On the Linux operating system, eviction was ensured by the hangcheck-timer kernel module.

When Clusterware was operational, both the oprocd and the hangcheck-timer were run at the same time. Although the hangcheck-timer remains a requirement for RAC at Oracle 11g Release 1, it is no longer a requirement for RAC at Oracle 11g Release 2. At this release, there is also no oprocd daemon, and the functionality has been implemented within Clusterware's cssdagent and cssdmonitor processes, without requiring the additional hangcheck-timer kernel module. The timeout value for resetting a node remains equal to Oracle Clusterware's misscount value. This configurable value is given in the file crsconfig_params and set when the root.sh script is run as part of the Grid Infrastructure software installation. By default, the value of CLSCFG_MISSCOUNT is left unset in Oracle 11g Release 2, and the parameter takes the default value of 30 seconds as confirmed with the crsctl command after installing the Grid Infrastructure software:

```
[oracle@london1 bin]$ ./crsctl get css misscount
30
```

If you do wish to configure an additional timer with respect to this misscount value in Oracle 11*g* Release 2, then we recommend evaluating and testing the optional functionality provided by IPMI, rather than using the hangcheck-timer kernel module (you'll learn more about this later in this chapter). An IPMI-based timer can provide functionality above and beyond Oracle Clusterware. This is because it can be implemented in a hardware-independent fashion from the operating system itself. In this case, it is possible to reset a system undergoing a permanent hang state. If activating an IPMI-based timer, we recommend a timeout value of at least double the configured misscount value. This will both complement Clusterware's functionality, but also enable Clusterware to serve as the primary agent in evicting failed nodes from the cluster.

Configuring the oracle user

As noted previously in this chapter, the oracle user is created by the Oracle Validated RPM. This user can be the owner of both the Oracle database and Grid Infrastructure software. If you do not need to explicitly create additional users for your environment, then we recommend maintaining this default ownership. However, if you wish to have a different owner for the Grid Infrastructure software, then you may also create the grid user using the methods detailed previously for the oracle user. You must also ensuring that the oinstall group is specified for the initial group. Next, we will focus on the configuration of the environment of the oracle user only as owner of all installed Oracle software, including the database software, the Grid Infrastructure software of Clusterware, and ASM.

Creating the Oracle Software Directories

Before installing the Oracle software, you need to create the directories to install Oracle 11*g* Release 2. These directories correspond to the environment variables you will set for the oracle user. The directories you create will depend on whether you wish to implement a configuration adhering to the OFA; unless you have a policy in place that prevents you from being OFA-compliant, then we recommend that you follow the OFA guidelines for directory configuration. For an OFA-compliant configuration, you will create a parent directory of /u01 or later or a separate /u01 disk partition under the root file system. All other directories containing Oracle software will be created under this directory.

When the Oracle software is installed, the OUI will search for an OFA directory configuration the oracle user has permission to write to, such as /u01/app. The OUI will use this directory for the Oracle software configuration. The OUI will create the oraInventory directory in this location with permissions set to the oinstall group. This ensures that if multiple users are configured, all users will be able to read and modify the contents of oraInventory. If the ORACLE_BASE environment variable is set, then this takes preference over the OFA-compliant directory structure. Of course, if ORACLE_BASE is set to the OFA-compliant directory of /u01/app/oracle, then the outcome is the same. If ORACLE_BASE is not set and an OFA directory structure is not available, then the oracle user directory is used for software installation. However, the default permissions in this configuration do more than prevent the oracle user having ownership of the Oracle software.

If basing your installation on OFA, then your directory structure will be based on an ORACLE_BASE for the oracle user, but on a separate ORACLE_HOME directory also termed the ORA_CRS_HOME for the Grid infrastructure software. For the Grid Infrastructure software, the subdirectory structure must be owned by the root user once it's operational. Therefore, the directory must be installed directly under ORACLE_BASE. The /u01/app should also be owned by root, but with a group of oinstall to permit access to the oraInventory directory. Similarly, installations owned by the oracle user should be under

285

the ORACLE_BASE directory. For the database ORACLE_HOME, the directory structure should be owned by the oracle user.

When configuring an OFA-compliant structure for both the Grid Infrastructure software and Oracle database software, we recommend that you create the ORACLE_BASE directory and allow the OUI to create the ORACLE_HOME and ORA_CRS_HOME to default specifications.

Issue the following commands as root to implement this minimum requirement:

```
[root@london1 root]# mkdir -p /u01/app/oracle
[root@london1 root]# chown -R root:oinstall /u01
[root@london1 root]# chmod -R 775 /u01
```

Using mkdir, the directories specified by ORA_CRS_HOME and ORACLE_HOME can also be pre-created to use the preferred directory structure instead of the default values from the OUI, which are /u01/app/11.2.0/grid/ for the Grid Infrastructure software and /u01/app/oracle/product/11.2.0/dbhome_1/ for the Database software. Initially, the permissions on these directories should be set to 775. After a successful default Grid infrastructure software installation, however, some of the directory ownership and permissions will have been changed to an owner of root, group of oinstall, and permissions of 755.

```
[root@london1 /]# ls -ld /u01
drwxr-xr-x 3 root oinstall 4096 Sep 17 14:03 /u01
[root@london1 /]# ls -ld /u01/app
drwxr-xr-x 5 root oinstall 4096 Sep 17 15:25 /u01/app
[root@london1 /]# ls -ld /u01/app/11.2.0/grid/
drwxr-xr-x 64 root oinstall 4096 Sep 17 15:32 /u01/app/11.2.0/grid/
```

Under the grid directory itself, some of the directories will be owned by root, such as bin, crs, css, and gns. However, the majority of the directory structure will retain ownership under the oracle user (or grid user, if you have chosen a separate owner for the Grid Infrastructure software). The default ORACLE_HOME and oraInventory directory will retain the following permissions after the Database software has also been installed:

```
[root@london1 /]# ls -ld /u01/app/oracle/product/11.2.0/dbhome_1/
drwxr-xr-x 72 oracle oinstall 4096 Sep 17 17:07
[root@london1 /]# ls -ld /u01/app/oraInventory/
drwxrwx--- 5 oracle oinstall 4096 Sep 17 17:10
```

Setting Environment Variables

With the oracle user created and the password supplied by the Oracle Validated RPM, it is possible to log in with the newly created oracle user account. The oracle user account will be configured with a default ~/.bash_profile in the oracle user's home directory, which will resemble the following:

```
[oracle@london1 oracle]$ cat ~/.bash_profile
# .bash_profile

# Get the aliases and functions
if [ -f ~/.bashrc ]; then
        . ~/.bashrc
fi
```

```
# User specific environment and startup programs

PATH=$PATH:$HOME/bin

export PATH
unset USERNAME
```

If you are using the OFA directory structure, you do not need to update the default ~/.bash_profile file with any environment variables before installing the Oracle Grid Infrastructure or Oracle database software. The installation will create the default directory structure detailed in the previous section. In fact, Oracle explicitly recommends not setting the environment variables ORA_CRS_HOME, ORACLE_HOME, ORA_NLS10, or TNS_ADMIN. And should you set the ORACLE_BASE environment variable only if you wish to change the installation locations from the default OFA.

Oracle has previously asserted that the ORACLE_BASE environment variable will become mandatory in future versions; however, at version 11g, it is not required if you are satisfied with the default such as /u01/app/oracle. Oracle recommends that you not set the additional environment variables because they are used extensively in the installation scripts. Therefore, not setting the variables ensures that there are no conflicting locations defined. If you do set the ORACLE_HOME environment variable, then your settings will override the default installation location for both the Grid Infrastructure software and Oracle database software. Thus, you should be aware of the correct relationship between the ownership and permissions of the different directory structures. You should also ensure that your settings comply with the appropriate guidelines.

After installation, you should set the required environment variables for the operation and administration of your system. Within the ~/.bash_profile file, you should also set the following set the value of umask to 022.

The umask command applies a default mask to the permissions on newly created files and directories. The value 022 ensures that these are created with permissions of 644; this prevents other users from writing to the files created by the Oracle software owner.

■ **Note** The ~/.bashrc file is primarily for setting user-defined aliases and functions with environment variables being added directly to the ~/.bash_profile file. Oracle does not require any additional aliases and functions, so there is no need to modify this file.

For Oracle 11g Release 2 RAC, the following environment variables should be set for the oracle user: PATH, ORACLE_SID, ORACLE_HOME, and ORACLE_BASE. Environment variables must be configured identically on all nodes except for ORACLE_SID, which is instance specific. The correct setting of the ORACLE_SID variable is dependent upon the chosen approach for workload management; you can learn more about this in Chapter 11. The following sections detail the purpose of the most relevant environment variables applicable to an oracle user installing and administering 11g Release 2 RAC on Linux.

Setting the ORACLE_BASE Variable

The ORACLE_BASE environment variable defines the root of the Oracle database software directory tree. If the ORACLE_BASE environment variable is not set explicitly, it will default to first to an OFA-compliant configuration. If such a configuration doesn't exit, it will default to the value of the oracle user's home directory. However, you should set your ORACLE_BASE environment variable to the setting defined by the OUI after installation is complete.

All Oracle database software installed on the system is located below the directory specified by ORACLE_BASE, which would be similar to /u01/app/oracle if you're using the recommended OFA-compliant directory structure. The oracle user must have been granted read, write, and execute privileges on this directory. If you're installing Oracle 11g Release 2 software on an ASM Cluster File System (ACFS), on an OCFS2 file system on SAN, or on NAS storage presented as an NFS file system, then the ORACLE_BASE and the directories below it can be located on this shared storage with a single directory. Also, the software installation should be shared between all of the nodes in the cluster. It is important to distinguish between the location of the Oracle 11g Release 2 database software and the Oracle Grid Infrastructure software, which must be installed on storage local to the node and not on a shared file system.

As noted previously, the Oracle Grid Infrastructure Software is not installed below ORACLE_BASE, but in a directory parallel to such as /u01/app/11.2.0/grid. This directory is known variously as the ORA_CRS_HOME, CRS_HOME, or GRID_HOME and ownership belongs to the root user. The /u01/app directory also belongs to the root user, but it goes under the oinstall group to enable the oracle user access to the oraInventory location. How you set ORACLE_BASE also determines the default location of the Oracle 11g Database DIAGNOSTIC_DEST parameter, which replaces the previous background, user, and core dump destinations.

Setting the ORACLE_HOME Variable

The ORACLE_HOME environment variable specifies where the Oracle database software is installed. The ORACLE_HOME location must not be the same as ORA_CRS_HOME. For the Oracle database software a typical default location would be /u01/app/oracle/product/11.2.0/dbhome_1 if the ORACLE_HOME environment variable is not set before installation, the actual default location is determined by the OUI in a path dependent on whether ORACLE_BASE is also set. If ORACLE_BASE is set the ORACLE_HOME environment variables can also be set temporarily to ORA_CRS_HOME before installing the Grid Infrastructure software to ensure that the Grid Infrastructure Software is installed in a separate location from the ORACLE_BASE. After installation the ORACLE_HOME is used in many configuration environments to identify the location of the Oracle database software and configuration files and if accepting the default OUI values you should ensure that it is set correctly to these values after the install is complete.

Configuring the ORACLE_SID Variable

The ORACLE_SID environment variable defines the Oracle system identifier (SID) of the database instance on an individual node. In a standard, single-instance Oracle environment, the ORACLE_SID is the same as the global database name. In a RAC environment, each node has an instance accessing the same database. Therefore, each instance should have a different value for ORACLE_SID. We recommend that these values should take the form of the global database name, which begins with an alphabetic character, can be up to eight characters in length, and has a suffix for which the default is the instance number. For example, a database with a global database name of PROD might have these corresponding ORACLE_SID values on different nodes: PROD1, PROD2, PROD3, and PROD4.

If you're configuring an administrator-managed approach to workload management, then you can set the ORACLE_SID statically set for each node in the cluster, as well as its corresponding instance. If you're configuring a policy managed database, however, then you don't want to fix the ORACLE_SID on a particular node. Instead, you want to allocate it dynamically to nodes according to the workload policy. For this reason, if the ORACLE_SID environment variable is statically set, it may not correspond to the instance running on a node at a particular point in time. Therefore, it should reference the name of the current running instance before being set accordingly. Alternatively, under a policy managed database, the instances may be pinned to their respective nodes to ensure that Clusterware maintains the same node number order. Thus, you might pin the same ORACLE_SID allocation with this command:

```
crsctl pin css -n
...
```

Setting the ORA_CRS_HOME Variable

The ORA_CRS_HOME environment variable specifies the directory located parallel to the ORACLE_BASE directory. This is the directory where the Oracle Grid Infrastructure software is installed, as in this example:

```
/u01/app/11.2.0/grid
```

The Grid Infrastructure software must not be installed on a shared file system, even if the ORACLE_HOME variable has been configured in this way. We do recommend adhering to the OFA standards in this case. However, if you do not wish to adhere to them, then the Grid Infrastructure software may be installed in any location that is not the existing ORACLE_HOME for the Oracle database software, as long as ownership can be set to the root user. The ORACLE_HOME environment variable may not be used directly by the OUI; instead, the ORACLE_HOME environment variable must temporarily be set to this value when installing the Grid Infrastructure software to a particular user-specified directory. Once operational, however, this environment variable provides a distinct value for identifying the directory where the Grid Infrastructure software is installed. The ORA_CRS_HOME should also be set in the PATH environment variable of the root user.

In the 11g Release 2 documentation, the ORA_CRS_HOME variable is also interchangeably referred to as CRS_HOME or GRID_HOME. ORA_CRS_HOME is an environment variable set and used by some Oracle configuration scripts, so some people advise that you should not set it. Conversely, you may see conflicting advice that provides guidance on how to set this environment variable. We recommend that you set ORA_CRS_HOME, but ensure that it is set to the correct location, such as /u01/app/11.2.0/grid. If you choose not to set ORA_CRS_HOME, then you should set an environment variable (such as GRID_HOME) to use as your environment reference to the Grid Infrastructure software.

Setting NLS_LANG and ORA_NLS10

The NLS_LANG environment variable specifies the client-side language, territory, and character set. This variable enables Oracle to perform automatic conversion between the client and database character sets. If NLS_LANG is not set, then the default value will be based on locale settings (and the value of LANG environment variable in particular):

```
[oracle@london1 ~]$ locale
LANG=en_US.UTF-8
LC_CTYPE="en_US.UTF-8"
LC_NUMERIC="en_US.UTF-8"
LC_TIME="en_US.UTF-8"
LC_COLLATE="en_US.UTF-8"
LC_MONETARY="en_US.UTF-8"
LC_MESSAGES="en_US.UTF-8"
LC_PAPER="en_US.UTF-8"
LC_NAME="en_US.UTF-8"
```

```
LC_ADDRESS="en_US.UTF-8"
LC_TELEPHONE="en_US.UTF-8"
LC_MEASUREMENT="en_US.UTF-8"
LC_IDENTIFICATION="en_US.UTF-8"
LC_ALL=
```

In this default setting, the client NLS_LANG configuration would be AMERICAN_AMERICA.AL32UTF8. Therefore, it is only necessary to set NLS_LANG if you wish the Oracle client-side localization settings to differ from the operating system environment. The environment variable ORA_NLS10 is set by default to the path $ORACLE_HOME/nls/data. This path determines the location of Oracle message-related data specific to a particular locale. In a default environment setting, ORA_NLS10 is not required unless the message files are located in a nondefault directory.

Configuring the TNS_ADMIN Variable

The environment variable TNS_ADMIN specifies the path of a directory containing the Oracle network configuration files, such as tnsnames.ora. If TNS_ADMIN is not set, then the default location for the network configuration files is used; that is, $ORACLE_HOME/network/admin will be used. Oracle recommends not setting TNS_ADMIN before software installation.

Setting the PATH Variable

The PATH environment variable defines the executable search path, and it should include both the $ORACLE_HOME/bin directory, the $ORA_CRS_HOME/bin directory for the oracle user, and the $ORA_CRS_HOME/bin directory. For example, this snippet defines the search path for the root user:

```
PATH=$PATH:$ORACLE_HOME/bin:$ORA_CRS_HOME/bin;
```

Setting the LD_LIBRARY_PATH Variable

The LD_LIBRARY_PATH environment variable specifies a list of directories that the runtime shared library loader searches for shared libraries. For security reasons, shared libraries found within this list take priority over default and compiled loader paths; therefore, only trusted libraries should be included in this list. Programs with the set-uid privilege always ignore the settings of LD_LIBRARY_PATH. You can also run the command ldconfig to set system-wide custom runtime library paths in the file /etc/ld.so.conf. For Oracle, the LD_LIBRARY_PATH environment variable is not required for the standard server software. However, it may be needed for other Oracle or third-party products that use shared libraries, such as the Oracle Orion tool (see Chapter 4 for more information about the Oracle Orion tool). If this variable is needed, it should be set to include the $ORACLE_HOME/lib and $ORA_CRS_HOME/lib directory.

Setting the JRE_HOME and CLASSPATH Variables

The JAVA_HOME and JRE_HOME environment variables are required for nondefault Java-based utilities such as jdbc or sqlj. These variables are typically set to the default locations of $ORACLE_HOME/jdk and $JAVA_HOME/jre/bin, respectively. The CLASSPATH environment variable specifies a list of directories and class libraries to be searched by the Java loader. In a default environment, these Java-related environment variables are not required. Therefore, they are ignored by utilities such as dbca because the location of the Oracle JDK is specified in the dbca script itself.

Configuring the ORACLE_PATH and SQLPATH Variables

The environment variables `ORACLE_PATH` and `SQLPATH` are set to a directory name that contains the location of a directory that SQL*Plus searches for SQL scripts. If these environment variables are not set, then no default value is enabled. The most useful script found in this location is `login.sql`, which enables the customization of the SQL*Plus profile for the oracle user.

Setting the DISPLAY Variable

The `DISPLAY` environment variable specifies an X Window display that graphics should be displayed to. This environment variable should be set to a server name followed by a colon, an X server number followed by a period, and a screen number. In most cases, when displaying directly onto the default X display of a system, the server number and screen number will both be zero. An example setting might be `london1:0.0`. The most common exception occurs when running multiple instances of software, such as Virtual Network Computing (VNC), for displaying graphics across the Internet.

Setting the TEMP and TMPDIR Paths

By default, the directory used for the storage of temporary files on Linux is usually the `/tmp` directory. In this directory, Oracle will create files, such as installation log files; and utilities will create files to track values, such as process identifiers. The `/tmp` directory should not be confused with the intended location of the Oracle `TEMP` tablespace, which must reside in a permanent storage area and not in `/tmp`. If you want Oracle to use a directory other than `/tmp` for temporary storage, both `TEMP` and `TMPDIR` should be set to the path of this directory.

Putting Environment Variables to Work

Now let's look at an example `~/.bash_profile` file that shows how to configure several environment variables and settings for a post-installation Oracle 11*g* Release 2 RAC node. Note that the export command is used on each environment variable line both to set the value of the variable and to ensure that this value is passed to all child processes created within the environment:

```
[oracle@london1 oracle]$ cat ~/.bash_profile
# .bash_profile

if [ -t 0 ]; then
stty intr ^C
fi

# Get the aliases and functions
if [ -f ~/.bashrc ]; then
        . ~/.bashrc
fi


# User specific environment and startup programs
umask 022
export ORACLE_BASE=/u01/app/oracle
export ORACLE_HOME=$ORACLE_BASE/product/11.2.0/dbhome_1
```

```
export ORA_CRS_HOME=/u01/app/11.2.0/grid
export ORACLE_SID=PROD1
export PATH=$ORACLE_HOME/bin:$ORA_CRS_HOME/bin:$PATH
```

These environment variables would be set automatically on login or directly with the following command:

```
[oracle@london1 oracle]$ source .bash_profile
```

Completing the Linux Configuration for RAC

In this section, we look at the actions not completed by the Oracle Validated RPM, but which are required to complete the Linux configuration in preparation for the installation of the Oracle Clusterware and Oracle database software for RAC functionality. This section pays particular attention to configuring the shared storage between the nodes in the cluster.

Configuring Hostnames and Name Resolution

After installation, the hostname of the system is set in the file /etc/sysconfig/network. The file will also contain content for enabling the network and for defining the gateway.

If you need to change the system hostname for any reason, then the recommended method is to do this through the graphical user interface. Begin by selecting Network from the System and then Administration menu, and the hostname can be modified under the DNS tab of this utility.

■ **Caution** On any Oracle 11*g* RAC system, neither the hostname nor the domain name should be modified after the Grid Infrastructure software has been installed.

If you provided the IP address of your working DNS Server during the operating system installation, then some of the hostname and name resolution information will have already been configured for you. If this is the case, you should verify the contents of the file /etc/resolv.conf. Alternatively, you could configure the file manually for a DNS Server added after the operating system has been installed on the cluster nodes. In both cases, the file should reference the search path for the domain in use. The following example for a GNS configuration shows both the domain and subdomain:

```
[root@dns1 named]# cat /etc/resolv.conf
search example.com grid1.example.com
nameserver 172.17.1.1
options attempts: 2
options timeout: 1
```

■ **Note** The subdomain is not required for a manual IP configuration.

You should also use the file /etc/nsswitch.conf to verify the order of name services that are queried. In particular, you want to ensure that references to NIS are not found before the DNS:

```
[root@dns1 ~]# vi /etc/nsswitch.conf
#hosts:     db files nisplus nis dns
hosts:      files dns
```

You should use the nslookup command to verify that the DNS name resolution, as explained earlier in this chapter's "Drilling Down on Networking Requirements" section.

For both GNS and manual IP configurations, we recommend that the /etc/hosts file be kept updated with the public and private interconnect addresses of all the nodes in the cluster. This file should also include the domain name extension to be included as an alias in the host file for the fixed public IP addresses.

Keeping the file updated ensures that there is no break in operations during any temporary failure of the DNS service. Again, the preferred method is to modify the settings using the graphical user interface. Navigate to the same utility used to set the hostname and select the Hosts tab. At this point, you have the option to add, edit, or delete the address, hostname, and aliases of hosts relevant to the cluster. You should also modify the default hostnames, removing the configured hostname from the 127.0.0.1 loopback address to prevent potential name resolution errors in the Oracle software. For example, these kinds of errors can occur when using the srvctl utility. Only the local hostname should be associated with this loopback address. It is particularly important that you do not remove this loopback address completely; removing it will result in errors in Oracle network components, such as the listener. Therefore, you should also remove or comment out all of the special IPv6 addresses. The following /etc/hosts file shows the details for a two-node cluster for a manual configuration:

```
# Do not remove the following line, or various programs
# that require network functionality will fail.
127.0.0.1           localhost
172.17.1.101        london1.example.com london1
172.17.1.102        london2.example.com london2
172.17.1.201        london1-vip.example.com london1-vip
172.17.1.202        london2-vip.example.com london2-vip
192.168.1.1         london1-priv
192.168.1.2         london2-priv
```

For a GNS configuration, the VIP addresses should not be included in the /etc/hosts file. As noted previously in this chapter, SCAN addresses should not be configured in /etc/hosts for either GNS or a manual IP configuration.

Using NTP

All nodes in an Oracle cluster must have exactly the same system time settings. If the system clocks are not synchronized, you may experience unpredictable behavior in the cluster. For example, you might fail to successfully register or evict a node as required. Also, manually adjusting the clock on a node by a time factor of minutes could cause unplanned node evictions. Therefore, we strongly advise that you synchronize all systems to the same time and make no major adjustments during operation. ("Major adjustments" do not include local time adjustments, such as regional changes for daylight saving time.)

Within Linux, the most common method to configure time synchronization is to use the Network Time Protocol (NTP). This protocol allows your server to synchronize its system clock with a central server. Your preferred time servers will be available from your Internet service provider. Alternatively, if these are not available, you can choose from a number of open access public time servers.

In Oracle 11*g* Release 2 RAC, the Oracle Cluster Time Synchronization Service Daemon is always operational. However, if NTP is active, CTSS only monitors the status of time synchronization. If NTP is not available, then CTSS will synchronize the time between the nodes of the cluster itself without an external time source. For this reason, operating with NTP is preferable. After installing the Grid Infrastructure software, you can monitor the operation of CTSS in the octssd.log in the $ORA_CRS_HOME/log/london2/ctssd directory, as in this example:

```
[cssd(26798)]CRS-1601:CSSD Reconfiguration complete. Active nodes are london1 london2 .
2009-09-17 15:34:32.217
[ctssd(26849)]CRS-2403:The Cluster Time Synchronization Service on host london2 is in observer
mode.
2009-09-17 15:34:32.224
```

A good practice within a network environment is to configure a single, local dedicated time server to synchronize with an external source. You should also set all internal servers to synchronize with this local time server. If this method is employed, you can use the configuration detailed momentarily to set the local time server to be the preferred server. This approach configures additional external time servers in case of the local one fails. If you do not have NTP available, then you should ensure that the NTP service is disabled. You should not run NTP without an external time source available because the CTSS service will remain in observer mode for potentially unsynchronized times, as reported in the octssd.log.

You can instruct the Oracle server to use NTP on Oracle Enterprise Linux systems from the graphical user interface by right-clicking the Date and Time tab displayed on your main panel, and then selecting Adjust Date & Time. Next, select the second tab on this page and add your NTP servers using the process detailed previously during the installation process. You can also configure NTP manually using the chkconfig and service commands to modify the /etc/ntp.conf and /etc/ntp/step-tickers files. To do this, begin by first ensuring that the NTP service has been installed on the system by using the chkconfig command:

```
[root@london1 root]# chkconfig  --list ntpd
ntpd   0:off  1:off  2:off  3:off  4:off  5:off  6:off
```

Next, manually edit the /etc/ntp.conf file and add lines specifying your own time servers, as in the following examples:

```
server ntp0.uk.uu.net
server ntp1.uk.uu.net
server ntp2.uk.uu.net
```

If you have a preferred time server, add the keyword prefer to ensure synchronization with this system, if available:

```
server ntp0.uk.uu.net prefer
```

To use open-access time servers, enter the following information:

```
server 0.rhel.pool.ntp.org
server 1.rhel.pool.ntp.org
server 2.rhel.pool.ntp.org
```

You will also have a default `restrict` line at the head of your configuration file. However, another good practice is to include server-specific security information for each server. This prevents that particular NTP server from modifying or querying the time on the system, as in the following example:

```
restrict ntp0.uk.uu.net mask 255.255.255.255 nomodify notrap noquery
```

Next, modify your `/etc/ntp/step-tickers` and add the same servers listed in your `/etc/ntp.conf` file:

```
server ntp0.uk.uu.net
server ntp1.uk.uu.net
server ntp2.uk.uu.net
```

Now use the `chkconfig` command to make sure that the NTP daemon will always start at boot time at run levels 3 and 5:

```
[root@london1 root]# chkconfig --level 35 ntpd on
```

You're now ready to verify the configuration, which you accomplish using `chkconfig --list`:

```
root@london1 root]# chkconfig  --list ntpd
ntpd   0:off  1:off  2:off  3:on  4:off  5:on  6:off
```

The start-up options for the NTP daemon are detailed in the `/etc/sysconfig/ntpd` file. In normal circumstances, the default options should be sufficient. You can now start the service to synchronize the time using the following command:

```
[root@london1 root]# service ntpd start
```

Next, the date command can be used to query the system time to ensure that the time has been set correctly. The NTP daemon will not synchronize your system clock with the time server if they differ significantly. If the system clock and time server differ too much, the NTP daemon will refer to the systems in the `/etc/ntp/step-tickers` files to set the time correctly. Alternatively, the time can be set manually using the `ntpdate` command:

```
[root@london1 root]# ntpdate -u -b -s ntp0.uk.uu.net
```

Configuring Secure Shell

During the installation of Oracle 11*g* Release 2 RAC software, a secure shell (ssh) configuration is required on all nodes. This ensures that the node on which the installer is initiated can run commands and copy files to the remote nodes. The secure shell must be configured, so no prompts or warnings are received when connecting between hosts. During the installation of the Grid Infrastructure software, the OUI provides the option to both test and automatically configure a secure shell between the cluster nodes. Therefore, we recommend that you not configure a secure shell in advance, but instead permit the OUI to complete this part of the configuration.

You should review the following steps to troubleshoot and verify the actions taken by the installer *only* if the connectivity test following automatic configuration fails. Additionally, these steps for the manual configuration of ssh are required for the Oracle Cluster Health Monitor user called `crfuser` (you will learn more about this in Chapter 12).

To configure a secure shell on the cluster nodes, first run the following commands as the oracle user to create a hidden directory called ~/.ssh if the directory does not already exist (we use the standard tilde character [~] here to represent the location of the oracle user's home directory):

```
[oracle@london1 oracle]$ mkdir ~/.ssh
[oracle@london1 oracle]$ chmod 755 ~/.ssh
```

Now create private and public keys using the ssh-keygen command. Next, accept the default file locations and enter an optional passphrase, if desired:

```
[oracle@london1 ~]$ /usr/bin/ssh-keygen -t rsa
Generating public/private rsa key pair.
Enter file in which to save the key (/home/oracle/.ssh/id_rsa):
Enter passphrase (empty for no passphrase):
Enter same passphrase again:
Your identification has been saved in /home/oracle/.ssh/id_rsa.
Your public key has been saved in /home/oracle/.ssh/id_rsa.pub.
The key fingerprint is:
a7:4d:08:1e:8c:fa:96:b9:80:c2:4d:e8:cb:1b:5b:e4 oracle@london1
```

Now create the DSA version:

```
[oracle@london1 ~]$ /usr/bin/ssh-keygen -t dsa
Generating public/private dsa key pair.
Enter file in which to save the key (/home/oracle/.ssh/id_dsa):
Enter passphrase (empty for no passphrase):
Enter same passphrase again:
Your identification has been saved in /home/oracle/.ssh/id_dsa.
Your public key has been saved in /home/oracle/.ssh/id_dsa.pub.
The key fingerprint is:
dd:14:7e:97:ca:8f:54:21:d8:52:a9:69:27:4d:6c:2c oracle@london1
```

These commands will create four files in ~/.ssh called id_rsa, id_rsa.pub, id_dsa, and id_dsa.pub. These files contain the RSA and DSA private and public keys.

In the .ssh directory, copy the contents of the id_rsa.pub and id_dsa.pub files to a temporary file. This file will be copied to all other nodes, so you use the hostname to differentiate the copies:

```
[oracle@london1 oracle]$ cat id_rsa.pub id_dsa.pub > london1.pub
```

Repeat this procedure for each host in the cluster, and then copy the public key file to all other hosts in the cluster:

```
[oracle@london1 oracle] scp london1.pub london2:/home/oracle/.ssh
```

Next, concatenate all the public key files into /ssh/authorized_keys on each host in the cluster:

```
cat london1.pub london2.pub > authorized_keys
```

Finally, set the permissions of the authorized keys file on all nodes:

```
[oracle@london1 oracle]$ chmod 644 authorized_keys
```

If no passphrase was specified, ssh and scp will now be able to connect across all nodes. If a passphrase was used, then these two additional commands should be run in every new bash shell session to prevent a prompt being received for the passphrase for every connection:

```
[oracle@london1 oracle]$ ssh-agent $SHELL
[oracle@london1 oracle]$ ssh-add
```

Enter the passphrase, and the identity will be added to the private key files. You can test the ssh and scp commands by connecting to all node combinations, remembering to check the connection back to the node you are working upon. Connections should be tested across both public and private networks:

```
[oracle@london1 oracle]$ ssh london1
[oracle@london1 oracle]$ ssh london2
[oracle@london1 oracle]$ ssh london1-priv
[oracle@london1 oracle]$ ssh london2-priv
```

All combinations should be tested. On the first attempted connection, the following warning will be received, and the default of answer yes should be entered to add the node to the list of known hosts. Doing so prevents this prompt from stalling the Oracle installation:

```
[oracle@london1 .ssh]$ ssh london1
The authenticity of host 'london1 (172.17.1.101)' can't be established.
RSA key fingerprint is 6c:8d:a2:13:b1:48:03:03:74:80:38:ea:27:03:c5:07.
Are you sure you want to continue connecting (yes/no)? yes
Warning: Permanently added 'london1,172.17.1.101' (RSA) to the list of known hosts.
```

If the ssh or scp command is run by the oracle user on a system running an X Windows–based desktop from another user, then the session will receive the following warning unless X authority information is available for the display:

```
Warning: No xauth data; using fake authentication data for X11 forwarding.
```

This warning is received because, by default, ssh is configured to do X11 forwarding, and there is no corresponding entry for the display in the ~/.Xauthority file in the home directory of the oracle user on the system where the command was run. To prevent this warning from occurring during the Oracle software installation, edit the file /etc/ssh/ssh_config and change the line ForwardX11 yes to ForwardX11 no. Next, restart the sshd service, as shown here:

```
[root@london1 root]# servce sshd restart
```

X11 forwarding will now be disabled, and the warning should not be received for ssh or scp connections. Alternatively, you can use the following entries to disable X11 forwarding at a user level. Do this by creating a file called config in the .ssh directory of only the oracle user:

```
[oracle@london1 .ssh]$ cat config
Host *
ForwardX11 no
```

If X11 forwarding is disabled at the system or user level, you can still use the ssh or scp command with the -X option request to forward X Window display information manually, as in the following example:

```
[oracle@london1 oracle]$ ssh -X london2
```

If X11 forwarding is re-enabled after installation, then using ssh with the -x option specifies that X information is not forwarded manually:

```
[oracle@london1 oracle]$ ssh -x london2
```

Configuring Shared Storage

Before installing Oracle 11g Release 2 RAC, it is necessary, at minimum, for shared storage to be available for the Oracle Cluster Registry (OCR) and the Clusterware voting disk. Additional shared storage will also be required for the database files before creating the database. However, an Oracle software-only installation may be performed when creating a database at a later point in time.

This storage must present the same disk images to all of the nodes in the cluster for shared access; it must also be configured with this shared access in mind. For example, a file system type, such as ext3, can be used with a single mount point only. Therefore, it is not suitable for formatting the shared disk storage used in a clustered environment.

Configuring storage successfully is vital for providing a solid foundation for RAC. You can learn about the available storage options in general in Chapter 4; and you can learn more about OCFS version 2 in the context of virtualization in Chapter 5. We recommend OCFS version 2 as the key foundation for virtualized solutions; however, OCFS version 2 also remains a valid shared storage option for the OCR, the Clusterware voting disk, and database files.

In 11g Release 2, the OCR and voting disk can be stored in an ASM diskgroup. ASM, not OCFS2, is Oracle's recommend location for these at this release. Additionally, the Oracle 11g Release 2 database software may be installed in an ACFS, OCFS2, or NFS file system. However, the Grid Infrastructure software may not be installed on a shared cluster file system. Unless you're using a shared ORACLE_HOME, we recommend installing the database software on the same local file system in a location parallel to the Grid Infrastructure software, as explained previously in this chapter. You should review Chapters 4 and 5 in advance of configuring your Linux operating system because these chapters provide in-depth information on selecting the correct storage solution for a particular environment. Whichever option you select, in the context of configuring Linux, the distinction should be clearly understood between the storage used for installing the Oracle Grid Infrastructure software and the database server software, the storage used for the OCR and Clusterware voting disk and the storage used used for holding the Oracle database files.

The OCR and Clusterware voting disk may reside on a shared configuration of ASM (but not ACFS), OCFS2, or NFS. In contrast to how things worked in previous releases, block or raw devices are not supported by the OUI in 11g Release 2. While block or raw devices are supported by the software itself, they cannot be used for installation. We recommend that you protect against disk failure by using RAID storage. and with this in place the minimum number of copies required of each is one. If RAID storage is not available, then the OCR and Clusterware voting disk must have an odd number of multiple copies; this makes three copies of each the minimum required if there is no external redundancy. Each copy of the OCR and Clusterware voting disk requires 280MB of disk space. We recommend ensuring that sufficient disk is allocated initially. You can accomplish this by reserving 500MB for each copy; this value means you won't run up against space constraints from such things as disk formatting or ASM metadata. For example, if you wish to create an ASM diskgroup with external redundancy solely for the use of the OCR and Clusterware voting disks, then this diskgroup should be a minimum of 1GB in size to accommodate both.

Oracle database files may be installed on ASM (but not ACFS), OCFS2, or NFS. Block or raw devices are not supported by the OUI for Oracle database files; however, database files can be created on block or raw devices after installation. Regardless, the recovery area cannot be created on block devices or ACFS, and none of the Oracle database files can be created on locally configured storage for RAC.

If you're using a NAS-based solution, you should refer to the vendor-specific information for your certified storage to learn the relevant details such as mount options. This will help you correctly present the NFS file systems to the nodes in the cluster. For SAN-based installations (we include iSCSI NAS in this description), additional steps are required to discover and partition the LUNs presented by the SAN storage.

Discovering and Configuring SAN Disk

The host-level component of the SAN infrastructure is the HBA, and the storage vendor compatibility matrix should be observed to ensure full system support for the card and server chosen. The HBA itself carries a significant level of the processing intelligence for the protocols it implements. In other words, the HBA performs much of the processing of these protocols itself, without consuming resources from the host CPU. The HBA determines the bandwidth supported by the host for communication with the storage. Therefore, it must be considered in terms of the bandwidth supported by the switched fabric infrastructure and storage itself. This helps ensure compatibility at the performance levels attainable. Most HBAs have the ability to auto-negotiate the speed at which they operate with the storage.

With the HBA physically installed on the PCI bus of the server, the command lspci can be used to confirm that is has been correctly seated. The following truncated output from lspci illustrates that this host has a single Emulex FC HBA:

```
0b:00.0 Fibre Channel: Emulex Corporation Zephyr LightPulse Fibre Channel Host Adapter (rev
02)
```

If the adapter is physically established before the operating system installation takes place, then the most appropriate driver will usually be installed for the HBA as a kernel module at this time. If the HBA is added after installation, then the most appropriate driver will be installed dynamically. The driver is identified and configured within the file /etc/modprobe.conf:

```
[root@london1 ~]# cat /etc/modprobe.conf
alias eth0 e1000e
alias eth1 e1000e
alias scsi_hostadapter ata_piix
alias scsi_hostadapter1 lpfc
```

The loaded driver can be confirmed with the lsmod command, and the driver version and the particular options supported at this release can be viewed with the command modinfo:

```
[root@london1 ~]# modinfo lpfc
filename:       /lib/modules/2.6.18-128.el5/kernel/drivers/scsi/lpfc/lpfc.ko
version:        0:8.2.0.33.3p
author:         Emulex Corporation - tech.support@emulex.com
description:    Emulex LightPulse Fibre Channel SCSI driver 8.2.0.33.3p
license:        GPL
```

Additional information regarding the driver may also be recorded in /var/log/messages at driver load time. For example, the following snippet confirms the link status:

```
Jul 27 12:07:12 london1 kernel: scsi2 :  on PCI bus 0b device 00 irq 90
Jul 27 12:07:12 london1 kernel: lpfc 0000:0b:00.0: 0:1303 Link Up Event x1 received Data: x1
x1 x10 x2 x0 x0 0
```

As discussed in Chapter 4, the LUNs can be added as SCSI devices dynamically. You do this by removing and reinserting the FC driver module or by rebooting the system. If the operation is successful, the disks will appear in /proc/scsi/scsi, as shown by the following output:

```
[root@london1 ~]# cat /proc/scsi/scsi
Attached devices:
Host: scsi0 Channel: 00 Id: 00 Lun: 00
  Vendor: ATA      Model: Hitachi HDT72505 Rev: V560
  Type:   Direct-Access                    ANSI SCSI revision: 05
Host: scsi1 Channel: 00 Id: 00 Lun: 00
  Vendor: ATA      Model: Hitachi HDT72505 Rev: V560
  Type:   Direct-Access                    ANSI SCSI revision: 05
Host: scsi2 Channel: 00 Id: 00 Lun: 00
  Vendor: DGC      Model: RAID 0           Rev: 0324
  Type:   Direct-Access                    ANSI SCSI revision: 04
Host: scsi2 Channel: 00 Id: 00 Lun: 01
  Vendor: DGC      Model: RAID 0           Rev: 0324
  Type:   Direct-Access                    ANSI SCSI revision: 04
Host: scsi2 Channel: 00 Id: 00 Lun: 02
  Vendor: DGC      Model: RAID 0           Rev: 0324
  Type:   Direct-Access                    ANSI SCSI revision: 04
```

At this stage, the SAN disks are successfully configured and presented with the hosts. Note that in this example the disk model is shown as RAID 0 for a performance and testing configuration. You should ensure that your disks have a RAID level to ensure more data protection than then level shown here. Next, you need to partition them using the utility fdisk or parted.

Partitioning Disks

The first step in preparing the disks for both the Clusterware and Database files irrespective of how they are to be used is to first create partitions on the disks. The example commands used to illustrate the creation of partitions on these disks is fdisk and parted.

The command fdisk -l displays all of the disks available to partition. The output for this command should be the same for all of the nodes in the cluster. However, the fdisk command should be run on one node only when actually partitioning the disks. All other nodes will read the same partition information, but we recommend adopt one of the following pair of approaches. First, you can run the partprobe command on the other nodes in the cluster to update the partition table changes. Second, you can reboot these nodes for the partition information, so they are fully updated and displayed correctly.

The following example shows the corresponding disk for one of the SCSI devices detailed previously. In this example, /dev/sdd is the external disk to be partitioned:

```
[root@london1 ~]# fdisk -l /dev/sdd

Disk /dev/sdd: 1073 MB, 1073741824 bytes
34 heads, 61 sectors/track, 1011 cylinders
```

```
Units = cylinders of 2074 * 512 = 1061888 bytes

   Device Boot      Start       End     Blocks   Id  System
```

To partition the drives, use fdisk with the argument of the disk device you want to partition:

```
[root@london1 root]# fdisk /dev/sdd
```

In the preceding example, the shared device /dev/sdd has been selected as the disk where a copy of the OCR and Clusterware voting disk will reside under an ASM diskgroup. We will create the single required partition of 1GB in size, passing it to the ASM configuration.

At the fdisk prompt, enter option n to add a new partition; p, to make it a primary partition; and 1, the number of the next available primary partition. Next, accept the default value for the first cylinder and enter the size of the partition in the form of the number of cylinders. In this case, that number is half of the available value. The reported number of cylinders may vary even for exactly the same disks connected to different architecture systems. Therefore, you can also specify the partition size, such as +500M for a 500MB partition. For these selections, the fdisk dialog will resemble the following:

```
[root@london1 Desktop]# fdisk /dev/sdd

Command (m for help): n
Command action
   e   extended
   p   primary partition (1-4)
p
Partition number (1-4): 1
First cylinder (1-1011, default 1):
Using default value 1
Last cylinder or +size or +sizeM or +sizeK (1-1011, default 1011):
Using default value 1011

Command (m for help): w
The partition table has been altered!

Calling ioctl() to re-read partition table.
Syncing disks.
```

The newly created partition can now be displayed as follows:

```
[root@london1 Desktop]# fdisk -l /dev/sdd

Disk /dev/sdd: 1073 MB, 1073741824 bytes
34 heads, 61 sectors/track, 1011 cylinders
Units = cylinders of 2074 * 512 = 1061888 bytes

   Device Boot      Start       End     Blocks   Id  System
/dev/sdd1              1       1011   1048376+   83  Linux
```

Now either run partprobe or reboot the remaining nodes in the cluster, and then use fdisk -l to verify that all of the nodes can view the partition tables written to the disk.

We noted during Linux installation that MBR partitioning stores data in hidden sectors at the start of the disk, whereas GPT partitioning does not do this. Therefore, when using MBR partitioning either with fdisk or parted, it is important to take this data into account when creating disk partitions, especially on the disks where the Oracle database files will reside. The modifications required are dependent upon the storage type and configuration, and the aim here is to ensure that, for a RAID striped configuration, disk I/O is aligned with the storage RAID stripe size. Depending on the I/O characteristics, failure to do this may lead to an increase in disk or stripe crossing in some cases. For example, this may occur in cases where a single logical read or multiple write operations from the system will result in multiple stripe operations on the storage, thus proving detrimental to performance. In MBR formatting, the hidden sectors occupy the first 63 sectors of the disk. In a case where this storage stripe size is 64kB, it is necessary to realign the partition boundary to sector 128, where 128 sectors of 512 bytes align with the 64kB stripe size. This should be done for each disk on which the database data files will reside, as well as for the first partition on a disk. All subsequent partitions should align with the new boundary. The following example illustrates the additional fdisk commands (run in expert mode) required to realign the partition boundary for the partitioning dialog shown previously:

```
Command (m for help): x

Expert command (m for help): b
Partition number (1-4): 1
New beginning of data (63-1044224, default 63): 128
```

fdisk can still be used to format disks with the MBR formatting scheme; however, parted must be used to take advantage of GPT partitioning. Like fdisk, parted is invoked with the argument of the disk to partition. On starting, it prints the version of the software and licensing information to the screen. Next, it presents the (parted) prompt:

```
[root@london1 ~]# parted /dev/sdd
GNU Parted 1.8.1
Using /dev/sdd
Welcome to GNU Parted! Type 'help' to view a list of commands.
(parted)
```

If the disk label type is not already specified as gpt (the default), then use the mklabel command to specify the new disk label type:

```
(parted) mklabel
Warning: The existing disk label on /dev/sdd will be destroyed and all data on
this disk will be lost. Do you want to continue?
Yes/No? Yes
New disk label type?  [msdos]? gpt
```

The print command is used to display the partition table. We have just created the partition table, so this example shows that the disk label type is gpt and no partitions have yet been created:

```
parted) print

Model: DGC RAID 0 (scsi)
Disk /dev/sdd: 1074MB
Sector size (logical/physical): 512B/512B
```

```
Partition Table: gpt

Number  Start  End  Size  File system  Name  Flags
```

To create a partition, use the mkpart command. At the prompts, enter a value for the partition name and accept the default file system type. Although mkpart can be used for creating a local file system at the same time as the partition, it does not support any clustered file systems that can be shared between nodes or ASM. For the partition sizes, enter the starting value for the partition in megabytes. The first value will be 0, and the ending value will be in megabytes. The following example creates a 1074MB partition:

```
(parted) mkpart
Partition name?  []? crs1
File system type?  [ext2]?
Start? 0
End? 1074
(parted)
```

Use mkpart to create the subsequent partitions, and then enter the values for partition and file system type. Next, enter the ending point of the previous partition as the starting point of the new one; for this partition's ending point, enter the value (in MBs) of the disk size detailed in the disk geometry section. Printing the partition table now displays the created partition. You do not need to call an additional write command, and the partition table will remain on exiting the parted application:

```
(parted) print

Model: DGC RAID 0 (scsi)
Disk /dev/sdd: 1074MB
Sector size (logical/physical): 512B/512B
Partition Table: gpt

Number  Start   End     Size    File system  Name  Flags
1       17.4kB  1074MB  1074MB               crs1
```

GPT partitions are not visible with the fdisk command, and one partition will be displayed, regardless of the number of partitions created:

```
[root@london1 ~]# fdisk -l /dev/sdd

WARNING: GPT (GUID Partition Table) detected on '/dev/sdd'! The util fdisk doesn't support
GPT. Use GNU Parted.

Disk /dev/sdd: 1073 MB, 1073741824 bytes
255 heads, 63 sectors/track, 130 cylinders
Units = cylinders of 16065 * 512 = 8225280 bytes

   Device Boot      Start         End      Blocks   Id  System
/dev/sdd1               1         131     1048575+  ee  EFI GPT
...
```

Therefore, if you have created multiple partitions, you should view /proc/partitions to see whether the partitions have been successfully created and are available for use.

If you're using an OCFS2 cluster file system method to store the OCR and Clusterware voting disk, then the Grid Infrastructure software installation will create the OCR and Clusterware voting disk as files during the installation process. Thus the only requirement is to format the disk partitions you created previously with OCFS2, as discussed in Chapter 5. You may then specify suitable file names to be created at the time of the Grid Infrastructure installation process (see Chapter 7 for more information on this). If you wish to use ASM, there are additional configuration steps required to prepare the partitions either with ASMLIB or manually.

I/O Multipathing with Device-Mapper

I/O multipathing is a concept similar to network channel bonding, which is covered later in this chapter. Like channel bonding, I/O multipathing support requires at least two storage HBAs per server that connect to the target storage to display the LUNs through two independent paths. To completely eliminate any single point of failure, each path should also be accessed through a separate storage switch. In the event of an HBA, cable, or switch failure, a path to the storage is maintained. During regular operations, such a configuration provides load balancing in addition to redundancy.

Typically storage vendors have provided multipathing software solutions dedicated for their range of storage products. In contrast, device-mapper provides a generic solution for I/O multipathing across a range of vendors' products, including Oracle Enterprise Linux 5. Notwithstanding the generic nature of multipathing with device-mapper, you should check with your storage vendor to determine its support for this form of multipathing. You should also inquire about the specific software and configuration settings for a complete multipathing solution at both the server and storage levels.

As its name implies, device-mapper provides a method to redirect I/O between block devices. It also provides the foundation for a number of storage configurations that you have already encountered in this chapter, such as LVM and RAID.

The device-mapper-multipath is included in a default installation, or it can be installed from the installation media with the rpm or yum commands. The module is loaded with the command modprobe dm-multipath. Before proceeding with multipath configuration, it is necessary to install and configure the storage and HBA, so that the two paths to the disk devices are visible to the Linux operating system. The following example illustrates the same storage approach shown in the previous example, but with the additional, visible path to the same devices:

```
[root@london1 ~]# cat /proc/scsi/scsi
Attached devices:
Host: scsi0 Channel: 00 Id: 00 Lun: 00
  Vendor: ATA      Model: Hitachi HDT72505 Rev: V560
  Type:   Direct-Access                    ANSI SCSI revision: 05
Host: scsi1 Channel: 00 Id: 00 Lun: 00
  Vendor: ATA      Model: Hitachi HDT72505 Rev: V560
  Type:   Direct-Access                    ANSI SCSI revision: 05
Host: scsi2 Channel: 00 Id: 00 Lun: 00
  Vendor: DGC      Model: RAID 0           Rev: 0324
  Type:   Direct-Access                    ANSI SCSI revision: 04
Host: scsi2 Channel: 00 Id: 00 Lun: 01
  Vendor: DGC      Model: RAID 0           Rev: 0324
  Type:   Direct-Access                    ANSI SCSI revision: 04
Host: scsi2 Channel: 00 Id: 00 Lun: 02
  Vendor: DGC      Model: RAID 0           Rev: 0324
```

```
    Type:   Direct-Access                    ANSI SCSI revision: 04
Host: scsi3 Channel: 00 Id: 00 Lun: 00
  Vendor: DGC       Model: RAID 0            Rev: 0324
    Type:   Direct-Access                    ANSI SCSI revision: 04
Host: scsi3 Channel: 00 Id: 00 Lun: 01
  Vendor: DGC       Model: RAID 0            Rev: 0324
    Type:   Direct-Access                    ANSI SCSI revision: 04
Host: scsi3 Channel: 00 Id: 00 Lun: 02
  Vendor: DGC       Model: RAID 0            Rev: 0324
    Type:   Direct-Access                    ANSI SCSI revision: 04
```

The additional devices will also be visible with the fdisk command; depending on the storage, however, they may not be accessible.

The multipathing setup is configured in the file /etc/multipath.conf. The following example is specific to the EMC CLARiiON storage; other storage vendors can supply examples specific to their products. Begin by removing or commenting out the following section:

```
#blacklist {
#        devnode "*"
#}
```

Next, add the following to the end of the file:

```
defaults {
path_grouping_policy failover
user_friendly_names yes
}
multipaths {
multipath {
wwid 360060160a5b11c00420e82c83240dc11
alias       crs
mode        640
uid         500
gid         500
 }
}
devices {
    device {
        vendor "DGC"
        product "*"
        product_blacklist "(LUNZ|LUN_Z)"
        path_grouping_policy group_by_prio
        getuid_callout "/sbin/scsi_id -g -u -s /block/%n"
        prio_callout "/sbin/mpath_prio_emc /dev/%n"
        path_checker    emc_clariion
        path_selector   "round-robin 0"
        features        "0"
        hardware_handler        "1 emc"
        features "1 queue_if_no_path"
        no_path_retry 300
        hardware_handler "1 emc"
        failback immediate
```

```
}
```

The device-mapper creates a number of devices to support multipathing. A device name such as /dev/dm-* indicates the kernel device name, and it should not be accessed directly:

```
[root@london1 ~]# ls -l /dev/dm-*
brw-rw---- 1 root root 253, 2 Aug  5 15:32 /dev/dm-2
brw-rw---- 1 root root 253, 3 Aug  5 15:32 /dev/dm-3
brw-rw---- 1 root root 253, 4 Aug  5 15:32 /dev/dm-4
brw-rw---- 1 root root 253, 5 Aug  5 15:32 /dev/dm-5
brw-rw---- 1 root root 253, 6 Aug  5 15:32 /dev/dm-6
brw-rw---- 1 root root 253, 7 Aug  5 15:32 /dev/dm-7
```

Devices names such as /dev/mpath/mpath2 are created as symbolic links, according to udev rules defined in /etc/udev/rules.d/40-multipath.rules. It is possible to modify these rules to set the correct permissions (as detailed in the previous section). However, these modified rules will only impact these symbolic links. Instead, the device to use for access is listed under the directory /dev/mapper/, as in this example: /dev/mapper/mpath2. For this reason, the syntax for the section to define persistence is based on the WWID; the LUN unique ID; and the alias, mode, and ownership. The upcoming example illustrates the approach for explicitly naming and changing the ownership of the OCR and Clusterware voting disk. At the same time, it leaves the other devices with their default naming, which means you can apply these changes to as many devices as you wish. This is the preferred method for configuring the correct permissions of multipathed devices, as opposed to using udev rules directly, an approach you'll learn about later in this chapter. You should ensure that the ownership and permission is set equally in /etc/multipath.conf for all of the nodes in the cluster.

To verify your configuration, run the multipath command with the –d option, as in this example: multipath -v3 -d. The verbose output gives considerable detail. In particular, the paths list section is useful for identifying the devices, their paths, and their current status. If the output is satisfactory, you can run the same command without the –d option to active the configuration. Checking the /dev/mapper directory shows the created multipath devices available for use:

```
[root@london1 ~]# ls -l /dev/mapper*
total 0
crw-r----- 1 root   dba       10, 63 Aug  5 15:31 control
brw-r----- 1 oracle dba      253,  3 Aug  5 15:32 crs
brw-r----- 1 oracle dba      253,  6 Aug  5 15:32 crsp1
brw-rw---- 1 root   disk     253,  2 Aug  5 15:32 mpath2
brw-rw---- 1 root   disk     253,  5 Aug  5 15:32 mpath2p1
brw-rw---- 1 root   disk     253,  4 Aug  5 15:32 mpath3
brw-rw---- 1 root   disk     253,  7 Aug  5 15:32 mpath3p1
brw-rw---- 1 root   disk     253,  0 Aug  5 15:32 VolGroup00-LogVol00
brw-rw---- 1 root   disk     253,  1 Aug  5 15:31 VolGroup00-LogVol01
```

Note the updated name and permission for the OCR and Clusterware voting disk in the preceding example. The multipath command also shows the active paths to the devices:

```
root@london1 ~]# multipath -ll
mpath2 (360060160a5b11c006840e1703240dc11) dm-2 DGC,RAID 0
[size=102G][features=1 queue_if_no_path][hwhandler=1 emc][rw]
\_ round-robin 0 [prio=0][active]
 \_ 3:0:0:0 sdc 8:32  [active][undef]
```

```
\_ round-robin 0 [prio=0][enabled]
 \_ 2:0:0:0 sdf 8:80  [active][undef]
crs (360060160a5b11c00420e82c83240dc11) dm-3 DGC,RAID 0
[size=1.0G][features=1 queue_if_no_path][hwhandler=1 emc][rw]
\_ round-robin 0 [prio=0][active]
 \_ 3:0:0:1 sdd 8:48  [active][undef]
\_ round-robin 0 [prio=0][enabled]
 \_ 2:0:0:1 sdg 8:96  [active][undef]
mpath3 (360060160a5b11c0046fd4df53240dc11) dm-4 DGC,RAID 0
[size=299G][features=1 queue_if_no_path][hwhandler=1 emc][rw]
\_ round-robin 0 [prio=0][active]
 \_ 3:0:0:2 sde 8:64  [active][undef]
\_ round-robin 0 [prio=0][enabled]
 \_ 2:0:0:2 sdh 8:112 [active][undef]
```

You can test the multipath configuration by disabling access to the active path:

```
[root@london1 ~]# echo offline > /sys/block/sdd/device/state
```

In the next example, the failing path is identified by the major and minor device number combination. In this case, the system logs the path failed over in response to the path being disabled:

```
device-mapper: multipath: Failing path 8:48.
device-mapper: multipath emc: emc_pg_init: sending switch-over command
```

The multipath command shows the currently active path:

```
[root@london1 ~]# multipath -l
...
crs (360060160a5b11c00420e82c83240dc11) dm-3 DGC,RAID 0
[size=1.0G][features=1 queue_if_no_path][hwhandler=1 emc][rw]
\_ round-robin 0 [prio=0][enabled]
 \_ 3:0:0:1 sdd 8:48  [failed][faulty]
\_ round-robin 0 [prio=0][active]
 \_ 2:0:0:1 sdg 8:96  [active][undef]
...
```

The preceding example includes more actions than simply changing paths to the devices. In EMC CLARiiON terminology, the LUN is automatically trespassed between storage processors on the storage itself in response to the switch over command to enable access through the alternate path. This additional functionality reiterates the importance of ensuring that multipathing with device-mapper is a supported configuration throughout the entire system, including the HBA and storage.

To return the device back to an active state, you should echo running instead of offline to the device state.

Partitioning on multipath devices can be performed with the fdisk command, exactly as detailed previously on the /dev/mapper/mpath0 device. However, an additional step is required to then register the created partitions with the command kpartx.

Preparing the Partitions for ASM with ASMLIB

After presenting the shared storage to the operating system and partitioning the disks, no additional software is required to use them for ASM. If you're using ASM either for the OCR and Clusterware voting disk partition or for database storage, then you may also wish to configure ASMLIB on the underlying devices beforehand. One of the main benefits of ASMLIB is that it provides persistence in the naming and permissions of the disks to be used for ASM. And while udev can also provide this functionality without requiring additional package installations beyond the default operating installation, ASMLIB was always intended to provide additional benefits for Oracle environments. As noted previously in this chapter, the use of ASMLIB reduces the requirement for file descriptors across the system. ASMLIB also implements asynchronous I/O, bypassing the standard Linux implementation of asynchronous I/O. However, the main benefits of ASMLIB are in the area of manageability and flexibility.

Once configured, ASMLIB provides a standard method for identifying the presence of ASM disks on the system. It is also possible to add additional nodes to the cluster or transfer the disks between different architecture systems. Subsequently, scanning the disks will detect the ASM configuration and maintain the configured permission for ASMLIB installed locally on each node. This stands in contrast to udev, which requires manual identification and configuration of the ASM disks for each individual system. Therefore, the main benefits of ASMLIB are ease of use and the ability to identify ASM disks. If you are comfortable with the benefits of having udev implement this solution for the OCR and Clusterware voting disk partitions, then ASMLIB is not an essential requirement. However, ASMLIB may provide additional identification benefits for the ASM diskgroups that contain database files. This is especially true in cases where disks are often transferred between systems, thereby reducing the possibility of errors resulting in data loss.

ASMLIB requires the installation of three RPM packages: the ASM library, tools, and driver. The RPM packages for the tools and driver are included with the installation media; however, the ASM library is not. Customers of the Unbreakable Linux Network can retrieve the library from there. The library (and the other packages) can also be downloaded from the following location:

www.oracle.com/technology/software/tech/linux/asmlib/rhel5.html

You can install all three ASMLIB RPM packages, as follows:

```
[root@london1 ~]# rpm -ivh oracleasm*
Preparing...                ######################################### [100%]
   1:oracleasm-support      ######################################### [ 33%]
   2:oracleasm-2.6.18-164.el#################################### [ 67%]
   3:oracleasmlib           ######################################### [100%]
```

Your first action is to configure the driver. This action sets the ownership of the device as a functional equivalent of udev configuration:

```
[root@london1 asmlib]# /etc/init.d/oracleasm configure
Configuring the Oracle ASM library driver.

This will configure the on-boot properties of the Oracle ASM library
driver.  The following questions will determine whether the driver is
loaded on boot and what permissions it will have.  The current values
will be shown in brackets ('[]').  Hitting <ENTER> without typing an
answer will keep that current value.  Ctrl-C will abort.
```

```
Default user to own the driver interface []: oracle
Default group to own the driver interface []: dba
Start Oracle ASM library driver on boot (y/n) [n]: y
Scan for Oracle ASM disks on boot (y/n) [y]: y
Writing Oracle ASM library driver configuration: done
Initializing the Oracle ASMLib driver:                    [  OK  ]
Scanning the system for Oracle ASMLib disks:              [  OK  ]
```

Next, you use the createdisk command to mark the disks as ASM disks:

```
[root@london1 ~]# /etc/init.d/oracleasm createdisk VOL1 /dev/sdc1
Marking disk "VOL1" as an ASM disk:                       [  OK  ]
```

The configured disks can be deleted with the deletedisk command. In the process of deleting the disk metadata, this command will also delete access to any data configured on the disk. The listdisks command shows the configured volumes, while the querydisk command shows the mapping between the ASM disk and the system disk device:

```
[root@london1 asmlib]# /etc/init.d/oracleasm querydisk /dev/sdc1
Device "/dev/sdc1" is marked an ASM disk with the label "VOL1"
```

After configuring the first node in the cluster, you can use the scandisks command to detect the configured disks on the other nodes:

```
[root@london1 asmlib]# /etc/init.d/oracleasm scandisks
Scanning the system for Oracle ASMLib disks:              [  OK  ]
```

If you have configured multipath devices as explained previously in this chapter, then an additional configuration step is required. A multipath configuration will present three views of the same disk device. These views represent both channels and the multipath device itself. By default, on scanning ASMLIB will select the first channel scanned, which may not be the multipath device. To ensure that it is the multipath device that ASMLIB uses, you can add a section that excludes scanning the non-multipath devices to the /etc/sysconfig/oracleasm configuration file. For example, you can exclude scanning the disk devices that represent the channels for the OCR and Clusterware voting disk partitions given in the previous example, as shown here:

```
ORACLEASM_SCANEXCLUDE="sdd sdg"
```

Explicitly excluding the channels from direct use means that ASMLIB will be configured with the multipath device, thereby ensuring that ASM will benefit from the underlying redundancy of the I/O configuration.

Preparing the Partitions for ASM with udev

Due to Linux's Unix-based heritage, devices in Linux are traditionally files created by the mknod command. This command directs input and output to the appropriate device driver identified by the major device number. One of the challenges with the static configuration of devices is that the number of devices pre-created to support a wide range of hardware connectivity is significant. This makes it difficult to identify which devices are connected to the system and active. With the 2.6 kernel, an in-memory virtual file system implementation called sysfs was introduced to present a rationalized view of the connected hardware devices to processes running in user space. The sysfs virtual file system is mounted on /sys; a driver loaded as a module registers with sysfs when the module is loaded, and the udevd event management daemon dynamically creates the corresponding devices under /dev. This implementation reduces the created devices down from many thousands of pre-created static devices to only the devices connected to the system. The device configuration enables device creation and naming, according to defined rules in the main configuration file, /etc/udev/udev.conf. This file includes an entry for the directory that defines the rules for device creation; by default, it is located under the directory /etc/udev/rules.d.

Familiarity with udev is important because previously, attributes such as device ownership and permissions could be modified and would be persistent across reboots due to the static nature of the configuration. Under udev's dynamic configuration, the device is created every time the corresponding driver module is loaded. Therefore, rules must be defined to ensure this configuration sets the desired attributes each time. Configuring devices with udev means that operating system standards can be used for correctly preparing a partition for ASM, but without requiring ASMLIB.

Configuring Udev Permissions

Due to the dynamic nature of device configuration with udev, it is necessary to configure udev so it changes the permissions of the disk devices for the OCR and Clusterware voting disk to the correct owner for purpose of installing and operating Clusterware. As shown in the following example, the devices are owned by the oracle user, which is also the grid infrastructure software owner with 660 permissions. Similarly, for any devices to be used by ASM for Database files, the ownership should be set to the database software owner. In this case, that is the same oracle user. To change both the owner and the group, the permissions can be modified by writing a udev rule. You can do this in the directory /etc/udev/rules.d by modifying the file, 50-udev.rules. However, introducing a syntax error into this file may prevent the system from booting; therefore, it is best practice to create a new rules file to be read after 50-udev.rules, such as 55-udev.rules. In this example, the rules shown change the ownership for the OCR and Clusterware voting partition previously created. The new name is the device name without the /dev directory:

```
# There are a number of modifiers that are allowed to be used in some of the
# fields.  See the udev man page for a full description of them.
#
# default is OWNER="root" GROUP="root", MODE="0600"
#
KERNEL=="sdd[1-9]", OWNER="oracle" GROUP="dba", MODE="0660"
```

Subsequently, you can reload the udev rules and restart udev:

```
[root@london1 rules.d]# udevcontrol reload_rules
[root@london1 rules.d]# start_udev
Starting udev:                                          [  OK  ]
```

The permissions are now preserved across system reboots:

```
[root@london1 rules.d]# ls -l /dev/sdd1
brw-r----- 1 oracle dba 8, 49 Jul 29 17:20 /dev/sdd1
```

Finally, you should ensure that the settings are applied to all of the nodes in the cluster.

Enabling Udev Persistence

Here's something else to consider if you're not using ASMLIB. In addition to using udev to set permissions, you should also consider using it to configure device persistence of the OCR and Clusterware voting disk partition, as well as the database storage partitions used for ASM. Similar to the setting of permissions, the dynamic nature of device discovery with udev means that there is no guarantee that devices will always be discovered in the same order. Therefore, it is possible that device names may change across reboots, especially after adding new devices. For this reason, we recommend that you also configure udev to ensure that the same devices are named consistently whenever udev is run.

The first step is to identify the physical devices that correspond to the logical disk names configured by udev. The physical device names are derived on the storage itself, and these typically correspond to the Network Address Authority (NAA) worldwide naming format to ensure that the identifier is unique. Figure 6-9 illustrates the identifier for a LUN under the heading of Unique ID.

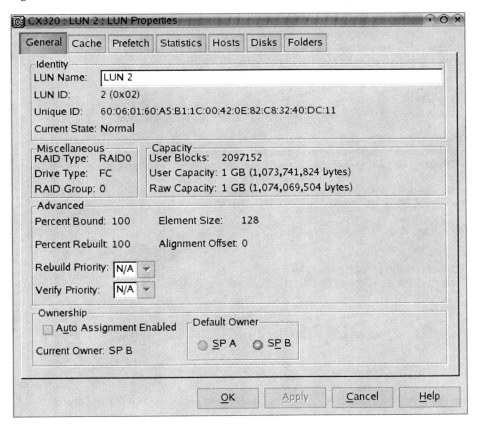

Figure 6-9. The LUN Unique ID

The identifier can also be determined with the commands udevinfo or /sbin/scsi_id when run against the devices in the /sys directory. With the /sbin/scsi_id command, the arguments -p 0x80 and

-s return the SCSI Vendor, model, and serial number to cross reference against the storage. However it is the optionally specified -p 0x83 and the -s arguments that return the unique identifier. In this case, that identifier is prefixed by the number 3, which identifies the device as an NAA type 3 device; this identifier also corresponds to the unique ID from the storage:

```
[root@london1 ~]# /sbin/scsi_id -g -s /block/sdd
360060160a5b11c00420e82c83240dc11
```

The identifier being determined by the storage is based on the entire LUN, as opposed to the individual disk partitions configured by the systems. Therefore, the identifier is the same for multiple partitions on the same device. Additionally, the identifier will also be the same for the same device shared between nodes in the cluster:

```
[root@london2 ~]# /sbin/scsi_id -g -s /block/sdd
360060160a5b11c00420e82c83240dc11
```

The file /etc/scsi_id.config enables you to set options to modify the default behaviour of the scsi_id command. In particular, the option -g is required for the scsi_id command to produce output. Therefore, we recommend that you add the line options=-g to this file, as follows:

```
# some libata drives require vpd page 0x80
vendor="ATA",options=-p 0x80
options=-g
```

The following example for setting udev rules assumes that this addition has been made. If you do not wish to make the preceding addition, then you should be aware that the -g option must be given to the scsi_id command when specified in the udev rules. If not, the command will generate no output, causing the rule to fail.

You can also retrieve the device information using the command udevinfo in conjunction with the identifier shown under the heading, ID_SERIAL:

```
[root@london1 ~]# udevinfo -q all -p /block/sdd
P: /block/sdd
N: sdd
S: disk/by-id/scsi-360060160a5b11c00420e82c83240dc11
S: disk/by-path/pci-0000:0b:00.0-fc-0x5006016b41e0613a:0x0001000000000000
E: ID_VENDOR=DGC
E: ID_MODEL=RAID_0
E: ID_REVISION=0324
E: ID_SERIAL=360060160a5b11c00420e82c83240dc11
E: ID_TYPE=disk
E: ID_BUS=scsi
E: ID_PATH=pci-0000:0b:00.0-fc-0x5006016b41e0613a:0x0001000000000000
```

Once you have the unique identifier, you can edit the file created previously for setting device permissions, 55-udev.rules. The following entry corresponds to the device name identified previously and uses /sbin/scsi_id with the -g option that was set in the /etc/scsi_id.config file. Also, the %n substitution variable is specified so that the partitions for this device are correctly named in numerical order. At this point, the owner, group, and permissions are preserved, as previously described:

```
KERNEL=="sd*", BUS=="scsi", PROGRAM=="/sbin/scsi_id",
RESULT=="360060160a5b11c00420e82c83240dc11", NAME="crs%n", OWNER="oracle", GROUP="dba",
MODE="0660"
```

You can verify the validity of the rules with the command, udevtest:

```
[root@london1 rules.d]# udevtest /block/sdd
main: looking at device '/block/sdd' from subsystem 'block'
run_program: '/bin/bash -c '/sbin/lsmod | /bin/grep ^dm_multipath''
run_program: '/bin/bash' (stdout) 'dm_multipath           55257  0 '
run_program: '/bin/bash' returned with status 0
run_program: '/lib/udev/usb_id -x'
run_program: '/lib/udev/usb_id' returned with status 1
run_program: '/lib/udev/scsi_id -g -x -s /block/sdd -d /dev/.tmp-8-48'
run_program: '/lib/udev/scsi_id' (stdout) 'ID_VENDOR=DGC'
run_program: '/lib/udev/scsi_id' (stdout) 'ID_MODEL=RAID_0'
run_program: '/lib/udev/scsi_id' (stdout) 'ID_REVISION=0324'
run_program: '/lib/udev/scsi_id' (stdout) 'ID_SERIAL=360060160a5b11c00420e82c83240dc11'
run_program: '/lib/udev/scsi_id' (stdout) 'ID_TYPE=disk'
run_program: '/lib/udev/scsi_id' (stdout) 'ID_BUS=scsi'
...
```

Finally, reload the udev rules and restart udev. The devices that can be specified for the OCR and Clusterware voting disk have been created as devices, and they are now available for use. This ensures that a given name will preserved for a particular device across reboots:

```
[oracle@london1 ~]$ ls -l /dev/crs*
brw-r----- 1 oracle dba 8, 48 Jul 31 15:44 /dev/crs
brw-r----- 1 oracle dba 8, 49 Jul 31 15:44 /dev/crs1
```

You can also use the command udevinfo to query the created device based on its name, as in this example:

```
udev udevinfo -q all -n /dev/crs
```

Network Channel Bonding

As explained in Chapter 4, we recommend using a teamed network interface configuration implemented on the private interconnect network because it can protect against the interconnect switch itself being a single point of failure for the entire cluster. To implement teaming, you will need two available network interfaces per node in addition to the external network interface (again, see Chapter 4 for more information). You will also need two network switches connected to each other with an interswitch link, and these switches must support this form of topology. If this is the case, after installing the Linux operating system according to the guidelines detailed previously in this chapter, then you will have an active external interface, an active private interconnect interface, and an additional, currently inactive private network interface.

Your goal when configuring bonding is to implement high availability and prevent the presence of a single point failure, whether that failure is in the NICs installed in the system, the interconnect switches, or the network cables. Any one of these components should be able to fail without impacting the availability of the interconnect. The aim of this configuration is *not* to increase bandwidth or interconnect performance, but to ensure there is no single point of failure due to the aforementioned components. In Chapter 4, we discuss the role of the interconnect in the context of performance of the entire cluster; you should always review the demands of interconnect traffic in this context, rather than in isolation.

The most widely deployed and supported solution for bonding occurs with the channel bonding module installed by default with the Oracle Enterprise Linux operating system. This module includes a number of bonding modes; you can find detailed summary of these modes and their roles in Table 6-7.

Table 6-7. Bonding Modes

Mode	Name	Details
0	balance-rr	Provides round-robin load balancing on packet transmission, regardless of load.
1	active-backup	Singe NIC is active with standby operational on failure of standby.
2	balance-xor	Provides load balancing on XOR value of the source and destination MAC address; this means that the same NIC is used between a particular source and its destination.
3	broadcast	Transmits network traffic transmitted on all interfaces. This mode isn't recommended for a high availability interconnect.
4	802.3ad	Provides 802.3ad dynamic link aggregation on supported network hardware.
5	balance-tlb	Transmits load balancing based on load.
6	balance-alb	Transmits and receives load balancing. ARP replies to other nodes are replaced with specific slave MAC addresses, so replies from these nodes are received on different NICs.

In conjunction with the teamed hardware configuration described in Chapter 4, we recommend that the interconnect be configured in mode 1. This mode utilizes active-backup with one switch by default. All of the NICs attached to that switch act as the primary and the secondary switch, and the NICs configured as the backup become active only in event of the failure of the corresponding primary component. A direct interswitch link is present for a topology with multiple switches. This link provides a form of external routing between the switches, ensuring that network traffic can be transmitted and received between all of the teamed NICs, regardless of which NICs or switches are active at any particular point in time. We also recommend mode 1 for active-backup as the most applicable high availability solution that applies to the widest possible range of networking hardware and software drivers deployed with multiple switches. Once you have configured the bonding devices on the private interconnect for all of the nodes in cluster, we recommend that you also test the setup thoroughly to gauge the system's response to failures at a NIC, cable, or switch level.

At your discretion, you may use another mode, such as one of the load balancing options. However, when doing so, we recommend that you conduct additional tests of your chosen solution to ensure its compatibility with your hardware and software configuration. These tests should also demonstrate that the prime goal of maintaining high availability is achieved. If you're considering this option, you should bear in mind that a wide range of the driver software and related documentation assumes that a teamed configuration will reside within a single switch. Such an approach increases bandwidth and provides failover at the NIC level, as opposed to switch level. For this reason, we advise thorough testing for compatibility before you deploy your solution.

We will assume that the interfaces' device names are eth0, eth1, and eth2, respectively. You may also have additional interfaces, especially if you're using a backup network. You may also consider teaming on the external interface. However, for the sake of simplicity, we will consider only the three devices listed here. To optimally implement bonding, all of the interfaces that are intended to communicate on the private interconnect should be configured in this fully redundant way with bonding, as well. Care should also be taken to ensure that all of the servers are connected to the active and backup switches with the same corresponding interfaces. In other words, if eth1 on london1 is connected to the active switch, then eth1 on all other nodes should also be connected to this same switch.

Because bonding is implemented through a loadable kernel module (similar to the hangcheck-timer module), you need to set configuration options in the file, /etc/modprobe.conf. You also need to explicitly load and set the bonding module options when you initiate the private network interface. Creating an alias for the interface name—bond0, in this case–enables parameters to be assigned to the bonding module:

```
alias bond0 bonding
options bond0 miimon=100 mode=1
```

Two options are of particular interest. First, you must specify either miimon or the combination of arp_interval and arp_ip_target. We recommend setting miimon because this is the most applicable solution for ensuring high availability, and this parameter determines how often Media Independent Interface (MII) link monitoring occurs (in milliseconds). In the previous example, the value is set to 100. In addition, all modern NICs should support MII link monitoring, which makes it a feasible default option.

As explained previously, the second parameter of mode must be set to the value of 1 or its text equivalent (active-backup), unless you have fully validated the operation of an alternative mode in your environment.

To configure the network devices so they can use the bonding module, you need to modify the file located in the directory, /etc/sysconfig/network-scripts. Assuming that you're using the eth1 and eth2 devices for the interconnect, you can copy the file that corresponds to the currently configured private interconnect interface, such as ifcfg-eth1, to a new file named ifcfg-bond0. Next, edit the device name in this file to reflect the alias name detailed in /etc/modprobe.conf. At this point, ifcfg-bond0 will contain entries similar to the following:

```
DEVICE=bond0
BOOTPROTO=none
ONBOOT=yes
TYPE=Ethernet
USERCTL=no
IPADDR=192.168.1.1
NETMASK=255.255.255.0
```

Next, modify the files ifcfg-eth1 and ifcfg-eth2 to configure the devices as slaves for the master device configured in ifcfg-bond0. Your entries should follow the example illustrated in the next results snippet. The files themselves will be identical, except for the line that specifies the device name that relates to the configuration file and the hardware address:

```
DEVICE=eth1
HWADDR=00:30:48:D7:D5:43
BOOTPROTO=none
ONBOOT=yes
MASTER=bond0
SLAVE=yes
USERCTL=no
```

For testing purposes, you can restart the network service with the following command:

```
service network restart
```

However, we recommend rebooting the system as part of the testing process; this helps ensure that the bonding module is loaded during the boot process.

With the bonded network interface activated, the following output from the ifconfig command shows that the private interconnect network is active with its master and slave devices:

```
[root@lonodn1 ~]#   ifconfig -a
bond0      Link encap:Ethernet  HWaddr 00:30:48:D7:D5:43
           inet addr:192.168.1.1  Bcast:192.168.1.255  Mask:255.255.255.0
           inet6 addr: fe80::230:48ff:fed7:d543/64 Scope:Link
           UP BROADCAST RUNNING MASTER MULTICAST  MTU:1500  Metric:1
           RX packets:1797 errors:0 dropped:0 overruns:0 frame:0
           TX packets:79 errors:0 dropped:0 overruns:0 carrier:0
           collisions:0 txqueuelen:0
           RX bytes:109087 (106.5 KiB)  TX bytes:15878 (15.5 KiB)

eth0       Link encap:Ethernet  HWaddr 00:30:48:D7:D5:42
           inet addr:172.17.1.101  Bcast:172.17.255.255  Mask:255.255.0.0
           inet6 addr: fe80::230:48ff:fed7:d542/64 Scope:Link
           UP BROADCAST RUNNING MULTICAST  MTU:1500  Metric:1
           RX packets:2917 errors:0 dropped:0 overruns:0 frame:0
           TX packets:1370 errors:0 dropped:0 overruns:0 carrier:0
           collisions:0 txqueuelen:1000
           RX bytes:237686 (232.1 KiB)  TX bytes:205579 (200.7 KiB)

eth1       Link encap:Ethernet  HWaddr 00:30:48:D7:D5:43
           UP BROADCAST RUNNING SLAVE MULTICAST  MTU:1500  Metric:1
           RX packets:1545 errors:0 dropped:0 overruns:0 frame:0
           TX packets:60 errors:0 dropped:0 overruns:0 carrier:0
           collisions:0 txqueuelen:1000
           RX bytes:93313 (91.1 KiB)  TX bytes:12420 (12.1 KiB)

eth2       Link encap:Ethernet  HWaddr 00:30:48:D7:D5:43
           UP BROADCAST RUNNING SLAVE MULTICAST  MTU:1500  Metric:1
           RX packets:252 errors:0 dropped:0 overruns:0 frame:0
           TX packets:19 errors:0 dropped:0 overruns:0 carrier:0
           collisions:0 txqueuelen:100
           RX bytes:15774 (15.4 KiB)  TX bytes:3458 (3.3 KiB)
```

The bonding mode, current status, number of link failures, and the current active link can be viewed at the /proc/net/bonding location, as in this example:

```
[root@london1 bonding]# cat bond0
Ethernet Channel Bonding Driver: v3.2.4 (January 28, 2008)

Bonding Mode: fault-tolerance (active-backup)
Primary Slave: None
Currently Active Slave: eth1
MII Status: up
MII Polling Interval (ms): 100
Up Delay (ms): 0
Down Delay (ms): 0

Slave Interface: eth1
MII Status: up
Link Failure Count: 0
Permanent HW addr: 00:30:48:d7:d5:43

Slave Interface: eth2
MII Status: up
Link Failure Count: 0
Permanent HW addr: 00:30:48:d7:d5:56
```

Details related to the configuration of the network are also reported in the system log, which can be viewed either in /var/log/messages or with the command, dmesg:

```
igb: eth1: igb_watchdog_task: NIC Link is Down
bonding: bond0: link status definitely down for interface eth1, disabling it
bonding: bond0: making interface eth2 the new active one.
```

Once bonding has been configured and is active on all of the nodes in the cluster, the interface—bond0, in this case—represents the private interconnect interface to use for the Oracle software during installation. The slave device names should not be used directly in any of the configuration steps required.

I/O Fencing with IPMI

The Intelligent Platform Management Interface (IPMI) introduced in Chapter 4 is a standard for remote server management, and it is available on a wide range of systems that support Oracle Enterprise Linux. The key aspect for support of IPMI is the presence of a Baseboard Management Controller (BMC), which is typically located on the motherboard of the server. The BMC includes a service processor distinct from the system processor, and this service processor has its own firmware, power, and network connection. The BMC receives power when the system is connected, even if the server itself is turned off. This means that it is always in a powered on state. Consequently, the BMC is active, regardless of whether the Linux operating system is installed or running. The BMC provides significant functionality. For example, it can monitor the system hardware sensors, such as the state of the processors, memory, fans, power supplies, and temperature. The BMC also enables you to administer the server, letting you power a server on or reset a server remotely. Again, this functionality remains available, regardless of the operating system's status or your access to the system event logs. The BMC also provides serial over LAN (SOL) functionality, enabling access to the server console across the network.

From the preceding description, it should be clear that IPMI provides improved functionality for I/O fencing capabilities. It also provides the ability for one node in the cluster to remotely reset another from which contact has been lost, regardless of whether contact with the operating system on the node to be reset has been lost. Thus IPMI can be used to reset a node even if the operating system is in a hung state. If you have IPMI available on your cluster nodes, then you should configure it so that it is used for I/O fencing by the Oracle Clusterware.

The BMC provides an additional feature relevant to clustered environments: a watchdog timer with functionality similar to the hangcheck timer. However, as noted previously, the system must recover to a suitable operational state before the hangcheck timer can be triggered. The BMC watchdog timer runs independently of the operating system. This means that, even if the system is in a permanently hung state, the timer can still be triggered and perform a hardware-level reset. The BMC watchdog timer operates by setting a timer that counts down from a user determined value to zero. On reaching zero, the system is reset. On the operating system, a daemon is run to periodically reset the timer. Obviously, the value of operating system's daemon is smaller than that for the BMC watchdog timer limit. Consequently, during normal operations, the BMC watchdog timer does not reach zero, and the system remains operational. However, if the operating system remains in a hung state, the timer is not reset, and the system is reset when the BMC timer reaches zero. This reset occurs regardless of the status of the operating system. You may wish to consider setting the BMC watchdog timer functionality only if you are absolutely aware of the necessary timings required for it to operate as an additional reset mechanism to the Clusterware timeout.

Before attempting to configure the BMC, you must ensure that it is connected to the network. Typically, the BMC connection shares the first Ethernet port for IPMI Channel 1, usually eth0. Therefore, the BMC can be reached as long as this port is connected. Regardless, you should keep in mind that the BMC has its own separate MAC address and IP address, so it is only the physical infrastructure that is shared. Also, in a teamed network configuration, the BMC interface will operate independently of the bonded driver. This means that configuring the bonded driver as described previously will not provide resilience at the BMC level.

If your system supports IPMI, then there will usually be a number of configurable options at the BIOS level. These options typically fall under a heading such as Server Management, and they might include the potential to automatically start the BMC-related functionality. However, if this functionality is not enabled automatically, you can begin configuring IPMI by starting the IPMI service. If the system has a BMC, then the service should start successfully, as shown in this example:

```
[root@london2 modules]# service ipmi start
Starting ipmi drivers:                              [  OK  ]
```

You can see the details displayed in /var/log/messages:

```
Jul 27 17:06:58 london2 kernel: ipmi message handler version 39.1
Jul 27 17:06:58 london2 kernel: IPMI System Interface driver.
Jul 27 17:06:58 london2 kernel: ipmi_si: Trying SMBIOS-specified kcs state machine at i/o
address 0xca2, slave address 0x20, irq 0
Jul 27 17:06:58 london2 kernel: ipmi: Found new BMC (man_id: 0x000157,  prod_id: 0x0028,
dev_id: 0x20)
Jul 27 17:06:58 london2 kernel:  IPMI kcs interface initialized
```

If however a BMC is not present, however, the service will fail to start:

```
Apr 20 07:34:23 london5 kernel: ipmi_si: Interface detection failed
Apr 20 07:34:23 london5 kernel: ipmi_si: Unable to find any System Interface(s)
```

If the service fails to start, then you should check your hardware configuration to verify whether a BMC is present and enabled. If the service is running, then you should also use the chkconfig ipmi on command to enable the service so it starts at the current run level:

```
[root@london2 ~]# chkconfig --list ipmi
ipmi            0:off   1:off   2:on    3:on    4:on    5:on    6:off
```

The service status should show the IPMI modules are running before you proceed with configuring IPMI:

```
[root@london2 modules]# service ipmi status
ipmi_msghandler module loaded.
ipmi_si module loaded.
ipmi_devintf module loaded.
/dev/ipmi0 exists.
```

To configure IPMI, it is necessary to install the RPM package OpenIPMI-tools. You can do this directly or by using YUM:

```
[root@london1 ~]# yum install OpenIPMI-tools.x86_64
Loaded plugins: security
Server                                                  | 1.3 kB        00:00
Setting up Install Process
Resolving Dependencies
--> Running transaction check
---> Package OpenIPMI-tools.x86_64 0:2.0.16-5.el5 set to be updated
...
Installed:
  OpenIPMI-tools.x86_64 0:2.0.16-5.el5

Complete!
```

Without further configuration, it is possible to communicate with the BMC on the local system with the ipmitool command. This command lets you view the system status and logs, or even power cycle the system:

```
[root@london2 ~]# ipmitool power cycle
Chassis Power Control: Cycle
[root@london2 ~]#
Broadcast message from root (Tue Jul 28 14:32:07 2009):

The system is going down for system halt NOW!
```

However, IPMI functionality is fully realized only when it is possible to access the BMC remotely. Enabling this functionality requires that you configure the IPMI user and the LAN channel. By default, a NULL administrator level user exists for all channels; the following example shows the details for the NULL user on Channel 1:

```
[root@london1 ~]# ipmitool user list 1
ID  Name            Enabled Callin Link Auth IPMI Msg  Channel Priv Limit
1                   true    true   false     true      ADMINISTRATOR
```

You can use the `ipmitool` command's `user set` argument to add another user. The user is created and visible for all channels, although the authority levels for that user can be different on different channels. In the following example, the user `oraipmi` is created with the default privilege levels shown for Channel 1:

```
[root@london1 ~]# ipmitool user set name 2 oraipmi
[root@london1 ~]# ipmitool user list 1
ID  Name            Enabled Callin Link Auth IPMI Msg  Channel Priv Limit
1                   true    true   false     true      ADMINISTRATOR
2   oraipmi         false   true   false     false     NO ACCESS
```

You can use the `user priv` arguments to change the privilege levels. In the following example, user 2 the `oraipmi` user is set to the privilege level of 4, Administrator on Channel 1:

```
[root@london1 ~]# ipmitool user priv 2 4 1
[root@london1 ~]# ipmitool user list 1
ID  Name            Enabled Callin Link Auth IPMI Msg  Channel Priv Limit
1                   true    true   false     true      ADMINISTRATOR
2   oraipmi         true    true   false     true      ADMINISTRATOR
```

Finally, you can complete the user configuration by setting the password for the newly configured user, and then set the channel to use password authentication for the Administrator level:

```
[root@london1 ~]# ipmitool user set password 2 oracle
[root@london1 ~]# ipmitool lan set 1 auth ADMIN PASSWORD
```

With the `oraipmi` user configured and the authority level set, it is necessary to configure the LAN channel to the preferred IP configuration. The following example illustrates how to configure a static IP address on Channel 1:

```
[root@london1 ~]# ipmitool lan set 1 ipsrc static
[root@london1 ~]# ipmitool lan set 1 ipaddr 172.17.1.10
Setting LAN IP Address to 172.17.1.10
[root@london1 ~]# ipmitool lan set 1 netmask 255.255.0.0
Setting LAN Subnet Mask to 255.255.0.0
[root@london1 ~]# ipmitool lan set 1 defgw ipaddr 172.17.1.254
Setting LAN Default Gateway IP to 172.17.1.254
[root@london1 ~]# ipmitool lan set 1 access on
[root@london1 ~]# ipmitool lan set 1 snmp gridcommunity
Setting LAN SNMP Community String to gridcommunity
```

Finally, we can print the channel status to show that the BMC is configured and available for testing remotely:

```
[root@london1 ~]# ipmitool lan print 1
Set in Progress        : Set Complete
Auth Type Support      : NONE MD5 PASSWORD
```

```
Auth Type Enable        : Callback :
                        : User     :
                        : Operator :
                        : Admin    : PASSWORD
                        : OEM      :
IP Address Source       : Static Address
IP Address              : 172.17.1.10
Subnet Mask             : 255.255.0.0
MAC Address             : 00:04:23:dc:29:52
SNMP Community String   : gridcommunity
...
```

■ **Note** You cannot test remote IPMI connectivity from the server itself; therefore, you must perform such testing from another node in the cluster or on an additional management server on the network.

In the following example, the ipmitool is used to verify the power status of the chassis from a remote server that specifies the password on the command line. If the password is not specified, then it is prompted for. Alternatively, the password can be set in the environment variable IPMI_PASSWORD and the -E option can be used to list the sensor data. In the following example, some arguments, such as -I for the LAN channel, resolve to the default setting:

```
[root@london2 ~]# ipmitool -H 172.17.1.10 -U oraipmi \
 -P oracle chassis power status
Chassis Power is on
[root@london2 ~]# export IPMI_PASSWORD="oracle"
[root@london2 ~]# ipmitool -H 172.17.1.10 -U oraipmi -E sdr list
BB +1.2V Vtt   | 1.20 Volts   | ok
BB +1.5V AUX   | 1.48 Volts   | ok
BB +1.5V       | 1.48 Volts   | ok
BB +1.8V       | 1.80 Volts   | ok
BB +3.3V       | 3.32 Volts   | ok
...
```

The following dialog illustrates that you can now use IPMI to let one node in the cluster or on an external management server control the chassis of another node. For example, the first node might power down the other node. Next, the communication established with the BMC can enable the first node to power up the server from a powered down state:

```
[root@london2 ~]# ipmitool -H 172.17.1.10 -U oraipmi -E chassis power off
Chassis Power Control: Down/Off
[root@london2 ~]# ping 172.17.1.10
PING 172.17.1.10 (172.17.1.10) 56(84) bytes of data.
64 bytes from 172.17.1.10: icmp_seq=3 ttl=30 time=3.16 ms
64 bytes from 172.17.1.10: icmp_seq=4 ttl=30 time=3.05 ms
64 bytes from 172.17.1.10: icmp_seq=5 ttl=30 time=2.94 ms
```

```
--- 172.17.1.10 ping statistics ---
5 packets transmitted, 3 received, 40% packet loss, time 4001ms
rtt min/avg/max/mdev = 2.943/3.053/3.161/0.089 ms
[root@london2 ~]# ipmitool -H 172.17.1.10 -U oraipmi -E chassis power on
Chassis Power Control: Up/On
```

At this stage, the basic IPMI configuration is complete. However, we still recommend exploring the capabilities of IPMI further, as your requirements dictate. For example, you might use this service to configure SOL to display the system console remotely. You should also complete IPMI configuration for all of the nodes in the cluster and pay particular attention to the IP Addresses for the BMC, as well as the IPMI username and password for the Oracle Grid infrastructure software installation. Another nice feature: The IPMI configuration will persist in your BMC even if you reinstall the host operating system.

Summary

In this chapter, we explored the actions required to install, configure, and understand the Linux operating system before installing the Oracle grid infrastructure software and 11*g* Release 2 RAC Database Server software. Along the way, we focused on explaining all of the available configuration options, as well as the meanings behind the configuration decisions. At this point, you should have the necessary foundation for to implement successful Oracle software installations that are optimized for your environment.

■■■

## CHAPTER 7

Grid Infrastructure Installation

In Oracle 10*g* and 11.1, installing Oracle RAC can be a two- or three-stage process. The recommended configuration is to install the Oracle Clusterware, ASM, and RDBMS software in three separate Oracle homes. Oracle Clusterware must be in a separate Oracle home for architectural reasons. However, Oracle recommends that ASM and RDBMS be separated to provide more flexible options during upgrades. For many sites, the ASM and RDBMS software is identical; however, it is still common for users not requiring this level of flexibility to install ASM and RDBMS in the same Oracle home.

Prior to Oracle 11.2, the order of installation was therefore Oracle Clusterware, ASM (if required), and finally, the RDBMS software. In Oracle 11.2, Oracle Clusterware and ASM have been merged together into a single Oracle home known as the Grid Infrastructure home. The RDBMS software is still installed into a separate Oracle home. In Oracle 11.2, the order of installation is therefore Oracle Grid Infrastructure (including Oracle Clusterware and ASM), followed by the RDBMS software.

It is no longer possible to install Oracle Clusterware and ASM separately. This change has particular relevance in single-instance environments, which now require a special single-node Grid Infrastructure installation that includes a cut-down version of Oracle Clusterware in addition to ASM.

Getting Ready for Installation

In this section, we discuss the basic installation. Your first step will be to obtain the software distribution. Next, you will configure your X-Windows environment. Finally, you will determine whether to configure the grid software manually or to let the installer configure the software automatically.

Obtain Software Distribution

The first step is to obtain the Grid Infrastructure software distribution. The software can be downloaded from the Oracle Technology Network at www.oracle.com/technetwork/index.html. Alternatively, it may be available on DVD-ROM. In Oracle 11.2, software is delivered as a zip file that can be unzipped into a staging area.

For example, this snippet creates a suitable staging area:

```
[oracle@london1]$ mkdir /home/oracle/stage
[oracle@london1]$ cd /home/oracle/stage
```

Next, download the software into the staging area and unzip the download file:

```
[oracle@london1]$ unzip linux_11gR2_grid.zip
```

This unzip process will create a directory called /grid below /home/oracle/stage that contains the installation files.

Configure X Environment

Both the Grid Infrastructure and the RDBMS software must be installed using the Oracle Universal Installer (OUI). This tool runs in both interactive and silent modes. In interactive mode, the OUI is a GUI tool that requires an X environment. Due to the complexity of the installation process, we recommend that you initially perform installations in interactive mode because this mode allows many errors to be corrected without restarting the installation process. The silent mode is intended for installations on large numbers of nodes and for sites where you wish to ensure a high level of standardization. The installer also allows a response file to be generated at the end of the interview process. This file can optionally be modified and used as the basis for subsequent installations.

Checking Prerequisites

In Oracle 11.2, the OUI has been completely rewritten and is more user-friendly than in previous versions. Checking of prerequisites has been improved, and the installer offers a facility where it can generate fixup scripts for a limited selection of configuration errors and omissions. These fixup scripts should be executed manually by the root user before the installation can proceed.

The Cluster Verification Utility (CVU) has been fully integrated into the OUI. It forms the basis of the prerequisite checks, and it is also executed as the final step of the Grid Infrastructure installation. Note that Oracle still recommends that the CVU still be executed in standalone mode prior to installation. It also recommends that you run CVU before and after operations that add or delete nodes.

As in previous releases, the OUI interactive installation installs the software onto the first node and then relinks the executables, if necessary. The linked executables are then copied to the remaining nodes in the cluster. To use the OUI in interactive mode, an X environment must be available. You can either run an X environment on the console of the installation node, or you can use VNC.

The simplest way to do this is to perform the installation in the console window of the first node. The most popular Linux desktop environments are GNOME and KDE. Either can be used for OUI installations, as well as for GUI-based configuration assistants such as DBCA and ASMCA.

Alternatively, a VNC server can be configured to run on the installation node that allows a desktop environment to be presented on a separate VNC client. Using VNC is a better solution if you are in a different location than the database servers.

Starting an X environment in a console window

X is started automatically in Linux run level 5. However, in Oracle 11.2 it is recommended that Linux servers use run level 3, so X will not be available. To start X, log in to a console session as the root user and enter this snippet:

```
[root@london1]# startx
```

This will start a GUI desktop session on the same terminal. By default, Linux has a series of virtual sessions. And by convention, the X environment runs in the seventh session. You can switch to the X environment by holding down the CTRL+ALT+7 keys simultaneously; you can switch back to the shell sessions using CTRL+ALT-1, CTRL+ALT-2, and so on. Sometimes, this can be useful for problem diagnosis. However, once the desktop session is running, you can also start a terminal window from within the desktop.

To allow any user to run an X session, first start a terminal session as the root user and enter this line:

```
[root@london1]# xhost +
```

Next, change to the oracle user:

```
[root@london1]# su - oracle
```

Starting an X environment using VNC

An alternative option is to use VNC. VNC is a free client/server product in which a VNC server session runs on the server and a VNC Viewer runs on the client.

On the server, VNC is supplied with the operating system in Red Hat and Oracle Enterprise Linux distributions. For OEL5R2, the VNC server RPM is vnc-server-4.1.2-9.el5. In Linux, VNC is implemented as a service. You can check whether it is currently installed using this line:

```
[root@london1]# rpm -q vnc-server
```

If the package is not installed, then install it from the Linux distribution, as in this example:

```
[root@london1]# rpm -ivh vnc-server-4.1.2-9.el5.rpm
```

The following line checks whether the vncserver service is currently running:

```
[root@london1]# service vncserver status
Xvnc is stopped
```

If the vncserver service is not currently running, then you can start it with this line:

```
[root@london1]# service vncserver start
```

If you receive the following message, then you need to configure VNC on the server:

```
Starting VNC server: no displays configured                    [ OK ]
```

To configure VNC on the server, log in as root and add the following lines to /etc/sysconfig/vncservers:

```
VNCSERVERS="1:oracle"
VNCSERVERARGS[1]="-geometry 1024x768"
```

Next, set the geometry to reflect the display size available on the client. Note that the server number must be specified when connecting from the client. The following example indicates that you are connecting to server 1:

```
server14:1
```

Now log in as the oracle user and run vncpasswd:

```
[oracle@london1]$ vncpasswd
Password: <enter password>
Verify: <enter password again>
```

And now log in as root:

```
[root@london1]# service vncserver start
Starting VNC server: 1: oracle xauth: creating new authority file /home/oracle/.XAuthority
```

New 'london1.example.com:1 (oracle)' desktop is london1.example.com:1

```
Creating default startup script /home/oracle/.vnc/xstartup
Starting applications specified in  /home/oracle/.vnc/xstartup
Log file is /home/oracle/.vnc/london1.example.com:1.log
```

Next, you need to modify /home/oracle/.vnc/xstartup by uncommenting the following two lines:

```
unset SESSION_MANAGER
exec /etc/X11/xinit/xinitrc
```

Now log in as root again and restart the vncserver service:

```
[root@london1]# service vncserver restart
```

The vncserver service can be permanently enabled using this line:

```
[root@london1]# chkconfig vncserver on
```

The preceding command will start vncserver at run levels 2, 3, 4, and 5.

For the client, VNC can be downloaded from a number of sources, such as www.realvnc.com. At the time of writing, the current version of VNC was 4.1.3. Versions are available for Windows, Linux, and several other UNIX-based operating systems.

For Windows-based clients, VNC can be downloaded as either a ZIP file or an executable file. In the following example, the zip file was called vnc-4_1_3-x86_win32.zip and contained a single executable file called vnc-4_1_3-x86_win32.exe. This executable runs the VNC Setup Wizard, which allows you to install the VNC server, the viewer, or both.

The next example adds VNC server to the Windows menus:

```
Start > Programs > RealVNC > VNC Viewer 4 > Run VNC Viewer
```

Enter the server name when prompted (e.g. london1:1), and then enter the vnc password for the oracle user.

■ **Note** Other connection options exist, such as using Hummingbird Exceed or Xming. However, in our opinion, the two connection methods just described provide the simplest ways to achieve the desired behavior.

Determining Configuration Type

In Oracle 11.2 you can either perform a manual configuration in which case you are responsible for assigning names and IP addresses to all components in your cluster, or you can perform an automatic configuration in which case Oracle can assign names and IP addresses to a limited number of components in the cluster. For the automatic configuration, Oracle can assign names and IP addresses for the private network (interconnect), VIP addresses and SCAN VIP addresses. Oracle often refers to the automatic configuration as a Grid Naming Service (GNS) configuration. If you choose to perform an automatic configuration, we recommend that you still continue to configure the private network manually in order to be able test the private network prior to installation of Grid Infrastructure. The VIP and SCAN VIP addresses use the public network which must be configured manually for individual nodes prior to installation.

For both manual and automatic configurations, we recommend that you configure a DNS server in your environment. It is still theoretically possible to install Grid Infrastructure without a DNS server. However, you will receive some error messages from the Cluster Verification Utility at the end of the installation session if you do this. If you do not already have a DNS server in your environment, then it is relatively simple to create one locally. This may be necessary if you are installing Grid Infrastructure in a test environment.

For the automatic configuration, a DHCP server must also be available in your environment. Again, if a DHCP server is not available, you can configure one locally for testing purposes. Chapter 6 covers how to configure both DNS and DHCP in detail.

Also in Oracle 11.2, you can perform either a Typical or an Advanced Grid Infrastructure installation. If you have configured your environment manually, then you can use either the Typical or Advanced installations; if you wish to use the automatic configuration, you must select the Advanced installation.

As you would expect, the Typical Installation makes a few assumptions about your installation decisions. The Advanced Installation allows you to override some default options and only requires a couple of additional steps. In particular, the Advanced Installation option allows you to specify a name for your cluster; as we will see later, the Typical Installation option derives the name of the cluster from the cluster SCAN name, and that name may not always be appropriate. It is also easier to troubleshoot installation errors in the Advanced Installation because you will have entered more of the configuration options yourself. Therefore, we generally recommend that you perform an Advanced Installation, regardless of whether you wish to use manual or automatic configuration.

In the following sections, we will describe all three installation types in the following order:

- Advanced Installation - manual configuration (without GNS)

- Advanced Installation - automatic configuration (with GNS)

- Typical Installation - manual configuration (without GNS)

We will also fully describe the Advanced Installation with manual configuration. For the remaining two installation types, we will only discuss the differences between these and the Advanced / manual installation.

Advanced Installation - Manual Configuration

In this section we will discuss how to implement an advanced installation using the manual configuration option. We will assume that DNS is installed and configured, as detailed in Chapter 6, but we will also include the actual network configuration used for the installation of a four-node cluster.

Network Configuration

The first step is to configure the network infrastructure. In this example, values are configured in DNS and /etc/hosts. Tables 7-1 through 7-6 show the various values that we used. The values are based on the example configurations described in Chapter 6.

Table 7-1. DNS Settings

Domain Name	example.com
Server Name	dns1.example.com
Server Address	172.17.1.1

Table 7-2. DHCP Settings

Server address	Not required
Address range	Not required

Table 7-3. DNS Settings

Sub domain	Not required
Host name	Not required
VIP address	Not required

Table 7-4. SCAN Listeners

SCAN Name	cluster1-scan.example.com
SCAN Addresses	172.17.1.205, 172.17.1.206, 172.17.1.207

Table 7-5. Public Network Settings

Network	172.17.0.0
Gateway	172.17.0.254
Broadcast address	172.17.255.255
Subnet mask	255.255.0.0
Node names	london1, london2, london3, london4

Public IP address	172.17.1.101,172.17.1.102,172.17.1.103,172.17.1.104
VIP names	london1-vip london2-vip london3-vip london4-vip
VIP addresses	172.17.1.201,172.17.1.202,172.17.1.203,172.17.1.204

Table 7-6. *Private Network Settings*

Network	192.168.1.0
Subnet mask	255.255.255.0
Names	london1-priv london2-priv london3-priv london4-priv
IP addresses	192.168.1.1,192.168.1.2,192.168.1.3, 192.168.1.4

DNS Configuration

Your next task is to verify that the bind package has been installed and is running. Chapter 6 shows you how to do that. In this example, /etc/named.conf has exactly the same format that is shown in Chapter 6.

For example, forward lookups are configured in master.example.com, as shown here:

```
$TTL 86400
@               IN SOA dns1.example.com. root.localhost
                       2010063000        ; serial
                       28800             ; refresh
                       14400             ; retry
                       3600000           ; expiry
                       86400 )           ; minimum
@               IN NS  dns1.example.com.
localhost       IN A   127.0.0.1
dns1            IN A   172.17.1.1
london1         IN A   172.17.1.101
london2         IN A   172.17.1.102
london3         IN A   172.17.1.103
london4         IN A   172.17.1.104
london1-vip     IN A   172.17.1.201
london2-vip     IN A   172.17.1.202
london3-vip     IN A   172.17.1.203
london4-vip     IN A   172.17.1.204
cluster1-scan   IN A   172.17.1.205
                IN A   172.17.1.206
                IN A   172.17.1.207
```

And reverse lookups for example.com are configured in 172.17.1.rev:

```
$TTL 86400
@       IN SOA dns1.example.com. root.localhost. (
```

```
                         2010063000           ; serial
                         28800                ; refresh
                         14400                ; retry
                         3600000              ; expiry
                         86400  )             ; minimum
@        IN NS  dns1.example.com.
1        IN PTR dns1.example.com.
101      IN PTR london1.example.com.
102      IN PTR london2.example.com.
103      IN PTR london3.example.com.
104      IN PTR london4.example.com.
201      IN PTR london1-vip.example.com.
202      IN PTR london2-vip.example.com.
203      IN PTR london3-vip.example.com.
204      IN PTR london4-vip.example.com.
```

Forward and reverse lookups for the local domain must also be configured; again, see Chapter 6 for more information on how to do this.

On each node in the cluster, /etc/resolv.conf was configured as follows:

```
search example.com
nameserver 172.17.1.1
options attempts:2
options timeout:1
```

In the next example, we configured the private network addresses in /etc/hosts on each node:

```
192.168.1.1        london1-priv.example.com london1-priv
192.168.1.2        london2-priv.example.com london2-priv
192.168.1.3        london3-priv.example.com london3-priv
192.168.1.4        london4-priv.example.com london4-priv
```

Note that, in the preceding example, it is not strictly necessary to include a fully qualified domain name for the private network addresses. However, we show both the fully qualified and unqualified names for completeness and compatibility with earlier releases.

Choosing an Installation Option

Now run the installer as the user who will own the Grid Infrastructure software and look at your installation options. If you are installing the Grid Infrastructure under a user called grid, then you should run the installer as the grid user. The following example starts OUI as the oracle user:

```
[oracle@london1]$ /home/oracle/stage/grid/runInstaller
```

The installer is written in Java, and it takes a couple of minutes to load. When it does load, you'll see the page shown in Figure 7-1.

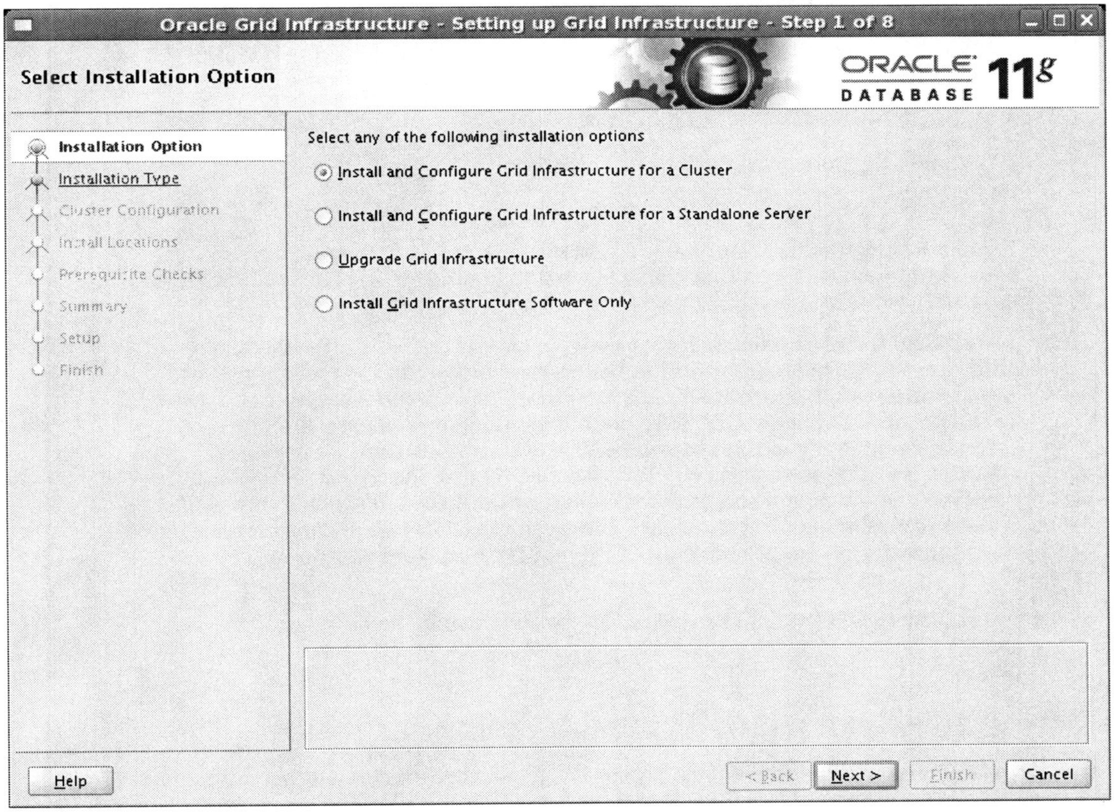

Figure 7-1. Choosing an installation option

The Installation Option page provides the following options:

Install and Configure Grid Infrastructure for a Cluster: If you are building a multimode cluster, we recommend that you select this option, which installs the Grid Infrastructure software (Clusterware and ASM) and configures the Clusterware files (OCR and Voting disks). If you choose to locate the Clusterware files in ASM, then an ASM disk group will also be created during installation. This option should also be used if you plan to deploy Oracle RAC One-node.

Install and Configure Grid Infrastructure for a Standalone Server: This option should be used if you want to build a single-node cluster. The Grid Infrastructure installation will include a cut-down version of Oracle Clusterware and ASM. This option is not appropriate for Oracle RAC One-node, which requires a minimum of two nodes in the cluster.

Upgrade Grid Infrastructure: This option should be selected if you have an older version of Oracle Clusterware installed on the cluster. The following versions of Oracle Clusterware can be upgraded directly:

- Oracle 10*g* Release 1 - 10.1.0.3 or above

- Oracle 10*g* Release 2 - 10.2.0.3 or above

- Oracle 11*g* Release 1 - 11.1.0.6 or above

If you are currently running Oracle Clusterware, and it is not one of the aforementioned versions, then you will need to upgrade to the latest patch set for your release before installing Oracle 11.2.

Install Grid Infrastructure Software Only: In Oracle 11.2, it is possible to perform a software-only installation of Grid Infrastructure and to run the root scripts that initalize the cluster environment at a later time. This option will be particularly useful for sites where the DBA does not have sufficient privileges, and the root scripts consequently have to be run by a system administrator. In previous releases, it was necessary to run the root scripts before the OUI session could complete, which meant some co-ordination was required between the DBA and system administrator. In this release, however, the OUI session can complete, and the administrator can be subsequently requested to run the root scripts.

Once you choose the desired option, press Next to continue to the next page.

Selecting an Advanced or Typical Installation Type

Now you can choose your installation type. Figure 7-2 shows the two choices that are available: Typical and Advanced. Both the Typical Installation and the Advanced Installation using manual configuration require the same amount of preparation prior to installation.

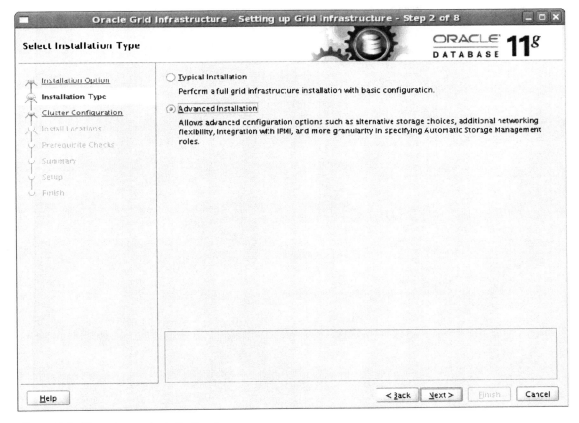

Figure 7-2. Choosing an installation type

In all cases, we recommend that a DNS server be available either within the enterprise or within the local network. Advanced Installation using the automatic configuration also requires that a DHCP server be similarly available.

In the next example, we will perform an Advanced Installation using manual configuration (without GNS). Be sure to select that option, and then press Next to continue to language section.

Selecting a Language

The next step in the install process is to choose your language. Oracle supports a wide number of languages, as shown in Figure 7-3.

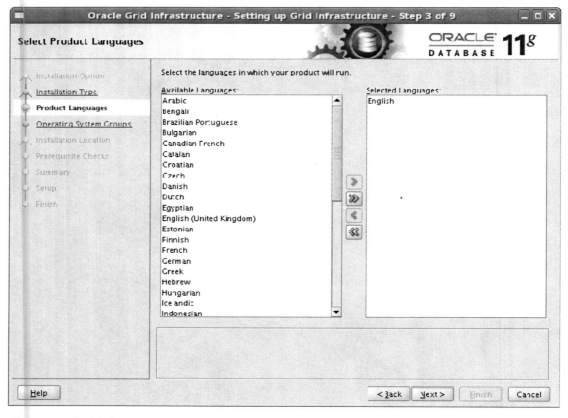

Figure 7-3. Grid infrastructure language choices

On the Language Selection page, (American) English will be preselected. If you wish error messages to be reported in other languages, then add these languages using the arrow buttons. We recommend that you do not attempt to remove American English.

Next, select any additional languages you want to use and press Next to continue to the Grid Plug and Play Information page.

Configuring the Grid Plug and Play

The Grid Plug and Play (GPnP) Information page requires some mandatory information about the cluster (see Figure 7-4). Take care when choosing a Cluster Name because it is very difficult to change this name later.

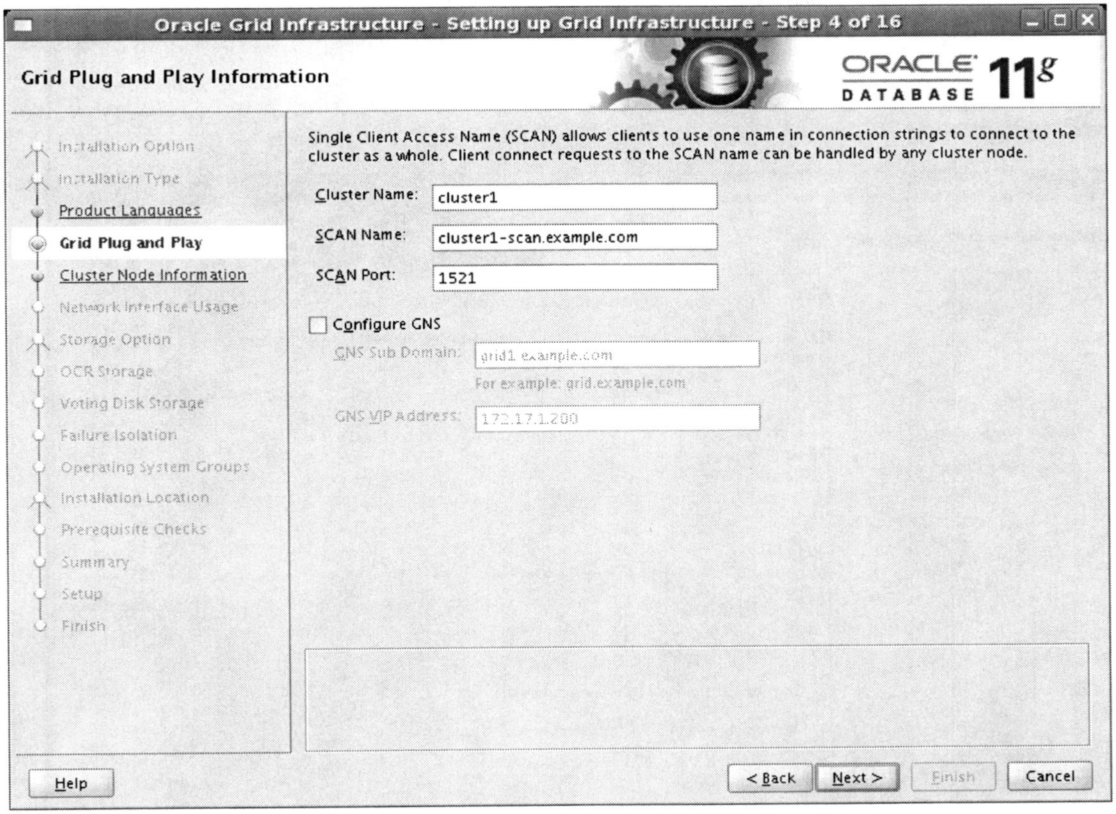

Figure 7-4. Configuring Plug and Play settings

The Single Client Access Name (SCAN) is a new feature in Oracle 11.2. The SCAN name effectively provides a network alias for the cluster. It replaces individual node names in the connection string and allows clients to connect to the cluster regardless of which nodes it is running on. The SCAN address is accessed via a SCAN VIP that typically runs on three nodes in the cluster. If less than three nodes are available, then multiple SCAN VIPs may be running on the same node. A dedicated SCAN listener process runs on each node that has a SCAN VIP. The SCAN listener is responsible for load balancing across the cluster, and the connection is forwarded to a local listener process running on one of the nodes currently in the cluster.

You will need to assign SCAN addresses in DNS prior to installing the Grid Infrastructure. Oracle recommends that three SCAN addresses be configured using addresses from the public network range.

In Figure 7-4, the SCAN name is cluster1-scan.example.com. The SCAN name generally takes this format: <cluster-name>-scan.<domain>. However, the precise format of the SCAN address appears to be an evolving naming convention, rather than a mandatory requirement.

The Grid Naming Service (GNS) is not required for the manual installation. Therefore, the GNS check box should not be checked.

Press Next to continue to the Cluster Node Information page.

Configuring the Cluster Node Information Page

On the Cluster Node Information page (Figure 7-5), enter the hostname and virtual IP name of each node in the cluster. You can either enter names individually using the Add button or you can specify a cluster configuration file that contains the names for all nodes.

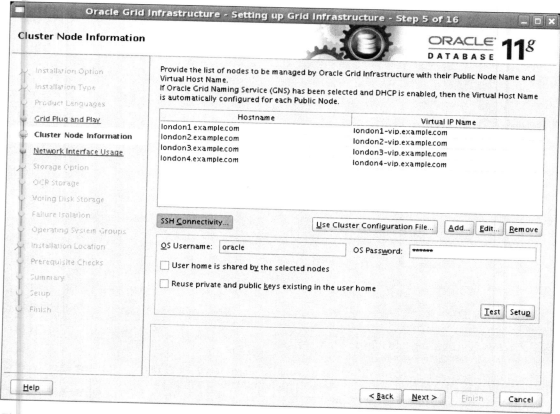

Figure 7-5. Configuring cluster node information

We recommended creating a cluster configuration file if there are more than two nodes. The format of the file looks like this:

```
<cluster_name>
<node_name> <vip_name>
[<node_name> <vip_name>]
```

A configured file might look like this:

```
cluster1
london1.example.com london1-vip.example.com
london2.example.com london2-vip.example.com
london3.example.com london3-vip.example.com
london4.example.com london4-vip.example.com
```

We named this file cluster1.ccf and stored it in /home/oracle, so that it will not be deleted in the event of a cleanup operation following a failed Grid Infrastructure installation.

The Cluster Node Information page also allows you to set up and test Secure Shell (SSH) connectivity between all the nodes in the cluster. If you do not need to customize your SSH configuration, then it is much simpler and quicker to allow Oracle to perform the SSH standard configuration at this point, especially if you have more than two nodes. We recommend that you allow the installer to configure SSH automatically at this stage, regardless of the installation type. Whether you configure SSH manually or automatically, the installer will test the SSH configuration at this stage to ensure there are no errors:

Press Next to continue to the Network Interface Usage page.

Configuring the Network Interface Usage Page

The next page you need to configure is the Network Interface Usage page (see Figure 7-6). You use this page to specify which interfaces should be used for the public and private networks.

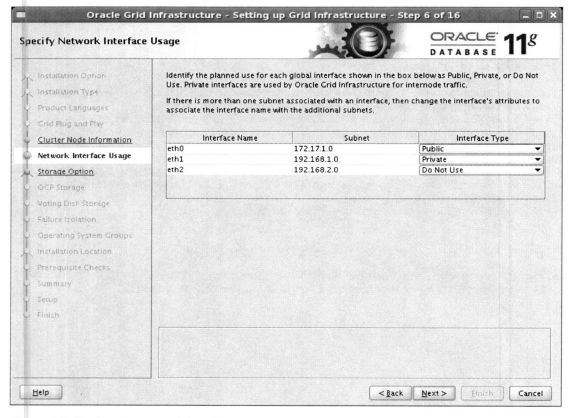

Figure 7-6. Configuring network interface usage

In Oracle 11.2, the installer makes some reasonable guesses at the proper settings to use. In the example shown in Figure 7-6, the public network will use the eth0 interface and the 172.17.1.0 subnet, and the private network will use the eth1 interface and the 192.168.1.0. subnet.

You can also specify which networks should not be used directly by Clusterware and RAC. For example, these might include storage, backup, or management networks. In the preceding example, the eth2 interface that uses the 192.168.2.0 subnet will not be used by Oracle Clusterware.

Press Next to continue to the Storage Option Information page:

Configuring the Storage Option Information Page

Your next step is to configure the Storage Option Information page (see Figure 7-7). In Oracle 11.2, you can place your Clusterware files (OCR and Voting disk) either in ASM storage or on a shared file system. In this version, you cannot create new Clusterware files on raw or block devices. However, you can upgrade existing Clusterware files on raw or block devices.

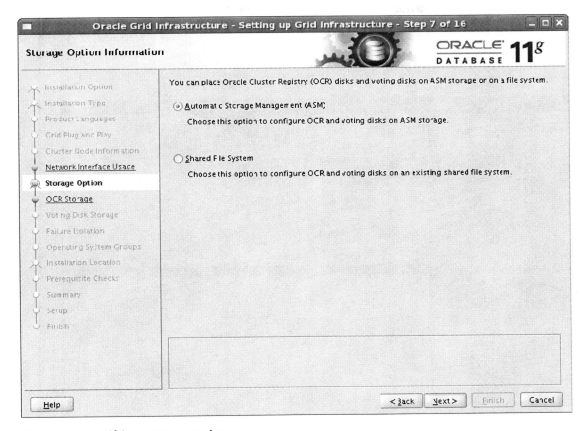

Figure 7-7. Specifying a storage option

If you specify ASM Storage in the Storage Option Information page shown in Figure 7-7 the LUNs must be provisioned and accessible with the correct permissions. ASM instances and ASM disk groups will be created later in the Grid Infrastructure installation process. If you specify Shared File System then a suitable cluster file system such as OCFS2 or a supported version of NFS must have already been installed.

Unless you have NAS-based storage, we strongly recommend using ASM to provide shared storage for RAC clusters. We also recommend placing the OCR and Voting disk in the ASM storage for newly created clusters.

Select the appropriate option and press Next to continue. If you have chosen ASM, then the Create ASM Disk Group page will be displayed.

Creating an ASM Disk Group

On the ASM Disk Group page (see shown in Figure 7-8), you can create an ASM disk group that will include the OCR and Voting disk. Additional ASM disk groups can be created later in the installation process.

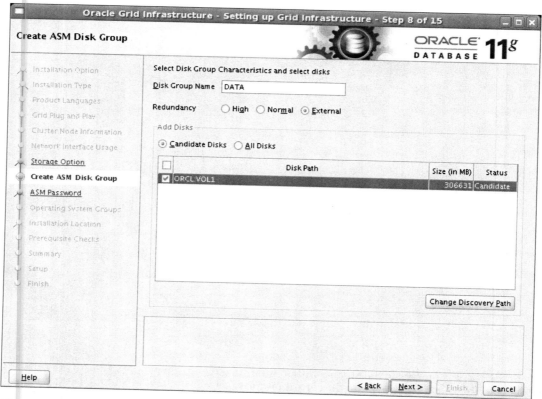

Figure 7-8. Creating an ASM Disk Group

If no candidate disks are displayed, then click Change Discovery Path... and modify the path.

Next, specify an ASM Disk Group name and the level of redundancy. If you select External Redundancy, you will need to specify one disk; if you select Normal Redundancy, you will need to specify three disks; and if you specify High Redundancy, you will need to specify five disks. The reason for the differing disk specification is that with Normal redundancy, three Voting disks will be created in the header of the ASM disks, so they will require three disks. In the case of High Redundancy, five Voting disks are created, so you will need five disks.

When you have specified the details for the ASM Disk Group, press Next to continue to the ASM Password page.

Specifying an ASM Password

The ASM Password page lets you specify passwords for the ASM SYS user and the ASMSNMP user (see Figure 7-9). The SYS user is used to administer ASM using the SYSASM privilege that was introduced in Oracle 11.1.

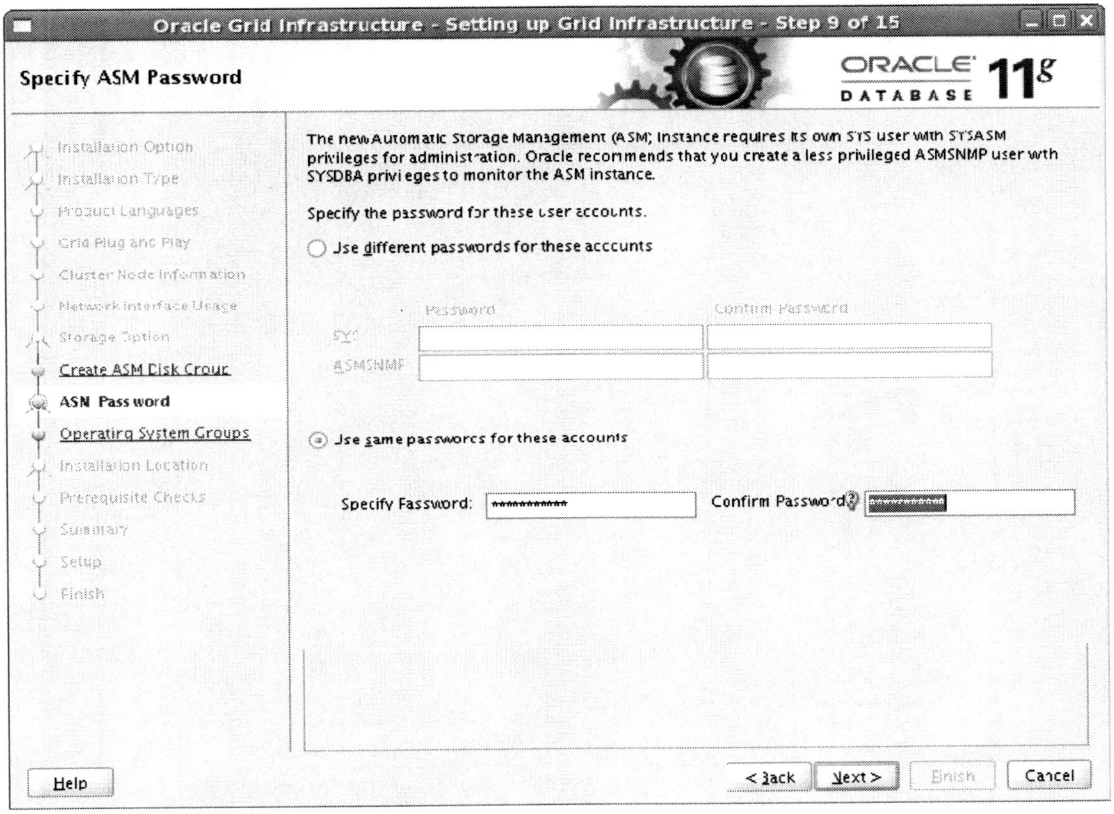

Figure 7-9. Specifying an ASM password

The ASMSNMP user is new to Oracle 11.2, and it includes SYSDBA privileges to monitor ASM instances. You can optionally use the same password for both accounts; however, we recommend that you use different passwords for each account.

Press Next to continue to the Failure Isolation Support page:

Specifying a Username and Password for IPMI

The Failure Isolation Support page lets you specify a username and password for the Intelligent Platform Management Interface (IPMI), as shown in Figure 7-10.

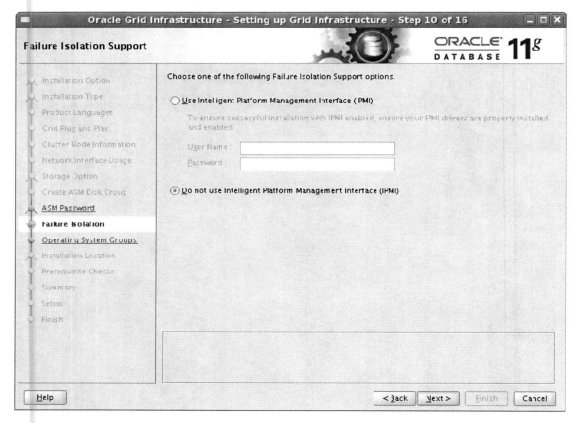

Figure 7-10. Failure Isolation Support

If you wish to use IPMI, you must ensure that you have appropriate hardware. You must also ensure that IPMI drivers are installed and enabled prior to starting the Grid Infrastructure installation process, as described in Chapter 6.

Press Next to continue to the Privileged Operating System Groups page.

Configuring Privileged Operating System Groups

The Privileged Operating System Groups page allows you to associate certain key Oracle groups with groups that you've defined at the operating-system level (see Figure 7-11).

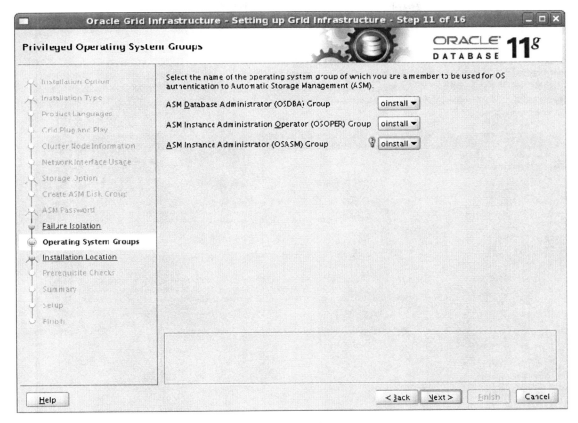

Figure 7-11. Creating associations for Operating System Groups

On the Privileged Operating System Groups page, you can specify operating system groups for the following Oracle groups:

- ASM Database Administrator (OSDBA)

- ASM Instance Operator (OSOPER)

- ASM Instance Administrator (OSASM)

Although different operating system groups can be specified for each Oracle group, the default operating system group (oinstall) is sufficient for most installations.

Press Next to continue. If you accepted the default values, you will receive the following warning:

INS-41813 OSDBA, OSOPER and OSADM are the same OS group.

Click Yes to ignore the warning and continue to the Installation Location page.

Setting the Installation Location

The Installation Location page lets you specify values for the Oracle base location ($ORACLE_BASE) and the Oracle Grid Infrastructure home location (see Figure 7-12). In Oracle 10g and above, Oracle recommends that you not locate the Oracle Grid Infrastructure home (Clusterware home) in a directory below the $ORACLE_BASE directory. This is mainly recommended for security reasons because the Grid Infrastructure home contains directories where scripts can be placed that are automatically executed with root privileges.

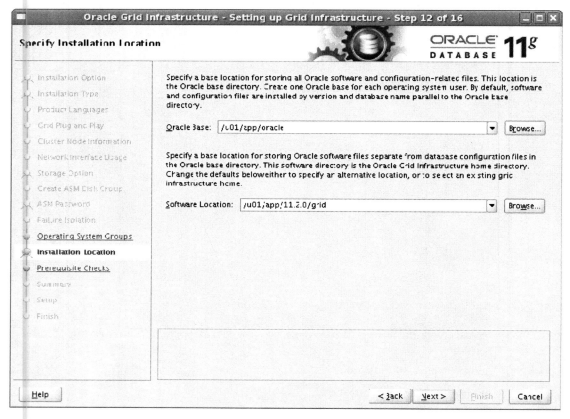

Figure 7-12. Specifying the installation location

In Oracle 11.2 and above, an out-of-place upgrade is used for the Grid Infrastructure. This means that a new Grid Infrastructure home is created for the upgrade software. Subsequently, Clusterware and ASM are switched over to use the new home. Therefore, in Oracle 11.2 and later, we recommend that you include the version number with the home directory path, so that two Grid Infrastructure homes can exist concurrently on the same node during the upgrade.

Press Next to continue to the Inventory page.

Specify the Central Inventory's Location

If you are making the first Oracle installation on the cluster, the Create Inventory page will be displayed (see Figure 7-13). This page lets you specify the location of the central inventory. A copy of the central inventory will be created and maintained in the same location on each node in the cluster.

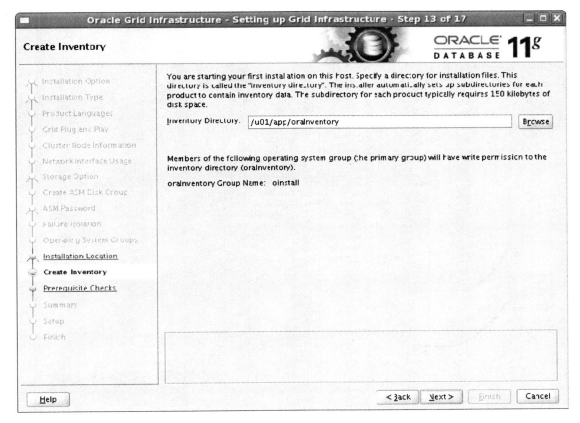

Figure 7-13. Creating the Inventory location

You can also specify the operating system group that will own the inventory, which defaults to oinstall. Members of this group can write to the inventory.

Press Next to continue to the Prerequisite Checks page.

Performing Prerequisite Checks

In Oracle 11.2, the Prerequisite Checks page (see Figure 7-14) has been enhanced to perform many of the checks previously performed only by the Cluster Verification Utility (CLUVFY).

If you have followed the Linux operating system installation and configuration steps covered in Chapter 6, then there should be no reported errors at this screen. However, in Figure -7-14 we deliberately did not configure kernel parameters on any nodes in the cluster. We chose to do this to illustrate a new feature of the OUI to identify and repair operating system configuration errors before proceeding with the Grid Infrastructure software installation. If you are satisfied that you have installed and configured Linux correctly and that you have no errors to repair, then you may proceed directly to the Summary page.

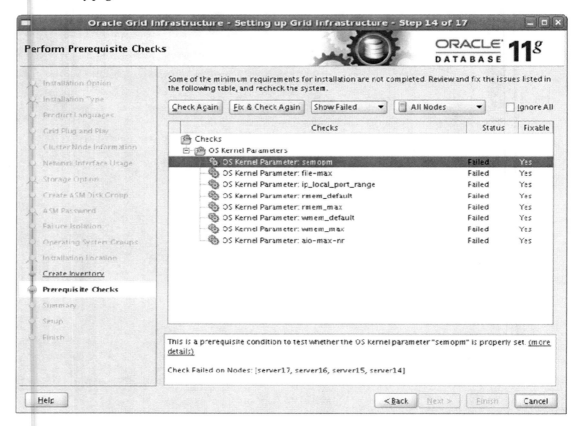

Figure 7-14. Performing Prerequisite Checks

If any prerequisite checks fail, then error messages will be displayed. In some circumstances, the page will generate scripts to fix the errors.

Identifying Typical Errors

Typical configuration errors identified by the prerequisite checks at this stage include the following:

- Insufficient swap space
- Incorrect run level
- Inadequate shell limits
- Inadequate kernel parameters

Getting More Detail

On the Prerequisite Checks page, the installer displays a list of errors. You can click on each error to get additional details. For example, if you click the failure message for the rmem_default kernel parameter, you'll see the additional information shown in Figure 7-15. Notice particularly that this page shows the cause of the error and recommended actions.

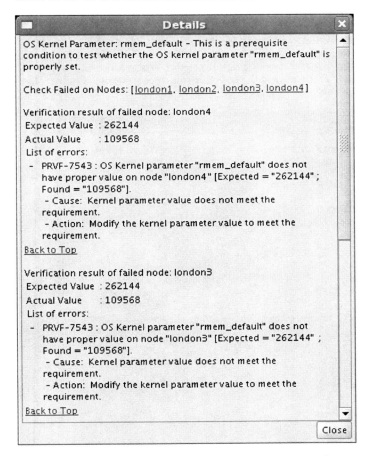

Figure 7-15. Viewing error messages, including causes and recommended actions

This message in Figure 7-15 shows that the rmem_default parameter was still at the default value of 109568 on each node in the cluster. The expected value is 262144 on each node in the cluster. The message is repeated for each node on which errors exist.

■ **Note** It is possible to select an error and press Fix and Check Again to resolve a number of errors, including kernel parameter errors.

Fixup Scripts

Depending on the nature of an error, the installer may generate a script to fix it. If you get such a script, you should run it as the root user before returning to the Prerequisite Checks page. If you cannot log in as the root user, then you should work with someone who can.

Fixup scripts can be generated for kernel parameter errors and user limits errors. In this release, fixup scripts cannot be generated for errors such as missing packages (RPMs) or insufficient swap space.

Figure 7-16 shows an example where the installer is telling you that you have an automatically generated script to run. Notice the instructions for running the script. Also notice that the installer tells you the nodes on which the script should be run.

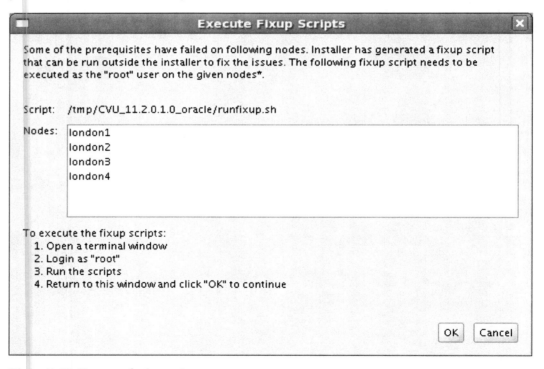

Figure 7-16. Error resolution scripts

Figure 7-16 also mentions a directory named /tmp/CVU_11.2.0.1.0. Fixup scripts are generated in directories created with this naming pattern:

/tmp/CVU_<release>_oracle

The installer will create that directory on each node in the cluster during the Grid Infrastructure installation process. Any fixup scripts will be written to that directory. Another script named runfixup.sh is created to run all the individual scripts.

Scripts generated include the following:

- runfixup.sh: This shell script creates a log file (orarun.log) and executes orarun.sh.

- orarun.sh: This shell script contains the functionality to perform all supported fixes.

- fixup.enable: This file specifies which types of fix should be applied.

- fixup.response: This file contains a set of parameters as name-value pairs.

Anatomy of Fixup Scripts

The orarun.sh script contains the functionality to perform all the supported fixes. It takes two parameters: the name of the response file (fixup.response) and the name of the enable file (fixup.enable).

Not all configuration errors can be fixed automatically in the first release. Currently, fixup scripts can be generated for the following kernel parameters:

- SHMMAX: kernel.shmmax

- SHMMNI: kernel.shmmni

- SHMALL: kernel.shmall

- SEMMSL: kernel.sem.semmsl

- SEMMNS: kernel.sem.semmns

- SEMOPN: kernel.sem.semopm

- SEMMNI: kernel.sem.semmni

- FILE_MAX_KERNEL: fs.filemax

- IP_LOCAL_PORT_RANGE: net.ipv4.ip_local_port_range

- RMEM_DEFAULT: net.core.rmem_default

- RMEM_MAX: net.core.rmem_max

- WMEM_DEFAULT: net.core.wmem_default

- WMEM_MAX: net.core.wmem_max

- AIO_MAX_SIZE: fs.aio-max-size

Fixup scripts can also be generated for the following shell limits:

- MAX_PROCESSES_HARDLIMIIT: hard nproc
- MAX_PROCESSES_SOFTLIMIIT: soft nproc
- FILE_OPEN_MAX_HARDLIMIT: hard nofile
- FILE_OPEN_MAX_SOFTLIMIT: soft nofile
- MAX_STACK_SOFTLIMIT: soft stack

The fixup.enable file is generated by the OUI, and it lists the types of fixes that should be applied by orarun.sh, as in this example:

```
SET_KERNEL_PARAMETERS="true"
```

The fixup.response file is generated by the OUI, and it contains a set of parameters listed as name-value pairs, as in this example:

```
FILE_OPEN_MAX_HARDLIMIT="65536"
INSTALL_USER="oracle"
SYSCTL_LOC="/sbin/sysctl"
SEMOPM="100"
IP_LOCAL_PORT_RANGE="9000 65000"
RMEM_DEFAULT="262144"
RMEM_MAX="4194304"
WMEM_DEFAULT="262144"
WMEM_MAX="1048576"
AIO_MAX_NR="1048576"
```

Note that fixup.response includes more than just kernel parameter values; it also includes security and other parameters required by orarun.sh.

Addressing Failed Checks

We recommend that you address all failed prerequisite checks to ensure that any errors occurring during the installation process are genuine problems. However, you can choose to ignore some errors. For example, if your cluster does not need to synchronize time with external servers, you may decide not to configure NTP, in which case Clusterware will perform time synchronization internally using CTSS. In such cases, you can click Ignore All on the Prerequisites Checks page to acknowledge the warning, as well as to instruct the installer that you are prepared to continue.

The following example shows the output generated by running /tmp/CVU_11.2.0.1.0_oracle/runfixup.sh on the first node:

```
[root@london1 oracle]# /tmp/CVU_11.2.0.1.0_oracle/runfixup.sh
Response file being used is :/tmp/CVU_11.2.0.1.0_oracle/fixup.response
Enable file being used is :/tmp/CVU_11.2.0.1.0_oracle/fixup.enable
Log file location: /tmp/CVU_11.2.0.1.0_oracle/orarun.log
Setting Kernel Parameters...
kernel.sem = 250 32000 100 128
```

```
fs.file-max = 6815744
net.ipv4.ip_local_port_range = 9000 65500
net.core.rmem_default = 262144
net.core.wmem_default = 262144
net.core.rmem_max = 4194304
net.core.wmem_max = 1048576
fs.aio-max-nr = 1048576
```

The installer will repeat the prerequisite checks, and if necessary, request that further errors be fixed. Although it is possible to ignore any warnings, we recommend that you attempt to resolve all errors identified during the prerequisite checks before continuing with the installation. Most errors can be resolved dynamically without exiting the installer.

When all prerequisite checks have succeeded, or you have indicated that you wish to ignore any failed checks, then the Summary page will be displayed:

Reviewing the Summary Page

The Summary page lets you review the installation you are about to unleash upon your cluster (Figure 7-17). You'll see the choices you've made so far, as well as some of the ramifications of those choices.

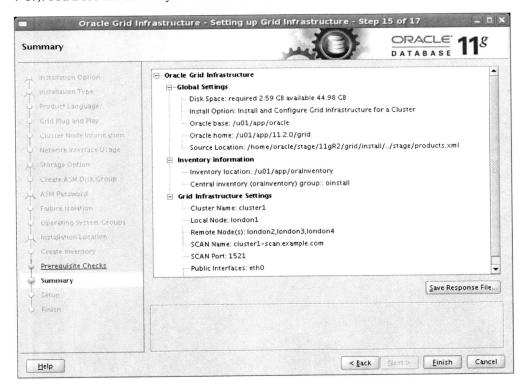

Figure 7-17. The installation summary

The Summary page saves a copy of the response file, if required. The response file can be used as input for silent installations.

Press Finish to start the installation, and the Setup page will be displayed.

Setup Page

The Setup page shows your progress through the following:

- Install Grid Infrastructure
  - Prepare
  - Copy files
  - Link binaries
  - Setup files
  - Perform remote operations
- Execute Root Scripts for Installing Grid Infrastructure

The installer will copy the software and supporting files from the staging area to the Oracle Grid Infrastructure home on the local cluster node. It will then replicate the Grid Infrastructure home from the local node to all remote nodes.

Reviewing Execute Configuration Scripts

When the remote copy is complete, the Execute Configuration scripts page will be displayed (see Figure 7-18 for an example of that page). This page will present you with a list of scripts that you will need to run while logged in as the root user. You may need to work with your system administrator to get the scripts run.

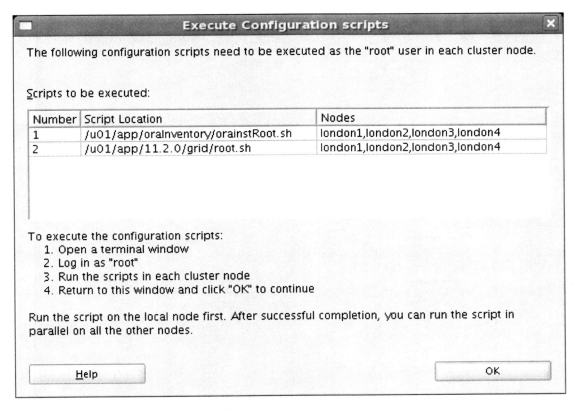

Figure 7-18. Reviewing post-install configuration scripts

Execution Order

The scripts should be executed in the order that the servers are listed. For example, Table 7-7 shows the correct order of execution given the data in Figure 7-18.

Table 7-7. Reviewing the Execution Order for the Post-Install Scripts Listed in Figure 7-18

Hostname	Script Name
london1	/u01/app/oraInventory/orainstRoot.sh
london2	/u01/app/oraInventory/orainstRoot.sh
london3	/u01/app/oraInventory/orainstRoot.sh

Hostname	Script Name
london4	/u01/app/oraInventory/orainstRoot.sh
london1	/u01/app/11.2.0/grid/root.sh
london2	/u01/app/11.2.0/grid/root.sh
london3	/u01/app/11.2.0/grid/root.sh
london4	/u01/app/11.2.0/grid/root.sh

It is particularly important that the root.sh scripts be executed in the specified order because the final script (london4, in this case) performs additional configuration after the OCR has been initialized on all nodes in the cluster.

Running the orainstRoot.sh Script

The orainstRoot.sh script initializes the Oracle inventory on the local node. It performs the following actions:

- Creates the directory (e.g., /u01/app/oraInventory)
- Creates the subdirectories
- Creates /etc/oraInst.loc, which contains the location of the Oracle inventory
- Sets the owner and group permission for the inventory files.

A sample orainstRoot.sh script looks like this:

```
[root@london1 oracle]# /u01/app/oraInventory/orainstRoot.sh
Changing permissions of /u01/app/oraInventory.
Adding read,write permissions for group.
Removing read,write,execute permissions for world.

Changing groupname of /u01/app/oraInventory to oinstall.
The execution of the script is complete.
```

Executing the root.sh script

The root.sh script configures the Clusterware daemons on each node.

On the first node, root.sh initializes the OCR. On the remaining nodes, root.sh adds the new node to the OCR. On the final node, root.sh also configures the VIP addresses for all nodes in the OCR. It is essential that root.sh be run successfully on the final node after it has been executed on all other nodes.

On the first node in the cluster, the output of root.sh looks like this:

```
[root@london1 ~]# /u01/app/11.2.0/grid/root.sh
Running Oracle 11g root.sh script...

The following environment variables are set as:
    ORACLE_OWNER= oracle
    ORACLE_HOME=  /u01/app/11.2.0/grid

Enter the full pathname of the local bin directory: [/usr/local/bin]:
The file "dbhome" already exists in /usr/local/bin.  Overwrite it? (y/n)
[n]:
The file "oraenv" already exists in /usr/local/bin.  Overwrite it? (y/n)
[n]:
The file "coraenv" already exists in /usr/local/bin.  Overwrite it? (y/n)
[n]:


Creating /etc/oratab file...
Entries will be added to the /etc/oratab file as needed by
Database Configuration Assistant when a database is created
Finished running generic part of root.sh script.
Now product-specific root actions will be performed.
2009-10-23 08:31:15: Parsing the host name
2009-10-23 08:31:15: Checking for super user privileges
2009-10-23 08:31:15: User has super user privileges
Using configuration parameter file: /u01/app/11.2.0/grid/crs/install/crsconfig_params
Creating trace directory
LOCAL ADD MODE
Creating OCR keys for user 'root', privgrp 'root'..
Operation successful.
  root wallet
  root wallet cert
  root cert export
  peer wallet
  profile reader wallet
  pa wallet
  peer wallet keys
  pa wallet keys
  peer cert request
  pa cert request
  peer cert
  pa cert
  peer root cert TP
  profile reader root cert TP
  pa root cert TP
  peer pa cert TP
  pa peer cert TP
  profile reader pa cert TP
  profile reader peer cert TP
  peer user cert
  pa user cert
 Adding daemon to inittab
 CRS-4123: Oracle High Availability Services has been started.
```

```
ohasd is starting
CRS-2672: Attempting to start 'ora.gipcd' on 'london1'
CRS-2672: Attempting to start 'ora.mdnsd' on 'london1'
CRS-2676: Start of 'ora.gipcd' on 'london1' succeeded
CRS-2676: Start of 'ora.mdnsd' on 'london1' succeeded
CRS-2672: Attempting to start 'ora.gpnpd' on 'london1'
CRS-2676: Start of 'ora.gpnpd' on 'london1' succeeded
CRS-2672: Attempting to start 'ora.cssdmonitor' on 'london1'
CRS-2676: Start of 'ora.cssdmonitor' on 'london1' succeeded
CRS-2672: Attempting to start 'ora.cssd' on 'london1'
CRS-2672: Attempting to start 'ora.diskmon' on 'london1'
CRS-2676: Start of 'ora.diskmon' on 'london1' succeeded
CRS-2676: Start of 'ora.cssd' on 'london1' succeeded
CRS-2672: Attempting to start 'ora.ctssd' on 'london1'
CRS-2676: Start of 'ora.ctssd' on 'london1' succeeded

ASM created and started successfully.

DiskGroup DATA created successfully.

clscfg: -install mode specified
Successfully accumulated necessary OCR keys.
Creating OCR keys for user 'root', privgrp 'root'..
Operation successful.
CRS-2672: Attempting to start 'ora.crsd' on 'london1'
CRS-2676: Start of 'ora.crsd' on 'london1' succeeded
CRS-4256: Updating the profile
Successful addition of voting disk 9e0f1017c4814f08bf8d6dc1d35c6797.
Successfully replaced voting disk group with +DATA.
CRS-4256: Updating the profile
CRS-4266: Voting file(s) successfully replaced
##  STATE    File Universal Id                    File Name Disk group
--  -----    -----------------                    --------- ---------
 1. ONLINE   9e0f1017c4814f08bf8d6dc1d35c6797 (ORCL:VOL1) [DATA]
Located 1 voting disk(s).
CRS-2673: Attempting to stop 'ora.crsd' on 'london1'
CRS-2677: Stop of 'ora.crsd' on 'london1' succeeded
CRS-2673: Attempting to stop 'ora.asm' on 'london1'
CRS-2677: Stop of 'ora.asm' on 'london1' succeeded
CRS-2673: Attempting to stop 'ora.ctssd' on 'london1'
CRS-2677: Stop of 'ora.ctssd' on 'london1' succeeded
CRS-2673: Attempting to stop 'ora.cssdmonitor' on 'london1'
CRS-2677: Stop of 'ora.cssdmonitor' on 'london1' succeeded
CRS-2673: Attempting to stop 'ora.cssd' on 'london1'
CRS-2677: Stop of 'ora.cssd' on 'london1' succeeded
CRS-2673: Attempting to stop 'ora.gpnpd' on 'london1'
CRS-2677: Stop of 'ora.gpnpd' on 'london1' succeeded
CRS-2673: Attempting to stop 'ora.gipcd' on 'london1'
CRS-2677: Stop of 'ora.gipcd' on 'london1' succeeded
CRS-2673: Attempting to stop 'ora.mdnsd' on 'london1'
CRS-2677: Stop of 'ora.mdnsd' on 'london1' succeeded
CRS-2672: Attempting to start 'ora.mdnsd' on 'london1'
```

```
CRS-2676: Start of 'ora.mdnsd' on 'london1' succeeded
CRS-2672: Attempting to start 'ora.gipcd' on 'london1'
CRS-2676: Start of 'ora.gipcd' on 'london1' succeeded
CRS-2672: Attempting to start 'ora.gpnpd' on 'london1'
CRS-2676: Start of 'ora.gpnpd' on 'london1' succeeded
CRS-2672: Attempting to start 'ora.cssdmonitor' on 'london1'
CRS-2676: Start of 'ora.cssdmonitor' on 'london1' succeeded
CRS-2672: Attempting to start 'ora.cssd' on 'london1'
CRS-2672: Attempting to start 'ora.diskmon' on 'london1'
CRS-2676: Start of 'ora.diskmon' on 'london1' succeeded
CRS-2676: Start of 'ora.cssd' on 'london1' succeeded
CRS-2672: Attempting to start 'ora.ctssd' on 'london1'
CRS-2676: Start of 'ora.ctssd' on 'london1' succeeded
CRS-2672: Attempting to start 'ora.asm' on 'london1'
CRS-2676: Start of 'ora.asm' on 'london1' succeeded
CRS-2672: Attempting to start 'ora.crsd' on 'london1'
CRS-2676: Start of 'ora.crsd' on 'london1' succeeded
CRS-2672: Attempting to start 'ora.evmd' on 'london1'
CRS-2676: Start of 'ora.evmd' on 'london1' succeeded
CRS-2672: Attempting to start 'ora.asm' on 'london1'
CRS-2676: Start of 'ora.asm' on 'london1' succeeded
CRS-2672: Attempting to start 'ora.DATA.dg' on 'london1'
CRS-2676: Start of 'ora.DATA.dg' on 'london1' succeeded
CRS-2672: Attempting to start 'ora.registry.acfs' on 'london1'
CRS-2676: Start of 'ora.registry.acfs' on 'london1' succeeded

london1     2009/10/23 08:38:45
/u01/app/11.2.0/grid/cdata/london1/backup_20091023_083845.olr
Configure Oracle Grid Infrastructure for a Cluster ... succeeded
Updating inventory properties for clusterware
Starting Oracle Universal Installer...

Checking swap space: must be greater than 500 MB.   Actual 4095 MB     Passed
The inventory pointer is located at /etc/oraInst.loc
The inventory is located at /u01/app/oraInventory
'UpdateNodeList' was successful.
```

On the final node in the cluster, the output of root.sh should look something like this:

```
[root@london4 oraInventory]#  /u01/app/11.2.0/grid/root.sh
Running Oracle 11g root.sh script...

The following environment variables are set as:
    ORACLE_OWNER= oracle
    ORACLE_HOME=  /u01/app/11.2.0/grid

Enter the full pathname of the local bin directory: [/usr/local/bin]:
The file "dbhome" already exists in /usr/local/bin.  Overwrite it? (y/n)
[n]:
The file "oraenv" already exists in /usr/local/bin.  Overwrite it? (y/n)
[n]:
The file "coraenv" already exists in /usr/local/bin.  Overwrite it? (y/n)
```

[n]:

Creating /etc/oratab file...
Entries will be added to the /etc/oratab file as needed by
Database Configuration Assistant when a database is created
Finished running generic part of root.sh script.
Now product-specific root actions will be performed.
2009-10-23 08:53:10: Parsing the host name
2009-10-23 08:53:10: Checking for super user privileges
2009-10-23 08:53:10: User has super user privileges
Using configuration parameter file: /u01/app/11.2.0/grid/crs/install/crsconfig_params
Creating trace directory
LOCAL ADD MODE
Creating OCR keys for user 'root', privgrp 'root'..
Operation successful.
Adding daemon to inittab
CRS-4123: Oracle High Availability Services has been started.
ohasd is starting
CRS-4402: The CSS daemon was started in exclusive mode but found an active CSS daemon on node
london1, number 1, and is terminating
An active cluster was found during exclusive startup, restarting to join the cluster
CRS-2672: Attempting to start 'ora.mdnsd' on 'london4'
CRS-2676: Start of 'ora.mdnsd' on 'london4' succeeded
CRS-2672: Attempting to start 'ora.gipcd' on 'london4'
CRS-2676: Start of 'ora.gipcd' on 'london4' succeeded
CRS-2672: Attempting to start 'ora.gpnpd' on 'london4'
CRS-2676: Start of 'ora.gpnpd' on 'london4' succeeded
CRS-2672: Attempting to start 'ora.cssdmonitor' on 'london4'
CRS-2676: Start of 'ora.cssdmonitor' on 'london4' succeeded
CRS-2672: Attempting to start 'ora.cssd' on 'london4'
CRS-2672: Attempting to start 'ora.diskmon' on 'london4'
CRS-2676: Start of 'ora.diskmon' on 'london4' succeeded
CRS-2676: Start of 'ora.cssd' on 'london4' succeeded
CRS-2672: Attempting to start 'ora.ctssd' on 'london4'
CRS-2676: Start of 'ora.ctssd' on 'london4' succeeded
CRS-2672: Attempting to start 'ora.drivers.acfs' on 'london4'
CRS-2676: Start of 'ora.drivers.acfs' on 'london4' succeeded
CRS-2672: Attempting to start 'ora.asm' on 'london4'
CRS-2676: Start of 'ora.asm' on 'london4' succeeded
CRS-2672: Attempting to start 'ora.crsd' on 'london4'
CRS-2676: Start of 'ora.crsd' on 'london4' succeeded
CRS-2672: Attempting to start 'ora.evmd' on 'london4'
CRS-2676: Start of 'ora.evmd' on 'london4' succeeded

london4   2009/10/23 08:57:40
/u01/app/11.2.0/grid/cdata/london4/backup_20091023_085740.olr
Configure Oracle Grid Infrastructure for a Cluster ... succeeded
Updating inventory properties for clusterware
Starting Oracle Universal Installer...

Checking swap space: must be greater than 500 MB.   Actual 4095 MB   Passed

```
The inventory pointer is located at /etc/oraInst.loc
The inventory is located at /u01/app/oraInventory
```

When the root.sh script has executed successfully on all four nodes in the cluster, press OK in the Execute Configuration Scripts page. The installer will return to the Setup page.

Monitoring Configuration Assistants

The Configuration Assistant page allows you to monitor the progress of the individual Configuration Assistants that are fired off by the installation (see Figure 7-19).

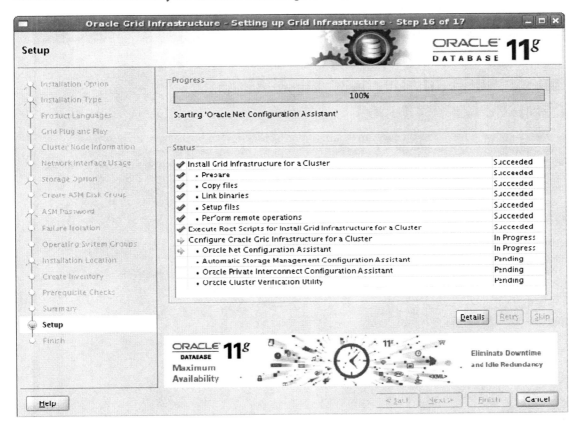

Figure 7-19. Executing the Configuration Assistant

The example installation shown in Figure 7-19 will continue as follows:

Configure Oracle Grid Infrastructure for a Cluster, which includes the following assistants:

- Oracle Net Configuration Assistant
- Automatic Storage Management Configuration Assistant
- Oracle Notification Server Configuration Assistant
- Oracle Private Interconnect Configuration Assistant
- Oracle Cluster Verification Utility.

For default installations, the Configuration Assistants should all execute silently. For non-default installations, the Configuration Assistants may display additional GUI windows to obtain further information.

When all of the Configuration Assistants are complete, the End of Installation page will be displayed. Press Close to terminate the installation.

Implementing an Advanced Installation for Automatic Configuration

In this section, we'll walk you through an example that shows how to implement an automatic configuration. We will describe an Advanced Installation of Grid Infrastructure using automatic configuration based on the Grid Naming Service (GNS). Again, we have assumed that DNS is installed and configured as detailed in Chapter 6; however, this example includes the actual network configuration used for the installation of a four-node cluster.

Configuring a Network Configuration

The first step is to configure the network infrastructure. Values are configured in DNS, DHCP, and /etc/hosts.

Tables 7-8 through 7-13 show the values that we used in our test environment; these are the same values we used to generate the subsequent screenshots and example code.

Table 7-8. The DNS settings

Domain Name	example.com
Server Name	dns1.example.com
Server Address	172.17.1.1

Table 7-9. The DHCP settings

Server address	172.17.1.1
Address range	172.17.1.201 - 172.17.1.220

Table 7-10. The DNS Subdomain Settings

Sub domain	grid1.example.com
Host name	cluster1-gns.grid1.example.com
VIP address	172.17.1.200

Table 7-11. The SCAN Listeners

SCAN Name	cluster1-scan.grid1.example.com
SCAN Addresses	Assigned by DHCP

Table 7-12. The Public Network Configuration

Network	172.17.0.0
Gateway	172.17.0.254
Broadcast address	172.17.255.255
Subnet mask	255.255.0.0
Node names	london1, london2, london3, london4
Public IP address	172.17.1.101,172.17.1.102,172.17.1.103,172.17.1.104
VIP names	Assigned by GNS
VIP addresses	Assigned by DHCP

Table 7-13. The Private Network Configuration

Network	192.168.1.0
Subnet mask	255.255.255.0
Names	london1-priv london2-priv london3-priv london4-priv
IP addresses	192.168.1.1,192.168.1.2,192.168.1.3, 192.168.1.4

Configuring DNS

Next, you need to verify that the bind package has been installed and is running. If the bind package is not available, then see Chapter 6 for details on installing and configuring the bind package.

When performing the manual configuration, /etc/named.conf is configured as detailed in Chapter 6. Forward lookups for example.com are configured in master.example.com as follows:

```
$TTL 86400
@               IN SOA dns1.example.com. root.localhost (
                        2010063000          ; serial
                        28800               ; refresh
                        14400               ; retry
                        3600000             ; expiry
                        86400 )             ; minimum
@               IN NS  dns1.example.com.
localhost       IN A   127.0.0.1
dns1            IN A   172.17.1.1
london1         IN A   172.17.1.101
london2         IN A   172.17.1.102
london3         IN A   172.17.1.103
london4         IN A   172.17.1.104
$ORIGIN grid1.example.com.
@               IN NS  cluster1-gns.grid1.example.com.
                IN NS  dns1.example.com.
cluster1-gns    IN A   172.17.1.200; glue record
```

For the automatic configuration, it is necessary to specify public addresses for each node in the cluster. It is also necessary to create a delegated subdomain (e.g., grid1.example.com), which is managed by the Grid Naming Service (GNS). There are several alternative syntaxes you can use to create a delegated subdomain; we have found the syntax shown to be the most effective.

Note that GNS is a cluster resource that requires its own VIP. The VIP is allocated within DNS. At any one time, GNS will only be active on one node in the cluster. If this node is shutdown, then Oracle Clusterware will automatically relocate the GNS VIP to one of the remaining nodes in the cluster.

In the automatic configuration, VIP addresses and SCAN addresses are allocated using GNS and DHCP. Therefore, it is not necessary to specify these addresses in DNS. Reverse lookups for example.com can be configured in 172.17.1.rev, as in this example:

```
$TTL 86400
@   IN SOA dns1.example.com. root.localhost. (
```

```
                    2010063000          ; serial
                    28800               ; refresh
                    14400               ; retry
                    3600000             ; expiry
                    86400 )             ; minimum
@       IN NS  dns1.example.com.
1       IN PTR dns1.example.com.
101     IN PTR london1.example.com.
102     IN PTR london2.example.com.
103     IN PTR london3.example.com.
104     IN PTR london4.example.com.
```

In the automatic configuration, VIP addresses are allocated using GNS and DHCP. Thus it is no longer necessary to specify reverse lookups for these addresses in DNS.

As with the manual configuration, forward and reverse lookups for the local domain must be configured in DNS (you can see how to configure these in Chapter 6).

On each node in the cluster, the /etc/resolv.conf is configured as follows:

```
search example.com grid1.example.com
nameserver 172.17.1.1
options attempts:2
options timeout:1
```

Note that you must also include the GNS subdomain in the search path, as covered in Chapter 6. Theoretically, GNS can also allocate addresses for the private network. However, in our opinion, it is advisable to continue to configure these addresses manually in /etc/hosts and/or DNS. Using manually configured private addresses allows you to maintain some mapping between public addresses, private addresses, and node numbers, which simplifies troubleshooting.

In this example, as with the manual configuration, we configured the private network addresses in /etc/hosts on each node:

```
192.168.1.1        london1-priv.example.com london1-priv
192.168.1.2        london2-priv.example.com london2-priv
192.168.1.3        london3-priv.example.com london3-priv
192.168.1.4        london4-priv.example.com london4-priv
```

The priv extension is not mandatory, but it has become a convention for RAC deployments.

Configuring DHCP

Next, you need to verify that the dhcp package has been installed and is running. If the dhcp package is not available, then see Chapter 6 for information on how to install and configure it. For our installation, we have configured DHCP to assign a range of 20 addresses that DHCP can allocate (172.17.1.201 to 172.17.1.220).

Setting up the Grid Plug and Play Information Page

If the Grid Infrastructure software is to be owned by a dedicated grid user, then start the OUI with that user. In our example, we will use the oracle user. As the oracle user, start the OUI using the following command:

```
[oracle@london1]$ /home/oracle/stage/grid/runInstaller
```

Note that the installer is written in Java, and it takes a couple of minutes to load. The installation procedure that uses the automatic configuration is similar to the procedure that uses the manual configuration—with a handful of exceptions. In the following pages, we will only describe those pages that are significantly different.

The first installer page of significance is the Grid Plug and Play Information Page (see Figure 7-20).

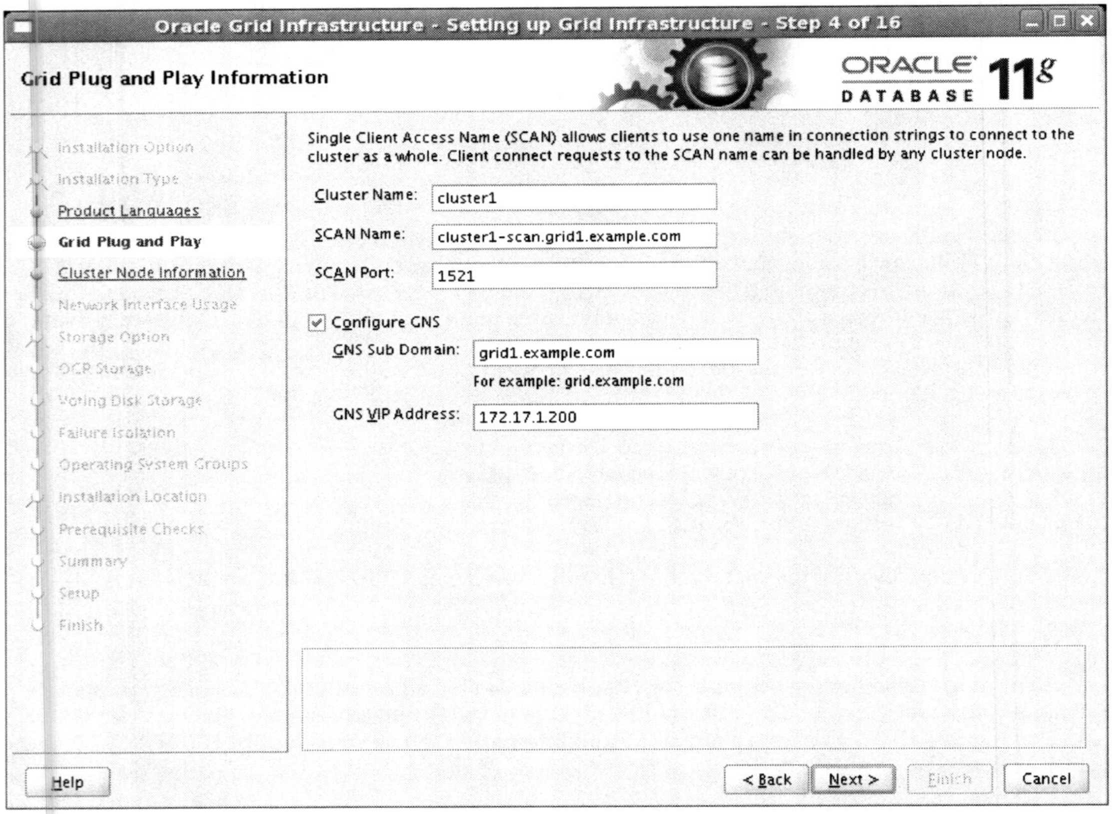

Figure 7-20. The Grid Plug and Play Information page

Several fields on the Grid Plug and Play Information page differ from the manual and automatic configuration. Unfortunately, in this release the fields are not displayed in an entirely intuitive order.

To use GNS, you should ensure that the Configure GNS box is checked. This will allow you to specify values for the remaining fields. The GNS sub domain is the name of the domain that will be delegated by DNS (e.g., `grid1.example.com`).

The GNS VIP address is single VIP address that is allocated to GNS. This address should be added to the DNS configuration.

In the example, we have also specified a SCAN name within the GNS sub domain (`cluster1-scan.grid1.example.com`). This is necessary because it allows SCAN VIP addresses to be allocated automatically by DHCP within the GNS subdomain.

Configuring the Cluster Node Information Page

The next page of note is the Cluster Node Information page (see Figure 7-21).

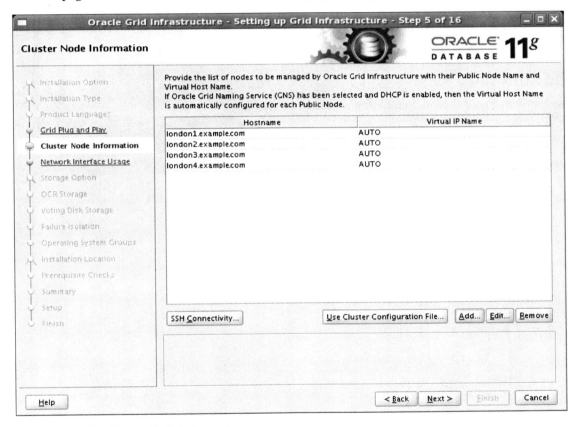

Figure 7-21. The Cluster Node Information page

For automatic configuration, it is only necessary to specify a list of host names on the Cluster Node Information page. The VIP addresses can be omitted because these will be allocated automatically by GNS.

If you have a large number of nodes or very long domain names, you can specify a list of nodes in a cluster configuration file. For the automatic configuration option, the syntax looks like this:

```
<cluster_name>
<node_name>
[<node_name>]
```

The following example shows four nodes in a cluster:

```
cluster1
london1.example.com
london2.example.com
london3.example.com
london4.example.com
```

The SSH connectivity configuration and testing functionality is identical to that for the Grid Infrastructure installation with manual configuration.

The Summary Page

After making all your choices, you'll come to the Summary Page (see Figure 7-22). This is where you can review your choices before committing to the installation.

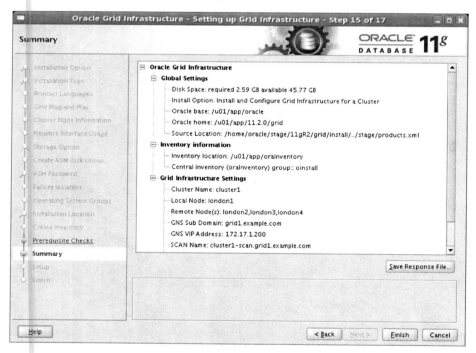

Figure 7-22. The Installation summary

The options we've discussed should appear in the Summary page for you to review. Options you'll see detailed on this page include the GNS Sub Domain, the GNS VIP Address, and the SCAN Name.

The remainder of the Grid Infrastructure installation with automatic configuration is identical to the Grid Infrastructure installation with manual configuration.

Typical Installation

Grid Infrastructure offers either a Typical Installation or an Advanced Installation. In reality, there is little difference between the Typical Installation and the Advanced Installation with manual configuration. Troubleshooting the Advanced Installation is simpler, so we recommend that you attempt that type of installation initially. When you are confident that your environment is correctly configured, then you may also attempt the Typical Installation.

Preparation for the Typical Installation is identical to the preparation required for the Advanced Installation with manual configuration. In this section, we discuss areas where the Typical Installation differs from the Advanced Installation with manual configuration.

▓ **Note** It is not possible to configure the Grid Naming Service using the Typical Installation.

Choosing the Installation Type

The Installation Type Page lets you choose whether to make a Typical or Advanced Installation (see Figure 7-23). Select Typical Installation, and then click Next to continue.

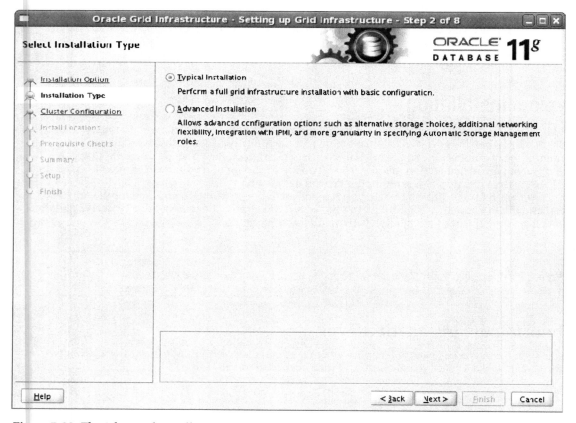

Figure 7-23. The Advanced Installation choice

Specifying the Cluster Configuration Page

You enter the SCAN name on the Cluster Configuration page (see Figure 7-24). The cluster name is automatically derived from the SCAN name, so it is not necessary to enter a cluster name.

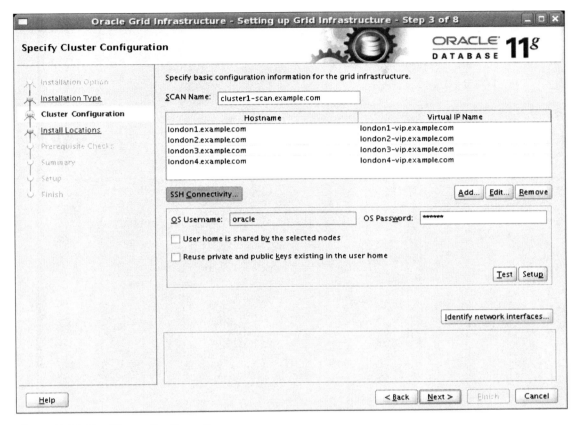

Figure 7-24. The Cluster Configuration page

The Typical Installation requires a manual configuration, so it is necessary to enter both the node name and VIP name for each node in the cluster. The SSH configuration is identical to that used in the Advanced Installation.

When you're done filling out the page, it is good practice to confirm that the network interfaces have been correctly assigned by the installer. Do that by clicking the Identify Network Interfaces button.

Install Locations Page

The Install Locations page (see Figure 7-25) is completely different for the Typical Installation. This page allows you to enter the following fields:

- Oracle Base location
- Software Location

- Cluster Registry Storage Type

- Cluster Registry Location (Cluster File System storage only)

- SYSASM Password (ASM storage only)

- OSASM Group

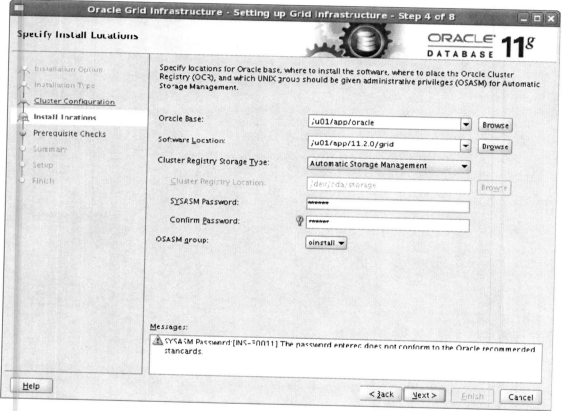

Figure 7-25. The Install Locations page

Reviewing the Summary Page for a Typical Installation

The Summary page shows the values entered during the interview session, along with the default values generated by the installer (see Figure 7-26). Check that the generated values are acceptable before continuing with the installation. If they are not acceptable, then cancel the installation and perform an Advanced Installation instead.

The remainder of the Typical Installation is identical to the Advanced Installation.

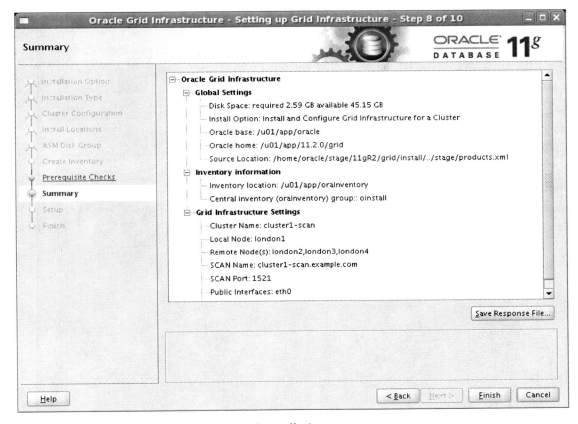

Figure 7-26. The Summary page for a Typical Installation

Installing a Standalone Server

It is also possible to install Grid Infrastructure on a standalone server. In Oracle 10*g* and Oracle 11*g*R1, it was possible to install ASM for a single instance database. In that case, the ASM instance would also include a cut down version of Cluster Synchronization Services (CSS), which ran in local mode and was configured in a local copy of the OCR.

In Oracle 11*g*R2, it is no longer possible to install Oracle Clusterware and ASM separately, so a complete Grid Infrastructure installation is required to run ASM for a single-instance database. However, both Oracle Clusterware and ASM are restricted to run on a single instance; this simplifies the preparation and installation process.

It is not possible to configure GNS with a Grid Infrastructure standalone server installation. It is not necessary to configure cluster names, SCAN names, SCAN VIPs, private network addresses, or public VIPs for a standalone installation.

In the remainder of this section, we will discuss some of the significant differences between the Grid Infrastructure installation for a standalone server and the Advanced Installation for a cluster.

Selecting an Installation Option

The Installation Option page lets you select the Install and Configure Grid Infrastructure option for a Standalone Server (see Figure 7-27).

■ **Note** It is not possible to convert a standalone installation into a cluster; if you wish to perform this operation, you will need to deinstall the node and then reinstall Grid Infrastructure for a cluster.

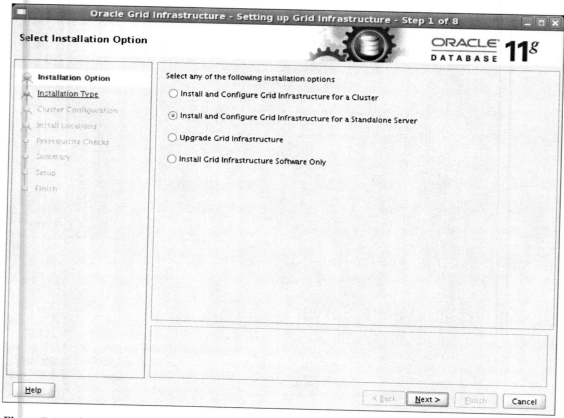

Figure 7-27. The Grid Infrastructure installation options

Creating an ASM Disk Group Page

ASM is mandatory for the Standalone Server installation. Figure 7-28 shows the configuration page. You will need to specify an initial ASM disk group at this stage. You can use the ASM Configuration Assistant (ASMCA) or SQL*Plus to add more disk groups later.

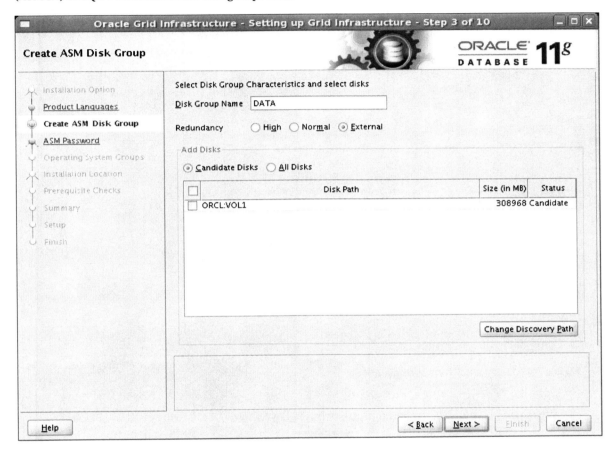

Figure 7-28. Configuring ASM configuration for a standalone installation

Reviewing the Summary Page for a Standalone Installation

The Summary page for a standalone installation shows the options specified during the interview process (see Figure 7-29). Press Finish to start the installation.

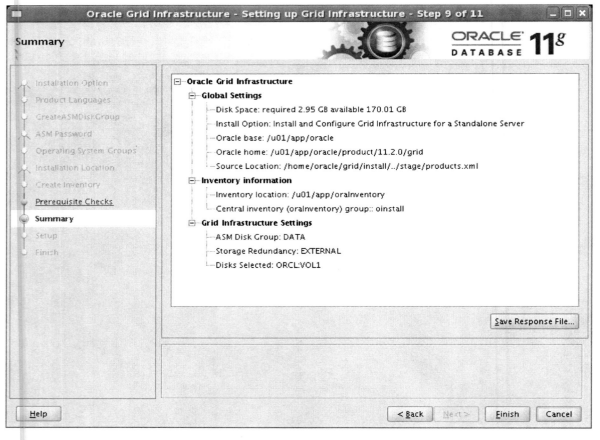

Figure 7-29. The Standalone Installation Summary page

Once, you press Finish, the Setup page will be displayed, and the following tasks will be performed:

1. Preparation
2. Copy Files
3. Link Binaries
4. Setup Files

Configuring the Execute Configuration Scripts

The Execute Configuration scripts dialog box lists one or more scripts that should be executed by the root user on the server (see Figure 7-30). You may need to work with your system administrator to execute those scripts.

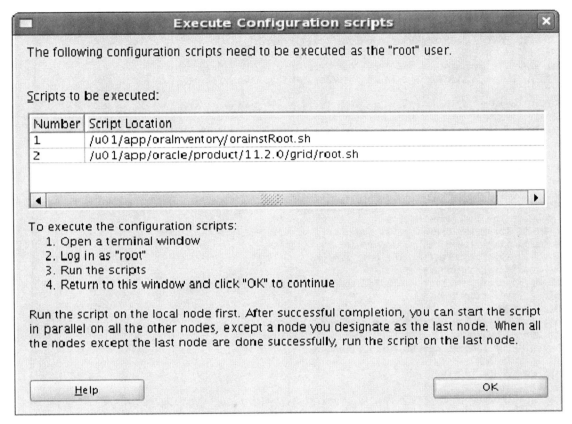

Figure 7-30. Configuration scripts for a standalone installation

If an Oracle inventory does not already exist, you will be asked to run the inventory creation script (orainstRoot.sh). The following example shows the results of running this script against the sample:

```
[root@london4]# /u01/app/oraInventory/orainstRoot.sh
Changing permissions of /u01/app/oraInventory
Adding read,write permissions for group,Removing read,write,execute permissions for world.
Changing groupname of /u01/app/oraInventory to oinstall.
The execution of the script is complete
```

The root.sh script configures Oracle Clusterware, initializes the OCR, and adds the OHASD daemon to /etc/inittab, as in this example:

```
[root@london4]# /u01/app/oracle/product/11.2.0/grid/root.sh
Running Oracle 11g root.sh script...

The following environment variables are set as:
    ORACLE_OWNER= oracle
    ORACLE_HOME=  /u01/app/oracle/product/11.2.0/grid

Enter the full pathname of the local bin directory: [/usr/local/bin]:
The file "dbhome" already exists in /usr/local/bin.  Overwrite it? (y/n)
[n]:
The file "oraenv" already exists in /usr/local/bin.  Overwrite it? (y/n)
[n]:
The file "coraenv" already exists in /usr/local/bin.  Overwrite it? (y/n)
[n]:

Creating /etc/oratab file...
Entries will be added to the /etc/oratab file as needed by
Database Configuration Assistant when a database is created
Finished running generic part of root.sh script.
Now product-specific root actions will be performed.
2009-08-02 12:41:11: Checking for super user privileges
2009-08-02 12:41:11: User has super user privileges
2009-08-02 12:41:11: Parsing the host name
Using configuration parameter file:
/u01/app/oracle/product/11.2.0/grid/crs/install/crsconfig_params
Creating trace directory
LOCAL ADD MODE
Creating OCR keys for user 'oracle', privgrp 'oinstall'..
Operation successful.
CRS-4664: Node london1 successfully pinned.
ohasd is starting
Adding daemon to inittab
2009-08-02 12:41:23
Changing directory to /u01/app/oracle/product/11.2.0/grid/log/server17/ohasd
Successfully configured Oracle Grid Infrastructure for a Standalone
```

As you can see, the standalone server configuration for Oracle Clusterware is much simpler than its cluster equivalent.

Deinstalling the Grid Infrastructure Software

If you wish to deinstall the Grid Infrastructure software, you should be aware that there is no provision to deinstall software within the OUI, nor can you cannot reinstall over an existing installation. Therefore, you should not delete directories manually. Instead, there is a deinstall script within the deinstall directory. You may run this to deinstall the Grid Infrastructure software either on the cluster as a whole or on the individual nodes in isolation. The deinstall script runs a check operation, and you are prompted to confirm the deinstallation before the script performs a clean operation, as shown in this example:

```
[oracle@london1 deinstall]$ ./deinstall
Checking for required files and bootstrapping ...
Please wait ...
Location of logs /tmp/deinstall2010-06-15_12-18-38-PM/logs/

############ ORACLE DEINSTALL & DECONFIG TOOL START ############


####################### CHECK OPERATION START #######################
Install check configuration START


Checking for existence of the Oracle home location /u01/app/11.2.0/grid
Oracle Home type selected for de-install is: CRS
Oracle Base selected for de-install is: /u01/app/oracle
Checking for existence of central inventory location /u01/app/oraInventory
Checking for existence of the Oracle Grid Infrastructure home /u01/app/11.2.0/grid
The following nodes are part of this cluster: london1,london2,london3,london4

Install check configuration END
...
Do you want to continue (y - yes, n - no)? [n]: y
```

The clean operation prompts you to run a script as the root user on the nodes as shown. It then returns to press Enter on the deinstall script:

```
root@london2 ~]# /tmp/deinstall2010-06-15_12-18-38-PM/perl/bin/perl -I/tmp/deinstall2010-06-
15_12-18-38-PM/perl/lib -I/tmp/deinstall2010-06-15_12-18-38-PM/crs/install /tmp/deinstall2010-
06-15_12-18-38-PM/crs/install/rootcrs.pl -force  -delete -paramfile /tmp/deinstall2010-06-
15_12-18-38-PM/response/deinstall_Ora11g_gridinfrahome1.rsp -lastnode
2010-06-15 12:22:39: Parsing the host name
2010-06-15 12:22:39: Checking for super user privileges
2010-06-15 12:22:39: User has super user privileges
Using configuration parameter file: /tmp/deinstall2010-06-15_12-18-38-
PM/response/deinstall_Ora11g_gridinfrahome1.rsp
...
CRS-2793: Shutdown of Oracle High Availability Services-managed resources on 'london2' has
completed
CRS-4133: Oracle High Availability Services has been stopped.
Successfully deconfigured Oracle clusterware stack on this node
```

After the deinstallation process is complete, you may reinstall the Grid Infrastructure software, if desired.

Summary

In this chapter, we have discussed the four main installation procedures for the Grid Infrastructure in Oracle 11gR2. This release includes both Oracle Clusterware and ASM. In the next chapter, we will describe how to install the RDBMS software.

CHAPTER 8

■■■

Clusterware

Oracle Clusterware is a software-based cluster manager that allows a group of physically separate servers to be combined into one logical server. The physical servers are connected together by a dedicated private network and are attached to shared storage. Oracle Clusterware consists of a set of additional processes and daemons that run on each node in the cluster and that utilize the private network and shared storage to coordinate activity between the servers.

This chapter describes Oracle Clusterware, discussing the components and their functionality. It also covers advanced topics such as the HA Framework and server-side callouts. Oracle has renamed the foundation for RAC and the high availability framework to Grid Infrastructure. Throughout the chapter, the terms Clusterware and Grid Infrastructure are used interchangeably.

Introducing Clusterware

The goal of Clusterware is to manage local and cluster resources. Oracle 11.2 has many different types of resources, including the following:

- Networks
- VIP addresses
- Local listeners
- SCAN listeners
- ASM instances
- Databases
- Database instances
- Services
- User-defined resources

Oracle Clusterware is responsible for determining the nodes on which resources should run. It can start, stop, and monitor resources; and it can optionally relocate resources to other nodes. Clusterware can also restart any processes that fail on their current node.

Oracle Clusterware protects against hardware and software failures by providing failover capabilities. In the event that a node or resource fails, Clusterware can be configured to relocate resources to other nodes in the cluster. Some resources that are tied to a specific node (an ASM instance, for example) cannot be relocated.

In addition to protecting against unplanned outages, Clusterware can be used to reduce or eliminate planned downtime for hardware and software maintenance.

For many applications, Oracle Clusterware can increase overall throughput by enabling the application to run on multiple nodes concurrently.

Oracle Clusterware is also responsible for monitoring which nodes are currently members of the cluster. When a node joins or leaves the cluster this event will be detected by Oracle Clusterware and reported to all other nodes in the cluster. Clusterware allows the number of nodes in a cluster to be increased or decreased dynamically, thereby providing application scalability.

In Oracle 10.1 and later, Oracle Clusterware is mandatory for RAC deployments. On Linux platforms, Oracle Clusterware is typically the only cluster manager that is deployed. On legacy UNIX platforms, however, Oracle Clusterware is often combined with third-party clustering solutions, such as IBM HA-CMP, HP ServiceGuard, Sun Cluster, and Veritas Cluster Manager. Oracle Clusterware and Veritas both operate in user-mode; proprietary vendor clusterware such as HA-CMP, ServiceGuard, and Sun Cluster operate in kernel-mode and can, therefore, potentially provide slightly higher levels of availability at the expense of increased support complexity.

You might recall from Chapter 3 that Oracle Grid Infrastructure uses two components on shared storage: the Oracle Cluster Registry (OCR) and the voting disk. In Oracle 10.2 and later, Clusterware can be configured to maintain mirrored copies of these files, protecting against media failure. The Oracle Cluster Registry (OCR) stores the cluster configuration of the including the current state of all resources. The voting disk maintains node membership information. In Oracle 11.2 and later, a copy of a third component known as the Oracle Local Registry (OLR) is stored on each node in the cluster. The OLR manages configuration information for the local node.

Examining the Hardware and Software Requirements

All servers in the cluster must contain at least two network interfaces: one for the public network and one for the private network. To ensure redundancy, Oracle recommends that both networks be bonded. In other words, there are at least two physical network adapters attached to separate physical networks. These are bonded together at operating system level for each logical network (you can learn more about this subject in in Chapter 6).

Each cluster must also be attached to shared storage. For multinode clusters, Storage Area Network (SAN), Network Attached Storage (NAS) and iSCSI are supported. For single-instance clusters, Direct Attached Storage (DAS) and NFS are additionally supported. Oracle recommends that there be at least two host bus adapters (HBAs) or network cards for each storage device attached to separate physical paths. These adapters should be managed using either the operating system or third-party multipathing software. When using Ethernet to connect to the storage (as in iSCSI and Fibre Channel over Ethernet (FCoE)), then it is strongly advised that you separate the interconnect traffic from the storage traffic to avoid collisions on the network layer. Additional storage connections may be required for applications with high I/O requirements.

Most contemporary servers are supplied with at least one physical disk or, alternatively, two mirrored disks. In a RAC environment, the physical disk is typically used to store the operating system, swap space, Grid Infrastructure home, and optionally, the Oracle RAC home. Although centralizing binaries on shared storage would appear to be more efficient, most users of clustered environments prefer to maintain separate copies of binaries on each node because this reduces the possibility of corruptions affecting multiple nodes. This approach also facilitates rolling upgrades that can reduce downtime.

Each node in the cluster should run similar operating system releases. In all cases, the operating system architecture and distributor should be identical. In most cases, the operating system version and patch level should also be identical. When adding new nodes to the cluster, occasionally it is necessary to install newer versions of the operating system that containing appropriate device drivers and other functionality. However, in this case, we would recommend upgrading the operating system on the older nodes, if possible. Doing so enables all nodes in the cluster to run similar versions. Adopting this approach will simplify problem resolution and reduce the possibility of human errors in the future.

Using Shared Storage with Oracle Clusterware

As mentioned in the preceding section, Oracle Clusterware uses two components on shared storage: the Oracle Cluster Registry and the voting disk. In Oracle 10gR2 and later, both components can be mirrored by Oracle and all copies of the associated files should be located on shared storage and accessible by all nodes. With Oracle 11.2, two new files have been introduced: the local registry OLR and the Grid Plug and Play profile (GPnP profile).

Storing Cluster Information with the Oracle Cluster Registry

The Oracle Cluster Registry (OCR) is used to store cluster configuration information. The OCR contains information about the resources controlled by Oracle Clusterware, including the following:

- ASM disk groups, volumes, file systems, and instances

- RAC databases and instances

- SCAN listeners and local listeners

- SCAN VIPs and local VIPs

- Nodes and node applications

- User-defined resources

- Its own backups

Logically, the OCR represents a tree structure; physically, each element of data is stored in a separate 4096 byte physical block.

The data in the OCR is essential to the operation of the cluster. It is possible to back up the contents of the OCR online, but restoring this data will almost always result in an interruption of service. Since Oracle 10gR2, it has been possible to configure two OCR mirrors that are automatically maintained by Oracle Clusterware. This helps ensure against media failure or human error. In Oracle 11gR2 and later, it is possible to configure up to five mirrored copies of the OCR. If there is more than one OCR mirror, then it is possible to replace a failed OCR mirror without an outage.

In 11gR2, the OCR can be stored in an ASM disk group or a cluster file system. The OCR can only be stored on raw devices or block devices if the cluster has been upgraded from an earlier version of Oracle. Also, Oracle has announced that raw devices and block devices are deprecated for Oracle 12—it is a good idea to migrate the OCR (and voting disks for that matter) off block devices and to either a supported cluster file system such as GFS or OCFS2 or follow the best practice to move these files into ASM.

The OCR should only be updated by Oracle Clusterware processes, Enterprise Manager, supported utilities such as `crsctl`, `srvctl`, `ocrconfig`; and configuration tools such as the `OUI`, `dbca,` and `netca`.

Storing Information in the Oracle Local Registry

The Oracle Local Registry is the OCR's local counterpart and a new feature introduced with Grid Infrastructure. The information stored in the OLR is needed by the *Oracle High Availability Services daemon* (OHASD) to start; this includes data about GPnP wallets, Clusterware configuration, and version information. Comparing the OCR with the OLR reveals that the OLR has far fewer keys; for example, ocrdump reported 704 different keys for the OCR vs. 526 keys for the OLR on our installation.

If you compare only the keys again, you will notice that the majority of keys in the OLR deal with the OHASD process, whereas the majority of keys in the OCR deal with the CRSD. This confirms what we said earlier: you need the OLR (along with the GPnP profile) to start the High Availability Services stack. In contrast, the OCR is used extensively by CRSD. The OLR is maintained by the same command-line utilities as the OCR, with the appended -local option. Interestingly, the OLR is automatically backed up during an upgrade to Grid Infrastructure, whereas the OCR is not.

Fencing with the Voting Disk

The voting disk is used to provide fencing and to determine cluster-node membership. During normal operations, the OCSSD daemon on each node in the cluster updates the voting disk once a second with the current status of that node. It then reads back the status structures of all other nodes in the cluster. In the event of an interconnect failure, all nodes in the cluster attempt to place a lock in the voting disk. If a node can lock a majority of the voting disks, then it gains control of the cluster.

In 11gR2, the voting disk can be stored in an ASM disk group or a cluster file system. As with the OCR, the voting disk can only be stored on raw devices or block devices if the cluster has been upgraded from an earlier version of Oracle. In any configuration, there should always be an odd number of voting disks. In the event of an interconnect failure in a two node-cluster, this ensures that one node always secures a majority of voting disks. For clusters containing three or more nodes, a more complex algorithm is used to determine which node ultimately controls the cluster.

If ASM is used to store the voting disks, then Oracle Clusterware automatically performs the mirroring. All copies are stored in the same ASM disk group. The number of mirrored voting disks copies stored in the disk group is dependent on the redundancy of the disk group (see Table 8-1).

Table 8-1. The Number of Voting Disk Mirrrors When Stored in ASM

Redundancy of the ASM Disk Group	The Number of Voting Disks Mirrored and the Minimum Number of Failure groups
External Redundancy	1
Normal Redundancy	3
High Redundancy	5

Within the ASM disk group, each voting disk must be stored in a separate failure group on physically separate storage. By default, each disk within an ASM disk group is a separate failure group. This translates into the requirement that, for normal redundancy, you need to define at least three failure groups. For high redundancy, at least five failure groups must use ASM for storing the voting disks. Also, the disk group attribute must be set to compatible.asm=11.2.

If a cluster file system is used to store the voting disks, then Oracle recommends that at least three copies be maintained on physically separate storage. This approach eliminates the possibility of a single point of failure. In Oracle 11*g*R2, up to 15 voting disk copies can be stored. However, Oracle recommends configuring no more than five copies.

Recording Information with the Grid Plug and Play Profile

The GPnP profile is an important part of the new 11.2 Grid Infrastructure, and it records a lot of important information about the cluster itself. The file is signed to prevent modifications, and administrators generally should not edit it by administrators. The profile is an XML document, which is the main reason why adding nodes requires a lot less input from the administrator. Here is a sample profile, shortened for readability:

```
<?xml version="1.0" encoding="UTF-8"?>
<gpnp:GPnP-Profile Version="1.0" xmlns="http://www.grid-pnp.org/2005/11/gpnp-profile"
    xmlns:gpnp="http://www.grid-pnp.org/2005/11/gpnp-profile"
    xmlns:orcl="http://www.oracle.com/gpnp/2005/11/gpnp-profile"
    xmlns:xsi="http://www.w3.org/2001/XMLSchema-instance"
    xsi:schemaLocation="http://www.grid-pnp.org/2005/11/gpnp-profile gpnp-profile.xsd"
    ProfileSequence="3" ClusterUId="002c207a7175cf38bffcea7bea5b3a49"
    ClusterName="ocfs2" PALocation="">
  <gpnp:Network-Profile>
    <gpnp:HostNetwork id="gen" HostName="*">
      <gpnp:Network id="net1" IP="172.17.1.0" Adapter="bond0" Use="public"/>
      <gpnp:Network id="net2" IP="192.168.1.0" Adapter="bond1"
        Use="cluster_interconnect"/>
    </gpnp:HostNetwork>
  </gpnp:Network-Profile>
  <orcl:CSS-Profile id="css"
    DiscoveryString="/u03/oradata/grid/vdsk1,/u03/oradata/grid/vdsk2,/u03/oradata/grid/vdsk3"
    LeaseDuration="400"/>
  <orcl:ASM-Profile id="asm"
    DiscoveryString="++no-value-at-profile-creation--never-updated-through-ASM++"
    SPFile=""/>
  <ds:Signature...>...</ds:Signature>
</gpnp:GPnP-Profile>
```

The preceding profile can be obtained by invoking gpnptool with the get option. This dumps the XML file into standard output. For better readability, we saved this to a local PC and opened it with Firefox, which displays the XML a lot more nicely. The cluster this profile is taken from uses OCFS2 for storing the voting disk and OCR.

We have also removed the signature information from the profile because it didn't provide information needed for this discussion. The example illustrates that the cluster has a unique identifier, and that the name is also recorded. The next item in the profile is the network profile, an important piece of information. Oracle uses the GPnP profile and the information stored in the OCR when adding a node to the cluster. The fact that the network interfaces are stored in the GPnP profile allows the administrator to specify less information on the command line. This is also a convenient place to look up which network interface is used for what purpose; here, the Use attribute on the Network tag gives the interface's purpose away.

Another important piece of information is recorded in the CSS-Profile tag, which records the location of the CSS voting disks. In the preceding example, there are three copies of the voting disks on a cluster file system /u03 in directory /u03/oradata/grid/. Because the voting disks are stored outside of ASM, the ASM information is not populated. Unless your database uses ASM specifically, no ASM instance will be brought online by Grid Infrastructure because it simply is not needed. If ASM is used, the relevant tags <orcl:CSS-Profile/> and <orcl:ASM-Profile/> will look something like the following:

```
<orcl:CSS-Profile id="css" DiscoveryString="+asm" LeaseDuration="400" />
<orcl:ASM-Profile id="asm" DiscoveryString=""
    SPFile="+DATA/prod/asmparameterfile/registry.253.699915959" />
```

The only supported case where the file should be modified is when the ASM instance's spfile is corrupted and must be changed.

Using Background Processes

Chapter 2 touched on the background processes used by Grid Infrastructure; the following sections pick up that thread and explain that process in much more detail. The all-important relationship between processes could not be discussed in the concepts chapter. In the authors' opinion, the documentation about Grid Infrastructure in general, but especially the startup sequence, is incomplete. This makes it very hard for anyone trying to adopt, implement, and troubleshoot Grid Infrastructure. Also, it took a while for Oracle Support to publish additional information in My Oracle Support that addressed the worst shortcomings. The following sections will fill in many of the important details that the official documentation neglects to cover or explains incorrectly.

Grid Infrastructure Software Stacks

Oracle re-architected Grid Infrastructure into two different stacks. The official documentation refers to them as the High Availability Services stack and the Cluster Ready Services stack. Other sources divide the software stack into the lower and upper stack. We will stick to Oracle's terminology in this chapter, to minimize confusion. Figure 8-1 provides an overview of the processes and their position in the stack.

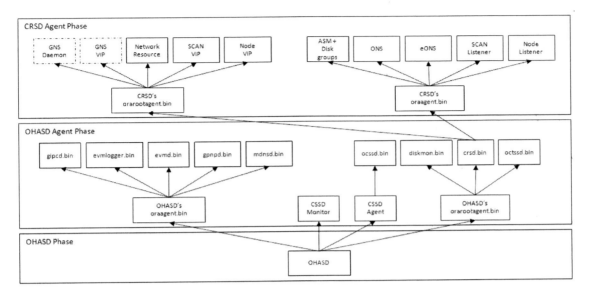

Figure 8-1. The Grid Infrastructure software stack and process dependencies

The High Availability Services stack consists of daemons that communicate with their peers on the other nodes. As soon as the High Availability Services stack is up, the cluster node can join the cluster and use the shared components (e.g., the OCR). The startup sequence of the High Availability Services stack is stored partly in the Grid Plug and Play profile, but that sequence also depends on information stored in the OLR.

Next, we will take a closer look at each of these processes in the context of their position in the software stack, beginning with the lower part of the software stack.

Drilling Down on the High Availability Stack

The high availability stack is based on the *Oracle High Availability Services* (OHAS) daemon. In previous versions of Oracle Clusterware, three processes were started by the operating system init process: CRSD, OCSSD, and EVMD. In Oracle 11gR2 and later, the only process under direct control of the init process is the Oracle High Availability Services (OHAS) daemon. This daemon is responsible for starting all other Oracle Clusterware processes. It is also responsible for managing and maintaining the OLR. In a cluster, the OHAS daemon runs as the root user; in an Oracle Restart environment, it runs as the oracle user.

In Unix systems, the Oracle High Availability Services Stack is managed by the init process. On Linux, the following entry is appended to /etc/inittab on each node in the cluster during Grid Infrastructure installation:

```
h1:35:respawn:/etc/init.d/init.ohasd run >/dev/null 2>&1 </dev/null
```

In previous releases, entries were added to /etc/inittab for the CRS daemon, CSS daemon, and EVM daemon. These background processes are now indirectly controlled by the OHAS daemon. The advantage of having the OHAS daemon do this is that the administrator can now issue cluster-wide commands. The OHAS daemon will start even if Grid Infrastructure is disabled explicitly. Indeed, you can use this to restart the cluster layer in a single command. In Grid Infrastructure 11.2, OHAS is comprised of the following daemons and services:

- *The Grid Plug And Play (GPnP) daemon*: This daemon maintains the Grid Plug and Play profile and coordinates distribution of updates across all nodes in the cluster. This helps ensure that all nodes have the current profile. The Grid Plug and Play profile essentially contains sufficient information to start Clusterware. In previous versions, this information could be stored directly in the OCR. However, in Oracle 11gR2, the OCR can optionally be stored in ASM, which means sufficient configuration information must be available to start ASM and to access the OCR. (The GPNP daemon is sometimes referred to by the initials, GPNPD).

- *The Grid Interprocess Communication (GIPC) daemon*: This daemon is new in Oracle 11gR2. The daemon process is gipcd, and it supports Grid Infrastructure Communication. Although this daemon is created when High Availability Services stack is started, GIPC has no functionality in this release. There are plans to activate GIPC in a future release.

- *The multicast DNS (mDNS) service*: This service manages name resolution and service discovery within the cluster. It resolves DNS requests on behalf of the Grid Naming Service (GNS). A separate daemon is created within the High Availability Services stack to support multicast DNS.

- *The Grid Naming Service (GNS)*: This service performs name resolution within the cluster. It is implemented by the gnsd daemon, and it provides a gateway between the cluster mDNS service and the external DNS servers.

Drilling Down on the Cluster Ready Services Stack

The Cluster Ready Services stack builds on the services provided by the High Availability Services stack and requires that its services to be up and running. It is hinged on the Cluster Ready Services daemon. The following daemons and services are part of the Cluster Ready Services stack:

- *Cluster Ready Services (CRS)*: This service manages high availability cluster operations. CRS is responsible for starting, stopping, monitoring, and failing over resources. The CRS service is implemented by the crsd daemon, which runs as the root user and is restarted automatically if it fails. The crsd daemon maintains the configuration information in the OCR, and it manages cluster resources based on that information. The OCR resource configuration includes definitions of dependencies on other cluster resources, timeouts, retries, assignment, and failover policies.

  If the cluster includes Oracle RAC, then CRS is responsible for monitoring Oracle RAC database instances, listeners, and services. It is also responsible for restarting these components in the event of a failure. In a single-instance Oracle Restart environment, application resources are managed by the ohasd daemon and crsd is not used.

- *Cluster Synchronization Services (CSS) service*: This service monitors and manages node membership within the cluster. It is implemented using the `ocssd` daemon. CSS monitors cluster membership of existing nodes and notifies all cluster members when a node joins or leaves the cluster. By default, CSS interfaces with Oracle Clusterware libraries. These libraries provide node membership and interprocess communication services. Alternatively, CSS can interface with a third-party cluster manager such as Sun Cluster or IBM HA-CMP; in these cases, a different set of cluster libraries must be linked into the cluster executables.

- *The Cluster Synchronization Services Agent (`cssdagent`)*: The `cssdagent` process starts, stops, and monitors the status of the `ocssd` daemon. If the `cssdagent` discovers that the `ocssd` daemon has stopped, then it shuts down the node to guarantee data integrity.

- *The Cluster Synchronization Services Monitor (`cssdmonitor`) process*: The `cssdmonitor` process monitors the scheduling of CPU on the node. If the `cssdmonitor` process discovers that the node has not hung, then it shuts down the node to guarantee data integrity. This behavior is known as I/O fencing. In Oracle 10.2.0.4 and later on the Linux platform, these services were provided by the Oracle Process Monitor daemon (`oprocd`). In Oracle 11.2 and later, `oprocd` is no longer implemented. The hangcheck-timer kernel module has been made obsolete in Oracle 10.2.0.4.

- *The Disk Monitor (`diskmon`) daemon*: The `diskmon` daemon monitors and performs I/O fencing for Exadata storage. On the basis that Exadata storage could be added to any RAC node at any time, the `diskmon` daemon is always started when `ocssd` starts. Therefore, the `diskmon` daemon will always be present, regardless of whether the cluster uses Exadata storage.

- *The Oracle Clusterware Kill (`oclskd`) daemon*: The `oclskd` daemon is used by CSS to stop processes associated with CSS group members for which stop requests have been received from other nodes in the cluster.

- *The Cluster Time Synchronization Service (CTSS)*: This service was introduced in Oracle 11gR2, and it provides time synchronization between all nodes in the cluster. CTSS can operate in two modes; observer mode and active mode. Most sites use Network Time Protocol to synchronize all servers in their estate to an external time source. If Oracle Clusterware detects that NTP has already been configured, then CTSS will automatically run in observer mode, obtaining time synchronization information from NTP. If NTP is not configured, then CTSS will run in active mode, in which case the first node to start in the cluster will become the master clock reference. All nodes subsequently joining the cluster will become slaves, adjusting their system date and time settings to those of the master. The mode in which the CTSS service is running is logged in the alert log when the service starts. This feature will probably be particularly useful in virtualized environments, where system clocks are notoriously inaccurate.

- *The Event Manager (EVM) service*: This service is implemented by the `evmd` daemon. It distributes information about some cluster events to all members of the cluster. Events of interest include the ability to start and stop nodes, instances, and services.

- *The Event Manager Logger (EVMLOGGER) daemon*: The evmlogger daemon is started by the evmd daemon. It subscribes to a list of events read from a configuration file, and it runs user-defined actions when those events occur. This daemon is intended to maintain backward compatibility.

- *The Oracle Notification Service (ONS, eONS)*: This publish-and-subscribe service distributes Fast Application Notification (FAN) events to interested clients in the environment. Oracle plans to merge ONS and eONS into the evmd daemon with one of the next patchsets for 11.2.

Using Grid Infrastructure Agents

In Oracle 11gR2 and later, there are two new types of agent processes: the Oracle Agent and the Oracle Root Agent. These processes interface between Oracle Clusterware and managed resources. In previous versions of Oracle Clusterware, this functionality was provided by the RACG family of scripts and processes.

To slightly complicate matters, there are two sets of Oracle Agents and Oracle Root Agents, one for the High Availability Services stack and one for the Cluster Ready Services stack.

The Oracle Agent and Oracle Root Agent that belong to the High Availability Services stack are started by ohasd daemon. The Oracle Agent and Oracle Root Agent pertaining to the Cluster Ready Services stack are started by the crsd daemon. In systems where the Grid Infrastructure installation is not owned by Oracle—and this is-probably the majority of installations—there is a third Oracle Agent created as part of the Cluster Ready Services stack. Similarly, the Oracle Agent spawned by OHAS is owned by the Grid Infrastructure software owner.

In addition to these two processes, there are agents responsible for managing and monitoring the CSS daemon, called CSSDMONITOR and CSSDAGENT. CSSDAGENT, the agent process responsible for spawning CSSD is created by the OHAS daemon. CSSDMONITOR, which monitors CSSD and the overall node health (jointly with the CSSDAGENT), is also spawned by OHAS.

You might wonder how CSSD, which is required to start the clustered ASM instance, can be started if voting disks are stored in ASM? This sounds like a chicken-and-egg problem: without access to the voting disks there is no CSS, hence the node cannot join the cluster. But without being part of the cluster, CSSD cannot start the ASM instance. To solve this problem the ASM disk headers have new metadata in 11.2: you can use kfed to read the header of an ASM disk containing a voting disk. The kfdhdb.vfstart and kfdhdb.vfend fields tell CSS where to find the voting file. This does not require the ASM instance to be up. Once the voting disks are located, CSS can access them and joins the cluster.

The high availability stack's Oracle Agent runs as the owner of the Grid Infrastructure stack in a clustered environment, as either the oracle or grid users. It is spawned by OHAS directly as part of the cluster startup sequence, and it is responsible for starting resources that do not require root privileges. The list of processes Oracle Agent starts includes the following:

- EVMD and EVMLOGGER

- the gipc daemon

- the gpnp daemon

- The mDNS daemon

The Oracle Root Agent that is spawned by OHAS in turn starts all daemons that require root privileges to perform their programmed tasks. Such tasks include the following:

- CRS daemon

- CTSS daemon

- Disk Monitoring daemon

- ACFS drivers

Once CRS is started, it will create another Oracle Agent and Oracle Root Agent. If Grid Infrastructure is owned by the grid account, a second Oracle Agent is created. The grid Oracle Agent(s) will be responsible for:

- Starting and monitoring the local ASM instance

- ONS and eONS daemons

- The SCAN listener, where applicable

- The Node listener

There can be a maximum of three SCAN listeners in the cluster at any given time. If you have more than three nodes, then you can end up without a SCAN listener on a node. Likewise, in the extreme example where there is only one node in the cluster, you could end up with three SCAN listeners on that node.

The oracle Oracle Agent will only spawn the database resource if account separation is used. If not—i.e., if you didn't install Grid Infrastructure with a different user than the RDBMS binaries—then the oracle Oracle Agent will also perform the tasks listed previously with the grid Oracle Agent.

The Oracle Root Agent finally will create the following background processes:

- GNS, if configured

- GNS VIP if GNS enabled

- ACFS Registry

- Network

- SCAN VIP, if applicable

- Node VIP

The functionality provided by the Oracle Agent process in Oracle 11gR2 was provided by the racgmain and racgimon background processes in Oracle 11gR1 and earlier.

Initiating the Startup Sequence

The startup sequence in Grid Infrastructure is not completely documented in the Oracle Clusterware Administration Guide 11.2. Therefore, this section will elaborate on some of the more elaborate aspects of managing that sequence.

The init process, father of all processes in Linux, spawns OHAS. This occurs in two stages: first, the /etc/init.d/init.ohasd script is invoked with the run argument. Second, this script then calls the /etc/init.d/ohasd script, which starts $GRID_HOME/bin/ohasd.bin. The init scripts log potential problems using the syslog facility present on all Linux systems. The ohasd.bin executable uses $GRID_HOME/log/hostname/ohasd/ohasd.log to report its activities. All processes mentioned so far run with root privileges. If the administrator has disabled the Grid Infrastructure, then the Grid Infrastructure high availability stack must be started manually; otherwise, the startup sequence continues.

The ohasd.bin process then spawns four processes, all of which are located in $GRID_HOME/bin. Note that that Grid Infrastructure can be installed to an operating system account other than oracle. This chapter refers to the owner of the software stack as the *Grid software owner*. This chapter also assumes that the RAC binaries were installed as the oracle user. Finally, this chapter assumes that $LOG_HOME points to $ORACLE_HOME/log/*hostname*

- oraagent.bin, started as the Grid software owner

- cssdmonitor, started as root

- cssdagent, started as root

- orarootagent.bin, started as root

It is important to remember that these processes are created by ohasd.bin, rather than the CRS daemon process, which has not been created yet. Next, the Oracle Root Agent starts the following executables, which are also located in $GRID_HOME/bin:

- crsd.bin: started as root

- diskmon.bin: started as the Grid software owner

- octssd.bin: started as root

The Oracle Agent (started as the Grid software owner) in turn will start these executables:

- evmd.bin: started as the Grid software owner

- evmlogger.bin: started as the Grid software owner

- gipcd.bin: started as the Grid software owner

- gpnpd.bin: started as the Grid software owner

- mdnsd.bin: started as the Grid software owner

The cssdagent executable is responsible for starting ocssd.bin, which runs as the Grid software owner. The cssdagent executable doesn't spawn additional processes.

Once the CRS daemon is created by the OHAS's Oracle Root Agent, the Cluster Ready Services stack will be started. The following actions depend on CRS to create additional Oracle Agents (owned by the Grid software owner and oracle) and another Oracle Root Agent. Again, it is important to note the distinction between these agents and the ones created by OHAS. You will also see that they are different because their log files are located in $LOG_HOME/agent/crsd/ rather than $LOG_HOME/agent/ohasd. You will see the following processes spawned by crsd.bin:

- oraagent.bin: started as the Grid software owner

- oraagent.bin: started as oracle

- oraarootgent.bin: started as root

These agents are henceforth responsible for continuing the start process. The Grid software owner's Oracle Agent (oraagent.bin) will start the following infrastructure components, all as the Grid Software owner:

- Clustered ASM instance

- ons

- enhanced ONS (eONS), a Java process

- tnslsnr: a SCAN listener

- tnslsnr: a node listener

The ONS binary is an exception because it is not started from $GRID_HOME/bin, but from $GRID_HOME/opmn/bin. The enhanced ONS service is a Java process. Therefore, it doesn't start from $GRID_HOME/bin, either; however, its JAR files are located there.

The oracle Oracle Agent oraagent.bin will start the database and services associated with the database resource, as defined in the Oracle Cluster Registry.

The Oracle Root Agent will start the following resources:

- The network resource

- The SCAN virtual IP address

- The Node virtual IP address

- The GNS virtual IP address if GNS is configured

- The GNS daemon if the cluster is configured to use GNS

- The ASM Cluster File System Registry

Managing Oracle Clusterware

Oracle provides a comprehensive set of tools that can be used to manage Oracle Grid Infrastructure, including the following:

- Enterprise Manager

- The crsctl utility

- The srvctl utility

- Cluster Verification Utility

- The oifcfg utility

- The ocrconfig utility

- The ocrcheck utility

- The ocrdump utility

The following sections will explain what these tools are and how to use them.

Using the Enterprise Manager

Both Enterprise Manager Database Control and Enterprise Manager Grid Control can be used to manage Oracle Clusterware environments. The functionality of Enterprise Manager Database Control is restricted to managing a single database that may have multiple instances. If Enterprise Manager Database Control is deployed, then the management repository must be stored in the target database. Enterprise Manager Database Control is often configured in test systems; it is less frequently deployed in production environments.

Enterprise Manager Grid Control provides a much more flexible management solution, and many Oracle sites now use this tool to manage their entire Oracle estate. The Enterprise Manager Grid Control management repository can be stored in a separate database, outside the cluster. Enterprise Manager Grid Control supports a wider range of administrative tasks, such as the ability to configure and maintain Data Guard.

If you do not already use Enterprise Manager Grid Control to manage your database environment, then we strongly recommend that you investigate this tool, which is subject to ongoing development. At the time of writing, a new version of the tool with a more user-friendly interface was planned for Oracle 11gR2.

■ **Note** Although Oracle promotes Enterprise Manager as the primary database management tool, the fact is that most users still use command-line tools to manage their clustered environments.

Using the Clusterware Control Utility

The Clusterware Control Utility crsctl is the primary command-line tool for managing Oracle Clusterware. It has existed since Oracle 10gR1; however, its functionality has been significantly enhanced in Oracle 11gR2.

In Oracle 11gR2, crsctl has been extended to include cluster-aware commands that can be used to start and stop Clusterware on some or all nodes in the cluster. It can also be used to monitor and manage the configuration of the voting disks and to configure and manage individual cluster resources. The crsctl utility also supports new functionality, such as the configuration of administrative privileges to ensure role separation.

As you saw in the startup section, the OHAS daemon always starts when the system boots. If the Oracle High Availability Services stack is disabled, then none of the daemons for the High Availability Services stack will start, and that node cannot join the cluster. To manually start and stop Oracle Clusterware on all nodes in the cluster, execute the following commands as the root user:

```
[root@london1]# crsctl start cluster -all
[root@london1]# crsctl stop cluster -all
```

Alternatively, you could use the -n switch to start Grid Infrastructure on a specific (not local) node. To check the current status of all nodes in the cluster, execute the following command:

```
[root@london1]# crsctl check cluster -all
**************************************************************
london1:
CRS-4537: Cluster Ready Services is online
```

```
CRS-4529: Cluster Synchronization Services is online
CRS-4533: Event Manager is online
*************************************************************
london2:
CRS-4537: Cluster Ready Services is online
CRS-4529: Cluster Synchronization Services is online
CRS-4533: Event Manager is online
*************************************************************
```

The documentation suggests that crsctl start cluster and crsctl start crs are identical when executed on the same node. We found that this is not the case. The start cluster option successfully starts any daemon that has not yet started. In other words, in cases where all daemons but the CRS daemon have started, crsctl start crs fails with an error that states: "High Availability Services is already active." When invoked with the start cluster option, crsctl detected that crsd was not started, and it brought it back online.

In Oracle 11gR2 and later, the crs_stat utility has been deprecated. However, this utility is still shipped to provide backwards compatibility. The functionality of crs_stat has been integrated into the crsctl utility. You can use crsctl status resource -t to list the current status of all resources, as in the following example:

```
[root@london1]# crsctl status resource -t
--------------------------------------------------------------------
NAME          TARGET  STATE     SERVER        STATE_DETAILS
--------------------------------------------------------------------
ora.ACFS1.dg
              ONLINE  ONLINE    london1
              ONLINE  ONLINE    london2
              ONLINE  ONLINE    london3
ora.DATA.dg
              ONLINE  ONLINE    london1
              ONLINE  ONLINE    london2
              ONLINE  ONLINE    london3
ora.LISTENER.lsnr
              ONLINE  ONLINE    london1
              ONLINE  ONLINE    london2
              ONLINE  ONLINE    london3
ora.RECO.dg
              ONLINE  ONLINE    london1
              ONLINE  ONLINE    london2
              ONLINE  ONLINE    london3
ora.acfs1.acfs1_vol1.acfs
              ONLINE  ONLINE    london1
              ONLINE  ONLINE    london2
              ONLINE  ONLINE    london3
...
```

In Oracle 11gR1 and earlier, similar output can be generated using crs_stat -t. Note that in Oracle 11gR2, this report no longer truncates resource names, and the output for each node appears on a separate line. An interesting fact about the state details field: If there is a severe problem with the database—if the online redo logs can't be archived, for example—then this will be reported in that column.

■ **Note** You should not use crsctl to modify the status of resources prefixed with ora. unless directed to do so by Oracle Support. The correct tool to modify such resources with is srvctl; this tool will be covered in its own section.

The output of the crsctl status resource command does not list the daemons of the High Availability Services stack! You must use the initially undocumented -init option to accomplish this:

```
[root@london1 ~]# crsctl status resource -t -init
--------------------------------------------------------------------------------
NAME            TARGET  STATE    SERVER              STATE_DETAILS
--------------------------------------------------------------------------------
Cluster Resources
--------------------------------------------------------------------------------
ora.asm
      1         ONLINE  ONLINE   london1             Started
ora.crsd
      1         ONLINE  ONLINE   london1
ora.cssd
      1         ONLINE  ONLINE   london1
ora.cssdmonitor
      1         ONLINE  ONLINE   london1
ora.ctssd
      1         ONLINE  ONLINE   london1             OBSERVER
ora.diskmon
      1         ONLINE  ONLINE   london1
ora.drivers.acfs
      1         ONLINE  ONLINE   london1
ora.evmd
      1         ONLINE  ONLINE   london1
ora.gipcd
      1         ONLINE  ONLINE   london1
ora.gpnpd
      1         ONLINE  ONLINE   london1
ora.mdnsd
      1         ONLINE  ONLINE   london1
```

The functionality of the deprecated crs_start, crs_stop, and crs_relocate utilities has been integrated into crsctl. User-defined resources are covered in more detail in the "Protecting Applications with Clusterware" section later in this chapter; for now, you can initiate a resource using crsctl start resource *resourceName* and stop it using crsctl stop resource *resourceName*. If Oracle Support recommends doing so, you can stop resources of the High Availability Services stack by appending the -init parameter to crsctl start/stop resource *resourceName*. Bear in mind that this command merely instructs the high availability daemons to perform the task; you still need to check the log file to see whether it succeeded past the start request.

Many of the remaining options of the crsctl utility will be discussed in different sections later this chapter. For example, to make applications highly available, crsctl commands can be used to create user-defined resources. Again, refer to the "Protecting Applications with Clusterware" section for more information on this topic. This section will cover how to access control lists, as well as how to set and get resource permissions. This section also covers how the framework works to protect resources.

crsctl is also required to move voting disks into ASM or to other storage options (see the "Maintaining Voting Disks" section for more information on this topic).

Managing Resources with srvctl

The srvctl utility is a command-line tool that manages Oracle resources configured in the cluster. srvctl has been available since Oracle 10gR1. Like crsctl, srvctl has been significantly enhanced in Oracle 11gR2. In Oracle 11gR1 and earlier, srvctl managed six object types: asm, database, instances, services, node applications, and listeners. Oracle 11gR2 adds an additional ten object types: GNS, VIP Addresses, SCAN VIP addresses, SCAN listeners, Oracle homes, OC4J, servers, server pools, ASM disk groups, and ASM file systems.

The same options are available in Oracle 11gR2 that were available in previous releases: enable, disable, start, stop, relocate, status, add, remove, modify, config, getenv, setenv, and unsetenv. Note that all options have not been implemented for all of the objects. Table 8-2 summarizes srvctl options available in Oracle 11gR2 for each object type.

Table 8-2. Options for the srvctl Utility

	enable	disable	start	stop	relocate	status	add	remove	modify	config	getenv	setenv	unsetenv
database	✓	✓	✓	✓		✓	✓	✓	✓	✓	✓	✓	✓
instance	✓	✓	✓	✓		✓	✓	✓	✓				
service	✓	✓	✓	✓	✓	✓	✓	✓	✓	✓			
nodeapps	✓	✓	✓	✓		✓	✓	✓	✓	✓	✓	✓	✓
vip	✓	✓	✓	✓		✓	✓	✓		✓	✓	✓	✓
asm	✓	✓	✓	✓		✓	✓	✓	✓	✓	✓	✓	✓
diskgroup	✓	✓	✓	✓		✓		✓					
listener	✓	✓	✓	✓		✓	✓	✓	✓	✓	✓	✓	✓
scan	✓	✓	✓	✓	✓	✓	✓	✓	✓	✓			
scan_listener	✓	✓	✓	✓	✓	✓	✓	✓	✓	✓			

	enable	disable	start	stop	relocate	status	add	remove	modify	config	getenv	setenv	unsetenv
srvpool						✓	✓	✓	✓	✓			
server					✓	✓							
oc4j	✓	✓	✓	✓	✓	✓	✓	✓	✓	✓			
home			✓	✓		✓							
filesystem	✓	✓	✓	✓		✓	✓	✓	✓	✓			
gns	✓	✓	✓	✓	✓	✓	✓	✓	✓	✓			

You need to keep a couple points in mind when shutting down an ASM instance using srvctl stop asm. In Oracle 11.1 and earlier, you could stop an ASM instance, which resulted in a dismount command and a shutdown of the instance. In Oracle 11.2 the srvctl stop asm command does not work, especially if voting disks and OCR are located in ASM itself. To stop ASM in Oracle RAC 11.2, you need to shut down all clients of ASM, including CSSD. The only way to do this is to stop the High Availability Services stack on the node. The same applies to the srvctl stop home command when the Oracle home is the ASM home (you can find more information about this topic in Chapter 9).

Another useful command to know is srvctl's config option. This option retrieves information about a system, reporting all database resources if no additional arguments are provided. If an object such as a database, asm, scans, or scan listener is passed, then this option provides detailed information about the specified resource. This functionality is essential for deployments that GNS where DHCP is responsible for assigning network addresses. For example, you could use the following to find out which IP addresses are used for the SCAN:

```
[oracle@london1 ~]$ srvctl config scan
SCAN name: cluster1, Network: 1/172.17.1.0/255.255.255.0/
SCAN VIP name: scan1, IP: /cluster1.example.com/172.17.1.205
SCAN VIP name: scan2, IP: /cluster1.example.com/172.17.1.206
SCAN VIP name: scan3, IP: /cluster1.example.com/172.17.1.207
```

The srvctl stop home command simplifies patching the RDBMS. This command records which resources are currently started from the current node. This information is stored in a state file that the administrator specifies. Upon patch completion, you can use the srvctl start home command when the Grid Infrastructure restarts, and then use the state file and all resources that were active before the patch application is brought online again.

Verifying the Cluster with the CVU

The Cluster Verification Utility (CVU) is a command-line tool that was introduced in Oracle 10gR2. The CVU checks the configuration of a cluster and reports whether each component is successfully configured. The CVU checks operating system versions and patches, kernel parameters, user limits, operating system groups and users, secure shell configuration, networking configuration, and shared storage devices. The CVU comes in three versions; be sure to run `cluvfy.sh` on the staging area of the Grid Infrastructure media. You can download this file from Oracle's Technet website; you will find the `cluvfy` file in `$GRID_HOME/bin` after a successful installation.

The CVU can be invoked at a number of stages during the installation and configuration process. Each step represents a set of components that should be configured at that time. In Oracle 11gR2 and later, the OUI automatically executes the CVU as part of the installation process. In our experience, however, it is still more efficient to run the CVU prior to starting the installer to address any oversights or errors in the initial configuration. The CVU should also be run following the completion of administrative tasks, such as node addition and deletion.

Table 8-3 shows the stages when you should run the CVU in Oracle 11gR2.

Table 8-3. Stages at which to Execute the cluvfy Utility

Stage	Description
-post hwos	After hardware and operating system configuration
-pre cfs	Before CFS setup
-post crs	After CFS setup
-pre crsinst	Before CRS installation
-post crsinst	After CRS installation
-pre hacfg	Before HA configuration
-post hacfg	After HA configuration
-pre dbinst	Before database installation
-pre acfscfg	Before ACFS configuration
-post acfscfg	After ACFS configuration
-pre dbcfg	Before database configuration
-pre nodeadd	Before node addition
-post nodeadd	After node addition
-post nodedel	After node addition

You can also invoke the CVU to check individual components. This functionality can be useful for isolating a problem. Table 8-4 lists the CVU components in Oracle 11gR2.

Table 8-4. *The CVU Component Checks*

Component	Description
nodereach	Reachability between nodes
nodecon	Node connectivity
cfs	Cluster file system integrity
ssa	Shared storage accessibility
space	Space availability
sys	Minimum space requirements
clu	Cluster manager integrity
ocr	OCR integrity
olr	OLR integrity
ha	HA integrity
crs	CRS integrity
nodeapp	Node application existence
admprv	Administrative privileges
peer	Compares properties with peers
software	Software distribution
asm	ASM integrity
acfs	ACFS integrity
gpnp	GPNP integrity
gns	GNS integrity
scan	SCAN configuration
ohasd	OHASD integrity

Component	Description
clocksync	Clock synchronization
vdisk	Voting disk udev settings

The CVU is implemented as a set of Java classes. On Linux, the CVU can be executed using the runcluvfy.sh shell script. This script configures the Java environment prior to starting the CVU off the installation media. After the installation has completed, the cluvfy file can be found in $GRID_HOME/bin (like any other executable).

The default form of the command includes a list of nodes that should be checked. For example, the following snippet verifies the configuration of the hardware and the operating system on nodes london1 and london2:

```
[oracle@london1 ~]$ cluvfy stage -pre hwos -n london1,london2
```

You can append the –verbose switch to generate more detailed output:

```
[oracle@london1 ~]$ cluvfy stage -pre hwos -n london1,london2 -verbose
```

It is good practice to keep the output of the execution as part of the installation documentation. In Oracle 11gR2 and later, the CVU can optionally generate fixup scripts to resolve a limited subset of errors. In Linux, fixup scripts can be generated to adjust kernel parameters and modify user limits. The resulting scripts must be executed by the root user.

The CVU is supplied with the Oracle Clusterware software distribution. Alternatively, it can be downloaded from the downloads section of the Oracle website at this location: www.oracle.com/technology/products/database/clustering/cvu/cvu_download_homepage.html.

The CVU must be executed by a regular user (e.g., grid or oracle; it cannot be executed by the root user).

Occasionally it is necessary to gather more than the verbose output from the CVU, especially before the software has been successfully instantiated on the cluster nodes. In this case, a little modification to the script is necessary. By default, the runcluvfy.sh script on the Grid Infrastructure staging location removes all the intermediate trace output in line 129:

```
128 # Cleanup the home for cluster verification software
129 $RM -rf $CV_HOME
```

To preserve the output, it is necessary to comment this line out. The script has hard-coded dependencies on files in the staging location. If your staging location is read-only (e.g., it is an NFS mount or DVD), then you can still make the change quite easily. Copy the runcluvfy.sh file to a writable location, such as /u01/software. Next, create cluster verification home and export this as an environment variable. Now change the script in line 129 and comment out this line:

```
RM -rf $CV_HOME
```

Also change the variable EXEC_DIR in line 29 so it points to the location where your Grid Infrastructure software is staged. Make sure to set CV_TRACE to another writable directory for the trace output, and then execute runcluvfy.sh.

...

Note that the CVU is only designed to verify that a configuration meets minimum installation requirements; in other words, it isn't foolproof. For example, it occasionally reports failures that can be safely ignored. In other cases, it misses some configuration errors that may subsequently cause an installation to fail.

Configuring Network Interfaces with oifcfg

The Oracle Interface Configuration Tool (oifcfg) is a command-line tool that can be used to configure network interfaces within Oracle Clusterware. The oifcfg utility can be used to add new public or private interfaces, as well as to modify existing subnet information.

Prior to Oracle 11gR2, oifcfg updated the OCR only. In Oracle 11gR2, oifcfg has been extended to update the OLR and the GPNP profile. Please refer back to the "Recording Information with the Grid Plug And Play Profile" section for more information on where the network information is stored in the profile.

Administering the OCR and OLR with ocrconfig

The Oracle Cluster Registry Configuration tool ocrconfig is a command-line utility that can be used to administer the OCR and OLR. The ocrconfig tool has a number of options, including the ability to add and delete OCR mirrors, perform manual backups of the OCR, restore OCR backups, and export and import OCR configuration data. Many of the options for ocrconfig are also applicable to maintaining the OLR; options that target the OLR use the -local switch.

Checking the State of the OCR and its Mirrors with ocrcheck

The Oracle Cluster Registry Check tool, ocrcheck, checks the state of the OCR and its mirrors. The behavior of ocrcheck is determined by the user that invokes it. When invoked by a regular user, such as grid or oracle, ocrcheck checks the accessibility of all OCR mirror copies. It also reports on the current size and free space in the OCR. When invoked by the root user, ocrcheck also performs a structural check on the contents of the OCR and reports any errors. The ocrcheck command is most useful when trying to determine logical corruption in the OCR.

Dumping Contents of the OCR with ocrdump

The Oracle Cluster Registry Dump tool, ocrdump, can be used to dump the contents of the OCR to a text or XML file. ocrdump can only be executed by the root user. If requested, ocrdump can also dump the OLR to a file. The dump file name will default to OCRDUMP; however, this name can be changed by specifying an alternative file name on the command line. If desired, ocrdump can write to standard output. A very useful option is to extract the contents of a backed up OCR or OLR. This enables you to perform before and after comparisons when applying patchsets, for example. If you are unsure where your backup files are located, consult the output of ocrconfig -showbackup [-local]. For very specific troubleshooting needs, ocrdump offers the option to print only a specific key from the registry.

Defining Server-Side Callouts

Grid Infrastructure and Clusterware offer the ability to define callout scripts. These are usually small shell scripts or other executables used for very specific tasks that are stored in $GRID_HOME/racg/usrco. Such scripts are invoked by Grid Infrastructure whenever a FAN event is published by the framework affecting the local node.

FAN events are generated in response to a state change, which can include the following:

- Starting or stopping the database

- Starting or stopping an instance

- Starting or stopping a service

- A node leaving the cluster

The changes can either be user-initiated or caused by failures. Example uses of these scripts are to relocate services to preferred instances after a failed node restarts, to send a page to the on-call DBA, or even to automatically raise a ticket with a trouble ticketing system. The recommendation in this case is to keep the scripts short and to ensure they execute quickly.

Each script deployed in $GRID_HOME/racg/usrco will be invoked and passed the specified parameters as name-value pairs (see Table 8-5).

Table 8-5. Parameters Passed to a User Callout Script

Parameter	Description
event_typ	The Node Event. Possible values are NODE, SERVICE, SERVICEMEMBER.
version	The event protocol. The only valid value is 1.0.
hostname	The host name the event applies to.
status	The status of the node, service, or service member. Valid values are UP, DOWN, NODEDOWN, RESTART_FAILED, NOT_RESTARTING.
timestamp	The date and time the event was published.
cardinality	The number of nodes providing service.
reason	The reason for the change in state. Values are USER, FAILOVER, FAILURE.

It is up to the script to determine which of these parameters are needed for it to perform the action. For example, the following perl script sends the on-call DBA an e-mail when prodserv service of PROD database goes down:

```perl
#!/usr/bin/perl

use strict;
use warnings;
use Sys::Hostname;
use Net::SMTP::OneLiner;

# constants
my $MONITORED_DB       = "PROD";
my $MONITORED_SERVICE  = "prodserv";
my $LOGDIR             = "/tmp";
my $LOGFILENAME        = $MONITORED_SERVICE . "_" . hostname() . ".log";

my $eventType;
my $service;
my $database;
my $instance;
my $host;
my $status;
my $reason;
my $timestamp;
my $dummy;              # needed for split()

# parse command line
$eventType           = $ARGV[0];
($dummy, $service)   = split /=/, $ARGV[2];
($dummy, $database)  = split /=/, $ARGV[3];
($dummy, $instance)  = split /=/, $ARGV[4];
($dummy, $host)      = split /=/, $ARGV[5];
($dummy, $status)    = split /=/, $ARGV[6];
($dummy, $reason)    = split /=/, $ARGV[7];
$timestamp           = $ARGV[8];

# Notify the DBA our monitored service of our monitored database is down
if ($database eq $MONITORED_DB && $service eq $MONITORED_SERVICE
        && $status eq "down" && $eventType eq "SERVICE")
{
  # we still want to receive an email even if the logging failed. Using the
  # eval {} block allows the script to continue even if the call to open()
  # failed
  eval {
    open FILE, ">>", "$LOGDIR/$LOGFILENAME";
    print FILE "service:   $service\n";
    print FILE "database:  $database\n";
    print FILE "status:    $status\n";
    print FILE "reason:    $reason\n";
    print FILE "timestamp: $timestamp\n";

    close FILE;
  };
  # uses Net::SMTP::OneLiner to send email. Call format is
  # send_mail($from, $to, $subj, $msg);
```

```
    send_mail("oracle\@" . hostname() ,
      "oncallDBA\@example.com",
      "Service $MONITORED_SERVICE on database $MONITORED_DB host " .
        $host is down",
      "The service went down at $timestamp");
}
```

The code in preceding example parses the command-line arguments passed to the perl script as the array, @ARGV. This script uses the split() function to extract the values from the name-value pairs. If the monitored service of the monitored database is down completely (the SERVICE event type indicates this), then the script logs the incident into the defined log directory. Finally, the script sends an email to the on-call DBA's pager at this email alias: oncalldba@example.com.

Protecting Applications with Clusterware

Few users of Oracle Grid Infrastructure or Clusterware are aware of the fact that, in addition to providing a foundation for RAC, Grid Infrastructure is also a full-blown high availability framework. Essentially, this boils down to the fact that resources are monitored by a framework. If a resource is detected to have failed, then the framework has the necessary information about what to do with a failed resource. In most cases, it is enough to restart the failed resource on the same node. For Oracle supplied resources such as services and database instances, restart attempts are predefined by a respective resource type. If the restarts of a resource fail and if a resource can relocate, then Grid Infrastructure will try and relocate the resource to another available node. Resources that can be relocated are services and virtual IP addresses (node VIPs). Some resources are tied to a node and cannot be relocated. Such resources include most of the daemons in the high availability framework, as well as ASM instances.

Managing Resource Profiles

The clusterwide shared OCR contains the information about a system's resources, called a resource profile. In pre-11.2 installations, the crs_stat utility was used to dump a resource profile. Grid Infrastructure uses the crsctl status resource resourceName -p command to achieve the same result. Resource profiles have changed significantly with Oracle 11.2 (you can see a few examples that illustrate these differences in this chapter's "Configuring Active/Passive Clustering for Oracle Database" and "Configuring Active/Passive Clustering for Apache Tomcat" sections). Depending on the complexity of your application, it can be made up of a single or multiple resources. You can also define dependencies between the resources, ensuring they all start up in the correct order.

The changes to the resource profiles in Oracle 11.2 are so significant that Oracle dedicated a new appendix—Appendix B—to its release guide, "Clusterware Administration and Deployment Guide 11g Release 2 (11.2)." While the Oracle-supplied resources come with dedicated resource profiles that do not need to be touched, user-defined resources need to include a resource profile to work correctly.

In addition to a resource profile, user-defined resources need a controller, which is called an action script in the documentation. Grid Infrastructure uses agent programs (agents) to manage resources, and these agents invoke the action script's functions. The most common agent used to protect user-defined resources is the scriptagent. This agent allows developers to use simple shell scripts as action scripts for a resource. When used with scriptagent, an action script must implement the following callbacks and interfaces between the user resource and the framework:

- Start: Starts the resource

- Stop: Tries to gracefully stop the resource

- Check: Checks for the resource's health

- Clean: Forcefully terminates the resource

- Abort: Called when any of the preceding callbacks and interfaces hang and do not return; defaults to terminating the process

For specific application needs, you can develop your own agent and provide callback functions for those entry points. If an agent does not provide a callback function for the entry point, the action script of the resource will be invoked to perform the required action.

■ **Note** The agent framework is beyond the scope of this chapter. Interested readers can learn more about this subject by reading Chapter 5 of the "Oracle Clusterware Administration and Deployment Guide 11*g* Release 2."

The high availability framework will invoke the action script (or the agent directly) with the start option whenever crsctl start resource is called with the resource name. Similarly, you can stop, clean, or check by invoking the desired option. How well you code these options has a direct impact on the overall stability and responsiveness of the resource.

Resources sharing common attributes can be grouped into resource types. Predefined resource types are local resources or cluster resources; however, developers can also write their own types. In previous versions of Clusterware, Oracle supported another resource type, called an *application resource*; however, that resource type has been deprecated. It is still implemented for backward compatibility, but it should no longer be used.

The distinction between the resource types is visible in the output of crsctl status resource. Note how there are "cluster resources" and "local resources" sections. As their names suggest, local resources are tied to the node they are defined for, and they do not fail over. Cluster resources, on the other hand, can fail over and do not necessarily execute on all cluster nodes.

Grid Infrastructure continuously monitors resources as defined in their resource profiles. Any given resource is assigned a state, which can one of the following:

- ONLINE

- OFFLINE

- PARTIAL

- UNKNOWN

Configuring Active/Passive Clustering for Oracle Database

The Oracle database can easily be configured to use the Clusterware framework for high availability. Using Grid Infrastructure to protect a database resource is a very cost effective way of setting up an active/passive cluster. As an added advantage, using only one vendor's software stack to implement the cluster can make troubleshooting easier. Staff already familiar with RAC will easily be able to set up and run this configuration because it uses an identical software stack: all commands and log files are in familiar locations, and troubleshooting does not rely on the input from other teams.

To set up an active/passive cluster with 11*g* Release 2, you need to initially install Grid Infrastructure on all nodes of the cluster. Grid Infrastructure will provide the user with a cluster logical volume manager: ASM. If for some reason another file system is required, you have the option of choosing from the supported cluster file systems, including ACFS. Using a cluster file system that is mounted concurrently to both cluster nodes offers the advantage of not having to remount the database files and binaries in case of a node failure. Some configurations we saw suffered from extended failover periods caused by required file system checks before the file system could be remounted.

On top of the Grid Infrastructure build, you perform a local installation of the RDBMS. It is important that you do not choose a cluster installation when prompted so; otherwise, you risk violating your license agreement with Oracle.

When completed, the software stack consists of the components listed in Figure 8-2.

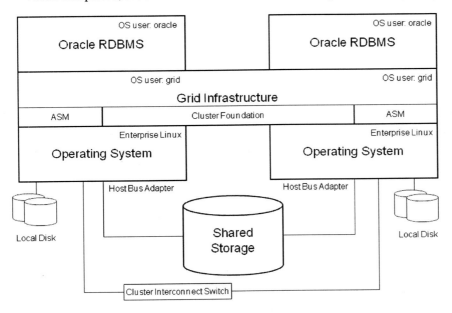

Figure 8-2. Oracle Software for an Active/Passive Cluster

After the binaries are installed and patched according to your standards, you need to create an ASM disk group or OCFS2/GFS mount point to store the database files. Next, start up the database configuration assistant from the first node to create a database. Please ensure that you store all the data files in ASM or the clustered file system. The same applies for the Fast Recovery Area: it should be on shared storage, as well.

After the database is created by dbca, it is automatically registered in the OLR. The profile of the resource is a good reference for the resource profile to be created in the next step. It is a good idea to save the resource profile in a safe location. You can extract the profile with the crsctl status resource ora.*databaseName*.db -p command. Next, remove the database resource from the OLR, as shown in the following example (this example assumes the database is named TEST):

```
[oracle@london1 ~]$ srvctl remove database -d TEST
```

Next, we need an action script that allows the framework to start, stop, and check the database resource. A possible action script might look like this:

```
#!/bin/bash

export ORACLE_SID=TEST
export ORACLE_HOME=/u01/app/oracle/product/11.2.0/db_1
export PATH=/usr/local/bin:$ORACLE_HOME/bin:$PATH
export ORACLE_OWNER=oracle

case $1 in
'start')
  su - $ORACLE_OWNER <<EOF
export ORACLE_SID=$ORACLE_SID
export ORACLE_HOME=$ORACLE_HOME
$ORACLE_HOME/bin/sqlplus /nolog
conn / as sysdba
startup
exit
EOF
    RET=0
    ;;
'stop')
  su - $ORACLE_OWNER <<EOF
export ORACLE_SID=$ORACLE_SID
export ORACLE_HOME=$ORACLE_HOME
$ORACLE_HOME/bin/sqlplus /nolog
conn / as sysdba
shutdown immediate
exit
EOF
    RET=0
    ;;
'check')
    # check for the existance of the smon process for $ORACLE_SID
    # this check could be improved, but was kept short on purpose
    found=`ps -ef | grep smon | grep $ORACLE_SID | wc -l`
    if [ $found = 0 ]; then
      RET=1
    else
      RET=0
    fi
    ;;
*)
    RET=0
    ;;
esac
# A 0 indicates success, return 1 for an error.
if [ $RET -eq 0 ]; then
```

```
  exit 0
else
  exit 1
fi
```

The preceding action script defines environment variables in the header section, setting the Oracle owner, the Oracle SID, and the Oracle home. It then implements the required start, stop, clean, and check entry points. The check could be more elaborate—for example, it could check for a hung instance—however, this example was kept short and simple for the sake of clarity.

The action script needs to be deployed to the other cluster node, and it must be made executable. Whenever there is a change to the script, the action script needs to be synchronized with the other cluster nodes! After defining the action script, you need to create a new cluster resource. Securing an Oracle database instance with Clusterware is simplified by the availability of the SCAN; users of the database do not need to worry about which node the database is currently started on because the SCAN abstracts this information from them. The communication of the SCAN with the local listener also makes a floating virtual IP (which other cluster stacks require) unnecessary. Using some values of the resource profile saved earlier, you need to configure the resource profile for the cluster resource next. It is easier to use a configuration file than to supply all the resource parameters on the command line in name-value pairs. To recreate the database cluster resource, you could use the following configuration file, which is saved as TEST.db.config:

```
PLACEMENT=restricted
HOSTING_MEMBERS=london1 london2
CHECK_INTERVAL=30
CARDINALITY=1
ACTIVE_PLACEMENT=0
AUTO_START=restore
DEGREE=1
DESCRIPTION="Oracle Database Resource"
RESTART_ATTEMPTS=1
ACTION_SCRIPT=/u01/app/crs/hadaemon/hacluster.sh
```

The preceding configuration file can be read as follows. Placement and hosting members go hand-in-hand; the restricted policy only allows executing the resource on the hosting members london1 and london2. The check interval of 30 seconds determines the frequency of checks, and setting active placement 0 prevents Oracle from relocating the resource to a failed node; a failed node could indicate a second outage in the system, and it would be better to let the DBAs perform the switch back to the primary node. The cardinality specifies that there will *always* be one instance of this resource in the cluster (never more or less); similarly, the degree of 1 indicates that there cannot be more than one instance of the resource on the same node. The parameters restart attempts and action script are self-explanatory in this context. Please note that the directory $GRID_HOME/hadaemon/ did not exist; it was created for this example.

Next, use the following command to register the resource in Grid Infrastructure:

```
$ crsctl add resource TEST.db -type cluster_resource -file TEST.db.config
```

If you get a CRS-2518 (invalid directory path) error while executing this command, you most likely forgot to deploy the action script to the other node.

> ■ **Note** You might be tempted to use the `ora.database.type` resource type here. Unfortunately, using this resource type repeatedly caused core dumps of the agent process monitoring the resource. These were in `$GRID_HOME/log/hostname/agent/crsd/oraagent_oracle`.

The permissions on the resource at this moment are too strict. At this moment, only root can effectively modify the resource at this time. Trying to start the resource as the oracle account results in a failure, as in this example:

```
[oracle@london1 ~]$ crsctl start resource TEST.db
CRS-0245:  User doesn't have enough privilege to perform the operation
CRS-4000: Command Start failed, or completed with errors.
```

You can confirm the cause of this failure checking the permissions:

```
[root@london1 ~]# crsctl getperm resource TEST.db
Name: TEST.db
owner:root:rwx,pgrp:root:r-x,other::r--
```

You would like the oracle user to also be able to start and stop the resource; you can enable this level of permission using the `crsctl setperm` command, as in the following example:

```
[root@london1 ~]# crsctl setperm resource TEST.db -o oracle
[root@london1 ~]# crsctl getperm resource TEST.db
Name: TEST.db
owner:oracle:rwx,pgrp:root:r-x,other::r--
```

The preceding snippet allows users logging in as oracle (or using `sudo su - oracle`) to start and stop the database, effectively transferring ownership of the resource to the oracle account. You need to ensure that the oracle account can execute the action script; otherwise, you will get an error when trying to start the resource. Members of the oinstall group have the same rights. All other users defined on the operating system level with privileges to execute the binaries in $GRID_HOME can only read the resource status.

> ■ **Note** All the resource attributes—and especially the placement options and start/stop dependencies—are documented in Appendix B of the "Oracle Clusterware Administration and Deployment Guide 11*g* Release 2 (11.2)" document.

The final preparation steps are to copy the password file and pfile pointing to the ASM spfile into the passive node's `$ORACLE_HOME/dbs` directory. You are in 11.2, so the ADR will take care of all your diagnostic files. You need to create the directory for your audit files however, which normally is in `$ORACLE_BASE/admin/$ORACLE_SID/adump`.

From this point on, you need to use `crsctl {start|stop|relocate}` to manipulate the database. Relocating the resource from london1 to london2 is easy after you implement the preceding steps, as the next example demonstrates:

```
[root@london1 ~]# crsctl status resource TEST.db
NAME=TEST.db
TYPE=cluster_resource
TARGET=ONLINE
STATE=ONLINE on london1
[root@london1 ~]# crsctl relocate resource TEST.db
CRS-2673: Attempting to stop 'TEST.db' on 'london1'
CRS-2677: Stop of 'TEST.db' on 'london1' succeeded
CRS-2672: Attempting to start 'TEST.db' on 'london2'
CRS-2676: Start of 'TEST.db' on 'london2' succeeded
[root@london1 ~]# crsctl status resource TEST.db
NAME=TEST.db
TYPE=cluster_resource
TARGET=ONLINE
STATE=ONLINE on london2
```

Configuring Active/Passive Clustering for Apache Tomcat

A slightly more complex example involves making Apache Tomcat or another web-accessible application highly available. The difference in this setup compared to the database setup described in the previous chapter lies in the fact that you need to use a floating virtual IP address. *Floating* in this context means that the virtual IP address moves jointly with the application. Oracle calls its implementation of a floating VIP an *application VIP*. Application VIPs were introduced in Oracle Clusterware 10.2. Previous versions only had a node VIP.

The idea behind application VIPs is that, in the case of a node failure, both VIP and the application migrate to the other node. The example that follows makes Apache Tomcat highly available, which is accomplished by installing the binaries for version 6.0.26 in /u01/tomcat on two nodes in the cluster. The rest of this section outlines the steps you must take to make Apache Tomcat highly available.

Oracle Grid Infrastructure does not provide an application VIP by default, so you have to create one. A new utility, called appvipcfg, can be used to set up an application VIP, as in the following example:

```
[root@london1 ~]# appvipcfg
Production Copyright 2007, 2008, Oracle.All rights reserved

  Usage: appvipcfg create -network=<network_number> -ip=<ip_address> -vipname=<vipname>
                     -user=<user_name>[-group=<group_name>]
               delete -vipname=<vipname>
[root@london1 ~]# appvipcfg create -network=1 \
> -ip 172.17.1.108 -vipname httpd-vip -user=root
Production Copyright 2007, 2008, Oracle.All rights reserved
2010-06-18 16:07:12: Creating Resource Type
2010-06-18 16:07:12: Executing cmd: /u01/app/crs/bin/crsctl add type app.appvip.type -basetype
cluster_resource -file /u01/app/crs/crs/template/appvip.type
2010-06-18 16:07:13: Create the Resource
2010-06-18 16:07:13: Executing cmd: /u01/app/crs/bin/crsctl add resource httpd-vip -type
app.appvip.type -attr USR_ORA_VIP=172.17.1.104,START_DEPENDENCIES=hard(ora.net1.network)
```

pullup(ora.net1.network),STOP_DEPENDENCIES=hard(ora.net1.network),ACL='owner:root:rwx,pgrp:roo
t:r-x,other::r--,user:root:r-x'

The preceding output shows that the new resource has been created, and it is owned by root exclusively. You could use crsctl setperm to change the ACL, but this is not required for this process. Bear in mind that no account other than root can start the resource at this time. You can verify the result of this operation by querying the resource just created. Note how the httpd-vip does not have an ora. prefix:

```
[root@london1 ~]# crsctl status resource httpd-vip
NAME=httpd-vip
TYPE=app.appvip.type
TARGET=OFFLINE
STATE=OFFLINE
```

Checking the resource profile reveals that it matches the output of the appvipcfg command; the output has been shortened for readability, and it focuses only on the most important keys (the other keys were removed for the sake of clarity):

```
[root@london1 ~]# crsctl stat res httpd-vip -p
NAME=httpd-vip
TYPE=app.appvip.type
ACL=owner:root:rwx,pgrp:root:r-x,other::r--,user:root:r-x
ACTIVE_PLACEMENT=0
AGENT_FILENAME=%CRS_HOME%/bin/orarootagent%CRS_EXE_SUFFIX%
AUTO_START=restore
CARDINALITY=1
CHECK_INTERVAL=1
DEGREE=1
DESCRIPTION=Application VIP
RESTART_ATTEMPTS=0
SCRIPT_TIMEOUT=60
SERVER_POOLS=*
START_DEPENDENCIES=hard(ora.net1.network) pullup(ora.net1.network)
STOP_DEPENDENCIES=hard(ora.net1.network)
USR_ORA_VIP=172.17.1.108
VERSION=11.2.0.1.0
```

The dependencies on the network ensure that, if the network is not started, it will be started as part of the VIP start. The resource is controlled by the CRSD orarootagent because changes to the network configuration require root privileges in Linux. The status of the resource revealed it was stopped; you can use the following command to start it:

```
[root@london1 ~]# crsctl start res httpd-vip
CRS-2672: Attempting to start 'httpd-vip' on 'london2'
CRS-2676: Start of 'httpd-vip' on 'london2' succeeded
[root@london1 ~]#
```

In this case, Grid Infrastructure decided to start the resource on server london2.

```
[root@london1 ~]# crsctl status resource httpd-vip
NAME=httpd-vip
TYPE=app.appvip.type
TARGET=ONLINE
STATE=ONLINE on london2
```

You can verify this by querying the network setup, which has changed. The following output is again shortened for readability:

```
[root@london2 source]# ifconfig
...
eth0:3    Link encap:Ethernet  HWaddr 00:16:36:2B:F2:F6
          inet addr:172.17.1.108  Bcast:172.17.1.255  Mask:255.255.255.0
          UP BROADCAST RUNNING MULTICAST  MTU:1500  Metric:1
```

Next, you need an action script that controls the Tomcat resource. Again, the requirement is to implement start, stop, clean, and check functions in the action script. The Oracle documentation lists C, C++, and shell scripts as candidate languages for an action script. We think that the action script can be any executable, as long as it returns 0 or 1, as required by Grid Infrastructure. A sample action script that checks for the Tomcat webserver could be written in plan bash, as in the following example:

```
#!/bin/bash

export CATALINA_HOME=/u01/tomcat
export ORA_CRS_HOME=/u01/app/crs
export JAVA_HOME=$CRS_HOME/jdk
export CHECKURL="http://172.17.1.108:8080/tomcat-power.gif"

case $1 in
'start')
   $CATALINA_HOME/bin/startup.sh
   RET=$?
     ;;
'stop')
   $CATALINA_HOME/bin/shutdown.sh
   RET=$?
     ;;
'clean')
   $CATALINA_HOME/bin/shutdown.sh
   RET=$?
     ;;
'check')
   # download a simple, small image from the tomcat server
   /usr/bin/wget -q --delete-after $CHECKURL
   RET=$?
     ;;
*)
   RET=0
     ;;
esac
# A 0 indicates success, return 1 for an error.
if [ $RET -eq 0 ]; then
```

```
  exit 0
else
  exit 1
fi
```

In our installation, we created a $GRID_HOME/hadaemon/ directory on all nodes in the cluster to save the Tomcat action script, tomcat.sh.

The next step is to ensure that the file is executable, which you can accomplish by running test to see whether the file works as expected. Once you are confident that the script is working, you can add the Tomcat resource.

The easiest way to configure the new resource is by creating a text file with the required attributes, as in this example:

```
[root@london1 hadaemon]# cat tomcat.profile
ACTION_SCRIPT=/u01/app/crs/hadaemon/tomcat.sh
PLACEMENT=restricted
HOSTING_MEMBERS=london1 london2
CHECK_INTERVAL=30
RESTART_ATTEMPTS=2
CHECK_INTERVAL=30
RESTART_ATTEMPTS=2
START_DEPENDENCIES=hard(httpd-vip)
STOP_DEPENDENCIES=hard(httpd-vip)
```

The following command registers the resource tomcat in Grid Infrastructure:

```
[root@london1 ~]# crsctl add resource tomcat -type cluster_resource -file tomcat.profile
```

Again, the profile registered matches what has been defined in the tomcat.profile file, plus the default values:

```
[root@london1 hadaemon]# crsctl status resource tomcat -p
NAME=tomcat
TYPE=cluster_resource
ACL=owner:root:rwx,pgrp:root:r-x,other::r--
ACTION_SCRIPT=/u01/app/crs/hadaemon/tomcat.sh
ACTIVE_PLACEMENT=0
AGENT_FILENAME=%CRS_HOME%/bin/scriptagent
AUTO_START=restore
CARDINALITY=1
CHECK_INTERVAL=30
DEFAULT_TEMPLATE=
DEGREE=1
DESCRIPTION=
ENABLED=1
FAILOVER_DELAY=0
FAILURE_INTERVAL=0
FAILURE_THRESHOLD=0
HOSTING_MEMBERS=london1 london2
LOAD=1
LOGGING_LEVEL=1
```

```
NOT_RESTARTING_TEMPLATE=
OFFLINE_CHECK_INTERVAL=0
PLACEMENT=restricted
PROFILE_CHANGE_TEMPLATE=
RESTART_ATTEMPTS=2
SCRIPT_TIMEOUT=60
SERVER_POOLS=
START_DEPENDENCIES=hard(httpd-vip)
START_TIMEOUT=0
STATE_CHANGE_TEMPLATE=
STOP_DEPENDENCIES=hard(httpd-vip)
STOP_TIMEOUT=0
UPTIME_THRESHOLD=1h
```

This example includes a hard dependency on the httpd-vip resource, which is started now. If you try to start the Tomcat resource, you will get the following error:

```
[root@london1 hadaemon]# crsctl start resource tomcat
CRS-2672: Attempting to start 'tomcat' on 'london1'
CRS-2674: Start of 'tomcat' on 'london1' failed
CRS-2527: Unable to start 'tomcat' because it has a 'hard' dependency
on 'httpd-vip'
CRS-2525: All instances of the resource 'httpd-vip' are already running;
relocate is not allowed because the force option was not specified
CRS-4000: Command Start failed, or completed with errors.
```

To get around this problem, you need begin by shutting down httpd-vip and then trying again:

```
[root@london1 hadaemon]# crsctl stop res httpd-vip
CRS-2673: Attempting to stop 'httpd-vip' on 'london1'
CRS-2677: Stop of 'httpd-vip' on 'london1' succeeded
[root@london1 hadaemon]# crsctl start res tomcat
CRS-2672: Attempting to start 'httpd-vip' on 'london1'
CRS-2676: Start of 'httpd-vip' on 'london1' succeeded
CRS-2672: Attempting to start 'tomcat' on 'london1'
CRS-2676: Start of 'tomcat' on 'london1' succeeded
```

The Tomcat servlet and JSP container is now highly available. However, please bear in mind that the session state of an application will not fail over to the passive node in the case of a node failure. The preceding example could be further enhanced by using a shared cluster logical ACFS volume to store the web applications used by Tomcat, as well as and the Tomcat binaries themselves.

Using Oracle Restart

Oracle Restart is a new feature in 11g Release 2. This feature could probably be best described as a single-instance version of the RAC command-line interface. To install Oracle Restart, you need to install Grid Infrastructure for a single node. Unlike clustered Grid Infrastructure, there is no prohibition against installing the software in the same Oracle base. Also, the administrator is free to install the software with different accounts for Grid Infrastructure and the database binaries. However, we've found that many administrators choose not do this, instead, they typically opt to use the oracle account to install both Oracle Restart and the database binaries.

ASM is only available as part of Grid Infrastructure. If you want to use it, then you must install Oracle Restart as well, in which case you might as well make most of it. From a database administrator's point of view, Oracle Restart is a blessing because it offers a single command-line interface into Oracle single-instance deployments and RAC. The automatic startup of resources registered with Oracle Restart solves a very old problem of having to provide startup scripts. This is a great advantage for companies running Oracle on many different hardware platforms. It is literally impossible to find a listener not started after a database server rebooted. Also, the administrator does not have to worry about the ASM instance or disk group not being mounted—this is also accomplished automatically.

After a fresh installation of Grid Infrastructure for a single server, you will find resources that are automatically managed by Oracle Restart. The resources managed by Oracle Restart after a fresh installation include the following:

- The CSS daemon
- The diskmon daemon
- Any ASM disk group(s)
- The listener
- The ASM instance

Identical to what you find in a full RAC installation, the aforementioned resources will automatically be protected from failure by the Grid Infrastructure software stack. In contrast to a RAC installation, Oracle Restart does not create resources for ONS and eONS daemons by default. If you would like to benefit from FAN events in an Oracle Restart environment, then you need to manually add and start these two processes, as in the following example:

```
[root@london1 ~]# srvctl add ons
[root@london1 ~]# srvctl start ons
[root@london1 ~]# srvctl add eons
[root@london1 ~]# srvctl start eons
```

Note that you can use server callouts the same way you do with RAC once the ONS/eONS processes are started (please refer to the "Defining Server-Side Callouts" section earlier in this chapter for more information about server callouts).

As with RAC, the Oracle High Availability Services daemon starts through the init process at system boot. And again, as with RAC, the OHAS daemon does not adhere to the standards of Red Hat's rc system in the 11.2.0.1 base release. This means that, even though a kill script is configured to stop OHASD in the relevant run level, the absence of a lock file in /var/lock/subsys/ means that the kill script is never invoked, which results in a database crash. The startup process from this point on differs from clustered Grid Infrastructure. For example, there are no cluster components started by CRSD (in fact there is no CRSD at all); instead, all you need to do is start ASM and the defined database resources, as well as any potentially registered services. In comparison with the clustered start sequence in RAC, you do not see a cssdmonitor process; rather, cssdagent will have to monitor ocssd.bin without the help of its clustered cousin. The OHAS daemon uses the OLR to read configuration information and resource dependencies; however, Oracle Restart does not use a GPnP profile.

All resources managed by Oracle Restart should preferably be controlled by the srvctl command-line tool. This ensures that the dependencies defined in the resource profile can be respected. This especially applies to the listener, database, and services. The main assistants—dbca, netca, and asmca—are Oracle Restart aware, and they will modify resource profiles. Any database created with dbca will automatically be registered in Oracle Restart, and it will have a dependency on the ASM disk group(s) it uses. With Oracle Restart, it is finally no longer necessary to modify the database service_name initialization parameter; indeed, it is actually no longer recommended. Instead, database services should be defined using the srvctl add service command. Neither should you use the deprecated CREATE_SERVICE in DBMS_SERVICE procedure.

You can query Oracle Restart meta-information much as you can with RAC. Many of the commands mentioned in the "Managing Oracle Clusterware" section can also be used for Oracle Restart. For example, the crsctl and srvctl command-line utilities support Oracle Restart with a non-clustered subset of their command-line arguments.

Troubleshooting Oracle Restart is almost identical to troubleshooting RAC; the daemons started in Oracle Restart use the same log file locations as their RAC counterparts. Thus, the primary location for troubleshooting log files is $GRID_HOME/log/hostname.

Troubleshooting

Troubleshooting is an art every database administrator should master. When working with Grid Infrastructure, administrators typically find themselves trying to troubleshoot startup and initialization issues.

Oracle provides a useful tool to collect troubleshooting information, called diagcollection.sh. It is located on all cluster nodes in $GRID_HOME/bin/diagcollection.sh. When called, this tool creates zip files that you can analyze yourself or attach to a service request.

Since Oracle 10.2, a central location is available for almost all log files related to the operation of Clusterware/Grid Infrastructure. This location is at $GRID_HOME/log/hostname. The alerthostname.log file is usually the first point of call in case of problems. SCAN listeners comprise one exception to this rule; their log files are stored in the ADR. The ADR_BASE for the SCAN listeners is either $GRID_HOME/log/ or $ORACLE_BASE/diag/.

The following sections provide more detail about ways to troubleshoot problems.

Resolving Startup Issues

Startup issues in RAC are usually caused by a change in the hardware setup and configuration, and they can sometimes be difficult to diagnose. For example, changes to routers and firewalls on the network layer can have a negative impact on the health of the cluster. Operating system upgrades should also not be underestimated. A simple upgrade of the running kernel can have devastating effects for a system using ASMLib if the system administrator forgets to install the matching kernel modules.

In our experience, the most common startup problem in Clusterware prior to version 11.2 issues concerned permissions on the raw (block) devices for the OCR and voting disk. Oracle 11.2 addresses this problem by storing OCR and voting disks in ASM. Should the cluster stack not start after a reboot or after stopping the cluster stack on a node, then there are a few locations to look for errors.

Oracle's cluster verification tool recommends the following settings for the OCR when block devices are used:

- *Owner*: the account under which Clusterware/Grid Infrastructure was installed

- *Group*: oinstall

- *Permissions*: 0640

Similarly, the following settings are expected for the voting files:

- Owner: the account under which Clusterware/Grid Infrastructure was installed

- Group: oinstall

- Permissions: 0640

How you should set the permissions and user/group attributes depends on how you defined the devices in the first place. That said, the most commonly used scripts to do this are udev or the /etc/rc.local scripts.

Clusters configured to use GNS will not start completely until communication with the DHCP and DNS servers is established.

A good first indication of the status of the cluster node is the output from the crsctl check crs command. Typically, you define your troubleshooting strategy based on its output. The following output shows what the command should return for a healthy cluster node:

```
[oracle@london1 ~]$ $GRID_HOME/crsctl check crs
CRS-4638: Oracle High Availability Services is online
CRS-4537: Cluster Ready Services is online
CRS-4529: Cluster Synchronization Services is online
CRS-4533: Event Manager is online
```

Several possible problems can be reported at this stage, including the following:

- *CRS-4639*: Could not contact Oracle High Availability Services

- *CRS-4535*: Cannot communicate with Cluster Ready Services

- *CRS-4530*: Communications failure contacting Cluster Synchronization Services daemon

- *CRS-4534*: Cannot communicate with Event Manager

Systematic troubleshooting of Grid Infrastructure follows a bottom-up approach because the resources have clearly defined dependencies (please refer to the "Startup Sequence" section for more information about the starting Grid Infrastructure in general). The generic troubleshooting document Oracle provides to resolve such issue is "My Oracle Support note 1050908.1 How to Troubleshoot Grid Infrastructure Startup Issues"; the following sections are loosely modeled on that support note.

Failing to Start OHAS

The first daemon to start in a Grid Infrastructure environment is OHAS. This process relies on the init process to invoke /etc/init.d/init.ohasd, which starts /etc/rc.d/init.d/ohasd, which in turn executes $GRID_HOME/ohasd.bin. Without a properly working ohasd.bin process, none of the other stack components will start. The entry in /etc/inittab defines that /etc/init.d/init.ohasd is started at runlevels 3 and 5. Runlevel 3 in Linux usually brings the system up in networked, multi-user mode; however, it doesn't start X11. Runlevel 5 is normally used for the same purpose, but it also starts the graphical user interface. If the system is at a runlevel other than 3 or 5, then ohasd.bin cannot be started, and you need to use a call to init to change the runlevel to either 3 or 5. You can check /var/log/messages for output from the scripts under /etc/rc.d/init.d/; ohasd.bin logs information into the default log file destination at $GRID_HOME/log/hostname in the ohasd/ohasd.log subdirectory.

The administrator has the option to disable the start of the High Availability Services stack by calling crsctl disable crs. This call updates a flag in /etc/oracle/scls_scr/hostname/root/ohasdstr. The file contains only one word, either enable or disable, and no carriage return. If set to disable, then /etc/rc.d/init.d/ohasd will not proceed with the startup. Call crsctl start crs to start the cluster stack manually in that case.

Many Grid Infrastructure background processes rely on sockets created in /var/tmp/.oracle. You can check which socket is used by a process by listing the contents of the /proc/pid/fd directory, where *pid* is the process id of the program you are looking at. In some cases, permissions on the sockets can become garbled; in our experience, moving the .oracle directory to a safe location and rebooting solved the cluster communication problems.

Another reason ohasd.bin might fail to start: the file system for $GRID_HOME could be either corrupt or otherwise not mounted. Earlier, it was noted that ohasd.bin lives in $GRID_HOME/bin. If $GRID_HOME isn't mounted, then it is not possible to start the daemon.

We introduced the OLR as an essential file for starting Grid Infrastructure. If the OLR has become corrupt or is otherwise not accessible, then ohasd.bin cannot start. Successful initialization of the OLR is recorded in the ohasd.log, as in the following example (the timestamps have been removed for the sake of clarity):

```
[ default][3046704848] OHASD Daemon Starting. Command string :reboot
[ default][3046704848] Initializing OLR
[  OCRRAW][3046704848]proprioo: for disk 0
 (/u01/app/crs/cdata/london1.olr),
 id match (1), total id sets, (1) need recover (0), my votes (0),
 total votes (0), commit_lsn (15), lsn (15)
[  OCRRAW][3046704848]proprioo: my id set: (2018565920, 1028247821, 0, 0, 0)
[  OCRRAW][3046704848]proprioo: 1st set: (2018565920, 1028247821, 0, 0, 0)
[  OCRRAW][3046704848]proprioo: 2nd set: (0, 0, 0, 0, 0)
[  CRSOCR][3046704848] OCR context init CACHE Level: 0xaa4cfe0
[ default][3046704848] OHASD running as the Privileged user
```

Interestingly, the errors pertaining to the local registry have the same numbers as those for the OCR; however, they have been prefixed by PROCL. The *L* can easily be missed, so check carefully! If the OLR cannot be read, then you will see the error messages immediately under the Initializing OLR line. This chapter has covered two causes so far: the OLR is missing or the OLR is corrupt. The first case is much easier to diagnose because, in that case, OHAS will not start:

```
[root@london1 ~]# crsctl check crs
CRS-4639: Could not contact Oracle High Availability Services
```

In the preceding example, ohasd.log will contain an error message similar to this one:

```
[ default][1381425744] OHASD Daemon Starting. Command string :restart
[ default][1381425744] Initializing OLR
[  OCROSD][1381425744]utopen:6m':failed in stat OCR file/disk
 /u01/app/crs/cdata/london1.olr,
 errno=2, os err string=No such file or directory
[  OCROSD][1381425744]utopen:7:failed to open any OCR file/disk, errno=2,
 os err string=No such file or directory
[  OCRRAW][1381425744]proprinit: Could not open raw device
[  OCRAPI][1381425744]a_init:16!: Backend init unsuccessful : [26]
[  CRSOCR][1381425744] OCR context init failure.  Error: PROCL-26: Error
 while accessing the physical storage Operating System
error [No such file or directory] [2]
```

```
[ default][1381425744] OLR initalization failured, rc=26
[ default][1381425744]Created alert : (:OHAS00106:) :  Failed to initialize
Oracle Local Registry
[ default][1381425744][PANIC] OHASD exiting; Could not init OLR
```

In this case, you should restore the OLR, which you will learn how to do in the "Maintaining Voting Disk and OCR/OLR" section.

If the OLR is corrupted, then you will slightly different errors. OHAS tries to read the OLR; while it succeeds for some keys, it fails for some others. Long hex dumps will appear in the ohasd.log, indicating a problem. You should perform an ocrcheck -local in this case, which can help you determine the root cause. The following output has been taken from a system where the OLR was corrupt:

```
[root@london1 ohasd]# ocrcheck -local
Status of Oracle Local Registry is as follows :
     Version                  :        3
     Total space (kbytes)     :    262120
     Used space (kbytes)      :      2232
     Available space (kbytes) :    259888
     ID                       : 1022831156
     Device/File Name         : /u01/app/crs/cdata/london1.olr
                                Device/File integrity check failed

Local registry integrity check failed

Logical corruption check bypassed
```

If the utility confirms that the OLR is corrupted, then you have no option but to restore it. Again, please refer to the "Maintaining Voting Disk and OCR/OLR" section for more information on how to do this.

Failing to Start Agents Created by OHAS

With ohasd.bin confirmed to be started and alive, you can proceed with checking the agents spawned by ohasd.bin, namely CSSDAGENT, CSSDMONITOR, ORAAGENT, and ORAAGENT_ROOT. We, the authors, have not encountered any problems with these agents yet; however, the generic piece of advice is to check file system permissions and the agent log files for clues. Do not confuse these agents with the ones created at a later stage by CRS. The log files are in $GRID_HOME/log/hostname/agent/ohasd/agentname. Note that the Oracle documentation and My Oracle Support do not take into account the fact that Grid Infrastructure can be installed with an account other than the oracle account. On systems where the grid user owns the software stack, you will find the following agent log directories in $GRID_HOME/log/hostname/agent/ohasd:

- oraagent_grid/

- oracssdagent_root/

- oracssdmonitor_root/

- orarootagent_root/

Failing to Start the Cluster Synchronization Services Daemon

The ocssd.bin process is spawned by the cssdagent process. You can check the agent's log file for any potential issues in $GRID_HOME/log/hostname/ohasd/oracssdagent_root. Once the initialization of the ocssd.bin process has started, you need to check its own log file, which is recorded in $GRID_HOME/log/hostname/cssd/ocssd.log. The log file is very verbose, so you should try to find the last occurrence of the following line after the initialization code:

```
[    CSSD][3412950784]clssscmain: Starting CSS daemon, version 11.2.xxx, in
(clustered) mode with uniqueness value xxx
```

Also note that occsd.bin will be started as often as defined in the resource profile's restart attempts. Successful initialization of the CSS daemon depends on the GPnP profile, the discovery and accessibility of the voting disks, and a functional network.

The GPnP profile is queried using interprocess communication IPC, as shown in this excerpt of the ocssd.log file (line breaks have been introduced for readability):

```
2010-06-25 09:43:19.843: [    GPnP][3941465856]clsgpnpm_exchange:
 [at clsgpnpm.c:1175] Calling "ipc://GPNPD_london1", try 4 of 500...
2010-06-25 09:43:19.853: [    GPnP][3941465856]clsgpnp_profileVerifyForCall:
 [at clsgpnp.c:1867] Result: (87) CLSGPNP_SIG_VALPEER. Profile verified.
prf=0x113478c0
2010-06-25 09:43:19.853: [    GPnP][3941465856]clsgpnp_profileGetSequenceRef:
 [at clsgpnp.c:841] Result: (0) CLSGPNP_OK. seq of p=0x113478c0 is '7'=7
2010-06-25 09:43:19.853: [    GPnP][3941465856]clsgpnp_profileCallUrlInt:
 [at clsgpnp.c:2186] Result: (0) CLSGPNP_OK. Successful get-profile CALL to
remote "ipc://GPNPD_london1" disco ""
2010-06-25 09:43:19.853: [    GPnP][3941465856]clsgpnp_getProfileEx:
 [at clsgpnp.c:540] Result: (0) CLSGPNP_OK. got profile 0x113478c0
```

This time it took four attempts to get the profile when CSSD started. In this case, the listening endpoint was probably not in place. If you get error messages indicating the call to clsgpnp_getProfile failed, you should check whether the GPnP daemon is up and running. You might see something similar to the following error message:

```
2010-06-25 10:25:17.057: [ GPnP][7256921234]clsgpnp_getProfileEx:
[at clsgpnp.c:546] Result:
(13) CLSGPNP_NO_DAEMON. Can't get GPnP service profile from local GPnP daemon
2010-06-25 10:25:17.057: [ default][7256921234]Cannot get GPnP profile. Error
CLSGPNP_NO_DAEMON (GPNPD daemon is not running).
2010-06-25 10:25:17.057: [ CSSD][7256921234]clsgpnp_getProfile failed, rc(13)
```

CSSD will abort if ocssd.bin cannot find a voting disk, if it is not accessible because of wrong file permissions, as well as for a handful of other reasons. If the voting disks are in ASM, then you will see the following messages in the log file, indicating successful detection of the disks:

```
2010-06-23 16:47:49.651: [    CLSF][1158797632]Opened hdl:0x32d5770 for
 dev:ORCL:OCRVOTE1:
2010-06-23 16:47:49.661: [    CSSD][1158797632]clssnmvDiskVerify: Successful discovery
for disk ORCL:OCRVOTE1, UID 84b990fb-73234f2b-bf82b7ae-c4d2e0a2,
Pending CIN 0:1276871678:0, Committed CIN 0:1276871678:0
```

```
2010-06-23 16:47:49.661: [    CLSF][1158797632]Closing handle:0x32d5770
2010-06-23 16:47:49.661: [   SKGFD][1158797632]Lib
:ASM:/opt/oracle/extapi/64/asm/orcl/1/libasm.so: closing handle 0x3280cc0
for disk :ORCL:OCRVOTE1:
2010-06-23 16:47:49.661: [    CSSD][1158797632]clssnmvDiskVerify: discovered a
potential voting file
```

If errors occur, then you will probably see the following string in the ocssd.log file:

```
2010-06-23 16:47:49.703: [    CSSD][1158797632]clssnmvDiskVerify: Successful discovery
of 0 disks
```

You will also see that the GPnP profile's discovery string has been used to scan available locations for voting files. If all possible options for the voting disk location have been exhausted and no disks were found, then CSSD will stop. You should check whether the file system permissions on the voting disks are correct if they are outside of ASM; this will solve this problem in the majority of cases.

The ocssd.bin daemon requires gipcd to be up and running for intercluster communication. The gipcd process in turn requires a working network. If that network is not started, then the gipcd process will bail out at this point. The failure message will look something like this: clssscmain: failed to open gipc endp. The cluvfy command-line utility can be used to verify whether the network is working.

Failing to Start the Cluster Ready Services Daemon

The node cannot join the cluster until the CRS daemon has successfully started. Therefore, CRSD is a milestone in the startup process. As noted earlier in this chapter's "Initiating the Startup Sequence" section, CRSD will create a new set of ORAAGENT and ORAROOTAGENT processes to create the virtual network resources, as well as to start the database and its associated services. The main log file for CRSD is found in the $GRID_HOME/log/*hostname*/crsd directory.

The successful start of CRSD depends on the discovery of the OCR and a fully functional CSS daemon. It also requires access to the GPnP profile (as discussed in the preceding section).

As with CSSD, a functional network and GIPC daemon are required for crsd.bin to work properly. If ocssd.bin has not been created, then the log file will show this as in the following example:

```
2010-04-30 10:34:01.183: [ CRSMAIN][3257705040] Checking the OCR device
2010-04-30 10:34:01.183: [ CRSMAIN][3257705040] Connecting to the CSS Daemon
2010-04-30 10:34:01.184: [ CSSCLNT][1111550272]clssnsquerymode: not connected to CSSD
2010-04-30 10:34:01.204: [ CSSCLNT][3257705040]clssscConnect: gipc request failed with 29
     (0x16)
2010-04-30 10:34:01.204: [ CSSCLNT][3257705040]clsssInitNative: connect failed, rc 29
2010-04-30 10:34:01.204: [  CRSRTI][3257705040] CSS is not ready. Received status 3 from CSS.
Waiting for good status ..
```

Problems related to file-system permissions should not happen with the OCR stored inside ASM; the user simply has no influence on these. If the OCR is stored outside ASM, then the permissions should be 0640, and the file should be owned by root, and the group should be oinstall. Whenever something goes wrong with the OCR, the system will return the PROT-26 error, which indicates an unsuccessful backend initialization. The error messages reported here are similar to the OLR error messages discussed previously in the "Failing to Start OHAS" section; however, this time the prefix *L* (as in PROTL) is missing. If the OCR is lost completely, then you will see the following error messages in the crsd.log file:

```
2010-06-30 22:13:40.251: [  CRSOCR][968725072] OCR context init failure.  Error:
  PROC-26: Error while accessing the physical storage ASM error
[SLOS: cat=8, o
pn=kgfoOpenFile01, dep=15056, loc=kgfokge
ORA-17503: ksfdopn:DGOpenFile05 Failed to open file +OCRVOTE.255.4294967295
ORA-17503: ksfdopn:2 Failed to open file +OCRVOTE.255.4294967295
ORA-15001: diskgrou
] [8]
2010-06-30 22:13:40.251: [    CRSD][968725072][PANIC] CRSD exiting: Could not init
 OCR, code: 26
2010-06-30 22:13:40.251: [    CRSD][968725072] Done.
```

In this preceding example, the PROC-26 error will be reported.

Failing to Start the GPnP Daemon

The Grid Plug and Play Daemon plays a central role in the startup process. If name resolution is not working, the daemon won't start. That poses severe problems, especially for systems using GNS, because CSSD and CRSD also will not start.
You can use the nslookup or host command line utilities to troubleshoot DNS setup. If you're using a dedicated name server separate from your corporate DNS server, you can issue the nslookup command as in the following example:

```
[oracle@london1 ~]$ nslookup - dnsServerName
```

This command enables the interactive mode of the nslookup utility. You can then interrogate the name server given on the command line by issuing the host hostname command in interactive mode. You can type exit at any time to leave the utility. If name resolution fails for a given host, then check with your networking team for help in resolving the problem.

Agents spawned by CRSD

Agents started by CRSD include ORAAGENT and ORAROOTAGENT. Note that these agents are different from the ones we discussed earlier in the chapter under the "Failing to Start OHAS" section. Depending on whether you chose to use a different operating system account to install Grid Infrastructure, then you may find two ORAAGENTS: one created by the Grid Infrastructure owner, and the other owned by the owner of the RDBMS binaries.
Failure to start these agents is rare, and you should consult the log files. The log files locations are all relative to $GRID_HOME/log/hostname/:

- ./agent/crsd/oraagent_grid/oraagent_grid.log

- ./agent/crsd/oraagent_oracle/oraagent_oracle.log

- ./agent/crsd/orarootagent_root/orarootagent_root.log

The authors have seen very few problems in this stage of the startup sequence, and most of these could be solved by checking the daemon log files. If the preceding does not help, then checking the started resource's log file(s) usually reveals the source of the problem.

> ■ **Note** Two components listed in the output of `crsctl status resource` are different from the ones mentioned in the preceding section. The `ora.gsd` resource is OFFLINE because it provides backward compatibility with Oracle 9*i*. We cannot imagine a case where 9*i* and 11.2 databases would coexist in the same cluster. The other resource that is always offline at the time of this writing is `ora.oc4j`. This resource is part of a new feature called Database Workload Management, and it has not yet been implemented.

Resolving Problems with Java Utilities

When troubleshooting problems, it might be necessary to enable additional output. Some command-line tools support tracing and debugging output. To enable additional output, set the SRVM_TRACE environment variable to `true`, as in the following example:

```
[oracle@london1 ~]$ export SRVM_TRACE=true
```

To disable tracing, use the built-in bash, unset SRVM_TRACE. A search in the $GRID_HOME/bin directory shows that several important utilities support additional trace information, including the following:

- `cluvfy`
- `netca`
- `srvctl`
- `srvconfig`

Even if it is impossible to get the meaning of the trace onscreen, this is always helpful information that can be sent to Oracle Support to speed up problem resolution.

Patching Grid Infrastructure

Applying one-off patches to Grid Infrastructure homes is a little different than patching an RDBMS home. The files in $GRID_HOME are protected with special permissions; if you try to apply a patch as the owner of the binaries, then you will be surprised to find that opatch fails with error code 73. Therefore, you need to follow this sequence of steps to perform a rolling patch:

1. Stop any resources started from the RDBMS home(s) on the local node to be patched. These resources might include the database and other services that can be stopped either by the Grid software owner or the RDBMS software owner in homogenous 11.2-only deployments. In heterogeneous deployments, the pre-11.2 database resources have to be stopped as the RDBMS owner.

2. Unlock the Grid Infrastructure home as root on the local node.

3. Apply the rolling patch as the Grid software owner. Do *not* roll the patch over to the other node yet! Sometimes, it might be necessary to specify the -local

flag; however, that depends on the patch. The PSU 11.2.0.1.1 for Grid Infrastructure required the local patching mode.

4. Lock the local Grid Infrastructure software home as root. This will bring the cluster stack back up.

5. Restart the resources that were running from the local RDBMS home(s).

6. Connect to the next node and repeat steps 1-5; i.e., stop the RDBMS resources and unlock the Grid Infrastructure home for each node.

7. When Grid Infrastructure has been unlocked on all nodes—and not before then—answer Y to the question that asks whether the next node is ready for patching.

8. Lock the Grid Infrastructure home and start all services of the patched node.

9. Repeat until all nodes are done.

This preceding sequence also applies for single-instance Oracle Restart deployments, although the commands you need to execute are slightly different. And you don't get a rolling patch, either. An example session demonstrates the application of the following patch: 8898852 "DATAFILE CORRUPTION WHEN FILE CREATED WITH COMPATIBLE.ASM LESS THAN 11 RESIZED."

The patch addresses a serious problem that occurs when a datafile created with a pre-11.2 ASM instance could become corrupted during a resize operation after its compatibility level was raised to 11.2. The example assumes that the patch is extracted to /mnt/db11.2/patches, a central patch repository.

The readme document supplied with the patch recommends checking that the version of $ORACLE_HOME/bin/perl/bin is greater than perl 5.00503. Oracle 11.2 is shipped with perl 5.10x, so this should not be a problem. Use this command to verify your version of perl is recent enough:

```
[oracle@london1 ~]$ $ORACLE_HOME/perl/bin/perl -v
```

On the authors' system, the preceding command returned the following:

```
This is perl, v5.10.0 built for x86_64-linux-thread-multi

Copyright 1987-2007, Larry Wall
...
```

It is always a good idea to check for inventory corruption before applying a patch. Oracle RAC maintains two inventories: a local one and a global one. Do not proceed with the application of the patch if your inventory is in any way corrupted! To check your inventory, use the lsinventory option with opatch and ensure that the last line of the command output reads "OPatch succeeded." Next, invoke opatch with the lsinventory -detail option against all installed Oracle homes. You can use the -oh argument to supply an Oracle home, as in the following example:

```
[~]$ $ORACLE_HOME/OPatch/opatch lsinventory -detail -oh $ORACLE_HOME
```

If all is well, proceed to patch the installation. In the first step, you record the status of the resources started from the RDBMS home(s) for later use. In this example, there is only one Oracle home; if there were more than one, then you'd need to invoke this command for all RDBMS homes:

```
[oracle@london1:]$ srvctl stop home -o $ORACLE_HOME -s /tmp/statusRDBMS -n london1
```

The state file in /tmp/statusRDBMS records all the resources executing out of $ORACLE_HOME. Later, you will see that its counterpart uses the same file to start the resources (you'll learn more about this later).

Next, you need to login as root to prepare for the process of stopping the local cluster stack. Export GRID_HOME to your Grid Infrastructure home, change the directory to $GRID_HOME/crs/install, and then invoke rootcrs.pl, as in the following example:

```
[root@london1 install]# ./rootcrs.pl -unlock -crshome $GRID_HOME
```

The output of the rootcrs.pl script is very similar to the output of the crsctl stop crs command; however, this script also changes permissions on the files in $GRID_HOME, so opatch can apply the patch. Consider the following output, which has been shortened for clarity:

```
2010-06-23 16:34:11: Parsing the host name
2010-06-23 16:34:11: Checking for super user privileges
2010-06-23 16:34:11: User has super user privileges
Using configuration parameter file: ./crsconfig_params
CRS-2791: Starting shutdown of Oracle High Availability Services-managed resources on
'london1'
CRS-2673: Attempting to stop 'ora.crsd' on 'london1'
...
CRS-2790: Starting shutdown of Cluster Ready Services-managed resources on 'london1'
...
CRS-2792: Shutdown of Cluster Ready Services-managed resources on 'london1' has completed
CRS-2793: Shutdown of Oracle High Availability Services-managed resources on 'london1' has
completed
CRS-4133: Oracle High Availability Services has been stopped.
Successfully unlock /u01/app/crs
```

Successfully unlocking $GRID_HOME prompts the beginning of the next stage. Now switch the user to the grid owner and apply the patch:

```
[oracle@london1 8898852]$ /u01/app/crs/OPatch/opatch apply
Invoking OPatch 11.2.0.1.2
Oracle Interim Patch Installer version 11.2.0.1.2
Copyright (c) 2010, Oracle Corporation.  All rights reserved.
Oracle Home       : /u01/app/crs
Central Inventory : /u01/app/oraInventory
   from           : /etc/oraInst.loc
OPatch version    : 11.2.0.1.2
...
OPatch detected the node list and the local node from the inventory.  OPatch will patch the
local system
then propagate the patch to the remote nodes.
This node is part of an Oracle Real Application Cluster.
Remote nodes: 'london2'
Local node: 'london1'
...
Please shutdown Oracle instances running out of this ORACLE_HOME on the local system.
(Oracle Home = '/u01/app/crs')
```

Is the node ready for patching [y/n]: y
...
The local system has been patched. You can restart Oracle instances on it.
Patching in rolling mode.
The node 'london2' will be patched next.
Please shutdown Oracle instances running out of this ORACLE_HOME on 'london2'.
(Oracle Home = '/u01/app/crs')
Is the node ready for patching? [y|n]

■ **Note** If you have not updated the base release's opatch to version 11.2, then you should do so before applying the first patch! Almost all patches released on My Oracle Support now require opatch 11.2.

At this point, it is critical that you stop do *not* continue further. Remember: Only the local node has been prepared for patching, so $GRID_HOME is still locked. Also, do not close the terminal session. To make this a rolling patch, you need to start the local resources before taking the remote node's resources down. Now log in as root again and patch $GRID_HOME:

```
[root@london1 ~]# cd $GRID_HOME/crs/install/
[root@london1 install]# ./rootcrs.pl -patch
2010-06-23 16:47:09: Parsing the host name
2010-06-23 16:47:09: Checking for super user privileges
2010-06-23 16:47:09: User has super user privileges
Using configuration parameter file: ./crsconfig_params
CRS-4123: Oracle High Availability Services has been started.
```

Wait a short while, check the cluster state (crsctl check crs), and then proceed when the software stack is up again. At this point, you are ready to start the RDBMS resources. The previously created state file plays a major role in this. Now log in as the RDBMS software owner again and start the resources with the following snippet:

```
[oracle@london1 ~]$ $ORACLE_HOME/bin/srvctl start home -o $ORACLE_HOME \
> -s /tmp/statusRDBMS -n london1
```

After all local resources are back up and running, you can shut down the resources on the remote node, london2. The sequence of commands to accomplish this is very similar to the sequence you used to patch the first node:

1. As the RDBMS owner, stop all resources from all RDBMS homes in use. Do so using this command: srvctl stop home. Be sure to pass the correct node name!

2. As root, execute rootcrs.pl -unlock -crshome $GRID_HOME.

3. Now answer Y to the question in london1's terminal session that asks whether the remote node is ready for patching. Again, don't continue with the next node yet.

4. After a successful patch application, lock $GRID_HOME again by invoking rootcrs.pl with the -patch option as root.

5. As the RDBMS user, start all the resources recorded in the state file using srvctl start home. Again, please ensure that you pass the correct hostname to srvctl.

6. Repeat steps 1-5 with any remaining nodes until all nodes are patched.

When all the nodes are patched, you should again verify the state of the inventory for the Grid software home by invoking $ORACLE_HOME/OPatch/opatch lsinventory -detail. In this example, the following result indicates a successful application of the one-off patch:

```
[oracle@london1 ~]$ /u01/app/crs/OPatch/opatch lsinventory
Invoking OPatch 11.2.0.1.2
...
Oracle Home        : /u01/app/crs
...
--------------------------------------------------------------------------------
Installed Top-level Products (1):
Oracle Grid Infrastructure                                          11.2.0.1.0
There are 1 products installed in this Oracle Home.
Interim patches (1) :
Patch  8898852      : applied on Wed Jun 23 16:41:01 BST 2010
Unique Patch ID:  11998663
   Created on 3 Dec 2009, 01:58:47 hrs PST8PDT
   Bugs fixed:
      8898852
Rac system comprising of multiple nodes
   Local node = london1
   Remote node = london2
--------------------------------------------------------------------------------
OPatch succeeded.
```

Adding and Deleting Nodes

Adding and deleting nodes from a cluster is one of the features that make RAC stand out from its competition. Nodes can be added to and removed from the cluster while all resources on the initial set of nodes are still up and running.

Adding Nodes

This special type of node maintenance is always performed in two steps:

1. The node is added to/removed from the Grid Infrastructure layer. All commands are to be executed as the Grid software owner (grid/oracle) or as root where specifically prompted.

2. The instance is added or removed from the cluster database. These steps must be performed by the owner of the RDBMS binaries, which is usually oracle.

When adding nodes into the cluster, it is imperative to ensure that all cluster nodes are properly cabled, the operating system is installed and patched, and that all user IDs across the cluster have the same value. Additionally, you need to ensure user equivalence for the Grid Infrastructure software owner and the RDBMS software owner across all nodes in the cluster. If you are using ASMLib, you should ensure that the driver is loaded and that all disks are discovered on the new nodes.

Note that the steps are slightly different depending on whether you decided to use a GNS setup or a more conventional configuration. In any case, you should run the cluster verification tool to ensure the cluster is ready for the node addition or deletion.

Oracle has made cluster maintenance a high priority in Oracle 11g Release 2. GNS enables dynamic provisioning of IP addresses for use as virtual IP addresses and SCAN VIPs. GNS is attractive when corporate DNS cannot easily be changed, or when administrators wish to assume more responsibility for their software stack. Without GNS, node additions require changes to the corporate DNS servers, and such changes can sometimes be difficult because of separate management chains in the organization.

Checking the Prerequisites

Before proceeding with the next set of steps, please ensure that the new node(s) to be added meet the stated requirements by running the cluster verification utility from one of the existing nodes of the cluster. The following example assumes that the cluster currently consists of nodes london1, london2, and london3; and that you want to extend the cluster by another node, london4. The following example also assumes that the Grid Infrastructure software stack is owned by the oracle user:

```
[oracle@london1]$ $ORACLE_HOME/bin/cluvfy stage -post hwos -n london4 -verbose
```

Again, it is good practice to keep the output of this command with the installation or maintenance documentation. The preceding command checks whether the operating system requirements on the new node to be added (london4) are fulfilled. We recommend running cluvfy one more time. This time, you're using it to check whether the steps before the node addition have been completed:

```
[oracle@london1 ~]$ cluvfy stage -pre nodeadd -n london4  -fixup -fixupdir /tmp
```

If any problems are reported on the london4 server, then you should run the generated fixup script as root. The exact path to the script will be printed by the cluvfy utility:

```
Fixup information has been generated for following node(s):
London4
Please run the following script on each node as "root" user to execute the fixups:
'/tmp/CVU_11.2.0.1.0_oracle/runfixup.sh'
```

Using the fixup scripts is a very convenient way to quickly fix the kernel parameters required for Grid Infrastructure to work. When this task has completed successfully, and the command output has been stored safely for later reference; then you are ready to begin the node addition. The actual node addition has always been performed using the $GRID_HOME/oui/bin/addNode.sh script.

Executing the addNode.sh Script

In previous versions of Oracle, the addNode.sh launched a graphical user interface, using a slightly modified Oracle Universal Installer. The administrator used this tool to specify the new public, private, and virtual IP addresses for the node(s) to be added, and OUI would finish the rest with the familiar interface. After the OUI completed the remote operations, it prompted the administrator to run a number of scripts as root. Oracle 11.2 has changed how this procedure works. The new addNode.sh script is headless; that is, it doesn't use a graphical interface. Thus, it resembles the pre-11.2 addNode.sh script when invoked with the silent option. The options to be passed to the addNode.sh script depend on whether GNS is in use in the cluster.

The Oracle Grid Infrastructure documentation states that executing the following command on one of the existing nodes in $GRID_HOME/oui/bin was enough to add a node to a cluster with GNS enabled:

```
[oracle@london1 bin]$ ./addNode.sh -silent "CLUSTER_NEW_NODES={newNodePublicIP}"
```

In the field, this proved to be untrue for the base release, 11.2.0.1.0. Bug 8865943 was filed against the problem, and a fix is expected. The preceding script consistently returned the following error:

```
SEVERE:Number of new nodes being added are not equal to number of new virtual nodes.
Silent install cannot continue.
```

Using the syntax you would use for a non-GNS setup works equally for GNS-enabled systems as a workaround to the aforementioned bug:

```
[oracle@london1 bin] $ ./addNode.sh -silent "CLUSTER_NEW_NODES={london4}" \
> "CLUSTER_NEW_VIRTUAL_HOSTNAMES={london4-vip}"
```

The output from this command will look something like the following:

```
Starting Oracle Universal Installer...

Checking swap space: must be greater than 500 MB.   Actual 3699 MB     Passed
Oracle Universal Installer, Version 11.2.0.1.0 Production
Copyright (C) 1999, 2009, Oracle. All rights reserved.
Performing tests to see whether nodes london2,london3,london4 are available
............................................................ 100% Done.
...
--------------------------------------------------------------------------------
Cluster Node Addition Summary
Global Settings
    Source: /u01/app/crs
    New Nodes
Space Requirements
    New Nodes
        london4
            /: Required 3.28GB : Available 48.00GB
Installed Products
    Product Names
        Oracle Grid Infrastructure 11.2.0.1.0
        Sun JDK 1.5.0.17.0
        ...
        Oracle Database 11g 11.2.0.1.0
--------------------------------------------------------------------------------

Instantiating scripts for add node (Friday, November 6, 2009 9:14:02 PM GMT)
.                                                           1% Done.
```

```
Instantiation of add node scripts complete
Copying to remote nodes (Friday, November 6, 2009 9:14:08 PM GMT)
..........................................................
..............                                96% Done.
Home copied to new nodes
Saving inventory on nodes (Friday, November 6, 2009 9:34:52 PM GMT)
.                                               100% Done.
Save inventory complete
WARNING:A new inventory has been created on one or more nodes in this session.
However, it has not yet been registered as the central inventory of this
system. To register the new inventory please run the script at
'/u01/app/oraInventory/orainstRoot.sh' with root privileges on nodes 'london4'.
If you do not register the inventory, you may not be able to update or patch
the products you installed.
The following configuration scripts need to be executed as the "root" user
in each cluster node.

/u01/app/oraInventory/orainstRoot.sh #On nodes london4
/u01/app/crs/root.sh #On nodes london4
To execute the configuration scripts:
    1. Open a terminal window
    2. Log in as "root"
    3. Run the scripts in each cluster node

The Cluster Node Addition of /u01/app/crs was successful.
Please check '/tmp/silentInstall.log' for more details.
```

Finishing the Node Addition

The output of the addNode.sh script indicates that two more scripts need to be run: orainstRoot.sh and then root.sh. The execution of the orainstRoot.sh script is not very remarkable because it only changes the permissions on the Oracle Inventory. The root.sh script performs the actual node addition, and its output is similar to the root.sh script you ran during the Clusterware installation.

Executing the aforementioned scripts on the new London4 node will show output like the following:

```
[root@london4 ~]# /u01/app/oraInventory/orainstRoot.sh
Creating the Oracle inventory pointer file (/etc/oraInst.loc)
Changing permissions of /u01/app/oraInventory.
Adding read,write permissions for group.
Removing read,write,execute permissions for world.
Changing groupname of /u01/app/oraInventory to oinstall.
The execution of the script is complete.
```

The real action takes place in the root.sh script, which must also be executed on the new node:

```
[root@london4 ~]# /u01/app/crs/root.sh
Running Oracle 11g root.sh script...
The following environment variables are set as:
    ORACLE_OWNER= oracle
    ORACLE_HOME= /u01/app/crs
```

Enter the full pathname of the local bin directory: [/usr/local/bin]:
The file "dbhome" already exists in /usr/local/bin. Overwrite it? (y/n)
[n]:
The file "oraenv" already exists in /usr/local/bin. Overwrite it? (y/n)
[n]:
The file "coraenv" already exists in /usr/local/bin. Overwrite it? (y/n)
[n]:
Creating /etc/oratab file...
Entries will be added to the /etc/oratab file as needed by
Database Configuration Assistant when a database is created
Finished running generic part of root.sh script.
Now product-specific root actions will be performed.
2009-11-06 21:41:31: Parsing the host name
2009-11-06 21:41:31: Checking for super user privileges
2009-11-06 21:41:31: User has super user privileges
Using configuration parameter file:
/u01/app/crs/crs/install/crsconfig_params
Creating trace directory
LOCAL ADD MODE
Creating OCR keys for user 'root', privgrp 'root'..
Operation successful.
Adding daemon to inittab
CRS-4123: Oracle High Availability Services has been started.
ohasd is starting
CRS-4402: The CSS daemon was started in exclusive mode but found an
active CSS daemon on node london1, number 1, and is terminating
An active cluster was found during exclusive startup, restarting to
join the cluster
CRS-2672: Attempting to start 'ora.mdnsd' on 'london4'
CRS-2676: Start of 'ora.mdnsd' on 'london4' succeeded
[some output has been removed for clarity]
CRS-2672: Attempting to start 'ora.asm' on 'london4'
CRS-2676: Start of 'ora.asm' on 'london4' succeeded
CRS-2672: Attempting to start 'ora.crsd' on 'london4'
CRS-2676: Start of 'ora.crsd' on 'london4' succeeded
CRS-2672: Attempting to start 'ora.evmd' on 'london4'
CRS-2676: Start of 'ora.evmd' on 'london4' succeeded
clscfg: EXISTING configuration version 5 detected.
clscfg: version 5 is 11g Release 2.
Successfully accumulated necessary OCR keys.
Creating OCR keys for user 'root', privgrp 'root'..
Operation successful.
london4   2009/11/06 21:46:12   /u01/app/crs/cdata/london4/backup_20091106_214612.olr
Preparing packages for installation...
cvuqdisk-1.0.7-1
Configure Oracle Grid Infrastructure for a Cluster ... succeeded
Updating inventory properties for clusterware
Starting Oracle Universal Installer...
Checking swap space: must be greater than 500 MB.   Actual 4095 MB   Passed
The inventory pointer is located at /etc/oraInst.loc

The inventory is located at /u01/app/oraInventory
'UpdateNodeList' was successful.

The important information here is recorded in the detection of an existing configuration, the addition of the necessary keys in the OCR, the creation of the ASM instance, and finally, the confirmation that the configuration of Grid Infrastructure for a cluster succeeded. The main part of the output is similar to the output of the crsctl start cluster command. The root.sh script automatically creates a backup of the OLR, but not of the OCR.

You can find more troubleshooting information in the $GRID_HOME/cfgtoollogs/crsconfig directory. With Grid Infrastructure, you no longer needed to execute root.sh with the -x switch to enable debugging output; the log files in the just mentioned directory are much more useful than anything that was available before.

The Oracle Universal Installer is invoked once more at the end of the root.sh script to update the central inventory. The installer adds the new node to the list of nodes in the inventory.xml file, which is shown in bold in the following example:

```
<HOME NAME="Ora11g_gridinfrahome1" LOC="/u01/app/crs"
 TYPE="O" IDX="1" CRS="true">
   <NODE_LIST>
      <NODE NAME="london1"/>
      <NODE NAME="london2"/>
      <NODE NAME="london3"/>
      <NODE NAME="london4"/>
   </NODE_LIST>
</HOME>
```

After the root.sh script finishes executing, /etc/oratab is updated with the necessary information for the n-th ASM instance. It is good practice to run a last cluvfy check from one of the initial nodes with the following arguments.

```
[oracle@london1 bin] ./cluvfy stage -post nodeadd -n london4
```

And with that, you've successfully completed adding a node to your Grid Infrastructure.

Adding the RDBMS Software

Next, you need to add the RDBMS home. This process is similar to the process for adding a node because it also uses the now headless addNode.sh script from $ORACLE_HOME/oui/bin. Remaining in the previous example, execute addNode.sh from one of the existing nodes, as shown in the following snippet:

```
[oracle@london1 bin]$ cd $ORACLE_HOME/oui/bin
[oracle@london1 bin]$ ./addNode.sh -silent "CLUSTER_NEW_NODES={london4}"
```

The output from this command will look something like the following:

```
Starting Oracle Universal Installer…
Checking swap space: must be greater than 500 MB.   Actual 3622 MB     Passed
Oracle Universal Installer, Version 11.2.0.1.0 Production
Copyright (C) 1999, 2009, Oracle. All rights reserved.
```

431

```
Performing tests to see whether nodes london2,london3,london4 are available
........................................................ 100% Done.
...
-------------------------------------------------------------------------------
Cluster Node Addition Summary
Global Settings
   Source: /u01/app/oracle/product/11.2.0/dbhome_1
   New Nodes
Space Requirements
   New Nodes
      london4
         /: Required 3.62GB : Available 44.95GB
Installed Products
   Product Names
      Oracle Database 11g 11.2.0.1.0
      Sun JDK 1.5.0.17.0
      Enterprise Manager Common Core Files 10.2.0.4.2
[some output removed]
      Enterprise Edition Options 11.2.0.1.0
-------------------------------------------------------------------------------
Instantiating scripts for add node (Friday, November 6, 2009 9:54:36 PM GMT)
.                                                      1% Done.
Instantiation of add node scripts complete
Copying to remote nodes (Friday, November 6, 2009 9:54:46 PM GMT)
..                     96% Done.
Home copied to new nodes
Saving inventory on nodes (Friday, November 6, 2009 10:28:22 PM GMT)
Save inventory complete
WARNING:
The following configuration scripts need to be executed as the "root" user in each cluster
node.
/u01/app/oracle/product/11.2.0/dbhome_1/root.sh #On nodes london4
To execute the configuration scripts:
   1. Open a terminal window
   2. Log in as "root"
   3. Run the scripts in each cluster node
The Cluster Node Addition of /u01/app/oracle/product/11.2.0/dbhome_1
was successful.
Please check '/tmp/silentInstall.log' for more details.
```

You should now execute the remaining root.sh script on the new node, london4. The output of that script does not differ from single-instance Oracle deployments, so it is not listed here.

With the RDBMS home successfully extended to the new cluster nodes, you can either manually add another database instance to the node or use the graphical dbca utility for this.

Deleting Nodes

Node deletion is an operation that few sites undertake lightly. In our experience, nodes were deleted from a cluster after catastrophic failures of multiple components of the underlying hardware. We have also seen unrecoverable driver updates on non-Unix platforms be responsible for having to remove the node from the cluster. The nodes that were removed are most often re-imaged by the system administrators and then added back into the cluster. The steps that follow show how to remove software from the RDBMS and Grid homes; however, in many cases, these tasks cannot be performed. From a DBA's point of view, it is important to have a clean OCR that does not reference the deleted node, and this can be achieved even without the node you need to delete being online.

Before a node can be removed from the cluster, you need to ensure that no database instance or other custom resource type uses that node. Also, you need to ensure that you have a backup of the OCR before continuing. Create one, if necessary, using this command:

```
ocrconfig -manualbackup
```

The dbca utility can help you remove database instances from a node, a task that beyond the scope of this chapter. By the time dbca finishes, it has updated the OCR and removed the redo thread and undo tablespace of that instance. It has also updated the tnsnames.ora files if there were no errors during the execution of the operation. Once the database instances and custom resources are deconfigured, you can proceed to removing the node from the cluster.

The following subsections take you through a node deletion process. In this example, the london2 node will be removed from a cluster that initially consists of two nodes: london1 and london2. We assume that the node to be removed from the cluster is still actively forming a part of the cluster. The node deletion process is the inverted equivalent of the node addition:

3. Remove the clustered RDBMS home.

4. Remove the node from the cluster layer.

Removing the Clustered RDBMS Home

The upcoming sections walk you through how to remove a node. You begin by removing disabling and removing the targeted node's listener, as in this example:

```
[oracle@london1 ~]$ srvctl config listener -a
Name: LISTENER
Network: 1, Owner: oracle
Home: <CRS home>
  /u01/app/crs/ on node(s) london2,london1
End points: TCP:1521
```

Now disable and stop the listener on london2 as the owner of the resource:

```
[oracle@london1 ~]$ srvctl disable listener -l LISTENER -n london2
[oracle@london1 ~]$ srvctl stop listener -l LISTENER -n london2
```

Next, you need to update inventory on the node to be deleted. You can skip this step if the node to be deleted no longer exists. The inventory.xml file showed this content before the updateNodeList command (this example has been shortened to show the RDBMS home only):

```
[oracle@london2 ContentsXML]$ cat inventory.xml
<?xml version="1.0" standalone="yes" ?>
<!-- Copyright (c) 1999, 2009, Oracle. All rights reserved. -->
<!-- Do not modify the contents of this file by hand. -->
<INVENTORY>
<HOME NAME="OraDb11g_home1" LOC="/u01/app/oracle/product/11.2.0/dbhome_1"
```

```
    TYPE="O" IDX="2">
    <NODE_LIST>
       <NODE NAME="london1"/>
       <NODE NAME="london2"/>
    </NODE_LIST>
  </HOME>
 </HOME_LIST>
 </INVENTORY>
```

As part of the process for preparing a node for deletion, you then execute the update Node List command, as shown in the following example (note the local flag):

```
[oracle@london2 bin]$ ./runInstaller -updateNodeList \
ORACLE_HOME=$ORACLE_HOME CLUSTER_NODES={london2} -local
Starting Oracle Universal Installer...

Checking swap space: must be greater than 500 MB.   Actual 1023 MB     Passed
The inventory pointer is located at /etc/oraInst.loc
The inventory is located at /u01/app/oraInventory
'UpdateNodeList' was successful.
[oracle@london2 bin]$
```

Running the preceding snippet changes the inventory so that it now reads as follows:

```
[oracle@london2 ~]$ cat /u01/app/oraInventory/ContentsXML/inventory.xml
<?xml version="1.0" standalone="yes" ?>
<!-- Copyright (c) 1999, 2009, Oracle. All rights reserved. -->
<!-- Do not modify the contents of this file by hand. -->
<INVENTORY>
...
<HOME NAME="OraDb11g_home1" LOC="/u01/app/oracle/product/11.2.0/dbhome_1"
    TYPE="O" IDX="2">
    <NODE_LIST>
       <NODE NAME="london2"/>
    </NODE_LIST>
  </HOME>
 </HOME_LIST>
 </INVENTORY>
```

The node london1 node is removed at this point. To physically remove the RDBMS home on the node to be deleted, you need to use the deinstall tool—OUI no longer has a deinstall option in version 11.2. You can either download the deinstall tool from Oracle's OTN website or find it in $ORACLE_HOME. As the RDBMS software owner, execute the deinstall command with the -local switch:

```
[oracle@london2 deinstall]$ ./deinstall -local
Checking for required files and bootstrapping ...
Please wait ...
Location of logs /u01/app/oraInventory/logs/

############# ORACLE DEINSTALL & DECONFIG TOOL START #############
[...]
```

A log of this session will be written to:
'/u01/app/oraInventory/logs/deinstall_deconfig2010-07-02_10-40-54-PM.out'
Any error messages from this session will be written to:
'/u01/app/oraInventory/logs/deinstall_deconfig2010-07-02_10-40-54-PM.err'

############# ORACLE DEINSTALL & DECONFIG TOOL END #############

We, the authors, have found that the deinstall tool does not always reliably clean out the RDBMS home on the node to be deleted.

■ **Note** If you installed the RDBMS binaries on a shared home, then you need to detach it using
`$ORACLE_HOME/oui/bin/runInstaller -detachHome ORACLE_HOME=$ORACLE_HOME`.

The failure to deinstall the RDBMS binaries on the node to be deleted does not matter. However, it is important not to leave erroneous inventory entries on the nodes *not* deleted. The following snippet updates the node list for the remaining nodes, passing a comma separated list of nodes that remained in the cluster to the CLUSTER_NODES parameter:

```
[oracle@london1 ~]$ $ORACLE_HOME/oui/bin/runInstaller -updateNodeList \
> ORACLE_HOME=$ORACLE_HOME "CLUSTER_NODES={london1}"
Starting Oracle Universal Installer...

Checking swap space: must be greater than 500 MB.   Actual 1023 MB     Passed
The inventory pointer is located at /etc/oraInst.loc
The inventory is located at /u01/app/oraInventory
'UpdateNodeList' was successful.
```

You specify the remaining cluster nodes in the CLUSTER_NODES parameter (i.e., you specify all nodes except the one(s) you are deleting in this parameter). This operation concludes the node removal from the RDBMS home.

Removing the Node from the Cluster

Next, you need to update the OCR and remove the node from Grid Infrastructure. We recommend making another manual OCR backup at this time! You need to connect as root to the node *you want to delete* and execute the rootcrs.pl script. This script is located in $GRID_HOME/crs/install and requires the -deconfig -force options, as the following output demonstrates:

```
The Oracle base for ORACLE_HOME=/u01/app/crs/ is /u01/app/oracle
[root@london2 ~]# crsctl check crs
CRS-4638: Oracle High Availability Services is online
CRS-4537: Cluster Ready Services is online
CRS-4529: Cluster Synchronization Services is online
CRS-4533: Event Manager is online
[root@london2 ~]# cd /u01/app/crs/crs/install/
[root@london2 install]# ./rootcrs.pl -deconfig -force
```

```
2010-07-03 10:16:08: Parsing the host name
2010-07-03 10:16:08: Checking for super user privileges
2010-07-03 10:16:08: User has super user privileges
Using configuration parameter file: ./crsconfig_params
VIP exists.:london1
VIP exists.: /london1-vip/172.17.1.201/255.255.255.0/eth0
VIP exists.:london2
VIP exists.: /london2-vip/172.17.1.202/255.255.255.0/eth0
GSD exists.
ONS daemon exists. Local port 6100, remote port 6200
eONS daemon exists. Multicast port 18904, multicast IP address 234.187.14.127,
listening port 2016
ACFS-9200: Supported
CRS-2673: Attempting to stop 'ora.registry.acfs' on 'london2'
CRS-2677: Stop of 'ora.registry.acfs' on 'london2' succeeded
CRS-2791: Starting shutdown of Oracle High Availability Services-managed
resources on 'london2'
CRS-2673: Attempting to stop 'ora.crsd' on 'london2'
CRS-2790: Starting shutdown of Cluster Ready Services-managed resources
on 'london2'
CRS-2673: Attempting to stop 'ora.OCRVOTE.dg' on 'london2'
CRS-2677: Stop of 'ora.OCRVOTE.dg' on 'london2' succeeded
CRS-2673: Attempting to stop 'ora.asm' on 'london2'
CRS-2677: Stop of 'ora.asm' on 'london2' succeeded
CRS-2792: Shutdown of Cluster Ready Services-managed resources
on 'london2' has completed
CRS-2677: Stop of 'ora.crsd' on 'london2' succeeded
[some output removed for clarity]
CRS-2677: Stop of 'ora.gipcd' on 'london2' succeeded
CRS-2677: Stop of 'ora.diskmon' on 'london2' succeeded
CRS-2793: Shutdown of Oracle High Availability Services-managed resources
on 'london2' has completed
CRS-4133: Oracle High Availability Services has been stopped.
Successfully deconfigured Oracle clusterware stack on this node
[root@london2 install]#
```

At this point, the Grid Infrastructure stack has been deconfigured on the local node.

■ **Warning** Be careful not to specify the -lastnode option unless you completely deconfigure *all* nodes of the cluster.

We have occasionally seen problems from removing the Clusterware home when custom resources (e.g., an active/passive Tomcat server) were executing on the node to be deleted. Therefore, we recommend removing the node to be deleted from the custom resource profile.

Finishing the Node Removal

Now switch to *one of the remaining* cluster nodes. Next, connect as root and remove the node to be deleted from the configuration, as in the following example:

```
[root@london1 ~]# crsctl delete node -n london2
CRS-4661: Node london2 successfully deleted.
```

As soon as you query the resource status, you will see that the node you deleted is no longer listed.

Next, you can delete the Grid software from the node to be removed. Back on the node removed from the cluster, execute the following steps to update the inventory and remove the grid home from the host. Begin this process by executing the following command as the owner of the Grid software stack:

```
[oracle@london2 ~]$ /u01/app/crs/oui/bin/runInstaller \
> -updateNodeList ORACLE_HOME=$ORACLE_HOME "CLUSTER_NODES=london2" CRS=TRUE \
> -local
Starting Oracle Universal Installer...

Checking swap space: must be greater than 500 MB.   Actual 1023 MB      Passed
The inventory pointer is located at /etc/oraInst.loc
The inventory is located at /u01/app/oraInventory
'UpdateNodeList' was successful.
```

You can now use the deinstall tool to remove the software from the node in exactly the same way that you removed the RDBMS binaries. The deinstall command-line utility is located in $ORACLE_HOME/deinstall/. The following command illustrates how to run this utility:

```
[oracle@london2 deinstall]$ ./deinstall -local
```

On *any one of the remaining* nodes, you need to update the node list as well. You do this by passing a comma-separated list of nodes to the CLUSTER_NODES parameter list that forms the cluster (minus the one you deleted), as in the following example:

```
[oracle@london2 bin]$  ./runInstaller -updateNodeList ORACLE_HOME=$ORACLE_HOME
"CLUSTER_NODES={london1,london3}" CRS=TRUE
```

Don't forget the CRS=TRUE parameter; this serves as an important indication of the Grid software home to the Oracle Universal Installer.

Exploring More Advanced Topics

We have saved some of the more advanced topics for the rest of this chapter. These topics include tasks administrators don't usually carry out every day, such as changing the listener ports for node listener and SCAN listeners. We also look at how to change the SCAN address after the installation has completed.

Grid Infrastructure will not run if there are problems with the OCR, OLR, or voting disks. We explained the importance of these files in the "Initiating the Startup Sequence" section earlier in this chapter. In this part of the chapter, we will explain how to recover from severe problems with the essential Clusterware files. Finally, we will cover how to move the OCR and voting disks into ASM.

Selecting non-Default Listener Ports

Some sites require using a different port than 1521 for the listener. When initially installing Grid Infrastructure, the administrator is not given the choice of which port she wants to use. This means that changing the listener port must happen after the installation has completed successfully.

The netca network configuration assistant provides the easiest way to change the listener port. Start netca as the owner of the Grid Infrastructure home. The following series of screen shots documents how to change the listener port from 1521 to 1526. Figure 8-3 shows the Welcome screen.

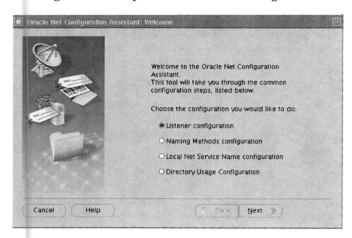

Figure 8-3. *The Welcome screen*

Next, select the Listener Configuration option and click Next. This brings up the options screen shown in Figure 8-4.

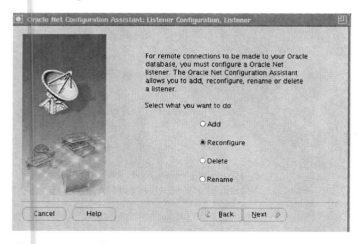

Figure 8-4. *The Listener options*

Now select Reconfigure and click Next to advance to the Listener Selection screen (see Figure 8-5).

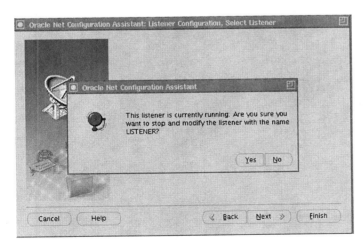

Figure 8-5. The Listener Selection screen

Unlike previous versions, the current version of Oracle Grid Infrastructure no longer uses the LISTENER_hostname naming convention for node listeners. Instead, all listeners are simply called LISTENER. Select LISTENER and proceed; most systems probably do not have additional listeners in place at this stage.

The netca utility warns you that it will shut down the listener with name LISTENER (see Figure 8-6). This is a clusterwide shutdown, which means that no new connections can be established to the listener you are changing. Existing connections are not affected. Acknowledging the warning prompts netca to shut down the listener.

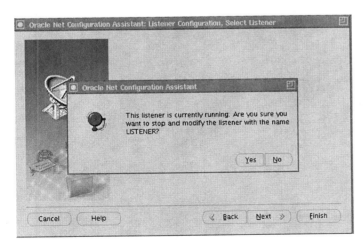

Figure 8-6. Shutdown Warning

The Protocol Selection screen lets you select the protocol the listener should support (see Figure 8-7). For most deployments, this should be TCP/IP.

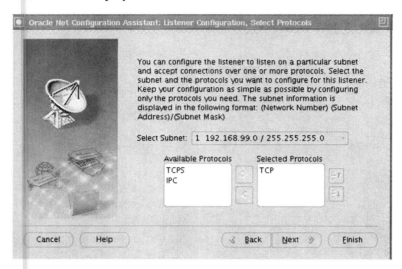

Figure 8-7. *The Protocol Selection screen*

The Select Subnet dropdown box at the top of the screen is useful only if you have multiple public networks in use. We will discuss this option in the "Configuring the Network" section later in the chapter. For now, select the protocols you would like to use and click Next. You will land on the Port Number screen shown in Figure 8-8.

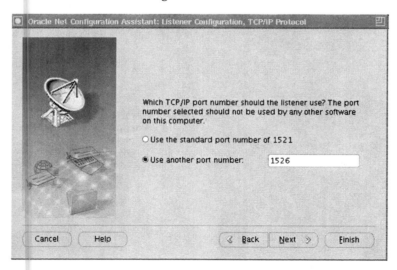

Figure 8-8. *The Port Number screen*

It is finally time to change the port from the default number 1521 to your preferred port number. The example in Figure 8-8 uses port 1526.

Click Next to complete the reconfiguration. The utility does not always reliably start the listener resource in the cluster, so you should ensure that the listener resource is up on all nodes before completing the work.

To verify that the listeners are really listening on the correct port, issue the srvctl command, as shown in the following example:

```
[oracle@london1 ~]$ srvctl config listener
Name: LISTENER
Network: 1, Owner: oracle
Home: <CRS home>
End points: TCP:1526
[oracle@london1 ~]$ srvctl status listener
Listener LISTENER is enabled
Listener LISTENER is running on node(s): london1,london2
```

The messages here indicate that the listener is enabled, and that it is running on two nodes. You can also see that they are listening on port 1526, which is the correct port for our example.

Selecting a non-Default SCAN Listener Endpoint

Changing the SCAN listener endpoint is simpler than changing the database listener endpoints. The srvctl command line utility offers following option for modifying the SCAN listener endpoints:

```
[oracle@london1 log]$ srvctl modify scan_listener -h

Modifies the SCAN listeners so that the number of SCAN listeners is the same
as the number of SCAN VIPs or modifies the SCAN listener endpoints.

Usage: srvctl modify scan_listener

{-u|-p [TCP:]<port>[/IPC:<key>][/NMP:<pipe>][/TCPS:<sport>] [/SDP:<port>]}
    -u Update SCAN listeners to match the number of SCAN VIPs
    -p [TCP:]<port>[/IPC:<key>][/NMP:<pipe>][/TCPS:<sport>] [/SDP:<port>]
         SCAN Listener endpoints
    -h Print usage
```

You should keep the current configuration for your change record manual for the cluster. The cluster can be queried using the srvctl config listener command, as shown in the following example:

```
[oracle@london1 log]$ srvctl config scan_listener
SCAN Listener LISTENER_SCAN1 exists. Port: TCP:1521
SCAN Listener LISTENER_SCAN2 exists. Port: TCP:1521
SCAN Listener LISTENER_SCAN3 exists. Port: TCP:1521
```

Now you need to stop the SCAN listener, change the configuration, and then start it up again:

```
[oracle@london1 log]$ srvctl stop scan_listener
[oracle@london1 log]$ srvctl modify scan_listener -p  1526
```

```
[oracle@london1 log]$ srvctl config scan_listener
SCAN Listener LISTENER_SCAN1 exists. Port: TCP:1526
SCAN Listener LISTENER_SCAN2 exists. Port: TCP:1526
SCAN Listener LISTENER_SCAN3 exists. Port: TCP:1526
[oracle@london1 log]$ srvctl start scan_listener
[oracle@london1 log]$ srvctl status scan_listener
SCAN Listener LISTENER_SCAN1 is enabled
SCAN listener LISTENER_SCAN1 is running on node london2
SCAN Listener LISTENER_SCAN2 is enabled
SCAN listener LISTENER_SCAN2 is running on node london1
SCAN Listener LISTENER_SCAN3 is enabled
SCAN listener LISTENER_SCAN3 is running on node london1
```

Changing the SCAN After Installation

The SCAN can take up to three IP addresses that have to resolve round-robin style in DNS. If the system has been set up with less than the maximum possible number of IP addresses, you can easily add more IP addresses after the installation. First, you need to change the DNS so it reflects all the IP addresses. Second, you check the current IP address list, as in the following example:

```
oracle@london1:~> host cluster1.example.com
cluster1.example.com has address 172.17.1.205
cluster1.example.com has address 172.17.1.206
cluster1.example.com has address 172.17.1.207
```

As the Grid software owner (oracle, in this example, but it could be any operating system account), you need to stop the SCAN and SCAN listener:

```
[oracle@london1 ~]$ srvctl stop scan_listener
[oracle@london1 ~]$ srvctl stop scan
```

Next, you should verify that the both SCAN and SCAN listener have indeed stopped:

```
[oracle@london1 ~]$ srvctl status scan_listener
SCAN Listener LISTENER_SCAN1 is enabled
SCAN listener LISTENER_SCAN1 is not running

[oracle@london1 ~]$ srvctl status scan
SCAN VIP scan1 is enabled
SCAN VIP scan1 is not running
```

With the SCAN and SCAN listener down, modify the SCAN as root:

```
[root@london1 ~]# srvctl modify scan -n cluster1.example.com
[root@london1 ~]# srvctl config scan
SCAN name: cluster1, Network: 1/172.17.1.0/255.255.255.0/eth0
SCAN VIP name: scan1, IP: /cluster1.example.com/172.17.1.205
SCAN VIP name: scan2, IP: /cluster1.example.com/172.17.1.206
SCAN VIP name: scan2, IP: /cluster1.example.com/172.17.1.207
```

Updating the SCAN listener itself is straightforward:

```
[root@london1 ~]# srvctl modify scan_listener -u
[root@london1 ~]# srvctl config scan_listener
SCAN Listener LISTENER_SCAN1 exists. Port: TCP:1521
SCAN Listener LISTENER_SCAN2 exists. Port: TCP:1521
SCAN Listener LISTENER_SCAN3 exists. Port: TCP:1521
```

Finally, you need to restart the SCAN and SCAN listener:

```
[root@london1 ~]# srvctl start scan
[root@london1 ~]# srvctl start scan_listener
```

The log files for the SCAN listeners are somewhat hidden in the $GRID_HOME/log directory. To view them, you need to point the ADR_BASE to $GRID_HOME/log, as in the following example:

```
[oracle@london1 ~]$ adrci

ADRCI: Release 11.2.0.1.0 - Production on Sat Jul 3 11:26:11 2010

Copyright (c) 1982, 2009, Oracle and/or its affiliates.  All rights reserved.

ADR base = "/u01/app/oracle"
adrci> set base /u01/app/crs/log
adrci> show homes
ADR Homes:
diag/tnslsnr/london1/listener_scan1
diag/tnslsnr/london1/listener_scan2
diag/tnslsnr/london1/listener_scan3
diag/clients/user_root/host_3052993529_76
diag/asm/+asm/+ASM1
adrci> set home diag/tnslsnr/london1/listener_scan1
```

With the ADR base set, you can view the log. Bear in mind that the SCAN listener can migrate. Even though there is a log file, that does not mean that this particular SCAN listener is currently running on that node. The srvctl status scan_listener command tells you which node a particular SCAN listener is running on.

Maintaining Voting Disks

Prior to Oracle 11.2, voting disks were stored on block devices or, alternatively, on raw devices. Block devices such as /dev/mapper/ocrvote1p1 provided an easier interface to the voting disks because no (deprecated) raw devices had to be created during the operating system's boot process. Nevertheless, and as you saw in the earlier "Troubleshooting" section, the CSSD process requires specific permissions and ownership of the voting disks. You set that ownership either through udev or the rc.local script.

In Oracle 10.2 and 11.1, we recommended that you create multiple voting disks to eliminate a potential single point of failure. Oracle 10.1 did not support this feature; in that version, there was always only one voting disk. Even with multiple voting disks, you should still back these disks up on a regular basis and test your recovery procedures. To back up a voting disk for these releases prior to version 11.2, you could use the dd operating system utility:

```
[root@london1 ~]# dd if=voting_disk of=backup_file_name
```

You did not need to shut down the database or Oracle Clusterware before backing up the voting disk. Although the voting disks were (in theory) identical, backing up each configured voting disk was recommended. Because voting disk locations were configured in the OCR, modifying them during any recovery process was difficult. Therefore, the most straightforward strategy was to back up all of the voting disks and, if recovery was necessary, restore each copy to its original location.

To recover the voting disks, you had to ensure that all databases and Oracle Clusterware were shut down. You could then restore the voting disks using the dd operating system utility:

```
[root@london1 ~]# dd if=backup_file_name of=voting_disk
```

With Oracle 11.2, you no longer need to back up voting disks because the contents of the voting disks are automatically backed up in the OCR. When a new voting disk is added, the contents of the voting disk will be copied to the new voting disk.

Restoring Voting Disks

In the unlikely event that a voting disk becomes corrupted, it must be restored from a backup. This can be further complicated if the OCR becomes corrupted, as well. Should this be the case, you need to restore the OCR before proceeding. How to restore the OCR was described previously in this chapter's "Maintaining the Local and Cluster Registry" section.

The exact recovery process depends on whether you used ASM or a cluster file system to store your voting disks. In the ASM scenario, you follow these steps to restore the voting disks as root:

1. Use `crsctl stop cluster -all -f` to stop the Clusterware stack on all nodes.

2. On an arbitrary node, start the Clusterware stack in exclusive mode, and then use the -excl flag as follows: `crsctl start crs -excl`. If this does not work, and you get CRS-4640/CRS-4000 errors, then you can use `crsctl disable crs` to disable the automatic starting of the Clusterware stack. With this option set, reboot the node. When it comes back online, you should be able to successfully execute the `crsctl start crs -excl` command. This will start the required background processes that make up a local ASM instance, which is one of the last things you see before the start is completed.

3. If the diskgroup containing the voting files was lost, then create a new one with exactly the same name (important!) and mount it if it is not mounted. Don't forget to set the ASM compatibility to 11.2 for the diskgroup. Also, if you are using ASMLib, then don't forget to execute /etc/init.d/oracleasm scandisks on the nodes for which you did not create the disk. Doing so makes those disks available to those nodes.

4. If you lost the OCR as well, then restore it first (see the "Dealing with a Corrupt or Inaccessible OCR" section later in this chapter for more information)

5. Restore the voting disks using this command: `crsctl replace votedisk + disk_group_name`. Remember that this diskgroup name must be identical to the one you lost.

6. Stop the partially started cluster stack using this command: `crsctl stop crs`.

7. Restart the cluster stack completely with the following command: `crsctl start crs`.

8. Start the cluster on the remaining nodes. If you have disabled the automatic start of the Clusterware stack in Step 2, re-enable it using `crsctl enable crs`.

The situation is slightly different if your voting disks are located outside of ASM. In that case, you will need to follow these steps to restore the voting disks:

1. Stop the cluster on all nodes using the following command: `crsctl stop cluster -all -f`.

2. Identify the status of your voting disks with the following command: `crsctl query css votedisk`.

3. Start the local node's cluster stack in exclusive mode: `crsctl start crs –excl`. You may have to disable the automatic start of Clusterware and reboot the node, as described in the previous ASM example if Clusterware states it is already started.

4. The File Universal ID (FUID) from the preceding output is important for the next step. Delete the damaged voting disk using this command: `crsctl delete css votedisk FUID`.

5. Replace the lost disk by adding another disk straight away using `crsctl add css votedisk /path/to/deletedVotingDisk`.

6. Stop the partially started Clusterware stack on the local node using this command: `crsctl stop crs`.

7. Restart the cluster using the following command: `crsctl start cluster -all`. If you disabled CRS in Step 2, then re-enable it.

Moving Voting Disks into ASM

ASM is the preferred location for the voting disks and OCR. Oracle Universal Installer no longer offers administrators the choice of storing voting disks on raw or block devices for new installations.

However, upgraded clusters still use block or raw devices to store the OCR and voting disks. Moving these into ASM requires a handful of steps. First, we recommend using a dedicated ASM diskgroup for the shared files. The separate ASM disk group is optional, but you might as well store the OCR in the same disk group as your data files. The reason we suggest a separate disk group has to do with LUN cloning. Assume that your storage array can create copies of the ASM disks—it would make sense to use this functionality to rapidly clone a database. If the OCR and voting disks are in the cloned disk groups, then the success of the clone operation might be in question.

Space requirements for the diskgroup are modest, and many sites use individual partitions of 1G each to form the diskgroup. The following example assumes that you are using ASMLib to label the disks. If you were to use udev instead, that would require a different setup. Please refer to the Chapter 9 on "Automatic Storage Management" for more information about udev and ASMLib.

Next, the storage team should present 1, 3, or 5 LUNs, depending on whether your new disk group will use external, normal, or high redundancy. Most systems should be fine with normal redundancy, given the fact that most storage arrays use some sort of internal protection. We do not recommend using a diskgroup with external redundancy because doing so would not allow you to have multiple voting disks. Furthermore, you cannot store the voting disks by specifying multiple diskgroups with external redundancy. Also, you cannot use a setup of disk group +DG1 to store the first voting file, +DG2 to store the second, and +DG3 to store the third voting file. There can only ever be one diskgroup that contains all the voting disks for a cluster. When requesting the storage for the voting diskgroup, you can provide additional protection by requesting that this storage not come from the same shelf in the array. Last but not least, the individual LUNs presented to the cluster for the new diskgroup should be of equal size.

The newly acquired storage then needs to be discovered and partitioned. Each of the new partitions should be marked as an ASM disk, as in the following example:

```
[root@london1 ~]# /etc/init.d/oracleasm createdisk OCRVOTE1 /dev/mapper/ocr1p1
[root@london1 ~]# /etc/init.d/oracleasm createdisk OCRVOTE2 /dev/mapper/ocr2p1
[root@london1 ~]# /etc/init.d/oracleasm createdisk OCRVOTE3 /dev/mapper/ocr3p1
```

■ **Note** The actual device name will be different if you are not using device-mapper multipath. Your system administrator should be able to provide you with the device name to use.

In the preceding example, the administrator created three ASM disks: OCRVOTE1, OCRVOTE2, and OCRVOTE3. The device-mapper multipath configuration in the /etc/multipath.conf file maps three block devices to the names OCRVOTE1, OCRVOTE2, and OCRVOTE3 in the /dev/mapper directory. Once the ASM disks are created, execute the /etc/init.d/oracleasm scandisks command on all remaining nodes of the cluster.

Next, connect to the local ASM instance as SYSASM and create the new diskgroup, as follows:

```
SQL> create diskgroup OCRVOTE normal redundancy disk
  2    'ORCL:OCRVOTE1','ORCL:OCRVOTE2','ORCL:OCRVOTE3';

Diskgroup created

SQL> alter diskgroup OCRVOTE set attribute  'compatible.asm'='11.2';

Diskgroup altered.
```

Alternatively, you can use asmca to accomplish the same. You should start the diskgroup resource on all nodes of the cluster; the -srvctl start diskgroup -g OCRVOTE command will do this for you. The final step is to get the voting disks into ASM. An interesting fact is that, regardless of how many voting disks were used in the cluster before, Grid Infrastructure will always create the number of voting disks based on the ASM diskgroup redundancy. The final command, which does not require the Clusterware daemons to be shut down, is to move the voting disks into ASM. We recommend making a backup of all voting disks beforehand, as described in the "Maintaining Voting Disks" section. The following example illustrates how to move the voting disks:

```
[root@london1: ~]# crsctl replace votedisk '+OCRVOTE'
```

You can check the location of the voting disks to ensure a successful execution of the command. If there were any problems during the execution, they will be reported on the command line and in the ASM instance's alert.log.

Maintaining Local and Cluster Registry

As noted in the "Storing Cluster Information with the Oracle Cluster Registry" section earlier in this chapter, voting disks and the OCR are located on shared storage. Your options are to use either ASM or a supporting cluster file system. Using block or raw devices is not recommended for Oracle 11.2. The fact that block and raw devices are deprecated should be a strong indicator of the future direction of the tool. During normal operation, you do not normally have to deal with the OLR and OCR because they work in the background, enabling the cluster to function correctly. The following sections will cover how to deal with OLR and OCR corruption, while the last section explains how to move the OCR into ASM.

Dealing With a Corrupt or Inaccessible OLR

If the OLR is corrupt or otherwise inaccessible, the OHAS daemon cannot start. The output on the server's console will show this message:

```
CRS-4124: Oracle High Availability Services startup failed.
CRS-4000: Command Start failed, or completed with errors.

Enterprise Linux Enterprise Linux Server release 5.4 (Carthage)
Kernel 2.6.18-164.el5 on an x86-64
```

When logged in as root, you can check the OLR using the ocrcheck command line utility (note the -local flag):

```
[root@london1 ohasd]# ocrcheck -local
Status of Oracle Local Registry is as follows :
        Version                  :           3
        Total space (kbytes)     :      262120
        Used space (kbytes)      :        2232
        Available space (kbytes) :      259888
        ID                       :  1022831156
        Device/File Name         : /u01/app/crs/cdata/london1.olr
                                   Device/File integrity check failed

        Local registry integrity check failed

        Logical corruption check bypassed
```

The "Device/File integrity check failed" message clearly indicates there is corruption in the OLR; the "Local Registry integrity check failed" message provides ample additional evidence of the same. In this case, there is no other option except to restore the OLR. Luckily, there is at least one backup, which was taken during the execution of the root.sh script when you installed or upgraded Grid Infrastructure.

By convention, the OLR backups are stored in $GRID_HOME/cdata/hostname/backup_date_time.olr, unless another backup location has been chosen. The OLR stores its own backup information, but that is not helpful in this case because it is corrupt. Don't let the message that no local backups are available trick you!

Find the most recent OLR backup and restore it in a runlevel other than 3 or 5, as in the following example. With the /etc/init.d/init.ohasd process started, it is not possible to perform the restore. You will get the following message if you try to do so anyway:

```
[root@london1 ohasd]# ocrconfig -local -restore \
/u01/app/crs/cdata/london1/backup_20091010_211006.olr
PROTL-19: Cannot proceed while the Oracle High Availability Service is running
```

Instead, you need to change to runlevel 2; you can do this using the init command:

```
[root@london1 ohasd] init 2
```

Now log back in and restore the OLR:

```
[root@london1 ~]# ocrconfig -local -restore \
> /u01/app/crs/cdata/london1/backup_20091010_211006.olr
```

Each call to ocrconfig creates a log file in $GRID_HOME/log/hostname/client. This log file can provide additional information about the output of the command; it can also be helpful when troubleshooting problems. At this point, you should return to the previous run level, either 3 or 5. If you successfully restored the OLR, then you will see the following message:

```
CRS-4123: Oracle High Availability Services has been started.
```

If case the local registry is lost completely—if the file system is corrupt, for example—then the scenario plays out slightly differently. The error reported by ocrcheck looks like the following:

```
[root@london1 ohasd]# ocrcheck -local
PROTL-602: Failed to retrieve data from the local registry
PROCL-26: Error while accessing the physical storage Operating System error
  [No such file or directory] [2]
```

The "no such file or directory" message is what gives it away. In this case, you cannot restore the OLR as you did in the previous example. The ocrconfig command fails, but it does not give you a reason for the failure; to find that, you need to check the log file in $GRID_HOME/log/hostname/client/ocrconfig_pid.log:

```
[root@london1 client]# cat ocrconfig_11254.log
Oracle Database 11g Clusterware Release 11.2.0.1.0 - Production
Copyright 1996, 2009
Oracle. All rights reserved.
2010-06-25 09:21:24.866: [ OCRCONF][3905760784]ocrconfig starts...
2010-06-25 09:21:24.867: [  OCROSD][3905760784]utopen:6m':failed in stat OCR
file/disk /u01/app/crs/cdata/london1.olr, errno=2, os err
string=No such file or directory
2010-06-25 09:21:24.867: [  OCROSD][3905760784]utopen:7:failed to open
any OCR file/disk, errno=2,os err string=No such file or directory
[ default][3905760784]u_set_gbl_comp_error: OCR context was NULL
2010-06-25 09:21:24.867: [  OCRRAW][3905760784]phy_rec:1:could not
open OCR device
2010-06-25 09:21:24.867: [ OCRCONF][3905760784]Failed to restore OCR/OLR from
[/u01/app/crs/cdata/london1/backup_20100625_085111.olr]
2010-06-25 09:21:24.867: [ OCRCONF][3905760784]Exiting [status=failed]...
```

The "No such file or directory" message means that because there is no file in the OCR location, so it cannot be replaced. Now change to runlevel 2 before continuing; this prevents any Oracle processes from interfering with the restore operation. Before restoring the file, you need to touch it first and set the correct permissions, as in this example:

```
[root@london1 client]# touch /u01/app/crs/cdata/london1.olr
[root@london1 cdata]# chown oracle:oinstall london1.olr
[root@london1 ~]# ocrconfig -local -restore \
> /u01/app/crs/cdata/london1/backup_20100625_085111.olr
```

If you installed the Grid Infrastructure software stack under a user other than oracle, then change the chown command in the preceding example to use the Grid software owner instead. Next, check the client log file again to see whether your attempt succeeded:

```
Oracle Database 11g Clusterware Release 11.2.0.1.0 - Production Copyright 1996,
2009 Oracle. All rights reserved.
2010-06-25 09:42:01.887: [ OCRCONF][2532662800]ocrconfig starts...
2010-06-25 09:42:03.671: [ OCRCONF][2532662800]Successfully restored OCR and set
  block 0
2010-06-25 09:42:03.671: [ OCRCONF][2532662800]Exiting [status=success]...
```

The OHAS daemon will then proceed to start the remaining daemons. After a few minutes, you should check the status:

```
[oracle@london1 ~]$ crsctl check crs
CRS-4638: Oracle High Availability Services is online
CRS-4537: Cluster Ready Services is online
CRS-4529: Cluster Synchronization Services is online
CRS-4533: Event Manager is online
```

Dealing with a Corrupt or Inaccessible OCR

While a corrupt OLR has significant impact on the availability of an individual node, a corrupt OCR is far more severe in its effect on the cluster. As you learned in the "Troubleshooting" section earlier in the chapter, the OCR must be accessible for CRSD to start. Without a working CRS daemon, a node cannot join the cluster, which effectively breaks the cluster.

To honor the importance of the OCR, Oracle has always backed the OCR up on a regular basis. The ocrconfig -showbackup command lists the node where the automatic backup has been taken, as well as the time the backup occurred and the backup file name. For Oracle 11.1 and later, it is also possible to perform manual backups. We strongly recommend you to make a manual backup of the OCR using the ocrconfig –manualbackup command before modifying any cluster, such as by adding or deleting nodes or by performing other OCR-relevant maintenance operations.

If neither the OCR and nor any of its mirrors is accessible, then you need to restore the OCR to start the cluster. What steps you should take to do so depends partly on where your OCR is located. The OCR can either be in ASM, (the recommended approach) or outside of ASM on a cluster file system or block/raw devices.

If the OCR is in the ASM, the procedure to recover the OCR is very similar to the procedure for restoring the voting disks. In fact, if you have placed the OCR on the same ASM diskgroup as the voting disks and lost it, then you must restore the OCR before restoring the voting disks because the voting disk backups are in the OCR. Follow these steps to restore an OCR that is located in the ASM:

1. Stop the Clusterware stack on all nodes using the following command: `crsctl stop cluster -all -f`.

2. On an arbitrary node, start the Clusterware stack in exclusive mode using `crsctl start crs -excl`. If this does not work, and you get CRS-4640/CRS-4000 errors, then you can disable the automatic start of the Clusterware stack using `crsctl disable crs`. With this option disabled, reboot the node. When it comes back online, you should be able to successfully execute the `crsctl start crs -excl` command. Doing so will initiate the required background processes to start a local ASM instance, which is one of the last things you see before the start is completed.

3. If the diskgroup containing the voting files was lost, then create a new one with exactly the same name (important!) and mount it if it is not mounted. Don't forget to set the ASM compatibility to 11.2 for the diskgroup. Also, if you are using ASMLib, then don't forget to execute `/etc/init.d/oracleasm scandisks` on the nodes where you did not create the disk. This makes those disks available to those nodes.

4. Restore the OCR using `ocrconfig -restore backup_file_name`. Note how there is no option to specify a different destination, which is why it is important to recreate the diskgroup with the same name. Check the `$GRID_HOME/log/hostname/client/` directory for the latest trace file. Any problems should be reported there. If you get a PROT-19 error ("Cannot proceed while the Cluster Ready Service is running"), then you need to stop the CRS daemon using the `crsctl stop res ora.crsd -init` command before attemping to restore the OCR again.

5. Stop the partially started cluster stack using this command: `crsctl stop crs`.

6. Now run this command to restart the cluster stack completely: `crsctl start crs`.

7. Restart the cluster on the remaining nodes. If you disabled the automatic start of the Clusterware stack in Step 2, then re-enable it using `crsctl enable crs`.

If the OCR is not stored in ASM, then the steps to restore the OCR are similar. Again, you need to ensure that the OCR can be restored in the same location it existed before it was lost. You should touch the OCR file names and set the permissions correctly. The file name should be part of your installation documentation, or in an archived output from ocrcheck. For example, you could use these commands if your OCR was on `/u03/oradata/grid/ocr{1,2,3}`:

- `touch /u03/oradata/grid/ocr{1,2,3}`

- `chown gridOwner:oinstall /u03/oradata/grid/ocr{1,2,3}`

- `chmod 0640 /u03/oradata/grid/ocr{1,2,3}`

Begin by following Steps 1 and 2 from the ASM scenario to stop the cluster. Next, follow these steps to complete the process of restoring the OCR:

1. Recreate the block device or the cluster file system where the OCR was located if it was lost.

2. Touch the OCR files and set permissions as just described.

3. Run the `ocrconfig -restore backup_file` to restore the OLR.

4. Bring the cluster up as described in Steps 5-7 of the ASM scenario.

Moving the OCR into ASM

Moving the OCR into ASM is simpler than the procedure for moving the voting disks into ASM. We recommend that you use at least one dedicated ASM diskgroup to store the shared Clusterware files. The following example moves the OCR to the OCRVOTE diskgroup:

```
[root@london1: bin]# ./ocrconfig -add +OCRVOTE
[root@london1 ~]# ocrcheck
Status of Oracle Cluster Registry is as follows :
 Version                  :          3
 Total space (kbytes)     :     292924
 Used space (kbytes)      :       8096
 Available space (kbytes) :     284828
 ID                       :  209577144
 Device/File Name         : /dev/raw/raw1
 Device/File integrity check succeeded
 Device/File Name         : +OCRVOTE
 Device/File integrity check succeeded

 Device/File not configured

 Device/File not configured

 Device/File not configured

 Cluster registry integrity check succeeded

 Logical corruption check succeeded
```

Next, you need to remove the raw device (or whatever other storage method was used out of ASM):

```
[root@london1 ~]# ocrconfig -delete /dev/raw/raw1
[root@racupgrade1 ~]# ocrcheck

Status of Oracle Cluster Registry is as follows :
 Version                  :          3
 Total space (kbytes)     :     292924
 Used space (kbytes)      :       8096
 Available space (kbytes) :     284828
 ID                       :  209577144
 Device/File Name         :    +OCRVOTE
 Device/File integrity check succeeded
```

```
Device/File not configured

Device/File not configured

Device/File not configured

Device/File not configured

Cluster registry integrity check succeeded

Logical corruption check succeeded
```

Unfortunately, it is not possible to have more than one copy of the OCR in the same diskgroup. The redundancy level of the diskgroup should provide protection from disk failure. Unlike with the voting disks, you are not limited to having all copies of the OCR in the same diskgroup, so you could choose to spread the OCR copies over other existing diskgroups.

■ **Tip** For the sake of safety, you should also run the `cluvfy comp ocr` command to check the OCR consistency across all cluster nodes.

Summary

We have covered a lot of ground in the chapter. We began by examining the hardware and software requirements, and then moved on to cover the most important files in the cluster stack. Some of the files were already known to us from previous Oracle versions; however, the Grid Plug and Play profile and Oracle Local Registry are new in 11.2.

We also discussed the main Grid Infrastructure daemons and the correct startup sequence. The number of log files maintained by Grid Infrastructure has increased quite dramatically, thanks to the additional background processes. We also briefly touched on inter-resource dependencies.

Next, we looked at the main utilities used for maintaining the software stack. These are most likely the tools the administrator will have to work with when it comes to resolving problems. We tried to group these utilities together in a logical fashion in the relevant troubleshooting sections.

We also covered how Clusterware allows developers to define callout scripts that can be used to notify administrators when UP and DOWN events are published by the Fast Application Notification framework. For example, we mentioned that one potential use of these callouts would be to send an e-mail to the on-call DBA's pager or to raise a ticket.

Next, we explained how Grid Infrastructure also allows administrators to set up cost efficient active/passive clusters, protecting Oracle databases (or third party applications) with the requirement to run on only one node with a floating virtual IPs.

Another useful topic that we covered is Oracle Restart, which is an interesting new option that brings you a lot of the "feel" of Oracle RAC to a single instance. Resources such as ASM, the listener, and databases are protected by the Grid Infrastructure. Such resources will be automatically started (but not stopped at the time of this writing due to a bug) when the server reboots.

Next, we dealt with troubleshooting the startup sequence and Java utilities, then segued into a discussion of how to patch Grid Infrastructure.

The ability to adding and remove nodes to the cluster is one of the great features offered by Grid Infrastructure in both its current and previous iterations. We discussed how that process differs in current and other recent releases.

We also delved into advanced topic such as changing the SCAN post installation and using non-default listener ports, before concluding the chapter with by explaining how to maintain (and restore) voting disks and the OCR/OLR.

■ ■ ■

## CHAPTER 9

Automatic Storage Management

In this chapter, we will describe ASM, which was introduced in Oracle 10.1 and is intended to simplify storage administration by automating disk and file management tasks to reduce management overhead and deployment costs.

ASM is a generic alternative to a clustered file system (CFS)/cluster logical volume manager that works on all platforms. ASM provides similar functionality to a classic CFS but includes volume management capabilities, such as disk balancing and redundancy. If you are using the Oracle Database 10g Standard Edition with the free RAC option, you must use ASM to store database files.

In our experience, since the introduction of Oracle 10.2, ASM has become the most popular choice for storage management on new deployments and has reached relative maturity in a remarkably short period of time. ASM is possibly the single most widely adopted feature after its initial release. Documentation and functionality have increased, and while initially documentation consisted of a chapter in the Administrator's Guide in 10g, it has now got a manual of its own, called Oracle® Database Storage Administrator's Guide, 11g Release 2.

Introducing ASM

We strongly recommend that you use ASM for new RAC deployments and also consider migrating existing RAC databases to ASM where the opportunity arises. The only exception to this recommendation is RAC databases running on supported NFS file systems such as Network Appliance. The number of deployments on NFS appliances, however, is not large.

ASM was introduced in Oracle 10.1 and has rapidly become the preferred database storage option for RAC deployments. Earlier versions had significant design issues, particularly in the areas of user interfaces and assignment of management responsibilities. These issues have largely been resolved in more recent releases, and ASM has become a much more user-friendly entity.

Unusually for an Oracle product, one of the main reasons for the rapid acceptance of ASM was due to licensing, but also due to the tight integration with the Oracle software stack. In Oracle 10.1 and above, Standard Edition users do not need to purchase the RAC option for small clusters. A number of conditions apply; there can be only two nodes in the cluster, there are limits on the number of processors in each node, and the database must use ASM. A significant number of users deployed Standard Edition clusters to take advantage of the lower licensing costs, and, as a result, ASM was implemented and tested by a larger number of sites than would normally have been expected.

> ■ **Caution** Oracle licensing terms change with reasonable frequency. If you decide to implement RAC for a small cluster, be sure to double-check the conditions we list in the preceding paragraph. Verify the licensing terms for yourself, for the specific release of Oracle Database that you are running.

ASM uses a technology introduced in Oracle 9.0.1 by the Oracle Managed Files (OMF) feature, which automates the creation and deletion of database files including data files, control files, and online redo logs. Under OMF, tablespaces can be managed without reference to file names.

Although primarily used in clustered environments, ASM can be used with both single-instance and RAC databases. The evolving design of ASM incorporates many storage best practices, and it has become the preferred choice for most RAC deployments.

ASM Terminology

Conceptually, ASM resembles the classical logical volume manager (LVM) we know from Linux, but it can do a lot more and—most importantly—it is cluster aware. Individual physical volumes, called ASM disks, are aggregated into volume groups, referred to as ASM disk groups. In a RAC environment, the ASM disks have to be located on shared storage accessible from all nodes in the cluster. The administrator can define redundancy levels for the disks in a disk group.

Unlike Linux LVM, there are no logical volumes based on a disk group. Instead, the disk group as a whole can be used to create and store database files. A list of supported database files is listed in the next section. Figure 9-1 demonstrates the difference between LVM and ASM:

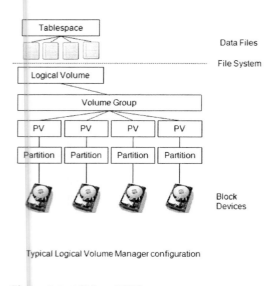

Figure 9-1. ASM vs. LVM

Note that Figure 9-1 lists partitions as part of the block device. Partitions were mandatory in ASM 10g but are no longer required from 11.1 onwards. We listed partitions here anyway to acknowledge the fact that manual partitioning can make use of the outer part of the spindle for optimal disk performance.

Besides the non-existing logical volume, ASM does not suffer the overhead of a file system layer—all database files reside directly on an ASM disk group. The analogy to raw devices is intentional.

ASM files are organized in extents, which are spread across the disks in the disk group, depending on the redundancy level of the disk group.

Supported File Types

The list of supported file types has increased steadily, initially with a focus on database-related files. Oracle ASM's intrinsic file system supports the following file types:

- Files usually found in the Fast Recovery Area

    - Archived online redo log files

    - Flashback logs

    - RMAN backup piece

    - RMAN image copy

    - Data pump dump file

    - Block change tracking file

- Files usually found in the main database storage area

    - Control files and control file automatic backups

    - Data files

    - Temp files

    - Online redo log files

    - Server parameter file

ASM also supports storing the voting disk and OCR. While the OCR location is externalized and visible in the disk group, the voting files are stored internally in ASM disks and cannot directly be modified by the user. The ASM disk headers will specify where a voting file starts and where it ends within the ASM disk.

In Oracle 11.2, the new ASM Clustered Filesystem (ACFS) can manage any file type including shared Oracle database homes, trace files, and external application files. Note that database files are not supported in ACFS. We understand from the ASM development team that this limitation has been imposed primarily for performance reasons. Files stored in ACFS can be accessed using traditional Linux O/S commands such as ls, pwd, and more, since ACFS supports a classic vnode interface. In this aspect, ACFS in our opinion is better than the initial OCFS release, which required special tools for administration and was furthermore plagued by problems.

ASM Management

ASM was originally designed to reduce management overhead. The DBA can perform storage-related tasks directly without involving storage administrators. This does not imply that storage administrators or system administrators become obsolete; they still perform essential tasks in managing a RAC cluster. It does mean, however, that the departments work more closely together. For many sites, ASM can potentially replace third-party Logical Volume Managers. It can also implement redundancy, replacing expensive external RAID storage. Most of the sites, however, still use external redundancy and rely on the storage array to protect from individual disk failures.

However, experience has shown that for many larger users, ASM offers fewer benefits, as the complexity of storage management and the related network infrastructure still requires specialist knowledge. Most users still require storage administrators to manage legacy Oracle databases running on file systems and also to manage non-Oracle storage. In Oracle 11.1 and above, therefore, the roles of the DBA and storage administrator have been separated within ASM, allowing responsibilities to be assigned to different teams or even different organizations if necessary.

ASM simplifies management of large numbers of disks by allowing groups of disks sharing similar characteristics to be assigned to disk groups. In ASM, the basic unit of administration is normally the disk group.

ASM can perform some of the tasks traditionally performed by third-party management procedures such as striping and mirroring, providing increased reliability and performance. By default, ASM implements two-way mirroring to maintain a redundant copy of data providing fault tolerance, but for particularly important data, ASM can also implement three-way mirroring. If the storage layer already provides mirroring capabilities or implements RAID, then ASM can utilize these features instead.

ASM automatically stripes data across all disks in a disk group, providing improved I/O performance. The default stripe size is determined by the class of database file. ASM also performs limited load balancing of files between disks. Rebalancing operations that uniformly distribute file extents that make up a file across all available disks are automatically performed whenever disks are added or dropped from the disks group. Rebalancing is intended to eliminate physical disk hotspots. In Oracle 10.2 and above, rebalancing operations can also be managed manually.

ASM and RDBMS Support

It is important to remember that much of the functionality within ASM is implemented by the RDBMS kernel. Therefore, for example, if you wish to take full advantage of Oracle 11.2 functionality, you would need to upgrade both ASM and the RDBMS to that release; it is not sufficient or possible simply to upgrade the ASM component. You also need to raise the compatibility level of your ASM disk group to make use of more advanced features.

ASM supports all versions of the RDBMS from Oracle 10.1 upwards. The ASM version must be more recent or the same as the RDBMS version. If the version differs between ASM and the RDBMS, then only the older functionality will apply. In Oracle 10.2 and above, ASM supports multiple database versions. For example, Oracle 11.2 ASM can support one database running Oracle 11.2 and another running 10.2 in the same cluster.

Prior to Oracle 11.2, the Clusterware version must also be more recent or the same as the ASM version. In Oracle 11.2, ASM has been integrated into the Grid Infrastructure. It now shares an Oracle Home with Clusterware. Future patch sets will include both components. This also eliminates the discussion about the number of ASM instances per RAC node—with Grid Infrastructure, there will be only one. Grid Infrastructure patches will apply to all components within the Grid Infrastructure home, including ASM, but also ACFS and Clusterware.

In Oracle 10.1, ASM typically shared the RDBMS Oracle Home. In Oracle 10.2 and 11.1, Oracle recommends that ASM was installed in a separate Home to the RDBMS, providing increased flexibility during upgrades. Note that this separation is not mandatory and many users, particularly those running smaller databases, continue to use the same Oracle Home for ASM and RDBMS. For systems with limited memory, combining the ASM and RDBMS Homes significantly reduces memory usage, as only one version of the oracle executable will be loaded. In Oracle 11.2 and above, the separation of ASM and RDBMS is enforced by the new Grid Infrastructure architecture. But contrary to the earlier releases, Grid Infrastructure includes the cluster software stack as well as ASM in one single Oracle home.

ASM Installation

In Oracle 11.2, ASM has been integrated with Oracle Clusterware and is now part of the new Grid Infrastructure. Both components are installed together, and Chapter 7 describes this installation in detail.

We recommend that you use local storage for the Grid Infrastructure home on each node in the cluster. This increases space usage and theoretically imposes a management overhead. However, in practice, most users have found that using local Oracle Homes provides increased flexibility and ultimately results in higher availability. Since Oracle 10.1.0.3, it has been possible to perform a rolling upgrade of Oracle Clusterware. In Oracle 11.1 and above, it is also possible to perform a rolling upgrade of ASM. Rolling upgrades allow individual nodes to be upgraded without affecting other nodes in the cluster. Clusterware rolling upgrades are already proven technology in production systems, reducing downtime and minimizing risk during the upgrade. Shared Oracle Homes limit this flexibility; therefore we recommend that local storage is always used for the Grid Infrastructure home.

In earlier versions of Linux running the 2.4 kernel, we recommended deployment of the ASM library (ASMLib), which is a set of three open source RPMs supplied by Oracle for Linux systems. With the introduction of the udev system, which is part of kernel 2.6–based distributions, the administrator has another choice. A third option exists with the device-mapper-multipath package. We discussed each of these in Chapter 6.

ASM Components and Concepts

ASM consists of the following main components: the ASM instance, failure groups, and ASM files. Along with these components, we are going to look at redundancy level, striping and mirroring, Intelligent Data Placement, and access control in detail.

ASM Instances

In order to use ASM in a RAC cluster, a separate ASM instance must be running on each node. The ASM instance maintains metadata in the ASM disk groups and supports with the database instances. The ASM instance must be started before other database instances can access files located in ASM storage. If the ASM instance is terminated, all client database instances will also be terminated. The ASM instance also handles adding and dropping disks and rebalancing operations,

The database instance communicates with the ASM instance to obtain information about files stored in ASM. However, the ASM instance does not perform I/O directly for applications. Application I/O is still performed by the server processes and background processes associated with the database instances. The ASM instance performs I/O only during rebalancing operations.

The ASM instance is a stripped-down version of a standard instance that is now referred to as an RDBMS instance. The instance type is defined by the INSTANCE_TYPE that takes the values RDBMS (default) or ASM.

You can connect to a running ASM instance and query it using dynamic performance (V$ and X$) views. Unlike a database instance, an ASM instance does not mount or open the database. Consequently, it does not have access to a data dictionary—the ASM instance does not have persistent information stored, and no data files of its own. Therefore it does not support queries against DBA/ALL/USER views.

In Oracle 10g, connections to the ASM instance required the SYSOPER or SYSDBA privilege. In Oracle 11.1, the SYSASM privilege was introduced, allowing separator groups of storage administrators and DBAs to be defined. In Oracle 11.2, you must have SYSASM privilege to perform most administrative tasks in ASM. SYSOPER privilege is required to start up and shut down the ASM instance, to mount, dismount, check and offline disks groups, and to access ASM dynamic performance views. Users with SYSASM privilege can also perform these tasks and in addition can create disk groups and add or drop disks.

Instance Names

Prior to Oracle 11.2, it was possible to have more than one ASM instance on each node, even though this was considered bad practice by most Oracle professionals and it was not supported by Oracle. Administrators could also specify names for ASM instances. By default Oracle will name instances +ASM<nodeNumber>, e.g., +ASM1, +ASM2, etc. While these instance names are not mandatory, we recommend that you follow these naming conventions if you create ASM instances manually.

In Oracle 11.2, there can be only one ASM instance on each node and it is not necessary to modify the instance names. Instance names are defined inside the resource profile of the ASM resource, which can be queried using the crsctl status resource ora.asm -p command. You see that the instance names are generated on your behalf in the following example:

```
[oracle@ondon1 ~]$ crsctl stat res ora.asm -p
NAME=ora.asm
TYPE=ora.asm.type
[...]
GEN_USR_ORA_INST_NAME@SERVERNAME(london1)=+ASM1
GEN_USR_ORA_INST_NAME@SERVERNAME(london2)=+ASM2
```

SGA

The ASM instance maintains a separate SGA. Additional ASM background processes introduced in Oracle 11.2 increase the SGA requirement. ASM automatically defaults to Automatic Memory management. Oracle strongly recommends that you stick with this, but you are, of course, free to change the spfile to match your requirements. It is entirely possible to revert back to Automatic Shared Memory Management as in Oracle 10g. In this case, you should consult the Oracle® Database Storage Administrator's Guide 11g Release 2 to for recommendations about manually setting instance memory parameters.

The same document suggests that the default value for the memory_target parameter is sufficient for most environments. In our 11.2.0.1.0 64bit Linux ASM instance, memory_target was set to 272MB. The breakdown of components is visible in the view (G)V$MEMORY_DYNAMIC_COMPONENTS:

```
SQL> select component,current_size,min_size,max_size
  2    from V$MEMORY_DYNAMIC_COMPONENTS
  3  where current_size <> 0
  4  /
```

COMPONENT	CURRENT_SIZE	MIN_SIZE	MAX_SIZE
shared pool	142606336	142606336	142606336
large pool	4194304	4194304	4194304
SGA Target	180355072	180355072	180355072
PGA Target	104857600	104857600	104857600
ASM Buffer Cache	25165824	25165824	25165824

Background Processes

We said in the introduction section that ASM is a special type of Oracle database. Therefore you can expect to find most of the background processes typical for an RDBMS instance in the ASM instance as well. In a single-instance Oracle Restart environment, an ASM instance has a number of background processes, including PMON, SMON, DBWO, LGWR CKPT, and MMAN. In a RAC environment, additional background processes support clustering, including LMON, LMDO, LMSO, LCKO, and DIAG.

The following background processes were found in our 11.2 ASM instance with a mounted ASM cluster filesystem:

```
SQL> select name,description
  2  from v$bgprocess
  3  where paddr <> '00';

NAME  DESCRIPTION
----- ----------------------------------------------------------------
PMON  process cleanup
VKTM  Virtual Keeper of TiMe process
GENO  genericO
DIAG  diagnosibility process
PING  interconnect latency measurement
PSPO  process spawner O
DIAO  diagnosibility process O
LMON  global enqueue service monitor
LMDO  global enqueue service daemon O
LMSO  global cache service process O
LMHB  lm heartbeat monitor
MMAN  Memory Manager
DBWO  db writer process O
LGWR  Redo etc.
LCKO  Lock Process O
CKPT  checkpoint
SMON  System Monitor Process
RBAL  ASM Rebalance master
ASMB  ASM Background
GMON  diskgroup monitor
VBGO  Volume BG O
VBG1  Volume BG 1
VBG2  Volume BG 2
VDBG  Volume Driver BG
VMBO  Volume Membership O
ACFS  ACFS CSS
MMON  Manageability Monitor Process
```

MMNL   Manageability Monitor Process 2

28 rows selected.

Different from an RDBMS instance, each ASM instance has additional background processes. Some of these are not shown in the preceding listing as they are not always active. The following background processes can be found with an ASM instance:

- The ASM rebalance master background process (RBAL) coordinates disk rebalancing activity. It also exists in RDBMS instances.

- The ASM Background process (ASMB) is used for interactions between the CSS daemon, mainly during the initial connection to the ASM instance and a heartbeat mechanism.

- The disk group monitor process (GMON) manages disk group compatibility and monitors disk groups for offline disks in diskgroups. If it finds offline disks in a disk group, it will create up to five slave processes (B*nnn*) to keep track of the time it was offline. If the offline disk can be brought online within the specified disk repair time, it can be prevented from being dropped. The Disk Resynchronization Slave processes (DRnn) are responsible for resynchronizing the previously offline disk. Another background process, "MARK," keeps track of extents in need for resynchronization. This process is started in the RDBMS instance.

- The Volume Background process (VBGn) is related to the ACFS functionality. It handles the communication between the OS volume driver and ASM instance. There can be up to nine VBGn processes.

- The Volume Driver process (VDBG) passes ASM commands on disk groups to the ASM Dynamic Volume Manager (ADVM).

- The Volume Membership process (VMB0) maintains cluster membership on behalf of ADVM.

- The ASM Cluster File System CSS Process (ACFS) keeps track of which nodes form part of the cluster. In case of node evictions, these are passed on to the ACFS via the ACFS process. The process is mainly used to ensure consistency on the file system level.

- The ASM rebalancing slave processes (ARB*n*) perform the actual rebalancing by moving data extents between disks. When completed, the Disk Expel Slave processes (Xnnn) will remove dropped disks from a disk group.

- Metadata operations are handled by the Onnn and OCFn background processes.

- The Interconnect Latency Measurement Process PING measures the latency of the interconnect every few seconds.

- ASM automatically reads the secondary extent in normal/high redundancy disk groups if it finds that the primary extent is corrupt. ASM will try to perform the read asynchronously by spawning a Rnnn slave process.

Parameters

Oracle ASM 11.2 changed the way it stored its initialization parameters. Versions prior to Oracle 11.2 allowed you to store initialization parameters either in a parameter file ("pfile") or server parameter file ("spfile"). Per convention these files were located in the Oracle ASM software home in the dbs sub directory.

ASM 11.2 only ever uses a server parameter file—but on RAC you will not find it in $GRID_HOME/dbs, which can be a surprise. Instead, clustered ASM uses the GPnP profile (see Chapter 8 for more information about the GPnP profile) to locate the spfile. If it does not find it there, it tries to locate it in $GRID_HOME/dbs. On our cluster, the ASM server parameter file was located in +OCRVOTE/cluster1/asmparameterfile/:

```
ASMCMD> ls -l
Type                Redund  Striped  Time            Sys  Name
ASMPARAMETERFILE    HIGH    COARSE   APR 27 00:00:00  Y    REGISTRY.253.717382259
```

■ **Note** Single instance Oracle ASM relies on the OLR to locate the server parameter file.

There are only a handful of parameters in use in an ASM instance. Smaller sites do not normally have to modify them, but if you do, you can use either the SQL "alter system" command or, alternatively, Enterprise Manager. The only required parameter is "instance_type", which has to be set to "ASM". Other parameters worth considering are the following:

> **CLUSTER_DATABASE:** Required setting for RAC deployments is "TRUE".
>
> **INSTANCE_TYPE:** Every ASM instance requires that the instance_type parameter is set to ASM.
>
> **ASM_DISKSTRING:** This parameter specifies a set of disk locations used by Oracle during disk discovery. When a new disk is added to a disk group, the ASM instance discovers the new disk by searching in the directories specified by this parameter. The default value is NULL. When using ASMLib, you don't need to change the parameter as the disk discovery string is set correctly and uses "ORCL:*". You need to change the parameter only when you are using udev or device mapper multipathing for ASM disks.
>
> **ASM_PREFERRED_READ_FAILURE_GROUPS:** The preferred mirror read feature first appeared in Oracle 11.1. Mainly useful for extended distance clusters where it can help reducing latency, it is a comma-separated list of failure groups that should be read by the local instance. When specifying this parameter, it is important to set the scope-clause in the alter system command correctly.
>
> **ASM_POWER_LIMIT:** When disks are added to or removed from disk groups, ASM moves file extents between disks to balance I/O equally between all disks in the group. The asm_power_limit parameter determines how aggressively the rebalancing operation is performed. The parameter takes a numeric value ranging from 1 (slowest) to 11 (fastest).

ASM_DISKGROUPS: The asm_diskgroups parameter is dynamic and updated when a disk group is created, dropped, or mounted. The mount operation does not have to be executed within ASM, but can also be initiated by `srvctl start diskgroup -g` *diskgroupName*. The disk groups specified in the asm_diskgroups parameter will automatically be mounted when the ASM instance starts.

Note When using a parameter file, the administrator is responsible for maintaining the ASM_DISKGROUPS parameter.

DIAGNOSTIC_DEST: The ASM instance uses the ADR exactly as databases do. In our cluster, the local ASM instance had its ADR home in $GRID_HOME/log/, but you can also commonly find the ADR_HOME under $ORACLE_BASE/diag. When using the adrci command line utility, make sure to set the base to the correct location.

PROCESSES: The default value for the processes parameter should suit most environments. However, if many databases access the ASM instance, you might need to increase the parameter. Keep in mind that the background processes of the ASM instance also need to fit into the processes parameter.

Note Memory parameters (shared_pool_size, large_pool_size, etc.) usually do not need adjusting if you stick to Automatic Memory Management as suggested.

Failure Groups

If a disk controller fails, then all disks that are connected to it will be inaccessible. ASM defines failure groups, which are groups of disks that are dependent on a single point of failure, such as a controller. To ensure redundancy, each mirror should be located on a different failure group. In the event of a controller failure, ASM can, therefore, guarantee that it can reconstruct the failed disk group from mirrored copies of extents in remaining disk groups.

A special type of failure group has been introduced in ASM 11.2, and it's called a quorum failure group. This type of failure group is used in the context of extended distance clusters, when the voting files are deployed in ASM. A quorum failure group does not contain user data, and it does not count for disk group redundancy requirements.

With stretched clusters, we need at least three voting files, one on each site plus a third that is normally deployed via NFS. Unfortunately, the OUI doesn't allow such a complex setup, so when configuring the extended distance cluster, you should start with a normal configuration—two voting disks on site A and one for site B—and add the third voting disk after the installation finishes.

Begin by exporting a file system on the NFS appliance, containing a zero-padded file to serve as the voting disk later. The file should be the same size as the ASM disks already used to store the voting files. This NFS export should then be concurrently mounted by the two sites. Continue by adding the new zero-padded file as an ASM disk, marked as a quorum failure group—for this you have to change the disk discovery string. Once the new disk is added to the disk group, ASM will automatically readjust the voting files and include the NFS "disk."

Oracle 11.1 introduced a new feature called "PREFERRED_READ_FAILURE_GROUP" to speed up access to storage in extended distance clusters. In stretched-RAC deployments with ASM, each local storage array forms its own failure group. This way, ASM can be used for providing redundancy. We said earlier that ASM always uses the primary extent when dealing with ASM files, which could potentially be on the remote site. Oracle 10*g* did not offer any possible way of instructing ASM to read the local extent instead. With ASM 11.1, this has changed for the better. Setting the COMPATIBLE.RDBMS parameter at the ASM disk group level to at least 11.1, and the ASM instances' initialization parameter PREFERRED_READ_FAILURE_GROUPS to the respective local site, ASM will try to prefer the local site over the remote site, potentially reducing latency.

ASM Files

Files created within ASM follow the naming standard set by the Oracle Managed File feature first introduced on Oracle 9*i*. This offers the significant advantage of not having to specifying file names and accidentally storing data files in the wrong directory. But it comes at a price—the administrator loses control over file names.

Naming Files

ASM files can be addressed in a number of ways. The most common is probably the fully qualified file name, which takes the following form:

```
+DiskGroupName/DBUniqueName/Filetype/FiletypeTag.file#.incarnation
```

To complicate matters, the fully qualified name is never used to create a file—this would produce an error. Instead, when creating a tablespace, for example, the administrator issues the following command:

```
SQL> create tablespace users datafile size 1g extent management local
  2   segment space management auto;

Tablespace created.
```

Note the absence of a file name in the command. The initialization parameter "DB_CREATE_FILE_DEST" is used by the RDBMS instance to determine the disk group to place the file in. If the administrator wants to specify a disk group to place a file in, she could change the command to read as follows:

```
SQL> create tablespace users datafile '+DATA' size 1g extent management local
  2   segment space management auto;

Tablespace created.
```

However, when modifying a file, you have to specify the fully qualified file name, as you always did before the introduction of ASM. To resize a data file, for example, you use the following syntax:

```
SQL> alter database datafile '+DATA/PROD/DATAFILE/users.259.679156903' resize 10G;
```

465

You have seen from the previous sections that it is not necessary to specify a file name in the create tablespace command. The same applies for online redo logs and control files. The Fast Recovery Area works in a similar way, and all three of them are defined in the initialization file as follows:

- DB_CREATE_FILE_DEST
- D B_CREATE_ONLINE_LOG_DEST_{1,2,3,4,5}
- DB_RECOVERY_FILE_DEST

The common case, where one disk group ("+DATA" or similar) is used to store the data files and a Fast Recovery Area ("+FRA") is employed, and no "DB_CREATE_ONLINE_DEST_n" clause is specified, will cause control files and online redo logs to be multiplexed to the FRA and DATA disk group. If you specified DB_CREATE_ONLINE_LOG_DEST_n, then the control files and online redo logs will be created in that location instead. Specifying multiple different destinations provides greater fault tolerance.

Aliasing Files

In addition to the incomplete syntax we have just demonstrated, it is also possible to create files with an alias, as in this example:

```
SQL> create tablespace users datafile '+DATA/PROD/myDataFile.dat' size 1G;

Tablespace created.
```

You should note, though, that the alias is just a pointer to the fully qualified name for the file created behind the scenes. Aliases can also be created for existing data files, but we do not see a reason other than convenience behind the creation of an alias.

Managing Control Files

Control files take a special role in ASM. We have explained earlier that Oracle complains when you try to use an Oracle Managed File name to create a new file. Control files, however, are recorded with their fully qualified name in the initialization file. This can cause a problem when you try to recreate the control file from a SQL script generated by an "alter database backup controlfile to trace" command. In this case, you need to reset the value of the "*.control_files" parameter in the initialization file, bounce the instance, and then issue the "CREATE CONTROLFILE" command. In earlier versions of Oracle, the restore of a control file also failed when the initialization parameter was not unset, a deficit that has been rectified in recent versions of the Oracle RDBMS.

Understanding Extents, Allocation Units, Types, and Templates

ASM files within a disk group are organized into extents, which are further subdivided into allocation units (AU). Similar to extents within an ASSM tablespace with an auto allocation policy, extents can be of variable sizes as the data file grows. Variable extent sizes require a compatible setting of at least 11.1 for the disk group.

Properties of files stored in ASM are determined by their type, which maps to a template. A template, in a nutshell, determines the storage characteristics of a file. This includes the redundancy level (usually based on the disk group's redundancy level), the stripe type (coarse/fine), and the file type. For the external redundancy disk group "DATA," the following templates were in use:

```
SQL> select redundancy,stripe,name,primary_region,mirror_region
  2  from v$asm_template
  3  where group_number = 3
  4  /

REDUND STRIPE NAME                             PRIM MIRR
------ ------ ------------------------------   ---- ----
UNPROT COARSE PARAMETERFILE                    COLD COLD
UNPROT COARSE ASMPARAMETERFILE                 COLD COLD
UNPROT COARSE ASMPARAMETERBAKFILE              COLD COLD
UNPROT COARSE DUMPSET                          COLD COLD
UNPROT FINE   CONTROLFILE                      COLD COLD
UNPROT COARSE FLASHFILE                        COLD COLD
UNPROT COARSE ARCHIVELOG                       COLD COLD
UNPROT COARSE ONLINELOG                        COLD COLD
UNPROT COARSE DATAFILE                         COLD COLD
UNPROT COARSE TEMPFILE                         COLD COLD
UNPROT COARSE BACKUPSET                        COLD COLD
UNPROT COARSE AUTOBACKUP                       COLD COLD
UNPROT COARSE XTRANSPORT                       COLD COLD
UNPROT COARSE CHANGETRACKING                   COLD COLD
UNPROT COARSE FLASHBACK                        COLD COLD
UNPROT COARSE DATAGUARDCONFIG                  COLD COLD
UNPROT COARSE OCRFILE                          COLD COLD
UNPROT COARSE OCRBACKUP                        COLD COLD
UNPROT COARSE ASM_STALE                        COLD COLD

19 rows selected.
```

Control files, for example, are unprotected by ASM. (The disk group in this example was set up with external redundancy) Control files will use fine striping, and are placed in the cold region of the disk. Please refer to the section "Intelligent Data Placement" for more information about hot and cold regions of an ASM disk group.

To change the characteristics of a file, you could create your own template. For example, to explicitly set files to be created in the hot region of the disk group, a new template needs to be created:

```
SQL> alter diskgroup data
  2  add template allhot attributes (hot);
```

Since the disk group uses external redundancy, we cannot define the mirror blocks to be placed in the hot region—there simply are no mirror blocks to store. The new template is a user template—the SYSTEM column in v$asm_template is set to "N" here:

```
REDUND STRIPE NAME                             PRIM MIRR S
------ ------ ------------------------------   ---- ---- -
UNPROT COARSE ALLHOT                           HOT  COLD N
```

To make use of the template, create a tablespace and specify the template to be used:

```
SQL> create tablespace hottbs datafile '+DATA(allhot)' size 10M;
```

The file name clause—together with the template information—instructs ASM to use the new template "ALLHOT." The V$ASM_FILE view reflects this:

```
SQL> select bytes,type,redundancy,primary_region,mirror_region,
  2  hot_reads,hot_writes,cold_reads,cold_writes
  3* from v$asm_file where file_number = 284
SQL> /

     BYTES TYPE        REDUND PRIM MIRR  HOT_READS HOT_WRITES COLD_READS COLD_WRITES
---------- ----------- ------ ---- ---- ---------- ---------- ---------- -----------
  10493952 DATAFILE    UNPROT HOT  COLD          4        127          0           0
```

Redundancy

ASM supports three types of redundancy for ASM disk groups:

- **External redundancy** does not involve any mirroring. It uses the existing operating system or storage array protection, such as RAID or LVMs. Note, however, that if you select external redundancy, it is your responsibility to ensure that the underlying storage is correctly configured; ASM cannot guarantee recoverability in the event of a failure. You do not need to define any failure groups if you are using external redundancy.

- **Normal redundancy**, which is the default, implements two-way mirroring, in which each file extent will be written to two disk groups using one primary extent and one mirrored extent. To guarantee redundancy, you must define at least two failure groups.

- **High redundancy** implements three-way mirroring, in which each file extent will be written to three disk groups using one primary extent and two mirrored extents. To guarantee redundancy, you must define at least three failure groups.

From our experience, the majority of ASM deployments make use of the external redundancy setting. Most enterprises use storage arrays with internal protection against disk failure. If a disk fails within a disk group in the array, the storage administrator is usually tasked with replacing the failed disk long before the ASM administrator even notices that an individual disk has been lost. Among the very few users of normal redundancy disk groups is CERN. The Centre for Nuclear Research has decided very early to leverage the power of ASM's mirroring to save on the cost of expensive storage arrays. Their setup has been in production for some time, and performance and user experience are excellent.

Striping

ASM implements striping of files across the disks within a disk group to optimize I/O performance. Therefore every disk within the group should have the same type and performance characteristics. Two types of striping—coarse and fine—are implemented depending on the database file type.

Coarse striping is used for most file types, including database files, transportable tablespaces, backup sets, dump sets, autobackup control files, change tracking files, Data Guard configuration files, and some others. The coarse stripe size depends on the size of the allocation unit. When setting the disk group compatibility to 11.1 for RDBMS and ASM, variable extent sizes can be used for coarse striping. The first 20,000 extents always equal the allocation unit (AU) size. The next 20,000 extents are 4 times the size of the AU, and the extents thereafter will use 16 times the AU size.

By default, fine striping is used only for control files, online redo logs, and flashback logs. The stripe size is 128KB. Also by default, eight stripes are created for each file; therefore, the optimum number of disks in a disk group is a multiple of eight.

Mirroring

ASM uses mirroring to provide data redundancy, and it mirrors extents at the file level. This differs from most operating system mirroring, which is performed at disk level. If an ASM disk is lost, the extents mirrored on other ASM disks can be used to continue operations without data loss or interruption to service. In the event of a disk failure, ASM can reconstruct the failed extents using the mirrored extents from other disks in the same group. The use of striping means that the I/O required to reconstruct the new disk is spread evenly across the remaining disks in the group. If the disk error is transient, and the failed disk can be brought online again within a time threshold, the Fast Mirror Resync feature can help speed up the resynchronization operation. The requirement is to have a disk group with COMPATIBLE.RDBMS set to ≥ 11.1, and optionally a DISK_REPAIR_TIME. A so-called Staleness Registry keeps track of changes to the AUs within the offline disk. When the disk is brought online again, the Staleness Registry is used to recover the contents of the disk. If a disk cannot be repaired in time, it will automatically be dropped from the disk group, resulting in a full rebalance operation. This was the default behavior in 10g. Another rebalance operation occurred when the disk was eventually repaired and added back into the disk group.

Read errors are not a severe problem with mirrored ASM extents. Remember that ASM by default always reads the primary extent first. In case of a read error on the primary extent, ASM tries to read its mirrored extent. In high redundancy disk groups, it also tries to read the second mirror copy. Only if none of the mirrored copies are readable does ASM bail out; all other failures are merely recorded in the ASM instance's alert.log.

Write errors are more severe. A write operation issued by the ASM client is successful only if at least one extent copy can be written to an ASM disk. Additionally, the disk containing the primary extent will be taken offline, and the RDBMS instance has to acknowledge that fact for the write to complete successfully. If none of the mirrored extents can be written, the RDBMS instance has to take action and offlines the data file. The ASM instance, upon receiving a write error notification from the RDBMS, checks whether to offline the ASM disk only, or even the whole disk group. Once the disk is taken offline (or dropped, depending on COMPATIBLE.RDBMS), the algorithm is the same as in the foregoing read error example.

Intelligent Data Placement

For high performance storage architecture, it has always been recommended to partition individual hard disks into an outer and an inner part. Data in the outer part of the spindle is accessed faster and generally speaking offers best performance.

Intelligent Data Placement is a new 11.2 feature, and it allows the administrator to divide the ASM disk into a hot and cold region. The outmost tracks of a disk are referred to as the hot region, and the innermost tracks make up the cold region. The Intelligent Data Placement feature requires the disk group's RDBMS and ASM compatible flag to be set to 11.2, otherwise the options discussed here won't be available.

Intelligent Data Placement is unlikely to provide any benefit for disk groups filled to less than a quarter—the management overhead is not likely to outweigh the benefit offered by specifying a special disk region. Furthermore, the feature does not seem to apply to LUNs provided by a storage array, as the disk geometry is masked from ASM. We see the greatest potential for IDP with deployments where every disk in the storage backend is mapped to a LUN and presented to the database server.

By default, all files are created in the COLD region of the disk, as shown in the PRIMARY_REGION and MIRROR_REGION columns in the V$ASM_TEMPLATE view. Additional views with information about data placement are VASM_DISK, VASM_DISK_IOSTAT, V$ASM_FILE and the aforementioned V$ASM_TEMPLATE views. You can either use templates or make use of the alter diskgroup modify file command to change the placement policy. We discussed the use of templates in the section "Understanding Extents, Allocation Units, Types, and Templates" earlier in this chapter.

Access Control

ASM can optionally be instructed to grant access to the content of a disk group based on explicitly assigned access control lists. These ACLs limit the power of connections using the SYSDBA privilege, i.e., RDBMS instances in most cases.

Oracle 11.1 began separating super user access to ASM from super user access to the RDBMS instance. In 10g the SYSDBA role was the all-powerful role, both for ASM and the RDBMS. With 11.1 Oracle introduced a new privilege, called SYSASM. The SYSDBA privilege previously used still exists, but it has been redesigned.

Understanding Access Privileges

Users are granted access to the SYSASM role through membership of the operating system "OSASM" group. SYSDBA and SYSOPER roles for the ASM role are granted through membership of the operating system OSDBA and OSOPER group. The mapping of operating system group to role is performed during the installation of the Grid Infrastructure software. Most sites use the DBA group for OSASM, OSDBA, and OSOPER privileges. However, to successfully implement ASM access control, separate groups should be considered for each Oracle installation. This configuration step should be planned well and in advance if separation of duties is wanted. Table 9-1 demonstrates the case where two 11.2 RDBMS homes are installed on a cluster, in addition to the Grid Infrastructure. Assume the following users and groups:

Table 9-1. Example Cluster Configuration for ASM ACLs

Software Home	Software Owner	DB Name	Group Mapping
Grid Infrastructure	oracle	ASM	ASM Database Administrator Group (OSDBA) Group: asmdba
			ASM Instance Administration Operator (OSOPER) Group: asmdba
			ASM Instance Administrator (OSASM) Group: asmowner

Software Home	Software Owner	DB Name	Group Mapping
RDBMS home 1: "Finance"	orafin	FIN	Database Administrator (OSDBA) Group: dbafin
			Database Operator (OSOPER) Group: dbafin
RDBMS home 2: "Reporting"	orareport	REP	Database Administrator (OSDBA) Group: dbareport
			Database Operator (OSOPER) Group: dbareport

The "software owner" in this table maps to the operating system account under which the binaries have been installed. We have omitted the primary group for the account—oinstall—for the sake of clarity. You can use the id command line utility to verify user and group mapping; the "-a" option prints more information

```
[root@london1 ~]# id -a orafin
uid=503(orafin) gid=502(oinstall) groups=502(oinstall),504(asmdba),505(dbafin)
context=root:system_r:unconfined_t:SystemLow-SystemHigh
```

If the groups are not set already, the administrator can use the usermod command to change secondary groups for a user:

```
[root@london1 ~]# usermod –G asmdba,dbareport orareport
```

The RDBMS software owners absolutely require membership of the ASMDBA group, otherwise they cannot access the ASM instance at all. Furthermore, separate operating system groups "DBAFIN" and "DBAREPORT" separate access to the database instances. As with all user and group mappings in RAC, the UIDs and GIDs must be identical across all nodes.

The SYSASM role replaces the previously used SYSDBA role as the all-powerful role in ASM from 11.1 onwards. Users logging in with this privilege can perform any maintenance operation. Users connecting with the SYSDBA role, which in most cases are ASM clients, have fewer privileges now than they had pre–Oracle 11.1.

Preparing the ASM Disk Group

To prevent unauthorized ASM clients from performing unwanted activities, ASM can set privileges on the disk group level. Making use of the access control feature requires that the disk group uses the following disk group attributes:

- COMPATIBLE.ASM = 11.2
- COMPATIBLE.RDBMS = 11.2
- ACCESS_CONTROL.ENABLED = true

The ASM file access control feature limits the power of the SYSDBA connection. File access is based on the triple user-group-others, just as with file system permissions. An optional umask value can be specified. With it, the ASM administrator can change the default permissions for newly created files. This is a feature very similar to the shell's umask command, and it is controlled via the disk group's ACCESS_CONTROL.UMASK attribute. The default umask value is 066, setting file system permissions to full control for the owner, and no control for the group and others for newly created files. Permissions can be set to none, read-only, and read-write. These map to the numeric values 0, 2, and 6.

ASM derives the owner information from the operating system—in our foregoing example, the operating system accounts. "ORAFIN" and "ORAREPORT" can be owners of files, since they own their respective RDBMS installation. As you would expect, the owner of a file has full permissions, including changing the file's group setting.

User groups can be collections of databases that share similar storage requirements. Unlike the owner information, which is derived from the operating system, the group is optional, and has to be specifically created. You can use the "ALTER DISKGROUP … ADD USERGROUP" command to create a user group.

To retrospectively introduce access control to a disk group, use the alter diskgroup commands to enable access control. Log into an ASM instance with the SYSASM role enabled and change the attributes to the required settings:

```
SQL> ALTER DISKGROUP DATA set attribute 'compatible.asm' = '11.2';

Diskgroup altered.

SQL> ALTER DISKGROUP DATA set attribute 'compatible.rdbms' = '11.2';

Diskgroup altered.

SQL> ALTER DISKGROUP DATA set attribute 'access_control.enabled' = 'TRUE';

Diskgroup altered.
```

Enabling access control at this stage does not change ownership of any existing file! It does, however, enable access control for any new file in the disk group. In our system, after enabling access control, the following permissions were set after a new tablespace "HOTTBS" with data file "HOTTBS.284. 725562071" had been created. Our disk group's files were listed as follows:

```
SQL  select name, permissions,user_number,usergroup_number
  2    from v$asm_file f natural join v$asm_alias t
  3   where group_number = 3
SQL> /
```

NAME	PERMISSIONS	USER_NUMBER	USERGROUP_NUMBER
SYSTEM.256.722359017	rw-rw-rw-	0	0
SYSAUX.257.722359017	rw-rw-rw-	0	0
TEMP.278.723575013	rw-rw-rw-	0	0
[...]			
spfile.283.723575205	rw-rw-rw-	0	0
spfilePROD.ora	rw-rw-rw-	0	0
HOTTBS.284.725562071	rw-------	1	0

31 rows selected.

Only the newly created file has had adjusted permissions, respecting the UMASK value of 066. This UMASK setting removes permissions from the group and all "others."

Also, the V$ASM_USER view is now populated—group number 3 maps to the DATA disk group. User number 1 from the foregoing output maps to user "orafin," as the following example shows:

```
SQL> select group_number,user_number,os_id,os_name
  2  from v$asm_user;

GROUP_NUMBER USER_NUMBER OS_ID      OS_NAME
------------ ----------- ---------- -----------
           3           1 503        orafin
```

This corresponds to the output of the id command:

```
[root@london1 ~]# id -a orafin
uid=503(orafin) gid=502(oinstall) groups=502(oinstall),504(asmdba),505(dbafin)
context=root:system_r:unconfined_t:SystemLow-SystemHigh
```

Changing File Ownership and Permissions

Next you need to change the ownership of files using the alter diskgroup set permission and alter diskgroup set ownership commands. You should ensure that the user you are assigning the privileges does indeed exist. Then use the alter diskgroup command again to set the ownership and permissions:

```
SQL> alter diskgroup data set ownership
  2  owner = 'orareport'  --case sensitive!
  3  for file '+DATA/PROD/DATAFILE/users.259.679156903';

Diskgroup altered.
```

This can easily be scripted for data files by using the following scriptlet when connected to an RDBMS instance:

```
SQL> select 'alter diskgroup data set ownership owner = ''orareport'' ' ||
  2  'for file ''' || name || ''';' from v$datafile;
```

The output can be spooled into a file for later execution using a SYSASM connection against the ASM instance. Don't forget to set the ownership for all other database files such as online redo logs, temporary files, and all other files belonging to your database. The server parameter file is a special case. During our tests with the new functionality, it turned out that the spfile has to be owned by the Grid software owner rather than the RDBMS software owner. Failure to change ownership to the Grid Software owner repeatedly resulted in the following errors:

```
SQL> startup
ORA-01078: failure in processing system parameters
ORA-01565: error in identifying file '+DATA/fin/spfilefin.ora'
ORA-17503: ksfdopn:2 Failed to open file +DATA/fin/spfilefin.ora
ORA-15056: additional error message
ORA-17503: ksfdopn:DGOpenFile05 Failed to open file +DATA/fin/spfilefin.ora
ORA-17503: ksfdopn:2 Failed to open file +DATA/fin/spfilefin.ora
```

ORA-15260: permission denied on ASM disk group

```
ORA-06512: at line 4
SQL> exit
```

Once the permissions are set, the database will start again. You can use the asmcmd command to verify the permissions on the file:

```
ASMCMD> cd +data/fin
ASMCMD> ls --permission
User    Group  Permission  Name
                           spfilefin.ora =>
   +DATA/FIN/PARAMETERFILE/SPFILE.270.726353479
ASMCMD> ls --permission  +DATA/FIN/PARAMETERFILE/SPFILE.270.726353479
User    Group  Permission  Name
oracle         rw-------  SPFILE.270.726353479
```

The ascmd command also allows you to change ownership of a single file (the wildcard character "*" did not work at the time of this writing). Use "chown owner[:group] filename" to change ownership. In this configuration the Grid software stack was owned by oracle.

■ **Note** The data file must not be online to perform a change of ownership or permissions. It is good practice to assign ownership and privileges as soon as enabling access control, or the database instance may not start!

With the ownership set, you can connect as SYSDBA to the RDBMS instance to set permissions—remember that the owner of the file has the privilege to do so. Again, a small scriptlet can make this a lot easier for databases with many data files:

```
SQL> select 'alter diskgroup data set permission owner = read write, ' ||
  2  'group = read only, other = none' ||
  3  ' for file ''' || name || ''';' from v$datafile;
```

To change permissions of the EXAMPLE tablespace's data file, you would use this command:

```
SQL> alter diskgroup data set permission owner = read write,
  2  group = read only, other = none
  3  for file '+DATA/FIN/datafile/example.279.723575017';

Diskgroup altered.
```

The new settings are reflected in the V$ASM_FILE view, as shown in the output here:

```
SQL> select name, permissions,user_number,usergroup_number
  2  from v$asm_file f natural join v$asm_alias t
  3  where group_number = 3
  4 and name = 'EXAMPLE.279.723575017'
  5 /
```

NAME	PERMISSIONS	USER_NUMBER	USERGROUP_NUMBER
EXAMPLE.279.723575017	rw-r-----	1	0

Optionally, you can create a group of ASM clients sharing similar requirements. The alter diskgroup add usergroup command allows you to perform this task. Information about users and groups is stored in the dynamic performance views V$ASM_USER and V$ASM_USERGROUP.

Maintaining ASM

In the last edition of this book, this has been a longer discussion—how to add and remove ASM instances from cluster nodes. Up to Oracle 11.1 this was still true, as one of the Oracle homes was usually dedicated for ASM. The integration of ASM into Grid Infrastructure has fundamentally changed this: from now on, Oracle Database 11g makes maintenance much easier, in that adding and removing ASM instances is now part of the node addition and deletion process. The Oracle Universal Installer will automatically create an ASM instance when a node is added to the cluster. Conversely, when a node is removed from the cluster, OUI will also remove the ASM instance. This approach makes dealing with ASM very simple.

Creating an ASM Disk Group

Disk groups can be created using asmca, asmcmd, or Enterprise Manager. Disk groups can also be created manually using the CREATE DISKGROUP command in SQL*Plus when connected to the ASM instance, as in the following example:

```
SQL> create diskgroup DATA
> normal redundancy
> failgroup controllerA disk 'ORCL:DATA01', 'ORCL:DATA02', 'ORCL:DATA03', 'ORCL:DATA04'
> failgroup controllerB disk 'ORCL:DATA05', 'ORCL:DATA06', 'ORCL:DATA07', 'ORCL:DATA08';

Diskgroup created.
```

■ **Note** In the foregoing example, we assumed disk provisioning via ASMLib. We discussed SAN Disk Discovery and Configuration in Chapter 6 in detail.

The redundancy clause in the preceding example specifies which level of redundancy should be provided by ASM. If no FAILGROUP clause is specified, then each disk will be in its own failure group. In this example, two failgroups were explicitly created for two storage controllers. Since you are using a server parameter file in ASM 11.2, the disk group name will be added automatically to the ASM_DISKGROUPS parameter. Clusterware will also detect a new ASM disk group and add it as a resource.

Oracle 11.1 added attributes to the ASM disk group, which were extended in Oracle 11.2. At the time of this writing, the following attributes could be set.

- COMPATIBLE.ASM
- COMPATIBLE.RDBMS
- COMPATIBLE.ADVM
- AU_SIZE
- SECTOR_SIZE
- DISK_REPAIR_TIME
- ACCESS_CONTROL.ENABLED
- ACCESS_CONTROL.UMASK

The ASM compatibility flag sets which features are available with a disk group. It also specifies the minimum version of the ASM to access the disk group. By default, the ASM compatibility is set to 10.1 when a disk group is created, except for asmca, which defaults to 11.2. Many features of Grid Infrastructure such as ACFS volumes and storing the OCR and voting disk in ASM require the COMPATIBLE.ASM flag to be 11.2.

The database instance's "compatible" parameter has to be at least the same as or higher than the RDBMS compatibility flag of the disk group. It defaults to 10.1.

The final compatible flag, COMPATIBLE.ADVM, is new to ASM 11.2 and defines whether a disk group can store an ASM Dynamic Volume. COMPATIBLE.ADVM requires COMPATIBLE.ASM to be set to 11.2 as well. By default the value for COMPATIBLE.ADVM is blank.

The compatible attributes just described can be set either during the creation of the disk group or at a later stage. The CREATE DISKGROUP and ALTER DISKGROUP commands take the settings in the attribute clause, as shown in this example:

```
SQL> ALTER DISKGROUP ocrvote SET ATTRIBUTE 'compatible.asm' = '11.2';

Diskgroup altered.

SQL> ALTER DISKGROUP ocrvote SET ATTRIBUTE 'compatible.advm' = '11.2';

Diskgroup altered.
```

■ **Caution** Once a "compatible" attribute has changed, it is not possible to revert back to the old setting.

Table 9-2 maps features against minimum compatible settings.

Table 9-2. Required Compatible Settings Mapped to Features

Feature	Min. ASM Compatibility	Min. RDBMS Compatibility	Min. ADVM Compatibility
User defined allocation unit size up to 64MB	11.1	11.1	n/a
Population of the V$ASM_ATTRIBUTE view	11.1	Not applicable	Not applicable
Faster recovery from transient disk failures	11.1	11.1	Not applicable
Support for non-uniform extent sizes	11.1	11.1	Not applicable
Hot and cold regions for data placement	11.2	11.2	Not applicable
Support for storing Cluster Registry and voting disks in a disk group	11.2	Not applicable	Not applicable
Support for 4096 bytes sector size	11.2	11.2	Not applicable
Support for storing the ASM server parameter within ASM itself	11.2	Not applicable	Not applicable
Support for Access Control Lists (ACLs)	11.2	11.2	Not applicable
Support for ASM Cluster File System (ACFS)	11.2	Not applicable	11.2

Beginning with Oracle 11.1, the administrator has the option to specify a larger allocation unit than the default size of 1M. This was possible in 10.2 as well but required setting an underscore parameter. The larger a file gets, and a big file tablespace can grow to considerable size, the more extents have to be managed by the ASM instance. Increasing the ASM AU size, which is responsible for the extent size, can be greatly beneficial. The AU is set as an attribute to the disk group, and it can be set only during disk group creation. Use the attribute "AU_SIZE" to specify any of the following allocation unit sizes in the range of 1M to 64M; increments are to be in powers of 2. Oracle has also extended the maximum file sizes with ASM 11.1. If your compatibility level is set to greater than version 11.1, then file sizes can range up to the petabyte scale.

ASM takes into account that new hard disks are manufactured now with support for larger than the previously default sector size of 512 bytes. If all disks specified in the create diskgroup statement support the new sector size of 4k, then the disk group can make use of it. To enable larger sector sizes, use the attribute SECTOR_SIZE, which can take either the default value of 512 or, alternatively, 4096/4k. You should not use 4k sector size when you intend to create an ADVM volume on the disk, as there is a performance penalty associated with this.

The DISK_REPAIR_TIME attribute has been introduced in Oracle 11.1 to prevent transient disk failures to cause a disk to be dropped after it goes offline. In Oracle 10.2 a transient disk failure caused the disk to be dropped, followed by a rebalance operation. The algorithm employed in Oracle 10.2 made this a costly operation, and the amount of data moved during a rebalance operation usually is a multiple of the failed disk size.

With Oracle 11.1 and later, a transient disk failure still causes a disk to go offline, but if the failure is rectified within the DISK_REPAIR_TIME, the disk can be brought online again. ASM keeps track of the changes made to the offline disk, and can quickly rebuild it when it's brought online again. Use the "alter diskgroup diskgroupName online disk diskName" command to bring a disk online again.

▪ **Note** The foregoing example assumes that no failgroups have been explicitly created, resulting in a 1:1 mapping between disk and failgroup.

Other new features include ACCESS.CONTROL_ENABLED and ACCESS_CONTROL.UMASK. These two are related to ASM access control and are discussed in the section "Access Control", earlier in this chapter.

Once the CREATE DISKGROUP command is initiated, ASM will automatically mount the newly created disk group. You can query the dynamic performance view GV$ASM_DISKGROUP to check the status of the new ASM disk group on all cluster nodes.

The disk group attributes are visible in the V$ASM_ATTRIBUTE view, for example:

```
SQL> select name,value from v$asm_attribute where group_number=3
  2  and name not like 'template%'
  3> /
```

NAME	VALUE
disk_repair_time	3.6h
au_size	1048576
sector_size	512
compatible.asm	11.2.0.0.0
compatible.rdbms	11.2
cell.smart_scan_capable	FALSE
access_control.enabled	TRUE
access_control.umask	066

8 rows selected.

Output not printed here is related to the ASM file templates.

Extending an ASM Disk Group

Even with the most careful planning, there might be the need to extend an ASM disk group. Extending an ASM disk group is a relatively simple task once the underlying block devices have been presented to all cluster nodes. When adding a new LUN to ASM, it is recommended to use performance and size characteristics identical (or as close as possible to) to the existing ASM disks.

The device-mapper-multipath utility we discussed in Chapter 6 does not format the logical device in /dev/mapper, but rather requires the administrator to format the underlying block device, usually /dev/sd*. This operation should be performed on only one node of the cluster. With the device partitioned, the administrator can use either partprobe or kpartx to re-read the partition table on the other cluster nodes. A restart of the multipath daemon ("service multipathd restart") should show the new partition in /dev/mapper. We have seen cases where it was necessary to flush the unpartitioned multipathed device temporarily using multipath -f, followed by a reload of the multipath daemon. Alternatively, a cluster reboot will certainly detect the new partition tables.

With the new block devices detected on all nodes, you could use ASMLib to mark the disk as an ASM disk on one node of the cluster. On the remaining nodes, issue /etc/init.d/oracleasm scandisks to detect the new disk. With the operation completed, connect to the ASM instance as SYSASM and add the new disk to the disk group as in the following example, where the ASMLib disk "DATA11" is added to the disk group:

```
[oracle@london1 ~]$ sqlplus / as sysasm

SQL*Plus: Release 11.2.0.1.0 Production on Tue Jul 13 11:48:21 2010

Copyright (c) 1982, 2009, Oracle.  All rights reserved.


Connected to:
Oracle Database 11g Enterprise Edition Release 11.2.0.1.0 - 64bit Production
With the Real Application Clusters and Automatic Storage Management options

SQL> alter diskgroup DATA add disk 'ORCL:DATA11' rebalance power 6 nowait;

Diskgroup altered.
```

The command prompt will return almost immediately, triggering a rebalance operation in the background. You can check V$ASM_OPERATION for an estimate of how long the rebalance will take. Alternatively, a script to add a disk to a disk group could specify WAIT instead of NOWAIT, with the effect that the control is not returned to the script until the rebalance operation finished.

Dropping Disks from an ASM Disk Group

In some rare occasions, it is necessary to drop a disk from a disk group. The only times we have seen the need to drop a disk were during a SAN migration (more on that later in this section) or when an ASM disk with different, non-matching performance characteristics had to be removed from a disk group.

Dropping a disk triggers a rebalance operation. It is safe to remove the ASM disk physically from the cluster only when the HEADER_STATUS of the V$ASM_DISK view shows "FORMER" for the disk you dropped. Use the alter diskgroup command to drop a disk from a disk group:

```
SQL> alter diskgroup data drop disk 'DATA11' rebalance power 3;

Diskgroup altered.
```

Control is returned to the user almost immediately, and the rebalance operation starts in the background. Again, check V$ASM_OPERATION for information about a time remaining estimate.

SAN MIGRATION EXAMPLE

SAN migrations can be performed by ASM as well. The following example takes into account that adding and dropping disks can be performed in one single command. Using the same command saves time because only one rebalance operation is needed. The approach is fully supported by Oracle.

Consider the following example:

```
SQL> alter diskgroup data add disk 'ORCL:NEWSANO1', 'ORCL:NEWSANO2', 'ORCL:NEWSANO3',
drop disk 'ORCL:OLDSANO1', 'ORCL:NEWSANO2', 'ORCL:NEWSANO3' rebalance power 11;

Diskgroup altered.
```

The rebalance operation was deliberately started with a high priority to speed the process up. The clause `rebalance power 11` is what specifies that higher priority.

The same procedure could be used to migrate from slow to fast storage—just ensure that new LUNs allocated to the servers are on fast storage, and add them into the disk group while at the same time dropping the slow ones.

You need to watch out for the common pitfall of forgetting to properly present the new LUNs to all cluster nodes. This is a manual process, and the more nodes form part of the cluster, the easier it is to forget a node. You should also execute an /etc/init.d/oracleasm listdisks command on all cluster nodes using ASMLib to ensure that the new and old disks are properly discovered.

Enabling Disk Discovery

We discussed how to make ASM disks available to the operating system in Chapter 6. Depending on which method you choose to provide the ASM disks, you may need to instruct ASM to look at different places for disks.

The most important parameter during disk discovery is the initialization parameter "ASM_DISKSTRING". When using ASMLib, you do not need to modify it at all—the ASMLib-provided disks are automatically discovered.

The asm_diskstring variable needs to be adjusted to reflect the location of the ASM candidate disks if you are still using block or raw devices. Similarly, NFS volumes require zero padded files to be used as ASM disks, in which case the asm_diskstring should point to the mountpoint of the ASM disks.

Understanding the ASM Header

ASM places a lot of meta-information into each ASM disk's header. The header information can be made visible using the kfed utility. In versions prior to 11.1, kfed had to be linked manually, but manual linking is no longer necessary. To show the ASM header, use the kfed utility as shown here:

```
[oracle@london1 ~]$ kfed read /dev/oracleasm/disks/OCRVOTE1
```

You should adjust your path if you are not using ASMLib to provide disks to your ASM instance. When executing the command, you should consider diverting the output to another location for inspection. Once saved, you can view it with any editor you like. In the header, you can find a lot of interesting information that is also externalized through the various V$-views. In the dump of my OCRVOTE1 disk, I found the following useful information, summarized in Table 9-3.

Table 9-3. Example Cluster Configuration for ASM ACLs

Header Field	Value	Corresponding Information
kfdhdb.driver.provstr	ORCLDISKOCRVOTE1	The ASMLib provider string
kfdhdb.grptyp	KFDGTP_HIGH	Disk is member of a disk group with high redundancy
kfdhdb.hdrsts	KFDHDR_MEMBER	Member of a disk group
kfdhdb.dskname	OCRVOTE1	The ASM disk name
kfdhdb.grpname	OCRVOTE	The disk group name
kfdhdb.crestmp.*		Creation timestamp
kfdhdb.mntstmp.		Timestamp from when the disk was mounted
kfdhdb.secsize	512	512 byte sector size
kfdhdb.blksize	4096	Block size
kfdhdb.ausize	1048576	1M allocation units
kfdhdb.dsksize	964	Disk size (OS)
kfdhdb.dbcompat		Compatible.RDBMS

Although kfed can also be used to write a modified header back into the disk header, this should be done only under *the explicit request and supervision of Oracle Support.*

Installing the Grid Infrastructure

When installing Grid Infrastructure under a different operating system account than the RDBMS, you need to take some extra care when configuring ASMLib. Recall from Chapter 6 that prior to using ASMLib you have to configure it. Consider the following example, where the Grid Infrastructure software is installed by using the operating system account "grid." The operating system user "grid" has the primary group "oinstall," and secondary groups "asmowner" and "asmdba." In this case, you should configure ASMLib as shown here:

```
[root@london1 grid]# /etc/init.d/oracleasm configure
Configuring the Oracle ASM library driver.
```

This will configure the on-boot properties of the Oracle ASM library driver. The following questions will determine whether the driver is loaded on-boot and what permissions it will have. The current values will be shown in brackets ('[]'). Hitting <ENTER> without typing an answer will keep that current value. Ctrl-C will abort.

```
Default user to own the driver interface []: grid
Default group to own the driver interface []: asmdba
Start Oracle ASM library driver on boot (y/n) [n]: y
Scan for Oracle ASM disks on boot (y/n) [y]: y
Writing Oracle ASM library driver configuration: done
Initializing the Oracle ASMLib driver:                    [  OK  ]
Scanning the system for Oracle ASMLib disks:              [  OK  ]
```

Any other setting is likely to provoke a failure during the creation of the ASM instance and associated disk groups during the execution of the root.sh script.

Re-creating the ASM Disks

The ASM metadata area is re-created at the start of each ASM file and contains details of all the extents contained in the file. If you need to re-create the ASM instance on disks that have previously been used for ASM, then you will need to reinitialize the ASM metadata area using the dd utility. For example, you might use the following commands to initialize the disks after having very carefully verified that these are indeed the disks you intend to erase:

```
[rootglondonl ~] # dd if=/dev/zero of=/dev/mapper/mpathOp1 bs=4096 count=1
[root@londonl ~] # dd if=/dev/zero of=/dev/mapper/mpath1p1 bs=4096 count=1
[root@londonl ~] # dd if=/dev/zero of=/dev/mapper/mpath2p1 bs=4096 count=1
```

Note that this command applies to shared storage, making the disks wiped by dd unusable across all cluster nodes! Please be extra careful not to wipe out the wrong disks. Once the metadata has been removed from the ASM disk, it can be unpresented from the host and reused. After the storage has been unpresented from the node, it is recommended to remove the devices from the SCSI bus.

ASM Cluster File System

Before Oracle 11.2, ASM was used to store database-related files (with some exceptions), but was not suitable to act as a general purpose file system to store Oracle binaries, core dump files, parameter files or traces, and other dumps generated by the RDBMS and the operating system.

The situation has changed with Grid Infrastructure 11.2 and Oracle's introduction of the ASM Cluster File System (ACFS). ACFS is a POSIX-compliant general purpose cluster file system, built on top of the ASM Dynamic Volume Manager (ADVM). ADVM provides so-called volumes on which the ACFS (or another, non-Oracle file system) can be created. An ADVM volume is created as part of an ASM disk group. Volumes are not partitioned, which is equivalent to using a LVM "logical volume" in classic Linux LVM. Ultimately, ADVM leverages the underlying functionality provided by the ASM disk group and benefits from the same striping and mirroring capability as any other database file would.

▨ **Note** ACFS requires Red Hat Enterprise Linux 5.x or Oracle Enterprise Linux 5. Other Linux distributions are not supported at the time of this writing.

ACFS and the underlying supporting technology are another step in the direction of a "one vendor" solution—ACFS has the potential to make other cluster file systems used together with RAC obsolete. A current design limitation at the time of this writing prevents an ACFS volume to be used as the root file system for Linux. The availability for Linux, UNIX, and Windows with a common set of utilities is a great advantage. Admittedly, there are some differences in the Windows world. To use ACFS, you need to run a certified platform, and at the time of this writing, it was available only on Linux and Windows. The toolset installed with Grid Infrastructure consists of three loadable kernel modules:

- oracleacfs.ko

- oracleadvm.ko

- oracleoks.ko

Additionally, the following command line utilities are installed as well:

- mkfs.acfs

- acfsdbg

- acfsutil

- advmutil

- fsck.acfs

- mount.acfs

An ACFS mount point can be used as an installation target for a shared RDBMS home. The tight integration into Grid Infrastructure ensures that the necessary file system is mounted as part of the Grid Infrastructure startup sequence, preventing the failure of the database startup due to missing binaries.

▨ **Note** Database files are explicitly not supported in ACFS.

When opting to install a shared RDBMS home—which we do not recommend as it prevents the administrator from applying rolling patches—then the mount point for the ACFS should be in $ORACLE_BASE/acfsmounts/, where $ORACLE_BASE refers to the RDBMS owner's environment variable. After the successful installation of the RDBMS binaries to the $ORACLE_BASE/acfsmounts/ directory, the administrator needs to add the ACFS as a Grid Infrastructure resource—it is explicitly discouraged to use the ACFS mount registry. We will discuss the mount registry later in this section. To add the $ORACLE_HOME as a Grid Infrastructure resource, use the following commands:

```
[oracle@london1 ~]$ srvctl add filesystem -d ADVMVolumeDeviceName \
> -v ADVMName -g underlyingDiskGroupName -m PathToMountPoint \
> -u RDBMSSoftwareOwner    \
```

As this is fairly abstract, here's a real life example. We are registering the volume "orahomevol" of disk group "DATA" into the cluster registry for the RDBMS owner "oracle":

```
[oracle@london1 ~]$ srvctl add filesystem -d /dev/asm/orahomevol-942 \
> -v orahomevol -g DATA -m /u01/app/oracle/product/11.2.0/dbhome_1 \
> -u oracle
```

A second option in addition to using ACFS for shared Oracle homes is to use ACFS to store application data that previously could not be stored in ASM. We see the main benefit of such a clustered file system in providing a common location for external tables or any other directory object in the database. External tables refer to a directory object to load the data from the file system into the database. If the directory on the file system exists on the first node, while the user is on the third node of the cluster, the read operation will fail. If we move the external table's underlying directory to an ACFS mount, this problem goes away, as the directory in the file system is shared across all cluster nodes.

We already mentioned the ACFS mount registry in the context of ACFS for shared RDBMS homes. The mount registry can be compared to the Linux /etc/fstab file: any ACFS registered with it will be mounted automatically after a system start. The mount registry extends this concept to the cluster and will ensure that the file systems are mounted on all nodes in a clustered environment. Mounting a file system in Linux requires root privileges. The absence of an orarootagent process in Oracle Restart therefore causes registered file systems not to be mounted automatically. See the section "ACFS and Oracle Restart" for more information on how to overcome this limitation.

ACFS supports snapshots as well, which might be an incentive to use ACFS in single node installations. A snapshot is a read-only point-in-time copy of an ACFS file system, using COW technology for space efficiency. See the section "ACFS Snapshots" later in the chapter for more information about ACFS snapshots.

More than one way exists to create a cluster file system based on ACFS: graphical user interfaces include the ASM configuration assistant (see ahead) and Enterprise Manager Grid Control. Supporters of the command line find support for creating and working with ACFS in SQL*Plus and asmcmd. The following two sections will explain the use of asmca and the command line to give you an overview of how to create an ACFS in Linux.

Creating and Mounting an ACFS Using ASMCA

The easiest way to create an ASMCFS is to use the ASM Configuration Assistant asmca. We recommend creating a separate ASM disk group for the ADVM volume, although this is optional.

Start the asmca utility from the $GRID_HOME/bin directory to begin the ACFS creation. As with all GUI tools, you need to have access to an X11 server to run it—refer back to Chapter 7 for more information about starting the graphical user tools. Once the initial screen completes loading, click on the "Create" button to begin the creation of a new disk group on the "Disk Groups" tab. Figure 9-2 shows the "Create Disk Group" configuration dialog.

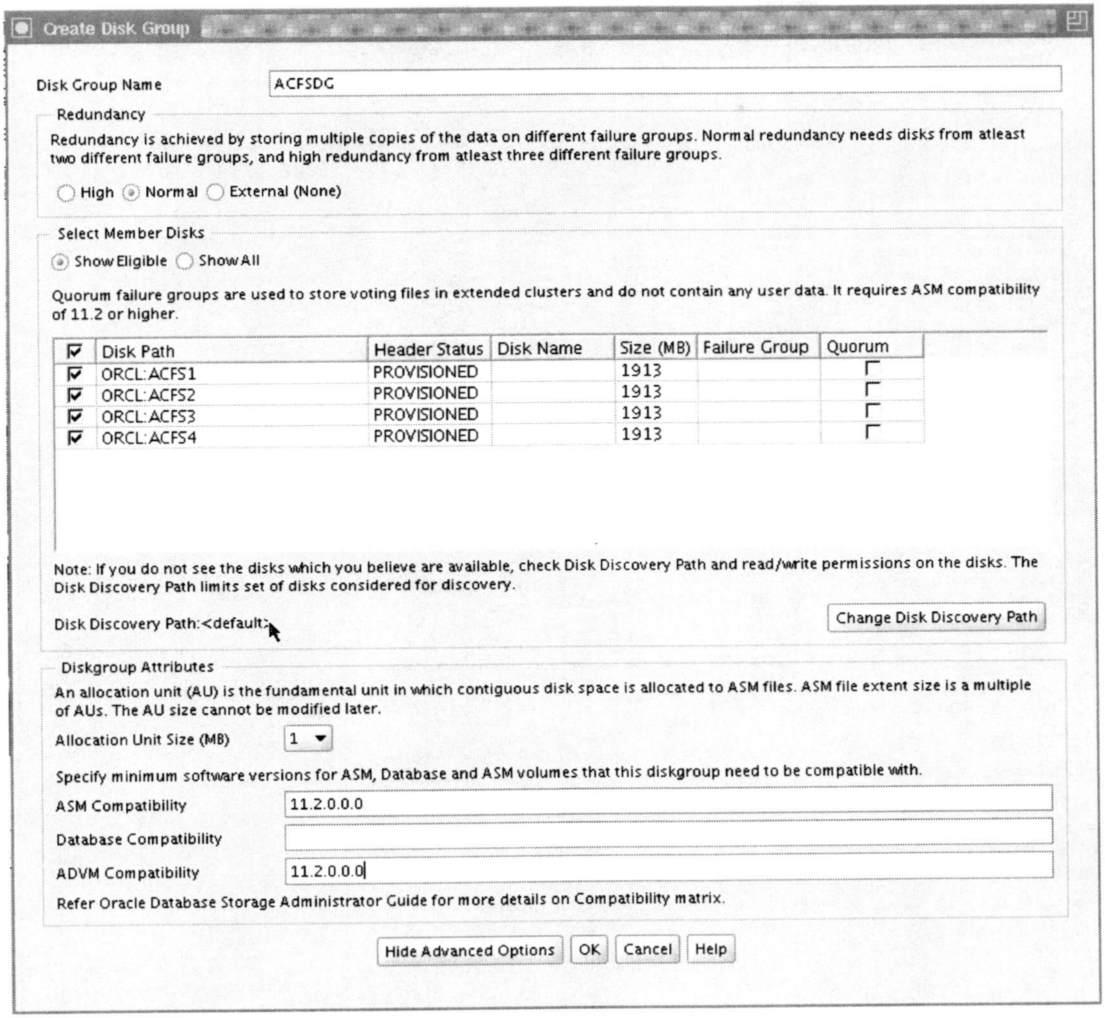

*Figure 9-2. **Create Disk Group configuration dialog***

The important information in Figure 9-2 is the new disk group name, which should take a user-friendly, non-cryptic name, and the redundancy level plus the ASM disks to form the disk group. You should choose the redundancy level based on your storage array. You also need to set the ASM and ADVM compatibility to 11.2.0.0.0 at least. The disk group attributes are accessible as part of the advanced options. Define failure groups if appropriate; in our example we didn't need to. Click OK to finish the disk group creation. The command will then execute in the background, and if all went well, you are rewarded with a success message, as shown in Figure 9-3.

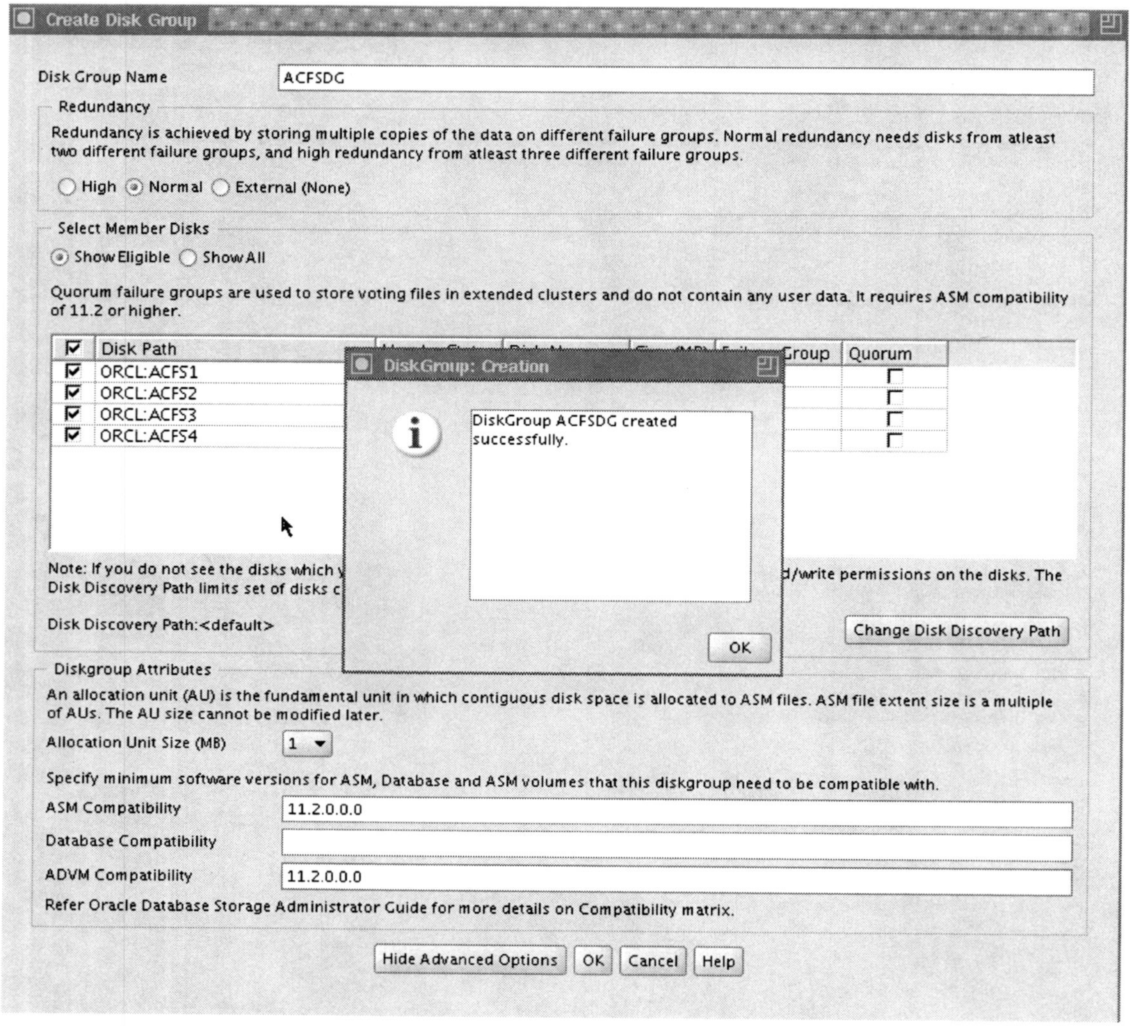

Figure 9-3. Disk Group created successfully

The new disk group can then be used to store an ADVM volume. On the main screen of the asmca tool, click on the "volume" tab. You are shown the screen as in Figure 9-4.

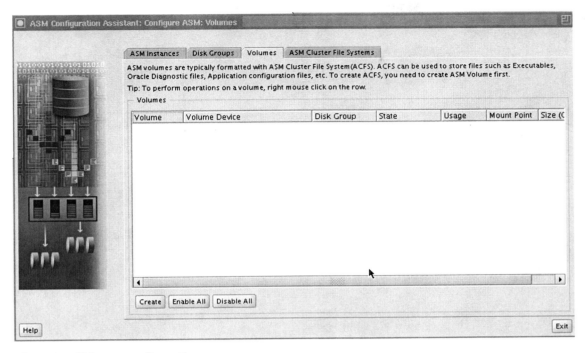

Figure 9-4. Volumes configuration screen

Click on the "Create" button to bring up the "Create Volume" dialog. This dialog is shown in Figure 9-5.

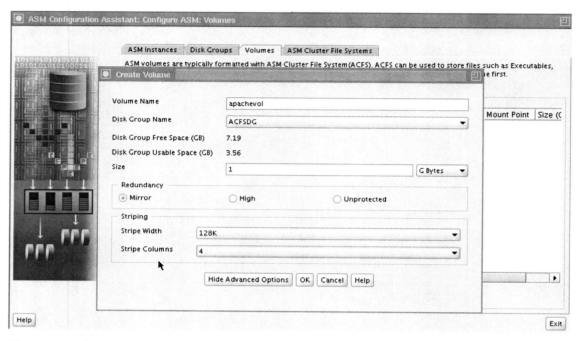

Figure 9-5. Volumes creation screen

We placed the new ADVM volume on the disk group ACFSDG we just created, assigned the name "apachevol," and created it with 1G of available space. Unlike classical LVM, the volume we create will not need to be partitioned. It can be dynamically resized when needed, which is a one-step operation, i.e., thanks to the absence of a classic ext3 or ext4 file system, no calls to `resize2fs` are needed.

■ **Note** If your disk group does not show up in the "Disk Group Name" dropdown box, then it's compatible attributes for ASM and ADVM are most likely not set to 11.2.0.0.0.

The advanced options shown in the lower half of the configuration screen allow you to fine-tune the new ADVM volume. You can optionally specify a stripe width in the range of 4k to 1M, and also define the number of columns in the stripe set. The range of columns specifiable is 1 to 8, and defaults to 4. If you have a disk group with normal redundancy and would like to specify a different redundancy level than the one of the disk group, make sure to set it accordingly. After you confirm the creation of the volume by clicking "OK," `asmca` creates the volume and displays it in the overview screen. This is shown in Figure 9-6.

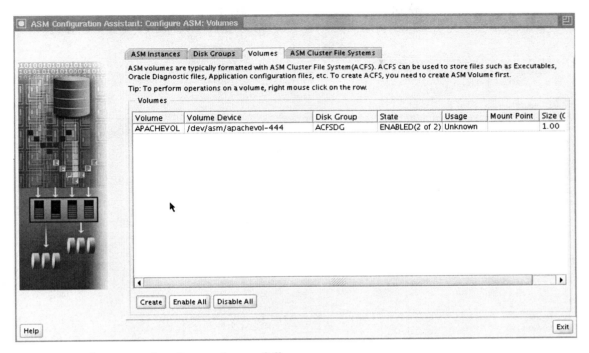

*Figure 9-6. **Volumes apachevol created succesfully***

The new volume is enabled by default and can be used for the next step. In its current state, the volume needs an ACFS file system. Select the "ASM Cluster File Systems" tab to proceed with its creation. Figure 9-7 shows the ACFS creation dialog.

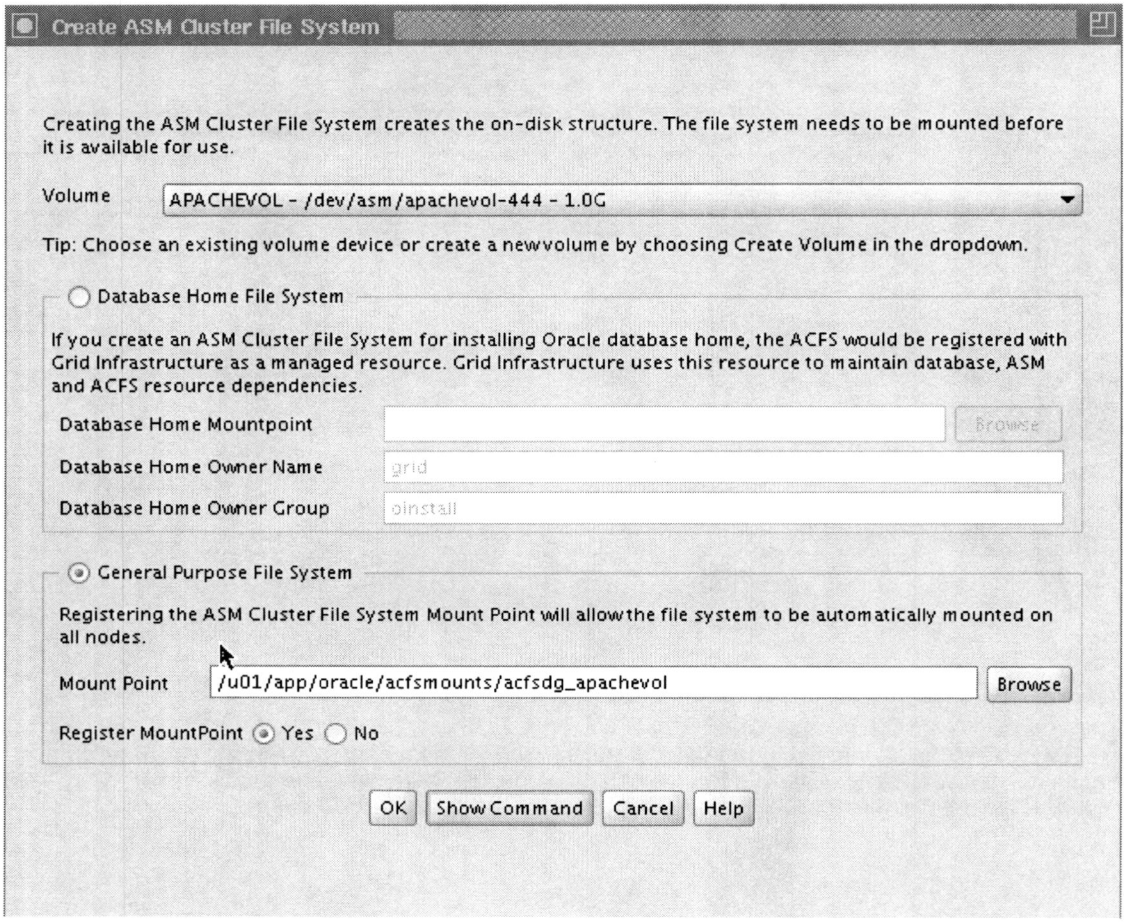

Figure 9-7. ACFS creation

The user has two options in this dialog: either specify the ACFS home as a shared home for an Oracle RDBMS installation, for which approx 4.6 GB are required, or create a general purpose file system. At the time of this writing, we do not recommend storing the RDBMS binaries in the ACFS home.

When creating a general purpose file system, you have the option to specify a mount point and to register that mountpoint. If you choose not to register the mount point, you can always do so at a later stage. Registering the mountpoint offers the advantage that the file system is mounted automatically when Grid Infrastructure starts. The ACFS will be mounted on all cluster nodes. Clicking OK initiates the creation of the ACFS volume and optionally registers it on all cluster nodes. The final screen in asmca with the file system created is shown in Figure 9-8.

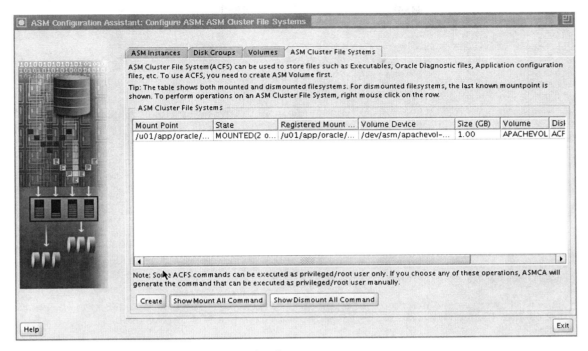

Figure 9-8. ACFS creation successfully completed

As you can see from the output, the ACFS volume is mounted with its registered mount point on all cluster nodes.

Creating and Mounting an ACFS Using the Command Line

The previous example showed how to create an ACFS volume and how to mount it automatically on all nodes of the cluster. The same procedure can also be completed by using the command line. The example in this section walks you through the creation of the same ACFS, but this time from the command line.

First of all, a new disk group is to be created. This can be done in SQL*Plus, for example. Connect to your local ASM instance as SYSDBA, as shown here:

```
[oracle@london1 ~]$ sqlplus / as sysasm

SQL*Plus: Release 11.2.0.1.0 Production on Wed Jul 14 21:10:54 2010

Copyright (c) 1982, 2009, Oracle. All rights reserved.

Connected to:
Oracle Database 11g Enterprise Edition Release 11.2.0.1.0 - 64bit Production
With the Automatic Storage Management option
```

After connecting, issue the CREATE DISKGROUP command to create a new group:

```
SQL> CREATE DISKGROUP ACFSDG normal REDUNDANCY
  2   DISK 'ORCL:ACFS1', 'ORCL:ACFS2', 'ORCL:ACFS3', 'ORCL:ACFS4';

Diskgroup created.
```

Next, issue some ALTER DISKGROUP commands to set the two compatibility parameters:

```
SQL> ALTER DISKGROUP ACFSDG SET ATTRIBUTE 'compatible.asm'='11.2',;

Diskgroup altered.

SQL> ALTER DISKGROUP ACFSDG SET ATTRIBUTE 'compatible.advm'='11.2';

Diskgroup altered.
```

You should mount the newly created disk group on all cluster nodes. You can use the srvctl start diskgroup command to do so:

```
[oracle@london1 ~]$ srvctl start diskgroup -g ACFSDG
```

Once the group is mounted on all nodes, you can use either SQL*Plus or asmcmd to create the new ADVM volume. For the sake of simplicity, we performed this step in SQL*Plus again:

```
SQL> alter diskgroup acfsdg add volume apachevol size 1g
  2   /

Diskgroup altered.
```

The add volume clause to the alter diskgroup command can also take additional parameters, exactly the same way as the asmca if the disk group uses normal redundancy. Consider this example:

```
SQL> ALTER DISKGROUP ACFSDG add volume apachevol size 1G
  2   mirror stripe_width 128k stripe_columns 4;

Diskgroup altered.
```

The dynamic performance view V$ASM_VOLUME then displays information about the newly created volume:

```
SQL> select volume_name,state,usage,volume_device,mountpath
  2   from v$asm_volume
  3   /

VOLUME_NAME      STATE      USAGE  VOLUME_DEVICE          MOUNTPATH
---------------- ---------- ------ ---------------------- --------------------
APACHEVOL        ENABLED           /dev/asm/apachevol-444
```

Future commands require the volume device, so it's a good idea to note it down somewhere.

As an alternative to issuing the "alter diskgroup... add volume" command in SQL*Plus, you could use the volcreate command in asmcmd, as the following example demonstrates:

```
[oracle@london1 ~]$ asmcmd
ASMCMD> volcreate -G ACFSDG -s 1G apachevol
```

If you don't see an error message, the command succeeded. You can verify success with the volinfo command:

```
ASMCMD> volinfo -G ACFSDG -a
Diskgroup Name: ACFSDG

        Volume Name: APACHEVOL
        Volume Device: /dev/asm/apachevol-444
        State: ENABLED
        Size (MB): 1024
        Resize Unit (MB): 256
        Redundancy: MIRROR
        Stripe Columns: 4
        Stripe Width (K): 128
        Usage:
        Mountpath:
```

The next step is to create an ACFS file system on the volume we just created. The following command creates that file system. Notice the reference to the volume device in the command:

```
[oracle@london1 ~]$ /sbin/mkfs -t acfs /dev/asm/apachevol-444
mkfs.acfs: version                 = 11.2.0.1.0.0
mkfs.acfs: on-disk version         = 39.0
mkfs.acfs: volume                  = /dev/asm/apachevol-444
mkfs.acfs: volume size             = 1073741824
mkfs.acfs: Format complete.
```

Before we can mount the file system, a mount point is needed. Ensure that you create the mount point on every node of the cluster where you like to mount the file system. The following commands create a mountpoint "acfsdg_apachevol" under $ORACLE_BASE/acfsmounts. The "mkdir" commands need to be executed on each node.

```
[oracle@london1 ~]$ mkdir $ORACLE_BASE/acfsmounts
[oracle@london1 ~]$ mkdir $ORACLE_BASE/acfsmounts/acfsdg_apachevol
```

Mount the file system as root:

```
[root@london1 ~]# mount -t acfs /dev/asm/apachevol-444 \
>  /u01/app/oracle/acfsmounts/acfsdg_apachevol/
```

Optionally, register the ACFS with the mount registry:

```
[oracle@london1 ~]$ /sbin/acfsutil registry -a /dev/asm/apachevol-444 \
>  /u01/app/oracle/acfsmounts/apachevol/
```

493

```
acfsutil registry: mount point /u01/app/oracle/acfsmounts/acfsdg_apachevol successfully
added to Oracle Registry
```

At the end of the ACFS creation, the file system is created:

```
[oracle@london1 ~]$ /sbin/acfsutil info fs
/u01/app/oracle/acfsmounts/acfsdg_apachevol
    ACFS Version: 11.2.0.1.0.0
    flags:         MountPoint,Available
    mount time:    Wed Jul 28 16:20:02 2010
    volumes:       1
    total size:    1073741824
    total free:    998002688
    primary volume: /dev/asm/apachevol-444
        label:
        flags:                  Primary,Available,ADVM
        on-disk version:        39.0
        allocation unit:        4096
        major, minor:           252, 227329
        size:                   1073741824
        free:                   998002688
        ADVM diskgroup          ACFSDG
        ADVM resize increment:  268435456
        ADVM redundancy:        mirror
        ADVM stripe columns:    4
        ADVM stripe width:      131072
    number of snapshots:  0
    snapshot space usage: 0

[oracle@london1 ~]$ df -h /u01/app/oracle/acfsmounts/acfsdg_apachevol/
Filesystem              Size  Used Avail Use% Mounted on
/dev/asm/apachevol-444
                        1.0G   39M  986M   4% /u01/.../acfsdg_apachevol
```

From this point onwards, you can use the ACFS like any other Linux file system.

Maintaining the ACFS

A number of maintenance operations can be performed with each of the ACFS components. Resizing a file system is trivial, and the new file system size is changed instantaneously on all cluster nodes—for example:

```
[root@london1 ~]# acfsutil size +256M /u01/app/oracle/acfsmounts/tomcatvol
acfsutil size: new file system size: 536870912 (512MB)
```

You can see the new size of the volume straightaway:

```
[root@london1 ~]# df -h /u01/app/oracle/acfsmounts/tomcatvol
Filesystem              Size  Used Avail Use% Mounted on
/dev/asm/tomcatvol-32
```

```
                     512M   73M  440M  15% /u01/app/oracle/acfsmounts/tomcatvol
[root@london1 ~]# ssh london2  df -h /u01/app/oracle/acfsmounts/tomcatvol
Filesystem           Size  Used Avail Use% Mounted on
/dev/asm/tomcatvol-32
                     512M   73M  440M  15% /u01/app/oracle/acfsmounts/tomcatvol
```

Mounting and unmounting an ACFS are identical to any other Linux file system:

```
/bin/mount -t acfs -rw /dev/asm/deviceName mountPoint
```

Unmounting the file system is even easier:

```
/bin/umount mountPoint
```

Snapshots can be taken using the acfsutil command, as in the following example:

```
 [root@london1 ~]#  mkdir /u01/app/oracle/acfsmounts/snap

[root@london1 ~]# acfsutil snap create prerelease \
> /u01/app/oracle/acfsmounts/acfsdg_apachevol/
acfsutil snap create: Snapshot operation is complete.
```

Using the acfsutil command, you can verify that the snapshot was indeed taken:

```
[root@london1 ~]# acfsutil info fs
/u01/app/oracle/acfsmounts/acfsdg_apachevol
    ACFS Version: 11.2.0.1.0.0
    flags:        MountPoint,Available
    mount time:   Wed Jul 28 16:20:02 2010
    volumes:      1
    total size:   1073741824
    total free:   930897920
    primary volume: /dev/asm/apachevol-444
        label:
        flags:                 Primary,Available,ADVM
        on-disk version:       39.0
        allocation unit:       4096
        major, minor:          252, 227329
        size:                  1073741824
        free:                  930897920
        ADVM diskgroup         ACFSDG
        ADVM resize increment: 268435456
        ADVM redundancy:       mirror
        ADVM stripe columns:   4
        ADVM stripe width:     131072
    number of snapshots:  1
    snapshot space usage: 49152
```

The snapshots don't have to be mounted by the administrator; they are available under the mountpoint's ".ACFS/snaps/" directory (note the dot in .ACFS). Each snapshot gets its own name:

```
[root@london1 ~]# ls -l /u01/app/oracle/acfsmounts/acfsdg_apachevol/.ACFS/snaps/
total 4
drwxrwx--- 4 root dba 4096 Jul 28 18:17 prerelease
```

To delete a snapshot, use the `acfsutil snap delete <snap_name> <mountpoint>` command.

Using ACFS with Oracle Restart

Unlike Grid Infrastructure for clusters, Oracle Restart does not have an orarootagent process owned by root in the 11.2 base release. Since loading kernel modules and mounting file systems require root access in Linux, Oracle Restart cannot perform the tasks normally performed by the agent in a cluster. If you are using ASM Cluster File systems in your Oracle Restart environment, you need to add the following code to /etc/rc.local for Red Hat–based systems, which should load the needed kernel modules during the boot process.

```
# modification to automatically load the ACFS kernel modules
# and to automatically mount registered file systems
# change ORACLE_SID to match the ASM SID for your cluster node!
ORACLE_SID=+ASM1; export ORACLE_SID
ORAENV_ASK=NO;    export ORAENV_ASK

source /usr/local/bin/oraenv

$ORACLE_HOME/bin/acfsload start -s
sleep 15
mount -t acfs acfsVolumeName fileSystemMountPoint
```

The kernel modules are required for the subsequent mount operation to succeed. We added a 15-second delay to allow the kernel to load the drivers before mounting the file system.

Administering ASM

ASM administration can be performed from a number of different places. Oracle offers command line utilities and graphical user interface tools to interact with the software. You have the following options for administering ASM:

- SQL*Plus

- The srvctl command line utility

- Enterprise Manager database Console/Grid Control

- The asmcmd utility

- The ASM Configuration Assistant, asmca

In contrast to previous versions, the main configuration utility, dbca, no longer has support to administer ASM. Instead, it has been superseded by the new asmca utility.

Using SQL*Plus to Administer ASM

The SQL*Plus command interpreter has always been available for administering ASM. In Oracle 10.1, when the asmcmd utility was not available, the use of SQL*Plus was mandatory for many tasks.

The CREATE, ALTER, and DROP DISKGROUP commands allow you to create and manage ASM disk groups and their contents. A number of ASM-specific dynamic performance views are available and populated in the ASM instance.

Setting the Environment

We discussed the ASM disk group creation in great detail earlier in this chapter—see section "Creating an ASM Diskgroup" for more information. In addition to working with disk groups, you can start and stop ASM using SQL*Plus, but in a RAC environment, SRVCTL is the preferred command line utility for instance management. In order to use SQL* Plus to start and stop ASM, you must set your environment variables to the Grid Infrastructure home, as in the following example:

```
[oracle@london1 ~]$ . oraenv
ORACLE_SID = [+ASM1] ?
The Oracle base for ORACLE_HOME=/u01/app/crs is /u01/app/oracle
```

Determining the User and Privilege

Before Oracle 11.2, only one user existed to connect to the ASM instance, and that was the "sys" user, using the SYSDBA privilege. In Oracle 11.1, the SYSASM privilege has been introduced, and it essentially replaced SYSDBA for the super user privilege as far as ASM is concerned. SYSDBA connections will be made by Oracle database instances, or by human users explicitly connecting with that role. Oracle 11.2 additionally introduced the ASMSNMP user for monitoring purposes. The following is how that user appears when you query v$pwfile_users:

```
SQL> select * from v$pwfile_users;

USERNAME                        SYSDB SYSOP SYSAS
------------------------------- ----- ----- -----
SYS                             TRUE  TRUE  TRUE
ASMSNMP                         TRUE  FALSE FALSE
```

For most administrative tasks, you log in as SYS with the SYSASM role. Although not recommended in a RAC environment, you can use the STARTUP and SHUTDOWN commands to start and stop an ASM instance. The shutdown will succeed only if your voting disks and OCR are *not* stored in an ASM disk group. Also, remember to shut down all databases connected to the ASM instance before shutting the instance down.

Knowing Your Options

The following options exist for the STARTUP command:

- STARTUP FORCE: The equivalent to the RDBMS startup force command first aborts the instance before starting it up again. The effect of the instance aborting is described in the SHUTDOWN ABORT bullet point.

- STARTUP NOMOUNT: Starts the ASM instance but does not mount any disk groups.

- STARTUP [MOUNT | OPEN]: Starts the ASM instance and mounts all disks registered in the ASM_DISKGROUPS initialization parameter.

And the following are the options for the SHUTDOWN command:

- SHUTDOWN NORMAL: The behavior is the same as with an RDBMS instance. The default shutdown mode waits for any ongoing operation such as a rebalance before continuing. If a RDBMS instance is still connected to the ASM instance, the command will fail. It will also wait for any connected user to disconnect. Mounted disk groups are all dismounted cleanly.

- SHUTDOWN IMMEDIATE: Ongoing operations are allowed to complete, but connected users will be disconnected from the ASM instance. Again, any RDBMS instance still connected to the ASM instance will cause the command to fail with an error.

- SHUTDOWN ABORT: With this option, the ASM instance aborts, and with it any connected RDBMS instance. ACFS volumes mounted will not be accessible and produce file system I/O errors.

Dealing with Connected Clients

Trying to shut down an ASM instance when the OCR is stored on a disk group results in an error:

```
SQL> shutdown immediate
ORA-15097: cannot SHUTDOWN ASM instance with connected client
```

The view (G)V$ASM_CLIENT lists the connected clients:

```
SQL> select db_name,status,instance_name from v$asm_client

DB_NAME  STATUS       INSTANCE_NAME
-------- ------------ ------------------------------
+ASM     CONNECTED    +ASM2
```

Unlike pre-11.2 deployments, the OCR can be stored within an ASM disk group, making the instance its own client. Even shutting down the disk groups mounted on the ASM instance doesn't solve this problem:

```
[oracle@london2 ~]$ srvctl stop diskgroup -g DATA -n london2
[oracle@london2 ~]$ srvctl stop diskgroup -g OCRVOTE -n london2
```

The foregoing commands completed without error.

```
SQL> select name,state from v$asm_diskgroup

NAME                             STATE
------------------------------   -----------
DATA                             DISMOUNTED
OCRVOTE                          QUIESCING
```

So although Grid Infrastructure reports the disk groups as stopped, the disk group storing OCR and voting disks is still accessible, but in a quiesced state. To recover from this state, you can issue the "startup" command again to start the instance and make it accessible to the database instances. Alternatively, to completely shut down ASM, you need to stop Grid Infrastructure on the node using the crsctl stop crs command.

Checking for Corruption

You can also use SQL*Plus to perform logical checks on the disk groups. This can become handy to check for corruption reported in the ASM instance's alert.log:

```
SQL> alter diskgroup DATA check;
```

The default action is to report any problems in the alert.log, but ASM does not attempt to fix them. If you specify the REPAIR keyword, ASM will try to address any reported problem.

Manually Mounting a Disk Group

If you would like to manually mount an ASM disk group, use the "alter diskgroup diskgroupName mount" command. We recommend not attempting this operation, but rather use srvctl for that purpose. See the section "ASM Administration Using SRVCTL" for examples.

Dropping a Disk Group

It is possible to drop disk groups via the command line. The command to be executed as sysasm is "drop diskgroup diskgroupName". This command will produce an error if the disk group is not empty. Either manually remove files or specify the including contents clause.

Creating ADVM Volumes

SQL*Plus also supports commands to create ADVM volumes in ASM disk groups. We discuss the creation of ACFS volumes using the command line in its own section—see "Creating and Mounting an ACFS Using the Command Line."

ASM Administration Using SRVCTL

We recommend the use of srvctl over other command line tools. Users of Oracle 11.1 and earlier will be surprised that it is not possible to entirely stop ASM using srvctl. In pre–Oracle 11.2, the command `srvctl stop asm -n nodeName` stopped an ASM instance. The same command in Oracle 11.2 produces the following error:

```
[oracle@london2 ~]$ srvctl stop asm -n london2
PRCR-1014 : Failed to stop resource ora.asm
PRCR-1065 : Failed to stop resource ora.asm
CRS-2529: Unable to act on 'ora.asm' because that would require stopping or
 relocating 'ora.registry.acfs', but the force option was not specified
```

The force option forces the command to execute, but some components won't stop, due to too many dependencies on other resources. The only option to completely stop ASM is to stop the Clusterware stack on the local node:

```
[root@london1 ~]# crsctl stop crs
```

In Oracle 11.1 and earlier, administrators used to create a dependency between local ASM and database instance. This ensured that the ASM instance was started together with the RDBMS instance when this was required. In Oracle 11.2, the dependency has been redefined. Instead of linking to the ASM instance, the dependency is created with one or more ASM disk groups. Consider the following example of database PROD (unneeded output not printed for clarity):

```
[oracle@london1 ~]$ crsctl status resource ora.prod.db -p
NAME=ora.prod.db
TYPE=ora.database.type
ACL=owner:oracle:rwx,pgrp:oinstall:rwx,other::r-
[...]
SPFILE=+DATA/prod/spfileprod.ora
START_DEPENDENCIES=hard(ora.DATA.dg) [...] pullup(ora.DATA.dg)
STOP_DEPENDENCIES=hard(intermediate:ora.asm,shutdown:ora.DATA.dg)
```

You can see that a start dependency has been created for the disk group DATA, which will also be started if needed as part of the database start. Similarly, a stop dependency exists for the same disk group. If you have multiple disk groups defined for the database, you will see additional dependencies for each dependent disk group.

We said earlier in the chapter that ASM disk groups are now resources within Grid Infrastructure. So instead of mounting the disk group via the "alter diskgroup mount all" commands, you should use the following syntax to mount a disk group in the cluster:

```
[oracle@london1 ~]$ srvctl start diskgroup -g diskgroupName
```

Alternatively the "-n" switch allows you to specify which host the disk group should be mounted on.

Accessing Files in ASM

In early versions of Oracle, ASM files within an ASM instance could not easily be accessed, and it could appear as a black box. This changed for the better with the introduction of asmcmd in Oracle 10.2. Alternatively, Enterprise Manager can be used to view files in ASM.

■ **Note** This discussion does not apply to ACFS—the vnode interface for ACFS allows standard Linux tools to view and manipulate files in an ASM Cluster Filesystem.

The ASM command line utility has been significantly enhanced with every release. In Oracle 11.2, it has reached a very mature state and supports many file-related commands. The asmcmd utility resides in $GRID_HOME/bin; therefore you need to point your $ORACLE_HOME and $ORCLE_SID accordingly. Start the utility by invoking $GRID_HOME/bin/asmcmd.

Navigation around the file structure within ASM follows the same technique you would use to navigate a standard Linux filesystem:

- Change directory using the "cd" command. This works both with fully qualified paths to directories as well as relative paths, much in the same way you'd navigate in an ext3 filesystem.

- The ls command prints the contents of a directory. Use the "-l" option for a long directory listing, and specify "--permission" to display file permissions (see the section "Access Control" earlier in this chapter for more information about this new feature).

- The "cp" command allows you to copy files from ASM to ASM or to the local file system. This is a very convenient way of moving files out of ASM.

- You can use the rm command to delete files, or use shell-like pattern matching. For example, rm * removes all files in the current directory. This command should be used only with great care.

- The du command calculates the disk usage from the current directory, very similar to its shell equivalent. The output shown is cumulative.

Oracle Enterprise Manager also offers a way to navigate around in ASM.

Using Files Instead of Devices

You can create an ASM file system based on operating system files instead of devices on Linux. You should not attempt this configuration on a production system except when on a supported NAS appliance, but it can be useful for testing or educational reasons. The following steps have been successfully tested on a RAC database but have limited applicability for RAC, as only one instance has access to the ASM disks that are created on the local disks of one node. The main focus is on single instance ASM.

Create a directory to contain the ASM files:

```
[root@london1 ~]# mkdir /asm
```

Create the ASM files using the dd command:

```
[root@london1 ~]# dd if=/dev/zero of=/asm/vol4 bs=1M count=1024
```

This command will create a file of 1GB in size. As the root user, associate a loop device with each file using the loset up command:

```
[root@london1 ~]# losetup /dev/loopl /asm/vol4
```

You can check if the loop device is properly presented to the host:

```
[root@london1 ~]# losetup /dev/loopl
```

Now use your favorite tool to mark this as an ASM disk; the ASMLib command createdisk can be used for this purpose, as shown in this example:

```
[root@london1 ~]# /etc/init.d/oracleasm createdisk VOL4 /dev/loop1
```

From this point on, you can make use of this file in the ASM instance, using your favorite tool to create a disk group on it. The command line option is shown here:

```
[oracle@london1 ~]$ sqlplus / as sysasm

SQL*Plus: Release 11.2.0.1.0 Production on Wed Jul 28 18:23:13 2010

Copyright (c) 1982, 2009, Oracle. All rights reserved.


Connected to:
Oracle Database 11g Enterprise Edition Release 11.2.0.1.0 - 64bit Production
With the Real Application Clusters and Automatic Storage Management options

SQL> create diskgroup FILEDG external redundancy disk 'ORCL:VOL4';

Diskgroup created.
```

Virtualization and Shared Disks

Oracle VM and other Xen-based virtualization software can mark block devices in the guest domain as shared storage. The simple solution is to use the graphical user interface, but the command line also allows the administrator to add shared storage to a running virtual cluster. The following example assumes that the virtual shared block device is a logical volume on the dom0. First create the logical volume from your volume group. The example volume group is named "data_vg" on the dom0.

```
[root@dom0 ~]# lvcreate --name virtcluster_112_asm_data01 --size 10G data_vg
```

Then add the logical volume to the running cluster, comprised of virtcluster_112_node1 and virtcluster_112_node2:

```
[root@dom0 ~]# xm block-attach virtcluster_112_node1 \
>  phy:/dev/data_vg/virtcluster_112_asm_data01 xvdd w!
[root@dom0 ~]# xm block-attach virtcluster_112_node2 \
>  phy:/dev/data_vg/virtcluster_112_asm_data01 xvdd w!
```

The foregoing command xm block-attach instructs the hypervisor to add a new block device called /dev/data_vg/virtcluster_112_asm_data01 in the backend (dom0) to the virtual machines virtcluster_112_node1 and 2 as frontend device xvdd. The new block device is presented in read-write mode, and is sharable across the cluster.

Once the command completed, the virtual machines feature a new shared block device, /dev/xvdd. You can use fdisk on any of the nodes to create a partition on the device, and either udev or ASMLib commands to make it an ASM disk.

Summary

This chapter provided a high-level overview of ASM, which is a lot of material to cover. We started the chapter by introducing the basic concepts behind ASM and related terminology. In Oracle 11.2, ASM has been improved greatly, providing support not only for database files (as it always did), but also for all file types, now with the extension of the ASM Cluster File System.

ASM in many ways resembles the LVM in Linux, but it doesn't suffer the overhead of maintaining volume groups and logical volumes, plus a system call for transitions from the file system to the kernel. And as an added benefit, it supports clustering by default.

The most fundamental change in ASM 11.2 is the integration into Grid Infrastructure. The best practices documents for 11.1 and 10.2 have become obsolete, and there is no longer a separate ASM installation for RAC.

Intelligent Data Placement and ACLs have also been introduced into ASM. With the correct compatible settings, it is possible to lock out ASM clients from accessing files in ASM disk groups. For certain deployments, the IDP feature can provide better throughput by moving data files to the outer area of disk platters. This feature might have only limited effect for LUNs masking the disk's platters from the OS.

ACFS deserves a longer discussion, and we provided ways of creating ACFS file systems using the GUI and command line.

Disk group creation, similarly, is an important topic, which we discussed in detail. The biggest change when comparing to ASM 10*g* is the introduction of attributes in 11.1, and extended in 11.2.

ASM can be administered in many ways: multiple options exist for the GUI and command line tools. We believe that the knowledge of the command line tools is essential for performing most maintenance tasks; therefore we dedicated a lot of space to the various ssh-friendly tools.

## CHAPTER 10

RDBMS Installation and Configuration

In this chapter, we will describe how to install the RDBMS software using the Oracle Universal Installer and the database management tools using the Database Configuration Assistant (DBCA). An important thing to bear in mind when reading this chapter is that the RDBMS software installed for a RAC database home is identical to the installation for a single-instance database home, with one exception: it must have the software for the RAC option linked in. At any stage, the RAC option can be unlinked to use the same home for single-instance Oracle databases.You can also run a single instance database from a RAC home by setting the init.ora parameter cluster_database to FALSE.

Installing the RAC Software

Since the introduction of ASM in Oracle 10g, the ASM and RDBMS software have shared a common code base. However, prior to Oracle 11g Release 2, the ASM and RDBMS software could be installed from a single OUI in the same Oracle home directory. Optionally, both sets of software could be installed in separate Oracle Homes. Separate Oracle homes improved manageability by enabling the separation of roles between database and storage management. This included the disadvantage of an additional Oracle home to maintain; however, unlike the RDBMS software, there could never more than one ASM instance operational on a node at a particular point in time. In Oracle 11.2, ASM is part of the Grid Infrastructure software. This means that it is installed in conjunction with the clusterware, as opposed to the RDBMS software. Such a separation enables you to group the ASM and clusterware that provides central management of your software. Note that only one installation can run on a node. You can learn how to install the Grid Infrastructure software in Chapter 7. The RDBMS software is now called the RAC software, and it requires a separate Oracle home and installation procedure.

As in previous versions, the RAC software is installed using the Oracle Universal Installer (OUI). Initial installations require an X-Windows environment. If you wish, you can create a response file to use in subsequent silent installations.

Start the Installer

You begin by starting in the installer. Do so as the oracle user in an X session, as in this example:

```
[oracle@london1]$ cd /home/oracle/stage/database
[oracle@london1]$ ../runInstaller
```

The installer takes a few moments to load; once it does, the Configure Security Updates page will be displayed.

Configuring the Security Updates Page

The Configure Security Updates page (see Figure 10-1) allows you to specify an email address to which security alerts and other product issues will be sent. This feature has also been included in Oracle 10gR2 and Oracle 11gR1 patchsets. Oracle recommends that you specify your My Oracle Support email address for this purpose.

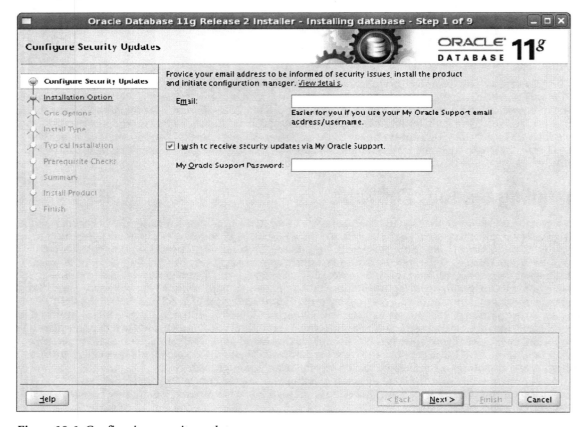

Figure 10-1. Configuring security updates

Specifying an email address is not mandatory. A warning message will be displayed f you do not specify an address; however, the installation will continue without any problem.

Configuring the Installation Options Page

The Installation Options page (see Figure 10-2) presents you with with three options:

- Create and configure a database

- Install database software only

- Upgrade an existing database

The first option will install the RAC software and then create a database. We recommend splitting that process into two separate steps. Doing so will make it easier to find and resolve any faults if an error occurs. Therefore, we recommend selecting the "Install database software only" option at this stage. You can create a database later, using the Database Configuration Assistant (DBCA).

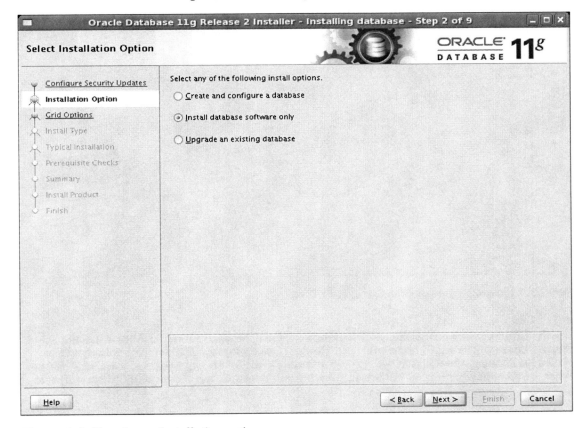

Figure 10-2. Choosing an installation option

Configuring the Node Selection Page

The Node Selection page (see Figure 10-3) lets you select between a single-instance database installation and a RAC database installation. This selection determines which libraries are linked into the executables during installation.

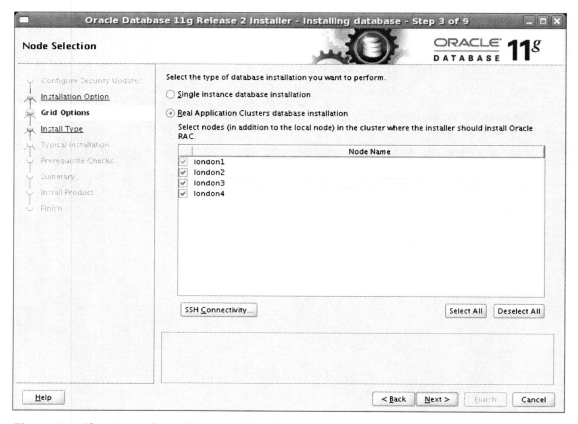

Figure 10-3. Choosing nodes and the type of install

If the Grid Infrastructure is detected, then the default will be set to a RAC database installation, and all known nodes will be added to the node list. This list is useful for verifying that Grid Infrastructure is installed on all nodes and that they are currently running. If any of the expected nodes are missing from this list, we recommend that you exit the installer, remedy the issue, and then restart the RAC software installation.

Configuring the Product Language Selection Page

Press Next to continue to the Product Language selection page. This is identical to the page used in the Grid Infrastructure installation. Select any additional languages you wish error messages to appear in, and then press Next to continue to the Database Editions page.

Configuring the Database Editions Page

The Database Edition page (see Figure 10-4) allows you to choose between the Standard Edition and Enterprise Edition of the Oracle database. In Standard Edition, the RAC option is included as part of the licensing. This version's licensing conditions mean that the cluster is limited to four processor sockets; note that these sockets may have multiple cores. The number of sockets is a restriction across the entire cluster. For example, you may have a cluster of four single-socket servers or two dual-socket servers. The RAC option is included in Standard Edition; however, other functionality is not included. For example, Standard Edition doesn't include the parallel execution (see Chapter 14 for more information on this feature).

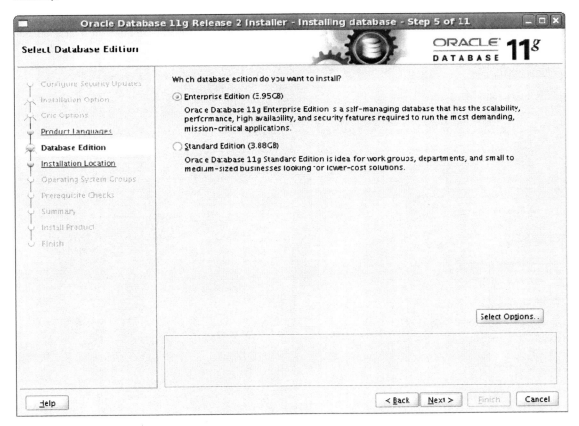

Figure 10-4. Choosing a database edition

Enterprise Edition provides more functionality, including physical and logical Data Guard, Flashback Database, Resource Manager, Oracle Streams, bitmap indexes, and parallel execution. If you are using Enterprise Edition, you can also purchase additional functionality, including the Partitioning option and Enterprise Manager options such as the Diagnostics Pack and the Tuning Pack.

It is possible to upgrade from Standard Edition to Enterprise Edition after installation. However, the upgrade process requires a software reinstallation, and it cannot be performed while the database is online. Downgrading from Enterprise Edition to Standard Edition requires all data to be exported and reimported into the recreated database. Consequently, the edition most applicable to your environment should be considered carefully before you select one.

Configuring the Installation Locations Page

The next screen you'll see is the Installation Location page (see Figure 10-5). The Oracle Base location should be identical to that used for the Grid Infrastructure installation. This holds true as long as the software is installed under the same user or if different users share the same operating system groups. Unlike the Grid Infrastructure installation, where ownership is changed to the root user as part of the installation process, the software location for the RAC software installation can be below the Oracle base and maintain ownership under the RDBMS software user.

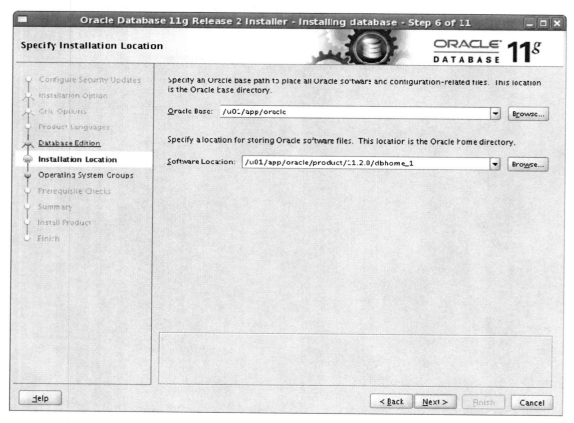

Figure 10-5. Choosing an Oracle base and an Oracle home

In Oracle 10gR2, the software location defaulted to $ORACLE_BASE/product/10.2.0/db_1. Additional homes were calle db_2, db_3, and so on. In Oracle 11gR2, the RDBMS homes are called dbhome1, dbhome2, and so on. If you planto create more than one database in the cluster, then we recommend retaining the recommended dbhome_1 directory name to allow for different versions of the RDBMS Oracle home to be installed. This approach will provide more flexibility during upgrades (e.g., dbhome_2, dbhome_3, and so on).

Configuring the Privileged Operating Systems Group Page

The Privileged Operating System Groups page (see Figure 10-6) lets you optionally specify groups for the Database Administrator (OSDBA) group and the Database Operator (OSOPER) group. The default for both groups is dba. In practice, most sites use the OSDBA group; it is very rare to see the OSOPER group used, although it can provide a useful separation of duties if you are concerned about security, or you wish to split responsibilities between different teams or companies.

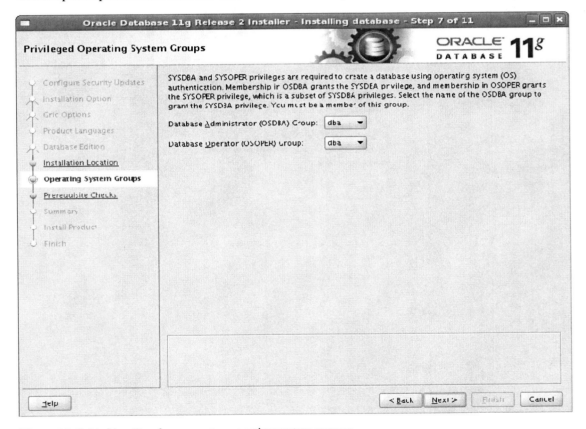

Figure 10-6. Linking Oracle groups to operating system groups

Configuring the Prerequisites Check Page

Press Next to continue to the Prerequisites Checks page. This page is similar to the Prerequisites Checks page in the Advanced Installation. When all prerequisite checks failures have been resolved or ignored, press Next to continue to the Summary page.

Reviewing the Summary Page

The Summary page (see Figure 10-7) displays the details of the options selected during the interview process. You can optionally save these options to a response file that can be used as input for subsequent silent installations.

Press Finish to start the installation process.

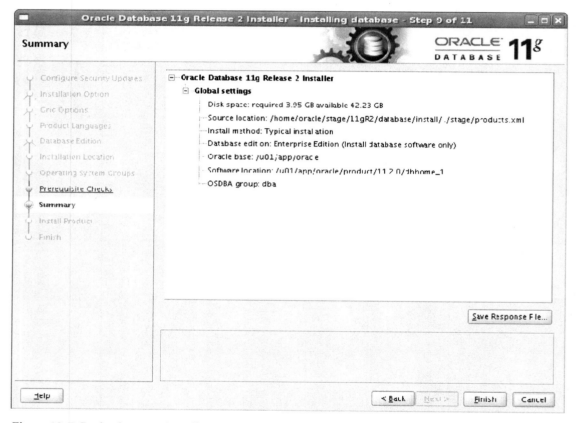

Figure 10-7. Reviewing your installation choices

Executing Configuration Scripts

At the end of the installation process, the Execute Configuration Scripts page will be displayed (see Figure 10-8).

We recommend that the scripts should be executed separately, in the order that the servers are listed. You should do this even though scripts other than the first may be executed in parallel or not in the listed order. We recommend running them one-at-a-time because it can ease troubleshooting. It can also help you ensure that the last script is run separately because it activates the new code version.

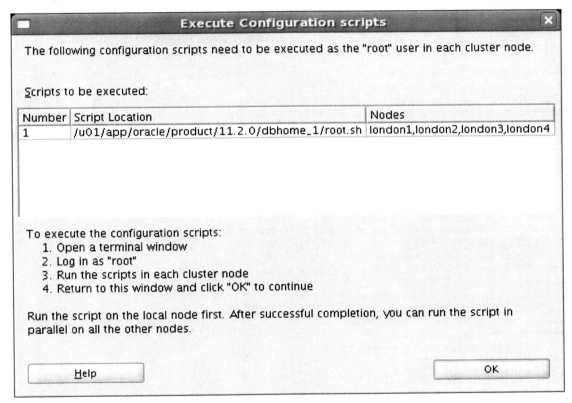

Figure 10-8. Executing configuration scripts

Press OK when the root scripts have been executed on all nodes.

The Finish page should be displayed, indicating a successful installation.This completes the RAC Software installation procedure.

Using the Database Configuration Assistant (DBCA)

In Oracle 10*g* and later, the Database Configuration Assistant (DBCA) has been the preferred tool for creating and dropping databases. DBCA allows supports limited modification of the database.

In Oracle 10*g* and 11.1, DBCA also supported maintaining ASM instances and diskgroups; in Oracle 11.2, this functionality has been moved to the new ASM Configuration Assistant (ASMCA).

In Oracle 10*g*, DBCA also provided limited support database services, including the ability to create, delete, and specify preferred and available instances. In Oracle 11*g*, this functionality was moved to the Enterprise Manager Database and Grid controls.

Starting the DBCA and Choosing an Operation

Before running DBCA, you need to ensure that any ASM diskgroups required by the database have been created. In Oracle 11.2, disk groups can be created using ASMCA or SQL*Plus commands. For most ASM configurations, we would recommend creating two ASM disk groups: one for the database files and another for recovery files. For production systems, these disk groups should be on physically separate disks. For non-production systems, a single ASM disk group may be sufficient. If you are using a cluster file system, then no ASM configuration is required.

DBCA is installed in the RAC Software home. It can run in GUI or silent mode. The GUI mode requires an X session. We recommend that you initially use the GUI interface to specify new databases. It is possible to save the results of the interview process as a database template that can be used as a basis for subsequent database creation. Alternatively, you can create a set of database creation scripts that, with minor modifications, can subsequently be used to build new copies of the database.

Prior to running DBCA, you need to ensure that the $ORACLE_HOME and PATH environment variables are set correctly to specify the RAC software home, as in this example:

```
export ORACLE_HOME=/u01/app/oracle/product/11.2.0/db_1
export PATH=$ORACLE_HOME/bin:$PATH
```

Next, start DBCA as the oracle user:

```
[oracle@london1]$ $ORACLE_HOME/bin/dbca
```

The Welcome page will be displayed.

Configuring the Welcome Page

The Welcome page (see Figure 10-9) allows you to choose whether you wish to create or administer a RAC database or a single-instance database. If the Grid Infrastructure and RDBMS Software has been successfully installed, then the default will be RAC.

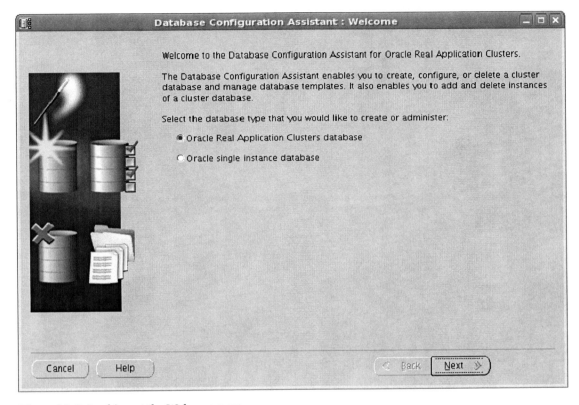

Figure 10-9. Looking at the Welcome page

Configuring the Operations Page

The operations page (see Figure 10-10) is where you tell DBCA what operation you wish to perform. We'll be creating a database, but it provides other choices, as well.

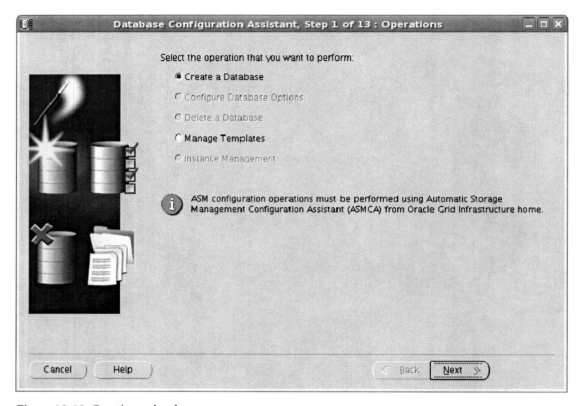

Figure 10-10. Creating a database

In Oracle 11.2, DBCA supports five options:

- Create a database
- Configure database options
- Delete a database
- Manage templates
- Instance management

Initially, you can only create a database or manage templates. The remaining options will become available once a database has been successfully created.

Creating a Database

When you select the Create a Database option from the DBCA Welcome page, the Database Templates page will be displayed. This launches the database creation process.

Configuring the Database Templates Page

The next screen you see is the Database Templates page (see Figure 10-11). In Oracle 10g, DBCA supported four default database templates:

- General Purpose
- Transaction Processing
- Data Warehouse
- Custom Database

The General Purpose and Transaction Processing templates were very similar, so these templates were combined in Oracle 11.1. Therefore, Oracle 11.2 lists only three default templates.

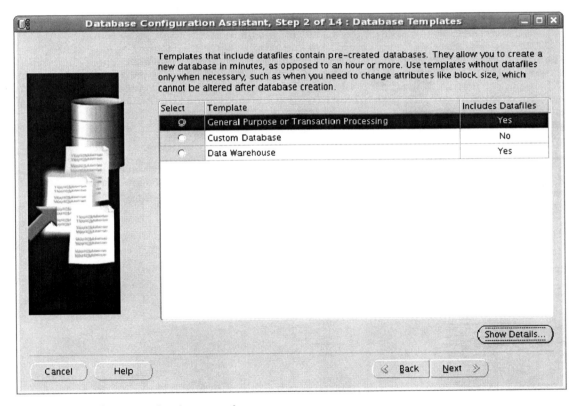

Figure 10-11. Choosing a database template

The templates are defined by XML files in $ORACLE_HOME/assistants/dbca/templates, as shown in Table 10-1. (There is no template file for the Custom Database template.)

Table 10-1. Templates and their Corresponding XML Files

Template	Template File Name
General Purpose and Transaction Processing	General_Purpose.dbc
Data Warehouse	Data_Warehouse.dbc

The General Purpose and Data Warehouse templates create an initial database that is based on the contents of the files, Seed_Database.ctl and Seed_Database.dfb. These files are also located in $ORACLE_HOME/assistants/dbca/templates. The RMAN utility is used to recover the contents of the seed database backup files into the newly created database.

At the time of writing, the only difference between the General Purpose and the Data Warehousing templates in Oracle 11.2 is that the STAR_TRANSFORMATION_ENABLED parameter is FALSE in the former and TRUE in the latter.

The Custom Database template creates a database and then executes the catalog scripts in $ORACLE_HOME/rdbms/admin, including catproc.sql and catalog.sql. Although the resulting database is smaller, the Custom Database template takes significantly longer to create due to the time required to execute the scripts. Databases created using the General Purpose template may present a higher security risk than those created using the Custom Database template. Therefore, we recommend that you use the faster General Purpose template to create test databases and the Custom Database template to create production databases.

Configuring the Database Identification Page (Admin-Managed)

The Database Identification page (see Figure 10-12) allows you to select between an Admin-Managed and a Policy-Managed database. The default is Admin-Managed. If you select Policy-Managed, then the page is redisplayed with a different set of fields.

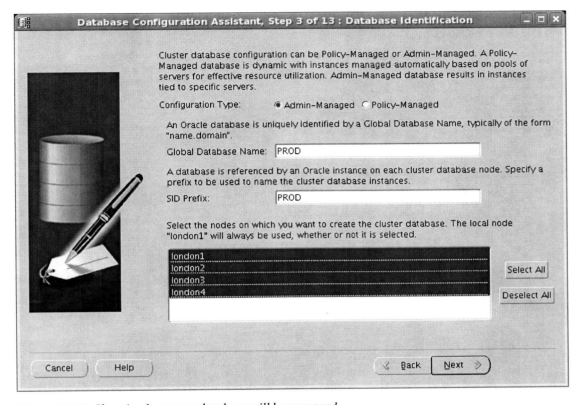

Figure 10-12. Choosing how your database will be managed

The Admin-Managed page allows you to enter a Global Database Name. By default, the name you enter will also be used as the prefix for instance names. Consequently, we recommend that you choose a Global Database Name that does not end in a digit. In other words, don't use PROD1 as a Global Database Name because the instance names will be PROD11, PROD12, which could be confusing down the road.

The Admin-Managed page also allows you to specify which nodes you wish to create the cluster database in. We would always recommend that instances be created on all nodes in the cluster; this maximizes operational flexibility in the future, especially during upgrades, migrations, and following node failures. Remember that instances can always be stopped and disabled to reduce resource usage.

Configuring the Database Identification Page (Policy-Managed)

If you select a Policy-Managed configuration, then the Database Identication page will be redisplayed (see Figure 10-13). Notice that the fields are different this time you see it.

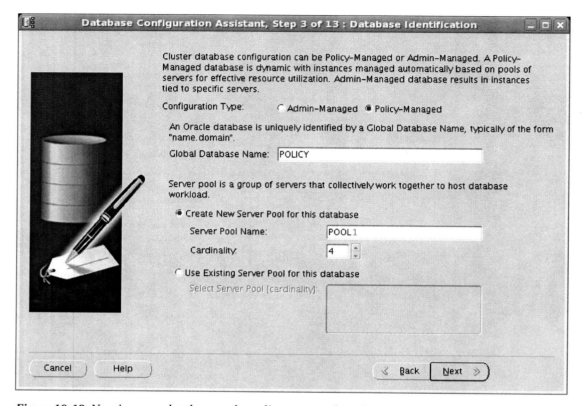

Figure 10-13. Naming your database under policy-managed configuration

The Policy-Managed Database Identification page also allows you to specify a Global Database Name. However, the naming issues discussed in the preceding section do not apply to Policy-Managed databases. In a Policy-Managed database, the instance name includes an underscore between the prefix and the instance number. Therefore, if the database name is PROD, the instance names will be PROD_1, PROD_2, and so on. It may still be necessary to manage these instances explicitly occasionally, but there is less possibility of confusion.

The Policy-Managed Database Identification page also allows you to specify a server pool in which to create the database. The concepts behind server pools are discussed in Chapter 2. You can either create a new server pool or specify the name of an existing pool. For new server pools, you can also specify the cardinality; this will default to the number of nodes in the cluster. For example, specifying a cardinality of 4 will result in a new pool with the attribute values shown in Table 10-2.

Table 10-2. The Server Pool Attribute Values for a Policy-Managed Database

Attribute	Value
Minimum	0
Maximum	4
Importance	0

If you select an existing server pool, the cardinality will be displayed, and that cardinality cannot be altered within DBCA.

If any of the selected nodes are unavailable, a warning message will be displayed. Nodes are reported as being unavailable if they are down or if Oracle Grid Infrastructure is not running on them. We recommend that you resolve such problems before continuing with the DBCA session.

Management Options Page

The Management Options page (see Figure 10-14) lets you optionally configure Enterprise Manager. If an Enterprise Manager Grid Control Agent is detected, then you will be prompted to register the database with the Enterprise Manager Grid control. Otherwise, DBCA will offer to install the Enterprise Manager Database control; in this case, a Management Repository will be installed in the newly created database.

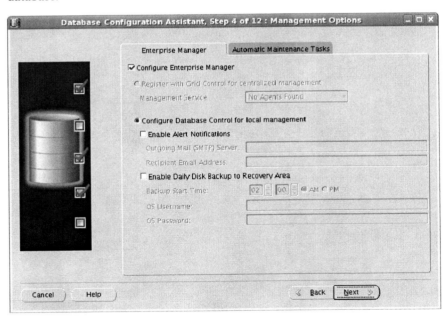

Figure 10-14. Choosing local management with the Enterprise Manager

On this page, you can specify an SMTP mail server and e-mail address for alert notification. You can also enable a daily backup of the database to the recovery area.

If you do not wish to configure the Management Options at this time, this page is also included in the Configure Database Options operation, which is accessed from the Operations page in DBCA. However, note that this page will no longer be available once the Management Options have been configured. To alter Enterprise Manager settings after configuration, you must use the emca tool instead.

The Automatic Maintenance Task tab allows you to enable or disable automatic tasks such as optimizer statistics collection and advisor reports. By default, these tasks are performed during the maintenance window that runs from 10:00pm to 6:00am on weekdays and all day on Saturdays and Sundays. If these times are not appropriate, then you can modify the maintenance window using Enterprise Manager.

Database Credentials Page

The Database Credentials page (see Figure 10-15) lets you specify passwords for the users required to create the database. If you have enabled Enterprise Manager, then you will be asked for passwords for the SYS, SYSTEM, DBSNMP, and SYSMAN users. For test databases, you can use the same administrative passwords for all accounts. However, for production databases, you should use a different password for each account to ensure robust security.

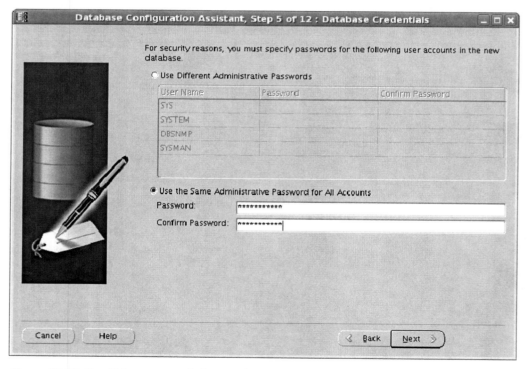

Figure 10-15. Specifying passwords for privileged users

Database File Locations Page

The Database File Locations page (see Figure 10-16) allows you to specify shared storage for the database. In Oracle 11.2, you can use Automatic Storage Management (ASM) or a Cluster File System. Note that raw devices and block devices are no longer supported for shared storage.

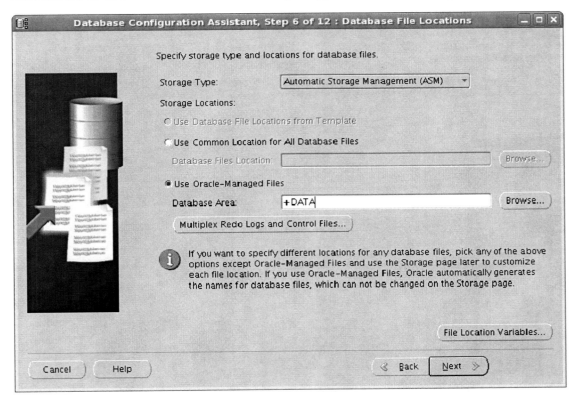

Figure 10-16. Choosing a storage management approach

You can choose from the following approaches when deciding a storage location:

- You can use a set of locations read from a DBCA template.

- You can specify a common location for all database files.

- You can let the database manage locations through the Oracle-Managed Files feature.

If you select Automatic Storage Management (ASM), then the default will be to use Oracle-Managed Files; if you select Cluster File System, then the default will be to use a common location for all database files. In either case, you can choose any of the three options.

If you choose to use Oracle-Managed Files, then you can optionally multiplex your redo logs and control files. You can choose up to five destinations; these should be spread across different physical disks to provide greater fault tolerance.

You can also display the file location variables. You cannot change the file location variables, but you can override them in the common location for all datafiles and the Oracle-Managed files options.

Setting up the Recovery Configuration Page

The Recovery Configuration page (see Figure 10-17) lets you specify a Flash Recovery Area. You can also choose to enable archiving.

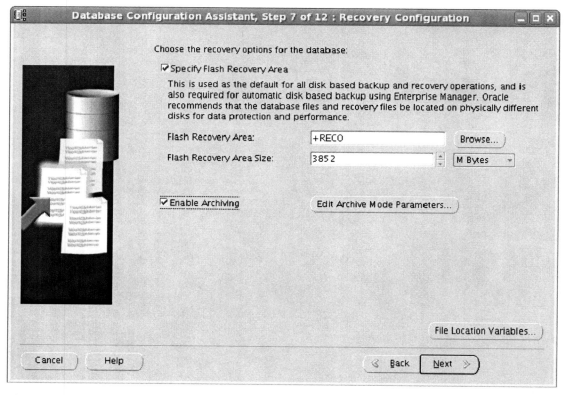

Figure 10-17. *Specifying a Flash Recovery Area*

The Flash Recovery Area was introduced in Oracle 10.1. If configured, it is used as the default location for all disk-based backup and recovery operations. File types stored in the Flash Recovery Area include archived redo logs, datafile copies, and flashback logs.

Space usage in the Flash Recovery Area is managed by Oracle. An initial allocation of space is specified. When this space is exhausted, Oracle will start to release space by deleting files based on a set of rules designed to ensure that the database can still be recovered. If no files can be deleted, then ultimately the database will hang. If that occurs, possible solutions are to increase the size of the Flash Recovery Area, to perform a backup, or to manually delete unnecessary files.

In our experience, the majority of users in Oracle 10.2 and later are now configuring the Flash Recovery Area to allow Oracle to manage database recovery files.

In addition to requesting a Flash Recovery Area, you may also choose to enable archiving on the Recovery Configuration page. By default, archiving is disabled during database creation. If you are building a database using the Custom Template database, it will be created be much more quickly with archiving disabled. If you are using the General Purpose or Data Warehouse Templates, then archiving has less impact because the initial database is created from an RMAN backup rather than SQL*Plus scripts.

If you enable archiving, then you can optionally specify multiple archive log destinations on this page. However, it is usually more efficient to specify multiple log destinations after the database has been created.

Configuring the Database Content Page

What you see on the Database Content page depends upon which template you selected. If you selected the Custom template or a template derived from the Custom template, then you will see the page shown in Figure 10-18.

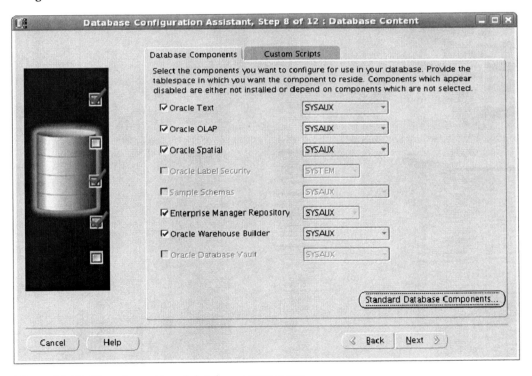

Figure 10-18. Choosing optional database components

You can optionally install the following components:

- Oracle Text
- Oracle OLAP
- Oracle Spatial
- Oracle Label Security
- Sample Schemas
- Enterprise Manager Repository
- Oracle Warehouse Builder
- Oracle Database Vault

You can also click the Standard Database Components button to display the Standard Database Components page.

Configuring the Standard Database Components Page

The Standard Database Components page (Figure 10-19) lets you to install the following components:

- Oracle JVM
- Oracle XML DB
- Oracle Multimedia
- Oracle Application Express

If you selected the General Purpose or Data Warehouse template, you can choose to install the sample schemas. This template will be stored in an additional tablespace called EXAMPLE that is approximately 130MB in size.

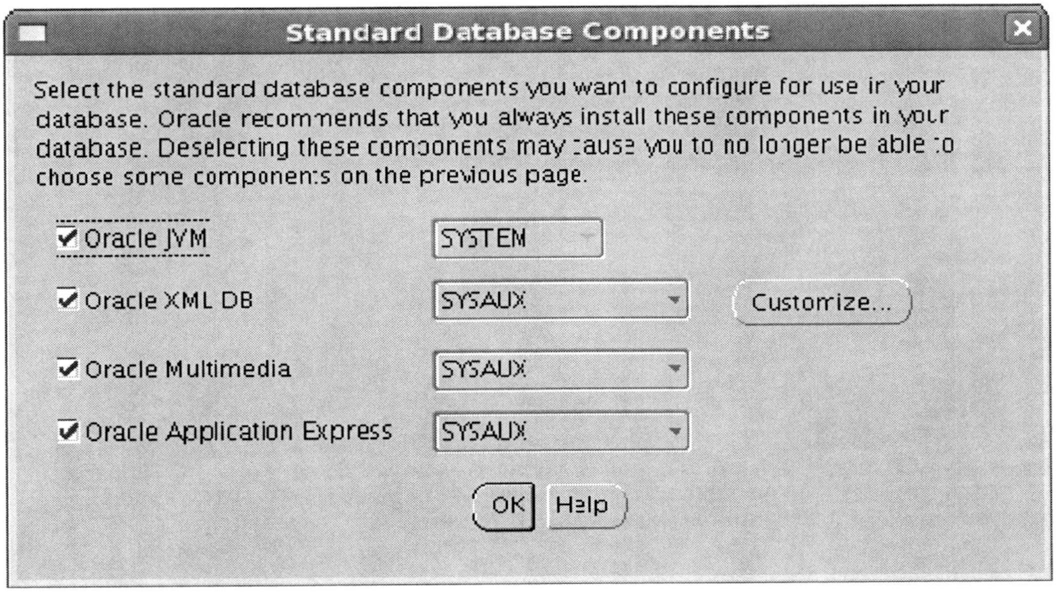

Figure 10-19. Configuring standard database components

In Oracle 11.2, the sample schemas are supplied as a transportable tablespace. The files are located at the following llcoation: $ORACLE_HOME/assistants/dbca/templates. The metadata file is example.dmp, and the datafile is example01.dfb.

The sample schemas include those listed in Table 10-3.

Table 10-3. Standard Example Schemas

Schema Name	Description
HR	Human Resources
OE	Order Entry
JMD Check	Online Catalog
PM	Product Media
IX	Information Exchange
SH	Sales History

On the Custom Scripts tab of the Database Content page, you can specify any Custom Scripts that you may wish to execute during database creation. However, we recommend that you defer running custom scripts until the database has been successfully created. This simplifies finding faults, should any errors occur.

Configuring the Initializations Parameters Page

The Initialization Parameters page includes four tabs:

- Memory
- Sizing
- Character Sets
- Connection Mode

On each tab, you press the All Initialization Parameters button to modify the 30 or so basic parameters, such as DB_BLOCK_SIZE. You can modify any supported parameter by pressing Show Advanced Parameters button on the All Initialization Parameters page. Oracle 11.2 has around 340 supported parameters; the actual number will vary by version and port.

Configuring the Memory Tab

The Memory tab (see Figure 10-20) defaults to using Automatic Memory Management, which was introduced in Oracle 11.1. This feature specifies Oracle will manage both SGA and PGA memory allocation. The concepts behind selecting Automatic Memory Management or Automatic Shared Memory Management are discussed in Chapter 4.

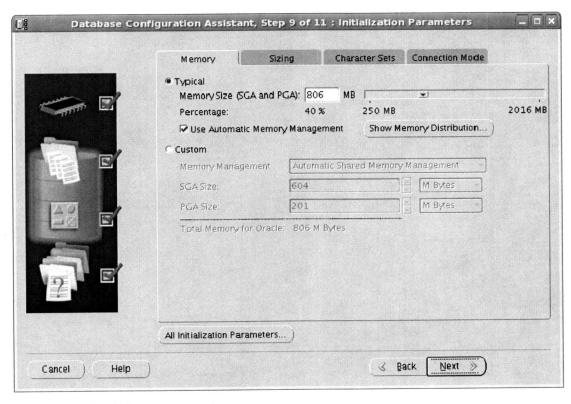

Figure 10-20. Specifying memory settings

Configuring the Sizing Tab

The Sizing tab (see Figure 10-21) allows you to specify the number of processes that each instance will support; the default is 150. The values of the TRANSACTIONS and SESSIONS parameters are derived from the PROCESSES parameter, if they have not been set manually.

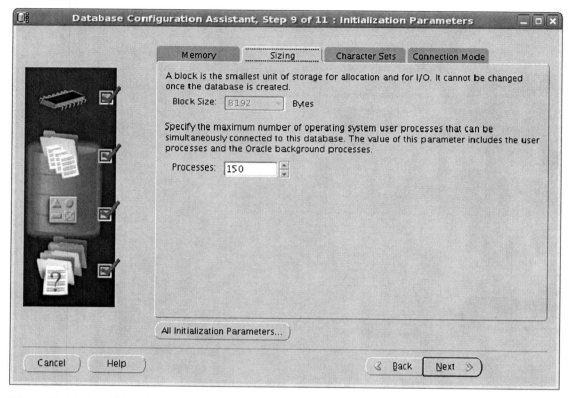

Figure 10-21. Specifying the number of processes

The Sizing tab also displays the database block size, but it does not allow you to change it. However, it can be modified if you press the All Intiialization Parameters button at the bottom of the page.

Configuring the Initialization Parameters Page

The Character Sets tab on the Initialization Parameters Page lets you specify a Database Character Set and a National Character Set. Figure 10-22 shows the Character Sets tab with the default choice selected.

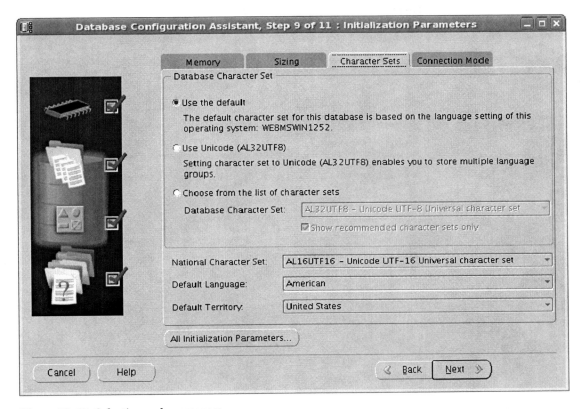

Figure 10-22. Selecting a character set.

The default Database Character Set will be derived from the character set selected when the operating system was installed. For example, the default character set in the UK is WE8MSWIN1252, which is a Microsoft Windows code page. Many sites with international applications are now chosing to use Unicode (AL32UTF8) for their Database Character Set because this provides more flexibility with multilanguage data. Alternatively, you can select from a list of about 30 other more localized character sets.

The National Character Set defaults to Unicode (AL16UTF16), which is a 16-bit universal character set. You can optionally use Unicode 3.0 (UTF8). The default language and default territory can also be modified on this page.

Configuring the Connection Mode Tab

The Connection Mode tab (see Figure 10-23) allows you to select between Dedicated Server mode and Shared Server mode. The default is Dedicated Server mode. We strongly recommend that you use this mode unless you are extremely short of memory. Shared Server mode may be required by certain Oracle features, but these will typically enable shared servers, if necessary. While Shared Server mode potentially uses less memory than Dedicated Server mode, experience has shown that it can cause severe serialization issues and contention between processes. Therefore, in our opinion, careful consideration and testing should be done before enabling Shared Server mode.

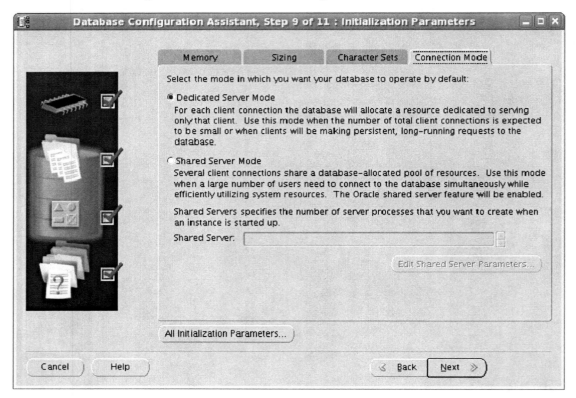

Figure 10-23. Selecting a connection mode

Configuring the Database Storage Page

Depending on the storage type selected, the Database Storage page (see Figure 10-24) allows you to specify locations and sizes for various database files, including the following:

- Control Files
- Data Files
- Redo Log Groups

You can override the locations of any datafiles. You can also change the data file sizes, unless you are using ASM with Oracle-Managed files. Finally, you can change the size of redo log groups and add new groups and members—again, unless you are using ASM with Oracle-Managed Files.

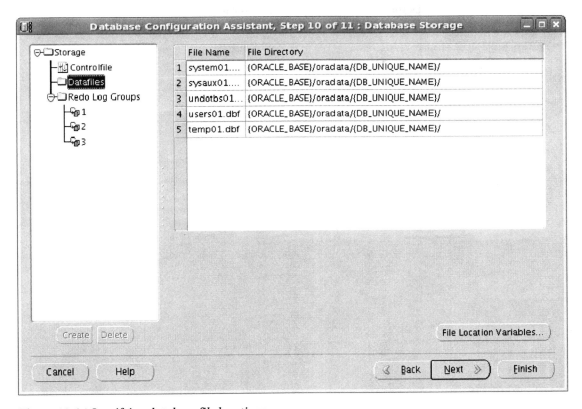

Figure 10-24.Specifying database file locations

Note that you can override the values for control files shown in Table 10-4.

Table 10-4. Overridable Storage Parameters

Parameter	Value
Maximum Datafiles	1024
Maximum Instances	32
Maximum Log History	1
Maximum Redo Log Files	192
Maximum Log Members	3

These values determine how large individual sections of the control file will be. They are difficult to modify after the database has been created, so take care that you anticipate whether your database will become very large in the future.

Configuring the Creation Options Page

The Creation Options page (see Figure 10-25) allows you to perform the following tasks:

- Create a new database (this is the default)

- Save as a Database template

- Generate database-creation scripts

You can only choose the Save as a Database Template option if you originally selected the Custom template or a user-defined template. This option will not appear if you originally selected the General Purpose or Data Warehouse template.

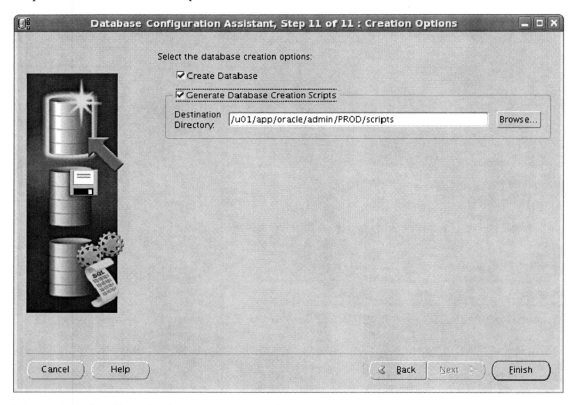

Figure 10-25. Specifying the database creation script options

If you choose to generate database creation scripts, you will be prompted for a location; the default is $ORACLE_BASE/admin/<DatabaseName>/scripts. Take care when accepting the default; if you subsequently use DBCA to delete the database, the scripts directory will also be removed, which may not be your intention. If you wish to preserve the creation scripts so that you can repeatedly build a database, then we recommend you save them to another directory, such as /home/oracle/<DatabaseName>/scripts.

Reviewing the Summary Page

Press Finish to continue after choosing the options described in the preceding section. You'll see a Summary page similar to the one shown in Figure 10-26. You may optionally save the page as an HTML file.

Press OK to return to the Creation Options page and begin the installation.

■ **Caution** Do *not* press Finish again on the Creation Options page; doing so will start a second installation process. If you do begin a second install process, it will run for a few minutes before causing both installation processes to fail.

A progress page is displayed while DBCA performs the following steps:

- Copying database files
- Creating and starting Oracle instance
- Creating cluster database views
- Completing database creation

When the installation has been successfully completed, you will see a message similar to the one shown in Figure 10-26. This message contains information about the new database. Make sure that you capture this information because you will need it to access the database.

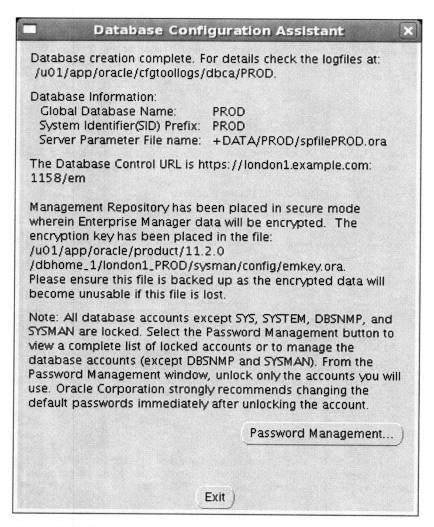

Figure 10-26. Reviewing the creation summary

This completes the database installation. If an Admin-Managed database has been created, one instance should by running on each specified node; if a policy-managed database has been created then the maximum number of instances that will be running is equivalent to the cardinality of the server pool.

Configuring the Database Options

After a database has been created, you can configure certain database options through DBCA. Ensure that the database is started, and then login to an X session as the oracle user and run dbca.

On the Welcome page, select Oracle Real Application Clusters Database; then, on the Operations page, select Configure Database Options. A list of cluster databases will be displayed. Select the database you wish to configure and press Next to continue.

If you have not previously configured Enterprise Manager, then the Management Options page will be displayed. If an Enterprise Manager Grid Control agent is detected on the node, then you can confirm that you wish to register your database with the Grid Control agent. Alternatively, you can install a management repository in the local database, so you can use Enterprise Manager Database control. The Management Options page also allows you to specify an e-mail address for alert notifications, as well as to configure a basic daily backup for the database.

Next, you will see the Database Components page. If you created the database from the General Purpose or Data Warehouse template, all options on the Database Components page will be disabled. If you created the database from the Custom Template, then you will be able to install the following additional components if they have not already been installed:

- Oracle Text

- Oracle OLAP

- Oracle Spatial

- Oracle Label Security

- Sample Schemas

- Enterprise Manager Repository

- Oracle Warehouse Builder

- Oracle Database Vault

You can also click the Standard Database Components button to display the Standard Database Components page. The Standard Database Components page allows you to install the following components:

- Oracle JVM

- Oracle XML DB

- Oracle Multimedia

- Oracle Application Express

The Database Credentials page comes next; it allows you to enter passwords for some or all of the SYS, SYSTEM, SYSMAN, and DBSNMP users, depending on which management options have been configured in the database.

Next, you will see the Connection Mode page, which allows you to select either Dedicated Server mode or Shared Server mode. As noted in the Database Creation selection, we strongly recommend that you use Dedicated Server mode whenever sufficient memory is available,

Press Next to continue. If any configuration options have been updated, a confirmation message will be displayed. Press OK to continue.

When the configuration is complete, a message is displayed. This message reports the actions that have been completed successfully. For example, if the Enterprise Manager Database control has been added to the database, you'll see the message shown in Figure 10-27.

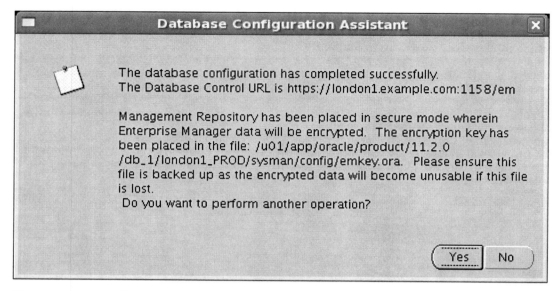

Figure 10-27. Completing the database configuration process

Deleting a Database

DBCA can delete any existing database, including its instances and administrative directories and files. To delete a new database, log in to an X session as the oracle user and run DBCA. On the Welcome page, select the Oracle Real Application Clusters Database option; and on the Operations page, select the Delete a Database optoin.

A list of existing databases will be displayed. Figure 10-28 shows an example list with only one database in it. Select a database to be deleted and press Finish.

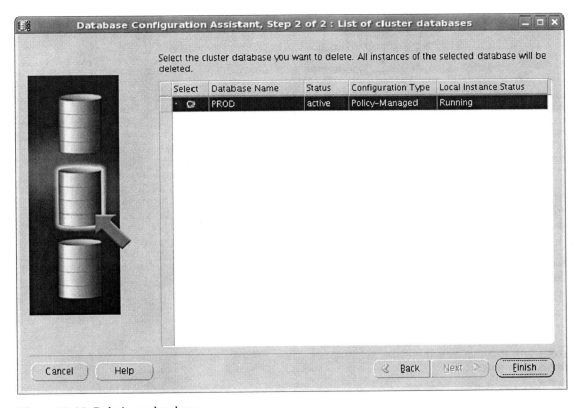

Figure 10-28. Deleting a database

This displays a confirmation message. Press Yes to delete the database; press No to exit.

If the any instances are currently running, these will be shutdown. The database files will be deleted, and a message will be displayed when the operation is completed.

Managing Templates

DBCA allows you to create, modify, and delete database templates that can subsequently be used to create new databases. To manage database templates, log in to an X session as the oracle user and run dbca. On the Welcome page, select Oracle Real Application Clusters Database; and on the Operations page, select Manage Templates.

Building Database Creation Scripts

In addition letting you creating a database directly, DBCA lets you generate database creation scripts. There are three main benefits to building databases using these scripts:

- The scripts can be customized using a command-line editor.

- The scripts can be used to rebuild identical copies of the database.

- The scripts can be used as documentation of the database build.

The default location for the DBCA scripts is `$ORACLE_BASE/admin/<database_name>/scripts`. However, this directory will be deleted if you drop the database using DBCA. Therefore, if you wish to use the scripts to rebuild the database more than once, you should store them in another location, such as `~/admin/<database_name>/scripts`.

The same scripts are generated for both Admin-Managed and Policy-Managed databases. However, the content differs significantly, depending on your choice of configuration type.

Scripts are generated on each node in the cluster. To simplify the database creation process, ensure that all nodes are running before generating the scripts. The scripts differ on each node. Those generated on the first node perform the actual database creation; on the remaining nodes, most of the commands in the SQL*Plus scripts are commented out using the REM clause. The scripts should be run on each node to complete the database creation.

The following sections describe the scripts generated for Admin-Managed and Policy-Managed databases. We also highlight differences between them. We generated the scripts in our examples using a four-node cluster created with the Custom template, and we used the default DBCA options whenever possible.

Setting up Admin-Managed Database Scripts

In the Admin-Managed example, the database was called ADMIN, and the following scripts were generated on each node:

- `ADMIN<InstanceNumber>.sh`

- `ADMIN<InstanceNumber>.sql`

- `init.ora`

- `CreateDB.sql`

- `CreateDBFiles.sql`

- `CreateDBCatalog.sql`

- `JServer.sql`

- `xdb_protocol.sql`

- `ordinst.sql`

- `interMedia.sql`

- `emRepository.sql`

- `apex.sql`

- `CreateClustDBViews.sql`

- lockAccount.sql

- postDBCreation.sql

The contents of these scripts are discussed in the upcoming sections.

Executing the ADMIN1.sh Script

The ADMIN1.sh script is the top level shell script; it should be executed on each node in the cluster. This shell script calls all other scripts generated by DBCA. Here is the code for our example script:

```
#!/bin/sh

OLD_UMASK=`umask`
umask 0027
mkdir -p /u01/app/oracle/admin/ADMIN/adump
mkdir -p /u01/app/oracle/admin/ADMIN/dpdump
mkdir -p /u01/app/oracle/admin/ADMIN/hdump
mkdir -p /u01/app/oracle/admin/ADMIN/pfile
mkdir -p /u01/app/oracle/cfgtoollogs/dbca/ADMIN
umask ${OLD_UMASK}
ORACLE_SID=ADMIN1; export ORACLE_SID
PATH=$ORACLE_HOME/bin:$PATH; export PATH
echo You should Add this entry in the /etc/oratab:
ADMIN:/u01/app/oracle/product/11.2.0/dbhome_1:Y
/u01/app/oracle/product/11.2.0/dbhome_1/bin/sqlplus /nolog
@/u01/app/oracle/admin/ADMIN/scripts/ADMIN1.sql
```

The preceding script overrides the default umask values, and then creates the administrative directories. In Oracle 11.2, foreground and background trace files and the alert log are written to directories in the Automated Diagnostics Repository (ADR). Thus only the four administrative directories listed in Table 10-6 are now required.

Table 10-6. *The Four Administrative Directories*

Directory	Purpose
adump	Auditing files
dpdump	Data Pump Files
hdump	High availability trace files
pfile	Initialization file

DBCA also creates a scripts directory for the database creation scripts, as well as a directory below $ORACLE_BASE/cfgtoollogs/dbca for DBCA trace and log files for the database.

After resetting umask, the script sets the ORACLE_SID. For Admin-Managed databases, the default SID is <database_name><instance_number> (e.g., ADMIN1). The script then invokes SQL*Plus to run the ADMIN1.sql, which will create the database and run the remaining SQL scripts.

Note that the shell script contains a reminder to add the database to /etc/oratab on each node in the cluster. If you create the database using the DBCA GUI, /etc/oratab will be updated automatically; if you create the database using DBCA-generated scripts, you will need to remember to update /etc/oratab manually.

Creating the ADMIN1.sql Script

The ADMIN1.sql script is the top-level SQL*Plus script. It is called by the shell script (in this case, ADMIN1.sh). Here is the code from our example ADMIN1.sql script:

```
set verify off
ACCEPT sysPassword CHAR PROMPT 'Enter new password for SYS: ' HIDE
ACCEPT systemPassword CHAR PROMPT 'Enter new password for SYSTEM: ' HIDE
ACCEPT sysmanPassword CHAR PROMPT 'Enter new password for SYSMAN: ' HIDE
ACCEPT dbsnmpPassword CHAR PROMPT 'Enter new password for DBSNMP: ' HIDE
ACCEPT asmSysPassword CHAR PROMPT 'Enter ASM SYS user password: ' HIDE
host /u01/app/oracle/product/11.2.0/dbhome_1/bin/orapwd
file=/u01/app/oracle/product/11.2.0/dbhome_1/dbs/orapwADMIN1 force=y
host /u01/app/11.2.0/grid/bin/setasmgidwrap
o=/u01/app/oracle/product/11.2.0/dbhome_1/bin/oracle
host /u01/app/oracle/product/11.2.0/dbhome_1/bin/srvctl add database
-d ADMIN -o /u01/app/oracle/product/11.2.0/dbhome_1
-p +DATA/ADMIN/spfileADMIN.ora -n ADMIN -a DATA,REDO
host /u01/app/oracle/product/11.2.0/dbhome_1/bin/srvctl add instance
-d ADMIN -i ADMIN1 -n london1
host /u01/app/oracle/product/11.2.0/dbhome_1/bin/srvctl add instance
-d ADMIN -i ADMIN2 -n london2
host /u01/app/oracle/product/11.2.0/dbhome_1/bin/srvctl add instance
-d ADMIN -i ADMIN3 -n london3
host /u01/app/oracle/product/11.2.0/dbhome_1/bin/srvctl add instance
-d ADMIN -i ADMIN4 -n london4
host /u01/app/oracle/product/11.2.0/dbhome_1/bin/srvctl disable database
-d ADMIN
@/u01/app/oracle/admin/ADMIN/scripts/CreateDB.sql
@/u01/app/oracle/admin/ADMIN/scripts/CreateDBFiles.sql
@/u01/app/oracle/admin/ADMIN/scripts/CreateDBCatalog.sql
@/u01/app/oracle/admin/ADMIN/scripts/JServer.sql
@/u01/app/oracle/admin/ADMIN/scripts/context.sql
@/u01/app/oracle/admin/ADMIN/scripts/xdb_protocol.sql
@/u01/app/oracle/admin/ADMIN/scripts/ordinst.sql
@/u01/app/oracle/admin/ADMIN/scripts/interMedia.sql
@/u01/app/oracle/admin/ADMIN/scripts/cwmlite.sql
@/u01/app/oracle/admin/ADMIN/scripts/spatial.sql
@/u01/app/oracle/admin/ADMIN/scripts/emRepository.sql
@/u01/app/oracle/admin/ADMIN/scripts/apex.sql
@/u01/app/oracle/admin/ADMIN/scripts/CreateClustDBViews.sql
```

```
host echo "SPFILE='+DATA/ADMIN/spfileADMIN.ora'" >
/u01/app/oracle/product/11.2.0/dbhome_1/dbs/initADMIN1.ora
@/u01/app/oracle/admin/ADMIN/scripts/lockAccount.sql
@/u01/app/oracle/admin/ADMIN/scripts/postDBCreation.sql
```

Although you will have entered passwords during the interview stage of DBCA, these passwords are not stored in the scripts for security reasons. Therefore, you will be prompted to enter the passwords again, in this case, you will need to enter them for the SYS, SYSTEM, SYSMAN, and DBSNMP users. Note that in Oracle 11.2, the ACCEPT command includes a HIDE clause to prevent passwords from being echoed.

The script then creates a password file on the local node using the orapwd utility. The default password file name is $ORACLE_HOME/dbs/orapw<instance_name>.

In Oracle 10.2, the DBCA scripts did not include the SRVCTL statements required to add a RAC database to the OCR. Consequently, these commands had to be executed manually after using scripts to create the database. In Oracle 11.2, the SRVCTL commands are included in the scripts generated by DBCA. The SRVCTL commands perform the following actions:

- Add the database to the OCR.

- Add each instance to the OCR.

- Temporarily disable the database.

Note that the srvctl statements are included in this version
The next part of the script invokes a series of SQL*Plus scripts that create the database and install various options. In this case, the following scripts were generated:

- CreateDB.sql

- CreateDBFiles.sql

- CreateDBCatalog.sql

- JServer.sql

- xdb_protocol.sql

- ordinst.sql

- interMedia.sql

- emRepository.sql

- apex.sql

- CreateClustDBViews.sql

These additional scripts are described in more detail in the upcoming sections.

The next step is to create a local init.ora file called init<instance_name>.ora with an SPFILE parameter that specifies the location of the Server Parameter file for the database. Two additional scripts are then executed. The first locks any unused accounts, while the second performs a series of post-database creation steps.

Generating the init.ora File

A default init.ora file is generated. This file contains default values for various instance parameters, as well as values for parameters that can be overridden during the DBCA interview phase (e.g., memory and block size).

The following code shows the parameters set in our `init.ora` example (the file has been modified for readability):

```
audit_file_dest=/u01/app/oracle/admin/ADMIN/adump
audit_trail=db
#cluster_database=true
compatible=11.2.0.0.0
db_block_size=8192
db_create_file_dest=+DATA
db_domain=""
db_name=ADMIN
db_recovery_file_dest=+REDO
db_recovery_file_dest_size=4294967296
diagnostic_dest=/u01/app/oracle
dispatchers="(PROTOCOL=TCP) (SERVICE=ADMINXDB)"
log_archive_format=%t_%s_%r.dbf
memory_target=845152256
open_cursors=300
processes=150
#remote_listener=cluster1-scan.example.com:1521
remote_login_passwordfile=exclusive

ADMIN1.instance_number=1
ADMIN2.instance_number=2
ADMIN3.instance_number=3
ADMIN4.instance_number=4
ADMIN1.thread=1
ADMIN2.thread=2
ADMIN3.thread=3
ADMIN4.thread=4
ADMIN1.undo_tablespace=UNDOTBS1
ADMIN2.undo_tablespace=UNDOTBS2
ADMIN3.undo_tablespace=UNDOTBS3
ADMIN4.undo_tablespace=UNDOTBS4
```

The `DIAGNOSTIC_DEST` parameter was introduced in Oracle 11.1, and it specifies the location of the ADR for the database. This defaults to the value of `$ORACLE_BASE`.

For Admin-Managed databases, several instance-specific parameters must be specified (as shown in the second part of the file):

- instance_number

- thread

- undo_tablespace

The contents of the init.ora file are used to start the instance and are subsequently stored in a central Server Parameter file (SPFILE).

Initially, the CLUSTER_DATABASE and REMOTE_LISTENER parameters are commented out. These parameters will not set to non-default values until configuration is complete and additional redo threads have been created for the database. If you wish to rebuild the database using these scripts, it will be necessary to remove any values set during previous database creations for these parameters, as well as for the CONTROL_FILES parameter.

Also, note that the REMOTE_LISTENER parameter now references the SCAN net service name, which resolves to a list of SCAN listeners. In previous versions, this parameter would specify a list of regular listeners.

Executing the CreateDB.sql Script

The CreateDB.sql script executes the CREATE DATABASE statement, as in this example:

```
SET VERIFY OFF
connect "SYS"/"&&sysPassword" as SYSDBA
set echo on
spool /u01/app/oracle/admin/ADMIN/scripts/CreateDB.log append
startup nomount pfile="/u01/app/oracle/admin/ADMIN/scripts/init.ora";
CREATE DATABASE "ADMIN"
MAXINSTANCES 32
MAXLOGHISTORY 1
MAXLOGFILES 192
MAXLOGMEMBERS 3
MAXDATAFILES 1024
DATAFILE SIZE 700M AUTOEXTEND ON NEXT  10240K MAXSIZE UNLIMITED
EXTENT MANAGEMENT LOCAL
SYSAUX DATAFILE SIZE 600M AUTOEXTEND ON NEXT  10240K MAXSIZE UNLIMITED
SMALLFILE DEFAULT TEMPORARY TABLESPACE TEMP TEMPFILE SIZE 20M AUTOEXTEND ON NEXT  640K MAXSIZE
UNLIMITED
SMALLFILE UNDO TABLESPACE "UNDOTBS1" DATAFILE SIZE 200M AUTOEXTEND ON NEXT  5120K MAXSIZE
UNLIMITED
CHARACTER SET WE8MSWIN1252
NATIONAL CHARACTER SET AL16UTF16
LOGFILE GROUP 1  SIZE 51200K,
GROUP 2  SIZE 51200K
USER SYS IDENTIFIED BY "&&sysPassword" USER SYSTEM IDENTIFIED BY
"&&systemPassword";
set linesize 2048;
column ctl_files NEW_VALUE ctl_files;
select concat('control_files='''', concat(replace(value, ', ', '''',''''), ''''))
 ctl_files from v$parameter where name ='control_files';
host echo &ctl_files >>/u01/app/oracle/admin/ADMIN/scripts/init.ora;
spool off
```

The preceding script starts an instance in NOMOUNT mode, and then executes the CREATE DATABASE statement. The statement creates three permanent tablespaces: SYSTEM, SYSAUX, and UNDOTBS1; it also creates one temporary tablespace called TEMP. In addition to the tablespaces, the script creates a single redo log thread. In this example, the redo log contains two logfile groups.

The CREATE DATABASE statement also creates the initial data dictionary tables, based on the contents of $ORACLE_HOME/rdbms/admin/sql.bsq. In Oracle 11.2, sql.bsq includes references to around 20 other *.bsq files that are also found in $ORACLE_HOME/rdbms/admin. These other *.bsq files contain definitions for various data dictionary components, such as dcore.bsq, dsqlddl.bsq, dmanage.bsq, dplsql.bsq, and so on.

For this database, we specified that ASM would be used for shared storage. ASM presents some interesting control file issues during database creation. When you create a file in ASM, you can only specify a partial path name; ASM will assign the next file number in the disk group to the new file. Therefore, you cannot know in advance what the file number will be assigned to a new file. Consequently, after the CREATE DATABASE statement has created the new database, including the controlfiles in the ASM disk group, this script selects the value of the CONTROL_FILES parameter from V$PARAMETER and appends this value to the init.ora file.

■ **Note** Before you can create the database again, you will need to use these scripts to delete the CONTROL_FILES parameter from the init.ora file.

Executing the CreateDBFiles.sql Script

The CreateDBFiles.sql script creates the remaining tablespaces that are initialized by the CREATE DATABASE statement. In this example, the tablespaces include the UNDO tablespaces for the remaining three instances and a USERS tablespace that is also the default permanent tablespace.

Oracle sets all tablespaces to auto extend by default, as in this example:

```
SET VERIFY OFF
connect "SYS"/"&&sysPassword" as SYSDBA
set echo on
spool /u01/app/oracle/admin/ADMIN/scripts/CreateDBFiles.log append
CREATE SMALLFILE UNDO TABLESPACE "UNDOTBS2" DATAFILE SIZE 200M AUTOEXTEND ON
  NEXT  5120K MAXSIZE UNLIMITED;
CREATE SMALLFILE UNDO TABLESPACE "UNDOTBS3" DATAFILE SIZE 200M AUTOEXTEND ON
  NEXT  5120K MAXSIZE UNLIMITED;
CREATE SMALLFILE UNDO TABLESPACE "UNDOTBS4" DATAFILE SIZE 200M AUTOEXTEND ON
  NEXT  5120K MAXSIZE UNLIMITED;
CREATE SMALLFILE TABLESPACE "USERS" LOGGING DATAFILE SIZE 5M AUTOEXTEND ON
  NEXT  1280K MAXSIZE UNLIMITED EXTENT MANAGEMENT LOCAL
SEGMENT SPACE MANAGEMENT  AUTO;
ALTER DATABASE DEFAULT TABLESPACE "USERS";
spool off
```

Note that the SMALLFILE clause is specified for each new tablespace. This optional keyword was introduced in Oracle 10.1; it is the default value, and it indicates that this is not a BIGFILE tablespace.

Executing the CreateDBCatalog.sql Script

Once the database has been created, the data dictionary must be populated. The `CreateDBCatalog.sql` script accomplishes this task:

```
SET VERIFY OFF
connect "SYS"/"&&sysPassword" as SYSDBA
set echo on
spool /u01/app/oracle/admin/ADMIN/scripts/CreateDBCatalog.log append
@/u01/app/oracle/product/11.2.0/dbhome_1/rdbms/admin/catalog.sql;
@/u01/app/oracle/product/11.2.0/dbhome_1/rdbms/admin/catblock.sql;
@/u01/app/oracle/product/11.2.0/dbhome_1/rdbms/admin/catproc.sql;
@/u01/app/oracle/product/11.2.0/dbhome_1/rdbms/admin/catoctk.sql;
@/u01/app/oracle/product/11.2.0/dbhome_1/rdbms/admin/owminst.plb;
connect "SYSTEM"/"&&systemPassword"
@/u01/app/oracle/product/11.2.0/dbhome_1/sqlplus/admin/pupbld.sql;
connect "SYSTEM"/"&&systemPassword"
set echo on
spool /u01/app/oracle/admin/ADMIN/scripts/sqlPlusHelp.log append
@/u01/app/oracle/product/11.2.0/dbhome_1/sqlplus/admin/help/hlpbld.sql
helpus.sql;
spool off
spool off
```

Next, the `CreateDBCatalog.sql` script executes several additional scripts (see Table 10-7).

Table 10-7. Data Dictionary Creation Scripts Executed by CreateDBCatalog.sql

Script Name	Description
$ORACLE_HOME/rdbms/admin/catalog.sql	Data dictionary views
$ORACLE_HOME/rdbms/admin/catblock.sql	Lock views
$ORACLE_HOME/rdbms/admin/catproc.sql	Procedural option scripts (PLSQL)
$ORACLE_HOME/rdbms/admin/catoctk.sql	Oracle Cryptographic Toolkit
$ORACLE_HOME/rdbms/admin/owminst.plb	Oracle Workspace Manager
$ORACLE_HOME/sqlplus/admin/pupbld.sql	SQL*Plus Product User Profile
$ORACLE_HOME/sqlplus/admin/help/hlpbld.sql	SQL*Plus Help

■ **Note** If you use the General Purpose or Data Warehouse templates, these scripts will have been pre-installed in the starter database.

Executing the JServer.sql Script

The JServer.sql script installs JServer, which is the optional Java Virtual Machine that runs within the database. The following snippet shows the script contents from our example:

```
SET VERIFY OFF
connect "SYS"/"&&sysPassword" as SYSDBA
set echo on
spool /u01/app/oracle/admin/ADMIN/scripts/JServer.log append
@/u01/app/oracle/product/11.2.0/dbhome_1/javavm/install/initjvm.sql;
@/u01/app/oracle/product/11.2.0/dbhome_1/xdk/admin/initxml.sql;
@/u01/app/oracle/product/11.2.0/dbhome_1/xdk/admin/xmlja.sql;
@/u01/app/oracle/product/11.2.0/dbhome_1/rdbms/admin/catjava.sql;
@/u01/app/oracle/product/11.2.0/dbhome_1/rdbms/admin/catexf.sql;
spool off
```

Executing the xdb_protocol.sql Script

The xdb_protocol.sql script installs the XDB database option, as in this example:

```
SET VERIFY OFF
connect "SYS"/"&&sysPassword" as SYSDBA
set echo on
spool /u01/app/oracle/admin/ADMIN/scripts/xdb_protocol.log append
@/u01/app/oracle/product/11.2.0/dbhome_1/rdbms/admin/catqm.sql
change_on_install SYSAUX TEMP;
connect "SYS"/"&&sysPassword" as SYSDBA
@/u01/app/oracle/product/11.2.0/dbhome_1/rdbms/admin/catxdbj.sql;
@/u01/app/oracle/product/11.2.0/dbhome_1/rdbms/admin/catrul.sql;
spool off
```

Executing the ordinst.sql Script

The ordinst.sql script installs the ORD components, which include Oracle Multimedia and Spatial:

```
SET VERIFY OFF
connect "SYS"/"&&sysPassword" as SYSDBA
set echo on
spool /u01/app/oracle/admin/ADMIN/scripts/ordinst.log append
@/u01/app/oracle/product/11.2.0/dbhome_1/ord/admin/ordinst.sql SYSAUX SYSAUX;
spool off
```

Executing the intermedia.sql Script

The `intermedia.sql` script uses the following commands to install Oracle Multimedia:

```
SET VERIFY OFF
connect "SYS"/"&&sysPassword" as SYSDBA
set echo on
spool /u01/app/oracle/admin/ADMIN/scripts/interMedia.log append
@/u01/app/oracle/product/11.2.0/dbhome_1/ord/im/admin/iminst.sql;
spool off
```

Executing the emRepository.sql Script

The `emRepository.sql` script installs and configures the Enterprise Manager Database control. The script creates an Enterprise Manager management repository in the local database. If you are using the Enterprise Manager Grid control, it is not necessary to create a local management repository. Our sample `emRepository.sql` script looks like this:

```
SET VERIFY OFF
connect "SYS"/"&&sysPassword" as SYSDBA
set echo off
spool /u01/app/oracle/admin/ADMIN/scripts/emRepository.log append
@/u01/app/oracle/product/11.2.0/dbhome_1/sysman/admin/emdrep/sql/emreposcre
/acfs1/product/11.2.0/dbhome_1 SYSMAN &&sysmanPassword TEMP ON;
WHENEVER SQLERROR CONTINUE;
spool off
```

The preceding script only creates the Enterprise Manager management repository; it does not configure the Enterprise Manager Database control.

Executing the apex.sql Script

The `apex.sql` script is new in Oracle 11.2. It installs objects for Application Express, which is a new rapid development tool that has been integrated with the database in Oracle 11*g* Release 2. Oracle Application Express (Apex) was formerly known as HTML DB. Here is the content of the script on our system:

```
SET VERIFY OFF
connect "SYS"/"&&sysPassword" as SYSDBA
set echo on
spool /u01/app/oracle/admin/ADMIN/scripts/apex.log append
@/u01/app/oracle/product/11.2.0/dbhome_1/apex/catapx.sql change_on_install
 SYSAUX SYSAUX TEMP /i/ NONE;
spool off
```

Executing the CreateClustDBViews.sql Script

The CreateClustDBView.sql script is only executed for RAC databases, and it creates a number of additional RAC-specific data dictionary views, as in this example:

```
SET VERIFY OFF
connect "SYS"/"&&sysPassword" as SYSDBA
set echo on
spool /u01/app/oracle/admin/ADMIN/scripts/CreateClustDBViews.log append
@/u01/app/oracle/product/11.2.0/dbhome_1/rdbms/admin/catclust.sql;
spool off
```

Chapter 12 discusses how to use these data dictionary views in more depth.

Executing the lockAccount.sql Script

The lockAccount.sql script is also new in Oracle 11.2. It locks and expires all unlocked user accounts with the exception of SYS and SYSTEM, as in this example:

```
SET VERIFY OFF
set echo on
spool /u01/app/oracle/admin/ADMIN/scripts/lockAccount.log append
BEGIN
 FOR item IN ( SELECT USERNAME FROM DBA_USERS WHERE ACCOUNT_STATUS IN
 ('OPEN', 'LOCKED', 'EXPIRED') AND USERNAME NOT IN (
'SYS','SYSTEM') )
 LOOP
  dbms_output.put_line('Locking and Expiring: ' || item.USERNAME);
  execute immediate 'alter user ' ||
    sys.dbms_assert.enquote_name(
    sys.dbms_assert.schema_name(
    item.USERNAME),false) || ' password expire account lock' ;
 END LOOP;
END;
/
spool off
```

Executing the postDBCreation.sql Script

This postDBCreation.sql script performs post database creation processing. Here is the content of the script from our example:

```
SET VERIFY OFF
connect "SYS"/"&&sysPassword" as SYSDBA
set echo on
spool /u01/app/oracle/admin/ADMIN/scripts/postDBCreation.log append
select 'utl_recomp_begin: ' || to_char(sysdate, 'HH:MI:SS') from dual;
```

```
execute utl_recomp.recomp_serial();
select 'utl_recomp_end: ' || to_char(sysdate, 'HH:MI:SS') from dual;
shutdown immediate;
connect "SYS"/"&&sysPassword" as SYSDBA
startup mount pfile="/u01/app/oracle/admin/ADMIN/scripts/init.ora";
alter database archivelog;
alter database open;
select group# from v$log where group# =7;
select group# from v$log where group# =8;
ALTER DATABASE ADD LOGFILE THREAD 4 GROUP 7  SIZE 51200K,
 GROUP 8  SIZE 51200K;
ALTER DATABASE ENABLE PUBLIC THREAD 4;
select group# from v$log where group# =5;
select group# from v$log where group# =6;
ALTER DATABASE ADD LOGFILE THREAD 3 GROUP 5  SIZE 51200K,
 GROUP 6  SIZE 51200K;
ALTER DATABASE ENABLE PUBLIC THREAD 3;
select group# from v$log where group# =3;
select group# from v$log where group# =4;
ALTER DATABASE ADD LOGFILE THREAD 2 GROUP 3  SIZE 51200K,
 GROUP 4  SIZE 51200K;
ALTER DATABASE ENABLE PUBLIC THREAD 2;
host echo cluster_database=true
  >>/u01/app/oracle/admin/ADMIN/scripts/init.ora;
host echo remote_listener=cluster3scan.juliandyke.com:1522
  >>/u01/app/oracle/admin/ADMIN/scripts/init.ora;
```

- connect "SYS"/"&&sysPassword" as SYSDBA

- set echo on

```
create spfile='+DATA/ADMIN/spfileADMIN.ora' FROM
pfile='/u01/app/oracle/admin/ADMIN/scripts/init.ora';
shutdown immediate;
host /u01/app/oracle/product/11.2.0/db_1/bin/srvctl enable database -d ADMIN;
host /u01/app/oracle/product/11.2.0/db_1/bin/srvctl start database -d ADMIN;
connect "SYS"/"&&sysPassword" as SYSDBA
alter user SYSMAN identified by "&&sysmanPassword" account unlock;
alter user DBSNMP identified by "&&dbsnmpPassword" account unlock;
host /u01/app/oracle/product/11.2.0/db_1/bin/emca -config dbcontrol db
-silent -cluster -ASM_USER_ROLE SYSDBA -ASM_USER_NAME ASMSNMP -CLUSTER_NAME
 cluster3 -LOG_FILE /u01/app/oracle/admin/ADMIN/scripts/emConfig.log
-DBSNMP_PWD &&dbsnmpPassword -SYS_PWD &&sysPassword -ASM_USER_PWD
&&asmSysPassword -SID ADMIN -ASM_SID +ASM1 -DB_UNIQUE_NAME ADMIN -EM_HOME
/u01/app/oracle/product/11.2.0/db_1 -SYSMAN_PWD &&sysmanPassword
-SERVICE_NAME ADMIN -ASM_PORT 1521 -PORT 1521
-LISTENER_OH /u01/app/11.2.0/grid -LISTENER LISTENER -ORACLE_HOME
/u01/app/oracle/product/11.2.0/db_1
-HOST server14 -ASM_OH /u01/app/11.2.0/grid;
spool off
exit;
```

The preceding script recompiles any packages that have not previously been compiled. It also recompiles any packages that do not depend on objects that have been modified during database creation.

The database is shutdown and mounted, archive logging is enabled, and the database is fully opened. The database still only has one redo thread, so at this point the remaining three redo threads are created and enabled. Creating the additional redo threads means that instances can be started on the other nodes.

You will remember that two parameters were commented out in the init.ora file; CLUSTER_DATABASE and REMOTE_LISTENER. Values for these parameters are now appended to the init.ora file because the database can now be started in cluster mode.

■ **Note** If you wish to rebuild the database using these scripts, you will need to remove the entries for these parameters from the init.ora file.

The next step is to create SPFILE based on the init.ora file. In this case, SPFILE will be stored in an ASM diskgroup. After SPFILE has been created, the instance is shutdown again.

In the OCR, the database is currently disabled, so the SRVCTL command is called first to enable the database and then to start the database. It will not be possible to start the instances on the remote nodes until the password file, init.ora file, and administrative directories have been created on those nodes.

Next, the SYSMAN and DBSNMP accounts are unlocked, and then the Enterprise Manager Configuration Assistant (EMCA) is executed to configure the Enterprise Manager Grid control.

Building Policy-Managed Database Scripts

For our example, we created a database named POLICY. Next, DBCA generated the following scripts on each node:

- POLICY<InstanceNumber>.sh
- POLICY<InstanceNumber>.sql
- init.ora
- CreateDB.sql
- CreateDBFiles.sql
- CreateDBCatalog.sql
- JServer.sql
- xdb_protocol.sql
- ordinst.sql
- interMedia.sql
- emRepository.sql

- apex.sql

- CreateClustDBViews.sql

- lockAccount.sql

- postDBCreation.sql

The files generated by DBCA for a Policy-Managed database are similar to those for an Admin-Managed database. There are but three exceptions, which are:

- POLICY_<InstanceNumber>.sh

- POLICY_<InstanceNumber>.sql

- init.ora

We will discuss these exceptions in more detail in the following sections.

Executing the POLICY_1.sh Script

The top-level shell script for a Policy-Managed database is similar to that for an Admin-Managed database, as in this example:

```
#!/bin/sh

OLD_UMASK=`umask`
umask 0027
mkdir -p /u01/app/oracle/admin/POLICY/adump
mkdir -p /u01/app/oracle/admin/POLICY/dpdump
mkdir -p /u01/app/oracle/admin/POLICY/hdump
mkdir -p /u01/app/oracle/admin/POLICY/pfile
mkdir -p /u01/app/oracle/cfgtoollogs/dbca/POLICY
umask ${OLD_UMASK}
ORACLE_SID=POLICY_1; export ORACLE_SID
PATH=$ORACLE_HOME/bin:$PATH; export PATH
echo You should Add this entry in the /etc/oratab:
POLICY:/u01/app/oracle/product/11.2.0/dbhome_1:Y
/u01/app/oracle/product/11.2.0/dbhome_1/bin/sqlplus /nolog
@/u01/app/oracle/admin/POLICY/scripts/POLICY_1.sql
```

The only significant change in a Policy-Managed database is that the $ORACLE_SID environment variable contains an underscore between the database name and the instance number. This convention provides more flexibility when choosing a name for a database.

Executing the POLICY_1.sql Script

The POLICY_1.sh shell script invokes the POLICY_1.sql script. Here is the content of the POLICY_1.sql script that we generated for this chapter's example:

```
set verify off
ACCEPT sysPassword CHAR PROMPT 'Enter new password for SYS: ' HIDE
ACCEPT systemPassword CHAR PROMPT 'Enter new password for SYSTEM: ' HIDE
ACCEPT sysmanPassword CHAR PROMPT 'Enter new password for SYSMAN: ' HIDE
ACCEPT dbsnmpPassword CHAR PROMPT 'Enter new password for DBSNMP: ' HIDE
ACCEPT asmSysPassword CHAR PROMPT 'Enter ASM SYS user password: ' HIDE
host /u01/app/oracle/product/11.2.0/dbhome_1/bin/orapwd
file=/u01/app/oracle/product/11.2.0/dbhome_1/dbs/orapwPOLICY force=y
host /u01/app/11.2.0/grid/bin/setasmgidwrap
o=/u01/app/oracle/product/11.2.0/dbhome_1/bin/oracle
host /u01/app/oracle/product/11.2.0/dbhome_1/bin/srvctl add srvpool
-g POOL1 -l 0 -u 4
host /u01/app/oracle/product/11.2.0/dbhome_1/bin/srvctl add database
 -d POLICY -o /u01/app/oracle/product/11.2.0/dbhome_1
-p +DATA/POLICY/spfilePOLICY.ora -n POLICY -g POOL1 -a DATA,REDO
host /u01/app/oracle/product/11.2.0/dbhome_1/bin/srvctl disable
database -d POLICY
@/u01/app/oracle/admin/POLICY/scripts/CreateDB.sql
@/u01/app/oracle/admin/POLICY/scripts/CreateDBFiles.sql
@/u01/app/oracle/admin/POLICY/scripts/CreateDBCatalog.sql
@/u01/app/oracle/admin/POLICY/scripts/JServer.sql
@/u01/app/oracle/admin/POLICY/scripts/context.sql
@/u01/app/oracle/admin/POLICY/scripts/xdb_protocol.sql
@/u01/app/oracle/admin/POLICY/scripts/ordinst.sql
@/u01/app/oracle/admin/POLICY/scripts/interMedia.sql
@/u01/app/oracle/admin/POLICY/scripts/cwmlite.sql
@/u01/app/oracle/admin/POLICY/scripts/spatial.sql
@/u01/app/oracle/admin/POLICY/scripts/emRepository.sql
@/u01/app/oracle/admin/POLICY/scripts/apex.sql
@/u01/app/oracle/admin/POLICY/scripts/owb.sql
@/u01/app/oracle/admin/POLICY/scripts/CreateClustDBViews.sql
host echo "SPFILE='+DATA/POLICY/spfilePOLICY.ora'" >
/u01/app/oracle/product/11.2.0/dbhome_1/dbs/initPOLICY_1.ora
@/u01/app/oracle/admin/POLICY/scripts/lockAccount.sql
@/u01/app/oracle/admin/POLICY/scripts/postDBCreation.sql
```

The most significant difference for this policy-managed database is the use of the SRVCTL command to create a new server pool for the database. Alternatively we could have used an existing server pool if a suitable one was available.

Note also that the SRVCTL add database also specifies the name of the server pool to which the database will be added.

Executing the init.ora File for a Policy-Managed Database

The initial init.ora file for a Policy-Managed database differs significantly from an init.ora file for an Admin-Managed database. We've reformatted the following example to improve readability:

```
audit_file_dest=/u01/app/oracle/admin/POLICY/adump
audit_trail=db
compatible=11.2.0.0.0
#cluster_database=true
```

```
db_block_size=8192
db_create_file_dest=+DATA
db_domain=""
db_name=POLICY
db_recovery_file_dest=+REDO
db_recovery_file_dest_size=4294967296
diagnostic_dest=/u01/app/oracle
dispatchers="(PROTOCOL=TCP) (SERVICE=POLICYXDB)"
log_archive_format=%t_%s_%r.dbf
memory_target=845152256
open_cursors=300
processes=150
#remote_listener=cluster1-scan.example.com:1521
remote_login_passwordfile=exclusive
```

The most obvious difference between the two versions of the file is that the instance-specific
parameters for INSTANCE_NAME, THREAD, and UNDO_TABLESPACE are no longer required. In a Policy-Managed
database, the management goal is to be able to add and drop instances automatically. Therefore, there
are no fixed values for redo threads and undo tablespaces; these are assigned dynamically based on
demand.

As with the Admin-Managed database, the CLUSTER_DATABASE and REMOTE_LISTENER parameters are
commented out initially. These are updated by the postDBCreation.sql script when the database is
capable of running in cluster mode.

Deinstalling the RDBMS Software

Deinstalling the RDBMS has some of the same caveats and issues as when deinstalling the Grid
Infrastructure software. For example, there is also no facility to deinstall software within the OUI.
Instead, you should use the deinstall script within the deinstall directory of the RDBMS home
directory. As with the Grid Infrastructure software, the deinstallation script runs a check operation, and
you are prompted to confirm the deinstallation before it performs a clean operation. As shown in the
following listing, the deinstallation operation will remove both the software from your RDBMS Oracle
home and any configured database environments:

```
oracle@london1 deinstall]$ ./deinstall
Checking for required files and bootstrapping ...
Please wait ...
Location of logs /u01/app/oraInventory/logs/

############ ORACLE DEINSTALL & DECONFIG TOOL START ############


####################### CHECK OPERATION START #######################
Install check configuration START
Specify a valid location of central inventory for the Oracle home
'/u01/app/oracle/product/11.2.0/dbhome_1' that you want to de-install:

The cluster node(s) on which the Oracle home exists are: (Please input nodes
separated by ",", eg: node1,node2,...)london1,london2,london3, london4

Checking for existence of the Oracle home location
```

```
/u01/app/oracle/product/11.2.0/dbhome_1
Oracle Home type selected for de-install is: RACDB
Oracle Base selected for de-install is: /u01/app/oracle
Checking for existence of central inventory location
Checking for existence of the Oracle Grid Infrastructure home
/u01/app/11.2.0/grid
The following nodes are part of this cluster: london1,london2,london3,london4

Install check configuration END


Network Configuration check config START

Network de-configuration trace file location:
/u01/app/oraInventory/logs/netdc_check3858909217437932248.log

Network Configuration check config END

Database Check Configuration START

Database de-configuration trace file location:
/u01/app/oraInventory/logs/databasedc_check7918207744133071457.log

Use comma as separator when specifying list of values as input

Specify the list of database names that are configured in this
Oracle home [PROD]:

###### For Database 'PROD' ######

RAC Database
The nodes on which this database has instances:
[london1, london2, london3, london4]
The instance names: [PROD1, PROD2, PROD3, PROD4]
The local instance name on node: PROD1
The diagnostic destination location of the database:
/u01/app/oracle/diag/rdbms/prod
Storage type used by the Database: ASM

The details of database(s) PROD have been discovered automatically.
Do you still want to modify the details of PROD database(s)? [n]:

Database Check Configuration END

Enterprise Manager Configuration Assistant START

EMCA de-configuration trace file location:
/u01/app/oraInventory/logs/emcadc_check.log

Checking configuration for database PROD
Enterprise Manager Configuration Assistant END
Oracle Configuration Manager check START
```

```
OCM check log file location : /u01/app/oraInventory/logs//ocm_check1251.log
Oracle Configuration Manager check END

######################### CHECK OPERATION END #########################


######################### CHECK OPERATION SUMMARY #########################
Oracle Grid Infrastructure Home is: /u01/app/11.2.0/grid
The cluster node(s) on which the Oracle home exists are:
(Please input nodes seperated by ",", eg: node1,node2,...)
london1,london2,london3,london4
Oracle Home selected for de-install is:
/u01/app/oracle/product/11.2.0/dbhome_1
Inventory Location where the Oracle home registered is:
The following databases were selected for de-configuration : PROD
Database unique name : PROD
Storage used : ASM
Will update the Enterprise Manager configuration
for the following database(s): PROD
No Enterprise Manager ASM targets to update
No Enterprise Manager listener targets to migrate
Checking the config status for CCR
london1 : Oracle Home exists with CCR directory, but CCR is not configured
london2 : Oracle Home exists with CCR directory, but CCR is not configured
london3 : Oracle Home exists with CCR directory, but CCR is not configured
london4 : Oracle Home exists with CCR directory, but CCR is not configured
CCR check is finished
Do you want to continue (y - yes, n - no)? [n]: y
```

Summary

In this chapter, we have explained how to install the RDBMS software in a RAC environment. We have also explained how to create and configure a RAC database using DBCA. In the process of explaining how to create a database with DBCA, we introduced the concepts behind and use of Admin-Managed and Policy-Managed databases. In the next chapter, we will look at practical examples of these concepts in the wider context of Workload Management.

CHAPTER 11

■ ■ ■

Workload Management

This chapter explores workload management options available with Oracle Real Application Cluster (RAC). There is a global trend in the industry to consolidate applications and workloads, and this is where Real Application Cluster shines. For a consolidation project to be a success, suitable mechanisms need to exist to allow these applications to coexist together. Administrators need to be able to define importance levels for applications served by Oracle, and less important applications must not starve out the ones with higher importance levels.

Database client sessions should not be disrupted in case of node failures; instead, they must be relocated to a surviving cluster node. Also, database sessions should be evenly distributed to all cluster nodes to prevent one node from being over-utilized, while another set of nodes remains idle. Sessions in a connection pool would ideally be able to move to less busy nodes at runtime, as well.

Last but not least, the database should provide accounting functionality based on application usage metrics. The infrastructure provider (whether internal or external) can use these metrics to charge the consumers of their services.

All the preceding concepts are available with Oracle Real Application Cluster databases. The central workload management concept—and the first we will discuss in this chapter—is database services. But workload management comprises a number of additional technologies as well, including the following concepts that will be covered in depth throughout this chapter:

- Load Balancing
- High Availability Framework
- Fast Application Notification (FAN)
- Fast Connection Failover
- Transparent Application Failover
- Resource Manager

Let's start by taking a look at the available database services.

Introducing Services

Services as we know them today have a long history. They were introduced to the Oracle user community back in 1999, with Oracle 8*i* Release 2. In its "Getting to know Oracle 8*i*, Release 2" manual, Oracle introduced services to the network stack. They did this alongside another feature, called *dynamic registration*; specifically, the process monitor background process (PMON) registered with the listener of a database. While the connection method using the SID is still available even in 11*g* Release 2, users are encouraged to use the SERVICE_NAME parameter in the CONNECT_DATA section of the local naming file.

Although services were introduced long ago, from a single-instance user's point-of-view, it wasn't entirely clear why one should prefer the service name to the ORACLE_SID. Indeed, using services seemed to introduce more problems! Most of the networking issues in an Oracle environment are caused by incorrectly specified service names on the database and/or the local naming configuration. The most common of these errors is possibly the infamous ORA-12514 error: "TNS: listener does not currently know of service requested in connect descriptor."

So what exactly are these *services*? In a nutshell, they are logical entities you can define in Oracle RAC databases that enable you to group database workloads and route connection requests to the optimal instances that are assigned to offer the service. In single-instance Oracle, services can be used to provide additional levels of granularity for statistics aggregation and tracing. However, the full potential of services is realized in RAC environments by controlling which instances in the cluster perform a specific workload at different times for a given priority.

In many consolidation projects, individual services are created per application consolidated in the cluster. Other than that, there is hardly a limit to the creativity of the users when it comes to defining services. For instance, you can create services on a departmental basis or to reflect a certain type of workload such as batch processing or online reporting. Users connect to the database service, not the database itself, and they can be directed to the best instance providing the service transparently.

As we will see later in this chapter, services form the basis of workload management in RAC. Effective capacity management is made possible by assigning services to specific instances in the cluster and further controlling resource consumption with the Resource Manager. In the event of planned or even unplanned outages, services can be relocated to different instances in the cluster to provide continued availability to the application. Technologies such as Transparent Application Failover and Fast Connection Failover can make failover seamless to the users in a correctly configured system.

There is more than one way to create services, and we will discuss the different options available in their own section later in the chapter.

Creating an Administrator Managed Database vs. Policy-Managed Database

Administrators have two options when defining services to RAC databases, depending on how a database is managed. For administrator-managed databases, preferred and optionally available instances are defined for a service. Think of preferred instances as "active" instances or the instance you want to provide the service under normal conditions. If a preferred instance is available, the service will be started on it. If a preferred instance fails, a service can relocate to an available instance, if so defined. Available instance are instances on "standby." Once the failed node comes back online, the service will not automatically move back to the preferred instance.

Policy-managed databases behave differently. Remember that administrators have less control over policy-managed database because they are mostly automated, and services are no exception to this general rule. Instead of manually defining preferred and available instances, you define whether a service should run on all or only one instance in the server pool. A service that is started on all nodes in a server pool is referred to as a "uniform" service. The opposite, a service started on one arbitrary instance only, is called a *singleton* service. When additional instances join the server pool, Oracle automatically extends uniform services to the newly joined instances without user intervention. Although we said in the RAC Concepts chapter that the transition to using a SCAN is not immediately needed, you definitely have to use a SCAN address when connecting to a policy-managed database. This is because the Oracle client can't know how at connect time on how many nodes a policy-managed database is running.

A startup policy can be assigned to services, regardless of database type. This feature is new with release 11.2. Services can start automatically when the database starts. Similarly, services can be configured to start depending on the database role in a Data Guard environment. Before this, a database trigger had to be deployed, firing after the startup of the database and activating services based on the detected database role. The database role is available in the V$DATABASE view, and it can even be queried while the database is mounted and not open.

Services play an important role in other parts of the database, as well. We'll explore how you can use services with the database scheduler, shared server, and parallel processing. Later in the chapter, we will explain how the Resource Manager can be used to control resource usage on a per-service basis.

Managing Services with the Database Scheduler

The Oracle database scheduler (also referred to as the *scheduler*), replaces functionality previously provided by the DBMS_JOB package. In a nutshell, the scheduler allows the execution of code, both inside and outside the database, in either an ad-hoc fashion or at defined intervals. One of the design goals of the scheduler was to provide (better) support for the execution of jobs in a clustered environment. The discussion of all the scheduler's features is beyond the scope of this chapter, but we will cover the necessary basics for you to understand how the scheduler and RAC services cooperate.

The first thing you will notice when dealing with the scheduler is that it is a lot more flexible than DBMS_JOB. Unfortunately, this flexibility comes at the cost of higher complexity. The scheduler uses a number of concepts to facilitate the creation of jobs. For example, metadata for jobs can be defined in a number of entities:

- Job classes
- Programs
- Schedules
- Windows

All of this sounds quite abstract, and it is, in a way. It helps to keep in mind that all the metadata serves only one purpose: the creation of a job. It's important to keep this in the back of your mind for the following discussion. The more metadata that is available about a job, the less coding that is required to instantiate it.

The procedure to create a scheduler job is heavily overloaded, and the parameters to be supplied depend on how much detail you have saved as metadata. So, instead of entering the same information repeatedly, in a heavily customized environment, you only need to refer to the job class, the program, and a scheduler to create the job.

Similar jobs can be grouped into job classes. Job classes are very important in the context of RAC and workload management in general. These entities can take attributes such as a resource consumer group and a database service, as well as some other attributes. The association with a service allows database administrators and developers to limit the execution of a job to a distinct subset of nodes in the cluster.

■ **Tip** Stopping a service will automatically will stop the jobs that rely on it from executing!

From a RAC administrator's perspective, this is one of the most sought-after improvements over DBMS_JOB: you have more control over which service a job executes. Add in the integration with a resource consumer group, and you have a very flexible tool for automating the execution of work.

A scheduler program saves meta-information about what is to be executed. The scheduler can execute anonymous PL/SQL blocks, stored procedures, or an executable stored outside the database, such as a shell script or C program. Stored procedures can of course take arguments; up to 255 arguments are supported.

A schedule defines the frequency of execution and the interval at which a job is to be executed. A very flexible syntax allows the creation of individual schedules, and it leaves little to be desired. Jobs can be executed only once, at a specific time. Or, they can be executed multiple times, as defined by the schedule.

Last but not least, scheduler windows work hand-in-hand with the resource manager. Windows are represented by a start timestamp and have a fixed duration. The important feature in the context of workload management is the integration with resource manager. A window can have a resource plan associated with it that becomes active as soon as the window opens.

These few paragraphs obviously can't provide a complete overview of the scheduler, but it should provide you with enough insight into the scheduler and its related objects to get you started. From the workload-management perspective, the most important concepts to remember are the scheduler's ability to use resource consumer groups and scheduler windows to change resource plans, as well as its ability to limit the execution of jobs to a service in job classes.

To bring theory to life, let's go through the definition of a scheduler job using a job class to limit its execution to the service batchserv. To keep the example simple, we will populate the parameters for the job creation manually, except for the job class. The following job purges data from a logging table older than two days by using the stored procedure, PURGELOGPROC:

```
BEGIN
  dbms_scheduler.create_job_class(
    logging_level => DBMS_SCHEDULER.LOGGING_RUNS,
    service => 'batchserv',
    comments => 'Limits execution to batchserv service',
    job_class_name => 'BATCHSERVCLASS');
END;
/

BEGIN
  dbms_scheduler.create_job(
    job_name => 'PURGELOGJOB',
    job_type => 'STORED_PROCEDURE',
    job_action => 'PURGELOGPROC',
    repeat_interval => 'FREQ=DAILY',
    start_date => to_timestamp('11.05.2010 19:00', 'dd.mm.yyyy hh24:mi'),
    job_class => 'BATCHSERVCLASS',
    comments => 'purge logs older than two days',
    auto_drop => FALSE,
    enabled => TRUE);
END;
/
```

The newly created database job will use BATCHSERVCLASS job class; it will limit its execution to the nodes utilizing the BATCHSERV service.

Using Services with Shared Server

Shared server is discussed less and less frequently in Oracle related publications. The majority of Oracle installations possibly use dedicated server connections and connection pools based on them. The days when hardware was not powerful enough to support a large number of users may be considered ancient history, which partly explains the absence of shared server-related subjects. An application deployed in a RAC environment does not usually have to deal with these problems; we can now scale to a larger user base by adding another node to the cluster. However, we still think it is useful to understand shared servers and services, as well as how they work.

A small number of systems that need to support thousands of connections can benefit from using a shared server configuration, especially in conjunction with connection pooling. But what exactly is a *shared server configuration*? And how does it relate to services? We will have a look at shared servers first, and then examine the link of shared servers to services.

In a shared server configuration, database sessions do not create a dedicated connection between the database client and the database. Instead, a so-called dispatcher process is initially contacted by the database client. The dispatcher in turn places the client request into a queue, from where an idle shared server from a pool of shared servers picks it up and processes it. The Oracle server process is called *shared* because there is no 1:1 mapping between it and a client. Once the request is completed, the result of the processing is placed into the dispatcher's response queue; from there, it is transmitted to the client.

To set up and manage connection with shared servers, a number of initialization parameters must be changed. You can do using the database configuration assistant dbca or Enterprise Manager if the standard SQL*Plus interface is not sufficient. The most important initialization parameters are shared_servers and dispatchers. With the latter parameter, we come full circle and create the link with services.

The dispatcher process in the shared server setup is the first component contacted by an Oracle client. By default, dispatchers accept all client connections; however, it is possible to create dispatchers to serve a specific service only. Consider this example for a configuration that uses two dispatchers for the service wikisrv and five dispatchers for all other connection requests:

```
*.dispatchers=(protocol=TCP)(dispatchers=5)
*.dispatchers=(protocol=TCP)(dispatchers=2)(service=wikisrv)
```

Prior to the introduction of Database Resident Connection Pooling (DRCP), the use of shared servers could solve problems created by legacy applications.

■ **Note** We will discuss the DRCP feature later in this chapter's "Database Resident Connection Pool" section.

Some CGI scripts created a dedicated connection each time a dynamic web page was requested; this caused unusually high overhead to the database CPUs. The dedicated server process creation does not happen in a shared server configuration; instead, the number of shared server processes and dispatchers is configured by the database administrator in the initialization files. This reduces CPU overhead and overall resource consumption on the database server.

The use of shared server and dedicated server processes is not mutually exclusive. The two coexist quite happily in an Oracle database. In fact, many administration tasks require the use of dedicated server connections, even if you set up shared server for user connections.

■ **Note** Services play an important role for parallel execution as well, for which a whole chapter has been dedicated. Please refer to chapter 14 for more information.

Managing Services

Managing services is an important aspect of any RAC project. As you will see in the "Balancing the Workload" section, defining services to run on the most appropriate subset of cluster nodes is essential in achieving an even workload distribution across nodes. Services are deeply integrated with Grid Infrastructure and Clusterware. Instead of setting the database initialization parameter service_names manually so it defines an instance-to-service mapping, you should use administrative tools such as the ones to be described below instead. In fact, bypassing the administration tools for service maintenance is strongly discouraged!

Next, we will explain how services are created and modified. There are three different tools you can use to create services:

- The server control srvctl command line tool

- Enterprise Manager

- The DBMS_SERVICE package

The Database creation assistant dbca used to be available to manage database services. However, this functionality was removed in Oracle 11.1. The remaining tools available to create, modify, and delete services are the ones mentioned previously in this chapter. We will discuss each of them independently. For learning the definitions of load balancing properties, we kindly refer the reader to the "Balancing the Workload" section later in this chapter; that section includes an extensive discussion of workload management.

Managing Services with SRVCTL

Using srvctl is probably the easiest way to define and manage services in a RAC environment. The syntax has changed a little in Oracle 11.2, allowing administrators to define workload management-related properties on the command line, rather than having to rely on the DBMS_SERVICE package. You will also find that some options refer to administrator-managed databases, while others are applicable to policy-managed databases only. The srvctl utility provides you a number of actions that you can execute against a service, including the following:

- Create a service

- Start and stop a service

- Modify a service

- Check service's define-time properties

- Check service's runtime properties

The syntax for the creation of services depends on whether the database type is administrator-managed or policy managed. For administrator-managed databases, the following options are available:

```
srvctl add service -d dbUniqueName -s serviceName
   -r preferredList [-a availableList] [-P {BASIC | NONE | PRECONNECT}]
   [-l [PRIMARY | PHYSICAL_STANDBY | LOGICAL_STANDBY | SNAPSHOT_STANDBY]
   [-y {AUTOMATIC | MANUAL}] [-q {TRUE | FALSE}] [-j {SHORT | LONG}]
   [-B {NONE | SERVICE_TIME | THROUGHPUT}] [-e {NONE | SESSION | SELECT}]
   [-m {NONE | BASIC}] [-x {TRUE | FALSE}]
   [-z failover_retries] [-w failover_delay]
```

The list of options is slightly different for policy-managed databases:

```
srvctl add service -d dbUniqueName -s serviceName
   -g serverPoolName [-c {UNIFORM | SINGLETON}]
   [-l [PRIMARY | PHYSICAL_STANDBY | LOGICAL_STANDBY | SNAPSHOT_STANDBY]
   [-y {AUTOMATIC | MANUAL}] [-q {TRUE | FALSE}] [-j {SHORT | LONG}]
   [-B {NONE | SERVICE_TIME | THROUGHPUT}] [-e {NONE | SESSION | SELECT}]
   [-m {NONE | BASIC}] [-P {BASIC | NONE }] [-x {TRUE | FALSE}]
   [-z failover_retries] [-w failover_delay]
```

Users of Oracle 11.1 will notice that a number of new options have been introduced into the latest version of the tool. The most important of these new features: You can now set connect-time load balancing parameters and enable the load balancing framework without having to call `DBMS_SERVICE.MODIFY_SERVICE()` to do so. Many of the arguments to srvctl are identical for other operations regarding services, so they will be listed only once. Table 11-1 shows the most common command-line options to srvctl.

Table 11-1. Command-Line Options for Adding Services

Option	Meaning	Comment
-d *dbUniqueName*	Specifies the unique name for this database, as defined during the addition of the database to Grid Infrastructure. If you are unsure about the name, you can query the OCR using srvctl config database for a list of defined databases	
-s *serviceName*	Specifies the name of the new service to be added.	
-r *preferredList* and -a *availableList*	Provides a comma-separated list of available and preferred nodes for a service.	Only for administrator-managed databases
-g *serverPoolName*	Specifies the server pool the service should be assigned to.	Only for policy-managed databases
-c UNIFORM or SINGLETON	Defines the service to run either on all nodes in the server pool (uniform) or only one (singleton).	Only for policy-managed databases

Option	Meaning	Comment
-l PRIMARY, PHYSICAL_STANDBY, SNAPSHOT_STANDBY, LOGICAL_STANDBY	Defines the service to start with the specified database role.	
-P NONE, BASIC, PRECONNECT	Allows you to define the Transparent Application Failover policy.	Only for administrator-managed databases
-y AUTOMATIC or MANUAL	Defines whether the service starts with the database or not.	
-q TRUE or FALSE	Enables notifications for clients sent through Advanced Queuing rather than FAN.	ODP.NET clients need this to receive load balancing information; some OCI clients need this, as well
- j LONG or SHORT	New in 11.2, the connection load balancing goal can be set via the command line rather DBMS_SERVICE	
-B NONE, SERVICE_TIME or THROUGHPUT	Disables or enables the load balancing advisory.	
-e NONE, SESSION, SELECT	Defines the type of failover operation.	
-m NONE, BASIC	Specifies the failover method.	
-z and -w	Overrides the default number of failover retries (-z) and the failover delay (-w).	

You should keep the separation between administrator-managed databases and policy-managed databases in mind. Only administrator-managed databases can have preferred and available instances!

Assume you want to add a service named reporting to your four-node administrator-managed database that normally uses the third node, but can alternatively run on the first node. You could use the following syntax to do so:

```
[oracle@london2 ~]> srvctl add service -d PROD -s REPORTING -r PROD3 -a PROD1 \
>    -P BASIC -e SESSION
```

Note that Transparent Application Failover should also be enabled for session failover with the basic method of reestablishing a session only when needed. The new service must be started before it can be used by clients. The syntax for starting services looks like this:

```
srvctl start service -d dbName [-s service [-n nodeName | -i instanceName ]]
```

The database name is the only mandatory argument here. If service names are omitted, then all services for the database will be started. The remaining parameters allow the administrator to start one or more services on a specific database instance. To start the preceding created service on its available node, you would use the following command:

```
[oracle@london1 ~]> srvctl start service –d PROD –s REPORTING –i PROD1
```

Conversely, you can stop services using the following command:

```
srvctl stop service -d dbName [-s service  [-n nodeName | -i instanceName] ] [-f]
```

For example, you can issue the following command to stop the reporting service on instance PROD3:

```
[oracle@london1~ ]> srvctl stop service –d PROD –s REPORTING –i PROD3
```

Service definitions can be modified after a service is created. You can also shuffle services around once they are created. Instances can also be upgraded from available to preferred. Of course, you can also modify the workload balancing attributes; we will cover how to do that in the "Configuring Server Side Load Balancing" section later in the chapter.

Moving a service from one set of nodes to another is also supported. You can do so using the following syntax:

```
srvctl modify service -d dbName -s service -i oldInstance -t newInstance [-f]
```

This syntax moves a service from the old instance to a new instance, optionally forcing session disconnects. For example, we could move the aforementioned reporting service from the preferred instance to the available instances using this syntax:

```
[oracle@london1~]> srvctl modify service –d PROD –s REPORTING –i PROD3 –t PROD1
```

It is also possible to upgrade instances from available to preferred instances:

```
srvctl modify service -d dbName -s service -i availableInst -r [-f]
```

To upgrade instance PROD1 to a preferred instance for the reporting service, use the following command:

```
[oracle@london1~]> srvctl modify service -d PROD -s REPORTING -i PROD1 -r
```

It is also possible to perform the mapping between preferred and available instances in one command:

```
srvctl modify service -d dbName -s serviceName -n -i preferredNodes
    [-a availableNodes] [-f]
```

Checking the status of services is important from time to time. This helps you identify which services are running on their available, rather than their preferred instances. Passing the relocate argument to srvctl allows the administrator to move the service back to where it should be. To compare the configuration against its current status, Oracle supplies the srvctl config service and srvctl status service calls. When invoked with the config option, Oracle displays configuration information about services, as in the following example:

```
[oracle@london1 ~]$ srvctl config service -d PROD -s reporting
Service name: reporting
Service is enabled
Server pool: prod_reporting
Cardinality: 1
Disconnect: false
Service role: PRIMARY
Management policy: AUTOMATIC
DTP transaction: false
AQ HA notifications: false
Failover type: SESSION
Failover method: NONE
TAF failover retries: 0
TAF failover delay: 0
Connection Load Balancing Goal: LONG
Runtime Load Balancing Goal: NONE
TAF policy specification: BASIC
Preferred instances: PROD1
Available instances: PROD3
```

You can see from the output that the service is defined to run on instance PROD1 as preferred instance, but with PROD3 as a backup. The service is set up neither for distributed processing (XA) nor for connection load balancing or AQ notifications.

The final option to cover in this section is the relocate command. As we said in the introduction, services will not automatically fail back from available instances to their preferred instances. However, you can use the srvctl relocate command to force a service to fail back to its preferred instance:

```
srvctl relocate service -d dbName -s serviceName
    {-c fromNode -n toNode |
    -i sourceInstance -t destinationInstance }
    [-f]
```

This is one of the few administrator-managed commands applicable to policy-managed databases, as well, but only for singleton services. The DBA would usually use the -i and -t arguments with administrator-managed databases. The use of the -c and –n flags is most appropriate for policy-managed databases.

Continuing with the example, let's say that we learned our service was running on the available node. Let's also say that we want to move our service back to the preferred instance. We can make that move using this snippet:

```
[oracle@london3 ~]$ srvctl status service -d PROD -s reporting
Service reporting is running on instance(s) PROD1
[oracle@london3 ~]$ srvctl relocate service -d PROD \
> -s reporting -i PROD1 -t PROD3
[oracle@london3 ~]$ srvctl status service -d PROD -s reporting
Service reporting is running on instance(s) PROD3
```

Managing Services with Enterprise Manager

Enterprise Manager DBConsole and Enterprise Manager Grid Control both offer the ability to modify services. Enterprise Manager 11*g* Release 1 is the latest release, and it includes almost complete support for Oracle 11*g* Release 2 databases. Enterprise Manager Grid Control 10.2.0.5 requires additional patches to support Oracle 11.2 as a managed target, and even then, it cannot use new 11.2 features. This section shows screen captures from an 11.1 Enterprise Manager Grid Control setup that monitors, among other targets, a four-node RAC system.

As with any well-designed graphical user interface, administration of Oracle is simplified, as is the creation and management of services. To access the service management interface, selecting the cluster database target, and then click on Availability tab. You should be presented with the page shown Figure 11-1.

Figure 11-1. The Availability tab in Enterprise Manager Grid Control for a cluster database

Next, click the Cluster Managed Database Services link. After specifying the login credentials for the database and host on the next page, you are redirected to the main service management console within Enterprise Manager (see Figure 11-2). If you installed Grid Infrastructure with a user other than the RDBMS binaries, then please enter those RDBMS account credentials. Otherwise, EM will spin forever trying to get the information. The options presented will differ, depending on the management type of your database. Figure 11-2 shows the resulting "Cluster Managed Database Services" page.

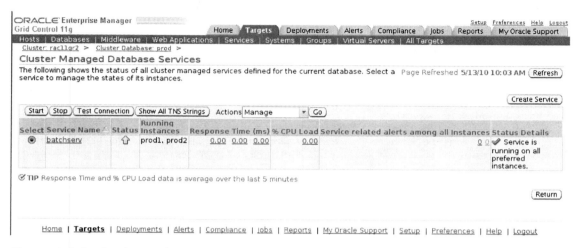

Figure 11-2. *Services in an administrator-managed database*

Next, click the Create Service button to create a new service. You'll be taken to the page in Figure 11-3, which presents you with the same options as with the command line interface; however, in this case, you don't have to remember the syntax.

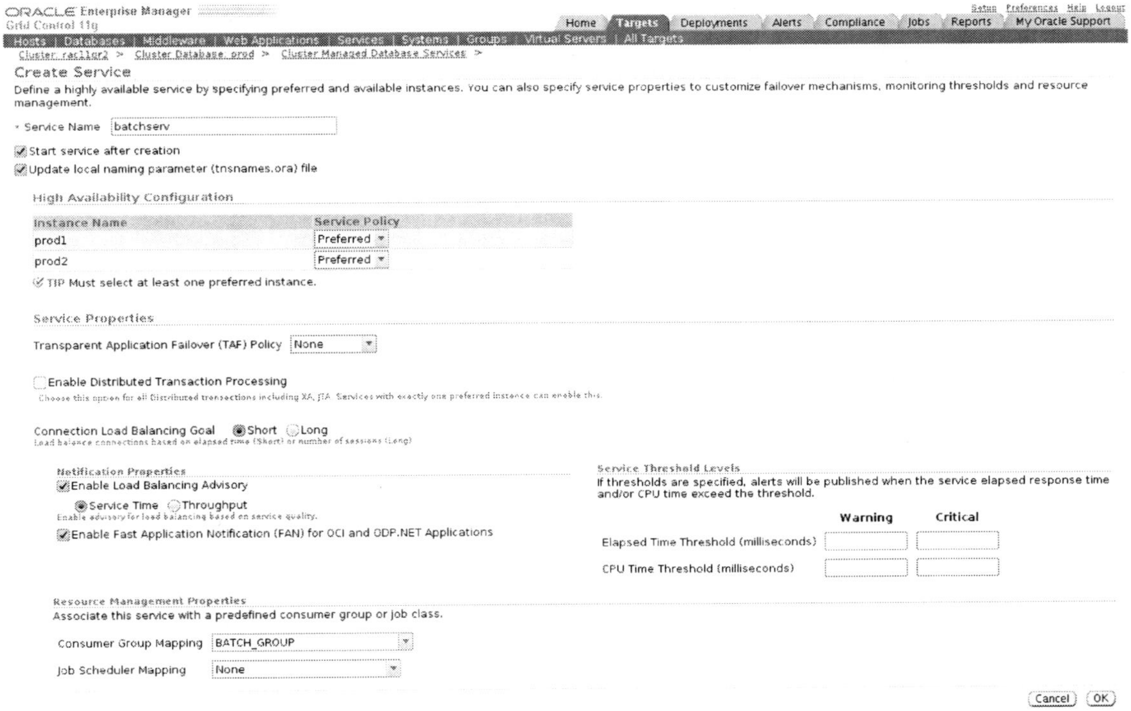

Figure 11-3. Creating a new service for an administrator-managed database

In addition to the options offered by srvctl, you can define custom alerts in cases where a service uses more CPU cycles than a specified threshold. Internally, this calls DBMS_SERVER_ALERT.SET_THRESHOLD(). Grid Control conveniently provides the option to update the server's tnsnames.ora file; it also starts the service after its creation.

Once you successfully add the service to the cluster database, it will appear in the Overview page. If you opted to start the service after its creation, it should be up on the preferred nodes. Another nice feature relates to maintaining the local tnsnames.ora file. This file will include the necessary entry to connect to the service. If this is not required, then the TNS settings can be obtained by clicking the Show all TNS strings button. The page that comes up next displays all TNS strings for the services defined, along with your TAF policies and load balancing settings (see Figure 11-4).

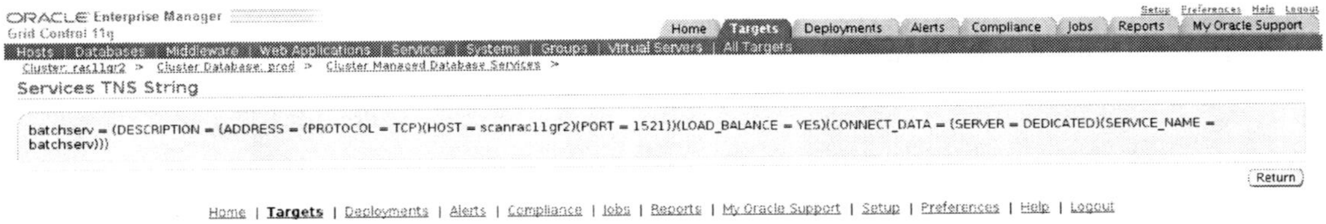

Figure 11-4. Displaying all TNS settings for the services defined in database PROD

Modifying the service settings is as simple as clicking the service name in the Overview page. You are then redirected to the same page you edited when creating the service. The Manage option in the service Overview page lets you start, stop, and relocate services.

Managing Services with DBMS_SERVICE

The DBMS_SERVICE package allows you to create and modify services in Oracle RAC and single-instance databases. In Oracle 11.2, most of this service's functionality is marked as deprecated in favor of the server control utility, srvctl. The following procedures in DBMS_SERVICE should no longer be used in RAC 11.2 and Oracle Restart environments:

- CREATE_SERVICE()

- MODIFY_SERVICE()

- START_SERVICE()

- STOP_SERVICE()

The documentation states the fact that the service definition and its modifications don't propagate into the metadata held in the OCR. Subsequent calls to srvctl would therefore overwrite settings made by calls to the deprecated subprograms. This is not only true for Oracle 11g, but also for 10g. Therefore, we do not recommend maintaining services with this package in 11.2. DBMS_SERVICE will update the data dictionary only, but Clusterware will not know about the service and cannot monitor it.

In Oracle 11.1 and earlier, calls to DBMS_SERVICE are still relevant, although this is mainly for the aforementioned reasons of modifying service attributes.

One of the more useful remaining functions in DBMS_SERVICE is DISCONNECT_SESSION, which disconnects all sessions from a service.

Balancing the Workload

Services are essential for load-balancing in a RAC environment. Making the optimal use of resources requires that you avoid situations where the majority of connection requests end up on one node, while the other nodes remain mostly idle. In Oracle 10g Release 2 up to, but not including 10.2.0.4, a number of bugs caused load balancing to fail in some cases. As far as we can tell, these problems have been resolved, and load balancing should work as expected in releases 10.2.0.4 and later.

Two types of load balancing exist with the Oracle database software stack: client-side and server-side load balancing. With client-side load balancing prior to Oracle 11.2, you choose a random listener out of the ADDRESS_LIST parameter in the local naming file to connect to. When using the Single Client Access Name with multiple IP addresses instead, connection requests will be spread across all SCAN listeners in a round-robin way. This is also the reason why you should have specified more than one IP address for the SCAN address during the installation. Server-side load balancing uses information provided by the load advisory framework. The SCAN listeners (or database listeners in Oracle 11.1 and earlier) direct connection requests to the most suitable instance providing the database service. The load balancing advisory keeps track of the load on individual instances; thus, it allows the listener to select (among other things) the least loaded node for a connection.

We will discuss the implementation of client-side and server-side load balancing, as well as the load advisory framework in the "Configure Client Side Load Balancing" and "Configure Server Side Load Balancing" sections later in this chapter.

Configuring Client-Side Load Balancing

Client-side load balancing, or *connection-load balancing*, is defined in the local naming file by setting the LOAD_BALANCE parameter to True or On, as in this example;

```
ebs.example.com =
  (DESCRIPTION=
    (ADDRESS_LIST=
      (LOAD_BALANCE = on)(FAILOVER = ON)
      (ADDRESS = (PROTOCOL = tcp)(HOST = london1-vip.example.com)(PORT = 1521))
      (ADDRESS = (PROTOCOL = tcp)(HOST = london2-vip.example.com)(PORT = 1521))
      (ADDRESS = (PROTOCOL = tcp)(HOST = london3-vip.example.com)(PORT = 1521))
      (ADDRESS = (PROTOCOL = tcp)(HOST = london4-vip.example.com)(PORT = 1521))
      (CONNECT_DATA =
        (SERVICE_NAME = ebs.example.com))))
```

In RAC 11.2, the LOAD_BALANCE setting has lost a little bit of its relevance with the introduction of the Single Client Access Name (SCAN). Remember that the scan resolves to a maximum of three IP addresses provided by the DNS server in a round-robin fashion. Prior to the 11.2 release, it was good practice to ensure that LOAD_BALANCE was enabled. It was also important to have all nodes' virtual IP addresses listed in the tnsnames.ora fileAn example for the new syntax using the SCAN is shown below.

```
ebs. example.com =
  (DESCRIPTION=
    (ADDRESS = (PROTOCOL = tcp)(HOST = cluster1.example.com)(PORT = 1521))
    (CONNECT_DATA =
      (SERVICE_NAME = ebs.example.com)
    )
  )
```

As you can see the 11.2 entry looks a lot less cluttered than the previous example, thanks to the SCAN "cluster1.example.com". There is no need to rush now and update all tnsnames.ora files in your environment when migrating from an older version to Oracle 11.2. In the transition phase, while upgrading from an older version of RAC to Oracle 11.2, it is not required to use SCAN straight away. The updating of the various tnsnames files on database clients can wait until the proper change control has been implemented. However, you must use SCAN if you intend to use policy-managed databases.

The FAILOVER directive is another important parameter. Set at the same level as the LOAD_BALANCE directive, the FAILOVER keyword instructs the Oracle client to try connecting to the next entry in the tnsnames ADDRESS_LIST section. For example, assume that node1 in the preceding example has failed and is currently rebooting. Its virtual IP address will have migrated to another node in the cluster, such as node4. Should a client request a connection through node1-vip, it will get a notification that the node failed, and it will immediately try another server thanks to the FAILOVER keyword.

The FAILOVER keyword has lost a bit of its relevance in RAC 11.2 because there is only one address specified in the local naming file. The DNS round-robin resolution will provide another IP address resolving to the SCAN should the initial connection request fail. The client will automatically try the next supplied IP address. However, it is possible to define multiple addresses pointing to standby databases in addition to the primary database. This means you might use a single tnsnames.ora file for the application, as in this example:

```
ebs.example.com =
  (DESCRIPTION=
    (FAILOVER=ON)
    (CONNECT_TIMEOUT=5)(RETRY_COUNT=3)
      (ADDRESS =
        (PROTOCOL = tcp)(HOST = prodcluster-scan.example.com)(PORT = 1521))
      (ADDRESS =
        (PROTOCOL = tcp)(HOST = drcluster-scan.example.com)  (PORT = 1521))
      (CONNECT_DATA=
        (SERVICE_NAME= ebs.example.com)
      )
  )
```

The preceding example illustrates yet again the usefulness of the SCAN option. You undoubtedly spotted the CONNECT_TIMEOUT and RETRY_COUNT parameters in the naming definition. These are new 11g Release 2 parameters, and they can be used in client connection strings, rather than a sqlnet.ora file where they are globally applicable.

Note the connect time load balancing is set to work on the Net*8 layer only, and it has nothing to do with session failover; FAN/FCF and TAF are responsible for handling these.

■ **Note** You might be surprised that LOAD_BALANCE and FAILOVER are enabled by default when an ADDRESS_LIST section is used in your tnsnames.ora file. If you don't want these to be enabled, you must specifically set LOAD_BALANCE to OFF and FAILOVER to FALSE.

Configuring Server-Side Load Balancing

SCAN listeners—or database listeners in Oracle releases prior to 11.2—route connection requests to the most suitable instance providing the service requested. To be able to do so, they need to regularly receive information from the database instances about their load. They also need to be instructed about what is actually most suitable for the application. Correct configuration of services is important to make maximum use of the load balancing feature.

The Oracle database has to register with the listener first. It does so using two important initialization parameters: local_listener and remote_listener. The local listener should be set to the node's *virtual* IP address, even when using the default port of 1521. A number of problems have been reported in versions up to and including RAC 11.1.0.7, where connection requests were re-routed to the hosts *public* IP instead of the virtual hostname. This rerouting can cause unwanted connection failures if the public hostname doesn't resolve on the client. Setting the local listener parameter is mandatory when using a different than the default port. The local_listener parameter can be hard-coded into the initialization parameter. Or, it can reference an entry from in the tnsnames.ora file. We have seen many sites leave the definition of local_listener and remote_listener to the local naming, as in the following example:

```
LISTENER_PROD1 =
  (DESCRIPTION=
    (ADDRESS_LIST=(ADDRESS=(PROTOCOL=TCP)(HOST=london1-vip.example.com)(PORT=1521))))
```

The way you set the remote listener changed in RAC 11.2. Instead of registering with the local listener, the database registers with SCAN listeners. The syntax instructing the database to communicate with the SCAN listener has also changed. It now uses the EZConnect keyword. To enable it, you need to update names.directory_path to include the ezconnect keyword in the sqlnet.ora file in _HOME/network/admin/:

```
names.directory_path=(ezconnect,tnsnames,ldap)
```

Instead of storing the remote_listener in the tnsnames.ora file, you usually hard-code it in spfile; you accomplish this using the is scanname:port syntax, as in this example:

```
SQL> alter system set remote_listener='cluster1-scan.grid1.example.com:1521'
 2*  scope=both sid='*';
```

The preceding statement will fail if the SCAN IP address cannot be resolved by all nodes in the cluster! Oracle explicitly discourages the use of a TNS alias for setting the remote listener setting.

If your RAC cluster operates with Clusterware pre-11.2, then you don't need to worry about this detail. Instead, all you need to do is add an entry in the tnsnames.ora file as in the following example:

```
LISTENERS_PROD =
  (DESCRIPTION=
    (ADDRESS_LIST=
      (ADDRESS=(PROTOCOL=TCP)(HOST=london1-vip)(PORT=1521))
      (ADDRESS=(PROTOCOL=TCP)(HOST=london2-vip)(PORT=1521))
      (ADDRESS=(PROTOCOL=TCP)(HOST=london3-vip)(PORT=1521))
      (ADDRESS=(PROTOCOL=TCP)(HOST=london4-vip)(PORT=1521))
    )
  )
```

The next step is to use the alter system command to set the remote_listener parameter to the TNS alias:

```
SQL> alter system set remote_listener='listeners_prod' scope=both sid='*';
```

Regardless of which version of Oracle you use, the listener.log files provide periodic service updates from all database instances.

> ■ **Note** A listener not providing service updates is a common cause for skewed load in RAC 10*g*. You should try to reload the listener a couple of times to see if that fixes the problem. The 10.2.0.4 patchset allegedly fixes these listener problems.

Cross-registration of listeners is the first step towards achieving a working server-side load balancing. In the next step, it is necessary to provide additional information about the expected connection duration for the service. The property to be used is called CLB_GOAL, and its setting is exposed in the DBA_SERVICES view. CLB_GOAL stands for *connection load balancing goal*, and it can be defined in Enterprise Manager by using srvctl or the DBMS_SERVICE package. Fortunately, Oracle simplified the setting of CLB_GOAL with Grid Infrastructure, as shown in the following example, which demonstrates how to use the -j switch:

```
$> srvctl modify service –d dbName –s serviceName –j {LONG|SHORT}
```

Prior to Oracle 11.2, you had to use DBMS_SERVICE or Enterprise Manager to modify CLB_GOAL, as shown in the following example:

```
BEGIN
  DBMS_SERVICE.MODIFY_SERVICE (
    service_name => 'SomeServiceName',
    clb_goal     => DBMS_SERVICE.CLB_GOAL_LONG -- or CLB_GOAL_SHORT
  );
end;
/
```

CLB_GOAL can take two parameters. These parameters tell Oracle about the expected duration of the session, which can be either short or long. The *short* parameter should be used for connections lasting only a few seconds to minutes in duration. In combination with the GOAL parameter to be discussed next, the short setting for CLB_GOAL is recommended for use with connection pools that include support for Fast Application Notification events.

Setting CLB_GOAL to long is suggested for dedicated connections that remain connected for longer periods of time. Oracle Application Express or Forms sessions are examples for these, as are some Excel plug-ins for database browsing. Setting only the connection load balancing goal will not activate the enhancements provided by the load advisory framework. However, setting this will instruct the listener to route connection requests based on metrics. Possible metrics available are load per node (as defined by the operating system's run queue) or the number of current connections. The load balancing framework provides additional benefits for load balancing, and we will discuss that framework next.

Exploring the Load Advisory Framework

The load advisory framework serves as the basis for runtime connection load balancing in RAC environments. It uses Fast Application Notification events to inform clients about changes to the infrastructure, such as node up or down events or changes to load on an instance. ODP.NET and other non FAN-aware clients can alternatively subscribe to messages sent through Advanced Queuing. To enable it, the GOAL parameter must be defined for a service. This parameter further describes the type of workload expected to connect to a service, and it can take three values:

- None

- Service time

- Throughput

Setting the goal to NONE disables the load balancing advisory for the particular service. Optimization for service time instructs Oracle to route requests to instances providing the best response time. The load balancing framework uses elapsed time and available bandwidth when considering which node to connect to. When optimizing for THROUGHPUT, Oracle will try to hand the connection off to the node providing the best overall throughput. Metrics such as the rate at which work is completed and available bandwidth are used. The recommended use for the SERVICE TIME goal is for web sessions where usage patterns are unknown. Batch processing workloads are candidates for a load balancing goal of THROUGHPUT. Enabling the load balancing advisory for a service is achieved by a call to srvctl in Oracle 11.2 or DBMS_SERVICE in earlier releases, as in this example:

```
[oracle@london1~]> srvctl modify service -d QA -s batchserv -B throughput
```

In Oracle 11.1 and earlier, you need to call DBMS_SERVICE:

```
BEGIN
  DBMS_SERVICE.MODIFY_SERVICE(
    service_name => 'batchserv',
    goal => DBMS_SERVICE.GOAL_THROUGHPUT
  );
END;
/
```

■ **Note** The preceding examples assume that a connect time load balancing goal has already been set.

The load balancing advisory is compatible with many key Oracle components, such as the listener, JDBC, and ODDP.NET connection pools. Applications not supported out-of-the-box can still use of it through a published API or OCI callback functions. With the load balancing advisory enabled for a service, FAN events are generated. These events enable clients to gracefully respond to changes in the RAC environment they are running on.

Oracle encourages the use of connection pools for connections to the database. From the point-of-view of the database, this means that a set number of long running transactions is created during application initialization. The application then borrows connections from the pool for short periods of time, performs work, and returns the connection back to the pool, where it can be reused. This removes the overhead of having to create a dedicated server process each time a dynamic web component connects to the database.

Using Transparent Application Failover

Transparent application failover (TAF) has been discussed in several other places in this book in detail. In this section, we will provide an overview that explains how to use it. Please refer back to Chapter 3 for a more complete discussion of the concepts behind TAF. As a reminder, TAF can be configured in two different ways:

- In a client side tnsnames.ora file

- As a property of a service

The second approach is the preferred one; it simplifies modifying a TAF policy and lets you manage it centrally instead of having to deploy a configuration file to all your servers.

Unfortunately the Oracle network administration tools network manager and network configuration assistant still aren't TAF-aware. Therefore, users who want to deploy this failover technique on the client side must manually edit the tnsnames.ora file. Alternatively, Enterprise Manager can be instructed to maintain the server's tnsnames.ora file, which can then be copied to clients.

■ **Note** Remember that TAF requires OCI libraries; thus, it will not work with the JDBC thin client!

Configuring Transparent Application Failover

To enable TAF, the alias for a TNS CONNECT_DATA section needs to be amended with a FAILOVER_MODE parameter, so it will support TAF when you define it in through local naming. A sample tnsnames.ora entry for select type failover using the basic connection method might look like this:

```
reporting =
 (DESCRIPTION=
   (ADDRESS=(PROTOCOL=tcp)(HOST=cluster1.example.com)(PORT=1521))
   (CONNECT_DATA=
     (SERVICE_NAME=REPORTING)
     (FAILOVER_MODE= (TYPE=select)(METHOD=basic))
   )
 )
```

In the preceding example, a RAC system is referenced through its single-client access name, and client-side load balancing and failover are implicitly enabled. The CONNECT_DATA section in the preceding example specifies that we would like to connect to a service called reporting. For this example, the reporting service can be assumed to run on all cluster nodes. As you can see the TAF-relevant information is inserted in the FAILOVER_MODE section.

The preconnect scenario is more complex to set up. Remember that you need two entries: the default and the backup entry. Consider the following setup:

```
tafpreconnect =
 (DESCRIPTION =
 (ADDRESS = (PROTOCOL = TCP)(HOST = cluster1.example.com)(PORT = 1521))
 (LOAD_BALANCE = YES)
 (CONNECT_DATA =
  (SERVER = DEDICATED)
  (SERVICE_NAME = tafpreconnect)
  (FAILOVER_MODE =
  (BACKUP = tafpreconnect_PRECONNECT)
```

```
  (TYPE = SELECT)(METHOD = PRECONNECT)(RETRIES = 180)(DELAY = 5)
  )
 )
)

tafpreconnect_PRECONNECT =
 (DESCRIPTION =
  (ADDRESS = (PROTOCOL = TCP)(HOST = cluster1.example.com)(PORT = 1521))
  (LOAD_BALANCE = YES)
  (CONNECT_DATA =
   (SERVER = DEDICATED)
   (SERVICE_NAME = tafpreconnect_PRECONNECT)
   (FAILOVER_MODE =
   (TYPE = SELECT)(METHOD = BASIC)(RETRIES = 180)(DELAY = 5)
   )
  )
)
```

You will notice that additional sessions are established when you connect using this TNS alias:

```
SQL> select inst_id,sid,failover_type,failover_method, failed_over
  2  from gv$session
  3* where username = 'APRESS'
14:22:10 MARTIN@tafpreconnect > /

   INST_ID        SID FAILOVER_TYPE FAILOVER_M FAI
---------- ---------- ------------- ---------- ---
         1         26 NONE          NONE       NO
         1        156 SELECT        PRECONNECT NO
         2        140 NONE          NONE       NO
```

■ **Note** When defining the TAF properties with the service directly, the FAILOVER_TYPE and FAILOVER_METHOD aren't populated in GV$SESSION.

Additional parameters are available to fine-tune the failover operation. In addition to the FAILOVER_METHOD and FAILOVER_TYPE parameters, administrators can set the RETRIES and DELAY parameters. The RETRIES parameter specifies the maximum number of attempts to failover and defaults to five if the DELAY parameter is specified. The DELAY parameter specifies the delay between connection attempts and defaults to one second if the RETRIES parameter is set. However, both the RETRIES and DELAY parameters are ignored when an application registers a TAF callback function, as in the next example we will discuss.

Using TAF with JDBC Applications

Once Transparent Application Failover-aware connection strings or services have been completed, it is possible to create applications that use this feature. There is no additional setup work required for session failover; you can use this feature straight away. For select type failover scenarios, a little more work is required. The next example demonstrates how to use TAF with JDBC applications. Oracle provides the interface OracleOCIFailover in the oracle.jdbc namespace; this enables you to leverage TAF in your applications.

Unfortunately, this interface is not well documented. The most important part of the interface defines a callback function and a number of constants that indicate the state of the failover, such as failover begin, end, abort, and so on. The exact definition is available in the Javadoc API documentation for JDBC.

You need to implement the interface and put any application logic into the CallbackFn() function. The class implementing the callback needs to be registered with the instantiated OracleDataSource object. The callback function will be invoked whenever a TAF event occurs, and it allows the developer to take action accordingly.

Remember that DML operations are not covered by TAF, nor the is session state preserved. However, the developer could intercept the failover and roll his transaction back when the FO_BEGIN event is raised. After receiving the FO_END event, the transaction can be restarted.

The following example demonstrates how to connect to an Oracle database with the OCI JDBC driver and register a TAF callback. The program then opens a cursor against the ALL_OBJECTS view and iterates over it. To extend the execution of the cursor, we added a 1000 millisecond delay before the next record of the result set is retrieved. The Oracle JDK installed with Oracle 11.2 (JDK 1.5) has been used to compile the code. Make sure your classpath argument or environment variable reference at least ojdbc5.jar. You also need to set your LD_LIBRARY_PATH to $ORACLE_HOME/lib. This is needed for the OCI driver. In Windows, you need to set the PATH environment variable instead:

```
// TNSNames.ora entry for this application:
reporting =
 (DESCRIPTION=
  (ADDRESS=(PROTOCOL=tcp)(HOST=cluster1.example.com)(PORT=1521))
  (CONNECT_DATA=
    (SERVICE_NAME=reporting)
    (FAILOVER_MODE=(TYPE=select)(METHOD=basic)))
 )

// File: TAF.java
import java.sql.*;
import oracle.jdbc.*;
import oracle.jdbc.pool.OracleDataSource;

public class TAF {
  private OracleDataSource ods;
  private static Connection conn;

  public TAF()
  throws Exception
  {
    ods = new OracleDataSource();
    ods.setURL("jdbc:oracle:oci:@reporting");
    ods.setUser("user");
    ods.setPassword("password");
  }
```

```java
public void connect() throws Exception {

  conn = ods.getConnection();
  ((OracleConnection) conn).registerTAFCallback(new TAFCallback(),
      new Object());
}

public void query() throws Exception  {
  Statement stmt = null;
  try {

    stmt = conn.createStatement();
    ResultSet rs = stmt.executeQuery(
      "select sys_context('userenv','instance_name') " +
        " from dual");
    rs.next();
    System.out.println("We are connected to instance " + rs.getString(1));
    rs.close();

    // now do some more work
    rs = stmt.executeQuery(
     "select object_id,object_name from all_objects");

    while (rs.next()) {
      System.out.println(rs.getInt(1) + "-" + rs.getString(2));

      // sleep a little bit to give us more time to simulate
      // instance failure
      Thread.sleep(1000);
    }

  } catch (SQLException e) {
    int sqlcode = e.getErrorCode();
    System.out.println("Error executing query " + e.toString());
  }
}

public static void disconnect()  {
  try {
    System.out.println("disconnecting");
    conn.close();
  } catch (Exception e) {
    System.out.println(e);
  }
}

public static void main (String[] args)
{
  System.out.println("starting..." );

  try {
    TAF t = new TAF();
```

```
        t.connect();
        t.query();
        t.disconnect();
      } catch (Exception e) {
        e.printStackTrace();
      }
    }
  }
}

// File: TAFCallback.java
import java.sql.*;
import oracle.jdbc.*;
import oracle.jdbc.pool.OracleDataSource;

public class TAFCallback implements OracleOCIFailover  {

  public int callbackFn (Connection conn, Object ctxt, int type, int event) {

    String failover_type = null;
    switch (type) {
      case FO_SESSION: failover_type = "SESSION"; break;
      case FO_SELECT:  failover_type = "SELECT";  break;
      default:         failover_type = "NONE";
    }

    switch (event) {

      case FO_BEGIN:
          System.out.println(ctxt + ": "+ failover_type +
            " failing over...");
          break;
      case FO_END:
          System.out.println(ctxt + ": failover ended");
          boolean doReconnect = true;
          break;
      case FO_ABORT:
          System.out.println(ctxt + ": failover aborted.");
          break;
      case FO_REAUTH:
          System.out.println(ctxt + ": failover.");
          break;
      case FO_ERROR:
          System.out.println(ctxt +
            ": failover error received. Sleeping...");
          // Sleep for a while-will be invoked again
          try {
            Thread.sleep(100);
          } catch (InterruptedException e) {
            System.out.println("Thread.sleep failed with: "
              + e.toString());
          }
          return FO_RETRY;
```

```
        default:
            System.out.println(ctxt + ": bad failover event.");
            break;
    }
    return 0;
  }
}
```

To see Transparent Application Failover in action, you need to simulate an instance failure. After starting the code execution, open a new terminal and issue a *shutdown abort* against the instance executing the code:

```
[oracle@london2~ ]> srvctl stop instance -d PROD -i PROD1 -o abort
```

You should now see the application reacting according to your instruction and fail over the second node providing the service:

```
[oracle@london1 taf]$ java TAF
starting...
We are connected to instance RAC1
20-ICOL$
...
40-I_OBJ5
java.lang.Object@1ac88440: SELECT failing over...
java.lang.Object@1ac88440: failover ended
26-I_PROXY_ROLE_DATA$_1
56-I_CDEF4
...
```

You can verify the connection from a different instance:

```
SQL> select sid,serial#,inst_id,failover_type,failover_method,
  2    failed_over,service_name
  3*  from gv$session where service_name = 'REPORTING';
```

SID	SERIAL#	INST_ID	FAILOVER_TYPE	FAILOVER_M	FAI	SERVICE_NAME
152	23	1	SELECT	BASIC	NO	reporting

Now when you abort instance 1, the session fails over and resumes the select:

```
[oracle@london1 taf]$ srvctl stop instance -d PROD -i PROD1 -o abort
```

```
SQL> select sid,serial#,inst_id,failover_type,failover_method,failed_over,
  2    service_name
  3*  from gv$session where service_name = 'REPORTING';
```

SID	SERIAL#	INST_ID	FAILOVER_TYPE	FAILOVER_M	FAI	SERVICE_NAME
41	91	**2**	SELECT	BASIC	**YES**	reporting

Transparent Application Failover feels a bit dated today, but it remains the easiest way to take advantage of a RAC deployment.

If you are considering using TAF, you should remember that it is not well suited to all types of applications. In fact, it only applies in very limited circumstances. While TAF works well for read-only applications, it presents issues for applications that modify the database. In the event of a failure, any uncommitted transactions will be rolled back or will need to be restarted by the application. Therefore, the application must be capable of detecting the failure and, if necessary, reapplying DML statements up to the point of failure. If this capability is a requirement, then the application must also be capable of recording all statements issued in a transaction, along with the values of any bind variables.

Also, note that while TAF can reauthorize a session, it does not restore the session to its previous state. Therefore, following an instance failure, you will need to restore any session variables, PL/SQL package variables, and instances of user-defined types. TAF will not restore these values automatically, so you will need to extend your applications to restore them manually.

For the reasons just discussed, you may find that the areas within your applications that can take advantage of TAF are fairly limited. In Oracle 10.1 and later, there has been some de-emphasizing of the capabilities of TAF in favor of FAN, especially for JDBC and .Net applications that use Fast Connection Failover (FCF). These are discussed in more detail in the next section.

Implementing Fast Connection Failover

Fast Connection Failover is based on events published by the Fast Application Notification framework that is part of every Real Application Cluster database installation. From a developer's point of view, it offers many advantages over Transparent Application Failover. First, no programmatic changes are needed for the application in most cases. It appears as if the age of fat database clients distributed to each user PC is slowly coming to an end. In an effort to reduce maintenance costs and increase efficiency, many businesses are consolidating their end-user PCs into terminal-server farms. The high maintenance PC might eventually be replaced by a thin client, and application deployment is going to be managed centrally. Many applications follow this trend and are developed with a web frontend that requires very few resources on the client side. Typically, a standard web browser is all that's needed to access the application.

Most of these types of applications use connection pools from which individual connections are borrowed for short periods of time. Fast Connection Failover, along with Fast Application Notification, provides the Oracle developer with the tools needed to successfully write multi-tiered applications. We are going to explore the use of FAN and FCF in this section.

Implementing Fast Application Notification

We introduced the Fast Application Notification Framework in Chapter 3. The framework forms the basis for many RAC specific features. It is mainly a notification mechanism that informs interested clients about state changes. These changes include node up and down events, service up and down events, and so on. FAN also serves as the basis of the runtime load balancing feature by communicating load advisory events.

■ **Note** The great advantage of FAN is that applications do not have to poll the database for information; instead, they receive events immediately after they occur.

You must use services if you want to take advantage of FAN. Many key Oracle components are already using FAN events under the covers. There are three different ways that you can use FAN events:

- *Use an Oracle client with integrated support:* No changes to the application are necessary when using JDBC, OCI, or ODP.Net clients. In most cases, these are connection pooled applications. To use the load balancing events, an Oracle database 10.2 or later is required. (You will see an example that relies on a Tomcat-based JDBC-connection pooled application later in the chapter.)

- *Use the FAN APIs:* Applications can use FAN events by leveraging the APIs provided. Unfortunately, the documentation regarding this feature for Java is incomplete and incorrect in many places, making it impossible to create an example. A documentation bug has been filed with Oracle to address this.

- *Use FAN callouts on the database server:* FAN callouts are small server-side executables in $GRID_HOME/racg/usrco/. Oracle executes them immediately after an event occurs. Their main use is to raise alarms for on-call DBAs or to automatically raise a ticket in a fault-tracking system. For services with a manual policy, a callout script could be employed to relocate or restart services when the preferred instance comes back on line.

Oracle RAC and Oracle Restart use the Oracle Notification Service (ONS) processes to send out the FAN events. The Oracle Notification Service (ONS) is used by Oracle Clusterware to propagate FAN messages both within the RAC cluster and to clients and application-tier systems. ONS uses a simple publish-and-subscribe method to generate and deliver event messages to both local and remote consumers.

ONS is automatically installed as a node application on each node in the cluster. In Oracle 10.2 and later, it is configured as part of the Oracle Clusterware installation process. ONS daemons run locally, sending and receiving messages from ONS daemons on other nodes in the cluster. In Oracle 11.2, ONS got company in the form of eONS, or *enhanced ONS*. In the base release, it was mainly used to handle user callouts. However, development efforts were underway to integrate eONS into EVMd directly. Unlike ONS, eONS is a java process that uses UDP multicast to communicate with all other cluster members.

Clients can subscribe to ONS events in either of two ways: by using a local ONS process or by specifying a remote ONS instance. Oracle Application Server typically had its own local ONS process; however, ONS is not normally present in an all-java middle tier. ONS and eONS are also available in Oracle Restart allowing developers to code for Data Guard broker events.

FAN events can broadly be categorized into three different event types:

- Node events

- Service events

- Runtime load balancing ("service metrics") events

Node events inform you about cluster membership states and nodes joining and leaving operations. Service events inform you about state changes in services. Finally, service metrics are used by the load balancing advisory to broadcast the load of instances to the client.

It is possible to dequeue the runtime load balancing events from their queue using a simple piece of code, as in the following excerpt:

```
CREATE procedure display_fan_events (
  po_service out varchar2,
  po_information out varchar2)
is
  v_dequeue_opts          DBMS_AQ.dequeue_options_t;
  v_message_properties    DBMS_AQ.message_properties_t;
  v_message_handle        RAW(16);
  v_event_msg             SYS.SYS$RLBTYP;
BEGIN
    v_dequeue_opts.consumer_name := '&V_GRANTEE';
    v_dequeue_opts.visibility    := DBMS_AQ.IMMEDIATE;
    v_dequeue_opts.dequeue_mode  := DBMS_AQ.REMOVEBROWSE;
    DBMS_AQ.dequeue(queue_name              => 'sys.SYS$SERVICE_METRICS',
                    dequeue_options   => v_dequeue_opts,
                    message_properties => v_message_properties,
                    payload            => v_event_msg,
                    msgid              => v_message_handle);
    po_service := v_event_msg.srv;
    po_information := v_event_msg.payload;
    COMMIT;
END;
/
```

It's easy to create a sample application that queries that data and dumps it to the standard output:

```perl
#!/usr/bin/perl

use strict;
use warnings;

use DBI;
use DBD::Oracle;
use Getopt::Long;

# define a cleanup routine for CTRL-C
$SIG{'INT'} = 'cleanupandexit';

# get the service name from the command line
my $service;
GetOptions ("service=s" => \$service);
die "usage: dequeue.sh -s <servicename>" if (!defined ($service));

# about to start...
print "Dequeue AQ events for Service $service\n";
my $dbh = DBI->connect ("dbi:Oracle:$service", "user", "password")
  or die ("Cannot connect to service $service: DBI:errstr!");

# prepare a cursor to loop over all entries in the queue
my $csr = $dbh->prepare(q{
  BEGIN DISPLAY_FAN_EVENTS(:po_service, :po_information); END;
});
```

```perl
# out variables to be bound to the cursor
my $po_service;
my $po_information;

$csr->bind_param_inout(":po_service", \$po_service, 4000);
$csr->bind_param_inout(":po_information", \$po_information, 4000);

eval {
  # just dequeue all the time, note that the procedure discards entries
  # from the queue after reading them!
  while (1) {
    $csr->execute();
    print "$po_information\n";
    sleep 1;   # give the eyes a break
  }
};
if ($@) {
  print "Error executing Cursor: $@";
  cleanupandexit();
}

# we are done - disconnect
$dbh->disconnect();

# called when user presses CTRL-C to clean up or an error occurs
# while exectuing the cursor
sub cleanupandexit {
  print "exiting...\n";
  $csr->finish();
  $dbh->disconnect();
  exit 0;
}
```

This sample output demonstrates the RLB feature very nicely. First, let's generate some load by continuously calculating random numbers:

```
[oracle@london2 ~]$ for i in 1 2 3 4 ; do
  sqlplus user/secretpwd@reporting @dothis.sql &
done

[oracle@london2 ~]$ cat dothis.sql
declare
 n number;
begin
  WHILE (TRUE)
  LOOP
    -- something silly burning CPU...
    n:= dbms_random.random();
  END LOOP;
end;
/
```

Oracle chose to distribute three of these four sessions to node 2, and one to node 1:

```
INST_ID SERVICE_NAME
---------- -------------------
         1 reporting
         2 reporting
         2 reporting
         2 reporting
```

Subsequently, instance two was hit harder:

```
[oracle@london1 ~]$ top
top - 16:58:06 up 6 days,  2:28,  7 users,  load average: 1.44, 0.74, 0.44
Tasks: 223 total,   7 running, 216 sleeping,   0 stopped,   0 zombie
Cpu(s):  1.1%us,  0.7%sy,  0.0%ni, 89.5%id,  8.5%wa,  0.0%hi,  0.0%si,  0.2%st
Mem:   4194304k total,  4119808k used,    74496k free,   104988k buffers
Swap:  1048568k total,   198792k used,   849776k free,   955824k cached

  PID USER      PR  NI  VIRT  RES  SHR S %CPU %MEM    TIME+  COMMAND
 4885 oracle    25   0  718m  29m  26m R 99.1  0.7   2:41.98 oracle
...

[oracle@london2 ~]$  top
top - 16:58:11 up 6 days,  2:28,  2 users,  load average: 3.49, 4.37, 2.29
Tasks: 213 total,   6 running, 207 sleeping,   0 stopped,   0 zombie
Cpu(s): 98.0%us,  0.3%sy,  0.0%ni,  1.5%id,  0.0%wa,  0.0%hi,  0.0%si,  0.2%st
Mem:   4194304k total,  4031568k used,   162736k free,   102356k buffers
Swap:  1048568k total,   344756k used,   703812k free,   822636k cached

  PID USER      PR  NI  VIRT  RES  SHR S %CPU %MEM    TIME+  COMMAND
 2304 oracle    18   0  718m  29m  26m R 92.3  0.7   2:30.08 oracle
 2306 oracle    25   0  717m  25m  23m R 87.6  0.6   1:28.14 oracle
...
```

The output of the dequeue application reflects this difference in load; it has been slightly reformatted for readability:

```
[oracle@london1 aq]$ ./dequeue.sh  -s reporting
Dequeue AQ events for Service reporting
service: reporting - VERSION=1.0 database=admindb service=reporting {
  {instance=admindb2 percent=13 flag=GOOD aff=TRUE}
  {instance=admindb1 percent=87 flag=GOOD aff=TRUE} }
     timestamp=2010-05-10 16:57:07
service: reporting - VERSION=1.0 database=admindb service=reporting {
  {instance=admindb2 percent=9 flag=GOOD aff=TRUE}
  {instance=admindb1 percent=91 flag=GOOD aff=FALSE} }
     timestamp=2010-05-10 16:57:37
service: reporting - VERSION=1.0 database=admindb service=reporting {
  {instance=admindb2 percent=7 flag=GOOD aff=TRUE}
  {instance=admindb1 percent=93 flag=GOOD aff=FALSE} }
```

```
timestamp=2010-05-10 16:58:07
exiting...
```

The relevant payload of the event is recorded in the instance, percent, and flag fields. Information pertaining to the instance is grouped. In the preceding example, you can see that instance 2 can take a lot less additional load ("percent") than instance 1, which still has resources to spare. The flag attribute states that, despite the load on the service, the load balancing goal (service time, in this example) is not violated.

Implementing a Fast Connection Failover Example

We chose an example based on JDBC connection pooling with the Apache Tomcat 6 servlet/JSP container. This example uses the new Universal Connection Pool (UCP) instead of the Implicit Connection Cache. The Implicit Connection Cache feature has been deprecated as of Oracle 11.2; new applications should no longer use this feature. This approach requires a little more work to set up; however, this is also a more work-relevant example because the majority of UCP demos are of little practical value.

The example uses JDK 1.6.0.18, Apache Tomcat 6.0.24, and Apache Ant 1.8, along with an Oracle 11.2 client for the remote ONS configuration. All software packages were downloaded from their respective websites and deployed into /opt/ on a machine separate from the cluster nodes. The oracle client software is installed to /u01/app/oracle/product/11.2.0/client_1 to conform to the Oracle Flexible Architecture.

Configuring Tomcat

You can download Apache Tomcat 6 from the project's website or a mirror near you, and then un-tar/gzip the file to /opt/apache-tomcat. This installation directory is henceforth referenced as $CATALINA_HOME. Before starting the web server in $CATALINA_HOME/bin/startup.sh, you should set some environment variables in your shell (please change them where necessary to reflect your environment):

```
export JAVA_HOME=/opt/jdk1.6.0_18
export CATALINA_HOME=/opt/apache-tomcat-6.0.24
export ANT_HOME=/opt/apache-ant-1.8.0
export ORACLE_HOME=/u01/app/oracle/product/11.2.0/client_1

export PATH=$CATALINA_HOME/bin:$JAVA_HOME/bin:$ANT_HOME/bin:$PATH
```

Next, you should copy the following required JAR files for the Universal Connection Pool, JDBC, and Oracle Notification Support from your $ORACLE_HOME into $CATALINA_HOME/lib:

- ojdbc6.jar

- orai18n.jar

- ucp.jar

- ons.jar

The Tomcat startup code will automatically make the JAR files available to all deployed applications. Finally, you need to add support for FAN events in Tomcat. To do so, edit

$CATALINA_HOME/bin/startup.sh and modify the line reading CATALINA_OPTS to include the following pointer to the Oracle client:

```
CATALINA_OPTS="-Doracle.ons.oraclehome=/u01/app/oracle/product/11.2.0/client_1 \
$CATALINA_OPTS"
```

The Oracle client's ons.config file contains the configuration for the remote Oracle Notification Service and its ports. Edit the file in $ORACLE_HOME/opmn/conf and ensure that you are making use of the correct ONS ports. In a default installation, the following should work for you after you change the host names in the line beginning with "nodes":

```
localport=6100
remoteport=6200
nodes=london1:6200,london2:6200,london3:6200
```

You can use onsctl debug in the Grid Infrastructure home on any of the Real Application Cluster nodes to find out which ports are in use by ONS. Therefore, the line beginning with "nodes" needs to list all the cluster nodes, as well as their remote ONS ports.

Preparing the Code

With all the preparation work completed, getting a data source from the pool is relatively simple. We need to look up the context where the data source is stored. By convention, this is in the jdbc sub namespace. We use a POJO (plain old java object) class to perform the lookup and connection management. A Java Server Page uses this class to retrieve a connection and display information about the server pool and various other statistics available in the UCP namespace. Here is the code behind the java class:

```java
package com.apress.racbook.wlm.ucp;

import java.sql.Connection;
import java.sql.SQLException;
import java.sql.Statement;
import oracle.ucp.jdbc.PoolDataSourceFactory;
import oracle.ucp.jdbc.PoolDataSource;

import javax.naming.Context;
import javax.naming.InitialContext;
import javax.naming.NamingException;

import java.io.Serializable;
import java.sql.ResultSet;
import java.util.Properties;

public class UCPDemo {

    private   Context        envContext, initContext;
    private   PoolDataSource pds = null;

    // look up a JNDI data source in the "comp/env" context root
    public UCPDemo(String jndiName)
```

```
    throws NamingException, SQLException
  {
    initContext = new InitialContext();
    envContext = (Context) initContext.lookup("java:/comp/env");

    pds = (PoolDataSource) envContext.lookup(jndiName);
  }

  // return a pooled connection from the pooled data source
  private Connection getConnection()
    throws SQLException
  {
    return pds.getConnection();
  }

  // get the instance the session was borrowed from. Retuns the
        //SQL Exception
  // if raised in the String as well.
  public String getInstance()
    throws SQLException
  {
    String instName = "";

    try {
      Connection conn = this.getConnection();
      Statement stmt = conn.createStatement();
      ResultSet rst = stmt.executeQuery(
        "select sys_context('userenv','instance_name') from dual");

      rst.next();
      instName = rst.getString(1);

      // return the connection to the pool
      stmt.close();
      conn.close();
      conn = null;
    } catch (SQLException sqlexception) {
      instName = sqlexception.toString();
    }

    return instName;
  }

  // public getter method for the private variable
  public PoolDataSource getPDS()  {
    return this.pds;
  }
}


// File: generic_connection.jsp
<%@ page language="java" contentType="text/html; charset=UTF-8"
```

```
      pageEncoding="UTF-8"%>
<%@ page import="com.apress.racbook.wlm.ucp.*" %>
<%@ page import="oracle.ucp.jdbc.oracle.*" %>

<!DOCTYPE html PUBLIC "-//W3C//DTD HTML 4.01 Transitional//EN"
  "http://www.w3.org/TR/html4/loose.dtd">
<html>
<head>
  <meta http-equiv="Content-Type" content="text/html; charset=UTF-8">
  <title>Generic Connection Page</title>
</head>
<body>

<table cellspacing="2" cellpadding="2" border="0">
<tr>
  <td><img src="images/proOracleRac11gOnLinux.gif" /></td>
  <td>

    <h1>Pro Oracle RAC 11g on Linux</h1>

    <h3>UCP Connection Pool Demo</h3>
  </td>
</tr>
<tr>
  <td colspan="2">
    <p>
      This demo uses a resource defined in $CATALINA_HOME/conf/context.xml to
      connect to a UCP connection pool using an Oracle 11.2 RAC database.
    </p>
  </td>
</tr>
</table>

<%
String jndiName = request.getParameter("jndiName");
// do processing if the user has entered a JNDI name previously
if (jndiName != null)  {

%>
<h2>Connecting to JNDI Name <%= jndiName %></h2>
<%

UCPDemo ucp;
ucp = new UCPDemo(jndiName);

%>

<p>You are connected to instance <%= ucp.getInstance() %></p>

<h3>Statistics</h3>

<table width="100%" cellspacing="2" cellpadding="2">
```

```
<tr>
  <th colspan="4">Pooled Data Source Connection</th>
<tr>
  <td> getAbandonedConnectionTimeout()    </td>
  <td> <%= ucp.getPDS().getAbandonedConnectionTimeout() %>  </td>
  <td> getAvailableConnectionsCount()      </td>
  <td> <%= ucp.getPDS().getAvailableConnectionsCount()  %>  </td>
</tr>
<tr>
...
<hr/>

<h3>Specify Connection Information</h3>

<form action="generic_connection.jsp">

<table>
<tr>
  <td>Connect to jndi Name: </td>
  <td><input type="text" name="jndiName" value="<%= jndiName %>"/></td>
  <td colspan="2"><input type="submit" /></td>
</tr>
</table>

</form>

</body>
</html>
```

■ **Note** You can download the complete source code for this example from the Apress website at www.apress.com. To deploy this code to your environment, simply drop the `workloadMgmt-1.0.war` file into `$CATALINA_HOME/webapps`.

The JSP page prompts the user for a JNDI name to connect to and then uses the UCPDemo class to initialize the connection pool. The user is rewarded with a wealth of statistics about the pool. The JNDI data source is defined in the web application's `context.xml` file. Beginning with Tomcat 5, JDBC data sources no longer need to be defined in `server.xml` or `context.xml` files that reside in `$CATALINA_HOME/conf`. Previously changes to the data source required a restart of the Tomcat instance. The `context.xml` relevant to this application is deployed as part of the META-INF directory. A sample data source configuration for a RAC data source can be defined as follows. This example has been reformatted for readability; when working with the context, it seemed to be required that all the information be one line:

```
<?xml version='1.0' encoding='utf-8'?>
<Context>
  <Resource name="jdbc/reporting"
    auth="Container"
```

593

```
    factory="oracle.ucp.jdbc.PoolDataSourceImpl"
    type="oracle.ucp.jdbc.PoolDataSource"
    description="FCF RAC database"
    connectionFactoryClassName="oracle.jdbc.pool.OracleDataSource"
    connectionWaitTimeout="30"
    minPoolSize="10"
    maxPoolSize="50"
    inactiveConnectionTimeout="60"
    timeoutCheckInterval="30"
    fastConnectionFailoverEnabled="true"
    onsConfiguration="nodes=node1:6200,node2:6200,node3:6200,node4:6200"
    user="databaseUser" password="databasePassword"
    url="jdbc:oracle:thin:@//cluster1.example.com:1521/reporting"
    connectionPoolName="FCF Connection Pool for service REPORTING"
    validateConnectionOnBorrow="true"
    sqlForValidateConnection="select 1 from DUAL"
    maxConnectionReuseTime="30"
  />
</Context>
```

Many of the attributes of the Resource tag reference setter functions in the PoolDataSource interface in the oracle.ucp.jdbc namespace. The most important attributes are listed in Table 11-2.

Table 11-2. Important Attributes for Creating Connection Pools

Attribute	Meaning	Comment
Name	The resource name	Use the resource name to look up the JDNI name in your application. In the sample code, this needs to be entered in the HTML form.
Type	The type of data source to be created by the servlet container	Use the suggested PoolDataSource here for Universal Connection Pool
minPoolSize	The minimum pool size	Allocated this when the connection pool is created.
maxPoolSize	The maximum pool size	Prevents the connection pool from growing beyond that specified number of sessions
fastConnectionFailoverEnabled	Controls the Fast Connection Failover	Enables Fast Connection Failover; obviously; this is the most important parameter for this demonstration!
onsConfiguration	Enables mapping between cluster nodes and their ONS ports	Required for Fast Connection Failover. Otherwise, the connection pool cannot receive FAN events.

Attribute	Meaning	Comment
user, password, URL	The database connection	
validateConnectionOnBorrow	Ensures the connection borrowed from the pool is valid	Relieves the developer of the responsibility of checking whether a connection is valid when borrowing it from the pool. This can create overhead if set to True.

When you point your web browser to the application (such as http://tomcathost:8080/workloadMgmt/generic_connection.jsp) and enter a valid JNDI name, the connection pool will be created and allocate sessions as specified per the minimum pool size. When refreshing the page, you should see the statistics change according to usage. You can use tools such as the Apache benchmark program (/usr/sbin/ab2) to stress the application a little and use the DISPLAY_FAN_EVENTS() function to find out how Oracle reacts to changes in load. You should see service up and down events when stopping and starting services, and you should also see sessions migrating from the instance where the service failed to other instances that provide the failed service.

Establishing Connection Affinity

When using connection pools, users grab a session from the pool, perform some work, and hand it back to the pool. It would be nice if the allocation of sessions could have some affinity to the instance a previous user allocated his session from. The rationale for this idea: Oracle's runtime load balancing previously selected an instance suitable for creating the initial session. If so configured, the initial and subsequent sessions will have an affinity to this instance, based on the assumption that the instance has spare resources. Sessions can incur performance penalties when relocated to a different instance after a load advisory event. The affinity hint tries to keep a session on the instance, regardless of the events received by the RAC instance.

The affinity hint does not guarantee that node affinity is going to be respected. If Oracle cannot satisfy an affinity request, it will break the affinity and reassign sessions from the connection pool to different instances. After this reshuffling of sessions, new affinities will be established.

Oracle supports connection affinity with the Universal Connection Pool and Oracle RAC from 11g Release 1 and later. Two types of affinity exist to choose from:

- Web session affinity

- Transaction-based affinity (also known as *XA-affinity*)

Web session affinity is often used for short lived sessions that do not incur a massive penalty when redirected to a different instance. Transaction-based affinity is used for the opposite—long-lived transactions that would incur performance penalties when relocated to a different instance if the cluster should use this type.

Connection affinity is based on Fast Connection Failover, run time connection load balancing, and a registered affinity callback. The first two points have already been discussed. The third and fourth requirements need some more explanation. The callback class has to implement the interface oracle.ucp.ConnectionAffinityCallback. During session initialization (such as in the constructor of class UCPDemo in the preceding example), the developer registers the instantiated callback with a PoolDataSource object. The following example demonstrates how to set an affinity. There are quite a few

595

lines of code in this example, but the important bit is in the affinityPolicy variable and the setAffinityPolicy() and getAffinityPolicy() functions. Although they have to be implemented, the context functions serve no specific purpose in the example:

```
package com.apress.racbook.wlm.ucp;

import oracle.ucp.ConnectionAffinityCallback;
import oracle.ucp.ConnectionAffinityCallback.AffinityPolicy;

public class ConnectionAffinity
  implements ConnectionAffinityCallback
{

  ConnectionAffinityCallback.AffinityPolicy affinityPolicy =
    ConnectionAffinityCallback.AffinityPolicy.WEBSESSION_BASED_AFFINITY;
    // use TRANSACTION_BASED_AFFINITY alternatively
  Object appAffinityContext = null;

  public AffinityPolicy getAffinityPolicy() {
    return this.affinityPolicy;
  }

  public void setAffinityPolicy(AffinityPolicy policy) {
    this.affinityPolicy = policy;
  }

  public Object getConnectionAffinityContext() {
    return appAffinityContext;
  }

  public boolean setConnectionAffinityContext(Object affinityContext)  {
    this.appAffinityContext = affinityContext;
    return true;
  }
}

// the modified constructor of UCPDemo now is defined as follows:
public class UCPDemo {

  private   Context         envContext, initContext;
  private   PoolDataSource  pds = null;

  public UCPDemo(String jndiName)
    throws NamingException, SQLException
  {
    initContext = new InitialContext();
    envContext = (Context) initContext.lookup("java:comp/env");

    pds = (PoolDataSource)envContext.lookup(jndiName);

    // set a little bit of connectivity
```

```
    pds.registerConnectionAffinityCallback(new ConnectionAffinity());
  }
...
```

When executing the sample application, you should now see that you are redirected to the same instance each time you refresh the page.

Reading FAN events using the FAN API

Oracle provides an API to register callbacks with FAN for applications that cannot use either the Universal Connection Pool or the Implicit Connection Cache. It also allows developers to create their own connection pools. However, only a subset of events is available through this API.

Speaking in pseudo-code, the application needs to connect (*subscribe*) to a service to receive FAN events. Event handler functions defined in oracle.simplefan.FanEventListener can be implemented by the developer to react to the following event classes:

- LoadAdvisoryEvent

- NodeDownEvent

- ServiceDownEvent

Depending on the event type, additional information is available. To enable this functionality in an application, you should place the simplefan.jar and ons.jar files into your class path. You should also configure the Oracle client's ons.config file as described previously to specify the remote ONS ports. Interestingly, the classes of the oracle.simplefan namespace are not part of the main JDBC javadoc documentation. Instead, these were described in the Oracle Database RAC FAN Events Java API Reference document. At the time of writing, the documentation regarding this feature was both incorrect in many places and incomplete. This is a new 11.2 feature, so we expect it to mature in future patchsets.

Using the Resource Manager

Database services and the Resource Manager form an ideal pair for workload management in RAC, especially in consolidated databases. Where services are used to logically subdivide the cluster into groups of similar workload, the Resource Manager allows the administrator to govern resource usage based on the service. When users connect through a dedicated service, a mapping within Oracle assigns these users a resource consumer group. Part of a resource plan, a resource consumer group has certain rights to consume resources on the database. The Resource Manager helps administrators prevent situations where less important workloads starve out the important ones, potentially endangering service-level agreements (SLAs).

The Resource Manager serves as a very strong argument in favor of consolidating multiple single-instance and RAC-databases into a single, more powerful cluster. Up until Oracle 11.1, the Resource Manager worked *horizontally* only—within a database. Beginning with Oracle 11.2, the so-called instance caging extends the Resource Manager's functionality *vertically* to multiple database instances on the same hardware.

The use of the Resource Manager is preferred over operating system management of application classes to govern their resource consumption. The operating system scheduler does not know about the different requirements of Oracle foreground and background processes, nor are operating systems able to provide the same granularity of control.

The Resource Manager relies upon the following concepts:

A resource consumer group: This is a group of users based on similar requirements. The Resource Manager allocates resources based on consumer groups. You can define your own custom mapping of sessions to resource consumer groups based on the service users connect to.

A resource plan directive: Plan directives associate how resources are allocated within a consumer group. Plenty of options exist to define which resources in what quantity are available to a consumer group. The the most important of these resources is probably the CPU quantity.

A resource plan: The resource plan is the top-level object in the Resource Manager. It brings resource consumer groups and their plan directives together. For the Resource Manager to work, a plan needs to be active. Resource plans can be assigned to scheduler windows (as discussed previously in this chapter), making it possible to have different plans for different times in the week.

Oracle comes with three pre-defined consumer groups: SYS_GROUP, DEFAULT_CONSUMER_GROUP, and LOW_GROUP. You will find that all user sessions other than SYS and SYSTEM in a default Oracle installation use the default consumer group. You can see that by checking the RESOURCE_CONSUMER_GROUP column in the GV$SESSION view.

The Resource Manager is very flexible, and it allows the creation of hierarchical plans and other advanced features. We'll work through a simplified example that demonstrates how to create a resource plan that supports two database services.

The high level steps to create the resource plan for our example are as follows:

1. Create a sandbox to verify the plan before activating it; this is called a pending area.

2. Add the consumer groups.

3. Create a resource plan.

4. Add plan directives to the plan.

5. Define mapping between consumer groups and services and grant privileges to users/roles to switch consumer groups.

6. Validate the sandbox.

7. Submit the sandbox after a successful validation.

8. (Optionally) Enable the plan.

Here is the PL/SQL code to implement the aforementioned steps:

```
-- Create the pending area
SQL> exec dbms_resource_manager.create_pending_area();

-- Add two consumer groups-reporting and batch (group "BATCH" already
-- exists in 11.1 and 11.2)

SQL> begin dbms_resource_manager.create_consumer_group(
  consumer_group => 'REPORTING_GROUP',
  Comment => 'group connecting through service reporting');
end;
/
```

```
-- this is not needed in 11g
SQL> begin dbms_resource_manager.create_consumer_group(
  consumer_group => 'BATCH_GROUP',
  comment => 'group connecting through service batch');
end;
/


-- Create the resource plan. We use the RATIO method to define the ratio of
-- CPU usage between resource consumer groups.
-- The ratio is 1:2:3:5:8 for low group, other group, reporting group, batch
-- group and sys group.

SQL> exec dbms_resource_manager.create_plan( plan => 'DAYTIME_PLAN', -
     mgmt_mth => 'RATIO', comment => 'Pro Oracle Database 11g RAC sample plan')

-- Create a plan directive for each consumer group. This is a very basic
-- example only using CPU allocation.

SQL> exec dbms_resource_manager.create_plan_directive( plan=>'DAYTIME_PLAN', -
  mgmt_p1 => 1, group_or_subplan => 'LOW_GROUP', comment => 'low group')

SQL> exec dbms_resource_manager.create_plan_directive( plan=>'DAYTIME_PLAN', -
  mgmt_p1 => 2, group_or_subplan => 'OTHER_GROUPS', -
  comment => 'others group')

SQL> exec dbms_resource_manager.create_plan_directive( plan=>'DAYTIME_PLAN', -
  mgmt_p1 => 3, group_or_subplan => 'REPORTING_GROUP', -
  comment => 'reporting group')

SQL> exec dbms_resource_manager.create_plan_directive( plan=>'DAYTIME_PLAN', -
  mgmt_p1 => 5, group_or_subplan => 'BATCH_GROUP', comment => 'batch group')

SQL> exec dbms_resource_manager.create_plan_directive( plan=>'DAYTIME_PLAN', -
  mgmt_p1 => 5, group_or_subplan => 'SYS_GROUP', comment => 'sys group')


-- Define mapping for service reporting to reporting group, same for batch
SQL> begin
  dbms_resource_manager.set_consumer_group_mapping(
    attribute => DBMS_RESOURCE_MANAGER.SERVICE_NAME,
    value => 'REPORTING',
    consumer_group => 'REPORTING_GROUP');
end;
/

SQL> exec dbms_resource_manager.set_consumer_group_mapping( -
  attribute => DBMS_RESOURCE_MANAGER.SERVICE_NAME, -
  value => 'BATCHSERV', -
  consumer_group => 'BATCH_GROUP')
```

```
-- Validate the pending area
SQL> exec dbms_resource_manager.validate_pending_area

-- Submit the pending area

SQL> exec dbms_resource_manager.submit_pending_area


-- Allow users REPORTING_USER and BATCH_USER to switch to their
-- consumer group. Must be done after the initial pending area has
-- been submitted.
BEGIN
  DBMS_RESOURCE_MANAGER.CREATE_PENDING_AREA;
  DBMS_RESOURCE_MANAGER_PRIVS.GRANT_SWITCH_CONSUMER_GROUP (
      GRANTEE_NAME    => 'REPORTING_RW',
      CONSUMER_GROUP  => 'REPORTING_GROUP',
      GRANT_OPTION    =>  FALSE);
  DBMS_RESOURCE_MANAGER_PRIVS.GRANT_SWITCH_CONSUMER_GROUP (
      GRANTEE_NAME    => 'BATCH_RW',
      CONSUMER_GROUP  => 'BATCH_GROUP',
      GRANT_OPTION    =>  FALSE);
  DBMS_RESOURCE_MANAGER.VALIDATE_PENDING_AREA;
  DBMS_RESOURCE_MANAGER.SUBMIT_PENDING_AREA;
END;
/
```

Your work is not yet done once you define the plan defined; you must also enable it. You do this either by assigning it to a window or by executing the following command:

```
SQL> alter system set resource_manager_plan = 'DAYTIME_PLAN' scope=both sid='*';
```

Next time a user connects to the database via services REPORTING or BATCH the automatic mapping to a consumer group should take place.

Caging an Instance

The Oracle Resource Manager has always been very good at managing resource consumption in the same database. It knows about the requirements of Oracle database foreground and background processes, and it can send individual processes to sleep more effectively than an operating system's scheduler. While the vertical management of resource usage was part of the Resource Manager very early on, it could not manage horizontally (i.e., across database instances).

Some large SMP machines, as well as RAC databases forming part of consolidation projects, have multiple databases running on the same host. Like any process in a runnable state, Oracle competes for available scheduling time. Resource Manager 11.2 has now finally been extended to prevent one of the databases from starving the others out for resources. In other words, the Resource Manager can now cage instance resource usage horizontally, while at the same time controlling resource usage within the database instance. This is a huge step forward, especially in cases where users cannot consolidate data in a single database for security or compliance reasons, yet still want to use one consolidated cluster.

■ **Note** Instance caging allows the administrator to partition the available CPU power between databases; however, instance caging does not prevent administrators from over-provisioning CPU power to databases.

Enabling instance caging, the marketing name for advanced capabilities of the Resource Manager, is simple. It requires an active resource plan on all the databases in the cluster. All that needs to be done at this point is to set the instance `cpu_count` initialization parameter to the desired value. For instance, on a RAC cluster with two databases (such as the production wiki and RMAN catalog), the available eight CPU cores could be allocated like this: six for the wiki and two for the RMAN catalog. The cpu_count parameter is a dynamic parameter that can be set at runtime, so corrections are possible without interrupting a service.

Database Resident Connection Pool

Applications not written either in Java or .Net often cannot use connection pools. In the past, this could lead to severe performance problems in cases where high throughput was required. Dedicated server processes simply could not be created quickly enough, and CPU overhead on servers could be significant. Shared server processes could somewhat help in the short term until the application was ported to a middle-tier solution capable of connection pooling.

In Oracle 11.1, this problem was addressed with database resident connection pools (DRCP). Instead of solely relying on a middle tier to provide connection pools, applications written in PHP or even classic CGI can use a connection pool provided by and inside the Oracle database. The use of a database resident connection pool is not limited to scenarios where no middle-tier connection pool is available; it can also be used to complement such a setup to scale into thousands of users.

A so-called pooled server combines a hybrid foreground process with a database session. Using a DRCP can result in a significant reduction of resource usage, mainly in terms of memory and CPU resources. Thus, it allows a large user base that would otherwise be impossible to support with the given hardware. The readily available pooled servers also reduce the cost of creating new client connections.

Connection handling is similar to a middle-tier connection pool. A connection broker will pick an available pooled server from the available servers to handle a client request. If there is no free pooled server, the server pool will be grown by a predefined value. if the pool reaches its maximum size, client requests will be placed into a queue. As soon as a client session has been released, the used pooled server is returned to the pool to serve additional client requests. Unlike with a shared server, the memory used by the pooled servers will be allocated from the PGA, rather than the shared pool. This is a tribute to the close relationship between pooled and dedicated server processes.

Administrators and developers can use the database resident connection pool either through OCI commands or a PL/SQL API in the form of `DBMS_CONNECTION_POOL`. Unfortunately, the PL/SQL package does not allow the creation of additional connection pools. The default database resident connection pool is the only pool available; it is named `SYS_DEFAULT_CONNECTION_POOL`.

To demonstrate the usefulness of DRCP, we set up a simple example. The performance improvements of using DRCP over dedicated sessions is quite dramatic, as you will see. The demonstration uses the typical single-threaded Apache 2.2.3/PHP 5.3.2/OCI 1.4.1 combination that is often found in open source-based development projects.

The two PHP scripts (named `drcp.php` and `dedicatedSever.php`) in this example are identical, except for the connection string used. In the DRCP case, the connection pool is tied to a policy-managed database's uniform service with connect-time load balancing goal of short and a service time goal. The TNS aliases are defined as follows:

```
drcp =
  (DESCRIPTION =
    (ADDRESS = (PROTOCOL = TCP)(HOST = cluster1.example.com)(PORT = 1521))
    (LOAD_BALANCE = YES)
    (CONNECT_DATA = (SERVER = POOLED)(SERVICE_NAME = drcp)))

nondrcp =
  (DESCRIPTION =
    (ADDRESS = (PROTOCOL = TCP)(HOST = cluster1.example.com)(PORT = 1521))
    (LOAD_BALANCE = YES)
    (CONNECT_DATA = (SERVER = DEDICATED)(SERVICE_NAME = nondrcp)))
```

Again, the full code suite can be downloaded from the Apress website (www.apress.com); the following snippet shows the relevant, very basic PHP code:

```php
<?php
if ( $conn=OCILogon("user", "password", "nondrcp")) {
  echo "Successfully connected to Oracle.\n";

  // get the instance information
  $stid = oci_parse($conn, "select sys_context('userenv','instance_name'), " .
    "sys_context('userenv','service_name') inst from dual");
  $r = oci_execute($stid);

  while (($row = oci_fetch_array($stid, OCI_BOTH))) {
    echo "<p>You are connected to instance ";
    echo $row[0] . " using service " . $row[1];
    echo "</p>";
    }

  oci_free_statement($stid);

  OCILogoff($conn);
  } else {
  $err = OCIError();
  echo "Error in connecting to the Oracle." . $err["message"];
  }
?>
```

The preceding example simply connects to Oracle (TNS alias, *nondrcp*) and queries the userenv context to learn which instance it runs on and the service name the session connected to. It then closes the session. We've kept this example deliberately simple to re-create the most common problem with non-pooled dedicated server connections.

The database resident connection pool uses the attributes described in Table 11-3.

Table 11-3. Important DRCP Properties for the Example Used

Property	Meaning	Comment
Pool Name	The database resident connection pool used	Only the default is supported.
Minimum pool size	The initial pool size	Do not choose this value; it's too low.
Maximum pool size	The maximum number of pooled sessions possible	
Pool increment	Increment the current pool size by n sessions until maximum pool size is reached	
Inactivity Timeout	Idle timeout before the session is returned to the pool	

Once the pool is defined per the preceding settings, it needs to be started:

```
SQL> exec dbms_connection_pool.start_pool;
```

We used the Apache benchmarking tool, *ab*, to test the effect a database resident connection pool has on the throughput and memory usage. The parameters used required 10000 requests with a concurrency level of 20. The benchmarking software was executed on the web server to eliminate potential network impact. The results of the test were quite telling. Here are the dedicated server results:

```
Document Path:          /dedicatedServer.php
Document Length:        699 bytes

Time taken for tests:   52.169972 seconds
Complete requests:      10000
Failed requests:        9252
   (Connect: 0, Length: 9252, Exceptions: 0)
Total transferred:      11324772 bytes
HTML transferred:       9404772 bytes
Requests per second:    191.68 [#/sec] (mean)
Time per request:       104.340 [ms] (mean)
Time per request:       5.217 [ms] (mean, across all concurrent requests)
Transfer rate:          211.98 [Kbytes/sec] received

Connection Times (ms)
              min  mean[+/-sd] median   max
Connect:        0    0   0.6      0      27
Processing:     3  103 489.2     30    8221
Waiting:        3  103 489.2     29    8221
Total:          3  103 489.2     30    8221
```

A large percentage of requests could not be served, and the total execution time was 52.167 seconds. By comparison, the DRCP example beats these statistics by miles—and ab did not report any failures during the execution. The whole 10000 requests were served by Oracle in 7.1 seconds, with an average of 14.213 ms per request. Compare that number to 104340 ms for the dedicated server. What follows are the results from the DRCP example:

```
Document Path:          /drcp.php
Document Length:        695 bytes
Concurrency Level:      20
Time taken for tests:   7.106642 seconds
Complete requests:      10000
Failed requests:        0
Total transferred:      8870000 bytes
HTML transferred:       6950000 bytes
Requests per second:    1407.13 [#/sec] (mean)
Time per request:       14.213 [ms] (mean)
Time per request:       0.711 [ms] (mean, across all concurrent requests)
Transfer rate:          1218.86 [Kbytes/sec] received

Connection Times (ms)
              min  mean[+/-sd] median   max
Connect:        0    0   0.2       0      7
Processing:     2   13 114.2       6   4530
Waiting:        2   13 114.2       6   4530
Total:          2   13 114.2       6   4530
```

Unfortunately, the use of any Advanced Security Option feature is not possible with DRCP. There are some other, less severe limitations, as well.

Summary

We covered a lot of ground in this lengthy chapter, and yet it in some ways this is only touching the tip of the iceberg. Oracle workload management and RAC were designed to work together, and you should invest a lot of effort in laying out the optimal configuration for services in consolidated databases. Database services are the key to successful workload management, and these can be configured by a number of tools. While the database configuration assistant was available in Oracle 10g, the local database console or Enterprise Manager Grid Control have taken over the reins. Most of the functions provided by DBMS_SERVICE have also been deprecated. This essentially leaves the server control utility srvctl and Enterprise Manager as the most useful configuration tools.

The aim of the workload balancing techniques described in this chapter is to spread the workload evenly over all instances of a cluster. For example, connect-time load balancing either uses round robin DNS resolution or multiple listener entries in the local naming file to spread the work across multiple (SCAN) listeners evenly. In a different vein, server-side load balancing tries to ensure that the listener initially contacted hands the connection request off to the least loaded node providing the requested service. Finally, runtime load balancing can be used to reassign sessions during their existence in a connection pool to less-loaded instances.

Oracle RAC uses the Fast Application Notification framework to broadcast information about load and node status. FAN-integrated clients can use the Fast Connection Failover technology to leverage this information and reassign database sessions in a connection pool when an instance fails. This is usually transparent to the end user. For some applications, Transparent Application Failover can be implemented providing session failover capability when instances fail. Open cursors can be salvaged when a session fails over, but any ongoing transaction will be rolled back. Neither can session state cannot be failed over; this combination makes TAF a less desirable option than Fast Connection Failover.

The previously used Implicit Connection Cache has been deprecated in favor of the new Universal Connection Pool, which offers many advanced features, including instance affinity. Oracle will try to keep sessions on the same instance if relocating them to a different instance would prove costly in terms of resources.

We also looked at the Resource Manager and how it can help assigning sessions to resource groups, governing their allowed resource usage. The Resource Manager has been extended in Oracle 11.2; now it not only manages resources within a database, but also within all the databases inside the same cluster node. Using the toolset provided by Oracle properly should enable you to consolidate projects on Oracle RAC; also, the extensive monitoring for services provides the business and the infrastructure teams with vital information about the use of their hardware.

Database Resident Connection pools are a great new addition to the Oracle software stack for single-threaded applications that do not use connection pooling. The Oracle database once more proves to be the one-stop solution for the developer's needs.

CHAPTER 12

■ ■ ■

Oracle Performance Monitoring

In this chapter, we will look at using the tools available for monitoring the performance of an Oracle 11*g* RAC cluster at the Oracle RAC level. In the next chapter, we'll look at performance monitoring under Linux. At an Oracle Database level, we concentrate on the tools and features provided under the framework of the 11*g* Manageability Infrastructure. These tools and features range from Oracle Enterprise Manager Database Control to the 11*g* Automatic Diagnostic Repository (ADR).

Within an Oracle 11*g* database, the Manageability Infrastructure is a collection of database features that enable you to realize self-tuning and self-management functionality directly within the Oracle database itself. The primary aspect of the Manageability Infrastructure is the automated gathering and processing of base statistics related to database operations. A key enabling feature of the Manageability Infrastructure is the background process called the *Manageability Monitor* (MMON). This process performs most of the manageability-related tasks on the database, a central part of which is to capture and store database statistics. The MMON process captures base statistics every 60 seconds. It also accesses the SGA directly, so it works efficiently and with minimal overhead. These statistics are compiled and initially stored in memory to be accessed by dynamic performance views. Subsequently, they are flushed to disk in the form of snapshots. Both the in-memory and on-disk collections of statistics are referred to as the *Automatic Workload Repository* (AWR). A number of performance views with the prefix DBA_HIST_ can be used to access the data; DBA_HIST_SNAPSHOT, for example, shows information regarding all of the snapshots that have been taken.

The MMON process is also assisted by the Manageability Monitor Light (MMNL) process. It is used primarily for performing tasks related to the *Active Session History* (ASH). The ASH contains session statistics sampled at one-second intervals to record what the sessions are waiting for. The information is stored in memory, where it can be accessed in the view V$ACTIVE_SESSON_HISTORY. The in-memory view is implemented as a rolling buffer, and older information is overwritten as newer information is added. Therefore, new information is also written to disk by the MMNL process every 30 minutes. By default, seven days of ASH information is retained on disk, and it can be seen in the view DBA_HIST_ACTIVE_SESS_HISTORY.

The MMON process also computes and stores metric values based on the statistics themselves, and these can be seen directly in the views V$SYSMETRIC and V$SERVICEMETRIC. For example, V$SYSMETRIC contains information such as the calculated buffer cache hit ratio and user transactions per second.

Given the features enabled by the Manageability Infrastructure, our focus for performance monitoring in an Oracle 11*g* RAC Database environment is on the tools that take advantage of this infrastructure. Therefore, we will cover performance monitoring using the standard Oracle graphical interface environment called Oracle Enterprise Manager Database Control. We will also review captured performance data with AWR reports and ASH, and then look at using the Automatic Database Diagnostic Monitor (ADDM) and analyzing the performance of individual statements using AWR SQL reports. Next, we will cover performance monitoring using SQL*Plus. Finally, we will look at some of the performance monitoring features and fault diagnosis available with the Automatic Diagnostic Repository (ADR).

Enterprise Manager Database Control

Oracle Enterprise Manager 11g Database Control is supplied and installed with the Oracle Database software, so it is available for all Oracle 11g RAC environments. Database Control is installed and configured wholly within the cluster to manage that cluster only, which distinguishes it from the separate Oracle Enterprise Manager 11g Grid Control that is installed and configured on a standalone management server. Database Control can be used to manage multiple Oracle and non-Oracle software environments.

If you are creating a new Oracle 11g database, and you wish to use Database Control, then we recommend that you install and configure it using DBCA. Provided that no Grid Control Management Agent is previously installed, DBCA will provide you with the option to automatically install, configure, and start all of the components you require, including a Management Repository schema owned by the user SYSMAN within the SYSAUX tablespace of the target database, a local Management Service (including an HTTP server), and Management Agents on all nodes.

EM Database Control uses the EM Agents installed on the nodes and associated Management Services to communicate with the database, instances, and other processes. You can use the emctl command to check whether these are currently running using the emctl command, assuming you have set your ORACLE_UNQNAME to your database name beforehand. The following example shows that EM is currently not running:

```
[oracle@london1 ~]$ emctl status dbconsole
Oracle Enterprise Manager 11g Database Control Release 11.2.0.1.0
Copyright (c) 1996, 2009 Oracle Corporation.  All rights reserved.
https://london1.example.com:1158/em/console/aboutApplication
Oracle Enterprise Manager 11g is not running.
------------------------------------------------------------------
Logs are generated in directory
/u01/app/oracle/product/11.2.0/dbhome_1/london1_PROD/sysman/log
```

If the Management Agent is not running, then you can start it, as follows:

```
[oracle@london1 ~]$ emctl start dbconsole
Oracle Enterprise Manager 11g Database Control Release 11.2.0.1.0
Copyright (c) 1996, 2009 Oracle Corporation.  All rights reserved.
https://london1.example.com:1158/em/console/aboutApplication
Starting Oracle Enterprise Manager 11g Database Control .......... started.
------------------------------------------------------------------
Logs are generated in directory
/u01/app/oracle/product/11.2.0/dbhome_1/london1_PROD/sysman/log
```

The Management Agent can be stopped again using the stop argument.

By default, DBCA configures Database Control on each node in the cluster. However, after installation, the Database Control Console is only started on the node where you ran DBCA. On the remaining nodes, only the Management Agent component is started, and these nodes upload their data to the Database Control Console node.

If you are upgrading an existing Oracle database, and have created a database without the use of DBCA or wish to reconfigure your Database Control, you can do so using the emca utility.

A wide range of configuration options can be performed with emca. The most straightforward method to install Database Control is to call the command emca, specifying -config dbcontrol db, while also ensuring that you use the -cluster argument.

In common with the way you configure Database Control with DBCA, you will be running the Database Control Console on the node where you ran emca only. Subsequently, calling emctl start dbconsole and emctl stop dbconsole will start and stop the Management Service on this node only. The same commands will start and stop the Management Agent only on the remaining nodes in the cluster.

If the Database Control Console could run on only one node, it would clearly not be a high-availability configuration. Therefore, you can reconfigure the Console to start on a different node (or on more than one if you desire) by using the command emca -reconfig dbcontrol -cluster. By default, running this command without additional arguments starts the Console on the node that you ran the command from, and it directs the Management Agents on all other nodes in the cluster to upload their data to this Console. You can customize the process by providing the arguments EM_NODE and EM_SID_LIST to start the Console on the list of nodes specified and instruct the Management Agents listed to upload data to these nodes. You can view the configuration at any time using emca -displayConfig dbcontrol -cluster, as in this example:

```
[oracle@london1 ~]$ emca -displayConfig dbcontrol -cluster

STARTED EMCA at Feb 15, 2010 5:56:27 PM
EM Configuration Assistant, Version 11.2.0.0.2 Production
Copyright (c) 2003, 2005, Oracle.  All rights reserved.

Enter the following information:
Database unique name: PROD
Service name: PROD1
Do you wish to continue? [yes(Y)/no(N)]: Y
Feb 15, 2010 5:56:42 PM oracle.sysman.emcp.EMConfig perform
INFO: This operation is being logged at
/u01/app/oracle/cfgtoollogs/emca/PROD/emca_2010_02_15_17_56_26.log.
Feb 15, 2010 5:56:44 PM oracle.sysman.emcp.EMDBPostConfig
showClusterDBCAgentMessage
INFO:
***************    Current Configuration    ***************
 INSTANCE          NODE              DBCONTROL_UPLOAD_HOST
 ----------        ----------        --------------------

PROD              london1           london1.example.com
PROD              london2           london1.example.com


Enterprise Manager configuration completed successfully
FINISHED EMCA at Feb 15, 2010 5:56:44 PM
```

Finally, if you have also added a new node to the cluster, you may use the command emca -addInst db to add it to the database configuration. Similarly, you can use the command emca -deleteInst db to remove it, as long as you remember to run the command to remove the instance from a different node in the cluster.

The Cluster Tab

Upon logging in to Database Control at the URL for the specified node, such as https://london1.example.com:1158/em, you are presented at the highest level with two tabs to view the database configuration or the cluster configuration, as shown in Figure 12-1. Your browser requires the Adobe Flash plugin to view the EM performance graphs.

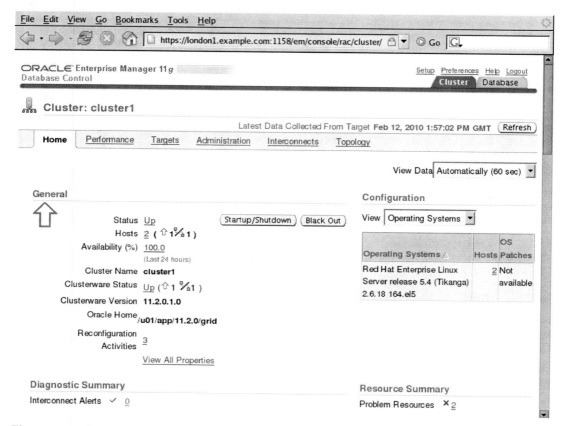

Figure 12-1. Cluster information from Database Control

The Cluster configuration provides details on the hosts in the cluster and clicking the Performance link drills down to a view of CPU, Memory, and I/O Utilization on all of the nodes in the cluster. It also provides a summary of the status of those nodes. You can use this Performance page to observe whether the cluster workload is evenly distributed across the cluster, as well as whether particular nodes are more heavily utilized than others. Similarly, the Interconnects link provides information on the Private Interconnect Transfer Rate in MB/sec for the cluster as a whole, and it shows the Total Error rate for the individual nodes. You should use this information in conjunction with the Linux operating system network performance utilities to ensure that the interconnect performance is not having a disproportionate impact on the performance of the cluster.

The Database Tab

The Database tab (see Figure 12-2) shows the performance of the cluster from a database, as opposed to the perspective from the host and operating system.

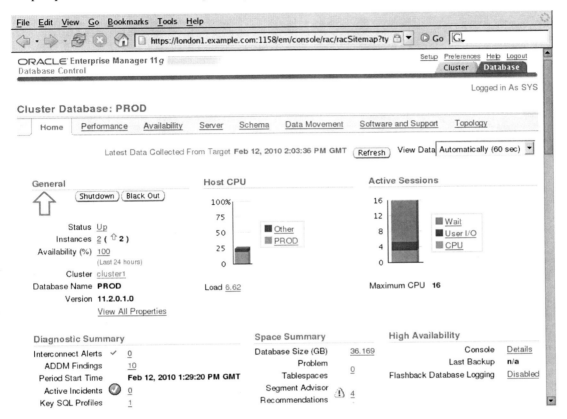

Figure 12-2. The Database tab from Database Control

The Performance Tab

The first two graphs on the Performance tab show the Cluster Host Load Average and the Global Cache Block Access Latency. The third graph shows the number of Average Active Sessions throughout the reporting period. The final graph on the Performance tab shows performance from the perspective of Database Throughput, I/O, Parallel Execution, Services, and Instances.

At the bottom of the Performance tab, there are six Additional Monitoring Links. The page you should use to monitor your inter-instance communication is the Cluster Cache Coherency page, as shown in Figure 12-3.

Figure 12-3. *Cluster Cache Coherency page*

The Cluster Cache Coherency page includes information on Global Cache Block Access Latency (this information also appears on the Performance tab), Global Cache Block Transfer Rate, and Global Cache Block Transfers and Physical Reads. Selecting the appropriate radio button makes the information available in both tabular numeric and graphical form. The Global Cache Block Access Latency is a useful initial statistic for observing the performance of your cluster. For releases of RAC, Oracle has typically recommended that the latency should be less than ten milliseconds before investigating potential performance issues; however, ideally you should expect these values to be no more than two milliseconds. If the latency is exceeding more than two milliseconds, we recommend investigating the performance in context of the workload, as well as looking at the latency of the entire hardware components of your cluster (see Chapter 4 for information on processing your workload more efficiently to reduce inter-instance traffic).

In addition to the overall interconnect latency, the metrics you will refer to most when reviewing your RAC's performance are observable within the Global Cache Block Transfer Rate view. In this view, you can observe the operation of Cache Fusion across the cluster. The constituent metrics are GC CR Blocks Received and GC Current Blocks Received.

The first metric, GC CR Blocks Received, reflects the implementation of read consistency across the entire cluster. In other words, when a SELECT statement is in operation on one node in the cluster, the session will request the data block that contained the data when the query began if another session on any node in the cluster has changed those rows since the query started. If the consistent read request cannot be satisfied from the local buffer cache, but it can be satisfied by shipping a data block from another instance in the cluster, then it is recorded in this metric.

The second metric, GC Current Blocks Received, shows the inter-instance transfer of data blocks that are in a current state. A data block is in a *current state* when it has been created or modified by an INSERT, UPDATE, or DELETE statement. The most recent data reflects that this action resides in the buffer cache of an instance. If this current block is requested and successfully transferred directly to another instance in the cluster, it is recorded in this metric.

The Global Cache Block Transfers and Physical Reads graph compares the number of block transfers across the interconnect with the number of physical reads. Block transfers across the interconnect are usually more efficient than physical reads, so they are favored by RAC, where possible.

The Global Cache Block Transfers and Physical Reads graph is the Active Session History (ASH) from a Cluster Cache Coherency perspective. Figure 12-4 shows an example of this graph. This data can be viewed in realtime or by dragging the shaded box to observe historical data. in the graph directly below on the same page the workload being processed is shown in relation to the events generated. Clicking a particular Cache Coherency event will drill down to a chart and summary data focused upon that particular event.

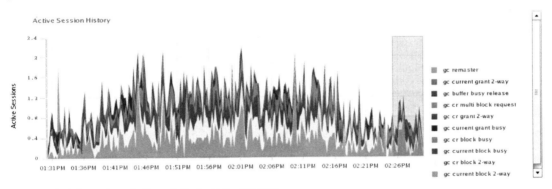

Drag the shaded box to change the time period for the detail section below.

Figure 12-4. The Active Session History graph.

In addition to viewing the Active Session History dynamically with EM, you can also generate reports for information related to time periods for which you are interested. The Active Session History (ASH) is a component of the AWR repository. In addition to reports that can be viewed with EM, the following types of reports can be generated directly: AWR reports, ASH reports, and Automatic Database Diagnostic Monitor (ADDM) reports. We will detail how to do so in the following sections; doing so will enable you to generate these reports, even if the EM graphical interface is not available in a particular environment.

AWR Reports

In this section, we describe the AWR and show how to generate reports from its contents. AWR snapshots of the current values of various database statistics are generated by the MMON background process using non-SQL kernel calls. AWR reporting tools allow you to generate a report in text or HTML format using either EM or SQL*Plus to compare the delta between two snapshots. This can help you determine the database workload during the intervening period.

The AWR is created automatically if you have created the RAC database using DBCA, as detailed in Chapter 10. Alternatively, you can create the AWR manually using the script, $ORACLE_HOME/rdbms/admin/catawr.sql.

A set of tables is created for the AWR under the SYS schema in the SYSAUX tablespace, and the AWR is implemented using three distinct sets of tables in the data dictionary. There are five control tables: WRM$_WR_CONTROL, WRM$_DATABASE_INSTANCE, WRM$_SNAPSHOT, WRM$SNAP_ERROR, and WRM$_BASELINE. There is also a DBA_HIST_% view for each of these tables.

There is also a set of tables to hold the snapshots. These tables have the WRH$ prefix, such as WRH$_SEG_STAT and WRH$_SQL_PLAN. There are approximately 60 of these tables, and each table has a DBA_HIST_% view with a similar name, such as DBA_HIST_SEG_STAT and DBA_HIST_SQL_PLAN.

Baselines are held in a separate set of tables, each of which has the same name as the snapshot table, but with a _BL suffix. For example, the snapshot table is called WRH$_LATCH, while the baseline table is called WRH$_LATCH_BL. There are no DBA_HIST_% views for the baseline tables.

At regular intervals, the MMON background processes trigger a snapshot of the current state of the database. The actual snapshot is performed by a MMON slave processes named M000. By default, snapshots are performed every 60 minutes and retained in the workload repository for seven days, after which they are automatically purged.

AWR snapshots are performed if the STATISTICS_LEVEL parameter is set to the default value of TYPICAL or to ALL. To disable AWR snapshots, you must set the STATISTICS_LEVEL parameter to BASIC; however, we do not recommended doing so because it disables all other forms of statistics gathering.

You can check the current snapshot interval and retention time with this snippet:

```
SQL> SELECT snap_interval, retention FROM dba_hist_wr_control;
```

You can modify these values using the MODIFY_SNAPSHOT_SETTINGS procedure in DBMS_WORKLOAD_REPOSITORY. For example, you can use this line to change the snapshot interval to 30 minutes and set the retention period to two weeks:

```
SQL> EXECUTE dbms_workload_repository.modify_snapshot_settings -
> (interval => 30, retention => 20160);
```

Both the interval and retention parameters should be specified in minutes. If you specify an interval of 0, Oracle will set the snapshot interval to 1 year; if you specify a retention period of 0, Oracle will set the retention period to 100 years.

You can take a snapshot manually at any time for the particular instance you are connected to using the CREATE_SNAPSHOT procedure at the SQL*Plus prompt, as in this example:

```
SQL> EXECUTE dbms_workload_repository.create_snapshot;
```

This procedure can accept a single parameter specifying the flush level for the snapshot, which is either TYPICAL or ALL. You can also create snapshots from within EM; you can access this functionality by navigating from the Administration page to the Workload Repository page, and then to the Snapshots page.

When you have a stable workload, you can take a baseline, which records the difference between two snapshots. First, identify a suitable pair of snapshot IDs using the DBA_HIST_SNAPSHOT view:

```
SQL> SELECT snap_id, instance_number, startup_time,
> begin_interval_time,end_interval_time
> FROM dba_hist_snapshot;
```

Both snapshots must belong to the same instance. They must also have the same instance start-up time. For example, assuming that the start and end snapshots for the period of interest are 234 and 236, you can generate a baseline:

```
SQL> EXECUTE dbms_workload_repository.create_baseline -
> ( -
>    start_snap_id => 234, -
>    end_snap_id => 236, -
>    baseline_name => 'Morning Peak' -
> );
```

You can check the current baselines in the DBA_HIST_BASELINE view. Unlike automatic snapshots, which will be purged at the end of the retention period, baselines will not be removed automatically. Baselines can be removed manually using the DROP_BASELINE procedure:

```
SQL> EXECUTE dbms_workload_repository.drop_baseline -
> ( -
>    baseline_name => 'Morning Peak' -
> );
```

You can extract reports from the AWR tables with the script, $ORACLE_HOME/rdbms/admin/awrrpt.sql. As shown in the following code example, this script asks whether you want the report output to be created in HTML or text format. It then asks you to specify the number of days of snapshots that you wish to view. Based on your response, it displays a list of the snapshots taken during this period. The script prompts you for the start and end snapshots for the report, as well as for a file name to write the report to:

```
SQL> @?/rdbms/admin/awrrpt

Current Instance
~~~~~~~~~~~~~~~~~

  DB Id     DB Name     Inst Num Instance
----------- ------------ -------- ------------
 121667269  PROD               1 PROD1

Specify the Report Type
~~~~~~~~~~~~~~~~~~~~~~~~~
Would you like an HTML report, or a plain text report?
Enter 'html' for an HTML report, or 'text' for plain text
Defaults to 'html'
Enter value for report_type:

Type Specified:  html

Instances in this Workload Repository schema
~~~~~~~~~~~~~~~~~~~~~~~~~~~~~~~~~~~~~~~~~~~~~~~

  DB Id     Inst Num DB Name     Instance     Host
----------- -------- ------------ ------------ ------------
 121667269         2 PROD         PROD2        london2.exam
```

```
                                                ple.com
 * 121667269          1 PROD         PROD1      london1.exam
                                                ple.com

Using  121667269 for database Id
Using            1 for instance number

Specify the number of days of snapshots to choose from
~~~~~~~~~~~~~~~~~~~~~~~~~~~~~~~~~~~~~~~~~~~~~~~~~~~~~~~~~~~
Entering the number of days (n) will result in the most recent
(n) days of snapshots being listed.  Pressing <return> without
specifying a number lists all completed snapshots.

Enter value for num_days:

Listing all Completed Snapshots

                                                        Snap
Instance     DB Name       Snap Id   Snap Started     Level
------------ ------------ --------- ------------------ -----
PROD1        PROD             110 08 Feb 2010 12:46        1
                              111 08 Feb 2010 14:00        1
...
                              278 15 Feb 2010 10:53        1
                              279 15 Feb 2010 10:58        1

Specify the Begin and End Snapshot Ids
~~~~~~~~~~~~~~~~~~~~~~~~~~~~~~~~~~~~~~~~~~
Enter value for begin_snap:278
Begin Snapshot Id specified: 278

Enter value for end_snap: 279
End   Snapshot Id specified: 279

Specify the Report Name
~~~~~~~~~~~~~~~~~~~~~~~~~~
The default report file name is awrrpt_1_278_279.html.  To use this name,
press <return> to continue, otherwise enter an alternative.

Enter value for report_name:

Using the report name awrrpt_1_278_279.html
...
Report written to awrrpt_1_278_279.html
```

If no file name is specified, a default name based on the start and end snapshots will be used. Keep in mind that you cannot create valid reports for a period during which an instance shutdown has been performed.

The awrrpt.sql script will only generate an AWR report for the instance to which you are connected. In a RAC environment, if you wish to generate an AWR report for another node in the cluster, you should use the awrrpti.sql script instead. This script prompts you for the same information as the standard script. However, it also gives you the option of specifying both the Database ID and the instance. Thus it lets you generate a report for any instance in the cluster without needing to run the command from the individual nodes:

```
SQL> @?/rdbms/admin/awrrpti
...
Instances in this Workload Repository schema
~~~~~~~~~~~~~~~~~~~~~~~~~~~~~~~~~~~~~~~~~~~~~~~

   DB Id    Inst Num DB Name      Instance     Host
------------ -------- ------------ ------------ ------------
  121667269        2 PROD         PROD2        london2.exam
                                               ple.com
* 121667269        1 PROD         PROD1        london1.exam
                                               ple.com

Enter value for dbid:121667269
Using  for database Id
Enter value for inst_num: 2
...
```

Interpreting the RAC Statistics of an AWR Report

You have now generated an AWR report to review the statistics captured across a period of time for an instance. If you're reviewing the performance, you can and should generate reports for all instances within the cluster. The statistics contained within a report are for one instance only, and this instance and the host environment will be recorded directly under the section heading, "WORKLOAD REPOSITORY report for":

```
WORKLOAD REPOSITORY report for

DB Name       DB Id        Instance     Inst Num Startup Time    Release      RAC
------------ ----------- ------------ -------- --------------- ----------- ---
PROD         121667269 PROD1                 1 12-Feb-10 13:36 11.2.0.1.0  YES

Host Name       Platform                             CPUs Cores Sockets Memory(GB)
--------------- ------------------------------------ ---- ----- ------- ----------
london1.example. Linux x86 64-bit                       8     8       2      15.66
```

Please take some time to examine the "Load Profile" section of this report. In particular, you should make sure that it covers the expected period and that meaningful activity has taken place on the database during this period.

■ **Note** In the following sections, we concentrate on the differences between an AWR report for a single-instance database and a RAC database. Much of the content of an AWR report is identical for both.

Within an AWR report, there are two main sections containing RAC statistics. The first section appears immediately after the "Top 5 Timed Foreground Events" and includes Global Cache Load Profile, Global Cache Efficiency Percentages, Global Cache and Enqueue Services (Workload Characteristics, Global Cache, and Enqueue Services), Messaging Statistics, and the Cluster interconnect. The second section appears at the end of the report, and it includes Global Messaging Statistics, Global CR Served Stats and Global CURRENT Served Stats, Global Cache Transfer Statistics and Transfer Times, Interconnect Latency, and Throughput and Dynamic Remastering Stats.

Top 5 Timed Foreground Events

The "Top 5 Timed Foreground Events" section will normally show the amount of CPU consumed in addition to the top four wait events. For a given workload, this list of events should be relatively stable; you should investigate any significant variation. You will generally see CPU at the top of the list. However, CPU usage is not necessarily an indication of a healthy system, as the application may be CPU-bound. The most common wait events are db file sequential read, db file scattered read, db file parallel read, and log file sync.

For RAC databases, watch for wait events related to Global Cache Service (GCS), which are identified by the prefix gc or the Cluster wait. In a RAC environment, you should expect to see GCS events, but they should not be consuming the majority of the time on the system. The following example shows the Top 5 Timed Foreground Events from a RAC system that is experiencing a degree of inter-instance activity:

```
Top 5 Timed Foreground Events
~~~~~~~~~~~~~~~~~~~~~~~~~~~~~~~~~~~~

                                              Avg
                                             wait   % DB
Event                         Waits  Time(s) (ms)   time Wait Class
----------------------------  ------ ------- ------ ----- ----------
DB CPU                                   588         28.4
enq: TX - row lock contention 41,498     293    7   14.2 Applicatio
log file sync                 126,489    231    2   11.1 Commit
gc current block 2-way        409,784    230    1   11.1 Cluster
gc cr block 2-way             407,726    220    1   10.6 Cluster
```

If your global cache events are prominent—and, in particular, if they appear above CPU time in the report—then this is an indication that you should drill down in the RAC statistics further to identify whether the amount of global cache traffic can be reduced.

Immediately after the "Top 5 Timed Foreground Events" section, the first RAC-specific section summarizes the number of instances for the start and end snapshots, as in this example:

```
                     Begin   End
                     -----  -----
Number of Instances:   2      2
```

Differing values indicate that an instance has been started or stopped during the snapshot period. If the number of instances is equal at the end of the period, this does not mean that one or more instances have joined or left the cluster during the snapshot period. Starting and stopping instances causes a higher than normal level of inter-instance messaging; therefore, the report should be treated with caution.

Global Cache Load Profile

This section of the AWR report presents a summary of the traffic across the interconnect in terms of blocks exchanged by GCS and messages exchanged by both GCS and Global Enqueue Service (GES). Consider this example:

```
Global Cache Load Profile
~~~~~~~~~~~~~~~~~~~~~~~~~~~~~             Per Second       Per Transaction
                                         ---------------   ---------------
      Global Cache blocks received:         3,510.45                  5.81
        Global Cache blocks served:         3,526.89                  5.84
         GCS/GES messages received:         7,447.04                 12.32
             GCS/GES messages sent:         6,774.80                 11.21
                DBWR Fusion writes:           578.61                  0.96
     Estd Interconnect traffic (KB)        59,076.44
```

Pay particular attention to the estimated interconnect traffic per second value at the end of this section. You should reference this value against the bandwidth of your network interconnect to ensure that your configuration has sufficient capacity for your requirements. In this example, utilization is 59MB/sec of a gigabit Ethernet interconnect, which has a theoretical maximum limit of 100MB/sec. Thus, this example shows a reasonably high level of utilization.

Global Cache Efficiency Percentages

This section of the AWR report shows the percentage of blocks accessed from local cache, remote cache, and disk. In an optimum system, the percentage of local cache accesses should approach 100%, while the percentage of remote cache accesses and disk accesses should both approach 0%. The following example shows a level of efficiency in terms of the percentages that you should expect to see:

```
Global Cache Efficiency Percentages (Target local+remote 100%)
~~~~~~~~~~~~~~~~~~~~~~~~~~~~~~~~~~~~~~~~~~~~~~~~~~~~~~~~~~~~~~~~~~
Buffer access -  local cache %:    94.38
Buffer access - remote cache %:     5.52
Buffer access -         disk %:     0.10
```

Bear in mind that it may take longer to read a block from disk than from a remote cache, although advancements in disk technology such as Solid State Disks (SSDs), are likely to reduce the margin of advantage towards the interconnect (see Chapter 4 for more information on SSDs). Therefore, you should concentrate on reducing both the amount of disk I/O and the global cache communication.

Global Cache and Enqueue Services - Workload Characteristics

This section of the AWR report describes the average times required to perform various GCS and GES tasks:

```
Global Cache and Enqueue Services - Workload Characteristics
~~~~~~~~~~~~~~~~~~~~~~~~~~~~~~~~~~~~~~~~~~~~~~~~~~~~~~~~~~~~~~~~
                Avg global enqueue get time (ms):     0.3
```

```
            Avg global cache cr block receive time (ms):       1.2
       Avg global cache current block receive time (ms):       1.0

             Avg global cache cr block build time (ms):        0.0
              Avg global cache cr block send time (ms):        0.0
        Global cache log flushes for cr blocks served %:       4.5
             Avg global cache cr block flush time (ms):        1.6

           Avg global cache current block pin time (ms):       0.1
          Avg global cache current block send time (ms):       0.0
   Global cache log flushes for current blocks served %:       3.2
         Avg global cache current block flush time (ms):       2.0
```

Of these statistics, the most significant are the enqueue get time, which should ideally be below 1 ms; and the global cache cr and current block receive times.

Global Cache and Enqueue Services - Messaging Statistics

The "Global Cache and Enqueue Services" section of the AWR report describes average time to exchange different categories of inter-instance messages, as in this example:

```
Global Cache and Enqueue Services - Messaging Statistics
~~~~~~~~~~~~~~~~~~~~~~~~~~~~~~~~~~~~~~~~~~~~~~~~~~~~~~~~~~~~
                      Avg message sent queue time (ms):      0.1
              Avg message sent queue time on ksxp (ms):      0.6
                  Avg message received queue time (ms):      0.0
                      Avg GCS message process time (ms):     0.0
                      Avg GES message process time (ms):     0.0

                          % of direct sent messages:        65.85
                          % of indirect sent messages:      33.18
                          % of flow controlled messages:     0.96
```

Cluster Interconnect

The "Cluster Interconnect" section of the report should be used to confirm that the interconnect network is running across the configured private interconnect, as opposed to a public network:

```
Cluster Interconnect
~~~~~~~~~~~~~~~~~~~~~~
                                    Begin                             End
            --------------------------------------------------   -----------
Interface   IP Address     Pub Source                            IP  Pub Src
----------  ---------------  ---  --------------------------------  --- --- ---
eth1        192.168.1.1     N    Oracle Cluster Repository
```

Foreground Wait Class

The "Foreground Wait Class" enables you to observe wait events in a grouped manner, as opposed to individual wait events. Thus it provides a simpler diagnosis on where performance issues may lie. In the following example, nearly 40% of all wait events are related to cluster activity; these events are likely to be impacting performance:

```
Foreground Wait Class                     DB/Inst: PROD/PROD1  Snaps: 278-279
```

Wait Class	Waits	%Time -outs	Total Wait Time (s)	Avg wait (ms)	%DB time
Cluster	1,068,216	0	814	1	39.3
DB CPU			588		28.4
Application	41,503	0	293	7	14.2
Commit	126,489	0	231	2	11.1
User I/O	17,300	0	73	4	3.5
Configuration	198	0	26	131	1.3
Other	1,050,015	0	20	0	1.0
Concurrency	8,493	2	4	0	0.2
Network	141,279	0	0	0	0.0
System I/O	87	0	0	0	0.0

Wait Event Histogram

The "Wait Event Histogram" section enables you to observe all RAC-related wait events. It shows the time consumed by the wait events, which are grouped into classes by the time consumed. These wait events range from less than 1 millisecond to longer than a second. In the following example, you can see that block busy and congested related events consume the most time on an individual event basis:

Event	Total Waits	<1ms	<2ms	<4ms	<8ms	<16ms	<32ms	<=1s	>1s
...									
gc cr block 2-way	407.3	91.3	5.9	2.4	.4	.0	.0	.0	
gc cr block busy	27.9K	25.4	50.1	16.8	3.3	2.3	1.8	.3	
gc cr block congested	644	66.5	9.0	15.5	8.9	.2			
gc cr block lost	2							100.0	
gc cr failure	377	91.5	5.6	2.7	.3				
gc cr grant 2-way	7309	91.8	5.6	2.2	.3	.0			
gc cr grant congested	13	53.8	7.7	15.4	23.1				
gc cr multi block request	77.3K	97.4	1.8	.8	.1	.0	.0	.0	
gc current block 2-way	410.2	91.1	6.1	2.4	.3	.0	.0	.0	.0
gc current block busy	18.6K	19.3	31.0	16.7	14.4	13.4	3.0	2.1	.0
gc current block congested	669	68.5	7.9	14.5	9.0			.1	
gc current block lost	1							100.0	
...									

"SQL Statement" Sections

The AWR report contains a series of sections listing SQL statements in the library cache that exceed predefined thresholds. The report does not show the statements per se, but it does show their statement ID numbers. Of particular interest to RAC users are the SQL statements ordered in the "By Cluster Wait Time" section, which details the amount of time a statement was involved in waits for cluster resources. The cluster wait time is reported as a percentage of total elapsed time for the statement, along with the elapsed time, CPU time, and number of executions.

For example, the statement being reported on in the following extract has experienced 384.3 seconds of cluster wait time over 61,113 executions, and the cluster wait time represents 47% of total elapsed time, which is significant enough to warrant further investigation. To do so, you should note the SQL Id used as input into the awrsqlrpt.sql script, as explained later in this chapter:

```
SQL ordered by Cluster Wait Time        DB/Inst: PROD/PROD1  Snaps: 278-279
      Cluster                     Elapsed
 Wait Time (s) Executions %Total  Time(s)  %Clu   %CPU   %IO    SQL Id
 -------------- ---------- ------ ---------- ------ ------ ------ -------------
        384.3      61,113   47.8     804.5   47.2   37.8    1.7  16dhat4ta7xs9
Module: wish8.5@loadgen1 (TNS V1-V3)
begin neword(:no_w_id,:no_max_w_id,:no_d_id,:no_c_id,:no_o_ol_cnt,
:no_c_discount,:no_c_last,:no_c_credit,:no_d_tax,:no_w_tax,:no_d_next_o_id,
TO_DATE(:timestamp,'YYYYMMDDHH24MISS')); END;
```

RAC-Related Segment Statistics

It is possible to observe the RAC-related segment statistics when viewed in combination with the SQL related data. These statistics include: global cache buffer busy, CR blocks received, and current blocks received. In the following example, you can observe that a large degree of the Global Cache Busy related statistics are generated by SQL running against the WAREHOUSE table and the CR and Current Blocks against the STOCK table:

```
Segments by Global Cache Buffer Busy      DB/Inst: PROD/PROD1  Snaps: 278-279

                                                          GC
           Tablespace                   Subobject  Obj.  Buffer   % of
Owner        Name    Object Name          Name     Type   Busy  Capture
--------   ---------- ------------------ ---------- ----- ------------ -------
TPCC       TPCCTAB    WAREHOUSE                     TABLE  6,199   55.66
TPCC       TPCCTAB    INORD                         INDEX  3,440   30.89
TPCC       TPCCTAB    ORDERS                        TABLE    630    5.66
TPCC       TPCCTAB    IORDL                         INDEX    441    3.96
TPCC       TPCCTAB    DISTRICT                      TABLE    251    2.25

Segments by CR Blocks Received            DB/Inst: PROD/PROD1  Snaps: 278-279

                                                           CR
           Tablespace                   Subobject  Obj.   Blocks
Owner        Name    Object Name          Name     Type  Received  %Total
--------   ---------- ------------------ ---------- ----- ------------ -------
TPCC       TPCCTAB    STOCK                         TABLE 321,799   54.74
```

TPCC	TPCCTAB	CUSTOMER		TABLE	97,031	16.51
TPCC	TPCCTAB	INORD		INDEX	61,230	10.42
TPCC	TPCCTAB	IORDL		INDEX	38,203	6.50
TPCC	TPCCTAB	ORDERS		TABLE	17,544	2.98

Segments by Current Blocks Received   DB/Inst: PROD/PROD1 Snaps: 278-279

Owner	Tablespace Name	Object Name	Subobject Name	Obj. Type	Current Blocks Received	%Total
TPCC	TPCCTAB	STOCK		TABLE	220,543	45.90
TPCC	TPCCTAB	IORDL		INDEX	57,394	11.94
TPCC	TPCCTAB	INORD		INDEX	42,573	8.86
TPCC	TPCCTAB	DISTRICT		TABLE	38,989	8.11
TPCC	TPCCTAB	CUSTOMER		TABLE	37,746	7.86

Dictionary Cache Stats (RAC)

For RAC instances, a subsection of the "Dictionary Cache Stats" section reports the number of GES requests, conflicts, and releases for each object type, as in this example:

Dictionary Cache Stats (RAC)   DB/Inst: PROD/PROD1 Snaps: 278-279

Cache	GES Requests	GES Conflicts	GES Releases
dc_awr_control	2	2	0
dc_objects	10	0	6
dc_segments	10	12	0
dc_sequences	26	3	0

In this report, you should look for an excessive numbers of GES conflicts, especially for sequences.

Library Cache Activity (RAC)

For RAC instances, a subsection of the "Library Cache Activity" section reports the number of GES lock requests, pin requests, pin releases, invalidation requests, and invalidations. Here's an example of that subsection:

Library Cache Activity (RAC)   DB/Inst: PROD/PROD1 Snaps: 278-279

Namespace	GES Lock Requests	GES Pin Requests	GES Pin Releases	GES Inval Requests	GES Invali- dations
BODY	0	69,471	69,471	0	0
CLUSTER	3	3	3	0	0

DBLINK	20	0	0	0	0
EDITION	18	18	18	0	0
INDEX	84	84	84	0	0
QUEUE	0	223	223	0	0
RULESET	0	4	4	0	0
SCHEMA	16	0	0	0	0
SUBSCRIPTION	0	2	2	0	0
TABLE/PROCEDURE	1,089	211,136	211,136	0	0
TRIGGER	0	89	89	0	0

Global Messaging Statistics

In the event that any serious Global Messaging problems appear in the "Top 5 Timed Foreground Events" or in the "Wait Events" sections, the "Global Messaging Statistics" section can be used to investigate further , as in this example:

```
Global Messaging Statistics          DB/Inst: PROD/PROD1  Snaps: 278-279

Statistic                          Total   per Second   per Trans
--------------------------------  -------  -----------  -----------
acks for commit broadcast(actual)   99,813       328.0         0.5
acks for commit broadcast(logical  191,511       629.2         1.0
broadcast msgs on commit(actual)   154,497       507.6         0.8
broadcast msgs on commit(logical)  159,559       524.3         0.9
broadcast msgs on commit(wasted)    36,032       118.4         0.2
broadcast on commit wait time(ms)    6,075        20.0         0.0
broadcast on commit waits            9,799        32.2         0.1
```

Global CR Served Statistics

The "Global CR Served Statistics" section contains the statistics for the number of blocks served by GCS. These statistics give an overview of GCS activity during the reporting period, and they are derived from the V$CR_BLOCK_SERVER dynamic performance view, as in this example:

```
Global CR Served Stats               DB/Inst: PROD/PROD1  Snaps: 278-279

Statistic                      Total
----------------------------  ------------------
CR Block Requests                566,707
CURRENT Block Requests            29,833
Data Block Requests              566,710
Undo Block Requests                3,317
TX Block Requests                 26,341
```

Global Current Served Statistics

The "Global Current Served Statistics" section of the AWR report contains histograms of the GCS operations required to support current read requests, including block pinning, flushing redo to disk, and write operations. The report is derived from the V$CURRENT_BLOCK_SERVER dynamic performance view. You should check this view if you believe that Cache Fusion is causing a bottleneck on systems with high levels of DML activity, as in this example:

```
Global CURRENT Served Stats             DB/Inst: PROD/PROD1  Snaps: 278-279
-> Pins    = CURRENT Block Pin Operations
-> Flushes = Redo Flush before CURRENT Block Served Operations
-> Writes  = CURRENT Block Fusion Write Operations

Statistic       Total   % <1ms  % <10ms % <100ms   % <1s   % <10s
----------  ----------  -------  -------  --------  -------  -------
Pins           477,147   99.65     0.32      0.02     0.01     0.00
Flushes         15,128   51.65    44.53      3.81     0.00     0.00
Writes         176,102    0.23    15.83     26.38    57.18     0.38
```

Global Cache Transfer Statistics

The "Global Cache Transfer Statistics" section of the report gives an overview of Global Cache transfer activity for each class of database buffer, as in the following example. This data is derived from the V$INSTANCE_CACHE_TRANSFER dynamic performance view; it is especially useful in diagnosing whether cache transfer activity is affected by contention or a high level of system load. You can use this data to analyze both circumstances. For Clusters with more than two nodes, these statistics can also be used to determine the impact of messaging between multiple nodes in the cluster:

```
Global Cache Transfer Stats             DB/Inst: PROD/PROD1  Snaps: 278-279
                            CR                        Current
                  ---------------------------  ---------------------------
Inst Block        Blocks    %      %     %     Blocks    %      %     %
No   Class        Received Immed Busy Congst Received Immed Busy Congst
---- ----------   -------- ------ ------ ------ -------- ------ ------ ------
  2 data block     556,975  95.6   3.2   1.2  478,247  95.8   3.7    .5
  2 undo header     27,929  66.7  33.2    .1    1,717  52.6  47.4    .0
  2 undo block       2,894  68.6  31.3    .0        0   N/A   N/A   N/A
  2 Others            181  97.8   1.7    .6      653  98.9    .6    .5
...

Global Cache DB/Inst: PROD/PROD1  Snaps: 278-279
-> Blocks Lost, 2-hop and 3-hop Average times in (ms)
-> ordered by CR + Current Blocks Received desc

                     CR Avg Time (ms)        Current Avg Time (ms)
                 ---------------------------  ---------------------------
Src  Block   Lost
Inst Class   Time  Immed   2hop   3hop    Immed   2hop   3hop
---- -------- -----  ----------  -------- --------  ----------  -------- --------
  2 data blo          1.1    1.1    N/A      0.8    0.8    N/A
  2 undo hea          0.6    0.6    N/A      0.7    0.7    N/A
  2 undo blo          0.6    0.6    N/A      N/A    N/A    N/A
  2 others            0.6    0.6    N/A      0.6    0.6    N/A
```

Interconnect Statistics

The "Interconnect Statistics" section enables you to observe the latency and throughput of your interconnect against the potential of the hardware selected for your cluster (see Chapter 4 for more information on this). You can use these statistics to determine whether the physical interconnect infrastructure is a bottleneck in your environment.

The following example shows the Interconnect Statistics section of the report. It provides ping latency statistics, throughput by client statistics, and device statistics:

```
Interconnect Ping Latency Stats          DB/Inst: PROD/PROD1 Snaps: 278-279
    Target 500B Pin Avg Latency      Stddev  8K Ping Avg Latency       Stddev
    Instance   Count    500B msg   500B msg    Count       8K msg      8K msg
    --------- -------- ----------- ----------- -------- ----------- -----------
           1       24         .14         .03       24         .12         .03
           2       24         .49         .56       24         .59         .54

Interconnect Throughput by Client        DB/Inst: PROD/PROD1 Snaps: 278-279
-> Throughput of interconnect usage by major consumers
-> All throughput numbers are megabytes per second

                          Send       Receive
Used By              Mbytes/sec    Mbytes/sec
----------------    -----------   -----------
Global Cache              24.93         24.78
Parallel Query              .00           .00
DB Locks                   1.88          2.04
DB Streams                  .00           .00
Other                       .00           .00
```

Dynamic Remastering Statistics

The "Dynamic Remastering Statistics" section gives you information on the internal Oracle workload in the mastering or ownership of the status of the Database objects. You also get information on Oracle workload reconfiguration, which you can use to help reduce the amount of messaging required by your workload, as in this example:

```
Dynamic Remastering Stats                DB/Inst: PROD/PROD1 Snaps: 278-279
-> times are in seconds
-> Affinity objects - objects mastered due to affinity at begin/end snap

                                              per      Begin      End
Name                          Total   Remaster Op      Snap     Snap
-------------------------   --------- ------------- -------- --------
remaster ops                        1          1.00
remastered objects                  2          2.00
replayed locks received        92,841     92,841.00
replayed locks sent           131,129    131,129.00
resources cleaned                   0          0.00
remaster time (s)                 3.3          3.30
quiesce time (s)                  1.6          1.55
```

freeze time (s)	0.0	0.01	
cleanup time (s)	0.4	0.36	
replay time (s)	0.6	0.58	
fixwrite time (s)	0.2	0.19	
sync time (s)	0.6	0.60	
affinity objects	N/A	7	5

Active Session History

The Active Session History (ASH) is a component of the AWR repository. ASH samples all sessions once per second and records information about those sessions that are currently waiting. This information is used by ADDM to classify any problems that have been identified.

For example, ADDM may be aware that a significant amount of time is being consumed waiting for I/O through waits for db file sequential read. ASH can identify the specific files and blocks that are causing the waits. This data is used by ADDM to produce more accurate recommendations.

ASH acquires information directly by sampling the session state objects. The default sampling interval is 1,000 milliseconds (1 second). ASH only records information about active sessions. It does not include information about recursive sessions or sessions waiting for idle events.

The information collected by ASH is flushed to disk periodically. By default, only one out of every ten active session samples is flushed to disk. Information flushed from the ASH buffer to disk is written to the workload repository history table, WRH$ACTIVE_SESSION_HISTORY, which is owned by SYS and stored in the SYSAUX tablespace.

Previously, you saw how you can use the EM interface to dynamically view ASH-based information. Additionally, a script is provided to report on the contents of the ASH repository. You can find this script in $ORACLE_HOME/rdbms/admin/ashrpt.sql. The script should be run in SQL*Plus, as in this example:

```
SQL> @?/rdbms/admin/ashrpt

Current Instance
~~~~~~~~~~~~~~~~~

  DB Id     DB Name      Inst Num Instance
----------- ------------ -------- ------------
 121667269 PROD                1 PROD1


Specify the Report Type
~~~~~~~~~~~~~~~~~~~~~~~~~
Enter 'html' for an HTML report, or 'text' for plain text
Defaults to 'html'
Enter value for report_type:

Type Specified:  html


Instances in this Workload Repository schema
~~~~~~~~~~~~~~~~~~~~~~~~~~~~~~~~~~~~~~~~~~~~~~~

  DB Id      Inst Num DB Name      Instance     Host
----------- -------- ------------ ------------ ------------
```

```
    121667269          2 PROD          PROD2          london2.exam
                                                      ple.com

  * 121667269          1 PROD          PROD1          london1.exam
                                                      ple.com


Defaults to current database

Using database id: 121667269

Enter instance numbers. Enter 'ALL' for all instances in a
RAC cluster or explicitly specify list of instances (e.g., 1,2,3).
Defaults to current instance.

Using instance number(s): 1
...
Summary of All User Input
-------------------------
Format          : HTML
DB Id           : 121667269
Inst num        : 1
Begin time      : 15-Feb-10 11:03:01
End time        : 15-Feb-10 11:18:02
Slot width      : Default
Report targets  : 0
Report name     : ashrpt_1_0215_1118.html
```

Much as when generating an AWR, by default ashrpt.sql will generate a report for the local instance only. To generate a report for an alternate instance, you can use the ashrpti.sql script. The script will generate output in HTML or text format, and you can specify a time-based interval for the duration of the period covered by the report. You specify this interval in minutes, which is 15 minutes by default. The following example shows the heading section of the generated ASH report:

```
ASH Report For PROD/PROD1

DB Name        DB Id       Instance      Inst Num Release       RAC Host
------------  -----------  ------------  -------- -----------   --- ------------
PROD          121667269 PROD1                  1 11.2.0.1.0  YES london1.exam

CPUs          SGA Size       Buffer Cache       Shared Pool      ASH Buffer Size
----  ----------------  ------------------  ------------------   ------------------
   8    8,155M (100%)      6,656M (81.6%)     1,344M (16.5%)        15.5M (0.2%)
```

The first section of the ASH report describes the environment in which the report was created, including the database, instance, release, node, and the number of CPUs. It also describes the sizes of the SGA, buffer cache, shared pool, and ASH buffer. The remainder of the report details the information specific to sessions active during the period of time for which the report was generated, and you should look for cluster-related activity within this session information.

Automatic Database Diagnostic Monitor

The Automatic Database Diagnostic Monitor (ADDM) uses data captured in the AWR to diagnose database performance, identify any problems, and suggest potential solutions. ADDM is built directly into the kernel, which minimizes any performance overhead.

ADDM analyzes database performance holistically. In other words, it considers all activity across the database before making recommendations about specific areas of the workload.

Executing an ADDM Report

ADDM runs automatically after each AWR snapshot, and the results are saved in the database. If ADDM detects any issues, then alerts are generated that can be inspected in the EM tools.

You can also run an ADDM report manually using the following script:

```
$ORACLE_HOME/rdbms/admin/addmrpt.sql
```

This script is similar to those used to generate AWR reports. It prompts for a start and end snapshot, as well as for the name of an output file. If no output file name is specified, then the report will be written to a file called:

```
addmrpt_<instance>_<start_snapshot>_<stop_snapshot>.txt
```

For example, the file name with its bracketed information filled in might look like this:

```
addmrpt_1_278_279.txt
```

Although the procedure for running ADDM reports is similar to that used with AWR reports, the content of an ADDM report is significantly different.

Controlling ADDM

The DBMS_ADVISOR and DBMS_ADDM packages allow you to control ADDM. The simplest way to access the DBMS_ADVISOR package is from EM, which shows a complete performance overview, including any recommendations, on a single page. The addmprt.sql script also calls the DBMS_ADVISOR package, allowing you to access ADDM manually. You can access the DBMS_ADVISOR API directly using PL/SQL calls. In addition to DBMS_ADVISOR, the DBMS_ADDM package enables the generation of reports for all instances of a RAC environment.

ADDM stores information in a set of tables owned by SYS in the SYSAUX tablespace. The base tables have a prefix of WRI$%. These tables are accessible through a number of views with the prefix, DBA_ADVISOR_%.

ADDM needs at least two snapshots in the AWR before it can perform any analysis. The ADDM report header describes the analysis period, database and instance names, hostname, and database version:

```
ADDM Report for Task 'TASK_875'
-------------------------------
```

```
Analysis Period
---------------
AWR snapshot range from 278 to 279.
Time period starts at 15-FEB-10 10.39.53 AM
Time period ends at 15-FEB-10 10.58.19 AM

Analysis Target
---------------
Database 'PROD' with DB ID 121667269.
Database version 11.2.0.1.0.
ADDM performed an analysis of instance PROD1, numbered 1 and hosted at
london1.example.com.

Activity During the Analysis Period
-----------------------------------
Total database time was 2068 seconds.
The average number of active sessions was 1.87.

Summary of Findings
-------------------
Description                              Active Sessions      Recommendations
                                         Percent of Activity
---------------------------------------  -------------------  --------------

1  Top SQL Statements                      1.1 |  59.02       8
2  Global Cache Messaging                   .72 |  38.46       1
3  Top Segments by "User I/O" and "Cluster" .71 |  37.74       5
4  Buffer Busy - Hot Objects                .29 |  15.73       0
5  Row Lock Waits                           .26 |  14.17       2
6  Commits and Rollbacks                    .22 |  11.72       2
```

The header specifies the measured time period, and the ADDM report is based on this statistic. The report header also summarizes the average database load during the snapshot period and a summary of the findings.

The DBMS_ADDM package provides similar functionality, except for multiple instances in a RAC environment. For example, calling DBMS_ADDM.ANALYZE_DB with the database name and start and end snapshot ids enables the analysis of all of the instances in the cluster. DBMS_ADDM.ANALYZE_INST does the analysis on one instance in the cluster, while DBMS_ADDM.ANALYZE_PARTIAL does the analysis on a selected number of instances in the cluster. For example, the following excerpt shows the generation of a partial report for instances 1, 2, and 3 of a 4-node cluster:

```
Begin
    :name := 'Partial ADDM RAC';   dbms_addm.analyze_partial(:name,'1,2,3',1012,1387);
End;
```

```
set long 1000000 pagesize 0;
select dbms_addm.get_report(:name) from dual;
```

The Report Format

An ADDM report is divided up into findings, which are listed in descending order of their perceived impact on database time. The following example shows a finding from an ADDM report. The finding highlights RAC-based wait events under the "Cluster wait" category. In this case, the recommendation was to investigate an UPDATE statement responsible for a significant proportion of the cluster wait time:

```
Finding 2: Global Cache Messaging
Impact is 2.62 active sessions, 38.46% of total activity.
------------------------------------------------------------
Inter-instance messaging was consuming significant database time on this
instance.

    Recommendation 1: Application Analysis
    Estimated benefit is .72 active sessions, 38.46% of total activity.
    ------------------------------------------------------------
    Action
        Look at the "Top SQL Statements" finding for SQL statements consuming
        significant time on Cluster waits. For example, the UPDATE statement
        with SQL_ID "82tfppq8s0dc2" is responsible for 20% of Cluster wait
        during the analysis period.

    Symptoms That Led to the Finding:
    ----------------------------------
        Wait class "Cluster" was consuming significant database time.
        Impact is .74 active sessions, 39.33% of total activity.
```

AWR SQL Report

If your performance monitoring investigations with AWR and ADDM reports reveal particular SQL Statements to investigate, you can view these in detail with this script:

```
$ORACLE_HOME/rdbms/admin/awrsqrpt.sql
```

You run the script just as you would to generate an AWR, except that in this case you specify a particular SQL ID. For example, this ID might be identified by the AWR report's "SQL Statements" section or an ADDM report:

```
SQL> @?/rdbms/admin/awrsqrpt

...

Specify the Begin and End Snapshot Ids
~~~~~~~~~~~~~~~~~~~~~~~~~~~~~~~~~~~~~~~~~
Enter value for begin_snap: 278
Begin Snapshot Id specified: 278
```

```
Enter value for end_snap: 279
End    Snapshot Id specified: 279

Specify the SQL Id
~~~~~~~~~~~~~~~~~~
Enter value for sql_id: 16dhat4ta7x

...
```

Viewing the SQL Report provides a summary of the AWR Report capture period, the SQL ID, and the Elapsed time. In following example, the SQL ID identified in the AWR report is a simple UPDATE statement:

```
WORKLOAD REPOSITORY SQL Report

Snapshot Period Summary

DB Name         DB Id     Instance     Inst Num Startup Time    Release       RAC
------------ ----------- ------------- -------- --------------- ----------- ---
PROD         121667269 PROD1                 1 12-Feb-10 13:36 11.2.0.1.0  YES

                 Snap Id     Snap Time       Sessions Curs/Sess
                 --------- ------------------- -------- ---------
Begin Snap:      278 15-Feb-10 10:53:14          55      2.9
  End Snap:      279 15-Feb-10 10:58:18          55      2.9
  Elapsed:              5.07 (mins)
  DB Time:             34.47 (mins)

SQL Summary                              DB/Inst: PROD/PROD1  Snaps: 278-279

                  Elapsed
   SQL Id        Time (ms)
------------- ----------
g5u7xuchhfu62   293,546
Module: wish8.5@loadgen1 (TNS V1-V3)
UPDATE WAREHOUSE SET W_YTD = W_YTD + :B2 WHERE W_ID = :B1
...
```

The remainder of the report details the SQL Plan statistics, the Execution Plan, and the full SQL Statement, which is useful when longer statements are truncated within the AWR report.

In our examples, we have used the information from the AWR to pinpoint a workload with significant cluster wait class activity. This activity is due to a number of UPDATE statements being processed by a several sessions simultaneously running the same UPDATE statement on multiple nodes at the same time.

Performance Monitoring Using SQL*Plus

Since early versions of Oracle 7, the two main sources of information for performance tuning an Oracle database have been system statistics and wait events. Both have been extended with additional statistics and events in subsequent releases. In releases up to and including 11g, the kernel has been much more thoroughly instrumented. This has resulted in a large increase in the number of latches and wait events that are individually reported. Execution time information is also available in the form of time-based metrics.

GV$ Views

Before reviewing the SQL*Plus queries, we will briefly review the relationship between the X$ tables, GV$ views, and V$ views. All are compiled into the Oracle executable and exist for both single-instance and RAC databases.

X$ tables present instance or session memory structures as tables. Although they still exist, RAC-specific X$ tables are not populated for single-instance databases; instead, X$ tables are defined in V$FIXED_TABLE.

GV$ views are also built into the Oracle executable. Therefore, they exist for all databases (including single-instance ones), and they reference the X$ tables.

The standard V$ views are also built into the Oracle executable. In general, V$ views do not directly reference X$ tables; instead, they generally use them indirectly through GV$ views, using queries of the following form:

```
SELECT <column_list>
FROM gv$<view_name>
WHERE inst_id = USERENV ('INSTANCE');
```

Both the GV$ and V$ views are defined in V$FIXED_VIEW_DEFINITION.

In a RAC environment, a number of additional synonyms for GV$ and V$ views are created by the script, $ORACLE_HOME/rdbms/admin/catclust.sql.

GV$ views include the instance number. When they are queried, the query is executed separately on all active instances using parallel execution. The results are merged on the instance initiating the query. GV$ views are not meaningful in a few cases because the views are derived from the control files. Because the control files are shared between all instances, the GV$ views return with duplicate sets of rows from each instance. For these views, we recommend using the local V$ dynamic performance views instead.

System Statistics

System statistics are maintained in each instance. They are reported in a number of dynamic performance views, including V$SYSSTAT, V$SESSTAT, and V$MYSTAT. In Oracle 11g, a subset of service statistics is also reported at a session level in V$SERVICE_STATS.

Segment Statistics

Segment statistics were introduced in Oracle 9.2. They provide a powerful mechanism you can use to identify which objects are subject to I/O or contention. Prior to the introduction of segment statistics, this information could only be obtained using an event 10046 level 8 trace or by polling the V$SYSTEM_WAIT dynamic performance view. The level of granularity is the object, so you may still need to use the 10046 trace if you need to identify a specific block or set of blocks.

Segment statistics are maintained in all databases when the value of the STATISTICS_LEVEL parameter is TYPICAL or ALL. Three statistics report global cache activity at the object level, and you can use these to quickly pinpoint the segments in your database that are experiencing the highest levels of inter-instance activity: gc cr blocks received, gc current blocks received, and gc buffer busy. You should be familiar with the first two statistics from the charts displayed in EM. The additional statistic, gc buffer busy, shows the segments that are experiencing levels of contention between instances.

The following example shows the global cache activity for the table segments of a schema named TPCC:

```
SQL> li
  1  SELECT
  2    table_name                AS "Table Name",
  3    gc_buffer_busy            AS "Buffer Busy",
  4    gc_cr_blocks_received     AS "CR Blocks Received",
  5    gc_current_blocks_received AS "Current Blocks Received"
  6  FROM
  7  (
  8    SELECT table_name FROM dba_tables
  9    WHERE owner = 'TPCC'
 10  ) t,
 11  (
 12    SELECT object_name,value AS gc_buffer_busy
 13    FROM v$segment_statistics
 14    WHERE owner = 'TPCC'
 15    AND object_type = 'TABLE'
 16    AND statistic_name = 'gc buffer busy'
 17  ) ss1,
 18  (
 19    SELECT object_name,value AS gc_cr_blocks_received
 20    FROM v$segment_statistics
 21    WHERE owner = 'TPCC'
 22    AND object_type = 'TABLE'
 23    AND statistic_name = 'gc cr blocks received'
 24  ) ss2,
 25  (
 26    SELECT object_name,value AS gc_current_blocks_received
 27    FROM v$segment_statistics
 28    WHERE owner = 'TPCC'
 29    AND object_type = 'TABLE'
 30    AND statistic_name = 'gc current blocks received'
 31  ) ss3
 32  WHERE t.table_name = ss1.object_name
 33  AND t.table_name = ss2.object_name
 34* AND t.table_name = ss3.object_name
SQL> /
```

Table Name	Buffer Busy	CR Blocks Received	Current Blocks Received
CUSTOMER	16	546039	180391
DISTRICT	537	10130	200367
HISTORY	238	11840	7000
ITEM	0	0	0
WAREHOUSE	13172	88643	113499
STOCK	159	1649497	1215391

ORDERS	1775	102103	94959

7 rows selected.

Pay particular attention to the buffer busy statistics, which can help you identify contention between instances. In this example, the STOCK table is responsible for the highest degree of inter-instance messaging. However, the WAREHOUSE table is responsible for the highest degree of contention, which confirms the findings previously noted in the sections that covered AWR, ASH, and ADDM.

If contention is high, it means there are a large number of rows per block, and sessions are updating multiple rows in that block, as opposed to a single row. Thus you may benefit from distributing the rows across a greater number of blocks by increasing the value of PCTFREE for the object in question.

Global Caches Services: Consistent and Current Reads

You can investigate GCS activity in terms of consistent reads and current reads. For example, you can use this formula to monitor the performance of consistent reads:

```
(gc cr block receive time X 10) / (gc cr blocks received)
```

The preceding formula returns the average time for consistent read block requests for the instance in milliseconds, and it is the GC CR metric of the Global Cache Block Transfer Rate that you observe within the EM RAC performance views. This is the most important value for determining interconnect performance because it usually reflects the largest constituent component of interconnect traffic.

Requests for global resources for data blocks originate in the buffer cache of the requesting instance. Before a request enters the GCS request queue, Oracle allocates data structures in the SGA to track the state of the request. It also collects statistics on these resource structures. The following query and output shows the consistent reads receive time, the blocks received, and the average latency:

```
SQL> li
  1  SELECT
  2    gc_cr_block_receive_time AS "Receive Time",
  3    gc_cr_blocks_received AS "Blocks Received",
  4    (gc_cr_block_receive_time * 10) /
  5      gc_cr_blocks_received AS "Average Latency (MS)"
  6  FROM
  7  (
  8      SELECT value AS gc_cr_block_receive_time FROM v$sysstat
  9      WHERE name = 'gc cr block receive time'
 10  ),
 11  (
 12      SELECT value AS gc_cr_blocks_received FROM v$sysstat
 13      WHERE name = 'gc cr blocks received'
 14* )
SQL> /

Receive Time Blocks Received Average Latency (MS)
------------ --------------- --------------------
      365718         3378788           1.08239404
```

The latency of a consistent block request is the time elapsed between the original request and the receipt of the consistent block image at the local instance. Using a Gigabit Ethernet interconnect, this value should normally be less than 2ms and should not exceed 10ms. However, this value can be affected by the system configuration and volume. In this example, you see that the average latency is 1ms; therefore, it lies within expectations. If latencies exceed 10ms, you should first use the Linux operating system utilities, such as netstat (see Chapter 13 for more information on this utility), to determine whether there are any network configuration issues, such as network packet send and receive errors. You should also use operating system utilities such as top and sar to measure the load on the nodes themselves.

If you have double-checked that the interconnect is configured correctly, and you are still experiencing high average latencies, you might consider reducing the value of DB_FILE_MULTIBLOCK_READ_COUNT. This parameter specifies the number of blocks a process will request in a single operation. The process will have to wait for all blocks to be returned; therefore, higher values may cause longer waits. Before you adjust this parameter, carefully assess its potential impact on the entire workload.

High average latencies may also be caused by a high number of incoming requests or multiple nodes dispatching requests to the LMS process. You can calculate the average LMS service time as follows:

```
average LMS service time = average latency
- average time to build consistent read block
- average time to wait for log flush
- average time to send completed block
```

Average latency is calculated as shown previously. Average time to build a consistent read block is calculated as follows:

```
gc cr block build time / gc cr block served
```

Similarly, average time spent waiting for a redo log flush is calculated as follows:

```
gc cr block flush time / gc cr blocks served
```

Average time to send a completed block is calculated as follows:

```
gc cr block send time / gc cr blocks served
```

The following query can be used to calculate the average LMS service time for consistent block reads:

```
SQL> li
  1  SELECT
  2  average_latency AS "Average Latency",
  3  average_build_time AS "Average Build Time",
  4  average_flush_time AS "Average Flush Time",
  5  average_send_time AS "Average Send Time",
  6  average_latency - average_build_time - average_flush_time - average_send _time
  7       AS "Average LMS Service Time"
  8   FROM
```

```
 9    (
10      SELECT
11  (gc_cr_block_receive_time * 10) / gc_cr_blocks_received AS average_latency,
12  (gc_cr_block_build_time * 10) / gc_cr_blocks_served AS average_build_time,
13  (gc_cr_block_flush_time * 10) / gc_cr_blocks_served AS average_flush_time,
14  (gc_cr_block_send_time * 10) / gc_cr_blocks_served AS average_send_time
15      FROM
16      (
17        SELECT value AS gc_cr_block_receive_time FROM v$sysstat
18        WHERE name = 'gc cr block receive time'
19      ),
20      (
21        SELECT value AS gc_cr_blocks_received FROM v$sysstat
22        WHERE name = 'gc cr blocks received'
23      ),
24      (
25        SELECT value AS gc_cr_block_build_time FROM v$sysstat
26        WHERE name = 'gc cr block build time'
27      ),
28      (
29        SELECT value AS gc_cr_block_flush_time FROM v$sysstat
30        WHERE name = 'gc cr block flush time'
31      ),
32      (
33        SELECT value AS gc_cr_block_send_time FROM v$sysstat
34        WHERE name = 'gc cr block send time'
35      ),
36      (
37        SELECT value AS gc_cr_blocks_served FROM v$sysstat
38        WHERE name = 'gc cr blocks served'
39      )
40*   )
SQL> /

Average Latency Average Build Time Average Flush Time Average Send Time
--------------- ------------------ ------------------ -----------------
Average LMS Service Time
-----------------------
    1.11967715        .012249408        .113152249        .030138924

         .964136572
```

The difference between the average latency time and the sum of the average build, flush, and send times represents the time spent in the LMS service and the time spent transmitting the messages across the interconnect. In the example just shown, the LMS Service Time is within expected boundaries.

Global Cache Services: Current Block Activity

You can also use SQL*Plus to determine the current block activity, which is the GC Current metric of the Global Cache Block Transfer Rate from the EM RAC performance views. You can calculate the overall average latency involved in processing requests for current blocks using the following formula:

(gc current block receive time X 10) / (gc current blocks received)

The latency is returned using the following query:

```
SQL> li
  1  SELECT
  2    gc_current_block_receive_time AS "Receive Time",
  3    gc_current_blocks_received AS "Blocks Received",
  4    (gc_current_block_receive_time * 10) / gc_current_blocks_received
  5    AS "Average (MS)"
  6  FROM
  7  (
  8    SELECT value AS gc_current_block_receive_time
  9    FROM v$sysstat
 10    WHERE name = 'gc current block receive time'
 11  ),
 12  (
 13    SELECT value AS gc_current_blocks_received
 14    FROM v$sysstat
 15    WHERE name = 'gc current blocks received'
 16* )
SQL> /

Receive Time Blocks Received Average (MS)
------------ --------------- ------------
      462110         4514548   1.02360192
```

You can calculate the amount of overall latency that can be attributed to the LMS process using the following snippet:

```
average LMS service time =
average latency
- average time to pin current blocks
- average time to wait for log flush
- average time to send completed block
```

The average latency is calculated as follows:

```
gc current block receive time / gc current blocks received
```

Similarly, the average time to pin current blocks is calculated as follows:

```
gc current block pin time / gc current block served
```

The average time spent waiting for a redo log flush is calculated as follows:

```
gc current block flush time / gc current blocks served
```

And the average time to send a completed block is calculated as follows:

```
gc current block send time / gc current blocks served
```

You can use the following query to calculate the average LMS service time for current block reads:

```
SQL> li
  1  SELECT
  2    average_latency    AS "Average Latency",
  3    average_pin_time   AS "Average Pin Time",
  4    average_flush_time AS "Average Flush Time",
  5    average_send_time  AS "Average Send Time",
  6    average_latency - average_pin_time - average_flush_time - average_send_time
  7    AS "Average LMS Service Time"
  8  FROM
  9  (
 10    SELECT
 11      (gc_current_block_receive_time * 10) / gc_current_blocks_received
 12        AS average_latency,
 13      (gc_current_block_pin_time * 10) / gc_current_blocks_served
 14        AS average_pin_time,
 15      (gc_current_block_flush_time * 10) / gc_current_blocks_served
 16        AS average_flush_time,
 17      (gc_current_block_send_time * 10) / gc_current_blocks_served
 18        AS average_send_time
 19    FROM
 20    (
 21      SELECT value AS gc_current_block_receive_time FROM v$sysstat
 22      WHERE name = 'gc current block receive time'
 23    ),
 24    (
 25      SELECT value AS gc_current_blocks_received FROM v$sysstat
 26      WHERE name = 'gc current blocks received'
 27    ),
 28    (
 29      SELECT value AS gc_current_block_pin_time FROM v$sysstat
 30      WHERE name = 'gc current block pin time'
 31    ),
 32    (
 33      SELECT value AS gc_current_block_flush_time FROM v$sysstat
 34      WHERE name = 'gc current block flush time'
 35    ),
 36    (
 37      SELECT value AS gc_current_block_send_time FROM v$sysstat
 38      WHERE name = 'gc current block send time'
 39    ),
 40    (
 41      SELECT value AS gc_current_blocks_served FROM v$sysstat
 42      WHERE name = 'gc current blocks served'
```

```
 43    )
 44* )
SQL> /

Average Latency Average Pin Time Average Flush Time Average Send Time
--------------- ---------------- ------------------ -----------------
Average LMS Service Time
-----------------------
    1.06117092      .148803422         .104628541         .028298863

              .779440094
```

High latency values may indicate server or interconnect performance issues; however, you should review your current block statistics against the possibility of contention for data between instances.

Global Enqueue Service

GES manages all the non-Cache Fusion intrainstance and inter-instance resource operations. High GES workload request rates can adversely affect performance. To calculate the average global enqueue time in milliseconds, use the following statement:

```
SQL> li
  1  SELECT
  2    global_enqueue_get_time AS "Get Time",
  3    global_enqueue_gets_sync AS "Synchronous Gets",
  4    global_enqueue_gets_async AS "Asynchronous Gets",
  5    (global_enqueue_get_time * 10) /
  6    (global_enqueue_gets_sync + global_enqueue_gets_async)
  7    AS "Average (MS)"
  8  FROM
  9  (
 10    SELECT value AS global_enqueue_get_time
 11    FROM v$sysstat
 12    WHERE name = 'global enqueue get time'
 13  ),
 14  (
 15    SELECT value AS global_enqueue_gets_sync
 16    FROM v$sysstat
 17    WHERE name = 'global enqueue gets sync'
 18  ),
 19  (
 20    SELECT value AS global_enqueue_gets_async
 21    FROM v$sysstat
 22    WHERE name = 'global enqueue gets async'
 23* )
SQL> /

  Get Time Synchronous Gets Asynchronous Gets Average (MS)
---------- ---------------- ------------------ ------------
    358597         27946887             115393   .127786124
```

Synchronous gets are usually locking events, whereas asynchronous gets are usually caused by nonblocking inter-instance process activity.

Library Cache

You can obtain further information about global enqueue activity caused by statement parsing and execution from the V$LIBRARYCACHE dynamic performance view. This view reports GES activity for locks, pins, and invalidations, as in this example:

```
SQL> li
  1  SELECT
  2    namespace                   AS "Namespace",
  3    dlm_lock_requests           AS "Lock Requests",
  4    dlm_pin_requests            AS "Pin Requests",
  5    dlm_pin_releases            AS "Pin Releases",
  6    dlm_invalidation_requests   AS "Invalidation Requests",
  7    dlm_invalidations           AS "Invalidations"
  8* FROM v$librarycache
SQL> /
```

Namespace	Lock Requests	Pin Requests	Pin Releases	Invalidation Requests
Invalidations				
SQL AREA	0	0	0	0
0				
TABLE/PROCEDURE	640720	5551128	5551128	0
0				
BODY	2	1965888	1965888	0
0				
TRIGGER	0	70915	70915	0
0				
INDEX	14849	14849	14849	0
0				
CLUSTER	2479	2503	2503	0
0				

If you see excessively high values in these columns, solutions include pinning packages in the shared pool using the KEEP procedure in the DBMS_SHARED_POOL package. Also, you might investigate methods of keeping cursors open either within the application or by using the SESSION_CACHED_CURSORS parameter.

Dictionary Cache

You can obtain additional information about global enqueue activity caused by statement pinning dictionary cache objects from the V$ROWCACHE dynamic performance view. This view reports GES lock requests, conflicts, and releases, as in this example:

```
SQL> li
  1  SELECT
  2    parameter      AS "Cache Name",
  3    dlm_requests   AS "Requests",
  4    dlm_conflicts  AS "Conflicts",
  5    dlm_releases   AS "Releases"
  6* FROM v$rowcache
SQL> /
```

Cache Name	Requests	Conflicts	Releases
dc_rollback_segments	99	0	0
dc_free_extents	0	0	0
dc_used_extents	0	0	0
dc_segments	7335	469	4158
dc_tablespaces	20	0	0
dc_tablespace_quotas	0	0	0
dc_files	6	0	0
dc_users	352	0	152
dc_objects	8712	106	1177
dc_global_oids	171	0	27
dc_constraints	2135	0	0
dc_sequences	733	43	5
dc_histogram_defs	56671	103	1828
kqlsubheap_object	0	0	0
dc_table_scns	121	0	0

...

You should look for high values in the Conflicts column. In the preceding example, there have been 43 conflicts for sequences. Uncached sequences are one of the most common causes of performance issues in RAC.

Lock Conversions

In Oracle 11g, most of the statistics related to lock conversions can be obtained from V$GES_CONVERT_LOCAL and V$GES_CONVERT_REMOTE. These views show the number of lock conversions on the local system and on remote systems, respectively:

```
SQL> li
  1  SELECT convert_type,average_convert_time, convert_count
  2* FROM v$ges_convert_local
SQL> /
```

CONVERT_TYPE	AVERAGE_CONVERT_TIME	CONVERT_COUNT
NULL -> SS	0	0
NULL -> SX	2	3
NULL -> S	1	24064
NULL -> SSX	5	627
NULL -> X	3	166358
SS -> SX	0	0
SS -> S	0	0
SS -> SSX	0	0
SS -> X	0	0
SX -> S	0	0
SX -> SSX	0	0
SX -> X	0	0
S -> SX	0	0
S -> SSX	0	0
S -> X	1	1693
SSX -> X	1	12

Lock conversions are essential to the efficient operation of a RAC database; moreover, they are not necessarily harmful. However, it is important to check that lock conversions, like lock requests, are not being blocked by instances holding incompatible locks.

To check which instances are currently blocking other instances, use the following query:

```
SQL> li
  1  SELECT
  2    dl.inst_id,
  3    s.sid,
  4    p.spid,
  5    dl.resource_name1,
  6    decode (substr (dl.grant_level,1,8),
  7      'KJUSERNL','Null',
  8      'KJUSERCR','Row-S (SS)',
  9      'KJUSERCW','Row-X (SX)',
 10      'KJUSERPR','Share',
 11      'KJUSERPW','S/Row-X (SSX)',
 12      'KJUSEREX','Exclusive',
 13    request_level) as grant_level,
 14    decode(substr(dl.request_level,1,8),
 15      'KJUSERNL','Null',
 16      'KJUSERCR','Row-S (SS)',
 17      'KJUSERCW','Row-X (SX)',
 18      'KJUSERPR','Share',
 19      'KJUSERPW','S/Row-X (SSX)',
 20      'KJUSEREX','Exclusive',
 21    request_level) as request_level,
 22    decode(substr(dl.state,1,8),
 23      'KJUSERGR','Granted','KJUSEROP','Opening',
 24      'KJUSERCA','Cancelling',
 25      'KJUSERCV','Converting'
 26    ) as state,
```

643

```
27    sw.event,
28    sw.seconds_in_wait sec
29  FROM
30    gv$ges_enqueue dl,
31    gv$process p,
32    gv$session s,
33    gv$session_wait sw
34  WHERE blocker = 1
35  AND (dl.inst_id = p.inst_id AND dl.pid = p.spid)
36  AND (p.inst_id = s.inst_id AND p.addr = s.paddr)
37  AND (s.inst_id = sw.inst_id AND s.sid = sw.sid)
38* ORDER BY sw.seconds_in_wait DESC

SQL> /

    INST_ID        SID SPID                    RESOURCE_NAME1
---------- ---------- ----------------------- -----------------------------
GRANT_LEVEL   REQUEST_LEVEL STATE
------------- ------------- ----------
EVENT                                                               SEC
------------------------------------------------------------- ----------
         2        127 5520                    [0x19][0x2],[RS]
Exclusive     Exclusive
rdbms ipc message                                                     2

         1        131 28215                   [0x1c000a][0x18a12],[TX]
Exclusive     Exclusive
gc cr request                                                         0

         2        126 5496                    [0x110012][0x5659b],[TX]
Exclusive     Exclusive
ges remote message
```

To discover which sessions are currently being blocked, first find this line in the preceding query:

```
>   WHERE blocker = 1
```

Once you locate the line, change it to this instead:

```
>   WHERE blocked = 1
```

Automatic Diagnostic Repository

In addition to proactively monitoring your Oracle Database performance, you should also be aware of any faults or errors in the software environment that may assist you in diagnosing the underlying reason for performance issues. In an Oracle 11g RAC environment, the Oracle Database Fault Diagnosability Infrastructure provides a central point for such fault diagnosis. Within this infrastructure, we will focus on the Automatic Diagnostic Repository (ADR), Trace Files, and the Oracle Database Health Monitor.

The ADR provides a framework for diagnosing faults in the Oracle Database software environment, even when the Database itself is unavailable. For this reason, the ADR is maintained as a directory structure external to the Database. The root of this directory structure is known as the ADR base, and it is defined by the DIAGNOSTIC_DEST init.ora parameter. If this parameter isn't set, then DIAGNOSTIC_DEST defaults to the ORACLE_BASE directory, as shown here:

```
SQL> show parameter diag

NAME                          TYPE        VALUE
----------------------------- ----------- --------------------------
diagnostic_dest               string      /u01/app/oracle
```

All of the nodes in the cluster may share a single ADR base on a shared cluster file system; however, this cluster file system should be separate from the Oracle Database environment. Therefore, OCFS2 would be preferable to ACFS because the ADR must remain available, even if the ASM instance is not. Alternatively, they can be maintained separately on all of the nodes in the cluster. Underneath the ADR base, each instance upon a node has an ADR home. Typically, in a RAC environment based on non-shared storage, this will mean that there is an ADR home for the ASM instance and an ADR home for the Database instance. All ADR homes are located under the diag directory and rdbms for the Database instance and asm for the ASM instance. The actual ADR home is defined by the database and instance names. You can set the ADR home at the operating system to a particular instance by setting the ADR_HOME environment variable. For example, this snippet sets the ADR home to a RAC database instance:

```
[oracle@london1 ~]$ export ADR_HOME=/u01/app/oracle/diag/rdbms/prod/PROD1
```

ADR homes share a common directory structure, and you can view the directory structure for a particular instance in the view V$DIAG_INFO or for all instances in GV$DIAG_INFO:

```
SQL> select name, value from v$diag_info;

NAME
----------------------------------------------------------------
VALUE
----------------------------------------------------------------
Diag Enabled
TRUE
ADR Base
/u01/app/oracle
ADR Home
/u01/app/oracle/diag/rdbms/prod/PROD1
Diag Trace
/u01/app/oracle/diag/rdbms/prod/PROD1/trace
Diag Alert
/u01/app/oracle/diag/rdbms/prod/PROD1/alert
Diag Incident
/u01/app/oracle/diag/rdbms/prod/PROD1/incident
Diag Cdump
/u01/app/oracle/diag/rdbms/prod/PROD1/cdump
```

```
Health Monitor
/u01/app/oracle/diag/rdbms/prod/PROD1/hm
Default Trace File
/u01/app/oracle/diag/rdbms/prod/PROD1/trace/PROD1_ora_2404.trc
Active Problem Count
1
Active Incident Count
1
```

The ADR is managed and the collected information viewed with the adrci command-line utility:

```
[oracle@london1 PROD1]$ adrci

ADRCI: Release 11.2.0.1.0 - Production on Wed Feb 17 09:40:32 2010

Copyright (c) 1982, 2009, Oracle and/or its affiliates.  All rights reserved.

ADR base = "/u01/app/oracle"
adrci>
```

If you have not set the ADR_HOME environment variable, then the adrci commands will report on all ADR homes underneath the ADR base directory. However, some commands do not support multiple ADR homes, as in this example:

```
adrci> show control;
DIA-48448: This command does not support multiple ADR homes
```

For commands that don't support multiple ADR homes, it is necessary to either set the ADR_HOME environment variable externally or within adrci using the set homepath command. The show control command details information about the ADR environment for an incident. For example, the variables SHORTP_POLICY and LONGP_POLICY show the incident files and metadata retention polices, which are set to 720 hours or 30 days and 8760 hours or 365 days, respectively:

adrci> show control

```
ADR Home = /u01/app/oracle/diag/rdbms/prod/PROD1:
*************************************************************************
ADRID                SHORTP_POLICY        LONGP_POLICY         LAST_MOD_TIME
LAST_AUTOPRG_TIME                         LAST_MANUPRG_TIME                       ADRDIR_VERSION
ADRSCHM_VERSION      ADRSCHMV_SUMMARY     ADRALERT_VERSION     CREATE_TIME
-------------------- -------------------- -------------------- ----------------------------
-------- ---------------------------------------- ---------------------------------------- ------
-------------- -------------------- ----------------- -------------------- ----------------------------
--------------------
2978996791           720                  8760                 2010-02-01 14:40:45.803438
+00:00           2010-02-15 02:08:41.049771 +00:00                                 1
2                    76                   1                    2010-02-01 14:40:45.803438 +00:00
1 rows fetched
```

These retention policies can be user-modified for a particular environment.

One interesting feature of adrci is that it provides a central tool to view the database alert log. If the ADR Home is not set, you have the option of selecting which alert log that you wish to view, as in this example:

```
adrci> show alert

Choose the alert log from the following homes to view:

1: diag/asm/+asm/+ASM1
2: diag/tnslsnr/london1/listener_scan2
3: diag/tnslsnr/london1/listener
4: diag/tnslsnr/london1/listener_scan1
5: diag/tnslsnr/london1/listener_scan3
6: diag/rdbms/prod/PROD1
Q: to quit
```

Alternatively, if the ADR Home is set, you will view the alert log for that instance. For example, the show alert command also supports standard Linux type options to tail the alert log for message in real time. The following example shows the alert log revealing an issue with "Checkpoint not complete" messages that will impact on performance (you can learn more about the reasons for this in Chapter 4).

```
adrci> show alert -tail -f
2010-02-16 22:00:39.917000 +00:00
Checkpoint not complete
  Current log# 2 seq# 1668 mem# 0: +DATA/prod/onlinelog/group_2.262.709828935
2010-02-16 22:00:42.928000 +00:00
Thread 1 advanced to log sequence 1669 (LGWR switch)
  Current log# 1 seq# 1669 mem# 0: +DATA/prod/onlinelog/group_1.261.709828935
2010-02-16 22:01:09.935000 +00:00
Thread 1 cannot allocate new log, sequence 1670
Checkpoint not complete
  Current log# 1 seq# 1669 mem# 0: +DATA/prod/onlinelog/group_1.261.709828935
2010-02-16 22:01:12.945000 +00:00
Thread 1 advanced to log sequence 1670 (LGWR switch)
  Current log# 2 seq# 1670 mem# 0: +DATA/prod/onlinelog/group_2.262.709828935
```

The alert log read by adrci is in XML format. for this reason, there is also a text version of the alert log in the trace directory that can be read with the standard Linux commands, as in this example:

```
/u01/app/oracle/diag/rdbms/prod/PROD1/trace/alert_PROD1.log
```

You may have also observed that the example information from V$DIAG_INFO revealed an active incident. You can view this incident and the time that it was raised with the show incident command, as in this example:

```
adrci> show incident

ADR Home = /u01/app/oracle/diag/rdbms/prod/PROD1:
*********************************************************************
INCIDENT_ID          PROBLEM_KEY  CREATE_TIME
-------------------- -------------------------------------------------------------- ---------------
------------------------
27729                ORA 29770   2010-02-09 00:45:35.477000 +00:00
1 rows fetched
```

You can also use `adrci` to create a package for this incident and create a zip file that includes all of the related information for it; this can be done either for your own benefit or to upload data to Oracle support:

```
adrci> ips create package incident 27729
Created package 1 based on incident id 27729, correlation level typical
adrci> ips generate package 1 in /tmp
cp: omitting directory `/u01/app/11.2.0/grid/log/london1/racg/racgmain'
cp: omitting directory `/u01/app/11.2.0/grid/log/london1/racg/racgeut'
cp: omitting directory `/u01/app/11.2.0/grid/log/london1/racg/racgevtf'
Generated package 1 in file /tmp/ORA29770_20100217094458_COM_1.zip, mode complete
```

In this next example, the incident trace file reveals that the incident is indeed cluster related. The file also provides a focus for investigating why performance was impacted at the point in time that the incident was raised:

```
ORA-29770: global enqueue process LMS0 (OSID 7419) is hung for more than 70 seconds

========= Dump for incident 27729 (ORA 29770) ========
----- Beginning of Customized Incident Dump(s) -----
====================================================
=== LMS0 (ospid: 7419) Heartbeat Report
====================================================
LMS0 (ospid: 7419) has no heartbeats for 100 sec. (threshold 70 sec)
  : Not in wait; last wait ended 64 secs ago.
  : last wait_id 1398345 at 'latch: gc element'.
==============================
Dumping PROCESS LMS0 (ospid: 7419) States
...
```

In addition to reactive incident response and monitoring, the ADR also provides a framework for proactively running verification checks against the database with a tool called *Health Monitor*. Health checks run a diagnosis to detect and report on faults such as datafile corruptions, and the list of checks can be viewed in V$HM_CHECK:

```
1* select name from v$hm_check
SQL> /
```

```
NAME
------------------------------------------------------------------
HM Test Check
DB Structure Integrity Check
CF Block Integrity Check
Data Block Integrity Check
Redo Integrity Check
Logical Block Check
Transaction Integrity Check
Undo Segment Integrity Check
No Mount CF Check
Mount CF Check
CF Member Check
All Datafiles Check
Single Datafile Check
Tablespace Check Check
Log Group Check
Log Group Member Check
Archived Log Check
Redo Revalidation Check
IO Revalidation Check
Block IO Revalidation Check
Txn Revalidation Check
Failure Simulation Check
Dictionary Integrity Check
ASM Mount Check
ASM Allocation Check
ASM Disk Visibility Check
ASM File Busy Check
```

Health checks can be run automatically in response to incidents. However, some health checks can be run manually with the DBMS.HM package, as in this example:

```
SQL> exec dbms_hm.run_check('DB Structure Integrity Check');

PL/SQL procedure successfully completed.
```

Details of the health check can be viewed with adrci:

```
adrci> show hm_run;
...
********************************************************
HM RUN RECORD 3
********************************************************
     RUN_ID                    61
     RUN_NAME                  HM_RUN_61
     CHECK_NAME                DB Structure Integrity Check
     NAME_ID                   2
     MODE                      0
     START_TIME                2010-02-17 10:54:29.982586 +00:00
     RESUME_TIME               <NULL>
```

```
END_TIME                    2010-02-17 10:54:29.985681 +00:00
MODIFIED_TIME               2010-02-17 10:54:29.985681 +00:00
TIMEOUT                     0
FLAGS                       0
STATUS                      5
SRC_INCIDENT_ID             0
NUM_INCIDENTS               0
ERR_NUMBER                  0
REPORT_FILE                 <NULL>
...
```

You can use adrci to create a report and view the findings:

```
adrci> create report hm_run HM_RUN_61;
adrci> show report hm_run HM_RUN_61;
<?xml version="1.0" encoding="US-ASCII"?>
<HM-REPORT REPORT_ID="HM_RUN_61">
    <TITLE>HM Report: HM_RUN_61</TITLE>
    <RUN_INFO>
        <CHECK_NAME>DB Structure Integrity Check</CHECK_NAME>
        <RUN_ID>61</RUN_ID>
        <RUN_NAME>HM_RUN_61</RUN_NAME>
        <RUN_MODE>MANUAL</RUN_MODE>
        <RUN_STATUS>COMPLETED</RUN_STATUS>
        <RUN_ERROR_NUM>0</RUN_ERROR_NUM>
        <SOURCE_INCIDENT_ID>0</SOURCE_INCIDENT_ID>
        <NUM_INCIDENTS_CREATED>0</NUM_INCIDENTS_CREATED>
        <RUN_START_TIME>2010-02-17 10:54:29.982586 +00:00</RUN_START_TIME>
        <RUN_END_TIME>2010-02-17 10:54:29.985681 +00:00</RUN_END_TIME>
    </RUN_INFO>
    <RUN_PARAMETERS/>
    <RUN-FINDINGS/>
</HM-REPORT>
```

You can also view the generated report under the ADR hm directory which in this example is /u01/app/oracle/diag/rdbms/prod/PROD1/hm, where the file HMREPORT_HM_RUN_61.hm was generated. This example didn't produce any findings, but if you do encounter findings in a run, their impact can also be seen in the V$HM_FINDING view:

```
SQL>  select description, damage_description from v$hm_finding where run_id = 62;
...
Datafile 4: '+DATA/prod/datafile/users.259.709828865' needs media recovery
Some objects in tablespace USERS might be unavailable
...
```

An additional feature provided by the ADR is the ability to view and search the database trace files gathered in the trace directory under the ADR home:

```
/u01/app/oracle/diag/rdbms/prod/PROD1/trace
```

The command show tracefile lists all of the trace files in this directory. adrci also supports searching for strings within trace file names and showing trace files related to a particular incident:

```
adrci> show tracefile -I 27729

diag/rdbms/prod/PROD1/incident/incdir_27729/PROD1_lmhb_7430_i27729.trc
```

Once a trace file has been found, its contents can also be viewed under adrci, as in this example:

```
adrci> show trace PROD1_lmhb_7430_i27729.trc
...
```

In addition to viewing system-generated trace files, you can also generate trace files of your own applications. The DBMS_MONITOR package provides a single API interface from which you can enable and disable trace for a specific session, module, action, or client identifier. In addition, DBMS_MONITOR provides other functionality to enable more granular collection of statistics for specified modules, actions, and client identifiers.

To enable tracing in a specific session, you first need to identify the SID and, optionally, the serial number of the session. This information can be obtained from V$SESSION:

```
SQL> SELECT sid, serial# FROM v$session WHERE username = 'TPCC';
```

Note that you may need to join V$SESSION to other dynamic performance views, such as V$SQL, to identify the session of interest.

To enable tracing for a specific session, use the SESSION_TRACE_ENABLE procedure. For example, you can use the following line to enable tracing for a session with a SID of 164:

```
SQL> EXECUTE dbms_monitor.session_trace_enable (session_id=>164);
```

This command will immediately enable tracing for the specified session; the result will be appended to the current trace file.

You can also include bind variable information in the same trace file:

```
SQL> EXECUTE dbms_monitor.session_trace_enable (session_id=>164,binds=>true);
```

By default, wait information is included in the trace file. You can specify that wait events should be traced using this snippet:

```
SQL> EXECUTE dbms_monitor.session_trace_enable (session_id=>164,waits=>true);
```

You can also include both bind and wait information in the same trace file. Tracing can be disabled for the same session with this snippet:

```
SQL> EXECUTE dbms_monitor.session_trace_disable (session_id=>164);
```

You can also enable tracing for all sessions connected to the database or instance with database_trace_enable. Similarly, you can enable tracing for a particular service or module with serv_mod_act_trace_enable.

Note that enabling tracing for all sessions will generate a large amount of trace output very quickly in the ADR trace directory. Enabling tracing globally will also slow down the database, so it is advisable not to enable it at the instance level on a production system.

Once you have generated your trace file, you can either view the contents directly or use the standard Oracle utility tkprof to provide a summary of the statements processed by the session when tracing was enabled and the events on which the statements waited. The following excerpt generated by tkprof illustrates how tracing permits you to view the activities of a session with finer granularity:

```
...
UPDATE DISTRICT SET D_YTD = D_YTD + :B3 WHERE D_W_ID = :B2 AND D_ID = :B1

call     count       cpu    elapsed       disk      query    current       rows
-------  ------  --------  ----------  ---------  ---------  ---------   --------
Parse        0      0.00       0.00          0          0          0          0
Execute    391      0.17       0.77          0        868        464        391
Fetch        0      0.00       0.00          0          0          0          0
-------  ------  --------  ----------  ---------  ---------  ---------   --------
total      391      0.17       0.77          0        868        464        391

Misses in library cache during parse: 0
Optimizer mode: ALL_ROWS
Parsing user id: 85      (recursive depth: 1)

Elapsed times include waiting on following events:
  Event waited on                              Times    Max. Wait  Total Waited
  ----------------------------------------     Waited   ---------- ------------
    ges message buffer allocation                291       0.00          0.00
    gc current block 2-way                       196       0.00          0.07
    gc cr block busy                               7       0.00          0.00
    enq: TX - row lock contention                 71       0.02          0.53
    gc cr block 2-way                             25       0.00          0.00
    gc current block congested                     1       0.00          0.00
    gc current block busy                          8       0.00          0.00
    gc buffer busy acquire                         3       0.00          0.00
    KJC: Wait for msg sends to complete            2       0.00          0.00
    buffer busy waits                              1       0.00          0.00
********************************************************************************
...
```

Summary

In this chapter, we described some of the tools and techniques available to you for monitoring the performance of your RAC cluster at the Oracle level. In particular, we looked at the tools integrated with the Oracle 11g Manageability Infrastructure.

In the next chapter, we'll look at what to do at the Linux level. For example, you'll learn about the most important of the built-in Linux commands and tools to help you diagnose server and interconnect performance problems.

CHAPTER 13

■■■

Linux Performance Monitoring

In the previous chapter, we looked at Oracle performance monitoring tools. However, performance problems often occur outside the Oracle environment at the processor and memory, network, or storage level. It is therefore important to understand the information provided, not only by the Oracle performance monitoring tools, but also by the standard operating system monitoring tools available on Linux. You can use the information provided by these tools to support the findings from Oracle tools to fully diagnose RAC performance.

There are a number of third-party performance monitoring tools that operate in the Linux environment. However, our focus here is on the operating system monitoring tools available by default with Oracle Enterprise Linux that complement the environment available with the Oracle tools. In this category, we cover the default tools available in the base Oracle Enterprise Linux installation—namely, the command line CPU and memory diagnostics with uptime, last, ps, free, ipcs, pmap, lsof, top, vmstat, and strace; and network tools of netstat, ss, and tcpdump. Additionally, if you have installed and configured Oracle Enterprise Linux as detailed in Chapter 6, you will have run the Oracle Validated RPM. One dependency for the latter is the RPM package, sysstat. sysstat includes the following Linux performance monitoring tools: iostat, mpstat, and sar. Consequently, a default Oracle-validated Enterprise Linux environment includes a number of command-line tools that, if mastered, can rapidly and comprehensively give you insight into the system-level performance.

We also provide an overview of additional optional Oracle-provided Linux monitoring tools, as well as information on another open source tool you may wish to investigate. The Oracle tools are called Oracle Cluster Health Monitor and OSWatcher, respectively. The additional open source tool, which is provided by IBM, is called nmon. These tools are easy to install, but provide both an alternative and complementary environment for monitoring Linux environments.

It is important to note that, as is the case with all software the performance monitoring tools covered in this section, the tools just mentioned all require system resources to run, and you should be aware of the level of resources required by each tool. This information should be considered when deciding upon your Linux performance monitoring toolset; therefore, we do not recommend running all of the tools detailed in this section at the same time. Instead, you should select the ones that will work best in your environment.

The uptime and last Commands

uptime is a standard Linux command that reports the amount of time that a system has been running. The following snippet shows you how to use this command:

```
[root@london1 ~]# uptime
 15:36:11 up 3 days,  3:50,  4 users,  load average: 0.13, 0.14, 0.10
```

uptime provides information on node availability, and it is useful as a command of first resort in diagnosing and troubleshooting node evictions across a RAC cluster. uptime also reports the system load over intervals of 1, 5, and 15 minutes.

In a similar vein, the last command and its -x argument provides a detailed log of system shutdowns and changes in run level, as in this example:

```
[root@london1 ~]# last
root     pts/2         172.17.1.81      Fri Feb  5 09:32   still logged in
root     pts/1         london2.example. Thu Feb  4 16:09   still logged in
root     pts/1         london2.example. Thu Feb  4 16:04 - 16:05  (00:00)
root     pts/0         172.17.1.81      Thu Feb  4 16:00   still logged in
reboot   system boot   2.6.18-164.el5   Thu Feb  4 15:52          (17:53)
root     pts/2         172.17.1.81      Thu Feb  4 15:36 - down   (00:13)
root     pts/1         172.17.1.81      Thu Feb  4 13:18 - down   (02:31)
root     pts/3         172.17.1.81      Mon Feb  1 14:37 - down   (3+01:11)
root     pts/1         172.17.1.81      Mon Feb  1 13:51 - 14:47  (00:55)
root     pts/2         172.17.1.81      Mon Feb  1 13:31 - 14:48  (01:17)
root     pts/1         172.17.1.81      Mon Feb  1 13:30 - 13:32  (00:02)
root     pts/0         172.17.1.81      Mon Feb  1 11:48 - down   (3+04:01)
reboot   system boot   2.6.18-164.el5   Mon Feb  1 11:46          (3+04:02)
root     pts/0         172.17.1.81      Fri Jan 29 15:48 - down   (00:09)
reboot   system boot   2.6.18-164.el5   Fri Jan 29 11:03          (04:54)
```

The ps Command

The ps command is one of the most basic, yet essential tools for analyzing performance on a Linux system. At its simplest, ps shows a list of processes; if called without arguments, it displays the list of processes running under the current session, as shown here:

```
[root@london1 ~]# ps
  PID TTY          TIME CMD
 6969 pts/2    00:00:00 bash
 7172 pts/2    00:00:00 ps
```

Fortunately, ps can do a lot more than this. For example, it accepts a wealth of arguments to present process listings in almost every conceivable form. The arguments to ps can take three forms: standard System V Unix-type options that must be preceded by a dash; BSD-type options that are not preceded by a dash; and GNU long options that are preceded by two dashes. In effect, you may use different combinations of arguments to display similar forms of output. The combination of arguments that you will use most regularly is that of a full listing of all processes that relies on the System V -ef arguments. The following shows the first ten lines of output:

```
[root@london1 ~]# ps -ef
UID        PID  PPID  C STIME TTY          TIME CMD
root         1     0  0 Feb04 ?        00:00:02 init [3]
root         2     1  0 Feb04 ?        00:00:00 [migration/0]
root         3     1  0 Feb04 ?        00:00:00 [ksoftirqd/0]
root         4     1  0 Feb04 ?        00:00:00 [watchdog/0]
root         5     1  0 Feb04 ?        00:00:00 [migration/1]
root         6     1  0 Feb04 ?        00:00:00 [ksoftirqd/1]
```

```
root        7    1  0 Feb04 ?       00:00:00 [watchdog/1]
root        8    1  0 Feb04 ?       00:00:00 [migration/2]
root        9    1  0 Feb04 ?       00:00:00 [ksoftirqd/2]
root       10    1  0 Feb04 ?       00:00:00 [watchdog/2]
```

To learn more details about each process, you can use the ps -elf command and its -l argument to see a longer, more complete listing. You can pipe the output through grep to restrict the number of lines returned, as in this example:

```
[root@london1 ~]# ps -elf | grep smon | grep -v grep
0 S oracle   13172    1  0 78   0 - 119071 -  Feb01 ? 00:00:00 asm_smon_+ASM1
0 S oracle   23826    1  0 75   0 - 1727611 - Feb01 ? 00:00:14 ora_smon_PROD1
```

However, you also have an alternative to using ps with grep. pgrep can provide you with the same functionality in a single command. For example, the following extract uses the -flu arguments to display the processes owned by the user oracle:

```
[root@london1 ~]# pgrep -flu oracle
6458 ora_pz97_PROD1
7210 ora_w000_PROD1
7516 ora_j000_PROD1
7518 ora_j001_PROD1
12903 /u01/app/11.2.0/grid/bin/oraagent.bin
12918 /u01/app/11.2.0/grid/bin/mdnsd.bin
12929 /u01/app/11.2.0/grid/bin/gipcd.bin
12940 /u01/app/11.2.0/grid/bin/gpnpd.bin
12970 /u01/app/11.2.0/grid/bin/diskmon.bin -d -f
12992 /u01/app/11.2.0/grid/bin/ocssd.bin
13138 asm_pmon_+ASM1
```

Another useful command is pidof, which can be used to identify processes. It can even be used without arguments. If you know the name of a process, you can quickly find its corresponding process identifier with this snippet:

```
[root@london1 ~]# pidof ora_smon_PROD1
23826
```

free, ipcs, pmap, and lsof

The free command, the /proc file system, the /meminfo file system, and the ipcs, pmap, and lsof commands are useful in diagnosing RAC performance problems. The following sections walk through how to use of each of these items.

The free Command

The free command displays the status of your system's virtual memory at the current point in time. There are three rows of output: the Mem: row shows the utilization of the physical RAM installed in the machine; the `-/+ buffers/cache:` row shows the amount of memory assigned to system buffers and caches; and the `Swap:` row shows the amount of swap space used.

The next example shows a system with 16GB of RAM after an Oracle RAC instance has started. At first, it may appear that nearly 13GB has been consumed, with just over 3GB free. However, with `free`, we can see that the operating system actually assigns memory to buffers and cache if it is not being used for any other purpose; therefore, the actual figure representing free memory is more than 4GB. If you are using any third-party system-monitoring tool that reports memory utilization is high on a Linux system, you should always confirm this with `free` to ensure that the memory is not simply free in buffers and cache instead:

```
root@london1 ~]# free
                total       used        free     shared    buffers     cached
Mem:         16423996   12813584     3610412          0     158820    1045908
-/+ buffers/cache:       11608856     4815140
Swap:        18481144          0    18481144
```

The preceding example also shows that the system is not using any of the configured swap space at this point in time. As we discussed in Chapter 6, unless you are creating a large number of processes on the system, swap space utilization should be minimal. If you monitor the memory utilization with `free`, and an increasing amount of swap space is being consumed, this will have a significantly negative performance impact.

By default, the values for `free` are expressed in kilobytes; however, you can specify the display to be used in bytes, megabytes, or gigabytes with the `-b`,`-m`, or `-g` flag, respectively. The `-s` flag can be used with an interval value to continually repeat the command according to the interval period. Alternatively, you can use the `watch` command to refresh the display in place. By default, running `watch free` will refresh in place every two seconds.

The /proc File System

When working with Oracle, you should also be familiar with the output of `/proc/meminfo`, which is the location from which the information for `free` is derived. Within `/proc/meminfo`, you can also see the amount of memory and swap that is free and used, and the amount of memory assigned to buffers and cache on an individual basis. In addition, `/proc/meminfo` includes the configuration of huge pages, the setting of which we discuss in Chapter 6.

The following example of `/proc/meminfo` shows the same system with a total of 16GB of RAM and 5,000 huge pages at 2MB each, which is a 10GB allocation in total. Of these, 3,442 huge pages remain as reserved after the Oracle instance has started. This indicates the difference between the number of pages not already used by the instance, but reserved for future use by the SGA and therefore not being available for standard small pages:

```
[oracle@london1 ~]$ cat /proc/meminfo
MemTotal:     16423996 kB
MemFree:       4079840 kB
Buffers:         29668 kB
Cached:         771924 kB
SwapCached:          0 kB
Active:        1509184 kB
Inactive:       456424 kB
HighTotal:           0 kB
HighFree:            0 kB
```

```
LowTotal:       16423996 kB
LowFree:         4079840 kB
SwapTotal:      18481144 kB
SwapFree:       18481144 kB
Dirty:               924 kB
Writeback:             0 kB
AnonPages:       1166644 kB
Mapped:           192576 kB
Slab:              39444 kB
PageTables:        38872 kB
NFS_Unstable:          0 kB
Bounce:                0 kB
CommitLimit:    21573140 kB
Committed_AS:    6138472 kB
VmallocTotal: 34359738367 kB
VmallocUsed:      284172 kB
VmallocChunk: 34359453879 kB
HugePages_Total:    5000
HugePages_Free:     4345
HugePages_Rsvd:     3442
Hugepagesize:       2048 kB
```

In this output, it's important to notice that 4,345 huge pages remain free. By default, the pages will be used on demand, which means the number of pages free will drop as they are used during normal Oracle SGA related database activity, such as when caching data in the buffer cache. Alternatively, setting the Oracle parameter PRE_PAGE_SGA to true will ensure that each process pages the SGA on startup, and all required pages will be allocated on instance startup. If unused pages remain available, these can be freed by setting the vm.nr_hugepages parameter to the utilized level (see Chapter 6 for more information on this).

The /sys/devices/system/node File System

When working on a system with a NUMA memory configuration, you should also be familiar with the meminfo data reported on a per memory node basis. For example, the following shows Node 0 of a 4-node configuration. In this case, a quarter of the total 70,000 huge pages are allocated on this node, which indicates an even distribution of pages across the nodes:

```
root@london5 node]# cat */meminfo
Node 0 MemTotal:    66036380 kB
Node 0 MemFree:     28338244 kB
Node 0 MemUsed:     37698136 kB
Node 0 Active:        454512 kB
Node 0 Inactive:      716248 kB
Node 0 HighTotal:          0 kB
Node 0 HighFree:           0 kB
Node 0 LowTotal:    66036380 kB
Node 0 LowFree:     28338244 kB
Node 0 Dirty:             76 kB
Node 0 Writeback:          0 kB
Node 0 FilePages:    1010516 kB
```

```
Node 0 Mapped:            80612 kB
Node 0 AnonPages:        169328 kB
Node 0 PageTables:        15504 kB
Node 0 NFS_Unstable:          0 kB
Node 0 Bounce:                0 kB
Node 0 Slab:              67836 kB
Node 0 HugePages_Total: 17500
Node 0 HugePages_Free:  15247
```

Additional NUMA-related commands that can influence and tune this allocation, such as the numactl and numastat commands (you can learn more about these commands in Chapter 4). It is also important to understand, not only how the memory is allocated, but also how it is used by the Oracle instance.

The ipcs Command

Regardless of whether you are using NUMA-based memory allocation, a significant proportion of your system memory will be allocated as shared memory for the SGA. This is true whether you are using manual shared memory management, automatic shared memory management, or automatic memory management. The ipcs command with the –m argument can be used to display the configured shared memory segments on the system. The following example shows a single shared memory segment has been allocated for the SGA:

```
[oracle@london1 ~]$ ipcs -m

------ Shared Memory Segments --------
key         shmid      owner      perms    bytes        nattch    status
0xed304ac0  32768      oracle     660      4096         0
0x90c3be20  1277953    oracle     660      8592031744   42
```

The corresponding command of ipcrm with the –M argument can be used to manually delete shared memory segments by a user with the appropriate permissions. However, you should use pmap and lsof beforehand to identify the processes using the shared memory segment.

The pmap Command

On an individual process basis, the pmap command details the memory mapped by that particular process, including the total memory utilization by process. The -x argument shows this information in an extended format. This can be used directly with a process number or in conjunction with the pgrep command, as described previously. Doing so returns the process number of a particular process that you can identify by name. For example, the following output illustrates the pmap information for a foreground process:

```
[root@london1 ~]# pmap -x 21749
21749:   oraclePROD1 (DESCRIPTION=(LOCAL=YES)(ADDRESS=(PROTOCOL=beq)))
Address            Kbytes     RSS     Anon  Locked Mode   Mapping
0000000000400000   155144       -        -       - r-x--  oracle
0000000009d81000    12404       -        -       - rwx--  oracle
000000000a99e000      280       -        -       - rwx--  [ anon ]
```

```
0000000015522000      556        -        -        - rwx--     [ anon ]
0000000060000000 8390656        -        -        - rwxs-   5 (deleted)
00000031a3600000      112        -        -        - r-x--   ld-2.5.so
00000031a381b000        4        -        -        - r-x--   ld-2.5.so
00000031a381c000        4        -        -        - rwx--   ld-2.5.so
00000031a3a00000     1332        -        -        - r-x--   libc-2.5.so
00000031a3b4d000     2048        -        -        - -----   libc-2.5.so
```

However, it is important to note that, as explained previously, some implementations of pmap under Oracle Enterprise Linux do not show the full extent of the listing. For example, compare the preceding output to the following example from SUSE Linux, which shows more complete information:

```
reading1:~ # pmap 7679
7679: oracle
START        SIZE     RSS     PSS    DIRTY   SWAP PERM MAPPING
08048000 136616K   9988K    683K      0K      OK r-xp
/u01/app/oracle/product/11.2.0/dbhome_1/bin/oracle
105b2000   1004K    208K     63K     56K      OK rwxp
/u01/app/oracle/product/11.2.0/dbhome_1/bin/oracle
106ad000    472K    320K    320K    320K      OK rwxp [heap]
20000000 309248K  76480K  71725K  42072K      OK rwxs /SYSVb0e4b134
b6dfe000    128K    128K     88K     88K      OK rwxp /dev/zero
b6e1e000    384K    384K      0K      0K      OK rwxp /dev/zero
...
b6e7e000    132K    132K    132K    132K      OK rwxp [anon]
bfbb9000     84K     36K     36K     36K      OK rwxp [stack]
ffffe000      4K      0K      0K      0K      OK r-xp [vdso]
Total:   465608K  93988K  77876K  47508K      OK

8704K writable-private, 147440K readonly-private, 309464K shared,
and 92528K referenced
```

In addition to reporting on shared memory, pmap can also be used to identify the private memory utilized by individual foreground processes to troubleshoot where memory has been allocated across the system on a process-by-process basis. Additional process-based memory utilization information is also available underneath the /proc directory and an individual process number. For example, the status information includes the following summary:

```
[root@london1 21749]# cat status
Name:     oracle
State: S (sleeping)
SleepAVG:       85%
Tgid:   21749
Pid:    21749
PPid:   21748
TracerPid:      0
Uid:    500     500     500     500
Gid:    501     501     501     501
FDSize: 64
Groups: 500 501
VmPeak:   8608684 kB
```

```
VmSize:    218028 kB
VmLck:          0 kB
VmHWM:      28616 kB
VmRSS:      28616 kB
VmData:      2920 kB
VmStk:        112 kB
VmExe:     155144 kB
VmLib:      12148 kB
VmPTE:        380 kB
StaBrk: 15522000 kB
Brk:     155ad000 kB
StaStk: 7fffac094010 kB
```

The lsof Command

lsof is an extensive command that lists the open files on the system. It can be used for diagnosing connectivity to a number of resources. For example, it provides information on the usage of standard files, shared memory segments, and network ports. Without arguments, the following example lists the processes under the oracle user attached to the shared memory segment; the id 1277953 is identified from the output of ipcs:

```
[root@london1 ~]# lsof -u oracle | grep 1277953
oracle    20508    oracle DEL    REG          0,13              1277953 /5
oracle    20510    oracle DEL    REG          0,13              1277953 /5
oracle    20514    oracle DEL    REG          0,13              1277953 /5
oracle    20516    oracle DEL    REG          0,13              1277953 /5
oracle    20518    oracle DEL    REG          0,13              1277953 /5
oracle    20520    oracle DEL    REG          0,13              1277953 /5
oracle    20522    oracle DEL    REG          0,13              1277953 /5
oracle    20524    oracle DEL    REG          0,13              1277953 /5
...
```

If you are also interested in the cached objects in the kernel, you can view them in the output of /proc/slabinfo; however, you will most likely be interested only in specific entries, such as kiobuf related to asynchronous I/O activity. In addition, a utility called slabtop can display kernel slab information in real time. The form of the output of slabtop is similar to that of the more general-purpose top.

top

ps and free are static commands that return information about system processes and memory utilization within individual snapshots. However they are not designed to track usage over a longer period of time. The first tool we will look at with this monitoring capability is top.

If top is called without arguments, it will display output similar to the following result. It will also refresh the screen by default every two seconds, but without requiring that you use watch to enable this functionality:

```
[root@london1 ~]# top
top - 11:15:54 up 19:24,  4 users,  load average: 1.27, 0.51, 0.23
```

```
Tasks: 285 total,   1 running, 284 sleeping,   0 stopped,   0 zombie
Cpu(s): 20.9%us,  2.8%sy,  0.0%ni, 49.2%id, 26.1%wa,  0.2%hi,  0.9%si,  0.0%st
Mem:  16423996k total, 12921072k used,  3502924k free,   162536k buffers
Swap: 18481144k total,       0k used, 18481144k free,  1073132k cached

  PID USER     PR NI  VIRT  RES  SHR S %CPU %MEM   TIME+  COMMAND
24725 oracle   16  0 8413m  27m  22m S 22.6  0.2  0:15.33 oraclePROD1 (LOCAL=NO)
24735 oracle   15  0 8413m  27m  22m S 21.9  0.2  0:16.28 oraclePROD1 (LOCAL=NO)
24723 oracle   15  0 8413m  27m  22m S 19.3  0.2  0:17.44 oraclePROD1 (LOCAL=NO)
24727 oracle   15  0 8411m  25m  20m S 18.9  0.2  0:16.22 oraclePROD1 (LOCAL=NO)
24729 oracle   15  0 8413m  27m  22m S 18.6  0.2  0:17.17 oraclePROD1 (LOCAL=NO)
24733 oracle   15  0 8413m  27m  22m S 17.9  0.2  0:15.29 oraclePROD1 (LOCAL=NO)
24737 oracle   15  0 8413m  27m  22m S 17.6  0.2  0:14.97 oraclePROD1 (LOCAL=NO)
24731 oracle   15  0 8413m  27m  22m S 15.9  0.2  0:15.63 oraclePROD1 (LOCAL=NO)
24743 oracle   15  0 8411m  25m  20m S 13.0  0.2  0:12.59 oraclePROD1 (LOCAL=NO)
20546 oracle   16  0 8424m  38m  19m D  7.3  0.2  0:09.99 ora_dbw0_PROD1
20548 oracle   15  0 8427m  41m  37m S  6.3  0.3  0:14.29 ora_lgwr_PROD1
20532 oracle   -2  0 8415m  31m  18m S  5.0  0.2  0:18.90 ora_lms0_PROD1
20536 oracle   -2  0 8415m  31m  18m S  4.3  0.2  0:19.49 ora_lms1_PROD1
```

The top display is divided into two main sections. Within the top-level section, the most important information in monitoring an Oracle RAC node is the load average, CPU states, and memory and swap space. The load average shows the average number of processes in the queue waiting to be allocated CPU time over the previous 1, 5, and 15 minutes. During normal operations, the load averages should be maintained at low values. If these values consistently exceed the processor core count of the server, this is an indication that the system load is exceeding capacity. When this is the case, there is the potential that the GCS background processes (LMSn) could become starved of CPU time, resulting in a detrimental effect on the overall performance of the cluster.

The CPU states show the level of utilization for all of the CPUs installed on the system. The oracle user workload will be shown as user time; however, there will be additional levels of system time and iowait time related to Oracle activity. A high level of iowait time may indicate that you should investigate the disk performance because the CPUs are spending the majority of their time simply waiting for I/O requests to be processed. An overall indicator of CPU is the idle value showing spare capacity on the system. A consistently low idle time in conjunction with a high load average provides additional evidence that the workload exceeds the ability of the system to process it.

The memory-related section displays information that bears a close resemblance to the output of free.

The bottom-level section includes statistics related to the processes running on the system. You can use this section to pinpoint which processes are using most of the CPU and memory on the system. In terms of memory, as well as the total percentage utilization on the system, the VIRT field shows how much memory an individual process has allocated, and the RSS field (the Resident Set Size) shows how much memory the process is using at the current time. For Oracle processes, these values should ordinarily be at similar levels.

From the example top output, we can see that the system is processing Oracle activity but is not under excessive workload at the present time.

top is an interactive tool that accepts single-letter commands to tailor the display. For example, you may use the u option to specify viewing processes solely for the oracle user by typing u or *oracle*, or you may sort tasks by age by typing A. Typing c also lets you also display the full process listing, which is useful in identifying the Oracle processes utilizing the highest levels of CPU. You should remember not to neglect monitoring system process tasks. For example, observing the kswapd process in top output on a regular basis would indicate a potential performance impact from utilizing swap space.

An important aspect of top is that, in addition to displaying information, you may also interact with the processes themselves, such as altering their relative priorities or killing them altogether. Therefore, the Help screen accessed by ? is useful for familiarizing yourself with the capabilities of the tool. You can terminate top by pressing the q key or Ctrl+C.

vmstat

As its name suggests, the vmstat utility focuses on providing output about the usage of virtual memory. When called without arguments, vmstat will output information related to virtual memory utilization since the system was last booted. Therefore, you are most likely to call vmstat with two numerical arguments for the delay between sampling periods and the number of sampling periods in total. If you specify just one numerical argument, this will apply to the delay, and the sampling will continue until the command is canceled with Ctrl+C. For example, the following will produce ten lines of output at three-second intervals:

```
[root@london1 ~]# vmstat 3 10
procs -----------memory-------- ---swap-- -----io---- --system-- -----cpu------
 r  b   swpd    free    buff   cache   si   so    bi    bo    in    cs us sy id wa st
 2  7    0 3498932 162972 1079928    0    0    18    23    66    59  0  0 99  0  0
 2  7    0 3495972 162972 1080028    0    0 13619  1277  8384 17455  8  3 66 23  0
 0  9    0 3499452 162972 1080164    0    0 15457  1821  9120 18800  9  3 64 24  0
 2  9    0 3498976 162972 1080240    0    0 16411  2451  9497 19562 11  3 61 25  0
 2  7    0 3498712 162972 1080368    0    0 15881  8385 10625 21277 12  3 60 25  0
 4  7    0 3498240 162972 1080480    0    0 14400  8495 10734 21287 12  4 58 26  0
 1  7    0 3497916 162972 1080620    0    0 12734 16371 10947 21363 13  4 57 26  0
 3  8    0 3503008 162972 1080668    0    0  9667 14266  9050 18520 11  3 57 28  0
 3  8    0 3503232 162972 1080788    0    0 11739  2818 11426 22608 15  4 54 27  0
 3  6    0 3502612 162972 1080848    0    0 10886  9531 11556 22593 16  4 52 28  0
```

Within the output, the first two fields under procs show processes waiting for CPU runtime and processes that are in uninterruptible sleep state. A traditional implementation of vmstat on many UNIX systems and earlier Linux versions also showed a w field under the procs section to indicate processes that are swapped out; however, entire processes are not swapped out under Linux, so the w field is no longer included. As with top, the next four fields under the memory section should be familiar from the output of free, which shows the amount of swap space in use, as well as the free and cached memory. The two fields under the swap section show the amount of memory being swapped in and out of disk per second. On an Oracle system, we would expect these values and the amount of swap in use to show a low or zero value. The fields under io show the blocks sent and received from block devices, and the fields under system show the level of interrupts and context switches. In a RAC environment, the levels of interrupts and context switches can be useful in evaluating the impact of the CPU servicing network-related activity, such as interconnect traffic or the usage of network attached storage (NAS).

Finally, the cpu section is similar to top in that it displays the user, system, I/O wait, and idle CPU time. The cpu section differs from top by including this information for all CPUs on the system.

In addition to the default output, vmstat also enables the display to be configured with a number of command-line options. For example, -d displays disk statistics, and -p shows the statistics for a particular disk partition specified at the command line. A summary of memory-related values can be given by the -s option.

strace

strace is a tool that can be used for diagnostics when performance monitoring reveals either errors or performance issues with a particular command or process. For example, if you suspect a particular process is not responding, you can use strace to determine the actions that the process is undertaking.

If the strace command is not available on your system, it can be installed as part of the strace RPM package from your install media:

```
[root@london1 ~]# yum install strace
Loaded plugins: security
Setting up Install Process
Resolving Dependencies
--> Running transaction check
---> Package strace.x86_64 0:4.5.18-5.el5 set to be updated
...
Installed:
  strace.x86_64 0:4.5.18-5.el5

Complete!
```

As its names implies, strace records and reports the system calls and signals of a process until the process exits. The information captured is either printed to the standard error channel or (more usefully) to a text file, the name of which is given as an argument to the -o flag. One of the most powerful additional strace options is available with the –e flag, which enables the tracing of particular system calls or groups of system calls, such as those that are network related. You can use strace in one of two ways. First, you can use it to precede a program run at the command line. Second, you can use -p to specify a process to attach to in order to perform the trace. For example, the following snippet shows a trace of the LMS process that is saved to a text file:

```
[root@london1 ~]# pidof ora_lms0_PROD1
20532
[root@london1 ~]# strace -p 20532 -o lms_strace.txt
Process 20532 attached - interrupt to quit
Process 20532 detached
```

If you examine the text file, you can observe that, on host london1, the LMS process is using the sendmsg and recvmsg system calls. Also, the process is communicating with the private interconnect address on london2 on 192.168.1.2:

```
sendmsg(12, {msg_name(16)={sa_family=AF_INET, sin_port=htons(42297),
sin_addr=inet_addr("192.168.1.2")}, msg_iov(3)=
[{"\4\3\2\1\273p\0\0\0\0\0\0MRON\0\3\0\0\0\0\0\0\206X\353\f\0\0\0\0"..., 76},
{"\1?\275E\377\177\0\0X\0\0\0\2\0\0\0\210@\275E\377\177\0\0\10k,K", 28},
{"\0\0\0\0\v\0\0\0\303\233\342\6\0\0\0\0\v\255\17\0\0\0\0\0:-\221\0\0\0\0\0"
..., 88}], msg_controllen=0, msg_flags=0}, 0) = 192
times({tms_utime=12192, tms_stime=6618, tms_cutime=0, tms_cstime=0})
= 436799560
getrusage(RUSAGE_SELF, {ru_utime={121, 924464}, ru_stime={66, 187937},
...}) = 0
times({tms_utime=12192, tms_stime=6618, tms_cutime=0, tms_cstime=0})
```

```
= 436799560
times({tms_utime=12192, tms_stime=6618, tms_cutime=0, tms_cstime=0})
= 436799560
poll([{fd=16, events=POLLIN|POLLPRI|POLLRDNORM|POLLRDBAND}, {fd=12,
events=POLLIN|POLLPRI|POLLRDNORM|POLLRDBAND}, {fd=20,
events=POLLIN|POLLPRI|POLLRDNORM|POLLRDBAND}, {fd=19,
events=POLLIN|POLLPRI|POLLRDNORM|POLLRDBAND}], 4, 30) = 1 ([{fd=20,
revents=POLLIN|POLLRDNORM}])
recvmsg(20, {msg_name(16)={sa_family=AF_INET, sin_port=htons(19552),
sin_addr=inet_addr("192.168.1.2")}},
```

netstat, ss, and tcpdump

You can use the netstat tool to display information related to the networking configuration and performance of your system, from routing tables to interface statistics and open ports. By default, netstat displays a list of all open sockets on the system. However, a wide variety of command-line options can be given to vary the details shown.

Looking at Interface Statistics

One form of output that you can produce with netstat relies on the -i argument to display interface statistics. This output shows the statistics for a typical RAC configuration:

```
[root@london1 ~]# netstat -i
Kernel Interface table
Iface   MTU Met    RX-OK RX-ERR RX-DRP RX-OVR  TX-OK TX-ERR TX-DRP TX-OVR Flg
eth0   1500   0   137371      0      0      0 582037      0      0      0 BMRU
eth0:1 1500   0      - no statistics available -                         BMRU
eth0:2 1500   0      - no statistics available -                         BMRU
eth1   1500   0  5858628      0      0      0 5290923      0      0      0 BMRU
lo    16436   0   991251      0      0      0 991251      0      0      0 LRU
```

In addition to the interface details, this command also provides information on the number of packets transmitted and received. You can also combine netstat with the ifconfig command to show errors and dropped packets. The following two examples for eth0 and eth0:1 confirm that, as a VIP address, eth0:1 shares the same hardware configuration as eth0. Therefore, in the netstat example, statistics are not duplicated for the interfaces used for the VIP configuration:

```
[root@london1 ~]# ifconfig eth0
eth0      Link encap:Ethernet  HWaddr 00:04:23:DC:29:50
          inet addr:172.17.1.101  Bcast:172.17.255.255  Mask:255.255.0.0
          inet6 addr: fe80::204:23ff:fedc:2950/64 Scope:Link
          UP BROADCAST RUNNING MULTICAST  MTU:1500  Metric:1
          RX packets:137503 errors:0 dropped:0 overruns:0 frame:0
          TX packets:627169 errors:0 dropped:0 overruns:0 carrier:0
          collisions:0 txqueuelen:1000
          RX bytes:34943895 (33.3 MiB)  TX bytes:220187041 (209.9 MiB)
          Memory:b8820000-b8840000
[root@london1 ~]# ifconfig eth0:1
```

```
eth0:1    Link encap:Ethernet  HWaddr 00:04:23:DC:29:50
          inet addr:172.17.1.209  Bcast:172.17.255.255  Mask:255.255.0.0
          UP BROADCAST RUNNING MULTICAST  MTU:1500  Metric:1
          Memory:b8820000-b8840000
```

The preceding information can assist you in diagnosing issues that you may suspect are resulting in poor network performance due to hardware errors. You can also observe continually updated values using the -c argument. Most importantly, you should see values in the RX-OK and TX-OK fields increasing on all interfaces as network traffic is communicated, with zero to low numbers in all of the other fields. In particular, increasing values in the RX-ERR and TX-ERR fields is an indication of a possible fault that requires further investigation.

Summary Statistics

For additional diagnostic information, you can run netstat with the -s argument to produce a summary report on statistics for all protocols configured on the system. For Cache Fusion traffic on Linux, you should pay particular attention to the UDP protocol-related information on the packets sent and received, as well as whether packet-receive errors are evident.

Listening Socket Statistics

The default output of netstat does not include listening sockets; these can be shown with the -l option. However, you will be more likely to prefer to display all established and listening socket-related information at the same time. You can accomplish this with the -a argument. The output of netstat -a can be somewhat lengthy; in particular, all information under the section Active Unix domain sockets relates to interprocess communication on the local host, and it is not network related. To restrict the output to network activity, you may also provide the additional --inet argument, as in this example:

```
[root@london1 ~]# netstat --inet -a | more
Active Internet connections (servers and established)
Proto Recv-Q Send-Q Local Address            Foreign Address      State

tcp        0      0 localhost.locald:bootserver *:*                LISTEN
tcp        0      0 localhost.localdomain:2208   *:*               LISTEN
tcp        0      0 *:cypress-stat              *:*                 LISTEN
tcp        0      0 192.168.1.1:59585           *:*                 LISTEN
tcp        0      0 192.168.1.1:62018           *:*                 LISTEN
tcp        0      0 london1.example.com:49795   *:*                 LISTEN
tcp        0      0 192.168.1.1:30056           *:*                 LISTEN
tcp        0      0 *:59468                     *:*                 LISTEN
tcp        0      0 192.168.1.1:62189           *:*                 LISTEN
tcp        0      0 *:sunrpc                    *:*                 LISTEN
tcp        0      0 172.17.1.209:ncube-lm       *:*                 LISTEN
tcp        0      0 london1.example.co:ncube-lm *:*                 LISTEN
tcp        0      0 172.17.1.208:ncube-lm       *:*                 LISTEN
```

The --inet argument provides a significantly more readable display and a snapshot of all network-related activity on the system. Within the fields, Proto refers to the protocol, which means we can observe the RAC-related communication established under the UDP protocol. As their names suggest, the Recv-Q and Send-Q fields relate to the receiving and sending queues, so they should almost always be zero. If these values are increasing—and increasing for the UDP protocol in particular—then you have evidence that your interconnect cannot sustain your desired workload. The Local address field shows your hostname and port number. Similar to the foreign address of the host to which you are connecting, this field will be *:* until a connection is established. The State field will usually show LISTEN or ESTABLISHED for the TCP protocol; however, UDP is a stateless protocol, so these connections have no state entries. If you also provide the -n argument, no name lookups will be done, and IP addresses for all connections will be displayed.

Looking up Well-Known Ports

If a port is defined as a well-known port in the /etc/services file, the port number will be replaced by the name. Referring to /etc/services, you can see that the port number shown as ncube-lm is in fact the standard Oracle listener port number of 1521:

```
[root@london1 root]# cat /etc/services | grep ncube-lm
ncube-lm        1521/tcp    # nCube License Manager
ncube-lm        1521/udp    # nCube License Manager
```

If you change this file so it is more meaningful for diagnosing Oracle network services, the output will be reflected the next time you run netstat, without having to restart any of the services. However, it is important to be aware that, from a strict standpoint, ncube-lm is the correct well-known port for 1521, as defined at the following location: http://www.iana.org/assignments/port-numbers.

Reporting on Socket Statistics Using ss

As an alternative to netstat, you can use the ss utility to report socket statistics. For example, the ss -l command displays listening sockets in a manner similar to that observed with netstat previously. Using ss without further arguments lets you rapidly determine the established connections on your system:

```
[root@london1 ~]# ss
State    Recv-Q Send-Q    Local Address:Port        Peer Address:Port
ESTAB    0      0         127.0.0.1:61876           127.0.0.1:6100
ESTAB    0      0         127.0.0.1:61861           127.0.0.1:6100
ESTAB    0      0         127.0.0.1:61864           127.0.0.1:6100
ESTAB    0      0         172.17.1.208:1521         172.17.1.102:39393
ESTAB    0      0         172.17.1.209:1521         172.17.1.209:11402
ESTAB    0      0         172.17.1.209:25333        172.17.1.209:1521
ESTAB    0      0         127.0.0.1:2016            127.0.0.1:10911
ESTAB    0      0         172.17.1.208:1521         172.17.1.208:16542
ESTAB    0      0         127.0.0.1:6100            127.0.0.1:61876
ESTAB    0      0         172.17.1.101:62822        172.17.1.203:1521
ESTAB    0      0         172.17.1.208:16542        172.17.1.208:1521
ESTAB    0      0         127.0.0.1:6100            127.0.0.1:61861
ESTAB    0      0         127.0.0.1:6100            127.0.0.1:61864
ESTAB    0      0         127.0.0.1:10911           127.0.0.1:2016
ESTAB    0      0         172.17.1.209:11402        172.17.1.209:1521
ESTAB    0      0         172.17.1.209:1521         172.17.1.209:25333
```

```
ESTAB      0      0        172.17.1.101:17046        172.17.1.102:11585
ESTAB      0      0        192.168.1.1:35959         192.168.1.2:21965
ESTAB      0      0        192.168.1.1:61659         192.168.1.2:27582
```

Capturing and Displaying Network Packets

You should consider using the tcpdump command for detailed analysis of network traffic. This command's functionality is similar to that provided by strace for an application communicating with the operating system kernel. tcpdump enables you to capture and display the network packets running on the entire system or a particular interface. The tcpdump command's -D option will display the interfaces available to you, as in this example:

```
[root@london1 ~]# tcpdump -D
1.eth0
2.eth1
3.any (Pseudo-device that captures on all interfaces)
4.lo
```

The following example shows the default summary information you see when running tcpdump against the private interconnect interface. Specifically, it shows the packets being transferred across this network:

```
[root@london1 ~]# tcpdump -i 2 | more
tcpdump: verbose output suppressed, use -v or -vv for full protocol decode
listening on eth1, link-type EN10MB (Ethernet), capture size 96 bytes
11:43:36.045648 IP 192.168.1.2.7016 > 192.168.1.1.sds-admin:UDP, length 192
11:43:36.046217 IP 192.168.1.2.19552 > 192.168.1.1.26976:UDP, length 224
11:43:36.046237 IP 192.168.1.1.sds-admin > 192.168.1.2.19552:UDP, length 192
11:43:36.046279 IP 192.168.1.1.sds-admin > 192.168.1.2.asc-slmd:UDP,length 256
11:43:36.046368 IP 192.168.1.2.7016 > 192.168.1.1.sds-admin:UDP, length 192
11:43:36.047215 IP 192.168.1.2.19552 > 192.168.1.1.26976:UDP, length 224
11:43:36.047231 IP 192.168.1.1.sds-admin > 192.168.1.2.19552:UDP, length 192
11:43:36.047260 IP 192.168.1.1.sds-admin > 192.168.1.2.asc-slmd:UDP,length 256
11:43:36.047413 IP 192.168.1.2.7016 > 192.168.1.1.sds-admin:UDP, length 192
11:43:36.047762 IP 192.168.1.2.11403 > 192.168.1.1.20890:UDP, length 520
11:43:36.047784 IP 192.168.1.1.18929 > 192.168.1.2.11403:UDP, length 192
11:43:36.047863 IP 192.168.1.1.18929 > 192.168.1.2.22580:UDP, length 8328
11:43:36.047865 IP 192.168.1.1 > 192.168.1.2: udp
11:43:36.047867 IP 192.168.1.1 > 192.168.1.2: udp
11:43:36.047868 IP 192.168.1.1 > 192.168.1.2: udp
11:43:36.047869 IP 192.168.1.1 > 192.168.1.2: udp
11:43:36.047870 IP 192.168.1.1 > 192.168.1.2: udp
11:43:36.048689 IP 192.168.1.2.11403 > 192.168.1.1.20890:UDP, length 448
11:43:36.048704 IP 192.168.1.1.18929 > 192.168.1.2.11403:UDP, length 192
11:43:36.048754 IP 192.168.1.1.18929 > 192.168.1.2.22580:UDP, length 8328
```

Similar to the strace -o option, the -w option can be used to write the data to an output file. Subsequently, the -r option can be used to read from that file, while -A can be used to print the contents of each packet.

iostat

iostat is the first of a number of utilities we will discuss that are installed with the sysstat RPM package. Other utilities we will discuss include mpstat and sar. The iostat utility also displays information related to CPU utilization, but it focuses on providing detailed I/O statistics. Like vmstat, iostat can be run without any command-line arguments to report statistics for average CPU utilization and disk devices since the most recent boot time. The format of the CPU utilization contains the same fields we have seen with top and vmstat. The disk statistics show the device name, the number of I/O operations per second, the number of 512-byte blocks read and written per second, and the total number of 512-byte blocks read and written. iostat can also be supplied with one or two numerical arguments to represent the interval between sampling periods and the number of sampling periods in total. You may also specify statistics for a specific device using the -p argument, such as -p sde for device sde. If you only wish to view disk utilization information, you can use the -d option. Alternatively, you can use the -c option to view information for the CPU only. The -k option displays disk information in kilobytes, as opposed to blocks. The following example shows the results from running iostat against an individual disk device:

```
[root@london1 ~]# iostat -p sde 3 10
Linux 2.6.18-164.el5 (london1.example.com)    02/05/2010

avg-cpu:  %user   %nice %system %iowait  %steal   %idle
           0.56    0.00    0.24    0.42    0.00   98.77

Device:            tps   Blk_read/s   Blk_wrtn/s   Blk_read   Blk_wrtn
sde              46.02       376.57       676.68   26774930   48113635
sde1            389.43         0.54        63.60      38074    4522265

avg-cpu:  %user   %nice %system %iowait  %steal   %idle
          15.52    0.00    2.88   17.72    0.00   63.88

Device:            tps   Blk_read/s   Blk_wrtn/s   Blk_read   Blk_wrtn
sde            4122.00     20955.67     72453.00      62867     217359
sde1          21653.33         0.00      1863.67          0       5591

avg-cpu:  %user   %nice %system %iowait  %steal   %idle
          25.88    0.00    4.75   20.79    0.00   48.58

Device:            tps   Blk_read/s   Blk_wrtn/s   Blk_read   Blk_wrtn
sde            3096.33      9361.67     58477.67      28085     175433
sde1          9752.00         0.00      2734.67          0       8204
```

When using iostat to observe disk statistics in a RAC environment, you should be keenly aware of the infrastructure that lies between the operating system and the actual disk devices. For example, the levels of abstraction can range from multipathing device drivers and host bus adapters to cache on the storage and a disk RAID configuration. The disk devices you're most interested in using are shared between all of the nodes in the cluster, and any useful information that you can derive on any individual node is likely to be limited. Therefore, iostat may prove useful in providing a highly generalized overview of disk activity on the system; however, there is no substitute for using the specialized storage analysis tools provided by the vendor of your chosen storage subsystem.

mpstat

By default, the `mpstat` command shows a CPU utilization report similar to that produced by `iostat` for all statistics since boot time. It also includes an additional field that shows the number of interrupts per second. `mpstat` also accepts the same number and type of numeric arguments as `vmstat` and `iostat`, which it uses to produce output at sampled intervals, as in this example:

```
[root@london1 ~]# mpstat 3 10
Linux 2.6.18-164.el5 (london1.example.com)      02/05/2010

11:38:12 AM  CPU   %user   %nice   %sys %iowait    %irq   %soft %steal   %idle    intr/s
11:38:15 AM  all   18.47    0.00   2.54   15.76    0.21    0.76   0.00   62.25   6977.00
11:38:18 AM  all   28.65    0.00   3.44   22.62    0.25    1.19   0.00   43.85   9674.75
11:38:21 AM  all   22.21    0.00   2.71   20.09    0.17    0.93   0.00   53.88   7495.99
11:38:24 AM  all   30.91    0.00   3.78   20.68    0.30    1.44   0.00   42.89  10392.59
11:38:27 AM  all   31.62    0.00   3.78   20.37    0.34    1.23   0.00   42.66  10206.08
11:38:30 AM  all   12.40    0.00   1.69   19.35    0.21    0.76   0.00   65.58   6710.37
11:38:33 AM  all   17.24    0.00   2.33   15.97    0.21    0.76   0.00   63.49   8070.23
11:38:36 AM  all   27.96    0.00   3.65   18.33    0.30    1.15   0.00   48.62   8732.89
11:38:39 AM  all   17.35    0.00   2.42   14.76    0.17    0.72   0.00   64.59   7200.34
11:38:42 AM  all   30.41    0.00   3.73   14.89    0.25    1.19   0.00   49.53   9328.86
Average:     all   23.72    0.00   3.01   18.28    0.24    1.01   0.00   53.74   8475.07
```

By default, `mpstat` reports CPU statistics averaged for all processors; however, the most significant difference compared to `iostat` is that `mpstat` uses the `-P` argument in conjunction with either the CPU number starting at 0 or with `-P ALL`, which displays output for all processors on an individual basis. When analyzing CPU performance with `mpstat` or other monitoring tools, you need to keep in mind that if you have a system equipped with multicore CPUs, each CPU core will be presented to the monitoring tool as a distinct CPU, even though the cores share some system resources (see Chapter 4 for more details on multicore CPUs). Similarly, Intel's hyperthreaded CPUs will also present each CPU physically installed in the system as two CPUs for each physical core. This enables processes to be scheduled by the Linux operating system simultaneously with the same core. `/proc/cpuinfo` should be your first reference for CPU architecture (Chapter 4 explains how to precisely map the CPU architecture to the representation by the operating system). The following example shows an extract of the first processor of `/proc/cpuinfo`:

```
[root@london8 ~]# cat /proc/cpuinfo | more
processor       : 0
vendor_id       : GenuineIntel
cpu family      : 6
model           : 46
model name      : Intel(R) Xeon(R) CPU        X7560  @ 2.27GHz
stepping        : 5
cpu MHz         : 2261.066
cache size      : 24576 KB
physical id     : 0
siblings        : 16
core id         : 0
cpu cores       : 8
apicid          : 0
fpu             : yes
```

```
fpu_exception   : yes
cpuid level     : 11
wp              : yes
flags           : fpu vme de pse tsc msr pae mce cx8 apic sep mtrr pge mca
cmov pat pse36 clflush dts acpi mmx fxsr sse sse2 ss ht tm syscall nx rdtscp
lm constant_tsc ida nonstop_tsc pni monitor ds_cpl vmx est tm2 cx16 xtpr
popcnt lahf_lm
bogomips        : 4522.13
clflush size    : 64
cache_alignment : 64
address sizes   : 44 bits physical, 48 bits virtual
power management: [8]
```

sar and kSar

The system activity reporter (sar) is a powerful tool that can encompass virtually all of the performance information generated by the other performance tools discussed in this chapter. In fact, some of the statistics from sar may look familiar to users of Oracle EM because sar underpins most of the host-based performance views. This is why the sysstat package must be installed on managed targets.

Configuring sar

As its name suggests, the system activity reporter is the front-end reporting tool. This tool is accompanied by the system activity data collector (sadc). Reports can be generated by sar in an interactive manner or written to a file for longer-term data collection. When you install the sysstat package, it sets sadc to run periodically by configuring the sa1 script from the cron scheduled script, /etc/cron.d/sysstat, as in this example:

```
[root@london1 root]# cat /etc/cron.d/sysstat
# run system activity accounting tool every 10 minutes
*/10 * * * * root /usr/lib/sa/sa1 1 1
# generate a daily summary of process accounting at 23:53
53 23 * * * root /usr/lib/sa/sa2 -A
```

By default, this script is run every ten minutes, capturing all system statistics for a one-second period. Next, the script appends the data to the current data file in the /var/log/sa directory, where the file is named sa, with a suffix that corresponds to the current date, as in this example:

```
[root@london1 sa]# ls
sa01  sa02  sa03  sa04  sa05  sar01  sar02  sar03  sar04
```

At the same location as sa1, you can find the file sa2, which by default runs once per day. sa2 runs sar to generate a full report on all of the data captured during the previous day by sadc.

A sar report presents system performance data divided into 17 separate sections. Each section contains data related to a specific aspect of system performance; this information is ordered by time throughout a 24-hour period, based on the ten-minute collection interval.

Invoking sar Directly

The standard statistics collection is useful for long-term performance monitoring and capacity planning trending activities; however, the one-second collection period at ten-minute intervals may not be sufficient for pinpointing specific performance issues. For this reason, you can also invoke sar directly to produce performance information on one or more of the specific performance-related areas to the screen.

This interactive performance requires two numerical arguments: one for the interval between sampling periods and one for the number of sampling periods in total. sar is different from the statistics commands that we have already seen, such as vmstat. For example, if you specify just one numerical argument, sar will report statistics for the time interval specified by the argument once, and then exit. You may also provide arguments to specify the type of performance information to view. If you do not provide any arguments, by default you will be shown performance information for all CPUs. The following extract shows the first output of the CPU performance information for a three-second sampling period, which will be collected ten times:

```
[root@london1 sa]# sar 3 10
Linux 2.6.18-164.el5 (london1.example.com)        02/05/2010

12:01:36 PM     CPU     %user     %nice   %system   %iowait   %steal     %idle
12:01:39 PM     all     12.30      0.00      3.31     19.51      0.00     64.89
12:01:42 PM     all     14.53      0.00      3.82     22.78      0.00     58.86
12:01:45 PM     all     14.98      0.00      3.70     23.53      0.00     57.79
12:01:48 PM     all     14.39      0.00      3.91     24.08      0.00     57.62
12:01:51 PM     all     13.65      0.00      3.57     23.35      0.00     59.42
12:01:54 PM     all     14.40      0.00      3.57     22.81      0.00     59.22
12:01:57 PM     all     12.95      0.00      3.86     24.19      0.00     59.00
12:02:00 PM     all     15.86      0.00      3.14     20.40      0.00     60.60
12:02:03 PM     all      8.93      0.00      0.21      0.72      0.00     90.14
12:02:06 PM     all     15.52      0.00      4.00     20.79      0.00     59.69
Average:        all     13.75      0.00      3.31     20.21      0.00     62.73
```

You can view additional or alternative performance information by providing other arguments, such as sar -n for network statistics or sar -b for I/O statistics. The full range of options is detailed in the sar man page. To produce performance information on all sections interactively, you can call sar -A; however, be aware that the output is extensive. In conjunction with sar -A, you may also find the -o option useful in directing the output to a file. The default file location is the same as the regularly sampled sar data. Therefore, we recommend that you specify a file name for detailed sar performance analysis work. For example, the following command collects all sar statistics at three-second intervals for a five-minute period into the london1.sa file:

```
[root@london1 root]# sar -A -o london1.sa 3 100
```

The file generated is in the sar binary format. This means sar will need to read the results file at a later point, which can be accomplished using the -f option:

```
[root@london1 root]# sar -f london1.sa
```

As you would expect, using the -f option excludes also using the -o option. However, it accepts the same command-line arguments, such as when called in an interactive manner. Thus, the following example shows the CPU-information only:

```
[root@london1 root]# sar -A -f london1.sa
```

To display all of the information collected in the file, you will need to specify the -A option.

Graphing the Results

The text-based sar output provides you with all of the recorded performance information you require. However, simply browsing sar -A output may prove difficult when attempting to diagnose any system performance issues that have occurred.

Fortunately, there are a number of tools available for graphing the output from sar. For example, the Interactive System Activity Grapher (isag) utility is available for graphing the data recorded in sar files. isag is no longer included automatically with the systtat RPM package, primarily due to its additional dependence on the gnuplot package. However, you can easily download and install the latest versions of isag and gnuplot to view your sar statistics, and isag is still included with current versions of the sysstat source code.

Alternatively, the kSar tool can be used to graph captured sar information; you can download this tool at http://ksar.atomique.net/. To use kSar, unzip the downloaded zip file, change the directory to the extracted kSar directory, and run the tool with the following command:

```
[root@london1 kSar-5.0.6]# java -jar kSar.jar
```

In the graphical interface, click the Data menu option and select *Run local command* to display the dialog window shown in Figure 13-1.

Enter local command

sar -A -f /var/log/sa/london1

OK   Cancel

Figure 13-1. Executing a local command from kSar

Next, specify the command to extract the sar data from your captured file, as in this example:

```
sar -A -f /var/log/sa/london1.sa
```

If the extraction is successful, after a short period of time kSar will report that the data import is finished. It will also display summary information, as well as potential system bottlenecks. The example shown in Figure 13-2 reports that CPU utilization is more than 25%, which makes it worth investigating further.

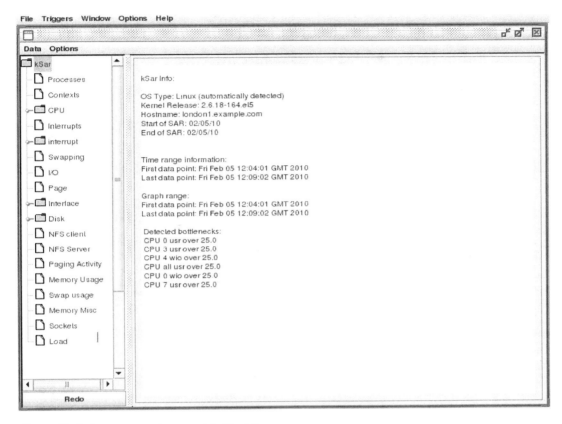

File   Triggers   Window   Options   Help

Data   Options

kSar

   Processes
   Contexts
   CPU
   Interrupts
   interrupt
   Swapping
   I/O
   Page
   Interface
   Disk
   NFS client
   NFS Server
   Paging Activity
   Memory Usage
   Swap usage
   Memory Misc
   Sockets
   Load

Redo

kSar Info:

OS Type: Linux (automatically detected)
Kernel Release: 2.6.18-164.el5
Hostname: london1.example.com
Start of SAR: 02/05/10
End of SAR: 02/05/10

Time range information:
First data point: Fri Feb 05 12:04:01 GMT 2010
Last data point: Fri Feb 05 12:09:02 GMT 2010

Graph range:
First data point: Fri Feb 05 12:04:01 GMT 2010
Last data point: Fri Feb 05 12:09:02 GMT 2010

Detected bottlenecks:
CPU 0 usr over 25.0
CPU 3 usr over 25.0
CPU 4 wio over 25.0
CPU all usr over 25.0
CPU 0 wio over 25.0
CPU 7 usr over 25.0

Figure 13-2. A summary view provided by kSar

At this point, you can select from the options in the Menu tab on the left of the screen to display information for particular areas. Subjects you can drill down on include I/O, interface traffic by interface, and CPU utilization. Figure 13-3 shows an example summary of CPU utilization across the capture period.

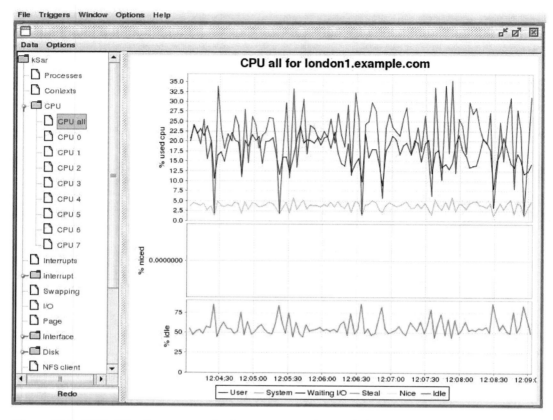

Figure 13-3. CPU utilization summarized across a reporting period

Oracle Cluster Health Monitor

The Oracle Cluster Health Monitor is an Oracle-provided tool for monitoring resource utilization on a cluster basis. In particular, the Oracle Cluster Health Monitor runs in one of two modes. In the first, it observes the system in real time. In the second, it collects data in a Berkeley DB repository on a node-by-node basis, enabling the review of data collected over time. This data can be used to pinpoint the causes of performance issues.

Installing the Oracle Cluster Health Monitor

The Oracle Cluster Health Monitor for Linux can be downloaded from the Oracle Technology Network web site at the following location: www.oracle.com/technology/products/database/clustering/ipd_download_homepage.html. The resulting downloaded is called crfpack-linux.zip. To install the tool, begin by creating a dedicated user for the tool on all nodes in the cluster. The following example illustrates how to create crfuser on the london1 node:

```
[root@london1 ~]# useradd -g oinstall crfuser
[root@london1 ~]# passwd crfuser
Changing password for user crfuser.
New UNIX password:
Retype new UNIX password:
passwd: all authentication tokens updated successfully.
```

Once the user has been created on all nodes, secure shell (ssh) must be configured without password prompts or warnings received when connecting between hosts. This can be performed with the same manual configuration steps required for configuring ssh for the oracle user (see Chapter 6 for information on the steps required to do this). Once you have tested ssh connectivity between nodes, copy and unzip the file crfpack-linux.zip into the /home/crfuser/ directory, designating ownership by the crfuser:

```
[crfuser@london1 ~]$ unzip crfpack-linux.zip
[crfuser@london1 ~]$ ls
admin  bin  crfpack-linux.zip  install  jdk  jlib  lib  log  mesg
```

Before installing the software, it is necessary to have a non-root file system available on which you can create the Berkeley DB database. If you opt for a default file system configuration (as we recommend), then you will not have a non-root file system available. Therefore, you can either mount a directory from an external source such as iSCSI; or, if you are using ASM, you can create an ACFS file system (see Chapter 9 for more information on how to do this). In the example shown in Figure 13-4, a 10GB ACFS file system is created for a two-node cluster, allocating 5GB of storage per node for that two-node cluster.

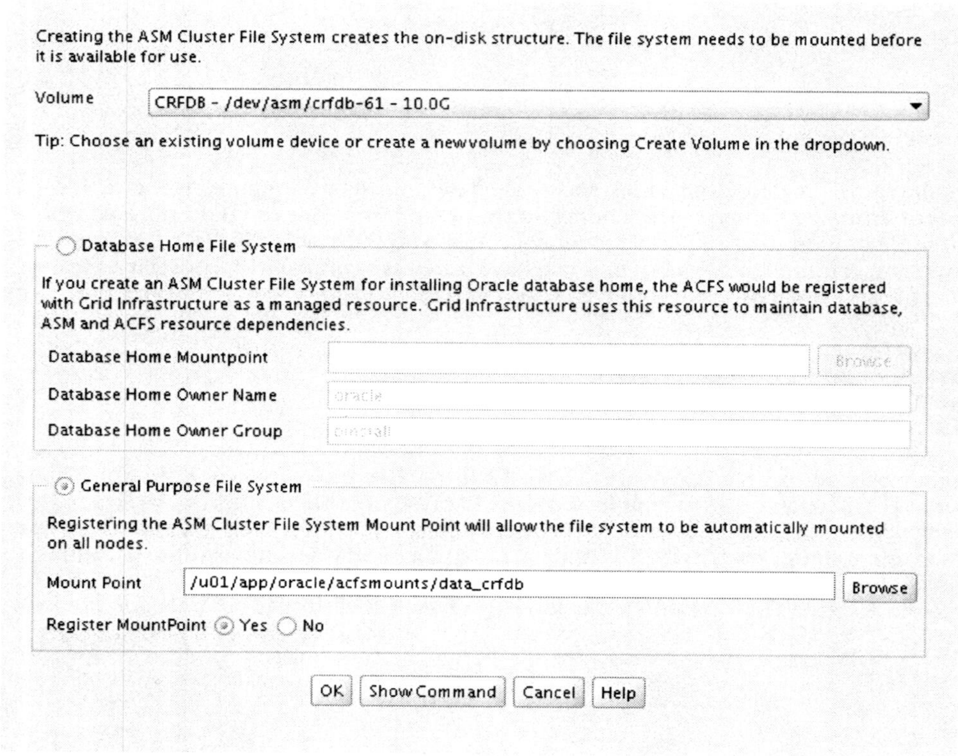

Creating the ASM Cluster File System creates the on-disk structure. The file system needs to be mounted before it is available for use.

Volume   CRFDB - /dev/asm/crfdb-61 - 10.0G   ▼

Tip: Choose an existing volume device or create a new volume by choosing Create Volume in the dropdown.

○ Database Home File System

If you create an ASM Cluster File System for installing Oracle database home, the ACFS would be registered with Grid Infrastructure as a managed resource. Grid Infrastructure uses this resource to maintain database, ASM and ACFS resource dependencies.

Database Home Mountpoint   Browse

Database Home Owner Name   oracle

Database Home Owner Group   oinstall

◉ General Purpose File System

Registering the ASM Cluster File System Mount Point will allow the file system to be automatically mounted on all nodes.

Mount Point   /u01/app/oracle/acfsmounts/data_crfdb   Browse

Register MountPoint ◉ Yes ○ No

OK   Show Command   Cancel   Help

Figure 13-4. A 10GB ACFS file system for the Oracle Cluster Health Monitor

You must then mount the ACFS file system on all nodes in the cluster:

```
[root@london1 ~]# /sbin/mount.acfs -o all
[root@london1 ~]# df -h
Filesystem          Size  Used Avail Use% Mounted on
/dev/mapper/VolGroup00-LogVol00
                    886G   19G  822G   3% /
/dev/sda1            99M   13M   82M  14% /boot
tmpfs               7.9G  192M  7.7G   3% /dev/shm
/dev/asm/crfdb-61    10G   85M   10G   1% /u01/app/oracle/acfsmounts/data_crfdb
```

Next, you need to make a separate directory for the Berkeley DB Database for all nodes in the cluster. Note that, although the file system is shared between the nodes, the Berkeley DB Database is not cluster-aware, so it cannot be shared between nodes. The following example creates the directory for the first node only:

```
[crfuser@london1 install]$ mkdir \
> /u01/app/oracle/acfsmounts/data_crfdb/oracrfdb1
```

On the first node, run the installation script from the install directory as the crfuser. Do this in conjunction with the -i option, specifying the nodes to be installed, the location of the Berkeley DB database, and the name of the master node, as shown here:

```
[crfuser@london1 install]$ ./crfinst.pl -i london1,london2 -b
/u01/app/oracle/acfsmounts/data_crfdb/oracrfdb1 -m london1

Performing checks on nodes: "london1 london2" ...
Assigning london2 as replica

Generating cluster wide configuration file...

Creating a bundle for remote nodes...

Installing on nodes "london2 london1" ...

Configuration complete on nodes "london2 london1" ...
```

Once the initial installation has completed on the first node, you can finish the installation by rerunning the install script as the root user with the -f option on all nodes, including the first node in the cluster, where you specify the Berkeley DB directory for each node. If the Berkeley DB directory is local, then it can have the same name on each node. In this example, which uses ACFS, the directory name is distinct per node. For example, the installation is completed as follows on node 1:

```
[root@london1 install]# ./crfinst.pl -f -b /u01/app/oracle/acfsmounts/data_crfdb/oracrfdb1
Removing contents of BDB Directory
/u01/app/oracle/acfsmounts/data_crfdb/oracrfdb1

Installation completed successfully at /usr/lib/oracrf...
```

Similarly, the installation is completed as follows on node 2:

```
[root@london2 install]# ./crfinst.pl -f -b  /u01/app/oracle/acfsmounts/data_crfdb/oracrfdb2/
Removing contents of BDB Directory
/u01/app/oracle/acfsmounts/data_crfdb/oracrfdb2/

Installation completed successfully at /usr/lib/oracrf...
```

A log of installation activity is maintained in the crfinst.log file in the crfuser home directory.

Starting and Stopping the Oracle Cluster Health Monitor

After installation is complete, the Oracle Cluster Health Monitor can be started on all nodes with the /etc/init.d/init.crfd script, as in this example:

```
[root@london2 init.d]# ./init.crfd enable
```

You can verify a successful startup by issuing the command again with the status argument:

```
[root@london1 init.d]# ./init.crfd status

OSysmond running with PID=3571.
OLoggerd running with PID=3623.

oproxyd running with PID=3626.
```

To stop the Oracle Cluster Health Monitor from running, use init.crfd with the disable argument. disable is preferable to the stop argument in this case because the daemons will be restarted when stop is used.

Understanding the Architecture

The Oracle Cluster Health Monitor starts three daemon processes: osysmond, ologgerd, and oproxyd. osysmond collects the monitoring data from the local system, while ologgerd receives the data from all nodes and populates the Berkeley DB database. Thus, ologgerd is only active on the master node with another node acting as a standby. You may also observe that the Berkeley DB database directories are now populated with data:

```
[root@london1 data_crfdb]# ls *
lost+found:

oracrfdb1:
crfalert.bdb   crfcpu.bdb     crfts.bdb    __db.003   __db.006
crfclust.bdb   crfhosts.bdb   __db.001     __db.004   log.0000000001
crfconn.bdb    crfloclts.bdb  __db.002     __db.005   london1.ldb

oracrfdb2:
crfalert.bdb   crfloclts.bdb  __db.002     __db.006
crfclust.bdb   crfrep.bdb     __db.003     log.0000000001
crfcpu.bdb     crfts.bdb      __db.004     london2.ldb
crfhosts.bdb   __db.001       __db.005     repdhosts.bdb
```

Installing the Client-Side GUI

In addition to the server-side installation, it is also possible to use the same installation software to install a client-side graphical interface. Oracle recommends installing this graphical interface on a separate node from the cluster. On the server, the daemon process oproxyd listens for network connections, such as connections from this interface. The client installation should be performed as the root user and not the crfuser, as in this example:

```
[root@london5 install]# ./crfinst.pl -g

Installation completed sucessfully at /usr/lib/oracrf...
```

The installation locates the files in the /usr/lib/oracrf directory, and the graphical client can be run from within the bin directory by specifying the cluster node to connect to:

```
[root@london5 bin]# ./crfgui -m london1
Cluster Health Analyzer V1.10
        Look for Loggerd via node london1
...Connected to Loggerd on london1
Note: Node london1 is now up
Cluster 'MyCluster', 2 nodes. Ext time=2010-02-08 12:30:57
Making Window: IPD Cluster Monitor V1.10 on nehep1,
Logger V1.04.20091223, Cluster "MyCluster"  (View 0), Refresh rate: 1 sec
```

Viewing Current and Captured Activity

By default, the client-side graphical tool runs in real-time mode, displaying the current activity across the cluster (see Figure 13-5).

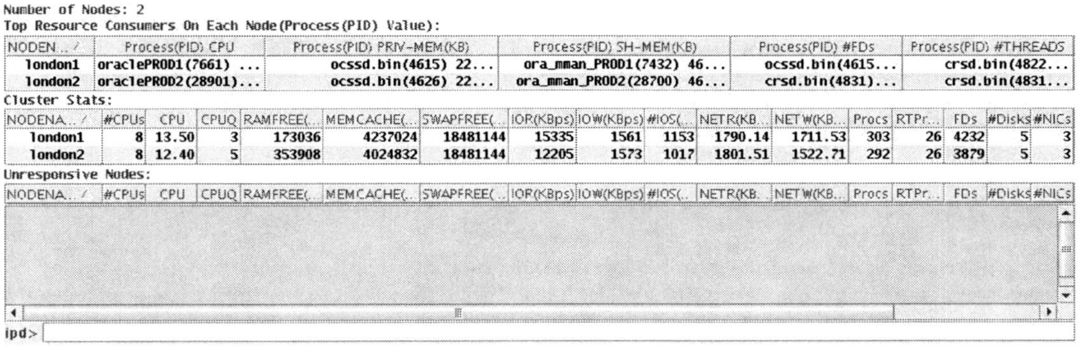

Number of Nodes: 2
Top Resource Consumers On Each Node(Process(PID) Value):

NODEN.. /	Process(PID) CPU	Process(PID) PRIV-MEM(KB)	Process(PID) SH-MEM(KB)	Process(PID) #FDs	Process(PID) #THREADS
london1	oraclePROD1(7661) ...	ocssd.bin(4615) 22...	ora_mman_PROD1(7432) 46...	ocssd.bin(4615...	crsd.bin(4822...
london2	oraclePROD2(28901)...	ocssd.bin(4626) 22...	ora_mman_PROD2(28700) 46...	crsd.bin(4831)...	crsd.bin(4831...

Cluster Stats:

NODENA.. /	#CPUs	CPU	CPUQ	RAMFREE(	MEMCACHE(	SWAPFREE(	IOR(KBps)	IOW(KBps)	#IOS(.	NETR(KB.	NETW(KB..	Procs	RTPr..	FDs	#Disks	#NICs
london1	8	13.50	3	173036	4237024	18481144	15335	1561	1153	1790.14	1711.53	303	26	4232	5	3
london2	8	12.40	5	353908	4024832	18481144	12205	1573	1017	1801.51	1522.71	292	26	3879	5	3

Unresponsive Nodes:

NODENA.. /	#CPUs	CPU	CPUQ	RAMFREE..	MEMCACHE(	SWAPFREE(	IOR(KBps)	IOW(KBps)	#IOS(.	NETR(KB.	NETW(KB..	Procs	RTPr..	FDs	#Disks	#NICs

ipd>

Figure 13-5. The current activity, as shown in the client-side GUI

There is also the option to replay captured data from a previous period of time. For example, the following command replays the data from the previous five minutes:

```
[root@london5 bin]# ./crfgui -d "00:05:00" -m london1
```

In addition to the graphical tool, there is a command-line tool called oclumon that can be used either in real time or to browse historical data. oclumon can be called either from the server or from the client environment. By default, oclumon reports data in real time for the local node, as in this example:

```
[root@london1 ~]# oclumon dumpnodeview

----------------------------------------
Node: london1 Clock: '02-09-10 12.08.01 UTC' SerialNo:77669
----------------------------------------
```

```
SYSTEM:
#cpus: 8 cpu: 8.66 cpuq: 3 physmemfree: 1506256 mcache: 3318060 swapfree: 17141300 ior: 12474
iow: 882 ios: 994 netr: 785.5 netw: 862.11 procs: 291 rtprocs: 26 #fds: 3752 #sysfdlimit:
6553600 #disks: 5 #nics: 3  nicErrors: 0

TOP CONSUMERS:
topcpu: 'oraclePROD1(8943) 7.75' topprivmem: 'ocssd.bin(4615) 224436' topshm:
'ora_mman_PROD1(26453) 462752' topfd: 'ocssd.bin(4615) 95' topthread: 'crsd.bin(4822) 54'
```

With the –allnodes option, oclumon will report data from all of the nodes in the cluster. Additionally, you can use the –v option for verbose output. oclumon also accepts querying for historical data. For example, the following command will report verbose output for all nodes for the previous five minutes:

```
[root@london1 ~]# oclumon dumpnodeview -v -allnodes -last "00:05:00"
```

If oclumon is entered with no arguments, it returns a query prompt to enter commands interactively. From this, you can conclude that the strength of the Oracle Cluster Health Monitor lies in two things. First, it can review historical data to diagnose issues such as node evictions that may have occurred at a previous point in time. Second, it can provide a central location for recording performance monitoring data for all nodes in the cluster simultaneously.

OSWatcher

OSWatcher is not really a performance monitoring tool in its own right. Rather, it is a framework for capturing, storing, and analyzing data generated by a number of the standard command-line performance monitoring tools that we have previously covered in this chapter. OSWatcher also includes a utility called OSWg that graphs the captured data. As such, it offers similar functionality to the combination of sar and kSar. OSWatcher has been developed by Oracle, and it can be downloaded from the My Oracle Support web site as a .tar archive.

Installing OSWatcher

Follow these steps to install OSWatcher. Begin by extracting the archive into a directory of a user with permissions to run the standard command-line performance monitoring tools, such as the oracle user:

```
[oracle@london1 ~]$ tar xvf osw3b.tar
./
./osw/
./osw/Exampleprivate.net
./osw/OSWatcher.sh
./osw/OSWatcherFM.sh
./osw/OSWgREADME.txt
./osw/README.txt
...
```

Starting OSWatcher

Next, start OSWatcher with the startOSW.sh script. This script can take a couple arguments. The first argument specifies a snapshot interval for how regularly the command-line tools should be run to gather the data. The second argument specifies the number of hours of data to collect. If no arguments are given, the default values are selected. The following example collects information using the default values:

```
[oracle@london1 osw]$ ./startOSW.sh
[oracle@london1 osw]$

Info...You did not enter a value for snapshotInterval.
Info...Using default value = 30
Info...You did not enter a value for archiveInterval.
Info...Using default value = 48

Testing for discovery of OS Utilities...

VMSTAT found on your system.
IOSTAT found on your system.
MPSTAT found on your system.
NETSTAT found on your system.
TOP found on your system.

Discovery completed.

Starting OSWatcher v3.0    on Tue Feb 9 15:25:49 GMT 2010
With SnapshotInterval = 30
With ArchiveInterval = 48

OSWatcher - Written by Carl Davis, Center of Expertise, Oracle Corporation

Starting Data Collection...

osw heartbeat:Tue Fe b 9 15:25:49 GMT 2010
osw heartbeat:Tue Feb 9 15:26:19 GMT 2010
osw heartbeat:Tue Feb 9 15:26:49 GMT 2010
osw heartbeat:Tue Feb 9 15:27:19 GMT 2010
```

Stopping OSWatcher

To stop the data collection, run the stopOSW.sh script as the same user. At this point, the captured data can be browsed manually within the archive directory, as in this example:

```
 [oracle@london1 archive]$ ls *
oswiostat:
london1.example.com_iostat_10.02.09.1500.dat
oswmeminfo:
london1.example.com_meminfo_10.02.09.1500.dat
...
```

Viewing Results Graphically

Alternatively, the extracted files include a Java utility for viewing the data in a graphical form. First, Java must be specified in the user's PATH environment variable, and the utility must be run as follows, by specifying the archive directory that contains the collected data:

```
[oracle@london1 osw]$ export PATH=$ORACLE_HOME/jdk/bin:$PATH
[oracle@london1 osw]$ java -jar oswg.jar -i archive

Starting OSWg V3.0.0
OSWatcher Graph Written by Oracle Center of Expertise
Copyright (c)  2008 by Oracle Corporation

Parsing Data. Please Wait...

Parsing file london1.example.com_iostat_10.02.09.1500.dat ...

Parsing file london1.example.com_vmstat_10.02.09.1500.dat ...

Parsing Completed.
```

When the parsing of data is complete, OSWg presents a number of options in the terminal window that you can use to choose the graph to display:

```
Enter 1 to Display CPU Process Queue Graphs
Enter 2 to Display CPU Utilization Graphs
Enter 3 to Display CPU Other Graphs
Enter 4 to Display Memory Graphs
Enter 5 to Display Disk IO Graphs

Enter 6 to Generate All CPU Gif Files
Enter 7 to Generate All Memory Gif Files
Enter 8 to Generate All Disk Gif Files

Enter L to Specify Alternate Location of Gif Directory
Enter T to Specify Different Time Scale
Enter D to Return to Default Time Scale
Enter R to Remove Currently Displayed Graphs
Enter P to Generate A Profile
Enter Q to Quit Program

Please Select an Option:
```

Selecting an option displays a graph in an individual window, as shown in Figure 13-6.

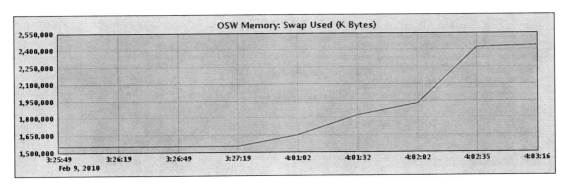

Figure 13-6. Results from OSWatcher

If you choose to run OSWatcher on a regular basis, it is important to be aware that, by default, the tool will not restart after the system reboots. Therefore, Oracle also provide an RPM package downloadable from My Oracle Support to install a service to start OSWatcher when the system boots.

nmon

In contrast to the Oracle Cluster Health Monitor and OSWatcher, nmon is a performance monitoring tool developed by IBM initially for AIX-based systems, but which has been extended to Linux environments. nmon was released as open source, and it is available for download from the following location: http://nmon.sourceforge.net. Available downloads include precompiled binaries and the standard x86 32-bit binary for Red Hat systems. Once downloaded and given executable permissions against, the binary file will run against the standard Oracle-validated RPM installation for both x86 and x86-64 environments.

By default, nmon runs in interactive mode; pressing the h key displays the information available (you can see nmon's menu in Figure 13-7). Figure 13-8 shows how nmon can provide detailed output for the processor, memory, network, and storage with multiple sections simultaneously.

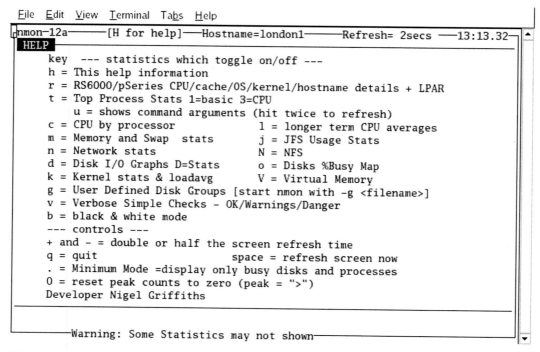

Figure 13-7. *nmon's menu*

For example, pressing n displays information related to network traffic, thus enabling the RAC DBA to observe the utilization levels of the cluster interconnect.

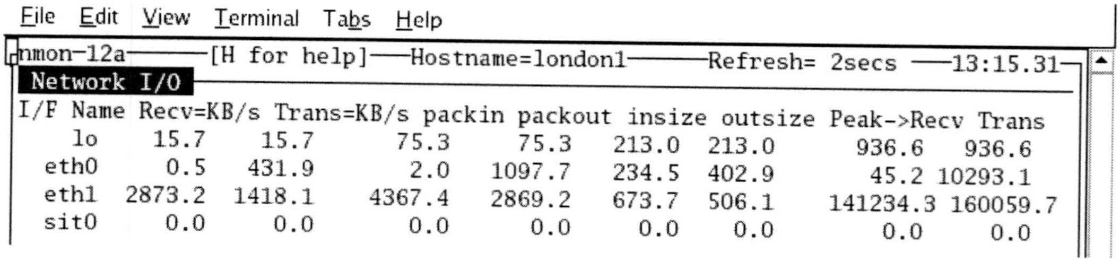

File   Edit   View   Terminal   Tabs   Help

nmon—12a———[H for help]——Hostname=london1———Refresh= 2secs ——13:15.31								
Network I/O								
I/F Name	Recv=KB/s	Trans=KB/s	packin	packout	insize	outsize	Peak->Recv	Trans
lo	15.7	15.7	75.3	75.3	213.0	213.0	936.6	936.6
eth0	0.5	431.9	2.0	1097.7	234.5	402.9	45.2	10293.1
eth1	2873.2	1418.1	4367.4	2869.2	673.7	506.1	141234.3	160059.7
sit0	0.0	0.0	0.0	0.0	0.0	0.0	0.0	0.0

Figure 13-8. *nmon's detailed statistics output*

Additionally, nmon enables the capture of information over periods of time. Later, you can use this information to graph the data with spreadsheet tools. Thus, nmon is a useful open source tool that is easy to install, while also providing comprehensive coverage that complements the standard Linux- and Oracle-provided performance-monitoring tools.

Summary

In this chapter, we described some of the tools and techniques available to you for monitoring the performance of your RAC cluster at the Linux level. We also detailed the most common Linux command-line and graphical tools, which you can use to confirm your earlier findings gleaned from using the Oracle-specific performance monitoring tools described in Chapter 12.

CHAPTER 14

■■■

Parallel Execution

Parallel Execution is a feature of the Oracle Database that enables the division of certain database operations into multiple subtasks that operate simultaneously. The goal of this approach is to complete these tasks more quickly than if they were executed serially as a single task. Parallel Execution has the potential to improve performance and response times by harnessing more of a system's hardware resources (see Chapter 4 for more information on hardware resources) to complete the task at hand. Parallel Execution enables singe-instance environments by utilize more of a system's CPU cores, memory, and I/O in a single operation. However, Parallel Execution is particularly relevant to RAC because it enables operations to be processed beyond the resource capabilities of a single node, letting you leverage the CPU, memory, and I/O capability of the entire cluster (if desired) to complete a single operation.

The nature of Parallel Execution, where you utilize multiple resources to accomplish a single task, makes it applicable to processing resource intensive operations. However, it is not applicable to simple DML operations, such as SELECT, INSERT, UPDATE, and DELETE statements that manipulate a limited number of rows. For this reason, Parallel Execution is not associated with regular DML operations in OLTP environments. However, in an OLTP RAC environment with a high number of concurrent users, this type of utilization is the desired outcome. In this case, multiple users can fully utilize all server resources across the cluster, all without requiring parallel operations.

That said, Parallel Execution still may be used in OLTP environments for more resource-intensive maintenance and data load operations. For example, Parallel Execution makes sense for operations such as CREATE TABLE AS SELECT, CREATE TABLE for an index organized table, and CREATE INDEX. It also makes sense for Parallel Data Pump operations, RMAN backup, and recovery and gathering statistics. You should be aware that not all of these operations may be able to fully utilize parallel operations across the entire cluster. For example, Parallel Data Pump jobs can only run on a single node in a cluster, regardless of the number of nodes in the cluster and even though the worker processes may run on multiple instances.

Parallel Execution is most recognized as bringing benefits to RAC environments in cases involving data warehousing or decision support systems (DSS). In these cases, Parallel Execution lets you the process SELECT statements efficiently, retrieve a large number of rows using full table scans, index fast full scans, and partition index range scans. Used judiciously and configured correctly, Parallel Execution can result in orders-of-magnitude improvements in the time to complete these types of data warehouse query operations. Consequently, this chapter will focus on Parallel Query in RAC environments in particular. We will also cover the concepts behind Parallel Execution, configuring Parallel Execution, and the monitoring and tuning of such environments. Before doing so, it is important to note that Parallel Operations require the use of Oracle Enterprise Edition because Parallel Operations are not available in Oracle Standard Edition. Therefore, if operating in a Standard Edition environment, features such as Parallel Query, Parallel DML, Parallel index builds, and Parallel Backup and Recovery will not be available to you.

Parallel Execution Concepts

At the most basic design level, executing an operation in parallel requires a controlling process to initially determine whether the operation will complete more quickly in parallel, as opposed to serially. Once the controlling process forecasts that it will complete an operation more quickly in parallel, it will then determine how the tasks required for the operation are to be allocated between a number of processes. These processes then simultaneously execute the tasks allocated to them before returning their subset of results back to the controlling process. The controlling process then serially assembles the results gathered from all of the parallel processes allocated to the subtasks, before returning the result set back to the user.

From the basic analysis, we can make a number of initial observations regarding Parallel Execution. First, it is not necessarily the case that all operations will complete more quickly in parallel than they will serially. Even when operating in parallel, there are serial components that will limit the performance gains available from parallelizing an operation. In fact, this premise is long established in computing as Amdahl's Law; and even though the level of impact varies between workloads, it is important to bear in mind when configuring Parallel Execution that allocating an increasing number of parallel subprocesses is unlikely to result in linear scalability. At some point, the allocation of subprocesses will reach an optimal level, beyond which more resources will be consumed, but the operation as a whole will take longer to complete. It also raises a related point that the optimal level for one parallel operation may not actually be the optimal level for multiple operations on a system in which all the processes are attempting to run in parallel. In other words, the resources consumed by adding additional parallel processes up to the point where the operation completes the quickest may be proportionally greater than the additional performance improvement warrants. Therefore, reducing the number of subprocesses to a level below where the operation would complete quickest may actually provide the most benefit to the system as whole. This raises an important point: the correct sizing, configuration, and testing of the software are vital to extracting the benefits of parallelism for the workload as a whole across the system. This sizing must be based on the administrator's knowledge of the available CPU, memory, and I/O resources—and Oracle Parallel Execution is no exception to this general rule.

Serial Execution

To understand Oracle Parallel Execution, we'll begin with an example involving serial execution. The following listing shows a formatted execution plan for a simple query that counts the number of rows in the LINEITEM table, which is executed serially:

```
SQL> explain plan for
  2  select count(*) from lineitem;

Explained.

SQL> select * from table(DBMS_XPLAN.DISPLAY);
Plan hash value: 2139482517
```

```
-----------------------------------------------------------------------
|Id| Operation             | Name            | Rows  |Cost(%CPU)| Time
-----------------------------------------------------------------------
|0 |SELECT STATEMENT       |                 |1      |3701   (1)| 00:00:45
|1 |SORT AGGREGATE         |                 |1      |          |
|2 |INDEX FAST FULL SCAN|I_L_ORDERKEY    |6002K  |3701   (1)| 00:00:45
-----------------------------------------------------------------------
```

In this example, the users foreground process executes an INDEX FAST FULL SCAN, performs the COUNT aggregate function, and returns the result to the user.

Parallel Execution

For the same statement using Oracle Parallel Execution, the user's foreground process becomes the parallel controlling process, which is called the *Parallel Execution Coordinator* (PEC). For Parallel Queries, this controlling process is also known as the *Query Coordinator* (QC). The PEC initially determines whether to parallelize the operation.

■ **Note** In some circumstances, the PEC will have been instructed to parallelize execution. For example, a DBA or developer can set a configuration that causes Parallel Execution, or a developer can force Parallel Execution manually.

When operating in parallel, the PEC allocates a number of Parallel Execution Servers (PES). The Parallel Execution Servers are also sometimes known for queries as *Parallel Query Slaves* (PQ Slaves). The Parallel Execution Servers are granted to the PEC from an available system-wide pool according to the Degree of Parallelism (DOP).

The DOP is calculated automatically by the Oracle Software, or it can be determined by the DBA or developer's configuration. Depending on the configuration, the Parallel Execution Servers may be allocated on the local node, or on one or more nodes across the entire cluster, where they utilize the available resources and distribute information across the private interconnect. The Parallel Execution Servers are implemented on the operating system by processes such as the following:

```
oracle    13955    1   0 16:49 ?      00:00:03 ora_p000_PROD1
oracle    13957    1   0 16:49 ?      00:00:02 ora_p001_PROD1
oracle    14232    1   4 16:55 ?      00:00:02 ora_p002_PROD1
oracle    14234    1   4 16:55 ?      00:00:02 ora_p003_PROD1
oracle    14236    1   4 16:55 ?      00:00:03 ora_p004_PROD1
oracle    14238    1   3 16:55 ?      00:00:02 ora_p005_PROD1
oracle    14240    1   4 16:55 ?      00:00:03 ora_p006_PROD1
oracle    14242    1   2 16:55 ?      00:00:01 ora_p007_PROD1
oracle    14244    1   2 16:55 ?      00:00:01 ora_p008_PROD1
oracle    14246    1   2 16:55 ?      00:00:01 ora_p009_PROD1
oracle    14248    1   2 16:55 ?      00:00:01 ora_p010_PROD1
```

Prior to Oracle Database 10*g* Release 2, the Parallel Execution Coordinator would generate a SQL statement for each Parallel Execution Server—hence the term PQ Slave. In those earlier releases, each slave would parse and execute a cursor to retrieve its allocated subset of data from the database. In Oracle Database 10*g* Release 2 and later, the Parallel Execution Coordinator parses a single cursor that is shared by all of the participating Parallel Execution Servers. On the additional nodes in the cluster, the SQL is compiled by one Parallel Execution Server, and the cursor is shared with the other Parallel Execution Servers. The Parallel Execution Coordinator divides the workload into units termed granules that are either based on ranges of data blocks or on allocation of partitions for partitioned objects. The granules are calculated dynamically and assigned to the Parallel Execution Servers. The Parallel

Execution Servers then act as Dataflow operators for the portion of the global Parallel Execution Plan assigned to them. When a task is complete, the rows are returned to the Parallel Execution Coordinator, and another granule is assigned until all granules have been consumed.

In the next example, the Parallel Execution Coordinator is returned, and the results of the COUNT aggregate function are completed by the Parallel Execution Servers. The Parallel Execution Servers then apply the COUNT aggregate function to all accumulated results as if the INDEX FAST FULL SCAN had been completed serially. This method of allocation ensures that if a particular Parallel Execution Server has not completed its workload as rapidly as another, it will be assigned a lower number of granules. This prevents one server from unduly slowing the response time for the entire operation. It also introduces the concept of *Table Queues* as the method by which data is distributed between processes. When a Parallel Execution Server has completed all of its assigned workload, it returns to the pool to be reallocated. Figure 14-1 shows an example of this, depicting a simple Parallel Query operation with a DOP of 3.

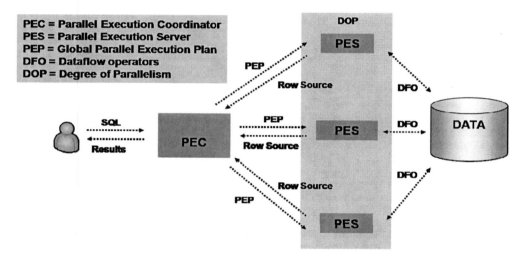

Figure 14-1. *A parallel query operation with three degrees of parallelism*

The following formatted execution plan shows exactly the same query you saw executed serially earlier in this chapter, except this time it is executed in parallel:

```
--------------------------------------------------------------------------------
|Id| Operation               | Name         | TQ     |IN-OUT | PQ Distrib
--------------------------------------------------------------------------------
|0 | SELECT STATEMENT        |              |        |       |
|1 | SORT AGGREGATE          |              |        |       |
|2 | PX COORDINATOR          |              |        |       |
|3 | PX SEND QC (RANDOM)     | :TQ10000     |Q1,00   |P->S   |QC (RAND)
|4 | SORT AGGREGATE          |              |Q1,00   |PCWP   |
|5 | PX BLOCK ITERATOR       |              |Q1,00   |PCWC   |
|6 | INDEX FAST FULL SCAN    | I_L_ORDERKEY |Q1,00   |PCWP   |
--------------------------------------------------------------------------------
```

Note

    - automatic DOP: Computed Degree of Parallelism is 2

In this parallel example, there is a single Dataflow operation that satisfies the query. The Dataflow operation is itself satisfied by two Dataflow operators, which in this case are shown as the PX BLOCK ITERATOR. The PX BLOCK ITERATOR or *granule iterator* operates upon granules allocated as block ranges that perform an INDEX FAST FULL SCAN on their allocated range of the I_L_ORDERKEY index. The columns PCWP for Parallel Combined with Parent and PCWC for Parallel are combined with the child. This example illustrates that the output from these stages is communicated within the same Parallel Execution Server and not between multiples processes. For these steps, the PX BLOCK ITERATOR is the parent, and the INDEX FAST FULL SCAN is the child. The aggregate function is performed by the Parallel Execution Servers, and the results are sent randomly using QC(RAND) to the Parallel Execution Coordinator process as a Parallel to Serial (P->S) operation. There is a single Table Queue, TQ1,00, that provides the communication between the Parallel Execution Servers and the Parallel Execution Coordinator. The Parallel Execution Coordinator process performs the COUNT aggregate function on the results, and then returns the results of the SELECT statement to the user.

Producers and Consumers

So far we have covered a simple example of the Parallel Execution. More complex examples introduce the concept of data redistribution. For example, if the Query contains a JOIN between two tables, the Parallel Execution Server operating on the block range of an allocated table might not contain sufficient information about either the entire block range of that table or, more importantly, the data retrieved from the other table in the JOIN.

To complete the JOIN, the information generated by both Parallel Execution Servers needs to be redistributed to a single process. From a design perspective, the simplest approach is to send all of the information to the Parallel Execution Coordinator. This single process may gather all of the data retrieved in parallel and perform the JOIN operation on it. Remember, however, that this two table JOIN is a simple example, and it may require multiple operations to process this task serially. This problem illustrates the factors previously identified in Amdahl's Law. That is, the time required for the operations to be processed in serial by the Parallel Execution Coordinator and then redistributed through all of the required data back to that single process would often negate the gains achieved in the portions of the operation that can be run in parallel. Consequently, for queries containing operations such as JOINs or SORTs, Oracle Parallel Execution deploys Producer and Consumer Parallel Execution Servers. The producer continues to serve the role of the granule iterator, processing its allocated range. However, the retrieved rows are then distributed to another Parallel Execution Server that retrieves all of the rows required to complete its operation. The number of Parallel Execution Servers deployed in such a scenario is double the Degree of Parallelism, as illustrated in Figure 14-2.

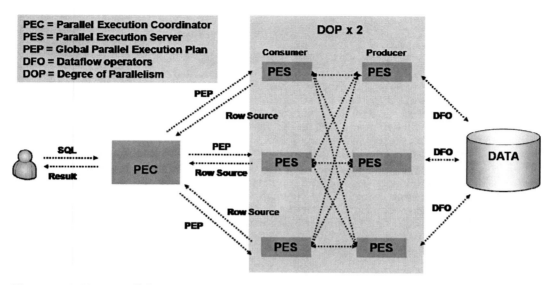

Figure 14-2. How Parallel Execution Servers communicate

Figure 14-2 shows that all of the Parallel Execution Servers establish a channel to all of the other Parallel Execution Servers. Within a RAC environment, these servers create four message buffers per channel and communicate asynchronously by passing the message buffers between them.

Let's look at a sample query that can be satisfied using Producers and Consumers Parallel Execution Servers. The following parts/supplier relationship query (Q16) from the TPC-H specification returns the number of suppliers who have not received complaints and who can supply the specified parts with certain attributes:

```
select
    p_brand,
    p_type,
    p_size, count(distinct ps_suppkey) as supplier_cnt
from    partsupp,
        part
where     p_partkey = ps_partkey
    and p_brand <> 'Brand#24'
    and p_type not like 'MEDIUM BURNISHED%'
    and p_size in (8, 27, 42, 9, 4, 13, 25, 19)
    and ps_suppkey not in (
        select
            s_suppkey
        from
            supplier
        where
            s_comment like '%Customer%Complaints%'
    )
group by
```

```
    p_brand,
    p_type,
    p_size
order by
    supplier_cnt desc,
    p_brand,
    p_type,
    p_size;
```

The following formatted execution plan shows how this query is executed in parallel:

```
-------------------------------------------------------------------------------
|Id  | Operation                   | Name              |  TQ    |IN-OUT | PQ Distrib
-------------------------------------------------------------------------------
|0   | SELECT STATEMENT            |                   |        |       |
|1   | PX COORDINATOR              |                   |        |       |
|2   | PX SEND QC (ORDER)          |:TQ10005           | Q1,05  | P->S  |QC (ORDER)
|3   | SORT ORDER BY               |                   | Q1,05  | PCWP  |
|4   | PX RECEIVE                  |                   | Q1,05  | PCWP  |
|5   | PX SEND RANGE               |:TQ10004           | Q1,04  | P->P  |RANGE
|6   | HASH GROUP BY               |                   | Q1,04  | PCWP  |
|7   | PX RECEIVE                  |                   | Q1,04  | PCWP  |
|8   | PX SEND HASH                |:TQ10003           | Q1,03  | P->P  |HASH
|9   | HASH GROUP BY               |                   | Q1,03  | PCWP  |
|10  | VIEW                        |VM_NWVW_1          | Q1,03  | PCWP  |
|11  | HASH GROUP BY               |                   | Q1,03  | PCWP  |
|12  | PX RECEIVE                  |                   | Q1,03  | PCWP  |
|13  | PX SEND HASH                |:TQ10002           | Q1,02  | P->P  |HASH
|*14 | HASH JOIN RIGHT ANTI        |                   | Q1,02  | PCWP  |
|15  | PX RECEIVE                  |                   | Q1,02  | PCWP  |
|16  | PX SEND BROADCAST           |:TQ10000           | Q1,00  | P->P  |BROADCAST
|17  | PX BLOCK ITERATOR           |                   | Q1,00  | PCWC  |
|*18 | TABLE ACCESS FULL           |SUPPLIER           | Q1,00  | PCWP  |
|*19 |  HASH JOIN                  |                   | Q1,02  | PCWP  |
|20  | PX RECEIVE                  |                   | Q1,02  | PCWP  |
|21  | PX SEND BROADCAST           |:TQ10001           | Q1,01  | P->P  |BROADCAST
|22  | PX BLOCK ITERATOR           |                   | Q1,01  | PCWC  |
|*23 | TABLE ACCESS FULL           |PART               | Q1,01  | PCWP  |
|24  | PX BLOCK ITERATOR           |                   | Q1,02  | PCWC  |
|25  | INDEX FAST FULL SCAN        |I_PS_PARTKEY_SUPPKEY| Q1,02 | PCWP  |
-------------------------------------------------------------------------------

Predicate Information (identified by operation id):
---------------------------------------------------

   14 - access("PS_SUPPKEY"="S_SUPPKEY")
   18 - filter("S_COMMENT" LIKE '%Customer%Complaints%')
   19 - access("P_PARTKEY"="PS_PARTKEY")
   23 - filter(("P_SIZE"=4 OR "P_SIZE"=8 OR "P_SIZE"=9 OR "P_SIZE"=13 OR "P_SIZE"=19 OR
"P_SIZE"=25 OR "P_SIZE"=27 OR "P_SIZE"=42) AND
            "P_BRAND"<>'Brand#24' AND "P_TYPE" NOT LIKE 'MEDIUM BURNISHED%')
```

Note

    - automatic DOP: Computed Degree of Parallelism is 2

Running the preceding execution plan produces output such as the following:

```
SQL> /
P_BRAND     P_TYPE                         P_SIZE SUPPLIER_CNT
----------  ------------------------------ ---------- ------------
Brand#54    STANDARD ANODIZED TIN               9           28
Brand#11    STANDARD PLATED TIN                25           24
Brand#12    PROMO ANODIZED COPPER             27           24
Brand#12    STANDARD BURNISHED COPPER         25           24
Brand#14    LARGE ANODIZED NICKEL             19           24
Brand#14    PROMO ANODIZED COPPER             19           24
Brand#21    LARGE ANODIZED COPPER             13           24
Brand#21    PROMO BURNISHED TIN                4           24
...
```

In this example, there are now six Table Queues that range from TQ1,00 to TQ1,05. These queues redistribute information between the Parallel Execution Servers and the Parallel Execution Coordinator. An individual operation or row source is identified under a particular Table Queue number. PX SEND and PX RECEIVE identify the distribution of rows between processes, while P->P under the IN-OUT column shows that the output is redistributed to another set of Parallel Execution Servers. The mapping of these operations to the operating system processes can be viewed in the V$PQ_TQSTAT table, which must be viewed in the session where the Parallel Query was run. The following view returns information only for the last query; it shows the previous execution plan in action:

```
SQL> select DFO_NUMBER, TQ_ID, SERVER_TYPE, PROCESS, INSTANCE from
v$PQ_TQSTAT order by TQ_ID;

DFO_NUMBER      TQ_ID SERVER_TYP PROCESS      INSTANCE
----------  ---------- ---------- -----------  ----------
         1           0 Producer   P000                1
         1           0 Producer   P001                1
         1           0 Consumer   P002                1
         1           0 Consumer   P003                1
         1           1 Producer   P000                1
         1           1 Producer   P001                1
         1           1 Consumer   P002                1
         1           1 Consumer   P003                1
         1           2 Consumer   P001                1
         1           2 Producer   P003                1
         1           2 Consumer   P000                1
         1           2 Producer   P002                1
         1           3 Producer   P001                1
         1           3 Producer   P000                1
         1           3 Consumer   P002                1
         1           3 Consumer   P003                1
         1           4 Ranger     QC                  1
         1           4 Consumer   P000                1
```

1	4 Producer	P003	1
1	4 Producer	P002	1
1	4 Consumer	P001	1
1	5 Producer	P001	1
1	5 Producer	P000	1
1	5 Consumer	QC	1

24 rows selected.

The preceding output illustrates that, from a conceptual standpoint, we have identified the distinct roles of producer and consumer processes. In this case, there are four processes, ranging from P000 to P003 according to the Degree of Parallelism of 2. In terms of implementation, it is important to note that a single Parallel Execution Server process can be both a producer and consumer for multiple operations in the Parallel Execution Plan. In this example, the Producer Parallel Execution Servers continue to serve the role of granule iterators against their allocated block ranges. Also, full table scans (TABLE ACCESS FULL) are performed against the PART and SUPPLIER tables, and an INDEX FAST FULL SCAN is performed against the I_PS_PARTKEY_SUPPKEY index on the PARTSUPP table. The results of both full table scans BROADCAST to all Parallel Execution Servers, which means you don't need to distribute the results of the index scan against the index on the comparatively larger PARTSUPP table.

The operations that are the consumer of these rows are identified by table queue TQ1,02. This queue is also the producer of the index scan. From the output of V$PQ_TQSTAT, it can be observed that the operating system processes P002 and P003 are the producers for this operation, as well as the consumers for the TQ1,00 and TQ1,01 Table Queue operations. These Parallel Execution Servers then perform the JOIN on the PART and PARTSUPP rows and the ANTI JOIN for the NOT IN operation on the SUPPLIER rows before redistributing the results to another set of Parallel Execution Servers. In this example, these servers are the operating system processes, P000 and P001. This form of redistribution continues for Table Queues ranging from TQ1,03 to TQ1,04. In this case, the operating system processes P000 and P001 and P002 and P003 alternate between producer and consumer roles, processing the GROUP BY operations in parallel. For the output and Table Queue TQ1,04, the Parallel Execution Coordinator acts as the RANGER to determine which ranges the producers will send to the Consumers at TQ1,05. This enables the Parallel Execution Servers to sort the rows in parallel for the ORDER BY operation. The results are returned to the Parallel Execution Coordinator serially, already in the sort order identified by QC (ORDER). Here, the Parallel Execution Coordinator returns the combined results shown previously to the user.

The execution plan will show the number of rows and bytes used to calculate each operation, and the V$PQ_STAT view can also be used to show the actual number of rows and the bytes redistributed between processes after the statement has executed. The following RAC example shows the same statement executed with a Degree of Parallelism of 14. It utilizes 14 Parallel Execution Servers per instance, distributing the producers and consumers across the cluster. Therefore, some of this data is transferred across the private interconnect, as opposed to using interprocess communication (IPC) on the same instance:

```
SQL> select DFO_NUMBER, TQ_ID, SERVER_TYPE, NUM_ROWS, BYTES,
PROCESS, INSTANCE from v$PQ_TQSTAT where TQ_ID = 2;
```

DFO_NUMBER	TQ_ID	SERVER_TYP	NUM_ROWS	BYTES	PROCESS	INSTANCE
1	2 Consumer		5716868	73913206	P011	1
1	2 Producer		6364469	82530761	P005	2
1	2 Consumer		5717580	73921160	P012	1

695

1	2 Consumer	5709740	73819091	P008	1
1	2 Consumer	5705592	73766961	P009	1
1	2 Consumer	5710244	73823988	P011	2
1	2 Consumer	5709316	73815808	P007	2
1	2 Consumer	5711992	73847887	P012	2
1	2 Consumer	5718760	73936753	P008	2
1	2 Consumer	5715084	73888517	P010	2
1	2 Consumer	5721996	73978570	P013	1
1	2 Producer	5117198	65998449	P003	1
1	2 Producer	5032410	65301516	P006	1
1	2 Producer	5473409	70611392	P001	1
1	2 Producer	5065132	65752161	P005	1
1	2 Producer	5210951	67171073	P004	1
1	2 Producer	5194921	67380186	P000	1
1	2 Producer	6342539	81829197	P001	2
1	2 Consumer	5713532	73868349	P013	2
1	2 Consumer	5719812	73953487	P009	2
1	2 Producer	4656192	60328063	P002	1
1	2 Producer	6440369	83128877	P006	2
1	2 Producer	6375671	82229038	P003	2
1	2 Producer	5944988	76978368	P002	2
1	2 Consumer	5721952	73977523	P010	1
1	2 Producer	6341648	81927190	P004	2
1	2 Producer	6440103	83137013	P000	2
1	2 Consumer	5707532	73791984	P007	1

Bloom Filters

Additionally—and of particular importance to RAC environments—you may also observe the use of Bloom Filters. You can identify such a filter in an execution plan easily; it takes the form of :BF0000. The step that creates and uses the first Bloom Filter in the plan looks like this:

```
-------------------------------------------------------------------------
|Id  | Operation           | Name                | TQ    |IN-OUT | PQ Distrib
-------------------------------------------------------------------------
...
|*19 | HASH JOIN           |                     |Q1,03  | PCWP  |
|20  | JOIN FILTER CREATE  | :BF0000             |Q1,03  | PCWP  |
|21  | PX RECEIVE          |                     |Q1,03  | PCWP  |
|22  | PX SEND HASH        | :TQ10001            |Q1,01  | P->P  |HASH
|23  | PX BLOCK ITERATOR   |                     |Q1,01  | PCWC  |
|*24 | TABLE ACCESS FULL   |PART                 |Q1,01  | PCWP  |
|25  | PX RECEIVE          |                     |Q1,03  | PCWP  |
|26  | PX SEND HASH        | :TQ10002            |Q1,02  | P->P  |HASH
|27  | JOIN FILTER USE     | :BF0000             |Q1,02  | PCWP  |
|28  | PX BLOCK ITERATOR   |                     |Q1,02  | PCWC  |
|29  | INDEX FAST FULL SCAN |I_PS_PARTKEY_SUPPKEY |Q1,02  | PCWP  |
-------------------------------------------------------------------------
```

A Bloom Filter implements an algorithm to test for membership in a set that requires considerably less space to implement than a 1 to 1 mapping detailing all of the members in the set. The trade off is that the Bloom Filter is probabilistic; in other words, when testing for set membership, an element is either *probably* a member of the set or *definitely* not a member of the set. However, the probable result does not confirm membership. If a test returns that an element is probably a member of the set when it is not, that result is termed a *false positive*. The implementation consists of two aspects. The first aspect involves constructing the Bloom Filter by adding members to a set. The second aspect involves querying whether elements are a member of that set. In the execution plan, these two aspects are represented by JOIN FILTER CREATE and JOIN FILTER USE, respectively.

To add an element to the set, a number of hash values are calculated for that element, and the bits in an array are set so they correspond to the computed positions. To test whether an element is a member of a set, the same hash values are calculated for the element. If all the corresponding bits are set, then it is probable that the element is a member of the set. The word *probable* is used because you cannot rule out the possibility that all of the bits were set for other elements. However, if one of the corresponding bits is not set, then it is guaranteed that the element is not a set member; otherwise, the bits would have been set when the element was added at the point the filter was created.

The benefit of the Bloom Filter is that it makes it possible to determine the probable mapping of values, but without requiring all of the values in a single location. In the execution plan example where the Bloom Filter was not used, this is exactly what occurred. All of the rows of the full table scan of the PART table were BROADCAST in order to JOIN with the rows of the PARTSUPP table. In this example, there are a comparatively greater number of rows. Consequently, at Table Queue TQ1,03, the results of the full table scan on the PART table are received, and the elements in the Bloom Filter are set on the values of P_PARTKEY. We can use this to determine the Predicate Information, as follows:

```
19 - access("P Partkey"="PS PARTKEY")
```

The operation at Table Queue Q1,02 uses this Bloom Filter to test the values of PS_PARTKEY from the rows retrieved from the PARTSUPP table. The Bloom Filter makes it possible to determine the rows where it is probable that "P_PARTKEY"="PS_PARTKEY"; it also makes it possible to reject rows where that is not probable without requiring that all of the rows retrieved be BROADCAST. Only the rows that are marked as probable are sent through the PX SEND HASH operation, and the HASH JOIN takes place on these rows. This enables the rejection of any false positives at this stage. Using the Bloom Filter enables you to significantly reduce the number of rows redistributed between Parallel Execution Servers. In a RAC environment, this translates to a reduction in the interconnect traffic required for Parallel Execution.

By default, Bloom Filters are enabled in the Oracle Database 11g Release 2, and the hidden or underscore parameter _bloom_filter_enabled is set by default to TRUE. The optimizer determines when to use of Bloom Filters, and such filters are more likely to be used for larger data sets where redistributing a large number of rows would be prohibitive.

The view V$SQL_JOIN_FILTER displays information about active filters. Contention is also reported within AWR reports, as in this example:

```
Enqueue Type (Request Reason)
------------------------------------------------------------------------
    Requests    Succ Gets Failed Gets     Waits  Wt Time (s) Av Wt Time(ms)
------------ ------------ ------------ ------------ ------------ --------------
BF-BLOOM FILTER (allocation contention)
      1,098          757          341          274            2           8.32
  . . .
```

Bloom Filters can be disabled by setting _bloom_filter_enabled to FALSE. Take care, however, because that is a hidden parameter that you are not supposed to set without guidance from Oracle support.

Partitioning

So far we have examined data retrieved based on allocated ranges of block-based granules, data redistributed between producer and consumer processes, and a technique to reduce the amount of data redistributed with Bloom Filters. An additional technique that can reduce the amount of data to be redistributed is *Partitioning*. For some operations, this technique can be used to eliminate data redistribution completely, which makes it particularly suited for scaling Parallel Execution in RAC environments.

At its most simple form of usage, Partitioning can be used for partition pruning where the optimizer is able to determine that a number of partitions need not be accessed to satisfy the query according to the values in the predicate list. Although simple to use, partitioning is a highly effective technique that can assist the optimizer in reducing the number of rows retrieved.

You can also use partitioning to perform Partition-Wise joins, where the single parallel join operation is able to be completed by a number of smaller join operations that operate against the partitions. The premise is similar to the one behind partition pruning: when the data is partitioned, the optimizer is able to identify the partitions that correspond to particular values. Consequently, for a Partition-Wise join, both objects in the join must be equipartitioned on the join key. To be *equipartitioned*, both objects must use either range or hash partitioning, and both objects must use the same type. Both objects must also have the same number of partitions and be partitioned on the same columns. While the objects themselves must use the same type, they do not have to be of the same type. For example, two tables can obviously be equipartitioned, but so too can an index and a table. When the two objects are equipartitioned, the join of a pair of equivalent partitions can be processed by a single Parallel Execution Server. This means that, even though the join operation takes place in parallel, it is not necessary to distribute any data between the objects to complete it. Without partitioning, you have seen that the allocation units for parallel processing are block-based granules. With partitioning, the units are partition-based granules where the minimum allocation unit is one pair of partitions per Parallel Execution Server. Thus the Degree of Parallelism that can be used is limited to the number of partitions. By definition, the number of partitions is always the same for both objects when using equipartitioning.

The previous example includes a JOIN operation between the PARTSUPP and PART tables, where P_PARTKEY is equal to PS_PARTKEY. The PARTSUPP rows are also accessed through the I_PS_PARTKEY_SUPPKEY index. This means we can use the following approach to equipartition the objects in question for the PART table for our example DOP of 2:

```
CREATE TABLE PART(
P_PARTKEY NUMBER NOT NULL,
P_TYPE VARCHAR(25),
P_SIZE NUMBER,
P_BRAND CHAR(10),
P_NAME VARCHAR(55),
P_CONTAINER CHAR(10),
P_MFGR CHAR(25),
P_RETAILPRICE NUMBER,
P_COMMENT VARCHAR(23)
)
```

```
PARALLEL
PARTITION BY HASH (P_PARTKEY)
PARTITIONS 2;
```

Similarly, we can use the following g approach to equipartition the PARTSUPP table:

```
CREATE TABLE PARTSUPP(
PS_PARTKEY NUMBER NOT NULL,
PS_SUPPKEY NUMBER NOT NULL,
PS_SUPPLYCOST NUMBER NOT NULL,
PS_AVAILQTY NUMBER,
PS_COMMENT VARCHAR(199)
)
PARALLEL
PARTITION BY HASH(PS_PARTKEY)
PARTITIONS 2;
```

We can also partition the I_PS_PARTKEY_SUPPKEY index:

```
CREATE UNIQUE INDEX I_PS_PARTKEY_SUPPKEY
ON PARTSUPP (PS_PARTKEY,PS_SUPPKEY) GLOBAL PARTITION BY HASH (PS_PARTKEY)
PARTITIONS 2;
```

With the preceding partitioning schema, the optimizer may now choose an execution plan, such as the following for the PART and PARTSUPP JOIN operation:

```
------------------------------------------------------------------------------
|Id  | Operation              | Name                 |Pstart|Pstop  |TQ     |IN-OUT
------------------------------------------------------------------------------
...
|20  | PX PARTITION HASH ALL  |                      |1     |2      |Q1,01  | PCWC
|*21 | HASH JOIN              |                      |      |       |Q1,01  | PCWP
|*22 | TABLE ACCESS FULL      |PART                  |1     |2      |Q1,01  | PCWP
|23  | INDEX FAST FULL SCAN   |I_PS_PARTKEY_SUPPKEY  |1     |2      |Q1,01  | PCWP
------------------------------------------------------------------------------
```

You can now observe that a partition iterator is used instead of a block range iterator. You can identify it in the plan by the additional Pstart and Pstop headings. No partition pruning is performed that can be identified by all of the partitions being iterated over. In this example, that is the 2 partitions for both objects. It is also possible to see that that the JOIN operation takes place in parallel, without any data redistribution having taken place, thus confirming the importance of partitioning for limiting interinstance traffic in Parallel Execution environments.

It is not possible to force the optimizer to use partition-based granules. Even against a partitioned schema, the optimizer may choose to use data redistribution if it determines that using a higher value for the Degree of Parallelism than the partitioning permits would result in a resolving the query faster. Additionally, the optimizer may also select an execution plan that utilizes a combination of the two approaches. Where a partition-wise join is available, but a higher Degree of Parallelism may be faster, the optimizer may use a Parallel Execution Server mapper against the objects. This mapper would use the partitioning scheme to optimize the redistribution of data to local-only redistribution; such an approach would minimize the traffic across the interconnect.

Parallel Execution Configuration

In addition to the configuration options at the schema level, features such as Partitioning mean that you have a number of alternatives at the instance and cluster level that you can use to implement and modify the behavior of Parallel Execution.

Next, you will learn about the configuration options with the relevant Parallel Execution parameters, and then look at how to configure your environment to match both your requirements and available hardware resources.

cluster_interconnects

We discussed setting the cluster_interconnects parameter in Chapter 4 in the context of hardware. Specifically, we discussed how this parameter enables the use of multiple private network interconnects to increase bandwidth availability for interconnect traffic.

This parameter can also enable you to increase the network capacity for interinstance messaging in a Parallel Execution environment. However, it is important to reiterate that the use of multiple interconnects will result in the failure of the entire interconnectsystem if any one network fails, which means it is not a high availability option. Consequently, we do not recommend setting cluster_interconnects. Instead, we recommend meeting demands for increased interconnect bandwidth with the appropriate hardware solution, such as 10 Gigabit Ethernet.

db_block_size, db_cache_size, and db_file_multiblock_read_count

As discussed in Chapter 12, using a smaller block size may be a solution for reducing interinstance traffic in transactional environments where multiple nodes are accessing the same rows in a single block. In a Parallel Execution environment, however, the emphasis is on high volumes of read activity. For example, there is no contention for the same rows for inserts, updates, or deletes. Neither is there contention for reading the same blocks because separate block ranges are allocated to separate Parallel Execution servers.

The emphasis on read activity means that data warehouse environments can benefit from using a larger block size for both table and index data. The block size can be schema-wide for a dedicated data warehouse database. Or, it can be set on a tablespace basis by following a couple steps. First, you create a buffer cache for a specific block size with a parameter such as DB_16K_CACHE_SIZE or DB_32K_CACHE_SIZE. Second, you set the corresponding block size by specifying BLOCKSIZE during the CREATE TABLESPACE statement. With an emphasis on reads where there is no additional insert activity, you should also set the value of PCTFREE for tables to a low value. This ensures that as many rows as possible are stored in these blocks. This configuration minimizes read activity by storing a defined number of rows in fewer blocks. The amount of data read in a single read operation is based upon the block size and the parameter, db_file_multiblock_read_count. db_file_multiblock_read_count is calculated automatically, and it should not be set manually. However, viewing the parameter can reveal the calculated value, as in this example:

```
SQL> show parameter db_file_multiblock_read_count

NAME                             TYPE         VALUE
-------------------------------- ------------ ------------------------------
db_file_multiblock_read_count    integer      128
```

The parameter db_file_multiblock_read_count may be calculated to different values on the nodes in the cluster if different workload characteristics are running on those nodes.

Now take a look at the db_cache_size parameter for sizing of the buffer cache. In this case, you also include the multiple block size caches and the buffer cache component for automatic shared memory management to distinguish the memory allocated to the SGA from that allocated to the PGA. However, you also handle Automatic Memory Management separately because memory can be reallocated between the SGA and PGA automatically.

In a Parallel Execution environment, rows are typically read with a direct path read event, as opposed to a db file scattered read event, which is usually associated with a full table scan operation. We discuss the importance of distinguishing between the two events in the context of Parallel Execution Performance later in this chapter. In the context of sizing the buffer cache, however, it is important to note that, when using a direct path read, the retrieved data blocks are not buffered in memory in the buffer cache component of the SGA. Instead, they are read directly in the user sessions memory allocated as PGA memory. Consequently, the emphasis of memory allocation for the Parallel Execution environment is focused more on the PGA, as opposed to the buffer cache component of the SGA. The notable exception to this is for In-memory Parallel Execution, which was introduced with the Oracle Database 11g Release 2. If enabled for a full table scan with db file scattered reads, in-memory Parallel Execution can calculate whether some data is in fact cached in the buffer cache and read. In-memory Parallel Execution is enabled with the parallel_degree_policy parameter, which you'll learn more about later in this section. However, it is likely that, if you're choosing to use In-memory Parallel Execution, then the decision will be made at the hardware sizing phase. This will enable you to specify a clustered environment with the appropriate levels of RAM and memory bandwidth for a dedicated buffered memory data warehouse environment.

instance_groups and parallel_instance_group

The instance_groups and parallel_instance_groups parameters were of particular relevance prior to Oracle 11g Release 1 because, before this release, Parallel Execution was not services-aware. In other words, the Parallel Execution Coordinator would be allocated to a node according to a defined service, but the Parallel Execution Servers could not be distributed across the other available nodes in the cluster. The solution to this problem was to use the INSTANCE_GROUPS parameter to assign instances to individual groups. The PARALLEL_INSTANCE_GROUP parameter could then be specified with, for example, an ALTER SESSION command. This command would allocate the instances within the cluster, so that a Parallel Query operation could run against in an individual session.

Parallel Execution has been services-aware since Oracle 11g, and we recommend using service configuration to distribute Parallel Execution Servers across the cluster (see Chapter 11 for more information on this topic). Although instance_groups and parallel_instance_groups are available and continue to provide the same functionality as in earlier releases, the parameters were deprecated in Oracle Database 11g, so a services configuration should be used instead.

When tracing Parallel Execution, it is necessary to use the trcsess utility to combine all of the trace files from the Parallel Execution Servers before using them with a utility such as tkprof. Once you have defined a service that you want to run Parallel Execution under, you can then specify that you want that service to extract the relevant trace data to combine, as in this example:

```
[oracle@london1 ~]# trcsess output="query16.trc" service=DSS *.trc
```

large_pool_size, parallel_execution_message_size, and shared_pool_size

By default, Parallel Execution-related memory is allocated in the shared pool. An exception to this rule is the largest memory component for Parallel Execution, the Parallel Execution Message Pool. This pool's memory will be allocated in the large pool when the SGA_TARGET parameter is set. You can view the memory allocations by executing the following query:

```
SQL> select * from v$sgastat where name like '%PX%';

POOL          NAME                      BYTES
------------  ------------------------  ----------
shared pool   PX subheap desc             140
shared pool   PX msg pool struct          692
shared pool   PX QC deq stats            1692
shared pool   PX server deq stats        1692
shared pool   PX subheap                33244
shared pool   PX QC msg stats            2816
shared pool   PX server msg stats        2816
large pool    PX msg pool              491520
```

■ **Note** When using Automatic Memory Management or Automatic Shared Memory Management, a large pool will be configured, and the Parallel Execution Message Buffers will be stored in that pool, regardless of whether you have explicitly set the large_pool parameter. The Parallel Execution Message Buffers will be store in the shared pool only if you meet this pair of conditions: first, you must have disabled automatic memory configuration; and second, you must not have set the large_pool parameter.

In any case, it is good practice to set the large_pool parameter, even if you're using automatic memory features to specify a minimum large pool requirement that Oracle can adjust upwards according to its current requirements.

The parallel_execution_message_size parameter determines the size of the buffers that constitute the Parallel Execution message pool, and this is the memory used for communication between the Parallel Execution Servers. In releases prior to Database 11*g* Release 2, the default value was 2148 bytes (or 2k). Consequently, it was typically reported that increasing the value of parallel_execution_message_size was beneficial. However, beginning with Oracle Database 11*g* Release 2, the default value of 16384 is usually sufficient, and increasing the amount to a value such as 32768 will result in more memory consumed from the large pool. Therefore, you should conduct tests to determine whether increasing the size is beneficial in a particular environment.

parallel_adaptive_multi_user

By default, the parallel_adaptive_multi_user parameter is set to TRUE. This parameter enables the rationing of available Parallel Execution Servers between multiple users executing Parallel Queries on the system. When a Parallel Query is issued, the Parallel Execution Servers will be assigned according to the requested Degree of Parallelism and the number of available Parallel Execution Servers not already in use. However, if multiple users are executing Parallel Queries and insufficient Parallel Execution Servers are available, then the parallel operation will be downgraded and run with a reduced Degree of Parallelism. This will occur whether `parallel_adaptive_multi_user` is set or not. Once a Degree of Parallelism is set for a particular query, it will not be downgraded while the query is running. If no Parallel Execution Servers are available, then a query will run serially or throw an error, according to the setting of `parallel_min_percent`, which will be discussed later in this section. This approach has the disadvantage that one or two queries may utilize all of the available Parallel Execution resources on the system, while the rest fail or run serially. Therefore, enabling `parallel_adaptive_multi_user` enables the system to downgrade a requested Degree of Parallelism. This downgrade is done according to an algorithm based upon the settings of the `cpu_count` parameter, which is multiplied by the `parallel_threads_per_cpu` to obtain a default Degree of Parallelism. Next, a reduction factor is applied according to predicted system load. This value is based on the number of active users on the system at the time that the query was started. This algorithm enables the Degree of Parallelism to be throttled below the requested amount, while the Parallel Execution Servers remain available for additional users. Over time, the algorithm is designed to provide an even distribution of resources. The potential disadvantage of setting `parallel_adaptive_multi_user` to TRUE is that it is difficult to predict the level of resources that will need to be allocated on anticipated future loads, especially in a clustered environment. Therefore, setting this parameter may have the unintended consequence of artificially limiting Parallel Execution performance, while also making it difficult to configure optimal performance for a particular individual query. Additionally, the number of CPUs on the system is a key input factor, but Parallel Execution is highly dependent on both memory and I/O resources.

For theses reason, we believe that `parallel_adaptive_multi_user` should typically be set to FALSE until its benefits have been tested and assessed in a particular environment. As an alternative, the DBA should investigate the features enabled by the `parallel_degree_policy` parameter for automating the Degree of Parallelism and enabling statement queuing. To limit resource usage on a per-user basis, we recommend using the `parallel_degree_policy` in conjunction with the `DBMS_RESOURCE_MANAGER` package to create a consumer group, map that consumer group to a data warehouse-focused service, and then create a plan to limit resource usage by users under that group. This approach offers a much finer degree of control than can be achieved using `parallel_adaptive_multi_user`.

parallel_automatic_tuning

The `parallel_automatic_tuning` parameter is a deprecated parameter. By default, it is set to FALSE; if this parameter were set to TRUE and the parallel clause was used when creating a table, then Oracle would automatically set the additional Parallel Execution parameters. However, this parameter's functionality was superseded first by `parallel_adaptive_multi_user`; and second by `parallel_degree_policy`.

parallel_degree_limit

The `parallel_degree_limit` parameter defaults to the value of CPU, and it is equal to the value of `cpu_count`, multiplied by `parallel_threads_per_cpu`, and multiplied again by the number of available instances. This parameter controls the maximum Degree of Parallelism that can be selected by any one statement. Alternatively, `parallel_degree_limit` can be set to the value of IO to limit the Degree of Parallelism according to the I/O capacity of the system, as measured by running `dbms_resource_manager.calibrate_io` (see Chapter 4 for more information on this). Finally, the parallel_degree_limit parameter can be set to an integer value to set a user defined limit for the maximum Degree of Parallelism. This parameter is enabled only when Automatic Degree of Parallelism is used by setting parallel_degree_policy to AUTO or LIMITED.

parallel_degree_policy, parallel_min_time_threshold, and parallel_servers_target

The parallel_degree_policy parameter introduced with Oracle Database 11g Release 2 is the most significant change to the configuration of Parallel Execution. Setting parallel_degree_policy enables three features: Automatic Degree of Parallelism, Statement Queuing, and in-memory Parallel Execution. The default setting for parallel_degree_policy is MANUAL, and it disables all of these features. Modifying this parameter to AUTO enables all three features, while setting it to LIMITED enables Automatic Degree of Parallelism, but also includes the option to manually override the calculated DOP for specific objects and statements.

Automatic Degree of Parallelism

Without Automatic Degree of Parallelism, when the parallel_degrees_policy parameter is set to MANUAL, the Degree of Parallelism can be set in order of precedence, as follows:

1. It can be set with a PARALLEL hint for a particular statement such as the following:

```
SQL> select /* parallel (lineitem,8) */ count(*) from lineitem;
```

2. It can be set with the ALTER SESSION FORCE PARALLEL command for an individual session, as in the following parallel query:

```
SQL> alter session force parallel query parallel (degree 8);
```

3. It can be set by specifying a PARALLEL value within a table or index definition, using an optional DEGREE clause.

The additional INSTANCES clause specified for RAC environments in previous versions of the Oracle Database is deprecated in release 11g, and it is no longer required. If the PARALLEL clause is used but the degree clause is not specified, then the Degree of Parallelism will default to the total of the number of CPUs, multiplied by the value of parallel_threads_per_cpu on all instances in the cluster. For example, if there are two nodes in the cluster with two sockets, eight cores in total on each, and a default value for parallel_threads_per_cpu of 2, then the default Degree of Parallelism will be 32, or 16 Parallel Execution Servers per instance.

Setting Automatic Degree of Parallelism to the AUTO level enables the optimizer to select a Degree of Parallelism that a statement will run against, without the DBA or developer needing to set the Degree of Parallelism explicitly at any level. It is important to reiterate that Automatic Degree of Parallelism, as the name implies, entirely overrides any manual settings of Parallelism, whether the settings are implemented with a hint, at the table level, or with a PARALLEL clause at the object level. The result is that parallelism may be used and a DOP selected entirely at the discretion of the optimizer. For example, an operation may be parallelized against an object without a PARALLEL clause or hint, or without a session-level parallel setting. The explain plan for such a statement specifies the calculated Degree of Parallelism, as shown in this example:

```
SQL> set autotrace on explain;
SQL> select count(*) from lineitem;

  COUNT(*)
----------
 599982790
...
Note
-----
   - automatic DOP: Computed Degree of Parallelism is 32 because of degree limit
```

The preceding example shows that the Degree of Parallelism has been set to the limit defined by parallel_degree_limit parameter, which is to the default to value of CPU. However, if the parallel_max_servers parameter is set to a value below this level (as discussed later in this section), then the computed DOP will remain at 32, but the statement will run with Parallel Execution Servers equal to parallel_max_servers on each instance. With an Automatic Degree of Parallelism in effect at the instance level, it is also possible to set a MANUAL policy at the session level, as in this example:

```
SQL> alter session set parallel_degree_policy=MANUAL;
```

To utilize object level definitions across the database, it is necessary to set the parallel_degree_policy parameter to LIMITED. At this setting, the optimizer will compute a Degree of Parallelism for objects for which the parallel clause has been used, as opposed to deciding whether to parallelize statements regardless of whether the target object has a PARALLEL clause defined. When Automatic Degree of Parallelism is enabled, the parameter parallel_min_time_threshold specifies the minimum time a query should take before Automatic DOP is used with the default value of AUTO.

We recommend testing Automatic Degree of Parallelism to determine whether it is beneficial in your environment. You can do this by examining the execution plan, recording the Degree of Parallelism against the performance of your queries, and comparing that degree of a parallelism to a manually calculated DOP. As noted previously, the DOP calculation is based on CPU or I/O, while the DBA will have superior knowledge about the resources available across the entire cluster. Notwithstanding the additional statement queuing and In-memory Parallel Execution features, the authors have observed that, while a manually calculated DOP can result in superior Parallel Query Performance, the Automatic DOP is accurate in calculating a near optimal level of performance. The parallel_degree_limit parameter is an important factor in the calculation.

Statement Queuing

When parallel_degree_policy is set to AUTO, a feature called Statement Queuing is enabled; this works in conjunction with Automatic DOP. As you have seen previously with the parallel_adaptive_multi_user parameter in releases prior to Oracle 11g Release 2, if insufficient Parallel Execution Servers are available to meet a requested DOP, then a Parallel Query may be downgraded, run serially, or throw an error. The disadvantage of this behavior is that it can prove suboptimal for the system as a whole, resulting in slower query times for all users and high utilization of resources. It also makes it difficult to tune, administer, and predict workloads. Statement Queuing provides a simple yet effective alternative to the previous behavior. Under Statement Queuing, if the requested Parallel Execution Servers are not available, then the new query is blocked from running and placed in a queue until the existing query holding the Parallel Execution Servers releases them. The next statement is then able to run at the requested DOP or the system enforced limit. This ensures that no statements are downgraded, run serially, or error. When this action occurs, the session waits on the JX enqueue event, as shown in the following extract from an AWR report:

```
                                            Avg
                                            wait    % DB
Event                          Waits  Time(s)  (ms)   time Wait Class
------------------------------ ------ ------- ------  ----- ----------
direct path read               5,180    1,942    375   71.1 User I/O
enq: JX - SQL statement queue      1      273 3.E+05   10.0 Scheduler
DB CPU                                    256           9.4
log file sync                      6        7   1166     .3 Commit
Parameter File I/O                 8        5    630     .2 User I/O
```

The parameter parallel_servers_target defines the number of running Parallel Execution Servers across the cluster before statements will be queued. parallel_servers_target cannot be more than the value of parallel_max_servers; and, by default, it is set to a lower value to ensure that statements are queued before all Parallel Execution Servers are utilized. For example, the default setting for a two-node cluster with eight CPUs per node is 32.

If Statement Queuing is implemented, then it enables more predictable behavior when analyzing and resolving issues in an environment where more Parallel Queries are consistently run compared to Parallel Execution Servers and system resources available.

In-memory Parallel Execution

In releases prior to Oracle 11g Release 2, a Parallel Query would almost always use a direct path read for full table scans, as opposed to a db file scattered read to read the data. As will be discussed later in this chapter in the context of performance, a direct path read bypasses the buffer cache. It also places a performance emphasis on the I/O capabilities of the system because the majority of objects subject to Parallel Queries would be larger than the buffer cache available. In-memory Parallel Execution has been made possible by advances in hardware capabilities, 64-bit computing, and memory performance (see Chapter 4 for more details). You can expect to see a number of competing in-memory data warehouse products coming to market that will harness these new hardware capabilities. In the Oracle Database, large memory capabilities give aggregated buffer caches in a RAC environment the potential to hold large objects in memory. This improves performance for buffered I/O, such as for db file scattered reads associated with full table scans in an OLTP environment.

When the parallel_degree_policy parameter is set to AUTO, the database may, depending upon an object's size, cache the data for subsequent reuse after initially reading from disk. However, this behavior diverges from the managing of data in a standard RAC environment. As discussed in Chapter 2, Cache Fusion enables the data blocks requested on one node in the cluster to be passed directly from the buffer cache on another node across the interconnect. If a block is requested on one node, that block will be always be cached on that node before access. This is a common shared-all clustering approach.

In-memory Parallel Execution differs from the preceding approach in this respect: if the sum total of the data blocks to satisfy the query will fit in the total buffer cache available across all nodes in the cluster, then they will be cached in a distributed fashion. Only a Parallel Execution Server on a particular node will be used to access the data blocks on that node, as opposed to passing block images between nodes with Cache Fusion. This concept can be thought of as simulating a shared-nothing cluster approach, which is typical in in-memory data warehouse products. The data is divided between the nodes in the cluster without sharing any of the data between them, and the resources on one node are dedicated to accessing the data only on that node. With this shared-nothing approach, it should also be clear why in-memory Parallel Execution, Automatic Degree of Parallelism, and Statement Queuing are enabled with a single parameter, as opposed to being enabled with separate parameters for each. With data cached on a per node basis and node affinity used to access this data, features such as Parallel Query table definitions, hints, query downgrading, and serialization would face significant design implementation challenges under such an approach. If In-memory Parallel Execution is to deliver benefits beyond a `direct path read` approach from any or multiple nodes in the cluster, then automating the entire In-memory Parallel Execution process is more likely to deliver optimal results when data is segmented on a per-node basis.

Once In-memory Parallel Execution is enabled, then the Oracle Database software will determine the caching of data for Parallel Query based on factors such as the size of the sum of the buffer caches across the nodes, the size of the objects subject to the Parallel Query, and the regularity with which they are accessed. Data is affinitized to the nodes based either on block ranges or partitions familiar from the Parallel Execution concepts discussed previously in this chapter. From these concepts, it is also possible to surmise that partitioning is particularly beneficial to In-memory Parallel Execution. This is because it enables Parallel Execution Servers on an individual node to operate on the rows contained within those partitions, while simultaneously minimizing the data redistribution and moving the implementation to something that closely resembles a clustered shared-nothing approach.

It should be clear that the `parallel_degree_policy` parameter brings great potential to implementing a high performance Parallel Execution environment where the full benefits of segmenting and affinitizing the data across the nodes are realized at the hardware selection and schema design phase. This approach may not benefit all environments, particularly environments where the data being queried changes on a regular basis. Therefore, we recommend adopting the following approach by default: `parallel_degree_policy` should remain at the MANUAL setting while you're reviewing the architectural design of the data warehouse and testing to determine whether In-memory Parallel Execution and its associated features will benefit your particular environment.

parallel_force_local

The `parallel_force_local` parameter defaults to the value of FALSE; however, when set to TRUE, this value restricts the Parallel Execution to utilizing the Parallel Execution Servers only on the node where the query was executed and nowhere else. `parallel_force_local` is particularly useful when enabled at the session level because it restricts the queries from a particular session to the local node. In previous releases, this result could only be achieved by setting the transaction isolation level to `serializable`.

parallel_io_cap_enabled

`parallel_io_cap_enabled` achieves a similar goal. It sets the `parallel_degree_limit` parameter to the value of IO to limit the Degree of Parallelism according to the I/O capacity of the system. However, `parallel_io_cap_enabled` is available even when Automatic Degree of Parallelism is not set. Before you can set the limit on the I/O, you must first calibrate the capacity by running `dbms_resource_manager.calibrate_io`.

parallel_max_servers, parallel_min_servers, parallel_threads_per_cpu, and processes

The parallel_max_servers parameter sets a limit on the number of Parallel Execution Servers available on an instance. By default, this parameter is equal to the value of cpu_count, multiplied by parallel_threads_per_cpu, and multiplied again by 5. parallel_min_servers sets the minimum value, and it must always be less than or equal to parallel_max_servers.

parallel_threads_per_cpu specifies the number of Parallel Execution Processes a CPU would be expected to process simultaneously. On an eight CPU server, the default values are as follows:

parallel_max_servers	integer	80
parallel_min_servers	integer	0
parallel_threads_per_cpu	integer	2

You should also ensure that the standard processes parameter is set to a value that permits the creation of the desired level of Parallel Execution Servers. parallel_max_servers sets the upper limit of the available Parallel Execution Servers for all users on an instance, which prevents the starvation of CPU resources. A query may request a higher Degree of Parallelism and use the CPU resources on multiple nodes in the cluster up to the level of parallel_max_servers, multiplied by all of the nodes in the cluster. However, the shared I/O resources available will remain the same. Thus it is important that you select an appropriate Degree of Parallelism or that you have it calculated automatically, without relying on parallel_max_servers to limit the DOP. parallel_min_servers should be set to a value of Parallel Execution Servers that you wish to be running on an instance permanently. The process will consume memory, but it will remain immediately available for Parallel Execution. Beyond parallel_min_servers, operating system processes will be started while the Oracle Database waits on the event os thread startup up to the limit of parallel_max_servers. This approach saves resources when they are not required at the expense of the ability to create Parallel Execution Servers when they are needed.

As you have seen, parallel_threads_per_cpu serves as an input value and multiplier for a number of additional Parallel Execution parameters. Therefore, even minor modifications can have a disproportionate effect on the configuration. Given the advances in CPU architecture and the performance available from even a single core on a multicore processor, we do not recommend increasing this value beyond the default value of 2, especially if the system is I/O bound. The only potential benefit from changing this parameter can be seen when reducing it to 1 for environments with a highly tuned I/O subsystem or when using In-memory Parallel Execution. However, we recommend tuning the parameters that depend upon it before modifying parallel_threads_per_cpu itself.

parallel_min_percent

The parallel_min_percent parameter defaults to the value of 0 and specifies the minimum percentage of Parallel Execution Servers that must be available on an instance for it to execute in Parallel; the query will fail if the availability does not meet the required percentage. The default value also means that a query will fail if insufficient Parallel Execution Servers are available to execute serially, as opposed to failing. The setting of this parameter is not required if Statement Queuing has been enabled.

pga_aggregate_target

In a default non-in-memory Parallel Execution environment, data is read directly into a Parallel Execution Server Process's private memory area. Consequently, the `pga_aggregate_target` parameter should be sized sufficiently to account for a work area big enough for all Parallel Execution Servers to be used. The amount of PGA memory required for a particular query on an instance is proportional to its Degree of Parallelism. You also need to provide enough memory for operations such as sorts and to minimize additional I/O by using the temporary tablespace. Your focus when memory sizing should be on the PGA before the SGA when using non-in-memory Parallel Execution.

We recommend using the PGA advisory section in an AWR report or viewing `V$PGA_TARGET_ADVICE` to ensure that sufficient PGA memory is available when sizing memory manually. Alternatively, you should also consider using Automatic Memory Management to enable the reallocation of memory between SGA and PGA. When the buffer cache is not being heavily utilized, there is less benefit in using operating system level Huge Pages for the SGA. This fact is one of the reasons for using Automatic Memory Management in Parallel Execution environments.

Parallel Execution Performance

The Monitoring of Parallel Execution performance can be done with all of the tools and utilities discussed in Chapters 12 and 13. The AWR report in particular is a useful tool for assessing the overall impact of Parallel Execution on each instance.

AWR Reports

The load profile provides a clear indication that the performance emphasis is on the physical reads. Also, it is important to note that the Transactions figure is typically low, so Parallel Query workloads are significantly different from OLTP environments, as illustrated by this example:

```
Load Profile           Per Second    Per Transaction   Per Exec   Per Call
~~~~~~~~~~~~         ---------------  ---------------   --------   --------
      DB Time(s):             38.4          8,358.2       9.28        0.41
       DB CPU(s):              1.5            317.9       0.35        0.02
       Redo size:          1,370.7        298,506.0
   Logical reads:         26,810.8      5,838,968.8
   Block changes:              3.7            794.0
   Physical reads:        24,061.6      5,240,243.8
  Physical writes:           380.7         82,907.4
       User calls:             94.1         20,483.5
          Parses:              2.1            466.3
     Hard parses:              0.2             45.3
  W/A MB processed:           22.8          4,973.6
          Logons:              0.9            185.2
        Executes:              4.1            901.1
       Rollbacks:              0.0              0.0
    Transactions:              0.0
```

This focus upon read performance is confirmed in the Top 5 Timed Foreground Events section. In the following example, the User I/O wait class dominates the top events:

Top 5 Timed Foreground Events
~~~~~~~~~~~~~~~~~~~~~~~~~~~~~~~~~~~~

Event	Waits	Time(s)	Avg wait (ms)	% DB time	Wait Class
direct path read	1,012,948	29,481	29	35.3	User I/O
db file scattered read	40,059	4,731	118	5.7	User I/O
DB CPU		3,179		3.8	
direct path read temp	13,605	1,828	134	2.2	User I/O
db file sequential read	6,081	148	24	.2	User I/O

As we have noted previously in this chapter, the most significant wait event is typically the direct path read. This wait event signifies that the Parallel Execution Server is reading data into its private memory area, bypassing the SGA. When doing direct path reads, you may observe fast object checkpoints, where a checkpoint is performed at the segment level to ensure that the any data blocks modified in the SGA are consistent with the data to be read on disk before the data blocks are read directly, as in this example:

```
Enqueue Type (Request Reason)
-------------------------------------------------------------------------
    Requests     Succ Gets Failed Gets      Waits  Wt Time (s) Av Wt Time(ms)
------------ ------------ ------------ ------------ ------------ --------------
KO-Multiple Object Checkpoint (fast object checkpoint)
        63           63           0           7            0         4.29
```

If In-memory Parallel Execution is enabled, then db file scattered read will indicate when it reads data that has been previously cached. As the previous example illustrates, you may see a combination where larger tables are not cached, but smaller ones may be. db file scattered reads may also of course continue be recorded for serial full table scan operations.

These statistics and concepts should make it clear that a significant contributing factor to Parallel Query performance is the availability of hardware resources, notably the CPU, memory, and I/O, which determine the rate at which data can be read. You should review Chapter 4 for more information on how to configure hardware in a RAC environment.

For Parallel Execution, the most significant of these factors is the CPU. Over time, the availability of processors with many high performance cores in a Linux environment means that considerable levels of I/O can be sustained by the CPUs across all nodes in an up-to-date RAC environment. Consequently, the emphasis on performance is invariably about providing sufficient I/O read capacity to match the level of performance available at the CPU level. Note that, when sizing Parallel Execution, some documentation may have been written against non-current, non-Linux systems where the available CPU resources were significantly below that of Linux systems available today. Also, some of that documentation advises increasing CPU usage to compensate for an I/O bound system. Contrary to this advice, where I/O is a limiting factor, the most viable alternative that will add a significant contribution to performance is to add the hardware resources necessary to increase I/O capacity. Other techniques will only provide limited results in cases where the available CPU is not being heavily utilized. You can use the AWR report to observe the relative usage of the CPU and I/O for an individual statement, as shown under the SQL ordered by User I/O Wait Time section in this example :

```
User I/O                    UIO per          Elapsed
Time (s) Executions         Exec (s) %Total  Time (s)   %CPU    %IO    SQL Id
-------- -----------        ---------- ------ ---------- ------  ------ -------------
   49.5            1            49.53   1.6      332.8   14.9    85.7  dqh4ks2qwcgs0
select p_brand, p_type, p_size, count(distinct ps_suppkey) as supplier_cnt
from partsupp, part where p_partkey = ps_partkey and p_brand <> 'Brand#35'
and p_type not like 'STANDARD BRUSHED%' and p_size in (29, 25, 16, 34, 6,
12, 36, 47) andps_suppkey not in ( select s_suppkey from supplier where
s_comment like '%Custom
```

This emphasis on I/O means that you should also pay attention to the operating system utilities discussed in Chapter 12. These utilities let you observe read performance, in addition to the AWR report data; they also run the desired configuration of Parallel Execution. In the following example, iostat is used to monitor the read performance of a single two-socket node executing a parallel query. The heading rMB/s shows a read rate of approximately 1 Gigabyte per second:

```
[root@london1 ~]# iostat -x -m sdb1 3 10
...
Device: rrqm/s  wrqm/s   r/s    w/s    rMB/s    wMB/s avgrq-sz avgqu-sz  await
svctm %util
sdb1     3.32     0.00 4150.50  0.66  1032.32    0.01   509.31   135.24  32.74
0.24   99.70

avg-cpu:   %user  %nice %system %iowait  %steal    %idle
            5.78   0.00    0.67   71.04    0.00    22.51

Device: rrqm/s  wrqm/s   r/s    w/s    rMB/s    wMB/s avgrq-sz avgqu-sz  await
svctm %util
sdb1     5.67     0.00 4689.67  0.67  1166.69    0.01   509.43   136.11  29.10
0.21  100.03

avg-cpu:   %user  %nice %system %iowait  %steal    %idle
            5.37   0.00    0.62   72.44    0.00    21.56

Device: rrqm/s  wrqm/s   r/s    w/s    rMB/s    wMB/s avgrq-sz avgqu-sz  await
svctm %util
sdb1     3.33     0.00 4352.33  0.67  1082.91    0.01   509.49   135.69  31.10
0.23  100.03
```

In a RAC environment, you should aim for the read rate to consistently be in the range of multiple gigabytes per second. If these rates are not achievable, then it is unlikely that you will be able to benefit from the full CPU potential of the all of the nodes in your cluster. In our experience, where sufficient capacity is not available, you should investigate some of the hardware technologies discussed in Chapter 4. For example, Solid State Disks (SSDs) can make a significant contribution to improving Parallel Query performance. Where I/O performance is maximized but CPU is underutilized, you may also consider some of the available techniques for data compression. These can reduce I/O usage at the expense of increasing the CPU usage required to decompress the data.

In an AWR report captured during a Parallel Execution workload, you may also observe wait events with the prefix PX Deq, such as PX Deq: Table Q Normal. From the earlier discussion of the concepts behind Parallel Execution, you might recall that producers and consumers communicate with Table Queues and that this type of wait event is recorded by a consumer process waiting for data from the consumer. As such, events in this class are considered idle events. This means that they cannot be explicitly tuned. Additional inspection should only be warranted if these events are recorded as consuming considerably more time than the I/O related events.

When previously discussing the pga_aggregate_target parameter, we noted that correctly sizing the PGA is the single most significant contributing factor for memory allocation in Parallel Execution environments. The following example shows a PGA aggregate target of 12 Gigabytes. It shows a size factor of 1 and estimates that the optimal size lies between 12 Gigabytes and 15 Gigabytes:

PGA Target Est (MB)	Size Factr	W/A MB Processed	Estd Extra W/A MB Read/ Written to Disk	Estd P Cache Hit %	Estd PGA Overallo Count	Estd Time
1,536	0.1	49,789.8	74,501.5	40.0	2	1.1E+08
3,072	0.3	49,789.8	48,597.1	51.0	1	8.8E+07
6,144	0.5	49,789.8	10,680.6	82.0	0	5.4E+07
9,216	0.8	49,789.8	7,668.8	87.0	0	5.1E+07
12,288	1.0	49,789.8	7,668.8	87.0	0	5.1E+07
14,746	1.2	49,789.8	0.0	100.0	0	4.5E+07
17,203	1.4	49,789.8	0.0	100.0	0	4.5E+07
19,661	1.6	49,789.8	0.0	100.0	0	4.5E+07
22,118	1.8	49,789.8	0.0	100.0	0	4.5E+07
24,576	2.0	49,789.8	0.0	100.0	0	4.5E+07
36,864	3.0	49,789.8	0.0	100.0	0	4.5E+07
49,152	4.0	49,789.8	0.0	100.0	0	4.5E+07
73,728	6.0	49,789.8	0.0	100.0	0	4.5E+07
98,304	8.0	49,789.8	0.0	100.0	0	4.5E+07

Given the focus on I/O driven by CPU performance, it is important to also ensure that the memory capacity is sufficient to match the capabilities of the I/O and CPU. For In-memory Parallel Execution, this also means correctly sizing the buffer cache. The following truncated buffer cache advisory shows advice for a dedicated 32k block cache that would benefit from being increased from its current 4 Gigabyte allocation.

P	Size for Est (M)	Size Factor	Buffers (thousands)	Est Phys Read Factor	Estimated Phys Reads (thousands)	Est Phys Read Time	Est %DBtime for Rds
...							
32k	3,456	.8	109	1.0	1,651	2	34.0
32k	3,840	.9	122	1.0	1,617	2	33.0
32k	4,096	1.0	130	1.0	1,593	2	33.0
32k	4,224	1.0	134	1.0	1,578	2	32.0
32k	4,608	1.1	146	0.9	1,492	2	30.0
32k	4,992	1.2	158	0.9	1,362	2	28.0
32k	5,376	1.3	170	0.7	1,150	2	23.0
32k	5,760	1.4	182	0.6	1,015	2	21.0
32k	6,144	1.5	194	0.6	983	2	20.0
...							

We noted previously that the interconnect plays an important contribution in Parallel Execution environments, especially when it comes to transferring data between producers and consumers on different nodes in the cluster. The AWR report includes a section on Interconnect Throughput by client, illustrating the level of bandwidth utilized by Parallel Query. The following example shows the interconnect throughput for one node in a two-node cluster:

```
Interconnect Throughput by Client        DB/Inst: PROD/PROD1  Snaps: 621-623
-> Throughput of interconnect usage by major consumers
-> All throughput numbers are megabytes per second

                     Send       Receive
Used By         Mbytes/sec  Mbytes/sec
--------------- ----------- -----------
Global Cache           .00         .00
Parallel Query         .70        2.93
DB Locks               .00         .00
DB Streams             .00         .00
Other                  .00         .00
```

The following example shows the throughput for the second node in the cluster:

```
Interconnect Throughput by Client        DB/Inst: PROD/PROD2  Snaps: 621-623
-> Throughput of interconnect usage by major consumers
-> All throughput numbers are megabytes per second

                     Send       Receive
Used By         Mbytes/sec  Mbytes/sec
--------------- ----------- -----------
Global Cache           .00         .00
Parallel Query        2.85         .70
DB Locks               .00         .00
DB Streams             .00         .00
Other                  .00         .00
```

The preceding example shows that Parallel Query consumed less than 3 MB/s for this two-node cluster. Therefore, it is well within the capabilities of a Gigabit-based interconnect. However, monitoring this MB/s value will indicate whether the bandwidth capacity is sufficient for Parallel Execution, particularly as the number of nodes in the cluster is increased.

SQL*Plus

In addition to the information based in an AWR report, you can also use SQL*Plus to observe Parallel Execution-related performance data. Previously, you saw an example at the session level with V$PQ_TQSTAT.

Statistics related to parallel operations can be monitored in the GV$PQ_SYSSTAT and GV$PQ_SESSTAT tables for system and session levels, respectively. More general information is also recorded in GV$SYSSTAT under events, with a name including the words parallelized, Parallel Operations, and PX. GV$PX_SESSION illustrates the status of the Parallel Execution Server processes available on the system, as in this example:

```
SQL> SELECT * FROM GV$PX_PROCESS;

    INST_ID SERV STATUS           PID SPID                SID SERIAL#
---------- ---- ---------  ---------- -------------- ---------- -------
          2 PO13 IN USE         56 29719                     4   14432
          2 POO5 IN USE         48 29703                     7   56722
          2 PO21 IN USE         64 29735                     9    3136
          2 PO29 IN USE         72 29751                    10      33
    ...
```

Advice on sizing the large pool adequately for the required message buffers can also be derived from the view, V$PX_BUFFER_ADVICE:

```
SQL>  select * from v$px_buffer_Advice;

STATISTIC                      VALUE
------------------------------ ----------
Servers Highwater                 36
Buffers HWM                     2575
Estimated Buffers HWM           1080
Servers Max                       64
Estimated Buffers Max           3264
Buffers Current Free             156
Buffers Current Total           2688
```

Trace Files

When discussing the applicability of configuring services, we also noted the uses of the trcsess utility, which you can leverage to combine Parallel Execution trace files. As shown in the following example, running tkprof against the generated trace file will also show detailed output of the events waited on during the execution of the particular queries traced:

```
Elapsed times include waiting on following events:
  Event waited on                               Times   Max. Wait  Total Waited
  ---------------------------------------       Waited  ---------  ------------
  PX Deq: Execution Msg                           659     0.88         13.41
  latch: cache buffers chains                      18     0.00          0.01
  direct path read                              11860     0.60        184.48
  latch free                                        6     0.00          0.00
  latch: library cache pin                          1     0.00          0.00
  PX Deq: Table Q Normal                        11910     0.41        192.58
  enq: BF - allocation contention                  18     0.00          0.03
  latch: enqueue hash chains                        1     0.00          0.00
  PX Deq Credit: need buffer                     1154     0.33         29.42
  PX Deq Credit: send blkd                       2370     0.64         54.86
  PX qref latch                                  1182     0.05          3.78
  PX Deq: Table Q Get Keys                         10     0.00          0.02
  PX Deq: Table Q Sample                           10     0.00          0.04
  SQL*Net message to client                      2786     0.00          0.00
  SQL*Net message from client                    2786     0.00          0.46
```

os thread startup	24	0.97	22.52
PX Deq: Join ACK	16	0.00	0.00
PX Deq: Parse Reply	15	0.00	0.01
PX Deq: Execute Reply	569	1.96	43.90
PX Deq: Table Q qref	6	0.01	0.02
PX Deq: Signal ACK	13	0.00	0.00
latch: session allocation	5	0.00	0.00

Summary

In this chapter, we have provided detailed information on the concepts, configuration, and performance of Parallel Execution in an Oracle Database 11g RAC environment. Along the way, we paid particular attention to some of the new features, such as in-memory Parallel Execution. If used appropriately, these features are particularly suited to helping clustered environments scale out to manage the largest of parallel operations.

CHAPTER 15

■■■

Upgrading to Oracle 11g Release 2

In this chapter, we will describe the process of upgrading to Oracle 11g Release 2. Unlike previous versions of RAC, where most deployments were to new systems, we believe there is now an established user base. Consequently, many Oracle 11.2 deployments will be upgrades from earlier versions of RAC.

At the time of writing, the vast majority of RAC installations are running Oracle 10g Release 2, so in this chapter we will discuss upgrading from that version to Oracle 11.2.

Two steps are involved in the upgrade process:

1. Upgrading Oracle Clusterware and ASM to Grid Infrastructure

2. Upgrading the RAC Software and the database

Oracle Clusterware and ASM should be upgraded to the Oracle 11.2 Grid Infrastructure at the same time. Although the installer gives you the option to defer the ASM migration, we strongly recommend performing it together with the Clusterware migration. The RAC software and database can be upgraded at a later date.

■ **Note** The RAC software version cannot be newer than the version of Grid Infrastructure.

Upgrading Grid Infrastructure Components

As just discussed, the Grid Infrastructure components, which are Oracle Clusterware and ASM, should be upgraded from earlier versions at the same time.

The following versions of Oracle Clusterware can be upgraded to Oracle 11.2:

- Oracle 10g Release 1: 10.1.0.3 or later

- Oracle 10g Release 2 - 10.2.0.3 or later

- Oracle 11g Release 1 - 11.1.0.6 or later

Upgrading earlier versions of Clusterware to Grid Infrastructure is always out of place; unlike previous upgrade paths, you will need to specify a new Oracle home for the grid software stack. Oracle Automatic Storage Management (ASM) can be upgraded in a rolling fashion if you are on ASM 11.1.0.6 or later and include a mandatory patch.

■ **Note** There is a known problem with rolling ASM upgrades on the 11.1 base release. Apply patch for bug 7436280 or the latest PSU on top of 11.1.0.7 to your configuration before attempting an ASM rolling upgrade.

If the Oracle Cluster Registry (OCR) and voting disk are currently installed on raw or block devices, the files for these components can be upgraded in place. You can optionally move the files to ASM or a cluster file system later. In Oracle 11.2, the OCR and voting disk are only supported on raw or block devices if they have been upgraded from a previous version; new installations must use ASM or a cluster file system (please refer to Chapter 8 for more information on how to move OCR and voting disks into ASM).

Installing the Prerequisites

Prior to upgrading a production system, we recommend that you rehearse the upgrade procedure on a test cluster. It is particularly important that you be confident in how the Grid Infrastructure upgrade procedure works because it is difficult to recover from a failure.

To test the upgrade process, we built a new cluster running Oracle 10.2 Clusterware, ASM, and RDBMS software and created an Oracle 10.2 database. We initially installed Oracle 10.2.0.1, and then patched all of the Oracle homes to 10.2.0.4 before creating the database. If you don't have physical hardware available, consider a virtualized environment. This isn't a like-for-like replacement of your production environment; however, it does give you the opportunity to practice using the upgrade process.

Upgrading Oracle 10*g* Clusterware is not seamless. We have encountered many minor OCR corruptions in Oracle 10*g*, most of these affecting node applications and database services. We strongly recommend that you resolve any corruptions in the OCR on your production cluster before attempting to upgrade to Oracle 11.2. Corruptions can often be resolved by deleting and re-adding services, instances, or databases. In the case of node applications, all four node applications must be removed and re-created together in Oracle 10*g* and Oracle 11.1.

Also, you should ensure that you have adequate backups of the OCR prior to attempting to fix any outstanding issues. We recommend that you shut down Oracle Clusterware on all nodes in the cluster, and then backup the OCR using the dd command, as in this example:

```
dd if=/dev/ocr1 of=/tmp/ocr1 bs=1M count=256
```

We typically make multiple copies of the file to different nodes or to shared storage. If you need to restore the OCR, then ensure that Oracle Clusterware is fully shutdown again before copying the file back (again, you do this using the dd command. Oracle 11.1 introduced the manualbackup option of ocrconfig, which you can use instead of the dd command to upgrade to 11.2.

Before starting an upgrade, make sure that you have backed up the following items:

- Oracle Clusterware home
- Oracle ASM home
- Oracle RDBMS software home(s)
- OCR
- Voting disk

- Database files

- Archived redo logs

- Control files

The Oracle homes should be backed up on each node in the cluster because the contents do vary between nodes. We recommend that you make multiple copies of the OCR and voting disk, but mirrored copies of these should be identical. If the database is stored in ASM, then you should use RMAN to backup the database files, control files, and archived redo logs.

If you are upgrading ASM diskgroups from Oracle 11.1, then we also recommend that you take metadata backups for each diskgroup using the md_backup command in the ASMCMD utility.

For Oracle 10.1 and later databases, you may consider enabling flashback logging for the database to restore the database more quickly if the upgrade fails. However, we still strongly recommend that you also make a full backup of the database.

Prior to the upgrade, the SCAN must be registered in DNS. We strongly recommend using three IP addresses for the SCAN (see Chapter 6 for more information about the SCAN).

You should ensure that all software components are downloaded and ready on the server(s) you intend to upgrade to 11.2. This way, networking problems that might occur should not affect you. Prior to installation, we downloaded the Grid Infrastructure software and unzipped the archive file into /home/oracle/stage/11gR2/grid on the first node in the cluster.

Running the Installer

The Grid Infrastructure upgrade is performed using the Oracle Universal Installer (OUI). This installer has a GUI interface and must be executed within an X-Windows session. Chapter 7 describes how to start the OUI in an X-Windows session, either at the console or as a VNC client. Before starting the installer, take a moment to unset all Oracle-related environment variables. The most common variables to unset are undefined in the following example:

```
[oracle@london1]$ unset ORACLE_HOME ORACLE_SID ORACLE_BASE ORA_CRS_HOME
```

Not unsetting ORA_CRS_HOME can cause the assistants upgrading the network configuration and ASM to fail. You should also ensure none of these variables are in the .bashrc and .bash_profile configuration files of the software owner on all nodes.

On the first node, log in as the Oracle user, navigate to the staging area, and run the installer:

```
[oracle@london1]$ cd /home/oracle/stage/11gR2/grid
[oracle@london1]$ ./runInstaller
```

The installer will take a couple of minutes to load the Java libraries before displaying the Installation Options page shown in Figure 15-1.

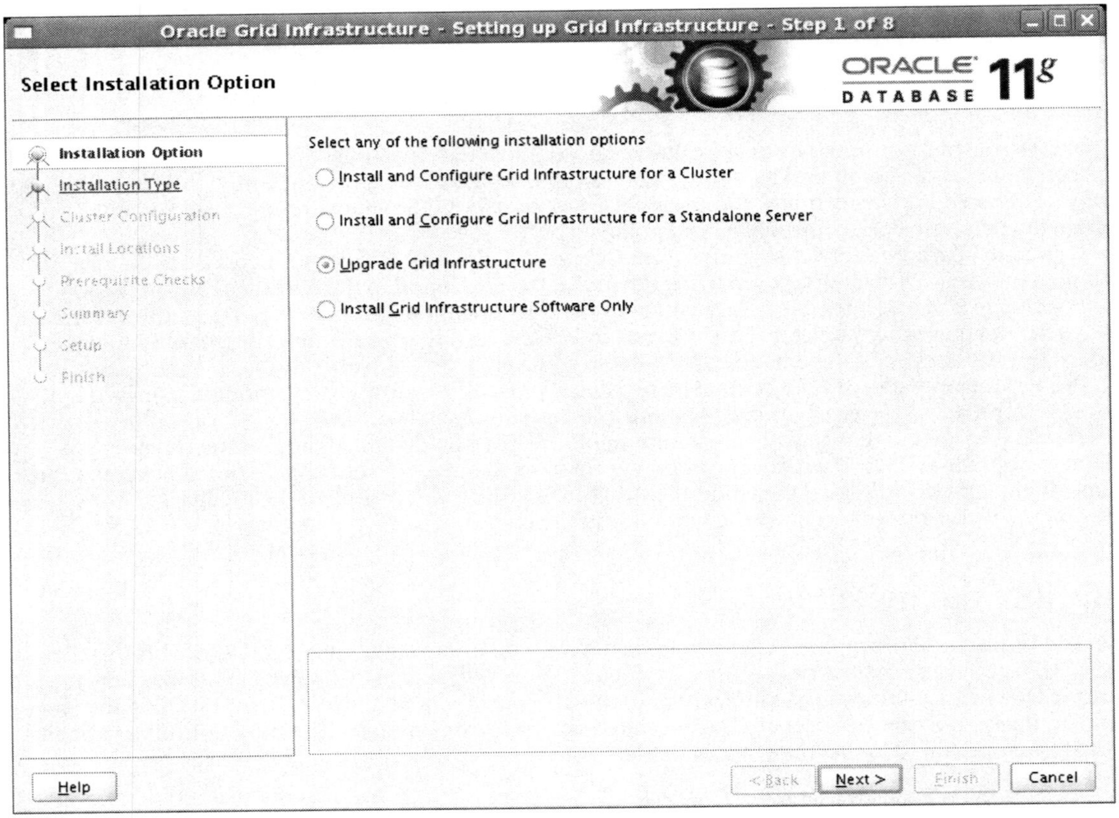

Figure 15-1. The Grid Infrastructure installation options

On some sites, we have seen very small root partitions that result in only little space available in the /tmp directory where OUI installs temporary files by default. You can set the TMP and TEMP environment variables to a directory with sufficient space to allow OUI to start. It is important to set both TMP and TEMP, not just one of them.

On the Installation Options page, select Upgrade Grid Infrastructure and press Next to continue.

Specifying Options

If the OUI detects an existing ASM instance, then a warning message will be displayed. Press Yes to continue if you are certain that you wish to upgrade the ASM instance at this time. If you choose not to upgrade ASM at this time, then you need to complete this task manually after the upgrade of Clusterware to version 11.2.

The Product Languages page will be displayed next. Select any additional languages that you want error messages to be displayed in, and then press Next to continue to the Grid Infrastructure Node Selection page (see Figure 15-2).

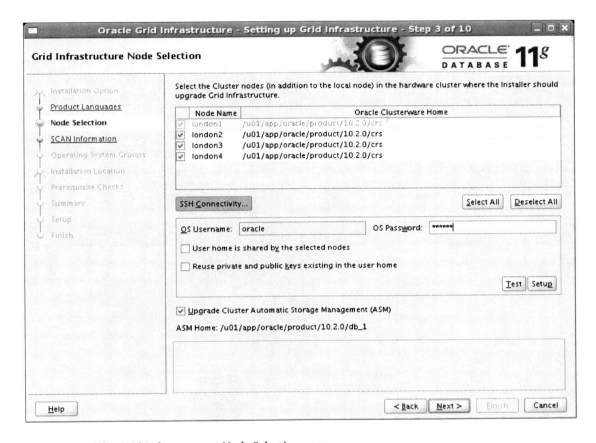

Figure 15-2. The Grid Infrastructure Node Selection page

On the Grid Infrastructure Node Selection page, the OUI will display the names of nodes already configured to be part of the cluster. If any nodes are missing from this list, then abort the installation and investigate why in the release you are upgrading from. If you find that all Clusterware daemons are running and that all nodes that should be part of the cluster are also up and running and registered in Clusterware, then you most likely have a corrupt global inventory.

If you wish to remove a node prior to performing the upgrade, we recommend that you do so using the original Oracle Clusterware software.

SSH connectivity should already be configured for the original installation, but there is always the possibility that the configuration has been subsequently modified. The OUI will test the SSH configuration before proceeding. If SSH was not used for the original installation (some early Oracle 10*g* installations continued to use RSH), then press the Setup button to instruct the OUI to set up a new SSH configuration. Note that, depending on the existing SSH configuration, the OUI automatic setup may fail. If this occurs, then we recommend that you abort the OUI session, delete the existing SSH configuration, and then try again.

The SSH configuration is stored in the `.ssh` directory of the `oracle` user on each node, and it can be deleted with the following line of code:

```
[oracle@london1]$ rm -rf /home/oracle/.ssh
```

Repeat this command on each node in the cluster. If you wish to retain a backup of the `.ssh` directory rather than simply deleting its contents, then we recommend renaming the directory, as in this example:

```
[oracle@london1]$ mv /home/oracle/.ssh /home/oracle/ssh_backup
```

If the OUI detects any existing ASM instances in the cluster, it will ask you to confirm that you wish to upgrade ASM. We strongly recommend that you upgrade Oracle Clusterware and ASM at the same time.

Press Next to continue to the Grid Infrastructure SCAN Information page (see Figure 15-3).

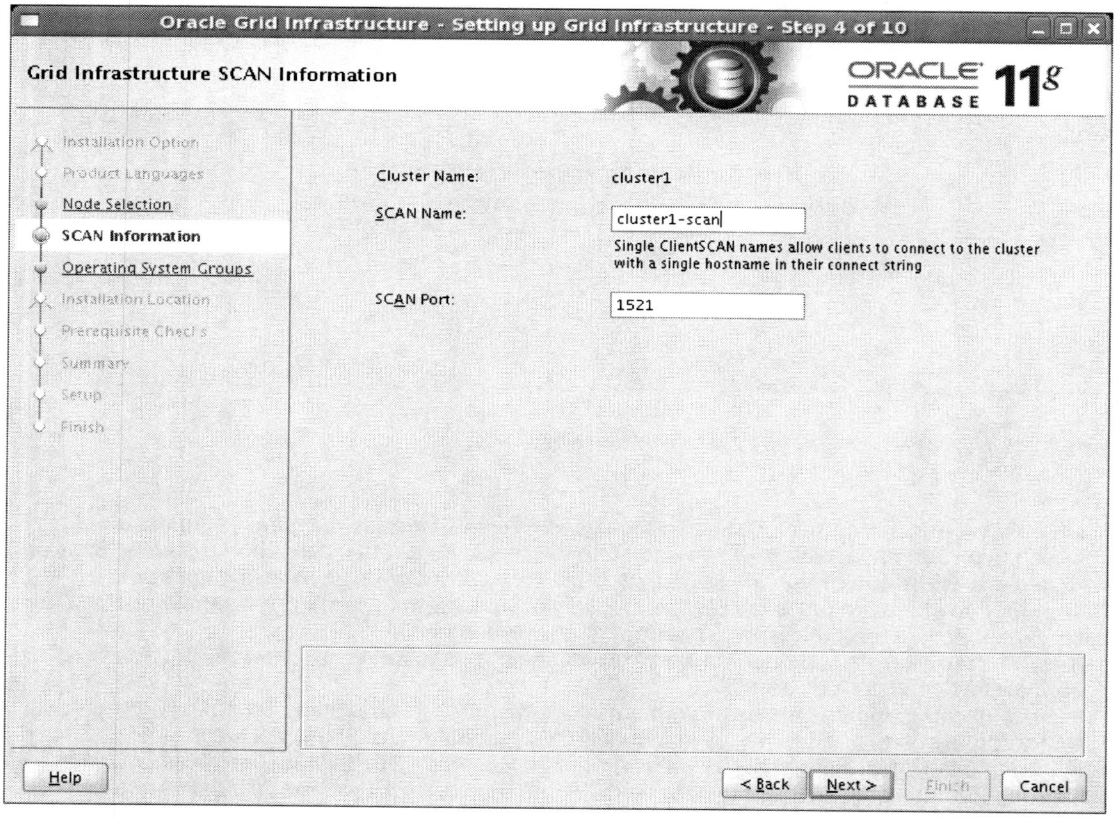

Figure 15-3. The Grid Infrastructure SCAN Information page

The Grid Infrastructure SCAN Information page displays the existing cluster name and recommends a SCAN name based on the cluster name. By convention, we have been creating the SCAN name by appending the -scan suffix to the cluster name.

■ **Note** The SCAN Information page also allows you to specify a SCAN port. The default port of 1521 is sufficient in most circumstances; in any case, this port can be changed post installation (see Chapter 8 for more information).

Press Next to continue to the ASM Monitor Password page. In Oracle 11.2 and later, a user with SYSASM privileges is required to perform administrative tasks on ASM diskgroups, such as creating and dropping disk groups or disks. In this release, an additional ASMSNMP user is created with SYSDBA privileges to monitor ASM. A password must be supplied for this user. The password must follow the new Oracle password requirements: it must be at least eight characters long, contain both upper- and lowercase letters, and include at least one numeric character.

Enter a password and press Next to continue to the Privileged Operating System Groups page. On this page, you can specify operating system groups that correspond to the following ASM groups:

- ASM Database Administrator (OSDBA) Group

- ASM Instance Administrator Operator (OSOPER) Group

- ASM Instance Administrator (OSASM) Group

The default value for all three groups is oinstall. Modify the groups as required, and then press Next to continue. If you accepted the default values, then a warning will be displayed stating that the OSDBA, OSOPER, and OSASM groups all have the same operating system group. The message will ask you to confirm this decision. Press Yes to continue to the Installation Location page (see Figure 15-4).

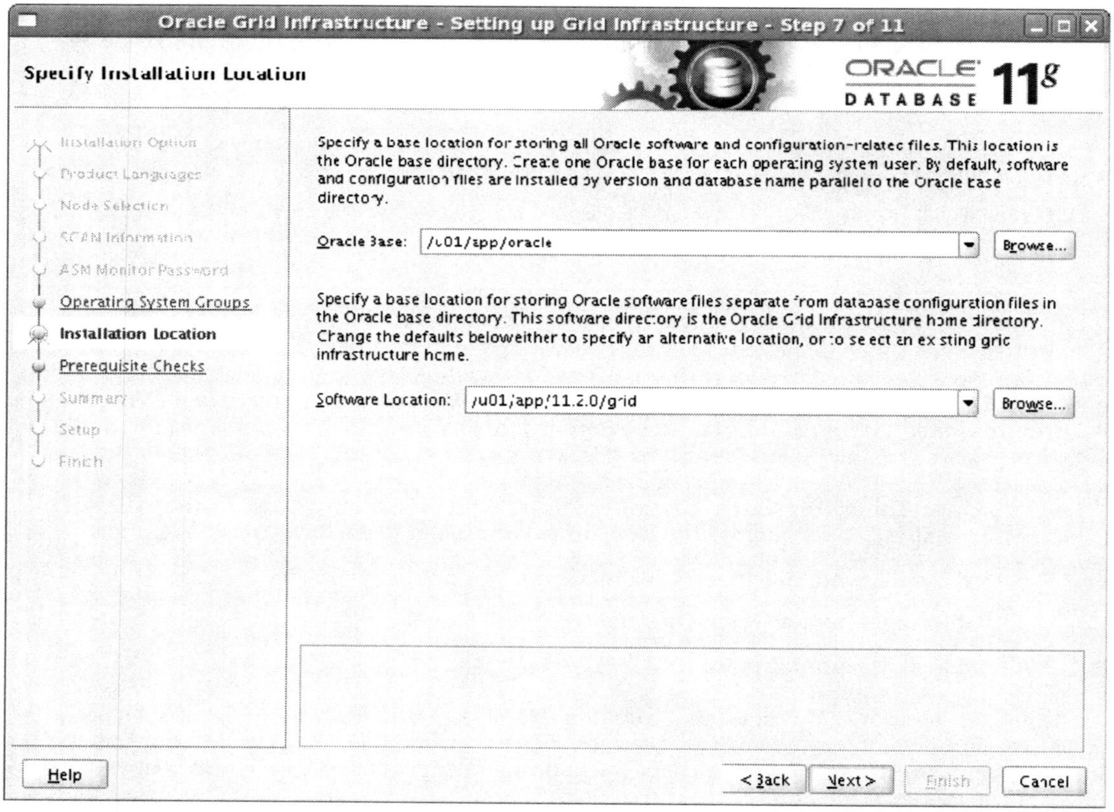

Figure 15-4. The Grid Infrastructure Installation Location page

The Installation Location page will suggest default values for the Oracle Base directory and the Grid Infrastructure software location. In this example, the Oracle Base directory defaulted to /u01/app/oracle. While the Grid Infrastructure software will not be stored below this directory, it will still be used by Grid Infrastructure as the default base for the diagnostic directory. All Grid Infrastructure-related log files will be stored in $GRID_HOME/log/hostname.

The Grid Infrastructure software location shown Figure 15-4 defaulted to /u01/app/11.2.0/grid. Note that the OUI performs an out-of-place upgrade from any supported previous release to Oracle 11.2. In other words, a completely new Oracle home will be created for the Grid Infrastructure software. This home includes both the Oracle Clusterware and ASM software.

Oracle recommends that the Grid Infrastructure software be installed in local Oracle homes on each node in the cluster. In other words, do not attempt to create a shared Oracle home for the Grid Infrastructure software because this will limit your options during upgrades and patching.

Press Next to continue to the Prerequisite Checks page. See Chapter 7 for a full description of this page. As the prerequisites have evolved between Oracle 10*g* and Oracle 11.2, you may find that several checks initially fail. We strongly recommend that you address all prerequisite check failures before attempting to continue with the upgrade. Do not ignore failures unless you are absolutely certain they will not cause the upgrade process to fail.

You can request that the Prerequisite Checks page generate fixup scripts for a limited number of check failures, including those related to kernel parameters and user limits. The fixup scripts must be run manually as the root user on each affected node.

When all prerequisite checks have been passed, the Summary page in Figure 15-5 will be displayed:

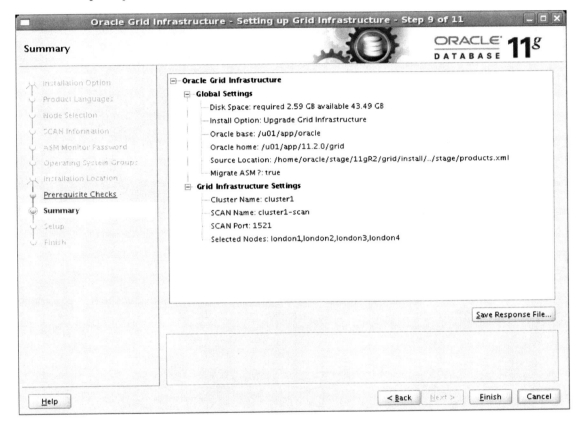

Figure 15-5. The Grid Infrastructure Installation summary

Running the Upgrade

Press Finish to terminate the interview process and to start the Grid Infrastructure upgrade process. The Setup page will be displayed; this page shows the current progress through the Setup. In this example, the following steps were performed:

1. Installed the Grid Infrastructure for a Cluster:

    a. Prepared the existing database for the upgrade process.

        b. Copied files.

        c. Linked binaries.

        d. Set up the file.

        e. Performed remote operations.

2.   Executed root scripts for Install Grid Infrastructure.

3.   Configured the Oracle Grid Infrastructure for a cluster, including the following items:

        a. The Oracle Net Configuration Assistant

        b. The Automatic Storage Management Configuration Assistant

        c. The Enterprise Manager Configuration Upgrade Utility

        d. The Oracle Cluster Verification Utility

After the Grid Infrastructure software is installed, you will see the Execute Configuration Scripts dialog box displayed (see Figure 15-6).

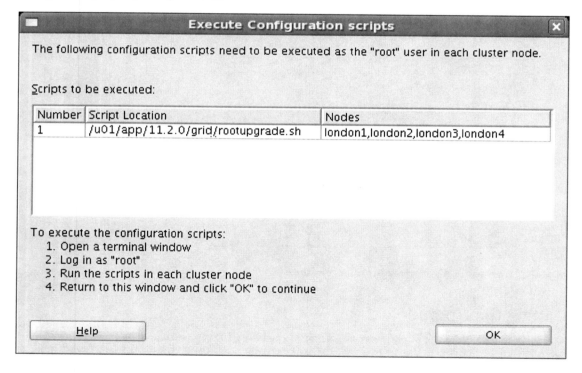

Figure 15-6. The Execute Configuration Scripts dialog

As the root user on each node in the cluster, run the rootupgrade.sh script. This script will upgrade the OCR and voting disk to the 11.2 format. It will also configure files such as /etc/inittab and the /etc/init.d scripts.

In our example, the output for the first node of the rootupgrade.sh script looked like this:

```
[root@london1]# /u01/app/11.2.0/grid/rootupgrade.sh
Running Oracle 11g root.sh script...

The following environment variables are set as:
    ORACLE_OWNER= oracle
    ORACLE_HOME=  /u01/app/11.2.0/grid

Enter the full pathname of the local bin directory: [/usr/local/bin]:
The file "dbhome" already exists in /usr/local/bin.  Overwrite it? (y/n)
[n]: y
    Copying dbhome to /usr/local/bin ...
The file "oraenv" already exists in /usr/local/bin.  Overwrite it? (y/n)
[n]: y
    Copying oraenv to /usr/local/bin ...
The file "coraenv" already exists in /usr/local/bin.  Overwrite it? (y/n)
[n]: y
    Copying coraenv to /usr/local/bin ...

Entries will be added to the /etc/oratab file as needed by
Database Configuration Assistant when a database is created
Finished running generic part of root.sh script.
Now product-specific root actions will be performed.
2009-12-22 21:34:38: Parsing the host name
2009-12-22 21:34:38: Checking for super user privileges
2009-12-22 21:34:38: User has super user privileges
Using configuration parameter file: /u01/app/11.2.0/grid/crs/install/crsconfig_params
Creating trace directory
CSS appears healthy
EVM appears healthy
CRS appears healthy
Shutting down Oracle Cluster Ready Services (CRS):
Dec 22 21:35:22.012 | INF | daemon shutting down
Stopping resources. This could take several minutes.
Successfully stopped CRS resources.
Stopping CSSD.
Shutting down CSS daemon.
Shutdown request successfully issued.
Shutdown has begun. The daemons should exit soon.
LOCAL ADD MODE
Creating OCR keys for user 'root', privgrp 'root'..
Operation successful.
  root wallet
  root wallet cert
  root cert export
  peer wallet
  profile reader wallet
  pa wallet
```

```
          peer wallet keys
          pa wallet keys
          peer cert request
          pa cert request
          peer cert
          pa cert
          peer root cert TP
          profile reader root cert TP
          pa root cert TP
          peer pa cert TP
          pa peer cert TP
          profile reader pa cert TP
          profile reader peer cert TP
          peer user cert
          pa user cert
Adding daemon to inittab
CRS-4123: Oracle High Availability Services has been started.
ohasd is starting
CRS-2672: Attempting to start 'ora.mdnsd' on 'london1'
CRS-2676: Start of 'ora.mdnsd' on 'london1' succeeded
CRS-2672: Attempting to start 'ora.gipcd' on 'london1'
CRS-2676: Start of 'ora.gipcd' on 'london1' succeeded
CRS-2672: Attempting to start 'ora.gpnpd' on 'london1'
CRS-2676: Start of 'ora.gpnpd' on 'london1' succeeded
CRS-2672: Attempting to start 'ora.cssdmonitor' on 'london1'
CRS-2676: Start of 'ora.cssdmonitor' on 'london1' succeeded
CRS-2672: Attempting to start 'ora.cssd' on 'london1'
CRS-2672: Attempting to start 'ora.diskmon' on 'london1'
CRS-2676: Start of 'ora.diskmon' on 'london1' succeeded
CRS-2676: Start of 'ora.cssd' on 'london1' succeeded
CRS-2672: Attempting to start 'ora.ctssd' on 'london1'
CRS-2676: Start of 'ora.ctssd' on 'london1' succeeded
CRS-2672: Attempting to start 'ora.crsd' on 'london1'
CRS-2676: Start of 'ora.crsd' on 'london1' succeeded
CRS-2672: Attempting to start 'ora.evmd' on 'london1'
CRS-2676: Start of 'ora.evmd' on 'london1' succeeded
clscfg: EXISTING configuration version 3 detected.
clscfg: version 3 is 10G Release 2.
Successfully accumulated necessary OCR keys.
Creating OCR keys for user 'root', privgrp 'root'..
Operation successful.

london1     2009/12/22 21:40:32
/u01/app/11.2.0/grid/cdata/london1/backup_20091222_214032.olr
Configure Oracle Grid Infrastructure for a Cluster ... succeeded
Updating inventory properties for clusterware
Starting Oracle Universal Installer...

Checking swap space: must be greater than 500 MB.   Actual 4095 MB     Passed
The inventory pointer is located at /etc/oraInst.loc
The inventory is located at /u01/app/oracle/oraInventory
'UpdateNodeList' was successful.
```

```
Starting Oracle Universal Installer...

Checking swap space: must be greater than 500 MB.   Actual 4095 MB      Passed
The inventory pointer is located at /etc/oraInst.loc
The inventory is located at /u01/app/oracle/oraInventory
'UpdateNodeList' was successful.
```

Output is similar on all nodes in the cluster. Although not specified in the Execute Configuration Scripts dialog box we recommend that the rootupgrade.sh scripts are run sequentially in node order on each node in the cluster. When you have executed the root scripts on all nodes in the cluster, press OK in the Execute Configuration Scripts dialog box to return to the Setup page. The files keep a detailed log in $GRID_HOME/cfgtoollogs/crsconfig/.

The Setup page will execute the remaining configuration assistants, including the Net Configuration Assistant (NETCA), ASM Configuration Assistant (ASMCA), Enterprise Manager Upgrade Utility (if Enterprise Manager Data Control is configured), and finally, the Cluster Verification Utility (CVU).

■ **Note** If the netca and asmca assistants fail at this stage, then you most likely had the environment variable ORA_CRS_HOME set, pointing to the 10.2 Clusterware home. In this case, skip the remaining assistants on the OUI page and execute configToolAllCommands in $GRID_HOME/cfgtoollogs/ after unsetting the ORA_CRS_HOME variable.

If any of the configuration assistants fails for a reason other than the one just noted, you are given the opportunity to resolve any issues and to retry the assistant. When all of the configuration assistants have completed successfully, the Finish page will be displayed. Press Close to terminate the installation session.

You should now have Oracle Clusterware and any ASM instances upgraded to Oracle 11.2. The databases will remain on their previous versions. In the next section, we will discuss the upgrade process for individual databases. If there are 10.2 database resources in the cluster, then Grid Infrastructure will work in compatibility mode. Any node with a 10.2 resource will be *pinned*, in Oracle terminology. You can use the olsnodes -s -t command to check whether a node is pinned. You should change this setting only when all pre-11.2 resources have been upgraded. Note that operating with pinned nodes in the cluster places some restrictions on the available options provided by Grid Infrastructure.

Upgrading RAC Software

The next step in the upgrade process is to install RAC software. It is possible to combine this step and the database upgrade into a single operation, in which case the OUI will invoke the Database Upgrade Assistant (DBUA) immediately following installation of the RAC software. However, we recommend that each step be performed separately; this simplifies any error detection and resolution.

As when performing the Grid software upgrade, you should download the RAC software and unzip the archive file into the /home/oracle/stage/11gR2/database directory on the first node in the cluster before initiating the upgrade process itself.

Running the Installer

Like the Grid Infrastructure software installation, the RAC software installation is performed using the Oracle Universal Installer.

Before launching the installer, ensure that the ORACLE_HOME, ORACLE_SID, and ORA_CRS_HOME variables are unset. Next, log in as the oracle user on the first node, navigate to the staging area, and run the installer:

```
[oracle@london1]$ cd /home/oracle/stage/11gR2/database
[oracle@london1]$ ./runInstaller
```

The installer will take a couple of minutes to load the Java libraries before displaying the Security Updates page. If necessary, you can use the TMP and TEMP environment variables if you are short on space on the /tmp directory.

The Security Updates page allows you to provide an email address that will be used by Oracle Support to supply information about security issues. You can optionally elect to receive security updates through My Oracle Support, in which case you should also supply your My Oracle Support password. The security updates are optional. If this is a test installation, then it is highly likely that you will not want to configure these security updates. If you do not specify an email address and optional password, then you will receive a warning that you will not receive critical patch updates; however, the installation will be allowed to continue. Next, the RAC Installation Options page will be displayed (see Figure 15-7).

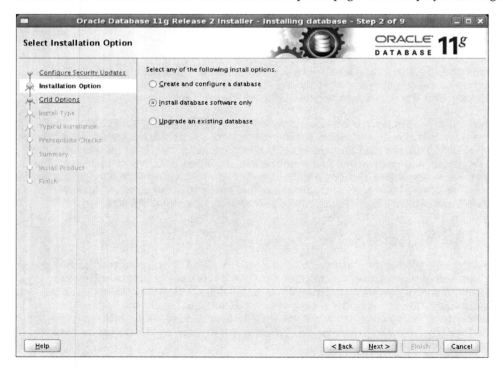

Figure 15-7. The RAC Installation Options Page

On the Installation Options page, we recommend that you select the *Install database software only* option. This option installs the RAC software on all nodes in the cluster, and then upgrades any databases. The remainder of the RAC software installation process for an upgrade is identical to the process described in Chapter 7 for a new installation. Even so, we will cover the remaining steps here as well, for the sake of completeness.

On the Node Selection page, ensure that all nodes in the cluster are included in the RAC software installation. If any nodes do not appear, then we recommend that you abort the installation, and then investigate and resolve the issue before restarting the installation.

The Node Selection page also allows you to configure SSH connectivity. This step should have been performed during the Grid Infrastructure software installation. However, the OUI will still test whether SSH connectivity is correctly configured before continuing to the next page.

The Product Languages page allows you to specify additional languages in which Oracle error messages can be generated, and the Database Edition page allows you to specify Enterprise Edition or Standard Edition. It is possible to change from Standard Edition to Enterprise Edition during the upgrade process; however, you should not attempt to change from Enterprise Edition to Standard Edition during the upgrade because this change can result in invalid or unusable objects in the data dictionary and/or database. If you wish to convert from Enterprise Edition to Standard Edition, you will need to export the database objects from the old Enterprise Edition database and import them into new the Standard Edition database.

The Installation Location page allows you to specify a location for the Oracle base directory and a location for the RAC Software Oracle home. In our example, the Oracle base directory defaulted to /u01/app/oracle, and the location of the RAC Software home defaulted to /u01/app/oracle/product/11.2.0/dbhome_1. Note that the RAC Software installation is an out-of-place upgrade; the software is installed into a new Oracle home and does not overwrite an existing Oracle home.

The Privileged Operating System Groups page allows you to specify operating system groups to be used by the Oracle Database Administrator (OSDBA) group and Database Operator (OSOPER) group. The default value for both groups is dba.

The next page is the Prerequisite Checks page. This page will perform all necessary checks prior to the RAC software installation. The checks are similar to those performed during the Grid Infrastructure installation; therefore, the checks should normally succeed for the RAC software installation.

When all prerequisite checks have been passed, the Summary page for the RAC installation will be displayed (see Figure 15-8).

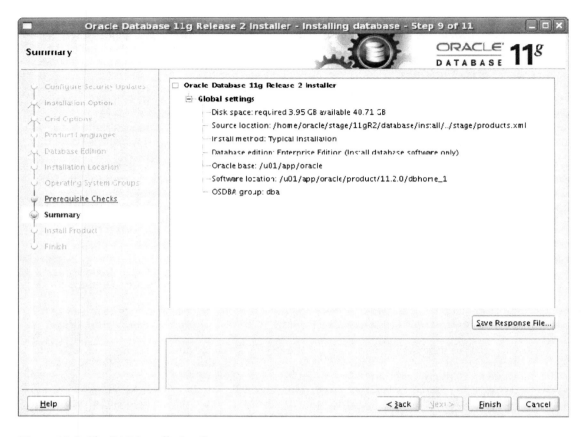

Figure 15-8. The RAC Installation Summary page

Press Finish to terminate the interview process and start the RAC software installation process. The Setup page will be displayed, showing the current progress through the setup process.

Running Configuration Scripts

Towards the end of the installation, the installer will prompt you to run some shell scripts as the root user. At the point, the Execute Configuration Scripts dialog box will be displayed (see Figure 15-9).

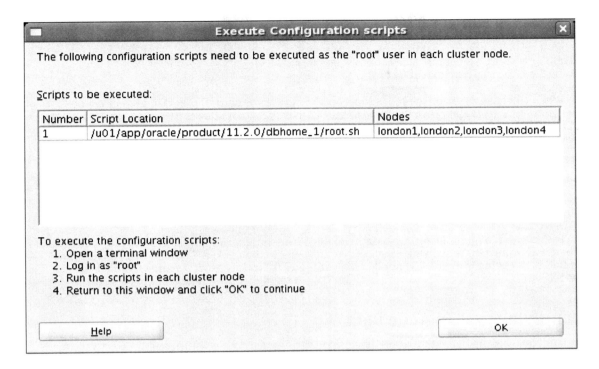

Figure 15-9. The Execute Configuration Scripts dialog

As the root user, run the specified root.sh script on each node in the cluster. In this case, the order of execution is unimportant, and the scripts can be executed concurrently. The following shows a sample of the output generated when running this script on one node:

```
[root@london1]# /u01/app/oracle/product/11.2.0/dbhome_1/root.sh
Running Oracle 11g root.sh script...

The following environment variables are set as:
    ORACLE_OWNER= oracle
    ORACLE_HOME=  /u01/app/oracle/product/11.2.0/dbhome_1

Enter the full pathname of the local bin directory: [/usr/local/bin]:
The file "dbhome" already exists in /usr/local/bin.  Overwrite it? (y/n)
[n]: y
   Copying dbhome to /usr/local/bin ...
The file "oraenv" already exists in /usr/local/bin.  Overwrite it? (y/n)
[n]: y
   Copying oraenv to /usr/local/bin ...
The file "coraenv" already exists in /usr/local/bin.  Overwrite it? (y/n)
[n]: y
   Copying coraenv to /usr/local/bin ...
```

```
Entries will be added to the /etc/oratab file as needed by
Database Configuration Assistant when a database is created
Finished running generic part of root.sh script.
Now product-specific root actions will be performed.
Finished product-specific root actions.
```

When you have executed the root scripts on all nodes in the cluster, press OK in the Execute Configuration Scripts dialog box to return to the Setup page. When setup is complete, the Finish page will be displayed. Press Close to terminate the installation session.

Preparing for the Database Upgrade

The final step in the upgrade process is to upgrade the databases within the cluster. It is possible to run Oracle 11.2 Grid Infrastructure with earlier databases, so this upgrade does not need to be performed immediately. If you have more than one database in the cluster, then each database can be upgraded separately and at different times, if necessary.

Before you can upgrade the databases, you must work through a number of preparatory steps; these steps are described in the following sections. At this point in the book, we assume that you have carried out sufficient testing to ensure the application continues to work as expected and within the SLAs of the new release.

Identifying the Upgrade Path

The complexity of the upgrade process depends on the original database. Upgrading directly to Oracle 11.2 is supported for the following database versions:

- 9.2.0.8
- 10.1.0.5
- 10.2.0.2 or later
- 11.1.0.6 or later

In our experience, most RAC users are running Oracle 10.2 or later. At the time of writing, a few Oracle 9.2 RAC databases remained in production.

If the current database version is Oracle 7.3, Oracle 8.0, Oracle 8.1, or Oracle 9.0, then the database must be upgraded to an intermediate release, and then upgraded from that intermediate release to Oracle 11.2. Table 15-1 shows the upgrade paths for earlier Oracle versions.

Table 15-1. RAC upgrade paths

Initial Version	Terminal Version	Intermediate Version	Final Version
7.3.3 (or below)	7.3.4	9.2.0.8	11.2
8.0.5 (or below)	8.0.6	9.2.0.8	11.2
8.1.7 (or below)	8.1.7.4	10.2.0.4	11.2
9.0.1.3 (or below)	9.0.1.4	10.2.0.4	11.2

Determine Upgrade Method

There are three commonly used upgrade methods:

- *The Database Upgrade Assistant (DBUA) method*: This GUI tool automates the Oracle 11.2 upgrade process, completing all of the tasks that would normally be performed manually. In Oracle 11.2, DBUA fully supports RAC database upgrades. We recommend using DBUA for smaller databases.

- *The Manual Upgrade Method*: The method uses SQL scripts and tools to perform the upgrade. The actual process has changed little since Oracle 10*g* though; however, and as you might expect, the process becomes slightly more complex with each successive release. Most DBAs prefer to have more control over the upgrade process, so they generally favor manual upgrades. We recommend using the manual upgrade method for larger databases and business-critical databases because this allows you to test and tune the upgrade process more comprehensively.

- *The Export / Import Method*: Upgrades can also be performed using the Data Pump export / import utility when the source database is Oracle 10.1. Or, you can use the original export / import utilities included with the earlier versions of your databases. In either case, a new target database must be created before the data is imported. The export / import method may be attractive for databases where the bulk of large tables are partitioned using date ranges or where a large percentage of the data is read-only. The Data Pump utility can also be parallelized, thereby achieving good transfer rates. Finally, the Data Pump's export ability can transport data directly to another database using Oracle Net Services, thereby avoiding any intermediate disk I/O. This can be a useful technique if space is at a premium or I/O is a bottleneck for you.

One of the main benefits of the export / import method is that it leaves the source database unchanged. Therefore, you can this method to develop and test without affecting the original database. Both the DBUA and manual methods update the target database; in order to test those upgrade approaches, it will be necessary to clone the database to a new location before attempting the upgrade.

Various other methods have been used by different sites to upgrade time-critical databases, including the Oracle Streams/Logical Standby database, Golden Gate, third-party tools such as Quest Shareplex.

In the remainder of this chapter, we will cover how to upgrade two databases in our example cluster. The PROD database will be upgraded automatically using the DBUA, while the TEST database will be upgraded manually using SQL scripts.

Testing the Upgrade Process

Once the upgrade process has been developed, it is important to test both the process and the resulting database to ensure that the database has been correctly upgraded. You also need to make sure that the software continues to function as required and expected.

Also, we strongly recommend that you attempt to perform some stress testing on the upgraded database. We realize this is not always possible in the real world, but in our experience, failing to perform stress testing is the most likely cause of bad performance in newly upgraded databases.

There are a number of Oracle and third party tools available for stress testing. Oracle introduced Real Application Testing (RAT) as a cost-option in Oracle 11*g* Release 1. The RAT toolkit consists of the SQL Performance Analyzer (SPA) and Database Replay. SPA is aimed at measuring performance of a SQL tuning set before and after a change to the database, while Database Replay has a broader focus. The reminder of this section will focus exclusively on Database Replay.

Database Replay consists of three parts:

- Capturing the workload

- Preprocessing the captured workload

- Replaying the captured workload

When initially released, only 11.1 database workloads could be captured by Database Replay. Subsequent patchsets or one-off patches have addressed this, so now you can capture workloads on 10*g* and 9*i* Release 2, as well. This makes RAT an attractive option, but users should bear in mind that it does not capture the entire software stack; rather, it captures only database workloads. Also, the capture process can add overhead to the production system. A system operating at its capacity limit should probably not be used to capture a representative workload; otherwise, you might encounter stability issues.

The capture process writes information into files in a directory object. Once the capture process has completed, the captured workload needs to be transferred to an 11*g* database for preprocessing. This process adds additional metadata to the captured files, making them suitable for replay.

The final step, which can be repeated as often as needed, is to replay the captured workload. Oracle clients now include a new utility called wrc (workload replay client). This utility replays the captured workload. If your source system has dependencies on remote objects such as external tables, directories, database links, then these need to be resolved first. You should also ensure that the test database you are replaying the workload against is restored or flashed back to the same SCN as the production database when you started the capture. Also, Oracle recommends setting the server's system time to match the production system's time when the workload was captured. If your application sends out information to customers in any way, shape, or form during the replay, you should ensure that none of this can happen!

After the replay finishes, you are presented with a report that compares the captured and replayed workload. This report should serve as the cornerstone of your investigation to determine whether the upgrade is likely to encounter performance issues. It is also a good test for the SQL Plan Baselines you will create during the migration (see the "Recommended Tasks" section later in this chapter for more information).

Running the pre-Upgrade Tool

The pre-upgrade tool must be run as part of the manual upgrade process. This tool is also run automatically by DBUA during the automatic upgrade process. However, Oracle recommends that you run the tool manually before initiating the automatic upgrade process, so you can preview its findings and address any issues before invoking DBUA.

The pre-upgrade tool is supplied as part of the new Oracle home. In our example, the pathname of the pre-upgrade tool looked like this:

```
/u01/app/oracle/product/11.2.0/dbhome_1/rdbms/admin/utlu112i.sql
```

We copied the utlu112i.sql script to the /tmp directory.

While the pre-upgrade tool is supplied as part of the Oracle 11.2 software, the tool must be run using the original Oracle environment, including the original ORACLE_HOME and PATH. In our example, we upgraded from Oracle 10.2.0.4 to Oracle 11.2; as part of this process, we ran the pre-upgrade tool as the oracle user:

```
export ORACLE_BASE=/u01/app/oracle
export ORACLE_HOME=/u01/app/oracle/product/10.2.0/db_1
export PATH=$ORACLE_HOME/bin:$PATH
```

The ORACLE_SID should be set to an appropriate value, as in this example:

```
export ORACLE_SID=PROD1
```

Note that the pre-upgrade tool is a SQL*Plus script; it can be executed in this fashion:

```
$ sqlplus / as sysdba
SQL> SPOOL upgrade1.log
SQL> @utlu112i.sql
SQL> SPOOL OFF
```

In our example, the following output was written to the upgrade1.log file:

```
Oracle Database 11.2 Pre-Upgrade Information Tool     12-26-2009 13:16:11
.
*********************************************************************
Database:
*********************************************************************
--> name:          PROD
--> version:       10.2.0.4.0
--> compatible:    10.2.0.3.0
--> blocksize:     8192
--> platform:      Linux IA (32-bit)
--> timezone file: V4
.
*********************************************************************
Tablespaces: [make adjustments in the current environment]
*********************************************************************
--> SYSTEM tablespace is adequate for the upgrade.
.... minimum required size: 731 MB
.... AUTOEXTEND additional space required: 251 MB
--> UNDOTBS1 tablespace is adequate for the upgrade.
.... minimum required size: 473 MB
.... AUTOEXTEND additional space required: 438 MB
--> SYSAUX tablespace is adequate for the upgrade.
.... minimum required size: 485 MB
.... AUTOEXTEND additional space required: 215 MB
--> TEMP tablespace is adequate for the upgrade.
.... minimum required size: 61 MB
.... AUTOEXTEND additional space required: 41 MB
.
*********************************************************************
Flashback: OFF
*********************************************************************
```

```
**********************************************************************
Update Parameters: [Update Oracle Database 11.2 init.ora or spfile]
**********************************************************************
WARNING: --> "java_pool_size" needs to be increased to at least 64 MB
  .
**********************************************************************
Renamed Parameters: [Update Oracle Database 11.2 init.ora or spfile]
**********************************************************************
-- No renamed parameters found. No changes are required.
  .
**********************************************************************
Obsolete/Deprecated Parameters: [Update Oracle Database 11.2 init.ora or spfile]
**********************************************************************
--> background_dump_dest          11.1      DEPRECATED    replaced by
"diagnostic_dest"
--> user_dump_dest                11.1      DEPRECATED    replaced by
"diagnostic_dest"
--> core_dump_dest                11.1      DEPRECATED    replaced by
"diagnostic_dest"
  .
**********************************************************************
Components: [The following database components will be upgraded or installed]
**********************************************************************
--> Oracle Catalog Views        [upgrade]  VALID
--> Oracle Packages and Types    [upgrade]  VALID
--> JServer JAVA Virtual Machine [upgrade]  VALID
--> Oracle XDK for Java          [upgrade]  VALID
--> Real Application Clusters    [upgrade]  VALID
--> Oracle Workspace Manager     [upgrade]  VALID
--> OLAP Analytic Workspace      [upgrade]  VALID
--> OLAP Catalog                 [upgrade]  VALID
--> EM Repository                [upgrade]  VALID
--> Oracle Text                  [upgrade]  VALID
--> Oracle XML Database          [upgrade]  VALID
--> Oracle Java Packages         [upgrade]  VALID
--> Oracle interMedia            [upgrade]  VALID
--> Spatial                      [upgrade]  VALID
--> Data Mining                  [upgrade]  VALID
--> Expression Filter            [upgrade]  VALID
--> Rule Manager                 [upgrade]  VALID
--> Oracle OLAP API              [upgrade]  VALID
  .
**********************************************************************
Miscellaneous Warnings
**********************************************************************
WARNING: --> The "cluster_database" parameter is currently "TRUE"
.... and must be set to "FALSE" prior to running a manual upgrade.
WARNING: --> Database is using a timezone file older than version 11.
.... After the release migration, it is recommended that DBMS_DST package
.... be used to upgrade the 10.2.0.4.0 database timezone version
.... to the latest version which comes with the new release.
WARNING: --> Database contains schemas with stale optimizer statistics.
```

```
.... Refer to the Upgrade Guide for instructions to update
.... schema statistics prior to upgrading the database.
.... Component Schemas with stale statistics:
....    SYS
....    SYSMAN
WARNING: --> Database contains INVALID objects prior to upgrade.
.... The list of invalid SYS/SYSTEM objects was written to
.... registry$sys_inv_objs.
.... The list of non-SYS/SYSTEM objects was written to
.... registry$nonsys_inv_objs.
.... Use utluiobj.sql after the upgrade to identify any new invalid
.... objects due to the upgrade.
.... USER PUBLIC has 1 INVALID objects.
.... USER SYS has 2 INVALID objects.
WARNING: --> Database contains schemas with objects dependent on network
packages.
.... Refer to the Upgrade Guide for instructions to configure Network ACLs.
WARNING: --> EM Database Control Repository exists in the database.
.... Direct downgrade of EM Database Control is not supported. Refer to the
.... Upgrade Guide for instructions to save the EM data prior to upgrade.
WARNING:--> recycle bin in use.
.... Your recycle bin turned on.
.... It is REQUIRED
.... that the recycle bin is empty prior to upgrading
.... your database.
.... The command:  PURGE DBA_RECYCLEBIN
.... must be executed immediately prior to executing your upgrade.
.
PL/SQL procedure successfully completed.
```

The pre-upgrade report includes the following sections:

- *Database*: This section contains basic information about the database, including the database name, operating system, version, and block size. The report will include a warning if the COMPATIBLE parameter needs to be modified prior to the upgrade.

- *Logfiles*: This optional section lists any redo log files that are smaller than 4MB. For the manual upgrade, any redo logs that are smaller than 4MB in size must be replaced by log files of at least 4MB prior to the upgrade. At the time of writing, most production sites typically use redo logs of between 100MB and 500MB.

- *Tablespaces*: This section reports current and required sizes for the SYSTEM, SYSAUX, temporary, and undo tablespaces. For manual upgrades, tablespaces must be extended manually. DBUA will attempt to extend undersized tablespaces, but most DBAs will want to extend these tablespaces themselves to maintain control over the database and to reduce the possibility of errors. Remember: If you are upgrading an Oracle 9.2 database, a SYSAUX tablespace is mandatory in Oracle 10.1 and later.

- *Flashback*: This section displays the current status of flashback logging. Even if you do not enable flashback logging during normal operations, you might consider using this feature during upgrades to allow the database to be quickly restored in the event of a failure.

- *Update Parameters*: This section lists any parameter values that should be updated before the database is upgraded.

- *Deprecated Parameters*: This section lists any parameters included in the current parameter file that are deprecated in Oracle 11.2. Parameters that have been deprecated between Oracle 10*g* and Oracle 11*g* include:

  - `BACKGROUND_DUMP_DEST`

  - `CORE_DUMP_DEST`

  - `USER_DUMP_DEST`

  All three deprecated parameters have been replaced by the new `DIAGNOSTIC_DEST` parameter, which was introduced in Oracle 11.1.

- *Components*: This section lists all components that will be upgraded.

- *Miscellaneous Warnings*: This section contains miscellaneous warnings. In the preceding example the following warnings were included:

  - `CLUSTER_DATABASE` *parameter*: This parameter must be set to FALSE prior to the upgrade. Effectively, the upgrade can only be performed against a single-instance database, so RAC must be disabled for the duration of the upgrade and subsequently re-enabled. DBUA will automatically update this parameter.

  - *Timezone file*: If the database is using a timezone file older than version 11, then the `DBMS_DST` package to upgrade the timezone file should be run after the database upgrade has been completed.

  - *Stale Optimizer Statistics*: This ensures that optimizer statistics have been collected for all objects in the `SYS` and `SYSMAN` schemas. In Oracle 10.1 and later, optimizer statistics can be collected for data dictionary objects using the `GATHER_DICTIONARY_STATS` procedure in the `DBMS_STATS` package.

  - *Invalid objects*: The pre-upgrade utility will check for invalid objects in the database. A list of invalid objects in the `SYS` schema is stored in the `REGISTRY$SYS_INV_OBJS` table; a list of invalid objects owned by other users is stored in the `REGISTRY$NONSYS_INV_OBJS` table. In our tests, the only invalid objects in these tables were the `DBA_REGISTRY_DATABASE` view and public synonym and the DBMS_REGISTRY package. These objects can be ignored because they will be recompiled during the upgrade process.

- *Objects dependent on network packages*: Oracle 11.2 supports fine-grained access control for the UTL_TCP, UTL_SMTP, UTL_MAIL, UTL_HTTP, and UTL_INADDR packages. To support fine-grained access control for these packages, Oracle XML DB must be installed. Before the upgrade, a list of current dependencies should be generated; following the upgrade, the DBMS_NETWORK_ACL_ADMIN package should be used to generate new access control lists for the affected objects.

- *Enterprise Manager Database Control*: During the upgrade process, the Enterprise Manager Database Control repository will be automatically upgraded if it exists. However, if the database is subsequently downgraded, then the Database Control repository will not be automatically downgraded. Therefore, the repository should be backed up using the emdwgrd utility prior to the upgrade. You can find this utility in $ORACLE_HOME/bin.

- *Purge recycle bin*: If the current database is Oracle 10.1 or later, then the recycle bin should be emptied immediately prior to the upgrade. Use this code to empty the recycle bin:

```
SQL> PURGE DBA_RECYCLEBIN;

DBA Recyclebin purged.
```

Performing Other Checks

The Oracle Database Upgrade Guide lists a number of other checks that should be performed prior to upgrading the database. Most checks are dependent on specific database features, as in these examples:

- Complete any outstanding materialized view refreshes.

- Check that no files require media recovery.

- Take out any files that are in backup mode.

- Clear out any outstanding distributed transactions.

- Synchronize any standby databases with the primary database.

Saving Current Database Parameters

Default values for both supported and unsupported parameters can vary between releases. Changes in parameter values can affect application performance. To reduce the time required to resolve performance issues caused by parameter changes, we recommend that you save the current database parameter values before upgrading the database. The saved values can subsequently be compared with the new parameter values to determine whether any have changed.

We recommend that you save both the supported and unsupported parameters that are externalized in the X$KSPPI and X$KSPPSV tables. The following script saves all parameter values to a text file called parameters.txt:

```
SET PAGESIZE 0
SET TRIMSPOOL ON
```

```
SET FEEDBACK OFF
SPOOL parameters.txt

SELECT i.ksppinm||';'||sv.ksppstvl
FROM x$ksppi i, x$ksppsv sv
WHERE i.indx = sv.indx
ORDER BY 1;

SPOOL OFF
```

Backing up the Database

Prior to running DBUA or starting the manual upgrade process, you should ensure that you have a full or intermediate backup of the database available. This will come in handy if the upgrade fails, and it is necessary to restore it to its original state. If you do not already back up the database regularly—for example, it is a test database—then you can back it up using RMAN.

The Oracle Database Upgrade Guide recommends a simple RMAN command that will perform a full backup. Unfortunately, in the versions we have seen, the syntax for the BACKUP CURRENT CONTROLFILE command is incorrect. The example that follows shows how to use the command with a valid syntax.

First, create a target directory for the backup:

```
[root@server14 ~]# mkdir /backup
[root@server14 ~]# chown oracle.dba /backup
```

Second, set the environment variables to the old environment:

```
export ORACLE_BASE=/u01/app/oracle
export ORACLE_HOME=/u01/app/oracle/product/10.2.0/db_1
export PATH=$ORACLE_HOME/bin:$PATH
```

Third, set the ORACLE_SID to an appropriate value:

```
export ORACLE_SID=PROD1
```

Fourth, start the RMAN client:

```
[oracle@london1]$ rman target=/ nocatalog
```

Fifth, execute an RMAN command similar to the following:

```
RUN
{
   ALLOCATE CHANNEL c1 TYPE DISK;
   BACKUP DATABASE FORMAT '/backup/%U' TAG pre_upgrade plus archivelog;
   BACKUP CURRENT CONTROLFILE FORMAT '/backup/control.bak';
}
```

Note that the preceding example allocates only one channel; you will need to add more channels, depending on the capability of your hardware.

Configuring the Listener Process

If the listener process is currently Oracle 9*i* or Oracle 10*g*, then it should be upgraded at this stage. The simplest way to upgrade the listener is to delete and re-create it using the NETCA utility. NETCA is the preferred tool for configuring listener processes in a RAC environment because it updates the OCR.

In our example, we had already upgraded the Grid Infrastructure to Oracle 11.2. This procedure also upgraded the listener processes to the new version. Therefore, it was not necessary to modify the listener processes in our example. Remember that the listener configuration is more complex in Oracle 11.2, which includes SCAN listeners (referenced by the REMOTE_LISTENER database parameter) and local listeners (referenced by the LOCAL_LISTENER database parameter).

Upgrading Automatically with DBUA

We recommend using the Database Upgrade Assistant (DBUA), which is a GUI tool, to upgrade smaller, non-critical databases automatically. In this section, we'll review an upgrade of the PROD database in our example cluster.

If you are upgrading a RAC database, then you need to ensure that the CLUSTER_DATABASE parameter is initially set to TRUE. DBUA will automatically update this parameter during the upgrade process.

We also recommend that the database you want to upgrade be running before DBUA is invoked. This ensures that the database has been started using the correct parameter files. Remember that DBUA will restart the database during the upgrade process using the default parameter files, so these need to be correctly configured.

The DBUA is a GUI tool that should be started in an X session (see Chapter 7 for more details on the different options for running X sessions in a Linux environment). The DBUA can be run by the oracle user or a user in the DBA operating system group.

The Oracle environment must be set to include the new Oracle 11.2 home, as in this example:

```
export ORACLE_BASE=/u01/app/oracle
export ORACLE_HOME=/u01/app/oracle/product/11.2.0/dbhome_1
export PATH=$ORACLE_HOME/bin:$PATH
```

Also, the ORACLE_SID environment variable must be set to the local instance name:

```
export ORACLE_SID=PROD1
```

Use this command to start the DBUA:

```
$ dbua
```

Firing up the DBUA will display the Welcome page (see Figure 15-10).

743

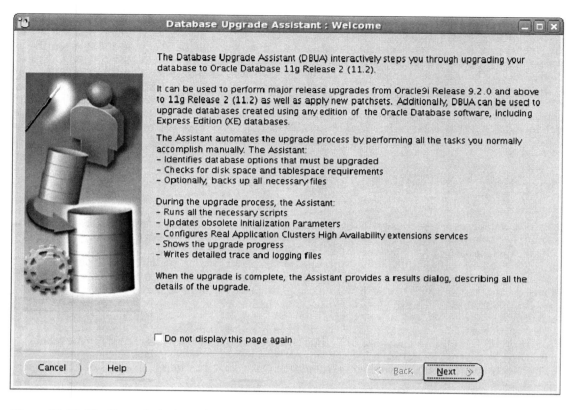

Figure 15-10. The Upgrade Assistant's Welcome page

Press Next to continue to the Select Database page (see Figure 15-11).

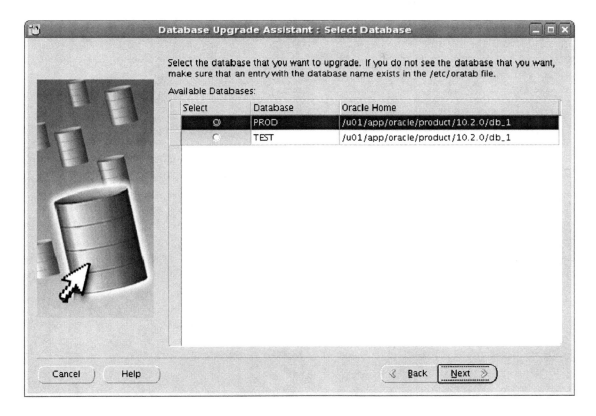

Figure 15-11. The Select Database page

On the Select Database page, you select the database you want to upgrade. In our example, we selected the PROD database. Our selection led to the warnings shown in Figure 15-12.

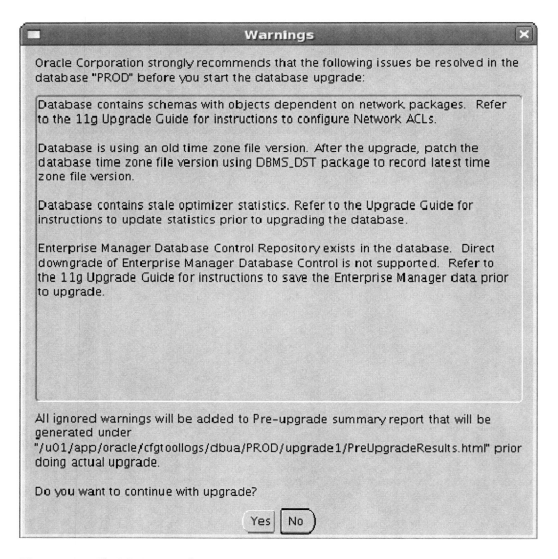

Figure 15-12. The DBUA upgrade warnings

These warnings were generated by the pre-upgrade report. In our example, we were satisfied that all issues identified by the warnings had been already been resolved or would be addressed after the upgrade, so we chose to continue with the upgrade.

Press Yes to continue to the first Upgrade Options page (see Figure 15-13).

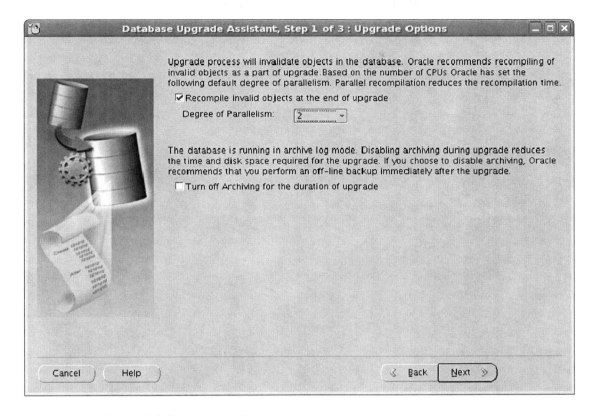

Figure 15-13. The DBUA's first Upgrade Options page

On the first Upgrade Options page, you can specify that invalid objects should be recompiled at the end of the upgrade. To reduce overall downtime, objects can be recompiled in parallel. The DBUA will recommend a degree of parallelism based on the number of CPUs detected. This value may need to be modified; for example, you may need to modify this if other production databases are currently running in the cluster.

DBUA can also disable the archive log mode for the duration of the upgrade process. This reduces the amount of disk space required for archived redo logs during the upgrade, and it may reduce the duration of the upgrade. If you choose to disable archiving, however, you should ensure that you make a full backup of the database immediately after the upgrade. This is normally not an option when standby databases are in place. If you do not choose to disable archiving, then the DBUA will display a warning that the upgrade will take longer and require more disk space. You should ensure that the local log archive destination has sufficient space before continuing.

Press Next to continue to the second Upgrade Options page (see Figure 15-14).

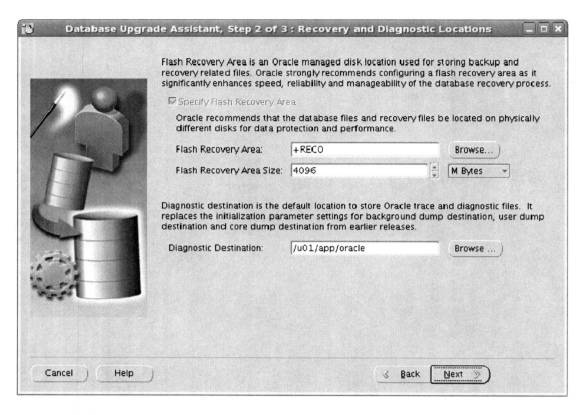

Figure 15-14. The second upgrade options page

On the second Upgrade Options page, you can specify a new size and location for the Flash Recovery Area. Remember that the upgrade will reinstall and recompile all PL/SQL and Java objects that can generate a large amount of redo.

In this example, the database is being upgraded from Oracle 10*g* to Oracle 11*g*. Therefore, the administrative and trace files will be moved from the Oracle 10*g* locations below the $ORACLE_HOME/admin/PROD directory to the new diagnostics area. In this case, the new area is created below /u01/app/oracle.

Press Next to continue to the upgrade's Summary page (see Figure 15-15).

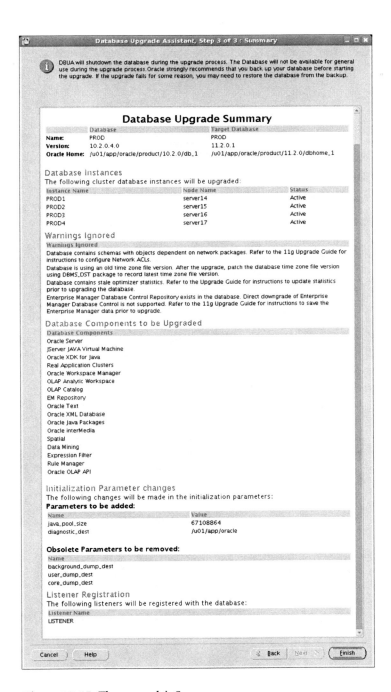

Figure 15-15. The upgrade's Summary page

Press Finish on the Summary page to initiate the upgrade. This brings up the Progress page, which displays the current progress of the upgrade. The upgrade is divided into a number of tasks. In our example, the following tasks were shown:

- Performing the pre-Upgrade

- Upgrading Oracle Server

- Upgrading JServer JAVA Virtual Machine

- Upgrading Oracle XDK for Java

- Upgrading Real Application Clusters

- Upgrading Oracle Workspace Manager

- Upgrading OLAP Analytic Workspace

- Upgrading OLAP Catalog

- Upgrading EM Repository

- Upgrading Oracle Text

- Upgrading Oracle XML Database

- Upgrading Java Packages

- Upgrading Oracle interMedia

- Upgrading Spatial

- Upgrading Data Mining

- Upgrading Expression Filter

- Upgrading Rule Manager

- Upgrading Oracle OLAP API

- Performing Post Upgrade

- Configuring Database with Enterprise Manager

- Generating Summary

When the upgrade is complete, the Upgrade Results page will be displayed (see Figure 15-16). This page summarizes the actions performed by DBUA during the upgrade. It also allows you to unlock and modify any passwords that have been affected by the upgrade.

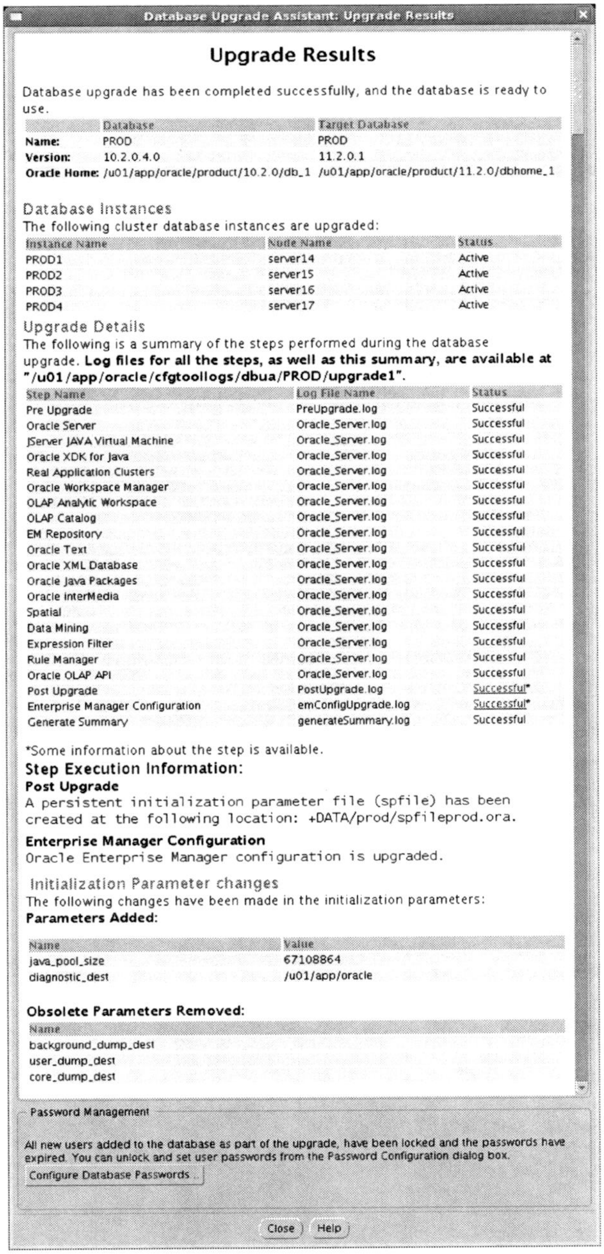

Upgrade Results

Database upgrade has been completed successfully, and the database is ready to use.

	Database	Target Database
Name:	PROD	PROD
Version:	10.2.0.4.0	11.2.0.1
Oracle Home:	/u01/app/oracle/product/10.2.0/db_1	/u01/app/oracle/product/11.2.0/dbhome_1

Database Instances
The following cluster database instances are upgraded:

Instance Name	Node Name	Status
PROD1	server14	Active
PROD2	server15	Active
PROD3	server16	Active
PROD4	server17	Active

Upgrade Details
The following is a summary of the steps performed during the database upgrade. **Log files for all the steps, as well as this summary, are available at "/u01/app/oracle/cfgtoollogs/dbua/PROD/upgrade1".**

Step Name	Log File Name	Status
Pre Upgrade	PreUpgrade.log	Successful
Oracle Server	Oracle_Server.log	Successful
JServer JAVA Virtual Machine	Oracle_Server.log	Successful
Oracle XDK for Java	Oracle_Server.log	Successful
Real Application Clusters	Oracle_Server.log	Successful
Oracle Workspace Manager	Oracle_Server.log	Successful
OLAP Analytic Workspace	Oracle_Server.log	Successful
OLAP Catalog	Oracle_Server.log	Successful
EM Repository	Oracle_Server.log	Successful
Oracle Text	Oracle_Server.log	Successful
Oracle XML Database	Oracle_Server.log	Successful
Oracle Java Packages	Oracle_Server.log	Successful
Oracle interMedia	Oracle_Server.log	Successful
Spatial	Oracle_Server.log	Successful
Data Mining	Oracle_Server.log	Successful
Expression Filter	Oracle_Server.log	Successful
Rule Manager	Oracle_Server.log	Successful
Oracle OLAP API	Oracle_Server.log	Successful
Post Upgrade	PostUpgrade.log	Successful*
Enterprise Manager Configuration	emConfigUpgrade.log	Successful*
Generate Summary	generateSummary.log	Successful

*Some information about the step is available.
Step Execution Information:
Post Upgrade
A persistent initialization parameter file (spfile) has been created at the following location: +DATA/prod/spfileprod.ora.

Enterprise Manager Configuration
Oracle Enterprise Manager configuration is upgraded.

Initialization Parameter changes
The following changes have been made in the initialization parameters:
Parameters Added:

Name	Value
java_pool_size	67108864
diagnostic_dest	/u01/app/oracle

Obsolete Parameters Removed:

Name
background_dump_dest
user_dump_dest
core_dump_dest

Password Management

All new users added to the database as part of the upgrade, have been locked and the passwords have expired. You can unlock and set user passwords from the Password Configuration dialog box.

[Configure Database Passwords ...]

[Close] [Help]

Figure 15-16. *The Upgrade Results page*

At this point, the DBUA upgrade is complete. However, some additional post-upgrade steps remain; we'll cover these later in this chapter. First, however, we'll explain how to upgrade a database manually using SQL scripts.

Upgrading a Database Manually

We recommend that you use SQL scripts to upgrade larger and business-critical databases manually. In this section, we will walk you through the process we used to upgrade the TEST database in our example cluster from Oracle 10.2 to Oracle 11.2.

In previous versions of Oracle, executing the pre-upgrade utility script, utluVersion.sql, was optional. Beginning with version 11.2, however, executing this is now mandatory; otherwise, the catupgrd.sql script will fail with an error. Refer to this chapter's earlier "Running the pre-Upgrade Tool" section for more information about executing this script on the non-upgraded database.

The Oracle environment must be set to include the new Oracle 11.2 home, as in this example:

```
export ORACLE_BASE=/u01/app/oracle
export ORACLE_HOME=/u01/app/oracle/product/11.2.0/dbhome_1
export PATH=$ORACLE_HOME/bin:$PATH
```

Also, the ORACLE_SID environment variable must be set to the local instance name:

```
export ORACLE_SID=TEST1
```

As mentioned previously, we did not need to upgrade the Oracle 10.2 listener process because new SCAN listeners and local listeners were created during the Oracle 11.2 Grid Infrastructure installation process. However, we did need to update the listener.ora file in the Oracle home for the new Oracle 11.2 RAC software ($ORACLE_HOME/network/admin/listener.ora). This is necessary because the REMOTE_LISTENER database and LOCAL_LISTENER database parameter reference entries in the listener.ora file.

We also added the following entries to $ORACLE_HOME/network/admin/listener.ora:

```
LISTENERS_TEST =
  (ADDRESS_LIST =
    (ADDRESS = (PROTOCOL = TCP)(HOST = cluster1-scan.example.com)(PORT = 1521))
    (ADDRESS =
      (PROTOCOL = TCP)(HOST = london1-vip.example.com)(PORT = 1521))
    (ADDRESS =
      (PROTOCOL = TCP)(HOST = london2-vip.example.com)(PORT = 1521))
    (ADDRESS =
      (PROTOCOL = TCP)(HOST = london3-vip.example.com)(PORT = 1521))
    (ADDRESS =
      (PROTOCOL = TCP)(HOST = london4-vip.example.com)(PORT = 1521))
  )

LISTENER_TEST1 =
  (ADDRESS = (PROTOCOL = TCP)(HOST = london1-vip.example.com)(PORT = 1521))

LISTENER_TEST2 =
  (ADDRESS = (PROTOCOL = TCP)(HOST = london2-vip.example.com)(PORT = 1521))
```

```
LISTENER_TEST3 =
  (ADDRESS = (PROTOCOL = TCP)(HOST = london3-vip.example.com)(PORT = 1521))

LISTENER_TEST4 =
  (ADDRESS = (PROTOCOL = TCP)(HOST = london4-vip.example.com)(PORT = 1521))

TEST =
    (ADDRESS = (PROTOCOL = TCP)(HOST = cluster1-scan)(PORT = 1521))
    (ADDRESS =
      (PROTOCOL = TCP)(HOST = london1-vip.example.com)(PORT = 1521))
    (ADDRESS =
      (PROTOCOL = TCP)(HOST = london2-vip.example.com)(PORT = 1521))
    (ADDRESS =
      (PROTOCOL = TCP)(HOST = london3-vip.example.com)(PORT = 1521))
    (ADDRESS =
      (PROTOCOL = TCP)(HOST = london4-vip.example.com)(PORT = 1521))
    (LOAD_BALANCE = yes)
    (CONNECT_DATA =
      (SERVER = DEDICATED)
      (SERVICE_NAME = TEST)
    )
  )

TEST1 =
  (DESCRIPTION =
    (ADDRESS =
      (PROTOCOL = TCP)(HOST = london1-vip.example.com)(PORT = 1521))
    (CONNECT_DATA =
      (SERVER = DEDICATED)
      (SERVICE_NAME = TEST)
      (INSTANCE_NAME = TEST1)
    )
  )

TEST2 =
  (DESCRIPTION =
    (ADDRESS =
      (PROTOCOL = TCP)(HOST = london2-vip.example.com)(PORT = 1521))
    (CONNECT_DATA =
      (SERVER = DEDICATED)
      (SERVICE_NAME = TEST)
      (INSTANCE_NAME = TEST2)
    )
  )

TEST3 =
  (DESCRIPTION =
    (ADDRESS =
      (PROTOCOL = TCP)(HOST = london3-vip.example.com)(PORT = 1521))
    (CONNECT_DATA =
      (SERVER = DEDICATED)
      (SERVICE_NAME = TEST)
```

```
      (INSTANCE_NAME = TEST3)
    )
  )

TEST4 =
  (DESCRIPTION =
    (ADDRESS =
      (PROTOCOL = TCP)(HOST = london4-vip.example.com)(PORT = 1521))
    (CONNECT_DATA =
      (SERVER = DEDICATED)
      (SERVICE_NAME = TEST)
      (INSTANCE_NAME = TEST4)
    )
  )
```

Preparing the Parameter Files

If you are currently using an SPFILE, it should be converted to a text file for the duration of the upgrade. You can verify whether your database is using an SPFILE by running the following SQL*Plus command, which returns the pathname of the SPFILE if there is one in use:

```
SQL> SHOW PARAMETER SPFILE
```

Our test database was created in Oracle 10.2 using DBCA with an SPFILE. The location of the SPFILE is stored in the $ORACLE_HOME/dbs/init<instance_name>.ora file on each node in the cluster. For example, our $ORACLE_HOME/dbs/initTEST1.ora file contains the following information:

```
SPFILE='+DATA/TEST/spfileTEST.ora'
```

In the preceding example, the SPFILE is stored in the +DATA ASM diskgroup. Next, we converted the SPFILE to a text file using the following command:

```
SQL> CREATE PFILE='/tmp/init.ora' FROM SPFILE;
```

```
File created.
```

The resulting file was stored in the /tmp directory to avoid overwriting any files in the $ORACLE_HOME/dbs directory. It is only necessary to perform this conversion on one node in the cluster.

If $ORACLE_HOME/dbs/init<instance_name>.ora files exist in the old Oracle home, then copy these as the oracle user to the same directory in the new Oracle home on each node in the cluster, as in this example:

```
[oracle@london1]$ cp /u01/app/oracle/product/10.2.0/db_1/dbs/initTEST1.ora \
/u01/app/oracle/product/11.2.0/dbhome_1/dbs/
```

Preparing Password Files

Next, copy the password file as the oracle user on each node in the cluster from the dbs directory in the old Oracle home to the dbs directory in the new Oracle home. The password file name has the format of orapw<instance_name>, as you can see in this example:

```
[oracle@london1]$ cp /u01/app/oracle/product/10.2.0/db_1/dbs/orapwTEST1 \
/u01/app/oracle/product/11.2.0/dbhome_1/dbs/
```

Modifying the Initialization Parameters

You need to ensure that the CLUSTER_DATABASE parameter is set to FALSE. In our example, we modified the temporary parameter file in /tmp/init.ora:

```
cluster_database = FALSE
```

Also, if you are upgrading an Oracle 10.2 or earlier database, then you need to comment out the BACKGROUND_DUMP_DEST, CORE_DUMP_DEST, and USER_DUMP_DEST parameters from the temporary parameter file because these parameters are deprecated in Oracle 11.1 and later.

Restarting the Database in UPGRADE Mode

Next, shut down the database using this syntax:

```
SQL> SHUTDOWN IMMEDIATE
```

Do *not* use the SHUTDOWN ABORT command because this would require instance recovery when the database is restarted. Next, restart the database in UPGRADE mode and use the PFILE parameter to specify the location of the temporary parameter file, as in this example:

```
SQL> startup upgrade pfile='/tmp/init.ora';
ORACLE instance started.

Total System Global Area   602619904 bytes
Fixed Size                   1338168 bytes
Variable Size              163579080 bytes
Database Buffers           432013312 bytes
Redo Buffers                 5689344 bytes
Database mounted.
```

Running the Catalog Upgrade Script

The catalog upgrade script will upgrade most objects in the data dictionary and associated Oracle schemas. We typically run this script from the /tmp directory and spool the output to a local file, as in this example:

```
[oracle@london1]$ sqlplus / as sysdba
SQL> SPOOL upgrade2.log
```

```
SQL> @?/rdbms/admin/catupgrd.sql
.....
SQL> SPOOL OFF
```

The $ORACLE_HOME/rdbms/admin/catupgrd.sql script can take several hours to run, depending on the CPU clock speed, amount of available memory, I/O bandwidth, and the number of components that must be upgraded.

In the preceding example, output is spooled to the /tmp/upgrade2.log file. This log file can become very large (it contained more than 67 million bytes in our example!). The Oracle documentation suggests that you inspect this file for errors. We recommend that you use the grep utility to search for errors. Use the -B and -A arguments to include a couple of lines of context around any errors that the utility discovers.

We also recommend that you monitor the alert log of the database being upgraded. In our case, the text alert log was written to this file:

```
/u01/app/oracle/diag/rdbms/test/TEST1/trace/alert_TEST1.log
```

During one of our tests, we did not disable archive redo logging. Subsequently, we ran out of archive redo log space. The catalog upgrade script simply hung. It can quite difficult to detect if this happens because the output is very repetitive. However, an error was written to the alert log, and we were able to release some more space for new archive log files. We did this using the rm command in the ASMCMD utility, deleting some old files from the affected diskgroup. If you have dependent standby databases, then please back the archived log files up before removing them.When sufficient space becomes available, the upgrade script will continue to execute without further intervention.

When the upgrade script completes successfully, restart the database:

```
SQL> SHUTDOWN IMMEDIATE
SQL> STARTUP PFILE=/tmp/init.ora
```

Configuring SPFILE

The next step is to recreate SPFILE with the new parameter settings. In our example, we used the following command:

```
SQL> CREATE SPFILE='+DATA/TEST/spfileTEST.ora'
FROM PFILE='/tmp/init.ora';

File created.
```

Next, you restart the database again to ensure that the new parameter file has been successfully created:

```
SQL> SHUTDOWN IMMEDIATE
SQL> STARTUP
```

Running the post-Upgrade Status Tool

Your next step is to run the post-upgrade status tool. This tool is implemented using the following SQL*Plus script:

```
$ORACLE_HOME/rdbms/admin/utlu112s.sql
```

Again, we executed this script from the /tmp directory:

```
[oracle@london1]$ sqlplus / as sysdba
SQL> SPOOL upgrade3.log
SQL> @$ORACLE_HOME/rdbms/admin/utlu112s.sql
.....
SQL> SPOOL OFF
```

For our example, this script generated the following output:

```
Oracle Database 11.2 Post-Upgrade Status Tool          12-26-2009 19:06:17
.
Component                     Status          Version    HH:MM:SS
.
Oracle Server
                              VALID       11.2.0.1.0   00:32:55
JServer JAVA Virtual Machine
                              VALID       11.2.0.1.0   00:11:04
Oracle Real Application Clusters
                              VALID       11.2.0.1.0   00:00:02
Oracle Workspace Manager
                              VALID       11.2.0.1.0   00:01:24
OLAP Analytic Workspace
                              VALID       11.2.0.1.0   00:01:12
OLAP Catalog
                              VALID       11.2.0.1.0   00:02:01
Oracle OLAP API
                              VALID       11.2.0.1.0   00:01:03
Oracle Enterprise Manager
                              VALID       11.2.0.1.0   00:19:10
Oracle XDK
                              VALID       11.2.0.1.0   00:03:43
Oracle Text
                              VALID       11.2.0.1.0   00:01:45
Oracle XML Database
                              VALID       11.2.0.1.0   00:07:21
Oracle Database Java Packages
                              VALID       11.2.0.1.0   00:00:54
Oracle Multimedia
                              VALID       11.2.0.1.0   02:30:31
Spatial
                              VALID       11.2.0.1.0   00:13:22
Oracle Expression Filter
                              VALID       11.2.0.1.0   00:00:25
```

```
Oracle Rules Manager
.                                      VALID      11.2.0.1.0  00:00:36
Gathering Statistics
.                                                             00:11:22
Total Upgrade Time: 04:19:05

PL/SQL procedure successfully completed.
```

In the preceding example, the Oracle Multimedia upgrade took two and a half hours. Much of this time was due to the aforementioned issue where we ran out of archive log space.

Running post-Upgrade Scripts

At this point, you're ready to run post-upgrade scripts. These scripts are stored in the catuppst.sql file, which is located in the $ORACLE_HOME/rdbms/admin directory. Connect to the database as sysdba, using SQL*Plus and execute the file:

```
[oracle@london1]$ sqlplus / as sysdba
SQL> SPOOL upgrade4.log
SQL> @?/rdbms/admin/catuppst.sql
.....
SQL> SPOOL OFF
```

In our example, the preceding script generated the following output (note that we have abridged and reformatted this output slightly to save space and make it easier to read):

```
TIMESTAMP
-------------------------------------------------------------------
COMP_TIMESTAMP POSTUP_BGN 2009-12-26 19:07:49


PL/SQL procedure successfully completed.

This script will migrate the Baseline data on a pre-11g database
to the 11g database.

Move BL Data SYS.WRH$_FILESTATXS
Move BL Data SYS.WRH$_SQLSTAT
Move BL Data SYS.WRH$_SYSTEM_EVENT
Move BL Data SYS.WRH$_WAITSTAT
Move BL Data SYS.WRH$_LATCH
Move BL Data SYS.WRH$_LATCH_CHILDREN
Move BL Data SYS.WRH$_LATCH_PARENT
Move BL Data SYS.WRH$_LATCH_MISSES_SUMMARY
Move BL Data SYS.WRH$_DB_CACHE_ADVICE
Move BL Data SYS.WRH$_ROWCACHE_SUMMARY
Move BL Data SYS.WRH$_SGASTAT
Move BL Data SYS.WRH$_SYSSTAT
Move BL Data SYS.WRH$_PARAMETER
Move BL Data SYS.WRH$_SEG_STAT
Move BL Data SYS.WRH$_DLM_MISC
```

```
Move BL Data SYS.WRH$_SERVICE_STAT
Move BL Data SYS.WRH$_TABLESPACE_STAT
Move BL Data SYS.WRH$_OSSTAT
Move BL Data SYS.WRH$_SYS_TIME_MODEL
Move BL Data SYS.WRH$_SERVICE_WAIT_CLASS
Move BL Data SYS.WRH$_INST_CACHE_TRANSFER
Move BL Data SYS.WRH$_ACTIVE_SESSION_HISTORY
...                                    ...
... Completed Moving the Baseline Data  ...
...                                    ...
... If there are no Move BL Data messages ...
... above, then there are no renamed    ...
... baseline tables in the system.      ...
...                                    ...
Drop Renamed Baseline Table SYS.WRH$_FILESTATXS_BR
Drop Renamed Baseline Table SYS.WRH$_SQLSTAT_BR
Drop Renamed Baseline Table SYS.WRH$_SYSTEM_EVENT_BR
Drop Renamed Baseline Table SYS.WRH$_WAITSTAT_BR
Drop Renamed Baseline Table SYS.WRH$_LATCH_BR
Drop Renamed Baseline Table SYS.WRH$_LATCH_CHILDREN_BR
Drop Renamed Baseline Table SYS.WRH$_LATCH_PARENT_BR
Drop Renamed Baseline Table SYS.WRH$_LATCH_MISSES_SUMMARY_BR
Drop Renamed Baseline Table SYS.WRH$_DB_CACHE_ADVICE_BR
Drop Renamed Baseline Table SYS.WRH$_ROWCACHE_SUMMARY_BR
Drop Renamed Baseline Table SYS.WRH$_SGASTAT_BR
Drop Renamed Baseline Table SYS.WRH$_SYSSTAT_BR
Drop Renamed Baseline Table SYS.WRH$_PARAMETER_BR
Drop Renamed Baseline Table SYS.WRH$_SEG_STAT_BR
Drop Renamed Baseline Table SYS.WRH$_DLM_MISC_BR
Drop Renamed Baseline Table SYS.WRH$_SERVICE_STAT_BR
Drop Renamed Baseline Table SYS.WRH$_TABLESPACE_STAT_BR
Drop Renamed Baseline Table SYS.WRH$_OSSTAT_BR
Drop Renamed Baseline Table SYS.WRH$_SYS_TIME_MODEL_BR
Drop Renamed Baseline Table SYS.WRH$_SERVICE_WAIT_CLASS_BR
Drop Renamed Baseline Table SYS.WRH$_INST_CACHE_TRANSFER_BR
Drop Renamed Baseline Table SYS.WRH$_ACTIVE_SESSION_HISTORY_BR
...                                    ...
... Completed the Dropping of the       ...
... Renamed Baseline Tables             ...
...                                    ...
... If there are no Drop Table messages ...
... above, then there are no renamed    ...
... baseline tables in the system.      ...
...                                    ...

PL/SQL procedure successfully completed.

<Output edited here>

TIMESTAMP
----------------------------------------------------------------------
COMP_TIMESTAMP POSTUP_END 2009-12-26 19:08:00
```

Recompiling Invalid Packages

The next step is to use the utlrp.sql script in the $ORACLE_HOME/rdbms/admin directory to recompile any invalid packages:

```
[oracle@london1]$ sqlplus / as sysdba
SQL> SPOOL upgrade5.log
SQL> @?/rdbms/admin/utlrp.sql
SQL> SPOOL OFF
```

In our example, the preceding script generated the following output:

```
TIMESTAMP
---------------------------------------------------------------------------  --
COMP_TIMESTAMP UTLRP_BGN  2009-12-26 19:09:30
DOC>   The following PL/SQL block invokes UTL_RECOMP to recompile invalid
DOC>   objects in the database. Recompilation time is proportional to the
DOC>   number of invalid objects in the database, so this command may take
DOC>   a long time to execute on a database with a large number of invalid
DOC>   objects.
DOC>
DOC>   Use the following queries to track recompilation progress:
DOC>
DOC>   1. Query returning the number of invalid objects remaining. This
DOC>      number should decrease with time.
DOC>         SELECT COUNT(*) FROM obj$ WHERE status IN (4, 5, 6);
DOC>
DOC>   2. Query returning the number of objects compiled so far. This number
DOC>      should increase with time.
DOC>         SELECT COUNT(*) FROM UTL_RECOMP_COMPILED;
DOC>
DOC>   This script automatically chooses serial or parallel recompilation
DOC>   based on the number of CPUs available (parameter cpu_count) multiplied
DOC>   by the number of threads per CPU (parameter parallel_threads_per_cpu).
DOC>   On RAC, this number is added across all RAC nodes.
DOC>
DOC>   UTL_RECOMP uses DBMS_SCHEDULER to create jobs for parallel
DOC>   recompilation. Jobs are created without instance affinity so that they
DOC>   can migrate across RAC nodes. Use the following queries to verify
DOC>   whether UTL_RECOMP jobs are being created and run correctly:
DOC>
DOC>   1. Query showing jobs created by UTL_RECOMP
DOC>         SELECT job_name FROM dba_scheduler_jobs
DOC>            WHERE job_name like 'UTL_RECOMP_SLAVE_%';
DOC>
DOC>   2. Query showing UTL_RECOMP jobs that are running
DOC>         SELECT job_name FROM dba_scheduler_running_jobs
DOC>            WHERE job_name like 'UTL_RECOMP_SLAVE_%';
DOC>#
```

PL/SQL procedure successfully completed.

```
TIMESTAMP
--------------------------------------------------------------------------    --
COMP_TIMESTAMP UTLRP_END  2009-12-26 19:12:54

DOC> The following query reports the number of objects that have compiled
DOC> with errors (objects that compile with errors have status set to 3 in
DOC> obj$). If the number is higher than expected, please examine the error
DOC> messages reported with each object (using SHOW ERRORS) to see if they
DOC> point to system misconfiguration or resource constraints that must be
DOC> fixed before attempting to recompile these objects.
DOC>#

OBJECTS WITH ERRORS
-------------------
                  0

DOC> The following query reports the number of errors caught during
DOC> recompilation. If this number is non-zero, please query the error
DOC> messages in the table UTL_RECOMP_ERRORS to see if any of these errors
DOC> are due to misconfiguration or resource constraints that must be
DOC> fixed before objects can compile successfully.
DOC>#

ERRORS DURING RECOMPILATION
---------------------------
                         0


PL/SQL procedure successfully completed.


PL/SQL procedure successfully completed.

SQL> spool off
```

You can use the following query to verify manually that all objects are valid:

```
SQL> SELECT COUNT(*) FROM dba_invalid_objects;

  COUNT(*)
----------
         0
```

You can use the post-upgrade invalid objects tool to identify post-upgrade invalid objects, as in this example:

```
SQL> @?/rdbms/admin/utluiobj.sql
.
Oracle Database 11.1 Post-Upgrade Invalid Objects Tool 12-26-2009 19:22:36
```

```
•
This tool lists post-upgrade invalid objects that were not invalid
prior to upgrade (it ignores pre-existing pre-upgrade invalid objects).
•
Owner                        Object Name                    Object Type
•

PL/SQL procedure successfully completed.
```

■ **Note** The post-upgrade invalid objects tool ignores objects that were invalid before the upgrade.

Updating /etc/oratab

DBUA automatically updates /etc/oratab. However, when using the manual upgrade method, it is necessary to update /etc/oratab by hand.

In our example, the original entry for the TEST database looked like this:

```
TEST:/u01/app/oracle/product/10.2.0/db_1:N
```

In our example, we changed this entry so it referenced the new Oracle home:

```
TEST:/u01/app/oracle/product/11.2.0/dbhome_1:N
```

Updating Environment Variables

If you do not use the .oraenv family of scripts to configure your environment, then you may also wish to update the $ORACLE_HOME environment variable in /home/oracle/.bash_profile. The original file looked like this in our example:

```
export ORACLE_HOME=/u01/app/oracle/product/10.2.0/db_1
```

The revised file looks like this:

```
export ORACLE_HOME=/u01/app/oracle/product/11.2.0/dbhome_1
```

Updating the Oracle Cluster Registry

After the update, the Oracle Cluster Registry will contain some incorrect entries for the database, such as the location of the Oracle home.

In theory, the OCR can be updated using the SRVCONFIG utility. In early versions of Oracle 11.2, however, we have found the SRVCONFIG command to be susceptible to bugs and errors in the OCR. Therefore, we recommend that you delete and re-create the entries for the upgraded database in the OCR.

The database should be removed from the OCR using the SRVCTL utility in the old Oracle home:

```
[oracle@london1]$ export ORACLE_HOME=/u01/app/oracle/product/10.2.0/db_1
[oracle@london1]$ export PATH=$ORACLE_HOME/bin:$PATH
```

Use the following command to delete any existing entries for the database; note that the -d option specifies the database name:

```
[oracle@london1]$ srvctl remove database -d TEST
```

You should use the SRVCTL utility to add the upgraded database and instances to the OCR in the new Oracle home:

```
[oracle@london1]$ export ORACLE_HOME=/u01/app/oracle/product/11.2.0/db_home1
[oracle@london1]$ export PATH=$ORACLE_HOME/bin:$PATH
```

Next, you need to add the new database:

```
[oracle@london1]$ srvctl add database -d TEST -o $ORACLE_HOME -p '+DATA/TEST/spfileTEST.ora' \
> -y AUTOMATC -a "DATA,RECO"
```

In the preceding example, the -d option specifies the database name, while the -o option specifies the new Oracle home. Also, the -p option specifies the path to SPFILE, and -y indicates that the database should be started automatically as part of the start process for Clusterware. The final option, -a, lists the diskgroups that the database depends on. If you specify the spfile command-line parameter, then you do not need to create the $ORACLE_HOME/dbs/init$ORACLE_SID.ora file. In this case, the agent will automatically create it for you.

Use this code to add the new instances:

```
[oracle@london1]$ srvctl add instance -d TEST -i TEST1 -n london1
[oracle@london1]$ srvctl add instance -d TEST -i TEST2 -n london2
[oracle@london1]$ srvctl add instance -d TEST -i TEST3 -n london3
[oracle@london1]$ srvctl add instance -d TEST -i TEST4 -n london4
```

In the preceding example, the -d option specifies the database name, the -i option specifies the instance name, and the -n option specifies the node name.

Setting the Initialization Parameters for the New Release

Before touching any other parameter, it is recommended that you convert the database to a RAC database. At the present time, the database is still running as a single-instance database. To reconfigure the database to use all nodes, set the CLUSTER_DATABASE parameter to TRUE:

```
SQL> ALTER SYSTEM SET cluster_database = TRUE SCOPE = SPFILE;
System altered.
```

Next, shut down the local instance:

```
SQL> SHUTDOWN IMMEDIATE
```

Now restart all instances in the database using the SRVCTL utility:

```
[oracle@london1]$ srvctl start database -d TEST
```

Finally, verify that all nodes have started:

```
[oracle@london1]$ srvctl status database -d TEST
Instance TEST1 is running on node london1
Instance TEST2 is running on node london2
Instance TEST3 is running on node london3
Instance TEST4 is running on node london4
```

If you have problems starting the remaining instances, you should double-check that the password files exist and that the init$ORACLE_SID.ora file points to SPFILE in ASM.

The compatible initialization parameter has a special role in Oracle. We recommend leaving it at its current pre-11.2 value for a transition period. This enables you to allow for a downgrade of the system without having to restore a backup and losing data. We also strongly recommend taking a full level 0 backup of the database before raising this parameter to 11.2.0. When starting with the new compatibility level, internal data structures are changed, which makes a downgrade impossible from that point forward. If you have physical standby databases in place, you need to ensure that you use the same compatibility setting for all databases in the Data Guard configuration.

And with this, you have completed the manual upgrade process.

Performing the Necessary post-Upgrade Steps

A number of post-upgrade steps should be performed. The first step is to back up the database. Once you've obtained the security of a backup, you can move forward with the following mandatory and optional tasks.

Completing Mandatory post-Upgrade Tasks

In this section, we'll outline some mandatory post-upgrade steps that you should consider. You do not need to execute the steps in the order listed; however, you should consider implementing each step, and then execute those steps that apply to your environment:

- Upgrade the timezone file version if the existing timezone file is earlier than version 11.

- Statistics tables created by a call to DBMS_STATS.CREATE_STAT_TABLE - typically used to transfer or backup statistics - need to be updated.

- Upgrade the RMAN recovery catalog schema if this is used for RMAN backups.

- If the source database was either Oracle 9.2 or 10.1 then you need to upgrade SSL users using external authentication.

- Users of the Oracle Text option need to install the supplied knowledge base from the companion products.

- If your database makes use if the Application Express (APEX) option, and the APEX version is lower than 3.2 it will automatically be upgraded to 3.2. Subsequently you will have to run a few more configuration steps.

- Additional security measures were introduced in version 11.1 for network related packages such as UTL_TCP, UTL_SMTP and others. You need to define specific access criteria to allow developers and code to make use of them

- If your system makes use of the Database Vault, you need to enable it.

The Oracle Database Upgrade Guide describes all these steps in detail.

Performing the Recommended Tasks

The Oracle Database Upgrade Guide also recommends a number of tasks that can be performed after the database has been upgraded. For example, it recommends updating passwords to enforce case-sensitivity. It also recommends configuring thresholds for server alerts. These steps tend to be database-specific, so we recommend that you consult the Guide for tasks relevant to your environment. One thing we would like to draw your attention to is the concept of plan stability. In the days of the rule-based optimizer, performance was predictable and the rules were simple. With the current, cost-based optimizer, things are a little different and having stable plans in the new version of the database is important. One way to achieve this is to use stored outlines to capture the most important statements in the non-11.2 database, and then transform them into entities managed by SQL Plan Management.

The first step is to identify the important SQL statements relevant to your business. You should take your time and discover these together with your key business users. Once you determine what these are, you can capture them as outlines. This can be a lengthy process, especially for systems not developed in-house. Some systems resist all such tuning efforts because they rely on a lot of dynamic SQL, which is literally impossible to capture in SQL outlines. Once identified, the essential list of SQL statements is extracted from the V$SQL view. The DBMS_OUTLN package has been extended in 10*g* to allow administrators to capture SQL statements by using the hash value and child number. Once you identify an essential SQL statement, you need to get its hash value and SQL ID from GV$SQL, as in this example:

```
SELECT inst_id,
  sql_text,
  sql_id,
  hash_value,
  plan_hash_value,
  child_number
FROM gv$sql
WHERE ...
```

Next, you can create an outline for the SQL statement:

```
begin
 DBMS_OUTLN.CREATE_OUTLINE (
   hash_value    => hashValue,
   child_number  => childNumber,
   category      => 'MIGRATION');
end;
/
```

You supply the values from the previous resultset for the hash value and child number. The MIGRATION category is only a suggestion; you can use any other outline category you like. However, to make the migration of the captured outlines easier, you should all group them under the same outline category. Prior to the migration, you should have captured all the important statements in outlines. The difficulty in using outlines is that, as soon as the hash value of a statement changes, it will no longer be used.

The DBA_OUTLINES view should now list your new outline. In a migration test database, you should try and convert this outline to a SQL Plan baseline after the database has been migrated to 11.2:

```
SQL> set serveroutput on
SQL> set long 1000000 trimspool on linesize 120
SQL> declare
  2    migrationReport clob;
  3  begin
  4    migrationReport := DBMS_SPM.MIGRATE_STORED_OUTLINE(
  5      attribute_name => 'CATEGORY',
  6      attribute_value => 'MIGRATION');
  7  dbms_output.put_line(migrationReport);
  8  end;
  9  /

before migrate:
after migrate:

---------------------------------------------------------------------------

                    Migrate Stored Outline to SQL Plan Baseline
Report
---------------------------------------------------------------------------

Summary:
--------
Total outlines to be migrated: 175

Outlines migrated
successfully: 175


PL/SQL procedure successfully completed.
```

In the preceding example, we instructed Oracle to migrate all outlines of the MIGRATION category to SQL Plan Baselines. The contents of the migrationReport variable returned by DBMS_SPM.MIGRATE_STORED_OUTLINE provides a detailed report about the migration status, as well as information about failed migrations.

The DBA_SQL_PLAN_BASELINES view should now list all the new SQL Plan Baselines that previously were stored outlines. To use the SQL Plan Baselines, set the optimizer_use_sql_plan_baselines parameter to true, either per session or through the alter system command.

When a baseline has been used, the LAST_EXECUTED field in DBA_SQL_PLAN_BASELINES will be updated. You should also see a value in GV$SQL.SQL_PLAN_BASELINE for statements using the baseline.

From a security point of view, it is good practice to change passwords so they are case sensitive. When set to true, the new initialization parameter, sec_case_sensitive_logon, makes passwords case sensitive. Only newly created accounts benefit from this straight away; existing accounts do not. For existing accounts, you need to prompt the user to change the password or, alternatively, execute an `alter user` command. The new `PASSWORD_VERSIONS` column in `DBA_USERS` indicates whether a password is case sensitive.

The command to create the password file has been changed to take an additional parameter: `ignorecase`. This parameter can be set to either n or y.

You should review any operating system jobs with hard-coded environment variables that would fail to connect because the database now runs from a different `ORACLE_HOME` than it did previously. If you changed passwords, you should also ensure that any automatically started job still connects to the database. Database links are another area you need to pay special attention to. For example, sometimes the `tnsnames.ora` file in the new Oracle home does not contain the information required to connect to the remote system.

If you are using database console, you should upgrade it to the new Oracle home. From the *new* Oracle home, you can execute the `emca -upgrade db -cluster` command and follow the instructions on the screen to provide the necessary information to connect to the database.

■ **Note** If you chose not to upgrade the database to 11.2, then you do not need to upgrade the database console.

Resolving Problems in Mixed-Database Environments

As we noted in our introduction, Oracle 11.2 fully supports continuing to use non-11.2 databases on a cluster that has been upgraded to 11.2. However, you should be aware that the Oracle 11.2.0.1 base release contained a number of problems that could affect users with a 10.2 database.

If you did not choose to remove and re-add the database resource into the OCR after upgrading Clusterware, then you might run into bug 9257105 after removing the now unneeded 10.2 Clusterware home from your machine. Although the OCR has been upgraded successfully, the action script parameter still references a file in the 10.2 Clusterware home. You can change this easily with the `crsctl` command, as in the following example:

```
[oracle@london1 ~]$ crsctl modify resource ora.PROD.db \
> -attr "ACTION_SCRIPT=$GRID_HOME/bin/racgwrap"
```

In this case, you need to replace the database name (PROD) with your database name. Note that this is one of the very rare occasions where you use `crsctl` command instead of `srvctl` to modify an Oracle resource. The command should be executed with the environment set to the 11.2 Grid Infrastructure home.

Another common problem with brand new installations of Grid Infrastructure 11.2 and pre-11.2 RDBMS instances is related to node pinning. During the upgrade, the nodes containing 10.2 RDBMS software will be pinned, allowing pre-11.2 databases to run on them. Non-upgraded clusters are not automatically pinned, which causes problems with `emca` and `dbca` when executed from the pre-11.2 Oracle homes.

The golden rule to remember here is that you should use the utilities from the `$GRID_HOME` to manage resources provided by the same Oracle home. Similarly, when managing pre-11.2 resources, you can use the commands from their respective homes.

You can find more information about problems with 10.2 databases and 11.2 Grid Infrastructure documented in My Oracle Support note, 948456.1.

Using a Swing Kit

Where possible, we recommend using swing kit to perform the upgrade. This allows you to install Grid Infrastructure instead of upgrading it, eliminating many potential points for failure. If Grid Infrastructure is installed and patched to match your standards from the outset, then a time-consuming task becomes greatly simplified.

One option is to use a physical standby database created on the new cluster. For example, Oracle 10.2/11.1 RDBMSs are fully supported on Grid Infrastructure. To create the standby database, all you need to do is create an identical home (in terms of patches) on the new hardware, in addition to the 11.2 RDBMS home you've already created. The standby database initially runs out of the original RDBMS home; on the day of the migration, a switchover first makes it the primary database, and from there, you follow the standard steps to migrate it to 11.2. Figure 15-17 shows the process graphically; note that this figure omits additional standby databases for the sake of simplicity and clarity.

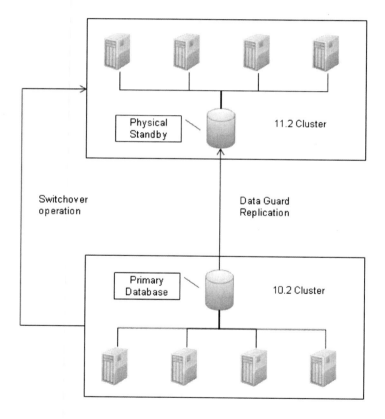

Figure 15-17. An alternetive upgrade strategy employing Data Guard switchover

This strategy can be very desirable on sites with many cluster nodes because executing the rootupgrade.sh script on many nodes can take a while to finish. If you want to keep the old hardware, then you should migrate the old cluster at your convenience to Grid Infrastructure 11.2. At this point, you could install the new RDBMS home before mounting the database under the new 11.2 home, and then wait for it to be synchronized with the primary database.

Summary

This chapter explained different strategies for migrating a pre-11.2 cluster to the latest release of the Oracle software. Most sites we have seen remain on Oracle 10.2.0.4, which is a very stable release. However, premium support for Oracle 10.2.0.4 comes to an end in mid-2011, so many sites should begin thinking about a migration strategy more seriously. Although extended (and lifetime) support are available to customers wishing to remain on their current release, this support comes at an extra cost.

Depending on their budget and other organizational concerns, some sites will perform an upgrade of the clusterware stack on the existing hardware. This is a proven approach, but it also has its problems, especially if you encounter OCR corruption.

Where possible, we recommend using a new cluster when you install Grid Infrastructure. We also recommend creating a fresh OCR and voting disks. You should then create a physical standby database for the database to be migrated, using exactly the same patch level that you use in your production database. On the migration day, you perform a switchover, start the database in the new home, and upgrade it.

Regardless of which method you choose, you need to migrate the database to 11.2 at some point. Oracle offers a GUI tool, called DBUA to take care of this task. We think it is suitable for smaller databases, but control over the migration process is important, which makes it less suitable for larger or business-critical databases.

With the rule-based optimizer marked as deprecated, DBAs now have to try their best to guarantee plan stability. Using stored outlines that you transform into a SQL Plan Management could be a new solution to this old problem.

Index

■ Special Characters and Numbers

■ A

▓ G

■ H

■ T

▒ U

You Need the Companion eBook

Your purchase of this book entitles you to buy the companion PDF-version eBook for only $10. Take the weightless companion with you anywhere.

We believe this Apress title will prove so indispensable that you'll want to carry it with you everywhere, which is why we are offering the companion eBook (in PDF format) for $10 to customers who purchase this book now. Convenient and fully searchable, the PDF version of any content-rich, page-heavy Apress book makes a valuable addition to your programming library. You can easily find and copy code—or perform examples by quickly toggling between instructions and the application. Even simultaneously tackling a donut, diet soda, and complex code becomes simplified with hands-free eBooks!

Once you purchase your book, getting the $10 companion eBook is simple:

❶ Visit **www.apress.com/promo/tendollars/**.

❷ Complete a basic registration form to receive a randomly generated question about this title.

❸ Answer the question correctly in 60 seconds, and you will receive a promotional code to redeem for the $10.00 eBook.

THE EXPERT'S VOICE™

233 Spring Street, New York, NY 10013

Offer valid through 3/11.

CPSIA information can be obtained at www.ICGtesting.com

261856BV00003B/13/P